MANGA
THE COMPLETE GUIDE

MANGA
THE COMPLETE GUIDE

Jason Thompson

BALLANTINE BOOKS NEW YORK

A Del Rey Trade Paperback Original

Published in the United States by Del Rey Books,
an imprint of The Random House Publishing Group,
a division of Random House, Inc., New York.

DEL REY is a registered trademark and the
Del Rey colophon is a trademark of Random House, Inc.

ISBN 978-0-345-48590-8

LIBRARY OF CONGRESS CATALOGING-IN-PUBLICATION DATA
Thompson, Jason.
Manga : the complete guide / Jason Thompson.
p.   cm.
"A Del Rey Trade Paperback Original."
Includes bibliographical references and index.
ISBN-13: 978-0-345-48590-8 (pbk.)
1. Comic books, strips, etc.—Japan—History and criticism.
2. Comic books, strips, etc.—United States—
History and criticism.   I. Title.
PN6790.J3T56 2007
741.5'952—dc22   2007009328

FRONT COVER: *Negima* © 2004 Ken Akamatsu/KODANSHA LTD. (top left)
Fullmetal Alchemist © Hiromu Arakawa/SQUARE ENIX (top right)
Fruits Basket © 1998 Natsuki Takaya (lower left)
Naruto © 1999 Masashi Kishimoto/SHUEISHA, Inc. (lower right)

BACK COVER: *Astro Boy* © Tezuka Productions (left)
Little Butterfly © Kaiohsha (middle)
Akira © 1998 Katsuhiro Otomo/KODANSHA LTD. (right)

Printed in the United States of America

www.delreybooks.com

9 8 7 6 5 4 3 2 1

Book design by Casey Hampton

*To Satoru Fujii, Seiji Horibuchi, Trish Ledoux, and Toshifumi Yoshida,
for getting me into the industry;*

*and to David Mills,
for getting me into manga in the first place*

ACKNOWLEDGMENTS

In addition to the many paid freelancers who assisted me with writing, research, translation, and scanning, I would like to thank the following people for their time, cooperation, and ideas: Trina Anderson, Adam Arnold, Steve Bennett, Dean Blackburn, Casey Brienza, Urian Brown, Peggy Burns, Chris Butcher, Jim Chadwick, Jay Chung, Yuki Chung, Dirk Deppey, Pancha Diaz, Lillian Diaz-Przybyl, Michael Dowers, Evelyn Dubocq, Izumi Evers, Bill Flanagan, Kit Fox, Shaenon Garrity, Evan Hayden, Matt High of Cold Cut Distribution, Carl Gustav Horn, Amy Huey, Anne Ishii, Dan Kanemitsu, Masae Kellogg, Jason King, Alexis Kirsch, Andy Kitkowski, Erik Ko, Chris Kohler, Henry Kornman, Matthew Lane, Rachel Livingston, Alvin Lu, Shie Lundberg, Evan Ma, Tomoko Machiyama, Patrick Macias, Akane Matsuo, Dallas Middaugh, Andy Nakatani, Robert Napton, Akito Neculai, Douglas Nerad, Tran Nguyen, Chris Oarr, Yuji Oniki, Michelle Pangilinan, Frank Pannone, Reginald Rhoades, Ian Robertson, Mee-Lise Robinson, Stephen Robson, Annette Roman, Jeremy Ross, Tomoko Saito, Jan Scott-Frazier, Eric Searleman, Stephanie Shalofsky, Jason Shiga, Allison Sima, Toren Smith, Jaime Starling, Jonathan Tarbox, Matt Thorn, Colin Turner, Frances Wall, Marc Weidenbaum, James Welker, Drew Williams, Stevie Wilson, Elin Winkler, David Wise, Benjamin Wright, Suzuki Yamashita, and Masayoshi Yasuda. I could not have finished this book without you. The number of casual conversations, interviews, and message-board postings that contributed to this book are innumerable, and unfortunately, I've probably forgotten many more names that should be listed here. If you were left off this list, it is entirely due to my own error, and I extend to you the deepest thanks and apologies.

Lastly, special thanks to Rory Root and the entire staff of Comic Relief in Berkeley, the San Francisco Bay Area's greatest comic book store. Your incredible manga selection came to my aid many times.

RESEARCH AND TRANSLATION

AISEI Japanese Language Services, Inc., Mayumi Kobayashi, Egan Loo, Mari Morimoto, Lillian Olsen, Mark Simmons, Akira Watanabe, Yoko Morihiro

ART AND SCANNING ASSISTANCE

Sean McCoy

WRITERS

Ronald Bog (RG), Rebecca Brown (RB), Julie Davis (JD), Patti Duffield (PD), Erica Friedman (EF), Shaenon Garrity (SG), Derek Guder (DG), Carl Gustav Horn (CGH), Patrick Macias (PM), Robert McCarthy (RM), Sean McCoy (SM), Dale Readings (DR), Ryan Sands (RS), Hannah Santiago (HS), Matt Segale (MJS), Mark Simmons (MS), Adam Stephanides (AS), Chuck Tang (CT), Mason Templar (MT), Aaron Tynes (AT), Karen Twelves (KT), Chris Vaillancourt (CV), Jen Wang (JW), Leia Weathington (LW)

CONTENTS

INTRODUCTION

In the early twenty-first century, a sight began to appear in American bookstores that was familiar to anyone from Japan: crowds of people reading books in the manga section. In Japan they call it *tachiyomi*, "stand-reading," and it is strongly discouraged, but in America it seems slightly more acceptable, perhaps because bookstore staff are too overworked, or perhaps because no other phenomenon has brought so many young adults and teenagers into the stores. Ten years ago most American bookstores had no manga section, and ten years before that most video stores had no anime section. Manga, comics made in Japan for Japanese audiences, have been embraced in America. We love them more than any test-marketed, focus-group products designed for us. If we can accept stories told with pictures, we can read manga. If we read comic books, newspaper strips, or online comics, we can read manga. If we can look the characters in their (sometimes) big eyes and take their stories at face value, we can read manga. And more and more of us do.

What are manga like? The question is like asking "What are books like?" or "What are DVDs like?" Manga aren't a single genre, like superhero comics or fantasy novels. They don't have a single style, with big eyes or speedlines or samurai swords. The term "manga" covers all Japanese comics, including stories for men and women, children and adults. Historical drama, comedy, romance, horror, sci-

Japanese *tachiyomi* perpetrators peruse the stacks of Mandarake, a popular used-manga store. *Photo courtesy of Patrick Macias*

ence fiction, sports, experimental works—manga span every genre imaginable. You may think you know "the manga style," but there are manga that look nothing like it.

Manga have been in America for more than twenty years; the first full-length manga were translated in 1987, and one of those books, *Lone Wolf and Cub,* is still in print. Latin America, Europe, and most of Asia have been reading translated manga for decades. The United States is one of the last places for the phenomenon to hit, but hit it has. As of 2007, more than one thousand manga series have been translated; not individual books, but epic stories often running twenty volumes or more. (If it sounds intimidating, there are many one-volume manga as well.) More than one hundred volumes of manga are now released in America every month, not counting similar-looking books published in the same format, such as manga-influenced American comics and Korean *manhwa*. Manga has surpassed anime as the up-and-coming export of Japanese pop culture (video games are the only possible competition). Anime conventions have taken place in America for years, but in October 2006 the first manga convention, Manga Next, was held in New Jersey.

Manga: The Complete Guide lists every manga that has ever been translated for American audiences, as well as a few that were made for Americans by Japanese artists. Here you'll find the new bestselling series with the covers bent back from *tachiyomi,* but you'll also find rare manga that were translated in the 1980s and 1990s, e-books, and even bilingual books printed in Japan. From the mainstream to the underground, from family-friendly to adult, this book has everything. Are you looking for a particular manga? Look it up in the title or artist index. Or maybe you don't have a manga in mind, but you're a fan of a particular genre, such as mystery, fantasy, or sports. In the table of contents are listed more than thirty articles on different topics. The amount of translated material is still a fraction of what is produced in Japan, but today there are translated examples of almost every manga genre, including rarely seen ones such as *pachinko* comics, military comics, and comics for businessmen.

Manga is popular around the world and has inspired comic artists everywhere. But no one is influenced by manga in general; people are influenced by specific artists, specific works. If you're already familiar with manga, you may know what you want to look up. But I think I envy the newbies more this time. More than one thousand manga await you. Jump in.

Check out http://www.delreymanga.com/mangaguide for periodic online updates to *Manga: The Complete Guide* and to give us your feedback. The Web site includes manga that were announced too late to make it into the book.

SIXTY YEARS OF JAPANESE COMICS

Manga (**漫画** or **まんが**) is Japanese for "comics." Coined in the 1800s by the Japanese artist Hokusai to refer to doodles in his sketchbook, the term can be translated as "whimsical sketches" or "lighthearted pictures." The same term is the root of the Korean word for comics (*manhwa*) and the Chinese word (*manhua*). Today, most Japanese people use the English word "comics" (*komikku*) as well.

Almost as soon as modern printing technology was introduced to Japan in the late 1800s, comics were published: first European-style satirical cartoons, then American-style newspaper strips, and eventually monthly comics magazines aimed at young readers. The oldest manga available in translation, *The Four Immigrants Manga,* was drawn by Henry (Yoshitaka) Kiyama while he was living in San Francisco in 1931. After World War II, the Japanese manga industry was quick to rise out of the ashes. TV was not common in Japan until the late 1950s, and movies were always expensive, so comics were cheap, accessible entertainment. Some artists developed self-contained comic stories for *kashibonya*—professional book lenders or "pay libraries"—who loaned hardbound comic books for a small fee. Others drew manga for a new crop of children's magazines, now printed in black and white instead of color because of postwar economic realities. The most popular magazine series were collected and repackaged as graphic novels (or, in Japanese, *tankôbon*). In this environment of frantic experimentation, today's "classic" manga artists established the styles that future generations would mimic.

As the Japanese economy improved, manga adapted. *Kashibonya* became a thing of the past, but monthly and biweekly manga magazines could be purchased at any

Osamu Tezuka helped establish the styles that would define modern manga. His *Lost World* was published in 1948.

newsstand. To compete with the fast pace of TV, the biggest publishers introduced weekly magazines, starting with *Weekly Shônen Magazine* in 1959. Manga were licensed for anime, toys, and live-action movies. At the same time, the form began to achieve critical respect; Sanpei Shirato's epic *Ninja Bugeichô* ("Ninja Military Chronicles," 1959–1962) was a favorite with student radicals due to its revolutionary themes. Art and stories became more diverse: sports, horror, war stories, science fiction, occupational manga, manga for adult readers. Sales rose throughout the 1970s and 1980s until the bestselling boys' magazine *Weekly Shônen Jump* sold more than five million copies a week. As manga became a bigger and bigger business, a flourishing fan community began drawing and trading *dôjinshi* (self-published comics and zines) based on their favorite characters. Publishers produced subculture magazines and direct-to-video animation for the fan market, and the fans, aka *otaku,* became Japan's equivalent of hard-core comic book collectors. But for most readers, manga were simply a part of their everyday lives, something they enjoyed casually, like movies or TV.

In the mid-1990s, the Japanese economy went into a recession, which affected manga as well. Sales dipped, and publishers were forced to rely more heavily on licensing, as well as finding new niche markets: video game manga, *pachinko* manga, Boys' Love manga. As everywhere around the world, the rise of the Internet and other new technologies changed reading and buying habits; newsstand magazine sales slumped. Publishers fretted about a rise in *tachiyomi* (reading manga in the store without buying it), *mawashiyomi* (loaning manga to your friends), used-book chains, and all-you-can-read manga cafés. But graphic novel sales remain strong; in 2002, the latest volume of the manga series *One Piece* broke records with an initial print run of 2.52 million copies. In Tokyo today, subway commuters may carry more cell phones than manga magazines, but comics are still more widely read and respected in Japan than anywhere else in the world.

American comics had their day in the sun. In the 1930s, newspaper comic strips such as *Dick Tracy, Little Orphan Annie,* and *Li'l Abner* featured long, melodramatic stories and were read by millions of people of all ages. In 1934, comic books were invented (originally as reprint collections of newspaper strips), and for years they enjoyed incredible popularity, with genres such as crime, Westerns, superheroes, romance, humor, and science fiction. But by 1954, the violent content of horror and crime comics attracted unwelcome attention from a public anxious about juvenile delinquency. *The Seduction of the Innocent,* a bestselling book by psychiatrist Fredric Wertham, claimed that comics exposed children to sex and violence (arguments that would be repeated fifty years later about video games). After a public backlash, the surviving publishers instituted strict self-censorship, limiting comics to superheroes and other "safe" entertainment. Over the next twenty years, comics gradually regained their sophistication, but they never recovered their sales or public image.

Meanwhile, in Japan, manga were booming. As early as the 1970s, a tiny number of outlets imported untranslated manga for American buyers, most of whom were already familiar with Japanese styles from watching early anime such as *Astro Boy* on American TV. With the first appearance of mass-market VCRs in 1975, American anime fandom began to grow. Frederik Schodt's 1983 *Manga! Manga! The World of Japanese Comics* was the first English-language book on the subject. By the early 1980s, manga artists such as Monkey Punch and Osamu Tezuka had appeared to small but enthusiastic groups at American comic book conventions, but almost no manga had been translated, except for a few short stories and English-language vanity projects printed overseas. To the vast majority of Americans, "comics" were full-color superhero stories. Black-and-white, foreign comics were not even on the radar.

Then, in the mid-1980s, American comics stores experienced the "black-and-white boom"—a sudden interest in black-and-white, small-press comics, based on the explosive success of the self-published *Teenage Mutant Ninja Turtles.* In this more receptive environment, two separate companies produced the first serious translated manga in 1987: First Comics with *Lone Wolf and Cub,* and Viz/Eclipse with several titles: *Area 88, Mai the Psychic Girl,* and *The Legend of Kamui.* Founded by Seiji Horibuchi with Satoru Fujii as editor in chief, Viz was the U.S. branch of the Japanese manga publisher Shogakukan. For its first releases Viz formed a partnership with Eclipse Comics, an American small-press comics publisher, whose employee James Hudnall had previously written to Shogakukan encouraging them to enter the American market. Toren Smith, another early manga fan, helped get Viz off the ground, then went on to found Studio Proteus, a major manga translation and localization company. Viz later parted ways with Eclipse, while Smith's Studio Proteus (who did work for both companies) went to Dark Horse Comics and built their manga division.

A BRIEF HISTORY OF MANGA

pre-1960s

In the immediate postwar period, manga are mostly children's adventure stories and family newspaper strips. The vastly influential and prolific Osamu Tezuka tries his hand at science fiction, *shôjo* (girls') manga, and more.

The Wonderful World of Sazae-san (Machiko Hachigawa) (1946) • *Lost World* (Osamu Tezuka) (1948) • *Metropolis* (Osamu Tezuka) (1949) • *Next World* (Osamu Tezuka) (1951) • *Astro Boy* (Osamu Tezuka) (1952) • *Princess Knight* (Osamu Tezuka) (1953) • *Phoenix* (Osamu Tezuka) (1954)

1960s

Anime TV shows are produced for the first time, and manga go wild with speedlines, fast cars, and action heroes. Meanwhile, artists in the *gekiga* (dramatic pictures) movement attempt to create manga for adults: hard-boiled crime stories such as *Golgo 13*, and on the less commercial end of the spectrum, existential dramas such as *The Push Man.*

Cyborg 009 (Shotaro Ishinomori) (1964) • *Speed Racer* (Tatsuo Yoshida) (1967) • *The Genius Bakabon* (Fujio Akatsuka) (1967) • *Lupin III* (Monkey Punch) (1967) • *Wild 7* (Mikiya Mochizuki) (1969) • *The Push Man* (Yoshihiro Tatsumi) (1969) • *Golgo 13* (Takao Saito) (1969)

1970s

The golden age of manga. Working within commercial magazines ostensibly for young readers, artists produce epic space operas, horror stories, historical dramas, romances, and even works on politics and religion. The *gekiga* movement morphs into *seinen* manga, sometimes trashy, over-the-top comics aimed at young men. Sports manga become more and more popular. *Shôjo* manga produce classic works of drama and science fiction, with women rather than men creating the majority of the stories for the first time.

Lone Wolf and Cub (Kazuo Koike & Goseki Kojima) (1970) • *Doraemon: Gadget Cat from the Future* (Fujiko F. Fujio) (1970) • *The Rose of Versailles* (Riyoko Ikeda) (1972) • *Devilman* (Go Nagai) (1972) • *The Drifting Classroom* (Kazuo Umezu) (1972) • *Barefoot Gen* (Keiji Nakazawa) (1972) • *Buddha* (Osamu Tezuka) (1972) • *Black Jack* (Osamu Tezuka) (1973) • *They Were Eleven* (Moto Hagio) (1975) • *Swan* (Kiyoko Ariyoshi) (1976) • *From Eroica with Love* (Yasuko Aoike) (1976) • *To Terra* (Keiko Takemiya) (1977) • *Lum*Urusei Yatsura* (Rumiko Takahashi) (1978)

1980s

Manga become big business, with publishers and editors relying on readers' polls to guide the direction of stories, sometimes at a creative cost. Female artists such as Rumiko Takahashi bring a new style to previously super-macho boys' magazines, while Katsuhiro Otomo and Hayao Miyazaki up the standard of realistic draftsmanship. The *otaku* fan market develops, along with many of the things stereotypically associated with anime: science fiction and mecha stories, RPG-style fantasy, cute big-eyed girls. Anime exerts a growing influence on manga character designs: eyes get bigger, hair gets wilder, bodies get slimmer. As the manga-reading audience ages, *jôsei* (women's) manga become an established market, and *seinen* manga branch out into comics about businessmen, golf, fishing, and other topics of interest to adult men.

Dr. Slump (Akira Toriyama) (1980) • *Maison Ikkoku* (Rumiko Takahashi) (1980) • *Akira* (Katsuhiro Otomo) (1982) • *Nausicaä of the Valley of the Wind* (Hayao Miyazaki) (1982) • *Fist of the North Star* (Tetsuo Hara) (1983) • *Dragon Ball* (Akira Toriyama) (1984) • *Appleseed* (Masamune Shirow) (1985) • *City Hunter* (Tsukasa Hojo) (1985) • *Banana Fish* (Akimi Yoshida) (1985) • *Knights of the Zodiac* (Masami Kurumada) (1986) • *Here Is Greenwood* (Yukie Nasu) (1986) • *Ranma ½* (Rumiko Takahashi) (1987) • *JoJo's Bizarre Adventure* (Hirohiko Araki) (1987) • *Please Save My Earth* (Saki Hiwatari) (1987) • *Short Program* (Mitsuru Adachi) (1988) • *Berserk* (Kentaro Miura) (1989) • *Even a Monkey Can Draw Manga* (Kentaro Takekuma & Koji Aihara) (1989)

1990s

After peaking in 1995, manga magazine sales begin to drop. In the same year, the critically acclaimed anime TV series *Neon Genesis Evangelion* increases mainstream awareness of *otaku,* giving nerdiness a certain hipster appeal. Although *dôjinshi* (fan-produced comics) are technically illegal, their audience booms, and major publishers increasingly scout *dôjinshi* artists for new talent. Boys' Love (*shônen ai*) magazines, featuring idealized guy-guy romances, are the latest craze with female readers.

Slam Dunk (Takehiko Inoue) (1990) • *The Walking Man* (Jiro Taniguchi) (1990) • *Boys over Flowers* (Yoko Kamio) (1992) • *Sailor Moon* (Naoko Takeuchi) (1992) • *Fushigi Yugi* (Yuu Watase) (1992) • *Black & White* (Taiyo Matsumoto) (1993) • *Fake* (Sanami Matoh) (1994) • *Rurouni Kenshin* (Nobuhiro Watsuki) (1994) • *Red River* (Chie Shinohara) (1995) • *Happy Mania* (Moyoco Anno) (1995) • *Cardcaptor Sakura* (CLAMP) (1996) • *One Piece* (Eiichiro Oda) (1997) • *GTO* (Tohru Fujisawa) (1997) • *Parasyte* (Hitoshi Iwaaki) (1997) • *Love Hina* (Ken Akamatsu) (1998) • *Pure Trance* (Junko Mizuno) (1998) • *Fruits Basket* (Natsuki Takaya) (1999) • *Naruto* (Masashi Kishimoto) (1999)

2000s

The manga market continues to fragment into subcultures, although hit graphic novels still sell in the millions. Classic series such as *Fist of the North Star, Kinnikuman,* and *Knights of the Zodiac* are revived as nostalgic spin-offs for aging fans. Gothic fashion provides new visuals and dark themes. The spirit of *kashibonya* (pay libraries) is reborn in the growing trend of manga cafés, where customers can read all they want for an hourly fee. As the North American manga market grows, large publishers think more and more in global terms, while some think outside of print altogether and begin digitizing their comics to distribute through new media.

Hot Gimmick (Miki Aihara) (2000) • *The Wallflower* (Tomoko Hayakawa) (2000) • *Nodame Cantabile* (Tomoko Ninomiya) (2001) • *Monokuro Kinderbook* (Kan Takahama) (2001) • *Cromartie High School* (Eiji Nonaka) (2001) • *Nana* (Ai Yazawa) (2002) • *Fullmetal Alchemist* (Hiromu Arakawa) (2002) • *Death Note* (Tsugumi Ohba & Takeshi Obata) (2005)

The way things used to be: the American comic market of the 1990s, as depicted in Tomoyuki Saito's *Dame Dame Saito Nikki.*

For years, Viz and Dark Horse were America's two largest manga publishers. Several other companies launched small manga lines, including Antarctic Press, Studio Ironcat, and Central Park Media. In the mid-1990s, the American comic market entered a slump, which hit superhero publishers hardest. Manga got a proportionally larger slice of a smaller pie. However, it still played by the rules of the American comics market and was sold mostly in specialty comics stores. Manga were printed left to right, in the thin pamphlet format of American comics, and only later (if at all) collected as graphic novels. Publishers experimented with colorization and even "collectible variant covers" to get attention from a dwindling audience of American comics readers. Since those readers were mostly male, virtually all translations were of *shônen* (boys') or *seinen* (men's) manga.

Then came *Sailor Moon.* The anime TV series was not a hit when it came to America in 1995, but it developed a passionate subculture of female fans. In 1997 the original manga was translated, along with several other titles, in the English manga anthology magazine *MixxZine.* The brainchild of former lawyer and Web designer Stuart Levy, *MixxZine* attempted to break out to non–comics readers (the first issues referred to manga as "motionless picture entertainment" in order to avoid the stigma associated with "comics"). The magazine lasted only a few years, but the *Sailor Moon* graphic novels were a hit, demonstrating that *shôjo* (girls') manga could succeed in America. Viz and other companies started their own *shôjo* lines, but Mixx Entertainment dominated the market for years under their new name, Tokyopop.

The manga market grew rapidly, pushed along by the growing popularity of anime and Japanese video games, but soon was standing on its own feet. Using scanners and the Internet, manga fans distributed unlicensed "scanslations," the same way that anime fans had copied videotapes ten years before. In 2002 two Japanese publishers launched major magazines in the United States: Gutsoon Entertainment with the short-lived weekly anthology *Raijin Comics,* and Shueisha with

Founded by artists and editors who defected from Enix in 2002, Ichijinsha's *Comic Zero-Sum* and Mag Garden's *Comic Blade* feature a mix of *shôjo* and *shônen* styles.

the official English version of their boys' magazine *Weekly Shônen Jump*. To bring *Weekly Shônen Jump* to America (as simply *Shonen Jump*), Shueisha partnered with Viz, which was now connected to two of Japan's three largest manga publishers. In 2004, the third major publisher, Kodansha, stepped in, partnering with science fiction publisher Del Rey. More American manga publishers sprang up, publishing titles from small and mid-sized Japanese manga companies.

Today most bookstores have manga sections, and in 2005 the pop culture retailers Web site ICv2 estimated the size of the American manga market at between $155 million and $180 million. Manga dominate the graphic novel bestseller list and frequently appear in the weekly lists of bestselling young-adult fiction. Their success has paved the way for Korean *manhwa* and Chinese *manhua* as well as a growing number of manga-influenced American comics. The very alienness that once turned away readers—the stylistic differences, the right-to-left format—is part of the appeal. For years, America has exported its movies, TV, and pop culture to Japanese audiences. Now the tables have turned—America is part of the manga world.

WHAT MAKES MANGA DIFFERENT

So why are manga so popular, anyway? Looking for answers, people have pointed to Japan's high literacy rate, the relatively late introduction of TV, and in the past the large number of commuters in cities such as Tokyo, who used to read manga magazines on the train. (In recent years, cell phones and handheld video games have eaten up people's commute time, and now readers are more likely simply to buy their favorite graphic novels at the store.) The true answer is as much about publishing smarts as it is about artistic techniques.

Two Facts About Manga

1. Manga are stories. Long stories. With endings.

Outside of the small presses, the American comics market isn't about stories; it's about franchises. The classic superhero comics, from *Superman* to *Spider-Man,* have beginnings but no endings; they focus on one-shots, collectibles, and novelty items; they are owned by corporations and designed to be reinvented endlessly by "new creative teams."

By contrast, while not many manga are as tightly plotted as novels, they have at least the dramatic cohesiveness of long-running TV shows. In a typical manga, the first chapter is something like a pilot episode, which establishes the basic premise and the main character. If the story is a flop, it may end hastily, but if it is a hit, the author is invited (or pressured) to keep it going until the intended ending (or until readers grow sick of it). Thus, the most popular, and some of the best, manga tend to be the longest. Popular manga often run for ten or more volumes. *Dragon Ball/ Dragon Ball Z* (forty-two volumes total) and *Ranma ½* (thirty-eight volumes) are among the longest series that have been translated, but they don't have anything on *Kochira Katsushika-ku Kameari Kôen-mae Hashutsujo* ("This Is the Police Station in Front of Kameari Park in Katsushika Ward"), an untranslated comedy series that celebrated its 150th volume in 2006. (A pure sitcom rather than a story manga, *KochiKame* is a bit of an anomaly, but many story manga have run fifty volumes or more.)

Sometimes it's clear when manga have run past their expiration date, but other manga manage to keep it together for their entire run. How can manga *be* so long? Don't readers get tired of it? The typical Japanese reader skims a manga page in three seconds, and given such furious speed, most manga focus on quick, cinematic storytelling, as pioneered by Osamu Tezuka in the 1940s and 1950s. By contrast, the classic American comics of the same period are dense, text-heavy stories rarely more than eight pages in length. At some point, American comics chose fancy production values and detailed draftsmanship, while Japanese comics chose cliff-hanger stories and cheap black-and-white printing. There are exceptions, such as Katsuya Terada and Akihiro Yamada, but they're not the rule.

2. The artist is more important than the property.

Most manga artists, except for those doing spin-offs of existing games, novels, and anime, own at least part of the copyright to their work. This stands in stark contrast to American comics, which until the 1990s were almost totally dominated by corporate-owned properties that viewed artists as interchangeable cogs. (*Blade, Spider-Man,* and *X-Men* were all created as works for hire.) Manga artists occasionally switch publishers, as when *Weekly Shônen Jump* artists left to form *Comic Bunch* (known in America as *Raijin Comics*), or when numerous Enix artists left the company in 2002, forming new magazines such as *Comic Blade.* (They took their manga series with them, but for copyright reasons they had to change the names slightly.)

Japanese publishers are besieged by applications from manga artists, but not just anyone will do. To find the best, publishers run new-talent contests, often printing the winning entries in *zôkan* (special editions) of their magazines. Other artists become famous through *dôjinshi* (self-published comics) and are later picked up professionally. When an artist is selected, he or she is assigned an editor, who oversees the artist's work and frequently steers it in a more commercial direction. In the 1980s, editors started taking a heavier hand in manga production, and in the higher-selling magazines, they have major input regarding plots. But it is almost unheard of for a manga artist to be dropped from the series he or she created and replaced with somebody else.

Manga artists work under rigorous schedules. A typical weekly title is twenty pages, or a stunning eighty pages a month. Some artists draw more than one story at a time. In the artist's notes for *YuYu Hakusho,* a weekly manga, Yoshihiro Togashi calculates how much free time he has, based on a formula of four hours per page (not counting time spent scripting) and five hours of sleep per night. He comes to the conclusion that he has nineteen free hours per week ("subtract time spent for eating, bathing, biological functions, and other necessities, and I'd only be left with three to four hours"). Some manga artists go days without sleep to meet their deadlines, and burnout horror stories abound. In the 1990s, the magazine *Quick Japan* ran a series of stories about manga artists who had gone crazy as a result of their work.

To manage their workload, most manga artists employ multiple assistants, who lay down screentone (the black-and-white dot patterns used in manga), gather reference materials, draw backgrounds and crowd scenes, help with the inking and computer effects (if any), and generally do whatever the artist asks them to. Unlike in American comic books (but like many American newspaper comic strips), there is no shame in using assistants; most artists do not credit their assistants, but some do, and some even allow them to show off their own work in the extra pages of their graphic novels. The system serves as a sort of mentorship, allowing aspiring artists to practice the skills they need to go pro. Some artists, such as Takao Saito, have vast studios with dozens of assistants. Others do not; Akira Toriyama lived in his parents' house while drawing the megahit *Dr. Slump,* and Mihona Fujii, artist of *Gals!,* used her mother as her primary assistant.

A few manga artists create "art for art's sake," whether in self-published *dôjinshi* or in underground magazines such as *Ax* and the now-defunct *Garo.* But for most creators, manga is both an art and a business: a mass medium that, unlike TV or movies, can be created by one person with the most basic tools. While the art shines through, the business finds new ways to thrive; many publishers are now experimenting with online manga, e-books, and other new media.

PUBLISHERS, MAGAZINES, AND GRAPHIC NOVELS

The majority of manga are printed by four Tokyo-based publishers: Kodansha, Shueisha, Shogakukan, and Hakusensha. Midsized publishers include Akita Shoten, MediaWorks, Square Enix (better known for their video games), Kadokawa Shoten, Ohzora Shuppan, Futabasha, and Shônen Gahosha. A vast number of smaller publishers exist as well, often focusing on niche markets such as sex comics and so-called Boys' Love manga for girls.

Although reading habits are changing, most manga are still published in thick magazines containing anywhere from ten to forty different stories. Magazines are aimed at a particular gender and age group, and although they use many different artists, they often have a house style or theme. Some stories are self-contained, but most continue from issue to issue. Weekly and biweekly magazines are about 450 pages and cost 250–300 yen (about $3–$4). Monthly magazines and zôkan (special editions) range in size and price, all the way up to 600–700 yen and a whopping 800–1,000 pages. (In 2006, the typical American comic book cost $2 for 32 pages.)

Although almost all manga are printed in black and white, occasionally the first few pages of a chapter are printed in color, as a bonus to readers. These pages are usually reprinted in black and white when the story is collected as a graphic novel. Many magazines have some non-manga content, such as columns by the artists or guest writers, news articles, celebrity interviews, or promotions for upcoming books, movies, anime, and video games. Most magazines have prizes and giveaways—whether the prizes are Louis Vuitton bags (in *Young You,* a magazine aimed at college-age and twentysomething women) or *Yu-Gi-Oh!* cards (in the boys' magazine *Weekly Shônen Jump*).

After being serialized in magazines, individual manga are reprinted as graphic novels. If you wouldn't want to pay for a whole magazine just to read your one favorite manga, you're not alone; in 2005 in Japan, the total amount of graphic novel sales exceeded manga magazine sales for the first time. *Tankôbon* (usually called "graphic novels" in English) cost about 400 yen and contain about 184 pages of a single story. A few years after the *tankôbon* comes out, really popular series are reprinted as teeny *bunkoban* (pocket editions) or thick *kanzenban* (perfect editions) of 300 pages or more. Most translated manga are printed in a format close to *tankôbon*.

---

* As of April 2007, $1 = 118 yen

THE FOUR MANGA DEMOGRAPHICS

Almost all manga magazines (and the stories inside them) are clearly aimed at either men or women. Age groups are sometimes unclear, but the gender difference is right there on the cover and title. (In magazines aimed at *otaku* [hard-core fans], it's harder to tell: that cute girl on the cover of *Asuka* might be the reader's stand-in, while that cute girl on the cover of *Dengeki Daioh* is more likely the reader's fantasy.)

To Americans, this gender gap may seem old-fashioned. But although few American TV shows would openly label themselves "a boys' show" or "a girls' show," advertisers know the difference, and manga publishers are merely being open about their target audience. (Superhero comics, after all, have unofficially been a boys' club for decades.) The few manga magazines that intentionally cross the gender line, such as *Wings* and the short-lived *Duo* in the 1980s, tend to attract mostly female readers and ultimately become *shôjo* manga. However, the verdict is still out on recent gender-blurring magazines such as *Comic Zero-Sum* and *Comic Blade,* not to mention the androgynous *shôjo* fantasy magazine *Asuka*. In any case, the most popular manga, such as *Weekly Shônen Jump* and Ai Yazawa's manga *Nana* (2002), are read by both genders.

Shônen (Boys' Manga) (少年)

Aimed at boys from early elementary school to their late teens (it varies depending on the magazine), *shônen* manga spill over with action, sports, and battle scenes. Science fiction and fantasy elements are also common. The stories are sometimes formulaic, but the bestselling magazines, *Weekly Shônen Jump* and *Weekly Shônen Magazine*, sell more than two million copies per week.

Typical Shônen *Magazines:*
Dengeki Daioh ("Electric Shock Great King") · *Shônen Ace* · *Shônen Champion* · *Monthly Shônen Gangan* · *Shônen Jump* · *Shônen Sunday*

Shôjo (Girls' Manga) (少女)

The most popular subjects of *shôjo* manga are romance, comedy, and drama, often all three in the same story. Styles range from lighthearted magazines for elementary school students (*Nakayoshi, ChuChu*) to racy magazines for teenagers (*Shôjo Comic, Cheese, Cookie*) to more fantasy-oriented publications (*Wings, Asuka*). Female readers also consume a number of specialty magazines featuring mystery, horror, and Boys' Love stories.

Typical Shôjo *Magazines:*
Bessatsu Friend • *Ciao* • *Cookie* • *Hana to Yume* ("Flowers and Dreams") • *LaLa* •
Margaret • *Nakayoshi* ("Pals") • *Princess* • *Ribon* ("Ribbon")

Seinen (Men's Manga) (青年)

Seinen means "young man," but the term describes all manga aimed at older male
readers, from the respectable *Big Comic* series (read mostly by men from their twenties to middle age) to the trashy, sexy "young" magazines (aimed at older high
school boys and college-age men). Business, crime, and the occasional political
drama; historical and military adventures; and the occasional genre story give *seinen*
manga great highs and lows.

Typical Seinen *Magazines:*
Big Comic Spirits • *Business Jump* • *Manga Action* • *Ultra Jump* • *Young Animal* • *Young
Jump* • *Young King Ours*

Jôsei (Women's Manga) (女性)

For college-age to middle-aged women, *jôsei* manga deal mostly with work, family,
and romance. Outwardly the most sedate and down-to-earth of all manga, they
feature some of the most sophisticated writing. The subgenre of "ladies' comics"
(*redicomi*) features explicit sex stories for women.

Typical Jôsei *Magazines:*
Be Love • *Chorus* • *Dessert* • *Feel Young* • *Flowers* • *Kiss* • *Office You* • *Silky* • *Young You*

WHAT'S NOT IN THIS BOOK

Manga: The Complete Guide catalogs all the Japanese comics available in English at
the time of publication (early 2007). With a few exceptions, the book includes only
titles that were printed in Japan prior to their English-language release. Titles that
are not listed include:

- *Anime comics (aka film comics, Ani-Manga, Cine-Manga, or Anime Manga).* Anime
  comics are spin-offs of popular anime: color comics made by taking anime
  stills and positioning them like comic panels with sound effects and dialogue.
  For many years they were considered an easy way to appeal to Americans'
  preference for color comics over black-and-white ones, but now they are
  mostly sold for their own right. Although the process of arranging the panels
  and adding the sound effects requires some skill, anime comics are not truly
  an original work and as such are not discussed here.

Examples of the four types of manga (clockwise from upper left): Kodansha's *Monthly Shônen Magazine* (*shônen*), Kodansha's *Bessatsu Friend* (*shôjo*), Shueisha's *You* (*jôsei*), and Kodansha's *Evening* (*seinen*)

- *Korean comics* (manhwa). Many Korean comics are heavily influenced by Japanese manga, to the point that they are hard to tell apart with a casual glance. The first major *manhwa* series published in America was *Redmoon* by the now-defunct ComicsOne in 2001, but today many companies publish *manhwa,* including CPM, Tokyopop, Dark Horse Comics, Infinity Studios, Netcomics, and Ice Kunion, a joint venture by three major Korean publishers. Translated *manhwa* range from horror to action to comedy, both boys' and girls' titles, including *yaoi manhwa* (mostly published in English by DramaQueen). Since the Korean language reads left to right (unlike Chinese and Japanese), *manhwa* are printed left to right in the same format as English books. They are grouped with manga at most bookstores.

- *Chinese comics* (manhua). Chinese comics, mostly produced in Taiwan and Hong Kong, come from a different artistic tradition than manga. Most translated Chinese comics are full-color martial arts stories more similar to American comics, with legendary, fantasy, and science fiction themes, usually printed at American comic book size to show the extreme detail of the artwork. *Manhua* aimed at female readers are rarely translated, with a few exceptions such as I-Huan's *Real Fake Princess,* which is printed in black and white in manga-sized graphic novels. *Manhua* have been published in English since the 1980s, and today DrMaster and HK Comics Ltd. are America's primary Chinese comics publishers.

- *OEL (original English-language) manga, OGM (original global manga), or other comics by American, Canadian, South American, and European authors.* Although manga-influenced comics have been a major force in America only since 2003 or so, a small number of American comic artists have been aware of Japanese comics for a long time, and manga-style comics have been a recognized niche market since the 1980s. In recent years, companies such as Tokyopop and Seven Seas have strongly promoted original manga. Manga-influenced comics by Western authors are frequently sold alongside manga, although in most bookstores the decision is primarily a matter of format and packaging (i.e., whether the book is printed in the compact manga size or the traditionally larger American comic format). Rather than draw an arbitrary line between who's "truly" manga-influenced and who's not, this book includes only comics drawn in Japan for the Japanese market, as well as a few collaborations between Japanese and American artists.

- *Translated manga anthology magazines.* Although almost all manga are originally printed in Japanese anthology magazines, they are typically released in English directly as graphic novels. Translated anthology magazines do exist, but the purpose of this book is to discuss the work of the artists, not how they were packaged in America. Therefore, magazines such as *Shojo Beat, Raijin Comics, Manga Vizion, Game On! USA, Smile, Animerica Extra, Super Manga*

Blast!, Pulp, Newtype USA, Robot, Mangajin, and the English edition of *Shonen Jump* are not listed, although the manga that were printed in them may be.

- *Short, one-shot manga printed in Western comics anthologies.* Many short comics by Japanese artists have been published in American magazines and books, such as the Go Nagai story in Marvel's *Epic Illustrated* #18 (1980), or the very short Katsuhiro Otomo story in DC's *Batman Black & White* #4 (1996). Due to the shortness and obscurity of these works, only a few major collections have been included, such as Fanfare/Ponent Mon's *Japan as Viewed by 17 Creators.*
- *Light novels.* Young-adult novels generally printed at the same size as manga graphic novels, often with manga-style illustrations, "light novels" have been a major force in Japanese publishing since the 1980s. Several American publishers, including Viz, Seven Seas, DMP, Dark Horse, and CMX have translated light novels, including prose spin-offs of popular manga such as *Gravitation* and *Fullmetal Alchemist.* They are often identical to manga on bookstore shelves.
- *Scanslations and other unlicensed manga.* Only officially licensed and translated manga are included, although untranslated manga may be mentioned in the articles.

PARASYTE[1]

Kiseiju, "Parasite/Parasitic Beast"[2] (奇生獣)[3] • Hitoshi Iwaaki[4] • Del Rey (2007–ongoing)[5] • Kodansha (Afternoon, 1990–1995)[6] • 12 volumes[7] • Seinen, Science Fiction, Horror, Action[8] • Unrated/16+ (language, graphic violence, brief nudity)[9]

Wormlike aliens secretly appear on Earth, replacing people's heads and turning them into coldly emotionless cannibals whose heads split open into shape-shifting living weapons. Shin, a high school senior, is a fluke: instead of his head, a Parasyte takes over his left hand, and human and alien develop a wary symbiosis as they fight to protect Shin's friends and family from the new race of predators feeding on human beings. Like a science fiction novel, *Parasyte* takes a fantastic situation and applies realistic human behavior, playing out the logical consequences as humanity copes with the invaders. Iwaaki's writing is more memorable than his art, but his style suits the serious mood of the story better than more exaggerated artwork would. The violence is graphic but not sadistic. Prior to the Del Rey edition, the series was released by Tokyopop from 1997 to 2002.[10]

★★★★[11]

1. Official English title.
2. Japanese phonetic title and literal translation. If the Japanese phonetic title is identical to the English title, it is not included.
3. Japanese kanji/kana title (if available). English subtitles in the Japanese edition (when notably different from the kanji/kana title) and *furigana* double meanings are shown within parentheses. If the original Japanese title is in English, it is not included unless it differs substantially from the English edition title. See Appendix B: The Japanese Language.
4. Artist's name. All artists are listed English style: personal name first, family name last.
5. English-language publisher and date(s) of publication. Dates range from the first volume (or American-style comic issue) to the last volume. In the case of series that went out of print and were rereleased by a new publisher (such as the Viz and Dark Horse editions of *Crying Freeman*), the dates of the most current printing are used. Titles that have been canceled or are on indefinite hiatus—whether due to low sales, the publisher going out of business, or other reasons—are listed as "suspended." Titles that were still running in Japan at the time of publication are listed as "ongoing."
6. Original Japanese publisher, magazine, and date(s) of publication. Publication dates are from the beginning of the magazine serialization to the publication of the last graphic novel of the series (typically a few months after the end of the

magazine serialization). Some manga were published in several different magazines; others were released directly as graphic novels and were not serialized. In a few cases the original publication information is unavailable due to the age and obscurity of the manga.

7. Number of graphic novel volumes. In the case of series that have been reprinted in Japan as *bunkoban* or *kanzenban* editions (about 300+ pages per volume), the number of volumes follows the original *tankôbon* editions (about 184 pages per volume), unless noted. For older series that were printed as American-style saddle-stitched comics and never collected as graphic novels, the number of comic issues is listed. Most comic issues are 24 to 48 pages, so four to seven comics typically equal one graphic novel.

8. Genre. Many different manga genres are described in the accompanying articles.

9. Age rating and objectionable content. The ratings are All Ages, 13+, 16+, and 18+. If the publisher has not provided a suggested age rating, the manga is listed as unrated and *Manga: The Complete Guide* assigns an approximate age rating. For example, "unrated/16+" means the manga has no visible age rating but its content is in line with other titles rated for ages 16 and up. See Appendix A: Age Ratings.

10. Description. The initials of the reviewer (see Writers on page viii) are listed after the review. Reviews without initials are written by Jason Thompson.

11. Ranking from zero to four stars. For titles that were published too late for review, NR appears at the end of the description.

GENERAL MANGA REVIEWS AND TYPES OF MANGA

Yuzo Takada's *3x3 Eyes*

2001 NIGHTS

2001 Yamonogatari, "2001 Nights Stories/Tales of 2001 Nights" (2001夜物語) • Yukinobu Hoshino • Viz (1995–1996) • Futabasha (Monthly Super Action, 1984–1986) • 3 volumes • Seinen, Science Fiction • Unrated/16+ (mild violence, nudity, sexual situations)

This serious, even stodgy science fiction anthology consists of linked stories about the human exploration of space, starting from the space shuttle and the Cold War era, to the far future when humans use technological advances to colonize distant planets. The echoes of Arthur C. Clarke's *2001* are intentional; there's even a joke about HAL. The plots often involve cosmic meditations on future generations, life in the emptiness of space, and God; in one story the Vatican locates original sin among the stars, and announces its opposition to space exploration. Not all of the tales are great, but they gradually form a sort of novel-in-stories, returning full circle for a satisfying ending. Hoshino draws it all in a super-realistic, Western, *gekiga* style, focused on the human body, a bit more Ryoichi Ikegami than Katsuhiro Otomo. The Viz edition was published without numbers: the correct order is *2001 Nights, 2001 Nights: Journey Beyond Tomorrow,* and *2001 Nights: Children of Earth.* ★★★★

3x3 EYES

3x3 Eyes (Sazan Eyes) (3x3 EYESサザンアイズ) • Yuzo Takada • Dark Horse (1995–2004) • Kodansha (Young Magazine Pirate Edition/Young Magazine, 1987–2002) • 8 volumes, suspended (40 volumes in Japan) • Seinen, Occult, Action • Unrated/16+ (mild language, graphic violence, nudity, sexual situations)

Globetrotting pulp horror/action-adventure manga, a minor 1980s classic, midway between *Indiana Jones, Ghostbusters,* and H. P. Lovecraft. Teenage Yakumo dies and is reborn as the unkillable zombie servant of Pai, a cute Chinese girl with a split personality, who is actually one of the last survivors of a race of three-eyed beings from Tibet, immortals with awesome magical powers. Pai's goal is to lose her immortality and become human, but her uniqueness makes her the target of other monsters, not to mention paranormal investigators and half-human cultists, who seek to use her to resurrect the evil god Kaiyan Wang. Working in a light, anime-influenced style (with occasional love comedy), Takada successfully depicts a world where secret cults sacrifice naked virgins in skyscrapers and monster rampages are caught on the evening news by incredulous reporters. The supernatural creatures are original, the cliff-hanger plots are exciting, and the balance of horror and humor is just right, even if Pai's surface personality is your stereotypical "China girl" ditz. The English edition ends abruptly (some additional material was printed in *Super Manga Blast!* magazine but never collected), but it isn't that big a loss; the later Japanese volumes become badly repetitive and succumb to *shônen* manga power escalation. Prior to the 1995 Dark Horse edition, the first volume was released in monthly comics format by Innovation Comics (with the same translation and retouch by Studio Proteus) in 1991. ★★★

888

888 Three-Eight (888スリーエイト) • Kuwata Noriko • DrMaster (2005) • Gentosha (Comic Birz, 2001–ongoing) • 1 volume, suspended (2+ volumes in Japan, ongoing) • Comedy • 13+ (extremely mild sex references)

The Suehiro Detective Agency consists of three young adults: Hisago, the easygoing boss who survives on handouts from his father; Nagi, the secretary; and Shimeki, who looks professional and serious but whose sole purpose in life is to take care of his dog. Business is slow; their biggest cases are meddling with each other's private lives, solving Shimeki's kidnapping, and in one chapter moonlighting as relationship counselors (with a sign taped to their door like Lucy's psychiatric stand in *Peanuts*). Beneath its boring talking-heads exterior, *888* is a witty character-driven office comedy, with the sharp dialogue of a radio play or a newspaper comic strip. The cute *chibi* art makes the characters look as immature as they act.
★★★

A, A'

A-A' • Moto Hagio • Viz (1997) • Akita Shoten/Shogakukan (Princess/Petit Flower, 1981–1984) • 1 volume • Shôjo, Science Fiction • Unrated/16+ (sexual situations)

Moto Hagio is often considered second only to Osamu Tezuka in the annals of manga artists, but very little of her work has been published in English. *A, A'* is, to date, the largest chunk of her work available in official English translation: a one-volume trilogy of stories set in a shared science fiction universe. The connecting thread is the presence of the Unicorns, a rare race of humans genetically engineered for space travel. The Unicorns are technologically gifted but have difficulty with emotion; rather than being cool and collected Mr. Spocks, however, they come across as almost autistic. In the title story (pronounced "A, A-prime"), a Unicorn named Adelade is killed while working on a remote space colony, and a clone, implanted with her memories, is sent to replace her. The second story, "4/4," introduces a telekinetic teenager named Mori, who learns to control the power of his "kaleidoscope eye" through his relationship with a childlike Unicorn girl. In the last and longest story, "X+Y," Mori, now a young adult, meets a Unicorn savant named Tacto, and falls in love with him. Hagio's dense world building is in full effect in these stories, as are some of her signature themes: gender-bending, emotional isolation, and damaged children with strange and complicated family relationships. (SG) ★★★★

ABANDON THE OLD IN TOKYO

Yoshihiro Tatsumi • Drawn & Quarterly (2006) • various magazines (1970) • 1 volume • Gekiga, Drama • Unrated/18+ (language, violence, nudity, sex)

The second in a series of Tatsumi books by Drawn & Quarterly. Like *The Push Man and Other Stories,* these are gloomy tales of life in the big city, starring mute blue-collar everymen and worn-out failures who walk the dark streets of 1970 Japan. The settings—dingy bathrooms, factories, and sewers—are drawn with rich detail, while the protagonists are drawn in a simple style, but without cartoon exaggeration. In the straightforward title story, a garbageman grows resentful of taking care of his aged mother; in "Beloved Monkey," a factory worker uses his pet as a refuge from the outside world; in "The Hole," a man is trapped in a pit by a deformed woman determined to take revenge on the male gender. While this collection is not quite as powerful as *The Push Man*, Tatsumi is a great storyteller and his pessimism is profound. It's hard to imagine that there was a time when manga were so gritty that these stories were published in mainstream publications such as *Weekly Shônen Magazine* (as well as the classic underground magazine *Garo*). ★★★★

ABENOBASHI: MAGICAL SHOPPING ARCADE

Abenobashi Mahô Shotengai, "Abenobashi Magical Shopping Arcade" (アベノ橋魔法☆商店街) • Gainax (creator), Satoru Akahori (story), Ryusei Deguchi (art) • Tokyopop (2004) • Kodansha (Magazine Z, 2001–2002) • 2 volumes • Shônen, Science Fiction, Comedy • 16+ (crude humor, nudity, sexual situations)

Adaptation of the anime series of the same name. A preteen boy and girl, Sasshi and Arumi, are trapped in various parallel worlds centered around the Abenobashi Shopping Arcade, a run-down indoor mall built in the 1950s. They zip between an RPG world, a sci-fi world, a dinosaur world, and other bizarre genre universes, always encountering slightly modified versions of the same Abenobashi shopkeepers and silly characters. Like the anime, *Abenobashi* starts out sentimental but immediately turns into lowbrow slapstick, with enormous naked breasts, penis jokes, and fart jokes made more garish by Deguchi's hyperactive, googly eyed artwork. As it goes on, there's some fun old-school *otaku* in-jokes in the style of Ippongi Bang, but it's a long haul to get there. ★½

ABSOLUTE BOYFRIEND

Zettai Kareshi, "Absolute Boyfriend" (絶対彼氏) • Yuu Watase • Viz (2005–ongoing) • Shogakukan (Shôjo Comic, 2003–2005) • 6 volumes • Shôjo, Romantic Comedy • 16+ (sexual situations)

Riiko Izawa, a teenage girl who lives alone and worries she'll never get a boyfriend, meets a futuristic mail-order salesman and orders a handsome, naked man who is delivered to her apartment in a big cardboard box. Activated by a kiss, Night is indeed the absolute boyfriend: he cooks, beats up bad guys with his super-strength, responds to her emotions, and cheerfully offers to demonstrate his sexual techniques but is equally happy to just snuggle. Unfortunately, Riiko finds herself massively in debt, her female classmates and her handsome next-door neighbor are jealous, and Night has a flaw . . . he falls in love with whoever kisses him, but it's only *permanent* if you have sex. An entertaining romantic comedy, *Absolute Boyfriend* is essentially a gender-reversed version of the typical *shônen* manga robot girl fantasy, with fanservice in the form of shirtless men instead of girls' panties. The art is in Watase's usual precise style. ★★★

ADOLF

Adolf ni Tsugu, "Tell Adolf" (アドルフに告ぐ) • Osamu Tezuka • Viz/Cadence Books (1995–1996) • Bungei Shunjû (Shukan Bunshun, 1983–1985) • 5 volumes • Seinen, Historical Drama • Unrated/18+ (language, violence, nudity, sex)

Adolf was one of Tezuka's last manga, but the first published in English (apart from the brief *Phoenix* excerpt in Frederik Schodt's *Manga! Manga!*). The opening pages introduce it as "the story of three men named Adolf." One is Adolf Kamil, a German Jew raised in Japan in the years leading up to World War II. Another is Kamil's childhood friend Adolf Kaufman, a German-Japanese boy who becomes indoctrinated into the Hitler Youth. The third, Adolf Hitler, is a constant background presence in this bleak and bloody espionage story. Tezuka wrote and drew *Adolf* as an attempt at more serious, adult-oriented manga. As such, *Adolf* isn't entirely successful, tending more toward pulp action and melodrama than naturalistic depictions of life. But as a wartime thriller, it's both exciting and moving. Japan's gradual descent into fascism, based partly on Tezuka's own memories of growing up in

Kobe, is particularly believable and chilling. The five English volumes, published by the now-defunct Viz subsidiary Cadence Books, are, confusingly, given subtitles but not numbered. The correct order: *A Tale of the Twentieth Century, An Exile in Japan, The Half-Aryan, Days of Infamy,* and *1945 and All That Remains.* (SG)　　　★★★★

AD POLICE

AD Police Shûen Toshi, "Dead End City" (AD.PO-LICE終焉都市) • Toshimichi Suzuki (story), Tony Takezaki (art) • Viz (1994) • Bandai (B-Club, 1989–1990) • 1 volume • Science Fiction, Action • Unrated/16+ (violence, language, nudity)

In the mid-twenty-first century, Tokyo has been reconstructed into a rip-off of *Blade Runner:* an urban blight dominated by the secretive Genom corporation and plagued by their renegade experiments, hulking androids named Boomers. This cop-drama prequel to the *AD Police* and *Bubblegum Crisis* anime (two of the more popular OAV series of the early 1990s) combines black humor and science fiction philosophy in a functional plot. Both the art and the story are blatantly in the style of *Akira,* but Takezaki's creepy and technically skilled cyberpunk artwork makes it worthwhile.　　★★★

THE ADVENTURES OF HAMTARO: A HOUSE FOR HAMTARO

Tottoko Hamtarô, "Pitter-Patter Hamtarô" (とっとこハム太郎) • Ritsuko Kawai • Viz (2003) • Shogakukan (Shôgaku Ninensei, 1997) • 1 volume • Pets • All Ages

Midway between a children's book and a manga, this is the original "owning a pet hamster" book that spawned the *Hamtaro* franchise. Unlike the anime series, there aren't any other characters, and Hamtaro doesn't talk; he just looks cute, eats sunflower seeds, and behaves pretty much like a real hamster. There are no dialogue balloons, just narration—the story is meant to be read to children—but the multiple-panel page layouts are similar to *shôjo* manga. The book also includes color pages, info about hamsters, and the sheet music for the Hamtaro song.　　★★★

AFTERSCHOOL NIGHTMARE

Hôkago Hokenshitsu, "Afterschool Clinic" (放課後保健室) • Setona Mizushiro • Go! Comi (2006–ongoing) • Akita Shoten (Princess, 2004–ongoing) • 6+ volumes (ongoing) • Shôjo, Psychological Horror • 16+ (mild language, graphic violence, sexual situations)

Living up to its title, *Afterschool Nightmare* captures feelings of identity loss and cold terror, beginning with a brutal Freudian punch below the belt. Mashiro, a handsome, delicate-featured teenager, has a dark secret: although he considers himself male, he has "the upper body of a man and the lower body of a woman." After "he" menstruates for the first time, he is recruited for a strange dream experiment together with several of his unseen classmates, in which they fight disturbing versions of one another in a surreal dreamworld. Through the shared experiment, Mashiro becomes closer to some of his classmates, but this only brings more shame and anxiety when a relationship threatens to turn sexual. And his classmates have their own psychological problems as well . . . A well-drawn, creepy, surprising series.　　★★★½

A.I. LOVE YOU

A.I. ga Tomaranai!, "Love/I/A.I. Won't Stop!" (A.I.が止まらない!) • Ken Akamatsu • Tokyopop (2004–2005) • Kodansha (Weekly Shônen Magazine/Shônen Magazine Special, 1994–1997) • 8 volumes • Shônen, Science Fiction, Romantic Comedy • 16+ (language, comic violence, partial nudity, sexual situations)

Teenage computer programmer Hitoshi uses his mid-1990s Macintosh to create the ideal woman, who comes to life in a bolt of lightning and accompanies him to school. Saati, the magical A.I. girlfriend, is soon followed out of the computer by a big-sister seductress A.I. and a playful little-sister A.I., and together they fight troublesome computer viruses and explain elementary computer terms. Compared to Ken Akamatsu's later works, *A.I. Love You* both is more conventionally sentimental and lacks his characteristic visual polish; his early art is wretched, and the story starts out as a combination rip-off of *Video Girl Ai, Oh My Goddess!* and *Weird Science.* By volume 4 Akamatsu's genius for pervy slapstick jokes has begun to develop, with scenes such as the one in which Saati is forced to do limbo underneath Hitoshi's body, only to be thunked in the head by his clothed erection. However, it's still an immature work, of most interest to die-hard Akamatsu fans. ★½

AIR GEAR

(エア・ギア) • Oh! Great • Del Rey (2006–ongoing) • Kodansha (Weekly Shônen Magazine, 2002–ongoing) • 15+ volumes (ongoing) • Shônen, Street Action • 16+ (language, crude humor, violence, partial nudity, sexual situations)

After he is humiliated by a rival gang, thirteen-year-old gangbanger Itsuki rises to the next level in street combat: Air Trecks, super-high-tech inline skates, which allow their riders to jump and soar above the rooftops of the city. Soon, he finds himself in a world of bizarre, superpowered street fighters, the Storm Riders, who do battle with skating techniques. Basically a less explicit version of *Tenjho Tenge* with skates, *Air Gear* is an excuse for Oh! Great to do what he does best: draw cool teenagers in cool poses, with occasional undercurrents of sex and sadism. Rape is hinted at (although the dialogue was toned down in the English edition of volume 1), and Itsuki lives with four Storm Rider sisters who provide nippleless shower scenes. Even without the dialogue changes, however, the overall mood is more upbeat than *Tenjho Tenge,* focusing on the thrill of flight and the spirit of competition, despite all the weird freaks creeping and crawling around the story. Like many series in *Weekly Shônen Magazine,* the art is almost *too* polished and screentoned and crowded with extraneous background detail. (But check out the excellent graffiti-style Japanese sound effects.) ★★★

Air Gear by Oh! Great

AISHITERUZE BABY

Aishiteruze Baby, "I'm in Love with Ya, Baby" (愛してるぜベイベ) • Yoko Maki • Viz (2006–2007) • Shueisha (Ribon, 2002–2005) • 7 volumes • Shôjo, Romantic Drama • 13+ (violence, child abuse)

Kippei is a Casanova in the making, preferring to spend his time on the school roof making out rather than languishing in the classroom. But everything changes when his little cousin Yuzuyu comes to live with his family and he finds himself stuck as her primary caretaker. His exasperation quickly disappears as he learns to take pride in preparing Yuzuyu's lunch and joy in playing with her in the sandbox, and as he learns how to cherish someone, this new insight brings him closer to Kokoro, the girl he thought was forever out of reach. While *Aishiteruze Baby* has plenty of heartfelt scenes, it isn't sappy—in fact, many of the characters suffer from abuse of some kind, giving the story a dark undertone. The art is adorable without being mawkish. (HS) ★★★

AI YORI AOSHI

Ai yori Aoshi, "Bluer than Indigo" (藍より青し) • Kou Fumizuki • Tokyopop (2004–2007) • Hakusensha (Young Animal, 1998–2005) • 17 volumes • Seinen, Romantic Comedy • 16+ (mild violence, nudity, sexual situations)

College student Kaoru's life is turned upside down by the sudden appearance of his childhood fiancée, Aoi, a kimono-wearing, ultra-traditional Japanese girl who has lived the last eighteen years wanting only to be with him. Unfortunately, if he wants to marry her, he must reconcile with his abusive, ultrawealthy family. Apart from the weepy abuse story line, *Ai Yori Aoshi* is a stereotypically sexist wife fantasy stripped down almost to the point of having only two characters and no plot whatsoever. Aoi, who wants only to cook and clean and be a bride and mother, is described as "the epitome of Yamato Nadesico, the model of a Japanese woman." From volume 2 onward a few competing female characters are introduced, but the attempt at a harem manga is half-hearted at best; the characters quickly fall into subordinate roles of housekeepers and maids in Aoi and Kaoru's platonic household. The manga reads easily, partly due to the fact that almost nothing happens except for breast shots and the periodic reaffirmation of the female characters' (and by extension, the male reader's) neediness. The soft, anime-style, heart-shaped faces resemble the art of Kosuke Fujishima (*Oh My Goddess!*). ★

AKIRA

(アキラ) • Katsuhiro Otomo • Dark Horse (2000–2002) • Kodansha (Young Magazine, 1982–1990) • 6 volumes • Seinen, Science Fiction, Action • Unrated/16+ (language, graphic violence, nudity)

In the megalopolis of Neo-Tokyo, thirty-eight years after World War III, the government, military, and revolutionaries struggle for power behind the scenes. But two random factors soon trigger a disaster: a teenage biker gang and a secret psychic research program, whose ultimate success was sealed away forever under the name Akira. One of the most important manga of the 1980s, *Akira* influenced thousands of science fiction manga and anime with its dark urban future, its detailed renderings of cities and machinery (co-opted by lesser artists into the screentone cutout backgrounds of today), and its ever-escalating cycle of destruction. (The realistic, three-dimensional look of Otomo's characters was also trendsetting.) Prior to *Akira,* Otomo's most significant work was the untranslated collection of New York stories *Sayonara Nippon,* and perhaps owing to this experience in urban realism, *Akira* starts out with a realistically dense web of street crime, coups, and conflicting factions. When things finally get crazy, though, they get *crazy,* culminating in a possibly dragged-out conclusion of endless shocking battles and explosions. The visual similarity to the French artist Moebius, who also did a few stories about futuristic wild-goose chases, is strong, but Moebius never drew any stories of this length. Sadly, Otomo has never again produced another manga work of this scale—but he probably realized that he didn't need to draw another *Akira,* since everyone else was going to try to draw it for him. Prior to the Dark Horse edition, the series was released in a colorized edition by Marvel's Epic line from 1988 to 1995. ★★★★

AKKO-CHAN'S GOT A SECRET!

Himitsu no Akko-chan, "Secret Akko-chan" (ひみつのアッコちゃん) • Fujio Akatsuka • Kodansha International (2001) • Shueisha (Ribon, 1962) • 2 volumes • Shôjo, Magical Girl, Comedy • Unrated/All Ages (mild crude humor)

Akko-chan's Got a Secret! is most fondly remembered for its spin-off TV show, one of the first examples of "magical girl" anime. Akko-chan, whose mom draws picture books, is a fifth-grade girl who is first seen brushing her hair and looking into her mirror ("A mirror is a girl's greatest treasure!"). In thanks for taking such good care of her mirror, the Queen of Mirrorland gives her a magic compact, which she can use to turn herself into anyone she wants. As the plot summary indicates, *Akko-chan's Got a Secret!*

is definitely a product of an earlier age, but the episodic stories (written by male gag manga artist Fujio Akatsuka) are spirited and slapstick; Akko mostly uses her mirror to play pranks. The primitive 1960s *shôjo* art features eyes like big crude buttons. ★★½

ALICE 19TH

(アリス19th) • Yuu Watase • Viz (2003–2004) • Shogakukan (Shôjo Comic, 2001–2003) • 7 volumes • Shôjo, Fantasy, Romance • 16+ (mild language, nudity, violence)

Timid Alice lived in the shadow of her older sister, Mayura, until one day a strange bunny-eared girl initiates her in the Lotis Words, a form of magic secretly practiced by "neo-masters" around the globe. But Alice and Mayura both love the same man, the reserved upperclassman Kyô, and their romantic rivalry triggers the ultimate battle with the forces of Mara, the dark side of magic. Similar in outline to *Cardcaptor Sakura* (the heroines even look alike), *Alice 19th* has one interesting idea: the concept of the "inner heart," a sort of demon-haunted collective unconscious or virtual reality. However, the magical element is ultimately underdeveloped, even for a series for a younger audience; the Lotis words have neither a visual style nor an internal logic that the reader can follow. As usual, Watase does an adequate job of establishing the human relationships, and the art is functional, but compared to her other manga, the story is disappointingly clichéd. ★½

ALICE IN LOSTWORLD

Shuzilow Ha • Radio Comix (2000–2001) • Dôjinshi • 4 issues • Science Fiction, Action • Unrated/16+ (violence, nudity, mild sexual situations)

Lieutenant Alice and her all-female platoon live in a futuristic city, when not on missions fighting mysterious humanoid aliens. The story is heavy on exposition, which overexplains the simple plot, and the art is a crude imitation of Masamune Shirow, from the insect-like vehicles to the gun-wielding girls in skintight crotch-hugging suits. ★½

ALICHINO

(アリキーノ) • Kouyu Shurei • Tokyopop (2005) • Home-sha (Eyes, 1998–2001) • 3 volumes, suspended • Shôjo, Gothic, Fantasy • 13+ (mild language, violence, brief partial nudity)

"Their beauty is an illusion . . . a mere mask . . . hiding a most hideous and twisted face." In a vague fantasy setting, human beings are the prey of Alichino, attractive evil beings who can grant wishes, take the form of animals, and eat human souls. Their only weakness is also the thing they most desire: Tsugiri, a handsome, depressive young man whose soul is so pure that he can kill an Alichino, or provide one with a most delicious meal. Incredibly detailed, realistic artwork makes *Alichino* worth reading just for the visual polish; Shurei's art lacks outright monsters but abounds with gorgeous *bishônen* and Gothic Lolita women with sad, doll-like eyes. The plot is dominated by the angst-ridden relationships between Tsugiri and the Alichino, some of whom want to protect him, while others want to eat him. As of April 2007, the series is on hold in both the United States and Japan, with Shurei supposedly working on the fourth and final volume. ★★★

ALIEN NINE

(エイリアン9) • Hitoshi Tomizawa • CPM (2003) • Akita Shoten (Young Champion, 1998–1999) • 3 volumes • Seinen, Science Fiction, Horror • 16+ (graphic violence, partial nudity)

In the near future, grotesque aliens land on Earth every day. At one particular school, three inline-skating sixth-grade girls are chosen to become Alien Fighters, and forced to merge with symbiotic froglike aliens who squat on their heads like helmets and fight the silent invaders with dozens of drill-shaped tentacles. Not nearly as lighthearted as the cover art suggests, *Alien Nine* is a tale of posthuman transformation, similar to science fiction novels such as *Lilith's Brood* or *Childhood's End* on an elementary school scale. Exposition and dialogue are minimal. Full of slime and mutating bodies, the story comes across mainly as a creepy metaphor for puberty, padded out with wordless battle scenes where it's often not clear what's at stake. The characters are too cute for their own good; their identical, virtually noseless faces make them hard to tell apart. ★★★

ALIEN NINE: EMULATORS

(エイリアン9・エミュレイターズ) • Hitoshi Tomizawa • CPM (2003) • Akita Shoten (Champion Red/Young Champion/Young Champion AIR, 2003) • 1 volume • Seinen, Science Fiction, Horror • 16+ (partial nudity, graphic violence)

Unnecessary sequel to *Alien Nine,* following the original characters to junior high and introducing a new female character. Strange biological transformations take place, and increasingly strange aliens appear, but as in the original, it's often hard to tell what's going on beyond the surface of weird imagery and action violence. ★★

ALIVE

Alive Saishû Shinkateki Shônen, "Alive: Final Evolutionary Boy" (アライブ一最終進化的少年一) • Tadashi Kawashima (original story), Toka Adachi (art) • Del Rey (2007–ongoing) • Kodansha (Weekly Shônen Magazine, 2003–ongoing) • 9+ volumes (ongoing) • Shônen, Postapocalyptic Science Fiction • 16+

A mysterious virus causes a global outbreak of spontaneous suicides and ushers in a nightmarish week of mass death. In the wake of the epidemic, a handful of teenagers find themselves developing superhuman abilities, and try to understand why they were spared. (MS) NR

THE ALL-NEW TENCHI MUYÔ!

Shin • Tenchi Muyô! Ryo-Oh-Ki, "New • No Need for Tenchi!/Ryo-Oh-Ki" (新・天地無用!魎皇鬼) • Hitoshi Okuda • Viz (2002–2007) • Kadokawa Shoten (Dragon Junior/Dragon Age, 2001–2006) • 10 volumes • Shônen, Science Fiction, Romantic Comedy • 13+ (violence, nudity, sexual situations)

The *No Need for Tenchi!* manga series ended in 2000, only to be replaced almost immediately by this sequel, written and drawn by the same artist. The only noticeable differ-

ence is that the stories tend to be shorter and more comedy-oriented, with fewer of the space-opera adventures that dominated the previous series. The focus on romantic comedy drives home the impact of *Tenchi Muyô!* as fanboy wish fulfillment in its purest form: the hero has cosmic superpowers but is otherwise a perfect blank onto which the reader can project himself, the women represent the basic spectrum of manga dream-girl types (the sexy tough gal, the prim aristocrat, the innocent prepubescent), and they're all uniformly obsessed with making Tenchi happy and being his perfect mate. Okuda ends with a long, dramatic story line built on the events in the original *Tenchi Muyô* OAV, and leaves the franchise more than open to another sequel. The English edition censors nudity. (CT) ★★½

ALL PURPOSE CULTURAL CAT GIRL NUKU NUKU

Bannô Bunka Neko Musume, "All Purpose Cultural Cat Girl" (万能文化猫娘) • Yuzo Takada, Yuji Moriyama • ADV (2004) • Futabasha (Weekly Manga Action, 1990, 1998) • 1 volume • Science Fiction, Comedy • 13+ (mild violence, mild suggestive situations)

Short comedy manga primarily known as the basis—or, perhaps more accurately, the pitch—for the more manic anime of the same name. When a mad scientist and his young son Ryunosuke find a dying cat, they transfer its brain into a teenage female android chassis, creating Ryunosuke's ditzy, mouse-chasing big sister Atsuko "Nuku Nuku" Natsume. The 1990 manga is vapid and plotless, scarcely comprehensible to someone who hasn't seen the anime, despite being made beforehand. The graphic novel actually consists of only 40 pages of black-and-white manga; the other 56 pages consist of a set of postcards and "Cat Girl Nuku Nuku Phase 3½—Nuku Nuku Goes to Space," an original 1998 color film comic by OAV animator/character designer Yuji Moriyama. The film comic is more polished and slightly more interesting than Takada's original story. ★

THE AMAZING ADVENTURES OF PROFESSOR JONES

Atelier Lana (Kazuaki Ishida) • Antarctic Press (1996) • 2 issues • Comedy, Adventure • 18+ (cartoon violence, nudity)

An innocuous, old-school cross of 1980s gag manga and adventure stories in the style of *Uncle Scrooge*. Professor Jones, an absent-minded archaeologist, travels the globe with his assistant Junichi, their stereotypical Chinese guide Chan, and a cute, bat-winged demoness discovered in one of his digs. They encounter pop culture references, random historical information, and nefarious traps; although the series is rated "For Mature Audiences," there's nothing more offensive than a little cartoon nudity. ★★½

ANDROMEDA STORIES

(アンドロメダ・ストーリーズ) • Ryu Mitsuse (story), Keiko Takemiya (art) • Vertical (2007) • Asahi Sonorama (Manga Shônen, 1980–1981) • 2 volumes • Shôjo, Science Fiction, Drama • Not Rated Yet

Courtly science fiction saga, involving princes and princesses on a planet two million light-years away from Earth. Written by classic Japanese science fiction author Ryu Mitsuse and drawn by classic *shôjo* artist Takemiya. NR

ANGEL: See *Erica Sakurazawa: Angel*

ANGEL/DUST

(エンジェル／ダスト) • Aoi Nanase • ADV (2005) • Kadokawa Shoten (Newtype, 2001) • 1 volume • Science Fiction, Fantasy • 13+ (mild violence, mildly suggestive outfits)

A shy, glasses-wearing schoolgirl finds herself psychically linked to a "bioroid emulate," a winged angel girl in a skintight outfit who suddenly falls out of the sky. Like a superhero with a secret identity, she fuses with the extraterrestrial creature, at which point the plot gives her nothing to do but fight with one of her classmates, another socially awkward girl who is also linked to an emulate. The screentone-laden art is polished but generic, and the story is pointless, with

musings about self-esteem apparently aimed at younger readers. ★

ANGEL/DUST NEO

Angel/Dust Neo (エンジェル／ダストネオ) • Aoi Nanase • ADV Manga (2006–2007) • Kadokawa Shoten (2003) • 1 volume • Science Fiction, Fantasy, Romantic Comedy • 13+

Love comedy sequel/retelling of *Angel/Dust*. This time, the protagonist is a boy, Akido, who finds himself suddenly forced to choose between human girls and female "emulates" who want to "make a contract" with him. NR

ANGELIC LAYER

CLAMP • Tokyopop (2002–2003) • Kadokawa Shoten (Monthly Shônen Ace, 1999–2001) • 5 volumes • Shônen, Science Fiction, Action • All Ages (mild violence)

"Angelic Layer" is a tournament in which mind-controlled robot gladiators battle in futuristic arenas—sounds like pretty typical *shônen* manga fare so far, right? But this is CLAMP we're talking about—their first *shônen* series and they're already breaking all the rules. For one thing, the main character, Misaki Suzuhara, is a girl. And not a sexy girl or a grim, determined bad-ass girl, but a nice, sweet cares-about-her-neighbors kind of girl. Perhaps even more shocking, the heroine isn't determined to be the champ or to prove herself to anyone. Nope, she just wants to do her best and have a good time. It's a sports manga about sportsmanship—a rare beast indeed! While this tournament may not run on testosterone, that doesn't mean it's not full of heated competition. The battles are intense and well choreographed, made vivid with art that departs from lead artist Mokona's previous styles, using coarser inking and fewer tones than usual. Fans of CLAMP's baroque attention to detail might be disappointed by this, their most cartoony work, but the style fits the material perfectly. (It is also, in many ways, the precursor for their current *shônen* hit *Tsubasa*.) The fights and training scenes are punctuated by frequent comic interludes with mad scientist Icchan, Misaki, and her friends, who sometimes transform into super-deformed "squid people." *Angelic Layer* won't win any awards for originality, but it's got heart to spare and is a brisk, entertaining read for boys and girls of all ages. (MT) ★★★

ANGEL NEST: See *Erica Sakurazawa: Angel Nest*

ANGEL SANCTUARY

Tenshi Kinryôku, "Angel Sanctuary" (天使禁猟区) • Kaori Yuki • Viz (2004–2007) • Hakusensha (Hana to Yume, 1994–2001) • 20 volumes • Shôjo, Science Fiction, Fantasy, Gothic, Adventure • 16+ (language, graphic violence, sexual situations)

The archetypal 1990s goth manga. Teenage Setsuna Mudo discovers that he is the reincarnation of the female angel Alexiel, who rebelled against the absent God and his hypocritical, fascist angels. But Setsuna's main concern is not the evil angels or the forthcoming apocalypse; it's his tormented, incestuous love for his sister, with whom he struggles to reunite on a quest through Gehenna, Hades, hell, and heaven. A sprawling epic, *Angel Sanctuary* begins in high school but soon leaves reality behind for totally fantastic science fiction settings. Characters constantly reveal dark secrets, die, and reappear in new forms, sometimes behaving in an out-of-character manner for momentary shock value, and delivering overwrought inner monologues ("I've even thought that if I could kill you and embrace your body as I died, I'd be a happy man"). This manga has *everything*: drugs, Bible quotes, miniskirted demons, cybernetic horrors, gun battles in heaven. The screentone-heavy art is elaborate and stylish, but the story is often frustrating to follow because of confusing page layouts, the bewilderingly huge cast of androgynous characters, and the sheer barrage of events and names. However, the plot improves after the first few volumes, and *Angel Sanctuary* ultimately succeeds as a complicated, inconsistent, but interesting story. ★★★

ANGEL'S WING

Tetsuya Aoki • Plex Co., Ltd. (2002–2004) • 7 issues • Shônen, Magical Girl, Action, Comedy • Unrated/13+ (mild violence, mild sexual situations)

An inane story drawn for the American comics market, *Angel's Wing* involves a little angel girl in a nightie who tries to do good deeds, in the process clashing with a little demon girl, which culminates in an overblown final-issue fight sequence. The weak art is barely propped up by computer coloring courtesy of American Sotocolor Graphics. ½

+ANIMA

Natsumi Mikai • Tokyopop (2006–ongoing) • MediaWorks (Dengeki Gao!, 2001–2005) • 10 volumes • Shônen, Fantasy, Adventure • 13+ (mild violence, abusive parents)

+Anima are a type of people who can transform into half-animal forms and who are discriminated against by human beings. Cooro, a boy who can grow black crowlike wings, rescues a mermaid from the circus, and together they gather a small group of fellows: a bear-pawed man, a bat-winged girl, and so forth. In search of more of their kind, the heroes go on adventures over hill and dale, forest and grasslands. Intended for younger readers, the stories are simple but enjoyable; the anime-style art is generic but restrained. The pleasantly drawn setting has echoes of the Wild West—Cooro's design has a faint Native American look—and many of the plots involve prejudice and tolerance. ★★½

ANNE FREAKS

(アンネ　フリークスAnne Freaks) • Yua Kotegawa • ADV (2006–2007) • Kadokawa Shoten (Monthly Shônen Ace, 2000–2002) • 4 volumes • Shônen, Crime, Suspense • 16+ (language, graphic violence, sexual situations)

While he's disposing of the body of his mother, teenage Yuri is discovered by a mysterious girl, who keeps his secret and murders the innocent witnesses. The completely amoral Anna recruits Yuri and another troubled boy, using them in her personal vendetta against the Kakusei Group, a cultlike terrorist organization. Meanwhile, a female police sergeant pursues the three young killers. As much a dark dream as a cynical psychodrama, *Anne Freaks* starts with its young, attractive protagonists engaged in the most unsympathetic behavior imaginable and then spends the rest of the manga trying to justify and analyze it ("Can murderers like us really save people?" broods Yuri. "No. We're just trying to make ourselves feel better"). The plot is slow to develop, and more unfortunately, the cold, generic art can't deliver the action scenes and facial expressions that the story demands. ★½

ANTIQUE BAKERY

Seiyô Kotto Yôgashiten, "Western [Occidental] Antique Bakery" (西洋骨董洋菓子店) • Fumi Yoshinaga • DMP (2005–2006) • Shinshokan (Wings, 2000–2002) • 4 volumes • Shôjo, Jôsei, Romantic Comedy, Drama • 16+ (language, adult themes, sex)

A smart, mature comedy, a brilliant gem of a manga. In a residential area of Japan, in a former antique store, lies a small café/bakery run and staffed (initially) by three men: thirty-two-year-old manager Tachibana, twenty-one-year-old former tough kid Eiji, and thirty-two-year-old master pastry chef Ono, who seems shy in the kitchen but whose employment history of seducing every man he's worked with marks him as a "gay of demonic charm." However, gay relationships are only one of many parts of *Antique Bakery,* a rare manga genuinely written for adults (specifically women) with a cast of adults of all sexual orientations. The plot follows the main characters and their customers, avoiding clichéd sitcom plots while managing to be both character-driven and totally hilarious (as well as educating the reader about the finer points of delicious French pastries). A darker, more serious story runs underneath the main plot, coming to the surface in volume 4. The pacing is excellent, the art is simple but lovely, and the dialogue is equal to great prose fiction. ★★★★

ANYWHERE BUT HERE

Tôku he Ikitai, "Anywhere but Here (I Want to Go Far Away)" (遠くへ行きたい) • Miki Tori • Fantagraphics (2005) • Tokyo News Tsushinsha (TV Bros, 1988–2005) • 1 volume, suspended (5 volumes in Japan) • Comedy • Unrated/13+ (crude humor)

Bizarre, wordless nine–panel gag manga, printed in two colors. Comparisons to *The Far Side* are not entirely off, particularly when Miki ventures into creepy science fiction territory (a man checks into a hotel room with a human body stuck under the wallpaper; a woman's Afro grows and grows until it turns into a planet with its own gravitational field), but his humor is even stranger and subtler. In the best strips, the punch line is completely out of left field (four people gather at a table, silently whip out props, and start performing separate weird activities; then, in the last panel, we see that they're in a restaurant and their food's arrived, so they all stop what they're doing and eat). The English edition consists of selected strips from the Japanese graphic novels. ★★★½

APOCALYPSE MEOW

Cat Shit One • Motofumi Kobayashi • ADV (2004) • Softbank/World Photo Press (Combat Magazine, 1991–2002) • 3 volumes • Military, Action • 16+ (language, graphic violence, sexual situations)

Stories of a three-soldier unit in the Vietnam War, *Apocalypse Meow* is a close-up look at combat on the ground, told with anthropomorphic bunnies and other animals. Intended perhaps to make the story cuter and thus more digestible to casual readers (a side story with human characters, at the end of volume 1, is fairly dry), the effect is similar to Art Spiegelman's *Maus:* Americans are bunnies, Vietnamese are cats, Japanese are monkeys, etc. Beyond that, the story is painstakingly realistic, although the author can't resist having a Vietnamese street vendor yell, "G.I.! You want fresh carrots?" There are no speedlines, no exaggerated blood and gore, and no unearned melodrama here; Perky, Rats, and Botaski—team

Takayuki Yamaguchi's *Apocalypse Zero*

(11 volumes in Japan) • Shônen, Postapocalyptic, Action • 18+ (language, extreme graphic violence, nudity, sexual situations)

After disastrous earthquakes, human civilization is seemingly reduced to a single high school in Tokyo, where the students still attend classes despite being plagued by giant cockroaches and bug-eyed mutant cannibal perverts in bondage gear. Only one person can save humanity: Kakugo, a soldierly teenage martial artist with (1) iron balls painfully embedded in his body and (2) "Zero," a living armor shell inhabited by the souls of hundreds of dead test subjects from the World War II bioweapons experiment that created it. While it vaguely follows the *Fist of the North Star* formula, *Apocalypse Zero* is in fact closer to a Go Nagai balls-to-the-wall gross-out. (One monster attacks with its grossly enlarged genitals, and in another scene, Kakugo performs hara-kiri with his thumb.) Enjoyably disgusting, sick, immature, sappy, and just about every other bad/good thing you can imagine, this self-aware *shônen* manga pulp benefits from polished artwork (with old-school cartoony character designs) and well-done action scenes.

★★★½

name "Cat Shit One"—face death countless times in countless tactical engagements, doing their duty with conscience, courage (most of the time), and occasional military humor. Kobayashi jumps right into battle, with maps and pages of teeny-tiny text helping explain the details (although he assumes a basic high school knowledge of the war); the treatment of the war is remarkably evenhanded. The art style comes from an illustrative tradition, with accurate drawings of vehicles, weapons, uniforms, and backgrounds. It's a slow read and far more Western-influenced than most manga, but vivid and fascinating, and the work of a skilled artist. The series was drawn left to right with an eye toward eventual translation. ★★★★

APOLLO'S SONG

Apollo no Uta, "Apollo's Song" (アポロの歌) • Osamu Tezuka • Vertical (2007) • Shônen Gahosha (Weekly Shônen King, 1970) • 1 volume • Shônen, Drama, Romance • 16+

Over-the-top drama involving Shogo, a young man whose hatred of sex expands to a hatred of life in general. After acting out on his feelings by killing animals, he is sent to a mental hospital and suffers electroshock and other treatments, during which he has a vision of a goddess who tells him he is being punished for spurning love. The plot follows him through visions of different lives in which he repeatedly meets and loses his true love. NR

APOTHECARIUS ARGENTUM

APOCALYPSE ZERO

Kakugo no Susume, "Kakugo's Advice" (覚悟の ススメ) • Takayuki Yamaguchi • Media Blasters (2005–2006) • Akita Shoten (Weekly Shônen Champion, 1994–1996) • 6 volumes, suspended

Yakushi Argent, "Argent the Physician" (薬師アルジ ャン) • Tomomi Yamashita • CMX (2007–ongoing) •

Akita Shoten (Princess Gold, 2004–ongoing) • 4+ volumes (ongoing) • Shôjo, Fantasy • 13+

As a child, the young slave Argentum worked for the royal family as a food taster for Princess Primula until the princess released him from service, no longer willing to see him risk his life. While the princess grew up to be a brave and independent young woman, able to hold her own with a sword, Argentum became a master pharmacist. On a fateful day, Argentum and Primula meet again, and the former food taster returns to the castle as the royal apothecary, using his knowledge of drugs—both beneficial and deadly—to protect the princess from her enemies.   NR

APPLESEED

(アップルシード) • Masamune Shirow • Dark Horse (1993–1995) • Seishinsha (1985–1989) • 4 volumes • Seinen, Science Fiction, Action • Unrated/16+ (mild language, violence, nudity)

Unfinished sci-fi tale of a war-ravaged near future. A utopian city called Olympus, populated mostly by "bioroids," or artificial humans, is conceived of as the last, best hope for the human race. Computers and A.I.'s form the government, but society still needs humans such as the tomboyish riot-police grrrl Deunan and her hulking cyborg partner Briareos to fight global terrorism and plots against Olympus. *Appleseed* starts out as a fascinating sci-fi exegesis on planned societies but gradually degenerates into combat porn; volume 4 is little more than a you-are-there gunplay reality show punctuated by obsessive footnotes. Shirow's screentone-heavy artwork improves even as his storytelling deteriorates—the action sequences are impressively energetic, and the artist's trademark interest in the female form encased in battle armor is well on display by the end—but the squandered potential of the premise is depressing. A note included in the back of the *Appleseed Databook* (an artbook and fan data base that includes a brief manga story) promises a return to sci-fi for the yet-to-materialize volume 5. Prior to the Dark Horse release, a portion of the series was published by Eclipse Comics from 1988 to 1992. (JD)   ★★

AQUA

Kozue Amano • Tokyopop (2007) • Enix (Stencil, 2001–2002) • 2 volumes • Science Fiction • 13+

A mellow science fiction tale that adopted the new title *Aria* when it switched from Enix's *Stencil* magazine to Mag Garden's *Comic Blade,* making this effectively a prequel (although both manga are self-contained). The *Aqua* portion of the story depicts heroine Akari's arrival on the planet Mars, which has now been terraformed into a watery world where gondoliers paddle their craft through the canals of Neo-Venezia. (MS)
NR

AQUA KNIGHT

Suichû Kishi, "Underwater Knight" (水中騎士) • Yukito Kishiro • Viz (2000–2002) • Shueisha (Ultra Jump, 1998–2000) • 3 volumes • Fantasy, Adventure • Unrated/13+ (crude humor, mild violence, nudity)

This whimsical, tongue-in-cheek fantasy yarn represents a major departure in both style and narrative tone for the creator of the cyberpunk epic *Battle Angel Alita*. Instead of grungy cyborgs and splattered brains, Kishiro serves up a candy-colored storybook world of killer-whale-riding armored knights, daffy demons, and megalomaniacal mad scientists. There's a nominal main plot involving a filthy urchin devoid of either brains or pants, the buxom young aqua knight who recklessly promises to take him on as a squire, and the deranged inventor who abducts the lad instead, but for the most part the artist seems to be making up the story as he goes along, and having a grand old time doing so. It's aesthetically gorgeous, endlessly inventive, and completely loony, and the abrupt ending is disappointing less for its barrage of deus ex machinas than for the fact it brings the party to such an early close. (MS)

★★★½

AQUARIAN AGE: JUVENILE ORION

Aquarian Age: Orion no Shônen, "Aquarian Age: Boy(s) of Orion" (アクエリアンエイジオリオンの少年) • Sakurako Gakurakuin • Broccoli Books (2003–2004) • Square Enix (Stencil, 2001–2003) • 5 volumes • Occult, Action, Drama • All Ages

Spin-off of the *Aquarian Age* collectible card game. Mana is a "mind breaker," a teenage girl with the incredible power to control minds. She is drawn into an ancient battle between five rival groups with such names as Wis-Dom and Darklore, each represented by a student or teacher who ends up serving Mana in her battle against Kaoru, another mind breaker. Characterization is weak and the plot is uncompelling; characters appear for no reason and disappear when it is no longer convenient to have them around. In addition, the art is weak, with stiff and unpleasant anatomy. (MJS)   ★½

AQUARIUM

(アクエリアム) • Tomoko Taniguchi • CPM (2000–2003) • Jitsugyo no Nihonsha (1990) • 1 volume • Romance, Comedy, Anthology • 13+ (adult themes, violence)

An anthology of *shôjo* short stories, applying Taniguchi's cute but limited art style to different subject matter and moods with varying degrees of success. As in all Taniguchi's work, some of the most endearing aspects are her notes to the English-speaking readers. The uncharacteristically dark "Aquarium" focuses on a depressed girl. "The Flying Stewardess," an occupational comedy, is mostly a collection of observations about Japanese airline stewardesses, while "The Heart is Your Kingdom," a short romance with a religious theme, is more an idea than a story.   ★★

AREA 88

(エリア88) • Kaoru Shintani • Viz (1987–1991) • Shogakukan (Shônen Big Comic, 1979–1986) • 1 volume, suspended (23 volumes in Japan) • Military Drama • Unrated/13+ (language, violence)

"What about you, Shin? What are you fighting for?!" "The skies that betrayed me . . ." A gracefully drawn tale of romantic machismo, *Area 88* is the story of mercenary fighter pilots serving for money in a fictional North African country. (But with the desert setting, bombing raids, and nuclear weapons, modern-day readers may be reminded of the Middle East.) Tricked into enlisting for a three-year term in Area 88, Japanese pilot Shin Kazama risks his life every day, while yearning for the country and fiancée he left behind. Kaoru Shintani was an assistant to Leiji Matsumoto, and the melancholy war theme and aerial combat scenes— planes swooping over black impressionistic backgrounds—show Matsumoto's influence. More *Area 88* was printed by Viz in monthly comics format (and in *Animerica* magazine) but never collected.   ★★★★

ARIA

Kozue Amano • ADV (2004) • Mag Garden (Comic Blade, 2002–ongoing) • 3 volumes, suspended (10+ volumes in Japan, ongoing) • Science Fiction • All Ages

Stand-alone sequel to *Prima*. On the terraformed planet Aqua (once known as Mars), in the beautiful city of Neo-Venezia, lives Aria, a young, pretty gondolier. Although her all-female coworkers occasionally engage in rivalries with competing gondola companies, Aria herself is content with the "simple pleasures": looking at rainbows, warming herself in front of the fireplace, walking down an unexplored alley and stumbling across an unexpected view. *Aria* is a mood piece of lovely landscapes and day-to-day magic, comparable to *Spirit of Wonder* or a defanged Hayao Miyazaki. As if the readers themselves were tourists, there's not much to do but look at the scenery: the fragments of real-life Venice (complete with historical explanations), the sunsets on the water, the hot springs set in a crumbling ruin. Yet deep down, despite all this stargazing, Aria still occasionally thinks like a manga character: "When I go back to work tomorrow, I'm gonna give it my all." In addition to the suspended ADV edition, the series is also scheduled for publication by Tokyopop in 2008.   ★★★

ARM OF KANNON

Birth (バースBIRTH) • Masakazu Yamaguchi • Tokyopop (2004–ongoing) • Gentosha (Comic Birz, 2001–2003) • 9 volumes • Science Fiction, Action, Horror • 18+ (language, graphic violence, explicit nudity, sex)

Mao, a girlish teenager with an unhealthily close relationship to his sister, becomes the unwilling human host of the so-called Arm of the Buddhist Goddess Kannon, an H. R. Giger–esque artifact that fuses with his body and gives him unbelievable, horrible, omnipotent powers. One of the most graphically violent sci-fi horror manga, *Arm of Kannon* achieves almost Toshio Maeda–esque levels of gore and perversity, with rape and dismemberment on almost every page, often happening to the same person. The plot is little more than an excuse to draw a bunch of monsters and weird bad-ass characters: cyborgs, shady military types, monks, and the polymorphous, godlike Arm, which causes writhing snakes and lions and tentacles to pour out of Mao's possessed body. As if the story wasn't confusing enough, volumes 5–7 suddenly switch to what is apparently a parallel-universe story line in which the Arm is the "Angel Fist" and the Holy Grail is involved; then volumes 8–9 go back in time to medieval Japan, where samurai fight over the Arm's powers. As a story, it's completely frustrating and arbitrary, although it's intermittently entertaining for the detailed, Grand Guignol artwork: eyeshadow-wearing *bishônen,* hideous wrinkled creeps, and slimy blobs covered with hundreds of mouths and eyeballs.   ★

ARMS: See *Project Arms*

THE AROMATIC BITTERS: See *Erica Sakurazawa: The Aromatic Bitters.*

ASHEN VICTOR

Haisha, "The Ashen One" (灰者) • Yukito Kishiro • Viz (1997–1999) • Shueisha (Ultra Jump, 1995–1997) • 1 volume • Science Fiction, Sports, Drama • Unrated/13+ (graphic violence)

A self-contained spin-off that revisits the world of *Battle Angel Alita* for a thoroughly downbeat take on the brutal death game of motorball. *Ashen Victor* is a departure from the earlier story in both style and content, rendered in an experimental high-contrast art style reminiscent of Frank Miller's *Sin City* and headlined by a glum loser rather than a spunky warrior gal. After a string of racetrack wipeouts, cyberschmuck Snev has become infamous as the "Crash King" and begins attracting an audience of fans eager to vicariously experience the cathartic thrill of self-destruction. It's a bleak, angry tale, but tremendously well done, and quite possibly Kishiro's best work to date. (MS)

★★★★

ASTRA

(アストラ) • Jerry Robinson (original concept and story), Sidra Cohn (story), Kenichi Oishi (script), Shojin Tanaka (art) • CPM (2001–2002) • Media Factory (1999) • 1 volume • Science Fiction, Action, Romance • Unrated/13+ (mild language, violence, sexual situations)

Absurd international co-production based on a never-produced sci-fi musical by Jerry Robinson (one of the early *Batman* artists) and singer-songwriter Sidra Cohn. Astra, a Barbie-doll-like princess from the all-female planet Eros, goes into space in search of sperm (yes, literally) to allow her unisex planet to produce children. Landing on near-future Earth, she falls in love with Yosuke, a square-jawed trucker, who rescues her from exploitation by the evil Ministry of Science. Brain-dead, retro plot with decent art; the vaguely American "good girl"–style art is not bad, and the sci-fi backgrounds show the influence of the French artist Moebius.   ★

ASTRIDER HUGO

(アストライダー・ヒューゴ) • Hisao Tamaki • Radio Comix (2000–2001) • Shogakukan (Hyper Coro-Coro, 1999) • 2 issues • Science Fiction, Action • Unrated/All Ages (mild language, mild violence)

In the year 2175, "Astral Strider" Hugo is a lone-wolf space pirate, pursued by inspector Regina Bennett (a cute girl), Kinela (a catgirl warrior), and others. Looking cool in his skintight "phi-tec suit" and helmet, able to beat up robots with his maser-powered knuckles, he fights an evil conspiracy and saves the misguided good guys who want to arrest him. The enthusiastic, accomplished sci-fi art is reminiscent of Kenichi Sonoda, but more dense and detailed, as Tamaki tries to squeeze a lot of story (and cool poses) into a small number of pages. "Damn you, pirate Hugo! I'll get you next time!" But there isn't a next time; the story was never completed. ★★★

ASTRO BOY

Tetsuwan Atom, "Iron Arm Atom" (鉄腕アトム) • Osamu Tezuka • Dark Horse (2002–2004) • Kôbunsha (Shônen, 1952–1968) • 23 volumes • Shônen, Mecha, Science Fiction • Unrated/All Ages (mild violence)

The *Astro Boy* manga represents the early Tezuka at his best, crafting polished, fast-paced adventure stories crackling with energy and wit. Astro ("Atom" in the original Japanese) is a boy robot created by the embittered Dr. Tenma, then adopted by kindly Professor Ochanomizu of the Ministry of Science. With the professor's help, Astro learns to use his superhuman powers to protect humanity. Although the *Astro Boy* stories are simple, action-oriented, and aimed at children, they also touch upon some of Tezuka's favorite big issues, including the struggle for equality (here demonstrated by robots that are treated like second-class citizens) and the thin line dividing the human and nonhuman. Modeled after a Japanese reprint edition, the Dark Horse edition of *Astro Boy* prints the stories out of chronological order, in a "greatest hits" fashion, often with introductory manga sections by Tezuka. The entire series is excellent, but if you read only one volume, consider volume 3, featuring the long and famous story "The Greatest Robot on Earth." Published when the *Astro Boy* manga and anime were at the height of their popularity, this story is fondly remembered by generations of readers and was the inspiration for Naoki Urasawa's untranslated Tezuka-noir manga *Pluto.* (SG) ★★★★

AWABI

Awabi (泡日) • Kan Takahama • Fanfare/Ponent Mon (2007) • Junkudo (2004) • Underground, Drama, Comedy • 1 volume • Unrated/13+

Short story collection by underground artist Kan Takahama (*Monokuro Kinderbook*), known for her intelligent dialogue and portrayals of characters of different age groups. In the main story, a young woman is rescued from a pond by an old man, and ends up spending time in an old-folks' home with him, the other residents, and the staff. NR

AZUMANGA DAIOH

Azumanga Daioh, "Azumanga Great King" (あずまんが大王) • Kiyohiko Azuma • ADV (2003–2004) • MediaWorks (Dengeki Daioh, 1999–2002) • 4 volumes • Four-Panel Comedy • 13+ (language)

Charming comedy about a group of high school girls and their teachers (a ten-year-old child prodigy, a daydreamer, an obnoxious loudmouth, a teacher who's more immature than her students, etc.). The manga is mostly four-panel strips (with just a few traditional manga sequences), and Azuma proves to be a quiet master of the four-panel form, with extremely good timing and use of "story four-panel" running jokes. But the strip's greatest strength is its character-driven writing, and when the characters graduate at the end of the manga, the reader may wish it was longer. *Azumanga Daioh* is definitely a product of the *moe* "cult of cuteness," and newbies to manga may not enjoy the gags about the vaguely pedophilic teacher (all the characters hate him, too), but on the whole the strip never strays into exploitation. The title is a pun on the artist's name and the magazine where it was serialized. ★★★½

BABY & ME

Aka-chan to Boku, "Baby and Me" (赤ちゃんと僕) • Marimo Ragawa • Viz (2005–ongoing) • Hakusensha (Hana to Yume, 1991–1997) • 18 volumes • Shôjo, Comedy • 13+ (brief crude humor, mild violence)

When their mother dies, ten-year-old Takuya is forced to take care of his toddler brother Minoru. Adorable, big-eyed Minoru is past the age of diapers (there's almost no potty humor), but he bumps into things, cries, gets possessive and then ashamed of himself, and says what's on his mind in baby talk (his most common words are "I'm saw-wee" and "Bwaza!"). At first resentful of being a surrogate mother, Takaya soon comes to love his brother even more than before, and with the help of their thirty-three-year-old working dad, their family thrives. Like an American newspaper comic strip, *Baby & Me* doesn't have any great surprises or much of a plot, but it's a sweet episodic comedy with a large cast of characters. (It eventually gets so there's not much time for the baby.) The writing, not the art, is the strong point, but the babies look cute and the grown-up characters have variety. The series is suitable for all ages apart from some minor issues: a dark story in volume 2, some crooks with guns, some accidents, and a discreet flashback showing Minoru's parents lying in bed together.   ★★★

BABY BIRTH

(ベイビィバース) • Sukehiro Tomita (story), Haruhiko Mikimoto (art) • Tokyopop (2003) • Kodansha (Magazine Z, 2001) • 2 volumes • Shônen, Fantasy • 13+ (mild language, violence, nudity, brief sexual situations)

Most likely a failed anime pitch, *Baby Birth* is an unintentionally ridiculous mash-up of stereotypical plot elements. Hizuru, a teenage singer/figure skater, meets Takuya, an arrogant young pianist whose piano playing awakens her hidden power to fight demons by singing (and improves her self-esteem, etc.). As lizard monsters, big-nosed warlocks, and sleazy tentacled beings invade the earth, Takuya and Hizuru team up to musically fight them, vanquishing the enemies in a brilliant screentone lightshow, while a little winged angel gives them advice. As the artist, Mikimoto turns in his usual professional performance: attractive and individualistic in the anime style he helped pioneer, but hectic and hard to follow, the work of an illustrator rather than a manga artist.   ★

THE BACHELOR PRINCE: See *Harlequin Pink: The Bachelor Prince*

BACKSTAGE PRINCE

Gakuyaura Ôji, "Backstage Prince" (楽屋裏王子) • Kanoko Sakurakoji • Viz (2007) • Shogakukan (Betsucomi, 2004–2006) • 2 volumes • Shôjo, Performance, Romance • 13+ (mild sexual situations)

Akari is a regular, plain high school girl who gets lost one day and tumbles into the backstage of a kabuki theater. There, she meets kabuki heartthrob Ryusei Horiuchi, a misanthropic actor who can only connect with his cat, Mr. Ken—and now her. Akari becomes Ryusei's assistant and girlfriend, but everyone else seems to be out to stop their love. Each of the chapters in this short series could stand alone, and there isn't much variation on the *Romeo and Juliet* love obstacle plotline. But it's refreshing to see Akari playing an equal role in the romance, initiating the make-out scenes as often (if not more) than Ryusei. The story doesn't break any new ground, but it's a good choice for a quick, light read. The art is typical *shôjo*, with lots of kimono shots. (HS)   ★★½

BAKI THE GRAPPLER

Grappler Baki (グラップラー刃牙) • Keisuke Itagaki • Gutsoon! Entertainment (2002–2004) • Akita Shoten (Weekly Shônen Champion, 1991–1999) • 46 issues (42 volumes in Japan) • Shônen, Martial Arts, Action • Unrated/16+ (mild language, graphic violence)

Gruesome, stripped-down *shônen* fighting manga that, in Japan, was adapted into numerous spin-offs. The series is mostly non-stop fights, starring Baki (his name is the same as the sound effect for something breaking), a fearless and ever-smiling teenage martial artist, who fights in underground tournaments against opponents such as "cord-cutting Shinogi," who rips his opponents' nerves out of their bodies with his bare hands, leaving them paralyzed. The human figures—the focus of the manga—are drawn in contorted cartoony poses with thick lines delineating the major muscles, a more fluid (but not necessarily more attractive) art style than the stiff processed realism of *Fist of the North Star* or, worse, *Tough*. Blood splatters, veins pop, and the series chews on the edge of perversity like a dog gnawing a bone; Baki has a little boy's face on a ripped, scarred body, and his opponents are sadistic types with rouged-looking lips, who prior to fighting him think such thoughts as "I feel like a young boy about to lose his virginity to a beautiful woman." Although it was serialized in every issue of *Raijin* magazine, it was never released as graphic novels. ★★

BAKUNE YOUNG

(バクネヤング) • Toyokazu Matsunaga • Viz (1997–2002) • Shogakukan (Young Sunday, 1993–2000) • 3 volumes • Seinen, Action, Parody • 18+ (language, graphic violence, nudity)

An indulgent comedy of machismo and militarism, *Bakune Young* mixes cops, crooks, wanna-be ninjas, and cleft-chinned American soldiers into the kind of movie Takashi Miike might make with a cast of thousands. (The American translation also recalls rap music and blaxploitation films, with lines such as "Commence to squabble!" and "I gots to take care of some mo' bidness.") The plot wanders furiously but is initiated by Bakune Young, a mole-faced, brutal thug on a mission to rule the world, based on a plan he made in junior high. In volume 1, he challenges the *yakuza* on national TV, kidnaps their boss (the "Don of Nippon"), and takes his hostage to Osaka Castle, where Bakune dons antique samurai armor and obliviously awaits the arrival of thousands of angry *yakuza*, cops, and special forces. By volume 3, almost none of the original cast remains, a supernatural element has been introduced, and the story becomes ever more dreamlike. Matsunaga's caricatural artwork presents his quirky subjects, and their gruesome deaths, with gorgeous detail and a thousand experimental techniques. ★★★½

BAMBI AND HER PINK GUN

Bambi • Atsushi Kaneko • DMP (2005–2006) • Enterbrain (Comic Beam, 1998–2002) • 2 volumes, suspended (7 volumes in Japan) • Underground, Crime, Adventure • 18+ (language, graphic violence, nudity)

Bambi, an amoral kidnapper, shoots and drives her way through armies of bounty hunters, who want to kill her and return her human cargo—a little boy—to their master, a monstrous Elvis-like singer, Gabba King. With an art style that's about 10 percent manga and 90 percent American underground/indie comics (with visual references to *Tales from the Crypt* and Robert Crumb), *Bambi and Her Pink Gun* is a unique artistic accomplishment, looking literally like no other manga ever translated. The plot is also very American, consisting mostly of cynical, hip violence, with minimal exposition. Bambi is a violent, pissed-off health nut who introduces herself as "Me Bambi"; her enemies are a rogue's gallery of wartcovered perverts, cross-eyed cowboys, and masked wrestlers. Fascinating to look at, it coasts by on style points alone. ★★★

BANANA FISH

Banana Fish • Akimi Yoshida • Viz (1997–2007) • Shogakukan (Betsucomi, 1985–1994) • 19 volumes • Crime Drama • 16+ (language, violence, sexual situations, brief nudity)

One of the great *shôjo* manga epics—and yet on the surface, hardly a *shôjo* manga at all—*Banana Fish* expresses the Japanese perception of 1980s America, and specifically New York City, as a thrilling place of violence, corruption, and freedom. Ash Lynx, a beautiful and ruthless youth gang leader whose older brother went mysteriously insane while in Vietnam, stumbles across a clue that might explain his brother's condition . . . and which pits him against a massive conspiracy stretching from the Mafia to the very heights of power. The plot is hard crime, a male-dominated action story full of death, drugs, and child sexual abuse (the latter entirely offscreen). But, almost so subtly as to be invisible, there is a love story as well: the unspoken but clearly gay relationship between Ash and Eiji Okumura, the young Japanese reporter who dares to enter Ash's dangerous world. The story is consciously literary (the title is a reference to J. D. Salinger), and the plot is tight and to the point, like a good crime/geopolitical thriller. The manga's one weakness is Yoshida's dull artwork, which, although unique, seems inadequate to tell a story of this scale; her urban backgrounds, cars, and guns look like a failed attempt at Katsuhiro Otomo–esque realism, or the product of a high school drafting class. But the worldview of *Banana Fish* is so fully realized that art is almost redundant, and even when the panels are nothing but talking heads, we hang on every word.

★★★★

BANNER OF THE STARS: See *Seikai Trilogy*

BAOH

Baoh Raihôsha, "Baoh the Visitor" (バオー来訪者) • Hirohiko Araki • Viz (1989) • Shueisha (Weekly Shônen Jump, 1984–1985) • 2 volumes • Shônen, Action, Horror • Unrated/16+ (extreme graphic violence)

A young girl with telepathy and a teenage boy implanted with a parasite that turns him into a bio-organic killing machine fight back against the evil secret organization that created him. An over-the-top gorefest with exploding brains, laser-pierced eyeballs, and killer mandrills (not to mention the girl's cute koala-like pet), *Baoh,* even more clearly than Araki's later work *JoJo's Bizarre Adventure,* shows the influence of ultraviolent splatter movies. Memorably melodramatic dialogue keeps the story moving from one one-sided fight scene to another. Araki's early artwork is an acquired taste, mixing intentionally ugly caricatural faces with stiff he-men and 1980s fashions similar to Shin-Ichi Hosoma (*Demon City Hunter*). ★★½

BAREFOOT GEN

Hadashi no Gen, "Barefoot Gen" (はだしのゲン) • Keiji Nakazawa • Last Gasp (2004–ongoing) • Shueisha (Weekly Shônen Jump, 1972–1973) • 10 volumes • Shônen, Historical, Drama • Unrated/13+ (language, crude humor, nudity, violence)

A classic documentary manga with a powerful antiwar (and antiracism) message, *Barefoot Gen* is based on Keiji Nakazawa's personal experiences as a survivor of the atomic bombing of Hiroshima. In 1945 Hiroshima, second-grader Gen and his parents, brothers, and sisters endure the last months of World War II: food shortages, American air raids, and accusations of treachery directed against his father, an outspokenly pacifistic artist. Meanwhile, the terrible day of August 6, 1945, creeps ever closer, and toward the end of volume 1, the bomb drops, destroying the city. But this is not the end; after countless pages of burning bodies, maggots, and radiation sickness, Gen and the surviving members of his family must go on, and the rest of the manga follows Gen as he struggles to grow up in postwar Japan, a real-life postapocalyptic world. Although *Barefoot Gen* is a conscious political statement, it is also a manga for children, and some readers may be surprised by its moments of humor and earthiness (or its rough-and-tumble brutality; there's plenty of punching, kicking, and biting). Readers interested purely in the war may lose interest after the first three or four volumes, as politics fades into the background and the story becomes a very traditional old-school *shônen* manga: plucky kids enduring the unendurable with a song on their lips, working all day to make ends meet, getting in fights, and outwitting adults. The result is almost like two manga in one, both of historical interest, but for different reasons. Highly recommended. In 1972, prior to *Barefoot Gen,* Nakazawa drew a shorter, even more autobiographical account of his Hiroshima experiences under the title *Ore wa Mita!* ("I Saw It!"). *I Saw It!* was published as a one-shot comic book by Educomics in 1982. The first four volumes of *Barefoot Gen* were previously translated by New Society Publishing in the early 1980s. ★★★★

BARON: THE CAT RETURNS

Baron: Neko no Danshaku, "Baron: The Cat Baron" (バロン―猫の男爵) • Aoi Hiragi • Viz (2005) • Tokuma Shoten/Studio Ghibli (2002) • 1 volume • Fantasy • All Ages

COME GET SOME!

I'LL KILL YOU AGAIN!!

The most macho hero ever? Masayuki Taguchi's *Baron Gong Battle*

Commissioned by Studio Ghibli to act as a manga counterpart to the animated short created for a Japanese theme park (which eventually became the movie *Neko ga Ongaeshi,* aka *The Cat Returns*), *Baron: The Cat Returns* is the story of Haru, a high school girl who rescues a cat. But this cat just happens to be the son of the King of Cats, and soon Haru finds herself swept up in a calamitous adventure as the Cat Kingdom tries to thank her by marrying her off to the prince. The manga is much more enjoyable than the anime that is based on it, largely because of the pacing; while the cat parade was much more lavish in the anime, many scenes dragged on far too long. In the manga, things zip right along, the rapid succession of events helping to convey Haru's confusion. The art style is unusual for manga, blending stylistic aspects from many genres. The animal characters really shine; the facial expres-

sions on the cats are genius. Screentone is deployed to create some startlingly cinematic effects, and when necessary the background details are precise and elegant. (HS)
★★★

BARON GONG BATTLE

(バロン・ゴング・バトル) • Masayuki Taguchi • Media Blasters (2005–2006) • Akita Shoten (Weekly Shônen Champion, 1997–1999) • 6 volumes, suspended (8 volumes in Japan) • Shônen, Fighting, Action-Adventure • 18+ (constant language, extreme graphic violence, nudity, sexual situations)

Baron Gong Battle is basically an attempt to create the most extreme *shônen* manga action movie imaginable; volume 4 even contains tributes to Arnold Schwarzenegger, Steven Seagal, Bruce Willis, and other action stars. Baron Gong is a beloved Chicago bar owner, but he's also a motorcycle-riding, shotgun-slinging bad-ass who hunts the evil mutant super-beings who killed his girlfriend. He drives cars into elevators; he helps women and orphans; his every line of dialogue is either the F-word, the B-word, or "Shut your pie hole, you murderous freak!"; and in one scene he steals booze from a homeless person so he can use it to disinfect a wound before cauterizing it with a hot knife. The graphic gore and topless sex-doll women are drawn with polish, and only the occasionally ridiculous bad guys serve as a reminder that the manga was theoretically drawn for children. The story reaches a pulpy peak when the scene shifts to Africa, the site of Gong's origin story. Well-executed, earnest, trashy action.
★★½

BASARA

(バサラ) • Yumi Tamura • Viz (2003–2007) • Shogakukan (Betsucomi, 1990–1998) • 27 volumes • Shôjo, Fantasy, Adventure • 16+ (violence, nudity)

Sometime after an unspecified apocalypse has reduced Japan to a feudal state, a desert tribe rebels against the cruel Red King, placing their faith in Tatara, the "child of destiny." When Tatara is killed, his twin sister, Sarasa, wears boys' clothes and takes his place, but through a terrible twist of fate, Sarasa and the Red King—the two archenemies—meet in disguise and fall in love. A romance in the epic narrative sense, *Basara* at times shows the influence of RPGs such as the *Final Fantasy* series, as Sarasa meanders up and down the length of Japan and Okinawa to collect the "legendary four swords" and gather allies to join her party. Although the story begins in a pseudo-Arabian desert, the rest of Japan turns out to be divided into different exotic settings (so why is Sarasa's homeland so awful?), each with their own side stories and colorful characters. Tamura's unconventional artwork, with its bold, fluid strokes, creates an atmosphere of elegance and splendor, and the story has many powerful moments. But the central mistaken-identity love story is almost too heavy to be resolved in a satisfying way, and as the story proceeds, it becomes obvious that good-looking characters are incapable of dying. Sarasa's dual female and male identity—her struggles for self-reliance and moral leadership, knowing all the time that she could choose to fall back into a stereotypical "woman's role"—provide an interesting dimension to the imperfect but ambitious story of war and internecine struggle.

★★★½

BASILISK

Basilisk: Kôga Ninpôchô, "Basilisk: The Kouga Ninja Scrolls" (バジリスク〜甲賀忍法帖) • Masaki Segawa (art), Fûtaro Yamada (original creator) • Del Rey (2006–2007) • Kodansha (Young Magazine Uppers, 2003–2004) • 5 volumes • Seinen, Ninja, Action • 18+ (language, extreme graphic violence, nudity, sexual situations)

Manga adaptation of Fûtaro Yamada's novel *The Kouga Ninja Scrolls,* set in Tokugawa-era Japan. To settle a dispute, the Tokugawa rulers arrange a match between two rival ninja clans, each represented by their ten best ninja. The chapters proceed in a quick, bloody elimination, with each group plotting to eliminate the other in the most underhanded fashion (as opposed to the typical

ritualistic manga fighting tournament). Meanwhile, caught in the middle are Oboro and Gennosuke, star-crossed lovers torn apart by the war between their respective clans. The real attraction is Segawa's artwork, which uses obviously computer-generated backgrounds to focus attention on the foreground action involving grotesque superpowered ninja: a limbless ninja who crawls like a worm, a woman whose blood oozes from her pores and turns into fog, a spider ninja who spits gluelike phlegm. Solid, inventive action violence.   ★★★

BASS MASTER RANMARU

Bass Master Ranmaru (バスマスター嵐丸) • Taiga Takahashi (story), Yoshiaki Shimojo (art) • ComicsOne (e-book, 2001) • Sogotasho Publishing (1999) • 1 volume • Fishing • All Ages

Hobbyist manga involving a rebellious fishing pro who gives up the big time to go back to small-town life. Ranmaru competes in fishing competitions, provides readers with fishing tips and techniques, and promulgates a nostalgic, pseudo-mystical appreciation of the art of bass fishing. The manga does a good job of explaining key terms (heavy fishing jargon permeates every chapter), but as a general read it's predictable and uncompelling. The e-book also suffers from a number of glaring typos. (RS)   ★★

BASTARD!!:
HEAVY METAL DARK FANTASY

Bastard!! Ankoku no Hakaishin, "Bastard!! Destructive God of Darkness" (バスタード!!暗黒の破壊神) • Kazushi Hagiwara • Viz (2001–ongoing) • Shueisha (Weekly Shônen Jump/Weekly Shônen Jump Zôkan/Ultra Jump, 1988–ongoing) • 23+ volumes, ongoing • Shônen, Fantasy, Adventure, Comedy • 18+ (language, graphic violence, nudity, graphic sex)

Shônen manga meets Dungeons & Dragons meets *Heavy Metal.* Besieged by armies of orcs and lizard men, the defenders of the kingdom of Meta-Rikana (aka "Metallicana") unleash their secret weapon: the fiendish sorcerer Dark Schneider, whose powers can be unlocked only by a virgin's kiss. Although *Bastard!!*'s central character dynamic is similar to that of *Inu-Yasha*—a former villain is magically bound to obey a young girl—Dark Schneider is far more destructive, an extremely horny, *extremely* foulmouthed bad-ass who kills everybody and makes fun of his corny enemies in selfreferential "What's up, doc?" fashion. He also looks like a long-haired metalhead and frequently goes around naked. Originally published in *Weekly Shônen Jump* (watch Dark Schneider turn defeated enemies into pals), *Bastard!!* was later moved to magazines for an older readership, possibly because of Hagiwara's obvious pleasure at baiting censors with increasingly sleazy and finally pornographic humor. Halfway through the series, the story takes an abrupt turn into the realm of angels and devils, almost like *Angel Sanctuary*. The artwork starts out terrible but slowly improves after volume 4, eventually becoming unbelievably polished; however, the plot is a train wreck, and many important details are told only in Hagiwara's untranslated *dôjinshi*. Most of the names are heavy metal music references. In Japan, the early volumes of *Bastard!!* were rereleased in a "Complete Edition" with heavily redrawn art and much more explicit sex, but Viz's English edition uses the original, tamer art in places. ★★

BATMAN: CHILD OF DREAMS

Kia Asamiya • DC (2003) • Kodansha (Magazine Z, 2000) • 1 volume • Superhero • Unrated/13+ (mild language, violence, shower scene)

A solid one-shot manga adaptation of the American superhero franchise, set in the traditional DC universe rather than reinventing the character for Japanese audiences (as in *Spider-Man: The Manga*). Batman, the dark hero of Gotham City, finds himself encountering copycat versions of all his old enemies. The trail leads to a mysterious drug, Fanatic, which gives people the power to become whoever they want. This clever if self-congratulatory take on superhero fandom gives Asamiya the opportunity to draw most of the classic Batman villains, including Two-Face, the Riddler, Penguin, and the Joker. As usual in an Asamiya comic, his character designs are stiffly stylized and unrealistic, but the backgrounds are slick and the composition is at times iconic. Talky fights with villains, shadowy cityscapes, tough guys with square jaws and big noses: Asamiya's draftsmanship isn't up to the best of American superhero comics, but he's a good match for the material. The English rewrite by comic writer Max Allan Collins, much more long-winded than the original Japanese dialogue, sounds appropriately melodramatic bordering on cheesy ("How ironic, don't you think? That so dark a figure defends the light?"). ★★½

BATTLE ANGEL ALITA

Gunnm, "Gun Dream" (銃夢) • Yukito Kishiro • Viz (1992–1998) • Shueisha (Business Jump, 1990–1995) • 9 volumes • Seinen, Science Fiction, Action-Adventure • Unrated/16+ (graphic violence, partial nudity)

An intense, furiously inventive cyberpunk adventure set in a grubby future world of cynical cyborgs and street trash. The amnesiac Alita, rescued from a garbage pile by one of the Scrapyard's rare Good Samaritans, begins an odyssey of self-discovery by way of bounty hunting, blood sports, and hightech wetwork, interwoven with philosophical explorations of the relationship between brain and body and artistic depictions of what happens when they get splattered all over a motorball track. Kishiro's illustration and storytelling chops improve as the story progresses, but from the very start *Alita* is packed full of nervy sci-fi concepts and heartrending drama, and the plot rockets along at a most un-manga-like pace—our heroine goes through more than a decade of adventures, and at least half a dozen bodies, in the span of these nine volumes. The final hundred pages provide an abrupt conclusion that Kishiro subsequently discarded in favor of the sequel series *Last Order,* and this original ending was omitted entirely from the large-format reprint series released in Japan between 1998 and 2000. (MS) ★★★★

BATTLE ANGEL ALITA: LAST ORDER

Gunnm Last Order, "Gun Dream Last Order" (銃夢 Last Order) • Yukito Kishiro • Viz (2002–ongoing) • Shueisha (Ultra Jump, 2000–ongoing) • 9+ volumes, ongoing • Seinen, Science Fiction, Action-Adventure • 16+ (mild language, graphic violence)

A continuation of Kishiro's *Battle Angel Alita*—or more precisely, an alternative ending, since it substitutes a sprawling space epic for the somewhat rushed conclusion that took up the final hundred pages of the previous series. Revived in the sky city of Tiphares by her archnemesis, the flan-gobbling mad scientist Desty Nova, our cyborg warrior heroine ascends to the stars and discovers that the heavens are full of asses that need whupping. Kishiro's artwork is better than ever, with striking graphic design and hyperkinetic martial arts sequences that could make angels weep, but after a strong start and some promising stabs at Swiftian social satire, the story settles into a cycle of overextended fighting tournaments punctuated by big chunks of exposition. It doesn't help that the quirky supporting cast of the original series is quickly phased out in favor of a bland set of replacements, although Alita's bloody-minded, smack-talking doppelgänger Sechs does a fair job of stealing the show. (MS) ★★★

BATTLE CLUB

(バトルクラブ) • Yuji Shiozaki • Tokyopop (2006–ongoing) • Shônen Gahosha (Young King, 2004–ongoing) • 5+ volumes (ongoing) • Seinen, Martial Arts, Comedy • 18+ (language, violence, nudity, constant sexual situations)

After having his butt kicked by a busty girl wrestler, Mokichi, a wanna-be tough guy (and in fact he's pretty manly already), joins the school's girl-dominated wrestling club. Much rolling, grappling, and crotch shots ensue, accompanied by training journeys, lesbian fanservice, and she-males. Very similar to Shiozaki's *Battle Vixens, Battle Club* benefits from being less overtly sadistic and

not having the previous series' pointless fantasy/historical elements. The whole thing is intentionally sleazy and self-parodying—the title is a reference to *Fight Club*—but even if all the clichés are intentional, it's hard to drum up enthusiasm for a series that aims so low. ★½

BATTLE ROYALE

(バトル・ロワイアル) • Koushun Takami (story), Masayuki Taguchi (art) • Tokyopop (2003–2006) • Akita Shoten (Young Champion, 2000–2005) • 15 volumes • Seinen, Suspense, Action • 18+ (language, graphic violence, nudity, sex)

Koushun Takami's novel *Battle Royale* scandalized a nation when it was first published in 1999, but just as remarkable as its shock value is the sadistic elegance of its basic concept, a lethal reality show in which an entire class of junior high school kids is turned loose on an island with instructions to kill each other until only one survives. This manga adaptation, co-created by Takami himself, hews more closely to the original novel than did Kinji Fukasaku's movie version. Thanks to its abundance of flashback scenes it functions almost as an expanded remix of the novel, shedding more light on the complex web of loyalties and petty resentments that drive the life-and-death decisions of the game's unwilling participants, while downplaying the novel's heartfelt but pointless denunciations of the imaginary fascist government that controls Japan in this alternate universe. Taguchi's art shifts fluidly from cutesy romance to gore-splattered ultraviolence to bug-eyed psychodrama, while somehow managing to give every one of the game's forty-two players a distinctive look and personality, and Keith Giffen's lurid English-language dialogue adds to the over-the-top pulp atmosphere. Although the series loses some of its momentum in the final volumes, thanks to overlong martial arts duels and gun battles and huge chunks of sentimental blather, the brutal logic of the death game keeps everything ticking along toward the conclusion. (MS) ★★★½

BATTLE VIXENS

Ikki Tousen, "One Warrior Equal to a Thousand" (一騎当千) • Yuji Shiozaki • Tokyopop (2006– ongoing) • Wani Books (Comic Gum, 2000– ongoing) • 12+ volumes (ongoing) • Seinen, Martial Arts, Comedy • 16+/18+ (constant language, crude humor, graphic violence, nudity, sex)

In a small number of chosen high schools, the students possess *magatama*—gems that show that they are mighty fighters, possessed by the spirits of 108 ancient Chinese warriors. Hakufu, a girl with big breasts, a foul mouth, and incredible hidden powers, enrolls in Nanyo Academy and starts kicking ass, attracting a bevy of friends and rivals. Extremely similar to *Tenjho Tenge,* but more comedic and less well drawn (although it has a slick rubbery look), *Battle Vixens* is a mean-spirited, clichéd, but intermittently amusing succession of ripped-off clothes, kicked-in faces, and, to quote the editorial text, "more camel-toes than a desert caravan." For cynical readers, the main reason to read the series is Keith Giffen's increasingly irreverent rewrite, which gradually drifts further and further from the literal translation and turns into a sort of hilarious Adam Warren–esque self-parody that oozes contempt for the material ("I try to be nice and let a few live . . . but no! They always look at my boobs!"). ★½

B.B. EXPLOSION

Hajikete B.B., "Burst Apart B.B." (はじけてB.B.) • Yasue Imai • Viz (2004–2005) • Shogakukan (Ciao, 1997–1999) • 5 volumes • Shôjo, Performance, Drama • All Ages

Based on the real-life entertainment academy Okinawa Actor's School, *B.B. Explosion* follows young Airi Ishikawa as she rises to fame in Japan and then America. The artist spent a lot of time hanging out at the school for research, and even modeled some of the characters after people she met there; Imai's enjoyment of the experience shines through despite the dated art. The story does its best to express Airi's passion, but there are times when the static medium of manga falls flat in presenting the dynamic force of her song

and dance. Furthermore, the story is bogged down in every chapter by Airi's episodes of self-doubt, which last a page or two before she is rejuvenated by her love for entertainment. These crying jags quickly become tedious in their predictability, and ruin an otherwise enjoyable story. (HS) ★

BEAUTIFUL PEOPLE: See *Mitsukazu Mihara: Beautiful People*

BEAUTY IS THE BEAST

Bijo ga Yajû, "The Beautiful Woman Is the Beast" (美女が野獣) • Tomo Matsumoto • Viz (2006) • Hakusensha (LaLa, 2002–2005) • 5 volumes • Shôjo, Romantic Comedy • 13+

Eimi Yamashita is a kooky high school student with a love for snacks and the bad boy on campus. Through her faith in his better qualities, Eimi helps her love interest come out from under the burden of his bad rep and confront his painful past. The story is episodic, visiting the characters during times of high crisis and fun, such as a dorm blackout and the school festival, while skipping over chunks of boring time as needed. Although the sparse art might be a deterrent, the series is worth reading for the many laugh-out-loud moments; the artist's quirky sense of humor picks up the slack for the sketchy art style. (HS) ★★★

BEAUTY POP

(ビューティーポップ) • Kiyoko Arai • Viz (2006– ongoing) • Shogakukan (Ciao, 2003–ongoing) • 8+ volumes (ongoing) • Shôjo, Drama • 13+

Kiri Koshiba has a magic touch that helps people turn from ugly ducklings into beautiful swans by giving them excellent haircuts. But despite her genius skills, Kiri isn't interested in becoming a beautician and cuts hair only when she is moved by someone's plight (and even then she often balks). Not so Narumi, the coolest boy in school and leader of the three-man makeover squad Scissor Project. Narumi's dream is to become the best beautician in Japan, and he is enraged that the indifferent Kiri might be his competition. Although Kiri is ostensibly the main character, she's a little too sleepy and standoffish to really capture the reader's attention. It falls to the boys of the Scissor Project to hold things together between Kiri's manic-depressive bouts of magic. The story lines are, of course, makeover-oriented; the art is clean and cute with nice character designs and a very restrained but effective use of screentone. As can be expected from a hair-cutting manga, special attention is paid to the characters' hair, each flyaway strand carefully inked, each floppy cowlick lovingly delineated. (HS)   ★★½

BECAUSE I'M THE GODDESS

Kamisama da Mono, "Because I'm the Goddess" (神様だもの) • Shamneko • Tokyopop (2006–2007) • Wani Books (Comic Gum, 2003–2004) • 3 volumes • Seinen, Fantasy, Comedy • 16+ (mild language, frequent partial nudity, sexual situations)

Pandora, a big-breasted, dopey goddess who talks about herself in the third person, comes to Earth to show people the power of the gods, and attract large crowds of men. But using too much power causes her to transform into a little girl, after which only a kiss from Aoi—her unwilling young male protector—can turn her back into her normal bombshell self. Although there's a fair amount of T&A, the inane plot revolves around evil spirits sent to Earth to possess people. The art is crude and slightly old-fashioned, with a 1980s/early-1990s look. ★

BECK: MONGOLIAN CHOP SQUAD

Beck (ベック) • Harold Sakuishi • Tokyopop (2005–ongoing) • Kodansha (Monthly Shônen Magazine, 2000–ongoing) • 29+ volumes (ongoing) • Shônen, Rock and Roll, Comedy, Drama • 16+ (language, crude humor, frequent mild violence, partial nudity, sexual situations)

Beck: Mongolian Chop Squad represents the upper echelons of the *Weekly Shônen Magazine* house style: a cool, fast-paced comedy-drama with refreshingly unforced plot development. The plot follows two teenage musicians: Yukio, the reader's slightly-too-wimpy stand-in, a bullied nobody with hidden musical talent; and Ryusuke, an assertive

kid who grew up in America, and who owns Beck, a pooping, biting dog who looks like several different dogs stitched together. While Ryusuke tries to get his band (also named Beck) off the ground, the perpetually luckless Yukio learns to play guitar to impress a girl, practicing till his fingers bleed ("I'm gonna play my ass off!") and taking music lessons from a middle-aged swim coach whose apartment is full of porn and blow-up sex dolls. The plot has the good elements of an American teen movie (sharp humor, a rock-and-roll esteem-building moral, and just a bit of sleaze); as for the art, Sakuishi draws stiffly but pleasantly, with the self-assurance of a good caricature artist. One of the best features of the manga is that Sakuishi really knows his music, exclusively Western music; the Red Hot Chili Peppers, Led Zeppelin, Nirvana, and Offspring are just a few of the groups mentioned by name. As for the name of the manga/dog/band, when one character proposes calling their band Beck, another character protests, "There's *already* a Beck!" Evidently the real-life musician Beck Hansen is okay with the homage, since volume 4 of the manga was shrink-wrapped with a promotional code to download a Beck song (technically Super-thriller covering Beck's "Go It Alone") from Tokyopop's Web site.   ★★★½

BEET THE VANDEL BUSTER

Bôken o Beet, "Adventure King Beet" (冒険王ビィト) • Riku Sanjo (story), Koji Inada (art) • Viz (2004–ongoing) • Shueisha (Monthly Shônen Jump, 2004–ongoing) • 12+ volumes (ongoing) • Shônen, Fantasy, Battle • All Ages (violence)

In a postapocalyptic fantasy world ruled by monsters called Vandels, the endlessly optimistic young Beet becomes a Vandel Buster, a sort of paid Vandel assassin. He sets out to destroy all the Vandels in the world, accumulating teammates along the way. In Japan, creators Sanjo and Inada are best known for *Dai's Great Adventure,* a manga based on the *Dragon Quest* video game series, and *Beet* also reads like a role-playing game come to life. Busters get points for destroying Vandels and other monsters, and everyone's strength

Kentaro Miura's *Berserk*

the 1940s instead of the 1990s. The self-contained stories are frequently ghoulish, but Taniguchi's characteristically restrained artwork depicts the blood and death in a cool, calm fashion. On the front cover of the Japanese edition, it is appropriately labeled (in English) a "diabolical hard-boiled story." The wordless, sound-effects-free battle sequence in chapter 3 is particularly notable.

★★★

BERSERK

(ベルセルク) • Kentaro Miura • Dark Horse (2003–ongoing) • Hakusensha (Young Animal, 1989–ongoing) • 31+ volumes (ongoing) • Seinen, Fantasy, Horror, Adventure • 18+ (language, frequent extreme graphic violence, nudity, sex)

A blood-soaked sword-and-sorcery epic with elements of Clive Barker's *Hellraiser*. In a Dark Ages of ceaseless war, a lone warrior walks the land: Guts, a one-eyed, one-armed swordsman with a giant sword and an automatic crossbow grafted onto his prosthetic arm. Half mad, shunning human contact, Guts fights the literally demonic feudal lords of Midland, seeking revenge on the friend who betrayed him and opened the gates of hell into the world. Don't let the antiheroic violence of the opening chapters fool you—*Berserk* is no mere exploitation comic, it's an almost dead-serious, epic tragedy. A lengthy flashback from volumes 3 to 14 reveals Guts's past, from his birth under the gallows tree to his youth as a mercenary, when he fought in vast military battles and met the loves of his life. *Berserk*'s medieval European world of mud and blood is so realistic—and drawn in such realistic detail—that when dark fantasy elements begin to intrude upon it, they do so with a slow, dawning horror. (There are a few exceptions, such as Guts's sidekick Puck, a winged fairy-like creature.) The story is savage in the extreme, with sexual abuse (of both genders) and elements of tentacle rape, but the most explicit scenes are timed to hit the reader with maximum emotional impact. For once, this is a manga about an angry bad-ass in which you actually understand how he got that way. The art combines close-up violent scenes drawn in splattery

is judged by their "Levels." Bright, energetic artwork, a cheerful tone, and a focus on character development make *Beet* a bit better than most manga of this type. The Vandels are actually more interesting characters than the humans. The Viz edition censors some of the PG dialogue; most notably, a dirty-minded pilot's desire to grope girls' breasts is downgraded to wanting kisses. (CT)

★★★

BENKEI IN NEW YORK

N.Y. no Benkei, "Benkei of New York" (N.Y. の弁慶) • Jiro Taniguchi (art), Jinpachi Mori (story) • Viz (2001) • Shogakukan (Big Comic Original Zôkan, 1991–1996) • 1 volume • Seinen, Crime Drama • Unrated/18+ (language, graphic violence, nudity)

Japanese expatriate Benkei is a man for all seasons: he's both a mild-mannered painter and a cold-blooded hit man who specializes in cases of revenge. *Benkei in New York* has a deliberately retro film noir feel; with its fedoras, Mafia stooges, and wealthy art patrons, it might be set in the New York of brushstrokes, with wide-screen shots of castles and armies drawn in intricate detail.

★★★★

BEST OF POKÉMON ADVENTURES: See *Pokémon Adventures*

BETWEEN THE SHEETS: See *Erica Sakurazawa: Between the Sheets*

BEYBLADE

Beyblade Bakuten Shoot, "Beyblade Explosive Revolution Shoot" (ベイブレードー 爆転SHOOT) • Takao Aoki • Viz (2004–2006) • Shogakukan (Corocoro Comic, 1999–2004) • 14 volumes • Shônen, Game, Battle • All Ages

A manga based on the "battling tops" toy franchise, a smash hit in Japan that came stateside and fizzled out. The premise is simple: two players use spinning tops launched by a rip cord, the tops spin into a ring and bounce off each other, and whoever's top is the last one spinning is the winner. The manga takes this concept and builds a hyperactive story around it starring a plucky young "blader" named Tyson. One day after losing a match to the neighborhood Beyblade bully, Tyson meets a mysterious masked man who gives him a special Beyblade, the Blue Dragon. From there he faces many opponents in a series of crazy battles, each more and more outlandish. While it's clearly designed to cash in on the Beyblade craze, the art is just spastic enough to be enjoyable, and the dialogue sometimes gives a sincere chuckle. The pacing is designed for kids with zero attention spans. (RB) ★★

BEYOND THE BEYOND

Sono Mukô no Mukôgawa, "Beyond the Beyond" (その向こうの向こう側) • Yoshitomo Watanabe • Tokyopop (2006–ongoing) • Mag Garden (Comic Blade, 2004–ongoing) • 4+ volumes (ongoing) • Fantasy, Adventure • 13+ (brief language)

Futaba, a young boy, is surprised when a girl falls out of the sky and (more or less by random chance) teleports him to a fantasy world, where they meet a wizard in the form of a cute animal, a giant talking cat, the spirit of a city, and other strange characters. It turns out that the girl is actually a magical being, the wish-granting Amaranthine, whom the princes of the realm seek for ambiguous motives. *Beyond the Beyond* is a mellow, meandering fantasy series with a children's-book feel. The artwork is a gentle *shôjo/shônen* hybrid, and although the world around the characters feels unformed apart from the immediately surrounding forests and houses, the situations they encounter are interesting. No relation to the PlayStation game series of the same name. ★★★

THE BIG O

(THEビッグオー) • Hitoshi Ariga (story and art), Hajime Yatate (original concept) • Viz (2002–2004) • Kodansha (Magazine Z, 1999–2001) • 6 volumes • Shônen, Science Fiction, Mecha, Drama • All Ages (mild language, violence, brief sexual situations)

Sometime in the future, the known world has shrunk to the domed megalopolis of Paradigm City, where forty years ago everyone lost all their memories of the past. While the neurotic inhabitants of the city deal with their personal memory loss in various ways, strange remnants of forgotten super-science keep turning up in the catacombs beneath the city: the MegaDeus, giant robots that are used by human pilots for nefarious ends. The mightiest robot of all is the Big O, the secret possession of Roger Smith, a gentlemanly professional negotiator who lives a double life as a robot-piloting scourge of evil. The *Big O* anime TV series, whose first season this manga was based on, combined *Batman*-esque pulp visuals with robot-slamming action and unresolved mysteries in the style of *Dark City* and *The Prisoner.* The manga adaptation starts as a standard spin-off, but over the six volumes Ariga's artwork and writing improve dramatically, and the stories become increasingly original and surreal. The simple but iconic characters, the work of a born cartoonist, inhabit a world of light and shadow. By the end, it's one of the rare adaptations that may be even better than the original—although Ariga is ultimately limited by the fact that the anime had no real ending and he can provide only suggestions, not answers. A two-volume sequel manga by Ariga, *The Big O: Lost Memory,* was never translated. ★★★½

BIO-BOOSTER ARMOR GUYVER

Kyôshoku Sôkô Guyver, "Strength-Boosting Armor Guyver" (強殖装甲ガイバー) • Yoshiki Takaya • Viz (1992–1997) • Tokuma Shoten/Kadokawa Shoten (Monthly Shônen Captain/Monthly Ace Next/Monthly Shônen Ace, 1985–ongoing) • 7 volumes, suspended (24+ volumes in Japan, ongoing) • Shônen, Tokusatsu, Science Fiction, Action • 13+ (mild language, graphic violence)

When teenage Sho accidentally touches a strange artifact of alien technology, it comes alive and bonds to his body, forming an insect-like power suit—the Guyver. But now that he is linked to the mighty bio-armor (which vanishes when not needed), he and his friends become the targets of Chronos, an evil conspiracy that plans to rule the world using their armies of monsters, the Zoanoids and Zoalords. In America, *Guyver* was a popular anime and manga title of the early 1990s (it was even adapted into two American live-action movies), possibly because the premise and execution are so similar to an American superhero comic. (In fact, it is a superhero show one culture removed . . . it was intended as a slightly more squishy, slimy version of a *tokusatsu* show such as *Kamen Rider* or *Ultraman.*) The *shônen* manga plot has some memorable twists and turns, and plenty of heroic angst, in a plot that mostly involves eight-foot-tall monsters running around in the woods fighting one another. (Some of the monsters look pretty good; all look like rubber suits.) In Japan, the series has continued for more than twenty years from two separate publishers; however, the English edition ends at one of the most terrible points to end a manga ever, just as one character is powering up an energy attack to blast another. Some nudity is censored in the English edition. ★★½

BIRTHDAY: See *The Ring, Vol. 4: Birthday*

BLACK & WHITE

Tekkonkinkurito, "Iron/Muscle/Concrete" or "Ferro-Concrete" (鉄コン筋クリート) • Taiyo Matsumoto • Viz (1997–2000) • Shogakukan (Big Comic Spirits, 1993–1994) • 3 volumes • Seinen, Crime Drama • Unrated/18+ (mild language, violence, nudity)

In the sprawling, run-down metropolis of Treasure Town, two young orphans live on the streets, gleefully picking fights with gangbangers and *yakuza* twice their size. Part fairy tale, part superhero comic, *Black & White* contrasts the violent but hopeful world of the children (who, like Peter Pan, can fly with no explanation) with the sad, alienated adults around them. Matsumoto's hand-drawn art has its own visual vocabulary. A cartoon moon looks down on strip clubs and corpses. Changes in mood are expressed with free-associative glimpses of strange whimsy and beauty: nature, animals, plants, fish. If Matsumoto is inspired by Katsuhiro Otomo, *Black & White* is his mini-*Akira*: a comic about a city, given form with frequent fight scenes and a good-versus-evil plot. Some characters from *Blue Spring* reappear here. ★★★½

BLACK CAT (DHP): See *Hino Horror, Vol. 6: Black Cat*

BLACK CAT (VIZ)

(ブラック・キャット) • Kentaro Yabuki • Viz (2006–ongoing) • Shueisha (Weekly Shônen Jump, 2000–2004) • 20 volumes • Shônen, Crime, Action • 16+ (violence)

In this adventure manga clearly inspired by *Cowboy Bebop,* Train Heartnet, aka "Black Cat," is an easygoing bounty hunter who once worked as an assassin for the world-spanning super-organization Chronos. Together with Sven (a ladies' man with fedora and eye patch), Rinslet (a sexy thief), and Eve (a little girl with shape-shifting abilities), he roams the world, looking for his next meal and revenge on the people who did him wrong. For the first few chapters, *Black Cat* seems to take place in a world like our own (all the names are changed, but the Latin American cityscapes look interestingly familiar), but soon fantasy elements creep in among the heist scenes: nanotechnology, Taoists who use *chi*-based superpowers, dinosaurs. The banter between the characters flows nicely, but the heists are juvenile, and the generic artwork removes any anticipation of seeing what will come next. For a *shônen* manga about superpowered crooks, the later volumes of *Hunter x Hunter* are far superior. ★★

BLACK JACK

(ブラック・ジャック) • Osamu Tezuka • Viz (1997–1999) • Akita Shoten (Weekly Shônen Champion, 1973–1983) • 2 volumes, suspended (18 volumes in Japan) • Shônen, Medical Drama • Unrated/13+ (medical gore)

In Japan, *Black Jack* is arguably Tezuka's most popular manga. It placed second in *Comic Link* magazine's 1998 survey of readers' all-time favorite manga (*Banana Fish* came in first) and continues to inspire other manga, from a running parody in *Excel Saga* to an origin-story homage in *Ray*. (It's so archetypal that it's referenced in the title of Shûhô Satô's untranslated medical manga *Black Jack ni Yoroshiku,* "Say Hello to Black Jack," about a somewhat less experienced doctor.) Sadly, the Surgeon with the Hands of God has only made it to the English-speaking world via two out-of-print volumes from Viz. They're worth tracking down; *Black Jack* is Tezuka in full-throttle pulp mode, whisking the reader through outrageous, kinetic action and a generous helping of realistically rendered medical gore. The mysterious Black Jack, his stern two-tone face bisected by a scar, is a preternaturally gifted surgeon . . . but one who operates *outside the law*! He's assisted by the cute/creepy Pinoco, a half-synthetic little girl constructed from a patient's engulfed twin. Presumably Tezuka was inspired by his pre-manga education as a physician, but medical accuracy is not exactly paramount in these stories. Instead, Black Jack stoically performs such patently absurd surgical feats as, say, operating on his own intestines in the middle of the Australian outback while surrounded by ravenous dingoes. *Black Jack* is bizarre, intense, and melodramatic as only Tezuka can be, but also brilliantly told and immensely fun. (SG) ★★★★

BLACK MAGIC

(ブラックマジック) • Masamune Shirow • Dark Horse (1998) • Seishinsha (1983–1985) • 1 volume • Seinen, Science Fiction, Adventure • Unrated/13+ (violence)

Crude fanzine story that, if you squint hard, suggests the promise of the artist's later *Appleseed*. Shirow's earliest published work is a barely intelligible sci-fi story filled with a mix-and-match combination of random neat stuff: artificial life-forms, spider robots, aliens who look like *oni* (Japanese demons), flying vehicles, cyber-assassins, gunplay, swordplay, origins-of-humanity theorizing, and a goobledygook of Greek name references. The character designs bear a strong resemblance to Kaoru Shintani's *Area 88*. The anime version, *Black Magic M-66,* bears almost no resemblance to this story. Prior to the Dark Horse edition, the series was published by Eclipse Comics in the early 1990s. (JD) ★

BLACK SUN, SILVER MOON

Kuro no Taiyô Gin no Tsuki, "Black Sun, Silver Moon" (黒の太陽銀の月) • Tomo Maeda • Go! Comi (2007–ongoing) • Shinshokan (Wings, 2002–ongoing) • 6+ volumes (ongoing) • Shôjo, Fantasy, Comedy • 16+ (mild language, violence)

Because of his family's debts to the church, Taki becomes the servant of Shikimi, a priest. By day he does tons of chores—but by night he and Shikimi head out to the graveyard to fight the walking dead! NR

BLADE OF THE IMMORTAL

Mugen no Jûnin, "Inhabitant of Immortality" (無限の住人) • Hiroaki Samura • Dark Horse (1996–ongoing) • Kodansha (Afternoon, 1993–ongoing) • 20+ volumes (ongoing) • Seinen, Samurai, Drama • Unrated/18+ (language, frequent extreme graphic violence, partial nudity, sex)

Manji, a swordsman made immortal by "bloodworms" infesting his body (similar to

Hiroaki Samura's *Blade of the Immortal*

to the fact that good and evil are not always clear, and on the road of vengeance the heroes make uncomfortable choices and strange bedfellows. The villains' sadism is more suggested than shown (although the dialogue is grisly enough), and the gore of battle is strangely tasteful—in the early volumes, bodies are dismembered in elaborate freeze-frames composed to resemble traditional Japanese paintings. But it's the power of the writing (particularly as the story progresses) that makes it, at times, superior to the ultimate samurai manga *Lone Wolf and Cub*. Ogami Itto is a fascinating character, though two-dimensional, but Manji, Rin, Hyakurin, and Samura's other characters behave like real people faced with all of life's unpredictability. ★★★★

BLAME!

(ブラムBLAME!) • Tsutomu Nihei • Tokyopop (2005–2008) • Kodansha (Afternoon, 1997–2003) • 10 volumes • Seinen, Science Fiction, Action • 16+ (occasional language, graphic violence, suggestive imagery)

Influenced by the detailed architecture and wordless action scenes of French comics, this almost plotless manga follows a man's journey through endless metal catacombs, defending himself against biomechanical monsters. One of the greatest gothic/cyberpunk settings ever drawn, the world of *Blame!* is a dungeon thousands of levels deep, a colossal machine where giant larvae feed on the rusty walls and silicon-based life-forms hunt down the few human survivors. (It has a strong resemblance to *The Matrix*.) The colossal interiors convey an oppressive sense of scale, as the blank-slate hero, Killy, wanders for page after page through the darkness, falling into ravines, climbing back up again, sometimes encountering other humans, and becoming involved in bizarre, complicated scenarios with minimal explanation. (Mostly, though, he just shoots things with his gun, which can destroy almost anything.) It gets repetitive, but it looks great. Totally without humor or sentimentality, it's like an extended nightmare, or a really good video

the *Highlander* movies), roams Japan serving Rin, a girl seeking revenge on her parents' killers. Equally strong in both art and writing, this excellent series was praised in Japan as a marriage of "high" and "low" art (i.e., Samura's traditionally trained artistic skill and manga). The figure art has a fluid quality, showing tremendous skill at realistic life drawing, although the waif-thin women and anachronistically punk villains—wielding weird but plausible weapons—strike a pleasant balance between 1990s style and historical accuracy. The swordfighting action could carry the story by itself, but the plot is original as well; stories with immortal protagonists tend to wallow in angst-ridden puffery, but *Blade of the Immortal* avoids this by focusing on the fascinating side characters and skirting any "who is stronger than whom" debate. The earthy, cynical Manji (he's only been immortal for a few years) has vowed to kill one thousand evil men, but he's resigned

game. Perhaps appropriately, the title is pronounced "Blam!" in Japan.
★★★

BLEACH

(ブリーチ) • Tite Kubo • Viz (2004–ongoing) • Shueisha (Weekly Shônen Jump, 2001–ongoing) • 27+
volumes (ongoing) • Shônen, Occult, Samurai,
Battle • 13+ (violence)

Ichigo Kurosaki, a teenager with the ability
to see ghosts, is conscripted for duty as a
Soul Reaper—a spiritual being who exorcises good ghosts and fights evil ones, aka
Hollows, with a samurai sword. Starting
out as a monster-of-the-week manga (the
masked Hollows resemble Mexican Day of
the Dead figures), *Bleach* takes several 90-
degree turns; around volume 9 the heroes
travel to the Soul Society, the Soul Reapers'
home plane, which resembles feudal Japan,
and later they venture to other strange dimensions where even deadlier enemies
await. *Bleach* follows the conventional fight-
train-fight pattern of *Shônen Jump* manga,
with cinematic swordfighting combat; however, in addition to action, Kubo keeps things
entertaining with snarky Tarantino-esque
humor and weird ideas. This is a world of
occult Pez dispensers, TV spiritualists, animated teddy bears, and high-tech dimension
warping. Although the plot is not particularly character-driven, Ichigo's classmates
and the rest of the supporting cast are distinctive and occasionally sexy. More style
than substance, but a good read just the
same.   ★★★

BLIND DATE: See *Harlequin Violet: Blind
Date*

BLOOD ALONE

Masayuki Takano • Infinity Studios (2006–ongoing)
• MediaWorks (Dengeki Daioh, 2004–ongoing) •
3+ volumes (ongoing) • Shônen, Vampire, Drama •
Not Rated Yet/13+ (violence, mild sexual situations)

Misaki, a vampire whose mind is trapped in
the body of a little girl, lives with her friend
and guardian Kuroe, a twenty-something
writer. With the curtains drawn, they laze

From Shueisha's *Weekly Shônen Jump*

around their ornately furnished city apartment, quietly reading, writing, playing with
a cat, or simply enjoying each other's company. But when night falls, they go out on
the dark streets, where detectives pursue serial killers and evil vampires, not knowing
the truth of Kuroe and Misaki's strange relationship. Part suspense, part relationship story,
Blood Alone is slow-paced, but it's a well-
executed, quiet tale that handles its creepy
subtext of forbidden love in a tasteful manner. Masayuki Takano's art is conventionally
cute but restrained and atmospheric.   ★★★

BLOOD: THE LAST VAMPIRE 2002

BLOOD: THE LAST VAMPIRE 2000 • Benkyo
Tamaoki • Viz (2002) • Kadokawa Shoten (2001) • 1
volume • Seinen, Vampire, Action, Horror • 18+
(language, graphic violence, explicit nudity, sex)

A sequel to the *Blood: The Last Vampire*
anime, set in the modern day instead of the
1960s. Saya, the seemingly emotionless
vampire heroine, is still killing her own kind
at the behest of the U.S. government, but

Kiriko Nananan's *Blue*

iant effort to defeat the vampire but is bested and forced to watch as the creature drinks the woman's blood. The cop ends up in a loony bin, only to be rescued by a special cop squad that's trying to stem the tide of vampires. . . . While the premise isn't terrible, the execution falls short; the action's often poorly drawn and hard to follow, and the characters are uninteresting. (RB)   NR

BLUE

(ブルー) • Kiriko Nananan • Fanfare/Ponent Mon (2004) • Magazine House (Comic Are!, 1996–1997) • 1 volume • Yuri, Underground, Romantic Drama • Unrated/13+ (brief language, sexual situations)

Kayako, a teenager sheltered by her group of friends, becomes curious about her classmate Masami, a loner who hides her secrets behind an inscrutable smile. Desire for friendship soon turns into love, and the two develop a lesbian (or partly lesbian) relationship. Mostly told from inside Kayako's head, *Blue* is a realistic story of "sweet, painful love," whose characters rarely express their feelings directly or in the best ways. Nananan's high-contrast, harshly lit artwork contributes to the feeling of disconnect and detachment. The characters' faces are drawn like overexposed photographs, as if the light shining on them is too bright to bear; when the camera turns away from their faces, as it often does, it's because the unspoken emotions are too intense to look them in the eye.   ★★★½

the mood has grown colder and more sadistic. The antagonists are a vampire street gang who, as in the anime, transform into grotesque batlike monsters. A female character who looks identical to Saya provides adult manga artist Benkyo Tamaoki with an excuse to draw the heroine in graphic sex scenes. Tamaoki's heroin-chic artwork is distinctive but sparse, and the "origin of the vampires" plot is predictable.   ★★

BLOOD SUCKER: LEGEND OF ZIPANGU

Yato no Kamitsukai, "The Familiar Spirit of the Night Blade God" (夜刀の神つかい) • Saki Okuse (story), Aki Shimizu (art) • Tokyopop (2006–ongoing) • Gentosha (Comic Birz, 2001–ongoing) • 11+ volumes (ongoing) • Seinen, Vampire, Action, Horror • 18+ (language, graphic violence, nudity)

Mediocre cop-buddy/action-horror manga. In the opening scene, a cop tracks the woman he loves to a lonely warehouse, where he finds her in the grip of a vampire that has just arisen from a three-hundred-year sleep. Trying his best to save her, he puts up a val-

BLUE INFERIOR

(ブルー・インフェリア) • Kyoko Shitou • ADV (2004) • Ushio Shuppansha (Comic Tom) • 1 volume, suspended (4 volumes in Japan) • Science Fiction, Adventure • All Ages

In a pollution-ravaged future, only a few "blessed lands" lie on the coasts between vast deserts, and the surviving communities live in fear of the "subhumans" who dwell in the wasteland. One day Kazuya, a fourteen-year-old orphan who loves the sea, finds a girl washed up on the beach: Marine, a mysterious girl with no memory of her past.

Blue Inferior is an uneventful but solid young-adult science fiction story with impressive 1980s *shôjo* artwork. Palm trees stand in the bright sun, coral reefs and fish are drawn with beautiful detail, and the heroes spend much of their time exploring nature: snorkeling, digging for insects, and so on. Unfortunately, only one volume is available in translation, leaving the plot unresolved.

★★★

BLUE SPRING

Aoi Haru, "Blue Spring" (青い春) • Taiyo Matsumoto • Viz (2004) • Shogakukan (Big Comic Spirits, 1993) • 1 volume • Seinen, Crime Drama • 18+ (language, violence, sex, nudity)

A collection of melancholy short stories about teenagers on the edge of adulthood, mostly delinquents, engaged in self-destructive behavior. This early Matsumoto work shows his favorite subjects: youth and age, and the power of landscapes, particularly forgotten and neglected urban landscapes such as fast-food joints and graffiti-choked schools. While Matsumoto's *No. 5* and *Black & White* function as unconventionally drawn action comics, *Blue Spring* is more experimental, providing glimpses of worlds where nothing happens, and worlds where bad things happen for no reason. ★★★½

BOBOBO-BO BO-BOBO

(ボボボーボ・ボーボボ) • Yoshio Sawai • Viz (2005) • Shueisha (Weekly Shônen Jump, 2001—ongoing) • 1 volume, suspended (21+ volumes in Japan, ongoing) • Shônen, Comedy, Battle • 16+ (language)

Slapstick, short-attention-span parody of fighting manga in general and *Weekly Shônen Jump* in particular. Bobobo-bo, master of the "Fist of the Nose Hair," battles the deadly bosses of the Bald Empire, accompanied by his edible sidekicks (who exist mostly to be used as shields and gorily mutilated) and two "normal" spiky-haired manga kids (who exist mostly to deliver unnecessary reaction shots and say things like "Whoa, that's crazy!"). Impressively absurd and almost totally plotless, with some good cynical one-liners among the comic beat-downs, it reads better in small doses than as a whole book. To American readers, it's often difficult to tell what is an untranslatable pun, what is a pop culture reference (some preserved in translation, some not), and what is just randomness for its own sake. The Viz edition consists of an excerpted story line from volumes 9 and 10 of the Japanese edition, reportedly the artist's favorite part of the series. ★★½

BOMBER GIRL

(ボンバーガール) • Makoto Niwano • Gutsoon! Entertainment (2003) • Shueisha (Weekly Shônen Jump, 1994) • 1 volume • Shônen, Comedy, Action • 18+ (language, crude humor, graphic violence, sexual situations)

Incredibly stupid action-comedy manga, vaguely parodying *The Dirty Pair* and other 1980s/early-1990s anime and manga. In near-future Tokyo, Rashomon Emi is a money-hungry bounty hunter in a short skirt and spiked breastplate, who behaves like a dominatrix, extorts money from innocents, and smashes perps' brains with her customized *tonfa*s (a *tonfa* is similar to a nightstick). ("Look what you did to my outfit! Now you're *really* in for it!"). The ugliness of the art is clearly intentional, but there's no excuse for the horrible story, which ends on a cliff-hanger. 0 Stars

BOOGIEPOP DOESN'T LAUGH

Boogiepop wa Warawanai, "Boogiepop Doesn't Laugh" (ブギーポップは笑わない) • Kouhei Kadono (original creator), Kouji Ogata (art) • Seven Seas Entertainment (2006) • MediaWorks (Dengeki Animation Magazine, 2000–2002) • 2 volumes • Shônen, Occult, School, Horror • 16+ (violence, nudity)

Manga adaptation of *Boogiepop and Others,* the first in Kouhei Kadono's *Boogiepop* series of supernatural light novels, involving a spooky supernatural creature in the form of a girl in a weird purple hat. When girls start to disappear from school, many people wonder whether the elusive *shinigami* (death spirit) Boogiepop, a sort of urban legend, is responsible. But in fact, Boogiepop is actually trying to stop a creature named Manticore, who (with the help of a male student) lures the girls into its clutches to serve as food or as puppets for its evil scheme. The story is told in a nonlinear fashion, through short vignettes that leave readers to put together the whole gruesome story themselves. Apart from the color covers and inserts, the artwork is bland and sketchy. The characters are nearly identical to one another, and there's also little action to follow, as most of the book is dialogue. Luckily for new readers who are unfamiliar with the *Boogiepop* world, there is a comprehensive guide at the end of both volumes, but it's still hard to get into. (KT)   ★★½

BOOGIEPOP DUAL: LOSER'S CIRCUS

Boogiepop Dual: Make Inutachi no Circus, "Boogiepop Dual: Loser's Circus" (ブギーポップ・デュアル 負け犬たちのサーカス) • Kouhei Kadono (original creator), Masayuki Takano (art) • Seven Seas Entertainment (2006) • MediaWorks (Dengeki Daioh, 1999–2000) • 2 volumes • Shônen, Occult, School, Horror • 16+ (violence, partial nudity, sexual situations)

An original spin-off of the *Boogiepop* world, *Boogiepop Dual* introduces an entirely new cast of characters and a more linear story than the short vignettes in which the other manga series (and the anime) are told. A new Boogiepop emerges with a male host, once again called on to fight the spiritual displacements that threaten the everyday world. This time these disruptions are in the form of a teacher who sexually abuses his female students. Despite its chronological storytelling, the manga still makes the reader strain to put together all the clues, only tipping its hand at the very end. Takano's art is creepy and atmospheric, while still delivering the familiar anime-style character designs, and the plot is easier to jump into than the other *Boogiepop* manga. (KT)   ★★★

BOW WOW WATA

Gau Gau Wata, "Bow Wow Wata" (ガウガウわー太) • Kazumi Umekawa • Gutsoon! Entertainment (2003–2004) • Coamix (Weekly Comic Bunch,

2001–2005) • 2 volumes, suspended (11 volumes in Japan) • Pet, Comedy, Drama • 13+ (violence)

Tasuke, the reluctant son of a veterinarian, discovers that he can hear animals' thoughts because his father is the "Shinto god of dogs" Komainu-sama. When he develops a crush on Misato, the cute owner of the unfriendly old dog Wata, he enters a sort of human-dog romantic triangle. Primarily, though, this is a pet medical drama, with stories based on animal health problems, apparently based on the author's experience as a certified veterinarian ("You know what's the most important thing in summer, don't you? It's preventing filaria!"). The animals are drawn more realistically than the humans, and their behavior is more aggressive than any American cute-animal comic, with plenty of biting and scratching. More of the story was published in *Raijin* magazine but never collected.   ★★½

BOYS BE

Boys Be . . . • Masahiro Itabashi (story), Hiroyuki Tamakoshi (art) • Tokyopop (2004–ongoing) • Kodansha (Weekly Shônen Magazine, 1997–2000) • 20 volumes • Shônen, Romantic Comedy • 16+ (language, partial nudity, sexual situations)

A long-running anthology series of short romantic comedies, mostly involving shy guys and flirty girls, although the sheer quantity of the stories leads to some interesting variations. Most of the stories involve kisses or love confessions, or are excuses for women to pose in scanty outfits, but the hero does not always get the girl, and a few of the stories are impressively funny. In "Attention Please! Chameleon Boy!" the main character tries desperately to keep his girlfriend from breaking up with him through abrupt personality changes. In "Our Unique Turn-Ons," three guys talk about their favorite fetishes, such as the backs of women's necks, mohair sweaters, and (the weird guy's choice) the cross-section of an apple. Initially crowded with too many small panels per page, the art opens up and improves as it goes on; however, the repetitive character designs make it difficult to tell one girl from the others. In Japan, the series was printed as *Boys Be . . . 2nd Season,* a sequel to the original 32–volume (!) *Boys Be . . .* series. Historical trivia: the title is a reference to "Boys, be ambitous!", a famous out-of-context English-language catchphrase in Japan, spoken by visiting American professor William S. Clark when he departed Sapporo Agricultural College in 1877. ★★½

BOYS OF SUMMER

Chuck Austen (story), Hiroki Otsuka (art) • Tokyopop (2006–ongoing) • 3 volumes • Sports, Romantic Comedy • 16+ (language, mild violence, nudity, sexual situations)

When Bud Waterston starts his freshman year in college, he moves into dorms where sexy girls flash their breasts and invite him to parties. When he demonstrates his incredible pitcher's arm, Chrissie, the baseball coach's daughter, tries to get him to sign up for baseball . . . but Bud has given up on the sport ever since the death of his father. Drawn by adult-manga artist Hiroki Otsuka from a script by American comics writer Chuck Austen, *Boys of Summer* is a successful cross-cultural collaboration. Otsuka's art has a mature, *jôsei/seinen* look, with strong figure art and minimal use of screentone; the characters are full-lipped women and buff, chiseled guys who look like they could actually have sex with one another. The tone is subdued and the American setting is authentic, making effective use of photo backgrounds. ★★★

BOYS OVER FLOWERS

Hana Yori Dango, "Boys Before Flowers" (花より男子) • Yoko Kamio • Viz (2003–ongoing) • Shueisha (Margaret, 1992–2003) • 36 volumes • Shôjo, Romantic Drama • 13+ (language, violence, sexual situations)

Tsukushi, a girl from a lower-middle-class family, is bullied, beaten, ostracized—and romanced—when she stands up to her snobbish classmates at an elite private high school. In a bickering, tempestuous relationship, she is drawn toward two fabulously wealthy men: the kind Rui Hanazawa and the arrogant, temperamental (and sometimes physically abusive) Tsukasa Domyoji. Basically a vicarious Cinderella story full of mansions, yachts, Louis Vuitton bags, and international vacations, *Boys over Flowers* is distinguished by its strong heroine, the proudly "weedlike" Tsukushi, who always stands up to the powers that be. (As in many manga, rich people in *Boys over Flowers* constantly use words such as "pauper" and "peasant.") The story reads quickly, and although some subplots are more implausible than others, it never drifts into exploitation or betrays the characters' original personalities. Not a sappy love story, it's a character-driven tale of social and relationship struggles that keeps the reader wondering what will happen next. ★★★★

BRAIN POWERED

(ブレンパワード) • Yukiru Sugisaki (art), Yoshiyuki Tomino (original story) • Tokyopop (2003) • Kadokawa Shoten (Monthly Shônen Ace, 1998–1999) • 4 volumes • Shônen, Science Fiction, Mecha, Adventure • 13+ (underwear, violence)

A confusing but pretty adaptation of the pretty but confusing 1998 anime series from *Gundam* director Yoshiyuki Tomino. The world of the near future is wracked by typhoons, earthquakes, flash floods, and other disaster-movie effects as an immense, long-dormant alien spaceship slowly rises from the depths of the ocean. A multicultural cast of characters, piloting organic don't-call-them-giant-robots, fight to either stop the imminent disaster or survive it aboard the alien ship. Meanwhile, the reader struggles to keep track of who's related to whom and puzzle out the mystifying plot. The manga teeters entertainingly along the razor edge of comprehensibility, much like the source anime, and then tries to cram ten anime episodes' worth of plot into the final volume. It does all look gorgeous, though. (MS) ★★½

Speech bubbles within image:
STAY AWAY FROM ME!! WHO ARE YOU? YOU'RE NOT HUMAN, ARE YOU?!
WHAT'S WRONG, MINAKO ?
I AM...
ME?
ALSO CALLED THE GOD OF FEAR.
I AM DEIMOS.
DEIMOS... YOU'RE THE DEVIL!
I CAME HERE TO TAKE YOU BACK.
WHY...?

Etsuko Ikeda and Yuho Ashibe's *Bride of Deimos*

BRIDE OF DEIMOS

Akuma (Deimos) no Hanayome, "Bride of the Devil (Deimos)" (悪魔[デイモス]の花嫁) • Etsuko Ikeda (story), Yuho Ashibe (art) • ComicsOne (2002–2004) • Akita Shoten (Princess, 1975–1983) • 7 volumes, suspended (17 volumes in Japan) • Shôjo, Horror • 13+ (language, violence, partial nudity)

Schoolgirl Minako Ifu finds herself stalked by a terrifying figure, the black-winged, horned Deimos (the Greek god of panic or terror), who says she is the reincarnation of his bride. From story to story Deimos appears in various guises, occasionally pursuing Minako, but usually acting as an instigator and witness to supernatural tales of tainted love and random doom. A classic of purple *shôjo* horror, *Bride of Deimos* makes no concessions to realism; the hapless heroine witnesses a new tragedy in every chapter, and the better stories have an element of bleak, illogical gruesomeness. (Hint: when someone asks, "Can love's passion break through reason?" in a *shôjo* manga, the answer is always yes.) While not as accomplished as *Rose of Versailles* and *Swan,* the 1970s artwork is graceful and impressionistic, with cascades of hair, dripping blood, and the occasional satanic imagery or suggestive Beardsley-esque candles. The sloppy translation takes some of the class out of the story, which admittedly is written for younger readers.

★★★

BRIGADOON

Brigadoon: Marin to Melan, "Brigadoon: Marin and Melan" (BRIGADOONまりんとメラン) • Hajime Yatate and Yoshitomo Yonetani (original concept), Nozomi Watase (manga) • Tokyopop (2003) • Kadokawa Shoten (Monthly Ace Next, 2000–2001) • 2 volumes • Science Fiction, Fantasy, Mecha • 13+ (violence, brief partial nudity)

Cookie-cutter retelling of the *Brigadoon* anime. Marin is a spunky poor girl in 1969 Japan. One day she meets a talking cat and a powerful blue robot, who tells her that its name is Melan Blue and it was sent to protect her. Meanwhile, in the sky appears a giant floating city, Brigadoon, which is somehow tied to Marin and Melan Blue and the survival of the Earth. While the manga tells the same tale as the anime, it adds nothing new and doesn't look as good. The entire twenty-six-episode TV series is condensed into two volumes, so much of the story is left out. (RB)

★

BRINGING HOME THE SUSHI

Various artists • Mangajin (1995) • 1 volume • Salaryman, Comedy, Drama • Unrated/13+ (mild language)

Subtitled *An Inside Look at Japanese Business Through Japanese Comics, Bringing Home the Sushi* collects samples of nine different occupational manga, from family-newspaper cheerful (*Tsuri-Baka Nisshi,* "Diary of a Fishing Freak") to serious and even melancholy (*Ningen Kôsaten,* "Human Crossroads"). Explanatory essays accompany each manga segment. While the collapse of the early-1990s Japanese bubble economy makes the stories more or less into period pieces, the book contains fascinating insights into workplace culture, family roles, and sexism, as well as sights that only manga can provide, such as a drunken, flag-wearing American auto manufacturer, a parody of Lee Iacocca, giving piggyback rides to Japanese businessmen. The artists include Jirô Gyû, Kenshi Hirokane, Kenichi Kitami, Yôsuke Kondô, Tatsuo Nitta, Sadao Shôji, Hiroshi Tanaka, Kazuyoshi Torii, Masao Yajima, Jûzô Yamasaki, and the lone female voice, Risu Akizuki. Two of the manga have been translated elsewhere: Risu Akizuki's *Survival in the Office: The Evolution of Japanese Working Women* and Kenshi Hirokane's *Kosaku Shima*. A fascinating book, sadly out of print.

★★★★

BROKEN ANGELS

Kowarehajimeta Tenshitachi, "Angels Who Have Started to Break" (壊れはじめた天使たち) • Setsuri Tsuzuki • Tokyopop (2006–2007) • Kadokawa Shoten (Asuka, 1999–2003) • 5 volumes • Shôjo, Psychic, Fantasy • 16+ (language, nudity, sexual situations)

The story of an unusual girl named Fujiwara Sunao who likes to dress in boys' clothes and has the power to control water. She uses her powers and insights to help disturbed people around her; for instance, she helps a man realize that the reason his kid acts out is because he recently lost his mother. While helping out, Fujiwara rattles off trite philosophy such as "The only one who can reach your dreams is you" or "You won't find happiness with a closed heart." Unfortunately, in addition to weak writing, *Broken Angels* suffers from bad storytelling and confusing art. It's never clear what's happening from page to page due to the sometimes nearly incomprehensible panel layouts. (RB)   ★

B'TX

Masami Kurumada • Tokyopop (2004–ongoing) • Kadokawa Shoten (Monthly Shônen Ace, 1995–2000) • Shônen, Science Fiction, Battle • 16 volumes • 13+ (mild language, constant graphic violence, brief nudity)

From the creator of *Knights of the Zodiac, B'TX* is the same elementary-school action formula with science fiction trappings. In order to save his genius childhood friend Kotaro, teenage Teppei must fight the evil Machine Empire, an army of cyborg bad guys. Teppei's weapons are his Messiah Fist battle gear and his horselike robot mount B'TX, the most powerful of the B'Ts, intelligent robots based on mythological beasts and monsters. (The designs scream "toy line.") The story is 99 percent action, with the hero's big fist pointed at the camera as he fights bad guys with names such as Metal Face; the frequently gory battle scenes, with H. R. Giger–esque bio-organic blobs and melting faces, clash grotesquely with the bright-eyed, fresh-faced main characters. The art is inconsistent and the English rewrite is intentionally over-the-top, like a Saturday morning cartoon ("You pathetic excuse for a minion!" "Quit giving me metallic lip, X!").   ★★

BUDDHA

(ブッダ) • Osamu Tezuka • Vertical (2003–2005) • Ushio Shuppan (Kibô no Tomo/Shônen World/Comic Tom, 1972–1983) • 8 volumes • Shônen, Religion, Historical Drama • Unrated/16+ (violence, nudity, sexual situations)

Tezuka's Buddhist beliefs work their way into many of his manga, such as *Phoenix,* but this is his most overtly religious work, an ambitious retelling of the life of the Buddha. Written for children but enjoyable for all ages, *Buddha* spices up the story of Prince Siddhartha's journey toward enlightenment with heaping doses of action, intrigue, and even slapstick comedy. Tezuka faithfully follows the outline of Buddhist dogma but expands on the personalities of the key figures in the Buddha's life, also adding original characters whose lives demonstrate tenets of the Buddha's teachings (and, often, include some extra two-fisted action for readers tiring of saintliness). Western readers may be shocked or baffled by Tezuka's often irreverent take on his subject matter; it's hard to imagine a Christian comic about the life of Jesus featuring bloody fight scenes, anachronistic sight gags, and the occasional fart joke alongside transcendent depictions of religious enlightenment. But *Buddha* has all these and more, and is ultimately both an engrossing, densely layered story and an inspiring exploration of faith. (SG)   ★★★★

THE BUG BOY: See *Hino Horror, Vol. 2: The Bug Boy*

BUS GAMER

Kazuya Minekura • Tokyopop (2006) • Square Enix (Stencil, 2001) • 1 volume • Action • 16+ (language, violence)

Toki, Nobuto, and Kazuo are recruited to play in the Biz Game, a three-versus-three capture-the-flag match that dictates the future of Japan's biggest corporations. Minekura starts in the middle of the story, not showing the battles until after the reader has a chance to appreciate the absurdity of the game's rules and the inability of the team to escape from them. Once the game actually begins, the violence is surprisingly powerful; manga comic relief and Minekura's *bishônen* art style are welcome contrasts to the dark story line. This is not *Battle Royale*—it does not attempt to make us hate the game—but it does agree that a human is defined only by his actions. The manga ends abruptly, apparently on hiatus. (SM)   ★★★

BUSO RENKIN

Busô Renkin, "Armored Alchemy" (武装錬金) • Nobuhiro Watsuki • Viz (2006–ongoing) • Shueisha (Weekly Shônen Jump, 2003–2006) • 10 volumes • Shônen, Battle • 16+ (violence, mild sexual situations)

"Alchemic warriors" are the only ones who can fight the Homunculi, man-eating artificial humanoids who can transform into robot animals (snakes, eagles, frogs, etc.). Kazuki, a boy with a big lance, and Tokiko, a superhero-like tough girl with the Valkyrie Skirt, are the high school heroes who fight the silly-looking villains using weapons conjured out of nowhere. Dull and disappointing, *Buso Renkin* is the latest in a string of *shônen* manga failures (such as the untranslated *Gun Blaze West*) by *Rurouni Kenshin* creator Nobuhiro Watsuki. His American-

comics-influenced art is more simplified and angular than ever but looks merely generic, and the clichéd story could entertain only the youngest readers. Watsuki's notes on what he was and wasn't allowed to do (such as have a villain make fun of Tokiko's facial scars) are more interesting than the manga itself, albeit depressing to read.   ★

BY THE SWORD

Yô, "Enchanting/Bewitching" (妖YO-U) • Sanami Matoh • ADV (2005) • Akita Shoten/Biblos (Princess 2000, Magazine Zero 2003–2005) • 2 volumes, suspended (3 volumes in Japan) • Shôjo, Fantasy, Adventure • 13+ (violence, partial nudity)

A clichéd feudal Japanese fantasy manga borrowing heavily from *Inu-Yasha.* Asagi, a demon hunter with a magic sword, wanders Japan along with two demons: Kaede, a half-demon girl, and Kurenai, her father, who is bound in spirit form except when he possesses his daughter and turns her into a combat expert. Their journey takes them into episodic encounters with various ghosts and monsters. The monster designs are boring (fangs + elf ears + tattoos = demon), the screentone-heavy art is hard to follow, and the mixture of monster-fighting action and kvetching comedy is strictly by the numbers. Some nudity is censored from the English edition.   ★

CAFÉ KICHIJOUJI DE

Café Kichijouji De, "At Café Kichijouji" (Café吉祥寺で) • Kyoko Negishi (story and art), Yuki Miyamoto (original concept) • DMP (2005–2006) • Shinshokan (Wings, 2000–2003) • 3 volumes • Shôjo, Comedy • 13+ (mild language, mild violence)

Spin-off of a Japanese "drama CD" series, following the exploits of five waiters: a neat freak, a narcissistic ladies' man, a starving student, a creepy occultist, and a cute-little-boy type with an evil streak and super-strength. Although the slick artwork prepares the reader for a cute-boy-a-thon, *Café Kichijouji De* is an unexpectedly sarcastic, twisted sitcom. When not dealing with completely outrageous day-to-day threats such as running from bulls or digging up mandrake roots, the characters spend most of their time fighting with one another or dealing with their pathetically slim paychecks. The hijinks never reach the heights of anarchy and surrealism of *Excel Saga* (or the British TV show *The Young Ones*), but it's got a good sense of humor. *Chibi* interludes space out the main chapters. ★★★

THE CAIN SAGA

Hakushaku Cain Series, "Count Cain Series" (伯爵カインシリーズ) • Kaori Yuki • Viz (2006–2007) • Hakusensha (Hana to Yume, 1991–1994) • 5 volumes • Gothic, Mystery • 18+ (occasional graphic violence, sexual situations)

Episodic gothic mysteries set in late-nineteenth-century London. In its best moments *The Cain Saga* captures the genuine ghoulishness of the Victorian era, or at least of its stereotypes. Repetitive but entertaining pulp stories of madwomen, incest, murder, and premature burial, they are tied together by the presence of Earl Cain Hargreaves, a handsome young dilettante with a tortured family background and a vast knowledge of poisons. The fun here is in Yuki's classical plots, and in the pleasure of seeing good-looking *shôjo* characters commit evil deeds; the art is often rough and crowded, but it gets the story across. The final portion of the series was published as *Godchild*. The series is very conservatively rated "for mature readers," perhaps for themes of incest and suicide. ★★½

CALLING YOU: KIMI NI SHIKA KIKOENAI

Kimi ni Shika Kikoenai Calling You, "I Can't Hear Anyone but You: Calling You" (きみにしか聞こえない—CALLING YOU) • Otsuichi (story), Setsuri Tsuzuki (art) • Tokyopop (2007) • Kadokawa Shoten (Asuka, 2003) • 1 volume • Shôjo, Drama • 13+

Manga adaptation of the novel by Otsuichi. In the title story, a pair of high schoolers so lonely that they don't even have cell phones strike up a psychic friendship through the imaginary phones inside their minds. Also included is the short story "Kizu/Kids," in which a boy discovers that his friend has the power to heal other people. (MS)　　NR

CALL ME PRINCESS

Hime 'tte Yonde Ne!, "Call me Princess" (姫ってよんでねっ) • Tomoko Taniguchi • CPM (1999–2003) • Jitsuyo no Nihonsha (1993) • 1 volume • Shôjo, Romance • All Ages (brief sexual humor)

Makoto, a teenage romantic who views her older sister's marriage as the ideal relationship, finds herself attracted to Ryu, her troubled stepbrother, when he moves into her household. A simple but well-told story for young readers, *Call Me Princess* makes up in charm what it lacks in melodrama. Taniguchi's artwork is at its cutest, with clear, clean linework. ★★½

THE CANDIDATE FOR GODDESS

Megami Kôhosei, "Goddess Cadet" (女神候補生) • Yukiru Sugisaki • Tokyopop (2004) • Wani Books (Comic Gum, 1997–2001) • 5 volumes • Seinen, Science Fiction, Mecha, Drama • 13+ (mild language)

Tedious giant robot story, better known for its anime adaptation. In the future, humanity is under attack by mute, impersonal, rarely seen aliens, who have reduced humanity to a single planet and scattered space colonies. The hero is a cadet at the Goddess Operator Academy, where young men (and a few women) compete and train to pilot humanity's last defense: vaguely female-looking giant robots. The dull story line focuses on inter-cadet crushes and rivalries and ends abruptly. Sugisaki's early artwork is underdeveloped and generic-looking, albeit more detailed than usual, due to all the ships and robots. ★

CANNON GOD EXAXXION

Hôshin Exaxxion, "Gun/Cannon God Exaxxion" (砲神エグザクソン) • Kenichi Sonoda • Dark Horse (2001–ongoing) • Kodansha (Afternoon, 1998–2004) • 7 volumes • Seinen, Military, Science Fiction, Mecha, Action • 18+ (language, nudity, graphic sex, graphic violence)

You Higuri's *Cantarella*

Said to have been inspired by *Neon Genesis Evangelion, Cannon God Exaxxion* actually borrows little other than *Evangelion*'s sense of scale and collateral damage: the giant robot Exaxxion is unharmed by a cannon blast that levels Mount Fuji, and when it walks, it rips through freeways like tissue paper, inadvertently sending innocent bystanders screaming to their deaths. Part Go Nagai robot freakout, part realpolitik military science fiction, the story begins when fascist aliens break their ruse of peaceful coexistence and take over the earth, crushing the human military with superior high-tech weapons. Luckily, a dirty old mad scientist has prepared the Exaxxion, and his teenage descendant Hoichi is forced to pilot it to save humanity, while both sides wage a propaganda war to spin the casualties. *Exaxxion* takes Sonoda's technology fetishism (see *Gunsmith Cats*) into the realm of science fiction, with antimatter, nanotechnology, and robots ranging from giant city-smashers to human-sized sexdroids. All these guns and phallic imagery aren't unintentional; the series has a strong sexual element, which gets increasingly explicit as it goes on. The actual number of giant robot battles is fairly small—most of the action involves alien political dealings and the hero running around outside the robot—and the high level of dramatic tension is occasionally buried in the dense script. Sonoda's stylized art drifts ever further away from reality and into a plastic-and-rubber world of shapes, be it the streamlined robots or the women's unlikely physiques. A sex scene is censored in volume 5 of the English edition. ★★★

CANON

Chika Shiomi • CMX (2007–ongoing) • Akita Shoten (Mystery Bonita, 1994–1996) • 4 volumes • Shôjo, Horror, Drama • 16+

When a vampire attacks her school, young Canon is mysteriously spared. She embarks on a quest for revenge against the bloodsucker who slaughtered her fellow students, but along the way she must make strange alliances.... NR

CANTARELLA

(カンタレラ) • You Higuri • Go! Comi (2005–ongoing) • Akita Shoten (Princess Gold, 2000–ongoing) • 10+ volumes (ongoing) • Shôjo, Historical, Occult, Drama • 16+ (mild language, violence, sexual situations)

Full of poison, treachery and plotting, this historical drama is based on the life of master schemer Cesare Borgia, with supernatural elements added. Born in Rome in A.D. 1475, the illegitimate son of a high-ranking priest, Cesare begins life as a sensitive *bishônen* who loves his stepmother and his stepsister, Lucrezia Borgia. But our antihero is haunted by dark spirits (literally), and after a series of tragedies he succumbs to evil, undergoing an abrupt personality change and using the "power of the beast" in his quest to rule Italy and then the world ("I will be my own god!"). The papal power struggles and corrupt nobility of Renaissance Italy provide a solid young-adult novel plot. On the other hand, despite attractive main characters and authentic-looking historical trappings, Higuri's art lacks depth and the action is often unclear. In other words, the story is slightly beyond the artist's abilities but still engrossing. In Japan, the series went on hiatus in 2005 so Higuri could work on other projects, although she has said she plans to return to it. ★★½

CARAVAN KIDD

(キャラバン・キッド) • Johji Manabe • Dark Horse (1992–1999) • Shogakukan (Weekly Shônen Jump Zôkan, 1987–1989) • 3 volumes • Shônen, Science Fiction, Adventure • Unrated/16+ (language, violence, partial nudity, mild sexual situations)

A surprisingly entertaining iteration of Manabe's standard adventure plot, which as usual revolves around a scantily clad sword-swinging babe and a couple of hapless schmoes who get dragged along on her vendetta against an evil empire and its legions of faceless goons. In this case the warrior heroine is named Mian Toris and endowed with an inexplicable fox tail, and the pair of dingbats whom she tags with dog collars and claims as her pets include horny teen Wataru and a bloblike, moneygrubbing little critter named Babo who provides a steady supply of welcome comic relief. The inevitable romantic pairing between Mian and Wataru is built up slowly and plausibly, and although the settings and vehicles aren't as detailed as in *Outlanders,* Manabe's cartooning is perfectly adequate. The English-language version rearranges the five Japanese volumes into three large-format books of about 300 pages each. (MS) ★★★

CARDCAPTOR SAKURA

(カードキャップターさくら) • CLAMP • Tokyopop (1999–2003) • Kodansha (Nakayoshi, 1996–2000) • 12 volumes • Shôjo, Magical Girl, Fantasy, Romance • All Ages

Cardcaptor Sakura isn't just one of the best kids' manga in translation, it's one of the very best manga available in English, period. When ten-year-old Sakura Kinomoto opens a mysterious book in her father's study, she lets loose a deck of magical "Clow Cards." Cerberus (better known as Kero-chan), the diminutive Guardian Beast, gives Sakura a magic wand and a mission—she must find and seal the escaped Clow Cards before disaster befalls the world. Sakura is aided by her best friend, the camcorder-toting, ultrarich Tomoyo, and indirectly by her watchful brother, Toya. Soon, Sakura meets her greatest rival and eventual partner, Li Syaoran, a Chinese boy who is descended from the one who made the cards. Sounds like a perfectly conventional, utterly forgetable premise, right? CLAMP isn't just a talented creative team—its members are shrewd businesswomen, and *Cardcaptor Sakura* was clearly crafted with merchandising in mind (Sakura's dozens of outfits, the collect-'em-all Clow Cards, adorable mascots). But in spite of these calculated elements, the series is brimming with warmth and joy and wonder that make the series much more than the sum of its parts. At its core, *Sakura* is about love in all its many forms: sibling love, childhood crushes, unrequited love, true love. There are too many romantic pairings to mention here, and each is handled with respect and without judgment. (The relationship of one of Sakura's classmates with a teacher, if seen as wish fulfillment, is sweet, but if taken too seriously is a bit disturbing.) CLAMP seems so uninterested in the collection quest formula they set up that in the second story arc (called "Master of the Clow" in Tokyopop's release), the cards disappear for chapters at a time to make room for the relationships. The artwork was a huge departure for CLAMP at the time of its release, cutting down on tones and using much thinner lines—the antithesis of *X/1999* visually as well as thematically. A real treat for manga readers young and old. (MT) ★★★★

CARDCAPTOR SAKURA: MASTER OF THE CLOW: See *Cardcaptor Sakura*

CASE CLOSED

Meitantei Conan, "Master Detective Conan" (名探偵コナン) • Gosho Aoyama • Viz (2004–ongoing) • Shogakukan (Weekly Shônen Sunday, 1994–ongoing) • 57+ volumes (ongoing) • Shônen, Mystery, Comedy, Drama • 16+ (occasional graphic violence)

Teenage overachiever and amateur detective Jimmy Kudo follows a shady pair of "men in black" one day and ends up transformed, by an experimental poison, into a grade-school-age kid. Forced to hide the truth from his family and friends for fear of being discovered by the thugs who poisoned him, he assumes the fake name Conan Edogawa (a composite of two famous mystery authors, Arthur Conan Doyle and Rampo Edogawa) and takes up residence with his not-quite-girlfriend Rachel, the captain of their school karate team, and her father, the hapless private eye Richard Moore. Conan solves Moore's cases while using a knockout trick and ventriloquist device invented by a friend to fool people into thinking that the answers are really coming from the adult PI instead of a pipsqueak kid. Meanwhile, he has to attend grade school again and come up with excuses for his older self's absence—like Superman masquerading as Clark Kent,

Conan often gets to hear Rachel's feelings about Jimmy, and has to work hard to keep her from guessing his true identity. The majority of cases are gory murders, complete with sprays of inky blood (the first volume includes a decapitation on a roller coaster), and the deceptively child-friendly wide-eyed style of Aoyama's masterly comic art makes the violence seem that much more shocking, like a slasher film set in Disneyland. The overarching mystery of the men in black gives the story a depth beyond the whodunit-of-the-week. Some character names were changed in the English translation (Richard Moore was originally Kogoro Mori); the alterations are explained in the back of various volumes, along with Aoyama's data files on his favorite fictional detectives. (JD) ★★★½

CATEGORY: FREAKS

(カテゴリ：フリークス) • Gokurakuin Sakurako • DrMaster (2005–ongoing) • Gentosha (Comic Birz, 2002–ongoing) • 3+ volumes (ongoing) • Shônen, Action, Horror • 18+ (language, violence, nudity, sex)

When "freaks"—evil monsters that are part spirit, part flesh—tempt and possess human beings, a group of exterminators fights them. But even though they look like handsome teenagers in black suits, the exterminators are not human, either . . . they're "stands," the natural enemy of "freaks," and when their job is over one of them eats up the incriminating remains. Structured as a series of monster-of-the-month stories, *Category: Freaks* achieves some memorable dark imagery, such as the giant eyeball that opens in the hero's torso, and the "flesh dolls" that doomed individuals literally pull from between the legs of Hainuwele, a female super-monster. For the most part, however, the art is a weakness: the possessed people look more comical than frightening, and the characters float above obviously photo-traced backgrounds. The often sexual plot elements are viewed with genuinely adolescent disgust and awe; as one of the eternally teenage protagonists says, it's the *adult* world that's scary. The series contains eye candy for both genders, but the cute gay boys don't show as much skin as the women, which include a hapless victimized maid-type character with big breasts. ★★½

CENTRAL CITY

SAYA • Studio Ironcat (2003) • 1 volume • Science Fiction, Crime Drama • Unrated/13+ (mild violence, partial nudity)

One hundred years after World War III, Kaede is a *bishônen* "SA Disposer" (a sort of bounty hunter) with pyrokinetic powers, who roams the city looking for the man who killed his friend, while some kind of police detectives pursue him. Primitive art and incomprehensible story; the dialogue doesn't even seem to come from the characters, as if the art and text occupy parallel tracks.

0 Stars

CERES: CELESTIAL LEGEND

Ayashi no Ceres, "Bewitching Ceres" (妖しのセレス) • Yuu Watase • Viz (2001–2006) • Shogakukan (Shôjo Comic, 1996–2000) • 14 volumes • Shôjo, Science Fiction, Romance, Horror • 16+ (violence, nudity, sex)

On her sixteenth birthday, Aya Mikage discovers a shocking family secret: she is the reincarnation of a *tennyô,* a "celestial maiden" from Japanese folklore, with awesome psychic powers. But her newly reborn alter ego, Ceres, has a passionate grudge against Aya's family, the owners of a globe-spanning corporation that will do anything to contain and control Ceres's power. Similar in plot to an Ira Levin science fiction novel, *Ceres: Celestial Legend* is a surprisingly heavy story of family, sexuality, adulthood, and the struggles between men and women. Even brother and sister are pitted against each other, and Aya/Ceres's love triangle—between the blank-slate Tôya and the humanly fallible Yûhi—is hotly contested. Covered in bandages, the characters limp from hospital to hospital, and the action takes place mostly in cold inorganic settings (despite a series of subplots where the characters travel across Japan in search of clues to the legend, encountering little horror stories along the way). Watase's art suffers from sophomore slump (the faces don't always match the bodies, and her attempts at gore look goofy), but her storytelling is in top form, simultaneously addressing Big Ideas and uncompromising relationship drama. ★★★★

CHANGE COMMANDER GOKU

Shônen Saiyûki Commander Goku, "Boy Bravest Legend Commander Goku" (少年最勇記コマンダーゴクウ) • Ippongi Bang • Antarctic (1993–1996) • Bandai (Cyber Comix, 1992) • 1 volume • Tokusatsu, Action, Comedy • 18+ (language, violence, nudity)

Cute, macho teenagers in power suits fight bad guys and zombies in this indulgent combination parody of several 1970s anime and manga titles, including *Black Jack, Cutey Honey,* and the artist's favorite, the untranslated boxing manga *Ashita no Jo.* The series reads like the author was having fun (Bang solicits reader ideas for Goku's powers), but it's basically plotless and the inane jokes don't always work, even if you recognize the obscure references. Several additional issues were published in comics form (as *Change Commander Goku 2*) but never collected. ★★½

A CHEEKY ANGEL

Tenshi na Konamaiki, "Cheeky Angel" (天使な小生意気) • Hiroyuki Nishimori • Viz (2004–2007) • Shogakukan (Weekly Shônen Sunday, 1999–2003) • 20 volumes • Shônen, Romantic Comedy • 16+ (language, mild violence)

When he was nine years old, a strange genie transformed Megumi Amatsuka from a boy into a girl, wiping the male Megumi from the memories of everyone except Megumi and his/her best friend. Years later, in high school, Megumi is a beautiful, temperamental girl who claims she's a guy . . . which doesn't stop Genzo, the local tough guy, from falling in love with her. Although the incredibly slow-moving plot relies too much on an infinite supply of ugly jerks picking fights with the heroes, at times *Cheeky Angel* is strangely thoughtful, as the characters try to puzzle out gender issues (or at least Japanese stereotypes thereof). On the plus side, the central cast of characters is well defined, and the non-sequitur Japanese humor (including many faithfully untranslated puns) makes for a slow but quirky read. The stiff art is like a form of cartoonist's shorthand: effective but not pretty. ★★

LE CHEVALIER D'EON

"Chevalier" (シュヴァリエ) • Tow Ubukata (original story), Kiriko Yumeji (art) • Del Rey (2007–ongoing) • Kodansha (Magazine Z, 2005–ongoing) • 4+ volumes (ongoing) • Shônen, Fantasy, Historical, Adventure • 18+

Set in eighteenth-century France on the eve of the revolution, *Chevalier d'Eon* is inspired by the rather extraordinary historical figure Charles de Beaumont, a diplomat and spy who lived the latter half of his life as a woman. For dramatic purposes, this story posits that hero d'Eon de Beaumont is sharing a body with the spirit of his dead sister, which is frankly no less bizarre than the biography of the real version and lends itself to a lot of pretty artwork. (MS) NR

CHIBIMONO

Chibimono: Chibi no Mononoke, "Little Supernatural Being" (ちびのもののけ) • Mizuo Shinonome • Infinity Studios (2007) • Futabasha (Comic High!, 2005–2007) • 3 volumes • Moe, Comedy • 13+

Young Wakana, a cute junior high student, moves to the countryside where one day she stumbles across a tiny crying girl, no larger than her hand. The girl turns out to be Nanana, a bumbling goddess in training, who needs encouragement. Despite the 13+ rating, the story basically has nothing unsuitable for younger readers. NR

CHIBI VAMPIRE

Karin (かりん) • Yuna Kagesaki • Tokyopop (2006–ongoing) • Kadokawa Shoten (Dragon Age, 2003–ongoing) • 11+ volumes (ongoing) • Shônen, Vampire, Romantic Comedy • 16+ (mild language, blood, sexual situations)

Karin Maaka, the daughter of a family of vampires, undergoes a sort of "vampire puberty" and discovers that she has a very un-usual condition: instead of sucking blood, she *produces* it and has to inject it *into* victims with her fangs. (Everyone feels great afterward.) But her newfound feelings are embarrassing, and when her hot classmate Kenta Usui is around, she can hardly restrain herself from either biting him or gushing blood out of her nose. A fun romantic comedy that plays up all the imaginable "blood = periods, sex = vampirism" comparisons, *Chibi Vampire* manages to have the good guilty feeling of dirty pleasures without actually showing any nudity (despite Kagesaki's previous work as an adult manga artist). The anime-style artwork is appealing. ★★★

CHICAGO

(シカゴ) • Yumi Tamura • Viz (2002–2003) • Shogakukan (Betsucomi, 2000–2001) • 2 volumes • Shôjo, Crime Drama • Unrated/13+ (mild language, violence)

After narrowly surviving a mysterious cover-up, search-and-rescue workers Rei and Uozumi are recruited by a clandestine rescue organization run out of Chicago, a bar in Shinjuku. A modern-day noir story that throws out mentions of Rwanda and Somalia in an attempt to seem hard-hitting, *Chicago* shows the influence of Frank Miller's *Sin City,* with silhouetted action poses, simply suggested backgrounds, self-aware "cool moments," and narrow escapes. However, there's nothing beneath the surface: the series goes nowhere and has no resolution, and the art is so loose that it's difficult to tell what's going on. ★★

CHIKYU MISAKI

Chikyû Misaki, "(Planet) Earth Misaki" (地球美紗樹) • Yuji Iwahara • CMX (2005–2006) • Kadokawa Shoten (Monthly Ace Next, 2001–2002) • 3 volumes • Shônen, Science Fiction • 13+ (crude humor, brief violence, brief nudity, mild sexual situations)

This absolutely charming manga has the plot of an American family animated movie, such as *The Iron Giant* or *Lilo & Stitch* (which, coincidentally, it also visually resembles). Fourteen-year-old Misaki and her father move to her great-grandfather's house, a mysterious old mansion by a lake said to be inhab-

Yuji Iwahara's *Chikyu Misaki*

ited by Hohopo, a Nessie-like creature. Soon, Misaki encounters the legendary Hohopo, who looks like a baby plesiosaur, but whom a kiss transforms into an adorable mute little boy, whose habits include bed-wetting, group snuggling, and running around the house naked. But can she keep his secret safe from criminals and scientists who want to exploit him? The art has a pleasantly organic, hand-drawn look, and the characters' big-eyed faces reflect Iwahara's Western cartoon influence. It's an excellent short manga for young readers, although cautious parents may want to scrutinize it for brief nudity and oblique references to sexuality, mostly between the adult characters. ★★★½

CHIRALITY: TO THE PROMISED LAND

Chirality (キラリティ) • Satoshi Urushihara • CPM (1996–2000) • Gakken (Comic Nora, 1995–1997) • 4 volumes • Postapocalyptic, Shônen, Science Fiction • 18+ (graphic violence, nudity, graphic sex)

In a future ravaged by a techno-virus that turns humans into killer robots, a few survivors venture out of their protected shelter to defeat the mad computer that is the cause of it all. Shiori, the dewy-eyed heroine, is taken under the wing of Carol, a shape-shifting, gender-shifting organism. The plot is a fair-to-middling example of its genre until the last volume, at which point Urushihara's breast fetish goes wild and the series turns into a topless lesbian orgy. The English version divides the original three-volume Japanese release into four volumes. ★

CHOBITS

(ちょびっツ) • CLAMP • Tokyopop (2002–2003) • Kodansha (Weekly Young Magazine, 2000–2002) • 8 volumes • Seinen, Science Fiction, Romance • 16+ (mild language, partial nudity, sexual situations)

In the not-too-distant future, android technology has made it possible for almost anyone to afford a "persocom"—everyone, that is, but *ronin* student Hideki. One day, however, Hideki finds the adorable and childlike Chi bound and abandoned in a dark alley. After taking her home and finding her well-placed activation switch, Hideki finds himself torn between being Chi's guardian and reconciling his romantic feelings for the possibly-sentient android. At first glance, *Chobits* appears to be a cynical work of exploitation, pairing CLAMP's distinctive artwork, at the height of their popularity, with the *otaku*-favorite "robot girlfriend" genre. Indeed, lead artist Mokona outdoes herself with designs that combine the youthful innocence and *kawaii* cuteness of *Cardcaptor Sakura* with pinup and bondage imagery. In spite of this, *Chobits* is perhaps CLAMP's most mature work to date, and not just "mature" in the fanservice sense. This time, they take love into the twenty-first century, exploring humans' relationship with technology through five distinctive side stories in addition to Hideki and Chi's tragically charming romance. A story-within-the-story fairy tale is surprisingly effective, if not terribly subtle. The series is not only one of the sexiest manga in its genre, it is also one of the most endearing. For continuity fans, it is worth noting that *Chobits* features CLAMP's most audacious crossover to date, working in characters from their minor *shônen* hit *Angelic Layer* in surprising ways. (MT)   ★★★½

CHRONO CRUSADE

Chrno Crusade (misspelled in the Japanese version) (クロノクルセイド) • Daisuke Moriyama • ADV (2004–2006) • Kadokawa Shoten (Comic Dragon, 1998–2004) • 8 volumes • Shônen, Historical, Occult, Action-Adventure • 13+ (language, violence, partial nudity)

Good guys, demons, and monsters clash in 1924 America in this enjoyable pulp adventure with slick, screentone-heavy visuals. Sister Rosette is a gunslinging young nun who wears a dress slit to the thigh and fights evil beings with cross-infused bullets. Her companion is Chrono, a demon in the form of a young boy, who can tap tremendous powers at the cost of draining years from Sister Rosette's life. With the help of a few friends and the demon-monitoring Magdalan organization, the unlikely pair travels across the United States, trying to find Rosette's long-lost brother, Joshua, and save the world in the process. Few manga have ever looked, or read, so much like an anime series on the black-and-white page. The monsters range

from generic to imaginative (the lesser ones draw from Egyptian and Nepalese cultures, among others), and the story has fun *Raiders of the Lost Ark*–style action sequences, with biplanes, zeppelins, and Ford Model T's. The cinematic plotting is solid and the execution outweighs the clichés, making for solid entertainment.   ★★½

CHRONOWAR

Denmu Jikû, "Electric Dream Space-Time" (電夢時空) • Kazumasa Takayama • Dark Horse (1996–1997) • Kodansha (Afternoon, 1995) • 9 issues • Seinen, Science Fiction, Drama • Unrated/16+ (violence, nudity)

Ten months after an asteroid impacts in central Tokyo, one of the three people who'd been listed as missing in the crater turns himself in to the police and spins an outrageous tale of where he'd been, including alien probes that are able to stop time, invasive cyber-circuitry procedures, resurrections, and battles to the death with other altered humans. The characters' reactions to being covered in metal tubing that wraps around their bodies like a skateboarder's protective gear and then talks to them telepathically are charmingly naturalistic ("Oh, God . . . I must be losing my mind!"). The story veers back and forth from soap opera to alien first-contact theorizing like an episode of *The X-Files* in comic form. Very nicely drawn, with a better-than-usual sense of place and atmospheric renditions of nighttime Tokyo. A sequel volume titled *Denmu Jikû 2: Runner* was published in Japan in 1999. (JD)   ★★

CINDERALLA: See *Junko Mizuno's Cinderalla*

CIPHER

(サイファ) • Minako Narita • CMX (2005–ongoing) • Hakusensha (LaLa, 1985–1990) • 12 volumes • Shôjo, Romantic Drama • 13+ (mild language, adult themes)

Teenage art-school student Anise Murphy makes friends with two handsome young twins, Cipher and Siva, a famous actor/model. When she discovers that they share the same identity—one staying at home

CHILDREN AND FAMILIES (児童・家族)

Although most translated anime and manga are aimed at teenagers, some of the longest-running Japanese series are classic stories of families and children known as *kazoku manga* (family manga). Machiko Hasegawa's *The Wonderful World of Sazae-san* (1946) reassured readers with its peaceful vision of a Japanese extended family, with children, parents, and grandparents all living together in the same home. The anime, which began in 1969, is still running on Japanese TV. Masashi Ueda's *Kobo the Li'l Rascal* (1982) follows a similar formula. These old-fashioned comics, and others like them, are the equivalent of American newspaper comic strips (see the article on FOUR-PANEL MANGA). Somewhat more cynical is Yoshito Usui's *Crayon Shinchan* (1990), whose title character's innocently outrageous behavior stands out among more sedate family manga.

Although Japanese society is stereotypically male dominated, the flip side is that, in the traditional household, the mother is the center of the family. Fathers in manga, when they show up at all, are usually incompetent goofballs (i.e., *Bleach, Ranma ½, Shrine of the Morning Mist*) or as occasionally in *shônen* manga, mysterious role models whose heroic status is in direct proportion to their remoteness (i.e., *Hunter × Hunter, Shaman King, Yu-Gi-Oh!: Millennium World*). In contrast, as writers such as Anne Allison and Ian Buruma have pointed out, mothers are practically worshipped. In Kazuo Umezu's *Drifting Classroom* (1972), this is literally the case; when the homesick children build a shrine to pray at, they use a bust of the hero's mother for the centerpiece. Elsewhere in the same manga, a mother's love triumphs over the very laws of the universe, when the hero's mother finds herself able to telepathically communicate with her son across time and space. This ideal of unconditional love goes beyond mother/child relationships; in *shônen* romances such as *No Need for Tenchi!* and *Ai Yori Aoshi,* the love interests often have an explicitly maternal quality, and the stereotypical male romantic comedy lead is a motherless boy, who has never known a woman's affection in any form.

Debuting as a quarterly magazine in 1976, Shogakukan's *Corocoro Comic* went monthly in 1979. Its first big title was *Doraemon,* but when it acquired the *Pokémon* manga license it decisively surpassed its competition.

Another popular genre is *ikuji manga* (child-care manga). In Marimo Ragawa's *Baby & Me* (1991) a ten-year-old must help take care of his baby brother after his mother's death. In Yoko Maki's *Aishiteruze Baby* (2002) a teenage boy must take care of a little girl. Kiyohiko Azuma's delightful *Yotsuba&!* (2003), about a green-haired six-year-old who has adventures in her neighborhood, appears in *Dengeki Daioh,* a magazine aimed at teenage boys. Azuma's comics about young girls are perfectly innocent but the same cannot be said for all of Azuma's imitators, who belong to the *moe* movement (see the article on *OTAKU*).

Manga *about* children, of course, are not the same as manga *for* children. Originally, almost all manga were aimed at elementary school students, but in the 1960s publishers courted older audiences, resulting in the diverse manga market of today. As in America, Japanese children's magazines often feature comics; Shogakukan produces a famous series of six "learning magazines," *Shôgaku Ichinensei* ("First-Grader") through *Shôgaku Rokunensei* ("Sixth-Grader"), each one aimed at a different grade in elementary school. They feature a mix of comics, articles, activities, and exercises aimed at both genders. One of the most famous children's manga of all originated in these magazines, Fujiko F. Fujio's *Doraemon* (1969), starring a robot cat who comes from the future to solve a boy's problems. In 1976 Shogakukan used *Doraemon* to draw readers into a new magazine, a somewhat less educational comic magazine for elementary school boys, *Corocoro Comic. Corocoro Comic* (named after the sound of a ball rolling) is known for its cheerfully hyperactive house style and its countless tie-in manga made in association with video game and toy makers, such as *Beyblade, Zoids,* and *Pokémon.* Corocoro's traditional rival is Kodansha's *Comic Bombom,* (founded in 1981 and frequently focusing on *Gundam* tie-ins).

Girls' magazines aimed at elementary school to junior high audiences exist as well, including Kodansha's venerable *Nakayoshi* (founded in 1954), Shueisha's *Ribon* (founded in 1955), and Shogakukan's *Ciao* and *ChuChu* (founded in 1977 and 2005, respectively). They, too, rely heavily on merchandising, although not as much as the boys' magazines for the same age group. Magazines aimed at a slightly older age group, such as the weekly *shônen* magazines, are also generally considered family fare (see the *SHÔNEN* and *SHÔJO* articles), although more potentially adult content appears as the target audience gets older.

One type of children's manga of which little has been translated is educational manga for children, with the exception of the *Edu-Manga* series of historical biographies (2000). Recent years have seen manga translators dabbling in Japanese children's books, from board books for the youngest children (Viz's *Pokémon* board books and Tokyopop's *Stray Sheep* by Tatsutoshi Nomura) to more challenging books such as Katsuhiro Otomo and Shinji Kimura's *Hipira,* about a little vampire. Ritsuko Kawai's *The Adventures of Hamtaro* (1997), midway between manga and children's book, was first printed in *Shogaku Ninensei* ("Second-Grader"). Even Akira Toriyama, the creator of *Dragon Ball* (1984) and the charming if occasionally scatological children's manga *Dr. Slump* (1980), dabbled in the field with the untranslated *Toccio the Angel* (2003). Typically printed in color, like American children's books, such works span a vast range of art styles.

Children and Family Manga

The Adventures of Hamtaro: A House for Hamtaro • *Aishiteruze Baby* • *Akko-chan's Got a Secret!* • *Astrider Hugo* • *Astro Boy* • *Baby & Me* • *B.B. Explosion* • *Beauty Pop* • *Beyblade* • *Call Me Princess* • *Cardcaptor Sakura* • *Crayon Shinchan* • *Doraemon: Gadget Cat from the Future* • *Dream Saga* • *Dr. Slump* • *Edu-Manga* • *Full Moon o Sagashite* • *Gals!* • *Gentleman's Alliance†* • *Ghost Hunt* • *Granny Mischief* • *Instant Teen: Just Add Nuts* • *Ironfist* • *Jing: King of Bandits* • *Just a Girl* • *Kamichama Karin* • *Kamikaze Kaito Jeanne* • *Kilala Princess* • *Kingdom Hearts* • *Kingdom Hearts: Chain of Memories* • *Kitchen Princess* • *Kobo the Li'l Rascal* • *Kodocha* • *The Legend of Zelda: A Link to the Past* • *Let's Stay Together Forever* • *Magical Mates* • *Magical Pokémon Journey* • *Magic Knight Rayearth* • *Mamotte! Lollipop* • *Marmalade Boy* • *Medabots* • *MegaMan NT Warrior* • *Metal Guardian Faust* • *Mink* • *Miracle Girls* • *Miss Me?* • *Mobile Fighter G Gundam* • *Mobile Suit Gundam: The Last Outpost* • *Mobile Suit Gundam Wing* • *Panku Ponk* • *Pichi Pichi Pitch: Mermaid Melody* •

while the other goes to school or work under the name Siva—she challenges them to a bet that she can learn to tell them apart in two weeks. Set mostly in New York, *Cipher* is a wide-eyed *shôjo* look at America in the 1980s, filled with now-kitschy references to Michael Jackson, Hall and Oates, and the Thompson Twins. Street scenes, subways, and other settings are drawn with gusto, depicting a world that may be as foreign to modern readers as it was to Japanese readers in 1985. Although historically interesting, for long stretches, the manga seems satisfied to merely show what it's like to be an American teenager; the plot doesn't really get moving until several volumes into the series, when Anise begins to learn the twins' strange past. On another level, the appeal of the series is simply seeing two hot boys who are so close that they kiss each other good night on the lips. ★★★

CITY HUNTER

City Hunter (シティ・ハンター) • Tsukasa Hojo • Gutsoon! Entertainment (2002–2004) • Shueisha (Weekly Shônen Jump, 1985–1992) • 5 volumes, suspended (35 volumes in Japan) • Shônen, Crime, Action, Comedy • 16+ (language, crude humor, violence, partial nudity, sexual situations)

One of the most popular *shônen* manga of the 1980s; translated into Chinese, it was so popular it was adapted into a 1993 live-action Hong Kong movie starring Jackie Chan. In the gambling dens and hostess clubs of Shinjuku dwells the "City Hunter," Ryo Saeba—a suave, cool mercenary who takes down villains with his unbelievable skills with the .357 Magnum. However, he's also a childish, skirt-chasing jokester who's perpetually popping a boner and harassing women,

after which his boyish partner Kaori gets mad and flattens him with a giant cartoon hammer. (Since the manga ran in *Weekly Shônen Jump,* he can't actually have sex on-screen, but dirty jokes and horny guys abound.) The square-jawed, vaguely Tetsuo Hara–like art style may be a turnoff to modern manga fans, but the stories are well told and entertaining. Additional material was published in *Raijin* magazine but never collected. ★★★

CLAMP SCHOOL DETECTIVES

CLAMP Gakuen Tanteidan, "Clamp School Detective Agency" (CLAMP学園探偵団) • CLAMP • Tokyopop (2003) • Kadokawa Shoten (Asuka Mystery

Tsukasa Hojo's *City Hunter*

DX, 1992–1993) • 3 volumes • Shôjo, Comedy • All Ages

During their *dôjinshi* days, the women of CLAMP created a fictional kindergarten-through-college school in Tokyo for the gifted and brilliant, where extravagance trumped learning and grown-ups were all but absent. The elementary school division is dominated by three personalities: sixth-grader Nokoru Imonoyama, the class chairman, is heir to billions, has an IQ second to none, and can detect a woman in distress from two kilometers away. Fifth-grader Suoh Takamura is descended from a ninja clan and is a martial arts master. Akira Ijyuin seems like just a sweet-natured kid with a talent for cooking, but he's secretly the master thief 20 Faces (see *Man of Many Faces*). Together they are the Clamp School Detectives. Led by Nokoru, their mission is to help all women in need (one of the series' big jokes is that Nokoru fancies himself a passionate feminist, when really he's all about chivalry). The cases range from finding the owner of a lost stocking to helping a stuck-up girl find her heart. Mileage will definitely vary with this series—it's short, cute, and not too demanding. It's also a good pick for younger readers, with nothing racy and jokes that appeal to all ages. Others will likely be put off by the overly precocious cast and lack of a major story arc. The characters and Clamp School make an appearance in *Man of Many Faces, Duklyon: Clamp School Defenders, X/1999,* and *Tsubasa: Reservoir Chronicle.* (MT)   ★★½

CLAYMORE

(クレイモア) • Norihiro Yagi • Viz (2006–ongoing) • Shueisha (Monthly Shônen Jump, 2001–ongoing) • 10+ volumes (ongoing) • Shônen, Fantasy, Action • 16+ (violence, partial nudity, attempted rape)

In a vaguely European fantasy world, everyone lives in fear of Yoma—flesh-eating humanoids who can disguise themselves in human form. The only warriors strong enough to oppose them are the Claymore, human-Yoma half-breed swordswomen-for-hire, who are almost as feared as the monsters themselves. Clearly inspired by the medieval setting and limb-severing gore of *Berserk, Claymore* suffers from a slow pace, mediocre fight scenes, and uninspired, repetitive visuals; even when the monsters start turning truly monstrous, which takes several volumes, they aren't memorable. The sinewy, pale character designs blur the line between Yoma and humans. There are a few good scares, but beneath the solemn atmosphere, it's just a fighting manga with lots of silent brooding and none of the fun. Some nudity is censored in the English edition.   ★★

CLOVER

(クローバー) • CLAMP • Tokyopop (2001–2002) • Kodansha (Amie, 1997–1999) • 4 volumes • Shôjo, Science Fiction, Romance • 16+ (mild language, violence, mild sexual situations)

Clover was the flagship title of Kodansha's short-lived anthology *Amie,* which was intended to showcase edgy and genre-bending *shôjo* manga. *Clover* certainly challenges the people's perception of what *shôjo* manga should be, with its gritty cyberpunk setting, violent action scenes, and bold, high-contrast artwork. In a distant dystopian future, powerful psychics are both coveted and feared by clandestine government agencies. These psychics are called Clovers and are ranked according to their power. One-Leaf Clovers are the lowest, on up to Four-Leaf. There is only one Four-Leaf Clover known to exist—Suu—and she has lived her entire young life in compliant captivity. After bargaining with the government wizards who want her contained, Suu sets forth on a pilgrimage to Fairy Park with Kazuhiko, a former military agent, as her bodyguard. It wasn't chance that pulled him out of retirement for this job; while in her cage, Suu struck up a long-distance friendship with Ora, a torch singer who was Kazuhiko's lover, and through Ora, Suu fell in love with this older man she had never seen. While the plot might echo *Akira* or *Battle Angel Alita,* the execution is distinctively CLAMP. Lead artist Mokona outdoes herself with art deco stylings and fashions that defy gravity in eye-catching ways. The romantic pairings highlight many forms of romantic love, smashing barriers of age and gender. The first two volumes tell one stand-alone story, while volumes 3 and 4 are prequels. On their Web site CLAMP puts Clover on its "in-progress" list, although after eight years with no new work, a continuation seems increasingly unlikely. Don't let that dissuade you—the series more than stands up as a completed work. (MT) ★★★½

CLUB 9

Heba Hello-chan (へばハローちゃん) • Makoto Kobayashi • Dark Horse (2001–2005) • Kodansha (Mister Magazine, 1992–1994) • 2 volumes, suspended (5 volumes in Japan) • Seinen, Romantic Comedy • Unrated/13+ (mild language, mild violence, mild sexual situations)

Haruo, a naive country girl come to study in Tokyo, ends up working at a hostess bar but vows to stay loyal to the big-galoot boyfriend she left back home. Guileless and simple but self-reliant, she learns the ropes of the hostess business and struggles to resist temptation as she is wooed by handsome and wealthy men: baseball players, rich executives, and so on. A sort of reversal of the standard "one guy, many girls" *seinen* romantic comedy formula, *Club 9* is a delightful series. The artwork is nothing like "normal" manga style—the chubby, busty girls and square-jawed men are cartoon characters whose rubbery expressions are too hilarious to be bound by looking cute all the time. The English rewrite makes Haruo's heavily accented rural Japanese sound like she's a hick from the classic newspaper comic strip *Li'l Abner* ("Don't you talk laik a plumb fool, Kenji Nakamura!"). Additional material was serialized in Dark Horse's anthology magazine *Super Manga Blast!* but never collected. ★★★½

COBRA

(コブラ) • Buichi Terasawa • Viz (1990–1991) • Shueisha (Weekly Shônen Jump, 1977–1984) • 12 issues, suspended (18 volumes in Japan) • Shônen, Science Fiction, Pirate Adventure • Unrated/13+ (violence)

A lightweight but thoroughly entertaining sci-fi space adventure that served as Terasawa's debut work. In a twist reminiscent of the Hollywood action movie *Total Recall,* a futuristic salaryman signs up for a virtual fantasy vacation only to discover that he really *is* an infamous space pirate, lying low after a face change

and a memory wipe. Now that he's had a taste of normal life, our hero can't wait to get back to his old line of work, and who could blame him? Cobra himself is an endearing lout with a fondness for cigars and a unique "psycho-gun" installed in his forearm, and his interplanetary adventures always seem to involve plenty of foxy ladies wearing outfits that would make Barbarella blush. Terasawa's early artwork feels like an amateurish emulation of Leiji Matsumoto and Osamu Tezuka, but its energy and expressiveness more than make up for the lack of polish. (MS) ★★★

THE COLLECTION: See *Hino Horror, Vols. 7–8: The Collection*

COMIC PARTY (CPM)

(こみっくパーティー) • various artists • CPM (2003) • Ohzora Shuppan (2001) • 3 volumes • Otaku, Comedy • 13+ (mild language, mild sexual situations, brief nudity)

Easily confused with the identically named Tokyopop series, CPM's *Comic Party* is a collection of fan comics based on the *Comic Party* franchise, drawn by (and presumably solicited from) various Japanese small-press artists. The forgettable short stories have standard *dôjinshi* weaknesses: mediocre art, disinterest in drawing anything but faces, and pointless, sentimental stories centered around trivial incidents. For hard-core fans only. ★

COMIC PARTY (TOKYOPOP)

(こみっくパーティー) • Sekihiko Inui • Tokyopop (2004–2006) • MediaWorks (Dengeki Daioh, 2001–2005) • 5 volumes • Otaku, Comedy • 13+ (language, mild violence, occasional suggestive poses)

Slickly drawn manga adaptation of the "dating simulation" video game franchise of the same name, better known in the United States through the anime adaptation (which, like this manga, eliminated the sexual elements). Kazuki, rejected from a fine-arts college, becomes involved in the world of Comic Party (an undisguised version of Japan's Comic Market convention), drawing and selling *dôjinshi,* to the embarrassment of his girlfriend. He soon befriends countless

COMEDY AND GAG (コメディ・ギャグ)

Humor manga take many forms, not just romantic comedy and four-panel manga in the style of newspaper comic strips. Anarchistic humor manga are known as "gag manga" and appear in almost all magazines. Recent gag manga from *Weekly Shônen Jump* alone include Yoshio Sawai's *Bobobo-bo Bo-bobo* (2001), Akira Amano's *Reborn!* (2004), and Hideaki Sorachi's *Gintama* (2004). Then there are the humor-specific magazines and minor magazines with titles such as *Honto ni Atta Warachau Hanashi* ("Funny Stories That Really Happened"). If you think all comedy manga involve clichés such as food jokes (people who can't cook, arguments over food, etc.) and jokes about women's breast size, you are reading the wrong manga. There's better stuff out there.

Originally almost all manga were humor, but the postwar manga boom was primarily in dramas and adventure stories; children's humor comics remained at a low level. The first superstar comedy artist was Fujio Akatsuka, the "king of gag manga." Akatsuka achieved some fame for the early magical-girl manga *Akko-chan's Got a Secret!* (1962), but in *Osomatsu-kun* (1962) and *The Genius Bakabon* (1967) he unleashed his full powers, depicting a fast-paced, simply drawn world where anything could happen for a joke, where authority figures are just as dumb as everyone else, and where the physical laws of the universe are often suspended. *Osomatsu-kun* contained adaptations of Charlie Chaplin routines, and Akatsuka was also influenced by Abbott and Costello and by Jerry Lewis.

Akatsuka led the way for other, even crazier artists, including several of his former assistants. While the late 1960s *gekiga* movement made Japanese comics in general more serious, gag manga went right in the other direction. The title character of Mitsutoshi Furuya's *Dame Oyaji* ("No-Good Dad Day") (1970) was tormented mercilessly by his wife and kids, while Yoshiko Tsuchida's *Tsuruhime Ja!* ("It's Princess Tsuru!") (1973) was an irreverent parody of *shôjo* manga. Kazuyoshi Torii invented *Toilet Hakase* ("Professor Toilet") (1970), which eliminated any taboos that may have remained involving poo humor in children's comics. A classic element of humor manga from this period was wacky poses and catchphrases. Kazuyoshi Torii's "Seven Years of Death" gag—in which you poke your fingers up someone's butt—was parodied as the "Thousand Years of Death" ninja technique in Masashi Kishimoto's *Naruto* (1999). Kazuo Umezu gave the world the perpetually snot-nosed urchin *Makoto-chan* (1976), his most popular creation, and encouraged kids to make weird hand gestures while saying "Guwashi!" Tatsuhiko Yamagami's satirical *Gaki Deka* ("Kid Cop") (1974), starring an exhibitionistic man-boy who perpetually wore a policeman's cap and declared, "I sentence you to death!", is considered the weirdest, darkest, and most groundbreaking of all gag manga from the period. Yasuji Tanioka worked in both children's comics and adult sexual humor; his sometimes dark strips are translated in *Comics Underground Japan* and *Secret Comics Japan*. Akira Toriyama's *Dr. Slump* (1980), coming after the end of the wave, shattered no new taboos but distinguished itself by its beautiful art and frequent flights of science fiction and fantasy.

Modern comedy manga contains its share of dirty humor. Tohru Fujisawa's *GTO* (1997), the story of a panty-peeking, occasionally butt-kicking slacker who somehow becomes the greatest teacher in Japan, has more masturbation jokes and filthy dialogue than any Kevin Smith movie. *GTO* is your basic heartwarming sitcom, and unlike true gag manga, it has a story and lots of visual polish. The modern extreme of gross-out humor is Gataro Man, whose works contain the ugliest art, the most scatological humor, and the most ridiculous violence imaginable. The translated 2003 movie *Battlefield Baseball* is based on his manga *Jigoku Koshien* ("Hell Koshien" [Baseball Tournament]), serialized in the ultramainstream *Weekly Shônen Jump*, of all places. As one reviewer pointed out, little baseball is played, but lots of bats and balls are used in inventive and painful ways.

Eiji Nonaka's *Cromartie High School*

One common comedy subject is the humorous suffering of miserable wage slaves, the impossibly poor, and people enduring other extreme conditions. Examples include Masahiko Kikuni's *Heartbroken Angels* (1988), Rikdo Koshi's *Excel Saga* (1997), and Kyoko Negishi and Yuki Miyamoto's *Café Kichijouji De* (2000), as well as Japanese TV shows such as *Nasubi,* a 1998 show in which a man was forced to live in an apartment for a year with no food, clothes, or furnishings other than what he could win through mail-order sweepstakes. Masaharu Noritsuke's *Chûtai Afro Tanaka* ("Dropout Afro Tanaka") (2004), while not literally starving, is a comically pathetic *freeter,* someone without a career path who drifts from job to job, including a stint as a trucker. Such themes are classic, dating back at least to the hapless *ronin* (in modern Japanese slang, a would-be college student struggling to pass the university exams) in Leiji Matsumoto's 1971 *Otoko Oidon* ("I Am a Man"), although the Japanese recession of the 1990s must have given them extra sting.

In terms of satires, Kentaro Takekuma and Koji Aihara's *Even a Monkey Can Draw Manga* (1989) is acknowledged as the greatest manga satire ever. Eiji Nonaka's *Cromartie High School* (2001) also takes on classic clichés, specifically boys' high school comics of the 1970s, although most of the jokes depend less on knowledge of old manga than on hilarious dialogue delivered in the most deadpan manner. One of the most famous untranslated satirists is Kôji Kumeta, whose work began as fairly normal high school romantic comedies but became increasingly surreal and deconstructionist, often directly poking fun at his own life and other manga artists, notably his friend Ken Akamatsu. *Ike! Nangoku Ice Hockey Bu* ("Go! Southern Ice Hockey Club") (1991) and *Katte ni Kaizô* (1998) combine intelligent, twisted humor, parodies of *otaku* topics such as anime and dating simulations, and lots of penis jokes. Kumeta's work was eventually considered too cult for *Weekly Shônen Sunday,* and he moved to other magazines. Kumeta's ex-assistant Kenjiro Hata, creator of *Hayate the Combat Butler* (2004), shows the influence of Kumeta's anime-like art style and dark, sarcastic humor. The frequently formulaic nature of *yaoi* manga lends itself to parody as well, in titles such as Fumi Yoshinaga's stunning *Antique Bakery* (2000) and Homerun Ken's *Clan of the Nakagamis* (2005); indeed, many of the most popular *yaoi* manga, such as Sanami Matoh's *Fake* (1994) and Maki Murakami's *Gravitation* (1996), swing between drama and self-parody.

Dôjinshi and short anthology comics often rely on in-jokes and saccharine cuteness, but Koge-Donbo (best known as the creator of DiGi Charat) is usually willing to sacrifice cuteness for a gag, unlike many of her imitators. Adorable chibi characters doing vicious things is a classic. The horror-obsessed heroine of Tomoko Hayakawa's The Wallflower (2000), initially drawn in a semirealistic fashion, eventually spends most of the story as a lovable three-foot-tall cartoon goth; but when her fury is provoked she reverts to the proportions of the humans around her, her eyes glittering wildly, her hands often gripping a chain saw. Thus armed, she carves her way through the clichés of Gothic Lolita fandom.

Comedy Manga

888 • Abenobashi: Magical Shopping Arcade • Akko-chan's Got a Secret! • All Purpose Cultural Cat Girl Nuku Nuku • The Amazing Adventures of Professor Jones • Antique Bakery • Baby & Me • Bastard!! • Battle Club • Battle Vixens • Because I'm the Goddess • BECK: Mongolian Chop Squad • Bobobo-bo Bo-bobo • Bomber Girl • Café Kichijouji De • Change Commander Goku • Chibimono • City Hunter • Clan of the Nakagamis (yaoi) • Comic Party (CPM) • Crayon Shinchan • Cromartie High School • Dark Tales of Daily Horror • Di Gi Charat • Di Gi Charat Theater • Digiko's Champion Cup Theatre • Disgaea • Disgaea 2 • Dodekain • Dominion • Doraemon: Gadget Cat from the Future • Doubt!! • Dr. Slump • Duklyon: Clamp School Defenders • Eerie Queerie • Even a Monkey Can Draw Manga • Excel Saga • F-III Bandit • FLCL • Flower of Life • Full Metal Panic Overload! • Gals! • Gatekeepers • The Genius Bakabon • Gintama • Girl Got Game • Gon • Gravitation • GTO • Hayate the Combat Butler • Here Is Greenwood • High School Agent • High School Girls • Hurrah! Sailor • Hyper Dolls • Hyper Rune • Ichigeki Sacchu!! • Imperfect Hero • Iono-sama Fanatics • Jinki: Extend • Kanna • Kanpai! • Kodocha • Kon Kon Kokon • Loan Wolf • Louie the Rune Soldier • Lupin III • Lupin III: World's Most Wanted • Magical Pokémon Journey • Magical x Miracle • Masked Warrior X • Midnight Panther • Millennium Snow • Mitsukazu Mihara: Haunted House • My Heavenly Hockey Club • Mystical Prince Yoshida-kun • Ninin Ga Shinobuden • Noodle Fighter Miki • Nosatsu Junkie • Octopus Girl • Ohikkoshi • Omukae Desu • Pokémon: The Electric Tale of Pikachu • Popo Can • Princess Princess • Princess Resurrection • RA-I • Reborn! • Samurai Champloo • Sequence • Seven of Seven • Sgt. Frog • Shout Out Loud! (yaoi) • Silbuster • Slayers Medieval Mayhem • Slayers Premium • Slayers Special • Slayers Super-Explosive Demon Story • Star Trekker • St. Lunatic High School • Strawberry Marshmallow • Street Fighter Sakura Ganbaru! • Super Mario Adventures • Those Who Hunt Elves • Time Traveler Ai • Trash • Twin Signal • Ultimate Muscle: The Kinnikuman Legacy • Vampire Doll Guilt na Zan • The Wallflower • Weather Woman • Welcome to the NHK • What's Michael? • Wild Act • Yakitate!! Japan • Yoki Koto Kiku • Yotsuba&! • You're Under Arrest! • Zatch Bell

cute, big-eyed, nerdy girls, including a shy voice actress who goes to the convention incognito and a girl who works at the copy shop; however, rather than love, the story focuses on the how-to of being a Japanese small-press artist, told with a yasashii (gentle) mood. As a portrait of a subculture, it's not entirely inaccurate, merely dumbed-down, whitewashed, and incredibly self-congratulatory. Despite the story's constant refrain that passion is more important than talent, the anime-style slapstick enthusiasm feels forced, a transparent commercialization of geek culture.　　　　★½

COMICS UNDERGROUND JAPAN

Various artists • Blast Books (1996) • 1 volume • Underground • Unrated/18+ (language, graphic violence, nudity, sex)

The biggest, most diverse collection of Japanese underground comics available in English, *Comics Underground Japan* includes work from various sources from 1981 to 1993. The art ranges from highly technically skilled and detailed to intentionally crude *heta-uma* (good-bad) drafting, and the subject matter varies widely as well. Suehiro Maruo's "Planet of the Jap" and Takashi Nemoto's "Future Sperm Brazil" deal with the atrocities (and sexual associations) of Japanese World War II military imperialism, while Yoshikazu Ebisu briefly satirizes corporate culture. Kazuichi Hanawa's dream-like "Jiniku" almost belongs to the fantasy genre, and Hanako Yamada's work reads like misanthropic journal comics, while Pan Migawa provides a flash of introspective whimsy. The collection also includes Neko-jiru and Hajime Yamano's short story "Cat Noodle Soup," which was adapted into the "Cat Soup" anime. The overall impression is of incredible talent and diversity. Other artists include Masakazu Toma, Carol Shimoda, Yasuji Tanioka, Muddy Wehara, Hideshi Hino, and Suzy Amakane (cover illustration). ★★★★

CONFIDENTIAL CONFESSIONS

Reiko Momochi • Tokyopop (2003–2005) • Kodansha (Dessert, 1998–2002) • 6 volumes • Shôjo Drama • 16+ (mild language, mild violence, occasional partial nudity, sex)

A collection of short *shôjo* dramas, each centered around a different social issue facing teenage girls in Japan, like the old *After School Specials*. Although some of the details are specifically Japanese (such as volume 1's tale of *enjo kôsai* [teen prostitution], or volume 4's tales of bullying), the subjects are generally universal, such as sexual harassment, drug addiction, and AIDS. In their function as educational comics, the stories avoid the most obvious sins of preachiness and patronizing their audience. Sexism and "blam-

ing the victim" are recurring themes, and the victims of the stories are surprisingly proactive by manga standards, organizing petitions and filing lawsuits against their oppressors. A few forgettable noneducational stories are mixed in with the rest. The art is merely generic. The series was originally published in Japan as six stand-alone volumes: *Namida* ("Tears"), *Uwasa* ("Rumors"), *Itami* ("Pain"), *Tobira* ("The Door"), *Memai* ("Dizzy"), and *Himitsu* ("Secrets"). ★★

CONFIDENTIAL CONFESSIONS: DEAI

Reiko Momochi • *Deai,* "Phone Dating" (であい) • Tokyopop (2006) • Kodansha (Dessert, 2003) • 2 volumes • Shôjo, Suspense, Drama • 16+ (brief language, brief violence, nudity, sex)

The only *Confidential Confessions* story more than one volume long, *Deai* focuses on Japan's subculture of cell phone text-messaging dating services (*deai-kei*). Rika, a girl who lives with her father and step-mother, gets involved in phone dating and organizes a sort of not-quite-prostitution ring with her friends, selling their time and underwear to perverts and lonely old men. What starts almost innocuously soon goes horribly wrong, and the story takes a turn into crime and suspense. The story is hardly groundbreaking (compare to the sleazier, stupider, but more energetic *Voyeurs Inc.*), but the plot is decently told, and the art is generic but cute. ★★

LA CORDA D'ORO

Kiniro no Cord, "The Golden Cord" (金色のコルダ) • Yuki Kure • Viz (2006–ongoing) • Hakusensha (LaLa, 2003–ongoing) • 7+ volumes (ongoing) • Shôjo, Fantasy, Performance, Drama • 13+

An adaptation of the popular dating sim game of the same name, the manga follows Kahoko Hino, an average girl who one day sees the music fairy that lives on her high school campus. The fairy gives her a magic violin and enters her in the school's prestigious music competition, where Kahoko must learn to play her magical instrument while dealing with a veritable harem of accomplished young men. The first two vol-

COOKING (料理・グルメ)

The sushi, sashimi, and ramen served in Japanese restaurants in the United States is a tiny, misleading picture of Japanese cuisine. Japan has a diverse food culture, which includes dishes imported from China and Korea, Italian-inspired *yôshoku* (Western cuisine), curry dishes, and sweet pastries from Portugal and France. Unlike most Americans, whose food is shipped to supermarkets from thousands of miles away, most Japanese people are still very aware of when food is in season, or what regions are known for what dishes (such as milk from Hokkaido in northern Japan); when the characters of *Hana-Kimi* go on a field trip, they're most excited about the local delicacies they'll be able to eat when they get there. Elaborately decorated *obentô* lunch boxes are the stereotypical sign of love from mother to child, or from girls to boys they have a crush on. Street vendors sell traditional junk food such as *takoyaki* (fried octopus balls) and baked sweet potatoes. The countless manga and anime scenes in which characters discuss their favorite foods, or cook, or (the ultimate comedy cliché) fight over the last piece of food reflect a culture in which food is always appreciated and never invisible.

Manga specifically about food or cooking, known in Japan as *ryôri* manga (cooking manga) or "gourmet manga," is a recognized genre of comics. Food-themed manga range from Ayumi Komura's *Mixed Vegetables,* a *shôjo* manga about a boy and a girl pursuing rival disciplines of sushi and pastry, to Mai Kenna and Tadashi Katô's *The Chef,* whose enigmatic title character is comparable in mystery to Osamu Tezuka's famous surgeon *Black Jack.* Typically, each installment of a cooking manga story involves some tasty dish and the process of making it. One of the reasons for the appeal of cooking manga may be the primarily visual nature of manga; even non-cooking manga often feature lavishly drawn, photorealistic close-ups of food that look as if the reader could eat it off the page. Other, more writing-oriented manga, such as *Antique Bakery,* can make readers' mouths water with detailed descriptions of delicious foods.

The hard work required to become a chef makes cooking a good match for the work ethic of *shônen* manga. In Japan, cooking is one of the few professions to still follow the arduous traditional apprenticeship system, and many cooks come from professional cooking families. The untranslated *Hôchônin Ajihei* ("Ajihei the Cook") by Jirô Gyû and Jô Big, which ran from 1973 to 1977 in *Weekly Shônen Jump,* was one of the first in the genre: the story of a young boy, the son of a traditional Japanese

Cooking is combat in Shinji Saijyo's excellent *Iron Wok Jan.*

chef, who starts out as an apprentice and struggles to be the best. Similar stories include *Mister Ajikko* in the 1980s and *Shôta no Sushi* ("Shota's Sushi") in the 1990s. *Iron Wok Jan* and *Yakitate!! Japan* fall into this category, and both emphasize another *shônen* manga standby: cooking as competition. The idea of cooks facing each other in a televised battle to see who can make the better dish might seem unrealistic if not for tournament TV shows such as *Iron Chef*, the Japanese megahit that ran from 1993 to 1999. Similar cooking shows still run on Japanese TV, and in comparison to them the melodrama of *Iron Wok Jan* seems hardly exaggerated, although they never do explain how he pulls incredibly expensive ingredients out of thin air.

The best cooking manga often contain tips for the readers. Tetsu Kariya and Akira Hanasaki's *Oishinbo* ("Feast"), which has run since 1983 in the manga magazine *Big Comic Spirits,* is perhaps the most streamlined example; like an American newspaper strip, it has little if any ongoing plot, but in each chapter the food critic hero, and the reader, observes the preparation of a new meal. Tochi Ueyama's *Cooking Papa,* which has run since 1986 in the rival magazine *Morning,* has even more straightforward recipes, prepared by the fatherly title character for his wife and kids. Even *Iron Wok Jan* and *Yakitate!! Japan*, whose dishes verge on the impossible, include a recipe for baking bread in a rice cooker (*Yakitate!! Japan,* volume 2) and a solid introduction to making simple Chinese food such as green pepper beef (*Iron Wok Jan,* volume 6). In this way, perhaps, cooking manga is not only entertaining in its own right but the most successful example of educational manga.

Cooking Manga
Antique Bakery • Iron Wok Jan • Kitchen Princess • Yakitate!! Japan

umes lack energy as the premise and characters are introduced; however, the series begins to show promise in the later volumes as characters unveil their hidden depths. The art is quite nice, with loving attention paid to the character designs of the *bishônen*. (HS) ★★

CORRECTOR YUI

(コレクター・ユイ) • Kia Asamiya (story), Keiko Okamoto (art) • Tokyopop (2001–2002) • NHK Shuppan (1999) • 5 volumes • Shôjo, Magical Girl, Action • Unrated/All Ages

Spin-off of Kia Asamiya's "Internet magical girl" manga/anime franchise. Although Asamiya drew his own untranslated manga version of *Corrector Yui,* perhaps he felt it lacked some essential girliness, for he also hired artist Keiko Okamoto to draw this adaptation, retelling the story in a *shôjo* style. Obviously he didn't pay her enough, however, prompting her to sabotage it by drawing as few lines as possible on each page. The condescending story has all the requirements of a *Sailor Moon* rip-off: a ditzy heroine (she's no good with computers, until she transforms into her online persona, Corrector Yui), an evil villain, and lots of fight scenes at theme parks. A four-volume sequel also drawn by Okamoto, *Corrector Yui 2,* was never translated.   0 Stars

COSPLAY KOROMO-CHAN

CoroCoro Koromo-chan, "Roll Roll Koromo-chan" (ころころころもちゃん) • Mook • DrMaster (2005) • MediaWorks (Dengeki Gao!, 2001–2003) • 1 volume • Four-Panel Comedy • 13+ (brief partial nudity)

Four-panel, *chibi* gag strips involving a perky costume fanatic (whose regular clothes look like a maid outfit) and her friends. Like *Azumanga Daioh,* the cast consists mostly of cute girls, and the series ends with school graduation, but the comparison ends there: the characters are one-note and the jokes are pandering, not in a sexual way, but in a back-patting sense. The anime-style art is unmemorable. Still, there are good absurd moments, such as animals cosplaying as other animals, and the main character cosplaying as the Ebola virus. ★★

COWBOY BEBOP

(カウボーイビバップ) • Hajime Yatate (story), Shinichiro Watanabe/Sunrise (cooperation), Yutaka Nanten (art) • Tokyopop (2002) • Kadokawa Shoten (Asuka Fantasy DX, 1999–2000) • 3 volumes • Science Fiction, Crime, Comedy • 13+ (mild language, violence, mild sexual situations)

Licensed spin-off of the *Cowboy Bebop* anime; episodic stories of space bounty hunters with no particular ending. The anime-style art is competent but exposes deeper, subtler problems; instead of the understated professionals they were in the stylish anime series, Spike Spiegel, Jet Black, and Faye Valentine are portrayed here as typical overreacting anime crooks, involved in petty rivalries, slapstick, and fighting over food. Evidently the retro-1970s coolness and sophistication of the anime were simply beyond the artist's grasp, or the manga was intentionally dumbed down, or both. ★

COWBOY BEBOP: SHOOTING STAR

Shooting Star Bebop (シューティングスタービバップ) • Hajime Yatate/Sunrise (original concept), Cain Kuga (story and art) • Tokyopop (2003) • Kadokawa Shoten (Asuka Fantasy DX, 1998) • 2 volumes • Science Fiction, Crime, Comedy • 13+ (language, violence, mild sexual situations)

Slightly more interesting than the other *Cowboy Bebop* manga, this adaptation was produced before the TV series, allowing the artist more freedom. The resulting stories are still weak compared to the anime, but completists may find it interesting. The slightly more original, *shôjo* look to the art is offset by a general lack of drafting ability.
★½

COYOTE RAGTIME SHOW

Coyote Ragtime Show (コヨーテラグタイムショー) • ufotable (original story), Tartan Check (art), Haruo Sotozaki (manga design) • Broccoli Books (2007–ongoing) • Jive (Comic Rush, 2006–2007) • 3 volumes • Shônen, Science Fiction, Comedy • 13+

Adaptation of the anime TV series, inspired by *Cowboy Bebop*. Franka, the orphaned daughter of Pirate King Bruce, is bequeathed a massive treasure hidden somewhere on Planet Graceland, which the Milky Way Federation has marked for destruction. Now, Franka and the space pirates of the spaceship *Coyote* have a week to find the treasure, while outwitting the master criminal Madame Marciano and her twelve robotmaid assassins. NR

CRAYON SHINCHAN

Crayon Shin-chan (クレヨンしんちゃん) • Yoshito Usui • ComicsOne (2002–2004) • Futabasha (Weekly Manga Action/Manga Town, 1990–ongoing) • 10 volumes (45+ volumes in Japan, ongoing) • Gag Manga • 13+ (crude humor, nudity)

Simply drawn gag strips about an elementary school kids who makes life a living hell for his parents. Rightly famous for having created one of the most memorable brats since Dennis the Menace, *Crayon Shinchan* is really about adults: Shinchan's parents, who have to raise the little hellion, and an everexpanding cast of neighbors, teachers, and local merchants who have to deal with the kid on a daily basis. The jokes quickly become repetitive; in an average volume, Shinchan will take off his pants in public, pee or poop in an inappropriate manner, look up ladies' skirts, use Mommy's expensive lipstick for body paint or her expensive perfume for bug spray, make pointed remarks about Mommy's anatomy ("crotch mustache!") or play dress-up games with her underwear, refuse to listen to any kind of rules, and/or fail to understand money. Occasional forays into fantasy break up this routine, as in a run of strips where the family visits the world of Shinchan's favorite TV show, *Action Mask*, a parody of *tokusatsu* shows such as

Kamen Rider. In large doses, *Crayon Shinchan* almost reads like a commentary on modern Japanese society and how heavily it depends on artifical roles and rules and politeness to keep people from strangling each other. The crude, wobbly line drawings are deceptively sophisticated. (JD) ★★★

CRESCENT MOON

Mikan no Tsuki, "Incomplete Moon" (未完の月) • Red Company/Tokamura Matsuda (story), Haruko Iida (art) • Tokyopop (2004–2005) • Kadokawa Shoten (Asuka, 1999–2002) • 6 volumes • Shôjo, Fantasy • 13+ (mild language, violence)

After experiencing strange dreams of a princess and a demon, orphaned Mahiru discovers that she is the reincarnation of a princess who once befriended the Lunar Race, a motley assortment of vampires, werewolves, and traditional Japanese monsters such as fox spirits. She soon meets modern-day members of the Lunar Race, a band of young thieves who are in the big city seeking precious artifacts, the Teardrops of the Moon. A relationship blossoms between Mahiru and Mitsuru, a temperamental, violent boy who transforms into a somewhat ridiculous-looking Japanese *tengu* (monster). An intermittently interesting plot can't make up for the heroine's frequently passive role in the story and the unique but clunky artwork. ★★

CREST OF THE STARS: See *Seikai Trilogy*

CRIMSON HERO

Beniiro Hero, "Crimson Hero" (紅色HERO) • Mitsuba Takanashi • Viz (2005–ongoing) • Shueisha (Bessatsu Margaret, 2002–ongoing) • Shôjo, Sports • 13+ (mild violence, mild sexual situations)

Rebelling against her wealthy family, who run a traditional Japanese restaurant complete with flower arrangement and tea ceremony, fifteen-year-old Nobara leaves home to pursue her dream of playing high school volleyball. Unfortunately, her school has no girls' volleyball team, so she must form a team on her own while working as a sort of "den mother" to the boys' team, cooking and cleaning for four handsome but troublesome guys in exchange for room and board. Although the plot moves slowly (there's not a single volleyball game in volume 1), *Crimson Hero* is a satisfying sports drama that eventually develops a large cast of both genders. (The boys are depicted both as possible romantic interests and as tough opponents with longer reach and greater power.) The short-haired Nobara (one of several butch-looking female characters) is a fallible but basically strong heroine, even though she's forced to do a lot of housework for sloppy guys in the course of the story. The art is attractive and detailed, with unusually realistic, yet androgynous, character designs; the characters look pretty whether they're playing on the court or just hanging around. ★★★

CROMARTIE HIGH SCHOOL

Sakigake! Cromartie Kôkô, "Charge! Cromartie High School" (魁!!クロマティ高校) • Eiji Nonaka • ADV (2005–ongoing) • Kodansha (Weekly Shônen Magazine, 2001–2006) • 17 volumes • Comedy • 13+ (language)

Hilarious parody of old-fashioned "high school tough guys" manga. Cromartie High School is a school so notorious that its students include a gorilla, a robot, and a barechested man with a handlebar mustache. The nominal main character is a studious teenager who chose to go to Cromartie to prove that he can study *anywhere*. The manga consists of short, dense, dialogue-driven gag strips, usually only six pages long. The characters are talking heads drawn stiffly in the style of Ryoichi Ikegami (who drew many famous high school manga in the 1970s, a visual joke that may be lost on Ikegami-ignorant readers). Rarely relying on Japanese pop culture references or other in-jokes, it's just great deadpan comedy. With its postmodern humor and intentionally clichéd "clip art" look, the nearest American equivalent may be the comics of David Rees (*Get Your War On*). ★★★★

CRIME AND *YAKUZA* (罪・ヤクザ)

Stories of crime, cops, and detectives are among the earliest manga genres. Early postwar stories were mostly *shōnen* manga tales of young crime fighters, but the more adult *gekiga* aesthetic soon led to grittier, more hard-boiled crime dramas. James Bond was popular in Japan in the 1960s, and was adapted into manga in the *007 Series* by Takao Saito. Saito went on to create his own version of an international super-operative, *Golgo 13* (1969), an emotionless, infallible hit man who is involved behind the scenes in hundreds of geopolitical conflicts. In translated manga, a more recent take on the super-spy genre is Miyuki Takahashi's *Musashi No. 9* (1996).

Police and Detectives

The everyday image of Japanese cops is more mundane than dramatic. Unlike American cops, who often seem a sort of remote authority, Japanese police officers cultivate a presence in their communities; the majority serve in small *koban* ("police boxes") staffed by four police officers, who patrol the neighborhood on foot or bicycle. The most enduring image of Japanese police officers in manga may be Osamu Akimoto's comedy *Kochira Katsushika-ku Kameari Kōen-mae Hashutsujo* ("This Is the Police Station in Front of Kameari Park in Katsushika Ward") (1976), one of the longest-running manga ever. The hero, Ryotsu Kankichi, is a lazy, thirty-six-year-old cop who spends most of his time on inane moneymaking schemes or wasting his money on hobbies such as *pachinko* and video games; for his idiotic, good-natured obliviousness he has been compared to a Japanese Homer Simpson. *Kochi-Kame* (as the manga is commonly known) is the spiritual ancestor of other cop comedies, such as Kosuke Fujishima's *You're Under Arrest!* (1986), whose heroines spend most of their time giving out parking tickets.

In keeping with Japan's tough gun control laws, Japanese police officers are permitted to fire their guns only under very particular circumstances; the "good" characters in *Death Note* (2004) scrupulously refuse to use guns, perhaps an attempt to ward off criticism of the manga's high level of casual killings. But manga also have their share of trigger-happy Japanese crime fighters. The motorcycle cops of Mikiya Mochizuki's *Wild 7* (1969) cheerfully blast their prey to pieces ("I said *erase* . . . not arrest!"). Buronson and Shinji Hiramatsu's 1975 classic *Doberman Deka* ("Doberman Detective"), starring a young, fiery cop toting a .44 Magnum, was influenced by Western cinema such as the *Dirty Harry* movies. The star of Tsukasa Hojo's *City Hunter* (1985) packs equally heavy heat; the hero is a skirt-chasing, goofball bounty hunter who will blow a hole in his own hand to save an innocent victim. Tutomu Takahashi's *Ice Blade* (1992) and Tetsuya Koshiba's *Remote* (2002) also depict cool police officers facing ruthless criminals.

In keeping with the *Dirty Harry* tradition, one major subgenre of Japanese crime comics is stories set in America. In the 1980s, at the same time when Americans were becoming fascinated with samurai and ninja, the mean streets of New York City represented all that was dangerous and enticing about America to Japanese eyes. Kazuo Koike, who had previously depicted his native Japan as a place where life is cheap in *Lone Wolf and Cub* (1970), transported readers to a corrupt, ultraviolent New York in *AIUEO Boy* ("The Starving Man") (1973) and *Wounded Man* (1981), both with art by Ryoichi Ikegami, and again in *Mad Bull 34* (1986), drawn by Noriyoshi Inoue. Akimi Yoshida's *shōjo* manga *Banana Fish* (1985), in which a Japanese reporter goes to New

York and discovers a sprawling conspiracy between the Mafia and the U.S. military over the development of a deadly drug, has fewer graphic visuals but an equally hard-edged story line. Kenichi Sonoda's *Gunsmith Cats* (1991), the story of two female bounty hunters, revels in detailed depictions of American cars and weaponry. Jiro Taniguchi and Jinpachi Mori's *Benkei in New York* (1991) cultivates a film noir style. Sanami Matoh depicts the world of New York cops and detectives again and again in *RA-I* (1995), *Trash* (2004), and *Fake* (1994), one of many *yaoi* manga about criminals and detectives. In a more modern variation of the theme, Santa Inoue depicts a Tokyo full of drive-bys, homeboys, and stone-cold killers in the rap-influenced *Tokyo Tribes* (1997).

Kenichi Sonoda's *Gunsmith Cats*

Gangs and Youth Crime

Translated manga, being mostly anime-style works from the 1990s and later, have largely passed up what was once a huge element of Japanese culture: the blue-collar *yankii* culture of delinquent teens and lower-class brawlers. In the 1970s and early 1980s *shônen* manga was full of manly, sentimental stories of *banchô* (gang boss) types in ragged school uniforms, often with elaborately greased and pompadoured hair, as parodied in the character "Wooden Sword" Ryu in *Shaman King* (1998). A related subculture is *bôsôzoku* (violent running tribes), gangs of young men and women who ride souped-up cars and motorcycles and wear baggy clothes combining the style of kamikaze pilots and day laborers. (They were also infamous for sniffing paint thinner.) The hero of Tohru Fujisawa's *GTO: The Early Years: Shonan Junai-Gumi* (1990) is a *bôsôzoku* (or technically an ex-*bôsôzoku*), as is one of the heroines of Novala Takemoto's *Kamikaze Girls*. A female street punk, such as *Kamikaze Girls'* Ichiko, is nothing out of the ordinary. Japanese movie and manga audiences have loved sailor-suited, death-dealing ladies long before Quentin Tarantino tried his hand at the genre; one classic example is Shinji Wada's 1976 *Sukeban Deka* ("Delinquent Girl Detective"), whose teenage heroine fights crime with a razor-bladed yo-yo that doubles as a police badge. Although *yankii* and *bôsôzoku* were once a serious concern of Japanese parents and police, they are now more a subject of nostalgia, as seen in the popular Japanese retro band Kishidan.

The streets of Tokyo are one of the most frequently and accurately depicted settings in manga; the big manga publishers make their headquarters here, and Tokyo nightlife is a common subject. In the 1990s Japan was gripped with moral panic over *enjo kôsai*, "compensated dating," a euphemism for prostitution usually performed by teenage girls in search of spending money. *Voyeurs Inc.* (1994), *Short Cuts* (1998), *Gals!* (1999), *Confidential Confessions: Deai* (2003), and *IWGP: Ikebukuro West Gate Park* (2001) all depict the phenomenon with varying degrees of prurient interest. Other youth crime scares of the 1990s have appeared in manga as well, such as *oyaji-gari* (old-man hunting), in which gangs beat up middle-aged office workers for their paychecks. It was in such a climate that Koushun Takami wrote *Battle Royale,* his brutal 1999 satire in which a fascist Japanese government deals with youth unrest by forcing teenagers to kill each other in a survival game whose traumatized winners are shown on national TV.

Yakuza

One classic crime genre involves *yakuza,* the Japanese equivalent of gangsters. With their scars and sunglasses, colorful suits, and colorful tattoos, *yakuza* are instantly recognizable in manga, and often in real life, too. Although they sometimes clash with the authorities or citizen groups, they are considered (or at least consider themselves) a semilegitimate part of the community; after the 1995 Kobe earthquake, the local *yakuza* openly helped provide food and supplies to the victims. Today, they make most of their money from protection rackets and gray-area businesses such as *pachinko*, gambling, prostitution, and loan-sharking. *Yakuza* represent the extreme of traditional Japanese machismo; in the 1960s and 1970s *yakuza* movies were a massive genre, traditionally depicting their heroes as noble samurai warriors in a corrupt modern world, although later portrayals became more ironic and nihilistic, following Kinji Fukusaku's 1973 film *Jingi naki Tatakai* ("Battles Without Honor and Humanity"). While many manga are willing to use *yakuza* thugs as cannon fodder, others are more ambivalent. In Masaomi Kanzaki's *Gun Crisis: Deadly Curve,* before the heroic cop blows away the drug-dealing *yakuza*, it's made clear that he's a "bad" *yakuza* ("I met with your head boss earlier . . . I'm to inform you that you are banned for life from the Kanto-kai!").

Yakuza manga, usually serialized in men's magazines or rougher *shōnen* magazines such as *Weekly Shōnen Champion,* are traditionally a popular genre: some of the longest-running titles include Ayumi Tachihara's *Maji!* (1987) at 50 volumes, Kazumasa Kiuchi and Jun Watanabe's time-traveling *yakuza* story *Emblem Take 2* (1990) at 62 volumes, and Tatsuo Nitta's *Shizuka naru Don* ("The Quiet Don") (1989) at 80 volumes and still running. Possibly due to their generally old-fashioned themes and art styles, almost no *yakuza* manga have been translated, with the exception of Sho Fumimura and Ryoichi Ikegami's *Santuary* (1990). Kazuma Kodaka, a female artist, was forced to draw under a male pen name when working in the traditionally manly genre; perhaps in retaliation, she went on to create the *yaoi yakuza* manga *Kizuna: Bonds of Love* (1992).

Crime and Yakuza *Manga*

Bakune Young • Banana Fish • Battle Royale • Benkei in New York • Black & White • Chicago • City Hunter • Club 9 • Confidential Confessions • Confidential Confessions: Deai • Crying Freeman • Doing Time • Fake • Finder Series (yaoi) • Fist of the Blue Sky • Gals! • Golgo 13 • GTO • GTO: The Early Years—Shonan Junai-Gumi • Gun Crisis • Gun Crisis: Deadly Curve • Gunslinger Girl • Gunsmith Cats • Gunsmith Cats: Burst • Hotel Harbour View • Ice Blade • IWGP: Ikebukuro West Gate Park • The Judged (yaoi) • Juror 13 • Kamikaze Girls • Kids Joker • Kizuna: Bonds of Love (yaoi) • Lady Snowblood • Loan

Wolf • Lupin III • Lupin III: World's Most Wanted • Monster • MPD Psycho • Musashi No. 9 • Neighbour #13 • Old Boy • Pineapple Army • RA-I • Reborn! • Remote • Rose Hip Zero • Samurai Executioner • Sanctuary • Sexy Voice and Robo • Skyscrapers of Oz (yaoi) • Smuggler • Strain • Tokyo Tribes • Trash • Voyeurs, Inc. • Wild 7 • Wild Com. • Worst • Wounded Man • X-Day • X-Kai • Yellow (yaoi) • You're Under Arrest!

Science Fiction/Fantasy Crime Manga

AD Police • Appleseed • Bambi and Her Pink Gun • The Big O • Black Cat • Blood Alone • Blood Sucker: Legend of Zipangu • Central City • Cobra • Cowboy Bebop • Cowboy Bebop: Shooting Star • Coyote Ragtime Show • Crusher Joe • Cutie Honey '90 • Dead End • Death Note • Dominion • Domu: A Child's Dream • Geobreeders • Getbackers • Ghost in the Shell • Ghost in the Shell 1.5: Human-Error Processor • Ghost in the Shell Volume 2: Man-Machine Interface • Goku: Midnight Eye • Heat Guy J • Hellhounds: Panzer Cops • Hyper Police • Junk: Record of the Last Hero • Najica Blitz Tactics • NaNa-NaNa • Silent Möbius • Twilight of the Dark Master • Wild Adapter

CROSS

Jûji, "Cross" (十字—クロス—Cross Oneself) • Sumiko Amakawa • Tokyopop (2004–2006) • Kadokawa Shoten (Asuka, 1997–2001) • 5 volumes • Shôjo, Occult, Drama • 13+ (language, graphic violence, nudity, sexual situations)

A teenage Japanese Catholic priest, codenamed "Cross," is a master exorcist who produces a cross from his forehead when using his powers. When he meets a twenty-year-old teacher who has strange occult stigmata on her skin (the Scriptura), they feel a connection to each other, but Cross's priestly vows stand in his way, and he's also got plenty of demon slaying to do. A would-be shôjo horror spectacular, Cross is told in the form of episodic stories centered around a Catholic church in Kamakura, which is plagued by imps, demons, molested nuns, and Satanic cults, as well as more surreal supernatural phenomena such as a woman whose face reflects the desires of the viewer. The art is awkward but manages to get the point across and gets more accomplished as the series goes on, although the demons never look very interesting. ★★

CROSSROAD

Shioko Mizuki • Go! Comi (2005–2007) • Akita Shoten (Princess, 2003–2005) • 7 volumes • Shôjo,

Romance, Family Drama • 16+ (language, mild violence, sexual situations)

When her grandmother dies, fifteen-year-old Kajitsu is forced to move in with her long-lost stepbrothers Natsu and Toru (the breadwinner of the group); they are soon

Shioko Mizuki's Crossroad

Crying Freeman by Kazuo Koike and Ryoichi Ikegami

eight-year-old. Silly humor and inappropriate crushes, including brushes with incest, keep the wheels of the story turning. ★★★½

CRUSHER JOE

(クラッシャージョウ) • Haruka Takachiho (story), Fujihiko Hosono (art) • Studio Ironcat (2000) • Asahi Sonorama (Manga Shônen, 1979–1983) • 1 volume • Shônen, Science Fiction, Adventure • Unrated/All Ages (violence)

Interplanetary heroes-for-hire in tight white trousers who solve problems for a price, the Crushers are the other classic creation by *Dirty Pair* creator Haruka Takachiho. Yoshikazu Yasuhiko's animation character designs for the 1983 *Crusher Joe* movie are ably recreated in "The Legend of the St. Germi," the first story of this anime tie-in comic, but artist Fujihiko Hosono's art style for the other two stories in Ironcat's compilation, created before the animation and based only on the novel illustrations, are different enough to make a reader wonder if they're even by the same artist (they are). The action and technology are well executed, if old-fashioned in the 1970s school of space tech, but the stories are very dependent on the reader's foreknowledge of the *Crusher Joe* universe, and feel thin on their own. (JD)   ★★

CRYING FREEMAN

(クライングフリーマン) • Kazuo Koike (story), Ryoichi Ikegami (art) • Dark Horse (2006–ongoing) • Shogakukan (Big Comic Spirits, 1986–1988) • 9 volumes • Seinen, Crime, Action-Adventure • 18+ (language, graphic violence, constant nudity, sex)

Emu Hino, a beautiful twenty-nine-year-old virgin, has accidentally witnessed a gangland hit performed by a handsome assassin who sheds tears for his victims at the crime scene. Now Hino is marked for death by the Chinese Mafia and is soon visited by Yo Hinomura, better known as "Crying Freeman." But before he is supposed to kill her, Hino begs Hinomura to take her virginity. Afterward, Freeman finds that he cannot bring himself to complete his lethal task. Instead, the pair fall in love and together try to break the hypnotic conditioning that turned

joined by Kajitsu's irresponsible twenty-eight-year-old stepmother and her six-year-old daughter, all living together in a tiny run-down house. But Natsu has grown from a cheerful kid into a good-looking but distant teenager, and Kajitsu finds herself unexpectedly attracted to him, while simultaneously seeking a father figure—or something more—from Akai, her twenty-something guidance counselor. Depicting a struggling alternative family where almost no one is related by blood, *Crossroad* consciously tackles Important Social Issues; the pleasant surprise is that it's a well-written manga that allows its characters to grow and change, rather than just using them as idealized mouthpieces (though Kajitsu makes a few good speeches). Forced to grow up too fast, the characters struggle with themselves and with their own feelings. The art is sketchy and cartoony rather than polished, giving the series a warm, handmade look; the one possible complaint is that, as in most manga, it's hard to tell a cute teenager from a cute twenty-

Hinomura from a humble ceramics artist into a reluctant killing machine. But to do that, they will have to face crooked cops and gangsters, as well as the dreaded Chinese organization that created Freeman in the first place. Easily the best known of the Kazuo Koike–Ryoichi Ikegami collaborations (partially as a result of an internationally co-produced 1995 live-action B-film adaptation), *Crying Freeman* is full of the wild sex and violence that supercharges works such as *Offered* and *Wounded Man*. But the characterizations are stronger and more memorable here, even as the tale itself becomes wildly digressive in the later volumes. The result is a pulpy classic of macho 1980s manga from the men who defined the genre. Prior to the Dark Horse edition, the series was released in a now out-of-print edition by Viz from 1989 to 1994. (PM)   ★★★★

CULDCEPT

(カルドセプト) • Omiya Soft (original creator), Shinya Kaneko (manga) • Tokyopop (2004–ongoing) • Kodansha (Magazine Z, 1999–ongoing) • 6+ volumes (ongoing) • Shônen, Fantasy, Game, Adventure • 13+ (crude humor, graphic violence)

Based on the cult hit PlayStation 2 game, *Culdcept* is one of the rare video game–based manga that are really good, whether or not you've played the game. The story takes place in a fantasy world in which duelists called "cepters" battle each other with magical cards. The main character is a headstrong young cepter who goes to the big city to gain worldly experience, accompanied by her magic talking staff/old man/advisor. Soon after arriving, she saves the city from being destroyed, becomes a hero, meets a band of oddballs, and sets off on a grand adventure. The art is fabulous, the world is richly detailed, and the story is filled with humorous gags and larger-than-life characters. All in all, it's a wonderful title. (RB)   ★★★½

CUTEY HONEY '90

Cutie Honey (Cutie ハニー) • Go Nagai & Dynamic Planning • Studio Ironcat (1997–1998) • Fushosha (Spa, 1992–1993) • 12 issues • Science Fiction, Action, Comedy • Unrated/18+ (language, violence, nudity, sexual situations)

"Warrior of love" Cutey Honey is a buxom, sexy android created by the late Dr. Kisagari to combat the crime syndicate Panther Claw, led by Sister Jill, an interdimensional demoness. Jill is also responsible for the death of Dr. Kisagari and covets the secret of Honey's "Elemental Materializing Device," which allows her to instantly change powers and identities. But thirty years after Honey has defeated Panther Claw and Sister Jill, they return to wreak havoc on Tokyo once again. A lesser follow-up to Go Nagai's much-loved anarchic 1973–1974 comedy series, *Cutey Honey '90* is little more than a parade of borderline incoherent storytelling, spastic violence, and fanservice (regulations for the drawing of once-forbidden pubic hair had recently been lifted when the series began, a fact that Nagai can't help but note in the manga itself). In previous titles, such as *Abashiri Ikka* ("The Abashiri Family") and *Harenchi Gakuen* ("Shameless School"), Nagai and his Dynamic Planning assistants proved that they could excel at such low-brow material. But there's a sense, as with much of their 1990s output, that they are merely grinding it out here. Studio Ironcat's poor reproduction and lettering do not help elevate things much either. Things finally pick up toward the end of the series, as Honey leads a commando assault on Sister Jill's demon dimension, but only the most devoted fans will need to join her. (PM)

★★½

CYBER 7

Seven Bridge (セブンブリッジ) • Shuho Itahashi • Eclipse (1989–1990) • Ushio Shuppansha (Comic Tom, 1986–1992) • 17 issues, suspended (7 volumes in Japan) • Science Fiction, Fantasy • 13+ (mild language, violence)

Although the English title makes it sound like a robot action manga, *Cyber 7* is considerably weirder, a young-adult science fiction title with conscious echoes of fairy tales. The outwardly normal siblings Natsuko, Taki, and Tatsuki are actually two princes and a princess from the Crystal World, a parallel universe from which they were driven by the despotic Lord Kakuo. When Kakuo tracks them down, they must flee through the dimensions, assisted by the Cyber Seven, puppet-like robot creatures that link together to form a literal bridge between the worlds. The detailed, faintly Western artwork has the chiseled 1980s look of Katsuhiro Otomo or Jiro Taniguchi, while the surreal villains are reminiscent of a Grant Morrison or Peter Milligan comic. ★★★

CYBORG 009

(サイボーグ009) • Shotaro Ishinomori • Tokyopop (2003–2005) • various magazines (1964–1998) • 10 volumes, suspended (36 volumes in Japan) • Science Fiction, Action • 13+ (language, violence)

Shotaro Ishinomori's most famous manga, *Cyborg 009* is classic pulp sci-fi for children, a rock-'em-sock-'em action comic with an antiwar message. The Black Ghost, a secret organization of war profiteers, kidnaps people from around the globe to use as guinea pigs for a cyborg army. But the nine cyborgs rebel against their masters and use their superpowers to fight for peace, vowing, "We are all humans and brothers." (The Native American and African cyborgs are drawn in a stereotypical style, but the story's antiprejudice message is sincere.) The sketchy oldschool art shows the strong influence of Osamu Tezuka. Bold shapes zip across the page; the heroes rush from one action scene to another, jumping onto planes in midflight, fighting giant robots and robot spiders, breaking into secret bases, casually outracing bullet trains. Countless battles are fought on easy-to-draw rocks above crashing seas, countless pages are filled with falling rubble and explosions. Unlike the episodic adventures of *Astro Boy, Cyborg 009* tells an ongoing story, but it was serialized in several different magazines and has its mood swings and disjointed moments. In one sequence the narrator reflects on Hiroshima and humanity's warlike nature; then the heroes go to Vietnam; then, a few volumes later, they're fighting beast-men in an underground empire. The English edition has

a satisfying ending, perhaps the best point at which to stop the series; Ishinomori intended to stop the series with volume 10 in 1966, but it was resumed due to reader demand and was still being produced at the time of Ishinomori's death. (The portions published in English were originally printed in Shônen Gahosha's *Weekly Shônen King* and Kodansha's *Weekly Shônen Magazine.*)
★★★★

DAEMON HUNTERS: HYMN FOR THE DEAD

Akumagari: Jyakumetsu no Seishôkahen, "Devil Hunters: Chapter of the Hymn of Death/Nirvana" (悪魔狩り~寂滅の聖頌歌篇~) • Seiuchiroh Todono • ADV (2004) • Mag Garden (Comic Blade, 2002–2005) • 1 volume, suspended (7 volumes in Japan) • Shônen, Fantasy, Action • 13+ (mild language, graphic violence)

Boring, generic "wandering swordsman" *shônen* fantasy manga with an excessively long, portentous prologue. Todono rips off *Berserk*'s crosshatched style of drawing swords and armor, but his character designs are worse than derivative. Even the demons, while superficially cool-looking, have no personality and look like a mishmash of RPG monsters and Todd McFarlane action figures. Michael Largness, the stoic monsterfighting hero with a sword and cape, is saddled with sidekicks: an obnoxious kid wizard, a passive female healer, an animal mascot. The series is a sequel to the artist's untranslated *Akumagari* ("Devil Hunters"), serialized in *Monthly Shônen Gangan.* ★

DAME DAME SAITO NIKKI

Dame Dame Saito Nikki, "The No-Good Saito Diary" (だめだめ斉藤日記) • Tomoyuki Saito • Dark Horse (2008) • MediaWorks (Dengeki Daioh/ Dengeki Ôdama, 2000–2001) • 1 volume • Comedy • 16+ (nudity, sexual humor)

A collection of short works by *dôjinshi* artist Tomoyuki Saito (who has lived in San Francisco for many years), this book mostly consists of a short-lived 4-page feature from *Dengeki Daioh* magazine, in which Saito describes the United States for Japanese readers. These "essays in manga form" cover

American holidays such as Halloween and Valentine's Day, the Powerpuff Girls and other pop icons, American obesity, and the comics and anime scene circa 2000. Saito is a talented chameleon capable of swinging between several art styles (but always featuring lots of cute girls), and her observations are witty and personal. The rest of the book consists of *dôjinshi*, often dealing with American pop culture. ★★★½

DANCE TILL TOMORROW

Asatte Dance, "Day After Tomorrow Dance" (あさって Dance) • Naoki Yamamoto • Viz (1997–2003) • Shogakukan (Big Comic Spirits, 1989–1990) • 7 volumes • Romantic Comedy • Unrated/18+ (language, nudity, graphic sex)

"As long as there's sex scenes, I can draw whatever I want" might be the motto of Naoki Yamamoto, an offbeat *seinen* manga creator whose favorite American artists include Gary Panter and Robert Crumb. Suekichi, a college student who works at an avant-garde theater troupe, inherits a fortune in trust from his dead grandfather, but his future plans are complicated by a girl who might just be after his money: the inscrutable, protean, sexually insatiable Aya. The result is an occasionally pornographic comedy of love, money, and marriage, with a large supporting cast of weird characters. Yamamoto's art has a gangly, hand-drawn look, and the whimsical, self-referential story provides many opportunities for surreal, artsy humor (one of the minor characters wears a mask from the 1980 cult film *Forbidden Zone*). Loosely plotted but enjoyable and unpredictable. ★★★½

DAPHNE IN THE BRILLIANT BLUE

Ai-Hikari to Mizu no Daphne, "Ai-Daphne of Light and Water" (アイ─光と水のダフネ Daphne in the Brilliant Blue) • Satoshi Shiki • Tokyopop (2006) • Shônen Gahosha (Young King Ours, 2004) • 1 volume • Seinen, Science Fiction, Action • 16+ (language, mild violence, brief nudity, sexual situations)

Anime/manga/multimedia franchise set in a future society, where humans have retreated to domed undersea cities and everyone rides Jet Skis through canal streets. The manga focuses on a different main character than the anime does: Ai, a school-skipping Jet Ski test driver who becomes involved in an intrigue involving terrorists and female secret agents in skimpy bodysuits. Shiki's art is slick and detailed as always, with sleek, gleaming machines and sharp-featured human characters. The story is also well told and remarkably coherent by his standards. Unfortunately, it ends abruptly, and ultimately functions merely as a teaser for the anime. ★★

DARK ANGEL

Seijü Denshô Dark Angel, "Holy Beast Folktale Dark Angel" (聖獣伝承ダークエンジェル) • Kia Asamiya • CPM (1999–2004) • Kadokawa Shoten (Newtype, 1990–1997) • 5 volumes • Fantasy, Action • 13+/16+ (graphic violence, nudity)

Dark, a nice-guy swordsman who sometimes transforms into an evil psycho with angel wings, wanders a vaguely Chinese/Central Asian landscape of desert wastelands, encountering people who try to kill him (and his flying fairy companion) for no reason. *Dark Angel* demonstrates why explosions and fireballs are so popular in manga fight scenes: they're the first resort of artists who can't even draw people hitting one another. The backgrounds are gray smears that exist to be blown up, the characters come and go apparently as Asamiya grows tired of them, and the battles all involve people throwing their big final explosive attack at their opponent and then realizing *their opponent is actually standing behind them*! The series ends abruptly with no resolution, but the plot is so weak that you could open up any random volume and it'd make just as much sense. 0 Stars

DARK ANGEL: PHOENIX RESURRECTION

Phoenix Resurrection Dark Angel (フェニックスレサレクションダークエンジェル) • Kia Asamiya • Image (2000) • Enterbrain (2001–2002) • 4 issues • Fantasy, Action • Unrated/13+ (violence)

A retelling of *Dark Angel* drawn specifically for the American superhero comics market, colored by J. D. Smith. Asamiya's processed artwork works well with Image-style computer coloring, but the story is as vapid as the original, and stopped in midstory due to low sales. After being published in America, the book was later reprinted in two volumes in Japan. ★

DARK EDGE

Yu Aikawa • ComicsOne/DrMaster (2004–2006) • MediaWorks (Dengeki Gao!, 1999–2006) • 6 volumes, suspended (15 volumes in Japan) • Shônen, Horror, Action • 13+ (graphic violence, mild sexual situations)

When they stay after dark at Yotsuji Private High School, a group of students discovers the terror that lies within its walls: zombies and monsters controlled by a mysterious faculty of vampire teachers. *Dark Edge* combines the gothic visual shocks of a "survival horror" video game with the teenagers-versus-monsters plot of a movie such as *The Faculty* or *Fright Night* (together with a horror movie's illogical behavior; after barely surviving their first night at the school, the surviving students attend their classes as usual the next day). The art is unexceptional, despite a few memorable images, but the story is tense. ★★½

DARKSIDE BLUES

(ダークサイド・ブルース) • Hideyuki Kikuchi (story), Yuho Ashibe (art) • ADV (2004) • Akita Shoten (Bonita, 1988) • 1 volume • Shôjo, Occult, Science Fiction • 16+ (brief language, graphic violence, nudity, brief sexual situations)

An unfinished, surreal science fiction horror tale. In the future, the family-owned Persona Corporation owns 90 percent of the world, monitoring past, present, and future under the ominous sign of the spider. Suddenly, a gothic figure of rebellion appears: the mysterious Darkside, a gentleman with inhumanly piercing eyes, who drives a horse-drawn carriage out of a black mirror and sets up shop in the Mansion of Illusions in Shinjuku's slums. A group of rebels and street urchins (dressed in embarrassing 1980s fashions) courts Darkside's help in the battle against the Persona Corporation.

If Kikuchi's *Demon City Hunter* flirts with weird imagery in the context of a formulaic action manga, *Darkside Blues* is almost undiluted surrealism. Some of the vignettes are reminiscent of writers such as Ray Bradbury, Grant Morrison, or China Miéville: a miniature factory is shoved into a person's wound, causing them to turn to gold; an "appetite enhancer for inanimate objects" causes a house to come to life and eat the occupants. Unfortunately, the story has no buildup, ending, or resolution, and ultimately is little more than glimpses of a kind of anime opium dream. Yuho Ashibe's 1970s *shôjo* artwork is the perfect counterpart to Kikuchi's strange but specific concepts.
★★★

DARK TALES OF DAILY HORROR

Ippongi Bang • Antarctic (1994) • 1 issue • Comedy • Unrated/13+ (sexual situations)

Unfunny collection of short stories by the "international rainbow-haired rock-'n'-roll cartoonist" Ippongi Bang. An extremely light parody of the horror genre, the tales involve ironic punishments for various social ills (a girl makes a devil's bargain to lose weight; a guy who cuts in line on the subway suffers an awful fate; a girl who wants to be a "material girl" turns into a sex doll). ★½

DARK WATER

Honogurai Mizu no Soko Kara, "In the Depths of Dark Water" (仄暗い水の底から) • Koji Suzuki (story), MEIMU (art) • ADV (2004) • Kadokawa Shoten (2002) • 1 volume • Horror • 13+ (violence)

Based on a collection of short stories by author Koji Suzuki (*The Ring*), MEIMU's *Dark Water* manga offers a quartet of horror tales, all of which revolve around disquieting bodies of liquid. The title story, "Dark Water," is about a recently divorced mother who begins to suspect that something sinister is going on in her run-down apartment building (the tale also served as the inspiration for a *Dark Water* live-action film in Japan, later remade in Hollywood). The second story, "Island Cruise," preys on the fear of what may lie beneath the waves during a boat trip. "Adrift" is also set during a sea journey, and posits a theory behind ghost ship legends. The final (and best) story, "Forest Beneath the Waves," contains no overt supernatural elements but is still a journey into the dark side as a man suffering from a midlife crisis seeks the ultimate getaway during a sea dive. Reading like a manga collection of Stephen King stories, *Dark Water* is a slight but enjoyable collection. As the top adapter of J-horror tales, MEIMU's art and storytelling are more than up to the task of conveying physical terror and psychological dread. (PM)   ★★★

THE DAY OF REVOLUTION

Kakumei no Hi, "The Day of Revolution" (革命の日) • Mikiyo Tsuda • DMP (2006) • Shinshokan (South, 1999–2001) • 2 volumes • Shôjo, Romantic Comedy • 16+ (mild language, sexual situations)

Kei, a girlish boy who hangs with the tough kids on the school roof, discovers that he's a medical hermaphrodite, and (slightly against his will) undergoes the transition to become female. The first chapter is promising—a transgender manga about an actual sex change—but things become conventional when Kei shows up at school as "Megumi," and the manga turns into a typical "girl who feels like a boy inside" story. Meanwhile, her four best friends from when she was a guy all ask her out. Like Hiroyuki Nishimori's *A Cheeky Angel,* the story parodies teenage male machismo, but Tsuda's heroine is weaker, the plot is slow, and the page compositions are dull. Disappointing.   ★★

DAZZLE

Hatenkô Yugi, "Unprecedented Game" (破天荒遊戯) • Minari Endo • Tokyopop (2006–ongoing) • Square Enix/Ichijinsha (Monthly G-Fantasy/Comic Zero-Sum, 1999–ongoing) • 8+ volumes (ongoing) • Shôjo, Drama • 13+ (language, occasional graphic violence, mild sexual situations)

Buddy story involving the travels of Rahzel, a young, impulsive sorceress (her powers mostly involve blasting things), and her companion, Alzeid (a *bishônen* former military man with a dark past). From the outline it may sound like a *Slayers*-esque adventure, but the series isn't really in the fantasy genre; the heroes wear modern-day clothes and wander through nondescript towns encountering thugs with guns and knives. The plot takes a long time to get moving, focusing on the main characters' pointless bickering before eventually turning to the angst of Alzeid's backstory. The character art is pretty but the setting and stories are dull, overrelying on fights with random goons.   ★½

DEAD END

The End (ジ・エンド) • Shohei Manabe • Tokyopop (2005–2006) • Kodansha (Afternoon, 2001–2002) • 4 volumes • Seinen, Science Fiction, Suspense, Action • 16+ (language, violence, nudity)

Shirou is a young man in a rut, working a boring job as a construction worker, until a naked girl falls out of the sky and stirs up his life. The mysterious Lucy disappears as suddenly as she arrived, and Shirou learns that he intentionally wiped his own memories and must find a bunch of old "friends" in order to make sense of his past and reunite with Lucy. Making things difficult are some homemade zombies and psychotic telepaths, which soon send the story down the path of violence and near horror. Among all the action, Shirou and his buddies don't seem too surprised that people are dying and strange technology is blowing up their apartments. *Dead End* has the feel of a dream, with the promise of answers hidden somewhere in its pages; for the most part, though, it's simply action with no moral compass. The talented artist's unpretty art matches the disaffected characters and grim urban settings. (SM)   ★★½

DEARS

(ディアーズ) • Peach-Pit • Tokyopop (2005–2006) • MediaWorks (Dengeki Gao!, 2001–2005) • 8 volumes • Shônen, Science Fiction, Otaku, Romantic Comedy • 13+ (mild language, partial nudity, sexual situations)

Mysterious but friendly aliens called DearS have crash-landed on Earth, and everyone is fascinated with them ("Get with the times! Paranoid theories are out and hot alien chicks

Jump, 2004–2006) • 12 volumes • Shônen, Occult, Suspense • 16+ (violence)

One of the strangest manga ever published in *Weekly Shônen Jump* magazine, *Death Note* is an unrelenting mind game of guessing and second-guessing. Light Yagami, a megalomaniacal genius student, discovers a Death Note, a notebook with the power to kill anyone whose name is written inside. Accompanied by the notebook's original owner, a ghostly *shinigami* ("grim reaper" or "death god"), he attempts to improve the world by slaughtering criminals, until an equally super-intelligent teenage detective mobilizes worldwide resources to track him down. *Death Note*'s cat-and-mouse drama is unequaled, taking the supernatural premise to the most extreme logical conclusions, although most of the action takes place entirely within the main characters' minds. The pretense of plausibility wears thin in the later volumes, but even past its prime, *Death Note* is amazingly well written, with countless twists and turns. It's a rare case of a truly Faustian antihero in a *shônen* manga— no "let's all be friends" messages here. Takeshi Obata's art strikes the perfect balance for the material: friendly enough to make the characters look sympathetic, but photorealistic enough for the dark themes and cold, institutional settings of the story.
★★★★

DEATH'S REFLECTION: See *Hino Horror, Vol. 10: Death's Reflection*

DEATH TRANCE

Kana Takeuchi • Media Blasters (2005) • 3 volumes • Samurai, Action, Horror • 18+ (mild language, violence)

A prequel to the movie of the same name, *Death Trance* tells the tale of Grave, a young man who lives for the thrill of the fight and to protect his beloved Shirayuki. When a monk arrives in Grave's village on a quest to fight the Goddess of Destruction, Grave and his loved one are drawn into a bloody battle with evil spirits. The art and story veer between poignant and clear, muddled and

Hideyuki Kikuchi and Shin-Ichi Hosoma's *Demon City Hunter*

are in!"). Seventeen-year-old Takaya is skeptical until he has a close encounter with a "defective" DearS, Ren, who sticks to him like glue, calls him "master," and lies around his room like a pet. Turns out that DearS are a race of slaves who are naturally inclined to seek masters and bond with them. Despite all the science fiction pretensions and the characters' delicate expressions, *DearS* is basically a fanservice "maid manga," with a seemingly endless number of interchangeable alien women in skintight fetish gear. The attempts at serious drama are unconvincing and the story simply introduces new characters until Peach-Pit runs out of ideas. Starting in volume 2, the sexually suggestive plot and art push the edges of the 13+ rating. ★½

DEATH NOTE

(デスノート) • Tsugumi Ohba (story), Takeshi Obata (art) • Viz (2005–2007) • Shueisha (Weekly Shônen confusing, but for the most part *Death Trance* makes for an entertaining and interesting read. Commissioned by Media Blasters and drawn by a Japanese artist. (LW) ★★½

DEJIKO'S SUMMER VACATION: See *Di Gi Charat Theater: Dejiko's Summer Vacation*

DEMON CITY HUNTER

Makai Toshi Hunter, "Demon (Realm) City Hunter" (魔界都市ハンター) • Hideyuki Kikuchi (story), Shin-Ichi Hosoma (art) • ADV (2003–2004) • Akita Shoten (Weekly Shônen Champion, 1986–1989) • 4 volumes, suspended (17 volumes in Japan) • Shônen, Occult, Science Fiction, Action • 16+ (language, brief partial nudity, graphic violence)

Spirited, ludicrous *shônen* manga spin-off of Hideyuki Kikuchi's untranslated *Demon City Shinjuku* novels. After the "devilquake" of 198X, Tokyo's Shinjuku district was separated from the rest of the world by massive chasms, and the human residents of the city now coexist uneasily, to say the least, with man-eating amoebas, tentacled sea monsters, dinosaurs, and leering undead off the cover of an Iron Maiden album. When a mysterious old man who may or may not be God starts wandering through the city, two clashing teams of square-jawed bad dudes go after him—the evil Dark Order and the noble Super Soldiers of the Defense Agency. But the *real* hero is Kyoya Izayoi, a superpowered teenage martial artist with a wooden sword and the ever-so-slightly-chubby look common to mid-1980s anime characters. *Demon City Hunter* barely bothers to explain its setting, but the reader soon gets the point as Kikuchi unleashes a barrage of surreal fight scenes and inventive monsters. The dated anime-style art has a thick-lined, brushstroke vitality; the adults look like members of *G.I. Joe,* the monsters are impressive, and the kids have teeny-tiny noses and mouths in the middle of big, cute faces. It's completely silly, but the author's nonstop imagination makes it a good series for mayhem-loving young readers. Sample dialogue: "Damn! That missile saved us from the two-headed dog, but now *another* one has shown up!" In places the art is blurry and hard to follow. ★★★

DEMON CITY SHINJUKU

Makai Toshi Hunter Series: Makai Toshi Shinjuku, "Demon (Realm) City Hunter Series: Demon (Realm) City Shinjuku" (魔界都市ハンターシリーズ 魔界都市新宿) • Hideyuki Kikuchi (story), Shin-Ichi Hosoma (art) • ADV (2003–2004) • Akita Shoten (Susperia Mystery, 2002) • 2 volumes • Shôjo, Occult, Science Fiction, Action • 16+ (mild language, graphic violence)

A stand-alone prequel to *Demon City Hunter,* this manga follows the same plot as the 1988 anime movie *Demon City Shinjuku* and delves into the origin of Kyoya, the hero of the series. Sometime after the transformation of Shinjuku, the evil magician Levy Rah places a curse upon the president of Earth, and Kyoya—a sword-wielding street punk—is called upon to enter the foreboding demon city and defeat the evil wizard. Along for the ride are Kyoya's friend Sam, the president's daughter Sayaka, and the coolly mysterious Dr. Mephisto. Hosoma's artwork has changed with the times in the fifteen years since *Demon City Hunter;* his lines are thinner and the characters have the sharper features and spiky hair of the current anime fashion. Whether consciously or as a result of developing a faster drawing style, his work has a rougher look on the whole; the backgrounds and monsters look like sketches in a high school notebook. Originally based on an untranslated novel by Kikuchi. ★★½

THE DEMON ORORON

Akuma no Ororon, "The Devil/Demon Ororon" (悪魔のオロロン) • Hakase Mizuki • Tokyopop (2004) • Shinshokan (Wings, 1998–2001) • 4 volumes • Shôjo, Occult, Fantasy, Drama • 13+ (language, violence, brief nudity, sexual situations)

Chiaki, a lonely teenage girl, receives a single wish from Ororon, a handsome, brooding, cigarette-smoking demon prince in a black business suit. When she wishes for Ororon to stay with her, they develop an unspoken mutual attraction, but they also attract the unwelcome attention of his enemies, evil supernatural hipsters out for the bounty on Ororon's head. Bloody, sexy battles make up the bulk of the plot, as Ororon drips blood all over his suit and Chiaki has doubts about loving someone so ruthless . . . until her *own* supernatural powers are devastatingly revealed. The angst-ridden moral conundrums are slightly more genuine than in other manga of this sort, but the washed-out, simplistic artwork isn't adequate to the city-destroying fight scenes. Mizuki strives to be stylish with bold black areas and lanky, cool-looking characters (Ororon looks like Sanji from *One Piece*) but doesn't quite achieve it. ★★

DEMON PALACE BABYLON

Makai Toshi Hunter Series: Makyû Babylon, "Demon (Realm) City Hunter Series: Demon Palace Babylon" (魔界都市ハンターシリーズ魔宮バビロン) • Hideyuki Kikuchi (story), Shin-Ichi Hosoma (art) • ADV (2003–2004) • Akita Shoten (Susperia Mystery, 2001) • 2 volumes • Shôjo, Occult, Science Fiction, Action • 16+ (language, nudity, graphic violence)

In this stand-alone sequel to *Demon City Hunter,* a strange palace appears in the sky above Tokyo's demon-haunted Shinjuku district. The palace turns out to be the Hanging Gardens of Babylon, whose masked lord invites Tokyo's elite—and most especially the hero's female friend Sayaka—to a grand housewarming party. Soon, sword-wielding Kyoya is fighting to rescue Sayaka from the clutches of none other than Nebuchadnezzar II, ruler of Babylon. Shin-Ichi Hosoma, the ever-adaptable artist, yet again "modernizes" his character designs for Sayaka and Kyoya, who resemble their *Demon City Shinjuku* selves but with wilder hair and different outfits. Compared to Kikuchi's other manga, though, it's a mild letdown—the level of craziness is lower than usual (even lower than the level of historical research), and the formulaic, fighting-oriented plot has the feel of a low-budget anime. Originally based on an untranslated novel by Kikuchi. ★★½

DENSHA OTOKO: THE STORY OF THE TRAIN MAN WHO FELL IN LOVE WITH A GIRL

Densha Otoko: Demo, Ore Tabidatsu Yo., "Train Man: But, I'm about to Leave on a Trip." (電車男—でも、俺旅立つよ。) • Hitori Nakano (original story), Wataru Watanabe (manga) • CMX (2006–2007) • Akita Shoten (Champion Red, 2005–2006) • 3 volumes • Seinen, Romantic Comedy • 13+ (mild violence, mild sexual situations)

In an uncharacteristic moment of bravery, a nerdy *otaku* stands up to a drunk who's pestering a pretty girl on a train. She is moved by his courageous act and sends him expensive teacups as a thank-you along with her phone number. Knowing that he wants to see her again, but being too nerdy and shy to figure out how, he turns to a popular *otaku* online forum for advice. The people on the forum are touched by his plight and give him advice on how to court the girl, and they eventually fall in love. One of three translated manga based on the hit book *Densha Otoko* by Hitori Nakano, this manga is the clear winner of the three. The art is energetic and humorous. Most important, the main character really comes across well as being a hopeless *otaku:* he's nerdy, bumbling, and sympathetically clueless. While all three train-men manga have their merits, this one makes for the best overall read. See also *Train_Man: Densha Otoko* and *Train Man: A Shojo Manga.* (RB) ★★★½

DESCENDANTS OF DARKNESS

Yami no Matsuei, "Descendants of Darkness" (闇の末裔) • Yoko Matsushita • Viz (2004–2006) • Hakusensha (Hana to Yume, 1994–1997) • 11 volumes • Shôjo, Fantasy, Occult, Comedy • 16+ (language, graphic violence, sexual situations)

Question: Is *Descendants of Darkness* a police office comedy? A horror story about child molestation? Or an RPG-esque fantasy comic about summoned dragons, monsters, and talking animals? Answer: all of the above. Asato Tsuzuki (age of death: twenty-six) and Hisoka Kurosaki (age of death: sixteen) are partners at the Ministry of Hades, ghostly investigators who go to Earth to help lost souls. In their line of work they clash with the seductive sexual predator Dr. Muraki, who raped and killed Hisoka. This bizarre, schizophrenic manga starts out as a supernatural mystery series (similar to *YuYu Hakusho, Her Majesty's Dog,* etc.), ventures into the uncomfortable territory of sexual abuse and murder, and then backs off, turning into a fantasy comic. The mix of exploitative subject matter and comic relief is extreme even by manga standards, but a more serious flaw is *Descendants of Darkness*'s *dôjinshi*-esque feeling of total pointlessness. The prospect of a *yaoi* love triangle between the three main characters is the closest thing to a plot, but even this goes nowhere. The jokes are clichéd, the fantasy elements are awkwardly introduced, and the only real appeal is the artwork, which is admittedly attractive, particularly in the later volumes. The heroes are broad-shouldered, handsome men who inhabit a sumptuous world of *shôjo* flowers, Asian mythological monsters who leap off the page, and skillfully composited photo backgrounds. There's almost no actual sex, but a suggestive panel is censored from volume 4 of the Viz edition. The Japanese series is on an "extended break," with the possibility of more material being released sometime. ★

DESERT CORAL

(デザート・コーラル) • Wataru Murayama • ADV (2004) • Mag Garden (Comic Blade, 2002–2004) • 3 volumes, suspended (5 volumes in Japan) • Fantasy, Adventure • All Ages (violence, brief partial nudity)

In his dreams, Naoto is summoned into the parallel world of Orgos, where the evil Elphis prey on the peaceful Sand Dusts, and where his dream girl, Lusia, takes him as her "servant monster." At its best (such as the dusky landscapes and the evocative cover art), *Desert Coral* conveys the solemnly awestruck feeling of a traveler in a faraway world. However, the plot (apocalyptic prophecies) and character designs (elf ears and cat ears) soon turn clichéd, and you never really figure out what the characters are fighting for or why women randomly confess love for the hero. The interaction between the "real" world and Orgos is interesting. ★★

DEUS VITAE

D'V (ディーヴァ) • Takuya Fujima • Tokyopop (2004) • Kodansha (Magazine Z, 2000–2002) • Shônen,

Science Fiction, Fantasy, Action • 3 volumes • 16+ (language, violence, nudity, sexual situations)

In the year 2068, Earth is ruled by the android Selenoids (who look and act just like people), while humans are reduced to a dying slave race. Ash, your typical cool martial artist who can shoot power fireballs, rebels against Earth's mechanical masters, spurning the advances of the naked mother computer ("Enter me, Ash!") and breaking free into the outside world. But will Raschur, a human commander who hates Selenoids, destroy the chance for both sides to find true peace? And why are military battles being fought on horseback in this science fiction manga? And what about the little-girl Selenoid who loves our hero? With every page elaborately composed like a screentone tapestry of realistic nude women and cybermachinery, *Deus Vitae* has impressively polished art, but the pompous dialogue and clichéd plot are compounded by confused, incomprehensible storytelling. ½

THE DEVIL DOES EXIST

Akuma de Sôrô, "I Am the Devil" (悪魔で候) • Mitsuba Takanashi • CMX (2005–2007) • Shueisha (Bessatsu Margaret, 1998–2002) • 11 volumes • Shôjo, Romantic Drama • 13+ (mild language, mild violence, sexual situations)

Seventeen-year-old Kayano finds herself attracted to a sixteen-year-old rebel: Takeru Edogawa, the "prince of attraction," the delinquent son of the school principal. Their relationship is further complicated when their single parents become engaged, turning them into stepbrother and stepsister . . . and making his sexiness all the more sinful. Despite the title and a little blood, *The Devil Does Exist* is a formulaic light drama for younger teenagers, far from the genuinely abusive and troubling love interests of manga such as *Hot Gimmick* and *Boys over Flowers*. Takeru and most of the other male characters have an androgynously pretty look (his appearance is based on the Japanese "visual rock" musician Hyde), and the "devil" behaves like a moody, teasing little brother who has trouble expressing his feelings. One of the better aspects is the art, which improves quickly after the first volume; the characters (who dress like 1990s punks) are attractive and realistic, and their faces are reminiscent of Korean comics, with full lips, long eyelashes, and spiky hair. ★★

DEVIL IN THE WATER

Mizu ni Sumu Oni, "Devil Dwelling in the Water" (水に棲む鬼) • Akiko Hatsu • ComicsOne (e-book, 2000) • Asahi Sonorama (1992) • 1 volume • Drama • 13+ (violence, sexual situations)

A collection of short romance stories tinged with crime and the supernatural. Each individual story unfolds quickly, and most revolve around unsolved murders and unfulfilled longings for often-dead lovers. In a number of the stories, a ghost of a deceased lover returns to tie up loose ends, including one story that takes its plot directly from Kenji Mizoguchi's *Ugestu Monogatari*. While no individual stories stand out as exceptional, the blend of melodrama, spirit possessions, and a number of twist endings straight out of detective fiction make for a surprisingly satisfying read. (RS) ★★★

DEVILMAN

(デビルマン) • Go Nagai & Dynamic Production • Kodansha International (2002–2003) • Kodansha (Weekly Shônen Magazine, 1972–1973) • 5 volumes • Action, Horror • Unrated/16+ (language, graphic violence, nudity)

Millions of years ago, a race of demons led by the fallen angel Satan ruled planet Earth until the great ice age left them in a state of hibernation. But when an explorer in the Himalayas discovers these sleeping demons, their evil is reborn into the modern era. Back in Japan, teenager Ryo Asuka realizes through his late father's studies that a great war will soon erupt between humankind and the awakened demons that want their world back. Believing that "the only actual way to fight the demons is to become a demon yourself," Ryo convinces his mild-mannered friend Akira Fudoh to merge with a demon and become Devilman, a terrifying hybrid being with supernatural powers that

he uses to fight the demonic legions. One of Go Nagai's signature creations, *Devilman* is an envelope-pushing classic of 1970s-era manga. Developed at the same time as a more simplistic *Devilman* anime TV series, the manga contains everything from comedy to splatter, superheroics, and even dramatic pathos that rings loud and clear through Nagai's loose and cartoony style. As Akira faces one ingeniously conceived threat after another, the story escalates from simple horror set pieces to huge-scale panoramas of biblically inspired carnage. Along the way, Nagai ruminates on topics ranging from evolution and morality to humankind's penchant for self-destruction—heady stuff for a children's manga back then, perhaps unthinkable now. The only caveat with the terrific Kodansha International edition is the inclusion of material created for a "New Devilman" series that sees Ryo and Akira traveling back in time to meet the likes of Adolf Hitler and General Custer. Like computer graphics shoehorned into a classic film, this later material, drawn in a different style, never really meshes with the 1970s-era original. Still, it's hard to complain too much, as these five volumes contain the sum total of Nagai's *Devilman* manga output. Prior to the Kodansha Bilingual edition, a single volume was self-published in English by Nagai's Dynamic Productions in 1986, and three monthly comic issues—actually "New Devilman" material—were released by Verotik in the mid-1990s. (PM) ★★★★

DEVIL MAY CRY 3

(デビルメイクライ3) • Suguro Chayamachi • Tokyopop (2005–2006) • Media Factory (2005–2006) • 2 volumes, suspended • Gothic, Video Game, Action • 16+ (mild language, graphic violence)

Based on the characters from Capcom's stylish megahit video game by the same name. While the game was known for its cool characters, gothic horror, and over-the-top intense action, the adaptation is a subpar action manga that takes a cool video game character and turns him into a bad action movie chump. The story takes place in Italy, where Dante is a hit man who specializes in

taking out demons. He gets a job to find a girl named Alice. From there the story dwindles into a predictable gothic take on *Alice in Wonderland,* with Dante blowing away white rabbits and spouting off some of the worst action hero dialogue ever to find its way into a Japanese comic. The art, at least, is appropriately dark and spooky; using high-contrast black and white and no screentone, Chayamachi creates an almost woodcut-like effect. Though the series has no real ending, a third volume may or may not ever materialize. (RB)   ★

THE DEVIL WITHIN

Tenshi no Naka ni Akuma Ari, "The Devil Within the Angel" (天使の中に悪魔アリ) • Ryou Takagi • Go! Comi (2007) • Shinshokan (Wings, 2003–2005) • 2 volumes • Shôjo, Fantasy, Romantic Comedy • 16+ (sexual situations)

Rion thinks that all men are devils, which is too bad, since she's being pursued by a trio of hot guys. But the only man she loves is Tenshi (angel), who looks just like her childhood sweetheart . . . but who's actually a teenager trapped in the body of a ten-year-old!   NR

D.GRAY-MAN

(ディー・グレイマン) • Katsura Hoshino • Viz (2006–ongoing) • Shueisha (Weekly Shônen Jump, 2004–ongoing) • 10+ volumes (ongoing) • Shônen, Gothic, Action • 16+ (graphic violence)

On a parallel Earth, in the late nineteenth century, good and evil race to find the "innocence"—not an abstract quality, but a divine force left over from the Great Flood, now embodied in certain objects and people around the world. On the side of good are the exorcists of the Black Order, who make their headquarters in a dark mansion atop a towering cliff; on the side of evil are the Clan of Noah, who serve the Millennium Earl, a satanic cartoon figure who turns lost souls into twisted *akuma* or devils ("I shall obliterate your puny 'god' and lead the world to its death with my *akuma*"). Allen Walker, a teenager born with the power to morph his hand into a weapon, is one of the exor-

cists who roam the globe on superheroic missions, often involving time slips, ruined cities, vampires, and other strange phenomena. Visually inventive and polished (the art looks like Takeshi Obata drawing *The Nightmare Before Christmas*), *D. Gray-Man* has the same weaknesses as a modern American superhero comic: chaotic fight scenes, hasty transitions, and excessive weirdness without any time for readers to catch their breath. The immersion approach partly works, but the appeal of the story is still mostly visual—an over-the-top gothic slugfest for teenage readers.   ★★

DIABOLO

Diabolo-Akuma, "Diabolo-Devil" (Diabolo-悪魔) • Kei Kusunoki, Kaoru Ohashi • Tokyopop (2004–2005) • Sobisha (Crimson, 2001–2003) • 3 volumes • Action, Horror • 16+ (graphic violence, infrequent nudity, sexual situations)

Ten years ago, when they were children, Ren and Rai sold their souls to the unseen force called Diabolo, gaining powerful combat abilities. (Seems like a weird thing to sell your soul for, but . . .) They try to use their powers for good, to prevent other people from making the same mistake, all the while knowing that soon the devil will come to claim them. *Diabolo* begins as a series of episodic horror stories, similar to Kusunoki's *Ogre Slayer,* in which the focus is on other hapless characters and the heroes just show up at the end to kill things. Gradually it turns to a more ambitious apocalyptic plot. Unfortunately, the visuals and action scenes are weak, although the lack of on-screen monsters works as an artistic choice.   ★★½

DI GI CHARAT

Di Gi Charat Kôshiki Comic Anthology, "Di Gi Charat Official Comic Anthology" (デ・ジ・キャラット公式コミックアンソロジー) • Koge-Donbo, various artists • Viz (2003) • MediaWorks (2000–2001) • 4 volumes • Otaku, Comedy • All Ages

Originating as a four-panel manga in a promotional magazine for the Akihabara-based Gamers chain of anime stores in the 1990s, *Di Gi Charat* soon exploded into a massive

franchise. In brief, *Di Gi Charat* is the story of green-haired, cat-eared alien Princess Dejiko, who arrives on Earth with her companions Puchiko and Gemo, only to find themselves penniless and forced to work in Gamers. They quickly become popular store mascots. This four-volume anthology contains commissioned *dôjinshi* by series creator Koge-Donbo and other artists. (Volume 1 includes stories by Miyabi Fujieda and Kanan; volume 2 includes stories by Peach-Pit and Kanan; all volumes include stories by Koge-Donbo.) The stories range from four-panel gag strips to 3–8-page stories, some focusing on character emotion and others on comic violence and gags. The art is cute and all the stories are pretty light in plot. (MJS) ★★

DI GI CHARAT THEATER: DEJIKO'S ADVENTURE

Dejiko Adventure (でじこ☆あどべんちゃー) • Yuki Kiriga (story and art), Koge-Donbo (original concept) • Broccoli Books (2004–2007) • Kadokawa Shoten (Dragon Junior, 2000–2002) • 3 volumes • Otaku, Comedy • All Ages

Di Gi Charat spin-off manga, printed in *Dragon Junior,* a magazine aimed at readers in their early teens. The plot involves Dejiko and friends trying to find a mysterious treasure in order to rebuild Gamers after accidentally destroying it in the first volume. The books consist partly of 3–5-page stories about Dejiko's quest and partly of four-panel gag strips parodying other manga genres. The art is generally good and varied; it's perfect if you'd like to see the *Di Gi Charat* cast in a variety of costumes (pirates, samurai, etc.). However, the plot is frequently ignored; it's less like a manga than an art book with word balloons. (MJS) ★★

DI GI CHARAT THEATER: DEJIKO'S SUMMER VACATION

Koge-Donbo, various artists • Broccoli Books (2003) • 1 volume • Otaku, Comedy • All Ages

Di Gi Charat spin-off manga, consisting of 3–5-page stories by various artists, including Koge-Donbo and Miyabi Fujieda. The first few stories have a summer/beach theme, but then they turn to general topics. Art styles vary from clean and simple to rough; stories vary from cute and sentimental to comical and violent. The stories consist mostly of in-jokes. Also includes interviews with Koge-Donbo, early *Di Gi Charat* comic strips from the monthly promotional magazine *From Gamers,* and pages from a *Di Gi Charat* weekly desk calendar. (MJS) ★★

DI GI CHARAT THEATER: LEAVE IT TO PIYOKO!

Di Gi Charat Gekiga Piyoko no Omakase!!, "Di Gi Charat Theater: Leave It to Piyoko!" (デ・ジ・キャラット劇場ぴよこにおまかせっ!!) • Hina (story and art), Koge-Donbo (original concept) • Broccoli Books (2004–2007) • MediaWorks (2002–2003) • 2 volumes • Otaku, Comedy • All Ages

Strips of 3–5 pages about the *Di Gi Charat* cast, focusing on Piyoko and the Black Gema Gema Gang. The art is generally clean and strong; it's cute but doesn't use super-deformed characters. These stories focus less on Piyoko's evil schemes (opening a rival game store, Black Gamers, to drive Dejiko out of business) and more on her feelings of inadequacy as a gang leader and her yearning for Dejiko to be an older sister to her. The stories are structured and paced well, introducing elements of the *Di Gi Charat* universe slowly so as not to overwhelm the reader. A good introductory manga for those unfamiliar with *Di Gi Charat.* (MJS) ★★½

DI GI CHARAT THEATER: PIYOKO IS NUMBER ONE!

Koge-Donbo, various artists • Broccoli Books (2003) • 1 volume • Otaku, Comedy • All ages

Di Gi Charat spin-off manga, consisting of 3–5-page stories by various artists, including Koge-Donbo and Kanan. Most of the stories focus on Piyoko and the Black Gema Gema Gang, the antagonists of the series. Also includes rough sketches of the Gema Gema Gang, interviews with Koge-Donbo, and early *Di Gi Charat* comic strips from the monthly promotional magazine *From Gamers.* Similar in format to *Di Gi Charat Theater:*

Dejiko's Summer Vacation, although the books can be read independently of one another. (MJS) ★★

DIGIKO'S CHAMPION CUP THEATRE

Dejiko no Champion Cup Gekiba, "Dejiko's Champion Cup Theatre" (でじこのチャンピオンカップ劇場) • Koge-Donbo • Studio Ironcat (2003) • Akita Shoten (2002) • 1 volume • Otaku, Comedy • All Ages (mild language, cartoon violence)

Di Gi Charat strips from the *Shônen Champion* family of magazines, mostly half-page gag strips with the occasional longer story lines. Like most of Koge-Donbo's early *Di Gi Charat* work, the characters are violent and bickering, much ruder and snarkier than the cuter work that she, and fan artists, drew later. Unfortunately, most of the art is small and rough; while Koge-Donbo shows versatility and skill as an artist, most of the work here looks like super-deformed scribbles. Also difficult to stomach is Rabi-en-Rose's insipid Valley Girl–speak and Dejiko's bizarre speech patterns that combine Ebonics with dated slang, a translation decision that is seen in no other *Di Gi Charat* manga. (MJS) ★★

DISAPPEARANCE DIARY

Shissô Nikki, "Disappearance Diary" (失踪日記) • Hideo Azuma • Fanfare/Ponent Mon (2007) • East Press (2005) • 1 volume • Autobiography, Underground • Unrated/16+ (mild violence, mature themes)

Manga artists under pressure from personal problems and the industry's demand for constant product sometimes burn out and disappear from the public eye. *Disappearance Diary* chronicles three such episodes in the life of *lolicon* founder and gag manga legend Hideo Azuma. Opening with his failed 1989 suicide attempt, Azuma recounts his subsequent stint as a Dumpster-diving homeless vagabond, a 1993 stretch working surreptitiously as a gas-pipe fitter, and a hallucinatory late-1990s alcoholic binge-and-purge that landed him in rehab. Drawn in his usual cuddly style and eschewing self-pity or melodrama, Azuma renders his downward

spiral as a deadpan comedy flecked with off-beat asides and absurdist flourishes. Along the way, he also offers a desultory potted history of his own rise as a manga star. *Disappearance Diary* won the Grand Prize for manga at the 2005 Japan Media Arts Festival. (CV) ★★★★

DISGAEA

Makai Senki Disgaea, "Demon World War Chronicle Disgaea" (魔界戦記ディスガイア) • Arashi Shindo • Broccoli Books (2006) • Ichijinsha (Comic Zero-Sum, 2003) • 1 volume • Video Game, Action, Comedy • 13+ (cartoon violence)

Based on the tactical RPG *Disgaea: Hour of Darkness,* the *Disgaea* manga faithfully follows the game world and characters. Prince Laharl is rudely awakened from his two-year slumber by his vassal Etna and notified that the king of the Netherworld is dead. Prince Laharl boasts of his new kingship and sets off to rule the Netherworld, but no one will listen to him, due to the attitudes of the demons he's supposed to be ruling. Various demons challenge the prince and are comedically thwarted. The story is simple and the gags tend to recycle, but all in all, it's a cute comedy, laced with smarmy characters. The cover, by Takehito Harada, does not reflect the interior art. (DR) ★★½

DISGAEA 2

Makai Senki Disgaea 2, "Demon World War Record Disgaea 2" (魔界戦記ディスガイア2) • Hekaton • Broccoli Books (2007) • MediaWorks (Dengeki Maoh, 2006–ongoing) • 1+ volumes (ongoing) • Fantasy, Adventure • 13+

The manga companion to the RPG video game of the same title. Now that everybody in the world has been turned into a demon, it's up to Adell, the last remaining human being, to challenge Overlord Zenon and put things back the way they were. Too bad he conjures up Zenon's daughter Rozalin instead. The first volume also includes some original chapters explaining what happened between the original *Disgaea* and the sequel. (MS) NR

DIVISION CHIEF KOSAKU SHIMA

Buchô Shima Kosaku, "Division Chief Kosaku Shima" (部長島耕作) • Kenshi Hirokane • Kodansha International (2000–2001) • Kodansha (Morning, 1992–2002) • 5 volumes, suspended (30 volumes in Japan) • Seinen, Salaryman, Drama • Unrated/18+ (language, nudity, sex)

The *Kosaku Shima* series of business comics are the ultimate ambassador for socially acceptable corporate manga culture. *Division Chief Kosaku Shima* is the second of several manga following the main character through his life and promotions, including *Section Chief Kosaku Shima,* 1983–1992; *Managing Director Kosaku Shima,* 2002–2005; and the currently running *Executive Managing Director Kosaku Shima.* (There's even a spin-off about his early life, *Young Kosaku Shima.*) The hero is the perfect salaryman, a young-looking forty-something executive of the massive Hatsushiba Electric, who balances a corporate conscience, a pair of cute kids from his previous marriage, and a mistress/girlfriend twenty years younger than he is. His job takes Shima around the globe, overseeing projects from Paris to Vietnam, where he invariably makes the moral and profitable decision and makes speeches explaining basic business concepts for the benefit of the reader. (The hero's relationships with women, and the occasional sex scenes, are equally idealized.) Looking past the shameless wish fulfillment, the series is extremely readable, and the stories are full of interesting factoids. In Japan, the series has been both popular and heavily promoted. In a famous incident in 1992, a talent search was held in which readers were invited to find the "real" Kosaku Shima, the ideal salaryman. Unfortunately, the contest failed due to lack of nominations; Shima's perfection had already far surpassed the point by which the character had any real-world analogue, and he was, and remains, a middle-aged businessman's superhero fantasy.   ★★½

D.N.ANGEL

Yukiru Sugisaki • Tokyopop (2004–ongoing) • Kadokawa Shoten (Asuka, 1997–ongoing) • 11+ volumes (ongoing) • Shôjo, Fantasy, Phantom Thief, Romantic Comedy • 13+ (mild language, mild violence, mild sexual situations)

Phantom thieves, romantic comedy, spirits, cute animals, angels and devils, school hijinks . . . it's easier to list genres *D.N.Angel* doesn't belong to. Fourteen-year-old Daisuke, the heir to a family of thieves, finds himself suddenly possessed by the mysterious alter ego that has been passed through his family for generations: Dark, the phantom thief, who glides over the night on angel wings and morphs Daisuke's body into that of a suave, handsome young man. Daisuke soon discovers that love triggers his nightly transformations, and when Dark meets the twin sisters Risa and Riku, he finds himself in a love triangle with his own alter ego. As Dark's supernatural origin is gradually revealed, the story moves away from romantic comedy and into outright fairy-tale fantasy. Yukiru Sugisaki's slick artwork hits all the anime-style signifiers like a pro—spiky hair, questionable noses, cute chinless faces—and would look gender-neutral if not for the countless floating feathers and glowing nimbuses that mark it as a *shôjo* manga. For younger readers, it's a sweet series (and it has almost no sexual content), but for older teenagers and adults who have read more anime, the art barely props up the clichés. The story is meandering; the series has gone on hiatus several times in Japan, and its eventual fate is still in doubt.   ★★

DOCTOR!

(ドクトール) • Ippongi Bang • Studio Ironcat (1997–1998) • 6 issues • Fantasy, Medical Drama • Unrated/13+ (language, brief nudity, surgery)

An adorably silly tribute to Osamu Tezuka's *Black Jack,* Doctor is an eye-patch-wearing surgeon-for-hire who roams a Spanish-speaking fantasyland vaguely based on Bolivia, using his surgical skills to solve ailments that magical healing cannot cure. His companion is Medio Liquido, a cute blob who disinfects the operating area and who looks like a slime from the *Dragon Quest* video game series. The surgical scenes are a mix of earnest anatomical trivia ("Liver, the king of internal organs") and tentacled monsters erupting from patients' bodies, only to be cut down by Doctor's scalpels. Poor image quality and translation mar the English edition. ★★½

DODEKAIN

Saikyô Kyojin Dodekain, "Strongest Giant God Dodekain" (**最強巨神ドデカイン**) • Masayuki Fujihara • Antarctic (1994–1995) • Bandai (Cyber Comix, 1992) • 8 issues • Shônen, Mecha, Comedy • Unrated/13+ (language, brief nudity)

Simple but inspired parody of giant robot power-escalation anime and manga, particularly the Go Nagai *Mazinger Z* variety. With Earth under attack by the dreaded Zogelians, a mad inventor unleashes Dodekain, a 15,000–mile-high giant robot literally larger than the entire planet. Piloted by your typical hot-blooded hero, Dodekain demolishes the alien monsters by punching and slapping the Earth with his bare hands, in the process causing more damage than the aliens did. ★★★

DOING TIME

Keimusho no Naka, "In Prison" (**刑務所の中**) • Kazuichi Hanawa • Fanfare/Ponent Mon (2004) • Seirinkogeisha (Ax, 1998–2000) • 1 volume • Underground, Autobiography • Unrated/13+ (language, partial nudity)

In 1995, underground manga artist Kazuichi Hanawa was convicted for possession of illegally modified model guns and sent to prison for the next two and a half years. His experiences provided the basis for *Doing Time,* a dreamlike documentary art comic. The book is not a true narrative; it jumps around in time, doesn't show Hanawa entering or leaving prison, and doesn't focus on particular characters, not even Hanawa himself. Instead, it describes every aspect of the prison in exhaustive detail, creating a sort of timeless mental blueprint, occasionally drifting into surrealism. From the opening page, "How to dress in prisoner's clothes," to the close-ups of grass in the prison yard, almost every item, room, and

piece of furniture is meticulously described, especially the meals, which fill page after page. The book is far from an exposé—the author expresses guilt at how well he's treated—and the prison comes off as a peaceful, strangely school-like environment, where the convicts are forced to enact counless little rituals of obedience: sitting the proper way, speaking the proper way, cleaning their cells, and so on. The heavily cross hatched, hand-drawn artwork gives equal priority to the people and the backgrounds, suitable for a book in which the setting dominates everything. The book also contains an essay and interview with Hanawa describing the circumstances of his arrest. ★★★★

DÔJINSHI: THE WORLD OF JAPANESE FANZINES

Various artists • Antarctic (1992–1993) • 4 issues • Dôjinshi • Comedy • Unrated/16+ (brief nudity)

Kazuichi Hanawa's *Doing Time*

DÔJINSHI (同人誌)

Just as Japan's comic industry dwarfs America's, so Japan's small press output is bigger than the professional American comic industry. The basics of *dôjinshi* (literally "same-person publications") is much the same as the small-press areas at American anime or comics conventions, where people sell comics with a print run of anywhere from a few hundred to a few thousand. Like fan fiction, *dôjinshi* often pays tribute to, and parodies, mainstream manga.

Dôjinshi became a major subculture in the 1970s, not long after the collapse of the 1960s underground comics scene and alternative manga magazines such as *Com.* College manga clubs (*manga kekyûkai*) still needed an outlet for their works, and began to trade and sell books at conventions, such as Tokyo's twice-yearly Comic Market (Comiket for short), which began in December 1975. Such college groups were the prototypical "*dôjinshi* circles," small groups of friends who worked together on comics, often each contributing a short story. Unlike the gender-divided mainstream comic industry, *dôjinshi* conventions were attended by a mixture of male and female artists, with female groups in the majority. High school and college-age women, with less academic and career pressure (and fewer opportunities), had more time to draw than their male counterparts. In the 1980s, the spread of *yaoi dôjinshi* (see the YAOI section) and other pop-culture parodies attracted growing numbers of fans, and convention attendance rose rapidly. Today, Comic Market has an attendance of over 500,000 people, and smaller *dôjinshi* conventions, often based on particular shows or subsets of fandom, go on throughout the year.

Dealers sell their wares at a *dôjinshi* convention in Shinsuke Kurihashi's *Pretty Maniacs*.

Dôjinshi span all imaginable subject matter: autobiographies, travelogues, self-published art portfolios, religious and political commentary, and original works of drama, fantasy, and science fiction. By far the most popular *dôjinshi*, however, are fanzine-style parodies of established manga, anime, video games, and whatever else is popular. In the 1980s, thousands of *dôjinshi* were based on popular manga such as *Dragon Ball* and *Captain Tsubasa;* in the 1990s, *Sailor Moon;* in the early 2000s, *Naruto, One Piece,* and *Harry Potter.* Innumerable niche fandoms coexist alongside the hundreds of popular parodies. Many of these parodies have some sexual element, whether *yaoi* (the favorite subject of female artists) or the many varieties of nominally straight adult manga (in the case of male artists). Such material is normally tolerated by Japanese publishers even though it infringes on copyright. There are several reasons for this: Japanese copyright law, unlike American law, does not require the copyright holder to pursue every single violation or risk losing the copyright; Japanese copyright litigation is time-consuming and generally awards lesser amounts to the plaintiff; and cracking down on *dôjinshi* may anger fans and damage publishers' relationship with a huge section of the market. Most publishers would much prefer to have fans on their side; some exhibit at Comic Market (though they are confined to a small area), and many manga and anime are specifically scripted to be *dôjinshi*-friendly, such as Shinji and Kaoru's suggestive sleepover in *Neon Genesis Evangelion.* On the other hand, in 1999 Nintendo took legal action against a creator of *Pokémon dôjinshi,* and in 2006 Shogakukan sued an English-language group over *Inuyasha dôjinshi;* in both cases the material was adult.

Many manga artists divide their time between *dôjinshi* and professional work; some even make a living on *dôjinshi.* CLAMP were originally a *dôjinshi* circle. Kenichi Sonoda's long-running zine *Chosen Ame* attracted some of the top talent in Japanese men's comics, while Kazushi Hagiwara indulged in graphic sex scenes in *dôjinshi* versions of *Bastard!!* The relative lack of sex in *Excel Saga* and *Gravitation* may be due to the extremely explicit *dôjinshi* produced by the artists in their spare time. Creators of original (non-parody) *dôjinshi* still make up a subset of the community, and sometimes look back nostalgically to the early days of Comic Market when they were in the majority.

In the past ten years, *dôjinshi* and other *otaku* culture have become increasingly visible in the mass media, and what was once a subculture has become a big business. Manga such as Sekihiko Inui's *Comic Party* (2001) and Shinsuke Kurihashi's *Maniac Road* (2002) show readers how they, too, could draw *dôjinshi* and go to Comic Market. *Dôjinshi* retail shops such as Tora no Ana, K Books, and LL Palace have grown rapidly, competing successfully with traditional bookstores (which do not sell *dôjinshi*) and advertising openly in manga magazines. The Internet has also contributed to the growth of fandom, but online comics show no sign of replacing printed *dôjinshi.* One side effect of the growing commercialization of *dôjinshi* is the appearance of "anthology comics" and "fan books" based on licensed properties such as *Di Gi Charat* (2000) and *Gunparade March: A New Marching Song* (2003). Although technically not *dôjinshi* since they are published by mainstream publishers, they are essentially collections of commissioned comics drawn in a *dôjinshi* style. Some people worry that growing awareness of *dôjinshi* may lead to a crackdown, but so far the truce holds; the police have a presence at Comic Market, but mostly in a crowd control function, and "obscene" *dôjinshi* are technically prohibited, but this is even less of a restriction than in professionally published adult manga.

Due to the sketchy legal status of parody *dôjinshi,* few examples have been professionally translated; it's much easier to find them online or at anime conventions than at bookstores.

This short-lived anthology collected Japanese *dôjinshi* (self-published fan comics), each issue devoted to a specific property that was popular with American fans at the time: *Ranma ½, Transformers,* Hayao Miyazaki, *Nadia.* The mediocre material ranges from four-panel gag manga to straightforward fan fiction; the selections seem random and little context is provided.   ★

DOLIS

Die Tödliche Dolis, "The Deadly Dolis" (致死量 ドーリス) • Maki Kusumoto • Tokyopop (2006) • Shodensha (Feel Young, 1998) • 1 volume • Jôsei, Drama • 16+ (language, violence, nudity, sexual situations)

Kishi, a young player who works at a bookstore, hits on Mitsu, an attractive but deeply disturbed woman whose arms are scarred from cutting. They sink into a dangerous relationship, as Kishi falls in love with his dangerously masochistic partner—a former artist's model—who doesn't care whether she lives or dies. Kusumoto's barren, disaffected art style, incorporating lots of text and photographic backgrounds, resembles Kiriko Nananan; however, her character artwork is inferior, using standard, if anorexic, manga designs. Printed in partial color; the flat, sickly colors, used in a collage-like rather than representational fashion, accentuate the gloomy and angst-ridden mood.   ★★½

DOLL

Mitsukazu Mihara • Tokyopop (2004–2005) • Shodensha (Feel Young, 2000–2002) • 6 volumes • Jôsei, Science Fiction, Drama • 16+ (language, violence, nudity, sex)

Gothic artist Mihara plays it straight and serious in this intelligent anthology series involving people and their robot companions. Set in a recognizable near future where robot butlers, maids, and companions have begun to appear, the stories are unusual by manga standards in that doll ownership is not considered perfectly normal and healthy—in one story a boy is disgusted when his divorced father takes a doll for a partner, while in another story, a misogynist who buys a doll for a sex toy finds himself inching closer to humanity as a result. The psychology is well thought out, often involving themes of childbirth and family, and the best tales have impressive twist endings. Though most of the stories are self-contained, an ongoing plot gradually develops, involving corporate intrigue and the company that makes the dolls. The dolls' old-fashioned outfits are the one openly gothic element, although the occasionally dark stories go well with the wan characters and high-contrast art.   ★★★

DOLLS

Kanyô Shôjo (Plant Doll), "The Watching Girl(s) (Plant Doll[s])" (観用少女(プランツ・ドール) • Yumiko

Kawahara • Viz (2004–2005) • Asahi Sonorama (Nemurenu Yoru no Kimyô na Hanashi, 1994–1999) • 4 volumes • Shôjo, Science Fiction • 13+ (violence)

In a vaguely Victorian future, the ultimate luxury purchase is "plant dolls"—beautiful, childlike, mostly immobile creatures that serve their owners as substitutes for daughters, sisters, and wives, while barely moving a muscle. A collection of weird short stories—some disturbing, some funny, most melancholy and moralistic—*Dolls* anticipates the Japanese "dollers" phenomenon (in which actual people, such as *Ghost in the Shell* anime director Mamoru Oshii, purchase and clothe life-sized mannequins). The text has a literary feel, and the baroque artwork (reminiscent of Matsuri Akino) is perfect for this world of towering skyscrapers, luxurious interiors, and lush ferns.

★★★

DOMINION

(ドミニオン) • Masamune Shirow • Dark Horse (1993–1997) • Hakusensha/Seishinsha (1985–1995) • 2 volumes • Seinen, Science Fiction, Police, Action, Comedy • Unrated/16+ (nudity, violence)

Rubber bullets and miniature tanks are the tools used by police in a polluted, dystopian future. Shirow's political insights and observations about human nature are garbled as usual—violent criminals and equally violent cops fondle weapons and argue philosophy while peacenik civilians and authority figures are treated with contempt—but *Dominion* is often truly funny, if sometimes borderline offensive, with the Tank Police operating as only a slight exaggeration of modern-day debates over acceptable violence levels and civil rights. Shirow's scratchy-pen artwork has great energy and fantastic detail: the near-future tech is nifty and unusually practical, with communication cards, electronic notepads, and tape-dispenser-style handcuffing devices. Leona Ozaki, the overzealous female tank officer who names her tank *Bonaparte,* comes off like a steroid-pumped version of Noa Izumi

from *Patlabor,* and the cat-eared Puma sisters are entertaining despite being obvious fan bait. The second volume, *Dominion: No More Noise* (rereleased in 2007 as *Dominion: Conflict*) is far superior to the first, but a continuation of the story has yet to materialize. Prior to the Dark Horse edition, a portion of the series was published by Eclipse Comics in 1989–1990. (JD)   ★★★

DOMU: A CHILD'S DREAM

Dômu, "Child's Dream" (童夢) • Katsuhiro Otomo • Dark Horse (1995–1996) • Futabasha (Manga Action Deluxe, 1980–1983) • 1 volume • Seinen, Science Fiction, Mystery, Horror • Unrated/16+ (graphic violence)

Police investigate a run-down apartment complex haunted by strange deaths, unaware of the true shadow over the building: a senile old man with psychic powers, who toys with the fragile minds and bodies of his neighbors. Then a little girl with even stronger psychic abilities moves into the complex, challenging the old man in an unseen war that escalates into massive destruction. *Domu* reads like a dry run for the even more apocalyptic psychic battles of *Akira,* but the early parts of the story, before it turns into an action comic, have a gloomy feeling of urban nightmare. The two main characters—the girl and the man—are both inarticulate, making for a cold story, whose human characters are mere dominos waiting to be toppled. Otomo's art is beautifully detailed and fine-lined; his characters are realistic, and the omnipresent apartment complex is imbued with mundane hostility.   ★★★★

DORAEMON: GADGET CAT FROM THE FUTURE

Doraemon (ドラえもん) • Fujiko Fujio • Shogakukan English Comics (2002–2005) • Shogakukan (various magazines, 1970–1996) • 10 volumes, suspended (45+ volumes in Japan) • Comedy • All Ages (extremely mild violence, occasional toilet humor)

This classic children's sci-fi gag manga occupies the same position in Japan as the most revered comic strips in America; almost forty years after its creation, the franchise is still going strong, with new animation, toys, and pop culture appearances. The premise is simple: Nobita, a lazy boy who's good at neither school nor sports, is visited by Doraemon, an earless cat-robot sent from the future to keep him from becoming a screwup. In every 8-page episode, Doraemon, like a genie, produces some marvelous future device (such as a propeller beanie) intended to make Nobita's life easier, but which always produces unexpected results, usually as a result of Nobita's misuse. (Although Doraemon, too, occasionally messes up.) The result is the silliest topsy-turvy situations, made all the funnier by the old-fashioned, simple artwork; Doraemon's blankly happy grin and occasional deadpan comments add to the surrounding elementary-school mischief. The series has never been officially released in America, but ten volumes were translated in a bilingual edition. ★★★★

DOROTHEA

(ドロテア) • Cuvie • CMX (2008–ongoing) • Kadokawa Shoten (Dragon Age, 2006–ongoing) • 3+ volumes (ongoing) • Shônen, Historical Adventure • 16+

In the fifteenth-century German town of Nauders, albino children are considered holy and are raised in privileged seclusion. But the albino Dorothea wants to see the world, so she trains herself as a warrior and manages to join the military and leave Nauders for the first time. But beyond the sheltered environment of her hometown, the girl with white skin and red eyes faces prejudice and suspicions of witchcraft. Drawn by Cuvie, better known for his adult manga. NR

DOUBT!!

(ダウト!!) • Kaneyoshi Izumi • Viz (2005–2006) • Shogakukan (Betsucomi, 2000–2002) • 6 volumes • Shôjo, Romantic Comedy • 16+ (language, brief nudity, sexual situations)

Popular girl Ai Maekawa has a dark secret: she's a former nerd who painfully transformed herself (mostly offscreen) into a hot girl who can hang out with the cool promiscuous kids. If you think she'll discover that beauty is only skin deep, you're totally wrong about *Doubt!!,* an unusually cynical, unpretentious *shôjo* comedy full of petty power struggles and self-serving human behavior. *Doubt!!*'s strength is its refreshingly sharp sense of humor and aggressive heroine, but some readers may be turned off by the unsympathetic characters and constant catfighting. In addition, the plot is episodic and directionless. ★★½

DRAGON BALL

Dragon Ball (ドラゴンボール)• Akira Toriyama • Viz (1998–2004) • Shueisha (Weekly Shônen Jump, 1984–1995) • 16 volumes • Shônen, Martial Arts, Comedy, Adventure • 13+ (violence, sexual humor, nudity)

Son Goku, a super-strong monkey-tailed boy so naive he doesn't know the difference between men and women, is roped into a teenage girl's quest for the seven Dragon Balls, which when gathered will summon a dragon and grant any one wish. Starting out as a comic fairy tale loosely based on the Chinese legend *Saiyûki* (aka *Journey to the West*), in volume 3 the series undergoes a metamorphosis (apparently in reaction to reader demands), becoming more and more focused on Goku's training in the martial arts. *Dragon Ball* was the model for almost every *Shônen Jump* action series that followed; breaking away from the humorless machismo of the previous titleholder, *Fist of the North Star,* it chose a playful, Jackie Chan–like spirit, and instead of punishing his defeated opponents, Goku almost invariably befriends them, turning them into good guys. No matter how Herculean his exertions, no matter how strong he gets (eventually surpassing "kami-sama"— i.e., God himself), Goku never loses his childish spirit: clueless, obstinate, totally good-natured. Akira Toriyama's artwork was unique for an action series for its time, giving his mishmashed fantasy world a cartoony, welcoming look. While not nearly at the same level of detail and page-per-page inventiveness as *Dr. Slump,* it's an excellent series for younger readers (although parents may wish to prescreen the early volumes, which contain moments of dirty humor and nudity). Individual volumes are inconsistently censored; the earlier printings are generally uncensored, the later ones more so. ★★★★

DRAGON BALL Z

Dragon Ball (ドラゴンボール)・ Akira Toriyama ・ Viz (1998–2006) ・ Shueisha (Weekly Shônen Jump, 1984–1995) ・ 26 volumes ・ Shônen, Martial Arts, Battle ・ All Ages (violence)

Picking up with the first appearance of Goku's son Gohan, *Dragon Ball Z* follows Earth's (formerly) monkey-tailed champion as he discovers that he is an alien and must defend his adopted planet against increasingly powerful bad guys from space and beyond. Spaceships, time travel, aliens, and cyborgs give the series a children's sci-fi feel, but the bulk of every book is hand-to-hand and fireball-to-fireball fight scenes: page after page of brilliantly choreographed, eventually repetitive battles, usually set against a backdrop of deserted wastelands so the artist doesn't have to draw buildings or bystanders. Clearly produced in as quick and dirty a manner as possible (but without obvious assistant abuse), *Dragon Ball Z* alternates between brief periods of exciting unpredictability and long periods of tedium, reportedly because Toriyama's intentions for the series (such as the desire to phase out Goku and the desire to end the manga after the fight with Freeza) were repeatedly outvoted by his readers and the demands of the industry that depended upon him. Working under these conditions, Toriyama proves himself a master of retroactive explanations, playing with his readers' expectations and fixing plot holes as he goes along. (However, he is never able to find something to do with all the leftover characters from *Dragon Ball.*) The series thus works both as world-saving soap opera and, on a purely visual level, as a flip-book comic that almost requires no translation. Although never entirely humor-less, the art is more square-jawed and the mood more serious than *Dragon Ball,* with a few genuinely brutal moments. (Some violent scenes involving guns, as well as a single moment of nudity and the original name of the bumbling Mr. Satan, are censored in the Viz edition.) In Japan, *Dragon Ball Z* was published as volumes 17–42 of the 42-volume *Dragon Ball* series.   ★★★★

DRAGON DRIVE

(ドラゴンドライブ) ・ Ken-ichi Sakura ・ Viz (2007–ongoing) ・ Shueisha (Monthly Shônen Jump, 2001–2006) ・ 14 volumes ・ Shônen, Video Game, Fantasy, Adventure ・ All Ages (mild violence)

Reiji's a loser kid who isn't really good at anything. One day his best friend, Maiko, introduces him to a secret virtual reality game called Dragon Drive, in which each player fights by controlling a dragon. Reiji is instantly intrigued and becomes quite good at the game . . . until one day, he and his friends are suddenly sucked into the fantastic world of Rikyu, where the dragons are actually real! While the *Dragon Drive* manga sounds like a cookie-cutter title created for the sole purpose of making anime and video game tie-ins (which it did), it's actually much better than it had to be; the art is great and the writing is solid. The dragons' battles are fierce, and humorous characters help keep the story from going stale. The English rewrite takes some liberties with the story, adding American slang and video game references that might make manga purists feel uneasy. (RB)   ★★

DRAGON EYE

Ryûgan Dragon Eye, "Dragon Eye" (龍眼ードラゴンアイー) ・ Kairi Fujiyama ・ Del Rey (2007–ongoing) ・ Kodansha (Shônen Sirius, 2005–ongoing) ・ 6+ volumes (ongoing) ・ Shônen, Fantasy, Action ・ 13+

Decades after a strange disease has ravaged the world, turning people into monsters, the surviving humans live in vigilantly defended cities. Hoping to protect what's left of humanity from the monster hordes, a young girl and boy undergo training to become

Minetaro Mochizuki's *Dragon Head*

warriors in classic sword-swinging style. (MS)   NR

DRAGON HEAD

(ドラゴンヘッド) • Minetaro Mochizuki • Tokyopop (2006–ongoing) • Kodansha (Young Magazine, 1994–2000) • 10 volumes • Postapocalyptic, Seinen, Suspense, Action • 16+ (language, graphic violence, partial nudity, sexual situations)

When a bullet train struck by a mysterious wave of force crashes inside a tunnel while carrying students on a school field trip, only three students survive. In a situation reminiscent of *Lord of the Flies* or *The Drifting Classroom,* they find themselves trapped in the darkness with the corpses of their former classmates and are driven to madness and infighting. To their horror, after finally managing to escape, they discover that the outside world is in even worse shape. An extremely raw, powerful comic, *Dragon Head* creates agonizing tension with a tiny cast, logical plotting, and repeated images of bleak destruction, as if the author was personally beating the reader over the head with apocalyptic imagery. Although the later volumes never quite regain the claustrophobic power of the first two, it's an exceptional series.   ★★★½

DRAGON KNIGHTS

Dragon Kishidan, "Dragon Knights" (ドラゴン騎士団) • Mineko Ohkami • Tokyopop (2002–ongoing) • Shinshokan (Wings, 1990–ongoing) • 25+ volumes (ongoing) • Shôjo, Fantasy, Comedy • 13+ (brief language, violence, brief partial nudity)

A long-running RPG-style *shôjo* fantasy epic, starting out slapstick and quickly becoming semiserious. Rath, Rune, and Thatz are the Dragon Knights of Fire, Water, and Earth, who serve the Dragon Lord of Draqueen in the ongoing struggle against the neighboring demon empire. (In this world, demons, dragons, fairies, and humans are all stylized, pointy-cheeked, gem-eyed humanoids.) Although initially the heroes do nothing but cross-dress and argue over food, this soon gives way to a dark epic with worthy dramatic twists and turns, which yet remains witty and self-referential. In one moment the heroes proclaim, "Tonight the rivers of Dusis will run black with demon blood!" and the next they're saying, "What is this? Everybody pick on the elf day?" The plot is so complicated that it requires a map and a 6-page "story thus far" summary; character profiles at the start of the volumes likewise help tell apart the characters, as well as their ghosts, doppelgängers, evil split personalities, and so on. The artwork is attractive but not quite adequate to the story; the heroes sail to faraway realms and occasionally we get a glimpse of a dramatic landscape, but mostly the story is like a stage play, with the characters talking and talking and talking, making little use of their surroundings. Also, the *shôjo* cuteness sometimes gets in the way of clarity—if a major plot point hinges on a demon's severed head, you'd better be willing to show it. It's a slow, confusing read, but for those who like (or can see past) the art, it's an interesting soap opera.   ★★

DRAGON VOICE

(ドラゴンボイス) • Yuriko Nishiyama • Tokyopop (2004–ongoing) • Kodansha (Weekly Shônen Magazine, 2001–2003) • 11 volumes • Shônen, Music, Comedy, Drama • 13+ (mild language, mild violence, mild sexual situations)

Dragon Voice is one of the few *shônen* manga to deal with the performing arts, and the mysterious absent parental figure/role model (a standard of boys' manga) is the hero's mother, not his father. Teenage Rin has looks and dance moves, but his gruff, gravelly voice (he talks in an unusual font) has dashed his dreams of becoming a singer . . . until he somehow ends up in the Beatmen, a five-man singing group with which his voice harmonizes. Despite the hero's unique weakness, the plot doesn't develop momentum and turns into one silly thing after another; for one volume the characters are forced to play the Voice Rangers in a musical *sentai* kids' show, and later on they all conveniently enroll in the same high school as a rival band. As in *Harlem Beat,* however, Nishiyama's execution is very solid: the dance scenes are full of bodies in motion, and the characters are entertaining, with lots of hot male eye candy. As Nishiyama acknowledges, it's hard to express music through manga, but she does an excellent job—musical notes are visually represented like the energy blasts in a fighting manga, and the sound lyrics burst out of the page. The music references betray Nishiyama's 1980s sensibilities: the series began in 2001, and she's still talking about Michael Jackson and *Back to the Future.*   ★★★

DRAGON WARS: THE TALE OF LUFIAK DUELL

Ryukihei • Studio Ironcat (2000) • 1 volume • Fantasy • Unrated/13+ (mild language, brief nudity, violence)

Lufiak the warrior, Feenie the fairy, and Valdik the dragon (or technically, the dragon-headed, sword-wielding lizard man) join together to save their fantasy world from the Dark Force and the evil dragon that rules it. The 1980s art is occasionally imaginative, but the RPG-like plot is brain-dead and the dialogue is terrible (especially when it tries to be funny). Additional material—a separate story line about a female thief who teams up with a dragon—was published in monthly comics format as simply *Dragon Wars* but never collected.   ★

DRAKUUN

Drakuun Ryûhimehei, "Drakuun, Dragon Princess Warrior" (ドラクゥーン竜姫兵) • Johji Manabe • Dark Horse (1997–1999) • Fujimi Shobo/Kadokawa Shoten (1988–2003) • 3 volumes (5 volumes in Japan) • Shônen, Fantasy, Adventure • Unrated/16+ (language, violence, nudity, sex)

A tedious and uninspired fantasy yarn from the creator of *Outlanders* and *Caravan Kidd.* Unlike his previous works, Manabe plays this one as a straightforward sword-and-sorcery adventure, with warrior princess Karula hacking and slashing her way through the enemy ranks in between rounds of poorly drawn pillow talk with the macho furry who serves as her love interest. Meanwhile, her drippy sister Rosalia whines and loses her clothes a lot. There's some decent monster and setting design in here, but Manabe seriously overreaches with his attempts to draw more realistic characters—the later volumes are populated by grotesquely misproportioned freaks with tiny cartoon heads, making the frequent fanservice and softcore scenes more disturbing than erotic. The fourth volume was published in English as individual comic issues but never compiled in book format, and the fifth one wasn't released in Japan until 2003, suggesting that even Manabe couldn't sustain any interest in the proceedings. (MS)   ★

DREAM GOLD: KNIGHTS IN THE DARK CITY

(ドリムゴールドKnights in the Dark City) • Tatsurou Nakanishi • ADV (2004) • Mag Garden (Comic Blade, 2003–2005) • 1 volume, suspended (5 volumes in Japan) • Science Fiction, Fantasy • 13+ (mild language, violence)

A lot of style covering up a lot of awkwardness. In the metropolis of Dark City, 250 "knights" (the proud bearers of 250 "treasure keys") compete with one another by hook or crook, dueling and stealing in search of Dream Gold, the ultimate treasure hidden somewhere in the city. Like its clear influence *Jing: King of Bandits, Dream Gold* aims for a fanciful fairy-tale mood, but the art is inferior and the action is confusing, crammed with poorly explained gimmicks: "rei sourcers," "heresy cards," "night points," "mobile weapons," and a *shônen*-manga-esque competition to be the best. The noseless, stylized character art is more crude than charming. The characters' names are a good example of the manga's spirit of trying too hard: Dragon W. Fabulous, Shad Heavymate, Lostfraye J. Odysseus, Kurorat Jio Clocks. ★★

DREAM HOTEL

Yume Hotel, "Dream Hotel" (夢ホテル) • Memi Hoshino • ComicsOne (e-book, 2000) • Aoba Shuppan • 2 volumes, suspended (9 volumes in Japan) • Jôsei, Drama • 13+ (mild adult themes)

Short story anthology revolving around the small hotel Villa D'Etrangers and its new manager, the selfless Yutaro. The nice premise provides the potential for human drama, but *Dream Hotel* missteps in almost all areas, from the art and characters (which channel a high schooler's bad sketches) to the convoluted, melodramatic plots. ("What, you *do* love me? What, you *amazingly* recovered your hearing? What, you're finally ready to tell your mother that you love her but her plane crashed en route to Japan from America? No, wait, *amazingly* she decided to take an earlier plane!") The manga is a mess of simplistic resolutions, and the motley crew of badly drawn characters gets old quickly. (RS) ★½

DREAM SAGA

Mugen Densetsu Takamagahara, "Dream/Phantasmal Legend Takamagahara" (夢幻伝説 タカマガハラ) • Megumi Tachikawa • Tokyopop (2004–2005) • Kodansha (Nakayoshi, 1997–1999) • 5 volumes • Shôjo, Fantasy, Adventure • All Ages (mild violence, the word *boobs*)

Like *Fushigi Yûgi* for eight-year-olds, this simplified *shôjo* fantasy adventure combines an environmental theme and Japanese mythology. When the sun goddess Amaterasu is imprisoned, fifth-grader Yuuki must travel to the dreamworld of Takamagahara (the land of the gods in Shinto religion) to save the world from darkness. Her male classmates also have counterparts in the dreamworld, and they form her entourage, assisting her when her ability to talk to animals and plants is not enough. As it turns out, Takamagahara is much like the real world, in that

it is plagued by pollution (caused by the bad guys); all the "monsters" are actually friendly giant animals angered by human maltreatment, and the characters even discuss auto pollution and alternative energy sources. The plot ties together neatly by Tachikawa's standards, and the series has nice moments of silly, self-referential comedy, but it's too juvenile to hold the attention of any but the youngest readers. ★★

THE DRIFTING CLASSROOM

Hyôryu Kyôshitsu, "Drifting Classroom" (漂流教室) • Kazuo Umezu • Viz (2006–2008) • Shogakukan (Weekly Shônen Sunday, 1972–1974) • 11 volumes • Science Fiction, Horror • 18+ (graphic violence)

A Japanese elementary school is suddenly teleported into a lifeless postapocalyptic wasteland, where the students struggle to survive starvation, madness, and other dangers. Compared to *Lord of the Flies,* Umezu has a marginally more hopeful vision of human (or at least child) nature, but the world around them is a relentless nightmare, encapsulating every parent's fears of what the future might hold . . . and every child's dream of somehow surviving that future, without parents or adult authority. Umezu's stiff, flip-book artwork, with its constant gaping eyes and screaming mouths, conveys raw emotion in the most direct fashion. Compared to *Orochi: Blood,* his themes are more developed, his plot more original, his storytelling more pared to the bone. Originally written for children, *The Drifting Classroom* has the power and immediacy of the greatest juvenile literature, and despite the brutal violence, it's perfect for younger readers who can handle it. ★★★★

DR. SLUMP

(Dr。スランプ) • Akira Toriyama • Viz (2005–2008) • Shueisha (Weekly Shônen Jump, 1980–1985) • 18 volumes • Shônen, Science Fiction, Comedy • 13+ (mild language, crude humor)

A spontaneous megahit when it first appeared in 1980, *Dr. Slump* established Akira

Toriyama as one of Japan's greatest cartoonists. In the anything-goes town of Penguin Village, Dr. Senbei Norimaki (an incompetent inventor who wants a wife but is just as happy setting up a Rube Goldberg–esque chain of events in order to see a girl's panties) builds Arale, a superpowered little robot girl. Arale, who is strong enough to split the planet in half by stamping her foot, spends most of her time running around the village, playing with poo and causing chaos. The plots, reminiscent of *Mad* magazine or children's books, are dense with imagination and demonstrate a sheer joy of drawing: Toriyama fills the pages with aliens, dinosaurs, talking animals and appliances, giant monsters, planes, and *Star Wars* references. The characters frequently make fun of the manga itself, and sometimes pick up the sound effects and play with them. The only problem with *Dr. Slump* is that it's so good it makes Toriyama's later series look halfhearted by comparison. Anarchic, fun, beautifully drawn, and incredibly creative.

★★★★

DUCK PRINCE

Ahiru no Ôjisama, "Duck Prince" **(あひるの王子さま)** • Ai Morinaga • CPM (2003–2004) • Kadokawa Shoten (Asuka, 2001–2003) • 3 volumes, suspended (6 volumes in Japan) • Shôjo, Romantic Comedy • 13+ (mild language, crude humor, brief nudity, sexual situations)

Reiichi, a teeny-tiny nerd with glasses and a bowl cut, is hit by a car and (through a combination of plastic surgery and magic) awakens to find himself transformed into a hot *bishônen.* Hiding his former identity, he tries to ask out the one girl who was nice to him before, only to be harrassed by his evil stepsisters, a spell-casting talking dog, and random complications that turn him back into his old ugly self. *Duck Prince* combines pretty *shôjo/shônen* hybrid art, lots of sexual innuendo (but almost no nudity), and a gleefully cruel attitude toward its hapless protagonist. However, the humor is painted with a broad brush and has its hit-or-miss moments. ★★½

DUKLYON: CLAMP SCHOOL DEFENDERS

Gakuen Tokkei Duklyon, "School Defenders Duklyon") **(学園特警デュカリオン)** • CLAMP • Tokyopop (2003) • Kadokawa (Comic Genki, 1991–1993) • 2 volumes • Tokusatsu, Comedy • All Ages

Duklyon: Clamp School Defenders is a gut-busting send-up of the *sentai* superhero team genre. Kentarou Higashikunimaru and Takeshi Shukaido are high school students at the prestigious Clamp School, and employees of the Duklyon bakery, but when a patriotic song is piped through the school's speakers, they transform into the costumed champions of justice: the Clamp School Defenders! Together with their manager, the hotheaded and mallet-wielding Eri, the team battles their archnemesis, the "evil" Imonoyama Shopping District Association, which tries to disrupt school life with its menagerie of monsters (like the Evil Sheep Beast Wooltar, or Giant Elephant Beast Sucophant). *Duklyon* is a celebration of silliness. The rapid-fire puns and parodies will elicit much rolling of the eyes, but you'll likely find yourself laughing in spite of yourself. A must-read for comedy fans, but those looking for plot and character development should look elsewhere. (MT) ★★½

EAGLE: THE MAKING OF AN ASIAN-AMERICAN PRESIDENT

Eagle **(イーグル)** • Kaiji Kawaguchi • Viz (2000–2002) • Shogakukan (Big Comic, 1997–2001) • 5 volumes • Seinen, Political Drama • Unrated/16+ (language, violence, brief nudity, sex)

When New York senator Kenneth Yamaoka makes a bid for the Democratic presidential nomination, young Japanese reporter Takashi Jo comes to the United States to cover his campaign. Once in America, Takashi discovers a secret: he's Yamaoka's illegitimate son. *Eagle* is a family story (Yamaoka is married into a Kennedy-esque clan), a meditation on America's role in the world, and a ground-level, state-by-state look at American political primaries. At times, it has the depth of a good novel, whose central question boils down to Takashi's own mixed feelings about his father: is Yamaoka a "heartless bastard" or a driven idealist whose ends justify the means? But Kawaguchi's ambition demands that he be held to high standards, and politically savvy readers may be disappointed by *Eagle,* whose Clinton-era view of politics (a thinly disguised Bill and Hillary are characters) comes across as a liberal, specifically Japanese liberal, fantasy. In predictably unrealistic manga fashion, Yamaoka is portrayed as a politician who can appeal to *everybody,* a Democrat who can enter Texas cowboy bars and win them over to his side on gun control. The big issues are labor, the economy, and international affairs; religion is never mentioned, and Yamaoka's race, though addressed, still isn't addressed enough. The opposing candidates are undeveloped (except for Yamaoka's chief Democratic rival Al Noah, aka Al Gore), and the story is so focused on the primaries that the Republican candidate barely even appears. In short, *Eagle* succeeds more on a character level than as a political analysis.   ★★★½

EAT-MAN

Eat-Man (イートマン) • Akihito Yoshitomi • Viz (1997–1999) • MediaWorks (Dengeki Gao!, 1996–2003) • 2 volumes, suspended (19 volumes in Japan) • Shônen, Science Fiction, Action • Unrated/13+ (violence)

Repetitive superhero series in a vaguely Wild Western sci-fi setting. Bolt Crank, a mercenary good guy of few words, wanders the planet performing impossible missions; he has the power to eat metal objects and later cause them to reappear, assembled from scratch, in his hand. The stories are extremely repetitive; Bolt's powers act as a deus ex machina for every situation, as he produces guns, machinery, vehicles, boats, and so on out of his hand. At only two volumes, the English edition ends before Yoshitomo's stiff art reaches its peak of proficiency.   ★½

EDEN: IT'S AN ENDLESS WORLD!

Hiroki Endo • Dark Horse (2005–ongoing) • Kodansha (Afternoon, 1997–ongoing) • 14+ volumes (ongoing) • Seinen, Science Fiction, Military, Action •

18+ (language, frequent extreme graphic violence, nudity, sex)

A postapocalyptic hard science fiction manga in which combat is interspersed with discussion of Big Issues, *Eden* is comparable to Masamune Shirow's *Appleseed.* Thirty-five years after a deadly viral epidemic, parts of the Earth have reverted to nature, and the United Nations wars with various factions for control of remote parts of the world. While wandering the wilderness of South America, teenage Elijah is picked up by a UN military unit and becomes involved in their battles against Propater, a cultlike organization. *Eden* starts out as a postapocalyptic survival story; the landscapes are evocatively drawn, with detailed images of abandoned cities overgrown with grass and trees. Soon, however, the story turns to military action, with ill-defined factions fighting using robots, prepubescent cyborg hackers, bioengineered monsters, and other increasingly fantastic technology. If the point is to show the horror and arbitrariness of war, it succeeds, but the characters and themes are secondary to the combat, ultimately to the detriment of the story. The fact that the characters are named after Gnostic religious terms doesn't clarify matters for the casual reader, and the discussion of Christianity is likewise disconnected from the action, although the good art makes it an enjoyable read.   ★★½

EDU-MANGA

Atomu Poketto Jinbutukan, "Atom Pocket Biography" (アトムポケット人物館) • various artists • DMP (2005–2007) • Tezuka Productions (2000) • 5 volumes • Historical Nonfiction • All Ages

Educational manga from Tezuka Productions about the lives of historical figures, with the *Astro Boy* characters slotted in for kid appeal. Astro Boy and his friends (looking distinctly off-model) appear in the introduction and a series of Q&A pages; otherwise, these are straightforward manga adaptations of the lives of famous people, including Albert Einstein, Anne Frank, Mother Teresa, Ludwig van Beethoven, and

Helen Keller. The stripped-down, amateurish art and bland translation rob the stories of much of their strength, although it's impossible to totally destroy the emotional impact of a life such as Helen Keller's. The presence of Astro Boy is charming but, from a Western perspective, inescapably odd. The books also include text biographies and timelines, useful references for grade-schoolers writing reports. (SG)   ★½

EERIE QUEERIE

Ghost! (ゴースト!) • Shuri Shiozu • Tokyopop (2004) • Shinshokan (1998–2003) • 4 volumes • Yaoi, Occult, Comedy • 16+ (language, brief violence, sexual situations, brief partial nudity)

Innocent young Mitsuo has a problem: he's a natural medium, and he's constantly getting possessed by girl ghosts who want to use his body to hit on guys. His occult-savvy classmate Hasunuma saves him, only to become attracted to Mitsuo himself, and soon their boys' school turns into a den of *shônen ai* pairings between Shinto priests, male ghosts, cross-dressers in maid outfits, and other teenage boys of a supernatural disposition. Light on both plot and sex (although clothes do get ripped off), *Eerie Queerie* is more a collection of winking guy-guy jokes than a story, but it gets points for its tongue-in-cheek mood and for keeping Mitsuo and Hasunuma's relationship up in the air as long as possible. The art delivers the requisite hot, sultry guys (as well as big-eyed, impossibly cute Mitsuo), but not much else.

★★

EIKEN

(エイケン) • Seiji Matsuyama • Media Blasters (2005–ongoing) • Akita Shoten (Weekly Shônen Champion, 2001–2004) • 18 volumes • Shônen, Fanservice, Romantic Comedy • 18+ (nudity, graphic sexual situations)

Actual pornography disguised as romantic comedy pseudo-pornography. Densuke, a clumsy teenager, is enlisted into his school's all-girls Eiken club, which has no real purpose (the name is meaningless) other than to surround him with stereotypical women

into whose enormous, lemon-shaped breasts and giant butts he constantly stumbles. The main thing distinguishing this from other fanservice manga is the complete lack of plot and the revolting artwork, including a sixth-grader with breasts so large they look like giant testicles, and numerous obscene shots of women eating Popsicles, hot dogs, veiny chunks of beef, and the like. Probably intended as a parody of "normal" *shônen* romantic comedy manga, it's still almost unreadable. Early volumes were labeled 16+ before the series switched to the more appropriate older rating.   0 Stars

ELECTRIC MAN ARROW

Denjin Arrow, "Electric Man Arrow" (電人アロー) • Daiji Kazumine • ComicsOne (e-book, 2000) • Asahi Sonorama (Manga Shônen, 1964–1966) • 1 volume, suspended (3 volumes in Japan) • Shônen, Action, Adventure • All Ages

A ridiculous, swerving 1960s adventure comic, *Electric Man Arrow* reads like early Tezuka mixed in a blender with *Kamen Rider* and then farted on. The story revolves around a cyborg mystery man who protects a young boy and unravels intricate, nefarious schemes by his enemy, X Fighter. Electric Man Arrow's main powers involve generating big lightning bolts that he can toss and burn dudes with. The main story involves the identity of X Fighter, who carries out Luddite attacks on cars and trains. Along the way, the story delivers nonsensical dialogue, impossible "scientific" death-defying escapes, and many science fiction and adventure genre clichés. Flat characters, stilted art, and nonsensical story. (RS)   ★

ELEMENTAL GELADE

(エレメンタル ジェレイドElementar Gerad) • Mayumi Azuma • Tokyopop (2006–ongoing) • Mag Garden (Comic Blade/Comic Blade Masamune, 2002–ongoing) • 12+ volumes (ongoing) • Shônen, Fantasy, Action • 13+ (mild language, violence, partial nudity)

Edel Raids are humanoid weapons, capable of shifting their entire body and soul into destructive tools for a human to wield.

While participating in a raid on another ship, a young sky pirate, Cou, discovers an Edel Raid named Ren, a sullen girl who slowly becomes attached to her rescuer. Many people seek to possess Ren, and the pirate and the weapon soon encounter other Edel Raid users, fighting some, befriending others. *Elemental Gelade* is a fantasy action-adventure manga with decent art—sometimes stylistic, sometimes chaotic and confusing. The character designs bear some similarity to *Kingdom Hearts*. (DR)   NR

EL-HAZARD: THE MAGNIFICENT WORLD

Shinpi no Sekai El Hazard, "World of Mystery El-Hazard" (神秘の世界エルハザード) • Hidetomo Tsubura • Viz (2000–2002) • Tokuma Shoten (Monthly Shônen Captain, 1995–1997) • 3 volumes • Shônen, Fantasy, Adventure, Comedy • 13+ (sexual situations, violence)

Bland adaptation of the *El-Hazard* OAV series. Hidetomo Tsubura's rubbery art is occasionally funny, but the stripped-down story only has the bare bones of the anime: boring guy ends up in high-tech pseudo-Arabian fantasy world, where his face is magnetically attracted to women's cleavage. In place of character interaction, the manga introduces two new evil Ifurits (genie-like, superpowered robots) for pointless fight scenes.   ★

THE EMBALMER: See *Mitsukazu Mihara: The Embalmer*

EMMA

(エマ) • Kaoru Mori • CMX (2006–ongoing) • Enterbrain (Comic Beam, 2002–2006) • 7 volumes • Historical, Romance • 16+ (nudity, mild sexual situations)

In 1885 England, a young man from a wealthy merchant family falls in love with a maid: Emma, a quiet young woman with glasses, who works in the house of a kindly widow. But will his family ever approve of the marriage? A three-handkerchief love story with occasional light comedy, *Emma* (no relation to the novel by Jane Austen) has a novel-like plot and a unique organic art style that makes London's streets and drawing rooms glow with warmth. Wordless sequences follow the characters about their daily tasks and in the silent reflection of their hearts; it has minimal narration and, unlike most manga with such large-eyed characters, it rarely breaks the mood with caricatures or outright goofiness. Despite the artist's eventual hiring of a historical consultant (from volume 3 onward), *Emma* is not a realistic portrayal of the Victorian era; this is a romanticized world where rich men ask out poor maids, the streets are clean (more or less), and an East Indian prince can ride an elephant through the London streets to visit the hero. Sweet and old-fashioned though it may be, in its own way it fits well with present-day *otaku* manga trends: a "maid manga" set in a time when maids were actually common. The nudity is scarce and nonexploitative.   ★★★½

THE EMPTY EMPIRE

Kara no Teikoku, "The Empty Empire" (空の帝国) • Naoe Kita • CMX (2006–ongoing) • Hakusensha (Hana to Yume, 1994–1997) • 7 volumes • Shôjo, Science Fiction, Fantasy • 13+ (mild language, violence)

In the twenty-sixth century, the world was united under the benevolent Emperor Idea, until his death threw everything into chaos. When Rose—an amnesiac boy who looks just like the dead emperor—shows up in an alley somewhere, he is discovered by the emperor's followers and made into a puppet ruler. Is Rose actually a failed clone of the emperor? Religious fanatics and bandit sky captains go after him, while the people who installed him on the throne pass their time in occasionally comedic schemes and intrigue. As for Rose, he questions whether he has any reason to be alive at all, and whether he can live up to the reputation of his previous self. But there's no denying Rose's considerable psychic powers. . . . The loose, cartoony *shôjo* artwork makes it difficult to get into the supposedly futuristic setting, but the story is interesting.   NR

ENCHANTER

Kikô Majutsushi: Enchanter, "Machine Artisan Magician: Enchanter" (機工魔術士—Enchanter) • Izumi Kawachi • DMP (2006–ongoing) • Square Enix (Monthly Gangan Wing, 2003–ongoing) • 12+ volumes (ongoing) • Shônen, Fantasy, Action, Comedy • 16+ (mild language, violence, sexual situations)

A traditional but fun mix of fantasy action and *shônen* romantic comedy, in the style of Rumiko Takahashi. Haruhiko, a high school student with a knack for machines and a crush on his teacher Ms. Fujikawa, is visited by a demoness who informs him that he is the reincarnation of the enchanter/alchemist Fulcanelli. Warping him into Fulcanelli's extradimensional laboratory, the demoness inducts him into a secret world where enchanters and demons fight over powerful artifacts, while also offering to deflower him. This is well-trodden territory, and the agreeable anime-style art is nothing special, but the familiar elements (humor, action, light sexual teases) are well done. Kawachi is a sympathetic hero, and the sexual element is played for character-driven humor, with nothing more visually explicit than cleavage-baring costumes. ★★★

ENMUSU: PICTURE SCROLL TO PROMOTE LOVE

Renai Shusse Emaki En x Musu, "Love Promotion Picture Scroll En x Musu" (恋愛出世絵巻えんxむす) • Takahiro Seguchi • ADV (2004) • Akita Shoten (Weekly Shônen Champion, 2002–2003) • 1 volume, suspended (6 volumes in Japan) • Shônen, Test Taking, Romantic Comedy, Maid, Battle • 16+ (partial nudity, sexual situations)

A grossly fetishistic *shônen* manga substituting women in maids' outfits for the usual summoned monsters, mecha, spirits, *Poké-mon,* and so on. Gisuke, a masochistically wimpy teenager, suddenly inherits Sonya, a cheerfully subservient Russian maid who cooks, cleans, washes his back, and gives him one of fifteen talismans that are the key to fabulous wealth and power. (The talismans are modeled on actual over-the-counter *omamori* good-luck charms, often given to

When "maid manga" goes bad: Takahiro Seguchi's *Enmusu*

students before exams.) Gisuke's academic rivals (they must prove their worth for the talismans by *scoring high on standardized tests*) have maids as well, and like all bad guys in *shônen* manga, they treat their servants poorly, in this case with dog collars and pseudo-sexual humiliation. The artwork is juvenile (everyone is noseless and looks about ten years old) and the plot is nauseating, unless it's actually an incredibly cynical parody, in which case it's brilliant and nauseating. ★½

ERICA SAKURAZAWA: ANGEL

Tenshi, "Angel" (天使) • Erica Sakurazawa • Tokyo-pop (2003) • Shodensha (Feel Young, 1999) • 1 volume • Jôsei, Romantic Drama • 16+ (mild language, brief nudity)

Erica Sakurazawa draws skillfully executed, archetypal *jôsei* manga: adult women's manga with plots that might be marketed as "chick lit" in the West. Her relationship-oriented stories are rarely idealized, and her art has a cool, sophisticated, slightly sketchy look, opting for understatement rather than extreme passion or humor. *Angel,* subdued even by Sakurazawa's standards, looks into the lives of a series of characters—a depressed teenage girl, a convenience store worker, an alcoholic single mother—who are visited by a mute, smiling angel girl whom only certain people can see. The angel's metaphorical or story purpose never becomes entirely clear; the vignettes are interesting but (one of Sakurazawa's minor weaknesses) lack a strong direction or resolution. ★★½

ERICA SAKURAZAWA: ANGEL NEST

Tenshi no Su, "Angel Nest" (天使の巣) • Erica Sakurazawa • Tokyopop (2003) • Shodensha (Feel Young, 1999–2001) • 1 volume • Jôsei, Romantic Drama • 16+ (mild language, brief nudity, sexual situations)

Short story anthology. In the magical-realist title story, a woman breaks up with her cheating husband, only to end up as a sort of surrogate parent to the girl he cheated on her with; meanwhile, a silent angel girl (possibly the same one from *Erica Sakurazawa: Angel*) appears out of nowhere and moves in with them. "God Only Knows" stars a gay man, his straight friend, and a girl; in "Tea Time" a woman meets a man while on vacation; and in "A Gift from the Heavens" a teenager steals a car and finds a girl sleeping in the backseat. Sakurazawa's artwork has a clean, mature look and her writing is sharp. ★★★

ERICA SAKURAZAWA: THE AROMATIC BITTERS

Aromatic Bitters (アロマチック・ビターズ) • Erica Sakurazawa • Tokyopop (2004) • Shodensha (Feel Young, 2002–2003) • 1 volume, suspended (2 volumes in Japan) • Jôsei, Romantic Drama • 18+ (mild language, nudity, sex)

Sayumi, a dissatisfied thirty-one-year-old who lives with her boyfriend, has an affair with a bartender whom she meets on vacation. Meanwhile, her boyfriend also has another woman in his life, and her forty-year-old married friend, for whom everything seems stable, is approaching her own crisis. A fascinating look at marriage, love, and dissatisfaction, *The Aromatic Bitters* is told from several different viewpoints, as the three main characters all struggle with the same issues. The effect is heartbreaking, but unfortunately the second volume was never translated, leaving the English edition with an abrupt ending to a promising story. ★★★½

ERICA SAKURAZAWA: BETWEEN THE SHEETS

Sheets no Sukima, "Between the Sheets" (シーツの隙間) • Erica Sakurazawa • Tokyopop (2003) • Shodensha (Feel Young, 1995–1996) • 1 volume • Jôsei, Romantic Drama • 18+ (language, nudity, sex)

Shy Minako is best friends with Saki, an attractive girl whom she tries to protect from unsuitable guys. But Minako's feelings for Saki are more than friendship, and soon she finds herself doing the unthinkable, sleeping with Saki's boyfriends just to get closer to her. This adult relationship story strikes a believable tone: characters joke about being lesbian even as they repress their true feelings. The ending is slightly unsatisfying, but the writing is excellent and the story moves quickly. ★★★

ERICA SAKURAZAWA: NOTHING BUT LOVING YOU

Aishiau Koto Shika Dekinai, "We Can Only Love Each Other" (愛しあう事しかできない) • Erica Sakurazawa • Tokyopop (2003) • Shodensha (Feel Young, 1994–1995) • 1 volume • Jôsei, Romantic Drama • 18+ (language, nudity, sex)

Nanako, a model at a turning point in her career, has two men in her life: Mitsuhiko, a horny player whom she sleeps with casually, and Etsushi, a long-haired, bisexual man whom she loves. One of the few manga to attempt to depict realistic gay and bisexual characters, *Nothing but Loving You* is an understated, interesting romance. ★★★

ERICA SAKURAZAWA: THE RULES OF LOVE

Ai no Okite, "Rules of Love" (愛の掟) • Erica Sakurazawa • Tokyopop (2004) • Shodensha (Feel Young, 1993–1994) • 1 volume • Jôsei, Romantic Drama • 18+ (language, nudity, sex)

Taku is not an especially handsome man who moves casually from woman to woman, using them for money, sex, and a place to spend the night; his attitude is merely thoughtless rather than malicious. Chizu is the latest in a string of women who love him, unaware—or in denial—of his true nature. The art has a sexy, sketchy quality; the characters are drawn with a minimal number of lines, but they have attractive, adult faces and muscular, gestural bodies that seem to show real figure-drawing ability. A simple, effective, poignant story. ★★★½

ERIKO TADENO: WORKS

Eriko Tadeno • ALC Publishing (2004) • Michi Publishing, Oozora Shuppan (Phryne, Mist, 1994–2000) • Yuri, Romance • Unrated/18+ (language, nudity, graphic sex)

An anthology of realistic lesbian-themed stories, mostly involving older characters. In "My Sister's Wedding" the thirty-year-old protagonist goes home to attend her younger sister's wedding and confronts the expectations of her family; in "I Like You the Way You Are" a closeted college student struggles to deal with the memory of a high school love; and in "My Sweet One" and "Gentle Loving" a forty-one-year-old businesswoman has a relationship with her twenty-four-year-old subordinate. Although the sex scenes play out like fantasies and the art is average, the writing is personal and insightful. ★★★

ES

ETERNAL SABBATH • Fuyumi Soryo • Del Rey (2006–2008) • Kodansha (Morning, 2001–2004) • 8 volumes • Seinen, Psychic, Suspense • 16+ (violence, nudity)

A quiet, effective science fiction thriller. Mine Kujyou, a workaholic brain researcher at Tohou Medical University, discovers the existence of Shuro—a genetically altered superhuman who can effortlessly control people's minds and alter their memories. As one of the few people immune to his powers, she tries to learn more about Shuro, but their relationship turns dangerous when an evil superhuman enters the picture. Shuro's powers (which are more believable than in most psychic manga) include the ability to enter people's mental landscapes and to create illusions of their worst fears, which adds some strange imagery to an otherwise visually flat story. The cold, detailed art style is suited to the emotionally detached protagonists. ★★★½

E'S

(エス) • Satol Yuiga • Broccoli Books (2007–ongoing) • Square Enix (Monthly G-Fantasy, 1997–ongoing) • 14+ volumes (ongoing) • Science Fiction, Action • 16+

Kai Kudou is part of an elite organization of psychics called Ashurum, whose members are dispatched to the city of Gald to suppress a guerilla movement. After one of his own teammates turns on him, Kai finds shelter with a pair of mysterious strangers and begins to question his loyalty to Ashurum. (MS) NR

LA ESPERANÇA

Esperança (エスペランサ) • Chigusa Kawai • DMP (2005–2006) • Shinshokan (Wings, 2000–2006) • 7 volumes • Shôjo, Drama • 13+ (mild violence)

A tale of young angst and hypocrisy in a Catholic boys' school in an imaginary Esperanto-speaking country. Georges, a pious, idealistic boy who wants to be friends with everybody, clashes with Robert, a brooding rebel who seems to be his exact opposite ("There's nothing more entertaining than defiling something pure"). Other characters soon become involved in the struggle over Georges' faith and feelings, including Sir Frederic, the snobbish son of a nobleman, and Henri, Georges' childhood friend. Although the setup recalls classic 1970s Boys'

Love stories, *La Esperança* is not quite *shônen ai;* the sexual ambiguity stays mostly at the level of a platonically smoldering friendship. Written for young readers, it's a meandering, episodic soap opera. The anatomy and camera angles are haphazard. ★★

ET CETERA

(えとせとら) • Tow Nakazaki • Tokyopop (2004–2007) • Kodansha (Monthly Shônen Magazine, 1997–2001) • 9 volumes • Shônen, Historical, Fantasy, Adventure • All Ages (mild language, crude humor, violence, brief partial nudity)

In a tumbleweed town in a cartoon version of the Wild West, plucky Chinese orphan Mingchao dreams of going to Hollywood and becoming an actress. Adventure finds her when she discovers the power of her grandfather's inheritance: the magic Eto gun, which fires bullets powered by the twelve animals of the Chinese zodiac (the rabbit bullet hops around, the bull bullet is really strong, etc.). Thus armed (although she's too nice to kill anybody), Mingchao sets out on her quest, gathering an entourage of crooks, missionaries, and Indians, and pursued by an evil crime syndicate. Although the character designs are familiar manga types (similar to a cross between Tommy Ohtsuka and Tsukasa Kotobuki), the art has a welcome element of exaggeration; when people do a double take, their hearts pop out of their chests, their eyes bug out, their tongues loll. The backgrounds are well drawn, too, adding the necessary context to Western action scenes involving paddleboats, mine cars, and runaway trains. All in all, a slightly above-average comedy-adventure. ★★½

ETERNAL ALICE RONDO: See *Key Princess Story: Eternal Alice Rondo*

EUREKA SEVEN

Kôkyôshihen Eureka Seven, "Symphonic Psalm Eureka Seven" (交響詩編エウレカセブン) • BONES (original story), Jinsei Kataoka & Kazuma Kondou (story and art) • Bandai Entertainment (2006–2007) • Kadokawa Shoten (Monthly Shônen Ace, 2005–2006) • 6 volumes • Science Fiction, Mecha • 13+ (mild violence, mild language)

Manga adaptation of the anime series. When an LFO (a sort of giant robot on a flying surfboard) crashes into his grandfather's garage, fourteen-year-old Renton is immediately smitten with its pilot, the enigmatic Eureka. After proving his worth to her, he joins the Gekkostate, a plucky band of revolutionaries who pilot LFOs in defiance of the corrupt government. The plot involves epic sky battles and Renton's lovesick blunders over Eureka, as well as nonspecific religious undertones with much discussion of "belief." The manga simplifies the anime plot, in the process removing some of the explanation of the science fiction world the characters inhabit. A second manga adaptation, based on the spin-off video game *Eureka Seven TR1: New Wave,* was also produced in Japan. (KT) ★★½

EVANGELION: See *Neon Genesis Evangelion*

EVEN A MONKEY CAN DRAW MANGA

Saru Demo Kakeru Manga Kyôshitsu, "Even a Monkey Can Draw Manga Classroom" (サルでも描けるまんが教室) • Kentaro Takekuma (story), Koji Aihara (art) • Viz (2002) • Shogakukan (Big Comic Spirits, 1989–1990) • 1 volume, suspended (2 volumes in Japan) • Underground Comedy • Unrated/18+ (language, sex, nudity)

Jaw-droppingly cynical, hilarious parody/analysis of manga, in the form of a veteran writer teaching an amateur artist how it's done. The super-dense, intentionally ugly art may be an impenetrable turnoff for some readers, but those able to persevere will discover invaluable insight: the evolution of panty shots, the differences between male and female porn manga, even actual practical information such as how to draw straight lines. From magazines and genres to the grim realities of the business, it's a brilliant deconstruction of manga circa 1990. Unfortunately, many chapters were cut from the first volume, and the second volume was never translated, let alone the additional material published in a 2006 *21 Seiki Aizôban* ("21st Century Collector's Edition").

★★★★

EXAXXION: See *Cannon God Exaxxion*

EXCEL SAGA

Excel Saga (エクセル・サーガ) • Rikdo Koshi • Viz (2003–ongoing) • Shônen Gahosha (Young King Ours, 1997–ongoing) • 17+ volumes (ongoing) • Seinen, Science Fiction, Tokusatsu, Comedy • 13+ (violence, sexual situations, pedophilic mad scientists)

Beneath the midsized city of Fukuoka dwells Il Palazzo, an aspiring evil overlord with two henchwomen, the hyperenthusiastic Excel and the disturbingly sickly Hyatt. (Shrill, ringleted Elgala later completes the team.) They're devoted to world conquest, but they're willing to start very, very small, living off instant ramen and trying to take over local shopping centers. Onto this premise, Koshi piles manga parodies, broad-as-a-barn-door satire, and pop culture references galore. *Excel Saga* grew out of a very different (and adults-only) *dôjinshi* satirizing local politics, and its roots show, from the amateurish art in the early volumes to the many Fukuoka in-jokes left intact (Il Palazzo and his minions are named after downtown hotels). The art improves over time, largely thanks to Koshi's acquisition of a squadron of assistants. The thrown-together slapstick of the early volumes eventually gives way to a dense plot involving Il Palazzo's opposite number, civic bureaucrat Dr. Kabapu, and his own minions. The rewrite by Carl Horn, dense with erudite jokes and double meanings, probably retains the spirit of the manga better than would a more literal translation. The *Excel Saga* anime, although equally inspired, bears very little resemblance to the manga. (CT)

★★★½

EXECUTIVE MANAGING DIRECTOR KOSAKU SHIMA: See *Division Chief Kosaku Shima*

EYESHIELD 21

(アイシールド21) • Riichiro Inagaki (story), Yusuke Murata (art) • Viz (2005–ongoing) • Shueisha (Weekly Shônen Jump, 2002–ongoing) • 24+ volumes (ongoing) • Shônen, Sports, Comedy • 16+ (mild language, crude humor, mild violence)

A thrilling, enjoyable sports manga, *Eyeshield 21* is written for an audience unfamiliar with American football, such as most Japanese readers (and many American manga fans, for that matter). In archetypal manga fashion, the hero, Sena, isn't a big bruiser—he's a shy, short teenager whose incredible speed makes him the reluctant "secret weapon" of his team, the Devil Bats. Sena's superheroesque secret identity as Eyeshield 21 (the eyeshield covers his face) is only one of many American-comic-like twists, together with the dynamic camera angles, the joke-crammed backgrounds, and caricatures almost like those of Jack Davis. (Eventually, the characters actually travel to America, where they go from city to city encountering what can best be described as "friendly stereotypes.") The slapstick attitude keeps the story from getting too heavy, but it *is* a genuinely dramatic story, with characters who work together as a team and who grow from loss and experience. Bonus points for the animal mascots.

★★★★

F-III BANDIT

(FIIIバンディット) • Ippongi Bang • Antarctic (1995–1996) • Gakken (Comic Nora, 1992) • 10 issues • Fantasy, Otaku, Romantic Comedy • 18+ (language, brief violence, crude humor, nudity, sex)

A combination of love and guts, sex and action, Bang's work mixes the sweet love comedies of Rumiko Takahashi with the adolescent mania of Go Nagai; another distant comparison might be Vaughn Bodé, who also drew buxom women, strange animal-people, and trippy page compositions. Takahashi's heroes are normal folks; Bang's heroes are rebels, pseudo-punks, old-school *banchô* tough dudes, and girl gangbangers. All the characters have big eyes, big mouths, and wild shocks of anime hair, drawn from extreme camera angles with extreme ges-

Sanami Matoh's *Fake* © 1994 SANAMI MATOH. All Rights Reserved. First published in Japan in 1994 by BIBLOS Co. Ltd., Tokyo. Foreign sales arranged through Akita Shoten.

tures, while lightning bolts and impressionistic light effects spill across the pages around them. At its best, *F-III Bandit* feels like someone just drawing whatever they want to, and having fun doing it; however, some of the stories are simply too slight and confusing, and feel like drug-induced flashbacks of early 1980s anime. A few of the stories drift into anthropomorphic animal themes.

★★½

FAKE

Sanami Matoh • Tokyopop (2003–2004) • Biblos (Be x Boy, 1994–2000) • 7 volumes • Yaoi, Crime, Comedy • 16+/18+ (language, violence, nudity, sex)

This influential *shônen ai* title brings out the latent homosexuality in the "cop buddy" movie formula. Randy "Ryo" Maclean, a part-Japanese NYPD rookie, is partnered up with Dee Laytner, a bisexual detective who hits on him as they work together on various cases. Two cute street urchins, pickpocket Carol and the homophobic, roller-skating Bikky, fill the daughter and son roles of Randy and Dee's informal family. Like most *yaoi*, *Fake* is anything but realistic (the occasional racial elements are particularly poorly handled), but the 1980s cop-show hijinks are pleasantly cheesy, down to the foul-tempered police chief yelling at the heroes. The best aspect of the series is that Sanami Matoh is fully aware of how ridiculous it all is, and goes for *City Hunter*–esque comedy and funny dialogue as well as guy-on-guy sexiness ("I've seen whores with more shame than you, you horny ape! Oh, well . . . maybe just this once . . ."). The platonic first six volumes are rated 16+ for older teens; only the final volume delivers the long-awaited 18+-rated sex scenes. An untranslated sequel, *Fake: Second Season*, was begun in 2007. ★★½

FANTASTIC PANIC

Fantastic Panic (ふぁんたすてぃくPANIC) • Ganbear • Antarctic (1993–1996) • Dôjinshi • 1 volume, suspended • Furry, Fantasy, Comedy • Unrated/13+ (mild language, mild violence, brief nudity)

A generic fantasy RPG parody with anthropomorphic "furry" characters; the main character is Nee the heroic mouse, but the ever-changing supporting cast includes Taigar the warrior cat, Kyau the cow girl, and Onui the dog priestess, as well as horses, lizards, tigers, and so on. Everyone is happy and plucky, with dialogue like "It's my duty to help people! Because I'm the hero!" and lots of "woofs" and "meows" written in. The art is mediocre and looks washed-out, the dialogue is uninspired, and if they weren't animals it'd have no distinguishing points. Additional material was printed in monthly comics format but never collected. ★

FIGURE 17: TSUBASA & HIKARU

(フィギュア17つばさ＆ヒカル) • Genco-Olm (original creator), Guy Nakahira (story and art) • ADV Manga (2004) • MediaWorks (Dengeki Daioh, 2001–2002) • 2 volumes • Shônen, Science Fiction, Action • All Ages (mild violence)

Manga adaptation of the anime series. Tsubasa and her father move to Hokkaido, where Tsubasa is walking in the woods when

FANTASY (ファンタジー)

The Japanese word *bôken* means "adventure," and CMX's fantasy manga line labels itself *gensô* (fantasy, illusion), but when most Japanese people refer to the fantasy genre, they use the English word *fantasy*. Strange worlds, quests, magic, and monsters appear frequently in manga for children and teenagers, and occasionally in manga for adults. Fantasy novels and RPGs, which boomed in the 1980s, have had a huge influence on manga. A few manga magazines are particularly fantasy-oriented, such as Square Enix's *Monthly G-Fantasy* and *Monthly Shônen Gangan,* Hakusensha's *Melody,* Shinshokan's *Wings,* and Kadokawa Shoten's *Dragon Age, Asuka,* and the now-defunct *Asuka Fantasy DX.* But all *shôjo* and *shônen* magazines have their share of fantasy manga—defining fantasy in the broadest sense as supernatural and mythological stories which could not happen in the real world.

Myths and Legends

Traditional Japanese fantasy *is* Japanese mythology: stories of ancient monsters, legends, and gods. The *kami* (spirits) of Shinto mythology are said to be infinite in number; they are the "eight million gods" mentioned offhandedly in Hayao Miyazaki's animated movie *Spirited Away.* Spirits, *oni* (demons), and *yôkai* (monsters) frequently appear in manga, whether close to their traditional forms in Shigeru Mizuki's classic *GeGeGe no Kitaro* (1965) or in modernized incarnations in Rumiko Takahashi's *Inuyasha* (1996) and Sakura Kinoshita and Kazuko Higashiyama's *Tactics* (2001). If there seems to be little translated manga based directly on Japanese folklore, it is only because the stories are so widely known that they are diffused throughout manga and pop culture. Rumiko Takahashi's *Lum*Urusei Yatsura* (1978) contains parodies of many myths and legends.

A common element of Shinto belief is that everything has a spirit that can be placated or offended, and which must be befriended, tamed, or appeased rather than simply fought. Natural places—grassy meadows, trees, lakes—and shrines are often sources of magic and spiritual power, or the homes of creatures that may be offended by human intrusion in their domain. This intrusion often comes in the form of pollution or housing developments, as in Kaoru Ohashi and Kei Kusunoki's *Sengoku Nights* (1999) or the Studio Ghibli animated movie *Pom Poko.*

Manga often draw from Chinese mythology as well. The Four Symbols of the Chinese constellations—Byakko the tiger, Suzaku the phoenix, Seiryu the dragon, and Genbu the tortoise— appear as gods, spirits, or character

Sei Itoh's *Monster Collection,* based on the collectible card game by Hitoshi Yasuda and Group SNE

names in countless manga. The ancient Chinese novel *Saiyûki* ("Journey to the West," also known as "The Monkey King") has been adapted numerous times. The story of a group of Buddhist pilgrims who head from China to India encountering various monsters and perils, its best-known character is Son Goku, a prideful monkey whose martial arts powers grow so mighty that he challenges the gods. Goku is imprisoned by the Buddha for hundreds of years until he learns humility and converts to the side of good; he remains a popular, rebellious folk hero. The myth is very loosely adapted in Akira Toriyama's lighthearted *Dragon Ball* (1984) and Kazuya Minekura's *Saiyûki* (1997); Katsuya Terada's *The Monkey King* (1995) is a slightly more faithful, but considerably more gory and explicit, full-color sword-and-sorcery adaptation.

European fairy tales, usually known by the German word *märchen,* are also well-known in Japan; they sit easily alongside similar Japanese *dôwa* (nursery tales or fairy tales) such as CLAMP's *Shirahime-syo: Snow Goddess Tales* (1992). Translated manga examples include Junko Mizuno's bizarre trilogy of fairy-tale adaptations (*Cinderalla, Hansel and Gretel,* and *Princess Mermaid*). Nobuyuki Anzai's *MÄR* (2003) is a conventional *shônen* fighting action manga set in a loosely fairy-tale-based world.

Other mythological subjects in translated manga include Hindu (*Genju no Seiza, RG Veda*), Norse (*Oh My Goddess!, The Mythical Detective Loki Ragnarok*), Greek (*Bride of Deimos, Kamichama Karin, Knights of the Zodiac* [*Saint Seiya*], *Wedding Peach*) and Babylonian (*Demon Palace Babylon*).

Imaginary Worlds

Most fairy tales and mythology simply take place in the past, or in vague settings; exhaustively detailed imaginary worlds, with maps and place names and histories, are a relatively recent invention. Heroic fantasy in the modern sense came to Japan through the translated works of Western writers. Robert E. Howard's *Conan* inspired Kaoru Kurimoto's *The Guin Saga* (1979), a long (108+ volumes) series of sword-and-sorcery novels involving a leopard-headed warrior's quest for his lost memories. It in turn inspired Kentaro Miura's blood-soaked European fantasy manga *Berserk* (1989).

"High fantasy" epics involving the clash of good versus evil, epitomized by J. R. R. Tolkien's *The Lord of the Rings,* were even more influential. Seiki Nakayama's long-running 1987 *shôjo* manga *Alfheim no Kishi* ("The Knight of Alfheim") showed Tolkien's influence, as did Sei Takezawa's 1988 novel series *Kaze no Tairiku* ("The Weathering Continent"), set in the dying continent of Atlantis. Science fiction writer Yoshiki Tanaka ditched the elves and dwarves but kept the epic plot for his fantasy novel series *The Heroic Legend of Arslan* (1986), a war saga inspired by Persian mythology. When fantasy role-playing games became popular in the mid-1980s, along with spin-off manga and novels such as Ryo Mizuno's 1986 *Record of Lodoss War* series (see the article on RPGs), the secondhand medieval European influence became overwhelming. A few writers and manga artists tried to shake off the influence of Western fantasy and create something uniquely Japanese. Novelist Noriko Ogiwara, a fan of C. S. Lewis's Narnia books, took Lewis's Christian model and crafted a fantasy world based around Shinto mythology; the result was *Dragon Sword and Wind Child* (1988), the first in the so-called Magatama Series (known as the "Jade Trilogy" or "Tales of Magatama" in America). She later went on to write a Western-influenced fantasy novel series, *The Good Witch of the West* (1997). RPG-influenced fantasy manga gradually sputtered out into "low fantasy" self-parodies, such as Hajime Kanzaka's *Slayers* series (1989).

Shôjo manga frequently has a fantasy bent and an appreciation for exotic settings. Chieko Hosokawa's incredibly long-running 1976 manga *Ôke no Monshô* ("Crest of the Royal Family"), involving an American girl teleported back in time to ancient Egypt, is one of the most famous examples of a whole genre of *shôjo* manga in which the heroine is a stranger in a faraway land. Yuu Watase's *Fushigi Yûgi: The Mysterious Play* (1992) sends its heroine to a fantasy version of ancient China; Chie Shinohara's *Red River* (1995) is set in ancient Anatolia. Other fantasy manga drop their readers into historical fantasy settings without a modern-day character as a point of reference. Yuho Ashibe's epic *Crystal Dragon* (1982) is seen through the eyes of a young female druid, whose journeys take her to ancient Rome.

After European and pseudo-European settings, the most common fantasy settings are pseudo-Asian. Fuyumi Ono's *The Twelve Kingdoms* novel series (1992) shows the influence of the classic Chinese novel *The Romance of the Three Kingdoms.* The *Suikoden* manga (2002) and RPG series were inspired by yet another Chinese classic, *Suikoden* ("Water Margin"), whose cast of 108 legendary heroes is sometimes referenced in manga and anime. Aki Shimizu, the artist of *Suikoden,* also created *Qwan* (2002), an original fantasy epic set in historical China with the addition of monsters and magic. Ryu Fujisaki's *Hoshin Engi* (1996), a sci-fi/fantasy title with all the nonstop slug-fests and occasional comedy associated with *Weekly Shônen Jump,* was based on Tsutomu Ano's fantasy novels, which were in turn based on the ancient Chinese novel *Fengshen Yangyi* ("Creation of the Gods").

Fusing fantasy, history, martial arts battles, and science fiction, *Hoshin Engi* represents the new wave of fantasy manga that resist categorization into a single genre. The 1990s saw a boom in *shônen* storybook fantasy manga, set in fairy-tale worlds as fanciful and colorful as those of *The Wizard of Oz* or *The Arabian Nights* with the addition of slapstick humor and fight scenes. Examples include Yuichi Kumakura's *Jing: King of Bandits* (1995), Eiichiro Oda's *One Piece* (1997), Hiro Mashima's *Rave Master* (1998), Yukito Kishiro's *Aqua Knight* (1998), and Hitoshi Tomizawa's *Treasure Hunter* (1995). The fantasy manga from Mag Garden's monthly magazine *Comic Blade* represent a different take on the genre: quiet stories of subtle magic and dreamlike places, less visually oriented, with the introspective feel typical of *shôjo* manga. (And it's no surprise that many of the *Blade* artists were originally published in Enix's now-defunct *shôjo* fantasy magazine *Stencil.*) Such titles include Rin Asano's *Tengai Retrogical* (2002), Wataru Murayama's *Desert Coral* (2002–2004), Yoshitomo Watanabe's *Beyond the Beyond* (2004), and Moyamu Fujino's *The First King Adventure* (2002–2005). The artist team CLAMP, who have worked on fantasy series for both *shôjo* and *shônen* magazines, recently brought together characters from all their previous stories for a grand epic, *Tsubasa: Reservoir Chronicle* (2003), one of Japan's most popular current fantasy manga.

Magic and Wizards

Fantasy set in the real world frequently involves some supernatural or magical element intruding on everyday life. Often this magical element is the protagonist herself. Wish-fulfillment stories about people with magic powers are popular everywhere, and in Japan an entire genre, "Magical Girls," is devoted to little girls with secret identities and shape-shifting, spell-casting abilities. J. K. Rowling's Harry Potter series is extremely popular in Japan and inspired Ken Akamatsu's comedy hit *Negima!* (2003), in which a ten-year-old British wizard becomes a teacher at a Japanese girls' school. Other "magic school" manga, though set in imaginary settings rather than the real world, include Yuzu Mizutani's *Magical x Miracle* (2002) and Toshihiko Tsukiji's pandering manga/anime/novel franchise *Maburaho* (2003).

At its core, magic is simply the power to make the unreal real; the question is the "rules" the artist applies to it, the rituals, the atmosphere, the specifics. Yuri Narushima's gloomy *The Young Magician* (1996) envisions a world where secret cults of magicians wage war behind the scenes of reality. Given the popularity of "heroes with partners" in manga and Japanese pop culture, monster summoners are popular characters, in series such as Sei Itoh's *Monster Collection: The Girl Who Can Deal with Magic Monsters* (1998), and Shinya Kaneko's *Culdcept* (1999). Demonology is the subject of Nari Kusakawa's *The Recipe for Gertrude* (2001), while alchemy features in Izumi Kawachi's *Enchanter* (2003), Nobuhiro Watsuki's *Busô Renkin* (2003–2006), and the manga that started the trend, Hiromu Arakawa's *Fullmetal Alchemist* (2002). Of course, what European wizards do with spells, another person might do with Buddhist incantations or sheer mind power, and so magical fantasy manga often border on the Occult and Psychic genres.

See also MAGICAL GIRLS, OCCULT AND RELIGION, RPGS.

Magic and Illusions
Alice 19th • *Angel/Dust* • *Baby Birth* • *Because I'm the Goddess* • *Brigadoon* • *Cardcaptor Sakura* • *Cardcaptor Sakura: Master of the Clow* • *Chibimono* • *Crescent Moon* • *The Demon Ororon* • *The Devil Within* • *D.N.Angel* • *Enchanter* • *The First King Adventure* • *Flower of the Deep Sleep* • *GATE* • *Genju no Seiza* • *Guardian Angel Getten* • *Hibiki's Magic* • *Judas* • *Kami-Kaze* • *Kanna* • *Kekkaishi* • *Lagoon Engine* • *Legendz* • *A Little Snow Fairy Sugar* • *Maburaho* • *Mamotte! Lollipop* • *Millennium Snow* • *My Dearest Devil Princess* • *Mystical Prince Yoshida-kun* • *The Mythical Detective Loki Ragnarok* • *Negima!: Magister Negi Magi* • *Oh My Goddess!* • *A Patch of Dreams* • *Pichi Pichi Pitch: Mermaid Melody* • *Pieces of a Spiral* • *Pixie Pop: Gokkun Pucho* • *Princess Ai* • *Purgatory Kabuki* • *The Recipe for Gertrude* • *Rozen Maiden* • *Sengoku Nights* • *Shakugan no Shana* • *Shugo Chara!* • *Someday's Dreamers* • *Someday's Dreamers: Spellbound* • *Soul Rescue* • *Spirit of Wonder* • *St. Lunatic High School* • *Sugar Sugar Rune* • *Tengai Retrogical* • *The Time Guardian* • *Togari* • *Translucent* • *Ultra Maniac* • *Wish* • *xxxHOLiC* • *The Young Magician*

Strange Places and Times
Alichino • *Angel Sanctuary* • *+Anima* • *Apothecarius Argentum* • *Aqua Knight* • *Bastard!!* • *Beet the Vandel Buster* • *Berserk* • *Beyond the Beyond* • *By the Sword* • *Caravan Kidd* • *Claymore* • *Culdcept* • *Cyber 7* • *Daemon Hunters: Hymn for the Dead* • *Dark Angel* • *Dark Angel: Phoenix Resurrection* • *Dazzle* • *Descendants of Darkness* • *Desert Coral* • *D. Gray-Man* • *Doctor!* • *Dragon Ball* • *Dragon Ball Z* • *Dragon Drive* • *Dragon Eye* • *Dragon Wars: The Tale of Lufiak Duell* • *Drakuun* • *Elemental Gelade* • *El-Hazard: The Magnificent World* • *The Empty Empire* • *From Far Away* • *Fullmetal Alchemist* • *Fushigi Yûgi* • *Fushigi Yûgi Genbu Kaiden* • *The Good Witch of the West* • *.hack//Legend of the Twilight* • *Hoshin Engi* • *Hunter x Hunter* • *Inuyasha* • *Jing: King of Bandits* • *Jing: King of*

Bandits: Twilight Tales • Kabuto • Kagerou-Nostalgia: The Resurrection • Katsuya Terada's The Monkey King • Kazan • Key to the Kingdom • King of Wolves • Kurohime • Lagoon Engine Einsatz • Liling-Po • Louie the Rune Soldier • Magical x Miracle • Magic Knight Rayearth • Magic Knight Rayearth II • MÄR • Mazinger • Midnight Panther • Monster Collection: The Girl Who Can Deal with Magic Monsters • Mouryou Kiden: Legend of the Nymph • Murder Princess • Mushishi • Naruto • Nausicaä of the Valley of the Wind • One Piece • O-Parts Hunter • Orfina • Orion • Planet Ladder • Princess Ninja Scroll Tenka Musô • Qwan • Rave Master • Record of Lodoss War: Chronicles of the Heroic Knight • Record of Lodoss War: Deedlit's Tale • Record of Lodoss War: The Grey Witch • Record of Lodoss War: The Lady of Pharis • Red River • RG Veda • R² [Rise to the Second Power] • Saiyuki • Saiyuki Reload • Sand Land • Scrapped Princess • Seimaden • Shion • Slayers Medieval Mayhem • Slayers Premium • Slayers Special • Slayers Super-Explosive Demon Story • Stainless Steel Armadillo • Stray Little Devil • Suikoden III: The Successor of Fate • Sword of the Dark Ones • Tenryu: The Dragon Cycle • Testarotho • Those Who Hunt Elves • Treasure Hunter • Tsubasa: Reservoir Chronicle • Vaizard • Vampire Game • The Vision of Escaflowne • Welcome to Lodoss Island • The World Exists for Me • Yu-Gi-Oh!: Millennium World • Zyword

Japanese Myths
Dream Saga • GeGeGe no Kitaro • Japan as Viewed by 17 Creators • Kon Kon Kokon • Lum*Urusei Yatsura • Orion • Shirahime-syo: Snow Goddess Tales • Tactics

Fairy Tales
Alone in My King's Harem (yaoi) • Baron: The Cat Returns • Junko Mizuno's Cinderalla • Junko Mizuno's Hansel and Gretel • Junko Mizuno's Princess Mermaid • Key Princess Story: Eternal Alice Rondo • Kilala Princess • Kingdom Hearts • Kingdom Hearts: Chain of Memories • Lost Boys (yaoi) • Märchen Prince • Miyuki-chan in Wonderland • Moon Child • My Only King (yaoi) • Pretear: The New Legend of Snow White • Princess Prince • Princess Tutu • Revolutionary Girl Utena • Revolutionary Girl Utena: The Adolescence of Utena

an alien spaceship lands. During a battle between good and evil aliens, Tsubasa merges with the alien's biotechnological combat suit and saves the day; the suit then detaches and morphs into a nearly identical clone of the heroine. The good alien asks for Tsubasa's help tracking down and killing escaped monsters; meanwhile, when they're not in combat, the clone (Hikaru) goes to school with Tsubasa under the pretense that they are twin sisters. The message of the story seems to be that Tsubasa overcomes her shyness through her connection with her pseudo-friend Hikaru, but the story is dull and we never really see this character develop. (KT)　　　　　★½

FIREFIGHTER: DAIGO OF FIRE COMPANY M

Megumi no Daigo, "Daigo of 'Me' Company" (め組の大吾) • Masahito Soda • Viz (2003–2007) • Shogakukan (Weekly Shônen Sunday, 1995–1999) • 20 volumes • Shônen, Firefighting, Action • 13+ (mild language, mild violence)

Eighteen-year-old rookie Daigo, who has always wanted to be a fireman, finds himself assigned to disappointing desk work at the firehouse in sleepy Medaka-ga-hara (the "Me" of the original Japanese pun title). About thirty pages into the first volume, however, Medaka-ga-hara turns into the most disaster-prone area on Earth, and even when he's just trying to go on a date, Daigo finds himself recklessly saving people from chemical spills, floods, escaped tigers, and fires, fires, *fires*! An archetypal *shônen* occupational manga, *Firefighter* follows its big-eyebrowed young hero as he learns the ropes, endures player-haters ("He's a loose cannon, captain! How can you let a ticking time-bomb like that run loose!?"), and gradually becomes the world's most awesome fireman. The plot is basically a series of action scenes with a story loosely written around them; eventually Daigo joins the elite rescue division, but for most of the manga he just happens to be present at the scene of horrible disasters. Although the plot is repetitive, the action is well set up and has a real sense of danger and excitement. And between life-or-death situations, there's lots of info about fire prevention, the importance of emergency exit signs, and the like. The art is on the realistic side, with dynamic figures and nice caricatural faces.

★★★

THE FIRST KING ADVENTURE

Kenja no Nagaki Fuzai, "The Wise Man's Long Absence" (賢者の長き不在The First King Adventure) • Moyamu Fujino • ADV (2004) • Mag Garden (Comic Blade, 2002–2005) • 2 volumes, suspended (8 volumes in Japan) • Fantasy • All Ages (mild violence)

A slow-building, *shôjo*-influenced fantasy story set in the real world. A group of elementary schoolers encounters Varumu, a prince from another dimension who must prove his worth for his father's throne by making pacts with the "spirit masters." (The spirit masters are giant magical beasts of the summoned monsters/*Pôkemon* style, and in fact, Varumu's fairy servant Aramin looks like Pikachu wearing a hood.) This standard manga/video game plot plays out in a surprisingly wistful, emo manner, focusing on sadness and loneliness. Varumu is like an alien out of place on Earth, and the people he encounters—Mueno, an introverted latch-key girl, and Yutaka, a boy who pushes people away—are all lonely as well. The cute art has a misty, picture-book quality.   ★★★

THE FIRST PRESIDENT OF JAPAN

Nihonko Shodai Daitôryô • *Sakuragi Kenichiro*, "Japan's First President: Kenichirô Sakuragi" (日本国初代大統領・桜木健一郎) • Ryuji Tsugihara (art), Yoshiki Hidaka (story) • Gutsoon! Entertainment (2002–2003) • Shueisha (BART, 1998–1999) • 4 volumes • Military-Political Drama • 13+ (language, violence)

Japan holds its first American-style presidential election by popular vote (actually he's prime minister, but what the heck), electing the young, unmarried Kenichiro Sakuragi, who cuts through the red tape of the Japanese bureaucracy and kicks ass. Told on a global scale, with crowd scenes, newspaper headlines, and military battles, *The First President of Japan* bludgeons the reader with countless crises: assassination attempts, a war between North and South Korea, a Chinese invasion of Taiwan, and much more. Although exciting in a roller-coaster way, the implausible story is crippled by extreme cheesiness and generic art; depictions of emotions are strictly on the cartoon level, with flying sweat drops and gaping mouths. The story ends abruptly, leaving major plot threads unresolved.   ★★

FIST OF THE BLUE SKY

Sôten no Ken, "Fist/Technique of the Blue Sky" (蒼天の拳) • Tetsuo Hara (art), Nobu Horie (story), Buronson (advisor) • Gutsoon! Entertainment, (2002–2004) • Coamix (Weekly Comic Bunch, 2001–ongoing) • 4 volumes, suspended (16+ volumes in Japan, ongoing) • Historical, Martial Arts, Action • 18+ (language, crude humor, graphic violence, partial nudity, sexual situations)

A prequel to *Fist of the North Star,* set in 1935 and starring the uncle of Kenshiro from that series. Kenshiro Kasumi, a martial arts master also known as Yan Wang (god of death), is living undercover as a nerdy professor at a Japanese women's college, until he returns to Shanghai to settle old scores by fighting Chinese gangsters. Compared to its predecessor, *Fist of the Blue Sky* is more plot-driven and slightly less fighting-focused (despite his seeming omnipotence, the Kenshiro of this time period doesn't willingly jump out in front of dozens of gun-wielding soldiers), but the change in mood is not uniformly positive. As *Riki-Oh* is to *Tough,* the pure macho violence of the 1980s original has been infused with comedy, mostly in the form of grotesque, ugly villains who shoot their own henchmen, wear bad toupees, and do everything possible to deserve getting killed. Torture and a certain pre-World War II decadence makes the series just as gory as *Fist of the North Star,* despite fewer actual deaths per volume. Hara's art is polished: stiffly realistic but strangely compelling. Slightly more of the story was published in *Raijin* magazine but never collected. ★★½

FIST OF THE NORTH STAR

Hokuto no Ken, "Fist/Technique of the North Star" (北斗の拳) • Tetsuo Hara (art), Buronson (story) • Gutsoon! Entertainment (2003–2004) • Shueisha (Weekly Shōnen Jump, 1983–1988) • 9 volumes, suspended (15 volumes in Japan) • Shōnen, Postapocalyptic, Martial Arts, Action • 18+ (language, graphic violence, nudity)

Extremely influential—and infamously gory—in its time, *Fist of the North Star* is a 1980s adventure in violence influenced by *The Road Warrior* (hero in leather versus Mohawked bikers) and Bruce Lee (although the real-life Bruce Lee had more motion and facial expressions). In the year 199X, after a nuclear war has reduced the planet to dried-up seabeds and run-down skyscrapers, one man walks the Earth fighting for justice: Kenshiro, the only true heir of the martial art named Hokuto Shinken (Fist of the North Star). The Fist of the North Star can erase people's memories, cure blindness, destroy buildings, and in the series' trademark death scene, kill villains on time-delay by making their heads swell up and explode . . . usually right after he delivers his most famous line: *"You're already dead."* The overarching plot involves Kenshiro's struggle against the other heirs of Hokuto Shinken, but most of the series operates like a Clint Eastwood movie, as Kenshiro wanders in from out of town, perhaps weeps at the

pointless deaths of innocent little kids, and slaughters the ten-foot-tall goons who killed them. Since Kenshiro's invulnerability is never in doubt, the reader keeps reading for "Ooh, he got what was comin' to him" catharsis. Originally printed in black and white in Japan (Viz released four out-of-print volumes of this edition in the late 1980s and early 1990s), Gutsoon's "Master Edition" is printed oversized in glossy full color, in a style similar to Chinese comics. ★★★

FIVE STAR STORIES

Five Star Monogatari, "Five Star Stories" (ファイブスター物語) • Mamoru Nagano • ToysPress (1997–2004) • Kadokawa Shoten (Newtype, 1986–ongoing) • 26 issues (12+ volumes in Japan, ongoing) • Science Fiction, Mecha, Adventure • Unrated/16+ (language, graphic violence, nudity, mild sexual situations)

A thoroughly unique sci-fi epic, very loosely based on a 1984 anime series named *Heavy Metal L.Gaim* that Nagano co-created with *Gundam* director Yoshiyuki Tomino. In *Five Star Stories,* Nagano expands the bare-bones *L.Gaim* premise into a vast saga spanning thousands of years, several solar systems, and multiple dimensions, and packs it full of knights, dragons, demons, immortal emperors, androids, battle robots, psychic warriors, classic-rock in-jokes, and whatever else catches his eclectic fancy. You'd need a scorecard to keep track of the ever-expanding cast and elaborate backstory, and one is helpfully provided in the form of the full-color cast profiles and background essays included in each English-language issue. The nonstop barrage of obscure cross-references and frequent jumps in time and space make it a challenge to follow the story, but Nagano's finely detailed linework and obsessive world building are entertaining all by themselves. The first ten Japanese volumes have been repackaged into 26 large-format English issues comprising about 80–100 pages each and priced at $9–$10, and the typography and name transliteration choices are just as eccentric as the publication format. (MS) ★★★

FLAG FIGHTERS

Haôgai, "Street of Kings/Supreme Ruler Street" (覇王街) • Masaomi Kanzaki • Studio Ironcat (1997–1998) • Kodansha (Monthly Shônen Magazine, 1995–1996) • 6 issues, suspended (5 volumes in Japan) • Shônen, Martial Arts • Unrated/13+ (language, violence)

Excruciatingly generic martial arts manga. Reppa Kagura, a typically angry but atypically tiny Kanzaki protagonist with a *shônen* manga shock of hair, fights bigger enemies with names such as Death Gate and Funky Destroyer in an anything-goes street tournament to collect one thousand flags from one thousand defeated foes. Obviously no manga has room for a thousand separate fight scenes, but *Flag Fighters* get tiresome after just one; the characters are dull and the art is loose and hasty, relying on generic energy blasts and opponents who seem to be fifteen feet apart from each other at all times.   ★

FLAME OF RECCA

Rekka no Honô, "Flame of Rekka/Blazing Fire" (烈火の炎) • Nobuyuki Anzai • Viz (2003–2009) • Shogakukan (Weekly Shônen Sunday, 1995–2002) • 33 volumes • Shônen, Martial Arts, Ninja • 16+ (language, graphic violence, nudity)

Polished and quick-paced, *Flame of Recca* reads like a more carefully plotted, more extreme version of *YuYu Hakusho.* Recca, a teenage ninja who can blast flames from his hands, fights and then teams up with other high school martial artists, until a secret from his past sends him into battle with his evil half brother Kurei and the maniacal industrialist Kôran Mori. Starting out with an OAV-style plot of young ninjas in high school, the scene quickly shifts to one of the longest fighting tournaments ever (12 volumes!), in which the heroes face increasingly threatening opponents armed with *madogu,* transforming ninja accessories. The art is heavy-metal gothic, full of shrieking villains, grotesque masks, and evil grins. This "dark" style, plus T&A, swearing, and comedic breast grabbing, indicates the de-

sire to aim the series at an older readership than the *Weekly Shônen Jump* manga it imitates, but the predictable storytelling never manages to create the illusion of tension.

                                    ★★

FLCL

Furi Kuri (フリクリ) • Gainax (story), Hajime Ueda (art) • Tokyopop (2003) • Kodansha (Magazine Z, 2000–2001) • 2 volumes • Shônen, Comedy • 13+

Released simultaneously with the 2000 anime series, the *FLCL* manga follows a roughly similar story line revolving around a dweeby preadolescent named Naota and his weird hometown of Mabase—a town that gets even weirder with the arrival of the Vespa-riding, guitar-wielding hottie who calls herself Haruko. Then comes random violence, domestic robots, rampaging mechanical monsters, trippy dream sequences, and lots of pervasive sexual tension. It's all very entertaining, and Ueda's simple but visually sophisticated cartooning is frequently beautiful, but the manga somehow manages to be even less comprehensible than the anime version. And while the anime balanced its confounding plot with kinetic energy and relentless visual spectacle, the mood of Ueda's manga is more brooding and subdued, even when the mayor's daughter is sprouting a bowl-shaped flying octopoid from her forehead or robots are flying into outer space to wallop satellites with baseball bats. (Viewers of the anime should also note that Ueda's manga is very different from the occasional manga sequences that appear in the animation itself.) (MS)   ★★½

FLESH COLORED HORROR

Niku iro no Kai, "Flesh Colored Horror" (肉色の怪) • Junji Ito • ComicsOne (2000) • Asahi Sonorama (Monthly Halloween, 1988–1997) • 1 volume • Horror • Unrated/18+ (graphic violence, nudity)

This anthology of short horror stories ranges from conventional revenge-from-the-grave stories ("Beehive," "Long Hair in the Attic") to splatter-movie gorefests ("Headless Sculptures") to Ito's characteristic metaphors for human vanity, age, and beauty ("Dying Young" and the title story). The stories span a lot of time, allowing the reader to watch Ito's artwork become cleaner and more refined and at the same time more caricatural, embracing his absurdist side. As in all Ito's work, his storytelling is clear and his faces and figures are realistic. ★★★

FLOWER OF THE DEEP SLEEP

Fukai Nemuri no Hana, "Flower of Deep Sleep" (ふかい眠りの花) • Yuana Kazumi • Tokyopop (2005) • Kadokawa Shoten (Asuka, 2002–2003) • 2 volumes • Shôjo, Fantasy, Drama • 13+ (mild violence)

Yuuki, a girl who has sad dream visions of the future, is caught in a understated love triangle between her own sister, Yuuka, and two brothers who they are fated to marry: Ryuune, who can read minds, and Ryuunosuke, who has the psychic power to soothe. When a strange dream girl—perhaps the personification of the desire for oblivion—starts to drag people into a comalike sleep, Yuuki must enter people's dreams and save them. A wistful, vague tale of dreams and memories, *Flower of the Deep Sleep* has an interesting premise, but the story is confusing and poorly explained. The art has a soft, sketchy, breezy quality; it's hard to tell the dreamworld from the real world, the flashbacks from the present, or one page from any other page. ★★

FLOWER OF LIFE

(フラワーオブライフ) • Fumi Yoshinaga • DMP (2007–ongoing) • Shinshokan (Wings, 2004–ongoing) • 3+ volumes (ongoing) • Shôjo, Comedy • 16+

Fumi Yoshinaga (*Antique Bakery, Gerard & Jacques*), best known for her *yaoi* work, turns to the high school comedy genre. A serious illness forces Harutaro to miss the first month of high school, but with the help of his chubby friend Shota, he tries to get back into the swing of things. Manga clubs, high school plays, and romance, all written in Yoshinaga's exceptional style. NR

FLOWERS & BEES

Hana to Mitsubachi (花とみつばち) • Moyoco Anno • Viz (2003–2005) • Kodansha (Young Magazine, 2000–2003) • 7 volumes • Seinen, Romantic Comedy • 18+ (language, nudity, graphic sex)

Masao Komatsu, a high school student with bad hair and no fashion sense, stumbles upon the World of Beautiful Men salon, where a group of stereotypically gay stylists—and later two gorgeous, sadistic women—promise to turn him into a *bishônen* and teach him how to pick up girls. Only briefly reminiscent of the TV series *Queer Eye for the Straight Guy,* the plot changes direction almost as much as Komatsu's appearance, sending its virgin hero into endless humiliating encounters and doomed relationships. (Unlike other men's sex manga, there's hardly any flattering of the man's ego . . . or any successfully consummated sex, for that matter.) Directionless but full of great characters and scenes, it's almost like an adolescent male version of Anno's *Happy Mania,* but the art is more polished and appealing, and Carl Gustav Horn's English rewrite is hilarious (despite or because of the liberties it takes with the original).
★★★½

FORBIDDEN DANCE

Tenshi no Kiss, "Angel's Kiss" (天使のキス) • Hinako Ashihara • Tokyopop (2003–2004) • Shogakukan (Betsucomi, 1997–1999) • 4 volumes • Shôjo, Performance, Drama • 13+ (mild violence)

After an accident ends her ballet career, teenage Aya is reinspired by Ballet Cool, an all-male dance troupe of sweaty, muscular guys. (Specifically, she's inspired by Akira, the standoffish troupe leader.) She becomes the only girl in the troupe, but she must deal with sexist men and jealous female rivals. More angst-ridden than the simple, almost newspaper-strip art suggests, *Forbidden Dance* would be downbeat if the plot complications—indeed, the whole series—didn't go by so quickly. Ashihara's poor grasp of anatomy

"Don't get mad, that's real Japanese style of kind" is something almost every manga fan has to say at least once. From Henry (Yoshitaka) Kiyama's *The Four Immigrants Manga,* published by Stone Bridge Press.

makes the dance scenes dull, and the plot lacks internal continuity. ★

THE FOUR IMMIGRANTS MANGA

Manga Yonin Shosei, "The Four Students Manga" (漫画四人書生) • Henry (Yoshitaka) Kiyama • Stone Bridge Press (1999) • Self-published (1931) • 1 volume • Historical, Comedy, Drama • Unrated/All Ages (adult themes)

Rescued from obscurity by translator Frederik Schodt, this incredible curiosity, drawn by artist Kiyama while he was living in California, is one of the earliest graphic novels ever created. Drawn in a style influenced by American newspaper strips of the time (such as *Bringing Up Father*), this semi-autobiographical story concerns four middle-class, college-age Japanese friends (a businessman, a farmer, an artist, and an idle philosopher) who immigrate to San Francisco in search of opportunity. The story spans 1904 to approximately 1922, through the San Francisco earthquake, World War I,

and Prohibition, with countless fascinating and funny insights into American society, racism, and the immigrant experience. Although the story is told in the form of fifty-two separate "newspaper strips," it works as a complete narrative, following the four heroes from youth to marriage and fatherhood. Extensive historical annotation is the crowning touch to this charming story, which went unappreciated in its artist's lifetime.

★★★★

FOUR SHOJO STORIES

Keiko Nishi, Moto Hagio, Shio Sato • Viz (1996) • 1 volume • Shôjo, Science Fiction, Jôsei, Romance • Unrated/13+ (sexual situations)

A collection of short manga edited by *shôjo* manga scholar Matt Thorn. It's an odd mixture of genres and vintages, clearly the product of a time when very little *shôjo* manga was available in English, but all four pieces are excellent. Two are by Keiko Nishi, a *jôsei* artist and clearly a favorite of Thorn's (he also edited the Nishi anthology *Love Song*). "Promise" is an affecting story about a teenage girl's relationship with a mysterious boy who plays hooky with her. In "Since You've Been Gone," a philandering husband must choose between his wife and mistress. "The Changeling," by Shio Sato, is a sci-fi story in which a space pilot investigates a suspiciously utopian planet. The story is engaging despite Sato's sparse and uneven art. For fans of classic *shôjo* manga, however, the gem of the collection is "They Were Eleven," a much-loved story by the legendary Moto Hagio. A sci-fi story about ten Galactic Academy cadets whose field test is complicated by the presence of an eleventh member, it's not one of Hagio's more ambitious efforts, but it still packs more memorable characters and Big Ideas into 120 pages than some manga can manage in twenty volumes. Overall, this regrettably out-of-print book is one of the strongest collections of short manga available in English. *They Were Eleven* was previously printed on its own as a monthly comic series from Viz, while *The Changeling* was printed in *Animerica* magazine. (SG) ★★★★

FOUR-PANEL MANGA (4コマ)

Four-panel manga, known in Japan as *yon-koma manga,* are the direct Japanese equivalent of American newspaper comic strips. Format-wise, they resemble American newspaper comic strips, although the panels are usually stacked from top to bottom, befitting the Japanese language. They are not always four panels, but the name has stuck. Four-panel manga sometimes appear as *omake* (bonus materials) in regular "story manga" graphic novels, such as *Fullmetal Alchemist* and *Genshiken,* usually poking fun at the main story.

Translated American newspaper comic strips, such as George McManus's *Bringing Up Father* and Chic Young's *Blondie,* first came to Japan in the 1920s. Japanese artists soon responded with their own humor strips dealing with mischievous children, henpecked husbands, and other family-friendly topics. Kabushima's 1926 *Shô-chan no Bôken* ("The Adventures of Shô-chan") was an early hit for children, and Ryûichi Yokoyama's 1936 *Fuku-chan* became a classic. After the war, Machiko Hasegawa's *Sazae-san* (1946) quickly became one of the most popular comic strips. *Sazae-san* was the first hit Japanese comic strip drawn by a female artist, and its resourceful heroine was the head of her household. From the immediate postwar years of food rationing and poverty to the later years of comfortable middle-class existence, *Sazae-san* was always topical, optimistic, and relaxing—an ever-popular vision of the archetypal Japanese family.

The postwar manga boom mostly consisted of long-format, comic-book-style "story manga" for children. In contrast, four-panel manga began to skew toward adults, such as Kô Kojima's 1956 *Sennin Buraku* ("Hermit Village"), a mildly risqué adult strip set in historical Japan. (Still running as of 2007, *Sennin Buraku* is the longest-running manga ever, and recently surpassed *Peanuts* as the longest-running comic strip still drawn by the original artist.) Story manga were filled with children's action and adventure, while four-panel manga—printed in respectable newspapers and magazines instead of those crude comic books—became the domain of salarymen and housewives. Like American newspaper comic strips, four-panel manga rarely have any ongoing plot, and the characters never age; Japanese fans refer to this effect as "Isono time," after the never-aging Isono family of *Sazae-san.*

But unlike American comic strips, four-panel manga do not always appear one at a time, once per day; often they are printed in weekly or monthly magazines with several consecutive pages of strips by the same artist. Taking advantage of this format, in the 1970s four-panel manga artists began to tell ongoing stories from strip to strip and issue to issue, using the individual punch lines as elements in a longer story. This so-called story four-panel manga bridged the generation gap and made four-panel manga more popular with younger readers. A pioneer of the form was Hisaichi Ishii, creator of the baseball four-panel manga *Ganbare!! Tabuchi-kun!!* ("Go for It!! Tabuchi-kun!!"), based on the real-life Kôichi Tabuchi of the Hanshin Tigers. (In the United States, Ishii is best known for his untranslated comic strip *Tonari no Yamada-kun* ["My Neighbors the Yamadas"], which was adapted into a 1999 animated movie by Studio Ghibli. In the 1980s and 1990s, the story four-panel medium was expanded by untranslated artists such as Maya Koikeda (a lesbian artist whose work includes love stories and dramas) and Chino Kurumi (a former *dôjinshi* artist whose stories, based in the city of Osaka, are widely believed to be autobiographical).

WORRIED...

YES?

MISS YUKARI, I HAVE A QUESTION.

THAT'S WHAT I HEARD.

DO AMERICANS REALLY KEEP THEIR SHOES ON IN THEIR HOUSES?

BUT WHAT IF...

AND THEN WALK INSIDE? WHAT THEN?!

THEY STEP IN SOME DOG POO?

Kiyohiko Azuma's *Azumanga Daioh*

Today, four-panel manga appear in many forms. Traditional comic strips still appear in Japanese newspapers, such as Masashi Ueda's harmless *Kobo the Li'l Rascal* (1982). Regular manga magazines for all age groups, and both genders, often feature the occasional four-panel manga (both story four-panel and non-story-oriented) mixed in with the prevalent comic-style manga. Some magazines are devoted entirely to four-panel manga, such as Take Shobo's *Manga Life* and *Manga Club* and Houbunsha's enormous lineup of *Manga Home, Manga Time, Manga Time Special,* and numerous others.

Despite the introduction of story elements, most four-panel manga are still focused on humor and light entertainment. But if anyone thought that it was primarily for conservative older readers, that image was certainly destroyed in the late 1990s with the appearance of *moe* four-panel manga aimed at teenage and adult male fans. (See the article on OTAKU.) Pioneered by Kiyohiko Azuma's *Azumanga Daioh* (1999) and the untranslated strips of Hayako Gotô, *moe* four-panel manga focused on cute girls in gentle comedy situations. The plotlessness of *moe,* its focus on everyday life and character interaction (together with an ever-so-slightly fetishistic fascination with the lives of young girls), turned out to be a good match for the format of four-panel comic strips. Other fan-oriented four-panel manga involve traditional *bishôjo* (beautiful girls) and video game parodies. Today, several four-panel magazines, such as *Moeyon* (short for "Moe Yon-Koma"), *Manga Time Lovely,* and *Manga Time Kirara,* are focused on *moe* manga; Hai Ran's *Tori Koro* (2002) is a good example of the genre.

Short manga appear in other formats as well, such as the nine-panel grid of Miki Tori's *Anywhere but Here* (1988), and one-page strips such as Usamaru Furuya's *Short Cuts* (1998).

Four-Panel Manga

Azumanga Daioh • *Bringing Home the Sushi* • *Cosplay Koromo-chan* • *Granny Mischief* • *Heartbroken Angels* • *How to "Read" Manga: Gloom Party* • *Kobo the Li'l Rascal* • *Neconoclasm* • *Survival in the Office: The Evolution of Japanese Working Women* • *Tenchi Muyô!: Sasami Stories* • *Tori Koro* • *Welcome to Lodoss Island* • *The Wonderful World of Sazae-san*

FREE COLLARS KINGDOM

(フリーカラーズキングダム) • Takuya Fujima • Del Rey (2007) • Kodansha (Magazine Z, 2002–2004) • 3 volumes • Furry, Adventure • 16+

When his master falls ill, Cyan, a young cat, is left in the basement and makes friends with the other stray cats in Tokyo's East Ikebukuro district. The hook? All the cats in *Free Collars Kingdom* are drawn as hot anthropomorphic cat-girls and cat-boys, giving a unique twist to this tale of feline turf wars and romantic escapades.   NR

FROM EROICA WITH LOVE

Eroica yori Ai o Komete, "From Eroica with Love" (エロイカより愛をこめて) • Yasuko Aioke • CMX (2004–ongoing) • Akita Shoten (Princess, 1976–1988, 1995–ongoing) • 26+ volumes (ongoing) • Shôjo, Action, Comedy • 13+ (language, sexual themes)

This is the fabulous 1970s, *shôjo* style: leggy men in tight trousers and silk shirts, Cold War espionage in exotic locales, and, of course, endless guy-guy flirtation (coupled with a distinct scarcity of actual sex). *Eroica* begins as the story of three teens with ESP, but these bland heroes are almost immediately dumped in favor of their villain, who becomes the central character. He is Earl Dorian Red Gloria, aka Eroica, a flamboyant gentleman art thief who commits robberies by zeppelin—appropriate, as he's modeled physically after Led Zeppelin star Robert Plant (his henchmen resemble the other members of the band). By the end of volume 1, Eroica has met his antagonist and love interest, the stoic German NATO officer Major "Iron Klaus" Eberbach, and the series has found its formula. Each story line takes the characters to a different point on the globe, where, generally, Eroica is trying to steal a priceless masterpiece and the major is trying to save it. The two stiff-upper-lip it through the frankly ridiculous contortions of the plot, whether fighting wolves in the Alaskan wilderness or painting the Vatican with a hot-pink kiss. Aoike's somewhat stiff, draftsman-like art isn't the best that 1970s *shôjo* manga has to offer, but, like its antihero, *Eroica* triumphs through style, wit, and pure audacity. In Japan, it's an institution; the manga ran for over ten years, returned after a hiatus, and continues to update sporadically. (SG)

★★★★

Yasuko Aoike's *From Eroica with Love*

Natsuki Takaya's *Fruits Basket* Fruits Basket volume 1 by Natsuki Takaya © 1998 Natsuki Takaya. All rights reserved. First published in Japan in 1999 by HAKUSENSHA, INC., Tokyo. English language translation rights in the United States of America, Canada, and the United Kingdom arranged with HAKUSENSHA, INC., Tokyo, through Tuttle-Mori Agency, Inc., Tokyo.

FROM FAR AWAY

Kanata Kara, "From Far Away" (彼方から) • Kyoko Hikawa • Viz (2004–2007) • Hakusensha (LaLa/Zôkan LaLa Fantasy Special, 1991–2003) • 14 volumes • Shôjo, Fantasy, Adventure • 13+ (violence)

A tightly plotted "schoolgirl in a strange land" story. By a method similar to the protagonist of Rumiko Takahashi's *Fire Tripper* (see *Rumic World Trilogy*, volume 1), teenage Noriko is teleported to a pseudo-medieval parallel universe, where a brooding, superhuman swordsman immediately rescues her from giant worms. Noriko's culture shock is intensified by her inability to understand the language; for the first two volumes, until she learns to speak it, the reader can understand both Noriko and the

natives, but they cannot understand each other. Although the language barrier is the biggest novelty in the series, the plot has the feel of a good young-adult sci-fi/fantasy novel, with unexpected character development and intelligently handled fantasy elements: tree spirits, strange animals, psychic powers. The forested faraway world doesn't look too different from many 1980s anime, but it is drawn with fine, precise lines and has an internally consistent design. Gradually the story focuses on Izark, the swordsman with a dark past; despite the gathering tension, the story is surprisingly chaste and light on violence. ★★★½

FRONTIER LINE

(フロンティアライン) • Yoshihisa Tagami • CPM (2002) • Gakken (Comic Nora, 1987–1988) • 1 volume • Shônen, Science Fiction, Military, Mecha • Unrated/13+ (language, violence)

Six gritty military mecha stories set in the backdrop of a future war on a distant planet. The result is an awkward mix of front-line drama, pseudo-history, goofy names ("Ronnie Garps," "General Zecter," "Planet Sodom"), and stiffly drawn, speedline-heavy 1980s robot combat. The tales are presented as snippets of a much larger conflict, which is described through endless maps and exposition, to the point where the reader becomes grateful for the character descriptions included at the beginning of the English edition. ★★

FRUITS BASKET

(フルーツバスケット) • Natsuki Takaya • Tokyopop (2004–ongoing) • Hakusensha (Hana to Yume, 1998–2006) • 23 volumes • Shôjo, Fantasy, Romantic Comedy, Drama • 13+ (mild language, mild violence, mild sexual situations)

Tohru, a Pollyannaish teenage orphan who lives alone, one day meets a very strange family: the Sohma clan, who are cursed to transform into cute talking animals when hugged by a member of the opposite sex. (Since the Sohmas are mostly beautiful, girlish men, it's the perfect nonthreatening guy scenario.) Each of the cursed Sohmas is associated with an animal of the Chinese zodiac, and over the first 10 volumes of the series Tohru gets to know them all, especially Yuki, "the rat," a popular and princely boy, and his rival Kyo, "the cat," a trouble-making outcast, whose patron animal was excluded from the zodiac in an ancient legend. But as the Sohmas become her new family, Tohru discovers that each of them has secret sorrows, and that for some of them, the fairy-tale curse is much crueler than others. Despite the openhearted heroine and the simple, wide-eyed artwork, *Fruits Basket* is a surprisingly sad series, dwelling on themes of loneliness, growing up, and the need for family. ("Will I be able to find a good job?" wonders Tohru. "Can I really live by myself? Someday I'll leave this home. . . .") Rather than providing comedy in the style of *Ranma ½,* the transforming-animal aspect is almost forgotten as the series goes on, except as an ever-present secret that the Sohmas must keep from the rest of the world, a secret that destroys relationships and turns parents against their children. (The martial arts element in the early volumes also gradually fades out.) The cast of characters is large, but everyone is so well defined that the stories tell themselves . . . gradually, scene by scene, emotion by emotion. Neither particularly well drawn nor incredibly witty, it's nonetheless a fascinating manga, like a sweet, melancholy dream.

★★★½

FULLMETAL ALCHEMIST

Hagane no Renkinjutsushi, "Alchemist of Steel" (鋼の錬金術師) • Hiromu Arakawa • Viz (2005–ongoing) • Square Enix (Monthly Shônen Gangan, 2002–ongoing) • 16+ volumes (ongoing) • Shônen, Fantasy, Adventure • 13+ (mild language, violence)

Scarred by a tragic alchemical experiment in their youth, Edward Elric has a cybernetic arm and leg, and his brother Alphonse is nothing but a human soul in a walking suit of armor. In search of a way to turn themselves back to normal, Edward pledges his alchemical services to the military, and they travel the country searching for the legendary philosopher's stone . . . and dealing with the injustice, corruption, and war that plague their native land. *Fullmetal Alchemist* starts much like any other manga about wandering heroes, with action and comic relief, but the plot becomes more powerful as it unfolds. The setting—similar to early-twentieth-century Europe, with crude cyber-technology—is unique, and the manga succeeds in addressing tough questions of morality and religion within its young demographic. (It seems inspired by both *Star Wars* and America's involvement in the Middle East.) Despite the protagonists' incredible powers, the fight scenes are tense.

★★★★

FULL METAL PANIC!

Fullmetal Panic! (フルメタル・パニック!) • Shouji Gatou (story), Retsu Tateo (art), Shikidouji (character design) • ADV Manga (2003–2006) • Kadokawa Shoten (Comic Dragon/Dragon Age, 2000–2005) • 9 volumes • Shônen, Military, Mecha, Romantic Comedy • 13+ (language, violence, partial nudity)

Based on Shouji Gatou's light novel series and subsequent anime, *Full Metal Panic!* is a high school romantic comedy with military espionage replacing the usual fantasy or martial arts. Feisty teenager Chidori is irritated to find herself "guarded" by her classmate Sosuke, a stoic, paranoid military nut totally clueless about everyday life. The hook is that Sosuke *really is* a highly trained mercenary, protecting her on the orders of an international antiterrorist organization with access to experimental giant robots. Switching back and forth from action comedy to pure action, *Full Metal Panic!* is best in comedy mode, when references to North Korea, the Middle East, and terrorist hijackings coexist absurdly with predictable gags about crushes, teachers, and school lunches. Unfortunately, the designs are generic, stealing from popular 1990s anime such as *Martian Successor Nadesico* and *Neon Genesis Evangelion.* Sosuke's soldierly amorality is both the funniest and most disturbing thing in the series.

★★

FULL METAL PANIC OVERLOAD

Ikinari! Full Metal Panic!, "All of a Sudden! Full Metal Panic!" (いきなり!フルメタル・パニック!) • Shouji Gatou (story), Shikidouji (character design), Tomohiro Nagai (art) • ADV Manga (2005–2006) • Kadokawa Shoten (Dragon Junior, 2000–2003) • 5 volumes • Comedy • 13+ (mild language, cartoon violence, brief partial nudity, mild sexual situations)

Another spin-off of the *Full Metal Panic!* franchise, this manga is aimed at younger readers and lacks the mecha and serious plot elements of Retsu Tateo's series. Again, Sosuke is a "war-mongering idiot" obsessed with protecting his female classmate, but this time, the whole thing is a cartoon. Sosuke's face never changes expression as he pulls guns on little girls, practices sniping in study hall, and blows up trains so that the woman he protects can get to school on time. The art is awful; however, the jokes are decent, adding up to fun, fast-paced, dumb slapstick for younger readers. (In one gag, Sosuke blasts a rival character's word balloon to pieces, disrupting his monologue.)   ★½

FULL MOON O SAGASHITE

Mangetsu (Full Moon) o Sagashite, "Search for the Full Moon" (満月[フルムーン]をさがして) • Arina Tanemura • Viz (2005–2006) • Shueisha (Ribon, 2002–2004) • 7 volumes • Shôjo, Romantic Fantasy, Drama • 13+ (brief sexual situations, adult themes)

Twelve-year-old orphan Mitsuki wants to be a singer, but due to throat cancer, she has only one year left to live. The Harbingers of Death, wearing cute animal-themed costumes, give her a chance to fulfill her dream before she dies by transforming her into a sixteen-year-old pop star who sings chart-topping, sad songs about Eichi, the boy who abandoned her to move to America. But debate rages as to whether Mitsuki should be allowed to live, and when one of the Harbingers falls in love with her, things get really chaotic. Despite the cute art (which looks like more an accumulation of Print Club stickers than representational artwork)

and talking animals, *Full Moon o Sagashite* is a surprisingly sad story dealing with death, suicide, and grieving in an over-the-top fairy-tale manner for young readers. The plot twists are seemingly contradictory and the whole thing has a short-attention-span feeling (the characters constantly change their minds and switch roles), but the premise is imaginative and the ending is appropriately tear-jerking. The art is better than Tanemura's earlier work *Kamikaze Kaitou Jeanne.*   ★★

FUSHIGI YÛGI: THE MYSTERIOUS PLAY

Fushigi Yûgi, "Mysterious Game" (ふしぎ遊戯) • Yuu Watase • Viz (1998–2006) • Shogakukan (Shôjo Comic, 1992–1996) • 18 volumes • Shôjo, Fantasy, Action, Romance • 16+ (language, violence, partial nudity, sexual situations)

Miaka, a comically gluttonous junior high student, is in the school library when she is sucked, *The Neverending Story*–style, into a mysterious book: the *Universe of the Four Gods.* Within the book is a pocket universe similar to ancient China, where she becomes the priestess of Suzaku, god of the kingdom of Hong-Nan. Miaka's best friend, Yui, tries to save her, only to be sucked into the book herself and become the priestess of a rival kingdom. As friends become bitter enemies and empires prepare for war, Miaka must go on a quest to find the Seven Celestial Warriors of Suzaku, seven hot guys destined to protect her and do her bidding. But among the Celestial Warriors, there is only one she loves—the dashing but greedy martial artist Tamahome. *Fushigi Yûgi* successfully balances several different elements: *shôjo* romance and *shônen* action, real-world and fantasy-world subplots, life-and-death cliffhangers and goofy comedy. With *chi*-blasting action scenes and super-deformed comic relief, the artwork shows the influence of anime, while the backgrounds and monsters range from amateurish in the early volumes to somewhat slicker in the second half. The real star is the writing, however. The supporting cast is compact, with strong personalities and good backgrounds, and the plot is packed with romantic fanservice (both guy-guy and guy-girl), as well as tear-jerking moments of love and sacrifice. One of the best "schoolgirl in a strange land" *shôjo* fantasies. Note that *Fushigi Yûgi* has two parts: the main story line ends resoundingly in volume 13; volumes 14–18 form a slightly inferior sequel. ★★★★

FUSHIGI YÛGI GENBU KAIDEN

Fushigi Yûgi Genbu Kaiden, "Mysterious Game: Legend of Genbu" (ふしぎ遊戯玄武開伝) • Yuu Watase • Viz (2005–ongoing) • Shogakukan (Shôjo Comic/Shôjo Comic Zôkan: Yuu Watase Perfect World, 2004–ongoing) • 6+ volumes, ongoing • Shôjo, Romance, Adventure • 16+ (violence, nudity)

A prequel to *Fushigi Yûgi* using 1923 Japan as its jumping-off point, *Genbu Kaiden* tells the story of Takiko Okuda, daughter of the obsessed author who translated the magic book *Universe of the Four Gods*. Intended for older fans, *Genbu Kaiden* inverts many aspects of *Fushigi Yûgi*: instead of a lovestruck heroine, Takiko is a *naginata*-wielding tomboy who has issues with men and her father; the heroes are on the run from the authorities; and despite slightly more explicit nudity, the romantic element is relatively subdued. This time the male lead is Limdo, a Celestial Warrior who must change into a girl to use his wind powers. (The Celestial Warriors of Genbu are more blatantly supernatural than their *Fushigi Yûgi* counterparts.) Watase clearly enjoys returning to the *Fushigi Yûgi* world, but the theme of father-child angst and the lack of humor (even *Ceres: Celestial Legend* has more comic relief) make for a less welcoming read. This series has gone on and off hiatus, due to Watase's health problems. ★★★

FUTABA-KUN CHANGE

(ふたば君チェンジ) • Hiroshi Aro • Studio Ironcat (2000–2003) • Shueisha (Monthly Shônen Jump/Monthly Shônen Jump Original, 1990–1997) • 8 volumes • Shônen, Romantic Comedy • Unrated/16+ (mild language, mild violence, nudity, sexual situations)

While reading a porn mag, mild-mannered teenager Futaba Shimeru (pronounced "she-male" . . . and yes, it's intentional) discovers a secret about himself: he turns into a girl when sexually aroused! A more *hentai*, more juvenile version of *Ranma ½*, *Futaba-kun Change* is a polymorphously perverse transgender fantasy. Unlike Ranma, whose goal is to become a man as soon as possible, Futaba nervously but eagerly experiences the good and bad aspects of womanhood (according to this manga: lingerie shopping and being groped on the subway, respectively) while crushing on his/her female friend Misaki. The plot is filled with T&A and hit-and-miss weirdness: wrestling competitions, mad scientists, giant man-eating plants, and so on. ★★★

GACHA GACHA

(ガチャガチャ) • Hiroyuki Tamakoshi • Del Rey (2005–2006) • Kodansha (Weekly Shônen Magazine/Magazine Special, 2002–ongoing) • 5 volumes • Romantic Comedy • 16+ (nudity, sexual situations)

Kouhei, a teenage dork in love with his classmate Kurara, is dumbfounded when his dream girl develops split-personality disorder, transforming back and forth into a slutty version of herself, Arisa, who is eager to show Kouhei her panties. Aware of the existence of Arisa, Kurara confides in Kouhei and asks him to help keep her other self out of trouble, but soon she reveals even more ridiculous split personalities: a Lolita-fantasy little girl, a martial artist, a cat-girl, and so on. As boys' romantic comedies go, *Gacha Gacha*'s one innovation is to compress all the stereotypical female characters into one body (although there are a few non-Kurara women as well). The art is slick, like a generic-brand Masakazu Katsura, but the story line is pure episodic cheesecake, with little emotion or character development, except when Kurara has to deal with the consequences of her problem. (Kouhei's one character trait is a love of beef, and Kurara's multiple selves originate from a mad science experiment, not manga-level psychology.

Not to be confused with Yutaka Tachibana's *shôjo* manga *Gatcha Gacha*. ★★

GACHA GACHA: THE NEXT REVOLUTION

Gacha Gacha (ガチャガチャ) • Hiroyuki Tamakoshi • Del Rey (2006–ongoing) • Kodansha (Weekly Shônen Magazine/Magazine Special, 2002–ongoing) • 13+ volumes (ongoing) • Romantic Comedy • 18+ (nudity, sexual situations)

Originally published in Japan as *Gacha Gacha* volume 6 and onward, the new story line gets its own separate title (and an 18+ age rating) for the English-language version. The *Gacha Gacha* virtual reality game has now gone mainstream, but evidently there are still a few bugs in the system, such as the one that causes schoolboy Akira Hatsushiba to turn into a girl every time he sneezes. (MS) NR

GADGET

(がじぇっと) • Hiroyuki Eto • ADV (2004) • Mag Garden (Comic Blade, 2002–2005) • 1 volume, suspended (3 volumes in Japan) • Science Fiction, Romance • 13+ (mild suggestive situations)

A romance between an awkward boy who loves repairing machines and a girl who seems to have some strange connection to them. Soon, strange miniature UFOs appear, which turn out to be ramshackle, inorganic life-forms that form bonds with humans. Though the plot is standard, *Gadget* is distinguished by its innocent mood, its gradually revealed science fiction elements, and most of all its odd, thick-lined, almost underground art. Whatever their age, the characters all look like squat-bodied children, perhaps appropriate for the inhabitants of a world of mechanical toys. ★★½

GALAXY ANGEL

(ギャラクシーエンジェル) • Broccoli (original concept), Ryo Mizuno (supervisor), Kanan (manga) • Broccoli Books (2004–2005) • Kadokawa Shoten (Dragon Junior/Dragon Age, 2001–2004) • 5 volumes • Science Fiction, Comedy • 13+ (mild violence, mild sexual situations)

Based on Broccoli's anime/video game franchise of the same name. The Angel Troupe are five beautiful and talented spaceship pilots charged by the young Captain Takuto with the task of protecting Prince Shiva, the sole member of the royal family to survive a coup d'état. The comedy (and later drama) of the series comes from the Angel Troupe's interpersonal conflicts, rather than their space battles against a rarely seen group of enemies. A love triangle between Takuto and two of the Angels provides most of the plot. Although the early stories are disconnected, a deeper story line gradually grows, together with some decent characterization. The story ends on a cliff-hanger, which is continued in *Galaxy Angel Beta*. (MJS) ★★

GALAXY ANGEL II

Galaxy Angel 3rd (ギャラクシーエンジェル3rd) • Broccoli (original concept), Kanan (story and art) • Broccoli Books (2007–ongoing) • Softbank Creative (Comi Di Gi/Comi Di Gi Plus, 2005–ongoing) • 2+ volumes (ongoing) • Science Fiction, Comedy • 13+

The latest installment in the multimedia *Galaxy Angel* series, which logically enough was released as *Galaxy Angel 3rd* in Japan. The original Angel Troupe has been disbanded, and our previous heroine Milfeulle Sakuraba is now guarding the gateway that connects the galaxies of Eden and Neue. Milfeulle's sister Apricot joins a new team of adventurers, each with their own special powers, among them an android with the charming moniker of Nano Nano Pudding. (MS) NR

GALAXY ANGEL BETA

Galaxy Angel 2nd (ギャラクシーエンジェル2nd) • Broccoli (original concept), Ryo Mizuno (supervisor), Kanan (manga) • Broccoli Books (2005–2006) • Jive (Comic Rush, 2004–2005) • 3 volumes • Science Fiction, Comedy • 13+ (mild violence, mild sexual situations)

Following up the story line begun in *Galaxy Angel,* this series explores the past of the

Angel Troupe members, offering some insight into their characters. The love triangles around Captain Takuto get deeper, while one of the Angels betrays her comrades. Generally better than the original *Galaxy Angel,* the stories of *Galaxy Angel Beta* veer more toward characterization and drama rather than episodic antics. (MJS) ★★½

GALAXY ANGEL PARTY

Kanan, various artists • Broccoli Books (2005–2006) • 3 volumes • Science Fiction, Comedy • 13+ (mild violence, mild sexual situations)

Dôjinshi style anthology of *Galaxy Angel* stories by Kanan and other artists. *Galaxy Angel Party* features characters who do not appear in the manga but do appear in the *Galaxy Angel* anime, such as the Twin Star Team of ten-year-old brothers Kokomo and Malibu (the Angel Troupe's rivals) and Normad, a sentient computer in the body of an ugly stuffed animal. Other characters, such as Captain Takuto, appear little or not at all. The resulting stories tend toward wacky comedies, quick jokes, or watered-down drama with art ranging from good to awful. (MJS) ★½

GALAXY EXPRESS 999

Ginga Tetsudô 999, "Galactic Railroad 999" (銀河鉄道999) • Leiji Matsumoto • Viz (1997–2002) • Shogakukan (Monthly Big Gold, 1996–2000) • 5+ volumes (ongoing in Japan) • Science Fiction • Unrated/13+ (violence, partial nudity)

The Galaxy Express 999 is a high-tech space vehicle, designed to look like an old steam locomotive, that travels across the vastness of the universe. Back on Earth, humanity is being hunted down by the Machine People, whose mechanized bodies allow them to live forever. After his mother is killed by one of the Machine People, young Tetsuro Hoshino wants to travel to their home world to obtain a machine body and get his revenge. While Tetsuro seeks to obtain passage on the 999, he meets a mysterious woman named Maetel, who looks just like his dead mother. She becomes Tetsuro's guardian, and the pair make the long voyage to the planet Andromeda together aboard the Galaxy Express. Along the way, Tetsuro has many adventures, meets many different lifeforms, and begins to question the true value of an eternal life. Created by Leiji Matsumoto in 1977, the original anime and manga versions of *Galaxy Express 999* rank among the high points of Japanese space opera, a genre that Matsumoto himself often excelled at (*Space Battleship Yamato, Captain Harlock,* etc.). Confusingly, this Viz edition is not the first series, but rather a sequel-continuation that began publishing some two decades later. Tetsuro rejoins Maetel aboard the 999, this time headed for the mysterious destination Eternal, where time and space are said to come together. Soon after they leave Earth, the solar system is destroyed by the mysterious Darqueen, who is covering the universe with an enveloping darkness. Now Tetsuro must "run beyond the light, beyond the time" to complete his quest. Although occasionally guilty of computer-assisted shortcuts, Matsumoto's distinctive artwork (a mix of melancholy, machine worship, and long flowing hair) remains very much the same decades after the original series. However, his storytelling skills seem to have gone a bit slack; the exact nature of Maetel and Tetsuro's journey here is annoyingly vague, and a distinct sense of aimlessness sets in early. But while it lacks the strong narrative backbone of the original, Matsumoto can still deliver clever cosmic wonders, and the characters continue to be endearing. Given the huge amount of *999* backstory, it's advisable that would-be readers seek out the *Galaxy Express* anime feature film before stepping aboard the manga. The magazine serialization comes to a sort of conclusion after five volumes, but Matsumoto continues to serialize Tetsuro's adventures as an online comic (http://ginga999.shogakukan.co.jp/999toppage.html). (PM) ★★★

GALAXY GIRL, PANDA BOY

Ginga Girl, Panda Boy, "Galaxy Girl, Panda Boy" (銀河ガールパンダボーイ) • Junko Kawakami • Tokyopop (2005) • Shodensha (2002) • 1 volume • Jôsei, Drama • 16+ (sexual situations)

One of two books in Tokyopop's short-lived "Passion Fruit" line (the other is *Sweat and Honey*), this is a collection of short stories aimed at an older female audience. The title story involves a disaffected teenage girl coming of age in an offbeat, New Age-y village where "there are always rainbows in the sky. And there are old men here who say they've seen dinosaurs." In the second story, "The Laidback Person I Will Never Forget," a girl is frustrated by her relationship with a carefree surfer. In the longest story, "Club Hurricane Adventure," a brother and sister are abandoned by their parents at a strange, isolated boarding school in the countryside, where they bond uncomfortably with other kids who have been left to fend for themselves. Emotional distance and isolation reverberate through these stories, and Kawakami's dreamy, slightly surreal storytelling suggests fairy-tale fantasy even when she introduces no overtly unreal elements. Her evocative artwork suits the material well. (SG)   ★★★½

GALLERY OF HORRORS: See *Hino Horror, Vol. 11: Gallery of Horrors*

GALS!

Mihona Fujii • CMX (2005–2007) • Shueisha (Ribon, 1999–2002) • 10 volumes • Shôjo, Comedy • 13+ (mild language, mild violence, mild sexual situations, adult themes)

Kogals—city girls with deep tans, outrageous consumerist fashions, and suspicions of criminal activity—were the "what is the matter with today's youth?" topic du jour in 1990s Japan. But yesterday's menace to society is today's sitcom guest star, and the media scare must have died down in time for *Gals!*, which stars sixteen-year-old Ran, a spunky, trash-talking, super-tough *kogal* with a heart of gold and the fake nails and handbag to match. (She doesn't have the tan, though.) Ran's wild appearance and bad grades alarm her family, who are all police officers, but

like the song says, the kids are all right; she just wants to have fun, and with her fists and her strong moral sense, she helps her friends navigate through a world which is occasionally dangerous to teenagers and teenage girls in particular. (Among other things, *kogals* are infamously associated with prostitution, a business which Ran scorns.) A spectacular "girl power" comedy for young teenage readers, *Gals!* has busy, colorful art and high spirits, which carry the reader along from episode to episode. Ran and her friends go on platonic dates with boys, do lots of *parapara* dancing, fight rival gals from other neighborhoods in Tokyo, and help solve one another's problems. There's lot of dialogue, most of it loud and outspoken ("Hands off, meathead! You think just 'cause I let you buy me dinner, I'm gonna hop in the sack with you like some cheap ho?!"). Of all the *shôjo* manga with cheerful, big-eyed characters smiling from the covers, it's one of the best.
★★★½

GAMERZ HEAVEN

Gamerz Heaven! (ゲーマーズヘブン!) • Maki Murakami • ADV (2004–2005) • Mag Garden (Comic Blade, 2003–2005) • 2 volumes, suspended (4 volumes in Japan) • Science Fiction, Action-Adventure • 13+ (violence, mild sexual situations)

Suzuki, a teenager obsessed with video games (specifically RPGs), finds a mysterious CD that takes him and his friends into Gamerz Heaven, a sort of parallel universe that looks almost identical to ours, only inhabited by "area masters" (boss enemies) and video game versions of his real-life classmates. The art is attractive, but the plot is confusing and dull, and the opportunities for RPG parody are generally wasted (although you do get to see Suzuki take multiple bloody sword wounds without really minding it, evidently due to high hit points).
★½

GATCHA GACHA

(ガッチャガチャ) • Yutaka Tachibana • Tokyopop (2006–ongoing) • Hakusensha (Melody, 2001–ongoing) • Shôjo, Romantic Comedy • 7+ volumes ongoing • 13+ (mild language, mild violence, mild sexual situations)

People call Yuri a slut, but she's actually innocent in her own way; every time she's dated some total loser, she really loved him and thought it could work out. Her best friend, Motoko, is a butch girl who's as cynical and manipulative as Yuri is idealistic and good-natured. When two guys—Yabe, a seedy slacker, and Hirao, the shy but passionate school president—start hanging out with the girls, who will end up with whom? Starring some atypical character types for a *shôjo* manga (where heroines have rarely kissed anybody), *Gatcha Gacha* is an above-average, occasionally unpredictable teenage romantic comedy. The title refers to the *gatcha gacha* sound of something switching back and forth (in this case, presumably Yuri's boyfriends). Not to be confused with Hiroyuki Tamakoshi's *shônen* manga *Gacha Gacha*. ★★★

GATE

Hirotaka Kisaragi • ADV (2005) • Biblos (Magazine Zero, 2002–2004) • 1 volume, suspended (3 volumes in Japan) • Shôjo, Fantasy • 13+ (violence)

Four male friends are at ground zero when Shibuya is struck by strange lightning bolts from another dimension, causing them to be possessed by the four beast-gods of Chinese legend: Genbu, Suzaku, Seiryu, and Byakko. In true *shônen* manga superhero style, the heroes learn to befriend the haughty spirits inside them, then use their occult powers to fight evil ghost-type creatures. The art is attractive, but the plot is little more than *bishônen* platonic eye candy, with each character getting his own short story. Unfortunately, the English edition ends before all four characters are even introduced. ★½

GATEKEEPERS

(ゲートキーパーズ) • Hiroshi Yamaguchi (original story), Keiji Goto (manga) • Tokyopop (2003) • Kadokawa Shoten (Monthly Ace Next, 1999–2001) • 2 volumes • Shônen, Science Fiction, Mecha, Comedy • All Ages (violence)

Manga adaptation of the anime of the same name. In 1969 Japan, the A.E.G.I.S. organization is in charge of recruiting powerful psychic teenage students, also known as Gatekeepers, in order to help defend Earth from an alien invasion. Although the concept is nothing new, *Gatekeepers* refuses to take itself seriously, making it a fun read. (For example, one Gatekeeper has the power to summon a giant panda spirit to fight for her.) A glimpse of emotional depth to the main characters contrasts nicely with the overall silliness. Unfortunately, the manga ends abruptly, leaving several plot threads dangling. (MJS) ★★½

GEGEGE NO KITARO

GeGeGe no Kitarô/Hakaba no Kitarô, "Kitarô the Spooky/Kitarô of the Graveyard" (ゲゲゲの鬼太郎／墓場の鬼太郎) • Shigeru Mizuki • Kodansha International (2002) • Kodansha (Weekly Shônen Magazine, 1965–1969) • 3 volumes (9 volumes in Japan) • Shônen, Mythological Monster, Comedy • Unrated/All Ages (mild language, brief violence)

A classic children's manga, *GeGeGe no Kitaro* is a fascinating grab bag of monsters and spooks from Japanese mythology, not to mention weird ideas known only to the mind of Shigeru Mizuki. Kitaro is the boy heir of the Ghostly Tribe, who was born in a cemetery and who uses his supernatural powers to fight monsters and do good deeds. (The "GeGeGe" in the title is a creepy cackling laugh, one that Kitaro himself rarely utters.) His closest companions are Ratman, a whiskery goblin, and his dead father's eyeball, which has little arms and legs and lives in Kitaro's empty eye socket. The self-contained stories have the fast-paced vigor of the children's comics they are, but also have a surprising element of pathos, as in volume 1's "The Leviathang," in which Kitaro is transformed into a giant monster, shunned by his friends, and nearly killed by the Japanese military. In another story, Kitaro scares skeptical adults who don't believe in ghosts by sending them on a train ride through scary and lyrical sights that would be at home in the works of Ray Bradbury. As for Kitaro himself, he is a quiet but charm-

GAMES AND HOBBIES

Just as manga depict countless professions—doctors (*Black Jack, Nurse Call*), fire-fighters (*Firefighter: Daigo of Fire Company M*), lawyers (*Over the Rainbow*)—so it also depicts countless leisure activities.

Fishing manga (*tsuri manga*) is a popular genre about a popular pastime. The classic example is Kenichi Kitami and Jûzô Yamasaki's good-natured *Tsuru-Baka Nisshi* ("Diary of a Fishing Freak"), still running since 1980. It has not been translated, except for brief sections in the defunct *Mangajin* magazine and the anthology *Bringing Home the Sushi,* in which the hero gives an impassioned defense of fishing as an everyman's hobby even an underachiever such as himself can enjoy. Taiga Takahashi and Yoshiaki Shimojo's *Bass Master Ranmaru* (1999) focuses more on technique than on the hero's comedic struggle to balance his hobby, work, and family life.

Pachinko, a quasi-legal form of gambling similar to vertical pinball machines, is a major money guzzler in "*pachinko* parlors" throughout the country. In the early 1990s the small publisher Byakuya Shôbo expanded its range from "how to win" *pachinko* magazines to *pachinko* manga magazines, such as *Manga Pachinker* and *Manga Pachisuro Panic 7.* Increasingly flashy electronic *pachinko* machines—such as the popular *pachisuro*, short for "*pachinko* slots"—have taken much of the strategy away from the game, but it retains a following, and two manga have been translated: Shigeru Tsuchiyama's *Pachinko Player* and Tsutomu Shinohara's *Wild Boogie* (both 1999).

Board games make good competitive drama. Mahjongg manga magazines, ranging from gag comics to crime dramas worked around the traditional Chinese game, have been around since Take Shobo released *Kindai Mahjong* ("Modern Mahjongg") in 1972; they still publish it as well as the spin-off magazine *Kindai Mahjong Original.* Unfortunately, no mahjongg manga have been translated. Mahjongg has had difficulty attracting young players in recent years; the same problem afflicted Go, until Yumi Hotta and Takeshi Obata's *Hikaru no Go* (1998) became a megahit. Serialized in *Weekly Shônen Jump,* it avoided turning away readers by focusing more on the drama surrounding the game than on high-level moves and strategies, and it was embraced as a teaching tool by Go organizations in both America and Japan. *Shôgi* (Japanese chess) has not been so lucky, possibly due to the more complicated rules and large number of variants. Junichi Nôjô and Toshihiko Kawaguchi's 1993 *Gekka no Kishi* ("Shogi Pro in the Moonlight") was made into a TV drama, and Masaru Katori and Jiro Ando's 2004 *Shion no O* ("Shion's King") successfully combines *shôgi* and a murder mystery, but both are aimed at adults. *Shôgi* manga aimed at children have generally flopped, including *365 Ho no Yuki* (2002), despite being drawn by the master of melodrama Shinji Saijyo (*Iron Wok Jan*).

Collectible card games, whether those based on manga such as *Yu-Gi-Oh!* or original games such as *Aquarian Age* and *Monster Collection,* are popular in Japan but belong more to RPG/video game fandom (see the article on RPGs). The number game Sudoku, invented in the West but given its name in Japan in the 1980s, is a regular feature in Japanese newspapers. In 2006, Japanime Co. released *The Manga Guide to Sudoku,* a cross-cultural collaboration written by Jay Morrison with art by manga artist Atsuhisa Okura. Although not a full-length story manga, *The Manga Guide to Sudoku* contains 40 pages of sudoku-educational manga followed by 120 pages of puzzles.

ing hero, staring gloomily out at the world with his one good eye perpetually peeking through the part in his hair. The artwork is even better than the writing, mixing richly detailed, occasionally surreal backgrounds with cartoony, spooky characters in the foreground; the incredible linework shows why Mizuki was one of the forerunners of the 1960s *gekiga* movement, which sought to introduce more realistic artwork to Japanese comics. The only downside is that so little has been translated. ★★★★

THE GENIUS BAKABON

Tensai Bakabon, "Genius Bakabon/Genius Idiot" (天才バカボン) • Fujio Akatsuka • Kodansha International (2000–2001) • various magazines (1967–ongoing) • 3 volumes, suspended (21+ volumes in Japan, ongoing) • Shônen, Comedy • Unrated/All Ages (mild language, brief crude humor)

Today it seems quaint, but in 1967 Japan, *The Genius Bakabon* was revolutionary: fast-paced, silly, anarchistic cartoon humor. The classic plot: Bakabon and his father are the biggest idiots in town, and their neighbors, cops, and everyone else tries to fool them. (On the other hand, Bakabon's mother is of normal intelligence, and his baby brother is a genius.) Each minimalist page is crammed with good-natured gags, as Bakabon and his hippo-faced, buck-toothed dad try outrageous solutions to ordinary problems and attempt unlikely get-rich-quick schemes such as making shoes out of squid. High points include a policeman forced to dress like a baby, Bakabon's father dressing up like a robot, and Bakabon and his father attempting to do "rock, paper, scissors" while wearing boxing gloves (they're surprised that it keeps coming up "rock"). ★★★

GENJI MONOGATARI: See *The Tale of Genji*

GENJÛ NO SEIZA

Genjû no Seiza, "Constellation of the Illusionary Beast" (幻獣の星座) • Matsuri Akino • Tokyopop (2006–ongoing) • Akita Shoten (Susperia Mystery, 2000–2005) • 13 volumes • Shôjo, Occult, Fantasy • 16+ (mild language, graphic violence)

When a bird-headed man appears before him and calls him "master," Fuuto discovers that he is the reincarnation of the holy king of Dhalasar (a fictional Central Asian country mostly based on Tibet). Although Fuuto resists his destiny and often abuses bird-headed Garuda for comic relief, he can't deny his developing psychic powers, and soon he meets a number of occult researchers (including a beautiful girl in a wheelchair), solves several mysteries, and shows a fraction of his powers on national TV. But back in Dhalasar, where the Chinese government has set up a fake king, the evil gods led by Lord Naga are planning to assassinate Fuuto. At turns episodic and epic, *Genjû no Seiza* is an intelligent modern-day young-adult fantasy drawing heavily from Hindu mythology. Although the story meanders and the level of seriousness goes up and down, Matsuri Akino's imagination is impressive and her art is precise and often beautiful. ★★★

GENOCYBER

(ジェノサイバー) • Tony Takezaki • Viz (1993) • Byakuya Shobo (Comic Nova, 1991–1993) • 5 issues • Science Fiction, Mecha, Horror • Unrated/16+ (mild language, graphic violence, nudity)

Unfinished manga teaser for the *Genocyber* anime, drawn by Takezaki based on a concept by his boss, Toshimichi Suzuki of the anime studio Artmic. Two psychic sisters—one animalistic and instinctual, the other brilliant and crippled—are used in a cruel experiment by an evil cybernetics corporation staffed by faceless employees. The manga has some creepy moments, and Takezaki does a good job in his usual Katsuhiro Otomo–esque style, but the story was canceled in the middle after the anime came out. ★½

GENSHIKEN

(げんしけん) • Shimoku Kio • Del Rey (2005–ongoing) • Kodansha (Afternoon, 2002–ongoing) • 7+ volumes (ongoing) • Seinen, Otaku, Romantic Comedy, Drama • 16+ (language, sexual situations, partial nudity)

Genshiken, aka the Society for the Study of Modern Visual Culture, is a college club of nerds obsessed with all aspects of Japanese *otaku* culture: anime, manga, cosplay, *dôjinshi,* and pornographic video games. Neither an "*Otaku* unite!" fantasy in the style of *Maniac Road* nor a savage parody like Evan Dorkin's *Eltingville Club, Genshiken* is somewhere between the two: a mostly realistic, often hilarious portrayal of college-age geeks, down to the bad posture and pretentious over-analysis of pop culture. (The fake manga that the characters discuss, *Kujibiki Unbalance,* was spun off into a real ongoing manga in 2006.) The story initially focuses on Kanji Sasahara, a bland closet geek joining the club for the first time, but most of the other characters are more interesting, including Kousaka, a good-looking but shameless *otaku;* Saki, the girl who loves him but hates his hobbies; and Madarame, the scrawny, crafty club president. The skillful writing and character portrayals put *Genshiken* above average: the characters vary between sympathetic and unsympathetic, cruel and kind, struggling to draw and sell their *dôjinshi,* awkwardly pursuing their sometimes (but not always) unrequited loves. The art is highly polished and detailed, although mostly restricted to drawing cluttered rooms full of manga, which might hit some readers too close to home. ★★★

GENTLEMAN'S ALLIANCE †

Shinshi Dômei †, "Gentlemen's Alliance †" (紳士同盟†) • Arina Tanemura • Viz (2007–ongoing) • Shueisha (Ribon, 2005–ongoing) • 6+ volumes (ongoing) • Shôjo, Romance • 13+

Set in a fancy high school with an absolute social caste that determines not only the classes you take but where you can go on campus, *Gentleman's Alliance †* follows Haine Otomiya as she tries to get close to her true love, student council president "Emperor" Shizumasa. But Haine is a lowly Bronze badge student, destined to see her Gold badge love but once a day when he addresses the students. That seems to be the plot, but it's hard to tell since Tanemura seems to be throwing in whatever stuff occurs to her, regardless of whether it fits with what happened a few pages previously. The manga is also overburdened by Tanemura's tendency to bog down her pages in florid displays of screentone that bloat the otherwise nice linework. In short, this manga takes all the problems of *Full Moon o Sagashite* and compounds them, resulting in a tedious mishmash of plot and art that is a trial to read. (HS) ★

GEOBREEDERS

(ジオブリーダーズ) • Akihiro Ito • CPM (1999–2004) • Shônen Gahosha (Young King Ours, 1997–ongoing) • 5 volumes, suspended (12+ volumes in Japan, ongoing) • Action • 13+ (violence, nudity)

Vaguely like *Ghostbusters* with more guns and panty shots, *Geobreeders* is the story of Kagura Security, five cute girls (and one token guy) whose job is to capture the Phantom Cats, shape-shifting cat-people who can possess electronic equipment. Somewhere outside the readers' attention is a plot involving corporate conspiracies, but the manga mostly consists of amazing (albeit sometimes confusing) popcorn-movie action sequences, involving chaotic collisions of tanks, cars, speedboats, and Japanese Self-Defense Force soldiers. As one of the best examples of the girls-with-guns genre, it's comparable to *Gunsmith Cats,* but more lighthearted and less sleazy: a Hong Kong action movie rather than a gritty TV show. (Despite massive destruction, there are few on-screen casualties.) Unfortunately, the English edition suffers from poor image quality and censorship; towels and swimsuits are inconsistently drawn on naked women in the early volumes. ★★★

GETBACKERS

Getbackers Dakkanya, "GetBackers Recovery Service/Business" (GetBackers奪還屋) • Yuya Aoki (story), Rando Ayamine (art) • Tokyopop (2004–ongoing) • Kodansha (Weekly Shônen Magazine, 1999–2007) • 39 volumes • Shônen, Street Action • 13+/16+ (language, crude humor, graphic violence, nudity, sexual situations)

Ginji and Ban, two teenage goof-offs in search of girls and money, have special powers: former gang boss Ginji is the "lightning lord" with electrical powers, and breast-grabbing Ban wields the "evil eye," which can cause terrifying illusions. Despite their initially dorky appearance, they're agents of the GetBackers, a "retrieval agency" whose members hang out in the restaurant Honky Tonk and who accept missions such as finding a stolen Vincent van Gogh painting or rescuing an old man's long-lost daughter. *GetBackers* is an interesting example of a Japanese superhero story, set in the real world but starring characters with unexplained abilities. The crime cases, particularly the early ones, are cleverly plotted and the heroes make good use of their powers in over-the-top action scenes and car chases. Later on, however, the series turns into a standard fighting manga, as the heroes go to bizarre locations such as the Infinity Fortress (your typical *shônen*-manga tower full of enemies) and face recurring allies and villains with names like Lady Poison and Doctor Jackal. The series never entirely loses its comedy aspects, though the ghoulish gore (zombie attacks, scalpels slicing peoples to ribbons) gets more extreme. The female characters are mostly sex objects. The photorealistic backgrounds resemble the world of *GTO*, and with good reason; Rando Ayamine was Tohru Fujisawa's assistant. The early volumes were initially labeled T (13+) but the rating was later retroactively upped to OT (16+). ★★½

GETTER ROBO: See *Venger Robo*

GHOST HUNT

(ゴーストハント) • Fuyumi Ono (creator), Shiho Inada (artist) • Del Rey (2005–ongoing) • Kodansha (Amie/Nakayoshi, 1998–ongoing) • 9+ volumes (ongoing) • Shôjo, Occult, Mystery • 13+ (mild violence, occult themes)

Based on a spin-off of Ono's *Akuryô Series* ("Evil Spirit Series") young-adult novels, this is the manga equivalent of a reality show about ghost hunters or psychic detectives. Mai, a high school student, becomes the assistant of Kazuya Shibuya, a handsome teenage investigator of paranormal phenomena. They investigate hauntings, working and sometimes competing with investigators from other occult disciplines. The cases are treated as serious investigations, with plenty of high-tech equipment (thermographs, infrared cameras). The supernatural manifestations are also realistically low-key, at least initially, consisting mostly of spoons bending and chairs sliding around empty rooms. The self-contained plots (each volume is a different case) are decent, but the weak art somehow makes it look like a TV show with a low special-effects budget. ★★

GHOST SCHOOL: See *Hino Horror, Vol. 9: Ghost School*

GHOST IN THE SHELL

Kôkaku Kidôtai, "Attack Shell Riot Police" (攻殻機動隊Ghost in the Shell) • Masamune Shirow • Dark Horse (1995) • Kodansha (Young Magazine Pirate Edition, 1989–1991) • 1 volume • Science Fiction, Police, Action • 18+ (violence, nudity, sex)

The dichotomy of Masamune Shirow's best-known work, a cyberpunk classic, is right in the title: a ghost of human consciousness inside the shell of a body also describes the manga itself, a philosophically ambitious ghost inside a shell of shoot-'em-up cop drama. Lifelike robots are grown in tanks, cybernetic enchancements surpass plastic surgery, and the Net is like a 1–900 party line for cybernetic terrorists, A.I.'s wanting to breathe free, and virtual-reality lesbian sex. Despite copious footnotes, *Ghost in the Shell* really doesn't make a whole lot of sense, and is best enjoyed for its imaginative futurist visions and naked or near-naked female forms. The rogue A.I. of the anime version, directed by Mamoru Oshii, is only a single case file in the manga. Dark Horse's 2004 edition restores a sex scene that was deleted from previous English editions. (JD)   ★★★

GHOST IN THE SHELL 1.5: HUMAN-ERROR PROCESSOR

Kôkaku Kidôtai 1.5, "Attack Shell Riot Police 1.5" (攻殻機動隊 1.5) • Masamune Shirow • Dark Horse (2006–2007) • Kodansha (1991–2003) • 8 issues • Science Fiction, Police, Action • Unrated/16+

More Section 9 cop drama in an assortment of mini-stories following up on the original *Ghost in the Shell* universe (rather than its not-exactly-a-sequel, *Man-Machine Interface*). The first case has buddy-team Togusa and Azuma on stakeout, tailing a dead man who's been turned into a remotely piloted drone through the use of micromachines. The artwork seems a little rushed compared to the other *Ghost* productions, with sketchy pen work substituting for Shirow's normally lavish screentones, but lighter, zippier story-telling makes for a satisfying read. (JD)
NR

GHOST IN THE SHELL VOLUME 2: MAN-MACHINE INTERFACE

Kôkaku Kidôtai 2, "Attack Shell Riot Police 2" (攻殻機動隊 2) • Masamune Shirow • Dark Horse (2003–2005) • Kodansha (Young Magazine Pirate Edition/Young Magazine, 1991–2001) • 1 volume • Science Fiction, Police, Action • 18+ (violence, nudity)

Hacker fetishism reaches its height in this poorly executed sequel to Shirow's previous cyberpunk classic. Pneumatically breasted cyberlass Motoko Aramaki (not the same as *Ghost in the Shell*'s Motoko Kusanagi) spends an average day sitting in a plush office, displaying her panties in a short skirt while simultaneously dispatching her consciousness into android backup bodies to combat the ever-present terrorist threats. This involves either floating naked in cyberspace and/or kung-fu fighting while dressed in a sprayed-on jumpsuit. With approximately 85 percent more crotch shots than the original *Ghost in the Shell, Man-Machine Interface* is more pinup poster than story; Shirow's technobabble dialogue is more impenetrable than ever, and one does begin to wonder why the cyberfuture contains so few men. The computer-colored artwork now appears dated, with a high proportion of Photoshop blur filters and primitive 3-D models. (JD)
★

GINGA LEGEND WEED

Ginga Densetsu Weed, "Silver Fang Legend Weed" (銀牙伝説ウィード) • Yoshihiro Takahashi • Comics-One (2000–2001) • Nihon Bungeisha (Manga Goraku, 1995–2006) • 3 volumes, suspended (38 volumes in Japan) • Animal, Adventure • Unrated/13+ (language, violence)

Weed, a cute little dog, heeds his mother's dying wish and goes in search of his father, the legendary boss dog Ginga, who has founded a canine utopia somewhere in the forests of Japan. Although the premise is charming, the rough execution comes across as an unintentionally humorous transplantation of old-school manga clichés into dog form. To quote one dog: "Weed is so noble! What a big heart he has! He sure is the son of the boss of Ohu!" Another dog rather perceptively tells us, "My owner, an elite banker, was suspected of illegal investing. . . ." Apart from anthropomorphism issues, the manga also suffers greatly from generic art that results in endless similar-looking dogs on similar-looking backgrounds of grass and trees. On the plus side, the plot is action-packed, involving frequent dogfights, humans with guns, and a giant bioengineered killer dog, which ludicrously but successfully keeps things moving. For young readers. ★★½

GINTAMA

Gintama, "Silver Soul" (銀魂) • Hideaki Sorachi • Viz (2007–ongoing) • Shueisha (Weekly Shônen Jump, 2004–ongoing) • 17+ volumes (ongoing) • Fantasy, Action • 13+ (mild language, mild sexual situations)

The name Gintama, or Silver Soul, is a pun that, if spoken aloud, could be misinterpreted as a slang term for testicles. It sets the tone perfectly for Hideaki Sorachi's wacky samurai saga that centers on a hypoglycemic, Meiji Restoration–era *ronin* named Gintoki Sakata. As Japan joins the modern age, Gin and his sword-wielding ilk are a dying breed who must struggle to find their place in the world. There's a twist, of course: the impetus for cultural and political change in Japan is not Commodore Perry's "black ships" but an extraterrestrial invasion. In addition to the bizarre alien creatures, there are plenty of modern references—including the scooter Gin uses to get around, late-twentieth-century plumbing, and fluorescent lights—that signal Sorachi's anything-goes approach to samurai manga (purists looking for stoic, Bushido heroics should steer clear). Along with Shinpachi, a nerdy samurai, and Kagura, a fresh-off-the-spaceship alien who looks like a cute Chinese girl, Gin takes up odd jobs that invariably put him at odds with the authorities. *Gintama* throws every Japanese perversion and racial stereotype up against the wall to see what sticks, and the gags are often surprisingly subtle and funny. A word of warning, however: the English adaptation dilutes much of the off-color humor that made the title a hit in Japan. (RG) ★★★

GIRL GOT GAME

Power!! (パワーPower!!) • Shizuru Seino • Tokyopop (2004–2005) • Kodansha (Bessatsu Friend, 1999–2002) • 10 volumes • Shôjo, Sports, Romantic Comedy • 13+ (brief language, brief partial nudity, sexual situations)

Lighthearted *shôjo* gender-bending comedy. Kyo is forced by her basketball-crazy dad to enroll in high school as a boy so that she can play on the school's famous men's basketball team. As luck would have it, her roommate is ace basketball player Chiharu, a good-looking but rude guy who calls her a "creepy little freak" before eventually figuring out she's a woman. Although the premise is similar to *Hana-Kimi*, *Girl Got Game* is a much more slapstick, less pretentious, more fun series, aimed at a younger audience. The plot speeds along with numerous chaotic twists and turns, climaxing in a ridiculous basketball match with the school faculty (one of the few actual basketball games of the series). Kyo's attempts to disguise herself as a guy are played for comedy; when she's worried that people think she's female, she reacts by harassing women ("I'm crazy about boobies! Crazy, I tells ya!"). The art is functionally cute. ★★½

A GIRL IN A MILLION: See *Harlequin Pink: A Girl in a Million*

GIRLS BRAVO

(GIRLSブラボー) • Mario Kaneda • Tokyopop (2005–2007), Kadokawa Shoten (Monthly Shônen Ace/Ace Momo-gumi, 2000–2005) • 10 volumes • Shônen, Romantic Comedy • 13+/16+ (comedy violence, partial nudity, sexual situations)

Bottom-of-the-barrel slapstick *shônen* romantic comedy. Yukinari, a "wimpy, short, goofy, dull, stupid and clumsy" boy who breaks out in hives from contact with women, is teleported to an alternate world with a 90 percent female population, from which he escapes and brings Miharu, an agreeably clueless woman who somehow doesn't trigger his gyno-allergy. Other visitors from Miharu's world follow, as well as stock characters such as a handsome narcissist who has the hots for all the girls, and several women with crushes on Miharu. The plot aims for random one-shot adventures (a treasure hunt, a fake Miharu, duplicate Miharus, etc.), but the punch lines are nonexistent and the sexual content is equally bland and uninteresting. ½

GLASS WINGS

Hane Hari (Glass) no Kimi, "The Glass-Winged One" (羽根玻璃ノ君) • Misuzu Asaoka • Tokyopop (2006) • Kadokawa Shoten (Asuka, 2003) • 1 volume • Gothic, Fantasy, Romance • 13+ (language, violence, brief partial nudity)

Overwrought, fantasy-themed goth comics with stiff but appropriate art; the characters' childlike faces and enormous eyes are framed by chains and lace, and sometimes by bleeding sores. In the title story, a boy with toxic blood is kept in a mansion by a noblewoman, like a tainted bird in a gilded cage. In "Firefly" a rogue member of a cannibal race falls in love with a human woman. In the interesting "Jion Princess" the main character is a sort of scapegoat, a magical double of a princess created to protect her mistress from sickness and bad luck. The stories are varied, although the interior art doesn't live up to the cover.   ★★½

GLOOM PARTY: See *How to "Read" Manga: Gloom Party*

GODCHILD

God Child (ゴッド　チャイルド) • Kaori Yuki • Viz (2005–2008) • Hakusensha (Hana to Yume, 2001–2004) • Shôjo, Gothic, Mystery • 8 volumes • 16+ (graphic violence, mild sexual situations)

The further adventures of Victorian dilettante Earl Cain Hargreaves, *Godchild* is the continuation of Kaori Yuki's *The Cain Saga.* Accompanied by Riff, his faithful butler, and Merry Weather, his ten-year-old half sister, Cain solves crimes and has run-ins with the evil secret organization Delilah and his wicked half brother, Dr. Jizabel Disraeli. The names indicate the over-the-top feeling of the proceedings, but to its credit *Godchild* rarely degenerates into intentional distracting humor. The ornately drawn gothic plots involve séances, sinister nursery rhymes, sadism, and murder, and the heroes are as seductive and destructive as the villains. The art overcompensates in detail for what it lacks in clarity, and the storytelling is sometimes confused. Best line: "It's not really love when you kill people or make them living statues!"   ★★½

GODZILLA

(ゴジラ) • Kazuhisa Iwata • Dark Horse (1988–1995) • Shogakukan (1985) • 1 volume • Science Fiction, Tokusatsu, Action • Unrated/13+ (violence)

After a thirty-year slumber, the giant monster Godzilla is accidentally revived by an undersea eruption. While making a beeline for the mainland of Japan, the creature destroys a Russian submarine, and the Japanese prime minister must face an escalating geopolitical crisis. As both Godzilla and a rogue nuclear missile threaten to completely destroy Tokyo, a scientist, his assistant, and a newspaper reporter seek to lure the monster into the mouth of a volcano. Manga tie-ins with Godzilla movies are a tradition that go all the way back to the famous monster's screen debut in 1954. Yet Dark Horse's *Godzilla*—a straightforward adaptation of the film *Godzilla 1985*—is the only one that has been translated into English so far. Kazuhisa Iwata's style is textbook 1980s commercial manga with some Katushiro Otomo–inspired detail among the well-rendered war machines and crumbling cityscapes. The problems with the manga are the same as the movie it is based on. This is more of a disaster story and a political thriller, with the "monster eating Tokyo" thrills regulated to the backseat. Still, Iwata's manga moves forward at a more agreeable clip than the film does, and he draws a mean, devilish, and oddly joyful Godzilla. The graphic novel also includes a fun gallery of Godzilla art featuring contributions from such comic superstars as Geoff Darrow, Mike Mignola, and Alan Moore. (PM)   ★★★

GO GO HEAVEN

(ゴーゴーヘブン!!) • Keiko Yamada • CMX (2007–ongoing) • Akita Shoten (1994–1999) • 13 volumes • Shôjo, Fantasy, Romantic Comedy • 13+

When luckless high school girl Shirayuki dies in a car accident, she is neither good enough for heaven nor bad enough for hell. The handsome Prince of Hell obligingly grants her a few additional weeks on Earth to resolve her unfinished business. In order to keep an eye on her in the meantime, the prince and his minions move into Shirayuki's bedroom.   NR

GÔJIN

Kazuho Takizawa (story), Yutaka Kondo (art) • Antarctic (1995–1996) • 8 issues • Historical, Tokusatsu, Action • Unrated/13+ (language, graphic violence)

"What if *Ultraman* was set in 1780 Japan?" When Edo (old Tokyo) is attacked by aliens and mythological giant monsters, alien-in-disguise Kyoshiro Steren transforms into his secret identity: Gôjin, a giant masked warrior. Meanwhile, a group of ninja-like "science warriors" mops up the lesser bad guys, using rocket launchers and other cobbled-together technology invented by the local mad scientist. The best thing about *Gôjin* is the extremely distinctive crosshatched art, but the reading experience is offset by crowded page layouts.   ★★½

GOKU: MIDNIGHT EYE

Gokû (ゴクウ) • Buichi Terasawa (story and art) • ComicsOne (2001) • Kodansha/Scholar Publishing (1987–1992) • 3 volumes • Science Fiction, Crime, Adventure • 18+ (language, graphic violence, nudity, sexual situations)

A near-future *noir* liberally spiced with ninjas, robots, hovercars, psychic supersoldiers, ghosts, shape-changing mutants, flying cities, and whatever else happens to catch the artist's fancy. Our eponymous hero is a wise-cracking detective with a magic staff and a robotic eye that can hack into anything from toasters to spy satellites, but for all the superficial glamour, Goku is more Jake Gittes than James Bond—he's always getting beaten up, and every buxom babe he beds is either evil, mind-controlled, or hopelessly doomed. Terasawa's artwork is carefully rendered and realistic, but it's frequently stiff and unimaginative, and the tedious, bewildering plots are less than the sum of their wacky parts. A small portion of the series was published in monthly comics format by Viz in the late 1980s under the title *Midnight Eye Goku*. (MS)   ★★½

GOLDEN WARRIOR ICZER-ONE

Tatakae!! Iczer-One, "Fight!! Iczer-One" (戦え!!イクサ-1) • Toshihiro Hirano (creator/some art), Yasuhiro Moriki (primary art duties) • Antarctic (1994) • Amatoria (Lemon People, 1986) • 5 issues • Science Fiction, Action • Unrated/16+ (graphic violence, nudity)

Forgettable, plotless spin-off/prequel to the 1985 anime *Iczer-One*. Iczer, an elf-eared naked girl android, crash-lands on a generic sci-fi planet with no memory of her past, except that her purpose is to fight the evil planet-invading aliens known as the Kthulhu. (The low-ranking Kthulhu look like H. P. Lovecraft's octopus-headed alien god Cthulhu, but the in-joke isn't very deep; the ones with speaking parts are humanoids in battle armor, or cute girls with names like Blue and Magenta.) Iczer soon meets up with sword-wielding freedom fighters, who join her in her battle against the slimy, H. R. Giger–ish invaders. A promised part two to the manga was never created.   ½

GOLGO 13

(ゴルゴ13) • Takao Saito • Viz (2006–2008) • Shogakukan (Big Comic, 1969–ongoing) • 13 volumes (140+ volumes in Japan, ongoing) • Seinen, Crime, Military, Political Thriller • 18+ (language, violence, nudity, sex)

A Japanese institution, *Golgo 13* is like James Bond without the wink: an infallible, emotionless, sexually magnetic sniper-for-hire who can assassinate anyone, anywhere in the world. (His name is derived from Golgotha, the hill on which Jesus Christ was crucified.) Most of the stories focus on Golgo's clients or targets rather than the dreaded hit man himself, and each perfectly crafted plot converges inexorably on the moment of greatest tension, the moment when Golgo does his assigned job with just one shot. (Of course, he'll first kill anyone who gets in his way.) As there is no continuity between stories, the Viz edition reprints twenty-six stories chosen from the nearly forty-year Japanese run: each volume contains a story line based on current events and figures (such as Saddam Hussein or Tiananmen Square) and a "classic" story line chosen for sheer 1970s pulp value. The art is openly a studio product, the result of countless assistants drawing helicopters and hatchet-nosed faces, but it has a retro appeal. In American comic terms, think of it as the greatest newspaper drama strip ever, an unintentional heir to hard-boiled stories such as *Dick Tracy* and *Steve Canyon*. A few unrelated *Golgo 13* stories were released prior to Viz's 2006 edition: four volumes from Lead (Leed) Publishing in 1986–1987, two volumes from Leed Publishing and Vic Tokai in 1989–1990 (as cross-promotion for the *Golgo 13* NES video game), and a three-issue limited comic series, *The Professional: Golgo 13* from Viz in 1991. ★★★★

GON

(ゴン) • Masashi Tanaka • CMX (2007–ongoing) • Kodansha (Weekly Morning, 1991–2002) • 7 volumes • Wordless, Animal, Comedy • Unrated/All Ages (mild violence)

Completely wordless, sound-effects-free and human-free, *Gon* is pure visual comics: beautifully drawn, breakneck tales of the tough little dinosaur Gon, who waddles into thirty-two-page episodes of animal mayhem instigated by an acorn, a whim, or a flea on his nose. In American terms, he's almost like a Looney Tunes character; an unstoppable id who messes with everything that gets in his way, a friend of the meek and a killer of evil ("evil" in a food-chain sense). Like cartoons, it can get a little mean-spirited; typically Gon torments some large predator and plays with the little, cute animals. Unlike cartoons, the wildlife art is super-detailed and naturalistic, although there's a grotesque pleasure here in showing realistically drawn animals contorted in strange ways: Gon buried in a pile of penguins, Gon's mouth gaping within the mouth of a shark. Prior to the CMX edition, the series was published by DC's Paradox

Press imprint in the late 1990s. The Paradox edition lacked volume numbers, a small matter as there is no continuity between stories. ★★★½

GOOD-BYE AND OTHER STORIES: See *The Push Man and Other Stories*

THE GOOD WITCH OF THE WEST

Nishi no Yoki Majo, "The Good Witch of the West" (西の善き魔女) • Noriko Ogiwara (story), Haruhiko Momokawa (art) • Tokyopop (2006–ongoing) • Mag Garden (Comic Blade, 2004–ongoing) • 5+ volumes (ongoing) • Fantasy, Adventure • 13+ (infrequent violence)

Based on the young-adult fantasy novels by Noriko Ogiwara, *The Good Witch of the West* is a familiar story well told. Firiel Dee is a young girl raised in the remote highlands, with little attention paid to her by her father, an astronomer whose life revolves around forbidden books and the distant stars. When she attends a ball held by the nobility, she discovers that she may be of royal blood, and she is forced to become a fugitive as evil forces track her down. Set in a pseudo-European world with little outright magic and monsters, the story involves much intrigue; as in Ogiwara's *Magatama Series* novels, the central conflict is between characters and ideologies rather than simple good versus evil. The *shôjo*-style artwork is generic—Firiel looks like a standard ever-optimistic heroine, and the surroundings are barely sketched—but the story is solid. ★★★

GRANNY MISCHIEF

Ijiwaru Baasan, "Cantankerous Grandma" (いじめるばあさん) • Machiko Hasegawa • Kodansha International (2001–2002) • Mainichi Shimbun (Sunday Mainichi, 1966–1971) • 3 volumes, suspended (6 volumes in Japan) • Four-Panel Comedy • Unrated/13+ (mild language, brief crude humor, cartoon nudity)

Machiko Hasegawa's second-best-known newspaper strip manga, *Granny Mischief* has slightly more teeth than *Sazae-san,* unlike its aged protagonist. A clever old lady who does whatever she damn well pleases, the title character plays pranks on her daughter-in-law, says the meanest things with an innocent smile, and writes fake letters from her nephew so she can make her fellow seniors jealous. Although (to its credit) the strip doesn't dwell on it, she's also genuinely lonely, like many elderly people. A one-note but funny strip with a good central character. ★★★

GRAPPLER BAKI: See *Baki the Grappler*

GRAVITATION

(グラビテーション) • Maki Murakami • Tokyopop (2003–2005) • Gentosha (Kimi to Boku, 1996–2002) • 12 volumes • Yaoi, Performance, Comedy • 16+ (language, mild violence, sex)

Shuichi is a high school singer-songwriter with dreams of taking his band to the big time . . . until one day he meets Eiri Yuki, a twenty-two-year-old romance novelist who grouchily dismisses Shuichi's lyrics ("Is this what love is? Some stupid cliché?"). After getting pissed off and trying to prove himself, Shuichi finds himself uncontrollably attracted to Yuki, and soon Shuichi confesses his feelings and moves in with his gay lover, triggering a change in his character design that makes him look increasingly girlish. *Gravitation* starts out as a semirealistic Boys' Love music story, but as the band Bad Luck starts to climb the charts (helped along by its lead singer's scandalous gay relationship), it turns into a crazed comedy beyond the dreams of the wildest tabloid. Volumes 1–3 are witty and restrained; volume 4 takes an unnecessary dark turn with elements of rape and murder; and volume 5 onward trades the angst for anime-style absurdity, in which characters pull bazookas out of nowhere, wear bunny suits, and fly over the skyscrapers of New York in a giant robot panda. The art gets slicker and more anime-style, while the plot turns into indulgent chaos. But it's *fun* chaos, dense with good dialogue and quirky scenes that would be hard to imagine in a more tightly controlled manga; at one point, a depressed Shuichi visits a movie theater and inspires the audience to revolt against happy endings; later, he suffers writer's block for an entire volume. In the end, the fun outweighs the frustration. The sequel, *Gravitation EX,* was initially drawn as an online comic; the first print volume was released simultaneously in America and Japan in 2007. ★★★

GRENADIER

(グレネダー) • Sousuke Kaise • Tokyopop (2006–ongoing) • Kadokawa Shoten (Monthly Shônen Ace, 2002–2005) • 7 volumes • Shônen, Action • 16+ (mild language, graphic violence, partial nudity)

Cheerful but mediocre action manga. A busty, blond-haired cowboy gunslinger travels across a vaguely Japanese landscape, fighting mecha with machine guns and teaming up with a penniless samurai. The heroine's nippleless breasts are occasionally on display, but the main focus is semislapstick action. The designs are generic and the art is weak; the action scenes are crowded with too many lines and lack clear, strong images. ★

GREY

Grey • Yoshihisa Tagami • Viz (1988–1997) • Tokuma Shoten (Monthly Shônen Captain, 1985–1987) • 2 volumes • Shônen, Military, Mecha, Science Fiction, Action • Unrated/18+ (language, violence, nudity)

A grim dystopian manga. In a desertified future Earth, society runs as a war machine, where the only escape from the slums is to join the military and kill as many enemies as possible. Grey, a cynical soldier, goes AWOL and does battle with progressively higher-tech enemies (tanks, cyborgs, mecha), struggling to discover the truth and stay alive. Eventually, Grey is fighting for his life on almost literally every page; the endless video game–like battles are oddly appropriate to the antiwar message, and the story has the structure of a good sci-fi movie. Tagami's strange, mechanical art style works well with the cold story. ★★★½

Tohru Fujisawa's *GTO*

GTO

Tohru Fujisawa • Tokyopop (2002–2005) • Kodansha (Weekly Shônen Magazine, 1997–2002) • 25 volumes • Shônen, Comedy • 16+ (language, crude humor, violence, partial nudity, sexual situations)

Eikichi Onizuka is a twenty-two-year-old virgin bad-ass: a motorcycle-riding karate expert who works crummy blue-collar jobs, lives in a room full of porn, and generally alternates between being a superhuman idiot savant and being a complete loser. Motivated by the thought of scoring with teenage girls, he decides to become a high school teacher—GTO, "Great Teacher Onizuka"—and ends up winning over one of the worst high school classes in Japan. Shameless, frequently sexist, and totally hilarious, *GTO* has the plot of any number of American movies (*Stand and Deliver,* etc.) about wacky teachers who touch their students' hearts. (And in this case their panties, but not quite; the joke is that it always *seems* like he's going to succumb to jailbait temptation, but cir-

cumstances and his heart of gold invariably intervene.) The rule of the manga is that every time Onizuka does something cool and heartwarming (such as helping latchkey kids connect with their parents, or beating up child pornographers) he must immediately do something unbelievably retarded (such as teaching his class wearing an elephant suit with the trunk coming out of his crotch). Pubic hair, poop jokes, and masturbation abound. Although the formula eventually repeats itself, it stays fresh thanks to funny imagery, richly detailed art, and smutty, pop culture–laden dialogue. When Onizuka imagines his own downfall, he envisions newspaper headlines screaming, "Tawdry Teacher Sipping Sake with Slutty Schoolgirl!" The huge cast includes Saejima, a corrupt cop with shady moneymaking schemes, and Uchiyamada, the bald school principal, who channels all his failures in life into hatred for Onizuka ("He's a bug, an infection, a parasite! A wicked poison chewing away the foundation of our school!"). At its best moments, *GTO* goes beyond the level of an Adam Sandler movie and approaches true social satire. ★★★★

GTO: THE EARLY YEARS— SHONAN JUNAI-GUMI

Shônan Junai Gumi, "Pure Love Gang of Shonan (Beach)" (湘南純愛組!) • Tohru Fujisawa • Tokyopop (2006–ongoing) • Kodansha (Weekly Shônen Magazine, 1990–1996) • 15 volumes • Shônen, Romantic Comedy, Fighting • 18+ (language, crude humor, violence, nudity, sexual situations)

The prequel to *GTO* (which stands on its own), *GTO: The Early Years* is comparatively immature, and not just because of the dick jokes. Eikichi and Ryuji are mulleted teenage hooligans who spend all their time either fighting *yakuza* and gangbangers or desperately trying to lose their virginity. (The opening story line sees them pretending to be college students to pick up older women at a resort, only to find out that the women they're hitting on are their hot new schoolteachers.) When their plans fail, they sit in adjacent beds watching porn and masturbating under the covers with "stroke

stroke stroke" sound effects. At its best, it's a funny, lowbrow sex comedy; however, the macho *shônen* manga elements are less entertaining, and readers may skim through the chapters in which the heroes prove their friendship by beating up bad guys. The art is conventional, hasty 1980s *shônen* artwork.

★★

GUARDIAN ANGEL GETTEN

Mamotte Shugo Getten!, "Please Protect (Me), Guardian Getten!" (まもって守護月天!) • Minene Sakurano • Gutsoon! Entertainment (2002–2004) • Enix (Monthly Shônen Gangan, 1996–2000) • 4 volumes, suspended (11 volumes in Japan) • Shônen, Fantasy, Romantic Comedy • 13+ (mild sexual situations)

Poorly drawn rip-off of *Oh My Goddess!* Tasuke, a fourteen-year-old boy who lives alone, accidentally summons Guardian Angel Getten (i.e., Belldandy), a Chinese moon spirit who lives with him and protects him from harm. Getten's rival, Guardian Angel Nitten (i.e., Urd), soon shows up as well and tries to put the moves on Tasuke, causing magical chaos at home and at school. Getten's primary character trait is prim-and-proper incomprehension of everything. ½

GUN CRISIS

Masaomi Kanzaki • Studio Ironcat (1998) • Leed Publishing (1991) • 3 issues • Seinen, Military, Action • Unrated/16+ (language, graphic violence, brief nudity)

Akatsuki, a Japanese antiterrorist task force, defends Japan's interests against kidnappers, Palestinian terrorists (depicted in a borderline racist manner), and the CIA. This short collection of stiffly drawn *Rainbow Six/Counterstrike*–like action scenarios adds a realpolitik justification to Kanzaki's usual love of violent heroes: after a pleading terrorist is shot in the head, the hero gives an end-justifies-the-means lecture to the female rookie. Scenes like these are actually the most interesting parts of the manga, as for the most part the art and story operate on a strictly functional action-movie level.

★½

GUN CRISIS: DEADLY CURVE

Gun Crisis • Masaomi Kanzaki • Leed Publishing (1991) • Studio Ironcat (2000) • 4 issues • Seinen, Police, Action • 18+ (language, graphic violence, nudity, sex)

Mean-spirited vigilante cop drama. A fiery rookie officer goes up against the drug-dealing rapists responsible for his girlfriend's death, dispensing justice that makes *Dirty Harry* look like a pacifist. The sole female character is tied up, raped, and brutalized; the villains are vile, ugly, and stupid; and the hero's sole emotions are anger and joy when a bad guy dies. Pathologically unpleasant and predictable. The story has no connection to the original *Gun Crisis*, although in Japan, the two stories were published together in one volume. ½

GUNDAM THE ORIGIN

Kidô Senshi Gundam the Origin, "Mobile Warrior Gundam: The Origin" (機動戦士ガンダム THE ORIGIN) • Yoshikazu Yasuhiko (story and art), Hajime Yatate & Yoshiyuki Tomino (original story), Kunio Okawara (mechanical design) • Viz (2002–2004) • Kadokawa Shoten (Gundam Ace, 2001–ongoing) • 12 issues, suspended (14+ volumes in Japan, ongoing) • Science Fiction, Mecha, Adventure • 13+ (mild language, violence)

Not so much a retelling of the original *Mobile Suit Gundam* anime series as a fleshed-out reinterpretation by the show's character designer and animation director, who also happens to be a superstar manga artist in his own right. For fans of classic *Gundam*, it really doesn't get any better than this, as the legendary Yasuhiko retraces the journey of surly antihero Amuro Ray and the stray warship *White Base* through the chaos of the One Year War. The characters are expressive and convincing, the action is gritty and physical, and the sci-fi world setting is realized in more concrete detail than the anime ever managed. Although the series is still ongoing in Japan, the U.S. release petered out after twelve issues in a hybrid format resembling a hundred-page comic book, and was never collected into standard small-sized graphic novels. (MS) ★★★★

GUNDAM (OTHER): See *Mobile Suit Gundam*

GUNHED

(ガンヘッド) • Kia Asamiya • Viz (1990–1991) • Kadokawa Shoten (Newtype, 1989) • 1 volume • Science Fiction, Mecha, Action • Unrated/13+ (mild language, violence)

Manga adaptation of the 1989 Japanese live-action movie *Gunhed,* a forgettable attempt at a *Terminator*-style action movie. In the future, a planeload of scavengers lands on a deserted island, which is actually an abandoned robot factory controlled by the evil computer Kyron-5 and its "biodroids." When they are attacked by the island's defenses, their only hope is Gunhed, a faceless, lumbering tank-mecha that talks in baseball analogies and opposes Kyron-5's plans for world domination. Asamiya's early art is as generic and clichéd as the plot. The Viz edition was colorized in an attempt to appeal to American comic readers.   ★½

GUNPARADE MARCH

(ガンパレード・マーチ) • Hiroyuki Sanadura (story and art), Sony Computer Entertainment (original creator) • ADV (2004–2005) • MediaWorks (Dengeki Daioh, 2001–2003) • 3 volumes • Shônen, Science Fiction, Mecha, Action • 16+ (mild language, violence, brief nudity, sexual situations)

Based on the PlayStation game franchise, *Gunparade March* is set in an alternate history where, immediately after World War II, humanity was attacked by alien invaders. By the present day, the world has been fighting the aliens for more than fifty years. The manga starts off as a generic story about a group of teenage pilots battling monsters while trying to deal with their own interpersonal problems. The first volume is full of flat stock characters (the snotty rich girl, the hothead, the sensitive little girl) and juvenile situation humor where boys accidentally see girls naked and then get beaten up. In the later volumes these bland characters begin to show surprising depth and several tragic events make up for the earlier fluff. Despite an overabundance of similar-looking char-

acters and a number of unresolved subplots, it's an enjoyable manga. (MJS)   ★★½

GUNPARADE MARCH: A NEW MARCHING SONG

Dengeki Gunparade March Shin Tanaru, "Electric Shock Gunparade March New Marching Song" (電撃ガンパレード・マーチ〜新たなる) • various artists • Media Blasters (2005) • MediaWorks (2003) • 1 volume • Comedy, Anthology • 13+ (sexual situations)

Anthology comics collection starring the characters from *Gunparade March,* written and illustrated by a variety of artists, including Shizuru Hayashiya, Shinnosuke Mori, and Kaishaku. Brief tributes are drawn by Hiroyuki Utatane, Sakurako Gokurakuin, Shotaro Harada, Miki Miyashita and others. The art is generally very good, including some beautiful color pages at the beginning. However, the story lines are typical *dôjinshi*-style material, ranging from adolescent sexual humor to melodramatic pieces with no resolution. (MJS)   ★½

GUNSLINGER GIRL

Yu Aida • ADV (2003–2005) • MediaWorks (Dengeki Daioh, 2002–ongoing) • 3 volumes, suspended (7+ volumes in Japan, ongoing) • Shônen, Crime, Action • 13+ (language, violence, adult themes)

The Italian government recruits young girls—*very* young girls—with troubled pasts, turning them into brainwashed cyborg assassins. The artwork starts off rough and gradually improves, vaguely resembling Kenichi Sonoda's *Gunsmith Cats* (as much in themes as in style), but more cluttered and awkward. The stories are filled with action and tragic drama, focusing on the conflict between the desires of young girls and their violent, emotionless programming. Although the concept is interesting, the fact that all the girls are largely emotionless prevents the characters from developing. As a result, the most interesting characters are the side characters, who are free to develop and show emotion. Overall, a good read. (MJS)   ★★★

GUNSMITH CATS

(ガンスミスキャッツ) • Kenichi Sonoda • Dark Horse (1995–2007) • Kodansha (Afternoon, 1991–1997) • 9 volumes • Seinen, Crime, Action • 18+ (language, graphic violence, nudity, graphic sex)

Calling Kenichi Sonoda's art anime-like doesn't tell half the story; as an anime character designer, his work on series such as *Bubblegum Crisis* and *Gall Force* helped define the look of 1980s anime. His first major manga, *Gunsmith Cats,* proved that Sonoda is a talented writer as well. In Chicago two women run a gunsmith's shop: Rally, a noble bounty hunter with such good aim she can blow off people's thumbs to disarm them, and Minnie-May, an ex-prostitute explosives expert who's nineteen years old but looks about ten. Like an episodic TV show, the manga has little overarching plot, but it follows the heroes and their friends through cool, complex stories involving bounties, drugs, car chases, and sadistic vendettas. The American setting is shown with loving detail (even the deep-dish pizza), but Sonoda's favorite things about America are cars and guns, on whose technical specs the art and plot linger fetishistically. Also fetishistic are Sonoda's depictions of women. Although the heroines are a fairly strong lot, they're drawn like thin-hipped plastic toys with pubic hair, and some of the plot elements are frankly pedophilic. But the skilled storytelling and action scenes can't be denied, the English rewrite is excellent, and no manga has better car chases. The series was first released in a 9-volume left-to-right edition (1995–2002); the newer 4-volume right-to-left edition, *Gunsmith Cats Omnibus* (2007), collects the same material plus a few extra stories, and undoes some very minor censorship of sexuality.

★★★½

GUNSMITH CATS: BURST

(ガンスミスキャッツバースト) • Kenichi Sonoda • Dark Horse (2007–ongoing) • Kodansha (Afternoon, 2005–ongoing) • 3+ volumes (ongoing) • Seinen, Crime, Action • 18+

Continuation of *Gunsmith Cats.*　　　NR

Satomi Ikezawa's *Guru Guru Pon-chan*

GURU GURU PON-CHAN

Guru Guru Pon-chan, "Round and Round Pon-chan" (ぐるぐるポンちゃん) • Satomi Ikezawa • Del Rey (2005–2007) • Kodansha (Bessatsu Friend, 1997–2000) • 9 volumes • Shôjo, Romantic Comedy, Pet, Drama • 13+ (crude humor, mild language, mild violence, mild sexual situations, partial nudity)

Ponta, a playful Labrador Retriever, falls in love with her owners' teenage neighbor, Mirai. Although wiser dogs tell her, "A love between dogs and humans can never be," she develops the ability to transform into a human girl, and soon, after learning to wear clothes and understand human language (more or less), she follows him to school and innocently declares her love for him. But Mirai, who knows Ponta's secret, is understandably reluctant to become "the pervert who does it with dogs." If you can appreciate a mix of 5 percent bestiality jokes and 95 percent romantic comedy, you can appreciate this delightful story, told mostly from an animal's perspective. ("I don't understand because I'm a dog!" she cries desperately at one point.) Dog owners will recognize authentically canine behavior in Ponta, whose mix of canine loyalty and human love makes for an unusually poignant character. Ikezawa's candy-like art is flawlessly cute, with great drawings of dogs and Ponta's human-dog poses (catching Frisbees, licking faces, hyperactively skipping with glee . . . or, when things turn sad, gnawing at her own hand in depression). Genuinely touching and only slightly disturbing. ★★★★

GUYVER: See *Bio-Booster Armor Guyver*

GYO

Gyo: Ugomeku Fukimi, "Fish: The Wriggling Horror" (ぎょ～うごめく不気味～) • Junji Ito • Viz (2003–2004) • Shogakukan (Big Comic Spirits, 2000–2002) • 2 volumes • Seinen, Horror • Unrated/18+ (violence, nudity)

With a nauseating stench, fish around the world walk out of the ocean on insect-like legs, first frightening a couple on vacation in Okinawa, then invading Japan in a slimy tide of walking sea creatures. Like Ito's immediately previous work *Uzumaki,* but more openly apocalyptic, *Gyo* is based on a quirky premise gradually taken to the point of nightmare. However, *Gyo*'s imagery of stinking, bloated bodies doesn't lend itself to as much variety as the spirals of *Uzumaki,* and by the end of the meandering second volume the reader is left with an impression of mathematical repetition—like a big-budget movie with lots of CGI fish—rather than a buildup to a climax of terror. Volume 2 also includes one excellent short horror story. ★★★

.HACK//LEGEND OF THE TWILIGHT

.hack//Tasogare no Udewa Densetsu, ".hack//Legend of the Twilight Bracelet" (.hack//黄昏の腕輪伝説) • Tatsuya Hamazaki (story), Rei Izumi (art) • Tokyopop (2003–2004) • Kadokawa Shoten (Comptiq, 2002–2004) • 3 volumes • Video Game, Fantasy, Adventure • 13+ (mild language, mild violence, brief partial nudity)

.hack was a three-pronged multimedia attack on the world of *otaku:* a manga, video game, and anime all launched simultaneously. All three were based on the same concept: a pair of twins, Shugo and Rena, go on a quest in a popular online RPG simply known as The World. Whether luck or fate, the twins' experience in The World is anything but ordinary; early into the game, Shugo's character is killed and brought back to life by a mysterious woman who gives him a bracelet with strange powers. From there the plot thickens and the line between reality and the game blurs. While this sounds like a great premise, the actual manga falls short; where there should be mystery and intrigue, there's just poor storytelling compounded by spastic and confusing art. However, the rewriter Jake Forbes has done an outstanding job of incorporating MMORPG lingo into the dialogue. (RB) ★

HAMSTER CLUB

Various artists • ComicsOne (e-book, 2000–2001) • Aoba Shuppan • 2 volumes • Pets • All Ages

You're not going to love this manga if you don't *love* hamsters. Many of these short stories are strictly instructive—facts on how to raise hamsters—while others are anthropomorphized takes on a hamster's life and his saccharine thoughts and feelings toward his owner. The collections feel uneven, and add up to choppy books that can't tell if they want to be an FAQ or a comedic melodrama. Volume 2 is slightly more interesting than the first, as more of the stories are anecdotal. Interestingly, the manga is heavily peppered with product placements, such as recommended hamster wheels, and specific companies and pet stores to patronize. (RS) ★½

HANA-KIMI: FOR YOU IN FULL BLOSSOM

Hanazakari no Kimitachi He, "For You in Full Blossom" (花ざかりの君たちへ) • Hisaya Nakajo • Viz (2004–ongoing) • Hakusensha (Hana to Yume, 1996–2004) • 23 volumes • Shôjo, Romantic Comedy • 16+ (language, brief nudity, sexual situations)

Mizuki Ashiya, a Japanese American girl, disguises herself as a boy so she can transfer to a Japanese all-boys school and be with her favorite athlete, rising high-jump star Izumi Sano. Sano quickly realizes that his new roommate is a girl, but he is too shy and flustered to reveal that he knows her secret. With its dreamy artwork (in later volumes), its unspoken but at times jealous crushes, and its unrealistically idealized male behavior, *Hana-Kimi* uses many of the same elements that make *yaoi* manga so popular. (Volume 14 even contains a genuine *yaoi* story, involving the one out-of-the-closet gay character in the series.) The far-from-subtle writing is at its best when it plays with opposing stereotypes: male-female, straight-gay, America-Japan. However, the plot is less focused on self-identity or romance (even platonic-sleeping-in-the-same-bed romance) than on the wacky hijinks of life in a boy's dorm: sports meets, school dances, ghost stories. To like *Hana-Kimi,* you have to like the enormous supporting cast, who serve to act funny and kill time while the main characters' relationship moves at a snail's pace. Every accidental touch, every casual comment sends Mizuki's and Sano's minds whirling, but the relationship is essentially static and the side stories are of varying quality. Nakajo's art (and writing, to a lesser extent) improves as the series goes on, but in the end, it has more hot guys than plot. (AT) ★★

HANAUKYO MAID TEAM

Hanaukyo Maid Tai, "Hanaukyo Maid Squad/ Corps" (花右京メイド隊) • Morishige • Studio Iron-cat (2003) • Akita Shoten (Monthly Shônen Champion, 1999–2006) • 3 volumes, suspended (14 volumes in Japan) • Shônen, Romantic Comedy • Unrated/16+ (crude humor, comic violence, nudity, frequent sexual situations)

Tarou Hanaukyo, a typical nebbish, becomes the heir of his insanely wealthy grandfather and must move into the family mansion inhabited by hundreds of identical maids, who bathe him, rub their breasts in his face, and wait on him hand and foot. This crude, grotesquely drawn comedy can think of nothing to do with the maid-manga premise other than sheer numerical overkill. The

few maids with distinct personalities and appearances, who guard the house with sci-fi technology, are boring stereotypes. ½

HANDS OFF!

Sono Te wo Dokero, "Remove Your Hands!" (その手をどけろ) • Kasane Katsumoto • Tokyopop (2004–2006) • Kadokawa Shoten (Asuka, 1998–2001) • 8 volumes • Shôjo, Psychic, Mystery • 13+ (language, violence, sexual situations)

Three male students team up to solve crimes with their psychic powers and street smarts: Yuuto, a tall, sociable guy who can see auras; Kotarou, who has no powers and is sometimes mistaken for a girl, much to his irritation; and Tatsuki, Kotarou's standoffish cousin, who dislikes touching people because it triggers his power to see into the past. On cases that take them into the seedy underbelly of Tokyo, they help protect students who are drifting into a bad scene: potential suicides, victims of abuse, and so on. Despite the playful title and the "comedy" label on the back cover of the English edition, *Hands Off!* is a mostly dramatic series, which takes its heavy subject matter at face value. Humor is saved for the funny four-panel strips in the back of the book and the slightest *bishônen* teases about how much the heroes like one another. The English dialogue is good, and the plots are clever and interesting. ★★★

HANSEL & GRETEL: See *Junko Mizuno's Hansel and Gretel*

HAPPY HUSTLE HIGH

H³ School! (H³スクール!) • Rie Takada • Viz (2005–2006) • Shogakukan (Shôjo Comic, 2003–2005) • 5 volumes • Shôjo, Romantic Comedy • 16+ (mild language, brief crude humor, sexual situations)

When her girls' school merges with a boys' school and becomes coed, tomboyish Hanabi becomes the only girl on the new student council, and meets Yasuaki, a surfer who's shy around women. (When we see the world from Yasuaki's point of view, all the girls are little clucking chicks.) Of course, the first order of business is to get

Harlequin Magazine, from the publishers of the Harlequin line of romance novels.

rid of the new school's no-dating rule! Similar in spirit to an American teen movie, *Happy Hustle High* is a sweet, slapstick series with a great heroine: rowdy, frizzy-haired Hanabi. The plot is fast-paced, the characters are extroverted, and the art is pleasantly cartoony. (In Takada's world, guys and girls look like different species: the girls are all short, cute, and funny-faced, and the guys are all tall, slim, and hot.) ★★★½

HAPPY LESSON: MAMA TEACHER IS WONDERFUL!

Happy Lesson: Mama Sensei wa Saikô!, "Happy Lesson: Mama Teacher Is Wonderful!" (ハッピー ☆レッスン・ママ先生は最高!) • Shinnosuke Mori (art), Mutsumi Sasaki (story) • ADV (2004) • MediaWorks (Dengeki Daioh, 2003) • 1 volume, suspended (2 volumes in Japan) • Shônen, Video Game, Romantic Comedy • 18+ (sexual situations)

Wretched spin-off of the equally wretched *Happy Lesson* Dreamcast simulation game, in which you (the player) are home-schooled by five good-looking female teachers who all want to be your surrogate mother. Despite the 18+ rating, the level of sexual teasing is fairly light. The art is a crude *Love Hina* imitation. 0 Stars

HAPPY MANIA

(ハッピー・マニア) • Moyoco Anno • Tokyopop (2003–2004) • Shodensha (Feel Young, 1995–2001) • 11 volumes • Jôsei, Romantic Comedy • 18+ (language, nudity, graphic sex)

"There aren't any good guys out there!" "Is this what happiness is?" Shigeta, the never-satisfied twenty-four-year-old protagonist of *Happy Mania,* is one of the most original characters in translated manga, despite (or because of) the fact that her personality reads like an exaggeration of negative traits from women's magazines and TV shows. Selfish and unfaithful, she flits from goal to goal and man to man, frequently jobless, obsessed with her age, her future, boyfriends, and marriage. When she *does* meet guys (which is often), they often suck in bed or have other hidden flaws . . . but she can't bring herself to choose Takahashi, the seemingly perfect guy who honestly loves her. Of course, *Happy Mania* is a comedy, told with self-referential humor and manic melodrama. (At one point, a nude Shigeta turns to the camera and asks the readers for advice, then cheerfully ignores it.) The plot is meandering in the extreme (unwanted characters frequently go on long journeys for the convenience of the story), and the English rewrite is sometimes awkward, but the story is funny and the art is sexy, though it takes a few volumes to develop. ★★★★

HARLEM BEAT

(ハーレム・ビート) • Yuriko Nishiyama • Tokyopop (1998–2007) • Kodansha (Weekly Shônen Magazine, 1994–2000) • 27 volumes (29 volumes in Japan) • Shônen, Sports • Unrated/13+ (language, mild violence, mild sexual situations, brief partial nudity)

One of the first sports manga published in America, *Harlem Beat* is a winner, with versatile artwork and a team of strong characters. Nat Torres (Narase Tooru in the original Japanese) is an insecure benchwarmer on his high school basketball team, until he discovers three-on-three "street hoops" and plays in a vacant lot with tough guys, cool chicks, and criminals. (In case you're wondering, it's set in Japan, not Harlem.) The art is sometimes crowded, but Nishiyama has the requisite skill to draw bodies in motion, as well as very cute, very distinctive stick-figure *chibi* caricatures. Our hero encounters countless friends and foes (including several strong female characters); the relatively restrained *shônen* manga training-and-fighting elements reach their entertaining peak when Torres consults a basketball-playing hairstylist to learn the "legendary invincible lay-up," his secret weapon. The 29-volume *Harlem Beat* series was published in America as two separate series, *Harlem Beat* (volumes 1–9) and *Rebound* (volumes 12–29). Tokyopop skipped volumes 10 and 11 of *Harlem Beat* entirely, summarizing them in a one-page "epilogue" before starting *Rebound* with volume 12. In *Rebound,* the characters fly to Sapporo for a national basketball tournament, and the end of the series brings the core cast of characters back where they began—three-on-three street hoops—for an admittedly over-the-top story about an evil basketball cartel. Balancing character interaction with action, downtime with basketball, and lots of good-looking characters of both sexes, Nishiyama's basketball manga are done with such enthusiasm and high spirits that the reader is carried along. A single nude scene is censored in the English edition of *Harlem Beat; Rebound* has a few brief scenes of partial nudity starting in volume 9.

★★★½

HARLEQUIN GINGER BLOSSOM: See *Harlem Pink: The Bachelor Prince, Harlequin Pink: A Girl in a Million, Harlequin Pink: Idol Dreams, Harlequin Violet: Blind Date, Harlequin Violet: Holding on to Alex,* and *Harlequin Violet: Response*

Since 1998 Harlequin Enterprises, the publishers of the Harlequin line of romance novels, has licensed *shôjo*-style manga adaptations of their books, published in Japan by Ohzora Shuppan. In 2005, Harlequin began to translate the manga adaptations back into English for American audiences; first published and distributed by Dark Horse, later under their own imprint. The titles are divided into two categories by age group: Harlequin Pink titles contain nothing more explicit than kisses and embraces; titles in the short-lived Harlequin Violet line all have sex scenes, although the sex is discreet and no actual nudity is visible.

HARLEQUIN PINK: THE BACHELOR PRINCE

Cinderalla de naru Yoru, "Cinderella for a Night" (シンデレラになる夜) • Debbie Macomber (story), Misao Hoshiai (art) • Dark Horse/Harlequin Enterprises (2006) • Ohzora Shuppan (2001) • 1 volume • Shôjo, Romance • Unrated/13+ (extremely mild sexual situations)

Prince Stefano of San Llorenzo is forced to seek a rich bride to provide money to his impoverished country. On a date auction arranged by the "romance novel fan club of Seattle" (which, amusingly, consists mostly of gossipy old ladies), he accidentally misses the intended bachelorette and ends up on a date with an ordinary middle-class girl who runs a coffee shop. Your basic Cinderella story, *The Bachelor Prince* is entertainingly lighthearted: Stefano dresses up as various movie stars to sneak away from his chaperones, there's lots of light comedy, and the sound effect for the gleaming sun reads, simply, "SUN!" Based on a 1994 novel by Debbie Macomber.   ★★

HARLEQUIN PINK: A GIRL IN A MILLION

Itsuka Hanayome Ni, "Someday a Bride" (いつか 花嫁に) • Betty Neels (story), Kako Itoh (art) • Dark Horse/Harlequin Enterprises (2005) • Ohzora Shuppan (2003) • 1 volume • Shôjo, Romance • Unrated/13+ (extremely mild sexual situations)

Crudely drawn Harlequin manga involving a romance between a young British nurse and a handsome, mature Dutch doctor with a past. The art, which looks intended for younger readers, is best when it's cute and silly, but most of the time, Dr. Marius van Houben's warm smile looks merely dopey. Based on a 1993 novel by Betty Neels. ★

HARLEQUIN PINK: IDOL DREAMS

Ritz de Yûshoku, "Dinner at the Ritz" (リッツで夕食) • Charlotte Lamb (story), Yoko Hanabusa (art) • Dark Horse/Harlequin Enterprises (2006) • Ohzora Shuppan (1998) • 1 volume • Shôjo, Romance • Unrated/13+ (extremely mild sexual situations)

The most archetypal, boring Harlequin romance plot imaginable. Twenty-two-year-old Quincy, who lives with her parents, finds herself randomly selected for a date with movie star Joe Ardness. In mere hours she finds herself in London, where she is wined and dined and taken to a romantic evening, while she frets and worries that the date is just a publicity stunt and that Joe only wants her for a one-night stand. The polished art has lots of background detail, but the scenery doesn't make up for the wimpy heroine and the predictable story. Considering that it's a black-and-white comic, there's lots of dialogue about people's eye color: "Your green eyes look angry right now." "Are you sure you don't like me? Your green eyes seem to be telling a different story." Based on a 1985 novel by Charlotte Lamb. ★

HARLEQUIN VIOLET: BLIND DATE

Blind Date (ブラインド・デート) • Emma Darcy (story), Mihoko Hirose (art) • Dark Horse/Harlequin Enterprises (2006) • Ohzora Shuppan (2003) • 1 volume • Jôsei, Romance • 16+ (sex)

Blind Date is unusual in that it addresses the traditional gender roles of Harlequin novels directly (and ultimately finds nothing wrong with them, of course). Peggy, an inexperienced, feminist college student with a sarcastic tongue, finds herself on a "blind date" TV show and gets hooked up with pop star John Gale. One of the funnier Harlequin manga (at least at the beginning), it also has clear, straightforward artwork with minimal *shôjo* impressionistic effects. Based on a 1986 novel by Emma Darcy. ★★

HARLEQUIN VIOLET: HOLDING ON TO ALEX

Eien no Koi no Mahô, "Magic of Eternal Love" (永遠の恋の魔法) • Margaret Way (story), Misao Hoshiai (art) • Dark Horse/Harlequin Enterprises (2006) • Ohzora Shuppan (2002) • 1 volume • Jôsei, Romance • 16+ (sex)

"The woman I love is married to her dancing." After tearing a ligament, ballerina Alex returns home to her parents' ranch in the Australian outback, where she reencounters the boy she left behind to pursue her career. Will she give up her dancing, and will her lost love give up his new girlfriend to be with her? This Harlequin manga adaptation has awkward art, overindulging in screentone, and the Australian setting is poorly handled—it comes off as a sort of old-South plantation, complete with an Aboriginal housekeeper. Based on a 1997 novel by Margaret Way. ★

HARLEQUIN VIOLET: RESPONSE

Kaku no Rakuen, "The Imaginary Garden" (架空の楽園) • Penny Jordan (story), Takako Hashimoto (art) • Dark Horse/Harlequin Enterprises (2005) • Ohzora Shuppan (1999) • 1 volume • Jôsei, Romance • 16+ (sex)

Twenty-something Sienna is hired as a personal secretary to Alexis Stefanides, a handsome, arrogant Greek multimillionaire who seduces her for impure reasons (when they sleep together, he symbolically crushes a rose in his fist). After an accident, Sienna gets amnesia; when she regains her memories, she finds herself married to Alexis, and her feelings of betrayal and damaged pride manifest themselves in torrid sex. The closest thing to a nonconsensual Harlequin manga title, *Response*'s best point is the purple descriptions of sex scenes. ("Once I gave my quivering body to his touch, the pleasures intensified.") The art is done in an effective, mature *jôsei* manga style. Based on a 1984 novel by Penny Jordan. ★★

HAUNTED HOUSE: See *Mitsukazu Mihara: Haunted House*

HAYATE THE COMBAT BUTLER

Hayate no Gotoku!, "Like Hayate!" (ハヤテのごとく！ (Hayate the Combat Butler)) • Kenjiro Hata • Viz (2006–ongoing) • Shogakukan (Weekly Shônen Sunday, 2004–ongoing) • 11+ volumes (ongoing) • Shônen, Otaku, Comedy • 16+ (mild language, mild sexual situations)

The next evolution of *Weekly Shônen Sunday*'s hip, nerdy, anime-style comedies, *Hayate the Combat Butler* makes up in writing for what it lacks in art. (Among other things, it's a parody of the universally wretched maid-girl sex-fantasy manga.) While fleeing the *yakuza* (to whom his deadbeat parents sold his internal organs), sixteen-year-old Hayate gets a job as the butler of Nagi Sanzenin, an incredibly rich thirteen-year-old girl who has a crush on him and who likes to draw manga. For Hayate's part, he only has eyes for Maria, the head maid. It's clear from the beginning that none of this is to be taken seriously; Hayate's jobs as butler include fighting a giant talking tiger and assorted robots (although this is not a fighting manga), and at times he gets mad at the narrator, who disses him constantly. (He really doesn't deserve it, either; unlike most *shônen* romantic comedy leads, he's merely a victim of constant bad luck, not a panty-peeking lech or a wimpy loser.) The chapters are jam-packed with dialogue-driven humor, sitcom situations, and *otaku* in-jokes (referring to anime as well as to even more obscure subjects such as dating simulation games), but where other manga might handle this material with breathless craziness, Hata approaches it with a calm, tasteful, self-aware mood. Perhaps so as not to add to the visual density of the manga, the art is extremely flat and dull: outline drawings of anime-style figures with blue and pink spiky hair, who don't come alive except on the color cover illustrations, and even then look like horrible anime cel art. Is it intentional that a self-referential nerd manga should be drawn with the most archetypally nerdy, ge-neric art imaginable? Much better than it looks. ★★★

HEARTBROKEN ANGELS

Itadarake no Tenshitachi, "Wounded Angels" (傷だらけの天使たち) • Masahiko Kikuni • Viz (1999–2001) • Shogakukan (Young Sunday, 1988–1991) • 2 volumes, suspended (3 volumes in Japan) • Seinen, Four-Panel Comedy • 18+ (crude humor, language, violence, nudity, sex)

Four-panel adult gag manga with a few repeating characters (the secretly perverted teenage lovers; the manga artist with the small penis; the pathetically poor family). The humor is mostly at the elementary school level, focused on poop and kinky sex, but there are a few unexpected anti-punch lines; a certain intelligence occasionally creeps through beneath the trashiness. Many of the strips make fun of TV, manga, and movie clichés, while others are mock-melodramatic and end with characters weeping sarcastic tears of joy. The English edition falls short of the original Japanese: many strips are missing, and the Japanese version was originally printed in two colors, so the black-and-white English edition looks dark and muddy. ★★½

HEAT GUY J

(ヒートガイジェイ) • Kazuki Akane & Satelight (original story), Nobuteru Yuki (character design), Chiaki Ogishima (story and art) • Tokyopop (2005) • Kodansha (Magazine Z, 2002–2003) • 1 volume • Shônen, Science Fiction, Action • 13+ (violence, sexual situations)

Adaptation of the anime series. Cool and cocky heartthrob Daisuke and his undercover android partner Heat Guy J work as crime fighters in the city of Jewde. The art and shading are crisp and well-done, and the anime and manga look similar; however, in the anime Daisuke has more street cred and a gaggle of lovesick prostitutes to follow him around, while in the manga he is clearly moonstruck for Antonia, the curvy scientist who designed J in the image of her father.

Neither variation makes him a sympathetic character. A faithful adaptation of screen to script, down to individual lines of dialogue. (KT) ★★

HEAVEN!!

Shizuru Seino • Tokyopop (2007–2008) • Kodansha (Bessatsu Friend, 2003–2004) • 3 volumes • Shôjo, Romantic Comedy • 13+

A romantic comedy by the creator of *Girl Got Game.* Our heroine Rinne sees (and exorcises) dead people, and when a delinquent classmate ends up in a coma after saving her life, she does her best to stop the local ghosts from possessing his vacated body. But her efforts are for naught as an unwelcome intruder ends up seizing control of the comatose punk's body, leaving the do-gooding ne'er-do-well trapped in the body of a cute and very pink stuffed monkey. Like they say, no good deed goes unpunished. (MS) NR

HEAVY METAL WARRIOR XENON

Jûki Kohei Xenon, "Heavy Machine Gun Armed Warrior Xenon" (重機甲兵ゼノン) • Masaomi Kanzaki • Viz (1987–1992) • Shogakukan (Shônen Big Comic, 1986–1987) • 4 volumes • Shônen, Science Fiction, Action • Unrated/13+ (mild language, graphic violence, partial nudity)

After he is turned into a cyborg by the Bloody Sea, an all-powerful weapons developer, teenage Asuka Kano gathers a group of allies and vows revenge. (When cybered out and wearing his helmet, Asuka resembles a *tokusatsu* action hero, and his enemies are mostly square-jawed suits and goons with filed teeth.) With angst-ridden superhumans fighting the powers that made them, *Xenon*'s plot is similar to *Arms*—or more accurately, they both walk the well-trodden path of countless action movies, anime, and superhero comics. Car chases and military scenes abound, but Kanzaki's stiff art probably didn't look original even in 1986. The series was canceled abruptly in Japan; a continuation, begun in 2006 in Tokuma Shoten's *Comic Ryu,* has not been translated. ★½

HE IS MY MASTER

Kore ga Watashi no Goshujin-sama, "He Is My Master" (これが私の御主人様) • Mattsuu (story), Asu Tsubaki (art) • Seven Seas Entertainment (2007–ongoing) • Square Enix (Gangan Powered, 2002–ongoing) • 5+ volumes (ongoing) • Otaku, Romantic Comedy • 16+

Hot girls end up working as maids for a spoiled, lecherous, and voyeuristic fourteen-year-old millionaire orphan. Tons of fan-service, guns, and general lunacy. NR

HELL BABY

Kyôfu o Jigoku Shôjo, "Terror [of the] Hell Girl" (恐怖!地獄少女) • Hideshi Hino • Blast Books (1995) • Kôsaidô (1982) • 1 volume • Horror • Unrated/16+ (graphic violence)

A classic Hideshi Hino story of a monstrous outsider, *Hell Baby* is a powerful mixture of horror, sweetness, and awe. Twin girls are born, one normal, one horribly deformed. The deformed baby is discarded in a garbage dump, where it dies and is resurrected as a blood-drinking cannibal, who feeds on small animals until strange urges take her to the city and her destiny. As shown by evocative chapter titles such as "The World's Graveyard" and "Like the Worms That Crawl the Earth," the story has a poetic tone, and the cartoony yet gruesome Hell Baby is a truly sympathetic, tragic figure. Despite the similar Japanese title, it has no relation to the anime and manga series *Jigoku Shôjo* ("Hell Girl"). ★★★½

HELLHOUNDS: PANZER COPS

Kenrô Densetsu, "Dog-Wolf Legend" (犬狼伝説) • Mamoru Oshii (story), Kamui Fujiwara & Studio 2B (art) • Dark Horse (1994) • Nihon Shuppansha (Amazing Comics/Combat Comic, 1988–1990) • 1 volume • Science Fiction, Crime, Political Drama • Unrated/13+ (violence)

Overly ambitious sci-fi tale of an alternative Japan whose history took a different path after World War II. The "Hellhounds" of the title are the Capital Police Cerberus Teams, or the Panzers, armored storm troopers who come into conflict with other police units in tussles over authority. An interesting premise that never really jells into an interesting comic, *Hellhounds* is talky and ultimately pointless, with too many scenes of politicians arguing in boardrooms and individual Panzer Cops expressing their ennui; it ultimately reads like a dry run for ideas later explored in Oshii's script for the anime *Jin-Roh*. The comic itself does little to explain its universe: most information is provided in dense text that makes the opening crawl from *Star Wars: Episode 1* look like an advertising jingle. The design of the Panzer Cops, with their gas-mask faces and World War II–style helmets over Kevlar SWAT gear, and the hijacking plot of the final two issues, are the best the series has to offer. Kamui Fujiwara's art bears a vague resemblance to that of Katsuhiro Otomo (*Akira*), but without Otomo's touch for detail or cinematic storytelling. (JD) ★★

Kohta Hirano's *Hellsing*

HELLSING

(ヘルシング)・ Kohta Hirano ・ Dark Horse (2003–ongoing) ・ Shônen Gahosha (Young King Ours, 1998–ongoing) ・ 8+ volumes (ongoing) ・ Seinen, Military, Horror, Action ・ 13+/16+ (language, extreme graphic violence, mild sexual situations)

Although the *Hellsing* anime TV series (but not the later OAV series) took the safe route, the original *Hellsing* manga is savage, gleefully offensive pulp horror. Alucard, a vampire with seemingly limitless powers, and his protegée Seras Victoria (a former female police officer), are agents of Hellsing, an organization founded to protect Britain from bloodsuckers. This conventional premise quickly falls apart into apocalyptic chaos: a global war between British Protestants, an insanely fundamentalist Catholic Church (complete with inquisitors and brainwashed killer nuns), and legions of Nazi vampires who suddenly descend upon the civilized world, slaughtering everyone. Although the story is technically sex-free, the phrase "pornography of violence" doesn't begin to describe the fang-in-neck and gun-in-mouth action, lovingly drawn with gangly black silhouettes and rapacious, ghoulish faces. The story slows to a crawl as it goes on, with page after page of living corpses dismembering civilians, but this only cements *Hellsing*'s status as a masterpiece of fetishistic violence on a grand scale. ★★★½

HERE IS GREENWOOD

Koko wa Greenwood, "Here Is Greenwood" (ここはグリーン・ウッド) ・ Yukie Nasu ・ Viz (2004–2006) ・ Hakusensha (Hana to Yume, 1986–1991) ・ 9 volumes ・ Shôjo, Comedy ・ 16+ (language, sexual situations)

Kazuya, a teenage boy with an unrequited crush on his older brother's wife, nurses his sorrows by moving out of his brother's house and going to Greenwood, a boys' boarding school. There he meets Shun (his suspiciously female-looking roommate), Shinobu, and Mitsuru (*bishônen* upperclassmen who love to tease the freshmen), and various other quirky characters: religious

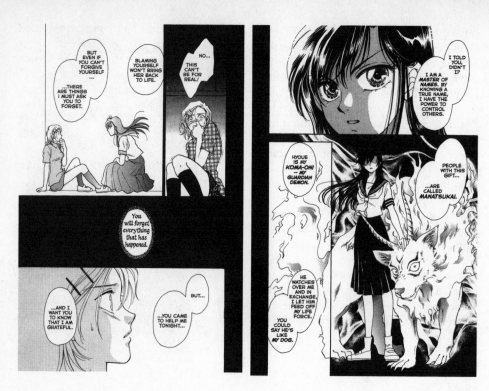

Mick Takeuchi's *Her Majesty's Dog*

proselytizers, gay students, and so on. Like *Hana-Kimi,* which it in many ways resembles, the purpose is not to tell a story so much as to develop an ensemble cast, and many of the chapters are one-shot parodies transplanting the characters to different genres (historical Japan, science fiction, fantasy, RPGs, etc.). The occasional alien or ghost adds to the sense of whimsy, and the humor is often self-referential, with the characters complaining about or talking to the artist ("I *knew* Yukie Nasu couldn't write a story without *some* kind of bizarre character coming to life!"). Although the character relationships are more interesting than *Hana-Kimi,* there is even less payoff and plot, which together with the dense text and flat 1980s artwork makes *Here Is Greenwood* an acquired taste. ★★★

HER MAJESTY'S DOG

Joôsama no Inu, "The Queen's Dog" (女王様の犬) • Mick Takeuchi • Go! Comi (2005–ongoing) • Akita

Shoten (Princess Gold, 2000–2006) • 11 volumes • Shôjo, Occult, Romantic Comedy, Action • 16+ (mild language, violence)

Since they kiss casually, their high school classmates think that Amane and Hyoue are lovers . . . but the truth is far stranger. Dark-haired, trusting Amane was raised in a remote Japanese village as a *manatsukai,* one who can cast magic with the power of words and names; handsome Hyoue is her obedient guardian demon, who kisses her for the power to transform into a horned dog-monster. Forced to keep their powers secret from normal humans, they deal with ghosts and rival animal demons . . . as well as romantic rivals who sense that Hyoue's unexpressed feelings for Amane are more than those of a pet for his master. *Her Majesty's Dog* successfully combines "monster of the week" action-horror with Rumiko Takahashi–esque relationship comedy. The art is in a generic but friendly anime style, occasionally venturing into the deep black areas and creepy images of a horror manga; in either case, the character relationships are strong. Anti-bullying and self-esteem themes mark it as a title for younger teenagers. ★★★

HIBIKI'S MAGIC

Hibiki no Mahô, "Hibiki's Magic" (ヒビキのマホウ) • Jun Maeda (story), Rei Idumi (art) • Tokyopop (2007–ongoing) • Kadokawa Shoten (Monthly Shônen Ace/Comp Ace, 2004–ongoing) • 2+ volumes (ongoing) • Shônen, Fantasy, Drama • 13+

The adventures of an apprentice magician in a world where science and magic coexist. Our heroine Hibiki is off to a poor start at magic school, since pretty much the only thing she's good at is brewing a tasty pot of tea. From the artist of the *.hack* manga and the scenario writer of the adventure games *Air* and *Clannad*. (MS) NR

HIGH SCHOOL AGENT

(ハイスクールAGENT) • Hitoshi Tanimura • Sun Comic Publishing (1992) • Scholar Publishing (Comic Burger, 1987–1988) • 4 issues, suspended (2 volumes in Japan) • Action • 16+ (language, violence, sexual situations)

Incredibly awful, possibly tongue-in-cheek manga involving a high school student who lives a double life as a secret agent: he goes to New York to blow things up, scuba-dives to retrieve gold bullion from a sunken U-boat, fights assassins, and so on. The art is weak and the stories are incomprehensible; at one point, the hero's companion is randomly molested by Nazi ghosts, although the scene is crudely censored in the English edition. 0 Stars

HIGH SCHOOL GIRLS

Joshi Kôsei, "High School Girls" (女子高生) • Towa Oshima • ComicsOne/DrMaster (2004–2005) • Futabasha (Manga Action/Comic High!, 2001–ongoing) • 8+ volumes (ongoing) • Comedy • 16+ (language, crude humor, nudity, sexual situations)

Crass, occasionally funny comedy series involving a group of friends at an all-girls high

school. Created by a woman for an audience of teenage boys, and apparently based on personal experience, *High School Girls* takes a tone of revealing "the shocking truth," with plenty of down-and-dirty information on feminine hygiene, social cliques (think of the movie *Mean Girls*), and the fact that women do not necessarily walk around naked when changing in the locker room. (De-glamorization doesn't mean de-fetishization, though, and there's also lots of sweaty panty shots.) The episodic stories drift between anime clichés and humorously recognizable high school behavior; the characters exchange inaccurate information about sex, deal with obnoxious teachers and embarrassing parents, and torment the one girl who has a boyfriend. After the temporary collapse of *Manga Action* magazine in 2004, the series was continued as *Joshi Kôsei—Baka Gundan* ("Girls' High School Students: Idiot Squad") in the magazine *Comic High!* (slogan: "Girlish comics for boys and girls). The English edition merges both versions under the same name. ★★½

HIKARU NO GO

Hikaru no Go, "Hikaru's Go" (ヒカルの碁) • Yumi Hotta (story), Takeshi Obata (art), Yukari Umezawa (Go consultant) • Viz (2003–ongoing) • Shueisha (Weekly Shônen Jump, 1998–2003) • 23 volumes • Shônen, Drama • All Ages

Hikaru, an elementary school student, is possessed by Sai, the so-handsome-he-looks-feminine ghost of a champion Go player from Japan's Heian era (794–1185). Driven by Sai's unfulfilled cravings, Hikaru grudgingly lets the ghost play a few games through his body, in the process beating Akira, an aspiring Go player of Hikaru's age, who is seriously rattled by the experience. But soon Hikaru develops his own interest in Go and tries to play the game by himself, joining a school club, meeting other players, and painstakingly developing his skills. Produced with the aid of the Japan Go Association, *Hikaru no Go* was a resounding success, reviving interest in the game among young people in Japan and elsewhere. The premise sounds like *Yu-Gi-Oh!* (ordinary boy possessed by game master), but this is not a manga of vicarious victory; Sai soon stops playing and settles into a role as Hikaru's trainer as well as the unattainable ideal toward which Akira strives. (The supernatural element is almost negligible, but is expertly handled on the rare occasions when it intrudes into the story.) As the manga is written for Go newbies, prior Go experience is not required; the story focuses not on specific strategies but on the psychological aspects. Nor is this a typical exaggerated manga where huge screaming crowds watch life-or-death Go matches in huge arenas. Instead, it's a realistic portrayal of life and ambition, following its characters as they grow from elementary school to near adulthood, with a rich cast of all ages and nationalities. Fascinating to read, dramatic without any violence or sexuality, this is one of the few all-ages manga that can truly be enjoyed by all ages (although one underage character's smoking habit is removed in the English edition). ★★★★

HINADORI GIRL

Hinadori Girl, "Fledgling Girl" (ひなどりGIRL) • Mari Matsuzawa • DrMaster (2005–2006) • MediaWorks (Dengeki Gao!, 2003–2005) • 3 volumes • Shônen, Moe, Romantic Comedy • 13+ (partial nudity, mild sexual situations)

In 2055 Japan (which looks just like the modern day), a brother and sister receive a gift from their scientist father: Support Robot Sally No. 1, a mute little girl-android who hugs things, cleans the house, and occasionally gets in trouble. Teenage Akira, a science nerd, is happy to act as a surrogate parent to the android, but Yoshiki, his little sister, is jealous of the affection he shows to it. With its platonic love triangle between a boy, his little sister, and an apparently prepubescent robot, *Hinadori Girl* is essentially a *moe* title, platonic but with enough suggestions of impure relationships to get the reader's imagination going. The series is predictable and cheesy, with generic art. ★½

Despite being numbered, these fourteen collections of Hideshi Hino horror stories are unrelated and can be read in any order (except for the two-volume *Oninbo and the Bugs from Hell* and *The Collection*). Volumes 15 (*The Experiment*) and 16 (*Who's That Girl?*) were announced but never released in English by DH Publishing.

HINO HORROR, VOL. 1: THE RED SNAKE

Akai Hebi, "Red Snake" (赤い蛇) • Hideshi Hino • DH Publishing (2004) • Hibari Shobo (1985) • 1 volume • Horror • Unrated/16+ (language, graphic violence, sexual situations)

One of Hino's best horror manga, this is a surreal nightmare seen from a child's-eye view. The nameless protagonist (one of Hino's archetypal bug-eyed, silent, traumatized children) dwells with his family in a dark house deep in the forest, in which he has spent all his life. His family is insane, sometimes comically so—his grandmother thinks she's a chicken—but the true horror doesn't begin until the hero goes into the house's forbidden rooms and unleashes the red snake, a demonic monster from a place "more wicked than hell itself." The claustrophobic setting and cartoony characters work well together, like inmates in an asylum, and the lurid and grotesque situations are as illogical as a dream. ★★★½

HINO HORROR, VOL. 2: THE BUG BOY

Dokumushi Kozô, "Poisonous Insect Boy" (毒虫小僧) • Hideshi Hino • DH Publishing (2004) • Hibari Shobo (1975) • 1 volume • Horror • Unrated/13+ (language, violence)

Sanpei, a lonely boy who loves animals, is bitten by a strange red bug and disgustingly transforms into a giant, speechless caterpillar. The plot was reportedly inspired by *The Metamorphosis;* Sanpei's family is revolted by their mutated son and drives him away, at which point the story diverges from Kafka and Sanpei becomes a vengeful monster who emerges from his lair in the sewer to eat people, thinking, "Die, you stupid humans!" The art is crude, but *The Bug Boy* is a sweet, sad, well-executed "sympathetic monster" story for children, aside from a little too much swearing. The scenes of the cute bug boy playing happily on piles of rotting corpses are priceless. ★★★½

HINO HORROR, VOLS. 3–4: ONINBO AND THE BUGS FROM HELL

Jigoku Mushi wo Kû! Oninbo, "Eat the Hell Bugs! Oninbo" (地獄虫を食う!鬼んぼ) • Hideshi Hino • DH Publishing (2004) • Rippu Shobo (1987–1988) • 2 volumes • Horror • Unrated/16+ (language, violence, cruelty to animals)

Oninbo, a pudgy kid with snot perpetually dripping out of his left nostril, is actually a demon, who feeds upon "bugs from hell" that live inside human souls. Eating the bugs has the effect of an exorcism, freeing the humans from terrible hallucinations, but Oninbo himself just wants food. He also clashes with rival demon-kids such as Mamushinbo, whose head splits open, unleashing swarms of flesh-eating caterpillars. *Oninbo and the Bugs from Hell* combines gross-out horror and goofy children's manga; Oninbo and his fellow demons look and act like Garbage Pail Kids or Campbell's Soup characters, much too malformed to be cute. The monsters are random masses of worms, snakes, tentacles, and swollen eyes. Ludicrous and formulaic but amusing. ★★½

HINO HORROR, VOL. 5: LIVING CORPSE

Shiniku no Otoko, "Carrion Man/Man of Dead Flesh" (死肉の男) • Hideshi Hino • DH Publishing (2004) • Hibari Shobo (1986) • 1 volume • Horror • Unrated/13+ (violence)

Simple, gruesome, but sincerely touching, *Living Corpse* starts out like an old *Tales from the Crypt* comic; the amnesiac protagonist staggers through the streets of an unknown town until he sees his reflection in the mirror and realizes he's dead. From there, things progress with surprising logic; he's arrested by cops and sent to jail, then a hospital, where scientists subject him to painful experiments and give him fake hands and a mask. Eventually, he escapes the laboratory and goes searching for his wife and son. An afterword by Hino, explaining how he wrote it in a state of severe depression, gives the story extra poignancy. ★★★

HINO HORROR, VOL. 6: BLACK CAT

Kuro Neko no Me ga Yami Ni, "The Black Cat's Eyes/Pupils in the Darkness" (黒猫の眼が闇に) • Hideshi Hino • DH Publishing (2004) • Rippu Shobo (1979) • 1 volume • Horror • Unrated/16+ (language, violence)

A black cat, who moves from owner to owner, is the narrator/observer of three (mostly) nonsupernatural tales of human misery. A failed circus clown becomes obsessed with a ventriloquist's dummy; an elderly couple abuses each other bitterly; and a boy takes revenge on his enemies with his vicious dog. (Wouldn't the dog go after the cat, though?) Hino's art is not at the level of his best works (*The Red Snake, Hell Baby, Panorama of Hell*) but the simple stories are decently done and almost gore-free. ★★

HINO HORROR, VOLS. 7–8: THE COLLECTION

M Collection (Mコレクション) • Hideshi Hino • DH Publishing (2004) • Bunkasha (1996) • 2 volumes • Horror • Unrated/16+ (mild language, graphic violence, nudity)

The story of an evil horror manga artist and his deranged family, *The Collection* shamelessly reuses images, characters, and whole story lines from Hino's superior horror manga *The Red Snake* and *Panorama of Hell*. The narrator, one of Hino's many alter egos, tells the story of his childhood in a bleak urban-industrial environment. As his family descends into madness, the narrator witnesses strange and creepy phenomena and is eventually possessed by an evil force that causes him to torture small animals to death and draw horror manga. An unsatisfying, juvenile retelling of familiar Hino themes. ★½

HINO HORROR, VOL. 9: GHOST SCHOOL

Hideshi Hino • DH Publishing (2004) • 1 volume • Shôjo, Horror • 18+ (graphic violence, mild sexual situations)

Illogical, gruesome, bloody *shôjo* horror. A girl is captured by an ex-teacher serial killer and forced to sit in his "class" along with the corpses of his previous victims; another girl is stalked by a doll maniac; a beauty contest winner is stricken with rapid aging; and in the worst story, the heroine falls prey to sailor-suit-obsessed perverts. Like all of his *shôjo* stories, *Ghost School* is one of Hideshi Hino's lesser works. His character designs substitute stiffly realistic female characters in place of his usual squat, iconic protagonists. Perhaps the supposedly cute (but in fact unpleasant) faces make the butchery and deformity more shocking, because the art crosses the line from horrifying to merely ugly, making it simply hard to look at.   ★

HINO HORROR, VOL. 10: DEATH'S REFLECTION

Hideshi Hino • DH Publishing (2004) • 1 volume • Shôjo, Horror • 18+ (mild language, graphic violence)

Graphic *shôjo* gross-out horror. In the title story, students who smoke in the school restroom are bloodily murdered by a ghost in the mirror. The other stories are predictable plots of stalkers and supernatural revenge, except for the best one, "The 3737 Mystery," a vaguely *Drifting Classroom*–like tale in which an entire classroom of students vanishes, to the bewilderment of those left behind. The stories frequently end with unsatisfying epilogues. Like the equally disappointing *Ghost School,* the art is inferior; the characters' faces look as if they were drawn by assistants, and the whole thing seems sloppy.   ★

HINO HORROR, VOL. 11: GALLERY OF HORRORS

Kyôfu Gallery, "Horror Gallery" (恐怖ギャラリー) • Hideshi Hino • DH Publishing (2004) • Leed Publishing (1998) • 1 volume • Horror • 18+ (mild language, graphic violence)

This children's horror anthology contains seven short color-themed stories, of which a few are effective (the mysterious crows in "Horror in Black") but most feel like weak attempts to write plots around certain

colors (in "Horror in Green" a boy turns into a plant; in "Horror in Yellow" the protagonist is afraid of chickens). The plots are silly and arbitrary, and Hino's art is unusually crude.   ★

HINO HORROR, VOL. 12: MYSTIQUE MANDALA OF HELL

Kaiki! Jigoku Mandala, "Mysterious/Eerie! Hell Mandala" (怪奇!地獄まんだら) • Hideshi Hino • DH Publishing (2004) • Rippu Shobo (1982) • 1 volume • Horror • 18+ (language, crude humor, graphic violence)

Sayoko Hoshi, a creepy, staring transfer student, has a secret: she's actually the immortal Mandala, the last surviving daughter of the Japanese underworld, who travels Japan seeking the Divine Crystal Eye of Hell. In order to get it, she must fight Western demons who have come to take over Japan. Vaguely similar in plot to *New Vampire Miyu, Mystique Mandala of Hell* is a stillborn premise that ends abruptly. Like a shy, pint-sized Miyu, Mandala is a mysterious figure who attracts human outcasts and gets in fights with rival monsters. In a more typical Hino touch, however, she eats centipedes and snakes, and frightens a bully into wetting his pants. Despite the 18+ rating, the cartoony horror is no more graphic than *Oninbo and the Bugs from Hell.*   ★★

HINO HORROR, VOL. 13: ZIPANGU NIGHT

Zipangu Night, "Zipangu [Japan] Night" (ジパングナイト) • Hideshi Hino • DH Publishing (2004) • Leed Publishing (1997) • 1 volume • Horror • 18+ (language, graphic violence, nudity)

Anthology of gross, childish (but graphic) horror stories. Judging solely from the narration, the stories are written as if by people in the future commenting on the social ills of present-day Japan ("It was an era of social disease; a time of greed and coldheartedness . . ."), but the theme is extremely tenuous; killer teachers and girls turning into giant rats don't offer much social commentary, although "Faceless" is a memorably disgusting treatment of plastic surgery. The most nauseating story is "Who the Hell?"

which begins with a girl waking up to find a baby in her arms. ★

HINO HORROR, VOL. 14: SKIN AND BONE

Hone Shôjo, "Bone Girl" (骨少女) • Hideshi Hino • DH Publishing (2004) • Souma Publishing (1997) • 1 volume • Horror • 18+ (graphic violence)

One of Hideshi Hino's later works, *Skin and Bone* suffers from obvious overuse of assistants and computer effects. The vaguely sickening art includes samples of both his stiff *shôjo* style and a version of his older style, with pudgy, cartoony characters who look like they came out of *The Family Circus.* Most of the contents are formulaic children's stories in which outcast girls get revenge via caterpillars, slugs, or skeletons. The standout is the vaguely *shôjo* "Two Sisters," in which an attractive sister is linked to an unbelievably hideous twin. ★

HOLDING ON TO ALEX: See *Harlequin Violet: Holding on to Alex*

HOROBI

Horobi, "Day of Destruction" (滅日) • Yoshihisa Tagami • Viz (1990–1991) • Tokuma Shoten (Monthly Shônen Captain, 1987–1990) • 15 issues • Psychic, Horror • 18+ (graphic violence, nudity, sex)

Flawed but ambitious, this creepy sci-fi drama suffers from a slow second act and a less-than-satisfying climax. Zen, a cynical misanthrope, and Shuichi, a handsome ladies' man, are twenty-something researchers at an institute studying the effects of pollution on amphibians. Suddenly, bizarre giant monsters start appearing throughout Japan, sending the population into fear and panic, while the heroes' paths cross with a pair of female researchers studying the myth of Idari, a legendary dragon-slaying hero from A.D. 645. The plot is too idea-driven for its own good, and too many pages are filled with talking heads, or scenes of cars driving while the characters within debate the environment, religion, and Japanese mythology. Tagami's glossy, oddly inorganic artwork takes a while to get used to but suits the dark mood. ★★★

HOSHIN ENGI

Hôshin Engi, "Creation of the Gods" (封神演義) • Ryu Fujisaki • Viz (2007–ongoing) • Shueisha (Weekly Shônen Jump, 1996–2000) • 23 volumes • Shônen, Fantasy, Action • 13+ (violence, brief nudity)

Over-the-top fantasy manga based on novels by Tsutomu Ano, themselves loosely based on the ancient Chinese novel *Fengshen Yangyi* (the original Chinese pronunciation of *Hoshin Engi*). The Shang dynasty is falling, thanks to the demoness Dakki, who has bewitched the emperor for her own selfish passions. The immortal masters recruit Taikoubou, an immortal-in-training, and his goofy flying steed Sibuxiang to hunt down evil demons and indirectly bring about the end to Dakki's reign. A mix of fantasy, sci-fi technology, and super martial arts, with plenty of humor, *Hoshin Engi* has a complicated plot and polished, extremely detailed anime-style artwork. Although theoretically set in ancient China, most of the action takes place in cyberworlds, floating sky castles, or other bizarre realms. The anime was released in English under the title *Soul Hunter.* NR

HOSHI NO KOE: See *The Voices of a Distant Star: Hoshi no Koe*

HOTEL HARBOUR VIEW

1997 nen no Ansatsusha, "1997 Assassin" (1997年の暗殺者) • Jiro Taniguchi (art), Natsuo Sekikawa (story) • Viz (1990) • Akita Shoten (Play Comic, 1985) • 1 volume • Crime • 18+ (violence, nudity, sexual situations)

Powerful, undiluted adult film noir. In the first story, a worn-out Japanese expatriate checks into a musty Hong Kong hotel inhabited by other outcasts, where the bartender talks endlessly about days gone by. In the second story, a female hit man stalks her prey in Paris. The plots focus on their gloomy subject matter like the lens of a camera, or like one of Taniguchi's incredible multiple-page wordless sequences, zooming in to stare at a bullet in the instant before death. The oversized format makes Tanigu-

HORROR (ホラー)

Horror manga are popular in Japan, where the genre is also known as *kaiki manga,* "shocking manga," or *kyôfu manga,* "terror manga." Monsters, frightening imagery, and violence often appear in science fiction, fantasy, and crime manga, but it takes a special kind of artist to write horror manga: to craft stories in which the protagonists suffer horrible fates, to close in on shocking scenes with excruciating slowness, panel after panel, until the reader is afraid to turn the page. The major publishers have steered away from horror-specific magazines, leaving the field to smaller publishers, although individual horror stories are quite welcome in even the most mainstream magazines.

The History of Horror Manga

Early horror manga were marginal works, mostly published in the *kashibonya* rental library market, rather than by major publishers. In the 1960s the monster boom, spurred largely by Japanese monster movies (see the article on TOKUSATSU), led to a proliferation of folkloric and modern creatures in children's comics. One successful formula was *shônen* manga stories starring spooky yet sympathetic characters, typically supernatural kids, who fought more sinister monsters. Examples include Shigeru Mizuki's *GeGeGe-no-Kitaro* (1965), Osamu Tezuka's *Dororo* (1967), and Kazuo Umezu's *Nekome Kozô* ("The Cat-eyed Kid," 1967). Hideshi Hino has drawn several manga in that vein, including *Oninbo and the Bugs from Hell* (1987). A modern example is Yoshiyuki Nishi's *Muhyo to Roji no Mahô Rishitsu Sôdan Jimushu* ("Muhyo and Roji's Magical Law Consultation Office") (2004), in which pint-sized wizard/lawyers fight ghoulish ghosts. At the same time, *shôjo* manga experimented with more psychological horror, largely due to the works of Kazuo Umezu. *Scary Book* collects his classic stories from that period, and *Orochi* (1969), although published in a boys' magazine, shows the same themes.

In the 1970s and 1980s, horror manga boomed. Small publishers such as Rippu Shobo and Hibari Shobo released stand-alone graphic novels aimed mostly at a female audience. The frequent deaths of protagonists made horror well suited for short stories, unlike the thousand-page epics common to other genres of manga. *Shôjo* readers took to horror like fish to water; lurid covers dripped with bright red blood and the greenish, screaming faces of horrified girls. The clash of

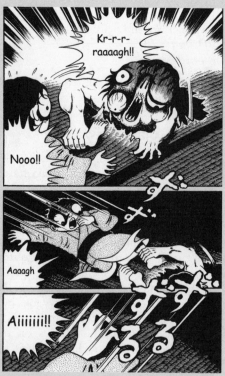

Hideshi Hino's *The Red Snake*

cute (perhaps sickly-cute) faces and violent, shocking imagery, as typified by cartoony artists such as Hideshi Hino and Kanako Inuki, was archetypal to the genre. From 1986 until its cancellation in 1995, Asahi Sonorama's *shôjo* horror magazine *Halloween* was the queen of the pure horror magazines, and printed the early works of artists such as Junji Ito, who combined Kazuo Umezu's shock techniques with a more realistic, detailed art style. Other magazines steered away from graphic gore and focused on suspense and suggestion. Many *shôjo* mystery magazines run works that could be considered horror, including Akita Shoten's *Susperia Mystery,* founded in 1987 under the name *Susperia,* and *Mystery Bonita,* founded in 1988.

Today, several magazines focus on horror manga. Asahi Sonorama's *shôjo* horror magazine *Nemuki,* short for *Nemurenu Yoru no Kimyô Hanashi* ("Strange Tales for Sleepless Nights"), specializes in evocative, creepy tales. Its spinoff, *Nemuki Zôkan Mugenkan* ("Dream Shop"), is currently running the untranslated sequel to Matsuri Akino's classic *Petshop of Horrors.* Bunkasha's *shôjo* magazine *Horror M,* short for "horror mystery," takes a more gruesome, ultraviolent approach; its most famous title is Rei Mikamoto's tongue-in-rotting-cheek gorefest *Reiko the Zombie Shop* (1999). Gentosha's primarily *seinen* magazine *Comic Birz* is not pure horror but rather a cocktail of historical, dark fantasy, and action comics, of which not all reach the extremes of Masakazu Yamaguchi's *Arm of Kannon* (2001).

Kazuo Umezu, Hideshi Hino, Junji Ito, Kanako Inuki, and Rie Mikamoto represent the purest of Japanese horror comics, but other artists flirt with horror as well. Kei Kusunoki and her twin sister, Kaoru Ohashi, are known for both horror and romantic comedies. Even Rumiko Takahashi, famous for the only occasionally scary fantasy comic *Inuyasha* (1996), began her career as an assistant to Kazuo Umezu, and her early work includes several straight horror tales.

Novels, Movies, and Manga

Prose horror novels are popular in Japan as well. In the 1980s, novelist Hideyuki Kikuchi wowed Japanese young adult audiences with his delirious combinations of science fiction, fantasy, horror, and action. His *Demon City Shinjuku* series (1982), set in a near-future Tokyo where modern-day evil wizards have unleashed bizarre monsters and aliens, was adapted into several *shônen* manga and anime series. *Vampire Hunter D* (1983), a tale of a postapocalyptic future where humans live under the oppression of vampire feudal lords, was equally successful. Kikuchi's work has an anything-goes quality influenced by horror movies and pulp fiction. Other authors were more restrained and suggestive, such as Kouhei Kadono, whose *Boogiepop* novels of surreal high school gloom were adapted into anime and manga in the late 1990s.

Horror movies have always been popular in Japan; due to the country's relative tolerance for violence and unhappy endings, foreign horror movies are sometimes available in uncut and more explicit versions. The extreme violence of 1970s and 1980s splatter movies inspired manga to new heights of goriness. *Baoh* (1984), *Warriors of Tao* (2001), and *Variante* (2004) show the touch of the "bio-horror" genre, with their slimy, fleshy transformations. In the late 1990s, in one of Japan's periodic horror booms, the country embraced a different kind of horror: creepy ghost stories, a classic theme updated by the addition of psychic elements and modern-day settings and technology. Movies such as *Ju-On* ("The Grudge"), the *Ring* series, and *Kairo* ("Pulse"), the latter two based on novels, were at the forefront of an international "J-horror" boom and were adapted into American remakes, as well as manga adaptations. Manga artist Shinichi Koga is best known in the United States for the mid-1990s movie adaptations of his manga *Eko Eko Azarak,* a 1970s "school horror" classic rife with black magic, witchcraft, and horrible deaths on school property. Numerous Junji Ito and Kazuo Umezu manga have been adapted into films as well.

American horror author H. P. Lovecraft enjoys a small cult following in Japan, but many seemingly Lovecraftian themes in manga, such as ancient dark gods and monsters hidden in remote shrines waiting to be unleashed, are in fact based on Shinto mythology. Kentaro Yano depicted Lovecraft's Great Old Ones in his untranslated five-volume *Jashin Densetsu* ("Evil God Legend") series, which ran in *Comic Nora* from 1988 to 1993. Junji Ito is also a fan, as seen in the story "The Village of Sirens" in *Museum of Terror* volume 3, and in plot elements in *Uzumaki* (1998). Lovecraft is one of many influences on Daijiro Moroboshi, one of the great untranslated horror artists, a cult favorite whose surreal, meticulously crosshatched works also deal with Chinese myths and legends.

Some of the most infamous anime and manga in the West is so-called tentacle porn, the brainchild of artist Toshio Maeda, who circumvented Japanese obscenity laws by depicting women ravished not by forbidden genitals but by tentacled monsters. Maeda's works—the most famous is *Urotsukidoji: Legend of the Overfiend* (1986)— represent the extreme fringe of manga, along with *ero-guro* (erotic grotesque) artists such as Shintaro Koga and Suehiro Maruo, whose work involves graphic sexual sadism. It's a long road from such artists to even the most disturbingly violent *seinen* manga, such as Eiji Otsuka and Sho-u Tajima's *MPD Psycho* (1997), or to psychosexual *shôjo* manga creep-outs such as Setona Mizushiro's *Afterschool Nightmare* (2004).

Pure Horror

Afterschool Nightmare • Boogiepop Doesn't Laugh • Boogiepop Dual: Loser's Circus • Bride of Deimos • Dark Water • Dolls • The Drifting Classroom • Flesh Colored Horror • Gyo • Hell Baby • Hino Horror (Black Cat • The Bug Boy • The Collection • Death's Reflection • Gallery of Horrors • Ghost School • Living Corpse • Mystique Mandala of Hell • Oninbo and the Bugs from Hell • The Red Snake • Skin and Bone • Zipangu Night) • Ju-On • The Kurosagi Corpse Delivery Service • Lament of the Lamb • Lullabies from Hell • Mantis Woman • Museum of Terror • Night of the Beasts • Octopus Girl • One Missed Call • Orochi: Blood • Panorama of Hell • Petshop of Horrors • The Ring • Scary Book • School Zone • Tomie • Urban Mirage • Uzumaki

Action Horror

3x3 Eyes • Apocalypse Zero • Arm of Kannon • Baoh • Baron Gong Battle • Category: Freaks • Cross • Dark Edge • Darkside Blues • Dead End • Death Trance • Demon City Hunter • Demon City Shinjuku • Demon Palace Babylon • Devilman • Devil May Cry 3 • Diabolo • Genocyber • Hellsing • Horobi • Innocent W • Inuyasha • JoJo's Bizarre Adventure • Kamiyadori • King of Thorn • Lycanthrope Leo • Mermaid Saga • MPD Psycho • Ogre Slayer • Onimusha: Night of Genesis • Princess Resurrection • Reiko the Zombie Shop • Sengoku Nights • Sister Red • The Sword of Shibito • Taimashin • Variante • Venus Versus Virus • Warriors of Tao • Wild Adapter • Witchblade Manga

Vampires

Although Japanese mythology is scarce on vampire tales, they are a popular modern subgenre, and Americans like them as well, so many vampire manga have been translated. The classic vampire manga is Moto Hagio's untranslated *Poe no Ichizoku* ("The Poe Clan," 1972). A gothic tale following two eternally teenage boy vampires from 1744 to the present day, it bears a strong resemblance to the work of Anne Rice. Narumi Kakinouchi's *Vampire Princess Miyu* (1988), originating as an anime tie-in and adapted into several sequels, takes a more Japanese approach, in which vampires and other monsters are essentially a part of the spirit world, rather than bloodthirsty beasts walking among humanity. Kei Toume's *Lament of the Lamb* (1996) strips vampirism to its bare essentials, while Kohta Hirano's *Hellsing* (1998) and Saki Okuse and Aki Shimizu's *Blood Sucker: The Legend of Zipangu* (2001) embrace all the classic Western vampire ideas. Lastly, there is a sub-subgenre of vampire comedies, including Yuna Kagesaki's *Chibi Vampire* (2003) and Erika Kari's *Vampire Doll Guilt na Zan* (2004).

Vampire Manga

Blood: The Last Vampire • *Blood Alone* • *Blood Sucker: Legend of Zipangu* • *Canon* • *Chibi Vampire* • *Crescent Moon* • *Dark Edge* • *D. Gray-Man* • *Hellsing* • *JoJo's Bizarre Adventure* • *Lament of the Lamb* • *Lunar Legend Tsukihime* • *Millennium Snow* • *Mitsukazu Mihara: Beautiful People* • *Negima!* • *New Vampire Miyu* • *Night Warriors: Darkstalkers' Revenge* • *Sequence* • *Sword of the Dark Ones* • *Trinity Blood* • *Tsukiyomi: Moon Phase* • *Until the Full Moon* • *The Vampire Dahlia* • *Vampire Doll Guilt na Zan* • *Vampire Game* • *Vampire Knight* • *Vampire Princess Miyu* • *Vampire Yui* • *The Wanderer*

chi's solid-looking, photographic artwork jump off the page. ★★★½

HOT GIMMICK

(ホットギミック) • Miki Aihara • Viz (2003–2006) • Shogakukan (Betsucomi, 2000–2005) • 12 volumes • Shôjo, Romance • 16+ (language, mild violence, nudity, sex)

Timid, virginal Hatsumi dwells with her family in a company housing complex, a cold world of family secrets and social ostracism. When her promiscuous little sister asks Hatsumi to buy her a pregnancy test, she is caught and blackmailed by her vicious neighbor Ryoki, a handsome but abusive and sex-hungry nerd who wants her for his "'goodbye-virginity' practice toy." Can Hatsumi's older brother Shinogu and her childhood friend Azusa save her? For some people, the heroine's constant victimization makes *Hot Gimmick* unreadable, but at its best, the story is an incredible page-turner, the manga equivalent of a bodice-ripper novel (though most of the abuse is psychological, not physical—this is a story of everyday torment, not explicit sadism). Hatsumi is forced to choose between one horrible relationship after another, and the plot undergoes shocking twists and turns, playing with the readers' sympathies. Eventually, though, the repeated plot twists strain the story's credibility. (Although the series has an actual ending, unlike *Tokyo Boys & Girls,* Aihara still manages to hedge her bets via the translated novelization, *Hot Gimmick S,* in which Hatsumi ends up with the other guy.) The story is well told and well drawn, however; Aihara's ultramodern, ultrastylish artwork wrings the maximum emotion and humor from the characters' almost stick-figure-like faces. ★★★

HOW TO "READ" MANGA: GLOOM PARTY

Gloom Party (グルームパーティー) • Yoshio Kawashima • DMP (2006) • Akita Shoten (Weekly Shônen Champion, 1995–1999) • 1 volume, suspended (5 volumes in Japan) • Shônen, Four-Panel Comedy • 18+ (language, crude humor, violence, nudity, sexual situations)

Here's a way to release dirty, strongly Japanese four-panel gag strips in English: annotate them and turn them into an "educational" reading experience! Translator G. Genki provides commentary on these salacious, occasionally nonsensical gag manga, helping explain numerous in-jokes about Japanese actors and celebrities, as well as samurai and crime movies of the 1970s. Unfortunately, most of the strips are still dumb and unfunny, often involving women being slapped or put in some humiliating situation. (On the other hand, the character on the cover, Sachiko the toddler housewife, is played mostly for absurdity.) Compared to *Heartbroken Angels,* the most similar thing available in translation, *Gloom Party* is both less explicit and less experimental. ★★

HUNTER X HUNTER

(ハンターxハンター) • Yoshihiro Togashi • Viz (2005–ongoing) • Shueisha (Weekly Shônen Jump, 1998–ongoing) • 23+ volumes (ongoing) • Shônen, Action-Adventure • 16+ (graphic violence, partial nudity, mild sexual situations)

A hard-to-describe, indulgent, strangely fascinating *shônen* manga. In order to find his long-lost father, Gon (a plucky young boy with a fishing pole) takes the legendarily impossible test to become a Hunter, a sort of super-skilled elite adventurer. After enduring endless tall-tale challenges (in which a pool of approximately four million applicants is winnowed down to eight people), Gon and his newfound friends join the Hunter ranks, at which point things get even weirder. On a chapter-by-chapter scale, *Hunter x Hunter* is an almost random collection of psych-outs, battles, puzzles, and trickery. But the plot somehow works on a larger scale as well: a grandiose mystery incorporating such seeming clichés as fighting tournaments, martial arts disciplines, and even collectible card games. Gon's friends Killua (a young assassin) and Kurapika (a boy seeking vengeance for the murder of his family) have roles almost as big as Gon himself, and between all their goals and subplots it seems the story could go on forever, but the series is unpredictable enough to sustain reader interest. Togashi's imaginary world is equal parts Dr. Seuss–esque whimsy and Charles Addams/Gahan Wilson morbidity, with occasional moments of shocking violence. The sketchy art ranges from extremely realistic to extremely crude, getting cruder and cruder as the series goes on. In Japan, the series is infamous for coming out at a slow pace, due to Togashi's poor work ethic, his desire to use few or no assistants, or both.

★★★½

HURRAH! SAILOR

Katsuwo Nakane • Infinity Studios (2005) • MediaWorks (Dengeki Daioh, 2004) • 2 volumes • Shônen, Science Fiction, Comedy • 13+ (language, nudity, sexual situations)

Enjoyable comedy about the adventures of a handful of military personnel who find themselves stranded when their ship crash-lands on a primitive planet. Most of the hijinks involve the five crew members coming up with plots to fix their damaged craft, meet the natives, and otherwise survive in their temporary home. The art is lacking in places, but the storytelling is clear and the visual gags are priceless. (LW) ★★★

HURRICANE GIRLS

Hiroshi Yakumo • Antarctic (1995–1996) • Dôjinshi • 6 issues • Action, Comedy • Unrated/13+ (mild language, violence)

Extremely amateurish, incomprehensible one-shot stories drawn with poor perspective and generic 1980s character designs. The subject matter is a potluck, ranging from female demon hunters and warriors (presumably the reason for the title) to a "ninja love triangle" and a comedy boxing match between an alien and a zombie. ½

HYPER DOLLS

Rakushô! Hyper Doll, "Easy Victory! Hyper Doll" (楽勝!ハイパードル) • Shimpei Itoh • Studio Ironcat (2000–2003) • Tokuma Shoten (Monthly Shônen Captain, 1995–1997) • 5 volumes • Shônen, Science Fiction, Tokusatsu, Comedy • Unrated/13+ (violence, partial nudity)

Hyper Dolls is a parody of *Ultraman* and other Japanese *tokusatsu* shows, in which costumed heroes fight giant monsters. Disguised as human schoolgirls to blend in, the Hyper Dolls are in reality a pair of super-strong alien cops, whose personalities combine the worst traits of bored clock watchers and condescending soldiers assigned to a base in a third world country. The self-referential sense of humor is much better than the overpowered-girls-bickering-while-destroying-stuff material requires, closer to Adam Warren's American *Dirty Pair* comics than, for example, *Slayers.* From science fiction in-jokes to digs at colonial politics, it's an enjoyable light series that's slightly smarter than it had to be.   ★★★

HYPER POLICE

(はいぱーぽりす) • Mee • Tokyopop (2005–ongoing) • Kadokawa Shoten (Dragon Magazine, 1994–ongoing) • 10+ volumes (ongoing) • Science Fiction, Fantasy, Crime, Comedy • 16+ (language, violence, nudity, sexual situations)

A sci-fi comedy with unusually good old-school art in the style of Masamune Shirow, this is one of the best "furry" manga available in English. *Hyper Police* is set in a future Tokyo, where trees grow on the overgrown skyscrapers and humans are a minority group outnumbered by monsters and anthropomorphic animals. Natsuki, a cute police officer with cat ears and a tail, investigates crimes with the help of Sakura, a fox-girl police officer who occasionally tries to eat her partner. Other recurring characters include a horny werewolf officer and a bewildered time-traveling samurai from historical Japan. The stories abound with pleasantly hand-drawn dragons, goblins, magic, cybertechnology, and all kinds of weapons (often modified with silver bullets, etc.). The plots are entertaining, and they never *quite* degenerate into close-ups of big-booty cat-girls in police uniforms . . . at least not for more than a few pages at a time. (At the end of volume 1, next to the weapon designs, the artist includes a diagram of the heroines' special underwear with tail holes.)   ★★★

HYPER RUNE

Cyber Planet 1999 Hyper Rune (サイバープラネット1999HYPER☆ルン) • Tamayo Akiyama • Tokyopop (2004–2005) • Kadokawa Shoten (Asuka, 1996–1997) • 4 volumes • Shôjo, Science Fiction, Fantasy, Magical Girl, Action • 13+ (mild language, mild violence, partial nudity)

Humanoid aliens land on Earth, trying to gather the five hidden elements that they need to carry out their apocalyptic master plan. Our planet's defender is Rune, granddaughter of a mad scientist, who supplies her with masked cybernoid battle suits and a fluffy mascot, Chat-kun, to fight the alien conspiracy! Will she become the space queen and save the planet? Will the aliens succeed in their plan to take over the school's student council? *Hyper Rune* is a mildly amusing comedy action series for young readers, combining elements of the *sentai/tokusatsu* costumed hero and the magical girl genres. The plot is nicely self-referential, and Akiyama's art—like a simplified version of CLAMP—is adequate.   ★★

ICE BLADE

Jiraishin, "Land Mine Earthquake" (地雷震) • Tutomu Takahashi • Tokyopop (1997–2000) • Kodansha (Afternoon, 1992–2000) • 3 volumes, suspended (19 volumes in Japan) • Seinen, Crime • Unrated/13+ (brief language, graphic violence, brief sex)

Stylish and effectively told, these cop dramas involve vengeful hitmen, Russian-Japanese smuggling on a remote north Japanese island, and subliminal messages inciting suicide and murder. The "Ice Blade" is the hero, Ky, a young, inscrutable cop of few words, who dresses in black and wields his gun with ruthless efficiency. (In the first story, he muses "No room for tears . . . in my next life . . . I'd rather be an emotionless flower," but for the most part his internal life is left to the reader's imagination.) In any case, the focus is not on Ky but on the police cases, which have interesting, far-out plots and a grim, hard-boiled feel, although the writing isn't as deep as it'd like to be. The action moves quickly, and the artwork is dark and moody. The English edition selects several self-contained stories from different parts of the Japanese run. ★★★

ICHIGEKI SACCHU HOIHOI-SAN

Ichigeki Sacchû!! Hoihoi-san, "One-Hit Bug Kill! Hoihoi-san" (一撃殺虫!!ホイホイさん) • Kunihiko Tanaka • Infinity Studios (2007) • MediaWorks (Dengeki Daioh, 2004) • 1 volume • Moe, Comedy • 13+ (mild violence)

Spin-off of a Japanese PlayStation 2 game. In the year 20XX, insects have developed a resistance to chemical pesticides, so scientists develop Hoihoi-san, cute doll-sized maid robots who go around and kill bugs with various teeny-tiny guns and weapons. (Naturally, what other solution is there?) The manga is told in the form of very short comics, mostly one page long. NR

IC IN A SUNFLOWER: See *Mitsukazu Mihara: IC in a Sunflower*

IDOL DREAMS: See *Harlequin Pink: Idol Dreams*

IMADOKI! NOWADAYS

Imadoki!, "Nowadays" (イマドキ!) • Yuu Watase • Viz (2004–2005) • Shogakukan (Shôjo Comic, 2000–2001) • 5 volumes • Shôjo, School, Romance • 16+ (mild language)

"I had zero interest in high school story lines for girl's comics," Watase writes in her notes for *Imadoki! Nowadays,* clearly intended as light entertainment for younger readers after her previous tightly plotted stories. Pollyanna-ish Tanpopo Yamazaki enrolls in a high-tech new high school in the big city, where she is bullied by her snobbish classmates, before making friends—and finding romance—through the gardening club. The structure is almost like a *Shônen Jump* manga,

as Tanpopo's infinite good nature turns rivals into friends, eventually gathering a small comedy ensemble of likable characters. The directionless plot is never outrageous enough to be really funny, however, and the attempts at social commentary (teen pregnancy, etc.) are weak. ★★

IMMORTAL RAIN

Meteor Methuselah (メテオ・メトセラ) • Kaoru Ozaki • Tokyopop (2004–ongoing) • Shinshokan (Wings, 1999–ongoing) • 8+ volumes (ongoing) • Shôjo, Science Fiction, Action, Drama • 16+ (language, violence, nudity, mild sexual situations)

In a faraway future world of sweeping deserts and seas, Rain, a six-hundred-year-old immortal with a metal cross in his chest, wanders the globe, carrying with him the sad knowledge that human life "vanishes as quickly as a shooting star." Machika, the granddaughter of a bounty hunter who once tried to collect the bounty on Rain's head, joins him on his adventures, trying to help him find a way to become mortal again. Meanwhile, everyone else wants the secret to immortality, particularly the massive Calvaria Corporation, which is excavating ancient ruins in search of long-lost bioweapons . . . and the secret of Rain's origin. Combining the complex character-driven plot of a *shôjo* manga with the action scenes and art of a *shônen* manga, *Immortal Rain* is a successful page-turner with many twists and turns, particularly in the later volumes once the series gets going. The backgrounds are well drawn, and the characters, particularly the antagonists, are well written and interesting. ★★★

IMPERFECT HERO

Akaten Hero!, "Red Mark Hero/Imperfect Hero!" (あかてんヒーロー!) • Nankin Gureko • ComicsOne/ DrMaster (2004–2005) • Gentosha (Comic Birz, 2002–2004) • 3 volumes • Comedy • 13+ (mild language, brief nudity, mild sexual situations)

A slapstick romantic comedy crossed with a *sentai* show parody. Wimpy teenager Yuji Midorikawa is secretly "G-Green," one of the less popular members of the color-coded masked hero squad Gakusei 5. Mayura is the buxom, vaguely dominatrix-like queen of the bad guys who are always trying to take over the world—until one day when she loses her horn, causing her to turn into a ditz who moves in with Yuji (not knowing his secret identity), raids places like chocolate factories, and decides that she wants a boyfriend. Clichéd but entertaining, *Imperfect Hero* tackles the old *Urusei Yatsura* "wimpy guy and crazy alien girl" plot with gusto, invigorated by the fact that the hero is sneaky and manipulative and deserves everything that happens to him. (At one point, Yuji disguises himself as one of the bad guys, only to get beaten up by his friends; then when he switches to his hero costume, the bad guys beat him up; and so on.)   ★★½

INDIAN SUMMER

Koharu Biyori, "Indian Summer/Balmy Autumn Weather" (こはるびより) • Takehito Mizuki • DrMaster (2004) • MediaWorks (Dengeki Daioh/Dengeki Teioh/ Dengeki Moeoh, 2004–ongoing) • 1 volume, suspended (2+ volumes in Japan, ongoing) • Moe, Comedy • 13+ (partial nudity, sexual situations)

Generically drawn Lolita-complex *moe* robot-maid fantasy; the main distinction from others of its kind (i.e., *Mahoromatic*) is that, instead of a blushing nebbish, the male lead is a creepily cute *chibi* guy who treats his innocent robot maid with cool, knowing perversion. (Sample dialogue: "The reason for my purchase was to dress you up and a lot of other things." "Noo, I'm worthless without my boobs.") Self-referential humor raises the manga from absolutely terrible to merely bad, as when the characters encourage the author to pursue his fetishes: "Dear Takehito Mizuki, please become an artist who will force the magazine to be discontinued."   ★

INFINITE RYVIUS

Mugen no Ryvius, "Infinite Ryvius" (無限のリヴァイアス) • Hajime Yatate (original story), Yousuke Kuroda (construction), Shinsuke Kurihashi (manga) • ComicsOne/DrMaster (2004–2005) •

MediaWorks (Dengeki Daioh, 2000) • 2 volumes • Shônen, Science Fiction, Drama • 13+ (mild language, partial nudity, brief sex)

Manga adaptation of the anime of the same name. In the year 2225, a group of teenage students are learning how to be pilots out in space when disaster strikes and their ship becomes lost in space without the help of any adults. The manga does a good job capturing the ways in which individuals respond to crisis, making this a type of *Lord of the Flies* in space. However, the condensed nature of the manga leaves out many scenes from the anime, and the manga comes across as dreamlike at best. Dramatic events happen right after one another with no transition, no clear idea of character, and little resolution. (MJS)   ★★

INITIAL D

Kashiramoji [*Initial*] *D,* "Initial D" (頭文字[イニシャル]D) • Shuichi Shigeno • Tokyopop (2002–ongoing) • Kodansha (Weekly Young Magazine, 1995–2005) • 32 volumes • Seinen, Racing, Action • 13+ (mild language, sexual situations)

In a small town in the shadow of Mount Akina, bored teenagers illegally race cars down winding mountain roads and talk about torque and RPMs while working at the gas station. Our hero, Takumi "Tak" Fujiwara, is the only one who doesn't get the fuss and can't tell an Enfini from a Trueno—but it turns out *that's because he's such a natural genius at racing he doesn't need to know anything about it!* When his secret comes out, Tak becomes a local celebrity and is challenged to one-on-one races by rich kids with high-powered cars, which he beats with his dad's 1986 Toyota. *Initial D* is a Japanese auto fan's dream, continual action painted with a limited palette of character designs and settings. The human characters have all the facial expression of walking rectangles, but the racing scenes have a rough, mechanical vigor. Cars screech down rural roads at night, drifting through curves at insane speeds, hugging the guardrails over black mountain valleys. On the rare occasion when the characters aren't thinking about cars, they're

Shuichi Shigeno's *Initial D*

2004–2006) • 3 volumes • Seinen, Occult, Horror • 16+ (graphic violence, nudity, sexual situations)

A group of young modern-day witches and occultists, of whom the only male is clairvoyant detective Makoto, are lured out to the wilderness and find themselves in a horrible trap: a modern-day witch hunt where vicious killers have been recruited to track them down and murder them! In a situation similar to *Battle Royale* or a snuff film with the addition of magic powers, the characters show poor teamwork, fleeing in different directions and fighting among themselves before being raped and killed or taking revenge on their torturers. Kusunoki's sadistic tendencies are more pronounced here than in any of her other manga. Her ghoulish art delights in showing cute anime-style faces maimed and mutilated; unfortunately, she doesn't do a good job of establishing the surroundings, making the violence seem especially arbitrary as the characters run around and get randomly assaulted. A strong, original premise, though.   ★★★

thinking about girls, such as Tak's maybe-girlfriend Natalie, who (when the story begins) is involved in a shady relationship with an "older gentleman." (After all, it's a *seinen* manga.) It's no surprise that the series was spun off into several successful video games (not to mention anime, a Hong Kong live-action movie, etc.); the plot has a video game–like structure, with the hero's hometown as the first "stage" and the subsequent towns and opponents as the later stages. A repetitive but extremely effective series, with an interesting "Nowheresville, Japan" setting and sympathetic blue-collar characters; the only thing it needs (in this reviewer's opinion) is more horrible car crashes. Some nudity is censored in the English edition; the first printing of the first volume was released uncensored and changed in reprints.   ★★★

INNOCENT W

(イノセントW) • Kei Kusunoki • Tokyopop (2006–2007) • Shônen Gahosha (Young King Ours,

INSTANT TEEN: JUST ADD NUTS

Otona ni Nuts, "Adult via Nuts" (おとなにナッツ) • Haruka Fukushima • Tokyopop (2004–2005) • Kodansha (Nakayoshi, 2000–2002) • 4 volumes • Shôjo, Romantic Comedy • All Ages (brief partial nudity, mild sexual situations)

Experimental nuts temporarily transform fifth-grader Natsumi into a sexy young adult woman with 33–22–33 measurements. For her, it's all fun—she gets taken to dinner by handsome guys and becomes a model—but her fifth-grade male friend Asuma gets flustered by her new body, and eventually she discovers that being grown-up has disadvantages too. *Instant Teen* is a playful, good-natured take on a just slightly racy premise, adapting teenage romantic comedy themes for a late elementary school audience—there's even an interlude in which Asuma and Natsumi swap bodies. The art is an above-average example of the sweet-and-light *Nakayoshi* magazine house style, with cheerful faces and leggy bodies.   ★★½

INUBAKA: CRAZY FOR DOGS

Inubaka, "Dog Crazy" (いぬばか We're Crazy for Dogs!) • Viz (2007–ongoing) • Shueisha (Young Jump, 2004–ongoing) • 9+ volumes (ongoing) • Seinen, Pet, Romantic Comedy • 16+ (mild language, crude humor, mild sexual situations)

The pet store Woofles has three employees: Teppei, the twenty-six-year-old manager; Kentaro, his scruffy slacker friend from high school; and Suguri, a naive eighteen-year-old girl from the countryside who loves dogs (she even wears a collar around her neck). Suguri's natural affinity for canines shines in these light episodic dramas about dogs and their owners. Despite being published in the sometimes spicy men's magazine *Young Jump, Inubaka* has relatively little romance or cheesecake. Instead there's plenty of dog poop and pee jokes, and lots of practical pet care information. The art is polished but generic: cute girls and cute dogs who look traced from photos. ★★

INUYASHA

Inuyasha, "Dog Demon" (犬夜叉) • Rumiko Takahashi • Viz (1997–ongoing) • Shogakukan (Weekly Shônen Sunday, 1996–ongoing) • 49+ volumes (ongoing) • Shônen, Historical, Fantasy, Adventure • 16+ (mild language, nudity, violence)

Below-average Takahashi is still better than most artists' best work, but *Inuyasha* explores well-trodden territory: cute, cleanly drawn heroes follow long story arcs of no clear termination and fight grotesque monsters-of-the-week. Kagome, a junior-high girl, travels back through time to feudal Japan, where she is taken for the reincarnation of a great priestess and becomes the master of Inuyasha, a surly dog-eared half-demon boy. When the magic Shikon Jewel—a demonic artifact—is shattered into a conveniently indefinite number of pieces, she and Inuyasha must travel across Japan to keep the fragments out of the hands of evil demons, and later hunt for Naraku, a spider-like evil manipulator with ties to Inuyasha and Kagome's previous incarnation. Of course, these are only the basics of an enormous cast of characters and demons, introduced in what feels like a make-it-up-as-she-goes-along fashion. Takahashi's only major non-romantic-comedy series (although there's a little of that, too) combines creepy folklore-horror with fight scenes: the heroes stumble upon a mysterious monster or legend, invariably escape death, and then Inuyasha cuts the monsters to pieces. The creatures are inventive, but it's obvious when the story is spinning its wheels; the best moments are when the character relationships assert themselves, but these moments are buried among thousands of pages of future TV-show episodes. Takahashi's art is simplified, and the story reads quickly. ★★★

IONO-SAMA FANATICS

Iono-sama Fanatics (いおの様ファナティクス) • Miyabi Fujieda • Infinity Studios (2007) • MediaWorks (Dengeki Teioh, 2005–2006) • 2 volumes • Otaku, Yuri, Romantic Comedy • 13+ (partial nudity, sexual situations)

Yuri (lesbian) romantic comedy. Iono, the queen of a faraway country, comes to Japan in search of beautiful dark-haired women for her harem of attendants. NR

I, OTAKU: STRUGGLES IN AKIHABARA:
See *Sota-kun no Akihabara Funtoki*

IPPONGI BANG'S CANVAS DIARY

Ippongi Bang • Antarctic (1994) • 1 issue • Comedy • Unrated/13+ (crude humor)

Intended for true Bang completists, this hyperactive one-shot comic introduces Ippongi Bang's "Studio Do-Do" and generally shows the artist goofing off with her assistants (Mio Odagi, Masayuki Fujiwara, Yutaka Kondo, Hiroshi Yakumo, and others). The comic opens with comments about the making of *Change Commander Goku* but soon moves to a trip to Taiwan, manga studio toilet etiquette, and other anecdotes. ★★

IRONCAT

Masaomi Kanzaki • Studio Ironcat (1999) • Dôjinshi (1996) • Comedy • 2 issues • Unrated/16+ (nudity)

"Every day, I have to wake up a half an hour early, not to wash my hair . . . but to hide my 'F-Cup' breasts! They're such a burden!" Unfinished, sloppily drawn, throwaway T&A manga starring a girl in a cat cosplay suit (just a bikini with a cat's tail, really) who fights animal-themed enemies. Inexplicably, it is reportedly one of Kanzaki's favorites of his own manga, and provided the name for the now-defunct U.S. publisher Studio Ironcat. 0 Stars

IRONFIST

Tekken Chinmi, "Ironfist Chinmi" (鉄拳チンミ) • Takeshi Maekawa • Bantam (1997) • Kodansha (Monthly Shônen Magazine, 1983–1997) • 2 volumes, suspended (35 volumes in Japan) • Shônen, Martial Arts • Unrated/All Ages (mild language, mild violence)

Ironfist has exactly what you'd expect in a children's martial arts manga set in ancient China, from speedline-filled (but basically bloodless) battles with bad guys to philosophical puzzles that the hero ponders on his way to inner strength. Chinmi, a cheerful boy with great martial arts abilities, journeys to Dailin Temple to train, accompanied by his pet monkey and an old martial arts master. The art and plot are simple and bland, but it's good-natured; the old master's wise sayings are clever, and it's fun to see Chinmi break logs into chopsticks with his bare hands. Although only two volumes were published in English ("Kung Fu Boy" and "Journey to Mount Shen"), the series was more successful in Britain, where twelve volumes were published under the title *Ironfist Chinmi*. ★★

IRONFIST CHINMI: See *Ironfist*

IRON WOK JAN

Tetsunabe no Jan!, "Jan of the Iron Pot!" (鉄鍋のジャン!) • Shinji Saijyo (story and art), Keiko Oyama (supervisor) • ComicsOne/DrMaster (2002–ongoing) • Akita Shoten (Weekly Shônen Champion, 1995–2000) • 27 volumes • Shônen, Cooking, Battle • 13+ (language, violence)

The Formula One racing circuit to *Iron Chef*'s stock-car rally, *Iron Wok Jan* takes the battle-cooking concept to the next level with *Street Fighter*–like competitions between charismatic chefs. On one hand, *Iron Wok Jan* is pure *shônen* manga, with cooking tournaments providing the meat of each book. On the other hand, main character Jan Akiyama is also a critique of *shônen* manga's typical train-to-be-the-best! philosophy—Jan is nothing short of a super-villain, a sociopath who doesn't give a damn about the customers who eat his food, the future of cuisine, or anything except humiliating his competitors. Jan's monomania is countered by the differing philosophies of his rivals and coworkers at Gobancho, Tokyo's premier Chinese restaurant. The artwork is intense and kinetic; in Saijyo's hands, even daily cooking is as dynamic as a karate demonstration match. The characters' appearance is video-game-like, and the size of women's torpedo breasts seems roughly proportional to their sense of passion for cooking. Real Chinese cooking techniques and recipes are packed into every volume—you'll learn something. An untranslated sequel, *Iron Wok Jan R,* was begun in 2006. (JD) ★★★★

I"S

(アイズ) • Masakazu Katsura • Viz (2005–2007) • Shueisha (Weekly Shônen Jump, 1997–2000) • 15 volumes • Shônen, Romantic Comedy • 16+ (crude humor, mild language, nudity, sexual situations)

Ichitaka, a teenager still hung up about being rejected in elementary school, has a crush on his classmate Iori, an aspiring actress/model. But other cute girls (whose names all begin with *I,* hence the title) keep chasing after him. More comedic than Katsura's other cheesecake romance, *Video Girl Ai, I"s* lacks that series' veneer of angst-ridden respectability. In its place are school stories: much of the action involves vacations and sleepovers with the supporting cast of Ichitaka's classmates (a horndog best friend, a gay guy, etc.). The other conventional plotline involves Ichitaka protecting Iori from sleazy guys who want to exploit her. Katsura's gorgeous artwork partly obscures the lame jokes, but nothing could obscure his real mission of finding any excuse to draw close-ups of women's barely clothed genitals. (To its credit, it may be the only boys' romance manga featuring both Twister *and* a form of Truth or Dare.) The Viz edition is inconsistently censored in the early volumes; nipples are mostly covered, but panties are exposed. ★★½

I SAW IT!: See *Barefoot Gen*

IWGP: IKEBUKURO WEST GATE PARK

Ikebukuro West Gate Park (池袋ウエストゲートパーク) • Ira Ishida (story), Sena Aritou (art) • DMP (2004–2006) • Akita Shoten (Young Champion, 2001–2004) • 4 volumes • Seinen, Street Crime, Comedy, Drama • 18+ (language, violence, nudity, sex)

A spin-off of a Japanese TV series set in Tokyo's Ikebukuro district (a popular nightspot), based on a mystery novel by manga author Ira Ishida. Makoto, a horny young scenester who can call on the services of various surveillance nerds and even a street gang, gets mixed up in mysteries always involving prostitution and hot girls. The closest comparison is *Voyeurs, Inc.,* but whereas Hideo Yamamoto goes for intentional ugliness and sleaze, *IWGP* goes for straightforward "let me pay you back with my body" titillation and non-ironic panty shots. The art is attractive but generic, with photos used for most of the backgrounds, and the stories involve various colorful characters and criminal subcultures, with varying levels of success. Volume 4 includes several unrelated *seinen* soft-core adult stories. ★★

JAPAN

(ジャパン) • Buronson (story), Kentaro Miura (art) • Dark Horse (2005) • Hakusensha (Young Animal, 1992) • 1 volume • Postapocalyptic, Seinen, Action • 18+ (language, graphic violence, nudity, sexual situations)

A group of Japanese tourists, together with an oxlike *yakuza* and the girl he has a crush on, are transported into a postapocalyptic future Europe, where Japanese people are refugees without a country, living under the heel of white Neo-Europeans. The *yakuza* organizes a resistance, whipping the wimpy, spoiled Japanese high school students into shape and fighting the bad guys in *Road Warrior*–esque desert combat. This perhaps entertainingly nationalist fantasy is 50 percent fighting and 50 percent meaningless ruminations like "What the hell does it mean to be Japanese anyway?" Kentaro Miura's bold action artwork gives a palpable sense of weight and impact. ★★

JAPAN AS VIEWED BY 17 CREATORS

Various artists • Fanfare/Ponent Mon (2005) • 1 volume • Underground • Unrated/18+ (language, nudity, sexual situations)

Japan as Viewed by 17 Creators is the most ambitious production (so far) of Frédéric Boilet's "Nouvelle Manga" movement, which seeks to bring together French and Japanese artists to produce personal stories of daily life. The book contains short vignettes by seven *mangaka* and ten French comic artists, most of whom were invited to visit Japan specifically for the project; each was assigned a particular city and location, and many of the stories are in the form of tourist diaries. With the possible exceptions of Jiro Taniguchi and Moyoco Anno (who uses her 6-page story as an excuse to draw some of her most detailed and beautiful art), none of the artists draw anything like a "typical manga" style, although they range from cartoony to hyperrealistic to experimental non-narrative. If the book has any flaw, it's that the multiple travel narratives are inherently repetitive. Aurélia Aurita's charming account of a visit to a hot springs succeeds because of its limited autobiographical nature, while Joann Sfar and Fabrice Neaud catalogue their culture shock in a more distant, general manner. Other stories have the feel of dreams: François Schuiten and Benoît Peeters briefly depict a science fiction Osaka in the style of their *Cities of the Fantastic* series, while Daisuke Igarashi and Taiyo Matsumoto spin fairy-tale fantasies. The other artists include Kan Takahama, Étienne Davodeau, Frédéric Boilet, Kazuichi Hanawa, Little Fish, David Prudhomme, Emmanuel Gilbert, and Nicolas de Crécy. ★★★★

Kan Takahama's short story in *Japan as Viewed by 17 Creators*

JAPAN INC.: AN INTRODUCTION TO JAPANESE ECONOMICS (THE COMIC BOOK)

Manga Nihon Keizai Nyûmon, "Manga Primer to Japanese Economics" (マンガ日本経済入門) • Shotaro Ishinomori • University of California Press/Lanchester Press (1988–1996) • Nihon Keizai Shimbun (1986–1988) • 2 volumes, suspended (4 volumes in Japan) • Educational, Business, Drama • Unrated/13+ (language, partial nudity, brief sex)

An educational business comic based on an introductory economics text, *Zeminaru Nihon Keizai Nyûmon. Japan Inc.* opens in 1980 Detroit with an anti-Japanese demonstration by angry U.S. auto workers, and subsequent chapters deal with outsourcing, trade deficits, the role of the elderly, and other issues. The main characters are two archetypal employees of the fictional Mitsutomo Trading Company: Tsugawa, the bad guy, a profit-minded businessman who neglects his family, and Kudo, the good guy, who always chooses the socially responsible

route. The plot has plenty of intrigue—sex, blackmail, a scandal involving the Vatican, a revolution in the Middle East—but it jumps around so rapidly in time and space that few scenes last for more than four pages. The action constantly stops for earnest, patronizing exposition; just picking up a pencil causes one character to ramble on for three pages ("To make pencils, we use the absolutely straight cedars of northern California or Oregon. We need many tools—chain saws and ropes and trucks to bring the felled trees to the railroad siding . . .") Copious text provides outdated statistics on the 1980s Japanese economy. The result is information overload. On the upside, Ishinomori draws a good Ronald Reagan. ★★

JERRY ROBINSON'S ASTRA: See *Astra*

JESUS

Iesu, "Jesus" (イエス) • Yoshikazu Yasuhiko • ComicsOne (e-book, 2000) • Japan Broadcast Publishing (1997) • 2 volumes • Religious, Historical Drama • 13+ (violence, partial nudity)

The life of Jesus of Nazareth, explored through the eyes of an original character, Joshua, a disciple of Jesus, a carpenter's son just like Jesus himself, who narrates the story. (Writer and artist Yasuhiko uses a similar trick in his manga *Joan* to discuss the life of Joan of Arc.) We meet Joshua in the opening pages just as he's being crucified right alongside Jesus, and in a series of flashbacks, we discover how he got there. Along with Joshua's first-person remembrances of Jesus' miracles and teachings, Yasuhiko delves into the political maneuverings of the various factions of the time, for whom Jesus' is-he-or-isn't-he messiah status was merely a useful tool for controlling the populace's hearts and minds. Yasuhiko accomplishes a rare feat with *Jesus:* a biblical story without preachiness, and no black-and-white villains. Jesus' divinity is left seriously open to question in a way that might offend devout Christians, but the treatment of his teachings is respectful and there's a great sense of empathy for the peaceful aims he was trying to achieve. The full-color artwork is

*R*ekishi manga, or history manga, are a favorite of many artists, including Yoshikazu Yasuhiko, Osamu Tezuka, and Tetsuo Hara. Europe and Britain are popular settings for historical stories such as Riyoko Ikeda's *The Rose of Versailles* (1972), the gothic romances of Kaori Yuki and You Higuri, and outright fantasies such as Toh Ubukata's *Pilgrim Jäger* (2002) and *Le Chevalier d'Eon* (2005).

Most historical manga, however, are set in Japan. Many belong to the genre of samurai period tales known as *jidai-geki* (period dramas), a term also used to describe movies, novels, and TV shows. Leed Publishing's manga magazine *Comic Ran,* founded with the support of venerable sumarai manga artists Takao Saito and Kazuo Koike, is devoted entirely to samurai dramas. The following list describes historical manga available in translation. Different historians measure eras by different factors. The dates listed are commonly accepted, but other sources may provide different dates, such as for the beginning of the Muromachi period.

Early Japan

Like all cultures, Japan's began as a hunter-gatherer society, though it also relied heavily on the sea. The Jômon era (11,000–300 B.C.) is known for its architecture, stone circles, and unique pottery. The introduction of the pottery wheel, metallurgy, and rice cultivation from China via Korea heralded the beginning of the Yayoi era (300 B.C.–A.D. 300). In the third century A.D., the legendary Queen Himiko ruled a state or group of tribes called Yamatai, arguably Japan's earliest attempt at centralized government. This period is depicted in Yû Terashima and Kamui Fujiwara's *Raika,* as well as Osamu Tezuka's *Phoenix Vol. 1: Dawn.*

The Kofun era (A.D. 300–538), depicted in *Phoenix Vol. 3: Yamato/Space,* is named for its distinctive, keyhole-shaped tumuli, or burial mounds. The mounds often contained *haniwa* pottery figures of people, animals, and cavalry (horses were introduced from mainland Asia around this time). During this time, the Yamato clan became dominant in central Japan, and the Asuka period (538–710) begins with the acceptance of Buddhism into the Yamato court. The imperial prince Shôtoku (574–622) is considered a pivotal figure in Japanese history; a proponent of Buddhism and the use of Chinese for a writing system, he has been attributed with adopting Confucian principles into a "constitution" that helped further centralize the government. His envoys to China brought back medicine, political concepts, civil engineering, and other advances. Ryôko Yamagishi's untranslated *shôjo* classic *Hi Izuru Tokoro no Tenshi* ("Son of Heaven in the Land of the Rising Sun") depicts Shôtoku as a sexually ambiguous *bishônen* with supernatural powers.

The Nara period (710–784), named after the capital city of the time, is depicted in *Phoenix Vol. 4: Karma.* Further bureaucratic reforms reinforced the government's power, and the writing of the histories *Kojiki* and *Nihon Shoki* backdated the legitimacy of the ruling family. The city of Nara was built based on the Chinese grid system; in 784 the capital was briefly moved to Nagaoka before being established in Heian (present-day Kyoto), which remained the imperial capital until the Meiji restoration.

Heian Era (794–1185)

The Heian era, the peak of the Japanese imperial court, was dominated by four clans vying for control over the royal family. Despite the infighting, court culture flourished, with great achievements in art and literature, and the spread of new schools of Buddhism. The Japanese syllabary of hiragana and katakana, developed at this time, liberated writers from the cumbersome Chinese kanji used by officials. Murasaki Shikibu's *The Tale of Genji,* Japan's first novel, was written in 1010. It has been repeatedly adapted into manga, including a translated *shôjo* version by Waki Yamato. Other translated manga set in the Heian court include *Otogi Zoshi* and *More Starlight to Your Heart.* While the court focused on itself, the warrior class gradually grew in experience and influence in outlying areas, serving as the distant hand of imperial rule.

Kamakura Era to Sengoku Era (1185–1568)

The Kamakura era (1185–1333) brought the first shogunate and the birth of the samurai as a ruling class. *Phoenix Vols. 7–8: Civil War* depicts the end of the Heian era, in which the Minamoto clan defeated its rivals and established a military capital in Kamakura. Ceremonial functions were left in Kyoto, but the new capital became the locus of the administrative, legal, and other practical aspects of governing. Cultural change accompanied the shift in power; Zen Buddhism was introduced and embraced by samurai, and art and literature began to favor martial themes. *Arm of Kannon,* volumes 8 and 9, though they hardly provide an accurate history, are the only translated manga set in the period.

    The Kamakura shogunate fell in 1333, and a debate over succession split the country in two for several decades. War did not stop the growth of culture, including Nô theater and new developments in Japanese architecture, as well as the tea ceremony, which spread beyond Zen monasteries for the first time. Takauji Ashikaga founded a new shogunate in Kyoto, launching the Muromachi era, but the nation's loyalties remained divided. Scattered conflicts continued, culminating in the Sengoku ("Warring States") era, which lasted from 1467 to 1568. Local lords severed ties with the central government, farmers launched armed uprisings in protest against taxes and oppression, and chaos reigned. This century of conflict has inspired many manga, its lawlessness lending itself to supernatural themes, as seen in Kei Kusunoki's *Sengoku Nights* and Rumiko Takahashi's *Inuyasha* and *Mermaid Saga.* Tezuka's *Phoenix Vol. 9: Strange Beings/Life* and his untranslated monster manga *Dororo* are also set in this period.

Reunification (1568–1600)

The introduction of firearms by the Portuguese in 1543 changed everything—no longer were traditional samurai tactics the most effective. Three successive military leaders cleared the way to the reunification of Japan, each dealing with different obstacles. Oda Nobunaga, both revered and reviled, ended the military power of Japan's many Buddhist sects through wholesale bloodshed. After his assassination, his most distinguished general, Hideyoshi Toyotomi, became regent. Although he himself was originally a commoner, Hideyoshi collected the people's weapons, giving samurai the exclusive right to bear swords and officially separating them from the peasant class. This era is also known as the Azuchi-Momoyama period, after the innovative castles each leader built.

Translated manga set in the period include *Keiji* and the Japanese-American collaboration *Samurai, Son of Death.*

Edo Era (1600–1867)

With Hideyoshi leaving a five-year-old to follow him, the most powerful remaining feudal lords began jockeying for power. Ieyasu Tokugawa (depicted in an unflattering manner in *Path of the Assassin*) quickly dominated the others and united the country. After assuming the shogunate, he moved the center of the military government to Edo, now known as Tokyo. His decisive victory came at the battle of Sekigahara in 1600, whose aftermath is shown in *Samurai Deeper Kyo* and *Vagabond.* The tale of the legendary swordsman Miyamoto Musashi, *Vagabond* explores the difficulties of the transition from lawlessness to order on a personal level.

The Edo era, also known as the Tokugawa era, is arguably the most successful example of feudalism in history. During more than 250 years of relative peace, a unique situation evolved. With their finances tied to the lands they administered, samurai became progressively poorer as the economy's commercialization caused wealth to accumulate in one of the lower classes, the merchants. The changing role of the samurai class is shown in *Satsuma Gishiden: The Legend of the Satsuma Samurai.* In classical times, only the upper classes could sponsor the arts, but prosperity created the opportunity for commoners to acquire luxury income. The result was the spread of literacy and education, and the genesis of popular arts, including Kabuki theater and woodblock printing. This affordable production method resulted in many new media, such as *ukiyo-e*, "pictures of the floating world," in which artists experimented with impressionistic drawings of fashionable topics and daily life. The humorous animal scrolls of the priest Toba had enjoyed half a millennia of popularity and inspired *toba-e*, bound collections of captioned drawings. Together with *kibiyoshi*, "yellow-cover" booklets of monochrome prints originally intended for children's stories, they are the precursors of manga.

A contributing factor to the era's success was Japan's isolation. While the rest of Asia was being colonized by Europe, Japan's physical separation and enforced exclusion of foreigners spared it the troubles of its neighbors. That ended in 1853 with the arrival of the U.S. Navy's Commodore Matthew C. Perry and a presidential demand for trading ports—Japan was the perfect pit stop for U.S. ships en route to Asia. This caused a division among the ruling class. Those who decided to open Japan won out by declaring that the shogunate was incapable of protecting Japan from the foreigners and that true power belonged to the emperor. The Meiji Restoration began when Emperor Meiji ascended the throne.

Translated manga set in the Edo era include *Basilisk, Blade of the Immortal, Gôjin, Kuro Gane, The Legend of Kamui Perfect Collection, Lone Wolf and Cub, Nemuri Kyoshiro, Onimusha: Night of Genesis, Oyayubihime Infinity, Samurai Champloo, Samurai Executioner, Samurai Legend, Samurai Shodown, The Sword of Shibito,* and *Tail of the Moon.*

Meiji Era (1868–1912)

Intent on attaining equality with the modern nations of the West, Japan sent emissaries to Europe and the United States. They brought back new ideas about government, medicine, industry, banking, education, the military, art, agriculture, and more. Alongside the implementation of these innovations was the dismantling of shogunate power. Japan's transformation from a feudal to a representative government is considered the least bloody in history, but it wasn't completely free of conflict. Castles were torn down, and samurai were stripped of their class privileges, their swords, and eventually their incomes. Some samurai fought the changes and lost; others found their way into leadership roles in the government's conscript army. *Rurouni Kenshin* explores the remarkable changes of the Meiji era from the perspective of a pro-government samurai. On the other hand, the heroes of *Kaze Hikaru, Peace Maker,* and *Peacemaker Kurogane,* which is set slightly before the Meiji era, are defenders of the shogunate. *Gintama* is a sci-fi comedy set in a sort of parallel-world Meiji era.

The Meiji constitution was announced in 1889. By the turn of the century, Japan had become an imperialist nation, taking control of Korea and gaining various Chinese islands in the Sino-Japanese War. When Russia became a threat, Japan allied itself with Britain, so as not to have all of Europe as an enemy, and defeated the Russians in the Russo-Japanese War. Further gains were made during World War I. Translated manga set in the late Meiji era include *Lady Snowblood, The Times of Botchan,* and *The Four Immigrants Manga.*

Taisho Period (1912–1926)

In 1912 Emperor Meiji was succeeded by his son, who suffered from poor health and neurological handicaps. While Japan's military was flexing its muscles, Japan's economy survived its complex adolescence and began to boom. Education, journalism, transportation, the expanding middle class, and an increasingly urban workforce combined to produce decades of affordable printed entertainment, both domestic and imported. This included political comics and the earliest modern manga, published in magazines and newspapers. At this time, publications specifically aimed at children began to appear, and their comics started to be reprinted in collected volumes. The sci-fi fantasy manga *Sakura Taisen* and *Steel Angel Kurumi* are nominally set in the Taisho period, as are many of the works of Suchiro Maruo, who reveled in the decadent spirit of the era.

The Road to War

The Showa period began in 1926 with Emperor Hirohito's ascension to the throne. Despite achieving universal male suffrage in 1925, Japanese society began to tip away from Westernization and progressive politics, toward militarism and austere traditional lifestyles. Deflation in the early 1930s, corruption, conflicts between the military and government, external pressures, and other issues combined to set Japan on the path to extreme nationalism and military expansion. The military are the bad guys of *Samurai Crusader,* while *Yoki Koto Kiku* refers briefly to the "February 26" incident of 1936, in which an ultranationalist military faction attempted a coup. Ironically, although that attempt failed, other military factions took advantage of the situation to amass power. In 1937, Japan—already having occupied Manchuria—invaded China, and the Second Sino-Japanese War began. The war forms the backdrop for *Fist of the Blue Sky.*

In an attempt to curb Japanese aggression, the Americans, British, and Dutch adopted an oil embargo in July 1941, effectively cutting off a vital component of Japan's military. Further economic measures exacerbated the situation, and the government responded with force, drawing the United States into World War II. During the war, the output of the whole nation was directed toward military success, often at the price of personal freedoms and limited resources. *Zipang, Adolf,* and *Who Fighter with Heart of Darkness* depict the war, although the last does so only peripherally. The atomic bombing of Hiroshima is the subject of *Town of Evening Calm, Country of Cherry Blossoms,* and *Barefoot Gen,* a classic manga that was actually written by a survivor of the bombing. The horror manga *Panorama of Hell* deals with the psychological aftermath.

The Modern Era

By the end of the war, many cities had been bombed to rubble. The reconstruction was a time of gradual recovery. Beginning in 1946, *The Wonderful World of Sazae-san* highlighted amus-

Keiji Nakazawa's *Barefoot Gen*

ing and bemusing aspects of everyday life, including the final years of the U.S. occupation. Political, social, and economic reforms accompanied the rebuilding of the cities. A new constitution was drafted under U.S. supervision. The Japanese written language was simplified, and manga, along with other cheap publications, blossomed, offering affordable entertainment to the long-deprived masses. The dimension-hoppers of *Abenobashi: Magical Shopping Arcade* travel back in time to the postwar reconstruction years when the arcade was founded.

Japan's path to an economic giant was not without bumps. Labor strikes occasionally became violent, and tensions over U.S. bases periodically flared. While the Socialist and Communist parties always had a role in Japanese politics, except during the war, more radical leftist groups formed among university students. The Vietnam War sparked these groups to violent protest in the 1960s. The classic manga *Abandon the Old in Tokyo, The Push Man and Other Stories,* and *Wild 7* express the anxious mood of their times, while *Brigadoon* and *Gatekeepers* are modern sci-fi robot manga set in the same period. Despite these troubles, the Japanese economy prospered until shortly after the death of Emperor Hirohito and the beginning of the Heisei period in 1989. The bursting of the "bubble economy" caused ripples that are still being felt, and with a rapidly aging population, Japan faces new challenges in the years ahead. (PD) gorgeous, simple watercolor paintings that showcase Yasuhiko's talent at its best. His depictions of the locations, including a double-page spread of old Jerusalem, are particularly impressive. (JD)   ★★★★

JING: KING OF BANDITS

Ôdorobô Jing, "King of Bandits Jing" (王ドロボウ JING) • Yuichi Kumakura • Tokyopop (2003–2004) • Kodansha (Comic Bombom, 1995–1998) • 7 volumes • Shônen, Fantasy, Adventure, Comedy • All Ages (mild language, cartoon violence, brief partial nudity)

A triumph of imagination and visuals over plot, *Jing: King of Bandits* is a slapstick fairy-tale fantasy, full of surreal imagery of strange places. Jing, the spiky-haired young hero, and Kir, his talking bird companion, travel from place to place on impossible heists, often acting as a force of anarchy, deposing evil kings and breaking out of prisons. They travel on flying turtles and magic trains; encounter goblins, dragons, and hook-nosed pirates; and go to haunted ghost ships and places such as Adonis, City of Clocks. No plot connects the individual stories, which range from a chapter to about a volume in length, but the premise stays remarkably fresh. Comparisons to *The Wizard of Oz* and other classic children's fantasies aren't inappropriate, although there's a Looney Tunes spirit here as well: there are big explosions and chaos, and Kir, the girl-crazy bird, has the squash-and-stretch look of Western animation. Human violence is minimal and stylized, and Jing is a friendly, kindly hero, although he does cheerfully flip off the camera once or twice.
★★★½

JING: KING OF BANDITS: TWILIGHT TALES

KING OF BANDIT JING • Yuichi Kumakura • Tokyopop (2004–2005) • Kodansha (Magazine Z, 1999–2005) • 7 volumes • Shônen, Fantasy, Adventure • 13+ (mild language, violence)

In contrast to the original *Jing: King of Bandits,* which was published in a magazine for preteens, this sequel was published in a magazine for teenagers. It continues a trend begun in the later volumes of the first series, away from hyperactive children's adventure and toward more wistful, melancholy fantasies. The faraway realms to which Jing travels are now gothic and gloomy, such as Rusty Nail, a city of organ dealers where Jing hunts for "God's brain," and Moulin Rouge, a city so sad that all visitors must pay a Love Tax enforced by ruthless storm troopers. Jing himself looks older, and the art is darker and more realistic. But the fairy-tale mood is the same: "Today's tale is about how the King of Bandits stole Main Street. What's that? Impossible, you say? Well . . . just keep reading." The episodic series has no real ending and, as of late 2006, the possibility remains that more volumes will be released.
★★★½

JINKI: EXTEND

(ジンキ・エクステンド) • Siro Tunasima • ADV (2004) • Mag Garden (Comic Blade, 2002–2006) • 3 volumes, suspended (9 volumes in Japan, suspended) • Science Fiction, Mecha, Action, Comedy • 13+ (language, mild violence, sexual situations)

In the future, war is waged in giant robots called Jinki, which only a select few are qualified to pilot. Enter Akao Hiiragi, a young woman determined to use the power of her Jinki for good. But a dangerous organization is hell-bent on using Jinkis for their own nefarious purposes, and it's up to Akao and her friends to save the day. The plot, characters, and fights are run of the mill for a mecha manga, but *Jinki: Extend*'s strength lies in its clever dialogue. Unfortunately, there is a constant undercurrent of misogyny, with rape themes and frequent insults directed at the female characters. Like several other Mag Garden titles, *Jinki: Extend* is actually the sequel to a title previously published by rival publisher Square Enix; the original series, titled simply *Jinki,* has not been translated. As for *Jinki: Extend* itself, the series went on hiatus in 2007 due to creative disputes between Tunasima and Mag Garden. (LW)
★★

Early images from Yuichi Kumakura's *Jing: King of Bandits*

JOAN

(ジャンヌ) • Yoshikazu Yasuhiko (story and art) • ComicsOne (2001) • Japan Broadcast Publishing (1995–1996) • 3 volumes • Historical, Drama • Unrated/13+ (violence, brief partial nudity)

Unique, intelligent, and sometimes horrifying examination of the life and death of Joan of Arc, as experienced by another French girl who begins seeing visions of Joan and is inspired to follow in her footsteps. As in Yasuhiko's manga *Jesus,* Emil (aka Emily) is a mirror-image character to Joan herself, even raised in Joan's own hometown, and who also wears men's clothes (in Emil's case, to hide from her family's political enemies). When she leaves home to fight for the king of France, just as Joan did, Emil likewise meets the kind of double-dealing and intrigue among nobles that Joan herself had to face, and she finds herself questioning her own spiritual and political commitments. Yasuhiko's full-color artwork is superlative, re-creating the historical details of fifteenth-century France with a sensitive eye for costuming and architecture, and his handling of Emil's story in a first-person narrative sums up all the confusion, exhilaration, and terror of Joan's experiences in a very up-close-and-personal manner. A sublime read. (JD)   ★★★★

JOJO'S BIZARRE ADVENTURE

Jojo no Kimyô na Boken, "JoJo's Bizarre Adventure" (ジョジョの奇妙な冒険) • Hirohiko Araki • Viz (2005–ongoing) • Shueisha (Weekly Shônen Jump, 1987–2004) • 80 volumes • Shônen, Horror, Action-Adventure • 16+ (crude humor, mild language, graphic violence)

Jotaro Kujo, a half-Japanese delinquent of the 1970s *banchô* (gang boss) type, is dragged out of jail by his Indiana Jones–esque British grandfather Joseph Joestar, to join him on a quest around the world to kill Dio—a megalomaniacal one-hundred-year-old vampire with a grudge against the Joestar family. Their journey from Japan to Egypt soon turns into a series of episodic battles against Dio's army of "Stand Users"—individuals who, like Jotaro and his friends, are possessed by tarot-themed spirits with a variety of shapes and abilities. Full of outrageous fashions, weird imagery, and graphic violence, *JoJo's Bizarre Adventure* with its idea of spirits-as-superpowers was an influence on manga as diverse as *Shaman King* and *Yu-Gi-Oh!* Araki's distinctive Western-influenced artwork (reminiscent of a glam combination of Burne Hogarth, Tetsuo Hara, and gag manga), while not "pretty," generally avoids the stiffness of other 1980s macho-man manga, and even the backgrounds and settings, which many manga artists leave entirely in the hands of their assistants, are filled with local color. The overall mood is of suspense and dread, even horror, alternating with unabashed self-referential cheesiness (many of the characters' names contain references to rock and pop music). From the over-the-top dialogue to the sheer gutsiness of the intergenerational story line, it's the signature work of a highly original artist. The Viz edition begins midway through volume 12 of the Japanese edition, skipping the more crudely drawn episodes of Joseph Joestar's early life and Dio's nineteenth-century origin story. Though the series "ended" in 2004, Araki quickly began *Steel Ball Run,* an untranslated pseudo-sequel set in the Wild West. Some violent scenes involving animals were redrawn by the artist for the English edition. ★★★★

JUDAS

Suu Minazuki • Tokyopop (2006–ongoing) • Kadokawa Shoten (Monthly Shônen Ace, 2004–2006) • 5 volumes • Shônen, Occult, Fantasy, Comedy • 16+ (language, graphic violence, brief nudity, sexual situations)

Disguised by the stark gothic covers of the English edition, *Judas* is a ridiculous, nearly incomprehensibly silly action comedy with tons of appropriated Christian imagery. Eve, a wimpy boy who looks like a cute girl, is the earthly vessel of Judas, the spirit of death, who emerges from his body in the form of a spiky-haired, foul-mouthed, killer macho man. (The split-personality dynamic is similar to *Bastard!!*) Mizuki, the girl who befriends Eve, becomes involved in an apocalyptic story involving the FBI, assassins, the Church, and scientific experiments that cause twisted mutant angels to emerge from people's bodies. The artwork is confusing and ugly, and the over-the-top plot isn't amusing enough to be worth the read. ½

JULINE

Kakutô Komusume Juline, "Fighting Girl Juline" (格闘小娘JULINE) • Narumi Kakinouchi • Tokyopop (2000–2002) • Kodansha (Amie/Amie Christmas Tokubetsu-gô, 1997–1998) • 5 volumes • Shôjo, Martial Arts, Fantasy • Unrated/All Ages (violence)

Juline and her two female friends are the teenage heirs of martial arts families in a setting that's half ancient China, half modern-day Japan. (Half of the scenes take place in generic modern schoolrooms, and the other half are set in silk-hung palaces and mysterious pagodas under the full moon.) While our blushing heroine nurtures a crush on her adult martial arts instructor, the three friends fight an evil clan ruled by the sinister Black Pearl, who, not coincidentally, looks a lot like Tamayo Black, their seductive new schoolteacher. A *shôjo* action title packed with an impressive number of fight scenes, *Juline* takes good advantage of Kakinouchi's experience as an animator, drawing the human body in motion. At times the art is sparse, but the panels drift across the pages like windblown leaves. The melodramatic

JÔSEI (女性)

Jôsei (adult women's) manga, the smallest of the four great manga categories, spans the same type of material covered in adult women's fiction in America. *Jôsei* manga started to appear in the late 1970s, when the first generation of *shôjo* manga readers was growing up. A few short-lived manga magazines had targeted older female readers, such as *Funny* (1969), *Jôsei Comic Papillion* (1974), and Shogakukan's still-running *Petit Comic* (1977). However, the market truly took off in 1980 with the appearance of Shueisha's *You,* Kodansha's *Be Love,* and Shogakukan's *Big Comic for Lady* (a spin-off of their popular *Big Comic* line).

Just as *seinen* manga of the time were directed at adult male salarymen, the *jôsei* boom was aimed at female office workers in their twenties and thirties. Perhaps experimenting with what was forbidden in *shôjo* magazines, early *jôsei* were heavy on sex, full of taboo love affairs and erotic fantasies. "Typical readers are working women, who get little attention from men, and housewives who are tired of their marriages," said Taiki Morohashi, who conducted a survey on women's comics in the 1990s. All *jôsei* had acquired a disreputable aura by the time the sex comics split off into their own magazines such as *Comic Amour.* Thus marginalized, and typically known as *redicomi* (ladies' comics), they soon became even more explicit. Less sleazy women's love manga were produced by Harlequin, the famous romance novel publishers, who in 1998 teamed up with Japanese publisher Ohzora Shuppan to produce manga versions of their books. Both sexual *redicomi* and Harlequin manga stories tend to be only one volume long, and none of the former has been translated. Manga romance imprints, with names such as Heartful and Missy, fill the used-books section of Japanese bookstores.

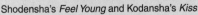
Shodensha's *Feel Young* and Kodansha's *Kiss*

In the late 1980s *jôsei* grew in variety. Adopting the English loanword *young,* which originally described *seinen* comics aimed at college-age men, publishers aimed at younger, hipper, more mobile women. Shueisha's *Young You* (1986), basically as conservative as its bestselling parent magazine, *You,* competed with more daring magazines such as Kodansha's *Kiss* (1992) and fashion magazine publisher Shodensha's *Feel Young* (1989). The ads in these magazines sell things such as jewelry, soaps, handbags, Internet services, and facial treatments. *Kiss* is best known in English for Tomoko Ninomiya's music-school drama *Nodame Cantabile* (2001) and Yayoi Ogawa's *Tramps Like Us* (2000), the story of a female professional who feels pressured to marry up for money and stability but takes in a younger, poorer, shorter man as her "pet." *Feel Young,* a spin-off of the canceled erotic magazine *Feel,* is the most groundbreaking of the three; it published the individualistic comics of Erica Sakurazawa, Mari Okazaki, and Mitsukazu Mihara, as well as Moyoco Anno's *Happy Mania* (1995), an outrageous comedy about a flaky, often jobless woman and the terrible men she sleeps with. *Young You* was canceled in 2005, but its star title, Chika Umino's *Hachimitsu to Clover* ("Honey and Clover") (2000), was transferred to Shueisha's more successful magazine *Chorus* for the remainder of its run. The story of students at an art college, *Hachimitsu to Clover* is seen through the eyes of Hagu, a shy student who looks much younger than her eighteen years; the series features beautiful, whimsical art and was popular enough to be animated, a rarity for *jôsei* manga.

Jôsei stories are mostly realistic: tales of jobs, families, relationships, animals. Period pieces are not uncommon, such as Taeko Watanabe's samurai drama *Kaze Hikaru* (1997), but fantasy elements are subtle and rare. However, many *jôsei* artists are former *shôjo* artists and bring their interests with them; Shogakukan's diverse magazine *Flowers* has run adventure stories by Yumi Tamura and European period melodramas by Chiho Saito, as well as Moto Hagio's *Otherworld Barbara* (2002), a labyrinthine science fiction psychodrama centered on a young girl who is discovered in a coma with her dead parents' hearts in her stomach. A more conventional artist is Yôko Shôji, creator of the classic 1977 school drama *Seito Shokun!* ("Attention Students!"), who took her characters into adulthood in a sequel published in *Be Love. Be Love* and *Flowers,* although very different, represent the most upscale *jôsei* magazines; the bottom rungs are occupied by magazines with names such as *Scandal,* the manga equivalent of tabloids. With artists from so many different time periods and backgrounds, the better *jôsei* magazines contain a fascinating mix of art styles, from detailed to sketchy, lavishly flowery to cool and restrained.

Unlike *shôjo, shônen,* and *seinen* manga, so little *jôsei* has been published in English that it is possible to list all of it in one place. It is one of the last great frontiers of manga translation. In 2007, *jôsei* manga publisher Ohzora Shuppan announced the formation of a U.S. branch named Aurora Publishing, the first *jôsei*-focused publisher to do so.

Jôsei Manga

Antique Bakery • *Awabi* • *Devil in the Water* • *Dolis* • *Doll* • *Dream Hotel* • *Erica Sakurazawa* (*Angel* • *Angel Nest* • *The Aromatic Bitters* • *Between the Sheets* • *Nothing but Loving You* • *The Rules of Love*) • *Galaxy Girl* • *Happy Mania* • *Harlequin Violet: Blind Date* • *Harlequin Violet: Holding on to Alex* • *Harlequin Violet: Response* • *Kaze Hikaru* •

story has an undercurrent of mystery reminiscent of Kakinouchi's horror work. ★★½

JUNK FORCE

(ジャンクフォース) • Kenichi Matukawa (mechanical design), Eiji Komato (character design), Hideki Kakinuma (DARTS) (story), Yusuke Ken (art) • ComicsOne (2004) • MediaWorks (Dengeki Gao!, 2002–2003) • 3 volumes • Shônen, Science Fiction, Mecha, Comedy • 16+ (language, violence, nudity)

A weak attempt at an anime/manga/novel multimedia franchise. As explained in the small print in the intro, the year is 2134, and Earth has become a scorched desert scarred by an ongoing war with the rebel human colonists of Mars. Four girls and one nebbishy guy (who keeps accidentally grabbing the girls' breasts and panties) roam the landscape in a hovertank, trying to shut down the automated Earth Purification System that threatens to wipe out what little life remains. Halfway decent mechanical designs are all that stand out among a formulaic plot and ugly, occasionally exploitative artwork.
½

JUNKO MIZUNO'S CINDERALLA

Mizuno Junko no Cinderalla-chan, "Junko Mizuno's Cinderalla" (水野純子のシンデラーラちゃん) • Junko Mizuno • Viz (2002) • Koushinsya (2000) • 1 volume • Underground, Fantasy, Romance • 18+ (nudity)

The first of pop/underground artist's Mizuno's three fractured fairy tales, *Cinderalla* is a goth version of the original story, drawn in Mizuno's usual style, which resembles *My Little Pony* meets Hideshi Hino. Cinderalla works at her father's *yakitori* restaurant, until her dad dies and returns as a zombie, bringing with him a zombie stepmother and stepsisters. The overall mood is of a delightful jewelry box, a cheerfully cute-creepy story full of Mizuno's favorite things to draw, like syringes and strange, bare-breasted women. Includes stickers and an interview with the artist. Printed in color on intentionally cheap, pulpy paper. ★★★

JUNKO MIZUNO'S HANSEL AND GRETEL

Mizuno Junko no Hansel & Gretel, "Junko Mizuno's Hansel & Gretel" (水野純子のハンセル&グレーテル) • Junko Mizuno • Viz (2003) • Koushinsya (2000) • 1 volume • Underground, Fantasy, Romance • 18+ (nudity)

Hansel and Gretel, redesigned as tough schoolkids from a 1970s manga, must save their happy hometown from a wicked spell. The goofiest and least faithful of Mizuno's three fairy-tale adaptations, *Hansel and Gretel* is focused on food and dieting, featuring such Mizuno-esque creations as a giant pink pig that considerately slices pieces off itself so people can eat them. Includes stickers, paper dolls, and other extras. Printed in color on intentionally cheap, pulpy paper. ★★★

JUNKO MIZUNO'S PRINCESS MERMAID

Ningyohime Den, "The Mermaid Princesses' Court" (人魚姫殿) • Junko Mizuno • Viz (2004) • Bunkasha (2002) • 1 volume • Underground, Fantasy, Romance • 18+ (violence, nudity, sex)

In keeping with Hans Christian Andersen's original story, *Princess Mermaid* is the most emotionally intense—not to mention violent and sexual—of Mizuno's fairy-tale adaptations. Three mermaid sisters run a brothel under the sea, until one of them falls in love with a human who works for the loathsome fish-processing plant that killed their mother. The well-written plot is red with rape, cannibalism, and mermaid spawn, and the undersea settings inspire Mizuno to some of her most beautiful artwork. Includes postcards and other extras. Printed in color on intentionally cheap, pulpy paper.

★★★★

JUNK: RECORD OF THE LAST HERO

Kia Asamiya • DrMaster (2006–ongoing) • Akita Shoten (Champion Red, 2004–2007) • 7+ volumes (ongoing) • Seinen, Tokusatsu, Action, Drama • 18+ (graphic violence, nudity, sex)

High school student Hiro receives a strange power suit in the mail. The Junk armored suit gives him incredible speed and strength. Eager to get revenge on the people who bullied him, he wears the suit on nightly rampages of sheer power, his identity concealed by his helmet. But as someone once said about another hero, "with great power comes great responsibility," and when Hiro encounters a woman with her own Junk suit, he must face the consequences of his actions.

NR

JU-ON

Jûon Video Side: Jogaku, "Grudge Video Side: Prelude" (呪怨序案) • Takashi Shimizu (story), Miki Rinno (art) • Dark Horse (2006) • Kadokawa Shoten (2003) • 1 volume • Horror • Unrated/16+ (language, graphic violence)

"Whenever someone dies in the grip of a powerful rage, a curse is born. That curse lingers in the place of death." Such a fearful condition afflicts a normal-looking suburban house in the Nerima ward of Tokyo. Years ago, a husband brutally murdered his wife, Kayoko, there, and their six-year-old son, Toshio, went missing soon after. Now whoever occupies the house is affected by a mysterious virus-like haunting and is sure to endure malevolent spectral appearances by the undead Kayoko and Toshio. Inspired by

the popular *Ju-On* film franchise (remade by Hollywood as *The Grudge*), *Ju-On* volume 1 (aka *Ju-On: Video Side*) follows the new owners, and teenage guests, of this haunted house as they come to grips with the horror that awaits them inside. Clearly designed for younger readers, Miki Rinno's underdeveloped *shôjo* art style seems at odds with the moody atmosphere of the rest of the *Ju-On* series. With new characters continually introduced, only to be dispatched a few pages later, the story is also a bit hard to follow. (PM)

★★

JU-ON VOL. 2

Jûon, "Grudge" (呪怨) • Takashi Shimizu (story), Meimu (art) • Dark Horse (2006) • Kadokawa Shoten (2003) • 1 volume • Horror • Unrated/16+ (language, graphic violence)

In this sequel to *Ju-On,* an aging horror film star is sent to investigate the dreaded house for a TV special. The second volume has much better art (courtesy of Meimu) and is much more successful at replicating the films' mix of unsettling psychological undercurrents and drop-kick gross-outs. (PM)

★★★

JU-ON: VIDEO SIDE: See *Ju-On*

JUROR 13

DJ Milky (story), Makoto Nakatsuka (art) • Tokyopop (2006) • 1 volume • Mystery, Suspense • 16+ (language, mild violence, sex, brief partial nudity)

The product of an American writer and a Japanese artist, *Juror 13* turns every adult's hassle into a paranoid nightmare: the dark chain of events begins when the main character receives a mysterious jury summons. Jeremy, an ordinary insurance claims investigator, starts to suspect that someone is plotting against him, and he follows the clues down a path of violence, passion, and car chases. A last-minute twist ending seems *too* sudden and leaves the reader expecting more. A less anime-influenced, more gritty art style would have served the material better.

★★

JUST A GIRL

Datte Onna no Ko na no Yo, "Even Though We're Girls" (だって女のコなのよぉ) • Tomoko Taniguchi • CPM (2003) • Jitsugyo no Nihonsha (1992) • 2 volumes • Shôjo, Romance • 13+ (brief partial nudity)

Taniguchi's longest and best-written story. Erica Fujita moves into the girls' dorm of a new high school, where she makes friends with Rena, a girl with a bad reputation. (They bond over a mutual love of stuffed animals.) Soon they both meet Sophie, a French girl from a local international college, and Rocky, a Japanese boy who wants to go to America and become a movie star. The pleasantly drifting plot, as much about friendship and new experiences as romance, feels like it could have been inspired by personal experience. Volume 2 also includes two unrelated short stories. ★★½

JUSTICE

Various • Antarctic (1994) • Dôjinshi (1981–1994) • 1 issue • Superhero • All Ages

This cross-cultural oddity translates assorted material from *Justice* and *Gadget,* Japanese *dôjinshi* fanzines devoted to American superheroes (mostly Batman, Iron Man, the X-Men, Teen Titans, and Alpha Flight). The entertaining and often well-drawn mishmash includes plentiful pin-ups, four-panel gag manga, and Japanese fanboy commentary on Howard Chaykin, Todd MacFarlane, John Byrne, and others. The Japanese artists include Toshihiro Ono (who drew the slick covers), Tommy Ohtsuka (as "Studio Zombie"), and Yujin Ishikawa, who wrote most of the articles. ★★★

JUSTY

(ジャスティ) • Tsuguo Okazaki • Viz (1988–1989) • Shogakukan (Shônen Sunday Zôkan-Gô, 1981–1984) • 9 issues, suspended (5 volumes in Japan) • Shônen, Psychic, Science Fiction • 13+ (violence)

Super ESPer Justy is a psychic agent of the Galactic Patrol, who uses his abilities (teleportation, power blasts, mind reading, etc.) to fight evil psychics around the universe. His companions include Astalis, a powerful psychic with the body of a grown woman and the mind of a five-year-old. Okazaki's art has the sparse backgrounds and figure-drawing ability of 1970s *gekiga* artists such as Ryoichi Ikegami, but his characters' child-like, cute faces foretell the anime style of the 1980s. The episodic stories are well told; only people familiar with the original Japanese edition will notice that the English edition skips around, rather than starting from the beginning. ★★½

JUVENILE ORION: See *Aquarian Age: Juvenile Orion*

KABUTO

Karasutengu Kabuto, "Crow Tengu Kabuto" (鴉天狗カブト) • Buichi Terasawa • ComicsOne (2001) • Shueisha (Fresh Jump, 1987–1988) • 2 volumes • Shônen, Occult, Ninja, Fantasy, Action • Unrated/16+ (mild language, nudity, violence)

Pitting a handful of valiant ninjas against all the legions of hell, this nutty fantasy yarn gives Terasawa a chance to display all the powers of creativity and imagination he evidently didn't feel like wasting on *Gokui: Midnight Eye.* The skimpy and incoherent story is merely a pretext for extended battle sequences in which our heroes slug it out with man-eating fish, demonic masks, haunted boats, and flying castles, and there are many moments of breathtaking spectacle. The second volume, in which Kabuto's team of ninja-god sidekicks inexplicably vanishes and the story starts over as a solo adventure, isn't nearly as entertaining as the first one. But at least we still have the ridiculous Dragon Manji Ship, not to mention ComicsOne's weirdly stilted English dialogue, which charmingly re-creates the feeling of a badly dubbed martial arts spectacular. (MS) ★★½

KAGEROU-NOSTALGIA: THE RESURRECTION

Kagerô Nostalgia: Shinshô, "Heat Haze Nostalgia: The New Chapter" (陽炎ノスタルジア〜新章) • Satomi Kubo • ADV (2004) • Mag Garden (Comic

Blade, 2002–2005) • 1 volume, suspended (3 volumes in Japan) • Fantasy • All Ages (violence)

The sequel to the untranslated *Kagerou Nostalgia,* this series fails to stand on its own without the original series, and comes across as frustrating, poorly plotted chaos. In a vaguely ancient-Japanese fantasy setting (with bazookas and the occasional monster), reincarnated warriors fight a war between good and evil clans, after briefly introducing themselves with catchphrases and snapshots. The plot would be incomprehensible if not for the explanatory text on the book cover, and the art consists of poorly drawn, melancholy pretty boys wearing costumes ripped off from RPG video games.   ½

KAGETORA

(カゲトラ) • Akira Segami • Del Rey (2006–ongoing) • Kodansha (Weekly Shônen Magazine/Shônen Magazine Special, 2001–2005) • 11 volumes • Shônen, Martial Arts, Romantic Comedy • 13+ (mild violence, partial nudity, mild sexual situations)

Kagetora, a young ninja kid of the ultra-traditional black clothes and throwing-stars variety, moves into the Toudou family dojo to help train and protect Yuki, the clumsy daughter of the family. Condescending love comedy situations for younger readers ensue, mostly involving Yuki bending down to expose badly drawn cleavage while looking up at Kagetora with big doe eyes. Weak artwork and derivative premise.   ½

KAMEN TANTEI

Kamen Tantei, "The Masked Detective" (仮面探偵) • Matsuri Akino • Tokyopop (2006–2007) • Akita Shoten (Susperia Mystery 1998–2000) • 4 volumes • Shôjo, Comedy, Mystery • 13+ (violence)

Haruko and Masato are high-schoolers who write mystery novels under a collective pen name. Suddenly they start running into murders and other mysteries in real life, and as they puzzle out the plot twists, a mysterious masked detective—who, strangely enough, goes by their pen name—shows up out of nowhere and explains how the crimes were committed. Ghosts and fictional characters coming to life are all part of the harmless weirdness. Though ultimately generic, the story is at its best when it's making fun of its own genre ("This is the dumbest thing ever! If ghosts solved crimes, there wouldn't be any police or detectives!"). In Japan it was followed by a short-lived sequel, *Shin Kamen Tantei* ("New Masked Detective").   ★★

KAMICHAMA KARIN

Kamichama Karin, "God Karin" (かみちゃまかりん) • Koge-Donbo • Tokyopop (2005–2007) • Kodansha (Nakayoshi, 2002–2005) • 7 volumes • Shôjo, Magical Girl, Fantasy • All Ages (mild comic violence)

Karin, an energetic elementary school orphan, uses a magic ring to become the Greek goddess Athena, in the process shouting her signature phrase: "I am God!" But actually, she's not the only god; several Greek gods eventually show up, most of them connected to her classmates, such as handsome but obnoxious Kujyou. Apart from the intentionally silly catchphrase, this well-made fluff has no religious elements, ancient Greek or otherwise. Koge-Donbo's very fun, very modern art style alternates polished prettiness with self-parodying, intentionally crude art. In their cute moments, the characters have big eyes like gumdrops and say things like "Criminy crumbs!" In their slapstick moments, they look as abstract as Internet emoticons.   ★★½

KAMI-KAZE

Kamikaze, "Divine Wind" (神・風) • Satoshi Shiki • Tokyopop (2006–ongoing) • Kodansha (Afternoon, 1997–2003) • 7 volumes • Seinen, Martial Arts, Fantasy, Action • 18+ (language, extreme graphic violence, nudity, sex)

Kamuro, the sword-swinging descendant of one of the five great elemental clans, comes to Tokyo to find the legendary "girl of water." When he finds her, he is just in time to rescue her from members of the other clans, who have turned evil and want to use her in a ritual to resurrect the monstrous "88 Beasts." Satoshi Shiki is an extremely polished, detailed artist who draws lavish photo backgrounds, acceptable humans (a rogue's gallery of cyborgs and weirdos), and interesting monsters possibly inspired by Japanese myth. But the plot is just an excuse to draw action and succeeds mostly as scattered interesting images with the occasional comprehensible fight scene. The characters don't make much sense or have consistent personalities, and the background of the warring clans is mostly explained in a lengthy text block in volume 2, between scenes of fighting and arguing. ★★

KAMIKAZE GIRLS

Shimotsuma Monogatari, "Shimotsuma Story" (下妻物語) • Novala Takemoto (story), Yukio Kanesada (art) • Viz (2006) • Shogakukan (2004) • 1 volume • Shôjo, Comedy, Drama • 16+ (language, mild violence, sex)

Adaptation of Novala Takemoto's novel of the same name. Gothic Lolita fashion fan Momoko lives in the sticks but still manages to live a baroque life in her heart. There's no reason she should become friends with boyish girl-gang member Ichiko, but despite their differences, Momoko and Ichiko's lives are drawn inextricably together. From Tokyo to the farthest corner of the boonies, Ichiko and Momoko travel through the worlds of "Goth-Loli" fashion and gang warfare, with side trips into romance, eventually becoming close friends. An amusing take on the *Odd Couple* formula, the manga lacks the punch of the *Kamikaze Girls* novel or the surrealism of the movie but makes a nice break from the usual girls' manga fare. The book also includes several non–*Kamikaze Girls* stories written by Yukio Kanesada. (EF) ★★½

KAMIKAZE KAITO JEANNE

Kamikaze Kaitô Jeanne, "Divine Wind Phantom Thief Jeanne" (神風怪盗ジャンヌ) • Arina Tanemura • CMX (2005–2007) • Shueisha (Ribon, 1998– 2000) • 7 volumes • Shôjo, Magical Girl, Phantom Thief, Romance • All Ages

Maron Kusakabe is the star of her school's rhythmic gymnastics team and the reincarnation of Jeanne d'Arc (Joan of Arc). In her magical form of Kamikaze Kaito Jeanne, accompanied by angel-in-training Finn, Maron "steals" paintings that have been possessed by demons, thus releasing the paintings' owners from the demon's enchantment. (So, like the very similar *Saint Tail,* she's doing *good* deeds by stealing.) Adding to the difficulty of her task is the appearance of Kaito Sinbad, a magical boy thief, who is her rival for the paintings but ends up falling in love with Maron (and vice versa). *Kaitou Jeanne* is a children's story about friendship, honor, and trust, with a background of betrayal, loneliness, and abandonment. Artistically, the style is reminiscent of Miho Obana's *Kodocha,* but lacks Obana's elegance: the necks become overlong, the heads sitting on top of them like carnival character faces. The action scenes are also occasionally hard to follow. *Chibi* characters are used to good comedic effect. (EF) ★★½

KAMIYADORI

(カミヤドリ) • Kei Sanbe • Tokyopop (2006–2008) • Kadokawa Shoten (Monthly Shônen Ace, 2004– 2006) • 5 volumes • Shônen, Gothic, Action • 18+

Think of it as extreme medical quarantine. With humanity threatened by a mutagenic virus that transforms people into monsters (the Kamiyadori of the title), an elite squad of peacekeeping officers are created to exterminate the victims of the disease and keep the contagion from spreading. These agents are known as the Right Arms, and you'll never guess which of their limbs are endowed with special superpowers to help them lay the smack down on rampaging Kamiyadori. Brought to you, with an extra helping of giant monster-chopping scissors, by the creator of *Testarotho.* (MS) NR

KAMUI

Shingo Nanami • Broccoli Books (2005–ongoing) • Square Enix (Stencil/Monthly Gangan Wing,

2001–2006) • 11 volumes • Postapocalyptic, Fantasy, Action • 13+ (violence, sexual situations)

In the future, Japan has been devastated by earthquakes, and civilization survives only in the ruins of Tokyo, where NOA—a military academy for superpowered teenagers—protects the people from mysterious giant monsters. From a faraway village comes Atsuma, a mysterious boy with a mission: to release the *kamui,* the nature spirits that are the source of NOA's power. Although the plot has echoes of the movie *Final Fantasy: The Spirits Within, Kamui* is basically an angst-ridden superhero comic in which good-looking characters fight one another and deliver clunky-sounding nihilistic dialogue. The art tries hard to be stylish, but Nanami's anatomy is weak, and her long-haired, long-legged, big-lipped character designs are unmemorable. The art gradually improves, but the story doesn't. ★½

KAMUI DEN: See *The Legend of Kamui Perfect Collection*

KAMUNAGARA: REBIRTH OF THE DEMONSLAYER

Kamunagara (カムナガラ) • Hajime Yamamura • Media Blasters (2004–2006) • Shônen Gahosha (Young King Ours, 2000–2006) • 6 volumes, suspended (11 volumes in Japan) • Seinen, Occult, Horror, Action • 16+ (brief language, graphic violence, brief nudity)

After a series of strange dreams, teenage kendo student Hitaka is attacked by a grotesque monster in broad daylight and defends himself with a sword that—to his surprise—emerges from his hand. Kanata, a troubled girl who claims to have known him in a past life, tells him that he is the last of the Clan of the Sword and that he alone can stop the (mostly) silent, body-possessing demons who are returning to the world. Dark conspiracies and withdrawn, weary protagonists mark *Kamunagara* as a product of the late 1990s angst-ridden hero generation, as epitomized by *Neon Genesis Evangelion.* The fight scenes are perfunctory, and the series errs on the side of not explaining

enough rather than explaining too much, but the horror intrudes on the real world in a gripping manner. The big shock moments in volumes 4 and 5, when the demons' origin is revealed, are genuinely disturbing.

★★★

KANNA

(神無) • Takeru Kirishima • Go! Comi (2007–ongoing) • MediaWorks (Dengeki Daioh, 2001–2005) • 4 volumes • Fantasy, Comedy • 16+ (violence, sexual situations)

Kagura, a college dropout, has strange dreams of the Tokugawa era, which come to life when he wakes up to find a mysterious mute girl in his bed! A sudden assault by monsters and demons leads him to realize that the girl, Kanna, is a visitor from a parallel world, and soon the pair must go on a strange quest in modern-day Japan. NR

KANPAI!

Kimi no Unaji no Kanpai!, "A Toast to the Nape of Your Neck!" (キミのうなじに乾杯！) • Maki Murakami • Tokyopop (2005) • Gentosha (Comic Birz, 2001) • 2 volumes • Comedy • 13+ (language, graphic violence, brief nudity)

Kanpai! has one great joke: the hyperactive main character is a "monster hunter hunter," who protects man-eating monsters from being overhunted by clichéd manga heroes. After the first twenty pages, it's hit-or-miss, although its best moments show Maki Murakami's talent for goofy facial expressions and absurd panel-by-panel comedy. Unfortunately, the second volume ends on a cliff-hanger, and as of December 2006 Murakami shows no signs of finishing the series, not that it had much plot to begin with. ★½

KARASUTENGU KABUTO: See *Kabuto*

KARE FIRST LOVE

Kare First Love, "He/My Boyfriend First Love" (彼 first love) • Kaho Miyasaka • Viz (2004–2006) • Shogakukan (Shôjo Comic, 2002–2004) • 10 volumes • Shôjo, Romance • 13+ (partial nudity, sexual situations)

Almost a relationship how-to book, *Kare First Love* is a shy girl's fantasy of having a boyfriend. Karin, a neurotically timid girl with glasses, is approached by Kiriya, a handsome student photographer who spontaneously kisses her, asks her out, buys her new clothes and lipstick, and promises not to leave her if she gets pregnant. Of course, obstacles stand between them, such as disapproving parents and . . . well, actually, there really aren't many obstacles. Graced with attractive, sexy artwork, *Kare First Love* is a very simple story, with really only two characters, and driven by the purest teenage emotions: anxiety, love, and the ever-present phantom of sex. ("It's all I ever think about. Maybe I'm *perverted* . . . ?") In that sense, it doesn't matter that both the hero and heroine are ciphers, or that Karin's passivity borders on depression; the characters exist simply so that the reader can vicariously experience the scenario. ★★½

KARE KANO: HIS AND HER CIRCUMSTANCES

Kareshi Kanojo no Jijô, "His and Her Circumstances/Situation" (彼氏彼女の事情) • Masami Tsuda • Tokyopop (2003–2007) • Hakusensha (LaLa, 1996–2005) • 21 volumes • Shôjo, Romantic Drama • 13+ (mild language, brief violence, sexual situations, adult themes)

Fifteen-year-old Yukino Miyazawa is the most popular girl in school, seemingly the nicest, loveliest, smartest student there is . . . except possibly for her male equivalent, the handsome, brilliant Soichiro Arima. But it's all a front; Yukino is a praise-hungry overachiever who sees school as a competition with Arima, and Arima has problems of his own, until they discover each other's secret sides and their rivalry turns into love. "Being perfect will not make people love you" is the moral of *Kare Kano,* a well-written high school love story that starts out as an exercise in romantic realpolitik before drifting into cliché. At its best, it's full of believable and funny relationship moments: people struggle to fill awkward pauses in conversation, girls put barrettes in boys' hair, and Yukino egomaniacally declares, "In the game of love, the adored one has all the power! Ha ha ha!" As it goes on, however, the series becomes cloying and predictable, beginning with several volumes of side stories in which Yukino's friends are paired off into romantic couples, two at a time. Then, starting from volume 13, the mood darkens and sinks into melodrama involving Arima's tortured past. As it turns out, "her circumstances" are basically those of a normal person, but "his circumstances" involve child abuse, trauma, and black despair, which jars with the previously established mood of the series. In place of realistic relationships, we get a melodrama about a girl who soothes the wounds of a tormented genius—a well-written but well-worn plotline. The 1998 anime adaptation, by *Neon Genesis Evangelion* director Hideaki Anno, emphasized the comedy elements and gag-style artwork of the early parts of the manga and was disliked by Tsuda as a result. ★★½

KASHIMASHI: GIRL MEETS GIRL

(かしまし〜ガール・ミーツ・ガール〜) • Satoru Akahori (story), Yukimaru Katsura (art) • Seven Seas Entertainment (2006–ongoing) • MediaWorks (Dengeki Daioh, 2004–ongoing) • 5+ volumes (ongoing) • Yuri, Romantic Comedy • 16+ (partial nudity, sexual situations)

"Even though I became a girl, I love her still." Hazumu, a delicate high school boy who has always been uncomfortable with his gender, confesses his love to his female friend Yasuna. He is rejected, but not long after, he is injured by a UFO crash and reconstructed by humanoid aliens, who accidentally give him a girl's body. A lesbian love triangle soon develops between the new "him" and two of his female classmates. More a romance than a comedy, *Kashimashi* is a pure body-swap fantasy into which the presumably male reader (it was serialized in a *shônen* magazine) can project himself; Hazumu's original "male" face is never shown. NR

KATSUYA TERADA'S THE MONKEY KING

Saiyukiden Daienô, "Legend of the Journey to the West: The Great Monkey King" (西遊記伝大猿王) • Katsuya Terada • Dark Horse (2005–ongoing) • Shueisha (Ultra Jump, 1995–ongoing) • 1+ volume (ongoing) • Seinen, Fantasy • 18+ (language, extreme graphic violence, nudity, sex)

Painted in feverish reds and purples, replete with gore and bare-breasted women, this loose full-color retelling of the Chinese legend *Saiyûki* has more in common with *Heavy Metal* magazine than with manga. Across strange wastelands travels the Monkey King, a savage, bestial monster who was imprisoned for five hundred years for defying the will of the Buddha. Sanzo the monk, who freed him from his shackles, takes the role of a gagged, blindfolded woman tied to the back of a horse. Instead of a repentant, merely mischievous villain, Terada's Monkey King is the id unbound. In 8-page segments with minimal dialogue and exposition, he spills the brains of the gods with his phallic staff, rapes and eats half-naked demon women, and fights the glistening insect/cyborg/angel inhabitants of Terada's imagination. Lengthy cultural and translation notes provide interesting reading; the story continuity is minimal, but fans of Richard Corben and Simon Bisley will recognize Terada as a talented kindred spirit. ★★★

KAZAN

Gaku Miyao • ComicsOne (2000–2002) • Shônen Gahosha (Young King Ours, 1997–2001) • 7 volumes • Shônen, Fantasy, Adventure • Unrated/All Ages (mild language, violence, brief partial nudity)

Kazan, a nomad warrior whose body is stuck in the shape of an eight-year-old boy, wanders the desert in search of the faraway land of Goldene, where he hopes to find a girl from his childhood . . . the only other survivor of his devastated tribe. His traveling companions include Kamushin (Kazan's pet eagle), Fawna (a girl with the power to conjure water), and Arbey (a crafty old crone who looks like a witch from a Disney movie). An adventure with an orig-inal setting, a touching story, and pleasant artwork, *Kazan* is comparable to the works of Hayao Miyazaki. Despite some blood and violence, the story is basically suitable for all ages. ★★★★

KAZE HIKARU

Kaze Hikaru, "The Shining Wind/The Wind Shines" (風光る) • Taeko Watanabe • Viz (2005–ongoing) • Shogakukan (Flowers, 1997–2006) • Shôjo, Historical Drama • 20 volumes • 16+ (mild language, mild crude humor, violence, sexual situations)

In 1863 Kyoto, with Japan divided between isolationism and modernization, peace is maintained by the *Miburôshi* ("Wolves of Mibu"), a group of semiofficial mercenary swordsmen. (The *Miburôshi* are better known by their later name: the *Shinsengumi,* "Newly Selected Squad.") Seeking to avenge the murder of her family by extremists, fifteen-year-old Sei disguises herself as a boy and joins the mercenaries, where she rubs shoulders with future historical figures and finds, to her dismay, that most of them are stinky guys who tell dirty jokes and don't live up to her ideals. Drawn in a simplified, gentle style, *Kaze Hikaru* at first glance looks like an old-fashioned children's manga. But it's an intelligent historical adaptation; Watanabe is aware that real events are always more surprising than scripted ones, and real people are rarely pure good or evil. (Only the main character comes off as morally uncomplicated.) At the same time, it follows a classic *shôjo* formula, the *Hana-Kimi* formula of the girl in a boy's world, who first admires and then loves her male companion. The plot moves slowly, focusing mostly on farming, household finances, and other nonglamorous activities, but the infrequent swordplay is treated seriously and usually ends in death (unlike in, say, *Rurouni Kenshin*). For readers who can get past the slow moments and the old-fashioned art, it's a well-written series. ★★★

KEDAMONO DAMONO

Kedamono Damono, "I'm a Beast" (けだものだもの) • Haruka Fukushima • Tokyopop (2007) • Kodansha

(Nakayoshi Lovely, 2004–2005) • 2 volumes • Shôjo, Romantic Comedy • 16+

Konatsu is the manager of the boys' basketball team, and she has a crush on Haruki, one of the players, who's older than her. Unfortunately, Haruki has a problem . . . he transforms from a boy by day to a pervy girl by night!　　　　　　　　　　　　NR

KEIJI

Hana no Keiji: Kumo no Kanata ni, "Keiji of the Flowers: Beyond the Clouds" (花の慶次—雲のかなたに) • Tetsuo Hara (art), Keiichiro Ryu (story), Mio Aso (scriptwriter) • Gutsoon! Entertainment (2003–2004) • Shueisha (Weekly Shônen Jump, 1990–1993) • 28 issues, suspended (18 volumes in Japan) • Shônen, Samurai, Comedy, Drama • Unrated/16+ (mild language, crude humor, graphic violence, nudity, sexual situations)

Fanciful historical drama loosely based on the life of Keiji Maeda, a seventeenth-century swordsman known for his flamboyance, love of song and dance, and personal code of honor. As a *shônen* manga drawn by the artist of *Fist of the North Star,* however, it comes across as a mix of samurai superheroism and low-comedy hijinks; Keiji leads armies, pees on the heads of his enemies, wins the hearts of women, and makes fools of ugly, blundering bad guys such as his villainous uncle (the local feudal lord) and his uncle's ninja assistant. The square-jawed, cheesy art dumbs down the subject matter, and the story is burdened with obtrusive historical narration. Serialized in *Raijin Comics* numbers 19–46; never collected in graphic novel form.　　　　　　　　　　　★½

KEKKAISHI

Kekkaishi, "Binding Boundary Master" (結界師) • Yellow Tanabe • Viz (2005–ongoing) • Shogakukan (Weekly Shônen Sunday, 2003–ongoing) • 16+ volumes (ongoing) • Shônen, Fantasy, Adventure • 13+ (mild language, violence)

Teenage Yoshimori is the modern-day heir to a family of demon hunters; his female neighbor Tokine is heir to a rival clan. Every night he and Tokine compete to hunt evil spirits, which they sniff out using talking demon dogs and fight with their powers of *kekkaishi*—the ability to create and destroy square force fields, which can be used as shields, cages, or bombs. *Kekkaishi* combines the traditional Japanese monsters of *Inuyasha* with the spiritualism and a bit of the funky humor of *Bleach.* (Yoshimori's big goal in life is to be a cake maker, and one of his friends is a ghostly chef, whom he eventually sends to a counselor who specializes in treating ghosts.) The pace is relaxed for a boys' manga, with the whimsical coolness of *Shônen Sunday* rather than the fiery urgency of *Shônen Jump;* the characters speak in actual dialogue rather than trading melodramatic declarations. Like puzzles in a video game, the hero conquers monsters and challenges by skillful use of his powers; meanwhile, he investigates mysterious demons, the "shadow organization," and the ancient shrine buried beneath his school. The art is in a smooth anime-influenced style.　　　　　　　　　　　★★★

KEY PRINCESS STORY: ETERNAL ALICE RONDO

Kagihime Monogatari Eikyû Alice Rondo, "Key Princess Story Eternal Alice Rondo" (鍵姫物語永久アリス輪舞曲[ロンド]) • Kaishaku • DrMaster (2006–ongoing) • MediaWorks (Dengeki Daioh, 2004–2006) • 4 volumes • Shônen, Fantasy, Adventure • 16+

Aruko Kirihara is a student obsessed with *Alice in Wonderland,* to the point of writing a sequel. One day he meets a girl who looks like his heroine, and he is pulled into a strange world of bunny-eared girls and unusual creatures, where he must go on a quest to discover the *true* sequel to the classic novel.　　　　　　　　　　　NR

KEY TO THE KINGDOM

Ôkoku no Kagi, "Key to the Kingdom" (王国の鍵) • Kiyoko Shitou • CMX (2007–ongoing) • Kadokawa Shoten (Asuka, 2003–2004) • 6 volumes • Shôjo, Fantasy, Adventure • 13+

When the kingdom of Laudeure loses its eldest prince in war, Asha, the only surviving son of the royal family, must take the throne. But first he must complete a quest to find the legendary Key to the Kingdom. Asha sets out on his journey, pursued by rivals, facing monsters and strange beasts. . . . NR

KIDS JOKER

(キッズ・ジョーカー) • Maki Fujita • ADV (2005) • Akita Shoten (Princess, 1998–2000) • 1 volume, suspended (6 volumes in Japan) • Shôjo, Detective, Romantic Drama • 13+ (violence)

Hotaru Yanagawa, a tough high school girl who gets in fights and wants to be a police detective, meets Yui Kajiwara, a good-looking, outwardly easygoing older guy who turns out to belong to a group of undercover crime fighters. Determined to solve cases on her own, she butts heads with him repeatedly ("Girls aren't supposed to do *dangerous* stuff like this!") as they become involved in increasingly risky cases. Unfortunately for this would-be "action love story," the plot is hard to follow and the art is flat. ★

KIKAIDER CODE 02

(キカイダー02) • Shotaro Ishinomori (story), MEIMU (art) • CMX (2005–2006) • Kadokawa Shoten (Monthly Ace Next/Monthly Shônen Ace/Ace Tokunô/Tokusatsu Ace, 2000–2004) • 6 volumes • Shônen, Tokusatsu, Science Fiction, Action • 18+ (graphic violence, nudity)

Mitsuko Komyoji is the daughter of the late Dr. Komyoji, a scientist forced to make powerful machine-monsters for an evil organization called DARK that wants to rid the Earth of humanity. Dr. Komyoji's most recent creation is an android equipped with a "conscious circuit" that gives the machine the ability to choose between good and evil. Created to fight against the DARK androids, this robot has two forms: a gentle human named Jiro and a machine warrior named Kikaider. One of the most popular live-action TV superheroes of the 1970s, Kikaider was the creation of Shotaro Ishinomori, who possessed a prolific imagination rivaled per-

haps only by that of Osamu Tezuka. Like many of Ishinomori's creations, Kikaider was a sentient android struggling to exist in a human world. Created after Ishinomori's death (although he still receives story credit), *Kikaider Code 02* is a remake of the original 1970s story updated with graphic violence. The impressively detailed artwork of MEIMU, better known for his horror titles, makes for an enjoyable experience for adults weaned on the rubber-suited original superhero. (PM) ★★★

KILALA PRINCESS

Kirara Princess (きららプリンセス) • Nao Kodaka (art), Rika Tanaka (story) • Tokyopop (2007–ongoing) • Kodansha (Nakayoshi, 2005–ongoing) • 3+ volumes (ongoing) • Shôjo, Fantasy, Romance • All Ages

Disney's master plan to capture the hearts and minds of little girls everywhere continues with this fantasy adventure revolving around the company's stable of iconic princesses. When Kilala awakens a sleeping prince, she gains the powers of all her beloved Disney princesses, which will surely come in handy when they set off to find a missing princess and rescue Kilala's kidnapped friend. (MS) NR

KINDAICHI CASE FILES

Kindaichi Shônen no Jikenbo, "Casebook of Young Kindaichi" (金田一少年の事件簿) • Fumiya Sato (art), Yozaburo Kanari (story) • Toykopop (2003–ongoing) • Kodansha (Weekly Shônen Magazine, 1992–2001) • 37 volumes • Shônen, Mystery • 13+ (graphic violence, brief nudity, sexual situations)

Cocky teenage sleuth Hajime Kindaichi, grandson of Japan's most famous detective, Kosuke Kindaichi, solves complicated murder mysteries on a regular basis, mostly gruesome multiple slayings involving decapitations and dismemberment. Formulaic as a TV mystery show, Kindaichi reliably solves one complete case per volume, but his own accompanying personal drama is rather bland. (Kindaichi's studious classmate Miyuki is clearly meant to be his Ms. Right, although he sees her merely as a childhood friend, so their interaction follows a boiler-plate pattern seen in countless other manga and anime: he acts like a slacker and ogles other girls, she nags him for neglecting his studies and gets jealous, rinse and repeat.) Fumiya Sato's art is a letdown considering the thrilling subject matter; the majority of panels are filled with close-up shots of plump faces, and tension is conveyed mostly by shocked reactions. Detailed background drawings are rare, and Kindaichi himself seems to have only a handful of expressions. The mystery scenarios, though, are inventive and intricate, offering genuine brain teasers, and elevate *Kindaichi* above its bland artwork. (JD)   ★★★

KING OF BANDITS JING: See *Jing: King of Bandits*

KINGDOM HEARTS

(キングダムハーツ) • Shiro Amano • Tokyopop (2005–2006) • Enterbrain (Famitsu PS2, 2003–2005) • 4 volumes • Fantasy, Adventure • All Ages

Kingdom Hearts, an RPG for the PlayStation 2, made history as the first collaboration between Disney and Japanese video game developer Square (now known as Square Enix). The plot involves Sora, a generic spiky-haired anime/manga hero, traveling through the worlds of different Disney movies, accompanied by Donald Duck and Goofy. Now from the very popular RPG comes an unabashed grab for cash, a condensed retelling of the game with very little added value for people who've already played it. That being said, the art is pleasant to look at and of course the Disney characters look adorable. Printed in 8-page installments in the video game magazine *Famitsu PS2*, the manga is a departure from the standard manga format in that it reads left to right, although the sound effects are still in Japanese. (RB)   ★

KINGDOM HEARTS: CHAIN OF MEMORIES

(キングダムハーツチェインオブメモリーズ) • Shiro Amano • Tokyopop (2006–2007) • Square Enix (Monthly Shônen Gangan, 2005–2006) • 2 volumes • Fantasy, Adventure • All Ages

Adaptation of the Game Boy Advance RPG of the same name. Sora and his friends have lost their memories and must go back to many of the same worlds they visited in *Kingdom Hearts*. This time, the Disney characters they meet don't seem to remember them. As they go through their adventures they begin to regain their lost memories. Not exactly gripping, and while the art is again great, the story doesn't make much sense unless you have firsthand knowledge of the game it's based on. (RB)   ★

KING OF THORN

Ibara no Ô, "King of Thorns" (いばらの王) • Yuji Iwahara • Tokyopop (2007–ongoing) • Enterbrain (Comic Beam, 2002–2005) • 6 volumes • Post-apocalyptic, Science Fiction, Horror, Adventure • 16+

When medical science is perplexed by a strange fossilizing disease known as Medusa, a group of victims are placed in cold sleep to await a cure. They awaken to find themselves in an abandoned facility overgrown with plants and surrounded by ferocious creatures, and their numbers soon dwindle further as the sleepers are picked off one by one. (MS)   NR

KING OF WOLVES

Ôrô, "King Wolf" (王狼) • Buronson (story), Kentaro Miura (art) • Dark Horse (2005) • Hakusensha (Monthly Animal House, 1989) • 1 volume • Seinen, Historical, Fantasy, Action • 18+ (graphic violence, nudity, sex)

While traveling along the ancient Silk Road, a Japanese historian/kendo champion and his fiancée are transported back in time to the thirteenth century, the golden age of the Mongol Empire. They soon discover that an old Japanese legend is actually true—Genghis Khan, the "King of Wolves," was *Japanese!* The only mildly amusing premise is basically an excuse for Miura to draw macho sword fights and hordes of cavalry. Miura's crosshatched art is not at the level of *Berserk* or even *Japan,* and the fight scenes are disappointing.   ★½

KINNIKUMAN: See *Ultimate Muscle: The Kinnikuman Legacy*

KITCHEN PRINCESS

Kitchen no Ohimesama, "Kitchen Princess" (キッチンのお姫さま) • Miyuki Kobayashi (story), Natsumi Ando (art) • Del Rey (2007–ongoing) • Kodansha (Nakayoshi, 2004–ongoing) • 5+ volumes (ongoing) • Shôjo, Cooking, Fantasy • 13+

Ever since her fateful encounter with the "Flan Prince," Najika (the orphaned daughter of patissieres) has wanted to make sweets in order to serve them to her beloved. But her prince vanishes almost as quickly as he first appeared, leaving only one clue to his whereabouts: a pudding spoon with the mark of a certain school. In order to find her prince, she transfers to the school and the story begins. . . . NR

KNIGHTS OF THE ZODIAC (SAINT SEIYA)

Seitôshi "Saint" Seiya, "Holy Warrior (Saint) Seiya" (聖闘士星矢) • Masami Kurumada • Viz (2003–ongoing) • Shueisha (Weekly Shônen Jump, 1986–1990) • 28 volumes • Shônen, Martial Arts, Battle • 13+ (partial nudity, graphic violence)

One of the most influential manga of the 1980s, *Saint Seiya* (together with *Dragon Ball*) is the baseline of all modern *Shônen Jump* manga. A calculated hit, it combines the earnest machismo (and bushy-browed, rosy-cheeked characters) of 1970s boys' manga with pure fantasy, using Greek myths (plus a little mixed-up Christianity) as the basis for its characters' godlike superpowers. Seiya and his friends are modern-day armor-clad warriors trained in hand-to-hand combat to serve the goddess Athena. With virtually no pause for plot, they jump into one insane one-on-one fight scene after another, undergoing shocking, often self-inflicted torture in the name of friendship and justice (eyes gouged out, limbs severed, chained to crosses upside down, etc.). The characters' "cloths" (basically super-armor) are toys the reader might imagine playing with, and the whole manga is painted with glowing screentone and bright, primary colors. The dated artwork consists mostly of giant perspective-free splash pages of characters hitting one another, often over cosmic backdrops of meteors, planets, the Buddha, etc. In other words, it's the perfect little boy's fantasy, even drawn as if a ten-year-old drew it. (Violence-wary adults be warned: the manga, unlike the anime, is gloriously uncensored.) Two sequel manga, one by Kurumada and one by Shiori Teshirogi, have not been translated. ★★★

KOBO THE LI'L RASCAL

Yorinuki Kobo-chan, "Pick of the Litter Kobo-chan" (よりぬきコボちゃん) • Masashi Ueda • Kodansha International (2000–2001) • Yomiura Shimbun (1982–ongoing) • 3 volumes, suspended (60+ volumes in Japan, ongoing) • Four-Panel Comedy • All Ages

Long-running family newspaper strip starring Kobo, a five-year-old boy who lives with a traditional Japanese extended family of parents and maternal grandparents. Kobo gets in minor mischief, plays with his food, says funny things, and plays with his grandfather (the strip's second most important character). Consistently mild and unchallenging, it's of most interest to those studying Japanese culture. ★★

KODOCHA

Kodomo no Omocha, "Children's Toys/Child's Toy" (こどものおもちゃ) • Miho Obana • Kodansha (Ribon, 1994–1999) • Tokyopop (2002–2003) • 10 volumes • Shôjo, Comedy, Drama • 13+ (mild language, mild violence)

A charming, witty elementary school comedy. Sana Kurata is a precocious eleven-year-old child actress who stars in a "show within the show," *Kodomo no Omocha.* Her time is mostly taken up by her acting career, but she's also the only person in her class who can stand up to the equally precocious class bully, Akita Hayama. The title of *Kodocha* sums up the underlying assumption of the series—that adults are helpless before children, who are the *real* movers and shakers and plotters. Parental authority figures are absent, questionable, or wacky: Sana's mother is an eccentric with chipmunks and snakes living in her perfectly coiffed hair, and her only father figure is her young manager, Rei, aka her "gigolo." And yet over time the series deals with serious issues such as abuse and adoption. Joyfully weird and full of non sequiturs, the manga is loaded with funny details and good lines (many courtesy of English rewriter Sarah Dyer). The quaint art is at its best in the classroom scenes, where cute kids go about their individual business like characters in a Richard Scarry book.

★★★½

KODOMO NO JIKAN: See *Nymphet*

KON KON KOKON

(こんこんここん) • Koge-Donbo • Broccoli Books (2007–ongoing) • Softbank Creative (Comi Di Gi, 2006–ongoing) • 1+ volumes (ongoing) • Comedy 13+

A new serial from the creator of *Di Gi Charat*. Ren's classmates know him only as a good-looking, levelheaded honor student, but he harbors a guilty secret from his early years in the countryside: he's a complete nerd when it comes to the spirits and creatures of Japanese folklore. When a fox girl named Kokon arrives to repay an old favor, Ren's cover may be blown for good. (MS) NR

KOSAKU SHIMA: See *Division Chief Kosaku Shima*

KURO GANE

Kuro Gane, "Black Steel" (黒鉄) • Kei Toume • Del Rey (2006–2007) • Kodansha (Morning, 1996–2001) • 5 volumes • Seinen, Samurai, Drama • 13+ (mild language, violence)

After dying on the battlefield, young warrior Jintetsu ("Man of Iron") is reassembled and brought back to life as a mute little cyborg, his thoughts and words locked away. Accompanied by Haganemaru, a talking sword, he becomes a lonely, haunted (yet strangely cute) drifter, wandering from place to place, never able to return to his life as a human being. Set in the Tokugawa era, *Kuro Gane* is a classically structured Japanese tale of a wandering swordsman; the supernatural/sci-fi element ultimately has little effect on the hero's adventures. The focus is not on the fight scenes, which are unexciting (although Jintetsu is not invulnerable), but on the dramas of the people Jintetsu encounters. Toume's art is sketchy, sometimes hasty, but improves as the series goes on. ★★★

KUROHIME

Mahô Tsukai Kurohime, "Magic/Demon Gun User Black Princess" (魔砲使い黒姫) • Katakura M. Masanori • Viz (2007–ongoing) • Shueisha (Monthly Shônen Jump/Monthly Shônen Jump Extra/online, 2000–ongoing) • 12+ volumes (ongoing) • Shônen, Fantasy, Action • 16+ (graphic violence, frequent partial nudity, sexual situations)

The "magic gunslinger" Kurohime, a tall, cool bombshell whose guns can blast things or summon monsters, roams a mixed-up fantasy world combining Japanese and Wild West elements. But even Kurohime has a weakness—she sometimes transforms from a curvy grown-up into a helpless young girl. At these times, she relies on her traveling companion Zero, a young boy who at other times finds his face buried in the adult Kurohime's cleavage. With its adoring images of torpedo-breasted, leggy women warriors in skintight suits, *Kurohime*'s style is vaguely similar to a modern American superhero comic. NR

THE KUROSAGI CORPSE DELIVERY SERVICE

Kurosagi Shitai Takuhaibin, "Kurosagi Corpse Delivery Service" (黒鷺死体宅配便) • Eiji Otsuka (story), Housui Yamazaki (art) • Dark Horse (2006–ongoing) • Kadokawa Shoten (Kadokawa Mystery/Monthly Shônen Ace, 2002–ongoing) • 6+ volumes (ongoing) • Shônen, Occult, Mystery • Unrated/18+ (language, graphic violence, explicit nudity, sexual situations)

"It all started when Numata found the body. . . ." Kuro Karatsu, a college-age Buddhist monk, has the ability to speak to the dead: not as friendly ghosts, but as muttering, barely mobile corpses. A group of hipster occultists (an embalmer, a dowser, a channeler who talks through a hand puppet, etc.) recruits him to join their "corpse delivery service," carrying out the last wishes of the unburied dead, which often requires confronting their killers. Although not quite as graphic as Otsuka's *MPD Psycho*, *Kurosagi Corpse Delivery Service* has more than its share of cringe-inducing gore, with sick serial killers and ghoulish "revenge from beyond the grave" scenarios. But the writing is sharp, and the occasional horrors are treated with a dry wit and a certain distance. Like Hitoshi Iwaaki (*Parasyte*), Yamazaki's art is outwardly plain and realistic, yet achieves a stiffly creepy effect. ★★★½

LADY SNOWBLOOD

Syurayuki Hime, "Princess Syurayuki" (修羅雪姫) • Kazuo Koike (story), Kazuo Kamimura (art) • Dark Horse (2005–2006) • Shueisha (Weekly Playboy, 1972–1973) • 4 volumes • Historical, Crime Drama • 18+ (language, graphic violence, nudity, sex)

In the first chapter of *Lady Snowblood,* the heroine is stripped and nearly raped, then kills four men with a blade in thick-falling snow, the blood splattering her naked body. She is Yuki the undercover assassin, born to take vengeance on the people who wronged her mother. The time and place is 1890s Japan, a setting medieval enough for secret sword battles but Victorian enough for sexual hypocrisy. Kazuo Koike knows that the best way to do a history lesson is to make it incredibly filthy, and *Lady Snowblood* is loaded with dildos, rape, and men's lesbian action; in one cliff-hanger, Yuki is menaced by a man tragically burdened with a penis so big he can't have sex. Yuki's obvious male counterpart is the assassin hero of *Lone Wolf and Cub,* but she is an even more inhuman character, the ancestor of the thousands of cyborg women and emotionless female hit men in modern-day anime and manga. Perhaps indicating her blank-slate nature, in the course of the story she disguises herself as a nun, prostitute, pickpocket, and life insurance salesman, and finally sells her own story as a newspaper serial to draw out her enemies, in a brilliantly ridiculous self-referential touch. Kazuo Kamimura's art is comparable to Takao Saito (*Golgo 13*), with powerful cinematic layouts but notably old-fashioned draftsmanship. The 1973 movie adaptation of *Lady Snowblood* was one of the inspirations for Quentin Tarantino's *Kill Bill*. ★★★½

LAGOON ENGINE

(ラグーンエンジン) • Yukiru Sugisaki • Tokyopop (2005–ongoing) • Kadokawa Shoten (Asuka, 2002–ongoing) • 5+ volumes (ongoing) • Shôjo, Occult, Action, Comedy • 13+ (mild violence, mild sexual situations)

Yen and Jin Ragun ("Ragun En Jin" . . . get it?) are brothers in elementary school who are secretly exorcists in training. To be precise, they fight and negotiate with *maga* (this manga's word for monsters and spirits) using all kinds of ritualistic equipment such as magical staffs, helper spirits, etc. The anime-style art is super-cute, with every page containing big close-ups of the characters' happy faces and glistening eyes; unfortunately the action is boring and visually confusing, with big power waves and close-ups making it impossible to tell what's going on. The school drama of angst and crushes and brotherly love is slightly more interesting, but not much. Like many Sugisaki works, the series has gone on several lengthy hiatuses and may or may not ever be completed. ★

LAGOON ENGINE EINSATZ

(ラグーンエンジンアインザッツ) • Yukiru Sugisaki • ADV (2005) • Kadokawa Shoten (Newtype USA, 2004–2005) • Fantasy • 1 volume • 13+ (violence)

Drawn for the American *Newtype USA, Lagoon Engine Einsatz* feels like the trailer for a stillborn anime concept. The book consists mostly of action scenes and ends on a frustrating cliff-hanger. Thirteen-year-old Sakis, the heir to the throne of Lagoonaria, rides with the sky knights in giant airships and wields the magic sword Lagoonverse to fight abominations, people infected with a plague that turns them into monsters. Copious production sketches and glossaries offset the lack of background information in the actual story. Despite the name, the story has no relation to *Lagoon Engine*. ★

LAMENT OF THE LAMB

Hitsuji no Uta, "Song of the Lamb" (羊のうた) • Kei Toume • Tokyopop (2004–2005) • Gentosha (Comic Burger/Comic Birz, 1996–2002) • 7 volumes • Seinen, Horror, Drama • 16+ (language, violence, mild sexual situations)

Kazuna, who lives with his aunt and uncle after his father's disappearance, starts developing strange cravings at the sight of blood. When he meets his long-lost sister, a lifelong invalid perpetually undergoing different medical treatments, he discovers the family secret: they are both vampires, a sort of hereditary disease that may one day drive them mad with bloodlust. Bound to his sister by their horrible secret, he starts to withdraw from society. A gloomy, claustrophobic drama set in ordinary, traditional Japanese households, *Lament of the Lamb* has a cast of perhaps half a dozen characters. Toume's dry art, although rougher than the color cover work suggests, is well suited to this slow-paced, often wordless tale in which virtually all violence and sexuality are kept offscreen. The plot, however, is more buildup than payoff. ★★★

LAND OF THE BLINDFOLDED

Mekakushi no Kuni, "Land of the Blindfolded" (目隠しの国) • Sakura Tsukuba • CMX (2004–2006) • Hakusensha (LaLa/LaLa DX, 1999–2004) • 9 volumes • Shôjo, Occult, Romance • All Ages (mild violence)

A strong premise disappointingly executed, *Land of the Blindfolded* involves three teenagers who have powers activated by touch: a girl who can see the future, a boy who can see the past, and another boy who can see

the future but uses his power unscrupulously. The series' greatest strength is its beautiful art, with a nice line and attractive characters of both sexes. However, the psychic idea is never satisfyingly explored, either in a science fiction "what if it really existed?" sense or for the role it might play in a romantic triangle. Given the theoretically significant power to predict the future, the characters use it mostly to prevent traffic accidents. Read one chapter at a time, it's a sweet, slow-moving story whose characters inhabit a pretty world of sunsets and puppy dogs and vegetable gardens; read in large chunks, it's boring and repetitive. ★★

THE LAST UNIFORM

Saigo no Seifuku, "The Last (School) Uniform" (最後の制服) • Mera Hakamada • Seven Seas Entertainment (2007–ongoing) • Houbunsha (Manga Time Kirara Carat/Manga Time Kirara Max, 2005–ongoing) • 3+ volumes (ongoing) • Yuri, Romance • 16+

Short stories of crushes and heartbreaks set in an all-girls' school. NR

THE LAW OF UEKI

Ueki no Hôsoku, "The Law of Ueki" (うえきの法則) • Tsubasa Fukuchi • Viz (2006–ongoing) • Shogakukan (Weekly Shônen Sunday, 2001–2005) • 16 volumes • Shônen, Battle • 13+ (violence)

Shueisha's adventure manga *One Piece* was so popular that Kodansha produced the suspiciously similar-looking *Rave Master*; Shogakukan produced *The Law of Ueki*, the least of the three comics. The art is clearly influenced by Eiichiro Oda, but the plot suggests *Shaman King*: Ueki, a teenager who is so mellow he has only one facial expression, is granted fighting powers to compete in a contest to determine the next King of the Celestial World. A more provocative translation might be "God," but the English edition has no desire to bring religion into what is in any case a manga almost completely disconnected from reality. Ueki has the power to turn trash into trees, and his opponents have the power to turn stuff into other stuff; when they win a fight, they gain a "talent" (such as the ability to rap, or the ability to do math homework), but Ueki is often penalized and loses as many talents as he gains. The action is decent, but the visuals are derivative and the tournament-battle plot feels equally arbitrary and generic. Moments of absurd humor fail to sustain interest. A sequel, *Ueki no Hôsoku Plus* ("The Law of Ueki Plus"), began in Japan in 2005. ★½

LEGAL DRUG

Gôhô Drug, "Legal Drug" (合法ドラッグ) • CLAMP • Tokyopop (2005–2006) • Kadokawa Shoten (Mystery DX, 2000–2003) • 3 volumes (suspended) • Shôjo, Occult, Drama • 16+ (mild language, mild violence, mild sexual situations)

CLAMP has beat around the *shônen ai* bush throughout their body of work. *Tokyo Babylon* and *Wish* are often considered honorary *shônen ai* titles, and even series such as *Rayearth* and *Clover* have strongly implied *shônen ai* relationships, but it wasn't until *Legal Drug* that the team fully commited to the conventions of the genre. The touching, the soulful glances, the pretense of animosity to hide attraction—CLAMP can be as coy as they want about the leads' relationship, but it's clear what they want readers to think. After collapsing in the snow one night, Kazahaya Kudo is rescued by the tall, dark, and handsome Rikuo Himuo. Kazahaya is taken in by Rikuo's boss, Kakei, owner of the Green Drugstore ("a drugstore with medicine and a danger"—yay Engrish!). During the day, Kazahaya and Rikuo man the store, but their boss is no ordinary pharmacist—Kakei is a clairvoyant who caters to a special clientele. The real reason he has taken the two young men in is because they have supernatural powers of their own, and soon Kakei has Kazahaya and Rikuo making house calls for those with spiritual ailments. The premise is quite similar to that of *xxxHOLiC,* and the supernatural stories in *Legal Drug* are every bit as magical, but often the "deliveries" are little more than a pretext for Kazahaya and Rikuo to have to hold hands, cross-dress, or be put in compromising situations. Tsubaki Nekoi, artist for *Wish* and *Suki,* again takes the lead on *Legal Drug,* and it is her best work. The chapter breaks, in particular, are guaranteed swoon inducers for fans of beautiful young men. The series is stalled at volume 3 (one-fifth of the planned story) after the magazine it is serialized in was canceled, but CLAMP has publicly said that they intend to resume publication soon. Even if that closure never comes, the great characters, gorgeous art, and fairly self-contained episodes make it a solid purchase. (MT) ★★★

THE LEGEND OF CHUN HYANG

Shin Shunkaden, "New Chun Hyang Legend" (新・春香伝) • CLAMP • Tokyopop (2004) • Hakusensha (Serie Mystery Special, 1992) • 1 volume • Fantasy • 13+ (mild violence)

Loosely based on a famous Korean folktale, CLAMP's "new" version takes the form of a Robin Hood story. Young Chun Hyang is the daughter of the village shaman and a master of martial arts, and she's not afraid to use her skills against the city guards who are in the employ of the corrupt Yang Ban (magistrate). When the Yang Ban crosses the line and kidnaps her mother, Chun Hyang sets off in search of the Amenosa, a government official who can defang her nemesis. She is joined by Mong Ryong, a handsome—and somewhat lecherous—stranger who shares Chun Hyang's passion for justice. The series lasted only a few chapters, so the book ends just as it really gets going, which is a shame. The formula is hardly groundbreaking, but Chun Hyang and Mong Ryong make a cute couple, and the Korean period setting gives Mokona a chance to show off her penchant for pretty costumes. As it stands, the book is like a stand-alone TV pilot for a show that never got off the ground. (MT) ★★

THE LEGEND OF KAMUI PERFECT COLLECTION

Kamui Gaiden Dainibu: Sugaru no Jima, "Kamui Side Story Part Two: The Island of Sugaru" (カムイ外伝第二部:スガルの島) • Sanpei Shirato, Akame Productions • Viz (1987–1998) • Shogakukan (Big Comic, 1981–1987) • 2 volumes, suspended (12 volumes in Japan) • Seinen, Historical Action, Drama • Unrated/18+ (graphic violence, nudity, sex)

Not the original *Kamui Den* ("Legend of Kamui"), which was one of the most influential manga of the 1960s, *The Legend of Kamui Perfect Collection* is an excerpt from a sequel series, drawn in the 1980s in a slicker style. (To be precise, *Kamui Perfect Collection* is drawn in the style of Goseki Kojima, who was an assistant on *Kamui Den* before going on to draw *Lone Wolf and Cub*.) The conservative panel layouts and heavy-handed narration mark it as the product of an earlier age of comics, but the backgrounds are beautifully detailed and the action scenes are well done, with Kamui fighting sharks and acrobatically flipping through the trees. Kamui (whose origin is not explained here), a fugitive ninja forever pursued by his former masters, finds himself in an island fishing village, where he considers settling down. More *Kamui* was printed by Viz in monthly comics format but never collected.

★★★½

LEGEND OF LEMNEAR

(レジェンドオブレムネア) • Satoshi Urushihara (art), Kinji Yoshimoto (story) • CPM (1998–2001) • Gakken (Comic Nora, 1991–1993) • 4 volumes • Shōnen, Fanservice, Fantasy, Adventure • 18+ (language, graphic violence, nudity, sexual situations)

Bad fantasy porn with blood. Lemnear, a swordswoman trained by her father, goes on a prophesied quest to defeat the ultimate evil, getting her shirt repeatedly torn off in the process. In this world, "power" obviously means "breasts," as judged by lines like "You've got more power than that . . . let's see *all* your power!" and "What amazing power she has!" Other clichés indulged here include slimy cancer-monsters, people who transform (ripping their clothes off in the process), and the ostensible heroine's need for constant reassurance from others. Urushihara's art gradually "matures" from boring and generic to full-on fetishism over the course of the series.

½

THE LEGEND OF MOTHER SARAH: TUNNEL TOWN

Sharyûra, "Sand, Current, Silk" (沙流羅) • Katsuhiro Otomo (story), Takumi Nagayasu (art) • Dark Horse (1995–1998) • Kodansha (Young Magazine, 1990–1997) • 1 volume, suspended (7 volumes in Japan) • Postapocalyptic, Seinen, Science Fiction, Adventure • Unrated/16+ (mild language, violence, brief nudity)

After a nuclear apocalypse, settlers from space stations—divided into the warring groups of "Epoch" and "M.E.," Mother Earth—recolonize the dried seabeds of the planet. Sarah, a battle-hardened mother roaming in search of her lost children, finds herself in a mining community where prisoners labor in the ruins of buried cities while their military overseers guard a secret. After an opening sequence set in space, *The Legend of Mother Sarah* turns into a low-tech, realistic action-adventure story, with less challenging writing than Otomo's *Akira* ("Since when does war make someone a 'real man,' Toki?!"). Also like *Akira,* the initially complicated plot turns out to be very simple and resolves with everything blowing up. But Sarah is a memorable heroine, and Nagayasu's art is a near-perfect imitation of Otomo's hyper-detailed art style. The single-volume Dark Horse graphic novel works as a complete story; additional material was published in monthly comics format but never collected.   ★★★

THE LEGEND OF ZELDA: A LINK TO THE PAST

Zelda no Densetsu, "The Legend of Zelda" (ゼルダの伝説) • Shotaro Ishinomori • Nintendo (1992–1993) • Shogakukan (1993) • 1 volume • Video Game, Fantasy, Action • All Ages (mild violence)

Uninspired full-color adaptation of the video game of the same name. The artwork is bland and the writing is routine. Originally printed in the American *Nintendo Power* magazine and later reprinted in Japan.   ★½

LEGENDZ

(レジェンズ) • Rin Hirai (story), Makoto Haruno (art) • Viz (2005–2006) • Shueisha (Monthly Shōnen

Jump, 2003–2005) • 4 volumes • Shônen, Science Fiction, Fantasy, Battle • All Ages

A multimedia phenomenon that wasn't, *Legendz* launched big in Japan, with a manga, anime, video game, and collectible card game. The franchise died quickly, with the manga ending abruptly at volume 4. It's a tournament manga in the *Pokémon/Yu-Gi-Oh!* mold, featuring kids battling with mythological monsters encased in containers called Soul Figures. The hero, Ken, is the maniacally enthusiastic trainer of the Windragon Shiron. His skill attracts the attention of more experienced Legendz users, and by the second volume he's enrolled in a massive tournament, while sinister forces lurk on the sidelines. The story doesn't deviate from the standards of the genre, although there is some effort to create a fairly elaborate universe for the Legendz. The manga's main strength is Haruno's appealing, slightly quirky artwork for the human characters; by contrast, most of the mythological creatures are disappointingly bland. (CT) ★★

LET'S STAY TOGETHER FOREVER

Zutto Issho ni Iyou Ne, "Let's Stay Together Forever" (ずっと一緒にいようね) • Tomoko Taniguchi • CPM (2003) • Jitsugyo no Nihonsha (1987–1989) • 1 volume • Shôjo, Romantic Comedy • All Ages

A collection of Taniguchi's oldest works, *Let's Stay Together Forever* includes her *shôjo* manga debut and other technically rough but charming romance comics. The title story involves a shy girl who goes out with Leo, a friendly Japanese metalhead who introduces her to Stryper, Skid Row, and Bon Jovi. Except for the last story, in fact, *all* the tales involve cute, big-haired boys and stadium metal, as well as cameos by A.L.F. dolls, Gremlins, and other aspects of 1980s American pop culture. (Taniguchi spent some time as an English major studying abroad in Michigan.) Enjoyably kitschy.

★★½

LIFE

(ライフ) • Keiko Suenobu • Tokyopop (2006–ongoing) • Kodansha (Bessatsu Friend, 2002–ongoing) • 14+ volumes (ongoing) • Shôjo, Drama • 16+ (language, violence, sexual situations)

"The only thing that makes me feel better is pain. If I want to know what it's like to get hurt . . . I have to experience it firsthand." Wracked with guilt over the accidental betrayal of a friend, high school freshman Ayumu becomes addicted to self-mutilation, carving grooves into her arms with an art knife. At the same time, she navigates the treacherous waters of high school society. *Life* is a catalog of edgy teen issues: in addition to cutting, it touches on suicide, sexual abuse, and systematic bullying. The early volumes are completely free of romance, focusing instead on the powerful relationships between the female characters. After a strong, stunningly naturalistic first volume, the manga dissolves into melodrama with the introduction of Katsumi, a teenage sadist whose over-the-top evil clashes with the realism of the opening scenes. Suenobu seeks out the dark corners of teenage life: the girls' friendships and enmities are painfully intense, and the cutting scenes are rendered in wince-inducing close-ups. The overall impression is of girls being physically torn apart by the brutality of adolescence. The Tokyopop edition ends each volume with an afterword by a clinical psychologist who talks about the issues raised in the manga. (SG) ★★★

LILING-PO

(リリン-ポ) • Ako Yutenji • Tokyopop (2005–ongoing) • Shinshokan (Wings, 1997–ongoing) • 9+ volumes (ongoing) • Shôjo, Historical, Thief, Drama • 13+ (brief language, brief graphic violence, mild sexual situations)

In ancient China, Liling-Po, a young master thief, is released from prison to gather eight stolen treasures, with a warrior and an aristocrat as his overseers. Visually overflowing with flowers, symbols, and crests, *Liling-Po* aims to be a sensual, sad fairy tale, but it succumbs to a feeling of ennui and cramped, dark artwork in which the emaciated main characters sit and brood. The story is a series of episodic adventures—if *adventures* isn't too strong a word—in which Liling-Po goes from place to place retrieving the treasures through gloomy character interaction. The storytelling improves as it goes on, however, and the tale of Liling-Po's origin—chiefly in volumes 3 and 4—has a suitable spirit of fairy-tale decadence. ★★

LINE

(ライン) • Yua Kotegawa • ADV (2006) • Kadokawa Shoten (Monthly Shônen Ace, 2003) • 1 volume • Shônen, Suspense • 16+ (language, violence)

When she picks up a strange cell phone in the street, a high school girl receives disturbing phone calls telling her about suicides before they happen. Similar to the Japanese movie *Suicide Club,* the hook is powerful, but the payoff is disappointing. The action is at least decently executed; Kotegawa's generic art is more refined than his earlier work in *Anne Freaks.* ★★

A LITTLE SNOW FAIRY SUGAR

Chitchana Yukitsukai Sugar, "A Little Snow Fairy Sugar" (ちっちゃな雪使いシュガー) • Haruka Arai (creator), Koge-Donbo (character designs), BH SNOW+CLINIC (art) • ADV (2006–2007) • Kadokawa Shoten (Dragon Junior, 2001–2002) • 3 volumes • Shônen, Comedy, Drama • All Ages

Based on the anime *Sugar: A Little Snow Fairy.* Saga is a no-nonsense eleven-year-old girl who is just trying to pass her classes and keep her job at the coffee shop. Sugar is an apprentice "season fairy" who is trying to practice her magic and find enough "twinkle" to become an adult. Saga is the only human who can see Sugar and the other fairies, so she ends up becoming a reluctant accomplice in Sugar's efforts to grow up. The comedy and drama come from the conflict between Saga's need for order and Sugar's clumsiness. What keeps them together is the fact that they are both trying to please and imitate their respective missing mothers. The stories are simple and sweet, going for maximum cuteness and melodrama; the art does the same. (MJS) ★★

LIVING CORPSE: See *Hino Horror, Vol. 5: Living Corpse*

LOAN WOLF

Shutaro Yamada • ComicsOne (e-book, 2000) • Shônen Gahosha (Young King Ours, 1999–2002) • 1 volume, suspended (3 volumes in Japan) • Seinen, Comedy • 13+ (gambling)

This manga starts with a doozy of a premise: two buddies are messing around on the tracks and accidentally cause a commuter train to derail. Years later, they are slapped into a 100 million yen debt, and the story follows their moneymaking schemes, with nonstop distractions along the way. *Loan Wolf* features a better than average English rewrite, with lots of contemporary-feeling references to Puff Daddy, the American kids' show *Reading Rainbow,* and Colonel Sanders (their rich relative is his spitting image). However, despite the promising premise, the story doesn't really go anywhere; the comic and characters feel squandered. (RS) ★★½

LODOSS WAR: See *Record of Lodoss War*

LONE WOLF AND CUB

Kozure Ôkami, "Wolf with Cub" (子連れ狼) • Kazuo Koike (story), Goseki Kojima (art) • Dark Horse (2000–2002) • Futabasha (Manga Action, 1970–1976) • 28 volumes • Seinen, Samurai, Action • 18+ (language, graphic violence, nudity, sex)

On a secret mission of revenge, a samurai turned assassin travels through feudal Japan, pushing a baby cart bearing his only surviving family: his infant son. In 8,000+ pages of mostly self-contained stories, this stoic killing machine eliminates his targets, his enemies, and entire armies, in the process encountering every aspect of Tokugawa-era Japan: farmers and merchants, samurai and ninja, rich and poor. Apart from the premise, the most famous thing about *Lone Wolf and Cub* is Goseki Kojima's painterly artwork: his wordless, cinematic action sequences influenced comics superstar Frank Miller, and his period architecture, clothes,

Kazuo Koike and Goseki Kojima's classic *Lone Wolf and Cub*

(1990) • 6 issues • Fantasy, Action • 13+ (brief language, graphic violence)

In 1956 Japan, a group of journalists and archaeologists discover evidence of a lost world beneath the earth's poles, guarded by an ancient conspiracy. Their investigations eventually take them by zeppelin to the underground world, where they encounter dinosaurs, ancient sorcerers, an evil god, and stereotypical natives. This interesting but ultimately formulaic pulp adventure consciously harks back to Edgar Rice Burroughs' *Pellucidar* and other classic Hollow Earth stories. Yamada's high-contrast, realistic, Western-style art starts out sketchily but visibly improves over the course of the series.

★★

LOST WORLD

(ロストワールド) • Osamu Tezuka • Dark Horse (2003) • Fujishobo (1948) • 1 volume • Science Fiction • Unrated/All Ages (mild violence)

Lost World is the first manga in Tezuka's early "science fiction trilogy," which also includes *Metropolis* and *Nextworld*. Together, they represent Tezuka's birth as a graphic novelist, learning to create book-length stories and to establish his own visual language. *Lost World* is the most primitive of the trilogy, written with a slapdash, almost stream-of-consciousness approach to plotting, and drawn in a style heavily influenced by early American animation. The first half of the manga assembles a motley group of characters; the second half sends them on a trip through outer space to the planet Mamango. This loose plot arc allows room for endless bizarre digressions: animal people, plant people, a shadowy gang, "energy stones," dinosaurs, mad scientists. Several of Tezuka's recurring "star system" characters make early appearances here, including the detective Shunsuke Ban (or "Mr. Mustachio") and the scheming Acetylene Lamp. By the story's surprisingly bleak and ambivalent end, Tezuka has made obvious strides as an artist and storyteller, although he's still far from his mature period. It's extremely unpolished and uneven (and the uncharacter-

and even trees and rocks glow with life. Despite its deserved reputation as a classic, *Lone Wolf and Cub* is first and foremost a pulp narrative, and there's plenty of sleaze among the death and gore. (Remember, this is by the author of *Wounded Man*.) The nearest equivalent may be *Golgo 13,* but *Lone Wolf and Cub* actually delivers an ending to its story of the ultimate assassin, however long in coming. In short, it's both an epic story and a successful franchise. Before Dark Horse, the series was partly released in English by First Comics in 1987, making it one of the first high-profile translated manga (partly thanks to original cover art by Frank Miller). In 2003, Kazuo Koike returned to the story with a sequel, *Shin Kozure Ôkami* ("New Lone Wolf and Cub"), published in the men's magazine *Weekly Post* with art by Hideki Mori.

★★★★

LOST CONTINENT

Last Continent (ラストコンチネント) • Akihiro Yamada • Eclipse (1990–1991) • Tokyo Sanseisha istically stilted Dark Horse translation doesn't help), but of definite interest to readers curious about the roots of manga. (SG) ★★½

LOUIE THE RUNE SOLDIER

Mahô Senshi Louie: Kôen no Bastard, "Magic Warrior Louie: The Bastard of Red Blazes" (魔法戦士リウイ紅炎のバスタード) • Ryo Mizuno (story), Jun Sasameyuki (art), Mamoru Yokota (character design) • ADV (2004–2005) • Kadokawa Shoten (Dragon Junior, 2000–2003) • 4 volumes, suspended (6 volumes in Japan) • Shônen, Fantasy, Comedy • 13+ (language, violence, partial nudity, mild sexual situations)

Manga adaptation of Ryo Mizuno's young-adult fantasy novels, produced as a tie-in to the anime. Louie, the alcoholic, fistfighting adult son of an esteemed wizard, is identified as the hero of a vague prophecy and finds himself the traveling companion of three mostly big-breasted female adventurers, who all dislike him to one extent or another. A vain attempt at injecting comedy into one of Mizuno's D&D-rip-off settings, the manga manages to steer a middle road avoiding both plot and humor. (The story is apparently set in the same world as *Record of Lodoss War,* but none of the same characters or settings appear.) Despite slapping barmaids' butts, Louie is actually fairly mild-mannered and thoughtful by the standards of boorish fantasy manga heroes (i.e., *Bastard!!, Sorcerer Hunters*). The art is competent but generic. ★½

LOVE♥COM

Lovely Complex (ラブ♥コンLovely Complex) • Aya Nakahara • Viz (2007–ongoing) • Shueisha (Bessatsu Margaret, 2001–ongoing) • 14+ volumes (ongoing) • Shôjo, Romantic Comedy • 15+ (mild sexual situations)

Risa Koizumi is the tallest girl in her class and Atsushi Ôtani is the shortest boy, and they are sick to death of being the butt of jokes. Everyone thinks they should hook up because it would be funny, but as Risa and Ôtani spend more time together they realize that they have a lot more in common than

being laughingstocks. While the basic premise is simple, all the characters are so well written that what could be a lackluster story becomes a rollicking good time. Reading about these characters and their daily lives is like hanging out with a group of your good friends. The art style is cute and simple, a good match for the comedy but strong enough for the drama scenes. Although the series is set in a high school, the characters rarely wear uniforms, and the oft-changing outfits and hairstyles are an entertaining relief from the monotonous costumes that otherwise dominate this genre. (HS) ★★★★

LOVE HINA

Love Hina, "Love Doll(s)/Fledgling(s)" (ラブひな) • Ken Akamatsu • Tokyopop (2002–2003) • Kodansha (Weekly Shônen Magazine, 1998–2002) • 14 volumes • Shônen, Romantic Comedy • 16+ (language, comic violence, constant partial nudity, constant sexual situations)

One of the most popular love comedies of the 1990s, *Love Hina* plays the "harem manga" premise for over-the-top physical comedy rather than the usual ego-stroking. Nineteen-year-old Keitaro is a wimpy, incompetent *ronin,* a high school graduate who has failed his all-important exam to get into Tokyo University. Like the hero of the vaguely similar *Maison Ikkoku,* he finds himself lodging with the opposite sex and falling in love . . . but due to "girl inflation" in the years since Rumiko Takahashi's classic romance, he ends up living with not one but *five* teenage women at a girls' boarding house/hot springs. The inventiveness of *Love Hina* is that it's less about merely flashing the reader with T&A and more about cramming as many sex jokes as possible into each chapter. The women are basically aware of how totally pathetic Keitaro is, and when he accidentally falls face-first in their panties or stumbles on them in the bath, they treat him like a human punching bag, cheerfully knocking him from panel to panel without any permanent damage. (Of course, they come to like him eventually . . . it's more like they express their affection through violence.) What makes this work is the smooth, good-looking art and the cheerfully pandering attitude, never descending into self-pity, excessive sentiment, or outright misogyny. It's a love comedy with the emphasis on *comedy,* and the humor is inventive and implausible. Gradually things get more and more over the top, with chase scenes and fight scenes, leading up to a dramatic ending that showcases Akamatsu's polished artwork: sexualized cartoon characters inhabiting a world of extraordinarily detailed backgrounds, with something happening on every panel of every page. ★★★

LOVELESS

Yun Kouga • Tokyopop (2006–ongoing) • Ichijinsha (Comic Zero-Sum, 2002–ongoing) • 7+ volumes (ongoing) • Fantasy, Romantic Drama • 16+ (violence, sexual situations)

Aoyagi Ritsuka, a sixth-grade latchkey kid, is in counseling due to child abuse and his brother's mysterious death. One day he encounters Soubi, a handsome twenty-year-old art student who once knew Aoyagi's dead older brother. Soubi kisses Aoyagi, tells him, "I love you," and vows to protect him, saying that Aoyagi's older brother told him to do so. Soon things get weirder as the two are linked by a collar and chain, and Aoyagi discovers that when they are connected, they develop strange powers, becoming a master-and-servant "fighter unit" and battling other linked couples who serve a strange organization, Septimal Moon. Did Septimal Moon murder his brother . . . or is something even stranger afoot? Attractively drawn but frustratingly slow-paced, mopey, and introverted, *Loveless* has one original idea: in the world of the story, all people are born with cat ears and a tail, which go away when they lose their virginity. It's a great metaphor, and an excuse to use cute anthropomorphic character designs. Unfortunately, the battle scenes are a less effective metaphor and fail as action scenes as well, with the characters mostly standing still and uttering "power words" as screentone explodes around them. (At least in *Revolution-*

ary Girl Utena the characters trade sword blows while working out their issues.) The mysteries are eventually resolved, but it's a slow, awkward journey. The suggestions of *yuri* and *yaoi* romance are mostly implied rather than shown. ★★

LOVE ROMA

(ラブロマ) • Minoru Toyoda • Del Rey (2005–2007) • Kodansha (Afternoon, 2002–2005) • 5 volumes • Seinen, Romantic Comedy • 16+ (mild sexual situations)

A feel-good, drifting romantic manga with a distinctive indie-comics art style, *Love Roma* breaks down a relationship into its component parts, as if its protagonist was a friendly space alien studying human emotions. Hoshino, a teenage boy who is always absolutely honest about his feelings, asks out his classmate Negishi, who soon overcomes her doubts and likes him back. (Although she occasionally hits him when he's *too* honest.) He asks her out on a date over the school intercom, they make declarations of love under sweeping skies, and their classmates, who are as charmed as they are, tag along and frequently erupt in applause. The art is blocky and crosshatched, and the people look like low-polygon video game characters; luckily, it comes across as a stylistic choice and fits the mood of sweet naïvete. The slightest sexual element enters the story beginning in volume 3. "You two really make being in love seem dull," one of their blunter classmates tells the lovers, but on the whole their self-assessment is more accurate: "Having a relationship is a wonder." ★★★

LOVE SONG

Keiko Nishi • Viz (1997) • 1 volume • Jôsei, Romance, Drama • Unrated/16+ (language, sexual situations)

A collection of short stories by *jôsei* artist Keiko Nishi, previously serialized in *Manga Vizion,* Viz's 1995–1998 first attempt at a manga anthology magazine. Nishi has a loose, sketchy art style that eschews *shôjo* cuteness, and her stories typically mix wistful romanticism with a sharp, cynical edge. The standout piece is the title story, the harrowing chronicle of a dysfunctional relationship between a masochistically loyal man and a beautiful, icy woman who has vowed that her experience of love will begin and end with the doomed affair she had with a female high-school classmate. The other three stories pale before the raw force of "Love Song," although all are solid work. "Jewels of the Seaside" is a slightly tongue-in-cheek Victorian horror story about three jealous sisters. In "The Signal Goes Blink, Blink," the longest story in the collection, a nerdy, introverted schoolboy develops healing powers and is peddled to the media as "The Miracle Boy." "The Skin of Her Heart" is an introspective science fiction story about a shy working-class woman living in a space colony. (SG)   ★★★½

Minoru Toyoda's *Love Roma*

LULLABIES FROM HELL

Jigoku no Komoriuta, "Lullabies of Hell" (地獄の子守唄) • Hideshi Hino • Dark Horse (2006) • various magazines • 1 volume • Horror • Unrated/16+ (graphic violence)

A collection of short horror stories from various points in Hino's career, *Lullabies from Hell* is an inconsistent but worthy introduction to this major artist. The title story, "A Lullaby from Hell," in which a death-obsessed artist tells his life story, is a primitive trial run for his later masterpiece *Panorama of Hell*. In the science fiction tale "Unusual Fetus—My Baby," a couple gives birth to a froglike creature. "Train of Terror," the weakest story, mixes snakes, roller coasters, paranoia, and twist endings into an illogical nightmare for young readers. The most interesting tale is "Zoroku's Strange Disease," an early Ray Bradbury–influenced fable in which an outcast artist rots into an oozing mass of sores in a lonely house in the forest. The latter story (clearly a strong influence on Junko Mizuno) achieves its goal of finding the beauty and pathos in the slimy and decayed.   ★★★

LUM PERFECT COLLECTION: See *Lum★Urusei Yatsura*

LUM*URUSEI YATSURA

Urusei Yatsura, "Those Annoying Aliens/Those Annoying People from Planet Uru" (うる星やつら) • Rumiko Takahashi • Viz (1989–1999) • Shogakukan (Weekly Shônen Sunday, 1978–1987) • 9 volumes, suspended (34 volumes in Japan) • Shônen, Science Fiction, Fantasy, Mythological, Romantic Comedy • Unrated/16+ (comic violence, nudity, mild sexual situations)

Ataru, a luckless teenage horndog, saves the Earth from an alien invasion and ends up engaged to Lum, a green-haired, horned alien princess who flies around in a tiger-striped bikini. But Lum is the one girl Ataru doesn't like, and Ataru spends most of his time avoiding her jealous wrath while hitting on her alien friends or anything else with XX chromosomes. *Lum★Urusei Yatsura* is a slapstick combination of sci-fi, fairy-tale, and ghost-story elements, with plenty of cute girls. Lum herself is the original *otaku* dream girl—a girl who'll either hit on you or zap you with lightning, but who'll never leave you alone—and after the manga ended, lovesick male fans kept up a steady demand for anime and merchandise. Compared to *Ranma ½,* the stories are more episodic and the art is busier, as Ataru and his friends become "weirdness magnets" for a steady stream of craziness. Starting with the pun title, there are many references to Japanese culture; some are rewritten in the English edition, some kept intact. *Lum Perfect Collection* contains the beginning of the story; the later graphic novels were released under the title *The Return of Lum.*   ★★★★

LUNAR LEGEND TSUKIHIME

Shingettan Tsukihime, "True Lunar Legend Moon Princess" (真月譚月姫) • TYPE-MOON/Tsukihime Project (original creators), Sasaki Shōnen (art) • DrMaster (2005–ongoing) • MediaWorks (Dengeki Daioh, 2003–ongoing) • 4+ volumes (ongoing) • Shōnen, Horror, Action • 16+ (graphic violence, sexual situations)

The anime/manga franchise *Lunar Legend Tsukihime* developed from the untranslated "visual novel" video game *Tsukihime.* For the first half of volume 1, the manga is awesomely creepy; in something almost like first-person video game perspective, it tells the story of Shiki Tohno, who wakes up in a hospital to find that he can see frightening fissures that run through all people and things. He, and he alone, has the power to cut the "death cracks," destroying any object, and potentially any living thing. Things get more conventional when Shiki encounters Arcueid, a female vampire who tells him that the world is secretly full of vampires, magicians, and supernatural creatures. The story is consistently gloomy and atmospheric, even when Shiki starts fighting vampires, but the generic character designs drag it down; Arceuid's "anime girl" look makes it difficult to take her seriously as an immortal creature of power.   ★★½

LUPIN III

Lupin Sansei, "Lupin the Third" (ルパン三世) • Monkey Punch • Tokyopop (2002–2004) • Futabasha (Weekly Manga Action, 1967–1972) • 14 volumes • Seinen, Crime, Comedy • 16+ (language, violence, nudity, sex)

Creeping out of the night in search of women, money, or thrills, a grinning rascal at home in dark castles and underground lairs, comes the master thief Lupin III—one of the most famous manga characters of all time. (His name is a homage to Maurice LeBlanc's master thief Arsène Lupin, although the homage was not appreciated by LeBlanc's estate, resulting in Lupin appearing in foreign editions under several pseudonyms, such as "Rupan" and "Wolf," until the name passed into the public domain in the 1990s.) Inspired mostly by *Mad* magazine and Mort Drucker, Lupin's episodic adventures bear little in common with any manga before or since. Each self-contained story involves some bizarre theft or heist, or opens with some shocking situation such as a train crash or Lupin on death row. The plots are full of clever twists; American comic readers may be reminded of the physical comedy of *Spy vs. Spy* and the devious plot constructions of Will Eisner's *The Spirit.* This is a crazy, groovy 1960s world of dynamite and backstabbing, hippies and gangsters, a world where guns kill people but bombs leave them as smoldering black silhouettes with surprised eyes staring out of their blackened faces. Men are gangly goons with big feet and narrow heads; women are buxom sex dolls who murmur dialogue like "Mmm, Lupin, you're an animal . . ." as boxers go flying off and knobby knees bump against the bedsprings. Fans of Hayao Miyazaki's animated film *Lupin III: The Castle of Cagliostro* should know that Monkey Punch himself disliked the movie; he felt that its altruistic, noble Lupin strayed from his own vision of Lupin as an amoral skirt-chaser. The original *Lupin III* is more like a cartoon from a men's magazine, which it was; a fascinating homage to *Mad* and a four-star example of comics as pure comedy.   ★★★★

LUPIN III: WORLD'S MOST WANTED

Monkey Punch • Tokyopop (2004–ongoing) • Futabasha (Weekly Manga Action, 1977) • 17 volumes • Seinen, Crime, Comedy • 16+ (language, crude humor, violence, nudity, sex)

The sequel to *Lupin III,* now more over the top and stylized than ever; Monkey Punch's art has matured from its sometimes cramped beginnings to a smooth, swinging style with crazy shapes and goofy caricatures. Lupin dodges boulders and leaps over spiked pits; one adventure opens with him in a cartoon shack perilously perched on a precipice, with only a female android for company; another sees him forced to achieve a simultaneous orgasm with a beautiful woman in order to find a hidden treasure. Yet another story parodies the legal issues surrounding the Lupin name, by having a lawyer dispute the hero's claim that he's Arsène Lupin's grandson. ★★★★

LYCANTHROPE LEO

Reô (Leo), "Violent/Mighty King (Leo)" (烈王レオ) • Kengo Kaji (story), Kenji Okamura (art) • Viz (1994–1999) • Shogakukan (Young Sunday, 1991–1993) • 1 volume, suspended (4 volumes in Japan) • Seinen, Horror, Action • Unrated/16+ (graphic violence, nudity)

When his own parents try to kill him, a hapless high school student discovers the terrible truth that he is a lycanthrope. But not a werewolf . . . a *were-lion!* A number of other bizarre, muscular shape-shifters soon show up, including were-oxen and were-flying-squirrels, in an action-oriented plot that involves the secret struggle between lycanthropes and humanity. The brawny, gory, 1980s-style artwork makes for a cheesy ultraviolent mood similar to *Fist of the North Star,* but the English edition of the series was canceled abruptly. ★★

MABURAHO

(まぶらほ) • Toshihiko Tsukiji (original creator), Miki Miyashita (art) • ADV (2005–2007) • Kadokawa Shoten (Dragon Age, 2003–2004) • Shônen, Fantasy, Romantic Comedy • 2 volumes • 13+ (sexual situations)

Manga adaptation of the light novel series by Tsukiji. Everyone has some magical power, but Kazuki, despite attending a prestigious magic academy, is relatively weak. However, his genetic makeup indicates that his child will be a powerful magician, and so three hot girls start hitting on him to "get his DNA." The characters and situations are stock, the girls are identical except for their hair, and the fanservice is tame. ½

MACROSS II: See *Super Dimensional Fortress Macross II.*

MADARA

Môryô Senki Madara, "Nature Spirit/Monster War Chronicle Madara" (魍魎戦記MADARA) • Eiji Otsuka (story), Sho-u Tajima (art) • CMX (2004–2005) • Kadokawa Shoten (Marukatsu Famicon, 1987) • 5 volumes • Shônen, Science Fiction, Fantasy, Action • 18+ (language, graphic violence, nudity)

An early game/manga/anime/"media mix" project, *Madara* has the simple plot and illogical weirdness of an 8-bit video game (including the requisite rip-offs of *Predator* and *Alien*). From his home in a remote forest village, the young cyborg boy Madara sets out on a quest to defeat the evil Emperor Miroku, whose eight generals each possess one of his original body parts. He slashes his way through armies of lizard-men, wolf-men, bunny-men, and other monsters, using his telescoping limbs, *chakra* fireballs, a magic sword, and other gimmicks. (Sample dialogue: "By placing the sword near your forehead, a dragon crest will appear, unleashing your spiritual aura and your battle gadgets.") In volume 3, Madara himself goes briefly out of the picture, and the cast expands, making the world of the series at least two-dimensional instead of one-dimensional. *Madara*'s messy mix of science fiction, fantasy, mythology, and big explosions has echoes in other 1980s manga and anime (notably *Bastard!!*). Given that it's written for kids, it's unfortunate that the occasional nudity and monster-gore gets the series an 18+ rating (16+ would probably do). Sho-u Tajima later developed into an impressive artist (see *MPD Psycho*), but his beautiful painted covers don't represent the primitive interior black-and-white artwork.

★★

MADE IN HEAVEN

Ami Sakurai (story), Yukari Yashiki (art) • Tokyopop (2006) • Gentosha (2003) • 2 volumes • Shôjo, Jôsei, Science Fiction, Romantic Drama • 16+ (language, brief violence, nudity, sex)

Known as *Made in Heaven Kazemichi* and *Made in Heaven Juri,* these are actually the first and second volumes of the same manga, based on two novels by Ami Sakurai. A skillful use of science fiction and mystery themes in a relationship story, it is the story of a man and a woman: Juri, a twenty-something psychologist with a history of abuse, and her snowboarder boyfriend Kazemichi, who, in the opening chapters before he meets her, suffers a horrible traffic accident and is turned into an outwardly lifelike cyborg with a limited life span and no sensation of touch. One is an emotional robot, the other is a literal robot; they participate in a troubled relationship until Kazemichi's disappearance forces Juri to discover the truth. The two volumes retell the same events from different perspectives. The story touches on love, death, and family, but there are no grand climaxes, no "bad guys," no scenes of humor or everyday life, just the distance between the main characters, the silence, and occasionally overwrought narrative ("Kazemichi seemed to exist on a plane . . . far from desire, evil or sin"). The art is mostly close-ups of beautiful characters, wrapped in a dark fog of screentone that seems to weigh them down.

★★★

MADE IN HEAVEN JURI: See *Made in Heaven*

MADE IN HEAVEN KAZEMICHI: See *Made in Heaven*

MAGICAL MATES

(マジカル☆メイツ) • Mio Odagi • Antarctic (1996) • Gakken (Gakken Chugaku 1, 1995) • 6 issues • Shôjo, Magical Girls • Unrated/All Ages (brief glimpse of panties, the word *slut*)

This slight but charming series has the honor of being the first *shôjo* manga for younger readers published in America. Three junior high girls with "real" magic powers—Rinko (a tarot reader), Noemi (a magician with a top hat), and Kana (a love charm specialist)—help their classmates deal with romantic troubles, ghosts, and other lighthearted problems. Includes bonus pages on tarot reading, stage magic, and so on. Originally announced as a 9-issue series, the last three issues were never published. ★★

MAGICAL POKÉMON JOURNEY

Pocket Monsters PiPiPi Adventure (ポケットモンスターPiPiPiアドベンチャー) • Yumi Tsukirino (story and art), Tsunekazu Ishihara & Satoshi Tajiri (original creators) • Viz (1999–2001) • Shogakukan (Ciao, 1997–2003) • 7 volumes, suspended (10 volumes in Japan) • Shôjo, Video Game, Comedy, Romance • Unrated/All Ages

A curious but enjoyable *shôjo* spin-off of *Pokémon,* not directly based on any anime or video game. The manga might as well not be about Pokémon at all, because the creatures here are all talking individuals with personality traits (unlike any other Japanese *Pokémon* spin-offs at the time when this manga came out), and the story involves a girl who has a crush on a guy who just wants to collect them. The jokes are funnier than the material demands; the stick-figure art is cute and clean. The original Japanese title, *PiPiPi Adventure,* is based on the original Japanese names of the heroine's main Pokémon (Clefairy, Pikachu, and Jigglypuff). ★★½

MAGICAL X MIRACLE

Yuzu Mizutani • Tokyopop (2006–ongoing) • Ichijinsha (Comic Zero-Sum, 2002–2006) • 6 volumes • Shôjo, Fantasy, Comedy • 13+ (mild sexual situations)

In the hopes of becoming a wizard, fourteen-year-old Merleawe travels to the capital city

MAGICAL GIRLS (魔法少女)

Who hasn't fantasized about wishing their desires into reality or becoming someone else? A seemingly evergreen genre with strong links to the girls' anime market, *mahô shôjo* (magical girl) series bring those fantasies to life with a veritable battalion of young heroines.

Two anime series defined the genre—*Mahô Tsukai Sally* ("Little Witch Sally," aka "Magic User Sally," 1966) and *Akko-chan's Got a Secret!* (1969). Debuting on TV in 1966, *Sally* was not only the first magical girl anime but also the first anime TV show specifically aimed at girls. With the heroine leaving her magic homeland for the more entertaining human world, *Sally* was inspired by the internationally famous television series *Bewitched*. Although the *Sally* anime series came before the *Akko-chan* series, the *Akko-chan* manga began serialization in 1962, making it the earliest magical girl manga. In contrast to Sally, Akko casts spells not on others but upon herself. Using a magical compact, Akko can change her identity as the needs of her various adventures dictate. This element of transformation became a major part of magical girl mythology, and with their secret identities and colorful costumes, the genre has much in common with superheroes. Often young girls transform into adult women, providing a metaphor for growing up.

For years, there was a string of magical girl TV series, each with its own twist and most with supporting manga. Some of the girls chose to live in the human world; others were sent there for training or punishment. There were also normal girls who discovered an enchanted item or learned of a magical past. Many magical heroines, such as *Mahô no Tenshi Creamy Mami* ("Magical Angel Creamy Mami," 1983) and *Mahô no Star Magical Emi* ("Magic Star Magical Emi," 1985), chose to use their talents to become idol singers (see MUSIC AND PERFORMANCE). Arina Tanemura's tearjerker *Full Moon o Sagashite* (2002) is a modern version of the same theme.

The global hit *Sailor Moon* (1992) reinvigorated the genre by introducing a team of dynamic heroines and plots that were more action-oriented. While there had been a 1985 crossover movie involving the leads of multiple magical girl shows, it was nothing like the color-coordinated, *sentai*-inspired Sailor Moon and her friends. Team titles *Magic Knight Rayearth* (1994), *Wedding Peach* (1994), and *Nurse Angel Ririka SOS* (1995) soon followed. *Revolutionary Girl Utena* (1996) turned the genre on its ear with gender-bending, psychological themes that offered a more mature take on the genre.

Any title with a magic-using female lead can be a "magical girl" series. Within this broad definition, many attributes have been added to the genre over the years, including animal mascots, ritualized transformations, special costumes, and teams of heroines. Beginning with an impish little witch and a girl with a magic mirror, the genre has expanded with time, yet always retained close ties to the anime market. Several American animated TV shows have magical girl elements, including the 1980s TV show *Jem* as well as *The Powerpuff Girls*, which was so popular in Japan that it was adapted into a 2006 licensed anime TV series, *Demashita! Powerpuff Girls Z* ("And They're Off! Powerpuff Girls Z").

Magical Girls for Men

The magical girl genre was created by men (as were many *shôjo* manga in the 1960s); Fujio Akatsuka created *Akko-chan*, and the *Mahô Tsukai Sally* manga adaptation was drawn by Mitsuteru Yokoyama. Other male creators soon had their own way with the genre, often sexualizing the characters. Go Nagai's camp classic manga *Cutey Honey*, serialized from 1973 to 1974 in *Weekly Shônen Champion*, introduced the concept of nude transformations: Honey, a busty crime-fighting girl android, loses her clothes whenever she changes to a new form. Nude transformations were later added to the *Sailor Moon* anime series, to the annoyance of original manga creator Naoko Takeuchi, who blamed the changes on "male animators." (In the censored English version of the anime, Sailor Moon's modesty is restored.) Other magical girl titles aimed at male audiences include the 1990s *Devil Hunter Yohko* anime series (created by manga artist Gaku Miyao) and Masakazu Katsura's *Shadow Lady* (1996). (PD)

Moyoco Anno's delightful *Sugar Sugar Rune*

Magical Girl Manga

Akko-chan's Got a Secret! • *Alice 19th* • *Angel's Wing* • *Because I'm the Goddess* • *Cardcaptor Sakura* • *Cardcaptor Sakura: Master of the Clow* • *Corrector Yui* • *Cutie Honey '90* • *Full Moon o Sagashite* • *Ironcat* • *Kamichama Karin* • *Kamikaze Kaito Jeanne* • *Magical Mates* • *Mamotte! Lollipop* • *Mink* • *Miracle Girls* • *Pretear: The New Legend of Snow White* • *Princess Tutu* • *Revolutionary Girl Utena* • *Revolutionary Girl Utena: The Adolescence of Utena* • *Sailor Moon* • *Sailor Moon StarS* • *Sailor Moon Super S* • *Saint Tail* • *Shadow Lady* • *Spellbound: The Magic of Love* • *Sugar Sugar Rune* • *Tokyo Mew Mew* • *Tokyo Mew Mew a la Mode* • *Ultra Maniac* • *Wedding Peach* • *Wedding Peach: Young Love*

of Viegald to study at a prestigious school for magic. Her plans are waylaid by a quartet of handsome young men who insist she is the exact doppelgänger of the kingdom's missing master wizard, Sylthfarn, and persuade her to act as Sylthfarn's stand-in to avoid causing a panic in the kingdom. The plot revolves around Merleawe's efforts to become a wizard in her own right while also posing as another person (a guy, to be precise). Unfortunately, the story is dull and the slick but generic *shôjo* art consists mostly of pretty outfits on pretty young people. (LW) ★

MAGIC KNIGHT RAYEARTH

Mahô Kishi Rayearth, "Magic Knight Rayearth" (魔法騎士レイアース) • CLAMP • Tokyopop (1999–2001) • Kodansha (Nakayoshi, 1993–1996) • 6 volumes • Shôjo, Fantasy, Adventure • All Ages (violence)

Hikaru, Umi, and Fuu, middle school girls with nothing in common, are brought together by fate when they find themselves magically transported from Tokyo Tower to the fantasy kingdom of Cephiro. The wise sage Guru Clef explains to the girls that they are the prophesied Magic Knights, who are destined to rescue Cephiro from impending doom. The kingdom's Pillar, the princess Emeraude, has been captured by the sinister Zagato. Our heroines must unlock their elemental magic powers (Fire, Water, and Wind to match the girls' colors and dispositions), upgrade their magic armor, and finally find their Mashin—demigods who look and fight like giant robots. Lots of action, comedy, and tears, all brought to life with CLAMP's trademark gorgeous art. *Rayearth* marks CLAMP's "major label debut." Up until its release, the team had been the darlings of the *dôjinshi* circles, but it was *Rayearth*'s publication in Kodansha's young girls' magazine *Nakayoshi* that really launched them into the big time. At the time, the blending of fantasy RPG elements with *shôjo* drama and all-ages humor, not to mention the shocking ending, was a breath of fresh air. Revisiting or discovering the series now reveals that it does not age particularly well; the clichés on which the series relies have been recycled and parodied too many times over the past decade. A sequel series, *Magic Knight Rayearth II,* which picks up right where the first three-volume series leaves off, introduces a slew of new characters from three invading kingdoms. The sequel pays more attention to love and romance (plus some strong *shônen ai* subtext), and Hikaru really shines, but the cumbersome cast makes for confusing action scenes and a criminal neglect of Umi and Fuu. Both series are solid, to be sure, but *Rayearth* falls short of classic status. Mokona, the mascot critter that made its debut in *Rayearth,* would go on to play a pivotal role in both *Tsubasa* and *xxxHOLiC.* (MT)   ★★½

MAGIC KNIGHT RAYEARTH II: See *Magic Knight Rayearth*

MAHOROMATIC

(まほろまてぃっく) • Bow Ditama (story), Bunjuro Nakayama (art) • Tokyopop (2004–2006) • Wani Books (Comic Gum, 1998–2004) • 8 volumes • Seinen, Science Fiction, Romantic Comedy • 16+ (language, graphic violence, nudity, explicit sexual situations)

If you want to see a girl in a maid's uniform jump-kicking mecha, played with a straight face, this is your manga. Mahoro, a combat android who once protected Earth from an alien invasion, chooses to spend her decommissioned days as a live-in maid to Suguru, a porn-reading, blushing orphan nerd to whom women are inexplicably attracted. The first few volumes are dominated by the artist's breast-centric sexual fantasies. Later on, however, things get more serious, and the main characters find themselves involved in an earth-shaking crisis. Do robots have souls? Can panty thievery, military drama, and the Cuban missile crisis coexist in the same manga? Somehow *Mahoromatic* manages to make the shift in mood, but there's only so much you can do with this material. The art, reminiscent of Shinsuke Kurahashi or early Hitoshi Okuda, is unmemorable; the characters and mecha are generic, but on the plus side, the action scenes move quickly.   ★

MAICO 2010

Toshimitsu Shimizu • ComicsOne (2000–2001) • Shônen Gahosha (Young King/Young King Ours, 1997–1998) • 4 volumes • Seinen, Science Fiction, Mecha, Romantic Comedy • 13+ (language, graphic violence)

Adaptation of the untranslated anime. Maico, a virginal prototype sex android, ends up becoming the first android DJ at

Japan Broadcasting, where the assistant director, Matsuo, has a crush on Maico's twenty-nine-year-old creator, Masudamasu. The manga is a typical *otaku* mix of sex and technology featuring strip mahjongg, off-screen robot rape, and Shimizu's trademark soft-looking, doll-like girls. (The women are drawn pin-up style, bulging out of swimsuits over symbolic backgrounds of flowering plants.) Later on, goofy-looking evil robots show up, and Maico participates in skyscraper-destroying battles in which her clothes are torn off. For what it is—softcore OAV fodder—the art's polished, and it feels like the product of a genuine nerd, rather than someone pandering to nerdy tastes. (Incidentally, Maico is a "cutie news announcer"–type DJ and definitely not a "get ready for some more phat beats"–type DJ.)   ★★

MAIL

Housui Yamazaki • Dark Horse (2006–2007) • Kadokawa Shoten (Monthly Shônen Ace, 2004–2005) • 3 volumes • Shônen, Occult, Mystery • 13+ (mild violence, disturbing scenes, brief nudity)

Vignettes of ghostly horror are effortlessly resolved by occult detective Akiba as he exorcises spirits terrorizing unfortunate residents of Tokyo, using his sanctified handgun. The stories vary in intensity and chill factor but maintain allegiance to the Japanese ghost genre that brought us *The Ring* and *Ju-On*. Though the stories sometimes lack depth, they never disappoint, holding the reader's interest as Akiba reveals the macabre specifics of each case, sometimes in a Rod Serling–type introduction. Any of the stories could be decompressed into a bone-chilling series of its own. The artwork is a satisfying marriage of clean character design and creepy detail. (SM)   ★★★

MAI THE PSYCHIC GIRL

Mai (舞) • Kazuya Kudo (story), Ryoichi Ikegami (art) • Viz (1987–1996) • Shogakukan (Weekly Shônen Sunday, 1985–1986) • 3 volumes • Shônen, Psychic, Action • Unrated/16+ (language, violence, nudity)

Mai Kuju looks and acts every bit like an average fourteen-year-old Japanese schoolgirl.

But, as the descendant of a family of legendary psychics, she is also gifted with enormous powers of telekinesis and telepathy, abilities that her father tells her to keep hidden. But Mai, along with several other psychic children around the globe, has fallen on the radar of the Wisdom Alliance, a secret organization that has been manipulating world events toward a doomsday scenario. Wishing to use Mai for their own ends, the Alliance dispatches various foes to capture her. Mai is suddenly forced to use her still-uncontrollable powers to defend her friends and family, even as she is shocked by her own capacity for inadvertently causing destruction. One of the best-known examples of ESPer manga in the United States, *Mai the Psychic Girl* is a solid page-turner with a very believable (and sometimes alarmingly nude) adolescent character at its center. But as various menacing men in black and psychic children shooting beams out of their eyes appear one after another, a fair amount of repetition sets in over the course of three volumes. Still, artist Ryoichi Ikegami does his best to keep things from ever getting too stale, and his scenes of Mai flying over the skyscrapers of Tokyo are magnificent. At one time, there was talk of director Tim Burton mounting a musical remake of the story with Winona Ryder in the lead. Like the *Mai* sequel that the conclusion of the manga clearly sets up, it has yet to materialize. (PM)   ★★★½

MAISON IKKOKU

(メゾン一刻) • Rumiko Takahashi • Viz (1993–2006) • Shogakukan (Big Comic Spirits, 1980–1987) • 15 volumes • Seinen, Romantic Comedy • 16+ (nudity, sexual situations)

Maison Ikkoku is Rumiko Takahashi's best series: the most touching, if not the most influential, of all her many romantic comedies. Set in a small boardinghouse inhabited mostly by comic relief (a peeping Tom, a bar hostess who sits around the house in lingerie, a drunken middle-aged housewife), *Maison Ikkoku* is the love story of Yusaku Godai, a struggling would-be college student, and Kyoko Otonashi, the building manager, a beautiful widow two years his senior. Perpetual loser Yusaku struggles to become a success and to tell Kyoko his feelings (or just make a pass at her), but both of them have other love interests as well. Although most of the early episodes are self-contained sitcoms, the story becomes more dramatic as the momentum builds, and the result is a long, genuinely touching soap opera. For Americans unfamiliar with manga, it might be the perfect starter series: the T&A isn't nearly as blatant as in most men's romantic manga, and Yusaku's male daydreams transcend cultural boundaries. (Contemplating whether to kiss a girl who's not Kyoko, he imagines her shotgun-wielding father catching them in the act and dragging him to the chapel.) The art is cute and attractive, with a noticeable development in style over the seven-year run.   ★★★★

MAMOTTE! LOLLIPOP

Mamotte! Lollipop, "Protect! Lollipop" (まもって! ロリポップ)・ Michiyo Kikuta・ Del Rey (2007–ongoing)・Kodansha (Nakayoshi/Nakayoshi Next, 2002–2005)・7 volumes・Shôjo, Fantasy・13+

When junior high student Nina accidentally swallows a magic "crystal pearl," a whole school full of teenage witches and wizards (some of them dressed up in Goth-Loli fashion) wants to catch her to get the magic inside. Two boy wizards, Zero and Ichi, go against the flow and decide to protect her from their classmates. Could one of them be her ideal boy?   NR

MANGA

Various artists・ Metro Scope (c. 1980–1982)・1 volume・ Science Fiction, Adventure, Historical Fantasy・Unrated/16+ (mild language, graphic violence, nudity, sexual situations)

Titles get no more basic than *Manga,* but for this 88-page anthology to call itself even that was bold for its time, coming out before Fred Schodt's first comprehensive 1983 survey of the field, *Manga! Manga!: The World of Japanese Comics. Manga*'s exact date of publication—it carries none—is in fact uncertain; its consulting editor Mike Freidrich

(see below) believes it was in late 1980 or early 1981, whereas Schodt's own citation for it in *Manga! Manga!* gives a date of 1982. Freidrich's sophisticated 1970s independent comics anthology *Star Reach* had included Japanese artists, which gave him the necessary connections to assemble this square-bound, magazine-sized album with Japanese managing director Tadashi Ookawara. A clear editorial afterword states the ambition of *Manga* to broaden awareness of Japanese comics abroad. Although solidly adapted into English, what strikes the contemporary reader is how little the pieces of *Manga* resemble popular notions of manga itself—aside from the unrepresentative short-story format, not one of its artists work in the "big-eye" lineage handed down from Osamu Tezuka. With its "sexy robot" cover by Hajime Sorayama, *Manga* gives an impression of a less lurid version of *Heavy Metal* magazine, despite its indisputably authentic Japanese lineup that includes a pre-*Domu* Katsuhiro Otomo's wordless "The Watermelon Messiah," Yukinobu Hoshino's "The Mask of the Red Dwarf Star," and *Manga*'s undoubted creative standout, the furious 20-page lead-in "Two Warriors" by Hiroshi Hirata (*Satsuma Gishiden*). The other artists included are Yosuke Tamori, Keizo Miyanishi, Noboru Miyama, Youji Fukuyama, Masaichi Mukaide, and Masayuki Wako. The ISBN of *Manga,* which may aid in tracking this rarity down, is 4–946427–01–5. (CGH)
★★★

MANGA ARTIST ACADEMY: See *Shôjo Beat's Manga Artist Academy*

MANIAC ROAD

Manii Road, "Maniac Road" (まにいロード)・Shinsuke Kurihashi・ComicsOne (2004–2005)・Media-Works (Dengeki Daioh, 2002–2003)・3 volumes・Shônen, Otaku, Comedy・13+ (brief partial nudity, mild sexual situations)

Takezou, a harmless adult *otaku* of uncertain age, moves into an Akihabara electronics store run by three sisters: Haruna, the gentle older sister; Aoba, a boyish teenager who hates nerds; and Isuzu, a little girl who's great at video games. He repays the sisters' kindness by converting their store into an *otaku* hotspot and initiating them into the world of military model building, cosplay, airguns, *dôjinshi,* and tabletop RPGs. The work of an older fan, *Maniac Road* explains its subject matter with the enthusiasm of someone telling you about his favorite things (including some truly old-school hobbies such as model trains and tactical board games). This "didja know" feel gives the comic its charm, although there is little plot and the art is slightly dated. ★★½

MAN OF MANY FACES

20 Mensô ni Onegai!!, "Please, 20–Faces!!" (20面相におねがい!!) • CLAMP • Tokyopop (2003) • Kadokawa Shoten (Comic Genki, 1989–1991) • 2 volumes • Shôjo, Phantom Thief, Romance • All Ages

One of CLAMP's first published works (along with *RG Veda*), *Man of Many Faces* wears its *dôjinshi* heart on its sleeve. By day, Akira Ijyuin is a mild-mannered fourth-grader at the fantastical Clamp School (see *Clamp School Detectives*), but by night he dons a mask and becomes the thief 20 Faces, who steals arbitrary objects for his two eccentric mothers (yup, two mothers—don't ask). One night, while fleeing from the cops, 20 Faces hides out in the bedroom of Utako Ohkawa, a spunky kindergarten student who is just getting over a painful "breakup" with her teacher. Soon the two kids fall in love, and the series follows their relationship from childhood crush to wedding bells. A warning—everything about this series is absurd. The loose-knit caper plots are arbitrary and underdeveloped. The pages are overdesigned, with an overabundance of ribbons and rolls of fabric and characters breaking the borders (too many cooks in the kitchen? This was drawn before CLAMP whittled itself down to four members). Romantic monologues spouted from the mouth of a kindergartner aren't just odd but a bit creepy. And yet the series is a charmer. While CLAMP would become more noted for their grim apocalyptic side in their early career, *Man of Many Faces* focuses on what would become their dominant theme, romantic love. As a guide to romance, *Man of Many Faces* contains some real gems of wisdom, and it's more genuine than the pretentious *The One I Love.* The Clamp School universe, first published here (it existed only as *dôjinshi* before), would be expanded in *Clamp School Detectives* and *Clamp School Defenders: Duklyon,* but this is the best manga of the lot, even if it is the least polished. (MT)
★★½

MANTIS WOMAN

Kamakiri Onna, "Mantis Woman" (カマキリ女) • Senno Knife • Studio Ironcat (2003) • Bunkasha (2000) • 1 volume • Horror • 18+ (mild language, graphic violence, nudity)

A collection of horror shorts by adult artist Senno Knife, connected by the school environment and a seemingly interchangeable female protagonist (her name and hair length change from story to story). Knife's vaguely *shôjo*-gothic style shines here, taking familiar horror formulas (mysterious packages, evil substitutes, possessed toys), infusing a creepy touch, and getting right to the meat. However standardly drawn his human characters, Knife more than makes up for it in his ghosts and creatures, such as an evil plush koala. (JW) ★★½

MÄR

Mär: Märchen Awakens Romance • Noboyuki Anzai • Viz (2005–ongoing) • Shogakukan (Weekly Shônen Sunday, 2003–2006) • 15 volumes • Shônen, Fantasy, Battle, Adventure • 13+ (violence, brief partial nudity)

Ginta, an enthusiastic young RPG fanatic, finds himself mysteriously transported into Mär Heaven, the fantasy world of his dreams, where rocks speak and castles float in the sky. Finding himself endowed with super strength and gifted with the magic weapon Babbo (a hammer attached to a snooty, talking ball and chain), he is called on to save the world from the Chess Pieces, an army of villains each with its own magic items. And since this is a *shônen* manga, what better way to save the world than a fighting tournament? *MÄR* is a predictable but fun, fast-paced manga with nice art: boldly drawn characters and interesting settings, to which the characters teleport back and forth. Anzai reuses many elements from *Flame of Recca* (masked and cloaked villains, magic accessories, extremely lopsided fight scenes), but *MÄR* is a slicker package, and its mood of youthful adventure works better within the limitations of mainstream *shônen* manga than *Flame of Recca*'s wanna-be edginess. Many of Ginta's friends and enemies are loosely based on fairy tales (for instance, Jack, as in Jack and the Beanstalk, has magic powers related to Earth and plants). One of the characters, Halloween, was censored in the English edition; originally a pumpkin-headed man chained to a cross, the cross was changed to a pole. ★★½

MARIKO PARADE

(まりこパラード) • Kan Takahama, Frédéric Boilet (collaborators) • Fanfare/Ponent Mon (2006) • Ohta Shuppan (2003) • 1 volume • Underground, Romance, Comedy, Drama • Unrated/18+ (nudity, graphic sex)

Inspired by the works of French expatriate Frédéric Boilet, Kan Takahama worked with Boilet to create *Mariko Parade,* a pseudo-sequel to Boilet's adult love story *Yukiko's Spinach.* Mariko, a young Japanese woman, and her middle-aged boyfriend, a French photographer/artist (a thinly disguised, fictionalized version of Boilet), go to a coastal resort, where they take photos and have sex. Compared to the male desire that permeates every page of Boilet's *Yukiko's Spinach, Mariko Parade* takes a funnier approach, lightly poking fun at the couple's differences, cultural and otherwise. But this snapshot of a relationship carries with it a poignant feeling that all things must pass; to quote Takahama, "Don't ask me why but the Japanese . . . are inclined toward that which is fleeting and sad . . ." Apart from scripting input and the cover art, Boilet's contribution consists of disconnected short pieces originally drawn for other magazines, which are plunked into the story like dream sequences or musical interludes. The resulting book is like a conversation between two artists with greatly different visual styles (photorealistic versus stylized) but similar interests: realistic human relationships and artistic experimentation for its own sake.

★★★½

MARIONETTE GENERATION

(マリオネットジェネレーション) • Haruhiko Mikimoto • Viz (2000–2004) • Kadokawa Shoten (Newtype, 1989–1998) • 5 volumes • Otaku, Romantic Comedy • 13+ (mild language, sexual situations)

Twenty-four-year-old "girl art" illustrator Izumi Morino wakes up one morning to find a two-foot-tall, talking female doll in his bed. The real story, however, is about his nebulous relationship with his underage assistant Kinoko, who has a crush on him. With its pseudo love triangle between a nerdy adult, a possessed doll, and a fourteen-year-old, *Marionette Generation* presages the *moe* movement. The potentially sleazy subject matter is treated whimsically and self-referentially, with the characters themselves debating whether the manga is based on Mikimoto's own life. The art is pretty, and the individual pages are beautifully composed. (The manga mostly consists of very short installments of 8 to 10 pages.) However, the story is uneventful, plotless, and hard to follow. ★★

MARMALADE BOY

(ママレード・ボーイ) • Wataru Yoshizumi • Tokyopop (2002–2003) • Shueisha (Ribon, 1992–1995) • 8 volumes • Shôjo, Romantic Comedy • 13+ (brief mild language, mild sexual situations)

Teenage Miki is (understandably) shocked when her parents cheerfully announce that they are divorcing and marrying another divorced couple so that they can all live happily together in a four-parent household. Worse still, the suggestions of polygamy are followed by suggestions of incest when Miki finds herself falling in love with Yuu, her new stepbrother. Flirting with taboos, but not nearly as risqué as it sounds, *Marmalade Boy* is a drama of love, family, and tennis,

Fuyumi Soryo's *Mars*

aimed at younger teens. Despite the lack of overt sexual content and the generally sweet mood, the love triangles are truly passionate, involving real *Romeo and Juliet*–level problems, not mere misunderstandings that could be solved if people talked to one another. (In fact, the hero and heroine are refreshingly smart by romantic comedy standards, and the unforced plot development doesn't insult the reader's intelligence.) Yoshizumi's notes in the final volumes reveal much about the editorial process of creating a hit manga. ★★★

MARS

(マース) • Fuyumi Soryo • Tokyopop (2001–2003) • Kodansha (Bessatsu Friend, 1995–2000) • 15 volumes • Shôjo, Romantic Drama • 13+ (language, violence, sex)

"Anger or sadness are different . . . they leave an indelible mark." Kira, a withdrawn artist, is both attracted and scared by Rei, a handsome, affectless rebel with a passion for motorcycle racing. When she asks Rei to model for her, they become closer, and she comes to understand his death wish, the secrets of his past that make him "strong and beautiful and sad." A well-written, tightly plotted romance, *Mars* deals successfully with powerful issues: trauma, child abuse, morality, the sacrifices of growing up. The story is written like a good novel, and the threat of violence, which lurks even in the "blood-colored sunset," is reserved for the most powerful moments. Police and psychologists are presented in a good light, but the story is never preachy or patronizing. The artwork is clear and attractive. The title refers to the Roman god of war. ★★★★

MARS: HORSE WITH NO NAME

Mars Gaiden: Namae no nai Uma, "Mars Side Story: Horse with No Name" (マース外伝:名前のない馬) • Fuyumi Soryo • Tokyopop (2004) • Kodansha (Bessatsu Friend, 1999) • 1 volume • Shôjo, Romantic Drama • 13+ (language, mild violence, mild sexual situations)

Anthology of three stories by Fuyumi Soryo, involving romances between cold, distant teenagers, gracefully bearing the scars of their pasts. Only the title story is *Mars*-related, a prequel showing how the heroine's friend Tatsuya met Rei, the violent hero of the manga. (And yes, the title is a reference to the song.) The art has a pleasing simplicity, but the stories pale in comparison to *Mars,* and the prequel adds little to the story. ★★★

MASAOMI KANZAKI'S IRONCAT: See *Ironcat*

MASKED WARRIOR X

Keiji Kenshi X-Calibur, "Crime/Detective Swordsman X-Calibur" (刑事剣士Xカリバー) • Masayuki Fujihara • Antarctic (1996) • Kadokawa Shoten (Comic Comp, 1988–1990) • 4 issues, suspended (4 volumes in Japan) • Shônen, Comedy, Action • Unrated/16+ (mild language, violence, nudity)

When a crime organization turns athletes into cybernetic "sports monsters" (like "Bowling Man" and "Sumo Man"), there's only one person to call: Dan Sabaki, aka "Kendo-Man," a swordsman who's never taken off his *kendo* gear in his entire life! This cheerfully dumb parody of *sentai* (costumed hero) TV shows and *shônen* manga hits its mark slightly more often than it misses. (When the hero recounts his origin story, a bystander asks him, "But weren't you a baby then? How could you remember that scene?") The 1980s-anime-style artwork has a crude energy. ★★½

MAXION

Totteoki Maxion, "Trump Card Maxion/The All-Important Maxion" (とっておきMAXION) • Takeshi Takebayashi • CPM (1999–2002) • Gakken (Comic Nora, 1996–1998) • 4 volumes • Shônen, Science Fiction, Romance • 18+ (language, mild violence, nudity, sexual situations)

A combination of psychic science fiction and T&A-packed male fantasy love triangle. Yusuke, a lecherous college guy, finds himself unable to choose between the girl-next-door Maki and Maki's mysterious cousin Shion (Maki + Shion = Maxion), who seemingly has no concept of emotions or sexuality (Stereotypical bad guy: "You've been poisoned by human emotions, haven't you?"). Psychic powers soon make the relationship between the three even stranger, but unfortunately, there's no ending; the manga was canceled in Japan just before the big reveal. The generic art and character designs are weaker than the occasionally interesting writing. ★★

MAZINGER

(マジンガー) • Go Nagai • First Comics (1988) • 1 volume • Science Fiction, Mecha, Action • Unrated/18+ (violence, nudity)

In this sci-fi rewrite of *Gulliver's Travels,* the pilot of a giant warrior robot named Mazinger is whisked away from a postapocalyptic battlefield to a fantasy realm populated by giant humans. The problems this presents to our protagonist are considerable: is Mazinger alone strong enough to defeat the army of evil lizards bent on making trouble for the giants? Will our hero overcome the considerable size difference to romance the nubile ruler of this strange country? And will the giant robot and its pilot make it back to Earth in time to win the final battle? Believed to be the first full-length manga created especially for the U.S. market, the 1988 *Mazinger* is an original story, not a translation of the classic 1972 *Mazinger Z* (sold in the United States as *Shogun Warriors*) that revolutionized the Japanese anime-manga-toy market. The only real concession to the American market is the beautiful artwork, which sees Mazinger erupting in color for the first time. Designed as a one-shot, the fun is over far too fast. It reads like something you'd find in a particularly good issue of *Heavy Metal,* which is probably the highest compliment you can give a purely escapist tale like this. (PM) ★★★★

MARTIAL ARTS (格闘)

Boxing, pro wrestling, kickboxing, karate . . . in the beginning, martial arts manga (*kakutô manga*) were considered a subgenre of sports stories. The first hit postwar martial arts manga was Eiichi Fukui's 1952 judo comic *Igaguri-kun,* which was cut short by his unexpected death in 1954. Ikki Kajiwara, the master of sports and competitive manga, repeatedly tried his hand at the genre.

By the time of Kajiwara's megahit *Karate Baka Ichidai* ("Fanatical First Generation of Karate," 1971), drawn by Jirô Tsunoda and Joya Hagemaru, martial arts manga were on the rise. Action stars such as Bruce Lee and Sonny Chiba were in the international spotlight, and martial arts manga had absorbed the gritty realism of the *gekiga* movement, in which blood and cracking bones were all part of the manga vocabulary. Based on the life of Mas Oyama, founder of the Kyokushin Karate School, *Ichidai* was so popular that new students flocked to Kyokushin in real life. Less formal but equally rough fighting techniques were practiced in "fighting high school students" manga such as Ryoichi Ikegami and Tetsu Kariya's 1974 *Otokogumi* ("Men's Gang"). The red-blooded machismo of *Otokogumi* was parodied in Eiji Nonaka's *Cromartie High School* (2001). Long before Nonaka, however, the "high school martial arts" genre had become the subject of lighthearted parody. Rumiko Takahashi's classic *Ranma ½* (1987) is set in a school where everyone seems to be a martial artist, and fights often incorporate school activities such as cheerleading, cooking, and rhythmic gymnastics.

Fist of the Blue Sky by Tetsuo Hara, Buronson, and Nobu Horie

Although realistic stories would always retain an audience, in the 1980s, martial arts stories moved into the realm of fantasy. The sometimes spiritual martial arts concept of *ki* (sometimes spelled *chi* or *qi* according to the Chinese pronunciation), internal life energy or breath power, became increasingly mixed with sci-fi ideas of energy blasts and cinematic special effects, and soon martial artists had the power of superheroes. Buronson and Tetsuo Hara's *Fist of the North Star* (1983) derived its techniques from acupuncture, in which the hero can kill his opponents in an instant just by touching the right pressure point. Far more influential, in the long run, were manga such as Akira Toriyama's *Dragon Ball* (1984), in which powerful martial artists unleash their internal *ki* power in the form of giant fireballs, blasting their enemies. Although absurdly exaggerated, such techniques were distantly based on the real claims of martial arts practictioners; the *reiki* that powers the hero's energy blasts in Yoshihiro Togashi's *YuYu Hakusho* (1990) has the same name as the *reiki* energy treatment used in real life as an alternative medicine. *Chakra* in *Naruto* and *nen* in *Hunter x Hunter* all amount to much the same thing: the ammo belt for the hero's powers.

The next escalation of martial arts manga came with fighting video games in the 1990s, such as Capcom's *Street Fighter* series, whose heroes regularly shot bolts of power. (Video game manga artists usually reserve such moves for special occasions, however, compared to the actual game mechanics, in which they may be just a button-push away.) As power levels rose and rose, martial arts manga artists became more aware of the trap of "strength inflation." The heroes of martial arts manga are always becoming stronger and stronger; thus, to maintain dramatic tension, they must face more and more powerful opponents, until the artist runs out of ideas or the series becomes totally ridiculous. The most extreme example may be *Dragon Ball* and its sequel, *Dragon Ball Z.* Toward the end of *Dragon Ball,* a mighty villain gathers up all his power to annihilate a city in a nuclear-bomb-like blast. A few volumes later, in *Dragon Ball Z,* an even mightier villain musters up his power to blow up the entire Earth, a process taking several pages of dramatic buildup. But by the end of *Dragon Ball Z,* the final villain in the series is able to destroy the planet merely by pointing at it. Modern martial arts manga artists can still come up with new fighting moves and inventive visual techniques, but for sheer power escalation, Akira Toriyama may never be beaten.

Martial Arts Manga
Apocalypse Zero • *Baki the Grappler* • *Battle Club* • *Battle Vixens* • *Crying Freeman* • *Dragon Ball* • *Dragon Ball Z* • *Fist of the Blue Sky* • *Fist of the North Star* • *Flag Fighters* • *Flame of Recca* • *Futaba-kun Change* • *Hoshin Engi* • *Hunter x Hunter* • *Ironfist* • *JoJo's Bizarre Adventure* • *Juline* • *Kami-Kaze* • *The Legend of Chun Hyang* • *Naruto* • *Punch!* • *Ranma ½* • *Samurai Girl Real Bout High School* • *Scryed* • *Shaolin Sisters* • *Shaolin Sisters: Reborn* • *Tenjho Tenge* • *Tough* • *Ultimate Muscle: The Kinnikuman Legacy* • *Warriors of Tao* • *Worst* • *YuYu Hakusho*

Fighting Game Manga
Night Warriors: Darkstalkers' Revenge • *Street Fighter II* • *Street Fighter II: The Animated Movie: Official Comic Adaptation* • *Street Fighter III Ryu Final* • *Street Fighter Alpha* • *Street Fighter Sakura Ganbaru!* • *Super Street Fighter II: Cammy*

MECHANICAL MAN BLUES

Awa • *Kidô Otoko,* "Sadness • Mechanical Man" (哀 • 機動男) • Tsukasa Kotobuki • Radio Comix (2000) • Dôjinshi • 1 volume • Science Fiction, Action • Unrated/16+ (violence, partial nudity)

An incomplete *dôjinshi* from the character designer of the video games *Battle Arena Toshinden* and *Saber Marionette J.* Heavily screentoned and detailed, with exaggerated, gangly bodies and rapacious-looking faces, the plot (humans versus machine oppres-

sors) is basically just a lot of skinny robots fighting almost-naked, jelly-breasted women in thongs. Good art, though.   ★½

MEDABOTS

Medarot 2 (メダロット2) • Horumarin • Viz (2002–2003) • Kodansha (Comic Bombom, 1999–2000) • 4 volumes • Video Game, Comedy, Action • Unrated/All Ages

This spin-off of the *Medabots* video game is crippled by horrible, extremely plain art, on the low end even for kids' manga. Blatant photocopier abuse is evident, and the characters have as little expression as the snarky robots they summon (who look like bundles of parts, totally lacking the cuteness or recognizability of, say, *Pokémon* or *Digimon*). The scenes of the main character begging his parents to buy him a Medabot are cringe-inducing. The English edition is actually the second series of Japanese *Medabots* manga.

½

MEGA COMICS

Various artists • General Products (1991) • 1 volume • Science Fiction, Crime • Unrated/13+ (mild language, graphic violence)

This 122-page one-shot anthology from General Products, the now-defunct merchandising arm of the famous fan-turned-pro anime studio Gainax, has high production values but lacks editorial polish, having sometimes decent but often comically broken English—even *translator* is misspelled in its credits. The dissonance is all the more sharp considering the book's boldly declared purpose ("This is the book you desired earnestly, and would brought you a great impressions!"), which was to present itself as an authentic voice straight from Japan on the subject of manga and anime, but whose actual core seemed to be a membership form within offering $25 annual memberships to Americans in the "General Products Club," in exchange for exceedingly vague-sounding benefits. Wrapped around this concept are three crime and sci-fi short manga stories, including a New York cop vignette by Akihiro Ito (*Geobreeders*) and Mamoru Ikeuchi's full-color "The Passenger," a hard-boiled future-city piece that would not look out of place in *Heavy Metal*. Ikuto Yamashita, later the primary mecha designer of *Neon Genesis Evangelion,* contributes "Attesa," the prologue to his as yet untranslated *Dark Whisper,* about an America that literally vanishes in the course of World War III. Among a 16-page profile of eight of Japan's "next generation" of artists are two who would actually obtain a certain following in English—Hitoshi Okuda (*No Need for*

Tenchi!) and Hiroyuki Utatane (*Countdown: Sex Bombs, Seraphic Feather*). (CGH) ★½

MEGAMAN NT WARRIOR

Rockman.EXE (ロックマンエグゼ) • Ryo Takamisaki • Viz (2005–ongoing) • Shogakukan (Corocoro Comic, 2001–2006) • 13 volumes • Shônen, Science Fiction, Action • All Ages

This is one of the most recent of many manga based on the long-running *MegaMan* video game franchise (*Rockman* in Japan). In this incarnation, MegaMan is a computer program called a NetNavi, charged with the task of defending cyberspace. MegaMan and his grade-school owner, Lan, have computer-themed adventures in high-tech DenTech City, eventually developing the ability to cross between the real world and cyberspace. Much time is spent on MegaMan's ability to merge with other Navis to form composite beings. The story builds toward an apocalyptic virtual conflict between good and evil, with a large cast of characters (many of them cameos from the various video games) showing up to help or hinder MegaMan and Lan. For a manga aimed at young children and based on a video game, it's well plotted and fairly engaging. Takamisaki's cute, blocky artwork, which makes all the characters look like preschool toys, is simple but appealing. (CT) ★★½

MEMORIES

Kanojo no Omoide . . . , "Her Memories . . ." (彼女の想いで . . .) • Katsuhiro Otomo • Marvel/Epic (1992) • Kodansha (1990) • 1 issue • Science Fiction • Unrated/13+ (language, mild violence)

This brief manga is best known as the basis for the "Magnetic Rose" sequence of Katsuhiro Otomo's 1995 anthology anime film *Memories*. Investigating a strange magnetic field within a Sargasso Sea of space, astronauts find a space station shaped like a giant metal rose, within which is an ornate, tomb-like structure, created by the robot servants of a lonely woman who went to space many years ago. The plot is considerably shorter and simpler than the anime version. Otomo's ultradetailed art is excellent as always,

MECHA AND ROBOTS (メカ・ロボット)

Of all the types and stereotypes that represent Japanese pop culture to the rest of the world, one of the most universally familiar is the giant robot, a mechanical samurai that stands ten or twenty stories high and swats down evildoers with its blazing sword of justice. Western anime and manga fans tend to refer to these as mecha, but Japanese audiences use this term—a contraction of the English word *mechanism*—to describe exotic machines of all kinds, from psycho-guns to space trains. In Japan, these metal titans are considered simply a species of robot, making them relatives of the android superheroes and cybernetic pets found in so many other sci-fi stories.

The roots of the robot family tree can be traced back to Osamu Tezuka's *Tetsuwan Atom* (1952) and Mitsuteru Yokoyama's *Tetsujin 28-gô* (1956), better known to Western audiences as *Astro Boy* and *Gigantor.* Tezuka's Atom was a lovable boy robot who inhabited a world of futuristic wonders, while Yokoyama's Tetsujin was a leftover superweapon created by imperial Japan in the last days of World War II, which now obeyed the commands of a plucky boy adventurer. While drawing on the themes of Western works such as *Frankenstein, Pinocchio,* Karel Capek's play *R.U.R.,* and Fritz Lang's film *Metropolis,* these two tales also laid the foundation for decades of later anime and manga. From Atom came a tradition of good-hearted robot heroes and companions, human in every way that mattered except for their amazing technological powers. (Manga scholar Frederik L. Schodt identifies the 1930s manga *Tanku Tankuro,* whose hero was a magical robot that defended Japan from foreign aggression, as an earlier variation on this theme.) From Tetsujin, a mindless behemoth created for war who would obey the commands of whoever held his remote control box, came the concept of the giant robot as neither hero nor rampaging menace, but as a tool that could be used for good or evil depending on the human intentions that drove it.

Many of the characters created in Atom's image were companions, pets, and domestic helpers, as in Kenji Morita's comedic *Marude Dameo* (1964) and *Robotan* (1966), or Fujiko F. Fujio's eternally popular *Doraemon* (1969), where a robot cat from the future livens up a boy's mundane life with his extra-dimensional bag of tricks. Arale, the klutzy android heroine of Akira Toriyama's *Dr. Slump* (1980), follows in this tradition, and more recently CLAMP's *Angelic Layer* (1999) and *Chobits* (2000) show that the appeal of the companion robot is as strong as ever. But Atom also prefigured a separate genre of superheroic robots and cyborgs, whose action-packed battles against the forces of evil were aimed at slightly older audiences.

An early example of the robot superhero was *8 Man,* created in 1963 by Kazumasa Hirai and Jiro Kuwata. Just like Hollywood's *Robocop, 8 Man*'s hero was a slain policeman whose mind had been transferred into an ultrapowerful mechanical body to continue his fight against crime. To prevent his electronic brain from overheating, he had to periodically dose himself with cigarette-shaped capsules stored in his belt buckle, making him look extra cool to impressionable kiddies. The tradition of the crime-fighting android continued with Shotaro Ishinomori's *Kikaider* (1972) and Go Nagai's *Cutie Honey* (1973), whose scientific powers included the kind of peekaboo transformation sequences that later became a staple of the "magical girl" genre.

Ishinomori was also the creator of *Cyborg 009* (1964), in which a group of ordinary humans were mechanically enhanced by an evil secret society, only to escape and use their technological powers to fight back against the bad guys. This particular premise proved enduringly popular, and it was recycled almost unchanged in Ishinomori's *Kamen Rider* (1971), Masaomi Kanzaki's *Heavy Metal Warrior Xenon* (1986), and Yoshiki Takaya's *Bio-Booster Armor Guyver* (1985). Takaya's *Guyver*, originally inspired by *Kamen Rider*, is still going strong twenty years later, and its biomechanoid aesthetics and soap-opera plots seem to have influenced later *Kamen Rider* sequels as well. More recently, advances in computing and the popularity of the cyberpunk genre have ushered in a new wave of cyborg heroes. Although the philosophical implications of placing human minds in mechanical bodies were being explored as early as 1977 via Leiji Matsumoto's *Galaxy Express 999*, a new wave of cybernetic fantasias arrived in the form of Yukito Kishiro's *Battle Angel Alita* (1990) and Masamune Shirow's *Appleseed* (1985) and *Ghost in the Shell* (1991).

Meanwhile, the giant robot was undergoing its own parallel evolution. *Tetsujin 28*'s Mitsuteru Yokoyama went on to create *Giant Robo* (1967), whose title robot had been developed by a sinister secret society, only to fall into the hands of a boy hero who used it to foil their evil plans—a twist reminiscent of *Cyborg 009* and *Kamen Rider*. And in 1972, Go Nagai unveiled *Mazinger Z*, a giant robot whose teenage pilot actually sat in its head and drove it around like a car. Although Nagai went to some lengths to invent a plausible scientific basis for Mazinger's abilities (if a miracle element named Japanium mined from Mount Fuji counts as plausible) and emphasized the practical difficulties of operating a giant robot with buttons and levers, the story was essentially a pretext for regular battles against rampaging enemy robots. Naturally kids loved it, the toys sold like hotcakes, and *Mazinger Z* kicked off a string of anime sequels and a whole genre of heroic "super robots." Go Nagai and his longtime assistant Ken Ishikawa added another wrinkle with 1974's *Getter Robo*, in which the title robot was made up of a trio of vehicles that transformed and recombined to create three different robots. By this point, the anime and toy industries were already overtaking the manga business as the creative forces behind the super robot genre, and *Getter Robo* became an early example of the "media mix" concept in which new franchises were launched in several formats simultaneously. Soon the manga aspect was merely an afterthought, the province of hack artists who created condensed and

Shotaro Ishinomori's *Cyborg 009* © ISHIMORI SHOTARO PRO, INC. All Rights Reserved. English publication rights arranged through Japan Vistec, Inc.

dumbed-down digests for kiddie magazines such as *Corocoro Comic* and *Comic Bombom*.

With the advent of the militaristic "real robot" genre introduced by the 1979 anime *Mobile Suit Gundam* (and its countless sequels and spin-offs), it seemed as if Tetsujin 28's descendants had left the realm of manga for good. In any event, a genre in which a dozen or more characters operate nearly identical mass-produced robots while sitting inside enclosed cockpits and wearing face-concealing helmets is ill-suited for a medium in which the artist can't use voices or color schemes to distinguish one player from another (which may be why manga of this type are so often visually incomprehensible). As the children who watched *Gundam, Macross* (one of three different mecha anime merged into the cobbled-together 1985 American TV show *Robotech*), and other real robot shows began to grow up, a new crop of titles combined the nostalgic appeal of these metal titans with the more sophisticated stories and higher-quality artwork expected by older readers. Mamoru Nagano's sci-fi fantasy epic *Five Star Stories* (1986) was an early example of the trend. *Mobile Police Patlabor* (1988) parodied the genre, while *Neon Genesis Evangelion* (1995) famously deconstructed it; both were accompanied by high-quality manga as part of their own "media mix" strategies. Meanwhile, *Macross* character designer Haruhiko Mikimoto crossed over into the manga field to create *Macross 7 Trash* (1995), an original spin-off of the 1994 anime series *Macross 7*.

At this point, manga titles have once again become partners in good standing as far as the real robot genre is concerned—particularly the *Gundam* portion of it, which now represents the lion's share of the market. The popular *Mobile Suit Gundam Seed* anime is accompanied by a complex array of interwoven text and manga serials grouped under the *Gundam Seed Astray* umbrella. Kadokawa Shoten's magazine *Gundam Ace* provides illustrated complements for all the latest model kit and video game releases, as well as ongoing serials like Haruhiko Mimoto's *Mobile Suit Gundam: Ecole du Ciel* and Yoshikazu Yasuhiko's *Gundam the Origin*. In an ironic example of recursion, Mine Yoshizaki's comedy manga *Sgt. Frog* (1999), whose diminutive alien invaders are passionate consumers of *Gundam* model kits, has now spawned its own line of toys and models from the same company that makes all the *Gundam* merchandise. Perhaps, twenty years from now, we'll be reading manga about the devoted fans of *that* toy series. (MS)

Androids and Cyborgs

Absolute Boyfriend • *AD Police* • *A.I. Love You* • *Alice in Lostworld* • *Angelic Layer* • *Appleseed* • *Ashen Victor* • *Astrider Hugo* • *Astro Boy* • *Battle Angel Alita* • *Battle Angel Alita: Last Order* • *Black Magic* • *Brigadoon* • *B'TX* • *Buso Renkin* • *Chobits* • *Cutie Honey '90* • *Cyber 7* • *Cyborg 009* • *Deus Vitae* • *Doll* • *Dolls* • *Dr. Slump* • *Eden: It's an Endless World!* • *FLCL* • *Gadget* • *Galaxy Express 999* • *Genocyber* • *Ghost in the Shell* • *Ghost in the Shell 1.5: Human-Error Processor* • *Ghost in the Shell Volume 2: Man-Machine Interface* • *Grey* • *Heat Guy J* • *Heavy Metal Warrior Xenon* • *Hinadori Girl* • *Hybrid Child* (*yaoi*) • *Ichigeki Sacchu Hoihoi-san* • *Indian Summer* • *Kikaider Code 02* • *Kuro Gane* • *Made in Heaven* • *Mahoromatic* • *Maico 2010* • *Mechanical Man Blues* • *Medabots* • *MegaMan NT Warrior* • *Metal Guardian Faust* • *Metropolis* • *My-HiME* • *NaNaNaNa* • *Phoenix, Vol. 1: Future* • *Phoenix, Vol. 5: Resurrection* • *Rizelmine* • *Saber Marionette J* • *Saikano* • *Sgt. Frog* • *Steam Detectives* • *Steel Angel Kurumi* • *Twin Signal*

The Big O • Brain Powered • The Candidate for Goddess • Cannon God Exaxxion • Dodekain • Eureka Seven • Five Star Stories • Frontier Line • Full Metal Panic! • Gundam the Origin • Gunhed • Gunparade March • Gunparade March: A New Marching Song • Jinki: Extend • Mazinger • Mobile Fighter G Gundam • Mobile Police Patlabor • Mobile Suit Gundam: Blue Destiny • Mobile Suit Gundam: Ecole du Ciel • Mobile Suit Gundam: The Last Outpost • Mobile Suit Gundam: Lost War Chronicles • Mobile Suit Gundam 0079 • Mobile Suit Gundam Seed • Mobile Suit Gundam Seed Astray • Mobile Suit Gundam Seed Astray R • Mobile Suit Gundam Seed Destiny • Mobile Suit Gundam Seed X Astray • Mobile Suit Gundam Wing • Mobile Suit Gundam Wing: Battlefield of Pacifists • Mobile Suit Gundam Wing: Blind Target • Mobile Suit Gundam Wing: Endless Waltz • Mobile Suit Gundam Wing: Episode Zero • Mobile Suit Gundam Wing: Ground Zero • Nadesico • Neon Genesis Evangelion • Neon Genesis Evangelion: Angelic Days • Q-ko-chan: The Earth Invader Girl • Rahxephon • Sakura Taisen • Stellvia • Super Dimensional Fortress Macross II • Venger Robo • The Vision of Escaflowne • The Voices of a Distant Star: Hoshi no Koe • Zoids Chaotic Century • Zoids New Century

and the English edition is nicely colorized. ★★★

MERMAID MELODY PICHI PICHI PITCH: See *Pichi Pichi Pitch: Mermaid Melody*

MERMAID SAGA

Rumiko Takahashi • Viz (1993–2004) • Shogakukan (Weekly Shônen Sunday, 1984–1994) • 4 volumes • Shônen, Horror, Adventure • 16+ (graphic violence, nudity)

Mermaids are real: cannibal creatures that share a strange life cycle with humans, and whose flesh, when eaten, either grants eternal youth or transforms you into a deformed monster. Yuta and Mana, an immortal man and woman who have survived eating the mermaid's flesh, wander Japan together, encountering the sinister mermaids and the hapless people cursed by their powers. Rumiko Takahashi's closest thing to a pure horror series, *Mermaid Saga* is a well-executed mix of gory horror and pseudo-folklore (some flashback stories take place in feudal Japan). Yuta's unresolved quest to become human again is similar to Anne Rice's vampire novels or the *Highlander* movies (as in *Highlander,* his one vulnerability is having his head cut off), but the characters are usually too busy dealing with the terrors at hand to dwell on their misfortune. In Japan and in the first English edition (1993–1996), the series was published as several books with different titles, including *Ningyo no Mori* ("Mermaid Forest"), *Ningyo no Kizu* ("Mermaid's Scar"), and *Yasha no Hitomi* ("Demon's Gaze," aka "Mermaid's Gaze" in the English edition). ★★★½

MERUPURI: MÄRCHEN PRINCE

(めるぷりメルヘン・プリンス) • Matsuri Hino • Viz (2005–2006) • Hakusensha (LaLa, 2002–2004) • 4 volumes • Shôjo, Fantasy, Romantic Comedy • 13+ (mild sexual situations)

Fifteen-year-old Airi, a perfectionist who dreams of the perfect marriage, meets Aram, a little-boy prince from a fantasy world who, thanks to a curse, turns into a hot teenager when it gets dark. (In either form, however, he's mentally a kid.) Starting out as a parody of a fairy tale, around volume 3 *MeruPuri* ditches the comedy elements and becomes a pure wish-fulfillment fairy tale as the scene shifts to Aram's world of *Harry Potter*–esque magic schools and frilly-dressed nobles. The art is attractive, with lots of screentone and handsome guys, but the plot is secondary. ★★

METAL GUARDIAN FAUST

Denjin Faust, "Electric Man Faust" (電人ファウスト FAUST THE ROBOT) • Tetsuro Ueyama • Viz (1997–1998) • Shogakukan (Corocoro Comic, 1994–1995) • 1 volume • Shônen, Mecha, Action • Unrated/All Ages (violence)

Well-drawn, serious children's tale about a *Robocop/Terminator 2*–esque helmeted android (or is he a cyborg?) who protects a little girl from nine enemy robots sent to kidnap her. (The bad robots are impressive and threatening, despite being named after Santa Claus' reindeer.) Ueyama's artwork is way above average for children's manga, and the action scenes in every chapter are well done. The only downside is the abrupt ending. ★★

METAMO KISS

(メタモ☆キス) • Sora Omote • Tokyopop (2007) • Kadokawa Shoten (Asuka, 2003–2005) • 3 volumes • Shôjo, Romantic Comedy • 13+

Here's a new one for the "odd family traditions" file. The people born into Kohamaru's family have the power to switch bodies with the person or animal they're destined to spend their lives with—a spouse, a pet, what have you. In Kohamaru's case, the lucky lifemate turns out to have strong feelings of her own, but unfortunately they're for his twin brother. One can see how that could be awkward. (MS) NR

METROPOLIS

Metropolis (Daitokai), "Metropolis (The Great City)" (メトロポリス(大都会) • Osamu Tezuka • Dark Horse (2003) • Fujishobo (1949) • 1 volume • Science Fiction • Unrated/All Ages (mild violence)

The second manga in Tezuka's early "science fiction trilogy." In a bustling future (pages burst with jam-packed crowd scenes), the evil Red Party forces a scientist to create an artificial superhuman who can be used as a weapon. The scientist and his creation, the androgynous child Michi, escape—but after the scientist's death, the Red Party tracks Michi down. Although still very crude compared to Tezuka's mature work, *Metropolis* represents a leap forward from the even rougher *Lost World,* while retaining the same breakneck energy and rush of ideas. Tezuka begins to explore themes to which he would return again and again: the struggle between fascism and humanism, the immense power of technology, the thin line between the human and nonhuman, the fight for equality. Michi is a clear prototype for Astro Boy, although he's a much darker and more conflicted character. *Metropolis* was loosely adapted into an anime feature film in 2002; the anime is less a faithful adaptation of the manga than it is a fond homage to Tezuka's vision of the future. (SG) ★★★

MIDNIGHT EYE GOKU: See *Goku: Midnight Eye*

MIDNIGHT PANTHER

(ミッドナイト・パンサー) • Yu Asagiri • CPM (1997–1999) • Gakken (Comic Nora, 1994–1997) • 4 volumes • Shônen, Sex Comedy, Adventure • 18+ (language, violence, nudity, sex)

Sonya, Kei, and Lou are "Midnight Panther"—performers by day, assassins by night. Accompanied by their manager, a toothless, money-hungry old crone, they travel the land seducing and killing evil men ("He was a great guy. Too bad I had to kill him"). Each of the trio has her own backstory (ditzy Kei can transform into a panther, boyish Lou is haunted by the horny ghost of her incestuous older brother, etc.), but the real point of the manga is to show them posing in lingerie and half-removed panties, their realistically proportioned bodies topped with wedge-shaped anime faces and big breasts. The extremely dumb plots require that the Panthers be disrobed and occasionally molested before kicking the guys in the nuts and decapitating them, but the women are mostly on top and the mood is lighthearted and winking. (To quote Asagiri: "I love nudity, sex and sleazy guys, so drawing these pictures is great fun.") The art is ugly and the stories are disconnected and episodic; it theoretically takes place in a postapocalyptic fantasy setting, but volume

3 takes place in a women's college, and volume 4 is set in feudal Japan. ★

MIDORI DAYS

Midori no Hibi, "Midori's Days" (美鳥の日々) • Kazurou Inoue • Viz (2005–2006) • Shogakukan (Weekly Shônen Sunday, 2003–2004) • 8 volumes • Shônen, Romantic Comedy • 16+ (nudity, sexual situations)

Seiji Sawamura, a macho high school student with no romantic experience, wakes up one morning to find his classmate Midori, a shy girl who had secretly wished "to be a part of his life," growing out of his right arm like a living hand puppet. Now it's literally true . . . *his only girlfriend is his right hand! Midori Days* is a perfect example of everything that's good about manga romantic comedies: taking a jaw-droppingly perverted idea and handling it in a light, cheerful manner, as though it were the most natural thing in the world. (Although in fact, *Midori Days* is fully aware of its own pervertedness.) More important, it's funny; most of the stories are short and fast-paced and deliver the goods. Around volume 5, the jokes become increasingly scattershot, but the story still delights. ★★★

THE MIGHTY BOMBSHELLS

Yûjin Ishikawa • Antarctic Press (1993) • Bandai (Cyber Comix) • 2 issues • Superhero • Unrated/All Ages (mild language, mild violence)

A short and sweet original superhero manga. Yujin Ishikawa clearly loves late-1970s–early-1980s American superhero comics. His spaceships are John Byrne's, as are the women's bodies, and the first words uttered by the heroes are a variant on Wolverine's early 1980s catchphrase: "We are the best at what we do!" However, what truly nails *Mighty Bombshells* to the 1970s, rather than some other time, is not art but plot, the old chestnut of the male members of the group mind-controlled to fight the females. It all has a glorious lack of irony, but lacks the emotional hook that really great superheroes have. (RM) ★★½

MILLENNIUM SNOW

Sennen no Yuki, "Millennium Snow" (千年の雪) • Bisco Hatori • Viz (2007) • Hakusensha (LaLa, 2001–2002) • 2 volumes • Shôjo, Fantasy, Drama • 13+ (violence)

Chiyuki has a heart defect, and on the day of her birth the doctors began to foretell her death. This sounds like the making for a very depressing melodrama, but toss in a finicky vampire, a werewolf obsessed with normality, and a talking sidekick bat and you have a recipe for a nice little comedy. The story toes the line between episodic and sequential as it follows Chiyuki and her paranormal pals through school and various adventures. Each chapter makes a point about the importance of being there for each other and believing in yourself. The art is recognizably Hatori, although her style is not as refined as it is in *Ouran High School Host Club.* The ending is abrupt; the series is on hiatus in Japan and theoretically may be continued someday. (HS) ★★½

MINK

Dennô Shôjo Mink, "Computer Girl/Cyber Idol Mink" (電脳少女☆Mink) • Megumi Tachikawa • Tokyopop (2004–2005) • Kodansha (Nakayoshi, 2000–2001) • 6 volumes • Shôjo, Magical Girl, Fantasy • 13+

Easily confused grade-schooler Mink acquires a computer program from the future, Wanna-Be, which allows the user to transform into "the person you Wanna-Be!" With it, she changes into singing star Cyber Idol Mink and immediately becomes Japan's biggest musical sensation. Her sole motivation for entering the music world is her crush on boy-band star Illiya, with whom she quickly gets up close and personal, but her true love soon emerges as teenage music mogul (no, really) Naoto Motoharu. Neither the boys nor the media manage to uncover her true identity, despite the fact that Cyber Idol Mink looks exactly like Mink and has the same name. Actually, all the characters have identical cute, big-eyed faces, so maybe it's understandable that no one makes the connection. Near the end, the manga develops a

MILITARY

In 1947, after the defeat of World War II, Japan became the only nation on Earth to forever renounce war. Article 9 of the postwar Japanese constitution, drafted by American army officers and influenced by Western and Japanese liberals, states that Japan will never maintain a standing army or settle international disputes through military force. The limitations on a standing army were eventually interpreted to permit a purely defensive force, the Japan Self-Defense Force (JSDF). Today, the JSDF is one of the world's most well-equipped "military" forces and has participated in international peacekeeping operations, but a deep ambivalence to war runs through Japanese culture: a prevailing pacifist tendency, coupled with occasional World War II revisionism, and a subculture of military fandom.

Children's war comics had existed before World War II, and during the war, artists produced jingoistic war comics and illustrations for the prototypical *shônen* manga magazines. One such illustrator was Shigeru Komatsuzaki, who went on to do thousands of paintings for plastic model kits, as well as conceptual art for Japanese science fiction films in the 1960s and 1970s. After the war, antimilitarism was forcibly imposed by the American occupation, as well as a genuine public backlash against the mind-set that had led to Japan's downfall. Of the few war comics from the period, all had an antiwar bent, such as Koremitsu Maetani's 1958 *Robot Santôhei* ("Robot, Private Third Class"). In the early 1960s, as part of a general mood of discontent sweeping Japanese society (see the article on POLITICS), pro-war views began to creep back into the media and comics. Young pilots and officers smiled innocently from the covers of boys' adventure comics such as Naoki Tsuji's *0–Sentarô* ("Zero Sentarô") and Ikki Kajiwara and Dan Tetsuya's *Shin Senkan Yamato* ("New Battleship Yamato"). Other artists, many of them veterans, responded to the trend with an antiwar viewpoint: Tetsuya Chiba's *Shidenkai no Taka* ("Taka of the Violet Lightning") (1963), Kenji Nakazawa's *Barefoot Gen* (1972), and Shigeru Mizuki's *Sôin Gyokusai Seyo!* ("Banzai Charge!") (1973) all told the stories of normal soldiers and their loved ones caught up in the horrors of World War II. Somewhere in the middle were comics such as Mikiya Mochizuki's 1964 *Saizensen* ("Front Line"), an action comic based on the true story of the 442nd Regimental Combat Team, Japanese American soldiers who fought in the battlefields of Europe.

At the same time, however, some artists told more romanticized war stories, such as Leiji Matsumoto's *Senjô Manga Series* ("Battlefield Manga Series," serialized from 1974 to 1980 in *Weekly Shônen Sunday*) and Kaoru Shintani's *Area 88* (1979–1986). Although these manga focus on the tragedy and senselessness of war, it is impossible not to detect a trace of revisionism in stories such as Matsumoto's "Stratospheric Currents," one of several plots adapted into the anime *The Cockpit*, in which a noble Nazi pilot chooses dishonor by allowing the British to shoot down a transport plane carrying Germany's secret atomic bomb. Matsumoto's work also dwelled lovingly on battleships, fighter planes, and other gadgetry; in the 1974 anime series *Uchû Senkan Yamato* ("Space Battleship Yamato"), designed by Matsumoto and known in the United States as *Star Blazers*, the World War II battleship *Yamato* is rebuilt as a space cruiser carrying the last heroes of the human race. Such subjects had a strong appeal: in the 1970s there was a boom in ultra-realistic plastic model kits, often based on real military hardware as well as robots and other imaginary mecha. Model magazines such as *Panther, Hobby Japan,*

Motofumi Kobayashi's *Apocalypse Meow*

and *Model Graphix* sometimes featured short manga on military topics. Other magazines focus on guns, which are almost entirely unavailable in Japan due to strict gun control laws—but paradoxically, that very unavailability allows the production of super-realistic model guns that look just like the real thing. Military *otaku*, stereotypically obsessed with military data and spending their spare time playing with paintball guns or doing "survival training," became an established part of fandom. (A typical character is Kensuke in *Neon Genesis Evangelion*.) At the same time, many military *otaku* stress that they are not pro-war and have no interest in real combat.

For years, Japan's premier military manga magazine—the *only* "pure" military manga magazine—was the monthly *Combat Comic*. Founded in 1984 by small publisher Nihon Shuppansha, *Combat Comic* rode a wave of interest in alternate history novels, including many variants of "what if Japan won World War II?" The comics also dealt with other past, present, and speculative military scenarios, generally treated with extreme realism, a lack of overt politicizing, and copious historical research. The magazine's most popular artist was Motofumi Kobayashi, an illustrator and former apprentice of Shigeru Komatsuzaki. However, in the 1990s Kobayashi angered his editors by his decision to draw his Vietnam War story *Apocalypse Meow* in a less than super-realistic style, using cats and rabbits in place of human characters. Kobayashi took *Apocalypse Meow* to the rival airsoft-gun publication *Combat Magazine* and eventually severed his ties with *Combat Comic,* which went out of business.

Beyond the subculture of military *otaku,* more character-oriented *sensō manga* (war manga) occasionally appears in mainstream magazines, where it is one genre among many. Kaiji Kawaguchi frequently deals with military topics, as in *Chinmoku no Kantei* ("The Silent Service"), his 1988 megahit about a rogue nuclear submarine piloted by an idealistic Japanese commander, and *Zipang* (2000), about a modern-day JSDF vessel transported back in time to the Battle of Midway. Stories also involve more distant conflicts: Tetsuya Egawa's 2001 *Nichirosensō Monogatari* ("The Story of the Russo-Japanese War") describes the war in text-heavy history-book detail, while Tetsuya Hasegawa's 2003 *Napoleon: Shishi no Jidai* ("Napoleon: Age of Lions") is a typical adventure manga full of action, heroism, and bloodshed.

As for the role of the armed forces in real-world Japan, it continues to change; in particular, regional conflicts with China and Korea lead to occasional movements to modify Article 9 and give the JSDF a freer rein. In 2004, at the request of the United

States, Japan deployed noncombat troops to Iraq; it was the first foreign deployment of Japanese troops since World War II. Current prime minister Shinzo Abe is in favor of expanding the military, and the JSDF, like many Japanese agencies, has employed cute manga-style mascots (the perky soldier "Prince Pickles") to improve its image. But pacifists have a strong voice as well. War in Japanese media, whether comics, books, or movies, is rarely pure escapism; and while guns and cannons may blaze away in more fantastical genres of manga, there are few manga that claim to represent the real world.

Military Manga

Adolf • Apocalypse Meow • Apollo's Song • Area 88 • Bakune Young • Barefoot Gen • Eden: It's an Endless World! • The First President of Japan • Frontier Line • Full Metal Panic! • Godzilla • Grey • Gun Crisis • Gunparade March • Gunparade March: A New Marching Song • Hellhounds: Panzer Cops • Hellsing • Mahoromatic • Maniac Road • Musashi No. 9 • Q-ko-chan: The Earth Invader Girl • Pineapple Army • Project Arms • The Rebel Sword • Red Prowling Devil • Revenge of Mouflon • Saikano • Sakura Taisen • Shadow Star • Striker • Who Fighter with Heart of Darkness • Zipang

rudimentary plot, as the creator of Wanna-Be pops up in cyberspace to harass Mink and her friends. The occasionally witty rewrite ("If I was afraid of ghosts, I wouldn't have become a talent manager!") can't add much interest to this flimsy, unimaginative fantasy of celebrity life. The art is typical Tachikawa: blandly cute smiling faces, busy collage layouts, and lots of screentone. (SG)   ★★

MIRACLE GIRLS

(ミラクル☆ガールズ) • Nami Akimoto • Tokyopop (1999–2003) • Kodansha (Nakayoshi, 1991–1994) • 9 volumes • Shôjo, Psychic, Magical Girl • All Ages

Toni and Mika (Tomomi and Mikage in the Japanese original) are identical girls with a secret: when they're together, they have telepathic powers! As the series begins, Toni is a tomboy stuck at an all-girls school, while Mika, who prefers science and reading, is dreading the upcoming athletic festival at her coed school. In typical identical twin story fashion, the two girls switch places, giving Toni a chance to fall in love with Jackson (Yuya), an outgoing boy from Mika's school. Mika's got a crush of her own—the

charming and scholarly Chris (Hideaki). For the first story arc, romance is at the forefront, with psychic powers used for comic effect. The twins' initial nemesis, the scheming Mr. K, is a bumbling buffoon, so there is never very much danger. As the four leads advance to middle school in the second and third story arcs, things get more serious, with the introduction of feuding twin princesses from a European kingdom, Mason Templar (Masaki), a handsome boy with psychic powers of his own, and the nefarious Mr. X, who will use any means necessary to control the powerful psychic twins. The story is timeless and charming—one of the best manga in English for the younger set. Older readers will probably be too turned off by the decidedly old-school art and the Westernized names. Finding a copy is another question altogether—a pity, as this older series is much better than Nami Akimoto's later work. (MT)   ★★½

MISS ME?

Tomoko Taniguchi • CPM (2003) • Jitsugyo no Nihonsha (1991) • 1 volume • Shôjo, Romantic Comedy • All Ages

Set in the same world as *Let's Stay Together Forever* (whose hero and heroine have cameos), *Miss Me?* is a romance set in the 1980s world of Japanese glam rockers and stadium metal bands (or at least teenagers who think metal bands look cool). Emyu, an innocent, pure-hearted club girl, is caught in a romantic triangle between two rockers, Shinkichi and Yasu. Mild but enjoyable. ★★

MITSUKAZU MIHARA: BEAUTIFUL PEOPLE

Mitsukazu Mihara • Tokyopop (2006) • Shodensha (2001) • 1 volume • Jôsei, Drama • 16+ (language, violence, sexual situations)

This collection of stories shows Mihara at her best: varied stories about love, vanity, and the supernatural, drawn in her usual high-contrast art style, starring sharp-featured, pale characters with long black hair. (Her figure drawings are frankly weak, but they get the job done.) Even the weaker stories have interesting premises, as when a man takes home a snow maiden in "Princess White Snow," or two bickering twenty-somethings find themselves the last two humans on Earth in "World's End." The more satisfying stories include "The Lady Stalker," about a stalker in a workplace, and "Blue Sky," about a vampire and his mortal female companion. ★★★

MITSUKAZU MIHARA: THE EMBALMER

Shigeshoshi, "The Embalmer" (死化粧師) • Mitsukazu Mihara • Tokyopop (2006–2007) • Shodensha (2003–2005) • 4 volumes • Jôsei, Drama • 16+ (language, violence, sexual situations)

In Japan, where most people are cremated, embalming is a rare profession and is considered even creepier than it is in America. This is the occupation of the main character of *The Embalmer,* an anthology of faintly gothic short stories focused more on death and bereavement than rotting flesh and formaldehyde. (Although the subject matter is morbid, it's neither graphic nor technically oriented.) The hero is a morose, handsome man with messy dark hair who sleeps around casually and lives in the back of a church, seemingly oblivious to the romantic interest of his young housekeeper. In typical manga fashion, the early stories focus on individual embalming jobs (in which the hero shows his sensitivity to the wishes of the deceased and their families), and later turns to the morbid origin of the hero himself. A solid hook and interesting stories. ★★★

MITSUKAZU MIHARA: HAUNTED HOUSE

Haunted House • Mitsukazu Mihara • Tokyopop (2006) • Shodensha (2002) • 1 volume • Gothic, Comedy • 16+ (language)

Gothic comedy similar to *The Addams Family,* drawn with Mihara's usual gangly, stark black-and-white art. Teenage Sabato is the only normal member of his family, who are all vampire-like, death-obsessed goths whose bathwater runs blood-red and who decorate their house with inverted crosses. Every chapter, he tries to get a girlfriend, and every chapter, his parents and sisters scare them off by intentionally acting as freakish as possible ("Please, for one day, act normal!" he begs). Even at just one volume, the joke quickly wears thin. ★★

MITSUKAZU MIHARA: IC IN A SUNFLOWER

Shûsekikairo no Himawari, "Integrated Circuit Sunflower" (集積回路のヒマワリ) • Tokyopop (2007) • Shodensha (1994–1997) • 1 volume • Gothic, Fantasy • 18+

A collection of seven early short stories from the pioneering Gothic Lolita artist, including her debut work, *The Children Who Don't Need Rubbers.* The subject matter covers sex, servant robots, cloning, murder, compulsive biting, and other wonders of the human condition. (MS) NR

MITSUKAZU MIHARA: R.I.P. (REQUIEM IN PHONYBRIAN)

R.I.P. (Requiem in Phonybrian) • Mitsukazu Mihara • Tokyopop (2006) • Asuka Shinsha (2000) • 1 volume • Gothic, Comedy, Drama • 16+ (language, violence)

An angel, sick of scrubbing heaven's gates, descends to Earth and takes pity on a handsome suicide, who is unable to enter heaven. She gives him one of her wings, trapping them both on Earth, where her new companion—the Brian of the title—keeps futilely trying to commit suicide, until his tragic past is revealed. Beneath its showy visuals, *R.I.P.* is a decent story. Although her figure drawing is sometimes questionable, Mihara's art is at its most gothic; everyone wears black suits or frilly petticoats, Mexican Day of the Dead skeletons creep across the panels, and the backgrounds are high-contrast photographs of cathedrals and churchyards.   ★★½

MIYUKI-CHAN IN WONDERLAND

Fushigi na Kuni no Miyuki-chan, "Miyuki-chan in Wonderland" (不思議の国の美幸ちゃん) • CLAMP • Tokyopop (2003) • Kadokawa Shoten (Newtype, 1993–1995) • 1 volume • Shônen, Comedy • 16+ (constant partial nudity, constant sexual situations)

Miyuki-chan in Wonderland is CLAMP's most minor work—both in page count and substance. The premise is this: Miyuki, a perpetually late uniformed schoolgirl, rushes off to class, only to find herself transported to a parallel world where lanky girls in miniskirts fawn over her in preparation for a PG-rated lesbian orgy. Miyuki-chan panics, tries to get away, then—*poof!* It was all a dream! Rinse and repeat for seven chapters. Even if you find the short-attention-span-*yuri* premise enticing, the book lacks value at under 100 pages of manga. If you buy it at all, buy it as an art book, as the book does showcase lead CLAMP artist Mokona's full range of sexy women. There are women with waist-length hair, women with shoulder-length hair—even women with cropped hair! The mind boggles. Miyuki-chan would go on to play "Where's Waldo?" as the recurring cameo in the dimension-hopping *Tsubasa* manga—her best role yet. (MT) ★

MOBILE FIGHTER G GUNDAM

Kidô Butôden G Gundam, "Mobile Fighting Legend G Gundam" (機動武闘伝Gガンダム) • Hajime Yatate & Yoshiyuki Tomino (original story), Koichi Tokita (art) • Tokyopop (2003) • Kodansha (Comic Bombom, 1994–1995) • 3 volumes • Shônen, Science Fiction, Martial Arts, Mecha, Action • All Ages (violence)

The first, and least accomplished, of the *Gundam* anime adaptations that Tokita produced for the kiddie magazine *Comic Bombom.* It's big and crude and loud, and frankly kind of dumb, but since *G Gundam* wasn't exactly a subtle show in the first place, the treatment almost works. In this particular alternate *Gundam* universe, the space colonies that orbit Earth resolve their political differences by sending giant robots down to the planet for a humongous martial arts tournament, little suspecting that sinister schemes revolving around the monster machine known as the Dark Gundam will require even more hitting than usual. As of the second volume, Tokita starts throwing in some of his four-panel gag strips, which are pretty much the highlight here. (MS) ★

MOBILE POLICE PATLABOR

Kidô Keisatsu Patlabor, "Mobile Police Patlabor" (機動警察パトレイバー) • Masami Yuki • Viz (1998) • Shogakukan (Weekly Shônen Sunday, 1988–1994) • 2 volumes, suspended (22 volumes in Japan) • Shônen, Science Fiction, Mecha, Police, Action • Unrated/13+ (mild violence, brief partial nudity)

A collection of good-natured yarns about a team of second-rate cops who bust the heads of robot-driving criminals and hippie eco-terrorists in the metropolitan Tokyo of the near future. Rather than a spoof of the giant-robot genre, *Patlabor* functions as a whimsical police drama with heavy doses of character-based comedy, and the construction and the police bots clattering around the streets of Tokyo seem like perfectly plausible additions to the landscape. Both the city settings and the ramshackle offices of the Special Vehicles Division are vividly realized, and the motley ensemble cast is a hoot, especially the brilliant but hopelessly lazy Captain Goto. Unfortunately, the plot barely progresses past the initial setup in the two volumes available in English, cutting the story off abruptly just as things start to get interesting. (MS) ★★★

MOBILE SUIT GUNDAM: BLUE DESTINY

Kidô Senshi Gundam Gaiden: The Blue Destiny, "Mobile Warrior Gundam Side Story: The Blue Destiny" (機動戦士ガンダム外伝 THE BLUE DESTINY) • Hajime Yatate & Yoshiyuki Tomino (original story), Tomohiro Chiba (cooperation), Mizuho Takayama (story and art) • Tokyopop (1999) • Kodansha (Haoh Magazine, 1997) • 1 volume • Science Fiction, Mecha, Action • Unrated/13+ (violence)

A spin-off manga set in the same One Year War time frame as the original *Mobile Suit Gundam* anime series. *Blue Destiny* brings some welcome changes to the standard Gundam formula, casting a regular soldier as its hero instead of a whining civilian and putting him at the controls of a mass-produced GM mobile suit instead of an exotic Gundam. Of course, he ends up becoming the ace pilot of a souped-up GM variant—the titular Blue Destiny—whose mysterious mind-machine interface transforms him into a ruthless killing machine, but it's still a step in the right direction. Based on a video game trilogy for the Sega Saturn, the manga version abruptly wraps up the story two-thirds of the way through. But it's still an entertaining read despite the truncated ending, and Takayama's artwork is crude but energetic. (MS)   ★★★

MOBILE SUIT GUNDAM: ECOLE DU CIEL

Kidô Senshi Gundam Ecole du Ciel, "Mobile Warrior Gundam Ecole du Ciel" (機動戦士ガンダム エコール・デュ・シエル) • Hajime Yatate & Yoshiyuki Tomino (original story), Yoshinori Sayama (mechanical design), Outasight (production), Haruhiko Mikimoto (story and art) • Tokyopop (2005–ongoing) • Kadokawa Shoten (Gundam Ace, 2002–ongoing) • 9+ volumes (ongoing) • Science Fiction, Mecha, Drama • 13+ (mild language, violence)

An original story set in the "Universal Century" world of the original *Mobile Suit Gundam* series, *Ecole du Ciel* begins two years after the events of the *Gundam 0083* anime and continues on to overlap with the sequel series *Zeta Gundam.* The narrative follows the adventures of Asuna Elmarit, a teenage pilot cadet at the Earth Federation's elite mobile suit academy, where an escalating series of training accidents gradually makes it clear that this school is actually a scheme to identify students with superhuman "Newtype" potential through a lethal process of elimination. The plot is surprisingly sophisticated, and while it may be daunting for *Gundam* novices because it hinges on points of Universal Century history and politics that aren't explained in the manga itself, it's actually one of the best-written *Gundam* manga to date. If anything, it's Mikimoto's artwork that falls short here—while he excels at drawing pretty girls, and his robot battles are dramatic and exciting, his visual storytelling is sometimes difficult to follow. (MS)   ★★★½

MOBILE SUIT GUNDAM: THE LAST OUTPOST

Shin Kidô Senki Gundam Wing G-UNIT, "New Mobile War Record Gundam Wing: G-UNIT" (新機動戦記ガンダムW G–UNIT) • Koichi Tokita (story and art), Hajime Yatate & Yoshiyuki Tomino (original story) • Tokyopop (2002–2003) • Kodansha (Comic Bombom, 1997–1998) • 3 volumes • Shônen, Science Fiction, Mecha, Action • All Ages/13+ (mild language, violence)

Best known for his workmanlike adaptations of whatever *Gundam* anime happens to be on the air at the time, artist Koichi Tokita finally gets to cut loose with an original story, and the results are a pleasant surprise. A spin-off story that takes place in parallel to the events of the *Gundam Wing* anime series, *The Last Outpost* recounts the adventures of a pair of hotheaded test pilot brothers as they defend their asteroid home from a rogue's gallery of mad scientists, megalomaniacs, and masked rivals. The story is as shallow as it is entertaining, with a lively and eccentric cast and even a touch of romantic comedy along the way. Unfortunately, the final volume degenerates into a tedious slugfest in which all crises are resolved by the hero mashing the button that makes his robot win. Volumes 1 and 3 are rated A, but volume 2 is rated T, for no discernible reason. (MS)   ★★½

MOBILE SUIT GUNDAM: LOST WAR CHRONICLES

Kidô Senshi Gundam Senki, "Mobile Warrior Gundam War Record" (機動戦士ガンダム戦記) • Masato Natsumoto (art), Tomohiro Chiba & Bandai Games Inc. (story), Hajime Yatate & Yoshiyuki Tomino (original story) • Tokyopop (2006) • Kadokawa Shoten (Gundam Ace, 2002–2003) • 2 volumes • Science Fiction, Mecha, Action • 13+ (violence)

A manga spin-off of the essentially plotless video game of the same name, which never saw a U.S. release. Set during the One Year War time frame of the original *Mobile Suit Gundam,* the story follows the adventures of two globetrotting teams of mobile suit pilots fighting on opposite sides, as well as the secondary dramas surrounding their respective mechanics and support teams. Natsumoto's art is polished and confident, and while his character drawings are perhaps a little cartoony for the grim and gritty subject matter, he has a knack for rendering the details of military hardware and for delivering clear, action-packed battle scenes. The writing has a similar feel to Chiba's *Gundam Seed Astray* serials, with its focus on team camaraderie and passionate, idealistic heroes. But something rings a little false about the characterizations of the team leaders here, as both Earth Federation officer Matt Healy and his Zeon rival Ken Bederstadt are soldiers of a type unique to anime, who fight for love and peace and don't actually want to kill anyone. (MS) ★★★

MOBILE SUIT GUNDAM 0079

Kidô Senshi Gundam 0079, "Mobile Warrior Gundam 0079" (機動戦士ガンダム0079) • Hajime Yatate & Yoshiyuki Tomino (original story), Kazuhisa Kondo (story and art) • Viz (2000–2003) • Bandai/MediaWorks (Cyber Comix/MS Saga/Dengeki Daioh, 1994–2005) • 9 volumes, suspended (12 volumes in Japan) • Shônen, Science Fiction, Mecha, Action • 13+ (mild language, violence)

A fairly straightforward adaptation of the original *Mobile Suit Gundam* anime series. Given the luxury of ample page space and a full decade to devote to his dream project, artist Kondo is able to cover pretty much every significant plot point from the anime, but the focus is very much on military action. Kondo renders the battle scenes in loving detail, devoting page after page to carefully rendered hardware and thundering gunfire accompanied by his trademark brand of eccentric English-language sound effects. But his character art is crummy and amateurish, and he generally rushes through the human elements of the story in his haste to get to the next big-budget combat spectacular. Viz released thirteen issues in a traditional comic book format between 1999 and 2000, then switched to graphic novels, eventually giving up on the series a couple of years before the final volume was finally released in Japan. (MS) ★★

MOBILE SUIT GUNDAM SEED

Kidô Senshi Gundam Seed, "Mobile Warrior Gundam Seed" (機動戦士ガンダムSEED) • Hajime Yatate & Yoshiyuki Tomino (original story), Masatsugu Iwase (art) • Del Rey (2004–2005) • Kodansha (2003–2005) • 5 volumes • Science Fiction, Mecha, Action • 13+ (underwear, mild language, violence)

An adaptation of the 2002 anime series *Gundam Seed,* which set out to bring the venerable franchise into the modern era with its lavish animation and angst-ridden pretty-boy pilots. Against the backdrop of a brutal space war, two childhood friends turned unstoppable superwarriors find themselves on opposite sides of the conflict, with an endless supply of cannon-fodder goons in between. The plot telescopes very nicely into five manga volumes, which probably says something about the amount of padding in the anime version, and the art is uniformly sleek and stylish. However, the battle sequences are nearly incoherent due to Iwase's interchangeable character faces and inability to depict mecha action clearly, ending up as a succession of robots striking cool poses while unknown objects explode for mysterious reasons. (MS) ★★

MOBILE SUIT GUNDAM SEED ASTRAY

Kidô Senshi Gundam Seed Astray, "Mobile Warrior Gundam Seed Astray" (機動戦士ガンダムSEED

ASTRAY) • Hajime Yatate & Yoshiyuki Tomino (original story), Tomohiro Chiba (story), Koichi Tokita (art) • Tokyopop (2004) • Kadokawa Shoten (Gundam Ace, 2003–2004) • 3 volumes • 13+ (language, violence)

Gundam Seed Astray is no mere spin-off or side story, but part of an elaborate multimedia project that was produced in parallel with the *Gundam Seed* anime series. Tokita's manga is just one of four interwoven *Astray* serials that continually cross over with one another, not to mention the main anime series, and since it was never intended to work as a self-contained story, it's not surprising that it doesn't. This title focuses mainly on the occasions when *Astray*'s two heroes—happy-go-lucky junk dealer Lowe Gear and grim soldier of fortune Gai Murakumo—cross paths and team up, so it manages to hit most of the story's key plot points. Tokita's art is clear and effective, making the action comprehensible even when the story isn't, and Tokyopop's editors have added a sprinkling of footnotes in an attempt to make the proceedings slightly less bewildering to readers who haven't seen the *Gundam Seed* anime. However, some of Tokyopop's additions—such as randomly claiming that characters are telepathic, or reversing the gender of the story's main villain—create more confusion than they dispel. (MS)   ★★½

MOBILE SUIT GUNDAM SEED ASTRAY R

Kidô Senshi Gundam Seed Astray R, "Mobile Warrior Gundam Seed Astray R" (機動戦士ガンダム SEED ASTRAY R) • Hajime Yatate & Yoshiyuki Tomino (original story), Tomohiro Chiba (story), Yasunari Toda (art) • Tokyopop (2005) • Kadokawa Shoten (Monthly Shônen Ace, 2003–2004) • 4 volumes • 13+ (language, violence, brief nudity)

Another of the serials produced as part of the *Gundam Seed Astray* multimedia project, *Astray R* focuses on the solo adventures of junk dealer Lowe Gear, the owner and operator of the sword-swinging Gundam Astray Red Frame. Toda's frenetic artwork is packed with energy and excitement, his characters are charming and full of personality, and he excels at drawing buxom babes,

but since clarity isn't really his forte, the obligatory mecha battles tend to be difficult to follow. While *Astray R* is generally a fun read, and a good complement to the main *Astray* serial by Koichi Tokita, the final volume—which centers on an extended battle between superpowered robots whose gimmicks and abilities are neither explained nor clearly depicted in the manga itself—is all but incomprehensible. (MS)   ★★

MOBILE SUIT GUNDAM SEED DESTINY

Kidô Senshi Gundam Seed Destiny, "Mobile Warrior Gundam Seed Destiny" (機動戦士ガンダム SEED DESTINY) • Hajime Yatate & Yoshiyuki Tomino (original story), Masatsugu Iwase (art) • Del Rey (2006–2007) • Kodansha (2005–2006) • 4 volumes • 13+ (mild language, violence)

A condensed adaptation of the sequel to the anime series *Gundam Seed.* As a new war breaks out between the Earth Alliance and the genetically enhanced Coordinators who inhabit the space colonies, a fresh set of heroes is introduced only to fall by the wayside as the focus gradually shifts back to the cast of the original series, leaving the new characters and situations rather underdeveloped. The storytelling of Iwase's manga is even more choppy and compressed than in the previous series, and the artwork no less stiff. The robot poses are still impressive, even if you can't tell what they're doing, but it's increasingly apparent that Iwase is just recycling the same pictures over and over. (MS)
★

MOBILE SUIT GUNDAM SEED X ASTRAY

Kidô Senshi Gundam Seed X Astray, "Mobile Warrior Gundam Seed X Astray" (機動戦士ガンダム SEED X ASTRAY) • Hajime Yatate & Yoshiyuki Tomino (original story), Tomohiro Chiba (story), Koichi Tokita (art) • Tokyopop (2006–2007) • Kadokawa Shoten (Gundam Ace, 2004) • 2 volumes • Science Fiction, Mecha, Action • 13+ (violence)

A continuation of Tokita's and Chiba's *Gundam Seed Astray* serial. While the previous *Astray* titles were part of a complex multimedia mosaic, *X Astray* is a more self-contained story that takes place during the final episodes of the *Gundam Seed* anime series and pushes the established characters into the background to focus on a couple of new arrivals. The protagonists this time are two teenage Gundam pilots with radically different personalities, the war-crazed Canard Pars and the idealistic do-gooder Prayer Reverie. (MS)   NR

MOBILE SUIT GUNDAM WING

Shin Kidô Senki Gundam Wing, "New Mobile War Record Gundam Wing" (新機動戦記ガンダムW) • Koichi Tokita (art), Hajime Yatate & Yoshiyuki Tomino (original story) • Tokyopop (2000–2001) • Kodansha (Comic Bombom, 1995–1996) • 3 volumes • Shônen, Science Fiction, Mecha, Action • All Ages (violence)

Utterly perfunctory adaptation of the 1995 anime series. Thanks to its colorful robots, memorable characters, and flowery philosophy, the *Gundam Wing* anime captured the imaginations of Western audiences in a way that no other story in the *Gundam* saga has ever managed, and made it possible for even hackwork like this to see the light of day. Artist Tokita phones in a choppy, ultracondensed remix of the story's highlights, made even less readable by the English edition's abominable taste in typography. The only saving grace is the wacky sound effects, which include such charmingly literal descriptors as "Whip," "Slide," "Stare," "Open," and "Quick." (MS)   ½

MOBILE SUIT GUNDAM WING: BATTLEFIELD OF PACIFISTS

Shin Kidô Senki Gundam Wing Battlefield of Pacifist, "New Mobile War Record Gundam Wing: Battlefield of Pacifist" (新機動戦記ガンダムW バトルフィールド・オブ・パシフィスト) • Hajime Yatate & Yoshiyuki Tomino (original story), Katsuhiko Chiba (scenario), Koichi Tokita (art) • Tokyopop (2002) • Kodansha (1997) • 1 volume • Science Fiction, Mecha, Action • All Ages (violence)

A *Gundam Wing* spin-off story that serves very nicely as a bridge to the events of the sequel anime *Endless Waltz.* As various interested parties race to seize control of the automated robot factory Vulkanus, the heroes are forced to consider the hypocrisy of disarming the rest of the world while retaining their own almighty Gundams. The well-constructed plot gives all the characters their share of attention, while touching on some interesting ideas about war and peace and technological development, and artist Tokita milks it for a number of great dramatic moments. (MS)   ★★★½

MOBILE SUIT GUNDAM WING: BLIND TARGET

Shin Kidô Senki Gundam Wing Blind Target, "New Mobile War Record Gundam Wing: Blind Target" (新機動戦記ガンダムW BLIND TARGET) • Sakura Asagi (art), Akemi Omode (story), Hajime Yatate & Yoshiyuki Tomino (original story) • Viz (2001) • Gakken (Anime V, 1999) • 1 volume • Science Fiction, Adventure • Unrated/All Ages (mild language, violence)

Another attempt to bridge the gap between the original *Gundam Wing* anime series and its sequel *Endless Waltz,* this one is based on a radio drama in which a shadowy conspiracy seeks to rekindle the flames of war between Earth and the space colonies. As usual, the Gundam pilots find themselves caught in the middle, but true to its radio roots, *Blind Target* has them resolving the crisis by standing around talking instead of kicking giant robot butt. The end result is rather tedious, and the superficially pretty art actually consists of the same handful of head shots duplicated over and over again. (MS)   ★

MOBILE SUIT GUNDAM WING: ENDLESS WALTZ

Shin Kidô Senki Gundam Wing Endless Waltz, "New Mobile War Record Gundam Wing: Endless Waltz" (新機動戦記ガンダムW エンドレスワルツ) • Hajime Yatate & Yoshiyuki Tomino (original story), Koichi Tokita (art) • Tokyopop (2002) • Kodansha (1997) • 1 volume • Science Fiction, Mecha, Action • Unrated/All Ages (violence)

Tokita's manga adaptation of *Endless Waltz,* the 1997 video series that served as an epilogue to the *Gundam Wing* anime, is more successful than his take on the original series. Not only does his artwork seem less rushed, but since the video series itself was only three episodes long, he doesn't have to compress everything to the point of incomprehensibility. The action sequences are still stiff and choppy, and a more ambitious artist might have put more mood and feeling into the flashback sequences that explore the traumatic pasts of the brooding pretty-boy Gundam pilots, but on the whole it gets the job done. (MS) ★½

MOBILE SUIT GUNDAM WING: EPISODE ZERO

Shin Kidô Senki Gundam Wing Episode Zero, "New Mobile War Record Gundam Wing: Episode Zero" (新機動戦記ガンダムW EPISODE ZERO) • Akira Kanbe (art), Katsuyuki Sumisawa (story), Hajime Yatate & Yoshiyuki Tomino (original story) • Viz (2002) • Gakken (1997) • 1 volume • Science Fiction, Mecha, Adventure • All Ages (mild language, violence)

The manga as info dump. *Episode Zero* is an anthology of short stories detailing the secret pasts of all the *Gundam Wing* heroes, based on flashback material originally meant to appear in the anime series but ultimately scrapped due to production issues. Perhaps that's for the best, because the stories here tend to rob the heroes of their aura of mystery and replace it with a fuzzy blanket of implausible coincidences. Dedicated fans of the *Wing* characters will want to seek this out, if only to see what the writers had in mind, but these choppy little vignettes don't really work as stories in their own right. Kanbe's art is stiff but serviceable, and although the storytelling tends to break down during the mecha battle sequences, these are fortunately kept to a minimum. A 16-page epilogue, titled "Preventer 5," serves as a teaser for a mercifully nonexistent follow-up story. (MS) ★★

MOBILE SUIT GUNDAM WING: GROUND ZERO

Shin Kidô Senki Gundam Wing Ground Zero, "New Mobile War Record Gundam Wing: Ground Zero" (新機動戦記ガンダムW グランドゼロ) • Reku Fuyunagi (story and art), Hajime Yatate & Yoshiyuki Tomino (original story) • Viz (2001) • Kadokawa Shoten (Asuka Fantasy DX, 1998) • 1 volume • Shôjo, Science Fiction, Adventure • Unrated/All Ages (mild violence)

A glorified *dôjinshi.* The title story is a self-contained adventure in which erstwhile human killing machine Heero Yuy goes on a psychological voyage with the help of his fellow *Gundam Wing* heroes, and the companion story "In Rose" gives Heero a chance to comfort his platonic love interest, Relena, over an ouchy twisted ankle. It's all the purest of fluff, but the art is lovely and everybody manages to stay in character, so for those who like this sort of thing, this is the sort of thing they'll like. (MS) ★★½

MÖBIUS KLEIN

(メビウスクライン) • Kia Asamiya • Fanboy Entertainment (2001) • MediaWorks (1994) • 1 issue, suspended (1 volume in Japan) • Shônen, Occult, Science Fiction, Action • 16+ (mild language, violence, nudity, sex)

Modern-day wizards duel over the fate of the Earth in this prequel to *Silent Möbius,* set in 1999 and starring the parents of several of the *Silent Möbius* characters (along with cameos from other Asamiya manga, such as the untranslated *Compiler*). Only one issue, about one-sixth of the complete story, was published in English. ★★

THE MONKEY KING: See *Katsuya Terada's The Monkey King*

MONOKURO KINDERBOOK

Kan Takahama • Fanfare/Ponent Mon (2006) • Seirindo (Garo, 2001–2002) • 1 volume • Romance, Drama • Unrated/16+ (sex)

A collection of literary short stories involving people in all stages of life: children, teenagers, the elderly, the middle-aged. Kan Takahama's artwork stands out first: computer-colored with gray washes and blur effects instead of screentone, it resembles Web comics more than anything in print in America or Japan. Her characters have the friendly eyes and simple features of manga characters, but Kan is realistic with the signs of aging, as in her debut story, "Women Who Survive," in which an elderly artist on the brink of retirement makes her peace with family and friends. The stories, which involve love, loss, and age, have strong dialogue and sharp, sometimes funny writing. In "Over There, Beautiful Binary Suns" a cheating couple has sex beside the seashore, while in another part of the beach, children draw dirty pictures. The title story, "Kinderbook," criticizes pedophilia and the exploitation of young women. "Show Our Generation the Way to Survive," an apparently autobiographical story, takes the form of a talk between Takahama and her friends about racism, reproduction, September 11, and other heavy topics. Most of the book was published in Japan under the name *Yellowbacks,* but some stories were removed and others added for the *Kinderbook* edition, a Western original. ★★★★

MONSTER

(モンスター) • Naoki Urasawa • Viz (2006–ongoing) • Shogakukan (Big Comic Original, 1994–2001) • 18 volumes • Seinen, Thriller • 16+ (graphic violence, sexual situations)

In Japan, Naoki Urasawa is a popular and critically acclaimed creator known for taking stale manga genres (inspirational sports drama in *Happy!,* apocalyptic sci-fi in *Twentieth Century Boys,* even the Astro Boy mythos in *Pluto*) and infusing them with new life through intelligent writing and a mature, sophisticated sensibility. *Monster* is Urasawa's foray into suspense thrillers, with a dash of medical drama. Dr. Tenma, a brilliant young Japanese surgeon working in Germany, sacrifices his career to save an orphaned boy rather than a powerful politician. Not until later does he learn that the boy, Johan, was already a cold-blooded murderer, the product of eugenics experiments behind the Iron Curtain. When Johan grows up to become a serial killer—and perhaps something worse—Tenma takes it upon himself to stop him, becoming the chief suspect for the murders in the process. Urasawa's quirkily naturalistic character designs add human warmth to the cold, morally gray universe of *Monster,* a grim world of eugenicists, neo-Nazis, assassins, and thugs illuminated only by the occasional small kindness. It's an engrossing, refreshingly smart thriller. (SG) ★★★★

MONSTER COLLECTION: THE GIRL WHO CAN DEAL WITH MAGIC MONSTERS

Monster Collection~Majûtsukai no Shôjo, "Monster Collection~The Girl Who Uses Magic Beasts/Monsters" (モンスターコレクション～魔獣使いの少女) • Sei Itoh (story and art), Hitoshi Yasuda/Group SNE (original concept) • CMX (2005–2006) • Kadokawa Shoten (Comic Dragon, 1998–2002) • 6 volumes • Shônen, Fantasy, Adventure, Comedy • 18+ (language, crude humor, sexual situations, nudity, graphic violence)

Based on an untranslated collectible card game, *Monster Collection* is much better than anyone could reasonably expect it to be. Kasche Arbadel, a female monster summoner, leaves her school of sorcery to retrieve a stolen tome and finds herself fighting an evil summoner and his dark master. On Kasche's side are Cuervo (a handsome young dervish), Natascha (a lamia: half-woman, half-snake), and Shin Men (a badass lizard man with John Lennon glasses). The first thing that stands out is the art: *Monster Collection* is drawn with genuine imagination and care. Bodies are anatomically accurate, backgrounds are detailed, and best of all, the monsters look great: hippogriffs, wyverns, fallen angels, giant insects, dragons. The writing manages to both wink at the reader and take its subject matter seriously: yes, there are sex jokes, manga in-jokes, and even pot smoking, but there's also a tidy plot and truly dramatic battle scenes. One of the best in its genre. ★★★½

MONSTERS, INC.

Hiromu Yamafuji • Tokyopop (2002) • 1 volume • Comedy • All Ages

Short and simple manga adaptation of the *Monsters, Inc.* animated movie. The smooth, elementary artwork is occasionally sweeter than the film (Boo, the human child, looks cute) but lacks many of the details—certain scenes, certain one-liners, and, of course, the detail and color of the CG visuals. A bland package aimed at manga newbies. ★½

MOON CHILD

Tsuki no Ko, "Moon Child" (月の子) • Reiko Shimizu • CMX (2006–ongoing) • Hakusensha (LaLa, 1988–1993) • 13 volumes • Shôjo, Science Fiction, Romance • 13+ (mild violence, partial nudity, mild sexual situations)

A weird *shôjo* science fiction series of the 1980s, *Moon Child* has a plot almost as strong as *Please Save My Earth,* with more impressive artwork and more aggressive flirting with taboo material. In 1985 New York, Art Gile, a male dancer in musicals, takes in a girlish amnesiac boy, Jimmy, whom he finds wandering the street one night. But strange phenomena follow Jimmy—telekinesis and visions of a variety of monsters and fish-creatures—and soon it turns out that Jimmy is an alien, one of a "mermaid" race who travel through the cosmos but must return to the planet Earth to spawn. Then one night Jimmy transforms into a beautiful adult woman who still has the mind of a little boy. . . . Loosely inspired by *The Little Mermaid, Moon Child* is a creepy, unearthly fairy tale with elaborate artwork of monsters and cityscapes. The best pages look less like a manga than book illustrations. Unfortunately, one secondary character—an old black woman—is drawn in an uncomfortably stereotypical fashion. ★★★★

MORE STARLIGHT TO YOUR HEART

Motto Kokoro ni Hoshi no Kagayaki wo, "More Starlight to Your Heart" (もっと心に星の輝きを) • Hiro Matsuba • ADV (2004–2005) • Mag Garden (Comic Blade, 2002–2005) • 2 volumes, suspended (8 volumes in Japan) • Shôjo, Historical, Japanese, Romantic Comedy • All Ages

Bland romantic comedy for younger readers, with one twist: it's set in the imperial court of Heian-era Japan. Akane, a clumsy young princess, disguises herself as a servant girl in order to be closer to her love interest, Aogi, one of the captains of the guard. The plot devices involve interesting bits of Japanese courtly custom, but the "disguise" element is irrelevant and the sheltered roles of the female characters limit them mostly to cleaning, gossiping, and playing with the cat. The English edition ends before anything really happens. ★★

MOURNING OF AUTUMN RAIN

Shûrin no Ki, "Mourning of Autumn Rain" (秋霖の忌) • Akiko Hatsu • ComicsOne (e-book, 2000) • Asahi Sonorama (Lady's Comic I/Mystery I, 1992) • 1 volume • Shôjo, Jôsei, Drama • 13+ (brief language, sexual situations)

A melodramatic collection of stories about loss, family, and gay love, with incest and netherworldly love thrown into the mix. The first story concerns a woman in mourning for her husband, who recently died in a car accident. Another story follows a husband trying to understand why his wife froze to death out in a field. Throughout the manga runs the theme that love and desire trump morality and social norms, but these moral indiscretions must be paid for, usually through suffering or death. Ultimately, the stories are unsatisfying and have no real motivation other than sensationalism. (RS) ★½

MOURYOU KIDEN: LEGEND OF THE NYMPH

Môryô Kiden, "Legend of the Nature Spirit/Monster Princess" (魍魎姫伝) • Tamayo Akiyama • Tokyopop (2004–2005) • Kadokawa Shoten (Asuka Fantasy DX, 1994–1995) • 3 volumes • Shôjo, Fantasy • 13+ (mild violence, nudity)

In the age of legend, warring spirit clans—the Mouryou, demons of darkness, and the Shiki, demons of light—fight in a land of perpetual mist. But that changes when Ayaka, the daughter of the Mouryou goddess, falls in love with Kai, the flute-playing prince of the Shiki. An overblown pseudo-mythical tragedy, *Mouryou Kiden* starts with a chaotic opening, becomes slightly more comprehensible when the star-crossed lovers take the stage, and pulls out all the melodramatic tricks and reversals before ending messily. Tamayo Akiyama's layouts and jeweled character designs resemble early CLAMP (she used to be part of the CLAMP collective), but her storytelling is weak, and her mediocre figure drawing is only partially concealed beneath long wavy hair and streams of vapor and generic backgrounds of rubble. ★½

MPD PSYCHO

Tajû Jinkaku Tantei Psycho, "Multiple Personality Detective Psycho" (多重人格探偵サイコ) • Eiji Otsuka (story), Sho-u Tajima (art) • Dark Horse (2007–ongoing) • Kadokawa Shoten (Monthly Shônen Ace, 1997–2006) • 11 volumes • Shônen, Crime, Horror • 18+ (language, extreme graphic violence, nudity, sexual situations)

Amamiya Kazuhiko is a police detective with several split personalities—some maniacal and ruthless. But when the city is plagued by sadistic serial killers who dismember their victims, eat their flesh, and plant flowers in people's still-living brains, the concept of insanity is very relative. Infamously gory mystery manga with slick, detailed art, from the author of *Mail* and *The Kurosagi Corpse Delivery Service.* NR

MUGEN SPIRAL

Mugen Spiral, "Dream Spiral" (夢幻スパイラル) • Mizuho Kusanagi • Tokyopop (2007) • Hakusensha (Hana to Yume, 2004–2005) • 2 volumes • Shôjo, Fantasy, Romance • 13+

In one corner we have high-schooler Yayoi, who uses her inherited mystical powers to protect people from malevolent spirits. In the other is the ambitious demon Ura, who aims to gobble up Yayoi's power to advance his own career. But Ura's not so scary now that he's been transformed into a little black kitty cat, is he? With the scheming demon reduced to a cute bewhiskered sidekick, magical adventures naturally ensue. (MS) NR

MURDER PRINCESS

Sekihiko Inui • Broccoli Books (2007) • MediaWorks (Dengeki Teioh, 2005–ongoing) • 1+ volumes (ongoing) • Shônen, Science Fiction, Fantasy, Comedy • 13+

When her father, the king, is murdered by a greedy drug manufacturer, Princess Alita prepares to inherit the throne—until a magical mishap causes her to switch bodies with Falis, a bounty hunter! Falis, in the body of Alita, and Alita, in the body of Falis, must somehow hold the kingdom together against deadly coups, rival heirs, and the evil Professor Akamashi and his android assassins. An original work from the artist of Tokyopop's *Comic Party* manga adaptation. NR

MUSASHI NO. 9

Kyûbanme no Musashi, "Musashi No. 9" (9番目のムサシ) • Miyuki Takahashi • CMX (2005–ongoing) • Akita Shoten (Kirara Seize/Mystery Bonita, 1996–ongoing) • 20+ volumes (ongoing) • Shôjo, Spy Thriller • 13+ (mild language, violence, brief sexual situations)

The androgynously handsome teenager Kou Shinozuka is Musashi No. 9 . . . one of the top agents of Ultimate Blue, the so-called Other United Nations, who preserves world peace and secretly decides the fate of entire countries. Equally deadly with guns, fists, and explosives, Musashi does battle with Chinese gun smugglers, Middle Eastern dictators, and rogue U.S. Army officers, usually while bodyguarding bewildered high school students. Like the title character of *Golgo 13* (but without the moral ambiguity), Musashi seems to be an emotionless mystery . . . but unlike Golgo, eventually the secret agent falls in love and is torn between duty and passion. (Although it might not be immediately obvious from its precise, drafting-table artwork, *Musashi No. 9* is a *shôjo* manga, albeit starring an incredibly butch protagonist.) The mostly disconnected stories deliver a variety of mini-dramas, but Musashi and Ultimate Blue are so powerful that the bad guys never really seem to stand a chance. Solidly executed but repetitive. ★★

MUSEUM OF TERROR

Itô Junji Kyôfu Hakubutsukan, "Junji Ito's Museum of Terror" (伊藤潤二恐怖博物館) • Junji Ito • Dark Horse (2006) • Asahi Sonorama (various magazines, 1987–2003) • 3 volumes, suspended (15

volumes in Japan) • Horror • 18+ (mild language, graphic violence, nudity)

One of the most prolific modern horror manga artists, Junji Ito often straddles the border between horror and surreal comedy; one of his untranslated tales involves people pursued by giant balloons shaped like human heads who strangle their victims with their "string." *Museum of Terror,* organized mostly chronologically from the beginning of Ito's career, contains dozens of his short stories, full of ghosts, slithery reanimated hair, obsessive behavior, and tastefully executed mutilation and butchery. Many of the early stories involve the recurring character Tomie, a fickle young femme fatale with long black hair, who cannot be killed but is often chopped into thousands of pieces that regenerate gruesomely into loathsomely beautiful clones. Like any artist who has produced so much work, Ito reuses similar faces and backgrounds, but his art is realistic and refined—his gloomy, lanky protagonists schlep into nightmare scenarios in drably ordinary villages and towns, and invariably they stay past the point of no return, unable to turn away from the ghoulish transformations and horribly logical escalation of events. You never know quite how an Ito story will end—comedically, cryptically, or full horror with its teeth in your throat. Volumes 1 and 2 contain the entirety of Ito's Tomie stories, including all the material from the out-of-print ComicsOne *Tomie* series as well as several new tales; volume 3 also includes one story, "Long Hair in the Attic," from the out-of-print *Flesh Colored Horror.*　★★★½

MUSHISHI

Mushi-shi, "Mushi Master" (蟲師) • Yuki Urushibara • Del Rey (2007–ongoing) • Kodansha (Afternoon Season/Afternoon, 1999–ongoing) • 8+ volumes (ongoing) • Seinen, Historical, Fantasy • 16+

An episodic serial whose hero is an expert in *mushi,* a word that normally means "bug" or "insect" but is here employed to refer to phantasmal spirit creatures. Our protagonist Ginko wanders the rustic Japanese landscape, studying these weird beings and helping strangers with their *mushi*-related problems. (MS)　NR

MW

(ムウ) • Osamu Tezuka • Vertical (2007) • Shogakukan (Big Comic, 1976–1978) • Seinen, Political/Psychological Drama • 18+

Michio, an elite banker from a wealthy family, has a secret: he's a serial killer. Furthermore, he's the closeted lover of the priest who hears his confessions. The whole twisted drama begins in Michio's youth, when he was exposed to a chemical weapon as a boy . . . a deadly chemical called MW (created by a foreign military power), which drives its victims insane.　NR

MY CODE NAME IS CHARMER

Code Name wa Charmer, "My Code Name Is Charmer" • (コードネームはCHARMER) • Narumi Kakinouchi (story and art), Aya Suzuka (original creator) • Studio Ironcat (2004) • Akita Shoten (Susperia, 1990–1997) • 2 volumes, suspended (4 volumes in Japan) • Shôjo, Psychic, School, Mystery • Unrated/All Ages (mild language, violence, mild sexual situations)

Boring sci-fi mystery based on an untranslated story by Aya Suzuka. Naomi, a psychic who can see evil "zeyrey" monsters from another dimension, spends her after-school hours with her friends in the Supernatural Phenomenon Research Team. Together, they get into romantic comedy hijinks and fight monsters that take bland forms like giant snakes and possessed puppies. The generic premise and execution make it a snoozer. Kakinouchi's art looks rushed as usual, and the dated character designs are totally 1980s.　★

MY DEAREST DEVIL PRINCESS

Hakoiri Devil Princess, "Devil Princess in a Box" (箱入りデビルプリンセス) • Makoto Matsumoto (original story), Maika Netsu (art) • Broccoli Books (2007–ongoing) • Jive (Comic Rush, 2004–ongoing) • 4+ volumes (ongoing) • Shônen, Fantasy, Romantic Comedy • Not Rated Yet

MUSIC AND PERFORMANCE

One of manga's greatest draws for American readers is the coverage of topics not found in domestic comics. Like sports, performing arts can offer the struggle of learning new skills, the drama of bringing talented people together, and the thrill of competition. Combine all that with the glamour and aesthetics of the performing arts, and the attraction is obvious. Through manga, performance has an extraordinary medium of expression in which ballerinas can float like feathers and musicians can be physically surrounded by the beauty and power of their songs.

Classic Arts

After its influences were all but wiped out during World War II, Western culture and the freedom and sophistication associated with it were enthusiastically embraced by many Japanese. While its popularity has waxed and waned over the years, the beauty of ballet makes it well suited for *shôjo* manga, dating back to manga such as Miyako Maki's *Hahakoii Waltz* ("Mother's Love Waltz") (1957). The most famous ballet manga is Kiyoko Ariyoshi's *Swan* (1976), although Hinako Ashihara's *Forbidden Dance* (1997) and the anime/manga project *Princess Tutu* (2002) are other translated examples.

Often urbane in her themes, Chiho Saito has written about ballet as well as other arts. Her untranslated series *Kanon* (1995–1997) involves a violin prodigy's quest to find her father as she journeys though the rarified world of professional music. Aspiring violinists, pianists, and conductors also appear in Keiko Yamada's *VS* (1999), Tomoko Ninomiya's *Nodame Cantabile* (2001), and Yuki Kure's *La Corda d'Oro* (2004).

As seen in series ranging from *Kare Kano* (1996) to *Ranma ½* (1988), most Japanese high schools have drama clubs. While they frequently play roles in manga, the plays depicted are rarely beyond the level of fairy tales such as Snow White and other excuses to get the characters to kiss onstage; the metaphorical science fiction play in *Kare Kano* volumes 7–9 is one of the few translated exceptions. Naoki Yamamoto's *Dance till Tomorrow* (1989) involves an avant-garde theater troupe. The drive to achieve professional theatrical greatness is explored with great detail in Suzue Miuchi's *Glass no Kamen* ("Glass Mask") (1976), one of *shôjo* manga's longest series. Although focused more on the lead's life than her TV career, Miho Obana's *Kodocha* (1994) offers hints of

Tomoko Ninomiya's *Nodame Cantabile*

the organizational structures beneath Japanese television production—the child actress Sana may have her own agent and jobs, but she's a loyal member of the theater group where she first learned her craft.

Less common than Western classical arts manga are those involving traditional Japanese performance. Aside from the cosmopolitan appeal of Western themes, one of the contributing factors may be that, as with Shakespearean theater, Nô, kabuki, and bunraku (a form of puppeteering) were originally, and mostly still are, performed only by men. Kanoko Sakurakoji's *Backstage Prince* (2005) involves a Kabuki performer. Haruka Nanami and Haruko Iida's untranslated *Fûshikaden + Cadenza* ("Flowery Cadenza") (2001) brings the Spartan elegance of Nô to life with a mystical flair. Exclusively Japanese, but with modern origins, the all-female Takarazuka theater troupe has both inspired and been inspired by manga. (See the article on TRANSGENDER.)

Popular Culture

Drama CDs and radio shows, voice-only dramas derived largely from anime and manga, are a unique aspect of Japanese media merchandising. (For the obvious reason that they would need to be rerecorded from scratch, no full-length drama CDs have been professionally translated.) A successful drama CD is a sign of marketability and can boost a manga's chances of becoming an anime; alternately, drama CDs are also used as an outlet for manga that aren't quite popular enough to be animated. While plenty of established *seiyû* (voice actors) perform in drama CDs, they also can be a good place for new actors and singers to make their start. Yuki Shimizu's *yaoi* title *Shout Out Loud!* (1996) offers an amusing look at the world of *seiyû* and radio dramas. The manga *Café Kichijouji De* (2001) is based on an original radio show.

"J-pop" has become a general term for Japanese popular music, but the term is broad, encompassing rap, techno-pop, R&B, punk, and hip-hop, among other genres. Some recent series that center on the struggle to make it in popular music include *Nana* (2000), *Beck: Mongolian Chop Squad* (2000), *Sensual Phrase* (1997), and Haruto Umezawa's *shônen* manga about a rock-and-roll band, *Bremen* (2000). Tourists returning from Japan in the late twentieth century often brought back wild stories about the continued popularity of 1980s American-style "stadium metal" and "hair bands"; a charming example is Tomoko Taniguchi's *Let's Stay Together Forever* (1987), a collection of *shôjo* short stories with titles such as "Big Brother Is a Naïve Metalhead." Today, heavy metal is still popular in Japan, as demonstrated by Kiminori Wakasugi's bestselling comedy manga *Detroit Metal City* (2006), starring a wimpy guy who lives a double life as a greasepainted, caped, screaming death metal vocalist.

"Idol singers"—young, cute, and usually female—dominated Japanese pop music in the 1980s. Talent has become more important, but originally their stardom relied primarily on their looks and persona. Naturally, they found their way into manga and anime, appearing in anime series as different as *Mahô no Princess Minky Momo* ("Magic Princess Minky Momo") (1982), one of countless "magical girl" idol shows, and *Super Dimensional Fortress Macross* (1982), as well as regular-life manga like Tsukasa Ôshima's soccer series *Shoot!* (1990). While female idol singers are usually individual performers, their male counterparts are mostly found in boy bands, as depicted in Yuriko Nishiyama's *Dragon Drive* (2001). Similar to 1980s glam rock groups in the United States, *visual kei* (visual style) bands rely on extreme fashion, heavy makeup, and androgynous male beauty. While *visual kei* has become ubiquitous in Japanese pop culture, it can be seen in the *bishônen* love interests of *The Devil Does Exist* (1998) and *The Wallflower* (2000). A related fashion movement is Gothic Lolita, which has produced manga artists such as Mitsukazu Mihara.

Although not a performance art per se, fashion is a major part of Japanese pop culture. Shodensha's fashion magazines *Boon* and *Zipper* include manga sections; *Boon* ran the hip-hop-influenced *Tokyo Tribes* (1997), while *Zipper* ran *Paradise Kiss* (2000). Set in trendy Harajuku around the fictional Yazawa School for the Arts, *Paradise Kiss* demonstrates the trials and tribulations of making it in clothing design and modeling. Minako Narita prefers the fashion world of New York City in her series *Cipher* (1985) and *Alexandrite* (1991). And, of course, there is an entire subgenre of *shôjo* manga based on cross-dressing male actors and models; translated examples alone include *W Juliet* (1997), *Never Give Up* (1999), *Tenshi ja Nai!* (2003), *Penguin Revolution* (2004), and *Nosatsu Junkie* (2004). Even the female lead of *Hana-Kimi: For You in Full Blossom* (1996) briefly goes under the spotlight in men's clothes. (PD)

Music and Performance Manga:

Amazing Strip • *Angel/Dust* • *Baby Birth* • *Backstage Prince* • *B.B. Explosion* • *Beauty Pop* • *BECK: Mongolian Chop Squad* • *Café Kichijouji De* • *Cipher* • *La Corda d'Oro* • *Dance till Tomorrow* • *The Devil Does Exist* • *Dragon Voice* • *Embracing Love* (*yaoi*) • *Femme Kabuki* (*adult*) • *Forbidden Dance* • *Full Moon o Sagashite* • *Il Gatto sul G* (*yaoi*) • *Gravitation* • *Hana-Kimi: For You in Full Blossom* • *Kodocha* • *Let's Stay Together Forever* • *Maico 2010* • *Mink* • *Miss Me?* • *Nana* • *Never Give Up* • *Nodame Cantabile* • *Nosatsu Junkie* • *Othello* • *Paradise Kiss* • *Pearl Pink* • *Penguin Revolution* • *Pichi Pichi Pitch: Mermaid Melody* • *Princess Ai* • *Princess Tutu* • *Sensual Phrase* • *Shout Out Loud!* (*yaoi*) • *Skip Beat* • *Strawberry 100%* • *Super Dimensional Fortress Macross II* • *Swan* • *Tenshi ja Nai!!* • *VS* • *The Wallflower* • *Wild Act* • *W Juliet* • *Wounded Man*

When Keita opens a mysterious box, he summons Maki, a busty princess from the demon world. Maki grants Keita three wishes in exchange for his soul—but she can't take his soul until he uses all three wishes. Unfortunately for her nefarious plans, Maki is an inexperienced demoness who doesn't even know how to be evil (*hakoiri* can also mean "raised in a box," implying that someone has a sheltered upbringing). She must live with Keita until she can trick him into making his third wish, while also teaching herself how to be demonic.   NR

MY HEAVENLY HOCKEY CLUB

Gokuraku Seishun Hockey-bu, "Heavenly Youth Hockey Club" (極楽青春ホッケー部) • Ai Morinaga • Del Rey (2007–ongoing) • Kodansha (Bessatsu Friend, 2005–ongoing) • 7+ volumes (ongoing) • Shôjo, Sports, Comedy • Not Rated Yet

You got your high school, you got your hockey club, you got your boys and girls mixing it up to comic effect. (Only there isn't really that much hockey.) From the creator of *Duck Prince* and *Your and My Secret.* (MS)   NR

MY-HIME

Mai-HiME (舞-HiME) • Noboru Kimura (story), Sato Ken-etsu (art) • Tokyopop (2006–2008) • Akita Shoten (Weekly Shônen Champion, 2004–2005) • 5 volumes • Shônen, Science Fiction, Battle • 18+ (violence, nudity, sexual situations)

Adaptation of the anime series. In what begins as a seemingly normal school transfer,

Yuuchi Tate quickly finds himself caught in a heated exchange between two curvy, heaving, sweating girls. When the fight turns supernatural, the girls discover that Yuuchi is a "key," a special person who can create a "child" (a sort of summoned combat creature) when paired with a HiME (highly advanced materializing equipment). The school is a facility for female HiMEs, who all want their hands on a male "key" like Yuuichi; he must endure not only their devastating squabbles but also the random attacks from huge monsters who periodically assault the campus. Lots of cheesecake. (DR) NR

MYSTICAL PRINCE YOSHIDA-KUN

Sore jaa Yoshida-kun!, "Well Now, Yoshida-kun!" (それじゃあ吉田くん!) • Natsuki Yoshimura • ADV (2004) • Mag Garden (Comic Blade, 2002–2003) • 1 volume, suspended (2 volumes in Japan) • Fantasy, Comedy • 13+ (mild sexual situations)

This *chibi* comedy manga follows the same structure as a *Looney Tunes* cartoon: the main character is almost totally unfazeable and overcomes his enemies by blissful ignorance. Yoshida, a sleepy-eyed boy dilettante who switches to a new hobby every chapter (his only true personality traits are wearing a *hanten* jacket and eating *karinto,* fried dough sticks), is unwittingly chosen to become the next King of the Demon World, after which cute demons show up on Earth to try to defeat him. ★★

MYSTIQUE MANDALA OF HELL: See *Hino Horror, Vol. 12: Mystique Mandala of Hell*

THE MYTHICAL DETECTIVE LOKI RAGNAROK

Matantei Loki Ragnarok, "Demonic/Magical Detective Loki Ragnarok" (魔探偵ロキRAGNAROK) • Sakura Kinoshita • ADV (2004–2005) • Mag Garden (Comic Blade, 2002–2005) • 2 volumes, suspended (5 volumes in Japan) • Mythological, Comedy, Drama • 13+ (mild language)

Unbeknownst to mortals, the Norse god Loki dwells on Earth in the form of an elementary school kid, with Fenrir as his pet and various other gods and giants also hanging around in the form of Japanese schoolboys and schoolgirls. Like the cutest Neil Gaiman comic ever, *Loki Ragnarok* is basically a domestic/school comedy that happens to involve obscure Norse mythology as well as the usual food jokes ("Loki, I'm finished. I'm not Thor anymore. I'm just a high school kid." "You didn't eat dinner last night, did you?"). Loki's actual detective work is minimal, although he *does* tackle a few surreal cases, such as the case of the stolen moon. Beautiful artwork and a gentle, mysterious mood add up to an enjoyable read. The series' rather abrupt beginning is due to the fact that, like several other *Comic Blade* series, it is a continuation of a series originally published in Square Enix's rival magazine *Monthly Shônen Gangan.* (The original series was called simply *Matantei Loki.*) ★★★

NADESICO

Chôgeki Uchû Senkan Nadesico, "Super Strike Space Battleship Nadesico," aka "Meteor Schlachtschiff Nadesico" (超撃宇宙戦艦ナデシコ) • Kia Asamiya • CPM (1999-2004) • Kadokawa Shoten (Monthly Shônen Ace, 1996–1999) • 4 volumes • Shônen, Science Fiction, Mecha, Comedy • 13+ (violence, partial nudity, sex)

A highly divergent manga adaptation of the *Martian Successor Nadesico* anime, apparently based on a discarded early plot outline. When Earth and Mars (Earth's colony) are attacked by mysterious invaders from Jupiter, the space cruiser *Nadesico* goes forth to fight. Akito, a wimpy cook, accidentally stows away and ends up both peeling potatoes and piloting a mecha while trying to evade the ditzy Captain Yurika, who has had a crush on him ever since they were children together. Although it sounds like slapstick, the excessively complicated plot involves corporate intrigue, parallel universes, shamanism, and anime references; there are many anime fans aboard the *Nadesico,* it turns out, and their shipboard lives soon become mixed up with their favorite 1970s shows, *Gekiganger 3* (a pseudo–Go Nagai robot anime) and *Space Pirate Captain Government* (a parody of Leiji Matsumoto's

MYSTERY (推理・ミステリー)

Japan's earliest examples of detective writing come from trial narratives of the Edo period, an era when accessibility to printed media was growing along with the luxury income of the lower classes. Despite nearly two hundred years of these unique Japanese narratives, the translated publication of Edgar Allan Poe's *The Murders in the Rue Morgue* (1887) changed everything, captivating readers in a way classic court cases never could. The genre was further encouraged with the translation of Arthur Conan Doyle's *Adventures of Sherlock Holmes* (1899) and the enthusiasm of tabloid publisher Ruikô Kuroiwa, who printed dozens of translated detective stories during the turn of the century. As inexpensive entertainment, Western mysteries engaged the imaginations of a generation.

Inspired by the West, Japanese writers began inventing their own detective stories, experimenting with the genre by creating distinctively Japanese sleuths and settings while occasionally drawing on sensational crimes of the past. In the Japanese publishing heyday of the 1920s, mysteries began to blossom and gain legitimacy as more literary authors tried their hand at crime stories. Rampo Edogawa, often called the father of Japanese mystery and horror writing (his pen name is a play on "Edgar Allen Poe"), flourished during this period, but all that ended with the rise of nationalism and the onset of war.

After being banned during World War II, mysteries came back with a bang, thanks to traditional whodunits by author Seishi Yokomizo. Manga were also a part of that boom, due in no small part to the groundbreaking and immensely popular *Shin Takarajima* ("New Treasure Island," 1947), written by Sakai Shichima and drawn by the legendary Osamu Tezuka. This new era of growth provided an unfettered creative freedom that allowed different genres to merge and transform, and mysteries and manga—known as *suiri manga* ("detection manga") or by the English-language term *mystery manga*—were included in the mix.

Originally a genre that favored older readers, crime stories began expanding their audience by aiming younger. The mystery publication *Tanteiô* ("Detective King") offered not only regular and illustrated tales but manga as well. Targeted specifically at boys, *Hayakawa Pocket Mystery* began publication in 1953, followed in 1956 by a surge in detective novels for adults. This symbiotic relationship between mystery novels and manga has continued over the decades. A modern example of mixing mysteries and other genres is the untranslated *Master Keaton* (1988), written by Hokusei Katsushika and drawn by Naoki Urasawa and serialized in the *seinen* manga magazine *Big Comic Original*. The title character is a middle-aged insurance investigator whose adventures range from missing persons to terrorism to archaeology, mixed with periodic glimpses of Keaton's complicated family life.

The 1990s saw a surge in the popularity of classically styled mystery manga with the success of Fumiya Sato and Yozaburo Kanari's *The Kindaichi Case Files* (1992). The lead is supposed to be the grandson of Seishi Yokomizo's famous gumshoe, Kosuke Kindaichi. This hit was soon followed by Gosho Aoyama's *Case Closed!* (1994), in which a teen detective is physically turned into a little kid. The son of a mystery writer, the newly transformed hero chooses an alias—Conan Edogawa—through desperation and an appreciation for past authors.

Fumiya Sato and Yozaburo Kanari's *Kindaichi Case Files*

Conan isn't the only brilliant pint-sized detective in manga. Others date back at least to Tezuka's *Kenichi Tanteichô* ("Chief Detective Kenichi," 1954), which borrowed its lead from *New Treasure Island*. Orphaned Narutaki of *Steam Detectives* (1994) offers traditional whodunits in a fictional art deco city where giant robots walk and technology is dominated by steam power. The *Clamp School Detectives* (1992) are a trio of charming preteen sleuths who attend a whimsical elite school where almost everyone is a super-genius.

With Conan and Kindaichi representing the most mainstream, traditional detective manga, other mysteries have used more unconventional settings, characters, and themes. *Karakurizôshi Ayatsuri Sakon* ("The Tales of Puppeteer Sakon") (1995) is the work of artist Takeshi Obata and writer Sharakumaro (a play on "Sherlock Marlowe"). Horror artist Yuzo Takada's *Genzô Hitogata Kiwa* ("Genzô's Demon Puppet Tales") (1998) is set during Japan's Warring States period. Both untranslated titles offer the unusual combination of detective work and puppeteering. The heroine of *Zodiac P.I.* (2001) uses astrology and magical transformation to solve crimes. The sisters of *Read or Dream* (2000) and one of the leads of *RA-I* (1995) have telekinetic powers. The series *888* (2003) and *Kamen Tantei* (1999) are as much about comedy as crime. The quirky cast of *The Kurosagi Corpse Delivery Service* (2002) use their paranormal talents to aid undead clients, often solving mysteries so their customers can move on to the next life. And *Death Note* (2004) features one of the most brilliant criminal minds ever depicted in manga, in an epic cat-and-mouse game with detectives of equal mind power. (PD)

Mystery Manga

888 • *Case Closed* • *Clamp School Detectives* • *Confidential Confessions: Deai* • *Death Note* • *Gorgeous Carat Galaxy* • *Hands Off!* • *Juror 13* • *Kamen Tantei* • *Kindaichi Case Files* • *The Kurosagi Corpse Delivery Service* • *Lupin III* • *Lupin III: World's Most Wanted* • *Mail* • *RA-1* • *Remote* • *R.O.D (Read or Dream)* • *Satisfaction Guaranteed* • *Secret Chaser* • *Steam Detectives* • *Voyeur* • *Voyeurs, Inc.* • *Yoki Koto Kiku* • *Zodiac P.I.*

Captain Harlock). Unlike the anime, the manga never fully embraces the element of mecha show parody, and the climax is conventional, but, at its best, it's entertaining pulp science fiction. ★★

NAJICA BLITZ TACTICS

Najica Dengeki Sakusen, "Najica Blitz/Lightning Tactics" (ナジカ電撃作戦) • Studio Fantasia/AFW/ Najica Project (original creators), Takuya Tashiro (manga) • ADV (2004) • Media Factory (Comic Flapper, 2001–2003) • 3 volumes • Action • 16+ (language, violence, nudity, sexual situations)

Manga adaptation of the anime series. Najica is a brilliant and sexy perfume creator, as well as a secret agent who goes on secret (and sexy) missions to stop evildoers. Her loyal partner, Lila, is an android. The stories are almost too short to be entertaining; almost all of them require the duo to wear incredibly revealing outfits, and each mission is executed amid a flurry of ridiculously short skirts and enough panty shots to desensitize even the most delicate of readers. (KT) ★

NANA

(ナナ) • Ai Yazawa • Viz (2005–ongoing) • Shueisha (Cookie, 2002–ongoing) • Shôjo, Jôsei, Romantic Drama • 16+ volumes (ongoing) • 16+ (mild language, nudity, sex)

The story of two very different twenty-year-old women with the same name, *Nana* is one of the most popular older-teens *shôjo* manga of the 2000s; its genius, perhaps, is to split its protagonist into both "who you might be" and "who you might *want* to be." In the self-contained first volume, we meet Nana Komatsu, a somewhat immature girl whose life has always revolved around men, and Nana Osaki, a sarcastic, independent punk rock vocalist, whose main goal is to make her band a success. In volume 2, the two Nanas meet on the train to Tokyo and become roommates and best friends. The drifting plot captures the feeling of being young and on your own: the two Nanas decorate their apartment, struggle from payday to payday, and deal with college and jobs,

parties and men. The plot focuses on the music scene and Nana Osaki's bandmates, and in volume 7 the narrator shifts from Komatsu to Osaki, although Komatsu remains vital to the story. What fashion was to *Paradise Kiss,* music is to *Nana*—a way for the characters to express themselves and for the artist to fill the pages with fine-lined drawings of stylish characters. The story wanders; the heroes' lives take new directions as people drift in and out, forcing them to choose among love, sex, art, and fulfillment. The English edition is very lightly censored; some references to prostitution are toned down, and nudity was obscured in the *Shojo Beat* magazine serialization but restored in the graphic novels. ★★★½

NANANANA

(なななな) • Show-Tarou Harada • Infinity Studios (2005–ongoing) • MediaWorks (Dengeki Daioh, 2002–2005) • 4 volumes • Shônen, Otaku, Romantic Comedy • 16+ (violence, partial nudity, sexual situations)

In the future, mankind has built Legions, a class of female androids to serve their human masters. Rescued as a boy from a burning factory by a Legion named Nana, the kindhearted Nanami decides to become a Legion paramedic for the police force. Fast-forward five years into the future, and Nanami finds himself suddenly promoted to chief of the crumbling Seventh Precinct. Along with his new position, he inherits an out-of-date Legion who bears a striking resemblance to the Legion who saved his life five years ago. . . . *NaNaNaNa* is not so much a bad manga as it is boring; like most manga about big-breasted robot women, it's rife with fan service and short on plot. The art is generic. (LW) ★

NAOKI URASAWA'S MONSTER: See *Monster*

NARUTO

(ナルト) • Masashi Kishimoto • Viz (2002–ongoing) • Shueisha (Weekly Shônen Jump, 1999–ongoing) • 37+ volumes (ongoing) • Shônen, Ninja, Fantasy, Action • 13+ (graphic violence)

The manga that made ninja cool again. In a vaguely feudal Japanese world where throwing stars coexist with motorboats and video cameras, clans of ninja (dressed in casual survival gear) hold the position of elite special ops forces. Twelve-year-old orphan Naruto, the trash-talking class clown of his ninja school, wants to become the most powerful ninja to prove himself to his peers ("Why am I always so different? I hate not fitting in!"). Teamed up with his classmates Sakura (the unusually well-written love interest) and Sasuke (the rival), he struggles to work with them and pass his exams, eventually becoming embroiled in vast intrigues involving competing clans and powerful rogue ninja. But Naruto's greatest strength is also his darkest secret, for a mighty demon is bound in his body, waiting to break free. To American readers, *Naruto*'s Japaneseness is certainly part of its appeal (Naruto is named after the spiral-shaped fish cakes often served with his favorite food, ramen), but in fact the manga has a Western feel, from its talky (but amazing) fight scenes and detailed art to the superhero-like position the ninja hold in their world. (The main difference from American superheroes is that, like most manga heroes, the ninjas in *Naruto* are basically ordinary kids who owe their powers to hard work, and the helpful diagrams that explain the *ninjutsu* might leave fans feeling that they, too, can use *chakra* to summon giant frogs and snakes, or split into multiple selves.) The characters are well defined, and the artwork is excellent, depicting Naruto's world with incredible detail and imagination. Like Naruto's personality, the story swings from self-consciously cool to weepy and melodramatic (even corny at times), but always takes its subject matter completely seriously. This irony-free, earnest spirit (as opposed to the more obviously over-the-top style of, say, *One Piece*) makes it a perfect manga for older children and teenagers . . . an all-absorbing, internally consistent world of self-sacrifice, heroism, and drama. The English edition has minor censorship, including partial nudity (Naruto's "ninja centerfold" illusion) and whenever Naruto flips somebody off. ★★★★

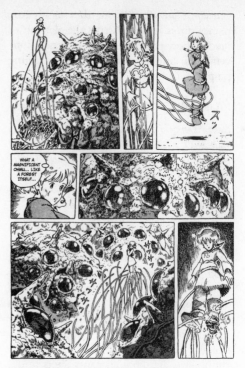

Hayao Miyazaki's *Nausicaä of the Valley of the Wind* diverged from the animated version of the story. © 1983 Nibariki Co., Ltd.

NAUSICAÄ OF THE VALLEY OF THE WIND

Kaze no Tani no Nausicaä, "Nausicaä of the Valley of Wind" (風の谷のナウシカ) • Hayao Miyazaki • Viz (1988–2004) • Tokuma Shoten (Animage, 1982–1994) • 7 volumes • Science Fiction • 13+ (violence)

The only major manga by famed animation director Hayao Miyazaki, *Nausicaä* is a science fiction epic, much longer and more complicated than the movie version (which was produced long before the manga was finished). In the unrecognizably far future, after an environmental collapse, humanity has reverted to a feudal state, living in the limited fertile land between vast deserts and toxic fungus forests inhabited by giant insects. Nausicaä, a profoundly empathic young girl from a small community, fights to save her people as the kingdoms around her go to war, unleashing devastating artifacts of ancient long-lost biotechnology. With gorgeous, dense, crosshatched artwork, Miyazaki depicts a completely original world, vaguely comparable to *Dune,* with its cultic science priests and giant worm monsters. In lesser hands, the story would be predictable—a hero prophecy, an environmental message—but Miyazaki burns through the clichés and into uncharted territory, pitting idealism against realism, and suggesting there are no easy answers. In terms of Miyazaki's movies, the closest comparison may not be *Nausicaä* at all but *Princess Mononoke,* which he worked on after the manga ended. The manga is printed oversized, befitting Miyazaki's extremely detailed artwork (more like a European comic than a manga). Like many translated manga of the 1980s and 1990s, it was released in several editions: first as a monthly comic series, then in a four-volume "Perfect Collection" edition, and finally in the original seven-volume edition.

★★★★

NECONOCLASM

(ネコノクラスム) • Asaki Yuzuno • Seven Seas Entertainment (2007) • France Shoin (Comics Papipo, 2005) • 1 volume (ongoing) • Four-Panel Comedy • 13+

Four-panel *bishôjo* gag manga starring countless cute girls (and one guy) with cat ears and a tail. (The *neco* in the title could mean *neko,* Japanese for "cat.") NR

NEGIMA!: MASTER NEGI MAGI

Mahô Sensei Negima!: Magister Negi Magi, "Magic Teacher Negima!: Magister Negi Magi" (魔法先生 ネギま!) • Ken Akamatsu • Del Rey (2004– ongoing) • Kodansha (Weekly Shônen Magazine, 2003–ongoing) • 18+ volumes (ongoing) • Shônen, Fantasy, Action, Romantic Comedy • 16+ (mild language, infrequent violence, constant partial nudity, constant sexual situations)

A calculated cross between *Harry Potter* and *Love Hina;* American fans call it "Love Hogwarts" after the magic school in J. K. Rowling's novels. Negi Springfield, a ten-year-old British genius wizard, is assigned to teach at a Japanese girls' school as part of his secret training in the arts of magic. Despite his efforts to be taken seriously, his teenage students treat him like an adorable little thing, and his magic often backfires and causes his students' clothes to fly off, or fills them with lusty desires to kiss his prepubescent lips. Nonetheless, Negi struggles to become a great wizard, going on quests and competing in martial-arts-style magic tournaments against evil sorcerers. Meanwhile, the thirty-one girls in Negi's class (including a robot girl, a vampire girl, a ninja girl, etc.) each gets her own turn in the spotlight, rising and falling in popularity based on the readers' poll results. The basic problem of *Negima!* is that the T&A doesn't mesh with the rest of the story; it's really about magic and wizard battles, not sex, and it doesn't make any sense for a ten-year-old boy to be the focus of so much hanky-panky, except for the ob-

Ken Akamatsu's *Negima!*

vious reason that he's the most harmless, nonthreatening male figure imaginable, taking the "harem manga" premise (wimpy guy surrounded by girls) to its illogical extreme. The *Negima!* franchise makers were obviously aware of this as well, as the original series was followed by a family-friendly anime/manga spin-off, Fujima Takuya's untranslated *Negima!? neo,* aimed at younger readers. For the intended teenage male audience, perhaps Akamatsu's original *Negima!* is simply the best of both worlds: reliable fantasy action and reliable cheesecake. Art-wise, there are simply too many characters and literally too much to look at, with *hundreds* of short-skirted girls running about, and lushly detailed backgrounds based on traced 3-D models. ★★½

NEIGHBOR #13

Rinjin Jûsan-gô, "Neighbor Number 13" (隣人13号) • Santa Inoue • Tokyopop (2008) • Scholar Publishing (Comic Scholar, 1993–1996) • 3 volumes • Psychological Thriller • Not Rated Yet

An infamous psycho-thriller from the creator of *Tokyo Tribes.* A timid man, mentally and physically scarred by childhood bullying, has developed a violent alternate personality. Now that he finds himself working and living alongside one of his former tormentors, his vicious, vindictive alter ego begins putting its own plan for revenge into effect. This manga was also the basis for an equally disturbing live-action movie. (MS) NR

NEMURI KYOSHIRO

(眠狂四郎) • Yoshihiro Yanagawa (art), Renzaburo Shibata (original creator) • Gutsoon! Entertainment (2003–2004) • Coamix (Weekly Comic Bunch, 2001–2003) • 13 issues, suspended (10 volumes in Japan) • Seinen, Samurai Drama • Unrated/18+ (graphic violence, sex)

Manga adaptation of the samurai novels by Renzaburo Shibata, best known in the United States through the spin-off movie series (1963–1969) translated under the title *Sleepy Eyes of Death.* In 1830 Japan, Nemuri Kyoshiro is a laconic blue-eyed swordsman who goes from master to master like an untameable wild beast, following his own inscrutable code. The adult artwork is detailed and polished, but the episodic plot is standard *seinen* bad-ass antiheroism. A major plot element involves Kyoshiro's love-hate relationship with Christianity (a forbidden religion in 1830 Japan); as the movies make clear, he's the offspring of a Japanese woman raped by a devil-worshiping Portuguese priest as part of the Black Mass. Serialized in *Raijin Comics* numbers 34–46; never collected in graphic novel form. ★★

NEON GENESIS EVANGELION

Shin Seiki Evangelion, "New Century Evangelion" (新世紀エヴァンゲリオン) • Gainax (original concept), Yoshiyuki Sadamoto (story and art) • Viz (1997–ongoing) • Kadokawa Shoten (Monthly Shônen Ace, 1995–ongoing) • 10+ volumes (ongoing) • Shônen, Science Fiction, Mecha • 16+ (language, violence, nudity, sexual situations)

Produced simultaneously with the *Neon Genesis Evangelion* anime, and continued sporadically long after the anime concluded, the *Evangelion* manga is character designer Yoshiyuki Sadamoto's alternate version of the story. In the year 2015, fifteen years after a mysterious explosion at the South Pole caused worldwide devastation, the planned city of Tokyo-3 finds itself under attack by strange giant creatures called Angels. Shinji Ikari, a neurotic fourteen-year-old, is one of a small group of teenagers chosen to defend Tokyo-3 by piloting the Evangelions, which appear to be giant robots but are actually bioengineered monsters, the products of the same super-science to which the Angels and the world's fate are linked. Taking the structure of your basic mecha story, and applying psychology, hard science fiction, and religious symbolism, *Evangelion* was one of the most controversial (and successful) anime of the mid-1990s. The toned-down manga version is relatively easy to follow, tending toward comedy and interaction between the teenage heroes (like the anime's early episodes), and the best parts reveal Sadamoto's unique ideas about the characters—he *did* design them, after all. The story diverges from the anime as it goes on, in ways that will be fascinating to *Evangelion* fans, and the art is polished and attractive. Whether or not it stands on its own without the anime, it's far superior to the average licensed adaptation. ★★★½

NEON GENESIS EVANGELION: ANGELIC DAYS

Shin Seiki Evangelion: Kôtetsu no Girlfriend 2nd, "New Century Evangelion: Girlfriend of Steel 2" (新世紀エヴァンゲリオン・鋼鉄のガールフレンド2nd) • Gainax (original concept/story), Fumino Hayashi (art) • ADV (2006–ongoing) • Kadokawa Shoten (Asuka, 2003–2005) • 6 volumes • Shôjo, Science Fiction, Mecha, Romance • 13+ (mild sexual situations)

A romantic comedy spin-off of the *Evangelion* anime, based on the "what if *Evangelion* were a generic high school anime" parody sequence in episode 26. Instead of traumatized characters in a depopulated future setting, the heroes of the series are all outwardly normal students with crushes on one another. Eventually a science fiction element intrudes, and the series progresses just like the original *Evangelion,* with the heroes piloting giant biomechanical monsters. This unnecessary retelling misses the entire point of the episode 26 parody (like the fact that it was a *parody*) and turns the plot into a clichéd love triangle; the action sequences, in particular, fail to hold up without the anime. The Japanese subtitle "Girlfriend of Steel 2" gives the misleading impression that it is a sequel to the untranslated *Evangelion* video game "Girlfriend of Steel," which in fact is a totally different story. ★

NESTROBBER

Blue Sky Blue (1992–1994) • Jo Duffy (story), Maya Sakamoto (art) • 2 issues • Science Fiction, Action • Unrated/13+

Unfinished action-espionage series, drawn by a Japanese artist and written by early manga fan and ex-Marvel editor Jo Duffy (she worked on the original Marvel edition of *Akira*). Additional material was published in *Dark Horse Presents.* NR

NEVER GIVE UP

Nebagiba!, "Never Give Up!" (ネバギバ!) • Hiromu Mutou • Tokyopop (2006–ongoing) • Hakusensha (Hana to Yume, 1999–2003) • 13 volumes • Shôjo, Drama • 13+ (mild language, brief partial nudity)

Kiri is a tall girl who looks so boyish that other girls confess their love to her. She's jealous of the feminine good looks of Tohya, a model, until she discovers . . . *Tohya's a guy!* Predictable romance and gender confusion ensue, as Kiri disguises herself as a *male* model in order to protect Tohya from "gay fashion photographers," and must protect her secret from her classmates as her picture appears on billboards and posters. More drama than comedy, *Never Give Up* has serious, refined *shôjo* artwork and a strong heroine; on the downside, the plot is formulaic and Tohya, while not as manipulative and domineering as the heroes of *Tenshi Ja Nai!* and *W Juliet,* is not very sympathetic. ★★

NEW LANCHESTER STRATEGY

Shin Lanchester Senryaku towa, "New Lanchester Strategy" (新ランチェスター戦略とは) • Shinichi Yano (script), Kenichi Sato (art) • Lanchester Press (1995–1996) • Waco (1986–1988) • 3 volumes, suspended (10 volumes in Japan) • Educational, Salaryman • All Ages

Western authors made a fortune selling business books based on the strategies of Sun Tzu; perhaps the reverse is the Lanchester Strategy, a Japanese sales strategy based on the military theories of British engineer Frederick William Lanchester (1868–1946). This polemic educational manga explains the Lanchester Strategy through the device of a resourceful Japanese salesman lecturing his colleagues; apparently the Lanchester Strategy even makes you popular with the ladies ("These days Mr. Sakamoto looks so handsome and self-assured!"). The writing is rudimentary, as if it were written for children or dumb adults; the cartoony art is like building blocks without the charm. ★

NEW VAMPIRE MIYU

Shin Kyûketsuki Miyû (Vampire Miyu), "New Vampire Princess Miyu" (新吸血姫美夕[ヴァンパイア ミユ]) • Narumi Kakinouchi (story and art), Toshiki Hirano (co-creator) • Ironcat (1997–2001) • Akita Shoten (Susperia, 1992–1994) • 5 volumes • Shôjo, Fantasy, Action • Unrated/13+ (mild language, graphic violence)

Spin-off of *Vampire Princess Miyu,* based on the plot of the anime TV series. The Western Shinma, a group of *very* loosely European supernatural creatures, arrives in the Japanese spirit world looking to take over. Miyu and her Eastern Shinma friends oppose them, while Larva, who was once a Western Shinma, finds himself targeted by his former comrades. A terrible series, *New Vampire Miyu* throws away the spooky mystery of the original manga in favor of pointless fight scenes between new characters (including Yui, who also appears in *Vampire Yui*). With Kakinouchi's hasty-looking art, there's also scarcely any detail in the costumes, the powers, or the personalities to tell them apart. The dialogue is barely translated, with characters constantly saying fragments of sentences, shouting one another's names, and so forth. Completely boring.

0 Stars

NEXTWORLD

Kitarubeki Sekai, "The World to Come" (来るべき世界) • Osamu Tezuka • Dark Horse (2003) • Fujishobo (1951) • 2 volumes • Science Fiction • Unrated/All Ages (mild violence)

The last manga in Tezuka's early "science fiction trilogy," published just a year before the first *Astro Boy* stories. In an indefinite near future, a world war is brewing, stoked by the feuding nations of Uran and Star. Meanwhile, a race of tiny superhumans called the Fumoon has evolved from nuclear radiation and arises to challenge mankind's supremacy. In the midst of these conflicts, scientists discover that the Earth is about to be destroyed by cosmic gas, and the Fumoon construct space arks to escape. This was Tezuka's longest and most ambitious manga to date, featuring a huge cast, a plot that jumps

around the world and across the galaxy, and an apocalyptic climax running for more than 30 chaotic pages. The title and concept were vaguely inspired by the movie *Things to Come,* just as the other manga in the trilogy, *Lost World* and *Metropolis,* were inspired by sci-fi movies Tezuka hadn't actually seen. *Nextworld* captures Tezuka at the end of the first phase of his creative career: manic, cartoony, illogical, and endlessly imaginative, with flashes of the mature brilliance to come. (SG)   ★★★

NIGHT OF THE BEASTS

Kemonotachi no Yoru, "Night of the Beasts" (獣たちの夜) • Chika Shiomi • Go! Comi (2006–2008) • Akita Shoten (Princess, 1996–1999) • 6 volumes • Shôjo, Occult, Action • 16+ (mild language, violence, mild sexual situations)

"Black demons" dwell secretly in the world, possessing humans and animals. Aria, a tough teenage girl who hangs out with the boys, encounters Sakura, a mysterious, handsome man whose demonic powers can be suppressed only by her touch. Low on body count and high on apprehension, *Night of the Beasts* is an effective story of *shôjo* occult horror. The character and demon designs are generic, but the art is fluid.   ★★

NIGHT WARRIORS: DARKSTALKERS' REVENGE

Vampire Hunter (ヴァンパイアハンター) • Run Ishida • Viz (1999) • 1 volume • Fighting, Video Game • Unrated/13+ (violence)

Poorly drawn short stories based on individual characters from the monster-themed Capcom fighting game. The disconnected, *dôjinshi*-like stories are predictable meet-and-fights (and barely even that), adding nothing to the characters, although vampire hunter Donovan and succubus Morrigan are slightly fleshed out.   0 Stars

NININ GA SHINOBUDEN

Ninin ga Shinobuden (ニニンがシノブ伝) • Ryoichi Koga • Infinity Studios (2005–ongoing) • Media-Works (Dengeki Daioh, 2000–2006) • 4 volumes •

Shônen, Otaku, Ninja, Comedy • 16+ (language, crude humor, sexual situations)

A fun, satirical romp through the clichés of ninja manga. Shinobu, a young *kunoichi* (female ninja) in training, is sent into the world by her master, Onsokumaru (who, for no explained reason, is shaped like a gum ball) to complete a great trial to pass into the next phase of her training. Her trial: to steal panties from high school girls, of course! During her trial, scatterbrained Shinobu crashes into the home of the equally clueless Kaede, and the two girls have a series of wacky adventures, Kaede acting as a sort of tour guide for the ninjas who are unfamiliar with modern society. The jokes fly fast, many of them dutifully footnoted, although most of the humor is spoken in the universal language of dick and fart jokes. The title is a complicated pun. (LW) ★★

NO. 5

Number Five Go, "Number Five" (ナンバーファイブ 吾) • Taiyo Matsumoto • Viz (2001–2003) • Shogakukan (Ikki, 2000–2005) • 2 volumes, suspended (8 volumes in Japan) • Seinen, Underground, Science Fiction • 18+ (violence)

In a strangely transformed future of low-rent bioengineering and ecological collapse, the super-sniper known as No. 5 flees into the wilderness, taking with him a nearly mute woman. Pursued by the other agents of the Rainbow Council, an international squad of peacekeepers/overlords, he fights back against his former comrades. If *Black & White* was Matsumoto's excuse to depict a city as a surreal playland, *No. 5* gives him the reins of the entire world, here depicted as a multicultural utopia/dystopia of outrageous costumes, animals, and scenery. The hand-drawn artwork and free-associative imagery is beautiful; however, the vaguely fighting-oriented story never comes together, particularly not in the small portion available in English. ★★★

NODAME CANTABILE

(のだめカンタービレ) • Tomoko Ninomiya • Del Rey (2005–ongoing) • Kodansha (Kiss, 2001–ongoing)

Chika Shiomi's *Night of the Beasts*

• 17+ volumes (ongoing) • Jôsei, Comedy, Drama • 16+ (mild language, mild sexual situations)

Shinichi, a college student at Momogaoka Music Academy, wants to become a conductor and conduct a great orchestra in Europe. His goals are hampered by his fear of flying and, more important, his snobbery and coldness to others—the last two of which improve slightly when he meets Megumi Noda ("Nodame"), his slovenly but pretty next-door neighbor, who can barely take care of herself but has a talent for the piano. While Nodame crushes on Shinichi, they make friends with other people at the college, including Ryutaro, a rocker violinist; Masumi, a gay student who loves Shinichi; and Franz von Stresemann, the musical equivalent of the dirty old martial arts master. Will they be able to work together to form a great orchestra, with Shinichi at the lead? Mixing the competitive spirit of *shônen* manga with the interpersonal relationships

NINJA (忍者)

"What does it mean to endure?"
"To withstand anything by holding a blade in one's heart."

—*Path of the Assassin*

The words *ninja* and *shinobi* derive from a kanji meaning "to go unperceived" or "to endure." As Kazuo Koike points out in *Path of the Assassin* and *Lone Wolf and Cub*, this kanji is made of a combination of the kanji for "knife" and "heart," suggesting the nearly superhuman toughness from which ninja derive their powers. Indeed, ninja are some of the classic heroes of Japanese comics and children's stories dating back to the prewar period, and their air of mystery dates back to the legends that surrounded them in real life.

The historical origin of ninja is obscure, but they were believed to exist from the Kamakura era (1185–1333) to the Edo era (1600–1857). In pop culture, they were traditionally depicted in all-black uniforms, symbolizing their invisibility, but most ninja probably spent most of their time undercover, in disguise. As spies and assassins, bodyguards and secret police, their greatest virtue was absolute loyalty to their feudal lord (*daimyô*); perhaps the most famous real-life ninja is Hattori Hanzô, whose service to Tokugawa Ieyasu is the subject of Kazuo Koike and Goseki Kojima's *Path of the Assassin* (1978). The most famous ninja clans, the Kouga and the Iga, are depicted perpetually warring with each other for the honor of serving the shogun. The clash of loyalty and compassion makes some of the greatest Japanese dramas. In Sanpei Shirato's classic manga *Ninja Bugeichô* ("Ninja Military Chronicles") (1959) ninja fought against corrupt feudal lords and became heroes of the people. Student protestors of the time saw *Ninja Bugeichô* as a metaphor for modern-day Japanese society; Shirato's follow-up was *Kamui Den* ("The Legend of Kamui") (1964), whose hero openly rebelled against his ninja masters. Shirato's Kamui lived the life of an outcast, surviving with the special techniques of his ninja training, but forever pursued by his former comrades.

In addition to their loyalty, the other defining ninja trait is their special techniques, their *ninjutsu*, an idea that may even predate ninjas as a group. (Yû Terashima and Kamui Fujiwara's *Raika* of 1987 takes this concept and runs with it, depicting the prehistoric ninja-before-there-were-ninja.) At the same time as Shirato was writing *Ninja Bugeichô,* he also wrote a more standard children's comic about ninja, *Sasuke* (1961), which focused on exaggerated ninja abilities such as splitting into multiple selves, jumping incredible heights, or appearing to be killed only to fool one's opponents with a log or a bale of straw. (Sasuke is a classic name for a ninja, referenced even in Masashi Kishimoto's *Naruto*.) Fûtaro Yamada, one of many popular ninja novelists of the period, upped the bar with *The Kouga Ninja Scrolls* (1958), a long series of novels depicting ninjas with monstrous, supernatural powers such as slithering like snakes, or bleeding poison, or bloating into rubbery blobs to deflect blades. *The Kouga Ninja Scrolls* inspired the 1993 anime *Ninja Scroll* and was directly adapted into the 2005 anime and manga *Basilisk*. Mitsuteru Yokoyama's manga/TV series *Red Shadow* (1967), although set in feudal Japan, starred ninjas in color-coded costumes with high-tech gadgetry. Ninjas were superheroes, and ninja manga were everywhere in the 1960s and 1970s.

Eventually trends changed, and by the 1980s, ninja were distinctly out of fashion.

Ninja were jokes and klutzes, the subject of self-parodies such as Fujihiko Hosono's *Sasuga no Sarutobi* ("Clever Sarutobi") (1982), set in a high school for ninja. (Of course, comedic ninja had appeared before, as in Fujiko Fujio's *Ninja Hattori-kun,* 1964.) When they did appear as heroes, they were often so fantastic that they were essentially just another kind of superpowered martial artists, as in Nobuyuki Anzai's *Flame of Recca* (1995). Straightforward historical ninja stories were still written—such as Yu Koyama's *Azumi* (1994), about a ninja-like female assassin—but tended to be aimed at older readers.

Ninja did not regain their essential coolness until Masashi Kishimoto's *Naruto* appeared in *Weekly Shônen Jump* in 1999. Kishimoto threw out the clichés of the genre, such as the black outfits, and focused on the core elements, making ninja into the highly trained commandos of a vaguely Japanese fantasy world. *Naruto* became a megahit and inspired a new generation of ninja fans.

Ninja Manga
Basilisk • La Blue Girl: The Original Manga (adult) • Flame of Recca • Gôjin • Kabuto • Kagetora • The Legend of Kamui Perfect Collection • Lone Wolf and Cub • Naruto • Ninin Ga Shinobuden • Path of the Assassin • Princess Ninja Scroll Tenka Musô • Raika • Rurouni Kenshin • Samurai Deeper Kyo • Shinobu Kokoro: Hidden Heart (yaoi) • Tail of the Moon

of *shôjo* manga, *Nodame Cantabile* seems like it can't lose, but it falls short of its potential. The plot is more adagio than allegro, with a slow pace and a shortage of overt passion, drama, or comedy. The dialogue suffers from clunky translation and rewrite. The art is generic and inexpressive, and never solves the essential problem that you can't show sound in a manga; unlike *Swan* and other classic *shôjo* manga, it rarely uses impressionistic effects. (In Japan, *Nodame Cantabile* soundtrack CDs were released, and indeed, the story reads better while listening to classical music.) As the characters express themselves and encounter one another through music, the series approaches themes that are beyond the artist's grasp, leaving the reader to fill in the gaps.　★★½

NO NEED FOR TENCHI!

Tenchi Muyô!, "No Need for Tenchi!/Unnecessary Tenchi! Ryo-Oh-Ki" (天地無用! 魎皇鬼) • Hitoshi Okuda • Viz (1996–2007) • Kadokawa Shoten (Comic Dragon, 1994–2000) • 12 volumes • Shônen, Science Fiction, Romantic Comedy • 13+ (violence, nudity, sexual situations)

The original *Tenchi Muyô!* anime was basically a slicker, more blatantly pandering update of Rumiko Takahashi's *Lum★Urusei Yatsura,* with the identical premise of an average teenage boy pursued by a sexy alien *oni* and lots of beautiful, short-tempered women from outer space. This was the first manga spin-off of the Tenchi anime, written and drawn by former *dôjinshi* artist Hitoshi Okuda, who does a respectable job of emulating the Tenchi house style. Following the continuity of the first OAV series (as indicated by the "Ryo-Oh-Ki" of the Japanese title), the manga boils down to two types of stories: short, slapstick comedies, typically featuring the Tenchi girls learning about Earth culture and/or getting into superpowered catfights, and longer science fiction dramas involving the elaborate mythos of the Planet Jurai. It's perky, polished, and engineered to please (especially if the reader happens to be a geeky teenage boy), but even more derivative and forgettable than the anime from whence it came. The series has run through several English editions, all from Viz; the most recent right-to-left edition censors some nudity that was allowed to pass in the earlier versions, including two cover images that have been covered up. (CT) ★★

NOODLE FIGHTER MIKI

Muteki Kanban Musume, "Invincible Signboard Girl" (無敵看板娘) • Jun Sadogawa • ADV (2005) • Akita Shoten (Weekly Shônen Champion, 2002–2006) • 1 volume, suspended (17 volumes in Japan) • Shônen, Comedy • 13+ (comic violence)

Not a cooking or fighting manga, *Noodle Fighter Miki* is a juvenile black comedy about a violent-tempered girl who helps out at her mom's ramen shop and has a rivalry with the girl who works at the bakery next door. The art is ugly but interesting, with big-headed, noseless characters making big evil grins and grumpy pouts; it has a surly, sketchy quality. A sequel series, *Muteki Kanban Musume N* ("Noodle Fighter Miki N"), was begun in 2006. ★

NOSATSU JUNKIE

Nôsatsu Junkie, "Charming Junkie" (悩殺ジャンキー) • Ryoko Fukuyama • Tokyopop (2006–ongoing) • Hakusensha (Hana to Yume, 2004–ongoing) • 8+ volumes (ongoing) • Shôjo, Romantic Comedy • 13+ (mild language, mild sexual situations)

Naka wants to be a teenage model, but she has a problem: whenever she smiles, she looks evil. Then one day she discovers a shocking secret about the cute model Umi: *she's a guy in drag!* Umi agrees to help Naka become a model in return for not spilling "her" secret, and so the two of them become close partners and share a room and undergo tough modeling training. More funny and snarky than romantic and angsty, *Nosatsu Junkie* is one of the better "cross-dressing male model" manga. Among other atypical points, the characters have to actually work hard to make it in the business, and both Umi and Naka have a refreshing mean-spirited streak. ★★★

NOTHING BUT LOVING YOU: See *Erica Sakurazawa: Nothing but Loving You*

NURSE CALL

Eriko Okamura • ComicsOne (e-book, 2000) • Aoba Shuppan • 2 volumes, suspended • Drama • 13+ (mature themes)

One of ComicsOne's better e-book releases, *Nurse Call* is a mature attempt to tackle contemporary issues in Japan. This episodic manga revolves around Dr. Kuraishi and Nurse Asami, an idealized doctor and nurse, who deal with visiting patients' physical and mental health issues. When not being strictly informative about the issue showcased in each chapter, the manga manages to touch on social topics: the way that the elderly are often devalued in Japan, older women having children, abusive environments for children, bullying, STD transmission between a married couple, and so on. The stories are well plotted, and the female-centric *jôsei* perspective is refreshing. Unfortunately, almost every story reinforces traditional family and gender roles and ends with the most appealing (and often improbable) resolution. (RS) ★★★

NYMPHET

Kodomo no Jikan, "The Children's Hour/Time" (こどものじかん) • Kaworu Watashiya • Seven Seas Entertainment (2007–ongoing) • Futabasha (Comic High!, 2005–ongoing) • 3+ volumes (ongoing) • Otaku, Romantic Comedy • 16+

Lolicon romantic comedy with cutesy art. Daisuke is an inexperienced twenty-three-year-old schoolteacher just assigned to his first class of third-graders. To his embarrassment, he finds himself pursued by his precocious student Rin. Note: Due to controversy over the content of the manga, *Nymphet* was cancelled by Seven Seas in June 2007. NR

OCTOPUS GIRL

Tako Shôjo, "Octopus Girl" (タコ少女) • Toru Yamazaki • Dark Horse (2006) • Leed Publishing (1994–2002) • 3 volumes, suspended (4 volumes in Japan) • Horror, Comedy • 18+ (language, crude humor, graphic violence, nudity)

OCCULT AND RELIGION (オカルト・宗教)

"Don't you think a Buddhist making the sign of the cross is bad form?"
"Huh? Oh . . . see, I don't remember the sutra all that well, so I thought I'd just throw that in."
— *The Kurosagi Corpse Delivery Service*

Manga dealing with the occult are not considered their own genre, perhaps because they are so widespread; tales of ghosts, reincarnation, and strange forces appear in almost all manga magazines, for purposes of comedy, drama, or horror. Relatively few manga deal with real-world religion (*shûkyô*), apart from *dôjinshi* and low-circulation magazines produced by religious groups. In mainstream manga, however, the distinction between "occult" and "religion" is often blurred.

Buddhism and Shinto

Shinto is Japan's native religion. Buddhism was introduced to Japan in the sixth century, which prompted local traditions to organize themselves in reaction; the name *Shinto* did not even exist until this time. The two have sometimes struggled, and at alternating times both have been promoted by the authorities; Shinto was the state religion from 1868 to 1945, in an attempt to promote nationalism and Emperor worship, which ended with Japan's defeat in World War II. For the most part, though, Shinto and the many Buddhist sects are inextricably mixed, and the influence of both religions is pervasive throughout Japanese society. Osamu Tezuka, who drew many comics on religion and history, explains the teachings of Buddhism in his historical biography *Buddha* (1972). *Phoenix* (1956) touches on the history of Shinto, although most Shinto stories fall under the domain of mythology. (See FANTASY article.) Hiroyuki Takei's untranslated *Butsu Zone* ("Buddha Zone") (1997) is a *shônen* action manga starring an emissary of a Bodhisattva; among other powers, he can subdue foes or catch bullets by producing the hundreds of arms often seen on Buddhist and Hindu statues. Masamune Shirow's sci-fi fantasy *Orion* (1990) combines elements of both religions. A few fantasy manga make speculations about the historical link between Shinto and the Japanese government, typically conspiracy stories where Japan is secretly protected by mystic powers: examples include *X/1999* (1992), *Shrine of the Morning Mist* (2000), and *Kamunagara: Rebirth of the Demonslayer* (2000).

Osamu Tezuka's *Buddha* is a thoughtful treatment of Buddhism, originally written for young readers.

In practical terms for the average Japanese person, Shinto is less a dogma than a set of traditions and holidays; if Buddhism concerns itself with death, transcendence, and morality, Shinto concerns itself with day-to-day life. Activites such as buying *omamori* (amulets) for good luck or safe birth and praying before shrines on New Year's and other auspicious occasions are commonly seen in manga. Buddhist and Shinto priests and Shinto "shrine maidens" (*miko*), while not on every street corner, are also part of life in Japan. *Miko*, with their distinctive robes, appear in *Silent Möbius* (1988), *Inuyasha* (1996), and again *Shrine of the Morning Mist* (2000). Male Buddhist and Shinto priests appear in manga too often to count, although as with *miko*, most translated examples show them in a fantasy context banishing demons and using other pseudo-magical powers. Reiko Okano's untranslated *jôsei* manga *Fancy Dance* (1984) is an unusually realistic story about a young man who inherits his father's position as a Zen Buddhist priest.

Foreign Religions

Besides Buddhism and Shinto, Christianity is the largest religion in Japan, but it is estimated that less than 5 percent of Japanese are practicing Christians. (Some estimate as few as 1 percent.) Of those Christians, most are Catholics, spiritual descendants of the original communities who were converted by Jesuit missionaries in 1549 and went underground during the Edo era (1600–1867), when Japan's borders were closed and all things foreign were forbidden. Modern-day missionaries, including Jehovah's Witnesses and Mormons, are active in Japan but have made little headway. It is not considered paradoxical for a Japanese person to express simultaneous belief in Buddhism, Christianity, and Shinto. Christmas is celebrated in Japan, but in a form almost entirely devoid of religious context; it is a "romantic holiday" where lovers spend a special night together, some private time before the entire extended family gets together for New Year's. In brief, the majority of Japanese are not Christians and have little knowledge of the religion. Manga such as Sumiko Amakawa's *Cross* (1997) and Yu Aikawa's *Dark Edge* (1999) include footnotes and glossaries explaining basic concepts such as Communion and the word *amen*.

Popular Japanese images of Christianity fall into two categories. On one hand, Japanese Christians have traditionally been active in social justice issues, and zealous priests and nuns appear in positive contexts in manga such as *One Pound Gospel* (1987) and the popular girls' school novel series *Maria-sama ga Miteru* ("The Virgin Mary Is Watching") (1998), although the latter is more famous for its intimations of lesbian romance between the characters. On the other hand, Christianity is often associated with magic and the occult, perhaps due to the more than 250-year-long Edo period in which Christianity was a secretive cult, whose practice is punishable by death. The numerous "magical girl" heroines who derive their powers from God or prayer may have been inspired by TV shows such as *The Flying Nun*, which was broadcast in Japan. There is little deep meaning in these portrayals. When asked by *Animerica* magazine why she used a nun in training as a character in *Saint Tail* (1994), Megumi Tachikawa replied, "I wanted the setting to feel a bit foreign."

For many Christians, the association with magic would be troubling enough, but countless horror, sci-fi, and fantasy manga involve wild, over-the-top visions of angels, devils, Satanism, and other loaded imagery. A classic example is Go Nagai's *Devilman*

(1972), an apocalyptic superhero story in which it is discovered that savage devils once ruled the Earth in prehistoric times and will rise again to destroy humanity. Go Nagai was inspired by Dante and Milton; later series to use demons, angels, and God include Kazushi Hagiwara's *Bastard!!* (1988), Kaori Yuki's *Angel Sanctuary* (1994), and the anime/manga series *Neon Genesis Evangelion* (1995), which takes imagery from Gnosticism and Kabbalah. For every one of these at least slightly researched, internally consistent fantasies, there are countless stories in which angels and devils appear for casual comedy purposes, or simply because manga artists like drawing feathery wings. In numerous children's TV shows and *shônen* manga, including Masami Kurumada's *Knights of the Zodiac* (*Saint Seiya*) (1986), bad guys tie good guys to crosses.

Japanese Christians are resigned to fanciful portrayals of their religion in the mainstream media. Manga, after all, are primarily escapism. More realistic depictions do exist, such as Osamu Tezuka's *Ode to Kirihito* (1968) and Yoshikazu Yasuhiko's thoughtful historical biographies *Joan* (1995) and *Jesus* (1997). In America, Christian fans of anime and manga, who may enjoy the visual style and storytelling techniques of manga but not the foreign themes, have produced original English-language "Christian manga" such as Buzz Dixon and Min Kwon's *Serenity* (2005). Online groups such as the Christian Anime Alliance and Anime Angels keep track of the content of particular series.

Other major religions—Judaism, Islam—make an even smaller showing in manga. Osamu Tezuka's *Adolf* (1983) includes a sympathetic but sometimes inaccurate portrayal of Judaism. Jewish groups in Japan and abroad have sometimes complained about the use of Stars of David as generic "mystic symbols" in manga, and have complained even more vocally about occasional appearances of the Buddhist *manji,* known to most Westerners as the swastika, an ancient religious symbol appropriated by the Nazis. (Technically, the *manji* is a swastika flipped left to right.) *Manji,* which have no anti-Semitic meaning in their original context, appear throughout Asia and in Japanese pop culture, including Hiroaki Samura's manga *Blade of the Immortal* (1993), whose hero is named after the symbol and wears a *manji* on the back of his clothes.

Ghosts and Superstitions

The predominance of supernatural themes in manga reflects a general Japanese interest in spiritualism—ghosts, palm reading, paranormal abilities, theories about life after death. Such beliefs come and go in fads; manga from the year 1999 often contain joking references to the prophecies of Nostradamus, such as the supposedly imminent arrival of the "King of Terror." Sakura Tsukuba, Naoko Takeuchi, and Shigeru Mizuki have professed belief in psychic phenomena, astrology, and the occult, respectively. During the publication of her science fiction epic *Please Save My Earth* (1987), Saki Hiwatari began getting letters from crazed fans claiming that they too were reincarnations of aliens who once lived on the moon. Hiwatari wrote an editorial stressing that the story was fiction and asking readers not to become obsessed. Some manga (among them *Yu-Gi-Oh!* volume 1 and *Love Roma*) contain skeptical depictions of astrologers and fortune-tellers, but whether the motivation is curiosity or pure escapism, manga readers are clearly interested in such themes.

Hiroyuki Takei's *Shaman King* (1998) shows numerous Japanese superstitions and folk beliefs, along with virtually every worldwide occult or religious tradition. One of

Takei's main characters is an *itako,* a sort of traditional female shaman who speaks with the dead. Other characters are *onmyôji,* practitioners of an ancient form of Japanese divination influenced by Taoism; they are sometimes referred to as "yin and yang masters." *Kokkuri* boards, the Japanese equivalent of ouija boards, are also used to tell the future. *Wara ningyo,* straw dolls that are nailed to walls or trees, can be used for good causes or to curse your enemies in a voodoo-doll fashion; Hikaru Gosunkugi, a creepy character from Rumiko Takahashi's *Ranma ½* (1987) who specialized in the practice, was considered inappropriate enough that he was largely replaced with a new character in the TV anime version.

Ghost stories are common in Japan, not all of them as horrific as Japanese horror movies such as *The Ring.* Hisaya Nakajo's *Hana-Kimi: For You in Full Blossom* (1996) is one of several *shôjo* manga to contain "real-life" ghost stories describing creepy events experienced by the author. The manga *Ghost Hunt* (1998) is based on a spin-off of Fuyumi Ono's *Akuryô Series* ("Evil Spirit Series") (1989), supernatural young-adult novels dealing with teenage paranormal investigators. Housui Yamazaki's *Mail* (2004) and *The Kurosagi Corpse Delivery Service* (2002), the latter with art by Eiji Otsuka, represent the even larger genre of mystery stories in which the protagonists are exorcists or use ghosts to help solve crimes. Reincarnation is another classic theme. It provides an element of mystery and identity crisis in tightly plotted dramas such as *Please Save My Earth* (1987), *Pieces of a Spiral* (1992), and *Oyayubihime Infinity* (2003), and explains the main characters' superpowers in mainstream action manga such as *Sailor Moon* (1992) and *Shaolin Sisters: Reborn* (2001).

Shinigami, "death gods" or "death spirits," originated in the late nineteenth century as the Japanese translation for Western images of the grim reaper. (The term is also used to describe gods such as the Greek Hades or the Egyptian Anubis.) In Japanese pop culture, they are usually depicted as spiritual beings who guide dead souls to their final destination, or protect the living from troublesome spirits and ghosts. Most *shinigami* stories are light comedies about the rules of the afterlife. They range from *shôjo* dramas such as *Descendants of Darkness* (1994), *Omukae Desu* (1999), and *Full Moon o Sagashite* (2002) to *shônen* action series including *YuYu Hakusho* (1990), *Bleach* (2001), and Atsushi Ohkubo's *Soul Eater* (2004). A very unusual portrayal appears in Tsugumi Ohba and Takeshi Obata's *Death Note* (2004), in which amoral *shinigami* grant the protagonist the power to kill anyone on Earth.

General Occult

3x3 Eyes • The Amazing Adventures of Professor Jones • Arm of Kannon • Crescent Moon • Diabolo • GATE • GeGeGe no Kitaro • Genju no Seiza • Geobreeders • Go Go Heaven • Hana-Kimi: For You in Full Blossom • Her Majesty's Dog • Horobi • Innocent W • Kamunagara: Rebirth of the Demonslayer • Kekkaishi • Lagoon Engine • Legal Drug • Lunar Legend Tsukihime • Magical Mates • Möbius Klein • Mugen Spiral • My Code Name Is Charmer • Night of the Beasts • Otogi Zoshi • Oyayubihime Infinity • Pieces of a Spiral • Platinum Garden • Please Save My Earth • Princess Resurrection • Purgatory Kabuki • Sailor Moon • Sailor Moon StarS • Sailor Moon Super S • Sengoku Nights • Shaman King • Shrine of the Morning Mist • Silent Möbius • Striker • Tactics • Tokyo Babylon • Tsukuyomi: Moon Phase • Twilight of the Dark Master • X/1999 • xxxHOLiC • Yu-Gi-Oh! • Yu-Gi-Oh!: Duelist • Yu-Gi-Oh!: Millennium World • Zodiac P.I.

Takako, picked on by other girls, finds herself transformed into a human head upon a regular-sized octopus body, which she uses to take gory revenge (and afterward, swim around the ocean encountering vampires and eel girls). In the same way that American comic artists sometimes parody horror and romance comics of the 1950s, *Octopus Girl* is a vicious slapstick parody of old-school *shôjo* horror manga, specifically Kazuo Umezu. With lolling tongues, wacky expressions, and popping eyeballs, it reads like a gory version of Umezu's untranslated gag manga *Makoto-chan,* although the intentionally ugly artwork and deep inky shadows might remind American readers of underground artists such as Basil Wolverton and Charles Burns. The filthy-tongued English rewrite goes along with the complete subversion of *shôjo* prettiness. ★★★

ODE TO KIRIHITO

Kirihito Sanka, "Ode to Kirihito" (きりひと讃歌) • Osamu Tezuka • Vertical (2006) • Shogakukan (Big Comic, 1968–1971) • 1 volume • Seinen, Drama • 16+ (violence, nudity, rape, adult themes)

Investigating a bizarre disease that turns humans into doglike creatures, Dr. Kirihito Osanai travels to a remote, snowbound Japanese village. There, he's infected with the "Monmow disease" himself, and leaves the village with the face of a dog. Met with horror everywhere he goes, Kirihito is sold to a black-market freak show and begins a long journey home by way of Taipei and Syria. Meanwhile, his schizophrenic colleague Dr. Urabi investigates an outbreak of a similar disease in South Africa. He meets a gentle Catholic nun, Helen, who has also been infected. Said to be Tezuka's favorite of his own works, *Ode to Kirihito* is part globetrotting adventure, part medical drama, set in a harsh, violent world where humans are only a step away from devolving into brute animals. The feverish narrative builds upon primal fears of atavism, mutation, ostracism, and literally "losing face." It's also a Christian story, drawing parallels to the humiliation of Christ on the cross and making numerous references to the Gospels ("Kirihito," in Japanese, sounds similar to "Kirisuto," the usual pronunciation of "Christ"). Tezuka's art here is loose but detailed, with some stunning hallucinatory sequences. The Vertical edition presents the entire saga in a single thick volume. (SG)

★★★★

OFFERED

(オファード) • Kazuo Koike (story), Ryoichi Ikegami (art) • ComicsOne (2001) • Shogakukan (Big Comic Spirits, 1989–1990) • 2 volumes • Seinen, Action-Adventure • 18+ (language, graphic violence, nudity, sex)

Young Yu Tachikawa is a top athlete, an MIT scholar, and an all-around combination of brains and brawn. While competing in South America, Yu is kidnapped by a seductive woman claiming to be the granddaughter of Adolf Hitler. She informs Yu that he is actually the spawn of an artificial insemination experiment involving the sperm of the ancient Babylonian king Gilgamesh. After an epic bout of copulation, the pair sets out to discover the legendary city of Agarti, where Yu is fated to become a modern-day hero-king. But a host of grotesque enemies stand in the way, and Yu discovers that he may not be the only descendant of Gilgamesh currently active in the modern world. Another over-the-top pairing between writer Kazuo Koike and artist Ryoichi Ikegami (see also their *Crying Freeman* and *Wounded Man*), *Offered* is a tidal wave of nudity, sex, and violent imagery broken only by outrageous dialogue played totally straight. The small but vocal cult of Koike and Ikegami is bound to lap up both volumes in a hurry, but anyone easily offended (or just under eighteen) had probably best steer clear of *Offered*'s blood-and-filth-packed fountain of lowbrow thrills. (PM)

★★★★

OGRE SLAYER

Onikirimaru, "Ogre Slasher" (鬼切丸) • Kei Kusunoki • Viz (1995–1998) • Shogakukan (Shônen

Sunday Chôzôkangô, 1992–2001) • 2 volumes, suspended (20 volumes in Japan) • Shônen, Horror • Unrated/16+ (graphic violence)

Short *shôjo*-esque horror stories, in which modern-day people are preyed upon by ravening ogres, then defended by a mysterious young man with a sword. Once the Ogre Slayer shows up, the ending is always the same, but the buildups are gruesome and genuinely disturbing, often involving human beings transformed into ogres through psychological stress and hatred. The horned, emaciated ogres are visually inspired by ancient Japanese "hell scrolls."

★★★

OHIKKOSHI

(おひっこし) • Hiroaki Samura • Dark Horse (2006) • Kodansha (Afternoon, 2001–2002) • 1 volume • Seinen, Romantic Comedy • Unrated/13+ (mild language, brief violence, brief partial nudity, sex)

One-shot romantic comedy by the creator of *Blade of the Immortal,* who here displays his talent for hip, modern characters in a setting of bands, dating, and drinking binges. Sachi, a poor college student, has a crush on a cool girl with a long-distance boyfriend and is oblivious to the affection of his childhood friend Koba. The writing is self-referential ("In a romantic comedy, the lead must of course be a virgin") and contains numerous subtle parodies of other manga. The side story is even more tongue-in-cheek: a silly piece about a young *shôjo* manga artist who suffers trials and tribulations after receiving bad advice from her editor. Samura's art is so detailed and precise it almost distracts from the lightheartedness of the story.

★★★½

OH MY GODDESS!

Aa! Megamisama!, "Aa! Great Goddess!" (ああっ女神さまっ) • Kosuke Fujishima • Dark Horse (1994–ongoing) • Kodansha (Afternoon, 1988–ongoing) • 34+ volumes (ongoing) • Shônen, Romantic Comedy, Science Fiction, Fantasy • Unrated/13+ (infrequent partial nudity, occasional sexual situations)

One of the classic *otaku* manga, *Oh My Goddess!* started out as a neutered *Lum★Urusei*

Yatsura and then fathered an entire genre of "shy guy living platonically with beautiful girls" manga, aka "harem manga" (such as *No Need for Tenchi!*). Tech-geek college student Keiichi Morisato attracts the attention of the Norse goddess Belldandy, who moves in with him and devotes herself to helping him in every way imaginable. Belldandy (the maid/housekeeper/mother figure) is soon followed by several of her sisters, each representing her own archetype, such as Urd (the seductress who toys with Keiichi) and Skuld (the "cute little sister" type). As in most sitcoms, the sexual potential of the situation is completely sublimated into PG scenarios in which Keiichi dreams of kissing Belldandy and the most cherished values are kindness and gentleness, occasionally aided by a little slapstick magic. This static formula has gone on for nearly twenty years as of the time of this writing, with little change except for the art, which has followed prevalent styles, from the plump, big-boned women of the 1980s to the slim, increasingly young-looking girls that are trendy in modern manga. (Fujishima, or his assistants, have an eye for elaborate clothes and finery and hair, meticulously detailed to the point of daintiness.) As the manga goes on, the already minor sexual element dwindles even further, and the story increasingly focuses on sci-fi scenarios, robots, and technology; Keiichi's main hobby is motorcycle mechanics, and even the goddesses are treated as programmers of a sort of massive heavenly computer. It's always sappy, but the witty English rewrite gets the most mileage out of this predictable confection, only rarely crossing the line from cute to insipid. Dark Horse has also printed *Oh My Goddess! Colors,* a one-volume collection of assorted *Oh My Goddess!* chapters colorized in Japan, together with bonus material. ★★★

OH MY GODDESS!: ADVENTURES OF THE MINI-GODDESSES

Kosuke Fujishima • Dark Horse (2000) • Kodansha • Four-Panel Comedy • 1 volume • Unrated/All Ages

Four-panel, plotless gag strips starring *chibi* versions of Belldandy, Skuld, and Urd, the

Kosuke Fujishima's *Oh My Goddess!*

three main women of *Oh My Goddess!* Shrunk down to miniature size for unspecified reasons, they take part in understated sight gags with household objects and small animals, and start a band with Gan, a scatterbrained rat. More for cuteness' sake than anything else, although Fujishima's art is as polished as always. ★★½

OLD BOY

(オールドボーイ) • Garo Tsuchiya (story), Nobuaki Minegishi (art) • Dark Horse (2006–ongoing) • Futabasha (Weekly Manga Action, 1996–1998) • 8 volumes • Seinen, Crime Drama • 18+ (language, violence, nudity, sex)

Ten years locked in a windowless room with a television, a bed, and food brought regularly from a panel in the door . . . Yamashita has spent a decade in this private prison, not knowing why he's there, what he did, or who put him there. After all this time, he finds himself back in the world, suddenly free with no answers. His goal: to find whoever did this to him. A small clue found in one of his meals while he was locked in that mysterious room—a shred of paper with a partial name of a restaurant—leads Yamashita on his mission. *Old Boy* is a hard-boiled manga that is as powerful and moving as its protagonist. Yamashita's "punishment" and his journey to find answers leaves you yearning for more, and with each answer, a maze of new questions arises. The manga was adapted into a box-office hit Korean film adaptation by Chan-Wook Park (*Sympathy for Mr. Vengeance*). (DR) ★★★★

OL SHINKARON: See *Survival in the Office: The Evolution of Japanese Working Women*

OMUKAE DESU

Omukae Desu, "(Here Is Your) Escort" (お迎えです) • Meca Tanaka • CMX (2006–2007) • Hakusensha (LaLa, 1999–2002) • 5 volumes • Shôjo, Occult, Comedy • 13+ (mild language, mild sexual situations)

Unfazeable college freshman Madoka takes a part-time job as a spiritual medium, who lets ghosts possess him so that they can take care of unfinished business (an old man wants to see his granddaughter's birth, a dead kid wants to go to the amusement park, etc.). His supervisor is a guy in a bunny suit, and his coworkers include several girls, all of whom work as *shinigami* (reapers, or spirit guides) for the same mysterious company. Similar to the early volumes of *YuYu Hakusho* but more understated, *Omukae Desu* is a *shôjo* comedy about the rules of the afterlife. However, blank-faced Madoka is an uninteresting character, and flat sentimentality outweighs the occasional absurdism. ★★

ONCE UPON A GLASHMA

Hajimari no Glashma, "Original Glashma" (はじまりのグラシュマ) • Kumiko Suekane • ADV (2007) • Kadokawa Shoten (Newtype, 2005–2006) • 1 volume • Fantasy • 13+

Vaguely *shôjo* set in a modern world where all women have vanished and the male population contains an ever-growing number of wizards. A few years after the women disappear, the Ministry of Internal Affairs and Communication calls for a national census to assess the growing wizard population. The main characters are "magic investigators" who go from household to household doing the census. NR

ONEGAI TEACHER

Onegai Teacher, "Please Teacher" (おねがい☆ティーチャー) • Please! (original creator), Shizuru Hayashiya (art) • ComicsOne (2003) • MediaWorks (Dengeki Daioh, 2002–2003) • 2 volumes • Shônen, Science Fiction, Romantic Comedy • 13+ (language, sexual situations)

Adaptation of the *Onegai Teacher* anime. Kei, a growth-stunted eighteen-year-old who's still a high school sophomore, discovers that his sexy new teacher is a half-human alien sent to observe humanity. For unlikely reasons, they end up getting married and living together to conceal her secret. The sci-fi element is arbitrarily dumped on top of the plot of this boring, saccharine marriage-fantasy manga featuring an unusually grouchy, bitter male lead. Shizuru Hayashiya's art looks hasty and generic compared to her work in *Sister Red*. ½

ONEGAI TWINS

Onegai Twins, "Please Twins" (おねがい☆ツインズ) • Please! (original creator), Akikan (art) • DrMaster (2006) • MediaWorks (Dengeki Daioh, 2005) • Shônen, Romantic Comedy • 1 volume • 16+ (nudity, sexual situations)

Adaptation of the *Onegai Twins* anime, a pseudo-sequel to *Onegai Teacher* (whose characters have minor roles in this manga). Maiku Kamishiro, a high school student who lives alone and supports himself, suddenly meets two girls, Miina and Karen. Based on the evidence of an old photo, one of them is his long-lost twin sister, but the photo is so vague they can't tell which one it is; thus they all end up living together, with the women doing the housework and both falling in love with the guy who might be their brother. The manga crams in pandering fan service as though the writers were working off a checklist: incest, lesbian teases, *yaoi* teases, and so on. Maiku is an unsympathetically cold protagonist, and the grayscale art is so heavily toned it looks ill-suited for black and white. ½

THE ONE I LOVE

Watashi no Suki na Hito, "The One I Love" (わたしのすきなひと) • CLAMP • Tokyopop (2004) • Kadokawa Shoten (Young Rose, 1993–1995) • 1 volume • Shôjo, Romance • 13+

A heartfelt but ultimately lacking novelty collection from future superstars CLAMP, *The One I Love* crams twelve stand-alone vignettes into a tight 120-page package. Each manga chapter is paired with a couple of pages of prose by Ageha Ohkawa and focuses on a different aspect of love, from crushes to dating insecurities to marriage, all from a distinctly female perspective. Despite the characters and situations being more adult than CLAMP's other works, this is perhaps the team's most juvenile work, depicting romance through pink-tinted glasses. The unifying theme, if there is one, is that girls should stop being so immature and just be themselves in a relationship—an admirable message, but one that comes off as almost anti-feminist in execution, as without exception, the boys in this manga are faultless and it's the women who need to change their behavior. *The One I Love* is the first manga to be illustrated by Tsubaki Nekoi, so fans of *Wish* and *Legal Drug* might want to give it a look to admire the art, but for everyone else, give this one a miss and check out *Man of Many Faces, Cardcaptor Sakura,* or *Chobits* to see CLAMP do romance right. (MT) ★½

ONE MISSED CALL

Chakushin Ari, "One Missed Call" (着信アリ) • Yasushi Akimoto (story), Mayumi Shihou (art) • Dark Horse (2007) • Kadokawa Shoten (2004) • 1 volume • Horror • 16+

Manga adaptation of the horror movie by Takashi Miike. College students begin receiving strange voice-mails dated from the future . . . their own voices screaming as they die! An epidemic of random death soon spreads, as the students die in horrible ways at the time and date predicted in the voice-mail. NR

ONE PIECE

(ワンピース) • Eiichiro Oda • Viz (2002–ongoing) • Shueisha (Weekly Shônen Jump, 1997–ongoing) • 44+ volumes (ongoing) • Shônen, Fantasy, Adventure • 13+ (violence)

The spiritual successor to *Dragon Ball* (the original series), *One Piece* combines unforgettable cartoon visuals with knockout fight scenes and an epic plot Akira Toriyama never aspired to. In a fantastic world of vast seas, teenage Monkey D. Luffy—possibly the most cheerfully stubborn *shônen* manga character ever—yearns to raise a crew, become the King of the Pirates, and find One Piece, a legendary lost treasure. His special ability is the power to stretch like rubber, used mostly to beat up opponents; his special weakness is that, thanks to the same magic fruit that gave him stretchy powers, he can never swim. Eiichiro Oda's gorgeous art resembles a cross between Disney and Peter Max (*Yellow Submarine*), gradually growing more detailed as the series goes on. The plot is set up like an RPG, as Luffy and his companions (which eventually include a skirt-chasing chef, the world's greatest swordsman, and a cute talking animal, among others) sail into a new area, become involved in the local troubles, fight the bad guys, and move on. Within this rough formula, however, grand plot threads are laid, and with each volume the world of *One Piece* becomes richer and more glorious: a tall-tale world of sea monsters, faraway kingdoms, cloud islands, and superpowered pirates of every shape, size, and description. The mood is sheer over-the-top melodrama—every line is weeping, laughing, or shouting—written with enough winking humor to be enjoyed by jaded hipsters as well as kids. The series is notable for its incredibly bloody and intense fight scenes in which, however, no one ever dies: the *shônen* manga updating of the *Looney Tunes* aesthetic. ★★★★

ONE POUND GOSPEL

1 Pound no Fukuin, "One Pound Gospel" (1ポンド
の福音) • Rumiko Takahashi • Viz (1994–1996) •
Shogakukan (Young Sunday, 1987–2007) • 3 volumes, suspended (4 volumes in Japan) • Seinen,
Sports, Romantic Comedy • Unrated/13+ (violence, brief nudity)

Kosaku, a novice boxer struggling with an
overeating problem, seeks moral support
from Sister Angela, a young Japanese Catholic nun. However, his love for her is more
than spiritual, and soon Sister Angela finds
herself torn between Kosaku and her vows.
(Meanwhile, Kosaku's coach, watching his
star boxer's weight shoot up, is concerned
with temptation of a different nature.) The
episodic stories center around Kosaku's opponents, mostly humorous small-potatoes
boxers with their own dreams and ambi-
tions; the boxing scenes are bloodless but
dramatic. The narrative is not as strong as
Takahashi's *Maison Ikkoku,* but the mix of
boxing, comedy, and light romance is charming. (Apparently "nun humor" is the same
in both America and Japan.) Begun in 1987,
the series was sporadically continued until
finally concluding in 2007.   ★★★½

ONIMUSHA: NIGHT OF GENESIS

Shin Onimusha: Night of Genesis, "New Onimusha: Night of Genesis" (新鬼武者NIGHT OF GEN-
ESIS) • Mitsuru Ohsaki • Udon Entertainment
(2006–2007) • Capcom (2005–2006) • 2 volumes •
Video Game, Samurai, Action • Unrated/13+ (violence)

Throughout history the demonic Genma
have worked with historical figures to dominate the world . . . but when the Genma
arise, an *onimusha* (oni warrior) is born to
stop them. Based on the video game *Onimusha: Dawn of Dreams,* this manga explores the
origin of the *onimusha* Soki and his quest to
destroy his father, the evil lord Tokugawa
Ieyasu. As Soki travels through feudal Japan,
he encounters many others who wield the
power of the *oni.* Pacing and plot are a little
on the slow side, and the story is predictable.
It's a decent historical action manga, and as a
prequel to the game, it's a good read for fol-

lowers of the series, but those unfamiliar
with the game may find it a little hollow.
(DR)   ★★

ONINBO AND THE BUGS FROM HELL: See
*Hino Horror, Vols. 3–4: Oninbo and the Bugs
from Hell*

O-PARTS HUNTER

666 Satan (666サタン) • Seishi Kishimoto • Viz
(2006–ongoing) • Square Enix (Monthly Shônen
Gangan, 2002–ongoing) • 16+ volumes (ongoing) •
Shônen, Science Fiction, Fantasy, Action-Adventure
• 16+ (mild language, infrequent graphic violence)

In addition to being one of the most amusing examples of a name changed for American audiences, *O-Parts Hunter* is a derivative
but strongly executed fighting adventure
manga for young readers. The art bears a
strong resemblance to Masashi Kishimoto's
Naruto, perhaps understandably, as Seishi
Kishimoto is his twin brother; in Japan, Masashi Kishimoto even addressed *Naruto* fans
to tell them to stop accusing his brother of
plagiarism. Set in a fantasy world where
treasure hunters seek ancient artifacts called
O-Parts, the story follows Ruby, a treasure-
hunting girl, and Jio, a young spiky-haired
boy who contains the split personality of
Satan (who's not nearly as bad as you'd expect). For the most part, the mood is light
and suitable for younger teenagers, with
Dragon Ball Z–influenced fight scenes and
imaginative otherworldly backgrounds. NR

ORFINA

(オルフィーナ) • Tennouji Kitsune • CMX (2007–
ongoing) • Kadokawa Shoten (Comic Dragon/
Dragon Junior, 1994–2004) • 12 volumes • Shônen,
Fantasy, Adventure • Not Rated Yet

European-style fantasy manga starring Orfina, a priestess of a country under assault by
its warlike neighbors.   NR

ORION

Senjutsu Chô-Kôkaku Orion, "Wizardry Super-
Attack Shell Orion" (仙術超攻殻オリオン) • Masamune Shirow • Dark Horse (1992–1994) •

Seishinsha (Comic Gaia, 1990–1991) • 1 volume • Science Fiction, Occult, Adventure • Unrated/16+ (violence, nudity)

Surprisingly readable sci-fi/fantasy hybrid story about a world of "psycho science," where magic and technology are combined. Basically one long fight scene livened up with lots of Buddhist theorizing about the mechanics of the universe, *Orion* is actually one of Shirow's most readable stories, with arguably some of his most imaginative visuals. An entertaining cast of gods and wizards plus a healthy dose of goofy, almost slapstick humor balance out the usual quotient of head-scratching terminology and mythological references. The heroine, Seska, is refreshingly free of deep thoughts or depression, and the "God of Destruction," Susano, is a cackling egomaniac. Simultaneously thoughtful and fun. (JD) ★★★★

OROCHI: BLOOD

Orochi, "Serpent" (おろち) • Kazuo Umezu • Viz (2002) • Shogakukan (Weekly Shônen Sunday, 1969–1971) • 1 volume, suspended (6 volumes in Japan) • Suspense, Horror • Unrated/16+ (violence)

In a moldering mansion, two aging sisters are locked in a bitter struggle over a hapless orphan girl, who suffers terrible abuse as the sins of the sisters' childhoods repeat themselves. Told partly through the eyes of the title character, Orochi, a sort of supernatural blank slate who is part immortal girl, part possessing spirit, this is a tale of V. C. Andrews–esque gothic horror written for children, operating on an almost purely emotional level with only the simplest dialogue. The old-fashioned artwork is almost enough to carry the story on its own—as stiff as it is oppressive, depicting the mansion and the equally claustrophobic exteriors with ornate detail and expressionistic darkness. Unfortunately, the plot is a blatant rip-off of the 1962 suspense movie *Whatever Happened to Baby Jane?* The Viz edition is a complete story but is only the last of 6 Japanese volumes of *Orochi* (later reprinted in a 4-volume edition); the Japanese edition consists of several self-contained stories with Orochi in the common role of observer. ★★½

ORPHEN

Majutsushi Orphen Haguretabi, "Orphen the Wandering Sorcerer" (魔術士オーフェンはぐれ旅) • Yoshinobu Akita (story), Hajime Sawada (art), Yuuya Kusaka (original character design) • ADV (2005–2006) • Kadokawa Shoten (Dragon Junior, 1998–2001) • 6 volumes • Shônen, Fantasy, Adventure, Comedy • 13+ (mild language, violence, brief partial nudity)

Spin-off of Yoshinobu Akita's young-adult fantasy novels (also known as *Sorcerous Stabber Orphen* or *Orphen: Scion of Sorcery*). Orphen, a young wizard raised as an assassin in the foreboding Tower of Fangs, now makes his living as a cash-starved wizard for hire; his companions include three tagalong boys and a girl who likes him. Aimed at young readers, *Orphen* alternates between tedious comedy and a more interesting serious plot involving the hero's past. The artwork is boring and hasty, the setting is generic, and the hero's magic consists of little more than firing power bolts from his hands. ★½

OTHELLO

(オセロ) • Satomi Ikezawa • Del Rey (2004–2006) • Kodansha (Bessatsu Friend, 2002–2004) • 7 volumes • Shôjo, Romantic Comedy, Drama • 16+ (mild language, mild violence, sexual situations, partial nudity)

A self-described "feel-good multiple personality story," *Othello* is almost like a *shôjo* version of the *Yu-Gi-Oh!* power fantasy, but never quite returns to the heights of its incredibly strong opening chapter. Yaya, a sixteen-year-old shy girl oppressed by false friends and feelings of self-hatred, is pushed over the brink and awakens her other self: Nana, a girl confident enough to beat up her enemies, flirt with the guy she likes, and jump off bridges onto moving trains. Unfortunately, like its protagonist, *Othello* has a split personality, in which Nana is sometimes treated as a violent psychological problem

OTAKU (オタク)

In Japan it's considered normal to read comics, but hard-core manga and anime fans have their own name: *otaku*. The term was invented by essayist Akio Nakamori, who in 1983 wrote a short-lived column in the adult manga magazine *Manga Burikko,* in which he complained about the nerdiness of modern manga fans. As Nakamori recounted from his experiences at Comic Market, this new crop of fans was so socially awkward, even among themselves, that they addressed one another with the stiff, pretentious word *otaku* (a very formal way of saying "you"). Thus, Nakamori titled his column *Otaku no Kenkyû* ("Otaku Studies"). *Mania,* short for "maniac," was the more polite Japanese slang for "fan," but *otaku* quickly became the new name for sheltered youths obsessed with their fantasy worlds.

The stereotypical *otaku* has much in common with American stereotypes of geeks and fanboys. In the early 1980s they drew their ranks from the sheltered, middle-class boys who were being groomed to pass tests and get good grades so as to get into the best schools and be prepared to participate in the newly booming Japanese economy. The classic *otaku* has poor social skills and hygiene; has obsessive collecting tendencies; is a know-it-all about his favorite topics; and loves anime, manga, science fiction and/or fantasy, and toy and model collecting. Individual interests vary; some *otaku* are obsessed with live-action *tokusatsu* movies, some with classic anime, some with giant robots, and some with model guns, battleships, and other military paraphernalia. (See the article on MILITARY.) *Otaku* can also be smart and creative. Many *otaku* participate in *dôjinshi* (self-publishing) circles, drawing their own comics or making their own computer games. (See the article on DÔJINSHI.) Some participate in cosplay, making costumes based on their favorite anime, manga, or game characters. Gainax, the famous anime studio founded in 1985, started out as a group of fans who did animated shorts for Japan's Daicon national science fiction convention. Former or current *otaku* have become successful manga artists, such as Kosuke Fujishima and Kenichi Sonoda. (Other artists, including Ippongi Bang and Hiroshi Aro, remained mostly cult followings.) In the mid-1980s *otaku* were the target audience, and often the creators, of the burgeoning new market in direct-to-video anime, featuring themes too niche for TV or theatrical animation, such as science fiction and erotica.

On a less positive note, *otaku* are also assumed to love pornography, particularly in the form of anime, manga, and adult video games. The *otaku* boom coincided with the early 1980s boom in *lolicon* anime and manga, in which, for the first time, graphic sex was coupled with the big-eyed, vaguely infantile character designs common to children's anime. Jokes about *otaku* being perverts or potential molesters were always common, but the jokes stopped in 1989 with the much-publicized arrest of Tsutomu Miyazaki, a twenty-seven-year-old man who had kidnapped, molested, and killed three preschool-age girls. When Miyazaki's apartment was searched, he was found to have thousands of videos, including numerous horror movies and several pornographic *lolicon* anime. The media latched on to Miyazaki's connection to fandom, exaggerating the size of his anime collection and turning *otaku* from mildly derogatory slang into a social disease creating a new generation of autistic monsters. The resulting moral panic led to new restrictions on the sale of adult anime and manga throughout Japan, and the term *otaku* became even more derogatory.

But the backlash died off, and Gainax promoted *otaku* pride in their famous anime *Otaku no Video* (1991), a satirical but loving depiction of the *otaku* lifestyle. *Otaku no*

MediaWorks' *Dengeki Daioh* ("Electric Shock Great King"); Kadokawa Shoten's *Monthly Shônen Ace* has made a business out of *Neon Genesis Evangelion* spin-offs.

Video paved the way for later works in the same vein, including Shimoku Kio's *Genshiken* (2002), Shinsuke Kurihashi's *Maniac Road* (2002) and *Pretty Maniacs* (2004), and the multimedia franchise *Comic Party.* Gainax's 1995 TV series *Neon Genesis Evangelion* was full of *otaku*-pleasing elements—cute girls, giant robots, intricate science fiction—but was also a self-analysis of Anno's own life up to that point, including his feelings of depression and social anxiety. *Evangelion,* with its many layers of meaning, made it cool to be an *otaku,* and soon mainstream commentators were discussing its meaning and confessing that they liked this or that giant robot anime. Nerds were hip or at least sympathetic, such as the robot-collecting hero of Iou Kuroda's *Sexy Voice and Robo* (2000). Stores specializing in *dôjinshi* and other *otaku* products, such as Mandarake and Tora no Ana, boomed. One such *otaku* chain store, Gamers, struck gold with *DiGi Charat,* a store mascot that became so popular it was spun off into anime and manga of its own. *Otaku*-friendly manga magazines, such as *Ultra Jump, Dengeki Daioh, Monthly Shônen Ace, Comic Gum,* and *Dragon Age,* increased in number. Newer artists such as Ken Akamatsu proudly proclaimed their *otaku* affiliations.

The term *otaku* retains a dubious edge, however. It remains associated with sexual fetishism, generally focused on the safest, most submissive female figures imaginable, as seen by the modern obsession with girls in maid outfits (*Hanaukyo Maid Team, He Is My Master, Sarai*). Another fetish is for dolls and robot women (*Chobits, Marionette Generation*); combining robots and maids, of course, is the best of both worlds (*Indian Summer, Mahoromatic, Steel Angel Kurumi*). The biggest trend of the late 1990s was named *moe* (pronounced *mo-eh*), after a word meaning "to sprout." In a general sense, the term describes a feeling of budding affection, somewhere between fetishism and enthusiasm

(as in, "I get *moe* from maids/girls with glasses/girls with eyepatches/etc."). However, *moe* also carries an implication of fresh young things, and the most popular *moe* manga, such as Kiyohiko Azuma's *Azumanga Daioh* (1999) and Barasui's *Strawberry Marshmallow* (2001), are everyday stories of very young girls, generally light comedies or sensitive dramas with few or no male characters, yet aimed at teenage and older men. In true *moe*, fans stress, there is no sexual element; the fans simply enjoy the cuteness and sweetness of the characters. Nonetheless, it has the potential to get readers' imaginations working. Publishers have released *moe*-specific magazines such as MediaWorks' *Dengeki Moeoh* and Futabasha's *Moeyon* (one of several magazines focused on *moe* four-panel comic strips). *Moe* is big business; in 2005 a Japanese market research group estimated that *moe* manga and merchandise made up one-third of the *otaku* market and had brought in $840.5 million in the year 2003.

In the late 1990s the media brought attention to a disturbing new trend: *hikikomori*, "acute social withdrawal," in which adolescents retreat from the world and refuse to leave their house or their room. The literal meaning of *otaku* is "your house"; now the most hard-core *otaku* were literally hidden away at home. The syndrome afflicts the protagonists of Peach Pit's *Rozen Maiden* (2002) and Tatsuhiko Takimoto's satirical novel *Welcome to the NHK* (2002), whose insane hero comes to the conclusion that the TV station NHK is plotting to turn the entire country into *hikikomori* by airing irresistibly nerdy anime TV shows. *Otaku* continue to receive both positive and negative press. The multimedia phenomenon *Densha Otoko* ("Train Man") is a heartwarming tale of an *otaku* who falls in love and comes out of his shell. In reaction to this kinder, cuddlier image of *otaku*, 2006 saw the publication of an anti-*otaku* satire, *Ken Otaku Ryû* ("Hating the Otaku Wave"). (The name was a parody of *Manga Kenkanryû*, "Hating the Korean Wave," an infamous anti-Korean screed.) Among other things, the book attacked the sexism of *moe* and *lolicon* manga. In interviews, the authors of *Ken Otaku Ryû* described themselves as *otaku*, but of an older type, defending their old-school science fiction fandom against the "new" *otaku* of porno video games and maid outfits.

The stereotypical *otaku* is male, but female *otaku* have always existed; women founded Comic Market and brought about the *dôjinshi* boom of the 1980s. Female *otaku* are stereotypically obsessed with *yaoi* manga. These fans are known as *fujoshi* ("rotten girls," a self-deprecating pun referring proudly to their "degenerate" interests) and have their own subcultures and hangouts, such as the *yaoi* bookstores along Otome Road in Tokyo; see the YAOI section.

Otaku Manga

Abenobashi: Magical Shopping Arcade • *A.I. Love You* • *Amazing Strip* • *Change Commander Goku* • *Chobits* • *Comic Party* (CPM) • *Comic Party* (Tokyopop) • *Cosplay Koromo-chan* • *Dame Dame Saito Nikki* • *Dark Tales of Daily Horror* • *DearS* • *Di Gi Charat* • *Di Gi Charat Theater* • *Digiko's Champion Cup Theatre* • *Doctor!* • *F-III Bandit* • *Futaba-kun Change* • *Genshiken* • *Hanaukyo Maid Team* • *Hayate the Combat Butler* • *He Is My Master* • *Ichigeki Sacchu Hoihoi-san* • *Indian Summer* • *Iono-sama Fanatics* • *Ippongi Bang's Canvas Diary* • *Love Hina* • *Lum*Urusei Yatsura* • *Maniac Road* • *Marionette Generation* • *Neconoclasm* • *Neon Genesis Evangelion* • *Oh My Goddess!* • *Popo Can* • *Pretty Maniacs* • *Sexy Voice and Robo* • *Sgt. Frog* • *Strawberry Marshmallow* • *Tori Koro* • *Virtual Bang* • *Welcome to the NHK* • *Yotsuba&!* • *You & Me*

and sometimes as a free-spirited cartoon prankster. Improbable slapstick revenge alternates with a more serious story involving Yaya/Nana's love triangle with a classmate and her career as a rock singer. In brief, it's an inconsistent manga, although the abrupt mood swings may not bother younger readers. ★★½

OTOGI ZOSHI

Otogi Zoshi, "Book of Stories for Women and Children" (**お伽草子**) • Narumi Seto • Tokyopop (2006) • Mag Garden (Comic Blade, 2004–2005) • Historical Drama • 2 volumes • 13+ (mild language, violence)

The *Otogi Zoshi* anime series involved reincarnation from the Heian era to the modern world, but the prequel manga is almost totally nonsupernatural, taking place entirely in the past. Hikaru, a sheltered girl of the Heian court trained in swordfighting, leaves the capital and is taken hostage by bandits who want revenge for injustices committed by the government. As Hikaru's worldview is shaken, evil forces behind the scenes set the stage for a bloody battle between the common people and the armies of the court. The art is detailed and the figure drawing is more than adequate for a historical action manga, but the drama feels forced and leaves major plot threads hanging, to be resolved only in the anime. ★½

OURAN HIGH SCHOOL HOST CLUB

Ôran Kôkô Host Bu (Club), "Ouran High School Host Club" (**桜蘭高校ホスト部[クラブ]**) • Bisco Hatori • Viz (2005–ongoing) • Hakusensha (LaLa, 2003–ongoing) • 10+ volumes (ongoing) • Shôjo, Comedy • 13+ (sexual situations)

Haruhi, an androgynous-looking scholarship student at the absurdly blue-blooded Ouran High School, finds herself forced to dress like a man and work for the Host Club, six gorgeous guys who entertain the school's female population for idle amusement and profit. The men of the host club, while drawn as more comic than sexy, span every *bishônen* and *shônen ai* fantasy: a gentleman

with glasses, a *shota* little-boy type and his caring protector, twins who play the incest card, and Tamaki, a handsome narcissist who vainly attempts to woo Haruhi. Having stocked the perfect male harem, *Ouran High School Host Club* has fun with every imaginable cliché; its characters even include a fangirl who rewrites the characters' relationships to make them more melodramatic. (In another scene, Tamaki draws a line on the floor, heartlessly separating the cast into "love comedy" and "sexless.") The levelheaded Haruhi, the "daughter" of this surrogate all-male family, provides the contrast to everyone else's craziness; she's even happy to be boyish, unlike the typical *shôjo* manga heroine in men's clothes. The text is as dense with jokes as the art is with screentone, and the English dialogue is appropriately over the top. A fun ensemble comedy. ★★★½

OUTLANDERS

(**アウトランダーズ**) • Johji Manabe • Dark Horse (1988–2000) • Hakusensha (Monthly Comicomi, 1985–1987) • 8 volumes • Science Fiction, Romance, Adventure • Unrated/16+ (mild language, nudity, sexual situations, violence)

A star-spanning epic adventure that gradually morphs into a drippy love story. *Outlanders* starts out splendidly, as an alien empire invades Earth with a fleet of monstrous biological warships in order to reclaim its legendary "sacred planet" from the worthless beasts that have polluted it (i.e., us). Fiery space princess Kahm crosses swords with everyman photojournalist Tetsuya, a shadowy secret society coordinates the response of Earth's governments, and alien warships shaped like armored slugs and pop-eyed goldfish blast the heck out of planes and tanks and major terrestrial land masses. Unfortunately, Manabe opts to focus on the least interesting of these plot threads—a lame and undermotivated romance between Kahm and Tetsuya, who go from star-crossed adversaries to swooning sweethearts in the space of the first couple of volumes, and then force the rest of the cast to spend the remainder of the story attesting to the awesomeness of their incomparable love. (MS) ★★½

OVER THE RAINBOW

Ame ni Nuretomo, "Even Though I'm Drenched in Rain" (雨にぬれても) • Keiko Honda • CPM (2004) • Shueisha (Office You, 1998–1999) • Jôsei, Romantic Drama • 13+ (language, sex)

A mediocre *jôsei* occupational manga. Two handsome young lawyers—Keita, a divorced father, and Bouya, his unmarried friend—leave their firm and start their own practice, accompanied by "Key," an amnesiac young woman whom they hire as their receptionist. Between cases, Bouya falls in love with Key, but Key is never more than a blank slate, and the manga is hampered by implausible behavior and weak writing, suggesting that, despite the thirty-something protagonists, it was written for young readers ("Poor Key. It's as if this empty room were a *metaphor* for your lost memories"). The legal cases are moralizing: divorce is bad, children come first, be nice to the elderly, and so on. ★½

OYAYUBIHIME INFINITY

Oyayubihime ∞ (オヤユビヒメ∞[インフィニティ]) • Toru Fujieda • CMX (2006–2007) • Akita Shoten (Princess, 2003–2006) • Shôjo, Occult, Romance • 6 volumes • 13+ (mild violence, mild sexual situations)

Kanoko and Maya are half sisters who, together, form the rising star "Mayu"; beautiful Maya is the actual actress, but her nerdy, lonely sister Kanoko is her coach and manager. They also have matching butterfly-shaped birthmarks on their bodies. One day they meet Tsubame, a tousle-haired teenage rock star with the same mark, who claims that it is the sign of his reincarnated lover from the Tokugawa period. But which sister? And what about all the other people with butterfly birthmarks? The characters respond with realistic skepticism to the idea, but soon strange dreams and visions make it clear that something is going on. Well drawn and well written, *Oyayuhibime Infinity* has echoes of *Please Save My Earth,* another manga about reincarnation in which it seems like everything would be solved if all the characters sat down together and shared all their information. It's an interesting story with strong characters and twists. ★★★½

PACHINKO PLAYER

Pachinker Atsushi, "Atsushi the Pachinko Player" (パチンカーアツシ) • Shigeru Tsuchiyama • Comics-One (e-book, 2000) • Sogo Tosho (1999) • 1 volume • Pachinko • 13+ (gambling)

One of the few translated examples of Japanese *pachinko* comics. Like most hobbyist manga, it functions as a how-to guide, advice column, and marketing device. The editing is bad, even by e-book standards, with entire speech bubbles left unlettered. Thankfully, the plot's arcs are so codified and generic that one can miss snatches of conversation without much disruption. The story follows celebrity gambler Atsushi as he helps down-on-their-luck females and catches crooked *pachinko* parlor owners. However, the focus on specific models of *pachinko* machines makes *Pachinko Player* feel stuck in a specific time and place years past. *Pachinko Player* would have benefited from a glossary and more footnotes, but as it is, it holds interest only as a peculiarity for the *pachinko* enthusiast. (RS) ★½

PANKU PONK

(パンク・ポンク) • Haruko Tachiri • Studio Ironcat (1999–2000) • Shogakukan (Shogaku Ninensei/ Pyonpyon, 1983–1994) • 6 issues, suspended (12 volumes in Japan) • Comedy • Unrated/All Ages (crude humor)

The English edition of this children's comic is actually bilingual; each issue contains the same manga pages printed twice, once in Japanese and once in English. Bonnie, a little girl, lives with her parents and Panku, a big fat talking rabbit (in one story he's mistaken for a pig). Panku's efforts to help Bonnie invariably end in a huge mess, sometimes funny and sometimes gross, as when he gets a pimple on his butt, or when he uses giant pancakes for pillows, only to wake up the next morning covered in mold. ★★

PANORAMA OF HELL

Jigokuhen, "Hell Transfiguration" (地獄変) • Hideshi Hino • Blast Books (1989) • Hibari Shobo (1983) • 1 volume • Horror • 18+ (language, graphic violence, sexual situations)

Hideshi Hino's masterpiece, this is the best horror manga available in English. Told directly to the reader by a ghoulish artist who paints with his own blood, *Panorama of Hell* is a surrealistic tale of nihilism on a personal and global scale. Although drawn in Hino's trademark cartoon style, with typical Hino scenes of ugly-cute children engaged in sadistic behavior, the story returns again and again to painfully serious and mature events: the Japanese invasion of Manchuria, the effects of generations of child abuse, and the threat of nuclear holocaust. Like a confessional underground comic, the story even borrows elements from Hino's actual life, building from a creepy opening to a climax of screaming terror. ★★★★

PARADISE KISS

(パラダイス・キス) • Ai Yazawa • Tokyopop (2002–2004) • Shodensha (Zipper, 1999–2003) • 5 volumes • Shôjo, Jôsei, Romance • 16+/18+ (language, nudity, sex)

After years of living up to her parents' expectations, Yukari's life changes when she meets a group of design students and becomes a model for their line of boutique clothes. Soon she is in a world of pierced, mohawked punks and transvestites, literally seduced by the world of fashion . . . and in particular by George, the blue-haired, bisexual leader of the pack. Originally published in a fashion magazine (to which the characters self-referentially refer), *Paradise Kiss* could have been just a stylish piece of nothing, but it's a gorgeous, sexy title that captures the anxiety and anticipation of growing up, making out, and breaking free. The plot features many of the same characters from Yazawa's untranslated *Gokinjo Monogatari* ("Neighborhood Story"), one of the mainstream *shôjo* hits of the early 1990s, but its status as a semi-sequel doesn't make it any less accessible to American readers, since the hero and hero-

Ai Yazawa's *Paradise Kiss* © 2000 Yazawa Manga Seisakusho. All Rights Reserved. First published in Japan in 2000 by Shodensha Publishing Co. Ltd., Tokyo, Japan. English publication rights arranged through Shodensha Publishing Co. Ltd. Original artwork reversed for this edition.

ine are both new. The writing consistently stays one step ahead of the reader, managing to be touching while avoiding romantic clichés. The art has the languid beauty and sensual figures of the British Aesthetic movement of the late nineteenth century (such as Aubrey Beardsley), and the reader can almost smell the smells: cologne, strawberries, champagne. ★★★★

PARASYTE

Kiseiju, "Parasite/Parasitic Beast" (奇生獣) • Hitoshi Iwaaki • Del Rey (2007–ongoing) • Kodansha (Morning/Afternoon, 1990–1995) • 12 volumes • Seinen, Science Fiction, Horror, Action • Unrated/ 16+ (language, graphic violence, brief nudity)

Wormlike aliens secretly appear on Earth, replacing people's heads and turning them

Uh oh, he's getting too wrapped up.

Hitoshi Iwaaki's *Parasyte*

into coldly emotionless cannibals whose heads split open into shape-shifting living weapons. Shin, a high school senior, is a fluke: instead of his head, a Parasyte takes over his left hand, and human and alien develop a wary symbiosis as they fight to protect Shin's friends and family from the new race of predators feeding on human beings. Like a science fiction novel, *Parasyte* takes a fantastic situation and applies realistic human behavior, playing out the logical consequences as humanity copes with the invaders. Iwaaki's writing is more memorable than his art, but his style suits the serious mood of the story better than more exaggerated artwork would. The violence is graphic but not sadistic. Prior to the Del Rey edition, the series was released by Tokyopop from 1997 to 2002. ★★★★

PASSION FRUIT

Short-lived *jôsei* manga imprint of Tokyopop. See *Galaxy Girl*, *Panda Boy* and *Sweat and Honey*

PASTEL

(ぱすてる) • Toshihiko Kobayashi • Del Rey (2005–ongoing) • Kodansha (Weekly Shônen Magazine/Magazine Special, 2002–ongoing) • 16+ volumes (ongoing) • Shônen, Romantic Comedy • 16+ (nudity, sexual situations)

Mugi, a depressed teenager who just broke up with his girlfriend, returns from a summer vacation to find that the hot girl he met at the beach has moved in with him! It turns out that Yuu (the girl) is a friend of the family, who is staying with Mugi since her parents died . . . and although Mugi keeps ending up with his face in her breasts, he can't bring himself to make her uncomfortable by asking her out. A by-the-numbers boys' romance comic (or rather, a fanservice comic), *Pastel* is less a story than a supplement to the swimsuit photos that often run in *shônen* manga magazines. The hero is passive and wimpy, and the girl is an inscrutable abstraction, occasionally sad or peeved, but mostly fawning over Mugi despite the fact that he's accidentally seen her naked umpteen times ("I guess that's just how girls are. They get bent out of shape over the tiniest things"). Other female love interests soon appear as well. The art is slick, with curvy bodies and detailed, photorealistic backgrounds. ★½

A PATCH OF DREAMS

Yume no Sorachi, "A Patch/Space of Dreams" (夢の空地) • Hideji Oda • Fanfare/Ponent Mon (2006) • Asukashinsha (2005) • 1 volume • Underground, Fantasy • Unrated/16+ (language, mild violence, nudity, sexual situations)

Renei, a twenty-two-year-old artist in an affair with a middle-aged professor, finds herself having recurring dreams in which she visits a surreal world inhabited by strange animals and dead people from her past. Renei and her acquaintances engage in long conversations about reality and the meaning of life, but soon her dreams start to interfere with her waking life. This metaphorical fantasy deals with death, suicide, and other heavy issues. The art consists of finely detailed, sketchy lines; tiny monsters and other fanciful things hide in the corners of otherwise realistic settings. The "patch of dreams" of the title refers to the vacant lots of the city, an entrance to the dreamscape, where a corkscrew-shaped mountain rises to Nirvana or oblivion. Although the book is a sequel to Oda's untranslated graphic novel series *Ku's World,* it stands on its own as an exercise in mood and surrealism. ★★★½

PATH OF THE ASSASSIN

Hanzo no Mon, "Hanzo's Gate" (半蔵の門) • Kazuo Koike (story), Goseki Kojima (art) • Dark Horse (2006–ongoing) • Kodansha (Weekly Gendai, 1978–1984) • 15 volumes • Seinen, Samurai, Drama • 18+ (language, graphic violence, nudity, sex)

Path of the Assassin is based on the mythologized exploits of the historical ninja Hattori Hanzô. It's also the story of Hanzô's master, Tokugawa Ieyasu, who unified Japan and founded the Tokugawa shogunate—but *Path* depicts Ieyasu as an idle, vain character, a comic schlub who relies on Hanzô's almost supernatural powers of stealth. The historical facts of Ieyasu's life would have been familiar to the original Japanese readers, but to many Americans, *Path of the Assassin* will be an insufficient introduction to its subject. Starting when the characters are teenagers (although, due to Kojima's unforgivingly uncute art style, they look about forty years old), the story meanders through countless subplots, many of them bawdy in nature, as when Hanzô helps his master with his marital problems. If the rambling story doesn't disappoint fans of *Lone Wolf and Cub* and *Samurai Executioner,* the lack of action might; it's certainly not as simple as a ninja equivalent to Koike and Kojima's more famous samurai stories. Compared to Kojima's earlier work, the art seems hastier. Still, Koike always spins an entertaining tale.

★★★

PEACE MAKER

Shinsengumi Imon Peace Maker, "Strange Tale of the Shinsengumi: Peace Maker" (新撰組異聞 PEACE MAKER) • Nanae Chrono • Tokyopop (2007–ongoing) • Square Enix (Monthly Shônen Gangan, 1999–2001) • 6 volumes • Shônen, Samurai, Drama • 16+

A nineteenth-century period piece following the adventures of a young upstart named Tetsunosuke as he wrangles his way into the ranks of the elite shogunate police force, known as the Shinsengumi, meeting various historical figures and training to avenge his parents' deaths. The series was renamed *Peacemaker Kurogane* when it moved from Square Enix's *Monthly Shônen Gangan* to Mag Garden's *Comic Blade,* so this is effectively a prequel to *Peacemaker Kurogane.* (MS) NR

PEACEMAKER KUROGANE

Peace Maker Kurogane, "Peace Maker Iron" (PEACE MAKER鐵) • Nanae Chrono • ADV (2004–2005) • Mag Garden (Comic Blade, 2002–2003) • 3 volumes, suspended (5 volumes in Japan, suspended) • Bishônen, Samurai, Drama • 13+ (graphic violence, sexual situations)

Sequel to *Peace Maker,* set in 1865 Japan and following the highly fictionalized adventures of the Shinsengumi, the *bushi* police force of Kyoto (at the time, the capital of Japan). The series gives no helping hand to new readers, jumping into a mob of characters with little explanation: Tetsunosuke, the spunky but haunted title character (his name is made with the same kanji as *kurogane*); Hijikata, his commander; Tatsunosuke, his older brother; and various other brooding samurai and ninja. Virtually every character has a historical basis, but the character designs are anime-ized to the extreme, with spiky *shônen* manga hair, dreadlocks, and supernatural villains with catlike eyes. The mix of history, comedy, and incongruously modern "cool factor" is similar to shows such as *Samurai Champloo* (which came later), but *Peacemaker* is far more convoluted, melodramatic, and adolescent. The artwork is agonizingly vague; sharp-featured, deep-shadowed people look decadent and pose with their swords but rarely ever fight or do anything. (Even when something *does* briefly happen—a *seppuku,* a murder—it's hard to tell what's happening beneath the buckets of blood.) There are moments of emotion and tragedy, but the story never adds up; to add another level of frustration, as of April 2007, the manga is on hiatus in Japan.   ★½

PEACH GIRL

(ピーチ・ガール) • Miwa Ueda • Tokyopop (2000–2003) • Kodansha (Bessatsu Friend, 1997–2004) • 18 volumes • Shôjo, Romantic Comedy, Drama • 13+ (mild language, brief violence, sexual situations)

Momo, an athletic swimmer, is a teenage girl with a problem: her naturally tanned skin and light hair make people assume she's a bimbo. (Specifically, she looks like a *ganguro,* a Japanese bad-girl fashion trend, although this term is not used in the English edition.) She has a crush on Toji, a strong, silent guy, but interference comes in the form of Kiley, an attractive, horny, good-natured goofball, and Sae, a jealous, conniving girl with a supernatural ability to meddle with Momo's relationships. A fun series with a strong heroine, good art, and lots of fast plot twists, *Peach Girl* reads like a junior high student's idea of what high school is like; the characters are tall, mature-looking, and extremely attractive, but when the story opens, most of them haven't had their first kiss yet. In the role of the "one person whom all your problems can be blamed on," Sae steals the show, a comically lovable villain often drawn in a more cartoony style than everybody else; when she's boasting, her head swells up like a balloon; when she gets deflated, she turns into a two-dimensional shadow of her former self, in which form she can flutter out of three-story windows. (Sae was so popular that she got her own series, *Peach Girl: Sae's Story.*) The story has a nice economy of characters, focusing on Momo, Toji, Kiley, and Sae, whose webs of lies catch all the others; enjoying the plot requires accepting that the romantic leads are unbelievably gullible and always stumble upon one another at the wrong mo-

ment. Sex enters the story in a fittingly melodramatic fashion in volume 5; the use of date rape as a plot element signals an irreversible change in mood, but the series as a whole remains extremely enjoyable, full of adolescent craziness. *Peach Girl: Change of Heart* was published in Japan as volumes 9–18 of the 18-volume *Peach Girl* series.

★★★★

PEACH GIRL: CHANGE OF HEART: See *Peach Girl*

PEACH GIRL: SAE'S STORY

Ura Peach Girl, "Reverse Peach Girl" (裏ピーチガール) • Miwa Ueda • Tokyopop (2006–2007) • Kodansha (Bessatsu Friend, 2004–2006) • 3 volumes • Shôjo, Romantic Comedy, Drama • 16+ (language, mild violence, sexual situations)

In this sequel to *Peach Girl*, Sae, the vain, jealous villain, has been held back a year in high school. Upwardly mobile as always, she tries to resume her modeling career and date a hot college guy, but her plans are complicated by the return of good-natured goofball Kanji Sawatori, or "monkey boy," her childhood sweetheart. The Sae of *Peach Girl* was a great character, but the predictable premise of *Sae's Story* makes it less fun; we don't necessarily *want* to see the world's most evil teenage girl redeemed by "the right guy" and explained away by a troubled home life. It's a well-told story but not a must-read, even for *Peach Girl* fans.   ★★½

PEARL PINK

Ten'nen Pearl Pink, "Natural Pearl Pink" (天然パールピンク) • Meca Tanaka • Tokyopop (2007–2008) • Hakusensha (LaLa, 2002–2004) • 4 volumes • Shôjo, Romantic Comedy • 13+

A second-generation office romance, in which the daughter of a star actress falls for the son of the man who runs her mother's talent agency. That's hard enough to read, and surely harder to live with, especially when peppy Tamoko has to keep her family situation under wraps. But perhaps those crazy kids will make it work somehow. (MS) NR

PETS AND ANIMALS (動物)

Snoopy, Garfield, Marmaduke—including pets in comics is only natural. A number of minor manga magazines, such as *Neko no Shippo* ("Cat's Tail"), *Nekodama, Nekopanchi,* and *Hamusupe,* are devoted to lighthearted pet-themed stories, but pets show up in mainstream manga as well. Exotic pets sometimes appear in manga, such as the hedgehog *Saint Tail* (1995) and the fox in *Imadoki* (2000), but they are usually treated as cute mascots more than actual animals. For stories focused on animals, a genre called *dôbutsu manga* (animal manga), dogs and cats are at the head of the pack.

Cute and Crafty

Cats outnumber all other pets in Japan, and many of them are the short-tailed breed known as Japanese bobtails. According to legend, a cat's tail caught fire while napping by a hearth and torched the city as it ran, causing the emperor to decree that all cats' tails be cut. One such short-tailed cat, the legendary Maneki-neko, is considered a sign of good luck; statues of him with an upraised paw greet customers at many restaurants and other businesses. In manga, cats range from devious, such as those in *Azumanga Daioh,* to loyal, like *Sailor Moon*'s talking cat Luna. Long-tailed cats are among the transforming animals of Japanese folklore, which lends them a mystical air and accounts for many of the cat-girls in anime and manga. Their ethereal nature is captured in Yumiko Ôshima's *shôjo* classic *Wata no Kuniboshi* ("Planet of Cotton") (1978). This enchanting tale of a kitten growing up is used as a metaphor for a girl becoming a woman. The amusing anecdotes of *What's Michael?* (1985) are close in mood to an American newspaper comic strip.

Manga's Best Friend

Cats may outnumber dogs in Japan, and cat manga drove the 2006 boom in specialty pet manga magazines, but dogs tend to be more successful as mainstream manga protagonists. (Even *Peanuts* is known simply as *Snoopy* in Japan.) It's due in part to the many canine adventure series of Yoshihiro Takahashi, whose untranslated classic *Ginga Nagareboshi Gin* ("Silver-fang Meteor Gin") (1984) tells the tale of a dog who must form a fighting pack to take down a killer bear. (Ginga's son is the star of a partially translated sequel series, *Ginga Legend Weed.*) Of course, there are more mild-mannered pet stories, such as Nobuko Hama's *Happy!* (1995), the heartwarming drama of a blind woman's life transformed by the addition of a seeing-eye dog, and Nichiho Higuchi's *Koharu Biyori* (2002), a dog-lover's answer to *What's Michael?* One of the oldest dogs in manga is *Norakuro* ("Black Stray"), Suihô Tagawa's amusing 1930s tale of a bumbling

Makoto Kobayashi's *What's Michael?*

stray dog who joins the army and participates in massive battles between armies of anthropomorphic animals.

The Winner's Circle

Heroic horses such as *Basara*'s (1991) Yato occasionally appear in action manga, but as exciting as horses in battle can be, there's a natural drama to racing. Horse racing is popular in Japan, and many equine manga revolve around the "sport of kings." Published almost exclusively in *seinen* and *shônen* magazines, horse-racing manga ranges from the stories about real-life horses such as Silence Suzuka to Tsunomaru's coarse comedy about a little horse that could, *Midori no Makibao* ("Green Makibao") (1995). Although he has drawn a wide variety of sports manga, Hiromi Yamasaki is arguably the leader of the horse-racing genre, with ten horse-oriented series to his name. Of course, race horses must be carefully raised. Masami Yuki's 1994 romantic comedy *Jaja Uma Grooming Up!* ("Grooming a Wild Horse!") involves a teenage boy who ends up working at a horse ranch with the rancher's four lovely daughters.

Fads and Fitting In

Most Japanese don't have room for large animals. This has provided the opportunity for less traditional pets—witness the recent fad for ferrets—to make their way into people's homes. Birds are a perennial favorite, and even the odd penguin such as in *Tuxedo Gin* (1997). Turtles—albeit talking and flying turtles—appear in series as varied as *Dragon Ball* (1985) and *Love Hina* (1998). Like fish, frogs, and other small reptiles, they make for manageable pets in real life. In school, children are often exposed to animals such as rabbits and guinea pigs, which students care for as part of their classroom chores. Although rodents will probably never be as prevalent as dogs or cats, the popularity of the *Hamtaro* multimedia franchise, based on Ritsuko Kawai's 1997 children's manga, highlights the Japanese hamster boom at the turn of the century. In sharp contrast to *Hamtaro*, Risa Ito's 1990 *Orochuban Ebichu* ("Ebichu Minds the House"), the story of a talking hamster who interferes with her twenty-five-year-old owner's relationships, is a cynical adult comedy.

Many manga also deal with people in animal-related careers, such as zookeepers, veterinarians, and even forensic entomologists. An animal-lover's classic, Noriko Sasaki's *Dôbutsu no Oishasan* ("The Animal Doctor") (1989) covers a vast array of unusual pets in its many thoughtful and amusing tales.

People love their pets, and while pampering them is on the rise in Japan, so too are their abuse and abandonment. This duality is not unique to Japan. Just as huskies became the most abandoned dogs after *Dôbutsu no Oishasan* made them popular, Dalmatians became the most abused dogs in the United States after the live-action remake of *101 Dalmations*. Currently, only dogs are required to be registered in Japan, so there are no definitive statistics on other pets, but with a third of outdoor-cat owners opting not to spay or neuter their pets, strays are common. Shelters are rare, and most don't even bother trying to find new homes for adult animals, only kittens and puppies. Owners who grow tired of their pets or must move to housing that doesn't permit them often have their pets put down or even set them loose. As a result, exotics such as raccoons, bass, and North American snapping turtles have become invasive species. *Inubaka: Crazy for Dogs* (2004), a comedy set in a pet store, addresses pet abandonment. (PD)

PENGUIN REVOLUTION

Penguin Kakumei, "Penguin Revolution" (ペンギン革命) • Sakura Tsukuba • CMX (2006–ongoing) • Hakusensha (LaLa, 2004–ongoing) • 5+ volumes (ongoing) • Shôjo, Romantic Comedy • 13+ (partial nudity, sexual situations)

Spoiler: not a manga about penguins. Yukari Fujimaru is a tireless teenage girl who harbors a strange gift: the ability to see wings on exceptional people. When she notices one of her schoolmates bearing a pair of wings, she learns that Ryoko is a model for the famous agency Peacock . . . not to mention a cross-dressing guy in disguise! When her father loses his job and Yukari must work, she finds herself working as Ryoko's manager and having to keep "her" secret. Peacock has harsh regulations: the models are ranked by birds and numbers, with "penguins" being lowest. (DR)   NR

A PERFECT DAY FOR LOVE LETTERS

Koibumi Biyori, "A Perfect Day for Love Letters" (恋文日和) • George Asakura • Del Rey • Kodansha (Bessatsu Friend, 1998–2001) • 2 volumes • Shôjo, Romance • 16+ (mild language, mild sexual situations)

An anthology of love stories, always involving secret crushes and usually involving anonymous love letters (or faxes, or text messaging, or the Japanese custom of exchanging notebooks with your loved one). The plots are rarely surprising, and sometimes feel false (as when a girl who works at a massage parlor falls in love with an abusive stalker), but the breezy, sophisticated artwork, similar to Moyoco Anno's, makes up for it somewhat.   ★★½

PETSHOP OF HORRORS

(ペットショップオブホラーズ) • Matsuri Akino • Tokyopop (2003–2005) • Ohzora Shuppan/Bunkasha (Monthly Apple Mystery/Horror M, 1995–1998) • 10 volumes • Shôjo, Horror • 13+ (language, graphic violence, brief nudity)

In Los Angeles' Chinatown is a curious pet shop run by Count D, an androgynous Chinese man of uncertain age. Although he has many satisfied customers, an unlucky few suffer horrible fates, killed by the exotic and mythological beasts that Count D has gathered from around the world. Attractively drawn with opulent, detailed artwork, *Petshop of Horrors* consists of episodic supernatural stories in the style of *The Twilight Zone.* (Another good comparison would be *Gremlins,* to which the first chapter of *Petshop* refers.) The stories are clever and unpredictable, swinging from melancholy to whimsy to horror. Yet they're rarely monster stories per se; Count D's creatures include mermaids, basilisks, and a three-headed dragon, but almost all the animals are capable of taking a human form, and they insinuate themselves into human relationships like the less visually interesting pets in Yumiko Kawahara's *Dolls.* The thread connecting these strange phenomena is a theme of environmentalism and animal rights, in which birdmen and cat-women are like white tigers, endangered species struggling to hang on against the march of humanity. Throughout the series the Count is followed and (very poorly) investigated by Detective Orcot, a skeptical, foul-mouthed police officer who provides most of the comic relief. (In fandom, the boyish Orcot and the girlish Count are the subject of much *yaoi* speculation, but their relationship in the manga is strictly platonic.) An imaginative, evocative series with a satisfying climax. An ongoing sequel series, *Shin Petshop of Horrors* ("New Petshop of Horrors"), has not been translated.

★★★½

PHOENIX

Hi no Tori, "Bird of Fire/Phoenix" (火の鳥) • Osamu Tezuka • Viz (2003–2007) • various magazines (1956–1989) • 12 volumes • Religion, Historical Fiction, Science Fiction • 13+/16+ (language, violence, nudity)

Described by Tezuka as "my life's work," *Phoenix* is epic in the extreme, spanning literally the whole of human history. It consists of twelve stories but was almost certainly unfinished at the time of Tezuka's death in 1989. The stories leap back and forth in time: the first takes place in the very distant past, the second in the very distant future, the third in the slightly less distant past, and so on, with past and future slowly converging toward the present. The stories are linked by the presence of the immortal Phoenix and the running themes of survival and immortality. Taken individually, they run the gamut from good to great, with the changes in style and tone that might be expected in a work serialized over the course of four decades. The best story may be volume 4, the stunning "Karma" (*Hô-ô* in Japanese editions), which follows the interlocking lives of two eighth-century sculptors, one a saintly Buddhist, the other a deformed and bitter bandit. The strangest may be volume 6, "Nostalgia," in which a woman left alone on a barren planet commits repeated incest with her descendants, only to be eventually relieved by shape-shifting aliens called Moopies (which also appear elsewhere in the series). Despite the periodic miss, all of the stories are the work of a master at the top of his form. The final volume of the Viz edition includes a selection of Tezuka's early work. (CT)

★★★★

PHOENIX RESURRECTION: See *Dark Angel: Phoenix Resurrection*

PICHI PICHI PITCH: MERMAID MELODY

(ぴちぴちピッチーマーメイドメロディー) • Michiko Yokote (story), Pink Hanamori (art) • Del Rey (2006–2007) • Kodansha (Nakayoshi, 2002–2005) • 7 volumes • Shôjo, Magical Girl, Romance • 13+

This incomprehensible magical girl manga involves a singing mermaid princess and her search for the missing pearl that is the source of all her power. Things are complicated when she falls in love with the young man who has her pearl, and to make things worse all of the seven seas are under attack by the evil Gackto. Or something. Despite the English edition's 13+ age rating, *Pichi Pichi Pitch* is insultingly juvenile, employing language, art, and story more fit for a seven-to-ten-year-old audience. The art is garbled and grating to the eye, and the writing is equally confusing. (LW)

★

PIECES OF A SPIRAL

Rasen no Kakera, "Pieces of a Spiral" (螺旋のかけら) • Kaimu Tachibana • CMX (2005–ongoing) • Shinshokan (Wings, 1992–1997) • 10 volumes • Shôjo, Occult, Fantasy • 13+ (mild language, violence)

Two identical but unrelated teenage boys, Sakuya and Wakyo, discover that they are the reincarnations of ancient warriors who served the half-human lord Bishu . . . who passed on his powers, and his violet eyes, to his two most faithful servants ("We truly are one person!"). The soulmates accept all this in the first 20 pages, after which they discover that Bishu has been reincarnated in the present as well, and that they must fight in the ongoing struggle between Bishu's human mother and his demon father, as well as other factions. *Pieces of a Spiral* is an uninspired treatment of reincarnation and psychic powers. The story flits confusingly back and forth from reality to the demon realm (which looks like ancient Japan), but little actually happens; the characters brood and internalize and plot against one another, but there's not much action, and the art is generic and dull. The psychic fight scenes consist of little more than posing followed by huge, hastily drawn explosions.

★½

PHANTOM THIEVES (怪盗)

Just as the investigations of genius detectives are compelling, so, too, are the exploits of master thieves. Largely inspired by the works of foreign writers, such as Maurice LeBlanc and Ernest William Hornung, but also drawing from the legends of Robin Hood–like Goemon Ishikawa and Jirokichi (aka Nezumi Kozô, "Rat Kid"), Japanese novelists created a unique genre of hero known as *kaitô* (mysterious/phantom thieves). These crafty crooks have developed a particular set of rules and an almost supernatural (or sometimes literally supernatural) ability to steal anything. They sometimes come from long lines of thieves and are merely carrying on a family tradition. Skilled in disguise and deception, phantom thieves usually announce their crimes ahead of time, avoid violence, and have dedicated police adversaries who are always just one step behind their quarry.

The lascivious, jet-setting title character of Monkey Punch's world-famous *Lupin III* (1967) is the grandson of the main character in Maurice LeBlanc's *Arsène Lupin: Gentleman Thief* novels (1907–1939). One of Lupin's cohorts is the laconic, sword-wielding Goemon Ishikawa, a descendant of Japan's legendary thief. Lupin steals for the thrill of it, while being perpetually chased by Interpol agent Koichi Zenigata. Like Lupin and Goemon, the often bungling detective has classic origins: his ancestor is au-

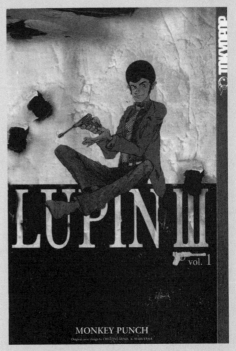

thor Kodo Nomura's Edo-era crime fighter Heiji Zenigata. Lupin is atypically adult for the genre, but in the very first chapter it's mentioned that he always sends his victims a letter announcing his crimes, a common *kaitô* plot device that was almost immediately dropped.

Not to be left out of the fun, a *shôjo*-styled super-thief arrived with flair in the form of British aristocrat Dorian of Yasuko Aoike's *From Eroica with Love* (1976). Motivated by beauty and desire, Dorian has only one true nemesis: Klaus, a handsome, straitlaced, sexually repressed NATO intelligence officer. In addition to espionage and action, the series focuses on campy sexual tension between the two rivals. Many other phantom thief manga also involve romance between the thief and his or her pursuer.

Phantom thieves are often art thieves, perhaps because it seems more noble than simply going after money. Tsukasa Hojo's untranslated *Cat's Eye* (1982) involves three sisters who illicitly

The original manga phantom thief: Monkey Punch's *Lupin III* LUPIN THE 3rd volume 1 © 1967 Monkey Punch. *Originally published in Japan in 1967 by CHUOKORON-SHINSHA, INC. English translation rights arranged with Monkey Punch through CHUOKORON-SHINSHA, INC., TOKYO, and TOHAN CORPORATION, TOKYO.*

reclaim their father's artwork, which starts showing up in the galleries of suspicious collectors after his mysterious disappearance. Another fatherless phantom thief, Kaito Kuroba, appears in Gosho Aoyama's untranslated *Magic Kaito* (1987), as well as occasional guest appearances in Aoyama's *Case Closed*. Discovering that his late father was not just a magician but also the notorious thief Kaitô Kid, Kuroba revives the legend to draw out those responsible for his father's death. Inspector Nakamori has been hunting Kaitô Kid for twenty years, and his daughter is Kaito's girlfriend. But what makes *Magic Kaito* distinctive is the introduction of a supernatural element in the form of a classmate who's a witch.

Three phantom thieves of the 1990s, all aimed at younger readers, take this supernatural theme in a divine direction. Meimi of *Saint Tail* (1994) is aided and blessed by a nun in training. Maron of *Kamikaze Kaito Jeanne* (1998) is the reincarnation of Joan of Arc, tasked by God to save the world . . . by stealing things, of course. Daisuke of *D.N.Angel* (1997) bears the genetic imprint of the mysterious, angelic Dark. Naturally, all three thieves must deal with detective adversaries and romantic complications, and none steal for reasons as crass as mere money.

The thrill of the heist, a costumed character with panache and verve, clever gadgets, complex traps, and the battle of wits between thief and detective: all these combine to create this specialized but diverse manga genre. (PD)

Phantom Thief Manga

Astrider Hugo • *D.N.Angel* • *Dream Gold: Knights in the Dark City* • *From Eroica with Love* • *Gorgeous Carat* • *Gorgeous Carat Galaxy* • *Jing: King of Bandits* • *Jing: King of Bandits: Twilight Tales* • *Kamikaze Kaito Jeanne* • *Liling-Po* • *Lupin III* • *Lupin III: World's Most Wanted* • *Man of Many Faces* • *Saint Tail* • *Shadow Lady* • *Steam Detectives* • *Treasure Hunter* • *Wild Act* • *Yoki Koto Kiku*

PILGRIM JÄGER

(ピルグリム・イェーガー) • Toh Ubukata (story), Mami Itoh (art) • Media Blasters (2004–2005) • Shônen Gahosha (Young King Ours, 2002–2006) • 3 volumes, suspended (6 volumes in Japan) • Seinen, Historical, Fantasy • 13+/16+ (graphic violence, nudity, sexual situations)

In 1521 Italy, the Renaissance is clouded by the dark reality of life on the ground: poverty, corruption, and religious persecution. Two pious female outcasts, Karin and Adele, make a living as street performers and exorcists, while hiding the strange powers that mark them as two of the "Thirty Silver Coins," superpowered religious warriors announced in the dying prophecy of the heretic Savonarola. *Pilgrim Jäger* transplants the *X/1999* "apocalyptic gathering of the superheroes" formula to a historical setting, operating on the premise that real-life figures such as Michaelangelo, Machiavelli, and Ignatius Loyola were actually hot, forward-thinking heroes with supernatural powers named after tarot cards. The mix of Italian history, theology, and superpowers is attention-getting, educational, and potentially hilarious, but the plot moves extremely slowly, and by the end of volume 3 (the last volume translated by Media Blasters) the two ostensible heroines have barely even encountered any of the other characters. Even in Japan, the story was forced to come to a hasty climax at the end of Part One of the planned epic. However, the kinetic artwork and gorgeous character designs, by Capcom video game–influenced manga artist Mami Itoh, make it worth reading just for the eye candy and ideological digressions. ★★★

PINEAPPLE ARMY

(パイナップルARMY) • Kazuya Kudo (story), Naoki Urasawa (art) • Viz (1988–1990) • Shogakukan (Big Comic Original, 1985–1988) • 1 volume, suspended (10 volumes in Japan) • Seinen, Crime, Military • Unrated/13+ (language, violence)

Japanese-American Jed Goshi, a grenade-toting veteran of Vietnam and numerous other war zones, makes a living from his combat expertise, but he's not exactly a mercenary—he's an instructor who teaches other people how to defend themselves. (Of course, he usually gets involved anyway.) Set mostly in New York and Central America, *Pineapple Army* is a prime example of the 1980s Japanese fascination with America as a place of violence and danger (but basically a good place nevertheless). The self-contained stories are a little predictable but well written, and Urasawa's friendly artwork keeps the mood from getting too heavy. ★★★

Mami Itoh and Toh Ubukata's *Pilgrim Jäger*

PITA-TEN

(ぴたテン) • Koge-Donbo • Tokyopop (2004–2005) • MediaWorks (Dengeki Gao!, 1999–2003) • 8 volumes • Shônen, Otaku, Romantic Comedy • 13+ (mild sexual situations)

Kotarou, an elementary school boy whose mother has died, one day meets Misha, a somewhat older, cute girl, who on her first appearance asks him, "Please go out with me!" But it turns out that Misha's intentions are not romantic—instead, she's an angel studying for her angel exam (just as Kotarou is studying to get into middle school), and she just wants to make him and everyone else happy. Soon they are joined by other supernatural women of mysterious provenance, but the story doesn't overload itself with too many characters; instead, it gradually goes from a self-consciously clichéd school comedy (blessed with Koge-Donbo's cute *chibi* artwork) to a touching story about growing up. As Kotarou's supernatural surrogate mother, Misha dances in the rain, hugs Kotarou, and occasionally makes memorably wistful observations. At the same time, she also talks in an unbearably cutesy speech pattern ("Gee whiz!" "That's a pwomise!" "Thank goodie goodie goodness!") It's an inconsistent work that doesn't reach its high points until the end—the early artwork has its rough spots—although some readers will prefer the goofy mood of the early episodes. ★★½

PITA-TEN OFFICIAL FAN BOOK

Pita-Ten Kôshiki Comic Fan Book, "Pita-Ten Official Comic Fan Book" (ぴたテン公式コミックファンブック) • various artists • Tokyopop (2005–2006) • MediaWorks (2002) • 3 volumes • Otaku, Comedy • 13+ (brief nudity, mild sexual situations)

Anthology comics collection based on *Pita-Ten.* Most of the stories are inferior imitations of Koge-Donbo's sugary style, with the subject matter mostly consisting of stories about food or characters getting sick and the other characters having to take care of them. The dominant mood is the light comedy of *Pita-Ten*'s early volumes, rather than the angst of the later volumes, although some are sad; in Mahide Ooya's story in volume 1, Kotarô suddenly finds that all his friends have grown up and forgotten him, while he remains a little boy. Other contributors include Mook (*Cosplay Koromo-chan*) and Koge-Donbo herself. ★½

PIXIE POP: GOKKUN PUCHO

Gokkun! Pûcho (ゴックン!ぷーちょ) • Ema Toyama • Tokyopop (2007) • Kodansha (Nakayoshi, 2004–2005) • 3 volumes • Shôjo, Fantasy, Romance • 13+

They say you are what you eat, but they usually don't mean it this literally. Thanks to Pucho, the magical beverage fairy, Mayu can take on the attributes of anything she drinks, from water to pork soup. Will being able to become invisible or transform into a piglet help her turn her love life around? Well, one imagines it couldn't hurt. (MS)   NR

PIXY JUNKET

Junket (ジャンケット) • PURE • Viz (1993–1997) • Seishinsha (1992) • 1 volume • Shônen, Science Fiction • Unrated/16+ (brief language, violence, nudity, mild sexual situations)

When they are the first on the scene at what appears to be a UFO crash site, two guys find a mute, friendly girl with insect wings—a pixy! But the government, genies, and other evil forces want to get their hands on the pixy, who may be the key to the mystic land of Chil Na Nug (presumably a mistranslated reference to the Irish fairyland Tir Na Nog). Set in a sci-fi/fantasy world inhabited by human and anthropomorphic animal characters, *Pixy Junket* is a shallow mishmash of chase scenes and stale sci-fi twists. The art looks like a bad imitation of early Masamune Shirow, perhaps understandably, as artist PURE was Shirow's former assistant. ★½

PIYOKO IS NUMBER ONE!: See *Di Gi Charat Theater: Piyoko Is Number One!*

PLANETES

(プラネテス) • Makoto Yukimura • Tokyopop (2003–2005) • Kodansha (Morning, 2001–2004) • Seinen, Science Fiction • 5 volumes • 13+ (language, mild violence, brief nudity)

Extremely realistic hard science fiction set in the late twenty-first century. The main characters are a small group of debris haulers who orbit the area between the Earth and the moon, cleaning up deactivated satellites and other hazardous space garbage. (The spaceships and lunar settings are drawn with amazing tactile detail, making the void of space look like the reader could step through the page and explore it.) Each of the haulers has his own reason for doing what he does, but the story focuses on Hachi, the son of a famous astronaut, whose goal is to join the first manned mission to Jupiter. There is no great melodrama or grand climax, despite a few action scenes; the stories involve space terrorism, politics, and the Jupiter expedition but always focus on the characters' families, loves, and lives. As the story progresses, Hachi drifts into inner space as well, conversing with spirits that speak to him about God and the cosmos. Dirty-old-astronaut jokes and occasional comedic touches maintain a not-entirely-serious manga spirit; the real strength of *Planetes* is telling human stories in a believable near-future setting, without slowing down the story for exposition. The last two volumes were released in America as volumes 4/1 and 4/2, instead of volumes 4 and 5. ★★★½

PLANET LADDER

(プラネット・ラダー) • Yuri Narushima • Tokyopop (2001–2005) • Soubisha (Crimson, 1998–2004) • Shôjo, Science Fiction, Fantasy • 7 volumes • 13+ (brief language, violence, partial nudity)

Teenage Kazuya is suddenly transported to a parallel world, where she is hailed as the prophesied "princess of the choosing," who will choose which one of the nine worlds will live and which ones will die. An interesting story told in an evocative fashion, *Planet Ladder* is reminiscent of prose science fiction such as Madeleine L'Engle's *A Wrinkle in Time* and Roger Zelazny's *Nine Princes in Amber*. When Kaguya finds herself alone and vulnerable in a strange environment, her reactions are realistic; she denies it as long as possible. (This is also the first sign that she's a fairly passive heroine.) When the worlds go to war over Kaguya, the battles take place mostly offscreen; instead, the focus is on the schemers in the different factions, who are numerous enough to make the reader grateful for the character charts at the beginning of each volume. At times Kaguya feels like a side character in her own story, and the story is slow and talky, but in the end it comes together . . . more or less. The series is marked by moments of spookiness and strange imagery: heaps of corpses and dead robotic dolls, a prince who has never been touched, a giant rooster with a human mind. However, the art itself is not great, with inconsistent designs, crude faces, and too much greasy-looking screentone.

★★★

PLASTIC LITTLE: CAPTAIN'S LOG

Plastic Little (プラスチックリトル) • Satoshi Urushihara • CPM (1998) • Gakken (Comic Nora, 1994) • 1 volume • Shônen, Science Fiction • 18+ (language, violence, nudity)

Spin-off of the *Plastic Little* anime (at one time infamous for its T&A content), for which Urushihara was the character designer. On a gas giant planet, Tita is the insecure teenage captain of a sort of high-tech whaling ship, which hunts rare animals in the cloud sea and captures them alive. Each self-contained chapter delves into the backstory of one of Tita's crewmates, while including at least a few panels of Tita's (or the other female characters') bare breasts drawn in photographic detail. Compared to Urushihara's other works, however, it's fairly restrained. The art is glossy and technically semicompetent, but the storytelling tends toward talking heads.

★½

PLATINUM GARDEN

(プラチナガーデン) • Maki Fujita • Tokyopop (2006–ongoing) • Akita Shoten (Princess, 2001–2006) • 15 volumes • Shôjo, Occult, Romance, Drama • 13+ (language, mild sexual situations)

A girl is forced by her grandfather's will to become the fiancée of a rich, handsome young man, who later turns out to have a secret: he's a medium who can bring back the souls of the dead. The supernatural element provides an interesting twist midway through the first volume, but it's almost impossible to recover from *Platinum Garden*'s unappetizing premise, in which the heroine seems destined to learn to love her arranged marriage and heal the wounded heart of her troubled fiancé, et cetera, et cetera. The rest of the plot continues the princess fantasy: the heroine must learn flower arranging and tea ceremony, she must attend a rich girls' school where everyone is jealous of her for marrying such a wealthy guy, and so forth. Average artwork.

★

PLEASE SAVE MY EARTH

Boku no Chikyû wo Mamotte, "(Please) Save/Protect My (Planet) Earth" (ぼくの地球を守って) • Saki Hiwatari • Viz (2003–2007) • Hakusensha (Hana to Yume, 1987–1994) • 21 volumes • Shôjo, Science Fiction, Romance, Drama • 16+ (language, violence, nudity, sex)

Alice, a girl who can hear the thoughts of plants, has strange dreams in which she is observing the Earth from the moon. Soon, she encounters other teenagers—and Rin, a bratty seven-year-old boy—who have had the "moon dreams," and they realize that they are the reincarnations of a group of humanoid alien scientists who observed twentieth-century Earth from a hidden moonbase. As their psychic powers from their former lives reawaken, their past and present identities become confused, and a tragic love triangle of the past comes back to haunt them, with potentially devastating consequences. Slow-paced but incredibly well plotted, *Please Save My Earth* is a masterpiece of young-adult science fiction. Hiwatari reveals the characters' secrets gradually, using overt psychic powers sparingly, before switching to multivolume flashbacks retelling the events of their alien pasts. The art is distinctive, full of plant life and flower symbolism, and becomes more polished and "modern" as it goes on. The writing is believable and dramatic with occasional comic relief (the early volumes have many in-jokes referring to 1980s anime and manga, scrupulously annotated by the editor). Initially the story is suitable for young readers, but things take a dark turn around volume 9. The adult elements come naturally from the story, however, and the plot is consistently rewarding and unpredictable.   ★★★★

POKÉMON: THE ELECTRIC TALE OF PIKACHU

Pocket Monsters Dengeki Pikachu, "Pocket Monsters Electric Shock Pikachu" (ポケットモンスター 電撃ピカチュウ) • Toshihiro Ono (story and art), Tsunekazu Ishihara & Satoshi Tajiri (original creators) • Viz (1998–2000) • Shogakukan (Corocoro Comic, 1997–1999) • 4 volumes • Video Game, Action, Comedy • Unrated/All Ages

Published as four unnumbered books (*The Electric Tale of Pikachu, Pikachu Shocks Back, Electric Pikachu Boogaloo,* and *Surf's Up, Pikachu*), this *Pokémon* spin-off roughly follows the plot of the anime, with some entirely new stories. Toshihiro Ono's sleek, friendly art is a good match for the material, although his fanboy tastes for big-breasted girls resulted in the series being censored in both the United States (where bustlines were reduced, swimsuits expanded, and dirty jokes rewritten) and Japan (where a few suggestive panels were redrawn between the original magazine publication and the graphic novel edition). Ono is clearly a science fiction fan as well, to judge from the futuristic technology and even mecha that he throws into the story.   ★★½

POKÉMON: PIKACHU MEETS THE PRESS

Gerard Jones (story), Ashura Benimaru (art), GAME FREAK (original creators) • Viz (2001) • 1 volume • Video Game Comedy • Unrated/All Ages

A collection of the short-lived *Pokémon* newspaper strip, created originally for American audiences. Gerard Jones, normally an excellent comic and book writer, here works in the "supposed to be funny but not really funny" school of strip writing,

while Ashura Benimaru (who used to draw comics in the back of *Nintendo Power*) draws in an awkward, big-footed "American" style. (Is this what it looks like when Americans try to draw manga?) Little advantage is taken of *Pokémon*'s unique qualities (the Pokémon talk, and certain characterizations seem to be based on *Magical Pokémon Journey*), and the plot follows a "kid and his imaginary friends/talking animal pals" formula.   ★½

POKÉMON ADVENTURES

Pocket Monsters Special (ポケットモンスター Special) • Hidenori Kusaka (story), Mato (art), Tsunekazu Ishihara & Satoshi Tajiri (original creators) • Viz (2000–2001) • Shogakukan (Shogaku Sannensei/Shogaku Yonnensei/Shogaku Gonensei/Shogaku Rokunensei, 1997–ongoing) • 7 volumes (25+ volumes in Japan, ongoing) • Video Game, Action • Unrated/All Ages

One of the weakest of the translated *Pokémon* spin-off manga, *Pokémon Adventures* is a direct adaptation of the original Game Boy games. Written for elementary school students, it has simple cartoony art with lots of big sound effects (apparently influenced by American comics), and the story lines are those of fighting manga, with Pokémon trainers constantly dueling one another. Despite some fun battles, the series adds nothing to the game and has little to appeal to older readers. (For that matter, you may want to give the kids something a little more challenging.) Selected stories were later repackaged under the name *Best of Pokémon Adventures*.   ★½

POKÉMON MYSTERY DUNGEON

Pokémon Fushigi no Dungeon: Ginji no Kyûjotai, "Pokémon Mystery Dungeon: Ginji's Rescue Team" (ポケモン不思議のダンジョン・ギンジの救助 隊) • Makoto Mizubuchi • Nintendo/Viz (2006–2007) • Shogakukan (Corocoro Comic, 2006) • 1 volume • Shônen, Video Game, Adventure • All Ages

Adaptation of the video game of the same name. Ginji, an ordinary kid, finds himself turned into a Pokémon and pushed into an

POLITICS (政治)

Japanese political comics (also known as *seiji manga*) fall into three types: (1) editorial cartoons, which have existed since the late 1800s; (2) mainstream story manga, usually aimed at adults, with political themes; and (3) a small number of "pundit manga" or "essay manga."

Japan is a parliamentary democracy, with much in common with the British government; power is concentrated in the legislature, known as the National Diet. Diet members elect the prime minister, who is then ceremonially appointed by the emperor, whose power is only symbolic. Since 1955, Japanese politics has been dominated by a single party, the Liberal Democratic Party (LDP). The LDP is composed of various factions but is generally conservative (despite their name), pro-business, and in favor of strong ties to the United States. The biggest opposition party, the Democratic Party of Japan, is a coalition of more left-wing forces.

Although political themes are now rare in manga, there was a time when manga were considered a subversive medium. Rocked with student protests, the early 1960s was the most turbulent period of postwar Japanese history, and many young radicals embraced manga (such as Sampei Shirato's ninja comics) as a blue-collar people's art form. During the late 1960s and early 1970s, even mainstream *shônen* manga often dealt with extremely adult political themes; *Weekly Shônen Sunday* ran *Mao Tse Tung,* a long, untranslated manga about the Chinese cultural revolution drawn by *Doraemon* creators Fujiko F. Fujio, while *Weekly Shônen Jump* ran stories such as *Barefoot Gen* and *Ningen no Jôken* ("The Human Condition"), protesting against American army bases in Japan. Action comics including *Cyborg 009* and *Wild 7* featured Vietnam War story lines; the *Cyborg 009* story is translated in the Tokyopop edition. The boxing manga *Ashita no Jo* ("Tomorrow's Joe"), whose dirt-poor rebel hero always pointed out the hypocrisy of the system, was also popular with student radicals. When the terrorist Japanese Red Army hijacked a plane to North Korea in 1970, they melodramatically proclaimed to the press, "We are Tomorrow's Joe!"

But as the Japanese standard of living rose in the 1970s, former protesters became apolitical and middle-class, and the same manga magazines that had pandered to the student movement gradually turned to other trends. Today, Japan has an even lower voting rate than the United States. When major manga publishers produce political stories, usually in *seinen* magazines, they are often traditional "one good man" stories calculated to restore the reader's faith in the political system. In Kenshi Hirokane's 1991 *Kaji Ryûsuke no Gi* ("Ryûsuke Kaji's Principles") the title character, a businessman, inherits the support of his dead father's LDP constituency and is pressured into accepting his father's Diet seat (not an uncommon event in Japan). He soon confronts, and struggles against, political corruption. A similar plot, aimed at younger readers, occurs in Masashi Asaki and Tadashi Aga's *Kunimitsu no Matsuri* ("Kunimitsu's Government"), which ran from 2001 to 2005 in *Weekly Shônen Magazine;* the fiery teenage hero starts out as a politician's secretary. In *Sanctuary* (1990) there's a twist; the idealistic politician also has support from an equally idealistic, and ruthless, *yakuza.* On a more satirical note, Kenny Nabeshima and Tsukasa Maekawa's 1989 *Hyôden no Tractor* ("Constituency Tractor") pokes fun at pork-barrel politics and fund-raising.

What issues do political manga involve? Although Japanese politicians do care about being perceived as morally upstanding (right-wing Tokyo governor Shintaro Ishihara, despite having gone on the record as a fan of mainstream anime and manga, triggered one of the periodic national campaigns against adult manga), many social issues that are controversial topics in the United States, such as abortion and gay rights, are not even on the radar. The economy is a frequent topic of debate, as is the environment, the latter even in mainstream *shôjo* and *shônen* manga. One of the most common topics in international politics, and one that stands out to American eyes, is the debate surrounding Japan's close ties to America, America's military bases on Japanese soil, and the modification of the postwar Japanese Constitution to permit a standing military independent of American aid. (See the article on MILITARY.) *The First President of Japan* (1998), picturing a powerful Japan breaking free of American interference and coming to prominence in a series of Asian military crises, is typical. Even *Eagle* (1997), by politically savvy manga artist Kaiji Kawaguchi, uses an American presidential election to deal with issues of interest to the Japanese public; after winning his party's nomination, the Vietnam-vet presidential candidate announces his intention to close all foreign U.S. military bases, to avoid another unwinnable war.

Japan's actual attitude toward America is more complex than these summaries suggest, but modern political manga are more often than not aimed at middle-aged businessmen, and international politics make better escapism than thorny domestic issues such as women's rights. *Japan* and *Strain,* outwardly apolitical action manga by Buronson, aka Sho Fumimura (the writer of *Sanctuary*), express the opinion that the younger generation is spoiled and that Japanese tourists should be concerned how they represent their country when abroad; the convoluted plot of *Strain* involves the heroes' pan-Asian racial alliance to control oil resources in the Pacific Rim. In 2003, *Weekly Shônen Magazine* ran a column and a manga about the effects of depleted uranium bullets on civilians in the Iraq war. In 2004, Hiroshi Motomiya's *Kuni ga Moeru* ("The Country Is Burning"), a manga dealing with the infamous World War II Nanjing Massacre, was pulled from Shueisha's mainstream *Young Jump* magazine after right-wing protesters and politicians complained that it used falsified photographs as source material and that there was no proof the massacre ever happened. In recent years, the venerable magazine *Manga Action* has become notable for its manga on current events and controversial historical subjects, such as *Town of Evening Calm, Country of Cherry Blossoms* (2003), a story about Hiroshima, and several other stories about the real-life kidnapping of Japanese citizens by North Korea.

In the early 1990s, a new kind of political manga appeared in Japan, in the form of Yoshinori Kobayashi's *Gômanism Sengen* ("The Arrogance Manifesto") in the weekly news magazine *Spa*. Kobayashi's manga was a multiple-page first-person opinion piece in comics form, and he took a funny but angry "shock jock" approach, combining anti-authoritarian and anti-American viewpoints, opposing censorship while expressing frequently right-wing views on subjects such as AIDS, foreigners, and women. In 1995, his revisionist attitude toward the Nanjing Massacre (like that of the right-wingers who protested *Kuni ga Moeru*) led to clashes with his publisher, and Kobayashi's strip moved to the rival magazine *Sapio*. *Spa* replaced Kobayashi with another "pundit manga" by conservative manga artist Tatsuya Egawa. Kobayashi's abrasive style has influenced other artists, such as Sharin Yamano, creator of the 2005 *Manga Kenkanryû* ("Hating the Korean Wave"). Mitsuru Kitano, of the Japanese embassy in Washington, responded to such controversies by pointing to polls indicating that Japanese feelings about South Korea have improved in recent years, and that nationalists and revisionists are merely more vocal.

Political Manga

Bakune Young • *Barefoot Gen* • *Cyborg 009* • *Eagle: The Making of an Asian-American President* • *The First President of Japan* • *Japan Inc.: An Introduction to Japanese Economics* (*The Comic Book*) • *Monster* • *The Rebel Sword* • *Revenge of Mouflon* • *Sanctuary* • *The Times of Botchan* • *Town of Evening Calm, Country of Cherry Blossoms* • *Wild 7*

---

all-Pokémon world, where he fights opponents and goes on a quest. Basic stuff for very young readers, with simple but competent art. Serialized in *Nintendo Power* magazine prior to the graphic novel edition. NR

POPCORN ROMANCE

Tôkibi Batake de Love & Peace, "Love and Peace in a Cornfield" (とうきび畑でラブ＆ピース) • Tomoko Taniguchi • CPM (2003) • Jitsugyo no Nihonsha (1992) • 1 volume • Shôjo, Romantic Comedy • All Ages

Zenta and Ryouta, two teenage brothers who star in a Japanese visual rock band, return to their grandpa's farm for health reasons and find themselves fighting to save the farm from developers. A predictable kids' story with a mild environmental theme. Most of the fun comes from cross-dressing Zenta's adjustment to farm life, and there is a nice plot involving Ryouta and Shima, the girl he left behind in the city. Also includes "The Magic of Love," a short story about acne. ★★

POPO CAN

(ポポ缶) • Masakazu Iwasaki • Infinity Studios (2005) • MediaWorks (Dengeki Daioh, 2003–2004) • 3 volumes • Shônen, Otaku, Comedy • 13+ (language, crude humor, mild violence)

One would think the greatest dream for a young male video game junkie is to buy a new game, pop it into the console, and then promptly have a sexy lady fall out of your television and into your lap. Unfortunately for Yasuharu, the sexy lady in question is Popomi, whose scatterbrained antics proceed to make his life an utter nightmare. *Popo Can* is a gag manga written in short chapters with little plot. The art is crisp and charming, if generic; the stories are sometimes funny, but the sheer randomness is difficult to get through at times. (LW) ★★

LA PORTRAIT DE PETITE COSSETTE

Cossette no Shôzô, "Cossette's Portrait" (コセットの肖像) • Cossette House/Aniplex (story), Asuka Katsura (art) • Tokyopop (2006) • Kodansha (Magazine Z, 2004) • 2 volumes • Gothic, Horror • 16+ (graphic violence)

Well-drawn but unexceptional gothic manga based on the anime of the same name. While working part time at an antiques shop, Eiri discovers a haunted portrait of a girl from eighteenth-century France and soon encounters her ghost. Cossette tells Eiri that her former possessions have been cursed to bring misfortune to those who own them; the plot involves the unfortunate fates of these owners as well as Cossette's own mysterious, disturbing motivations. The plot diverges from the anime. ★★

PRETEAR: THE NEW LEGEND OF SNOW WHITE

Shin Shirayuki-hime Densetsu Pretear, "New Snow White Legend Pretear" (新白雪姫伝説プリテイア) • Junichi Satou (original creator), Kaori Naruse (manga) • ADV (2004) • Kadokawa Shoten

(Asuka, 2000–2001) • 4 volumes • Shôjo, Fantasy, Drama • All Ages

In this magical girl blend of *Cinderella* and *Snow White and the Seven Dwarfs*, high school freshman Himeno balances the cruelty of her wicked stepmother and stepsisters with her duties to the seven *bishônen* Leafe Knights from the mystical realm Leafeania. Himeno is the Pretear, the legendary creater of Leafe, the source of all life and power in Leafeania and Earth. Himeno's power allows her to bond with the other Leafe knights and wield their elemental power; this also allows her to change into up to seven different magical girl costumes, which is a staple of any magical girl series. The story manages a decent plot twist in any given volume, which keeps the story interesting. However, some story elements feel rushed and unresolved by the end. (MJS)

★★½

PRETTY FACE

(プリティフェイス) • Yasuhiro Kano • Viz (2007–2008) • Shueisha (Weekly Shônen Jump, 2002–2003) • 6 volumes • Shônen, Romantic Comedy • 16+ (mild language, mild violence, nudity, sexual situations)

When teenage tough guy Rando gets into a horrible car accident, a mad plastic surgeon reconstructs his horribly burned face based on the photo in his wallet: *a photo of Rina, the girl he had a crush on!* Now bearing a cute female face atop an ectomorphic male body, Rando finds that his family has left him for dead and moved away, and he is mistaken for Rina's twin sister and adopted into her family. As insane as *Midori Days,* but sticking closer to the original premise, the laudably sick and twisted premise is played for all it's worth. There's every imaginable kind of cross-dressing, fake-breast wearing, pseudo-lesbian sexual tease (but no actual touching or pseudo-molestation), and countless scenes of the main character beating annoying guys to a pulp, possibly to the point of excess. The artwork is polished, funny, and titillating, with nice freak-out facial expressions; unfortunately, the conclusion is abrupt. (AT)

★★★½

PRETTY MANIACS

Pretty Maniis, "Pretty Maniacs" (ぷりてぃまにいず) • Shinsuke Kurihashi • DrMaster (2005–2006) • MediaWorks (Dengeki Daioh, 2004–2005) • 3 volumes • Shônen, Otaku, Comedy • 13+ (brief partial nudity, mild sexual situations)

Stand-alone sequel to *Maniac Road,* transplanting the same old-school *otaku* aesthetic into a cast of teenage girls. (Perhaps they were considered more reader-friendly than thirty-something male nerds.) Cute, geeky Shinano (the little sister of Takezou from the previous series) moves to a new high school and becomes president of the ailing manga club, which she must build from the ground up while trying to make friends with other nerds. Some of the geeky details are spot-on (such as intolerant art teachers who hate manga), while others feel slightly quaint (such as a lesson in old-fashioned bookbinding). Initially the cast is entirely female, but some male teenagers appear in volume 2, bringing romantic subplots with them. On the whole, though, the author's enthusiasm doesn't quite overcome the lack of plot and the generic, slightly old-fashioned art. ★★½

THE PRINCE OF TENNIS

Tennis no Ôjisama, "Prince of Tennis" (テニスの王子様) • Takeshi Konomi • Viz (2004–ongoing) • Shueisha (Weekly Shônen Jump, 1999–ongoing) • 37+ volumes (ongoing) • Shônen, Sports • All Ages (mild language, mild violence)

Seventh-grader Ryoma Echizen, the quietly smug son of a retired tennis master, joins his junior high tennis team and shocks everyone by trouncing bigger, older players. With Ryoma on their side (along with plenty of other good players), the Seishun Junior High team fights their way to the national tournament. *Prince of Tennis* is almost pure action, with a dizzyingly huge cast of good-looking boys whose lives off the court are left mostly to the readers' imagination. Each character has his specialized techniques, quirks, and signature phrases (Ryoma: "You've still got a ways to go"). The tennis details are authentic, and the straightforward art reads quickly, but the plot blurs into what feels like an endless tennis match, without humor or subplots to provide variety. If you're into cool boys and/or tennis, this is your manga, but it falls short of crossover appeal. In Japan, the manga was so popular with girls that it was adapted into a dating simulation video game allowing you to platonically spend time with the male characters. ★★½

PRINCESS AI

Princess Ai Monogatari, "The Story of Princess Ai" (プリンセス・アイ物語) • Courtney Love (co-creator), DJ Milky (co-creator and co-scripter), Misaho Kujiradou (co-scripter, art) • Tokyopop (2004–2006) • Shinshokan (Wings, 2004–2005) • 3 volumes • Shôjo, Musical, Romance, Fantasy • 13+ (language, violence, brief partial nudity)

One of the few U.S.-Japan manga collaborations actually published in Japan before it appeared in America, *Princess Ai* reinvents Courtney Love as a tousle-haired rock star bombshell with ripped-up Goth-Loli clothes, based on a guest character design by Ai Yazawa. (The manga itself is drawn by Misaho Kujiradou, whose best features are pretty faces.) Love's alter ego, Ai, wakes up with amnesia in a poorly drawn Tokyo alley, having forgotten that she is the princess of Ai-Land, a faraway realm where humans war with *dougen* (angels and demons). Wandering the streets feeling alone, she falls in love with a young guitarist, but she is pursued by miniskirted demonesses from her home world and exploited for her musical talent by an evil record company. The clichéd plot—whose movie-like three-act structure shows an American hand behind the wheel—has elements of a musical, with numerous singing scenes, mostly featuring original song lyrics written by DJ Milky. While the reader learns lessons about the power of love and the importance of tolerance, Ai tries to be every imaginable kind of heroine: one moment she's watching a cat give birth to kittens, the next she's in love, the next she's in angry rock star mode, complaining, "Screw H.T.A. and screw music!" and "I'm not some submissive sex slave!" More entertaining for its very existence than for the story, it's mostly of interest to younger readers. (AT) ★★

PRINCESS KNIGHT

Ribon no Kishi, "Knight of Ribbons" (リボンの騎士) • Osamu Tezuka • Kodansha International (2001) • Kodansha (Nakayoshi, 1963–1966) • 6 volumes • Shôjo, Magical Girl, Fantasy • All Ages

Often cited as the first modern *shôjo* manga, Tezuka's proto-feminist fantasy ran through four different serialized versions in the 1950s and 1960s. This is the third and best-known version, basically a more polished black-and-white retelling of the original series (a color comic that ran in *Shôjo Club* magazine in the 1950s). Princess Sapphire, born with both a male heart and a female heart due to a mix-up in heaven, disguises herself as a prince to inherit the throne. She enjoys swashbuckling adventures as a boy and Cinderella-style romantic escapades as a girl, while the scheming Duke Duralmin plots to expose the "prince's" true gender. A cherub named Tink follows her in mortal form, trying to convince her to give up her male heart and become an ordinary girl. Fairy-tale fantasy mixes with confused Christianity, as angels and devils get involved in Princess Sapphire's plight. *Princess Knight* introduces many elements that would become common in *shôjo* manga: a Western-style fantasy setting, a plucky heroine with extra-sparkly eyes, a cute supernatural sidekick, and, of course, female cross-dressing. The clean, stylized artwork, distinguished by simple shapes and bold patterns, represents some of the better work of Tezuka's middle period. (SG) ★★★½

PRINCESS MERMAID: See *Junko Mizuno's Princess Mermaid*

PRINCESS NINJA SCROLL TENKA MUSÔ

Himesama Ninpôcho Tenka • Mûsô, "Princess Ninja Scroll, Without Equal in the Whole World" • (姫様忍法著天下・無双) • Akane Sasaki • DMP (2005) • Square Enix (Monthly Gangan Wing, 2002–2003) • 2 volumes • Fantasy, Adventure, Comedy • 13+ (violence)

Hanzou Hattori, a little-girl ninja who "grows up" (i.e., gets bustier) when she uses her powers, goes on a quest against the evil Nobunaga and his legions of machine soldiers. The historical Japanese names are just tossed slapdash into this abysmal anime-style comedy-adventure, consisting mostly of giant explosions that wipe out the bad guys, with no buildup. **0 Stars**

PRINCESS PRINCE

(プリンセス・プリンス) • Tomoko Taniguchi • CPM (2002) • Jitsugyo no Nihonsha (1994) • 1 volume • Shôjo, Fantasy, Romantic Comedy • Unrated/13+ (violence, brief nudity)

In a fantasy kingdom live Prince Matthew, a handsome narcissist, and "Princess" Lori . . . actually Matthew's brother Lawrence, a long-haired but normal boy whose father raised him in the image of his dead mother ("See, I'm really a prince, too! I'm not a transvestite"). A lighthearted comedy-adventure for young readers, *Princess Prince* is entertaining and cutely drawn, but there is no resolution to most of the plot threads, which involve prophecies, magic gems, and Lori's identity. One of the stories has an antiracism message. Two interesting unrelated fantasy stories round out the volume: "Durga," a violent tale of a boy with a magic sword, and "The Tale of the Castle of Tears," a dramatic fairy tale that is the best story in the collection. **★★**

PRINCESS PRINCESS

(プリンセス・プリンセス) • Mikiyo Tsuda • DMP (2006–ongoing) • Shinshokan (Wings, 2002–2006) • 5 volumes • Shôjo, Comedy • 16+ (mild sexual situations)

Manga set in an all-boys school where the students deal with the lack of women by assigning certain students the roles of "princesses"—pretty boys who cross-dress at school events and serve as general-purpose cheerleaders. Of the three main characters, two enjoy playing girls, while one resents it, which unfortunately makes him even more popular when he's forced to put on Gothic Lolita clothes and parade around campus. A more than usually boring "guys' school" *shôjo* manga, the premise goes nowhere and the action is dialogue-driven, with the generically pretty characters talking and talking and endlessly explaining the school rules rather than actually doing anything. (Despite the 16+ rating, the series is light on *bishônen* innuendo, and even cross-dressing, for that matter.) For whatever reason, in Japan the series was popular enough to be adapted into a video game, an anime series, and a live-action TV drama. In 2006 Tsuda started a sequel series, *Princess Princess +*. **★½**

PRINCESS RESURRECTION

Kaibutsu Ôujo, "Monster Queen" (怪物王女) • Yasunori Mitsunaga • Del Rey (2007–ongoing) • Kodansha (Shônen Sirius, 2005–ongoing) • 4+ volumes (ongoing) • Shônen, Horror, Comedy • 16+ (graphic violence)

The good news is that young Hiro has been magically revived after a fatal accident. The bad news is that he's now the undead bodyguard of Princess Hime, a chain saw–toting member of the royal family who reigns over the creatures of the night, and her siblings are eager to thin out the waiting list for the throne. Gruesome hijinks and monster battles naturally follow. (MS) **NR**

PRINCESS TUTU

(プリンセスチュチュ) • Ikuko Itoh & Jun-ichi Satoh (story), Mizuo Shinonome (art) • ADV (2004–2005) • Akita Shoten (Champion Red, 2002–2003) • 2 volumes • Seinen, Magical Girl, Fantasy • 13+ (partial nudity)

Adaptation of the anime series of the same name. A magic necklace turns clumsy ballet student Arima into the graceful ballerina Princess Tutu, who uses her powers to restore the lost pieces of a prince's heart. Perhaps the strangest magical girl series outside of *Revolutionary Girl Utena, Princess Tutu* operates under a dreamlike logic all its own; there's never any context for the ballet-school setting, which seems to exist outside of time, and the shards of the heart have inexplicably turned into giant animals that

Princess Tutu has to tame. The second volume ramps up the weirdness, with girls turning into ducks, a cat ballet instructor who threatens his students with marriage, and the sinister Servants of the Raven. In an afterword, co-creator Satoh describes it as a "fairy tale," which is probably the best explanation. If Hans Christian Andersen had been a *shôjo* manga artist, he might have come up with something like this. A more expressive, daring art style might have turned this fable into a minor cult classic, but Shinonome's art is merely serviceable. (SG)   ★★

THE PROFESSIONAL: GOLGO 13: See *Golgo 13*

PROJECT ARMS

ARMS (アームズ) • Kyoichi Nanatsuki (story), Ryoji Minagawa (art) • Viz (2003–ongoing) • Shogakukan (Weekly Shônen Sunday, 1997–2002) • 22 volumes • Shônen, Military, Science Fiction, Action • 16+ (language, graphic violence)

Four teenagers, victims of childhood medical experiments by the seemingly omnipotent Egrigori organization, are ripped out of their everyday lives when they develop superpowers . . . first in the form of biomechanical arms and legs, then full-body transformations into ever-evolving, demonic monsters who may bring about the apocalypse. A grim, gory science fiction power fantasy, *Project Arms* manages to combine a complicated, onion-layered plot with near-constant fighting, although the ever-escalating ranks of bad guys (the cyborgs, the X-Army, the Red Caps . . .) must strain the resources of even the wealthiest global conspiracy. As the heroes travel across the world in search of revenge and the truth, their path is paved with angst, trauma, throwaway H. P. Lovecraft references, and *Akira*-esque massive destruction. Compared to *Spriggan*, Minagawa's artwork has become more stylized, his characters' faces distorted and lopsided almost to the point of inhumanity. The action is fast-paced and the monsters are imaginative, making for a predictable but effective page-turner.   ★★★

Akira Yokoyama's *Project X—The Challengers*

PROJECT X

(プロジェクトX) • various artists • DMP (2006) • Ohzora Shuppon (2003) • 3 volumes • Historical, Nonfiction • All Ages

Informative business manga are a subgenre of manga rarely seen in English translation. *Project X* is based on a Japanese TV series showcasing business success stories. The first volume follows the development and marketing of the Datsun 240 Z, or, as the cover puts it, "the legend of the most successful sports car in the world." The second volume dramatizes the development of Cup Noodle, and the third follows the history of the 7-Eleven franchise in Japan. It's the great-man model of history, white-collar style: a small group of visionary executives, salesmen, and engineers struggles to transform an area of Japanese industry. Despite vast enthusiasm for its subject matter, the series is fairly bland, consisting mostly of lightboxed drawings of products and close-ups of beaming employees shouting things like, "Yes!! I'll do my best!" But it may

PSYCHIC (超能力・エスパー)

Psychics, along with NINJA and MARTIAL ARTS characters, are one of the classic forms of native-grown Japanese superheroes; the term *chônôryoku,* "supernatural powers," is used to describe ESP as well as American-style superheroes.

The themes originated in the works of Japanese science fiction writers, who were themselves influenced by Western stories of psychic mutants such as A. E. Van Vogt's *Slan* (1946). Sakyo Komatsu's 1965 novel *ESPY* (about a team of ESP-using spies, of course) was an early hit that was adapted into a movie. Sci-fi writer Kazumasa Hirai created the series *Genma Taisen* ("The Great War with Genma"), in which a team of psychics of various backgrounds gather to save Earth from an all-powerful entity who roams the galaxy destroying planets; the premise has echoes of the alien superbeing Galactus from the *Fantastic Four.* Beginning as a manga drawn by Shotaro Ishinomori in 1967, *Genma Taisen* was adapted into several novels and sequel manga series, and the apocalyptic anime movie *Harmagedon* in 1983. Its visions of Tokyo demolished by psychic battles were an influence on CLAMP's *X/1999* (1992), and the anime movie adaptation of *X/1999* was handled by the same director, Rin Taro. Also in 1967 began Yuki Hijiri's still-running manga *Chôjin Locke* ("Locke the Superman"), originally a *dôjinshi,* the centuries-spanning story of a psychic superhero who travels through space fighting evil. Tsuguo Okazaki's *Justy* (1981) follows the same formula. In Keiko Takemiya's *To Terra* (1977), psychics are the one random factor in the computer-controlled space colonies of the future.

Although psychic powers, unlike magic, are theoretically measurable and have some pseudo-scientific explanation, most artists, such as the classic 1960s and 1970s artist Mitsuteru Yokoyama, treated them as essentially superpowers. Even a well-plotted story such as Saki Hiwatari's *Please Save My Earth* (1987) assumes that the reader knows how psychic powers "work," with much telekinetic clashing and energy blasts, whether the perpetrator is a human psychic or an alien being reincarnated in human form. On the other hand, some portrayals were more realistic and speculative, such as Yasutaka Tsutsui's 1975 science fiction novel *Nanase Futatabi* ("Nanase Once More"), which was adapted into a live-action TV series and later the manga *The Telepathic Wanderers.* Tsutsui's heroine can't leap to the top of skyscrapers or destroy things, but her ability to read minds is explored in detail. By far the most influential portrayal of psychic powers in manga, however, were the works of Katsuhiro Otomo. Otomo had already attracted attention with *Domu: A Child's Dream* (1980), in which a senile old man uses psychic powers to torment and kill the inhabitants of a rundown tenement, but in *Akira* (1982) he unleashed the whirlwind. Set in a near-future twenty-first-century Tokyo, *Akira* involved a government-sponsored experiment that created psychics so powerful they could unleash a force equal to nuclear bombs. But the power is too much for the human mind and body to bear, and madness and mass destruction result. Such themes had been handled before, but never with such jaw-dropping detailed, realistic artwork; *Akira* was the manga equivalent of a big-budget science fiction movie, and inaugurated a "psychic boom" in manga and anime of the 1980s. In the 1990s, the *Final Fantasy* video game series introduced Americans to the term *ESPer,* a popular Japanese term for a still-common manga archetype.

In their 1989 satire *Even a Monkey Can Draw Manga,* written when psychic manga were everywhere, Kentaro Takekuma and Koji Aihara claimed that psychics were the perfect replacement for ninjas in Japan's then-booming economy; whereas ninjas developed their powers through painstaking training and self-sacrifice, psychics didn't have to exert any effort. Instead, they joked, the most common scene in psychic manga was the "no, boom" scene, in which the heroes are goaded or tormented into some emotional outburst ("Nooo!"), whereupon their powers spontaneously activate and they kill the bad guys in a huge explosion (*"boom"*). Manga readers will have to determine the accuracy of Takekuma and Aihara's theory for themselves.

Psychic Manga

Akira • Aquarian Age: Juvenile Orion • Baoh • Broken Angels • Calling You: Kimi ni Shika Kikoenai • Central City • Ceres: Celestial Legend • Clover • Dead End • Domu: A Child's Dream • The Empty Empire • ES (Eternal Sabbath) • E'S • Gatekeepers • Genocyber • Hands Off! • Horobi • Justy • Kamui • Land of the Blindfolded • Mai the Psychic Girl • Maxion • Miracle Girls • Möbius Klein • Moon Child • My Code Name Is Charmer • Pieces of a Spiral • Please Save My Earth • Project Arms • Psychic Academy • Psychonauts • RA-I • The Ring • Rumic World Trilogy • Sakura Taisen • Secret Chaser • Seraphic Feather • Silent Möbius • Striker • Telepathic Wanderers • To Terra • Twilight of the Dark Master • Wild Com. • X/1999

intrigue Western readers curious about lesser-known genres such as "salaryman manga," and there's an inarguable oddball appeal to a manga about Cup Noodle. Each volume also includes bonus informational material like timelines and photographs (the "Trail of Cup Noodle" spread showcasing the history of noodle packaging design is particularly stunning). (SG)   ★½

PSYCHIC ACADEMY

Psychic Academy Oura Banshô, "Psychic Academy Universal Aura" (サイキックアカデミー煌羅万象) • Katsu Aki • Tokyopop (2004–2006) • Kodansha (Magazine Z, 1999–2003) • 11 volumes • Shônen, Psychic, Romantic Comedy, Action • 13+/16+ (language, mild violence, sexual situations, partial nudity)

This weakly drawn but adequately written series reads like a Japanese high school comedy version of *X-Men*. In the near future, science has discovered the existence of psychic mutants, who are trained at Japan's elite Psychic Academy, as well as other parts of the world. Ai, the shy little brother of the legendary superhero Zerodyme, transfers to the school and is caught in a love triangle. The plot includes corny dialogue and accidental breast groping, as well as a wisecracking telepathic rabbit, but there's also more serious sci-fi melodrama, involving prejudice against mutants, dream visions, and sinister scientific researchers. The superhero element comes through in the energy-blasting battle scenes, as well as the women's skintight outfits, which together with the anime-style pink hair, creates a kind of cultural train wreck. A decent series for younger teenage readers (although volume 11 contains nudity and is rated for older teens).   ★★

PSYCHONAUTS

(サイコノーツ) • Alan Grant & Tony Luke (story), Motofumi Kobayashi (art) • Marvel/Epic (1993–1994) • Nihon Shuppansha (1990) • 4 issues • Postapocalyptic, Psychic, Science Fiction • Unrated/13+ (mild language, graphic violence)

One of the first high-profile collaborations between Japanese and Western talent (though not *the* first; see *Samurai, Son of Death*). In the year 2199, the space colonies send a squad of six psychics (a samurai, a Native American mystic, etc.) on a mission to the polluted planet Earth, to see if it is once again capable of supporting human life. Once on the planet's surface, the Psychonauts encounter every sci-fi monster in the book, including zombie soldiers, dinosaurs, killer cyborgs, lizard men, slime mold, and a tentacled mutant overlord from another dimension. Motofumi Kobayashi's stiffly detailed style is just like a Western comic, and Tony Grant and Alan Luke's script reads like a fun comic from the British magazine *2000 AD*. In color. ★★★

PUNCH!

Rie Takada • Viz (2006–2007) • Shogakukan (Shôjo Comic, 2005–2006) • 3 volumes • Shôjo, Action, Romance • 13+ (mild violence, partial nudity, sexual situations)

Elle Nagahara is the granddaughter of the first Japanese Muay Thai champion and the daughter of the world's lightweight boxing champion and the world's wrestling champion—and she hates everything martial arts! Too bad she lives at her grandfather's gym and was engaged in the cradle to boxer Ruo. Elle tries to live a normal life and date normal guys, but her fiancé's gym goons always scare off her dates . . . until she meets street-fighting hoodlum Kazuki Shindo. Love soon flourishes as Elle becomes Kazuki's trainer. The art is typical Takada adorable, with the guys drawn super hot and Elle switching between cute and super-cute *chibi* as needed. At three volumes, the story avoids the common manga pitfall of dragging on too long, and instead serves up just the right portion of romantic fun. (HS) ★★★

PURE TRANCE

(ピュア・トランス) • Junko Mizuno • Last Gasp (2005) • East Press (1998) • 1 volume • Underground, Science Fiction • 18+ (language, violence, nudity, sexual situations)

Junko Mizuno's first major work, this genuinely underground manga was originally printed in a series of techno CD booklets. In the postapocalyptic future, humanity dwells in a city beneath the Earth's crust, and people eat synthetic food in the form of handfuls of pills. Keiko, the hypodermic-needle-covered, sadistic director of an Overeaters' Treatment Center, cruelly abuses her subordinates, until nurse Kaori escapes to the surface, pursued by Kimiko, a scarred security guard. *Pure Trance* combines the plot of a 1970s science fiction movie with the trashiness of Russ Meyer. As always in Mizuno's comics, the men are squat, potato-like ciphers and the women are violent, lusty dolls in lingerie and furs, gnawing hunks of meat, wielding whips and weapons. And the art, the *art!* Mizuno's mandala-like art is dense and delirious, with every inch of space crammed with hearts, test tubes, stuffed animals, sex toys, blood. But throughout all the madness, the story has a solid old-school quality, showing the influence of Osamu Tezuka, with lots of twists and turns and characters. A female-dominated playland of violence, addiction, and sex, Mizuno's work has both frightening and alluring qualities, like an exploitation story told with dolls. ★★★½

PURGATORY KABUKI

Yasushi Suzuki • DrMaster (2007) • 1 volume • Occult, Samurai, Action • 13+

Original manga project commissioned by DrMaster, featuring artwork by video game designer Yasushi Suzuki. Imanoturugi, a dead samurai, determines to leave the afterlife for purposes unknown. If he can gather one thousand blades from the other fallen warriors in the underworld, he will be allowed to return to the living world. NR

PURI PURI

Puri Puri: The Premature Priest (プリプリThe Premature Priest) • Chiaki Taro • DrMaster (2007–ongoing) • Akita Shoten (Monthly Shônen Champion, 2004–ongoing) • 6+ volumes (ongoing) • Shônen, Romantic Comedy • 16+

Masato, who wants to become a priest, finds his virtue tested when he becomes the only male student at an all-girls divinity school. Can he endure pranks and sexual temptation and follow his true calling? **NR**

THE PUSH MAN AND OTHER STORIES

Yoshihiro Tatsumi • Drawn & Quarterly (2005) • various magazines, 1969 • 1 volume • Gekiga, Drama • Unrated/18+ (language, violence, nudity, sex)

The first in a series of Tatsumi books by Drawn & Quarterly. Set in the dingy back alleys, factories, and bars of postwar Japan, these short (mostly eight-page) stories of urban alienation are created with incredible raw skill. Tatsumi, who allegedly coined the term *gekiga* ("dramatic pictures") to describe his comics, was inspired by police reports and news stories. The stories dwell on abortion, sexual dysfunction, miserable relationships, and financial troubles; women are mostly victims or villains; and the mood is depressing almost to the point of comedy. His blank-faced protagonists are invariably working-class outcasts, silent loners who bear the abuses of the world with little more than the occasional ". . ." until finally they snap, committing acts of passion, suicide, and murder. "Telescope" involves an impotent, crippled voyeur, "Test Tube" involves a sperm donor, and in "Piranha" a factory worker mutilates himself for insurance money. If they were drawn realistically, the stories would be almost too bleak to read, but the deft artwork combines bold-lined, cartoony characters (more reminiscent of 1950s magazine illustration than comics) with frequently realistic backgrounds. As short stories, they're masterful; with minimal dialogue and exposition, the panels carry the reader visually from deceptively simple setups to sad or shocking climaxes. Prior to the Drawn & Quarterly edition, portions of *The Push Man* (as well as other Tatsumi stories) were published in an unauthorized English edition in 1987 by Spanish publishing house Catalan Communications under the name *Good-Bye and Other Stories*.
★★★★

Yoshihiro Tatsumi's *The Push Man and Other Stories*

Q-KO-CHAN: THE EARTH INVADER GIRL

Q-ko-chan: The Chikyû Shinryaku Shôjo, "Q-Ko-Chan: The Earth Invader Girl" (QコちゃんTHE地球侵略少女) • Hajime Ueda • Del Rey (2006) • Kodansha (Magazine Z, 2002–2004) • 2 volumes • Shônen, Mecha, Action • 13+ (violence)

Sometime in the future, the world's powers are at war, strange aliens are landing, and terraforming "pure bombs" are causing portions of the Earth's ecosystem to travel back in time. Amid all this chaos (most of which is never explained), alien robot girls drop from the sky and find children to pilot them, like the standoffish hero Kirio, who first encounters Q-ko-chan in her humanoid form, begging him, "Please pilot me! I want you to board me!" Like *Alien Nine*, *Q-ko-chan* drops the reader into a bizarre science fiction scenario with no compass except for the relationships between its teenage heroes. Hajime Ueda's super-simplified, scratchy cartoon art is refreshingly simple, but his punk minimalism goes too far, making the story simply hard to follow. Flashes of humor are lost

Hajime Ueda's *Q-ko-chan: The Earth Invader Girl*

Shimizu's characters are realistic but attractive, and Qwan himself is no mere cute rascal; his childish energy has a mysterious, almost sinister quality. In addition to doing a fabulous job with the historical setting and fight scenes, Shimizu writes a good plot, combining historical palace intrigue with supernatural monsters. ★★★★

R² [RISE R TO THE SECOND POWER]

Maki Hakoda • ADV (2004) • Mag Garden (Comic Blade, 2002–2003) • 1 volume, suspended (2 volumes in Japan) • Science Fiction, Adventure • All Ages (brief partial nudity)

Kenta, a pizza delivery boy in the remote city of Lutzheim, lives an ordinary life until a terrorist attack on the city cathedral awakens memories of his forgotten past. Rushing to the scene, he rescues Kano, a sleeping girl whose powers are the target of a struggle between the military government and airship-riding rebels. Like *Desert Coral* and *The First King Adventure*, R^2 is a consciously classy adventure manga, aiming for a mood of gender-neutral storybook fantasy rather than over-the-top action. The art is sketchy but evocative, and the story flows smoothly enough to overlook the adventure-movie clichés (or, as the author puts it in her notes, the "old and familiar themes"). Unfortunately, the series ends abruptly in both America and Japan, leaving volume 1 like a movie trailer for an unfinished film. ★★

RAGNAROK GUY

(ラグナロック・ガイ) • Tsuguo Okazaki • Sun Comic Publishing (1992) • Shogakukan (Weekly Shônen Sunday, 1984–1991) • 6 issues, suspended (7 volumes in Japan) • Shônen, Science Fiction, Action • 13+ (graphic violence)

Guy Graybird, aka Ragnarok Guy, is a wanted man: a cool, tragic hero with the 1980s sci-fi fashion sense of a character from *Robotech* or *Crusher Joe*. He dutifully shoots and punches his way through space-port bars, jungles, and spaceships where everyone is out to get him, and no one will listen to his side of the story. *Guy* has almost no plot, particularly in the small portion avail-

in the incomprehensible, ultimately dull story, which ends so abruptly that the second volume has an epilogue from the translator titled "So What Happened?" ★

QWAN

Kai•Chikara•Ran•Kami Qwan, "Wondrous•Strong•Disruptive•God Qwan") (怪・力・乱・神　クワン) • Aki Shimizu • Tokyopop (2005–ongoing) • Media Factory (Comic Flapper, 2002–ongoing) • 5+ volumes (ongoing) • Historical, Fantasy • 13+ (mild language, graphic violence, mild sexual situations)

China's Han dynasty (206 B.C.–A.D. 220) is crumbling; the emperor is weak, there are ominous portents, and monsters and demons walk the land. Out of the heavens falls Qwan, a mysterious amnesiac boy with super strength, who blithely catches demons and devours them. Together with the medicine seller Chikei and other characters, Qwan goes in search of a sacred scroll said to contain the secrets of the heavens. The first thing to notice about *Qwan* is that the art is incredible; beautiful backgrounds, well-drawn humans, and imaginative monsters.

able in English, but it's a functional action comic. The questionable sound effects include the noises "SHACK" and "SHAT." ★★

RAHXEPHON

(ラーゼフォン) • Yutaka Izubuchi/Bones (original creator), Takeaki Momose (story and art) • Viz (2004) • Shogakukan (Sunday GX, 2001–2003) • 3 volumes • Shônen, Science Fiction, Mecha, Action • 16+ (language, mild violence, nudity)

Manga adaptation of the anime series of the same name, a rip-off of *Neon Genesis Evangelion.* Ayato is an average Japanese high school boy living with a girl named Reika who has a big crush on him. One day after school she is trying to put the moves on him when a tremendous explosion shakes their house, and they learn that reality is not what they thought; they are part of a great mystery involving a giant robot named Rahxephon, whom Ayato must pilot to save the world. Like Shinji from *Evangelion,* Ayato must pilot a robot he knows almost nothing about; also like Shinji, he suffers through a variety of personal problems and is surrounded by hot girls making his feelings and hormones go haywire. Throw in some cooked-up concept of the secret island of Mu and Tokyo being a whole world of its own, and you've got yourself a mystery. While the anime takes a rather serious tone and expands upon the *Rahxepon* mythos, the manga centers on boobies and fan service. (RB) ★

RA-I

Sanami Matoh • Tokyopop (2006) • Biblos (1995) • 1 volume • Shôjo, Psychic, Crime, Comedy • 13+ (mild language, brief violence)

Detective Al Foster gets more than he bargained for when two strange characters walk through his door one day: Rai, a teenager with telekinetic abilities, and Rei, his two-fisted adult big sister. Set in New York and visually almost identical to Sanami Matoh's *Trash* and *Fake,* this is the same formula with psychic powers added; in addition, a straight romantic comedy replaces *Fake's yaoi* dynamic. The mood is pleasantly tongue-in-cheek ("That was one helluva 'hello,' sister"), but Matoh's artwork is weak and her detective plots are uninspired. Rai's telekinesis is mostly used for blasting enemies with fireballs. ★½

RAIKA

Raika (雷火) • Yû Terashima (story), Kamui Fujiwara/Studio 2B (art) • Sun Comic Publishing (1992–1993) • Scholar Publishing (Comic Burger, 1987–1997) • 20 issues, suspended (12 volumes in Japan) • Historical, Ninja, Action • 13+ (mild language, partial nudity, graphic violence)

An action comic set at the dawn of Japanese history, when the historical shaman queen Himiko ruled the land of Yamatai somewhere on the islands of Japan. After Himiko's death, a virgin priestess is groomed as her successor, but Chinese spies and other factions compete to control her; meanwhile, a spiky-haired boy named Raika, who lives with his martial arts master in the nearby wilderness, is caught in the brewing conflict. Raika and his friends and foes fight with *shinsenjutsu,* "mountain magic," the precursor to *ninjutsu;* like the heroes of *The Legend of Kamui (Raika*'s obvious inspiration), they swing through the speed-blurred trees, fling daggers, and perform psychic-magic feats of power. The detailed, realistic artwork shows the influence of Katsuhiro Otomo, and the low-technology setting is interesting. A single graphic novel, collecting the first few issues of the comic, was also released in English. ★★★

RANMA ½

(らんま ½) • Rumiko Takahashi • Viz (1990–2006) • Shogakukan (Weekly Shônen Sunday, 1987–1996) • 38 volumes • Martial Arts, Shônen, Romantic Comedy • 16+ (mild violence, nudity)

Akane Tendo, the tomboyish heir of a karate dojo, finds herself engaged to Ranma Saotome, a macho teenage martial artist cursed to turn into a girl whenever he is splashed with cold water. *Ranma ½* virtually introduced sex changing into *shônen* manga, mathematically demonstrating that if your characters can change gender, you can in-

Hiro Mashima's *Rave Master*

ing, endlessly cute, endlessly enthusiastic . . . *Ranma ½* (together with Izumi Matsumoto's untranslated *Kimagure Orange Road*) is one of the classics of the *shōnen* romantic comedy genre. ★★★★

RAVE MASTER

Rave the Groove Adventure • Hiro Mashima • Tokyopop (2002–ongoing) • Kodansha (Weekly Shōnen Magazine, 1998–2005) • 35 volumes • Shōnen, Fantasy, Action • 13+ (mild language, violence)

Kodansha's answer to the hugely popular *One Piece, Rave Master* at first seems a pale imitation. For the first few volumes, Mashima's art is rough and inconsistent, and a clichéd story does not inspire much confidence. Here is a case, though, where readers' dedication is rewarded. Once Mashima hits his stride midway through the first story arc, the series is an absolute joy, with sexy-cool characters and contagious optimism. Protagonist Haru Glory grew up on idyllic Garage Island, sheltered from the growing military unrest in the outside world, when one day destiny washes up on his shores in the form of Plue—a doglike creature with a carrot for a nose—and the Ten Powers (aka the Ten Commandments), a magical transforming sword. Haru follows in his missing father's footsteps, venturing into the world in search of the lost Rave Stones in order to bring down the evil terrorist organization called Demon Card. His ever-growing band of allies includes Elie, a trigger-happy, amnesiac gambler; Musica, a gang leader with alchemical control over silver; Griffon Kato, a gelatinous eggplant/cartographer; and Ruby, a penguin philanthropist with burgeoning magic powers. Out there? You bet! Mashima's wild imagination leads to many chuckle-worthy characters, such as the flatulent Jiggle Butt Gang, a deluded superhero send-up named Lazenby, and an evil mastermind koala bear named . . . Koala. Particularly inspired is a choose-your-own-adventure chapter starring Plue and Griff on a quest for candy. The deadpan zaniness is not for everyone, and the Hot Topic–meets–Tolkien style will grate with some, but there

volve them in twice as many love triangles. The threat of a "serious" romance, or indeed serious anything, vanishes almost immediately after the first few volumes, as the focus shifts to a growing cast of rivals, all wanting to beat up or make out with Ranma, and mostly cursed to transform when wet . . . but into ducks, pigs, and other cute animals, not members of the opposite sex. *Ranma ½* is the manga equivalent of a successful sitcom; the plot always circles back to the same point, but as long as it's funny you don't care. Takahashi throws out an endless array of ridiculous Chinese-style martial arts, based on cooking, tea ceremony, rhythmic gymnastics, and what have you. Despite frequent bare breasts and the panty-stealing presence of Happosai (a dirty old man so stylized he belongs among the animal characters), the actual sexual element is surprisingly tasteful; this is a manga where the focus is on kissing and marrying, and the main male characters are either blushing romantics or spend the entire story running away from girls. Repetitive, teasing, charm-is little doubt that Mashima has proven himself every bit as talented as *Shônen Jump's* top artists. (MT) ★★★

RAY

Akihito Yoshitomi • ADV (2004–2005) • Akita Shoten (Champion Red, 2003–2005) • 3 volumes, suspended (7 volumes in Japan) • Seinen, Science Fiction, Medical Drama • 16+ (violence, graphic surgery, nudity, sexual situations)

When a mysterious doctor (Osamu Tezuka's *Black Jack,* in a cameo) restores her vision and gives her X-ray eyes, Ray becomes a miniskirted, scalpel-tossing master surgeon, performing impossible medical procedures ("You're the only one who can pull this off!"). *Ray* starts out as an episodic *Black Jack* homage but quickly turns into dark-conspiracy science fiction, pitting the heroine and her friends against mind-controlling parasites, a killer fungus, and a deadly organization that runs human organ farms. (At the same time, there's also pure goofiness in the form of kung-fu nurses and a peg-legged, cigar-chomping hospital director.) Yoshitomi's art is more developed and attractive than in *Eat-Man:* deep-shadowed, almost film noir, with American-influenced character designs. A sequel series, *Ray+* (aka *Ray the Other Side*), is currently ongoing in *Champion Red.* ★★★

READ OR DIE: See *R.O.D: Read or Die*

READ OR DREAM: See *R.O.D: Read or Dream*

REAL BOUT HIGH SCHOOL: See *Samurai Girl Real Bout High School*

THE REBEL SWORD

Kurd no Hoshi, "Star of the Kurds" (クルドの星) • Yoshikazu Yasuhiko • Dark Horse (1994–1995) • Tokuma Shoten (Comic Nora, 1986–1987) • 6 issues, suspended (3 volumes in Japan) • Shônen, Political, Action • Unrated/16+ (mild language, violence, nudity, sexual situations)

Sadly unfinished (in the English edition) story about a half-Japanese, half-Turkish

Akihito Yoshitomi's *Ray*

young man who is lured from Tokyo to Istanbul to see his estranged mother, only to be recruited instead by Kurdish guerrillas. Worth reading if only for a fresh look at Middle Eastern regional politics, albeit with its share of clichéd knife fights, a hookah-smoking belly dancer, and what looks to be the start of a contrived you-are-the-chosen-one plot. *Rebel Sword* features Yasuhiko's typical top-notch action—there are several really impressive chase scenes—and the artist's fondness for tough chicks riding motorcycles comes through yet again with Lira, a Honda-riding Istanbul resident in leather hot pants. The locations in Turkey and Kurdistan are gorgeously re-created. (JD) ★★

REBORN!

Katekyo Hit Man Reborn!, "Private Tutor Hit Man Reborn!" (家庭教師[かてきょー]ヒットマンRE-BORN!) • Akira Amano • Viz (2006–ongoing) • Shueisha (Weekly Shônen Jump, 2004–ongoing) • 13+ volumes (ongoing) • 16+ (violence)

"I was hired to teach you how to be a good Mafia boss." Wimpy teenager Tsuna is visited by Reborn, an adorably cartoony, expressionless baby hit man wearing a fedora and carrying various deadly firearms. Sent from Italy to groom Tsuna as the heir of the Vongola Mafia family, Reborn proves his power by shooting Tsuna between the eyes with the Deathperation Shot, which kills him and brings him back to life with the courage to carry out his dying regrets, such as telling a cute girl that he likes her. Reborn's bullets are later revealed to have other, less interesting special properties (such as making Tsuna stronger, or making him a good swimmer), and the series develops like a Mafia version of *Doraemon,* with a magic bullet for every occasion. The episodic comedy has its good moments, with goofy art like a poor man's *Eyeshield 21,* but the hero is too pathetic and there are too many new characters and bullets one after another. The supporting cast ranges from boring (such as a female assassin who kills with her bad cooking) to great (such as Lambo, a rival baby hit man in a cow suit, who looks like a Precious Moments character). The series has nothing unsuitable for younger teens; presumably it was rated for older audiences because of all the realistic weaponry. ★★½

REBOUND: See *Harlem Beat*

THE RECIPE FOR GERTRUDE

Gertrude no Recipe, "Gertrude's Recipe" (ガートルードのレシピ) • Nari Kusakawa • CMX (2006–2007) • Hakusensha (Hana to Yume, 2001–2003) • 5 volumes • Shôjo, Fantasy • All Ages (violence)

The opening scene establishes the weirdness level of *The Recipe for Gertrude:* Gertrude, a demon who looks like an ordinary boy (yes, Gertrude is male), floats in the sky fighting two giant animated rag dolls who have come to take back their ears. As Sahara, the human witness to the fight, soon discovers, Gertrude is a sort of man-made demon made of parts from other demons, whose "recipe"—the instructions on how to make

him—is sought by all kinds of evil creatures. The easygoing demon and the resourceful girl are drawn to each other as they deal with various creepy enemies, mostly taking the form of handsome men and cute but grotesque creatures. Bizarre images and action scenes make *Recipe for Gertrude* an interesting *shôjo* occult fantasy, but the simplistic art is not always up to the demands of the writing. ★★½

RECORD OF LODOSS WAR: CHRONICLES OF THE HEROIC KNIGHT

Lodoss Tô Senki: Eiyû Kishi Den, "Chronicles of the Lodoss Island Wars: Legend of the Heroic Knight" (ロードス島戦記英雄騎士伝) • Ryo Mizuno (story), Masato Natsumoto (art) • CPM (2000–2003) • Kadokawa Shoten (Monthly Shônen Ace, 1997–2000) • 6 volumes • Shônen, Fantasy • 13+ (violence, mild sexual situations)

Manga adaptation of Ryu Mizuno's young-adult fantasy novels, also adapted into the *Record of Lodoss War: Chronicles of the Heroic Knight* TV series. Five years after the events of *Record of Lodoss War: The Grey Witch,* the land is again at war, and a new generation of heroes must arise to fight the evil kingdom of Marmo, the dark elves, and the power-hungry sorcerer Vagnado. The *Grey Witch* heroes show up as guest stars, and everyone in the cast gets their moment to shine, but the focus is on the heroic knight, Spark, a sort of substitute for Parn from the original series (Can't the hero be the dwarf or the big scarred guy instead of the troubled but earnest young lad for once?). The plot is conventional, particularly the climax, but the pace is swift and the art is well drawn in a generic anime style. Like the anime it is based on, the manga rewrites the ending of the original *Record of Lodoss War* OAV series. ★★½

RECORD OF LODOSS WAR: DEEDLIT'S TALE

Lodoss Tô Senki: Deedlit Monogatari, "Chronicles of the Lodoss Island Wars: Deedlit's Tale" (ロードス島戦記ディードリット物語) • Ryo Mizuno (story), Setsuko Yoneyama (art) • CPM (2001–2003) •

Kadokawa Shoten (Asuka Fantasy DX, 1998) • 2 volumes • Shôjo, Fantasy • All Ages (partial nudity)

Shôjo manga adaptation of Ryu Mizuno's young-adult fantasy novel. Set after the events of *Record of Lodoss War: The Grey Witch,* this unmemorable fantasy-adventure aims for young readers, with nonviolent problem-solving scenarios such as human-elf prejudice and medieval class struggles. Estas, Deedlit's human-hating, childhood elf friend, attempts to be the third party in a romantic triangle with the two main characters but can't get his foot in the door. There are no strong emotions, ideas, or art to hold the interest of casual readers, but fans may appreciate some of the insights into the characters. ★★

RECORD OF LODOSS WAR: THE GREY WITCH

Lodoss Tô Senki: Hairo no Majo, "Chronicles of the Lodoss Island Wars: The Grey Witch" (ロードス島戦記灰色の魔女) • Ryo Mizuno (story), Yoshihiko Ochi (art) • CPM (1999–2002) • Kadokawa Shoten (Newtype/Ace Dash, 1994–1998) • 3 volumes • Fantasy • 13+ (violence, brief partial nudity)

Manga adaptation of Ryu Mizuno's young-adult fantasy novel, also adapted into the first eight episodes of the *Record of Lodoss War* OAV series. Written exactly like a generic Dungeons & Dragons adventure, the plot follows a party of adventurers (Parn the fighter, Deedlit the elf, Ghim the dwarf, etc.) from their first meetings in taverns to their final showdown with the ancient sorceress of the title. In the process they fight ogres and goblins, the thief picks locks, the cleric casts healing spells, and so on. The plot is an absolutely average, somewhat slow-moving example of its genre, but the drab artwork makes the manga an inferior experience to the colorful anime. ★★

RECORD OF LODOSS WAR: THE LADY OF PHARIS

Lodoss Tô Senki: Pharis no Seijo, "Chronicles of the Lodoss Island Wars: The Holy Woman of Pharis" (ロードス島戦記ファリスの聖女) • Ryo Mizuno

(story), Akihiro Yamada (art) • CPM • Kadokawa Shoten (Newtype, 1994–2001) • 2 volumes • Fantasy • 13+ (violence, nudity)

A manga adaptation of Ryo Mizuno's young-adult fantasy novel, this prequel to the entire *Record of Lodoss War* series is the only manga in the D&D-esque franchise to truly achieve a mood of high fantasy. Flaus, a female warrior-priest of the goddess Pharis, and Beld, a barbarian with a dark side, lead a crusade against a female demon lord who has plunged the land into war. Yamada's beautiful, classical artwork gives the story an epic feel, with Piranesian underground labyrinths and monsters that could have come from a Richard Corben comic. (The only problem is that Yamada's art is so detailed, it looks scrunched down at "manga size"; it was originally published in the Japanese *Newtype,* a large-format magazine.) ★★★

RED PROWLING DEVIL

Kurenai, "Crimson" (紅) • Toshimitsu Shimizu • ComicsOne (2002–2004) • Shônen Gahosha (Young King Ours, 1999–2002) • 8 volumes • Seinen, Military, Drama • 18+ (language, nudity, sex, violence)

Naomi O'Brien, a half-Japanese former IRA terrorist, must pay off her debt to society as a mercenary fighter pilot, serving a mysterious and ruthless organization. On her time off, she attends to her hospitalized brother and her artist boyfriend (who doesn't know about her job), but the "Red Prowling Devil" has many enemies, and Naomi and her fellow pilots soon find themselves at war with a competing mercenary group, which will do anything to bring them down. *Red Prowling Devil* starts out as a series of melancholy war stories similar to a sexed-up, awkwardly translated *Area 88* ("Blood red color paints the sky above Mount Alps. What hides inside the heart of the woman who saw the blossoming flowers there . . . ?"). In the end, however, it becomes almost nonstop aerial combat, with effective, exciting sequences of exploding planes and helmeted talking heads. (Shimizu is a huge fan of fighter planes, as seen in his untranslated manga

Rei Mikamoto's *Reiko the Zombie Shop*

Cecil B. DeMille historical epic, part Harlequin romance, the plot of *Red River* is more frankly titillating than *Basara* or even *Fushigi Yûgi,* with numerous scenes of the naked heroine being *almost* ravished in harems and lily-pad-choked pools. Minus the near-sex scenes, though, it is a surprisingly simple story, whose royal intrigues and military campaigns were clearly written for young readers. Despite the presence of magic as a plot device, *Red River* works well as a history lesson on ancient Egypt and the Middle East; unfortunately, the lanky, old-fashioned *shôjo* artwork can't do much with the generic character designs and endless ruler-drawn backgrounds of mud-brick houses. (The few bits of jewelry and decoration that seem to have been based on actual historical models stand out obviously.) To its credit, though, *Red River* has the courage to let its characters actually suffer and change, so the strong plotting provides a reason to keep reading.

★★★

801 T.T.S. Airbats, which was adapted into a translated anime.) Like all Shimizu manga, there are lots of full-page shots of limp nude women, and despite all her aeronautic skills, Naomi is a one-emotion character, a sad-looking sex doll. The ending is extremely abrupt.

★★

RED RIVER

Sora wa Akai Kawa no Hotori, "Heaven Is the Banks of the Red River" (天は赤い河のほとり) • Chie Shinohara • Viz (2004–ongoing) • Shogakukan (*Shôjo Comic,* 1995–2002) • 28 volumes • Shôjo, Fantasy, Romance • 16+ (violence, nudity, sexual situations)

To serve as a sacrifice for the evil sorceress-queen Nakia, teenage Yuri is teleported to Turkey's ancient Hittite Empire in the fourteenth century B.C. Escaping Nakia's clutches for the first of many times, she is taken under the wing of the handsome Prince Kail, whom she joins in his struggles for the throne, while being hailed by the common people as an incarnation of the goddess Ishtar. But how can they fall in love when she wants to return to her own time? Part

THE RED SNAKE: See *Hino Horror, Vol. 1: The Red Snake*

REIKO THE ZOMBIE SHOP

Zombieya Reiko, "Zombie Shop/Business Reiko" (ゾンビ屋れい子) • Rei Mikamoto • Dark Horse (2006–ongoing) • Bunkasha (1999–2004) • 11 volumes • Action, Horror • Unrated/18+ (language, graphic violence, nudity)

Businesslike schoolgirl Reiko Himezono has the power to turn the dead into zombies, which she uses to make money by solving mysteries. But the dead are hateful things, and Reiko's resurrections often result in maggot-infested ultraviolence. This fast-paced action-horror manga has the feeling of a tongue-in-cheek splatter movie, like the *Reanimator* or *Evil Dead* series. After the episodic first volume, the story turns into an ultraviolent battle manga, with Reiko and her team of zombie-summoning superheroines fighting Reiko's evil twin sister, a necromancer who wants to take over the world. Characters die right and left, bodies are chopped up by chain saws and plane propellers, and stiffly pretty anime-style faces transform into nightmarish evil grins. The plot is entertainingly trashy, and the art, while stylish, is primarily focused on telling the story in as clear and blood-soaked a manner as possible.   ★★★

REMOTE

(リモート) • Seimaru Amagi (story), Tetsuya Koshiba (art) • Tokyopop (2004–2006) • Kodansha (2002–2004) • 10 volumes • Seinen, Crime, Mystery, Romantic Comedy • 16+/18+ (language, graphic violence, nudity, graphic sex)

Ayaki, a ditzy twenty-two-year-old meter maid, is picked for a special role at the police department: the remote-control partner of Inspector Himuro, an emotionally crippled (but extremely hot) genius detective who dwells in a creepy underground lair. Himuro feeds advice to Ayaki via cell phone headset and forces her into dangerous cases despite her protestations ("I'm just a girl!" "You're a cop, Ayaki. You are not just a girl"). Meanwhile, Ayaki's new workload interferes with her fiancé's comedic attempts to sleep with her. It's hard to see how *Remote* was popular enough to be adapted into a Japanese TV drama; the mysteries involve graphic sex and violence but are essentially juvenile, depending on unlikely conicdences and clues purposely left by the killer. The art is detailed but crude; Ayaki looks like a photo of a real woman with a cartoon head awkwardly pasted on. Intermittently suspenseful, but shallow and hackneyed.   ★½

RESPONSE: See *Harlequin Violet: Response*

THE RETURN OF LUM*URUSEI YATSURA:
See *Lum★Urusei Yatsura*

REVENGE OF MOUFLON

Hôfuku no Mouflon, "Revenge of Mouflon" (報復の ムフロン) • Yoichiro Ono (art), Jiro Ueno (story) • Gutsoon! Entertainment (2002–2004) • Coamix (Weekly Comic Bunch, 2002–2004) • 2 volumes, suspended (7 volumes in Japan) • Political, Crime Drama • 16+ (language, crude humor, violence)

A fascinating over-the-top manga reaction to September 11. When a Japanese plane is hijacked by terrorists, Sano Yohei, a thirty-five-year-old TV comedian, takes the controls and tries to save the lives of those on board. But the U.S. government—essentially the bad guy of the story—has ordered American jets to shoot down the plane before it crashes into its target. Once you get over the ridiculous title ("Mouflon" are wild sheep, the alternative to living like domesticated sheep—get it?), *Revenge of Mouflon* is an idealistic melodrama about terrorism and the relation of the people to the government. Volume 1 is the most intense, but once the plane hits the ground in volume 2, the story heads into new geopolitical territory with hardly a stumble (no, Sano doesn't just *happen* to be present for *another* terrorist attack). Sano is one part average Joe, one part antiauthoritarian hero; at middle age, he still looks like a typical young manga protagonist, but sometimes you can see the lines in his face. The vigorous artwork is comparable to *Eyeshield 21,* combining good camera angles, intense action, and slightly caricatural faces; the plane crash is serious business, but when one character is flabbergasted, his jaw drops to the bottom of the page. More of the story was published in *Raijin* magazine but never collected.   ★★★½

REVOLUTIONARY GIRL UTENA

Shôjo Kakumei Utena, "Girl Revolution Utena" (少女革命ウテナ) • Chiho Saito (art), Be-Papas (concept) • Viz (2000–2004) • Shogakukan (Ciao, 1996–1998) • 5 volumes • Shôjo, Fantasy, Romance, Drama • Unrated/13+ (mild violence, mild sexual situations)

Illustrated by veteran girls' manga artist Chiho Saito, this manga adaptation was produced simultaneously with the *Revolutionary Girl Utena* anime TV series. When Utena Tenjou's parents died in an accident, she was sure her life had been saved by a prince—a memory sustained by the mysterious postcards she receives annually. The postcards lead her to exclusive Ohtori Academy, where she quickly finds herself embroiled in sword duels with the members of the Student Council for the hand of the "Rose Bride," Anthy Himemiya. Caught in the magic that surrounds the Rose Bride and the duels,

Utena must battle her way to find her own truth, save Anthy, and free the Student Council from themselves. Magic, symbolism, and surrealism crowd this tale but never detract from the characters. This basic idea of the girl who wants to be a prince and save the princess borrows heavily from early "girl prince" manga series, such as *Rose of Versailles* and *Princess Knight,* but stands alone on its own merits. (EF)   ★★★½

REVOLUTIONARY GIRL UTENA: THE ADOLESCENCE OF UTENA

Shôjo Kakumei Utena Adolescence Mokushiroku, "Girl Revolution Utena: Adolescence Revelation Record" (少女革命ウテナ～アドゥレセンス黙示録) • Chiho Saito (art), Be-Papas (concept) • Viz (2004) • Shogakukan (Bessatsu Shôjo Comic Special, 1999) • 1 volume • Shôjo, Fantasy, Romance, Drama • Unrated/16+ (sexual situations)

An alternate version of the *Revolutionary Girl Utena* story, *The Adolescence of Utena* is the manga adaptation of the *Utena* anime movie, produced simultaneously with the film. In this version, Utena enters Ohtori disguised as a boy, and her "prince" is an old boyfriend who now may or may not be alive. She is drawn immediately into the duels for Anthy's hand as Rose Bride and forced to fight her own prince in order to allow him—and herself—to move on. This self-contained story includes the same symbolism as in the original movie, remixed for a more desperate, faster pace. Ultimately, it has a more realistic and hopeful conclusion than the longer series. The ending draws on Japanese girls' literary sources such as the untranslated works of Yoshiya Nobuko. (EF)   ★★★½

RG VEDA

Seiden RG Veda, "Holy Legend RG Veda" (聖伝-RG VEDA-) • CLAMP • Tokyopop (2005–2006) • Shinshokan (Wings, 1989–1996) • 10 volumes • Shôjo, Fantasy • 13+ (violence)

CLAMP grew up in the 1980s—it's only fair to forgive them one big-hair-and-shoulder-pads manga. *RG Veda* is a loose reinterpretation of the myths in the Rigveda, the collection of Hindu hymns (that's loose with a capital *L,* and a lack of footnotes or glossary in the English edition means any semblances will be lost on most readers), reinterpreted through a fantasy lens. Three hundred years ago, the thunder god Taishakuten usurped the throne from the Heavenly Emperor, ushering in an age of violence. Lord Yasha, the greatest warrior in the land, learns of a prophecy that six stars shall descend from heaven and cause a schism that will split the heavens. Key to the prophecy is the childlike Ashura, who unites the six stars but hides a dark nature that threatens to destroy not only Yasha but the entire world. The series has not aged well, and for fans of any of CLAMP's work post-*Rayearth,* going back to *RG Veda* can be a painful and unrewarding experience. The artwork is dense and generic, looking more like You Higuri than later CLAMP manga. Despite much "happening," there is seldom any action, just screaming and melodramatic close-ups. The dialogue is both trite and repetitive. Only Ashura stands out as a truly classic character. There are some beautiful compositions, and a great ending rewards patient readers, but unless you are a CLAMP completist, the cons far outweigh the pros. (MT)   ★½

RICA 'TTE KANJI!

(りかって感じ!?) • Rica Takashima • ALC Publishing (2004) • Michi Publishing/Terra Publications (Phryne/Anise, 1995–2004) • 1 volume • Yuri, Romantic Comedy • Unrated/13+ (brief nudity, sexual situations)

Rica, an out but shy and inexperienced college student, moves to Tokyo and goes to the local bars and clubs to meet people. Gradually she becomes good friends with Miho, an art student who likes her. Comparable to the work of Elizabeth Watasin, this extremely enjoyable comic-strip glimpse inside Tokyo's lesbian scene has many interesting cultural tidbits. The art has a charming hand-drawn feel, and the pages are beautifully crowded with details, such as nightclub scenes filled with unique faces and bits of conversation. Some of the bonus material in the back of the book is untranslated, including a description of a gay pride event in New York City. A short sequel, *More Rica 'tte Kanji!*, appeared in the English-language magazine *Yuri Monogatari #4*.

★★★½

THE RING

Ring (リング) • Misao Inagaki (art), Koji Suzuki (original novel), Hiroshi Takahashi (script) • Dark Horse (2003) • Kadokawa Shoten (1999) • 1 volume • Horror • Unrated/13+ (language, violence)

An urban legend is drifting around Tokyo about a videotape connected to a series of mysterious deaths. According to the rumor, whoever watches this tape is fated to die one week later. When one of the deaths afflicts the family of a TV reporter named Reiko, she sets out to unravel the truth. But after watching the video for herself, Reiko realizes she is now the victim of a terrifying virus-like curse. With only a week to find a cure, she enlists the help of her ex-husband (who has also been exposed to the video) to try to find the source of the tape. The trail leads to the rural Izu peninsula, where they uncover the decades-old story of a very strange—and long-dead—girl named Sadako Yamamura. But will they find a way to stop the curse before their seven days are up? Koji Suzuki's 1991 horror novel *The Ring* and the subsequent 1998 feature film adaptation (remade by Hollywood) helped to kick off the "J-horror" boom, whose shockwaves continue to reverberate throughout the entertainment world. Misao Inagaki's manga adaptation of the film is a plain and crudely drawn piece of work. Yet the bare-bones artwork and storytelling mean that nothing gets in the way of the twists and turns of the plot. While there's not a lot of atmosphere, the *Ring* manga still works well as a quick way to catch up with the phenomenon. (PM)

★★

THE RING, VOL. 2

MEIMU (art), Koji Suzuki (original novel), Hiroshi Takahashi (script) • Dark Horse (2004) • Kadokawa Shoten (1999) • 1 volume • Horror • Unrated/16+ (language, violence)

The Ring, Vol. 2, is an adaptation of the 1999 sequel film of the same name. The franchise is now better served by artist MEIMU (later to handle other J-horror adaptations such as *Dark Water* and *Ju-On*), whose detailed art conveys the mix of psychological dread and alienation crucial to *The Ring*'s success. The story of *Ring 2* continues Reiko's quest to unravel the mystery of Sadako while a group of scientists seeks to find their own cure for the Ring curse. (PM)

★★★

THE RING, VOL. 3: SPIRAL

Rasen, "Spiral" (らせん) • Sakura Mizuki (art), Koji Suzuki (original novel) • Dark Horse (2004) • Kadokawa Shoten (1999) • Unrated/16+ (language, brief graphic violence, sex)

Author Koji Suzuki delivered the novel *Spiral* as the official sequel to his original *Ring* novel. But when *Spiral* was finally adapted as a feature film in 1998, it was marketed as a side story to be shoehorned in between the *Ring* and *Ring 2* movies. It's gotten a bit lost in the shuffle since then, which is too bad, since the story contains a number of fascinating ideas and concepts, if not out-and-out scares. *The Ring, Vol. 3: Spiral* begins after an autopsy, when a cryptic code written on a piece of paper is found on the body of a dead college professor. His old friend Takayama, who is recovering from the accidental death of his son, sets out to solve the puzzle. The clues lead him to the now-infamous cursed videotape that kills whoever watches it one week later. Takayama begins to follow his old friend's footsteps and soon finds himself haunted by a new incarnation of Sadako. A bit like the films of David Cronenberg, even in its manga incarnation *Spiral* comes across as a more philosophical and meditative take on J-horror than eventually became the norm, and it might even be closer to science fiction than horror. Sakura Mizuki's adaptation, while nothing dazzling to look at, does a solid job of conveying a very complex tale and hits just the right notes of dread and anxiety along the way. (PM)

★★

THE RING, VOL. 4: BIRTHDAY

Birthday (バースデイ) • MEIMU (art), Koji Suzuki (original novel) • Dark Horse (2004) • Kadokawa

Shoten (1999) • Unrated/16+ (language, violence, partial nudity, sexual situations)

A collection of three short stories by MEIMU and Mizuki, *The Ring, Vol. 4: Birthday* focuses on the character of Sadako herself and provides a much-needed new perspective on the whole *Ring* saga. The first tale, "The Casket Floating in the Sky," delves into the inner life of one of *The Ring*'s original supporting characters after she is exposed to the deadly Ring virus. The book's centerpiece, "Lemon Heart," is an adaptation of a short story by *The Ring*'s original author, Suzuki (itself stretched out to feature length for the 2000 film *Ring 0: Birthday*). It's a flashback tale that uncovers Sadako's teen years, when she tried to become an actress to escape her dark past only to become involved in a deadly affair with one of her teachers. The final entry, "Sadako," is a floating first-person narrative that adds a good deal of humanity to the single greatest J-horror spook of them all. (PM)   ★★★

RIOT

Satoshi Shiki • Viz (1995–1997) • Kadokawa Shoten (Newtype, 1993–1994) • 2 volumes • Fantasy, Action • Unrated/16+ (mild language, nudity, graphic violence)

Set in an undefined mishmash of Wild West, high fantasy, and cyberpunk motifs, this confusing fantasy manga ran for two volumes before going on permanent hiatus in both America and Japan. (Shiki eventually wrote a short untranslated sequel, *Riot of the World*.) While attempting to steal the ancient magic book *Riot*, Billy the Kid (a thief) becomes magically bound to the book's guardian, a young girl named Axel Rose. Random acts of mean-spirited violence alternate with never-resolved plot threads about megalomaniacal bad guys, warring churches, and female bounty hunters in buttless outfits. The screentone-laden artwork and exaggerated anatomy resemble the work of Kazushi Hagiwara and Tsukasa Kotobuki.   ★

R.I.P.: See *Mitsukazu Mihara: R.I.P. (Requiem in Phonybrian)*

RIZELMINE

(りぜるまいん) • Yukiru Sugisaki • Tokyopop (2005) • Kadokawa Shoten (Monthly Ace Next, 2000) • Shônen, Romantic Comedy • 1 volume • 13+ (sexual situations)

Formulaic robot-girl fantasy with two good points: (1) the art is fluid and (2) it's short. Tomonori, a fourteen-year-old boy who likes only older women, goes home from school and finds that he has a wife, Rizelmine, a twelve-year-old girl who is actually a top-secret nanomachine project. Rizelmine, who has the power to transform into an adult for short stretches, races around hugging and pestering Tomonori and occasionally blowing stuff up. The art is technically accomplished, but the story is inane and clichéd. ★

R.O.D (READ OR DIE)

Hideyuki Kurata (story), Shutaro Yamada (art) • Viz (2006) • Shueisha (Ultra Jump, 2000–2002) • 4 volumes • Seinen, Fantasy, Action • 16+ (language, violence, sexual situations)

Based on the light novels by Hideyuki Kurata, *Read or Die* has three things going for it: a great title, a great premise, and a very popular tie-in anime. Unfortunately, it doesn't live up to the promise of its packaging. The heroine, Yomiko Readman, is the Paper, a special agent for the British Library who carries out missions involving rare books. She has supernatural power over paper, which she can manipulate into any shape. It would seem impossible to develop such a premise into anything other than a fun action romp, but the manga manages to drain all joy from the concept, mainly by devoting much of the four-volume series to a tormented, angst-filled story line in which a vengeful rival Paper Master impersonates Yomiko's dead boyfriend, the saintly Donnie. Yomiko spends most of the manga wailing, whimpering, and watching helplessly as evil forces destroy the world around her. It's almost pornographically depressing and cruel. The screentone-heavy, crudely exploitative cheesecake art gives the manga an unwholesome feel. The English edition is slightly censored for nudity. (CT)   ★

ROMANCE AND LOVE COMEDY (恋愛・ラブコメディ)

"Why can't I have a normal relationship?"
—*The Devil Does Exist*

Romance manga, known in Japan as *renai* (love) manga, is popular among both sexes and all age groups. Girls' manga abounds with both comedic and serious love stories, while boys' manga tends toward "love comedies" with a heavy dose of sexual innuendo. Stories for adults are typically more explicit, with adult women's manga containing the most realistic relationship writing.

From a Western perspective, manga love stories may give the impression of a shy, even repressed culture. In contrast to American TV shows and novels where teenagers get into relationships, break up, and get into new relationships, characters in *shônen* and *shôjo* manga tend to be blushing virgins who obsess over things like their first kiss. Although things have changed in recent decades, the sexes traditionally mingle less in Japan than in America, and intense academic workloads and job pressures leave many people with no time for casual dating. In older love comedies from the 1980s, comical male characters sometimes produce how-to books explaining what to do on a date. Thanks to marketing by chocolate companies, Valentine's Day in Japan is a formal holiday on which women are expected to give chocolate to men they like (either romantically or platonically). Men who wish to return the favor must wait till White Day, March 14, originally named after the expected gift of white chocolate or marshmallows. If American teenagers stereotypically lose their virginity in the backseat of a car, Japanese teenagers and young adults often have sex in "love hotels," where couples can discreetly rent rooms by the night or by the hour.

Like all manga, romantic manga delight in flirting with bizarre and taboo scenarios, although the premise is often more extreme than the payoff. *Marmalade Boy* (1992) and *The Devil Does Exist* (1998) feature stepbrother-stepsister romances. Kei Kusunoki's untranslated comedy *Yagami-kun no Katei no Jijô* ("Yagami's Family Circumstances") (1986) takes the incest theme to the limit of absurdity; the protagonist has a hopeless, frustrated crush on his incredibly young-looking mother. Gender-bending and supernatural elements make the potential insanity even greater; in *Midori Days* (2003) the teenage hero wakes up to find his right hand replaced with a miniature, living girl growing out of his arm.

Miwa Ueda's *Peach Girl*

Shôjo *Romance*

In *shôjo* manga, romance is the dominant genre. In her notes for *Fushigi Yûgi: Genbu Kaiden,* Yuu Watase gripes about having to include love stories in her adventure manga to meet reader expectations. Serious romances are more common than love comedies; even manga that start with a light touch, such as *Kare Kano* (1996) and *Fruits Basket* (1998), often turn into sad, obsessive meditations on loneliness.

Love stories in *shôjo* manga were originally chaste schoolgirl romances, but this changed in the 1970s with the rise of young female artists with more daring sensibilities. Soon *shôjo* manga for teenagers began to feature impassioned romantic plots, sex scenes, and frank dialogue about love and sex. (On the other hand, magazines for younger readers, such as *Nakayoshi* and *Ribon,* still focus on pure-hearted crushes.) The magazine *Shôjo Comic,* which ran the work of groundbreaking artists Moto Hagio and Keiko Takemiya in the 1970s and is now the home of artists such as Mayu Shinjo and Rie Takada, has a long-standing reputation as the most explicit *shôjo* magazine for its junior-high age group, with stories that typically involve at least one flowery sex scene. *Explicit* is relative, however; the sex scenes in *Shôjo Comic,* although controversial enough to inspire irate letters from Japanese parents, are usually discreetly hidden under the bedsheets. *Cheese!* and *Renai Paradise* ("Love Paradise"), so far untranslated magazines aimed at slightly older teenage girls, are much racier, with typical stories involving sex on the school roof, in the gym equipment shed, and so on.

Shôjo manga have been accused of taking a reactionary view of male-female relationships; even in manga in which the characters consummate their love, sex is often portrayed as something a girl does primarily to make a boy happy. Some relationships border on abusive, with *Hot Gimmick* (2002) being one of the most extreme examples. But it would be inaccurate to say that all *shôjo* heroines are passive; the stars of *Gals!* (1999) and *Happy Hustle High School* (2003) take no guff from anyone and punch out creeps and stalkers, while the heroine of *Backstage Prince* (2005) takes the lead in the relationship.

In stories for younger teens, finding one's true love is usually the end of the story, but stories for older teens and college-age women give a more realistic picture of dating. The works of Ai Yazawa border on *jôsei,* adult women's manga, which traditionally focus on relationships. *Jôsei* is often stereotyped as love fantasies for bored housewives, but in recent years, artists such as Moyoco Anno and Erica Sakurazawa have given the genre a more modern chick-lit sensibility. *Jôsei* romances are now often contemporary romantic comedies in the Bridget Jones mold rather than old-fashioned bodice-rippers, although those still exist.

The *jôsei* subgenre of *redicomi* (ladies' comics), of which little has been translated, combines often idealized love stories with lavishly depicted sex scenes. In 1998, Harlequin, the famous Canada-based publisher of romance novels, teamed up with Japanese publisher Ohzora Shuppan to produce manga adaptations of their novels. Although formulaic and far tamer than homegrown *redicomi,* the stories proved successful, and the monthly manga magazine *Harlequin* is still published in Japan. In 2005, Harlequin began to translate their graphic novels back into English, first published by Dark Horse, and later under their own imprint.

One major subgenre of *shôjo* romance is *yaoi* (aka Boys' Love), manga featuring homosexual men in love. (See the introduction to YAOI.) Today pure *yaoi* manga are the domain of small specialty publishers, but mainstream *shôjo* manga often include wink-wink hints of love or sex between nominally straight male characters.

Shônen *Romance*

Although love interests in *shônen* manga are nothing new, romance only became a significant *shônen* genre in the 1980s. Boys' love stories tend toward comedy, with only a few (such as *Video Girl Ai*) focusing on angst and heartbreak. One of the most famous untranslated titles is Izumi Matsumoto's 1984 *Kimagure Orange Road* ("Whimsical Orange Road"), in which a boy with psychic powers is caught in a love triangle with two girls: one cute and stereotypically girlish, the other a cool, butt-kicking loner.

A number of *shônen* love comedies fall into the categories known to American fans as "harem" or "maid" manga. In these manga, an average-Joe protagonist is paired with either a large group of lovestruck girls who fight for his affections (the harem) or a single perfect, devoted, submissive girlfriend (the maid). The granddaddy of these subgenres is Rumiko Takahashi's early blockbuster *Lum*Urusei Yatsura* (1978), in which teenage horndog Ataru attracts the attention of bikini-clad demon girl Lum and a horde of sexy, short-tempered alien women. *Lum*Urusei Yatsura* emphasizes comedy over romance: Ataru is a hormone-addled buffoon, and most of the women treat him with contempt. Subsequent *shônen* love comedies made the women more lovelorn and the protagonist more shy, introverted, and bland, often to the point of becoming a complete cipher, so that the reader can ignore him or imagine, "Ah, if only I were in his shoes . . ." The title of the long-running harem anime and manga franchise *Tenchi Muyo!* (a pun on a common postal phrase, translatable as "No Need for Tenchi" or "Useless Tenchi") suggests how dismissible the heroes of these manga can be. Harem and maid manga with fantasy or sci-fi elements, making the dream girls into aliens, androids, or magical beings, are ubiquitous in *otaku*-oriented magazines such as *Dengeki Daioh* and *Dragon Age*. (See the article on OTAKU.) Harem romances exist in *shôjo* manga as well, with popular examples including *Fushigi Yûgi* (1992) and the tongue-in-cheek *Ouran High School Host Club* (2003).

The older the target audience, the more generous a *shônen* manga tends to be in doling out fanservice: cheesecake shots of breasts, butts, panties, and general nudity. The protagonists in male love comedies rarely have the courage to express their feelings, but they show a remarkable tendency to accidentally walk in on naked women, accidentally go into the women's bath at the hot springs, stumble and grab women's breasts, and the like. Fanservice usually takes the place of any depiction of actual sex; it's extremely rare for the hero of a *shônen* romance to consummate a relationship, as much due to *shônen* magazines' content restrictions as for any logical reasons. (Apparently random groping is more acceptable than sex.)

In *seinen* magazines, aimed at older male readers, more is permissible, although dramatic tension often demands that the hero and heroine not have sex till the end of the series. Some romance artists, such as Hidenori Hara and Rumiko Takahashi, take a tastefully discreet approach, while others go as far as the medium will allow. The manga satire *Even a Monkey Can Draw Manga* visualized the typical *seinen* love comedy as a sort of "sushi boat" restaurant where beautiful women continually throw themselves at the hero. In Rumiko Takahashi's *Maison Ikkoku* (1980), the hero struggles to get into a good college so he can be worthy of the woman of his dreams, while resisting temptation from other women. Similar stories with far more T&A include *Love Hina* as well as U-Jin's *Sakura Tsushin* ("Sakura Diaries") and Tatsuya Egawa's *Tokyo Daigaku Monogatari* ("Tokyo University Story"), both untranslated. Naoki Yamamoto's erotic comedy *Dance Till Tomorrow* is one of the few translated stories in which the protagonists have something like a normal sex life . . . not counting explicitly "adult" manga, of course, in which the sex is frequent but anything but normal. Not all *seinen* heroes are nebbishes; some are studs through and through, and their stories are outrageous, semi-pornographic fantasy scenarios, such as the many collaborations of Kazuo Koike and Ryoichi Ikegami.

Romance for Everyone

Although translated material skews toward teenagers and college-age readers, romantic manga for adults exist as well. Young adults in Japan face strong pressure to get married, particularly young women, such as the twenty-something protagonists of *Happy Mania* and *Tramps Like Us*. Although true arranged marriages are a thing of the past (except in melodramatic manga), many people still choose marriage partners through traditional *omiai,* in which two people are formally introduced to one another by their parents, a matchmaking service, or another third party. Concerned about Japan's dwindling marriage rate and birthrate, some local governments have even begun to fund matchmaking services, a depressing topic that does not come up in translated manga. Traditional romances have enjoyed a resurgence in popularity, such as the *Socrates in Love* movie and manga franchise, based on the weepy novel by Kyoichi Katayama. *Densha Otoko* ("Train Man"), the story of an antisocial *otaku* who overcomes his shyness and dates a lonely woman, is one of the biggest hit books, movies, and manga of recent years. Kenshi Hirokane's untranslated short story series *Tasogare Ryûseigun* ("Like Shooting Stars in the Twilight"), which began publication in 1995, is the first hit manga focused on love and sex among the elderly.

Romance manga have long been popular with Western audiences, possibly because of the dearth of romance comics in the modern American comics industry. Some of the earliest hit manga in America were *shônen* love comedies such as *Ranma ½* and *Oh My Goddess!* OEL (original English-language) manga are often influenced by romance manga, with popular examples including Fred Gallagher's harem romance *Megatokyo,* Chynna Clugston-Major's *Blue Monday,* and Svetlana Chmakova's *Dramacon.* To Americans raised on the idea that comics are about fantasy, science fiction, and action, manga romances may be quietly revolutionary.

SHÔJO AND JÔSEI LOVE STORIES

Romances

Backstage Prince • *Basara* • *Boys over Flowers* • *Call Me Princess* • *Cardcaptor Sakura* • *Cardcaptor Sakura: Master of the Clow* • *Ceres: Celestial Legend* • *La Corda d'Oro* • *Crossroad* • *The Devil Does Exist* • *Devil in the Water* • *Dolis* • *Emma* • *Erica Sakurazawa* (*Angel* • *Angel Nest* • *The Aromatic Bitters* • *Between the Sheets* • *Nothing but Loving You* • *The Rules of Love*) • *Full Moon o Sagashite* • *Fushigi Yûgi* • *Gentleman's Alliance†* • *Hana-Kimi: For You in Full Blossom* • *Harlequin Pink* (*The Bachelor Prince* • *A Girl in a Million* • *Idol Dreams*) • *Harlequin Violet* (*Blind Date* • *Holding on to Alex* • *Response*) •

Hot Gimmick • Imadoki! Nowadays • Just a Girl • Kare First Love • Kare Kano: His and Her Circumstances • Kaze Hikaru • Kitchen Princess • Land of the Blindfolded • Let's Stay Together Forever • Love Song • Made in Heaven • Man of Many Faces • Mariko Parade • Marmalade Boy • Mars • Mars: Horse with No Name • Miss Me? • More Starlight to Your Heart • Mourning of Autumn Rain • Nana • Neon Genesis Evangelion: Angelic Days • The One I Love • Oyayubihime Infinity • Paradise Kiss • Peach Girl • Peach Girl: Change of Heart • Peach Girl: Sae's Story • A Perfect Day for Love Letters • Platinum Garden • Please Save My Earth • Popcorn Romance • Princess Knight • Red River • Revolutionary Girl Utena • Revolutionary Girl Utena: The Adolescence of Utena • The Rose of Versailles • Sailor Moon • Socrates in Love • SOS • Sugar Sugar Rune • Suki • Tail of the Moon • The Tale of Genji • Tokyo Boys & Girls • Tower of the Future • Train Man: A Shojo Manga • Vampire Knight • X2 (Times Two)

Love Comedies

Absolute Boyfriend • Beauty Is the Beast • The Day of Revolution • The Devil Within • D.N.Angel • Duck Prince • Fruits Basket • Gatcha Gacha • Guru Guru Pon-chan • Heaven!! • Happy Hustle High • Happy Mania • Instant Teen: Just Add Nuts • Kedamono Damono • Lagoon Engine • Love♥Com • Magical Pokémon Journey • Mamotte! Lollipop • Metamo Kiss • Mugen Spiral • Othello • Ouran High School Host Club • Pearl Pink • Pixie Pop: Gokkun Pucho • Punch! • Sensual Phrase • Strawberry 100% • Tenshi ja Nai!! • Tramps Like Us • Ultra Cute • Ultra Maniac • Until the Full Moon • Wild Act • Wish • Yu-rara

SHÔNEN AND SEINEN LOVE STORIES

Romances

Ai Yori Aoshi • Astra • Densha Otoko • Gadget • I"s • Love Roma • Maison Ikkoku • Saikano • Suzuka • Train_Man: Densha Otoko • Video Girl Ai • The Voices of a Distant Star: Hoshi no Koe • Yubisaki Milk Tea

Love Comedies

A.I. Love You • The All-New Tenchi Muyô! • Amazing Strip • Boys Be • Boys of Summer • A Cheeky Angel • Chibi Vampire • Chobits • Club 9 • Dance till Tomorrow • DearS • Eiken • Flowers & Bees • Full Metal Panic! • Futaba-kun Change • Gacha Gacha • Gacha Gacha: The Next Revolution • Galaxy Angel • Galaxy Angel II • Galaxy Angel Beta • Galaxy Angel Party • Girls Bravo • GTO: The Early Years—Shonan Junai-Gumi • Guardian Angel Getten • Inubaka: Crazy for Dogs • Kagetora • Love Hina • Lum*Urusei Yatsura • Maburaho • Mahoromatic • Maico 2010 • Marionette Generation • Maxion • Midori Days • My-HiME • NaNaNaNa • Negima!: Magister Negi Magi • No Need for Tenchi! • Ohikkoshi • Oh My Goddess! • Onegai Teacher • Onegai Twins • One Pound Gospel • Outlanders • Pastel • Pita-Ten • Pretty Face • Psychic Academy • Puri Puri • Ranma ½ • Remote • Rumic Theater • Rumic World Trilogy • Saber Marionette J • Sakura Taisen • School Rumble • Short Program • Sorcerer Hunters • Time Traveler Ai • To Heart • Tuxedo Gin • You & Me • Your and My Secret

R.O.D (READ OR DREAM)

R.O.D—Read or Dream: We Are Paper Sisters Detective Company, aka *Shin ("New") Read or Die* • Hideyuki Kurata (story), Ran Ayanagi (art) • Viz (2006–2007) • Shueisha (Ultra Jump, 2003–2005) • 4 volumes • Seinen, Fantasy, Action • 16+ (brief nudity, sexual situations)

A semi-sequel to *Read or Die,* featuring the same basic premise—people with supernatural paper powers tracking down books—but a different cast of characters. *Read or Dream* became the loose basis for the 26-episode *R.O.D* TV anime (not to be confused with the earlier, three-episode OAV). The heroines are the Paper Sisters, three Hong Kong sisters who all possess the power to control paper. They own and operate Paper Sisters Detective Agency, which specializes in cases involving books (but also takes on more prosaic assignments to pay the bills). Although scripted by the same writer as the *Read or Die* manga, *Read or Dream* is completely different in tone: it's mostly a light, episodic action comedy, with the occasional tearjerker tossed in. Ayanagi's amateurish but cute anime-style art helps keep the mood cheerful, and she and Kurata work in plenty of fanservice for their young-adult male audience. (Kurata's preferred forms of cheesecake: busty women in snug outfits and girl-on-girl chumminess.) *Read or Dream* is unambitious, T&A-heavy fluff, but on its own level it's solid entertainment. (CT)   ★★½

ROSE HIP ZERO

Tohru Fujisawa • Tokyopop (2006–ongoing) • Kodansha (Weekly Shônen Magazine, 2005–2006) • 5 volumes • Shônen, Crime, Action • 16+ (language, violence)

Kido, a sharpshooting young police detective whose sister was killed by terrorists, is assigned a new partner: Kasumi, a cute, cool fourteen-year-old girl trained by the terrorist organization Alice to have incredible combat abilities. (In fact, Alice, the bad guys of the series, consists entirely of fourteen-year-old super-assassins.) In addition to fighting Alice's former comrades, the mismatched pair are forced to live together, leading to minor romantic hijinks. Drawn in a polished, detailed style with lots of two-page spreads of Alice looking cool, *Rose Hip Zero* is a well-executed manga, but the plot feels like Fujisawa is on autopilot. The story ties into two other action manga by the same artist, *Rose Hip Rose* and *Magnum Rose Hip.*   ★★

THE ROSE OF VERSAILLES

Versailles no Bara, "Rose of Versailles" (ベルサイユのばら) • Riyoko Ikeda • Sanyusha (1981) • Shueisha (Margaret, 1972–1973) • 2 volume, suspended (10 volumes in Japan) • Shôjo, Historical, Romantic Drama • Unrated/13+ (mild language, violence, sex)

One of the greatest classics of *shôjo* manga, this series is unfortunately available in English only in two hard-to-find volumes printed in Japan, and in a brief excerpt in Frederik Schodt's *Manga! Manga! The World of Japanese Comics.* Set before and during the French Revolution, this gorgeous costume epic follows the life of Marie Antoinette, as well as a fictional character, Oscar François de Jarjayes, a woman raised as a man, who serves as Captain of the Royal Guards. Over 9 volumes of courtly romance, revolution, and war (the 10th volume is a side story), Marie Antoinette turns from a sparkly-eyed young princess into a ruthless queen, while the noble Oscar finds it harder and harder to defend the established order. Meanwhile, Oscar comes to terms with her gender and her feelings for her manservant, Andre. The change in Ikeda's artwork over the course of the series epitomizes the 1970s change in *shôjo* manga styles; in their youth the characters are cute and childish, drawn with soft lines and plenty of comic relief, but as they grow up they develop sharp, androgynous, decadent features. The art is lavish, brilliantly depicting the palaces and gardens of Versailles and both nobles and commoners, but *Rose of Versailles* is more than just flowers and dresses. Like a great historical novel, it includes love and death, births and battle scenes—a true ground's-eye view of history.   ★★★★

ROZEN MAIDEN

(ローゼンメイデン) • Peach-Pit • Tokyopop (2006–ongoing) • Gentosha (Comic Birz, 2002–2007) • 8 volumes • Occult, Fantasy • 13+ (violence)

Jun, a pathologically withdrawn teenager who stays in his room all day and is rude to his caring older sister, one day stumbles across a very strange mail-order offer: a Rozen Maiden, one of a limited edition of rare European wind-up dolls made in the early twentieth century. The doll, Shinku, promptly comes to life and bosses Jun around, making him serve her tea and dragging him into a cryptic world where mirrors lead to alternate dimensions and dolls do battle over an ancient secret. Although the fight scenes are dull and visually unappealing, *Rozen Maiden* achieves a mysterious, evocative mood amid pleasantly crosshatched, gothic artwork of dim rooms full of Edwardian furnishings. The plot is formulaic, with the hero gathering an entourage of Rozen Maidens and coming out of his shell, but Peach-Pit takes the material seriously enough that the reader is inclined to follow suit. In early 2007, the series went on hiatus due to conflicts between Peach-Pit and their editor. ★★

THE RULES OF LOVE: See *Erica Sakurazawa: The Rules of Love*

RUMIC THEATER

Takahashi Rumiko Gekijô, "Rumiko Takahashi Theater" (高橋留美子劇場) • Rumiko Takahashi • Viz (1995–1998) • Shogakukan (various magazines) • 2 volumes • Comedy, Romance, Sports • Unrated/16+ (nudity)

A collection of Takahashi stories, mostly containing works from *seinen* magazines from the 1980s and 1990s (with one or two goofy older stories in the mix). Possibly her most adult work, the plots are primarily slice-of-life comedies and dramas, often with adult female protagonists. Magic realism occasionally intervenes in the form of ghosts and spirits, but the overall mood is restrained; it's a matter of taste whether you prefer these polished domestic stories to the chaos of her older work in *Rumic World Trilogy*. Some of the older stories in volume 2

Nobuhiro Watsuki's *Rurouni Kenshin*

have themes that were later used in *Ranma ½* (one about a boy who turns into a dog whenever his nose bleeds, and one body-swap gender-bender story). ★★★½

RUMIC WORLD TRILOGY

Rumiko Takahashi • Viz (1996–1997) • Shogakukan (various magazines) • 3 volumes • Comedy, Science Fiction, Horror • Unrated/16+ (violence, nudity)

A collection of Rumiko Takahashi's earliest short stories from the late 1970s and early 1980s. Most are similar to *Lum★Urusei Yatsura* (whose one-shot precursor appears here): fast-paced slapstick comedies with cute girls and science fiction elements, often ending with the protagonists bewailing their misfortune, or getting chased out of town by an angry mob. Other stories are straightforward science fiction (*Fire Tripper*) or psychic/ghost-story horror (*The Laughing Target*). As a minor curiosity, volume 3 contains Takahashi's only autobiographical piece, a 4-page story about taking care of a cat. ★★★½

Dragons and wizards, sword-wielding heroes with improbably large shoulder pads, terms such as *levels* and *hit points*—many of the trappings of Japanese fantasy can be traced to RPGs (role-playing games), the popular category of video and tabletop games that originated in America. RPGs are best known today as a video game genre, but their origin goes back to tabletop games played with pens, paper, and dice, beginning with Dungeons & Dragons in 1974. In their most basic form, RPGs involve playing the role of a fictional character, who gains power by surviving fights with monsters or other opponents, usually in a fantasy setting. The American tabletop RPG boom of the late 1970s and early 1980s made little impact in Japan, although some small publishers catered to tabletop fans, such as Hobby Japan with *Comic Master* and *RPG Magazine*. Translated computer games such as the Wizardry and the Ultima series also found a small audience.

The true form of Japanese RPGs, however, proved to be console video games for systems such as Nintendo. In 1986, the Japanese game and manga publisher Enix released Dragon Quest, a purposely simple RPG featuring playful artwork by Akira Toriyama. The game and its sequels converted millions of Japanese children into RPG enthusiasts. Long-running manga adaptations followed: Sanjô and Koji Inada's *Dragon Quest: Dai no Daibôken* ("Dragon Quest: Dai's Great Adventure") (1989–1996) and Chiaki Kawamata and Kamui Fujiwara's *Dragon Quest Gaiden: Roto no Monshô* ("Dragon Quest Side Story: The Crest of Roto") (1991–1997). It was partly to promote their RPGs that Enix launched the 1991 fantasy manga magazine *Monthly Shônen Gangan,* whose name comes from an attack in the Dragon Quest games, "Gangan ikouze!" ("Let's charge!").

The only RPG of comparable popularity was Square's Final Fantasy series, which began in 1987. In contrast to the kid-friendly Dragon Quest, Final Fantasy aimed for a mood of epic sci-fi/fantasy, expressed by the sophisticated artwork of Yoshitaka Amano. With its elaborate melodramas and lengthy dialogues between characters, Final Fantasy emphasized plot to an extent never before seen in RPGs, in a sense taking the genre away from its you-are-the-hero role-playing roots, but also receiving rave reviews for its scripting and artistry. In 2003, the long-term rivalry between the two companies ended with a merger into a new

Square Enix's *Monthly Shônen Gangan* is one of the heftiest monthly magazines, sometimes over one thousand pages. Its current hit title is *Fullmetal Alchemist.*

company, Square Enix. Today, *Monthly Shônen Gangan* also runs manga adaptations of games from the company's Square side, such as *Final Fantasy: Crystal Chronicles*.

Console RPGs gradually broke away from their European fantasy origins, venturing into science fiction (such as Sega's Phantasy Star series and the later Final Fantasy games), horror (Atlus' Shin Megami Tensei and its spin-offs), and mainstream products for younger audiences (Nintendo's Pokémon, Square's Kingdom Hearts). Many had manga adaptations. The late 1990s saw the rise of MMORPGs, massively multiplayer online RPGs, such as the anime/manga/game franchise .hack, or the hit American computer game World of Warcraft. For most manga artists, RPGs are a background influence at best, but the most consistent feature of all RPGs is a theme that also runs throughout *shônen* manga: if you fight hard, you can get stronger and stronger. A few artists, such as Saki Hiwatari (*Tower of the Future*), have gone beyond the superficial fantasy trappings of the genre to explore themes of escapism and identity.

Tabletop RPGs still enjoy a small cult following in Japan, as in America. The most successful homegrown RPG is Group SNE's Sword World, a Dungeons & Dragons/ RuneQuest imitation created in the 1980s by fantasy author/game designer Ryo Mizuno, better known for the *Record of Lodoss War* series. (*Record of Lodoss War* was based on transcripts of Mizuno's gaming sessions.) Kadokawa Shoten's manga magazines *Comic Dragon* and *Dragon Junior* (merged in 2003 into *Dragon Age*) originated as spin-offs of the fantasy "light novel" magazine *Dragon Magazine* (no relation to the American magazine of the same name). For a brief time, *Comic Dragon* ran manga based on American tabletop RPGs such as Shadowrun before focusing on Japanese fantasy licenses such as Slayers and Monster Collection.

In the 1990s, collectible card games (CCGs) stole much of the audience for traditional tabletop RPGs, thanks to the overwhelming popularity of the American game Magic: The Gathering. As with RPGs, a homegrown Japanese imitation proved more popular than the translated version; the card game introduced in Kazuki Takahashi's *Yu-Gi-Oh!* (1996) became a massive hit, and now virtually every major manga or anime series has a CCG spin-off.

See also FANTASY, GAMES AND HOBBIES, VIDEO GAMES.

RPG Video Game Manga
Disgaea • Disgaea 2 • .hack//Legend of the Twilight • Kingdom Hearts • Kingdom Hearts: Chain of Memories • The Legend of Zelda: A Link to the Past • Legendz • Magical Pokémon Journey • Medabots • Pokémon: The Electric Tale of Pikachu • Pokémon: Pikachu Meets the Press • Pokémon Adventures • Pokémon Mystery Dungeon • Suikoden III: The Successor of Fate

RPG-Themed Manga
Beet the Vandel Buster • Gamerz Heaven • Maniac Road • Tower of the Future • Yu-Gi-Oh! • Yu-Gi-Oh!: Duelist • Yu-Gi-Oh!: Millennium World

RUROUNI KENSHIN

Rurôni Kenshin, "Wandering Ronin Kenshin" (るろうに険心) • Nobuhiro Watsuki • Viz (2003–2006) • Shueisha (Weekly Shônen Jump, 1994–1999) • 28 volumes • Shônen, Samurai, Battle • 16+ (mild language, graphic violence)

Set in 1878 Japan, when the new world of business suits and locomotives coexists uneasily with the old world of samurai swords, *Rurouni Kenshin* combines an interesting setting, an adventure story for teenage readers, and lots of fight scenes. Kenshin, a former government assassin who has sworn never to kill again (instead he batters foes with a special blunt-edged sword), seeks a peaceful life at a dojo run by female swords instructor Kaoru, but he is constantly pursued by old enemies, corrupt revolutionaries (both left- and right-wing), and the consequences of his past misdeeds. Watsuki's art tends toward geometric faces and exaggerated musculature, and his bad guys show a love of 1990s American superhero comics, with several designs based directly on Jim Lee's *X-Men*. The plot mixes real historical figures with blatantly fantastic battles, frequently drifting into "string of fights" mode (most notably in the Kyoto story arc, volumes 8–17), but always maintaining some connection to history and the characters' motivations. The character writing is well done, the central characters have an endearing family structure, and the domestic comedy in the dojo scenes is enjoyable.   ★★★

SABER MARIONETTE J

(セイバー・マリオネットJ) • Satoru Akahori (original creator), Tsukasa Kotobuki (character design), Yumisuke Kotoyoshi (story and art) • Tokyopop (2003) • Kadokawa Shoten (Comic Dragon/Dragon Junior, 1996–1999) • 5 volumes • Shônen, Science Fiction, Romantic Comedy • 16+ (language, nudity, sexual situations)

Manga adaptation of Satoru Akahori's light novel series, better known in the United States for its anime spin-offs. Terra Two is a world populated only by men and buxom female androids called marionettes, who do household chores. Otaru Mamiya is the only male who treats marionettes with respect, and because of this he is granted three special marionettes of his own. Lime, Cherry, and Bloodberry all have the fabled maiden chip, which they refer to as their soul; but apparently a soul doesn't include free will, because they all fall in love with Otaru at first sight and do whatever they can to please their master. Together, they try to save their city-state from being conquered, and awaken the only real female on Terra Two. The art is well shaded, but the main characters all have eyes so large they slide down onto their drooping cheeks. A frustrating series, with slapstick comedy, blimplike breasts (Koyotoshi primarily works as an adult artist), and general degrading treatment of females. (KT)   ★½

SABER TIGER

(サーベル・タイガー) • Yukinobu Hoshino • Viz (1991) • Futabasha (various magazines, 1980–1981) • 1 volume • Seinen, Science Fiction • 13+ (brief graphic violence)

A collection of Yukinobu Hoshino's early works; the English edition includes only two stories out of several in the original Japanese edition. In the pulpy "Saber Tiger," time travelers in skintight bodysuits go from the year 2479 to the Ice Age to protect a small tribe of primitive humans. In the second story, "The Planet of the Unicorn," a group of space colonists lands on a seemingly hospitable planet of endless grasslands, only to face unexpected hardships. Although relatively primitive early works by Hoshino's standards, it's realistically drawn, interesting science fiction.   ★★★

SAIKANO

Saishu Heiki Kanojo, "Ultimate Weapon Girlfriend/She the Ultimate Weapon" (最終兵器彼女) • Shin Takahashi • Viz (2004–2005) • Shogakukan (Big Comic Spirits, 2000–2001) • 7 volumes • Seinen, Science Fiction, Military, Romance • 18+ (language, graphic violence, nudity, graphic sex)

Capturing the moments in adolescence when you feel the world might end, or the moment of adulthood when you realize you won't live forever, *Saikano* is a bizarre mix of apocalyptic war story and explicit sex, like a post-virginity *Neon Genesis Evangelion*. When the manga begins, grouchy Shuji is already going out with his classmate, the awkward (and underage-looking) Chise. However, the world intrudes on their relationship, in the form of a global conflict (whose cause and factions are never explained), and Chise's transformation into a godlike cyborg thing, a sort of death angel of the battlefields. The premise sounds like a bad anime, but the civilian-life-in-wartime elements, which dominate the plot, are shockingly realistic. *Saikano* is ultimately a tale of two people, an attempt to grapple with big issues of sex, death, and intimacy. Or you could say it's a porno tragedy. The art combines cute, lightly sketched characters with CG-enhanced photorealistic backgrounds, and the story is told with experimental layouts and heavy use of text.   ★★★½

SAILOR MOON

Bishôjo Senshi Sailor Moon, "Beautiful Girl Soldier Sailor Moon" (美少女戦士セーラームーン) • Naoko Takeuchi • Tokyopop (1997–2001) • Kodansha (Nakayoshi, 1992–1997) • Shôjo, Fantasy, Romance, Action • 18 volumes • Unrated/All Ages (violence, partial nudity)

The first successful *shôjo* manga and anime in the United States, *Sailor Moon* is a calculated combination of action and heartache, a formula possibly copied by American entertainment such as *Buffy the Vampire Slayer* (but without the sarcasm for adults). Serena (aka Bunny), a ditzy fourteen-year-old, encounters a talking cat and finds out that she is Sailor Moon, superpowered and short-skirted "Champion of Truth and Justice," whose mission is to save the world from evil witches, alien invaders, TV psychics, and other embodiments of ultimate evil. As she gathers her team of planet-themed Sailor Scouts, she travels to the moon and through time, and discovers that they are all the reincarnations of warriors who perished tragically in the distant past, including Tuxedo Mask, her handsome suitor. Fast-paced and formulaic, the early chapters are like episodes of a *sentai* TV show: diabolical villains cause trouble through evil front organizations (video stores, jewelry stores, afterschool programs, etc.), and then Sailor Moon and her friends show up and save the day. Like its influence *Saint Seiya,* the fight scenes consist mostly of disconnected poses over impressionistic screentone backgrounds, but unlike *Saint Seiya,* there is no gore to contaminate the prettiness, and the bad guys who get blasted to dust are usually not really humans at all. (For that matter, the fight scenes are much shorter and simpler than in any *shônen* manga.) The characters undergo power-ups and costume changes, and gather suspiciously marketable-looking accessories, but they also spend time as normal teenagers, and the character interaction continues to be fun after the repetitive bad guys start to get old (around volume 7). Although *Sailor Moon* is very much about love, marriage, and the baby carriage, and although the characters' super-moves have names like "Starlight Honeymoon Therapy Kiss," the gender roles are not entirely reactionary: Serena becomes less of a crybaby as the series goes on, and Tuxedo Mask, the sole male hero, exists mostly to get brainwashed and saved by the women. Despite weak art (at the beginning) and weak story lines (later on), it's sweet, effective entertainment. Beginning in *Sailor Moon,* the story continues in *Sailor Moon Super S* and concludes in *Sailor Moon StarS,* all of which were published in Japan as part of the same 18-volume series; the repetitive plots begin to wear thin in the later volumes.   ★★★

SAILOR MOON STARS: See *Sailor Moon*

SAILOR MOON SUPER S: See *Sailor Moon*

SAINT SEIYA: See *Knights of the Zodiac (Saint Seiya)*

SAINT TAIL

Kaitô Saint Tail, "Phantom Thief Saint Tail" (怪盗セイント・テール) • Megumi Tachikawa • Tokyopop (2001–2002) • Kodansha (Nakayoshi, 1994–1996)

• 7 volumes • Shôjo, Magical Girl, Phantom Thief, Romance • All Ages

Some writers of children's manga create stories that can be enjoyed by all ages; Megumi Tachikawa does not. With the guidance of her nun friend Seira, Catholic middle-schooler Meimi Haneoka transforms into Saint Tail—a ponytailed magical master thief who steals only for altruistic, romantic reasons. But she's in love with Asuka Jr., the young detective who's sworn to catch her! And soon enough, a rival thief shows up, also seeking Asuka's heart. With its predictable stories, *Saint Tail* is sweet stuff, but strictly for younger readers. Meimi's Catholicism-powered magic acts as a deus ex machina for every situation, and the art is as simple and fluffy as the stories. The characters are baby-like, with eyes like dinner plates. (In her notes, Tachikawa confesses, "My editor often tells me, 'Your faces are really smushed flat, aren't they?'") ★★

SAIYUKI

Saiyûki, "Journey to the Extreme" (最遊記) • Kazuya Minekura • Tokyopop (2004–2005) • Square Enix (Monthly G-Fantasy, 1997–2002) • 9 volumes • Bishônen, Fantasy, Action, Comedy • 16+ (language, occasional graphic violence, occasional nudity, mild sexual situations)

In this self-consciously cool take on the Chinese legend *Saiyuki* ("Journey to the West"; the manga title is a pun), Minekura retains little but the names of the main characters, here reinvisioned as hot guys who lounge around like fashion models with cigarettes dangling from their mouths. Sanzo, the priest, is a gun-toting, chain-smoking cynic; Gojyo is a foul-mouthed guy with a heart of gold; Hakkai is guilty of murder and incest; and little Son Goku is childishly good-natured. These four *bishônen* are on a mission to stop the resurrection of a demon king, and as they head from China to India by magic jeep (the time period is a mishmash), they argue constantly, stop in nameless towns, and get attacked by elf-eared *youkai* (demons) in jeans and T-shirts. Despite the generic designs, Mine-

kura's sharp-featured, screentoned art is easy on the eyes. The story strikes a balance between humor, fight scenes, and cooler-than-thou, darkly cynical pronouncements ("What's wrong with selfishness and egotism? We live to die smiling, don't we?"). However, it all feels aimless and padded out; the characters never really seem to *go* anywhere, and the plot only treads back into the heroes' tragic pasts, never forward. ★★

SAIYUKI RELOAD

Saiyûki Reload, "Journey to the Extreme Reload" (最遊記RELOAD) • Kazuya Minekura • Tokyopop (2005–ongoing) • Ichijinsha (Comic Zero-Sum, 2002–ongoing) • 7+ volumes (ongoing) • Bishônen, Fantasy, Action, Comedy • 16+ (language, occasional graphic violence, occasional nudity, sexual situations)

In 2002 Kazuya Minekura left Enix and was involved in the launch of a new magazine, *Comic Zero-Sum. Saiyuki Reload,* the continuation of *Saiyuki* under a new name, was the new magazine's flagship title. The four heroes continue their seemingly endless quest, with frequent digressions into origin story flashbacks, wisecracking arguments, and moody thoughts about loneliness. In between, they're attacked by bad guys, whom they dispatch while making cool poses. The art and storytelling are adequate, but the plot is little more than *bishônen* fanservice, content to go nowhere as long as the four heroes can take off their shirts and bicker suggestively with one another. ★★

SAKE JOCK

Various artists • Fantagraphics (1995) • 1 issue • Underground • 18+ (language, crude humor, nudity)

This short (72 pages) one-shot comic book anthology shows the work of a small number of avant-garde manga artists, mostly from the pages of the magazine *Garo,* although no historical perspective is provided. The standout is Imiri Sakabashira's "Horse Horse Tiger Tiger," a beautifully detailed glimpse of a dark urban-industrial dreamscape. The book also includes Naoto Yamakawa's indie-comics-esque slice-of-life "A

SALARYMAN (サラリーマン)

In the 1980s, in one of their periodic attempts to sell comics to adults, Marvel Comics ran a photo advertisement showing a businessman reading *The Incredible Hulk* on his lunch break. To Americans, the idea that "everyone reads manga in Japan" may conjure similar images of office workers openly reading boys' comics such as *Negima!* on the subway—but in fact, the image is almost equally unlikely. On the contrary, there are entire genres of manga aimed specifically at working adults: business dramas and office comedies that go under the collective name of "salaryman manga."

Comic strips about working life have existed in Japan since the dawn of four-panel manga in the 1920s, but salaryman comic strips first boomed in the 1960s. Japan's economy was on the rise, and as the growing class of white-collar office workers became recognized figures of the media, they soon appeared in comic strips in weekly newsmagazines and major daily newspapers. One of the first was Sampei Satô's *Fuji Santarô* (1965) in the *Asahi Shimbun*. The stars of these comics were typically figures of fun: low-ranked employees with amusingly pathetic lives, not entirely unlike American comic strip characters such as *Dilbert*. Sadao Shôji, creator of comics such as *Asatte-kun* (1974) in the *Mainichi Shimbun*, is credited with bringing more real-world observation and cynicism to the genre. Business comic strips are still read in Japan today, and the oldest strips are now considered classics, if a bit dusty; in 2006, Sampei Satô became one of a small number of manga artists to receive an Order of Culture award for contributions to Japan's art, literature, and culture.

In the late 1970s and early 1980s, Japan's economy again skyrocketed. As corporations became more important to the new economy, a new kind of salaryman manga appeared: long-running story manga with salaryman heroes, aimed at readers from college age on up. Salarymen were no longer drab, pathetic figures; they were elite businessmen, figures whom readers might want to become rather than laugh at. Publishers repositioned existing magazines to target them to office workers, and launched new magazines with names such as *Business Jump, Big Comic Business,* and *Big Comic Superior* (as in your superior at the office). In some cases, the branding didn't stick (*Business Jump* is now a typical cheesecake-oriented young men's magazine), but on the whole, the mood of *seinen* manga in this period was "settle down and get to work."

Kenshi Hirokane's *Division Chief Kosaku Shima*

311

The archetype of the new salaryman hero was Kenshi Hirokane's Kosaku Shima, who first appeared in *Section Chief Kosaku Shima* in 1983. Shima is an employee of the fictional Hatsushiba corporation, an idealized businessman who slowly climbs the corporate ladder while negotiating deals, exploring current hot-button issues, and getting hit on by gorgeous women. Judging from the lack of businessman heroes on American TV, career businessmen might seem unsympathetic, but Shima isn't in it for the money; he thinks only of the good of the company, its employees, and society as a whole. *Kosaku Shima* became so popular that it inspired a live-action TV series, a series of nonfiction business books, and countless imitators. The hero of Kimio Yanagisawa's *Tokumei Kakarichô Tadano Hitoshi* ("Mission Section Chief Hitoshi Tadano") pretends to be a shiftless clock puncher so that he can sniff out corporate corruption. Hiroshi Motomiya's more humorous *Salaryman Kintarô* (1994) approached the clash between old and new manga culture head-on: the star is a former gang member who saves a company president from a mugging and is given a job out of gratitude. Knowing only the tough life, Kintarô earnestly shouts, punches, and slugs his way through business disputes, while simultaneously trying to be a good single father for his young son. (In stereotypical Japanese fashion, no matter what he does, he can't be fired because his boss feels so indebted to him.)

But of course, not everyone can get promoted forever like Kosaku Shima. Another salaryman manga genre that developed in the early 1980s focuses warmheartedly on more modest, everyday businessmen, who care more about hobbies or their family than work. Kenichi Kitami and Jûzô Yamasaki's hit *Tsuru-Baka Nisshi* ("Diary of a Fishing Freak"), which began in 1980, involves a cheerful young salaryman who lives for the weekend when he can go fishing, to the occasional annoyance of his wife and boss. The protagonist of Mitsutoshi Furuya's *Genten Papa* ("Demerit Mark Papa") sucks at the office but awes his family with his knowledge of cooking, carpentry, and other useful topics. To some Japanese manga fans, the difference in attitude between *Section Chief Kosaku Shima* and *Tsuru-Baka Nisshi* (elite go-getters versus laid-back everymen) reflected the difference in editorial policy between publishers Kodansha and Shogakukan. In the spring of 1995, NHK's Sunday morning TV show *Keizai Scope* arranged a debate between the respective manga creators. Speaking to a studio audience, Yamasaki and Hirokane each gave the case for the lifestyles expressed in their manga. The audience voted more than two to one in favor of Hirokane, but perhaps it was an unfair trial; the audience consisted of executives, not rank-and-file employees.

Most salaryman manga protagonists are distinctly salary*men*. In Japan, most female office workers fall into the category of office ladies (OLs), typically single women in their twenties who serve as a clerical pool of secretaries, typists, and filing clerks. Risu Akizuki's popular four-panel strip *Survival in the Office: The Evolution of Japanese Working Women* (1989) depicts the culture with charm and demonstrates how office ladies feel about being asked to serve tea all the time. Most OLs have limited opportunities for promotion and typically quit when they get married; a scarcity of private or state-funded day care makes it difficult to balance work and motherhood. During the time of Kazuyoshi Torii's 1987 *Top wa Ore da!* ("I'm #1!"), a female boss was still rare enough to have a manga written around her, although the story is told from the perspective of her male subordinate. Today, women's roles are beginning to improve, and some women choose to start their own businesses as an alternative to the traditional, male-dominated Japanese corporate world.

In her book *Adult Manga: Culture and Power in Contemporary Japanese Society*, Sharon Kinsella argues that the 1980s salaryman manga trend was part of a conscious decision to make manga more "white-collar" and "respectable." According to Kinsella, this new "socially responsible" manga was promoted by upper-class editors at the major Tokyo-based manga publishers, in cooperation with cultural and educational institutions. If so, it partly succeeded. The use of manga as an educational tool became established at this time, and not just for children; Shotaro Ishinomori's influential *Japan Inc.: An Introduction to Japanese Economics* (1986) wrapped up grown-up economics lessons in a simple story. Inspirational stories about real-life businessmen and companies were commissioned in manga form, such as Takao Saito's *Gekiga Made in Japan* (1987), based on the autobiography of Sony president Akio Morita, and *Warren Buffett: An Illustrated Biography of the World's Most Successful Investor* (2003). But manga does not owe its popularity to being "good for you"; and for every manga about a brilliant businessman, there is one about a sympathetic goof-off.

Salaryman Manga

Bringing Home the Sushi • Division Chief Kosaku Shima • Japan Inc.: An Introduction to Japanese Economics (The Comic Book) • New Lanchester Strategy • Project X • Survival in the Office: The Evolution of Japanese Working Women • Warren Buffett: An Illustrated Biography of the World's Most Successful Investor

Hooker's Room," a cynical story about the elderly by Yoshiharu Mitsumoto, and works by Nekojiru, Kiriko Nananan, Naoki and Shunichi Karasawa, and Yasuji Tanioka.

★★★

SAKURA TAISEN

Sakura Taisen Manga Ban, "Cherry Blossom Wars: Manga Edition" (サクラ大戦漫画版) • Ohji Hiroi (story), Kosuke Fujishima (character design), Ikku Masa (art) • Tokyopop (2005–ongoing) • Kodansha (Magazine Z, 2002–ongoing) • 6+ volumes (ongoing) • Shônen, Video Game, Historical, Military, Fantasy, Romantic Comedy • 13+ (language, violence, mild sexual situations)

A dating simulation/tactical RPG franchise (yes, both at the same time) that started on the Sega Saturn, *Sakura Taisen* was spun off into several games, anime, an entire store filled with merchandise and costumes, and a manga series. Set in Tokyo during the Taisho era (1912–1926), the plot revolves around Ensign Ogami. Fresh from training in the Naval Academy, Ogami is assigned to doing menial tasks for Tokyo's all-female Imperial Theater Troupe. But these are not your ordinary actors; they are the Imperial *Fighting Theater Troupe*, women with psychic powers who defend Tokyo from automated steam-powered assault mecha! Although it captures both the action and dating aspects of the game, and the art is adequate, *Sakura Taisen* is of interest only to diehard fans. (DR)

★

SAMURAI CHAMPLOO

(サムライチャンプルー) • manglobe (original creator), Masaru Gotsubo (story and art) • Tokyopop (2005–2006) • Kadokawa Shoten (Monthly Shônen Ace, 2004) • 2 volumes • Shônen, Samurai, Action, Comedy • 13+ (mild language, violence)

An adaptation of the anime series by the director of *Cowboy Bebop, Samurai Champloo* mixes modern-day pop culture with Tokugawa-era Japan. The three main characters wander the countryside with little unified purpose: Jin, a reserved samurai searching for a motivation; Mugen, a short-tempered bad-ass mercenary; and Fuu, a sassy girl in search of "a samurai who smells like sunflowers." When Mugen and Jin aren't fighting each other, they're saving Fuu or getting in trouble with the local authorities. The manga has the same anarchistic spirit as the anime; while it lacks the great fight choreography and hip-hop soundtrack, the action scenes are fluid in their own way. (KT)   ★★★

SAMURAI CRUSADER

Ôritsuin Kumomaru no Shôgai, "The Life of Kumomaru Ôritsuin" (王龍院雲丸の生涯) • Hiroi Oji (story), Ryoichi Ikegami (art) • Viz (1995–1997) • Shogakukan (Weekly Shônen Sunday, 1991–1992) • 3 volumes • Shônen, Historical, Action • Unrated/16+ (language, violence, nudity)

Young Kumomaru is the heir to the powerful Oritsuin clan. Before assuming his familial responsibilities in pre–World War II Japan, he wants to get out and see the wide world beyond his nation's borders. After completing his training in the samurai arts, he heads for Europe, where he runs afoul of militant Japanese imperialists who are brokering for power with the growing Nazi regime. This cauldron of Japanese-German bad guys covets the ancient Kusanagi sword, said to contain the power of the gods. After the sword falls into Kumomaru's hands, the chase is on to get it back from him. While trekking across the globe to Paris, Shanghai, and Switzerland, Kumomaru befriends the likes of Ernest Hemingway, bumps into Pablo Picasso, and faces off against a psychically created ogre and an axe-wielding Aryan superman. Author Hiroi Oji (*Sakura Taisen*) delivers a satisfying, big-scale historical adventure story that reads like a mix between an Indiana Jones movie and a 1980s Hong Kong film. Artist Ryoichi Ikegami is in fine form throughout, with great action scenes and precise period detail. Seasoned Ikegami readers who've been through the torrid likes of *Crying Freeman* and *Offered* will notice that the thrills here stop just short of a PG-13 level of explicitness. Still, it's nice to have a straightforward Ikegami adventure yarn that doesn't require hiding the pages from plain sight from time to time. (PM)   ★★★½

SAMURAI DEEPER KYO

Akimine Kamijyo • Tokyopop (2003–ongoing) • Kodansha (Weekly Shônen Magazine, 1999–2006) • 38 volumes • Shônen, Historical, Action • 16+ (language, violence, partial nudity)

Akimine Kamijyo's samurai epic debuted in English just a few months before a little series called *Rurouni Kenshin*. Both are chock-full of swords and samurai, and both open with a seemingly sweet-natured protagonist with a sword he refuses to use; however it soon becomes clear that *Samurai Deeper Kyo* is cut from a wholly different cloth. When sexy bounty hunter Yuya Shiina finds the bumbling medicine peddler Kyoshiro Mibu, she plans to turn him in for a quick bounty. Her plans change when she discovers Kyoshiro is possessed by the infamous "Demon-Eyes" Kyo, a murderous samurai whose very name sends chills down people's spines. At first limited to short appearances in times of duress, Kyo soon takes over Kyoshiro's body completely and drags Yuya along on a quest to find his own body. As Kyo's power grows, so too does his posse of kings and killers, including such historical figures as Yukimura Sanada, swordmaker Muramasa, little ninja Sasuke Sarutobi, and Benitora, a Kansai country boy (and comic relief) whose true identity unfolds as the series progresses. The greatest fun of *Samurai Deeper Kyo* is seeing how Kamijyo takes liberties with some of Japan's most famous historical figures, circa A.D. 1600. Unfortunately, the series features many times more generic "bosses," each enemy knocked off in succession, only to be replaced by a new and stronger foe. It doesn't help the reader keep track of (or care about) who's who when dealing with similarly named reincarnations and creative faction names like The Four, The Ten, and The Twelve. What starts off as a series grounded in reality ends up as a Titanomachy of samurai gods, which isn't nearly as exciting as when the characters were mere human beings. The fights are certainly exciting, and there is no denying that Kamijyo's character designs are attractive (*bishônen* such as Yukimura have earned many female admirers), but at 38 volumes, the formula overstays its welcome. (MT) ★★½

SAMURAI EXECUTIONER

Kubikiri Asa, "Decapitator Asa" (首斬り朝) • Kazuo Koike (story), Goseki Kojima (art) • Dark Horse (2004–2006) • Kodansha (Weekly Gendai, 1972–1976) • 10 volumes • Seinen, Samurai, Crime Drama • 18+ (language, graphic violence, nudity, sex)

In Tokugawa-era Japan, certain crimes are punished by decapitation, and the greatest decapitator is Yamada Asaemon Yoshimitsu, who inherited his post from his father and his father's father. A spin-off of *Lone Wolf and Cub, Samurai Executioner* is a collection of tales of crime and punishment set in historical Japan (mostly in the same city), without the ongoing epic of Kojima and Koike's better-known series. The stories deal with individual criminal cases, the mysterious last words and deeds of the executed, and the minutiae of Asaemon's profession ("As the days warm, our skin takes on more fat, so there's more resistance to the blade"). The lurid crime dramas involve such subjects as prostitution, torture, urine drinking, and sadomasochism. At the center of all this chaos, however, is Asaemon, a superhumanly dedicated Buddhist (most of the time) who often finds ways to be merciful even when honor demands that he kill. Other tales center on "catcher" Kasajirô, a policeman who uses a hook and rope to capture fleeing criminals. The pulpy, yet humanistic artwork of Goseki Kojima transports the reader into the setting. ★★★½

SAMURAI GIRL REAL BOUT HIGH SCHOOL

Real Bout High School (リアルバウトハイスクール) • Reiji Saiga (story), Sora Inoue (art) • Tokyopop (2002–2004) • Kadokawa Shoten (Comic Dragon, 1998–2003) • 6 volumes • Shônen, Martial Arts, Comedy • 13+ (mild language, violence, partial nudity)

Manga adaptation of the Reiji Saiga novels, better known in the United States for their anime adaptation. Big-hipped "samurai girl" Ryoko is her school's champion kendo fighter, who spends her days defending her female friends from street punks, hoping to win the attention of the guy she likes, and dueling with her only serious competition, the macho, bandanna-wearing Shizumi. The characters are stock anime types, the art is polished but derivative, and you get exactly what you expect from the genre: thin skirts, ninjas, tournaments, and "shouldn't you be more ladylike?" jokes. ★★

SAMURAI LEGEND

Kaze no Shô—Byôki Hijô, "Paper of Wind—Twig/Treetop Life Secret Notebook" (風の抄一秒生秘帖) • Jiro Taniguchi (art), Kan Furuyama (story) • CPM (2003) • Akita Shoten (Young Champion, 1992) • Seinen, Historical, Samurai, Drama • 16+ (violence, nudity)

Opening with a brief framing story set in 1899 Meiji-era Japan, this what-if historical drama stars Yagyu Jubei, the famous swordsman. The Yagyu ninja clan—historically the defenders of the shogunate—is portrayed as secretly working to reform the system, while their enemy, the retired emperor Gomino, steals the Yagyu's secret writings in order to create a reactionary imperialistic regime. Historical exposition alternates with sword-fighting scenes, but the story feels condensed and lacks a human element, and Taniguchi's art is stiffer than usual. ★★

SAMURAI MAN

(サムライマン) • Naoki Serizawa • Media Blasters (2005–2006) • Akita Shoten (Weekly Shônen Champion, 2002–2003) • 3 volumes • Shônen, Fantasy, Action • 16+ (language, crude humor, graphic violence, sexual situations)

Ryouma's class field trip to Kyoto is interrupted by the appearance of giant armored samurai warriors, who appear out of nowhere in the middle of a city-destroying battle.

When Ryouma is possessed by one of the masked warriors, he must fight the ultimate evil and protect Japan from an extradimensional invasion. The art is decent and the juvenile premise is played mostly straight, although the villains are poorly developed, the dialogue is inane, and the heroine's panties manage to be visible just a bit more than perspective would allow. The manga was forced to end abruptly, so Serizawa unsuccessfully attempts to cram a big-budget apocalyptic plot into the last volume. ★½

SAMURAI SHODOWN

Samurai Spirits—Makai Bugeichô, "Samurai Spirits—Demon World Military Record" (魔界武芸著サムライスピリッツ)・ Kyoichi Nanatsuki (story), Yuki Miyoshi (art) • Viz (1997) • Shogakukan (Weekly Shônen Sunday Comics Special, 1995) • 1 volume • Shônen, Samurai, Video Game, Battle • Unrated/13+ (mild language, violence)

A prelude to the original *Samurai Shodown* video game. In 1787 Japan, easygoing samurai Haohmaru and Ainu priestess Nakoruru team up against the gathering forces of the Dark Kingdom, fighting female ninja Nagiri and sorcerer Madou Shiranui as well as a demonic battleship and an island of ogres. The rushed plot sounds better than it reads (the big battle raging across Japan takes place mostly offscreen), but the mediocre character designs and stiff artwork are what truly sink the story. Some nudity is censored in the English edition. ★

SAMURAI, SON OF DEATH

Sharman DiVono (story), Hiroshi Hirata (art) • Eclipse (1987) • 1 issue • Samurai, Drama • 16+ (violence, partial nudity, sex)

Billed as the first comics collaboration between an American writer and a Japanese artist, *Samurai, Son of Death* is chiefly of interest as a curiosity. In 1587 Japan, warlord Toyotomi Hideyoshi launches a military campaign against the forces of Shimazu Yoshihisa. Sadayasu, a samurai of Hideyoshi's forces, awakens among the corpses on the battlefield believing that he is undead, triggering many pretentious ruminations on death, religion, and the samurai code. Hirata's ultra-realistic *gekiga* artwork is excellent as always, but it's painful to see him forced to work under the incredibly cramped conditions of Sharman DiVono's script, which, in typical American comics fashion, crams dozens of characters and subplots into 48 pages. ★★½

SANCTUARY

(サンクチュアリ) • Sho Fumimura (story), Ryoichi Ikegami (art) • Viz (1993–1998) • Shogakukan (Big Comic Superior, 1990–1995) • 9 volumes • Seinen, Political, Crime Drama • Unrated/18+ (language, violence, nudity, sex)

Two Japanese survivors of the Cambodian killing fields return to their home country vowing to create a sanctuary for themselves at all costs. Akira Hojo becomes a gangster in the *yakuza*. Chiaki Asami enters the treacherous world of politics as a secretary to a member of the Japanese Diet. Believing the time is right to revolutionize Japan with their youthful energy, Hojo and Asami begin to maneuver for power in their respective areas of influence. Meanwhile, Kyoko Ishihara, the deputy chief of police, tries to uncover the truth about this unlikely alliance between a statesman and a gangster to whom she finds herself erotically drawn. Full of backroom deals, betrayals, and gangland bullet ballets, *Sanctuary* is adult-strength manga at its very best. Writer Sho Fumimura's meticulously researched plots make for feverish page-turners and are engrossingly complex without ever becoming confusing. The series is also blessed with a strong cast of supporting characters, among them loose cannon Tokai, an ultimate gangster in the *Scarface* mode, who ignites the pages whenever he appears. The superbly realistic art is among Ryoichi Ikegami's very best work; he can turn scenes of people simply sitting at a table talking into pulse-pounding drama. Entertaining and illuminating in equal amounts, *Sanctuary* leaves readers with a deeper understanding of the Japanese underworld and politics and thus a deeper understanding of Japan itself. (PM) ★★★★

SAND LAND

(サンドランド) • Akira Toriyama • Viz (2002–2003) • Shueisha (Weekly Shônen Jump, 2000) • 1 volume • Shônen, Science Fiction, Fantasy, Adventure • All Ages (violence)

Short but pleasant children's adventure series with a mild antiwar/environmental message. In a desert where all water is controlled by a greedy king, a grizzled sheriff seeks a lost oasis with the help of Beelzebub, the young prince of the demons (*mamono* in Japanese; despite Beelzebub's horns and tail, they're not devils so much as all-purpose monsters). *Sand Land* has brief moments of *Dragon Ball*–esque hand-to-hand fighting, but the majority of the action consists of lighthearted, quirky tank battles between the heroes and the military. ★★★

SARAI

(サライ) • Masahiro Shibata • ComicsOne (2001–2002) • Shônen Gahosha (Young King, 1998–ongoing) • 8 volumes, suspended (14+ volumes in Japan, ongoing) • Seinen, Science Fiction, Adventure • 18+ (language, graphic violence, graphic nudity, semi-graphic sex)

In the postapocalyptic, low-tech future, most people degenerate into mutated monsters after the age of 16, and unmutated children are the most precious commodity . . . for cannibalism and sex. Sarai is a "guard maid," a short-skirted, sword-and-machine-gun-wielding bodyguard who has a master-slave relationship with her employers. Although it goes through the motions of a postapocalyptic adventure story, *Sarai* is primarily a fetish manga. The atmosphere is sadistic in the purest sense of the word; in story after story, Sarai and her fellow guard maids go to a new location, only to discover that the world is divided into rapists and dewy-eyed victims and that the pillars of society (the clergy, the aristocracy) are only interested in spanking, lashing, and otherwise abusing our heroines. On the other hand, the stories are more than competently drawn; the interesting settings range from desert bazaars to Venice-like cities to flying airships, and the revolting mutants and dirty

old men wear the ugliness of their souls on their faces. In short, an imaginative, well-drawn mix of action and cynical fetishism. ★★½

SATISFACTION GUARANTEED

Yorozuya Tôkaidô Honpo, "General Store, Tokaido Head Office" (よろず屋東海道本舗) • Ryo Saenagi • Tokyopop (2006–ongoing) • Hakusensha (Hana to Yume Step Zôkan/Hana to Yume, 1998–2002) • 9 volumes • Shôjo, Mystery • 13+ (brief language, mild violence)

A pint-sized eighteen-year-old private eye, still tormented by his parents' death in a fire, teams up with a sixteen-year-old male supermodel with a split personality. A by-the-numbers *shôjo* mystery series with lots of angst and *bishônen* suggestions of love between the main characters ("I can't stand the thought of losing you," the model tells his partner). The cases are decent, but the setup and cute artwork are generic, and the mood is generally depressing. ★½

SATSUMA GISHIDEN: THE LEGEND OF THE SATSUMA SAMURAI

Satsuma Gishiden, "Legend of the Satsuma Samurai" (薩摩義士伝) • Hiroshi Hirata • Dark Horse (2006–2007) • Shônen Gahosha/Nihon Bungeisha (Zôkan Young Comic/Weekly Manga Goraku, 1977–1982) • 5 volumes • Seinen, Samurai, Action, Drama • 18+ (language, constant graphic violence)

In the opening sequence of *Samurai Gishiden,* teams of samurai execute a condemned criminal with a game called *hiemontori* ("grabbing something bloody"), tearing him apart from horseback and tossing his dismembered body back and forth in a contest to take his liver. Forty pages of this is sufficient introduction to this incredibly intense action manga by the famous samurai artist Hiroshi Hirata, whose work was praised by famous novelist Yukio Mishima for channeling "the violent warrior prints of the late Edo period." Set in the late 1700s, the story involves a rebellion by the lower-class samurai of Japan's Satsuma Province, who must work as craftsmen to make ends meet, while

Kazuo Umezu's *Scary Book*

in Japan) • Shôjo, Horror • Unrated/13+ (infrequent crude humor, violence)

Kazuo Umezu's horror stories from the 1960s and 1970s are classics, although they show their age, with dense, dark artwork and lots of narration. Some stories, such as volume 1's "Demon of Vengeance," hint at the gory streak that eventually consumed Umezu's work, but most of them are *shôjo* psychological horror: modern gothic tales set in a *Flowers in the Attic* world of ornate mansions and delicate, swooning beauties. In volume 1's "Mirrors," a girl is tormented by her reflection; in volume 2's "Insects," a girl is terrified by the sight of butterflies, which are somehow linked to the death of her mother. Impressionistic *shôjo* effects, such as swirling lines and amoeba-like blobs, reflect the heroines' shattered mental states. Written for children, the stories are occasionally silly, but at their best they strike primal themes such as rejection by one's parents and friends, loss of identity, and fear of madness. ★★★

the upper-class samurai enjoy privileges and kill the lower-class samurai for the slightest infraction. This powerful tale is told in a rugged fashion, with narration and historical info broken by sudden bursts of violence and rage. While similar to the work of Go-seki Kojima, the art is bolder and bigger, with giant full-page spreads of shouted oaths (hand-drawn in traditional Japanese calligraphy) and muscular men and horses in dynamic, gory action. A tale of a time when men were men and death was the solution to most problems, it's jaw-dropping in its passion and craftsmanship—a comic for people who think *Lone Wolf and Cub* is for wimps. ★★★★

SAZAE-SAN: See *The Wonderful World of Sazae-san*

SCARY BOOK

Umezu Kazuo Kowai Hon, "Kazuo Umezu's Scary Book" (楳図かずお こわい本) • Kazuo Umezu • Dark Horse (2006–ongoing) • Asahi Sonorama (various magazines) • 3 volumes, suspended (14 volumes

SCHOOL RUMBLE

(スクールランブル) • Jin Kobayashi • Del Rey (2006–ongoing) • Kodansha (Weekly Shônen Magazine, 2002–ongoing) • 16+ volumes, ongoing • Shônen, Romantic Comedy • 16+ (mild language, mild violence, sexual situations)

School Rumble wants to be a slapstick deconstruction of high school manga romantic comedies, but the problem is that this kind of material already parodies itself. The triangle setup is simple: Tenma is an ordinary shy girl who has a crush on an inscrutable guy, and Karasuma is a shy high school delinquent who has a crush on Tenma. Naturally, both of their crushes are doomed to perpetual failure; they overanalyze, they scheme, but whenever they're about to confess their love, they accidentally confess to the wrong person, or they get hit by a truck and knocked offscreen. The stories are short and the jokes are predictable. Tenma's sister Yakumo is memorable as a girl who can read men's minds and always knows their true motives. ★★

SCIENCE FICTION

The traditional definition of *science fiction* is: if it's something that might theoretically be possible according to known science, it's science fiction. If it's not, it's fantasy. But as with all genres, the feel is the most important thing, and so time travel, alien girls, and psychic heroes—not to mention robots, future societies, and spaceships—all fall into the category known in Japan by the English name "science fiction."

Science fiction, influenced by Western sci-fi writers such as Jules Verne and H. G. Wells, was one of many new genres embraced in rapidly modernizing late-1800s Japan. After World War II, writers such as Ray Bradbury and Isaac Asimov became popular in translation; even marginal sci-fi comedy manga such as *Hinadori Girl, Maico 2010*, and *Oh My Goddess!* make reference to Isaac Asimov's famous "Three Laws of Robotics." Homegrown science fiction fanzines and magazines appeared in the late 1950s, not long after the Japanese movie industry began producing tales of giant monsters, aliens, and fantastic future technology. (See the article on TOKUSATSU.) Famous writers who arose in the 1960s include Sakyo Komatsu, Shinichi Hoshi (a friend of Osamu Tezuka), Kazumasa Hirai (who also wrote several manga), and Yasutaka Tsutsui (author of numerous dark sci-fi satires and *The Girl Who Leapt Through Time,* which was adapted into a 2006 anime film).

Many famous postwar *shônen* manga were science fiction, such as Osamu Tezuka's 1948–1951 "science fiction trilogy" (*Lost World, Metropolis, Nextworld*) and *Astro Boy* (1952), Shotaro Ishinomori's cyborg heroes, and Mitsuteru Yokoyama's stories of psychics and robots. Robot stories became so popular that mecha became an established genre of its own. But sci-fi manga, like most manga of this period, were primarily aimed at children. Manga and science fiction struggled simultaneously for mainstream adult acceptance, and by the 1970s both had achieved a certain respectability. This coincided with a great creative period in *shôjo* manga, during which *shôjo* artists produced

Makoto Yukimura's *Planetes*

classic sci-fi works. Moto Hagio, who had drawn adaptations of Ray Bradbury stories, drew *They Were Eleven* (1975), a thriller about a group of young space cadets on a training exercise. Keiko Takemiya's *To Terra* (1977), set in the far future after humanity has deserted the polluted Earth to live in space colonies, follows a spaceship full of youngsters on a mission back to the abandoned planet. Such works expanded people's minds about the psychological potential and artistry of the genre. At the same time, *seinen* artists ventured into super-serious hard science fiction, such as Yukinobu Hoshino's *Saber Tiger* (1980) and *2001 Nights* (1984). With its combination of realistic space exploration and philosophical pondering, Hoshino's manga mirrored prose science fiction of the time. (A more recent example is Makoto Yukimura's *Planetes*, 2001.)

In the 1980s the mainstreaming of science fiction became complete, to the point that the genre lost identity; sci-fi manga became increasingly influenced by anime and movies, and sci-fi novels became dominated by illustrated "light novels" for teenagers. The always nebulous border between science fiction and fantasy became even fuzzier, and hard science fiction all but vanished, with the exception of the technology-oriented, merchandising-driven robot franchises. (Even a simple anime story such as Makoto Shinkai's *The Voices of a Distant Star: Hoshi no Koe,* about a relationship separated by light-years of space travel, includes the obligatory giant robots.) Today the occasional science fiction manga can be found in most *shônen* and *seinen* magazines (and in less mainstream *shôjo* magazines such as *Wings*), but in the 1980s and 1990s several magazines focused on science fiction themes: Kadokawa Shoten's now-defunct *Comic Comp* and its ongoing successor *Monthly Shônen Ace,* and Gakken's now-defunct *Comic Nora,* originally titled *SF Animedia.* In 2006 Tokuma Shoten, the former publishers of several science fiction prose magazines, announced the relaunch of *Comic Ryu,* a sci-fi manga magazine from the 1980s. The lineup of artists reads like a list of 1980s manga stars: Yoshikazu Yasuhiko, Kenji Tsuruta, Hideo Azuma, even Masaomi Kanzaki with a sequel to his canceled *Heavy Metal Warrior Xenon* (1986). Yesterday's vision of the future is today's nostalgia . . . but some themes are nearly universal.

Space Wars and Space Opera

One of the works that popularized science fiction in Japan, and loosened the definition of the genre, was *Star Wars.* Its vision of fantasy epics in outer space was quickly mimicked in the 1978 Japanese movie *Message from Space* (which was developed with design work, story credits, and a manga tie-in by Shotaro Ishinomori) and parodied in Akira Toriyama's *Dr. Slump* (1980), but its effects were far-reaching. Distant planets became the site of vaguely European duchies and baronies, exotic sci-fi fantasy settings for *shôjo*-influenced manga such as Keiko Takemiya and Ryu Mitsuse's *Andromeda Stories* (1980) and Mamoru Nagano's *Five Star Stories* (1986).

George Lucas was not solely responsible for space fantasies, however; the manga of Leiji Matsumoto had already combined grandiose science fiction themes with bold quests, storybook images, and an appreciation for retro machinery such as trains and World War II battleships. Military fans and science fiction fans are often the same (as proved by the popularity of military-themed mecha shows), and many sci-fi anime and manga deal with epic space wars, generally seen from the relative safety and comfort of the bridge of the officers' ships. The classic example is Yoshiki Tanaka's sprawling novel series *Ginga Eiyû Densetsu* ("Legend of the Galactic Heroes") (1981), in which two brilliant young commanders gradually rise through the ranks on opposite sides of the conflict. The manga adaptation was drawn by Katsumi Michihara, a popular *shōjo* science fiction artist. Hiroyuki Morioka's *Seikai Trilogy* novel series (1996) also follows this general theme, although the war is secondary to the hero and heroine's adventures on various planets.

Prose science fiction was still serious, and novelist Haruka Takachiho considered his work iconoclastic when he published *Crusher Joe* (1977), a lighthearted adventure story about a band of space mercenaries. Takachiho's follow-up was the even sillier and even more popular *Dirty Pair* novels (1979), about trigger-happy female space cops in silver bikinis; serialized in a Japanese science fiction magazine with illustrations by Yoshikazu Yasuhiko, it went on to spawn several anime and a long-running American comic adaptation by Adam Warren. Buichi Terasawa's *Cobra* (1978) featured even weirder interplanetary hijinks starring a big-nosed, wisecracking playboy with a cybernetic gun-arm. The anime/manga series *Cowboy Bebop* (1998), involving easygoing mercenaries in the year 2071, and the space pirates of *Coyote Ragtime Show* (2006) are the spiritual descendants of such space adventure comedies.

Future Earths

Another American movie, *Blade Runner,* could be credited with inspiring the many dystopian high-tech cities of anime and manga, but *Blade Runner* itself used Japanese cities as its model for a future Los Angeles. The anime series *Bubblegum Crisis* (1987) and its spin-off *AD Police* (1989), in which female mercenaries chase down rogue Boomer androids, was the most direct *Blade Runner* rip-off; the former featured character designs by Kenichi Sonoda, the latter was adapted into a manga by Tony Takezaki. In the 1980s, Japan *was* the future, the economy was booming, and anime and manga led the way in what would become known as the cyberpunk genre. The megacity setting of Katsuhiro Otomo's *Akira* (1982), drawn in stunning detail down to the last graffiti-covered wall and broken window, vaguely resembled the world of the present day; on the other hand, Masamune Shirow's *Appleseed* (1988), *Dominion* (1989), and *Ghost in the Shell* (1989) were set in stranger futures, when full-body cyborgs and genetically engineered cat-eared women could walk casually down the street. Both artists were incredibly influential, inspiring many manga, although few reached the level of Yukito Kishiro's *Battle Angel Alita* (1990).

Closely tied to cyberpunk is "steampunk," alternate histories or societies in which future and past levels of technology are mixed. The theme is seen in Hayao Miyazaki's animated film *Castle in the Sky* (1986), as well as the Miyazaki-influenced anime series *Nadia: The Secret of Blue Water* (1990–1991). Kia Asamiya's *Steam Detectives* (1994) is archetypal for the genre: a roughly 1930s world where men wear fedoras and women wear dresses, and where trains and steamships run alongside giant robots whose joints exhale hissing clouds of steam. Hiroi Oji's late 1990s video game/anime/manga franchise *Sakura Taisen* depicted 1920s Japan under attack by the forces of darkness and defended by women in steam-powered combat armor. Hiromu Arakawa's *Fullmetal Alchemist* (2002) is set in a world of roughly World War I–era technology, with the addition of clunky cybernetic body parts.

Manga, and Japanese pop culture in general, also have a powerful affinity for post-apocalyptic settings and disaster stories. Many things have been credited for this: Japan's real-life status as the only nation struck by nuclear bombs, Tokyo's frequent history of fires and earthquakes, even biologist Asajiro Oka's 1909 statement that the human race was doomed to extinction through a combination of Darwinist evolutionary theory and Buddhist ideas of transience. Sakyo Komatsu's bestselling 1973 novel *Japan Sinks* (adapted into several live-action movies and manga, the most recent in 2006) depicted Japan literally torn apart by earthquakes, a disaster that was borrowed by Go Nagai in *Violence Jack* (1973), in which warlords arise in the anarchy. Pollution causes the screaming deaths of billions in Kazuo Umezu's *The Drifting Classroom* (1972) and *Fourteen* (1990), while nuclear war provides a place where men can be men in Buronson and Tetsuo Hara's *Fist of the North Star* (1983), with its classic imagery of toppled skyscrapers and ships beached on the beds of dried-up seas. Yoshihisa Tagami's *Grey* (1985) is set in a nearly lifeless future of constant war, and Shin Takahashi's *Saikano* (2000) leads us down that path from the present day. Stories set long after an offscreen apocalypse are too common to list, but Hayao Miyazaki's *Nausicaä of the Valley of the Wind* (1982) depicts a truly original setting, a sci-fi/fantasy world of giant insects and fungus forests inhabited by feudalistic survivors. Non-sci-fi stories of large-scale disaster are popular as well, such as Minetaro Mochizuki's *Dragon Head* (1994) and Takao Saito's *Survival* (1976); even Kaiji Kawaguchi tried his hand at the genre with *Taiyô no Mokushiroku* ("A Spirit of the Sun," 2002).

Strange Creatures and Technology

Another idea popularized by Western pulp fiction was "lost worlds"—hollow Earths, jungle islands inhabited by dinosaurs, ruins of forgotten civilizations such as Atlantis and Agharta. Manga using this theme, with archaeologists bravely exploring the unknown, include Akihiro Yamada's *Lost Continent* (1990), Ryoichi Ikegami and Kazuo Koike's *Offered* (1989–1990), and Atelier Lana's *The Amazing Adventures of Professor Jones* (1996). Such stories are uncommon, and only marginally science fiction, but one "lost worlds" idea has become ubiquitous in Japanese pop culture: the idea of super-advanced ancient civilizations whose high-tech artifacts remain secretly buried around the globe. The theme appears in Hayao Miyazaki's animated film *Castle in the Sky* (1986), as well as countless video games and manga: Hiroshi Takashige and Ryoji Minagawa's *Striker* (1988), Kaori Ozaki's *Immortal Rain* (1999), and even marginally sci-fi *shônen* action manga such as Seishi Kishimoto's *O-Parts Hunter* (2002). ("O-parts" is short for "out of place artifacts," an English-language archaeological term better known in Japan than in America.) Even giant robot anime/manga such as *Neon Genesis Evangelion* (1995) and *The Big O* (1999) involve the unearthing of great and terrible secrets from the past.

Stories of scientific experiments creating monsters or mutant humans are common, but typically fit better in the mecha, psychic, or horror genres. Tales of aliens tend to fall into the categories of "super-advanced visitors who look just like people" or "incommunicative monsters," with a few exceptions such as comedies like Mine Yoshizaki's *Sgt. Frog* (1999) and Hideaki Sorachi's *Gintama* (2004), and aliens and pseudo-aliens who merge with humans, such as Hitoshi Iwaaki's *Parasyte* (1990), Mohiro Kitoh's *Shadow Star* (1998), and Hitoshi Tomizawa's *Alien Nine* (1998) and *Alien Nine Emulators* (1999). Seiho Takizawa's *Who Fighter with Heart of Darkness* (2004) shows that real-world UFO speculation is much the same in Japan as in America. Lastly, of course, there are the countless comedy manga and anime in which super-science or alien visitors are just a way to get the plot rolling. You'd think that aliens traveling across the galaxy would have better things to do than perform a sex-change operation (*Kashimashi~Girl Meets Girl~*) or flirt with teenage boys (*DearS, No Need for Tenchi!, Onegai Teacher, The World of Narue*), but in the world of manga, anything can happen.

See also: MECHA AND ROBOTS, PSYCHIC, TOKUSATSU.

Science Fiction Manga

2001 Nights • A, A' • AD Police • Akira • Alien Nine • Alien Nine: Emulators • Alive • Andromeda Stories • Appleseed • Aqua • Aria • Ashen Victor • Battle Angel Alita • Battle Angel Alita: Last Order • Blue Inferior • Cannon God Exaxxion • Central City • Ceres: Celestial Legend • Chronowar • Clover • Cyber 7 • Daphne in the Brilliant Blue • Darkside Blues • Doll • Dominion • The Drifting Classroom • Earthian (yaoi) • Eden: It's an Endless World! • The Empty Empire • ES (Eternal Sabbath) • Five Star Stories • Four Shôjo Stories • Frontier Line • Gadget • Galaxy Express 999 • Genocyber • Ghost in the Shell • Ghost in the Shell 1.5: Human-Error Processor • Ghost in the Shell Volume 2: Man-Machine Interface • Godzilla • Grey • Horobi • Immortal Rain • Infinite Ryvius • Justy • King of Thorn • The Legend of Mother Sarah: Tunnel Town • Lost Continent • Lost World • Made in Heaven • Manga • Mega Comics • Memories • Metropolis • Moon Child • Nausicaä of the Valley of the Wind • Neon Genesis Evangelion • Neon Genesis Evangelion: Angelic Days • Nextworld • No. 5 • Orion • Outlanders • Parasyte • Phoenix • Planetes • Planet Ladder • Plastic Little: Captain's Log • Please Save My Earth • Psychonauts • Pure Trance • Q-ko-chan: The Earth Invader Girl • Ray • Saber Tiger • Saikano • Seikai Trilogy • Seraphic Feather • Shadow Star • Standard Blue • Star Trek: The Manga • Star Wars: The Empire Strikes Back • Star Wars: A New Hope • Star Wars: Return of the Jedi • Star Wars Episode I: The Phantom Menace • Stellvia • To Terra • Tower of the Future • The Two Faces of Tomorrow • The Venus Wars • Version • The Voices of a Distant Star: Hoshi no Koe • Who Fighter with Heart of Darkness

Science Fiction Action Manga

Alice in Lostworld • Angel/Dust • Arm of Kannon • Astrider Hugo • Baoh • The Big O • Bio-Booster Armor Guyver • Black Cat • Black Magic • Blame! • Brain Powered • B'TX • The Candidate for Goddess • Chirality: To The Promised Land • Cobra • Crusher Joe • Cyborg 009 • Dead End • Demon City Hunter • Demon City Shinjuku • Demon Palace Babylon • Deus Vitae • Eat-Man • E'S • Gatekeepers • Goku: Midnight Eye • Golden Warrior Iczer-One • Gunhed • Gunparade March • Gunparade March: A New Marching Song • Heavy Metal Warrior Xenon • Japan • Kamiyadori • Kamui • Kikaider Code 02 • Möbius Klein • My-HiME • Nadesico • O-Parts Hunter • Pixy Junket • Project Arms • Ragnarok Guy • Sarai • Scryed • Silent Möbius • StONE • Striker • Super Dimensional Fortress Macross II • Train + Train • Trigun • Trigun Maximum • Twilight of the Dark Master • Twin Signal • Venger Robo • Warriors of Tao

Science Fiction Comedy Manga

A.I. Love You • The All-New Tenchi Muyô! • All Purpose Cultural Cat Girl Nuku Nuku • Astra • Chobits • Cowboy Bebop • Cowboy Bebop: Shooting Star • Coyote Ragtime Show • DearS • Excel Saga • Gacha Gacha • Gacha Gacha: The Next Revolution • Gal-

SCHOOL ZONE

(スクールゾーン) • Kanako Inuki • Dark Horse (2006) • Leed Publishing (1996–1997) • 3 volumes • Horror • Unrated/16+ (graphic violence)

A cursed elementary school is haunted by thirteen ghosts, who break free from their imprisonment and begin to terrify the students. Severed heads fly through the halls and bullying breeds supernatural evil; meanwhile, mild-mannered Nanka is possessed by an evil spirit in a mirror, giving him a twisted split personality. Drawn in a crude style similar to the work of both Kazuo Umezu (the dark backgrounds) and Hideshi Hino (the Cabbage Patch Kid character designs), *School Zone* is kitschy horror for younger readers. After a rocky start, the story proceeds with the breathless spirit of a campfire story. Not to be confused with Akiko Fujii and Michio Akiyama's one-volume adult manga *School Zone*.   ★★½

SCRAPPED PRINCESS

Scrapped Princess: Tôbôshatachi no Concerto, "Concert of Fugitives" (スクラップド・プリンセス 逃亡者達の協奏曲Concerto) • Ichiro Sakaki (original creator/story), Yukinobu Azumi (character design), Go Yabuki (art) • Tokyopop (2005–2006) • Kadokawa Shoten (Comic Dragon/Dragon Age, 2002–2004) • 3 volumes • Fantasy, Adventure • 13+ (violence, partial nudity, sexual situations)

Manga adaptation of the light novel series by Ichiro Sasaki. Due to a grim prophecy, the princess Pacifica was supposed to be killed as a child, but she survived only to be perpetually hunted by the forces of the kingdom. Luckily for her, Pacifica is protected by her fiercely loyal foster brother and sister, and together they race from adventure to adventure, usually one step ahead of their pursuers. The main cliché of *Scrapped Princess* is that all the characters, whether hapless bystanders or assassins on assignment to kill her, are all eventually won over by Pacifica's naive morality. The art is good, but the fight scenes are confusing. The manga ends abruptly, with no real conclusion; nor does it ever explain Pacifica's early life and background. (KT)   ★½

SCRYED

(スクライド) • Yosuke Kuroda (story), Yasunori Toda (art) • Tokyopop (2003) • Akita Shoten (Weekly Shônen Champion, 2001–2002) • Shônen, Post-apocalyptic, Science Fiction, Superhero, Battle • 5 volumes • 16+ (language, graphic violence, nudity, sex)

Over-the-top adaptation of the *Scryed* anime series. In the near future, Yokohama is struck by an earthquake and separated from the rest of the world. As a result, evolution somehow becomes "concentrated in one place," creating the Alter Users, superpowered mutant tough dudes. Kazuma, a rebelliously grinning hero with the power to punch things really hard with his mutated cyber-arm, fights the evil holier-than-thou super-stormtroopers of the police organization called Holy, while shouting things like "Atomic Massacre!" and "Death Bullet of Annihilation!" Completely ridiculous action chaos, *Scryed*'s best feature is enjoyably weird, exaggerated art vaguely similar to *JoJo's Bizarre Adventure,* with extreme foreshortening and blood sticking like icicles straight out of the characters' bodies. The hyper-gory, hyper-violent, juvenile mood is similar to *Apocalypse Zero,* with lots of absurd dialogue delivered with a straight face.   ★½

SECRET CHASER

(シークレット・チェイサー) • Tamayo Akiyama • To-kyopop (2006–2007) • Kadokawa Shoten (1999) • 2 volumes • Shôjo, Mystery • 13+

Former CLAMP member Tamayo Akiyama fails completely on this solo outing, with little to show for her effort but the trademark character designs made famous in *Magic Knight Rayearth*. The characters include a priest who may be the title character, a police detective who actually tries to do some mystery solving, and a red penguin that teleports. Wait, the penguin is actually just a hypnotic suggestion that is passed around like a virus among young boys and the celebrity girls who visit the aforementioned priest. This elaborate "mystery" is a "test" of the priest's powers to overcome mystical hypnotic powers . . . or was it all to find a missing kitten? It is impossible to follow who is talking at any given time because people speak without being graphically represented on the page, the story is so hard to follow that one looks at the page numbers to see if the pages are out of order, and the characters make so many absurd leaps of logic that you start to hate whoever it is that you think is talking. (SM) ½

SECRET COMICS JAPAN

Various artists • Viz (2000) • 1 volume • Underground • 18+ (language, graphic violence, nudity, sex)

A "post-underground" collection of manga published from 1996 to 2000, *Secret Comics Japan* makes its point in its introduction (written by former *Garo* editor Chikao Shiratori): the boundaries between high and low culture, underground and commercial, are a thing of the past. Unfortunately, the resulting book is scattershot, tending toward conventional art styles and narratives, with some comics (such as Benkyo Tamaoki's straightforward porn manga and Shintaro Kago's gorily effective horror story) seemingly included for shock value alone. Usamaru Furuya's exquisitely drawn gag comic "Palepoli" is pure formalistic experimenta-

tion, Hironori Kikuchi's pun-tastic "Gedatsu Man" needs annotation, and Makoto Aida's anime-schoolgirls-in-World-War-II fantasy "Mutant Hanako" is calculated pop trash of the "ha ha, look, comics can have sex and violence" variety. The best stories are Yuko Tsuno's surreal fairy tale "Swing Shell" and the sci-fi/horror story (in the style of *Pure Trance*) by Junko Mizuno and Norimizu Ameya. Other artists include Kiriko Nananan and Yoshitomo Yoshimoto.

★★★

SECTION CHIEF KOSAKU SHIMA: See *Division Chief Kosaku Shima*

SEIKAI TRILOGY

Seikai no Monshô, "Crest of the Stars"/*Seikai no Senki,* "Battle Flag of the Stars" (星界の紋章／星界の戦旗) • Hiroyuki Morioka (original creator), Aya Yoshinaga (composition), Toshihiro Ono (art, vols. 1–2), Wasoh Miyakoshi (art, vol. 3) • Tokyopop (2004) • MediaWorks (Dengeki Daioh, 1999–2002) • Shônen, Science Fiction, Adventure • 3 volumes • 13+ (brief language, violence, infrequent partial nudity)

Compressed manga adaptation of Hiroyuki Morioka's *Seikai* light novel series; volume 1 is subtitled *Crest of the Stars* and volumes 2–3 are subtitled *Banner of the Stars*. In the far future, humanity shares outer space with the Abh, a race of genetically modified, elflike, elite humans who are like benevolent parents to the rest of the galaxy. Jinto, a human with honorary Abh status, goes to officer training school and befriends Lafiel, an alien princess. But the human nations start a war with the Abh empire, and soon they must go into battle at the head of fleets of spaceships. As a sci-fi space opera, *Seikai Trilogy* is generic; the Abh are so infallible they're boring, and the space war plot (which alternates with planetside adventures) isn't presented in a way that the reader can follow the action. The Abh vocabulary is redundant: characters utter lines like "Release the hoksas!" and you flip to the glossary merely to find that "hoksas" means "mines." The artists each have their ups and downs. Toshihiro Ono's cutesy art reduces the series to a cartoon, with sexy girls and everyone else smiling all the time. Wasoh Miyakoshi's dignified, pompous artwork is a better match for the mood of the series, but Miyakoshi lacks Ono's underlying drawing ability. In either case, every other page consists of nearly identical people in uniforms standing on the bridges of starships. The novel series is still continuing in Japan, so the ending of the manga leaves it open for more. ★★

SEIMADEN

Seimaden, "Holy Magic/Demon Legend" (聖魔伝) • You Higuri • CMX (2005–2007) • Kadokawa Shoten (Asuka Fantasy DX, 1994–1999) • 10 volumes • Shôjo, Fantasy, Drama • 13+ (graphic violence, brief partial nudity)

Laures, a raven-haired demon prince, is in love with Hildegarde, a beautiful dancer who may be the reincarnation of his lost love. But the heroic Roddrick, one of the last survivors of the magic-using Azelle people, wants to save her from the demon. One of Higuri's early works, the first few volumes are difficult to read because of the immature, generic artwork and confusing storytelling. (The manga is a sequel to Higuri's untranslated one-shot *Azelle Seimaden,* which accounts for the lack of introductions to characters.) Things get juicier when the heroes are trapped in a castle by a mad count and Higuri discovers her true talents: *yaoi* teases and gothic sadism lite ("I long to profane you in the most painful way possible!"). Even at its best, however, the series always feels cobbled together from bits of other 1990s fantasy manga. ★½

SENGOKU NIGHTS

Sengoku Tsukiyo, "Warring States Era Moonlit Nights" (戦国月夜) • Kei Kusunoki, Kaoru Ohashi (co-creators) • Tokyopop (2006) • Sobisha (Crimson, 1999–2000) • 2 volumes • Shôjo, Occult, Fantasy • 13+ (brief language, graphic violence, sexual situations)

When Masayoshi's family property is marked for development—with golf courses built over ancient Sengoku-era battlefields—the evil spirits of the past are awakened. Nozuchi no Mikoto, the god of the land, appears as a handsome horned man in samurai garb and tells the teenage hero that he is the reincarnation of a sorcerous princess from hundreds of years ago. Furthermore, Nozuchi loved her, and he still loves "her" even though Masayoshi has a guy's body. Walking the line between *shôjo* and *shônen,* drama and comedy (with the expected boy-boy flirtation jokes), *Sengoku Nights* is a slight but enjoyable action series that takes advantage of Kusunoki's twin talents for romantic comedy and traditional Japanese monsters.

★★½

SENSUAL PHRASE

Kaikan Phrase, "Sensual Phrase" (快感フレーズ) • Mayu Shinjo • Viz (2004–2007) • Shogakukan (Shôjo Comic, 1997–2000) • 18 volumes • Shôjo, Romance • 18+ (language, nudity, sex)

Say you're a teenage girl who likes to write suggestive song lyrics . . . and say your lyrics catch the eye of Sakuya, glamorous lead singer of the rock band Lucifer, who wants you to write just for *him.* A completely over-the-top fantasy, *Sensual Phrase* is set in a world of media moguls, publicity stunts, drugs, and other celebrity perversions. Can Sakuya and Aine make it in the rock business, or will their jealous enemies tear them apart? Like a paperback romance novel, there's seduction in almost every volume, and the song lyrics really *are* sensual, or at least raunchy. The English rewrite turns it into camp ("You dirty little hussy!"), and one of the primary motivations to keep reading is to see what kind of outrageous lines the characters will say next. Shinjo's human anatomy is terrible—check out the giant hands and hot-dog-like fingers—but the story is consistently entertaining in a ridiculous way. ★★★

SEQUENCE

(シークエンス) • Ryo Saenagi • Tokyopop (2006) • Hakusensha (Hana to Yume, 2003) • 1 volume • Shôjo, Vampire, Comedy, Drama • 13+ (mild language, brief violence, mild sexual situations)

SEINEN (青年)

An enormous catch-all category, *seinen* (young men's) manga today refers to all manga aimed at men from their late teens to adulthood. Japanese story comics for adults, with realistic draftsmanship and hard-hitting social themes, first developed in the late 1950s in the *gekiga* (dramatic pictures) movement. In the 1960s, as the first generation of postwar manga readers began to reach adulthood, the major Tokyo-based publishers scouted talent from *gekiga* artists, whose primary market, the Osaka-based *kashibonya* (book rental) business, was drying up. Combining the cartoony escapism of *shônen* manga with the adult content and detailed art of *gekiga,* the result was a new type of manga: pulpy, violent, sexual, and popular.

Shônen magazines aimed at teenagers began to appear in the early 1960s, such as Shogakukan's *Boy's Life.* But Futabasha's *Manga Action* (1967), home of the smash hit *Lupin III,* is considered the first true *seinen* magazine. Other publishers responded almost immediately: Shônen Gahosha with *Young Comic* (1967), Akita Shoten with *Play Comic* (1968), and Shogakukan with *Big Comic* (1968). As the sales of these magazines climbed, children's magazines like *Weekly Shônen Sunday* and *Weekly Shônen Magazine* became more gritty and adult-oriented to compete. Amid the craze, only one *shônen* magazine, *Weekly Shônen Jump,* stuck to its original preteen target audience. As a result, it soon became the number one boys' magazine in Japan.

As *seinen* magazines proliferated, they soon expanded into new genres such as science fiction and erotic comics. But the overall trend was toward respectability; in the late 1970s and 1980s, as readers grew up and manga became increasingly big busi-

Kodansha's *Morning* is a weekly magazine aimed at white-collar adults in their twenties and up; Shogakukan's biweekly *Big Comic Superior,* part of their *Big Comic* line (also including *Big Comic, Big Comic Original,* and *Big Comic Spirits*)

ness, the major publishers responded with a new wave of magazines aimed at upper- and middle-class white-collar workers. Kodansha's *Morning* (1982) was one of the most successful of the new magazines, although *Big Comic* and its many spin-offs also followed the trend. This new, prime-time manga is marketed as "quality entertainment that compares favorably to novels and motion pictures," to quote the description of *Big Comic Original* on Shogakukan's Web site. But lurid action still sells comics, and even the largest publishers produce *seinen* manga that, by American standards, are more comparable to late-night cable TV.

Although modern-day *seinen* manga has incredible variety, most of the magazines fall into one of three categories:

Upscale Seinen *Magazines*

Japan's most respectable manga for adults are Shogakukan's *Big Comic* series and Kodansha's *Morning*, as well as men's lifestyle magazines that include short manga sections, such as *Weekly Post* and *Weekly Gendai*. They are sometimes known as *dansei* (adult men's) manga. In Japan, they are nearly as ubiquitous as the top weekly magazines in America, and they have similar bonus features and articles: previews of upcoming movies, interviews with actors and athletes, and the occasional editorial column. Aimed at adult, often middle-aged readers, their comics have topics similar to prime-time television: food, sports (such as golf), comedies, and dramas about people with interesting jobs and hobbies (mountain climbers, surgeons, policemen, financiers, politicians). Some stories may be violent and risqué by American standards, but on the whole they are considered mainstream entertainment. Typical advertisements are for cars, beer, cigarettes, PDAs, music, movies, and matchmaking services.

One sign of the magazines' popularity is that their manga are frequently adapted into live-action TV series. Recent examples from *Morning* alone include Sayaka Yamasaki's *Haruka 17* (2003), about a shy twenty-two-year-old talent manager who takes off her glasses and poses as a seventeen-year-old idol; Norifusa Mita's *Dragon Zakura* (2003), about a gang-member-turned-lawyer trying to tutor failing high school students; and Shûhô Satô's *Black Jack ni Yoroshiku* ("Say Hello to Black Jack") (2002), about a hospital intern struggling to become a full-fledged doctor. From *Big Comic Spirits* comes Hanaya Hanatsu's *CA to Oyobi!* ("Call Me Cabin Attendant!") (2005), a relationship comedy about an airline stewardess.

The Young Magazines

The rowdiest of the *seinen* manga magazines, the "young" magazines (*Young Jump, Young Sunday, Young Magazine,* etc.) are aimed at late-high-school- and college-age men. The most explicit, such as Futabasha's *Men's Young* and Wani Books' *Comic Kairakuten* ("Comic Pleasure Heaven"), are essentially sex comics. Big-breasted women, both photographed and drawn, pose provocatively on the covers; the stories inside typically involve sports, crime, crude humor, occupational dramas, and nervous nerds thrust into kinky sexual situations. Almost every "young" magazine features color photo spreads of attractive models and actresses in swimsuits; more explicit material is sometimes included in sealed inserts. Typical advertisements are for video games, cars, fitness equipment, skin care products, "men's health power-ups" for sex enhancement, and posters and collectibles featuring photos of the magazine's pin-up girls.

Otaku-*Oriented Magazines*

Although even mainstream *seinen* magazines run the occasional science fiction or horror story (*Battle Angel Alita* ran in *Business Jump*, and *Berserk* runs in the only slightly nerdy *Young Animal*), a few magazines focus on genre-oriented material. *Ultra Jump*, one of the older brothers of *Weekly Shônen Jump*, features science fiction, fantasy, and martial arts stories with lavishly detailed art. *Young King Ours* bristles with big guns and paramilitary action, while *Comic Birz* tends toward horror and dark fantasy. The most famous *seinen* magazine of this type is *Afternoon*, created in 1987 as the companion to Kodansha's *Morning*. In addition to featuring more obvious fantasy elements, these magazines also tend toward more anime-influenced artwork, with cute, childish, *lolicon* female characters. Typical advertisements are for video games, model kits, and anime and manga chain stores such as Mandarake and Tora no Ana.

As the manga readership continues to age, publishers have experimented with manga for even older age groups. *Big Gold* (as in "golden years"), a magazine aimed at aging baby boomers and featuring manga by classic creators such as Leiji Matsumoto and Shigeru Mizuki, was launched in 1992 but folded after a few years. But the audience for venerable magazines such as *Big Comic* and *Big Comic Original* continues to grow older, like Kenshi Hirokane's gradually aging super-salaryman *Division Chief Kosaku Shima*, and many series are clearly written by middle-aged artists for readers of their own generation. Another sign of the aging market are sequels to popular *shônen* series from the 1980s, such as *Ultimate Muscle* and *Fist of the Blue Sky*, aimed at the same fans who enjoyed them in their youth. In five or ten years, will today's *Naruto* and *Inuyasha* fans grow up to read manga about businesspeople and relationships? Or will they read sequels with names like *Naruto 2* and *Ultimate Inuyasha*? Only time will tell.

Pretty boy Kanata unwittingly releases the equally *bishônen* vampire Titi from a cross-shaped coffin in a deserted church. The gender-confused bloodsucker mistakes Kanata for the priest who betrayed him and promptly kills our protagonist. This starts the "sequence," a spell that revives Kanata by binding the two of them together so that each feels the other's pain; it also releases a collection of ne'er-do-wells known as "walks." Robbing vampirism and *bishônen* romance of all of their impact becomes the main focus of the manga as Kanata and Titi battle "walks" while the reader (and the licentious supporting character Ohji) wonders to what gender the effeminate Titi actually belongs. Generic artwork. A second volume was never completed in Japan, so the last three chapters are unlikely to be released stateside. (SM) ★½

SERAPHIC FEATHER

(セラフィック・フェザー) • Yo Morimoto (story, vols. 1–2), Toshiya Takeda (story, vols. 3+), Hiroyuki Utatane (art) • Dark Horse (2000–2006) • Kodansha (*Afternoon*, 1993–ongoing) • 6 volumes, suspended (9+ volumes in Japan, ongoing) • Seinen, Science Fiction, Action • Unrated/18+ (mild language, extreme graphic violence, nudity, sexual situations)

Contorted, spiderlike human bodies in clingy clothes, big-breasted girls with photorealistic nipples—you don't have to be told to figure out that Hiroyuki Utatane is primarily an adult comics artist. Set on a lunar city in the future, *Seraphic Feather* depicts a battle between UN forces and shadowy corporations, fighting over the "Emblem Seeds," alien artifacts of awesome power. In reality, however, the plot is just a clothes hanger for Utatane's artwork. Frustrating secrets and empty science fiction dialogue ("Whoever controls the seeds, controls the infinite worlds of quantum reality") alternate with psychic fight scenes and forced "surprises" designed to keep the reader's attention. (Part of the problem may be due to the fact that the series changed writers midstream, but Yo Morimoto's volumes are no different from Toshiya Takeda's.) The mood veers from fetishized cuteness to fetishized sadistic violence; in the original Japanese version of volume 2's cover, the heroine's sword was slicing through her own breast. Apart from the doe-eyed characters, the rest of the artwork is white noise; the multiple-page spreads of generic sci-fi walls and buildings do nothing but pad out the story. The series is still being produced in Japan on a very slow schedule, fourteen years after it first appeared; presumably by now even Utatane has forgotten what the plot was. ★

SEVEN OF SEVEN

Shichinin no Nana, "Seven of Seven" (七人のナナ) • Yasuhiro Imagawa (story), Azusa Kunihiro (art) • ADV (2003–2004) • Akita Shoten (Weekly Shônen Champion, 2002) • 3 volumes • Shônen, Fantasy, Comedy • 13+ (constant partial nudity, sexual situations)

Via a magic crystal, schoolgirl Nana Suzuki splits into seven copies of herself: original Nana, mean Nana, smart Nana, sexy Nana, and so on. After a brief "can't let the neighbors know" phase, in which Nana irrationally tries to keep people from finding out that she has six doppelgängers ("If Yuichi saw all seven of us, he would hate me!"), everyone finds out about the extra Nanas and the manga settles into the story of seven girls, six of whom have one-word personalities. This premise doesn't suggest many interesting plot possibilities, which may be why nearly all the story lines end up being about the Nanas studying for exams. It does, however, offer rich opportunities for fanservice, with the Nanas constantly cuddling together, tripping over one another to flash their panties, and so on. By volume 2, the

manga has abandoned all pretense of being about anything except pubescent cheesecake, and creators Imagawa and Kunihiro are building entire chapters around micro-miniskirts, cosplay outfits, and dissolving swimwear. (SG)   ★½

SEXY VOICE AND ROBO

(セクシーボイスアンドロボ) • Iou Kuroda • Viz (2005) • Shogakukan (Ikki, 2000–2003) • 1 volume • Seinen, Crime Drama • 16+ (language, brief nudity, sexual situations)

Nico Hayashi, a fourteen-year-old schoolgirl who impersonates voices for a telephone-dating service, finds her true calling as an all-purpose problem solver, working for a wealthy old man. Iichiro Sudo, a twenty-five-year-old robot-collecting hipster, is her unofficial sidekick. Together they are . . . Sexy Voice and Robo! A series of mostly disconnected crime stories involving lonely people, relationships, and the big city, *Sexy Voice and Robo* is really a love letter to Tokyo and its inhabitants, with rough, vigorous brush artwork comparable to that of American artists such as Craig Thompson. The closest thematic comparison is Taiyo Matsumoto, but Kuroda's stories are more understated and optimistic, and his art less self-consciously underground, but no less beautiful. The English edition compiles both Japanese volumes into one book.   ★★★½

SGT. FROG

Keroro Gunsou, "Sgt. Ribbet" (ケロロ軍曹) • Mine Yoshizaki • Tokyopop (2004–ongoing) • Kadokawa Shoten (Monthly Shônen Ace, 1999–ongoing) • 14+ volumes (ongoing) • Shônen, Otaku, Comedy • 13+ (mild language, sexual situations)

The Keroro Platoon—five amphibious invaders from the planet Keron—were sent to Pokopen (aka Earth) on a mission of intergalactic conquest. While the Keronians possess unimaginable military might, the "frogs" postpone planetary destruction, enamored as they are of such Earth inventions as *Gundam* model kits, iPods, and blogs. Instead the frogs become troublesome houseguests to the Hinata family, plotting harebrained

Mohiro Kitoh's *Shadow Star*

schemes from the titular Sgt. Keroro's bedroom, eventually becoming Earth's unlikely protectors. The highly episodic series combines sweetness, silliness, and a fetishistic love of *otaku* culture in a way that's hard to resist. Even though half the jokes will go over the heads of most American readers (there are more obscure pop culture references per page than in just about any other translated manga), there are more than enough sight gags and translatable puns to make this one of the funniest comedies to cross the Pacific. Sgt. Keroro is so unbearably cute, it's no wonder the series became a merchandising phenomenon throughout Asia. This real-world popularity manifests throughout the self-referential series, as characters wear their own merchandise, and the unpopular Keruru is mocked by his peers for failing to connect with readers. The formula, which works brilliantly for the first 8 or so volumes, eventually becomes stale, even tiresome, as the series becomes a victim of its own popularity. While the colorful covers and cute characters make *Sgt. Frog* seem like a kids' series, the humor definitely skews toward pop-culture-savvy teens and adults, as does the eye-pleasing fanservice. (MT) ★★★

SHADOW LADY

(シャドウレディ) • Masakazu Katsura • Dark Horse (1998–2001) • Shueisha (Weekly Shônen Jump, 1989–1992) • 3 volumes • Shônen, Phantom Thief, Fantasy, Action • Unrated/16+ (violence, frequent nudity)

In the ornate metropolis of Gray City lives Aimi Komori, a shy waitress . . . but when she puts on her magic eye shadow and calls forth her demon familiar De-Mo, she becomes Shadow Lady, a sexy cat burglar who teases the police. *Shadow Lady* shows Masakazu Katsura's dilemma: he wants to draw *Batman*-style superhero comics, but his readers demand cheesecake in the style of *Video Girl Ai* and *I"s*. The resulting compromise—slapstick action with the protagonist's clothes constantly getting ripped to pieces—proves only that Katsura wasn't meant to write comedy, and possibly not action either. The art, however, is beautifully slick, although more cartoony than his other work. ★★

SHADOW STAR

Narutaru-Mukuro naru Hoshi Tamataru ko-, "The Star That Died and the Jewel of a Girl" (なるたる-骸なる星珠たる子-) • Mohiro Kitoh • Dark Horse

(2000–2005) • Kodansha (Afternoon, 1998–2003) • 7 volumes, suspended (12 volumes in Japan) • Seinen, Science Fiction, Drama • Unrated/16+ (mild language, graphic violence, nudity, sexual situations)

Shiina, a junior-high-age dreamer who lives with her middle-aged pilot father, encounters Hoshimaru, a mute, starfish-shaped creature with great unblinking eyes. Although Hoshimaru is unable to communicate, he bonds to Shiina and follows her around, giving her rides in the night sky like a flying surfboard. But as she soon discovers, several other teenagers are also linked to "shadow dragons," near-omnipotent shapeshifting creatures who may be aliens, UFOs, or simply an extension of their partners' minds. The concept of children linked to companion monsters is a common one in anime and manga, but the abstract shapes of the Shadow Dragons (and the scrawny, anorexic appearance of their child partners) suggest *Neon Genesis Evangelion* as a specific inspiration. So too do the increasingly dark turns of the story, for apart from Shiina, virtually all the "dragon children" are severely disturbed, from her suicidal friend Akira to a conspiracy of amoral adolescents who plan to use their powers to rule the world. The vicious depictions of bullying and child abuse reach their peak in volume 7, whose sexual content was censored in the English edition. The art is crisp and detailed, with especial attention paid to the planes and military equipment that the JSDF sends to fight the Shadow Dragons. The writing is intelligent and the dialogue reads well, although it has a tendency toward pretentiousness, with multiple characters delivering variants of the same cynical rhetoric. Although it initially seems like young-adult science fiction, *Shadow Star* is more of a series *about* children written for adults . . . observing adolescence in hindsight and finding the sense of childlike wonder outweighed by pessimism and cruelty. ★★★

SHAKUGAN NO SHANA

Shakugan no Shana, "Shana of the Fiery Eyes" (灼眼のシャナ) • Yasuchiro Takahashi (original cre-ator), Noizi Ito (character design), Ayato Sasakura (art) • Viz (2007–ongoing) • MediaWorks (Dengeki Daioh, 2005–ongoing) • 2+ volumes (ongoing) • Shônen, School, Fantasy • 16+

Manga adaptation of Yasuchiro Takahashi's light novels, with big-eyed, anime-style art. Yuji Sakai, a high school student, discovers an unseen supernatural world overlapping our own: the Crimson Realm, where creatures of balance and imbalance fight over the Power of Existence. He befriends Shana, a cold young girl with a samurai sword (or perhaps a creature that simply looks like a girl), and while she defends him from evil threats, she gradually learns human emotions. The conspiratorial world of the series is complicated, with numerous supernatural creatures disguised as human beings, unbeknownst to the general populace. The English edition is slightly censored for near nudity. NR

SHAMAN KING

(シャーマンキング) • Hiroyuki Takei • Viz (2002–ongoing) • Shueisha (Weekly Shônen Jump, 1998–2005) • 32 volumes • Shônen, Occult, Battle • 13+ (violence, mild thematic material)

A mind-blowing mix of kids' fighting action, sarcastic humor, and intelligent writing. Yoh Asakura, an easygoing teenage shaman accompanied by a samurai ghost, is one of countless competitors in the Shaman Fight—a massive worldwide tournament that takes place every 500 years to determine the next savior of the human race. The Shaman Fight is sponsored by a Native American tribe, but the term *shaman* refers to all kinds of holy folk and wonder workers, and virtually every religion, mythology, and occult movement sends a representative to kick butt (even Jesus shows up, albeit only in a single panel). Clearly aware of the absurdity of it all, Hiroyuki Takei tosses out incredibly inventive ideas and characters within the simplest *shônen* manga formula, making a series that works on two levels. Like a fighting game, the emphasis is on the characters, a huge cast drawn in an exaggerated style influenced by American graffiti/

hip-hop art and 1990s superhero comics. The only problem is that *Shaman King* has distinct ups and downs; like many manga, it takes a few volumes to really get going, but more unfortunately, in the later volumes the art degenerates (becoming simpler and simpler), and the ending is so abrupt it has gone down as one of the great disappointments of *Shônen Jump* history. The English edition has many minor instances of censorship for crude humor, racial stereotypes, and drug references, including a *tanuki* spirit that squeezes opponents with its giant testicles, and the countless pot leaf designs on the hero's clothes (the name Yoh means "leaf").

★★★½

SHAOLIN SISTERS

Fûun-san Shimai Lin³, "The Three Winds and Clouds Sisters/The Three Elemental Sisters Lin³" (風雲三姉妹LIN³) • Narumi Kakinouchi • Tokyopop (2003) • Kodansha (Magazine Z, 1999–2001) • 5 volumes • Shônen, Martial Arts, Fantasy • All Ages (graphic violence, brief partial nudity)

Julin and Ko, orphans raised at Fighting Fang Hall, are separated when their home is attacked by villains. Julin's dying master tells her to seek out her father and her two sisters, and together they go on a quest to fight the evil mistress Bai Wang, ruler of the White Lotus Clan. A sort of parallel-universe version of *Juline* set in a Chinese fantasy setting, *Shaolin Sisters* was drawn for a *shônen* magazine rather than a *shôjo* magazine. Perhaps as a result, the story is simpler and more action-oriented, and the artwork is more representational, with real backgrounds in place of Kakinouchi's usual vague dreamscapes. Unfortunately, the fight scenes are weak—relying on anime-style power blasts—and the story is only average, despite a nice twist in the final volume.

★★

SHAOLIN SISTERS: REBORN

Shin Fûun-san Shimai Toku Lin, "New Three Winds and Clouds Sisters/New Three Elemental Sisters Special Lin" (新・風雲三姉妹特LIN) • Narumi Kakinouchi • Tokyopop (2005–2006) • Kodansha (Mag-

azine Z, 2001–2003) • 4 volumes • Shônen, Martial Arts, Fantasy • 13+ (brief language, violence, brief partial nudity)

Sequel to *Shaolin Sisters*. Julin, Seilin, and Kalin, the heroines of the previous series, are reincarnated as sisters in the modern world. Their old enemies are also reincarnated, and they send preening bad guys and mind-controlled students to try to steal the sisters' three magic bells, which may control the fate of the world. A by-the-numbers juvenile action series with energy-blasting martial arts and cute bunny rabbits; the modern-day setting removes one of the few points that made *Shaolin Sisters* stand out. ★

SHION: BLADE OF THE MINSTREL

Shion (シオン) • Yu Kinutani • Viz (1990) • Tokyo Sanseisha (1988) • 1 volume • Fantasy, Adventure • Unrated/16+ (violence, brief nudity)

Shion the Minstrel, a warrior who wields both a sword and music, travels through strange fantasy worlds encountering evil wizards and grotesque, frightening monsters. Extremely detailed and illustrative, with not a centimeter of paper unadorned with strange gems, jewelry, and crosshatched creatures, Kinutani's art looks like a cross between the work of Katsuhiro Otomo, Hayao Miyazaki, and American fantasy illustrators such as Frank Kelly Freas. The plots are less well constructed, and the story leaves open the possibility of sequels, which were never made. ★★

SHIRAHIME-SYO: SNOW GODDESS TALES

Shirahime-shô, "White Princess Tales" (白姫抄) • CLAMP • Tokyopop (2001–2002) • Kobunsha (1992) • 1 volume • Fantasy • 13+ (mild violence)

This stand-alone volume is a trio of tragic fairy tales about the Snow Goddess (Yuki-onna in Japanese) whose tears become snowflakes. In "Wolf Mountain," a young woman ascends a snowy mountain on a journey of revenge against a fearsome wolf; in "The Ice Flower," a young man and his lover make a fateful vow on the shore of an

SHÔJO (少女)

The tremendous success of Japanese girls' comics is considered by many to be the greatest difference between American and Japanese comics culture. Prewar *shôjo* (girls') magazines, such as the 1902 *Shôjo Kai* ("Girls' World") and Kodansha's long-running *Shôjo Club* (1923), contained more serialized prose stories than comics. After the war, new magazines appeared, and manga crowded out photo spreads, advice columns, and features on fashion; Kodansha's *Nakayoshi* (1954) and Shueisha's *Ribon* (1955) are still running today. Early *shôjo* magazines were monthly. In 1963, inspired by the success of the new boys' weeklies, publishers launched weekly magazines such as *Shôjo Friend* and *Margaret,* but the format proved unpopular, and today all *shôjo* magazines are biweekly, monthly, or more infrequent.

The short-lived weekly magazines created a demand for more artists, which changed *shôjo* manga in an even more significant way: actual women began to draw them. Early female artists included Miyako Maki and Toshiko Ueda, but in the 1940s and 1950s the field was dominated by men, including famous artists such as Osamu Tezuka, Leiji Matsumoto, and Kazuo Umezu. Early *shôjo* manga were conservative, even patronizing in tone: chaste, weepy tragedies about young girls and their beloved mothers, with the occasional Hollywood-style fantasy such as Osamu Tezuka's *Princess Knight.* Yoshiko Nishitani, one of the new female artists who debuted in 1965, brought modern-day school romance to the medium, expanding the audience from preteens to teenagers. Macoto Takahashi and other artists developed the trademark *shôjo* flowery backgrounds and sparkling eyes, influenced by the over-the-top glamor of Japan's Takarazuka theater troupe.

In the 1970s, *shôjo* manga boomed. Female artists were in the majority for the

Kodansha's *Nakayoshi*

first time, and artists such as Moto Hagio (*A, A'*), Ryôko Yamagashi, Riyoko Ikeda (*The Rose of Versailles*), and Keiko Takemiya (*To Terra, Andromeda Stories*) explored genres such as science fiction, sports, humor, horror, and the boy-boy love stories initially known as *shônen ai.* At a time when boys' and men's comics were dominated by the *gekiga* movement, with its focus on sociopolitical themes and ultra-realistic artwork, *shôjo* manga went into inner space. Moto Hagio's powerful writing caused her to be one of the first manga artists compared to "real" literature, while the works of Yumiko Oshima were closer to stream-of-consciousness poetry or essays. Some artists were influenced by the counterculture movement, which contributed to *shôjo* manga's impressionistic, dreamlike artwork. The trend toward emotion and psychology over plot contributed to a slump in *shôjo* manga in the 1980s, when the medium was perceived as esoteric and hard to understand. Subsequently, the artwork became more straightforward, and the major magazines became more down-to-earth. Still, *shôjo* art is often abstract or minimalist compared to the highly detailed (and often photo-traced) backgrounds seen in *shônen* and *seinen* manga.

Today, *shôjo* manga is aimed at many age groups and audiences. The bestselling *shôjo* magazines are those aimed at elementary school and junior high girls; Shogakukan's *Ciao* is in the lead with approximately 1 million copies per month (as of 2005), followed by *Ribon* at 537,000 and *Nakayoshi* at 457,000. All three are full of cheerful heroines with big smiles and even bigger eyes; the stories often involve anime and video game tie-ins, and each issue is bundled with goodies like toys and stickers. A separate strata of *shôjo* magazines are aimed at younger teens and midteens, including Kodansha's *Bessatsu Friend,* Akita Shoten's *Princess,* and Shogakukan's *Shôjo Comic* and *Betsucomi;* the bestseller is Shueisha's *Bessatsu Margaret* with a circulation of roughly 355,000. They mostly feature realistic school stories, and their non-manga pages contain articles and ads about fashion accessories, jewelry, manga illustration contests, and pictures of hot guys. Teenage female *otaku* may read magazines such as *Wings, Asuka, Comic Sylph,* and Hakusensha's borderline-nerdy *Hana to Yume* ("Flowers and Dreams") and *LaLa;* they focus more on fantasy and science fiction, and implications of *yaoi* romance between male characters. *Yaoi* itself is a subsection of *shôjo.* Virtually all of the many horror and mystery manga magazines target a *shôjo* demographic. Lastly, there are *shôjo* magazines for older teenagers, which border on the *jôsei* (adult women's) demographic. The most popular magazine of this type is *Cookie,* originally a spinoff of *Ribon,* which runs Ai Yazawa's hit relationship drama *Nana* (2002).

Shueisha's monthly *Bessatsu Margaret* and Hakusensha's biweekly *Hana to Yume*

Beginning in the 1980s with crossover hit artists like Rumiko Takahashi and Mitsuru Adachi, *shôjo* and *shônen* manga have increasingly swapped techniques and readers. Today, some female artists, such as CLAMP and Ai Morinaga, are equally comfortable in both worlds; some fans even worry about the *shôjo* talent drain as female artists go to work for higher-circulation boys' magazines. Gender expectations remain; in Masami Tsuda's *Kare Kano* a male letter writer complains about the embarrassment of having to buy *Kare Kano* from a female cashier at the bookstore. But just as women are some of the most devoted readers of the boys' magazine *Weekly Shônen Jump,* male *shôjo* fans prove that the appeal of manga goes beyond gender.

icy lake; and in "Hiyoku no Tori," a headstrong young lord, who craves battle more than love, has a tragic encounter with the Snow Goddess. For the most part, these are very traditional stories about a folk story icon, although CLAMP leaves a modern message in the epilogue ("The snow is not my tears . . . Snowflakes are the tears of man"). The watercolor shading is beautiful at times, but the character designs are CLAMP at their most generic. For most manga readers, *Shirahime-syo* is too quick and unsubstantial to warrant a purchase. (MT)   ★★½

SHOJO BEAT'S MANGA ARTIST ACADEMY

Mezase!! Manga no Hoshi, "Aim for It! Manga Star" (めざせ!!まんがの星) • Hiroyuki Iizuka (concept), Amu Sumoto (primary art), various artists • Viz (2006) • Shogakukan (2000) • 1 volume • "How to Draw" Book • All Ages

An excellent, comprehensive "how to draw *shôjo* manga" guide (in manga form), containing much information applicable to all forms of comic storytelling. Satomi, a girl panda who wants to draw manga, is instructed by Shogakukan's top *shôjo* artists, who show up as self-caricatures and share their tips. (At the end of the book, it literally shows Japanese readers where to go in Tokyo to drop off their submissions at the Shogakukan office.) Shoko Akira explains how to create memorable, easy-to-understand characters; Chie Shinohara talks about pacing, the importance of eliminating unnecessary

events, and the "show, don't tell" rule; Yuu Watase talks about basic drawing skills and advises against using too much screentone; and several other artists discuss subjects such as coloring, perspective, computer effects, and choosing a good title. A brief color section at the beginning shows coloring tips. It's a useful, entertaining guide for artists of all skill levels, although, as with all translated "how to draw" books, it often references hard-to-get brands of Japanese art supplies such as G-Pen and Prockey. The other artists include Mayu Shinjo, Rie Takada, Yukako Iisaka, Emiko Sugi, Masami Takeuchi, and Miyuki Kitagawa.   ★★★★

SHORT CUTS

(ショートカッツ) • Usamaru Furuya • Viz (2002–2003) • Shogakukan (Young Sunday, 1998–1999) • 2 volumes • Seinen, Underground, Comedy • Unrated/18+ (language, nudity, sex)

Technically brilliant, postmodern gag strips about *kogals* (trendy teenage girls) and the old men who want to have sex with them. The strips are one or two pages in length, with a few repeating characters, but no ongoing story. Furuya (whose origin is in underground comics) is an accomplished mimic, and his culturally literate strips reference various artistic movements, manga, and pop culture while still delivering the big-eyed, short-skirted cuteness. For those coming from outside Japan's prostitution subculture, lengthy cultural annotations are provided. The first volume includes color pages and an artist interview. ★★★

SHORT PROGRAM

(ショート・プログラム) • Mitsuru Adachi • Viz (2000–2004) • Shogakukan (various magazines, 1985–1995) • 2 volumes • Romance, Drama, Sports, Comedy • Unrated/16+ (mild language, mild violence, sexual situations, brief nudity)

Mitsuru Adachi, famed in Japan for his long-running baseball manga *Touch* and *H2*, gives a taste of his subdued, cute style in these collections of short (as few as 4 pages) stories from both *shôjo* and *shônen* magazines. The best ones are shy love stories with twist endings, although sports and comedy are also recurring themes. The humor sometimes falls flat (there are lots of puns), but Adachi's best work is impressively restrained, and his well-constructed tales rarely insult the readers' intelligence. The series is suitable for younger teenage readers, with virtually no T&A, and only the briefest bit of nudity in volume 2. ★★★½

SHRINE OF THE MORNING MIST

Asagiri no Miko, "Shrine Maidens of the Morning Mist" (朝霧の巫女) • Hiroki Ugawa • Tokyopop (2006–2007) • Shônen Gahosha (Young King Ours, 2000–2004) • 4 volumes • Shônen, Occult, Drama • 13+ (mild language, violence)

After being away for five years, teenage Tadahiro comes home to live with his cousins, three cute sisters who serve as traditional *miko* (Shinto shrine maidens, or priestesses) for a mountaintop shrine that looks down on a sea of mist in the valley below. An old crush rekindles with his cousin Yuzu, while Tadahiro's strange powers attract the attention of mysterious strangers and ghostly apparitions, who soon make life difficult at the local high school. Polished anime-style artwork, reminiscent of the work of Akihiro Ito or Kenichi Sonoda, makes an attractive look for this quiet, slow-paced story of Japanese occult conspiracies and monster-exorcising priestesses. The landscapes and cars are nicely drawn, and the monsters are drawn in a classical brush style, making them stand out boldly from everything else in the story. ★★★

SHUGO CHARA!

Shugo Kyara!, "Guardian Characters!" (しゅごキャラ!) • Peach-Pit • Del Rey (2007–ongoing) • Kodansha (Nakayoshi, 2006–ongoing) • 3+ volumes (ongoing) • Shôjo, Fantasy • 13+

Everyone in her elementary school thinks Amu is boyish and tough, but she just wants to be "normal" and date the school idol. Desperate to ditch her tomboy image, she makes a wish to her *shugorei* (guardian spirit) to help, and the next morning she wakes up to find three eggs in her bed. The three eggs hatch into three fairies, the Shugo Chara, who help her change various aspects of herself. She soon encounters other students with similar fairy helpers. NR

SILBUSTER

Ikkou Sahara • Antarctic (1993–1996) • 1 volume, suspended • Science Fiction, Tokusatsu, Comedy • Unrated/16+ (mild language, violence, nudity, sexual situations)

Giant girls in battlesuits protect the Earth from giant monsters sent by aliens in this slapstick parody of Japanese *tokusatsu* sci-fi films. Although the art is crude 1980s anime-style stuff, the story has its moments of humor: at one point, the Japanese military must occupy the monsters' attention long enough for the colossal, naked heroine to put on her clothes. Additional material was printed in monthly comics format but never collected. ★★

SILENT MÖBIUS

(サイレントメビウス) • Kia Asamiya • Viz (1991–2003) • Kadokawa Shoten (Comic Comp/Comic Dragon, 1988–1999) • 12 volumes • Shônen, Occult, Science Fiction, Action • Unrated/16+ (mild language, violence, nudity, sex)

Tokyo in 2026—your typical 1980s cyberpunk megalopolis—is plagued by Lucifer

SHÔNEN (少年)

Manga have a much more even gender split than American comics, but for sheer sales numbers, mainstream *shônen* (boys') manga still dominate the market. With their action-oriented story lines, *shônen* manga produce the bulk of licensed properties for anime, video games, and other media, and although they are typically aimed at boys in late elementary school and junior high, the bestselling magazines are read by all ages and genders.

Japanese boys' magazines existed before World War II, mostly publishing a mixture of humorous adventure comics and serialized prose stories, such as the monthly *Shônen Club*. After the war, one of the first manga-focused magazines was the monthly *Manga Shônen* (1947), which published the early works of artists such as Osamu Tezuka, Leiji Matsumoto, and Shotaro Ishinomori. The boys' comic market approached its modern form in 1959 with the near-simultaneous release of Japan's first two weekly comic magazines: Kodansha's *Weekly Shônen Magazine* and Shogakukan's *Weekly Shônen Sunday*. Finally, in 1968 arrived Shueisha's *Weekly Shônen Jump*. Other weekly *shônen* magazines have come and gone, but they are the three biggest *shônen* magazines from Japan's three biggest publishers.

A Japanese institution, *Weekly Shônen Jump* combines aggressive new-talent searching with a give-the-readers-what-they-want attitude, relying heavily on reader polls and feedback. As a result, it contains some of the most individualistic art styles and the most formulaic stories, usually involving fantastic battles or contests in which the hero extends the hand of friendship to defeated rivals. This dates back to a poll conducted by the early editors of the magazine, in which readers identified their core val-

Shueisha's *Weekly Shônen Jump* and Shueisha's *Weekly Shônen Magazine*

ues: *yûjo, doryoku, shôri* (friendship, perseverance, victory). In the 1980s, *Shônen Jump* became the bestselling manga magazine in history with titles such as *Dr. Slump, City Hunter, Fist of the North Star, Dragon Ball,* and *Knights of the Zodiac* (*Saint Seiya*). Sales peaked in the mid-1990s at 6.53 million copies per week, before dropping to approximately 3 million (as of 2004) with the general recession. Compared to *Sunday* and *Magazine,* it is aimed at a slightly younger audience, and it also has many female readers; unlike its competition, it never features photo spreads of swimsuit models. It is the only manga magazine with a direct U.S. counterpart.

In the late 1990s, *Weekly Shônen Jump* was briefly surpassed in sales by its closest rival, *Weekly Shônen Magazine,* which is aimed at slightly older readers than its competition and generally features cool, down-to-earth stories about high school guys (with only the occasional fantasy such as *Rave Master* and *Tsubasa: Reservoir Chronicle*). The artwork is generally slick and detailed, with photorealistic backgrounds.

Weekly Shônen Sunday's breezy, metropolitan tone was set in the early 1980s by the works of Rumiko Takahashi (*Lum*Urusei Yatsura, Ranma ½*), whose mixture of science fiction and romantic comedy made the magazine a forerunner of modern-day anime themes and a favorite of *otaku.* Takahashi's relationship-focused stories were complemented by the women-friendly sports romances of Mitsuru Adachi (*Short Program*). The fourth and lowest-selling of the classic weeklies is Akita Shoten's *Weekly Shônen Champion,* which was a major player in the 1970s and 1980s. In its heyday it focused on traditionally manly blue-collar subjects such as gangs and *yakuza,* but it always had an anarchistic streak. Today it is best known for over-the-top self-parodies such as *Iron Wok Jan, Apocalypse Zero,* and *Baron Gong Battle,* and bad-taste comedies such as *Eiken* and *Enmusu.*

Weekly *shônen* magazines are aimed at the casual reader, although their core demographic is boys in junior high. At approximately 450 pages for 240 yen (about U.S. $2), they are the best value in manga. Monthly and more infrequent magazines are much more numerous and are typically bigger and more expensive. For elementary-school-age boys, there are the hyperactive *Corocoro Comic* and *Comic Bombom,* which rely heavily on anime and game tie-ins. For teenage boys there are many monthlies that staddle the line with *seinen* manga, including *Monthly Shônen Gangan, Monthly Shônen Ace, Dengeki Daioh, Dengeki Gao!,* and *Shônen Fang.* They are generally aimed at hard-core fans and tend toward fantasy, science fiction, mecha, cute girls in costumes, and other *otaku*-oriented subjects. All *shônen* magazines make tremendous cross-promotional efforts, and the opening color pages often feature product coverage of video games, anime, toys, and occasionally live-action movies or TV series. Most weekly *shônen* magazines have monthly spin-off magazines as well.

Modern-day *shônen* manga have vast diversity, ranging from comedy to sports, romance to hobby/occupational stories, detective stories to battle manga. The last of these genres, possibly the biggest, ranges from modern-day martial arts stories to elaborate fantasy and science fiction. The heroes often have insanely spiky hair, the better to be recognized in silhouette. On the outside, they may be fiery or cool, earnest or cynical, clumsy or infallible. Often they are a combination of both—heroes who only *seem* like total goof-offs. Other heroes express their dual natures in a more literal fashion. The *henshin* (transforming) protagonists of manga such as *Yu-Gi-Oh!, Samurai Deeper Kyo,* and *Bastard!!* change from wimps to infallible superheroes, often becoming more unrestrained and savage in the process. Some heroes are more or less ordinary (and there-fore sympathetic) people who are strong by proxy, through alliance with familiar spirits, robots, or monsters, which reflect aspects of their personalities. *Yu-Gi-Oh!, JoJo's Bizarre Adventure, Shaman King,* and *Zatch Bell* all fall into this subgenre, which took off in the 1990s thanks to its most famous example, *Pokémon*.

Cliff-hangers are the basis of all story manga, but no matter how dark things may seem, *shônen* manga are ultimately optimistic. Defending a plot twist in his notes to *Rurouni Kenshin,* author Nobuhiro Watsuki writes, "The basics of a *shônen* manga are smiles and a happy ending." The success of most *shônen* manga depends on how well they play with these expectations, and the creativity they bring to the material.

Hawks, slimy demons from another dimension. The city's only hope is the A.M.P. ("Abnormal Mystery Police" or "Attacked Mystification P.D."), a *Charlie's Angels*–esque group of female cops, each with her own role: a sorcerer, a cyborg, a computer hacker, a psychic, and so on. Kia Asamiya's best-known series, *Silent Möbius* is very much a commercial confection. The early volumes borrow liberally from Masamune Shirow (*Appleseed*) and then-current anime, while the later volumes become increasingly overprocessed and computer-generated, as Asamiya trades his early generic 1980s character designs for his later distinctive, but awkward, triangle-nosed art style. The first several volumes focus one at a time on individual characters, eventually developing into a clichéd plot with lots of "Noooo! *Boom!*" moments (see the article on PSYCHIC) and speeches about how humans are better than demons because humans love one another. Production notes in the back of certain volumes reveal that the monsters, vehicles, and weapons were mostly designed by Asamiya's assistants. See also *Möbius Klein*. ★★

SISTER RED

(シスターレッド) • Shizuru Hayashiya • MediaWorks (Dengeki Daioh, 2001–2003) • ComicsOne (2004) • 2 volumes • Shônen, Horror, Action • 13+ (language, graphic violence)

After dying in a car crash, teenage Mahito is brought back to life as a humanoid creature of darkness, a Median (probably a misspelled reference to the city of Midian in Clive Barker's *Nightbreed*). She is soon embroiled in a battle between rival factions of Medians, who seek the power of the "sacred heart" implanted in Mahito's body. Although the opening chapters are promisingly dark and creepy, *Sister Red* ultimately settles into a conventional battle-of-the-superhumans plot, with unexciting character designs and an unsatisfying conclusion. ★★

SKIN AND BONE: See *Hino Horror, Vol. 14: Skin and Bone*

SKIP BEAT!

(スキップ・ビート!) • Yoshiki Nakamura • Viz (2006–ongoing) • Hakusensha (Hana to Yume, 2002–ongoing) • 15+ volumes (ongoing) • Shôjo, Comedy, Drama • 13+ (mild sexual situations)

A fun, unpredictable *shôjo* manga with a twist: instead of friendship or love, the heroine's motive is revenge. After being dumped by her musician boyfriend, whom she supported when he was a struggling nobody, Kyoko vows to become an even more popular celebrity than he is. Working crummy low-paying jobs, she fights to enter the talent business, encountering vain actresses and musicians, and the occasional weirdo with a heart of gold. Nakamura's figures and faces are good, and she comes up with great visuals to express the characters' feelings: when Kyoko sinks to the depths of despair, deep-sea fish swim in the air alongside her; when Kyoko gets mad, which is often, vengeful spirits pour out of her body. The celebrity-training sequences are like something out of a *shônen* manga. Some middle-finger gestures are censored in the English edition. ★★★

THE SKULL MAN

(スカルマン) • Shotaro Ishinomori (original concept/story), Kazuhiko Shimamoto (art) • Tokyopop (2002–2003) • Media Factory (Comic Alpha, 1998–2001) • 7 volumes • Science Fiction, Tokusatsu, Action • 13+ (graphic violence, nudity, sexual situations)

An expanded remake of a little-known 1970 manga by the late creator of *Kamen Rider* (who actually guest-stars), *The Skull Man* is a flawed but amazing tribute to the *tokusatsu* masked hero genre, done in a smooth retro style. Ishinomori worked with the artist just prior to his death in 1998, providing Shimamoto with notes and outlines. The title character is a masked avenger who dwells in a house in a cemetery and ruthlessly fights a secret organization of shape-shifters created by mad scientific experiments. Superpowered monsters do battle while the artist whips out the now-neglected manga techniques of the 1970s—a leisurely pace, impressionistic panel layouts, the use of visual effects to show psychological states. It's a little difficult to figure out what's going on, and the ending is unsatisfying, but you're spellbound from the first city scene to the last psychedelic montage of bats, flames, and skulls swirling over the moon. ★★★½

SLAM DUNK

(スラムダンク) • Takehiko Inoue • Gutsoon! Entertainment (2002–2004) • Shueisha (Weekly Shônen Jump, 1990–1996) • 5 volumes, suspended (31 volumes in Japan) • Shônen, Sports, Comedy • 13+ (language, mild violence)

Hanamichi Sakuragi, a high school delinquent with no girlfriend, joins the basketball team because Haruko, a cute girl, tells him, "I just love guys who play sports." Despite his bad temper, huge ego, and impatience, he slowly learns the basics of playing a team sport (miraculously without any dumb speeches about teamwork) while clashing with captain Gori (Haruko's big brother) and the other players. Great characters, comedy, and, most of all, intense basketball games stretching for volumes make *Slam Dunk* a terrifically fun *shônen* manga. With its muscular body types, clean lines, and chiseled faces, Inoue's art has a faint American look. (Evidently basketball wasn't entirely familiar to Japanese *Shônen Jump* readers at the time, since Inoue feels the need to explain basic basketball facts such as what a rebound is.) More of the story was published in *Raijin* magazine but never collected. ★★★½

SLAYERS: CITY OF LOST SOULS: See *Slayers Super-Explosive Demon Story*

SLAYERS MEDIEVAL MAYHEM

Slayers (スレイヤーズ) • Hajime Kanzaka (story), Rui Araizumi (art) • CPM (1999) • Kadokawa Shoten (Comic Dragon, 1992–1995) • 1 volume • Shônen, Fantasy, Comedy • Unrated/16+ (nudity, mild sexual situations)

Lina Inverse, a money-grubbing teenage sorceress, and Gourry Gabriev, her more or less platonic swordsman companion, wander a fantasy world doing odd jobs and getting in trouble. The first of many manga based on Hajime Kanzaka's *Slayers* novels, and the only one drawn by the original novel illustrator, *Slayers: Medieval Mayhem* is probably the funniest and smartest of the lot. (That isn't saying much, however; as "funny fantasy" goes, *Slayers* makes Terry Pratchett look like Dostoyevsky.) The disconnected stories provide no background for the characters, which doesn't matter much. ★★

SLAYERS PREMIUM

(スレイヤーズぷれみあむ) • Hajime Kanzaka (story), Tommy Ohtsuka (art), Rui Araizumi (character design) • CPM (2004) • Kadokawa Shoten (Dragon Junior, 2002) • 1 volume • Shônen, Fantasy, Comedy • 13+ (brief partial nudity, mild sexual situations)

This adaptation of the *Slayers Premium,* the last *Slayers* anime (at least as of 2007), reunites the entire cast for a fittingly cheesy finale. Ohtsuka's friendly, bold-lined cartoon art—every character seems to be smiling and winking at the camera in almost every panel—is a good match for the story, in which evil (but tasty) octopus people conspire to resurrect a sea monster. ★★

SLAYERS RETURN: See *Slayers Super-Explosive Demon Story*

SLAYERS SPECIAL

(スレイヤーズすぺしゃる) • Hajime Kanzaka (story), Tommy Ohtsuka (art), Rui Araizumi (character design) • CPM (2002–2003) • Kadokawa Shoten (Dragon Junior, 2000–2001) • 4 volumes • Shônen, Fantasy, Comedy • All Ages (mild violence, brief partial nudity, mild sexual situations)

Spin-off of Hajime Kanzaka's *Slayers Special* fantasy-comedy light novels. Lina Inverse, an overpowered teenage wizard, searches for food and adventure accompanied by Naga, her busty, thong-wearing rival. *Slayers Special* is targeted at slightly younger readers than the other *Slayers* manga, and the jokes are a more juvenile version of the same formula, with lots of food humor and *Tenchi Muyô!*–esque catfighting ("Naga's homemaker skills match mine!"). The two bickering heroines go on dungeon crawls, work as maids and waitresses, search for "bosom growth potions," and fight the occasional bad guy, such as a villainous math teacher. On the plus side, Ohtsuka's art is slick, a good match for the slapstick action and cartoon cheesecake. ★½

SLAYERS SUPER-EXPLOSIVE DEMON STORY

Chôbaku Madô Den Slayers, "Super Explosive Demon/Magic Story Slayers" (超爆魔道伝スレイヤーズ) • Hajime Kanzaka (story), Shoko Yoshinaka (art), Rui Araizumi (character design) • CPM (2001–2004) • Kadokawa Shoten (Comic Dragon, 1995–2001) • 8 volumes • Shônen, Fantasy, Comedy, Adventure • All Ages (mild violence, mild sexual humor)

Manga adaptation of the *Slayers* anime (which was itself inspired by Hajime Kanzaka's novels): the original TV series, *Slayers Return,* and *Slayers Next.* The only *Slayers* manga with an ongoing plot, it retells the story of boyish sorceress Lina, including her first encounters with Gourry the fighter, Zelgadis the half-human wizard, Amelia the spunky "champion of justice," and the other members of her adventuring party. Pure comedy stories alternate with longer plots and fight scenes involving nefarious bad guys and evil demons, usually vanquished by Gourry's magic sword or one of Lina's devastating spells. As a fairly direct adaptation, the series offers little new to fans of the anime. The art is muddy, and when the heroes aren't saving the world, the "comedy" is like a machine that makes two jokes: (1) "Your breasts are small!" "Gee, you have small breasts!" "You're flat-chested!" (2) "Boy, I'm hungry!" "Let's get some food!" "Boy, we ate a lot of food!" Actually, those are not *direct* quotes from *Slayers Super-Explosive Demon Story,* but this is: "It's a wonder you're so flat-chested when you eat that much." Several volumes in the series were released without numbers on the covers: *Slayers Return* is actually volume 4 of the series, and *Slayers: City of Lost Souls* is volume 5. ★½

SMUGGLER

(スマグラ) • Shohei Manabe • Tokyopop (2006) • Kodansha (Afternoon, 2000) • 1 volume • Seinen, Crime Drama • 16+ (language, graphic violence, partial nudity)

Ryosuke, a twenty-four-year-old *freeter* (someone with no career path who drifts between odd jobs and unemployment), gets into serious debt and ends up working with a pair of truckers who transport dangerous goods such as human corpses. Their path takes them into the urban underworld and encounters with *yakuza* and worse. Drawn in a realistic and distinctly unpretty style, with fishlike faces staring out of a background of urban gloom, *Smuggler* is a well-written, tightly plotted suspense story. ★★★

SOCRATES IN LOVE

Sekai no Chushin de Ai wo Sakebu, "Crying Out Love in the Center of the World" (世界の中心で愛をさけぶ) • Kyoichi Katayama (original creator), Kazumi Kazui (art) • Viz (2005) • Shogakukan (2004) • 1 volume • Shôjo, Romance, Drama • 16+ (partial nudity, sexual situations)

Manga adaptation of Kyoichi Katayama's bestselling novel of young love tested by sudden tragedy. The story remains basically intact and enjoyable, but many events from the novel have been condensed or removed in order to fit one volume of manga. The manga is missing most of Katayama's humorous observations about life and also a moving dialogue between protagonist Sakutaro and his grandfather about love and death. Although the removed material is not necessary to enjoy the story, without it *Socrates in Love* feels like any other saccharine romance manga. The characters are visually indistinct from one another and there are far too many panels without backgrounds. (MJS) ★★

SOMEDAY'S DREAMERS

Mahôtsukai ni Taisetsu na Koto—Someday's Dreamers, "The Things Important to Magic-Users—Someday's Dreamers" (魔法遣いに大切なこと—Someday's Dreamers) • Norie Yamada (story/original creator), Kumichi Yoshizuki (art) • Tokyopop (2006) • Kadokawa Shoten (Comic Dragon, 2002–2003) • 2 volumes • Shônen, Fantasy, Drama • 13+ (shower scene)

A calculated attempt at an anime/manga/book franchise with a cute female lead. (The manga, which has the same plot as the anime, came first by a narrow margin.) Teenage Yume (the name means "dream") moves to Tokyo to pursue a life as an apprentice magician, using her powers, like all magicians, to make people's dreams and wishes come true. Although you can smell a whiff of Harry Potter's "muggles" in an illogical plot element about anti-magician prejudice, *Someday's Dreamers* doesn't care in the slightest about castles or spell books or the other trappings of wizardry; magicians

are just the all-powerful instigators for predictably heartwarming stories such as a baseball player who gets his amputated leg back or a dying old woman who gets her final wish. The anime-style artwork is graceful, particularly the beautiful color covers, but it's merely a pretty execution of a shallow concept. ★

SOMEDAY'S DREAMERS: SPELLBOUND

Mahôtsukai ni Taisetsu na Koto Taiyô to Kaze no Sakamichi, "The Things Important to Magic-Users: Road of Sun and Wind" (魔法遣いに大切なこと太陽と風の坂道) • Norie Yamada (story), Kumichi Yoshizuki (art) • Tokyopop (2006–2008) • Kadokawa Shoten (Dragon Age, 2004–2006) • 5 volumes • Shônen, Fantasy, Drama • 13+

A follow-up to the previous *Someday's Dreamers* series with a new cast of characters. Our new protagonist is a high school student named Nami, an otherwise average teenager who happens to be not just a magician but an exceptionally inept one. As the story begins, her daily routine is disrupted by the arrival of a mysterious troubled transfer student. (MS) NR

SORCERER HUNTERS

Bakuretsu Hunters, "Explosive Hunters" (爆れつハンター) • Satoru Akahori (story), Ray Omishi (art) • Tokyopop (1998–ongoing) • Kadokawa Shoten/MediaWorks (Comic Comp/Dengeki Gao!, 1992–1998) • 13 volumes • Shônen, Fantasy, Comedy • 16+ (mild language, violence, nudity, sexual situations)

Tongue-in-cheek RPG fantasy. The Sorcerer Hunters' job is to fight evil magicians who rule the land like feudal lords. The male lead, Carrot Glacé, is a comedic lech who runs around hitting on every girl in sight; like Ataru in *Urusei Yatsura,* the only girls he doesn't like are the ones who throw themselves at him. He also has the uncontrollable power to turn into a giant rampaging monster, at which point only one thing can stop him: Tira Misu, his normally mousy girl companion, who throws off her glasses and cloak to reveal a dominatrix outfit and whips him into submission. The other Sorcerer Hunters, who are also named after food, include Marron (a *bishônen* wizard), Gateau (a musclebound exhibitionist), and Chocolat (Tira's sister, a fellow dominatrix who impales enemies with wire whips and wears the Nazi fetish outfit from the 1974 film *The Night Porter*). The series is at its best on the rare occasions when the kink and the action work together, as when Chocolat goes head to head with an evil sorceress in a bunny costume for the love of Carrot ("The only one who can grind Carrot beneath her high heels . . . *is me!*"). The rest of the time, it's just got attention deficit disorder, swinging between sex comedy (guy-girl and guy-guy), blood-splattered battles to save the world, cute childhood flashbacks, and little touching stories with morals such as "The heart is the strongest power of all." Perhaps the series' biggest disappointment is that none of the other characters is as audacious as Carrot, Tira, and Chocolat; most of the supporting cast and villains are your standard fantasy-anime designs. The original Japanese title uses the word *bakuretsu*, a trendy meaningless word used much like "extreme" in the United States. ★½

SOS

(エスオ・エス) • Hinako Ashihara • Viz (2005) • Shogakukan (Betsucomi, 2003) • 1 volume • Shôjo, Romance, Comedy, Drama • 16+ (mild language, brief violence, sexual situations)

A collection of romantic short stories, more bittersweet than the cute cover art suggests, involving compromises and unrequited love. In the title story, the main characters set up a dating service for their high school classmates. "That Sweet Organ Song" is a period romance set in 1922 Japan, and "The Easy Life" is the story of a girl and her inconsiderate boyfriend. The art is better than Ashihara's earlier *Forbidden Dance*. Despite occasionally serious subject matter, the stories are done in a tasteful way and are suitable for younger teenage readers.

★★★

SOTA-KUN NO AKIHABARA FUNTOKI

Sota-kun no Akihabara Funtoki, "Sota-kun's Akihabara Journal of Struggles" (壮太君のアキハバラ糞闘記) • Jiro Suzuki • Seven Seas Entertainment (2007–ongoing) • Square Enix (Monthly G-Fantasy/G-Fantasy Zôkan/G-Fantasy++, 2001–ongoing) • 5+ volumes (ongoing) • Otaku, Comedy • 16+

Otaku "coming out" story with lots of big-breasted women with dog ears. Sota, a high school student, is a closet *otaku* who loves *moe* anime starring the dog-eared girl character Papico. He tries to conceal his interests so he can get a girlfriend, but when he goes to a collectibles shop in Akihabara, the crazed owner forces him to come clean about his lifestyle. NR

SOUL RESCUE

(ソウルスレスキュー) • Aya Kanno (story and art) • Tokyopop (2006–2007) • Hakusensha (Hana to Yume, 2001–2002) • 2 volumes • Shôjo, Fantasy, Action • 13+

What happens when angels go too far? Apparently, community service. When the mighty but somewhat violent angel Renji gets carried away in battle with the forces of darkness, he's exiled to Earth to work off his debt to heavenly society by saving ten thousand souls. It's too bad that Renji is more of a *fighting* kind of angel. (MS) NR

SPEED RACER: THE ORIGINAL MANGA

Mach GoGoGo (マッハGoGoGo) • Tatsuo Yoshida (creator), Jiro Kuwata (art) • WildStorm (2000) • Asahi Sonorama (1968) • 1 volume • Racing, Action • Unrated/All Ages (mild violence)

Manga adaptation of the *Speed Racer* anime series, known as *Mach GoGoGo* in Japan. In "The Malanga," Speed must stop a murderous masked racer out to avenge his father's death. In "The Deadly Desert Race," he accepts a challenge to race in the desert and ends up facing scorpions, vultures, and camel-riding, scimitar-swinging desert tribesmen. The final story, "This Is a Racer's Soul!" involves the mysterious Racer X. These are simple children's comics from the 1960s, with cartoony art, fast-paced plots, and lots of fistfights and jumping in and out of speeding cars. Primarily of historical and fan interest. The same material was also printed in monthly comics form as *Speed Racer Classics* (1988–1989) by Now Comics. Though uncredited in the English edition, the manga was drawn by Jiro Kuwata (*8 Man*). ★★

SPELLBOUND: THE MAGIC OF LOVE

Tomoko Taniguchi • Fanboy Entertainment (2001) • 1 issue • Magical Girl, Romantic Comedy • All Ages

Original *shôjo* manga series made for American audiences by Tomoko Taniguchi, starring Ami, a teenage witch. The project was canceled after one issue. ★★

SPIDER-MAN: THE MANGA

Spider-Man (スパイダーマン) • Ryoichi Ikegami (story and art), Kôsei Ono and Kazumasa Hirai (story assistance) • Marvel Comics (1997–1999) • Kodansha (Bessatsu Shônen Magazine, 1970–1971) • 31 issues, suspended (5 volumes in Japan) • Shônen, Superhero, Action, Drama • Unrated/16+ (mild language, violence, mild sexual situations)

The costume may look exactly the same as the American Spider-Man, but the character inside the suit, an unlucky high school kid named Yu Komori, faced a very different set of problems. Set in a totally grim and depressing Tokyo, the manga Spider-Man (created by a fateful spider bite, much like Peter Parker) tangles with a delinquent teenage judo team and a womanizing playboy, as well as new and humorless versions of classic enemies such as Mysterio and the Lizard. Every single story sees Komori caught in the grip of a new moral and ethical nightmare (example: a Spider-Man impostor commits terrorist acts against companies guilty of pollution. Is it right to stop him?). It may not sound like much of a fun read, but the dark atmosphere and "only in the 1970s" touches will heroically remind you of a time when children's manga seemed to have absolutely no rules or restrictions. Ikegami's art is a bit rough around the edges, but the style perfectly matches the grimy nature of the downbeat stories. Although they are uncredited in the English edition, two writers assisted Ikegami on the series: first the American comic critic Kôsei Ono, and later the science fiction writer Kazumasa Hirai. (Thus the series undergoes a gradual change as familiar Marvel villains are phased out in favor of grittier stories where Spider-Man hardly even puts on his costume.) The complete series was never translated, reportedly due to Marvel balking at the sexual elements in the later parts of the Japanese edition. (PM) ★★★★

SPIRAL: See *The Ring, Vol. 3: Spiral*

SPIRIT OF WONDER

The Spirit of Wonder (ザ・スピリット・オブ・ワンダー) • Kenji Tsuruta • Dark Horse (1996–1998) • Kodansha (Comic Morning/Comic Morning Zôkan, 1986–1988) • 1 volume • Seinen, Historical, Science Fiction, Romance • Unrated/16+ (nudity, mild sexual situations)

In a seaside British town sometime in the early twentieth century, a young Chinese woman runs a restaurant and rents a room to a mad scientist, Dr. Breckenridge. Although the dirty old doctor is perpetually late on his rent, "Miss China" has a crush on his handsome assistant Jim, who in turn tries to show his feelings using the doctor's incredible inventions—teleporters, artificial shooting stars, and a device that allows him to write a message to China on the surface of the moon. Extraordinarily detailed artwork makes this manga live up to its name: a sweet if unresolved love story, similar to the comics of Kozue Amano (*Aqua, Aria*), in which the characters often stop and gaze at the scenery. The Jules Verne–esque science fiction isn't the only way in which *Spirit of Wonder* harks back to old-fashioned pulp; the heroine is a bit of a stereotype. Enjoyable but slight, with no real ending. ★★½

SPRIGGAN: See *Striker*

SPORTS (スポーツ)

Perhaps nothing shows the mainstream nature of Japanese comics better than the tremendous popularity of sports manga. Sports comics were once popular in America as well, but were wiped out in the 1950s and 1960s by the growing marginalization of comics and the rising tide of superheroes. Almost all major *shônen* and *seinen* magazines run sports stories; apart from a few small specialty magazines (such as Akita Shoten's *Golf Comic* and Shonen Gahosha's *Golf Comic Athlete*), there are no magazines devoted specifically to sports manga because they are ubiquitous in mainstream publications. Manga magazines often feature sports coverage or interviews with athletes in the articles in their text sections. Real-life stars sometimes appear in manga. The small number of translated sports manga are only the tip of the iceberg.

The History of Sports Manga

Traditional Japanese sports were chiefly martial arts such as judo, sumo, karate, kendo (swordfighting), and kyudo (archery). In the aftermath of World War II, the American occupation government banned these traditional sports for several years, believing that they had contributed to Japanese militarism. In their place, American sports such as pro wrestling, boxing, and baseball were encouraged. The transplantation was a success. In the years before private TV was introduced to Japan in 1953, some of Japan's earliest TV broadcasts were public screenings of sports matches. As Japan rebuilt itself from the ruins, people found heroes in the struggles of athletes.

Sports manga were regular features in *shônen* magazines and soon developed a popular formula, known as *spo-kon,* from the words *sports* and *konjô* ("guts" or "determination"). In a classic *spo-kon* story, the hero is from a poor family and suffers tragic hardship. Through intense training, he struggles to succeed in sports, although it is a long, hard road full of blood, sweat, and self-sacrifice. His coach or his father (sometimes the two are one and the same) is harsh and unforgiving, an archetype known in Japan as an *oni coach* (devil coach). Of course, he has the hero's best interests at heart . . . or at least the drive to win, no matter what the cost.

The gritty atmosphere of classic sports manga was influenced by *gekiga,* with its gloomy urban settings and impoverished lower-class characters. It also formed the basics of the "struggle to succeed" ethic seen in almost all modern-day *shônen* competition manga. Manga author Ikki Kajiwara is considered the master of the genre: working with an assortment of artists, he created such legendary works as the baseball comic *Kyôjin no Hoshi* ("Star of the Giants," 1966), the wrestling comic *Tiger Mask* (1968), and the boxing comic *Ashita no Jo* ("Tomorrow's Joe," 1968). All were published in *Weekly Shônen Magazine,* giving it a reputation as the best magazine for sports manga.

The 1964 Tokyo Olympics, in which Japan won sixteen gold medals, increased interest in sports throughout Japan. Sports stories began to appear in *shôjo* manga as well. Gradually, the unapologetic melodrama of *spo-kon* stories became moderated by a lighter, more humorous touch. Four-panel humor manga with sports themes grew in popularity. Mitsuru Adachi, a popular sports manga artist, is credited with demolishing the *spo-kon* formula; in his baseball romantic comedy *Touch* (1981), the hero is naturally gifted at the sport, cares as much about relationships as baseball, and lives in an affluent suburban setting. Adachi's manga were baseball stories for the new, comfortable, middle-class Japan. But the classic formula is still popular, and subsequent artists have spanned a wide range of comedy and drama.

Baseball

Baseball (*yakyû* in Japanese) was introduced to Japan in 1872, and the first formal team was established in 1878. It is the most popular sport in Japan; only soccer is a potential rival. Even high school baseball players can become celebrities; local high school tournaments culminate in the nationally televised annual tournament at Hanshin Kôshien Stadium in Nishonomiya, which draws crowds equal to or greater than professional baseball.

Baseball manga are some of the most popular manga in Japan. Shinji Mizushima has produced the longest-running baseball comics; his *Abu-san* has appeared since 1973 and is still running with 87 volumes, and his *Dokaben,* named after the bento boxes eaten by its stocky protagonist, first appeared in 1972 and now spans more than 100 volumes including various sequels. Ikki Kajiwara and Noboru Kawasaki's *Kyôjin no Hoshi,* about a young pitcher's struggle to join the real-life Yomiuri Giants, was adapted into Japan's first televised sports anime in 1968. *Kyôjin no Hoshi* pioneered the use of manga "special effects," time stops, slowdowns, and extreme close-ups to dramatize its baseball action. Baseball crept into the realm of outright superheroes in Norihiro Nakajima and Shirô Toozaki's over-the-top *Astro Kyûdan* ("Astro League," 1972), in which the heroes practice their batting on the rim of active volcanoes and eventually depart Japan in search of a remote tribe that practices a "purer," more primal form of baseball. Mitsuru Adachi's *Touch* and *H2* (1992) took a more sedate but still dramatic approach.

Given the tremendous popularity of the genre, it's surprising that as of 2006 no full-length baseball manga have been translated, with the exception of short stories in collections by Mitsuru Adachi and Rumiko Takahashi. Chuck Austen and Hiroki Otsuka's original English-language manga *Boys of Summer* (2006) is an attempt to rectify the situation.

Soccer

Japan, like nearly every country except America, takes soccer seriously. The sport was introduced to Japan in 1873; unlike most other countries, the English word *soccer* is used more commonly than *football,* a sign of American influence. A Japanese bronze medal in the 1968 Olympics led to a minor soccer boom and to the creation of Ikki Kajiwara and Mitsuyoshi Sonoda's famous soccer manga *Akakichi no Eleven* ("The Dark Red Eleven," 1970).

The most successful soccer manga ever is Yoichi Takahashi's *Captain Tsubasa* (1981), the straightforward story of a young boy who dreams of becoming a soccer star and eventually plays in tournaments around the world. *Captain Tsubasa* is credited with making soccer popular in Japan, but it was a smash hit in other countries as well, including Spain, Brazil, France, and Italy. It has seemingly been translated into almost every language except English, and sequels, spin-offs, anime, and video games continue to appear to this day. Other popular soccer manga include Tsukasa Oshima's long-running *Shoot!* (1990), which, like *Captain Tsubasa,* was followed by numerous sequels, and Motoki Monma's comedy *Buttobi Itto* ("Exploding Itto," 1999). As of April 2007, the only soccer manga translated into English is Daisuke Higuchi's *Whistle!* (1998).

Basketball

Basketball is a relatively recent addition to the Japanese sports scene; although Nobiru Kuroda's *Dash Kappei* (1979) was popular enough to be animated, the first megahit basketball manga were Hiroki Yagami's *Dear Boys* (1989) and Takehiko Inoue's *Slam Dunk* (1990). Although Inoue is also famous for the samurai manga *Vagabond* (1998), his first love is basketball; he wrote one of the first professional online manga, the basketball story *Buzzer Beater* (1997), and *Real* (1999), the story of a handicapped basketball player who takes to the court in a wheelchair. In 2006, Inoue sponsored the Takehiko Inoue Slam Dunk Scholarship, to send four Japanese basketball students to South Kent School in Connecticut in 2007.

Other popular basketball manga include Yuriko Nishiyama's *Harlem Beat* (1994), which has been translated, and Hiroyuki Asada's *I'll* (1996).

Yuriko Nishiyama's *Harlem Beat*

Other Sports

Sports adapted into manga include badminton, golf, dodgeball, ice hockey, and just about everything imaginable. Riichiro Inagaki and Yusuke Murata's *Eyeshield 21* (2002) may be the most popular manga ever to deal with what in Japan is called "American football." Full of outrageous gridiron action, parodying and embracing all the classic sports manga themes, it even includes a literal "devil coach"—the comically diabolical, fanged Yôichi Hiruma.

The Japan women's team won a gold medal in volleyball in the 1964 Olympics, prompting an interest in women's athletics, which was reflected in *shôjo* manga. Chikako Urano's volleyball manga *Attack No. 1* (1968) was one of the first successful *shôjo* sports comics, and a sequel, *Shin Attack No. 1* ("New Attack No. 1"), recently appeared in *Margaret,* the same magazine that ran the original. Mitsuba Takanashi's *Crimson Hero* (2002) is a modern *shôjo* volleyball manga. Sumika Yamamoto's tennis manga *Ace o Nerae!* ("Aim for the Ace!" 1973) became a classic and was adapted into multiple anime as well as a short-lived 2004 live-action TV series. More recently, Takeshi Konomi's *shônen* manga *The Prince of Tennis* (1999) developed a huge female following for the *bishônen* appeal of its cast of hot boys.

Racing and motorsports are considered a subcategory of sports manga, and race cars appear in *Speed Racer: The Original Manga* (1968), a spin-off of the anime, and Shuichi Shigeno's megahit *Initial D* (1995). Imaginary science fiction sports appear in series such as *Air Gear* (2002), *Ashen Victor* (1995), *Battle Angel Alita* (1990), and *The Venus Wars* (1987). Lastly, it is impossible to count the number of school-themed manga, particularly *shôjo* manga and romantic comedy manga, in which sports are a secondary aspect of the characters' lives. Motorcycling appears in *Oh My Goddess!* (1988) and *Mars* (1995), boxing in *One Pound Gospel* (1987) and *Tuxedo Gin* (1997), track and field in *Hana-Kimi: For You in Full Blossom* (1996) and *Suzuka* (2004), hockey (barely) in *My Heavenly Hockey Club* (2005). If a sport has been invented, it's in manga.

Sports Manga

Air Gear • *Apollo's Song* • *Ashen Victor* • *Boys of Summer* • *Crimson Hero* • *Eyeshield 21* • *Girl Got Game* • *Hana-Kimi: For You in Full Blossom* • *Harlem Beat* • *Initial D* • *Kimi Shiruya—Dost Thou Know?* (*yaoi*) • *Kizuna: Bonds of Love* (*yaoi*) • *Marmalade Boy* • *Mars* • *My Heavenly Hockey Club* • *Oh My Goddess!* • *One Pound Gospel* • *The Prince of Tennis* • *Rebound* • *Rumic Theater* • *Rumic World Trilogy* • *Short Program* • *Slam Dunk* • *Speed Racer: The Original Manga* • *Suzuka* • *Tuxedo Gin* • *The Venus Wars* • *Whistle*

STAINLESS STEEL ARMADILLO

Ryukihei • Antarctic (1995) • 6 issues • Fantasy • 18+ (graphic violence, nudity)

Pleasantly drawn but vapid 1980s RPG-style fantasy manga, apparently part of a longer story that was never completed or translated. Two sisters bearing a "dragon seal" (a sort of magic book) go in search of a wizard, in the process getting in fights with bad guys, such as soldiers strapped to small dragons, and a scantily clad necromancer. The plot seems to have been generated on a Dungeons & Dragons "wandering monster" table. ★

STANDARD BLUE

(スタンダードブルー) • Hiroki Ogawa • ComicsOne (e-book, 2000) • Shônen Gahosha (Young King Ours, 1998–1999) • 1 volume • Seinen, Science Fiction, Adventure • All Ages

Fully realized characters and the interesting, futuristic setting (Standard Blue, an artificial cityport floating in the ocean) make this an enjoyable, if short, adventure. After her father's death, Shiki runs away from her overbearing mother to work on her grandfather's salvage ship. Ogawa takes time to weave a compelling science fiction background that doesn't overrun the manga; in addition to Shiki, the other characters on the ship feel equally interesting, with hints of depth that are never expanded upon. At one volume, it's the beginning of what could have been a very successful ongoing story: an environmental science fiction tale that doesn't fall prey to eco-preachiness. (RS) ★★★

STAR TREK: THE MANGA

Shinsei Shinsei • Tokyopop (2006) • 1 volume • Science Fiction • 13+ (mild language, violence)

A licensed adaptation of *Star Trek* (the original 1960s TV series) produced and edited in America, containing short stories by several different writers and artists. The only Japanese manga artist in the group is Makoto Nakatsuka, who draws Chris Dows' story "Side Effects," a creepy story about the origin of the Borg. NR

STAR TREKKER

Atelier Lana • Antarctic (1991–1992) • Dôjinshi (1985) • 1 volume • Science Fiction, Comedy • Unrated/16+ (comic violence, infrequent nudity, sexual situations)

Unauthorized *dôjinshi* parody of *Star Trek,* set sometime after the Enterprise's adventures and starring a new crew of cute, anime-style humans and aliens. Hungover captain Aya Nakajima and her crew travel through the universe, encountering strange life-forms and silly threats, such as a disease that causes everyone to get naked and party. Old-school science fiction references and pop culture cameos (such as Robocop and Kamen Rider) add up to a sweet tribute to the TV series. In America, one graphic novel and two supplementary monthly comics were published before Paramount Pictures threatened Antarctic with legal action; as a result, the series is a collector's item. ★★★

STAR WARS: A NEW HOPE

Star Wars Aratanaru Kibô, "Star Wars: Hope Renewed" (スター・ウォーズ 新たなる希望) • Hisao Tamaki (art), George Lucas (original script) • Dark Horse (1998) • MediaWorks (1997) • 4 volumes • Science Fiction, Adventure • Unrated/All Ages (fantasy violence)

If you closed your eyes and tried to picture a *Star Wars* manga, this is exactly what you'd envision—an utterly faithful reenactment with lovingly detailed props and vehicles, plenty of scene-setting spectacle, a great abundance of speedlines, and simplified anime-style faces for all the principal characters. Tamaki's treatment doesn't offer any surprises, but it's polished and proficient, and the adaptation does a splendid job of capturing the movie's impressive vistas and the monolithic malevolence of archvillain Darth Vader. The four-volume English edition (featuring covers by American comic artist Adam Warren) was published in Japan as two volumes. (MS) ★★★

STAR WARS: THE EMPIRE STRIKES BACK

Star Wars Teikoku no Gyakushû, "Star Wars: The Empire's Counterattack" (スター・ウォーズ 帝国の逆襲) • Toshiki Kudo (art), Leigh Brackett and Lawrence Kasdan (original script), George Lucas (original story) • Dark Horse (1999) • MediaWorks (1998) • 4 volumes • Science Fiction, Adventure • Unrated/All Ages (fantasy violence)

The weakest of the manga adaptations of the original *Star Wars* trilogy. Kudo's character drawings waver uncertainly back and forth between wacky caricature and semi-realism, and the artist's aversion to drawing backgrounds means that there's often little sense of atmosphere; the swamp planet Dagobah, for example, is depicted as a white void decorated with a handful of sketchy tree roots. The end result is competent but uninspired, and one has to wonder if Kudo might have been better off giving up on realism entirely and rendering the whole thing in an impressionistic *shôjo* style. The four-volume English edition (featuring covers by American comic artist Adam Warren) was published in Japan as two volumes. (MS) ★½

STAR WARS: RETURN OF THE JEDI

Star Wars Jedi no Fukushû, "Star Wars: Revenge of the Jedi" (スター・ウォーズ ジェダイの復讐) • Shinichi Hiromoto (art), Lawrence Kasdan and George Lucas (original script), George Lucas (original story) • Dark Horse (1999) • MediaWorks (1998) • 4 volumes • Science Fiction, Adventure • Unrated/All Ages (fantasy violence)

As eccentric as the *New Hope* manga was orthodox, Hiromoto's adaptation of *Return of the Jedi* is a bizarre mishmash of scribbly pen work, dazzling spectacle, and impressionistic caricature. Although there are places where the art becomes a little *too* minimalist, and Hiromoto's style will probably strike many readers as just plain weird and ugly, the result is refreshingly original and in many places impressively dramatic. The artist also gives us an amusingly bestial Chewbacca, manages to make the infamous Ewoks charming, and wrings new depths of pathos from the demise of the Rancor and the final confrontation between Luke and Vader. The four-volume English edition (featuring covers by American comic artist Adam Warren) was published in Japan as two volumes. (MS) ★★½

STAR WARS EPISODE I: THE PHANTOM MENACE

Star Wars Episode 1 Phantom Menace (スター・ウォーズ エピソード1 ファントム・メナス) • Kia Asamiya (art), George Lucas (original story) • Dark Horse (1999–2000) • Shogakukan (Corocoro Comic,

1999) • 2 volumes • Science Fiction, Adventure • Unrated/All Ages (fantasy violence)

A workmanlike manga adaptation of the first movie in the *Star Wars* prequel trilogy. Asamiya's artwork is as slick and polished as usual, but the condensed format doesn't give the story much breathing space; with half the page count of the previous *Star Wars* adaptations, there's no room for splash pages or establishing shots, and given the movie's byzantine plot and long-winded dialogue, it's pretty much inevitable that we end up with page after page of talking heads and word balloons instead. When Asamiya has to resort to compressing an entire light saber duel between Qui-Gon and Darth Maul into *two panels* so as to leave room for more prattle about taxation of outlying trade routes, it's clear that something is badly out of whack. The two-volume English edition was originally published in Japan as one volume. (MS) ★★

STEAM DETECTIVES

Kaiketsu Jôki Tanteidan, "The Extraordinary Steam Detective Agency" (快傑蒸気探偵団) • Kia Asamiya • Viz (1998–2004) • Shueisha/MediaWorks (Monthly Shônen Jump/Ultra Jump/Dengeki Gao!, 1994–2000) • 8 volumes, suspended (13 volumes in Japan) • Shônen, Mecha, Mystery, Action • 13+ (violence, partial nudity)

On the fog-shrouded streets of Steam City, brilliant boy detective Narutaki runs a detective agency, assisted by his faithful butler Kawakubo, strong-and-silent robot Gouriki, and nurse Ling Ling, whose main function is to get her skirt ripped so you can see her garter belt. *Steam Detectives* is written in the style of a Saturday morning cartoon; in each episode, Narutaki solves mysteries, makes daring escapes, and fights recurring villains with names such as the Phantom Knight, Dr. Guilty, and the Boy Criminal Le Bread. The art is impressively iconic: an intentionally retro urban world of shapes and shadows, combining elements of *Batman,* Mike Mignola, and classic mecha shows such as *Gigantor.* (Unlike Asamiya's supposedly "mature" work on *Dark Angel* and *Silent Mö-*

bius, he doesn't try to disguise his basically simple character designs with excessive screentone and computer coloring.) The result is Asamiya's most enjoyable series: predictable, unpretentious, melodramatic fun. The English edition ends abruptly at the point when the manga's Japanese publication switched from Shueisha to Media-Works. ★★★

STEEL ANGEL KURUMI

Kôtetsu Tenshi Kurumi, "Steel Angel Kurumi" (鋼鉄天使くるみ) • Kaishaku • ADV (2003–2004) • Kadokawa Shoten (Ace Dash/Monthly Ace Next/Monthly Shônen Ace, 1997–2004) • 9 volumes, suspended (11 volumes in Japan) • Shônen, Science Fiction, Romantic Comedy, Action • 18+ (nudity, sexual situations, violence)

The best thing about *Steel Angel Kurumi* is that Kurumi herself voices the authors' motivations: "Hey, everyone! Let's all work hard so they'll make this series into an anime!" In Taisho-era Japan (1912–1926), Nakahito, a blushing, apparently neutered young mystic, accidentally becomes the master of Steel Angel Kurumi, a torpedo-breasted magic-powered maid robot designed for the Japanese imperial army. A fetishistic mishmash of fight scenes and fan-service, the plot jumps around erratically: the characters travel in time, participate in a global tournament to save the world from a demon invasion, and are distracted by endless comedy side stories. Countless "steel angels" appear, some apparently based on designs sent in by readers, but they all look the same. The art is muddy from too much screentone, and the series is too plotless to be engaging. ★

STELLVIA

Uchû no Stellvia, "Stellvia of the Cosmos/Stellvia of Outer Space" (宇宙のステルヴィア) • Xebec (story), Ryo Akizuki (art) • DrMaster (2005) • MediaWorks (Dengeki Daioh, 2003) • 2 volumes • Shônen, Science Fiction, Comedy, Adventure • 13+ (mild violence)

This adaptation of the *Stellvia* anime series follows the adventures of Shima, a young space pilot in training who, along with her fellow students at the Stellvia space academy, faces a generic threat to Earth. The bland background makes little impact, and readers can have no doubt that humanity can be saved by a cherubic smile and "believing in yourself." The characters' daily life and love stories fill in some of the gaps left by the plot, but there's little tension built by the apparently imminent destruction of the planet. It's typical fare for *Dengeki Daioh* magazine, focusing on the cute and sweet in the middle of what might otherwise be a ponderous story line. (EF) ★★

ST. LUNATIC HIGH SCHOOL

Yoru ni mo Makezu!, "Don't Give In Even to the Night!" (夜ニモマケズ!) • Majiko! • Tokyopop (2007) • Kadokawa Shoten (Asuka, 2004–2005) • 2 volumes • Shôjo, Fantasy, Comedy • 13+

Cute and energetic Niko Kanzaki enrolls in the prestigious St. Lunatic School, only to discover its secret . . . by day it's a human school, but by night it teaches special classes for demons! But of course, demons aren't quite as bad as they're cracked up to be, and some of them are cute guys. NR

STONE

Shin-Ichi Hiromoto • Tokyopop (2004) • Kodansha (Afternoon, 2001–2002) • 2 volumes • Seinen, Science Fiction, Adventure • 16+ (language, occasional graphic violence)

In the future, Earth's oceans have turned to a sea of liquid sand, and humans eke out a barren existence living on wrecked ships and fighting giant sand whales. Gigi, a young girl with strange powers who comes from a whaling tribe, joins up with pirates to go on a journey and to fight an evil empire. The movie-style plot is generic, but Hiromoto's feverish, scratchy artwork makes it worth reading just for the visuals—vivid black shapes and grotesque, caricatural faces. ★★½

STRAIN

(ストレイン) • Buronson (story), Ryoichi Ikegami (art) • Viz (1997–2002) • Shogakukan (Big Comic Superior, 1997–1998) • 5 volumes • Seinen, Crime, Action • 18+ (language, graphic violence, nudity, sex)

In the slums of Kuala Lumpur, Malaysia's capital city, Mayo is a cool and cynical Japanese hit man who offers his services for the low, low price of only five bucks a hit. The exact reason for his budget rates remains a carefully guarded secret. Mayo takes a shine to a teenage prostitute named Shion who is on the run from the local crime syndicate. But protecting Shion not only puts Mayo at odds with various gangsters, it also forces him to face his own troubled past and family relations. A deep well of corruption surrounds everything and the trail leads all the way to a bid to control the Asian oil market. A pairing between writer Buronson (*Fist of the North Star*) and artist Ryoichi Ikegami (*Wounded Man*) should have been a sure thing and should have resulted in—if not a Pulitzer Prize—at least another satisfying manly epic on par with *Crying Freeman.* Instead, *Strain*'s story continually fails to ignite and Ikegami's art routinely cuts corners on detail and variety. Disappointing. (PM) ★★

STRAWBERRY 100%

Ichigo 100%, "Strawberry 100%" (いちご100%) • Mizuki Kawashita • Viz (2007–ongoing) • Shueisha (Weekly Shônen Jump, 2002–2005) • 19 volumes • Shônen, Romantic Comedy • 16+ (partial nudity, sexual situations)

One day in high school, aspiring movie director Manaka accidentally startles a beautiful girl, who falls on top of him, exposing her strawberry panties. Although he's instantly smitten, he doesn't get a good look at her face before she runs off . . . so which of the school's several hot girls could it be? NR

STRAWBERRY MARSHMALLOW

Ichigo Marshmallow, "Strawberry Marshmallow" (苺ましまろ) • Barasui • Tokyopop (2006–ongoing) • MediaWorks (Dengeki Daioh, 2001–2005) • 5 volumes • Shônen, Moe, Comedy • 13+ (mild language, brief nudity)

In a quiet neighborhood live four quiet little girls. Sixteen-year-old Nobue, who smokes and drinks and likes to tease people, spends most of her time with her twelve-year-old sister and her junior high friends; they play video games, get sad and cry, send text messages, et cetera. (You know it's a *moe* manga when a sixteen-year-old has the role of the experienced older woman.) All of them are endearingly insecure and are ever so vaguely sexualized with occasional, discreet bath scenes and panty shots. The characterizations and dialogue are sometimes believable and funny ("I feel like half a sack of poo," one girl complains) and the art is decent, although it lacks variety, as you'd expect from a manga where the characters look the same and sit around the house all the time. ★½

STRAWBERRY PANIC!

(ストロベリー・パニック!) • Sakurako Kimino (story), Namuchi Takumi (art) • Seven Seas Entertainment (2007–ongoing) • MediaWorks (Dengeki G's Magazine, 2005–ongoing) • 3+ volumes (ongoing) • Yuri, Romantic Comedy • 16+

Lesbian romantic comedy set in an all-girls school, based on the short stories by Sakurako Kimino (also adapted into an anime and a series of light novels). NR

STRAY LITTLE DEVIL

(ストレイリトルデビル) • Kotaro Mori • DrMaster (2006–ongoing) • MediaWorks (Dengeki Gao!, 2004–2007) • 5 volumes • Shônen, Fantasy, Comedy • 13+ (mild violence, occasional partial nudity, occasional sexual situations)

Cute thirteen-year-old Pam Akumachi (*akuma* is Japanese for "devil") is whisked away to a fantasy world of angels and devils, where humans are just a fairy tale. She soon discovers that she, too, is part devil, and so she grows wings, horns, and a tail, and finds herself facing tests and challenges with a class of other infernal schoolkids. This is the start of her journey to devilhood! *Stray Little Devil*'s greatest strength is the pleasant polished art, with detailed backgrounds, cool monsters, and cute characters. The story is fluff, starting as if it might be for younger

Kotaro Mori's *Stray Little Devil*

readers, then vacillating between melodrama and bawdy, occasionally *yuri* humor. ★★

STREET FIGHTER II

Street Fighter II—Ryu (ストリートファイターII—RYU) • Masaomi Kanzaki • Udon Entertainment (2007) • Tokuma Shoten (Family Computer Magazine, 1993–1994) • 3 volumes • Video Game, Martial Arts, Action • Unrated/13+ (violence)

A straightforward adaptation of the original *Street Fighter II* arcade game, drawn in Kanzaki's square-jawed, big-boned, angry-looking style. Tough but fair martial artist Ryu arrives on the Shanghai-like man-made island of Shad, where a fighting tournament is under way. Meanwhile, Chinese Interpol agent Chun Li, she of the mighty legs, has also joined the tournament in order to investigate a mysterious mind-control drug peddled by the evil criminal organization Shadowlaw. A subplot involves Ryu helping out a poor girl who runs a Chinese restaurant. Kanzaki's fight scenes are stiff and the plot is predictable even by the standards of video game comics. Prior to the Udon release, a few issues of the series were published in colorized form in 1993–1994 by Tokuma's short-lived American comics division. ★½

STREET FIGHTER II: THE ANIMATED MOVIE: OFFICIAL COMIC ADAPTATION

Takayuki Sakai • Viz (1996) • 6 issues • Video Game, Martial Arts, Action • Unrated/13+ (mild language, violence)

The comic based on the movie based on the video game. Slightly divergent from the plot of the 1994–1995 anime movie, it's a crudely drawn, shoddy adaptation for very young readers. 0 Stars

STREET FIGHTER II: CAMMY: See *Super Street Fighter II: Cammy*

STREET FIGHTER III: RYU FINAL

Street Fighter III Ryu Final: Tatakai no Saki ni, "Street Fighter III Ryu Final: In Search of Battle" (STREET FIGHTER III RYU FINAL—闘いの先に) • Masahiko Nakahira • Udon Entertainment (2007) • Shinseisha (Gamest, 1997–1998) • Video Game, Martial Arts, Action • 2 volumes • 13+ (graphic violence)

Masahiko Nakahira's final *Street Fighter* comic, based on *Street Fighter III*. Ryu, now older and wiser, again roams the globe in search of powerful fighters. This time, however, he faces his deadliest opponent yet: Gouki, the killer who murdered Ryu's martial arts teacher and whose powers have transcended humanity. Nakahira's artwork is at its most dynamic, while the simple, portentous plot works mostly on a visual level—it *is* a fighting game manga, after all. ★★★

STREET FIGHTER ALPHA

Street Fighter Zero (ストリートファイターZERO) • Masahiko Nakahira • Udon Entertainment (2007) • Shinseisha (Gamest, 1995–1996) • Video Game, Martial Arts, Action • 2 volumes • 13+ (violence)

Manga adaptation of the video game, known as *Street Fighter Zero* in Japan. Ryu, the young martial artist always seeking the perfection of his craft, travels around the world fighting opponents and trying to come to grips with his own dark side. The plot is nominal— Ryu goes places and fights people—but Masahiko Nakahira's clean lines, strongly chiseled (yet attractively anime-style) character designs, and incredible talent for action scenes make this just about a perfect video game adaptation. As the fighting escalates, buildings, vehicles, and cities are trashed, culminating in a huge showdown; martial-artists-as-superheroes have never looked so good. Elements from Nakahira's comics were later incorporated by Capcom into the official *Street Fighter* mythology. ★★★

STREET FIGHTER SAKURA GANBARU!

Sakura Ganbaru!, "Go for It, Sakura!" (さくらがんばる!) • Masahiko Nakahira • Udon Entertainment (2007) • Shinseisha (Comic Gamest, 1996–1997) • Video Game, Martial Arts, Comedy • 2 volumes • 13+ (violence)

Fighting/comedy comic starring Sakura, the tomboyish schoolgirl martial artist from *Street Fighter Alpha*. With her thin arms and short skirts bearing powers beyond mortal men, she does battle with equally overpowered schoolyard opponents, demolishes her surroundings, et cetera. It's geeky stuff, but relatively innocent, and Masahiko Nakahira draws excellent action scenes. ★★½

STRIKER

Spriggan (スプリガン) • Hiroshi Takashige (story), Ryoji Minagawa (art) • Viz (1998–1999) • Shogakukan (Weekly Shônen Sunday, 1988–1996) • 3 volumes, suspended (11 volumes in Japan) • Shônen, Science Fiction, Military, Action • Unrated/13+ (graphic violence)

Yu Ominae is a high school student by day and a knife-wielding supersoldier by night, helping the Arcam Foundation (as in H. P. Lovecraft's Arkham) protect the world from the relics of a long-lost high-tech civilization. Part *Indiana Jones* pulp archaeology (including a brief appearance by a resurrected Hitler), part paramilitary action, the Viz edition of *Striker* consists of selected self-contained stories from different points in the Japanese run. As a result, there is little plot development, but even in the original Japanese the stories are repetitive. (Once you've seen one megalomaniacal psychic try to take over the world with an ancient superweapon, you've seen 'em all.) ★★½

SUGAR: A LITTLE SNOW FAIRY: See *A Little Snow Fairy Sugar*

SUGAR SUGAR RUNE

(シュガシュガルーン) • Moyoco Anno • Del Rey (2005–ongoing) • Kodansha (Nakayoshi, 2003–ongoing) • 7+ volumes (ongoing) • Shôjo, Magical Girl, Romance • All Ages

A pair of ten-year-old witches falls out of the sky into "the Human World of swirling desires," where (despite being best friends) they must compete to steal human hearts to determine who will become the next queen. Using magic glasses to see their classmates' hearts, they make people love them, then steal their crystallized emotions: orange hearts of crushes, red hearts of true love, violet hearts of forbidden love. Vanilla, a shy, timid witch, proves unexpectedly popular with the human boys, while the heroine Chocolat has less luck, because she's feisty and tough and has vampire-like fangs and her favorite things in life are frogs and spiders and "butt-whupping." This charming love story (with an element of fantasy intrigue) was written for elementary school students, but the fabulous art and strong writing make it just as enjoyable for adults. Although the series has its share of traditional magical girl accoutrements like sweets and magic perfume, there are charming and original ideas on every page: for instance, Pierre, a coldhearted, handsome boy, eats only cold foods, such as jellied caviar and cold pasta. The art is Anno's best: stars and moons and Halloween imagery cascade across the pages, the figures are lovely, and even the incidental details have personality,

such as the crooked trees. Like Anno's works for older readers (*Flowers & Bees* and *Happy Mania*), it's about love, in this case depicted with the perfect metaphor: it's all a game until you grow up and your own heart becomes vulnerable. ★★★★

SUIKODEN III: THE SUCCESSOR OF FATE

Gensô Suikoden III: Unmei no Keishôsha, "Fantasy Water Margin III: The Successor of Fate" (幻想水滸伝～運命の継承者) • Aki Shimizu • Tokyopop (2004–2006) • Media Factory (2002–2006) • 11 volumes • Fantasy, Adventure • 13+ (mild language, violence)

Based on Konami's popular RPG *Suikoden III* for the PlayStation 2, one of a series of popular games inspired by the ancient Chinese novel *Suikoden* ("Water Margin"). While most video game manga seem like just another way to get a little more money from fans, this series is a gripping read. The story centers on the conflict between two powerful kingdoms, and a third group of indigenous grassland-dwelling tribes caught in between. It's an epic story filled with intrigue, double-crossings, legendary heroes, mystical prophecies, and great characters. The art's solid, the pacing's good, and it's well written. If you've played the game, the manga provides more backstory to the characters. (RB) ★★★★

SUKI

Suki. Dakara Suki, "I Like You. Because I Like You" (すき。だからすき) • CLAMP • Tokyopop (2004) • Kadokawa Shoten (Mystery DX, 1999–2000) • 3 volumes • Shôjo, Drama, Romance • 13+ (mild violence, mild sexual situations)

Sixteen-year-old heiress Hinata "Hina" Asahi lives alone in a mansion with only her teddy bears Waka and Tono as company. Sweet and innocent to a fault, she is teased relentlessly by her peers for her childishness. When handsome new homeroom teacher Asou-sensei shows up in class, a new feeling blossoms in Hina—is it love? Hina's first crush only grows when she learns that Asou-sensei has moved in next door to her, and he seems all too willing to spend time together outside of class. Has Hina found love at last, or has her naiveté blinded her to a dangerous situation? *Suki,* one of CLAMP's shortest and most down-to-earth series, is also one of the team's best. The characters, as drawn by Tsubaki Nekoi and written by Ageha Ohkawa, are crafted with efficiency and depth rare in CLAMP's work. At three volumes, the series is tightly plotted but never rushed; in many ways, *Suki* bears more in common with a classic Hollywood thriller than it does with CLAMP's other works. (MT)   ★★★½

SUPER DIMENSIONAL FORTRESS MACROSS II

Chôjikû Yôsai Makurosu II Lovers Again, "Super-Dimensional Fortress Macross II: Lovers Again" (超時空要塞マクロスⅡ LOVERS AGAIN) • Sukehiro Tomita (original script), Tsuguo Okazaki (art) • Viz (1992–1994) • Shogakukan (Shônen Sunday Zôkangô, 1992–1993) • 1 volume • Science Fiction, Mecha, Adventure • Unrated/13+ (mild language, mild violence, revealing costumes)

In theory, the 1992 video series *Macross II* had the makings of a great follow-up to the original *Macross.* Eighty years after humanity defeats a race of giant alien warriors by soothing their savage hearts with Earth culture (as exemplified by pop ballads), our planet is menaced by a new wave of invaders who use martial songs to spur their soldiers into battle, setting the stage for a cosmic clash of cultures. Meanwhile, a wiseacre news reporter clashes with the bureaucrats of the Earth military and strikes up a tentative romance with an alien idol singer. The setup has potential, but this manga adaptation becomes as flat and lifeless as the anime version once the character drama gets elbowed aside in favor of tedious space battles. Artist Okazaki renders all the transforming jet fighters and biotechnological warships in faithful detail, and seems to particularly enjoy drawing the alien songstress Ishtar, whose costume amounts to little more than a couple of swatches of body paint. (MS)

★★

SUPER MARIO ADVENTURES

Mario no Daibôken, "Mario's Great Adventure" (マリオの大冒険) • Kentaro Takekuma (story), Charlie Nozawa (art) • Nintendo (1992–1993) • Shogakukan (1993) • 1 volume • Video Game, Adventure, Comedy • Unrated/All Ages

A full-color slapstick adventure story starring Mario, Luigi, Princess Toadstool, Bowser, and the other characters from *Super Mario World* (with a few elements from other games). The English localization is successful, and the jokes are funny and faithful to the game. Originally serialized in the American *Nintendo Power* magazine and later reprinted in Japan.   ★★★

SUPER STREET FIGHTER II: CAMMY

Super Street Fighter II Cammy Gaiden, "Cammy Side Story" (スーパーストリートファイターIIキャミィ 外伝) • Masahiko Nakahira • Viz (1997) • Shogakukan (Weekly Shônen Sunday Comics Special, 1994) • 1 volume • Shônen, Video Game, Martial Arts • Unrated/13+ (mild language, violence)

Masahiko Nakahira is a great fighting game artist, giving the impression of motion and impact together with attractive anime-style character designs, but *Super Street Fighter II: Cammy* is one of his earliest works and his art is undeveloped. Leotard-clad amnesiac Cammy, improbably long-legged agent of Britain's secret service MI6, fights terrorists around the globe as she discovers the truth of her dark connection to the evil organization Shadowloo. The simple plot has a military feel, with plenty of guns, a guest appearance by Guile, and even a *Predator*-like jungle sequence. Ultimately, however, it's little more than a lead-in to the game.   ★★

SURVIVAL IN THE OFFICE: THE EVOLUTION OF JAPANESE WORKING WOMEN

OL Shinkaron, "OL (Office Lady) Evolution" (OL 進化論) • Risu Akizuki • Kodansha International (1999–2000) • Kodansha (Morning, 1989–ongoing) • 5 volumes, suspended (26+ volumes in Japan, ongoing) • Four-Panel Comedy • All Ages (occasional adult themes)

SUPERHEROES

To Japanese readers, as to most of the world, American comics (*amecomi*) are synonymous with superheroes, the genre that has dominated American comics from the 1950s until recently. The bestselling American comics are available in translation but sell only to hard-core fans; most Japanese people know superheroes from other media, such as Capcom's licensed Marvel fighting games or translations of blockbuster superhero movies. (When Batman makes cameos in the works of Masakazu Katsura, it's always the Batman from the 1989 Michael Keaton movie.) Licensed adaptations of American comics have had mixed results, from Ryoichi Ikegami's interesting 1970s *Spider-Man: The Manga* (and a nearly forgotten *Hulk* adaptation written by Kazuo Koike during the same period) to the drab 1990s *X-Men: The Manga,* to the recent *Witchblade Manga.* Superhero artists such as Todd MacFarlane, Mike Mignola, and Jim Lee have small Japanese fan followings, providing readers with color art and visual spectacles unlike anything in manga.

Beyond the superficial trappings such as capes and secret identities, many *shōnen* manga are essentially superhero comics: tales of good guys and bad guys fighting with incredible powers. But American fans tend to enjoy those things that are specific to American comics, such as a shared universe of familiar characters that does not depend on particular artists or plotlines. In addition, character motivations are often different. Manga heroes generally fight for personal reasons, to protect the ones close to them—this line is repeated in countless manga—unlike American superheroes, who traditionally patrol the world looking for trouble. In series such as *Dr. Slump* and *Rave Master!,* American-style superheroes are parodied as arrogant buffoons. In manga, it is typically villains who are obsessed with abstract morality, whereas the good guys are concerned with their family and friends.

American comic publishers have not been unaware of the manga boom, and since the 1990s both Marvel and DC—America's two biggest superhero publishers—have experimented with hiring Japanese artists for their familiar properties. Katsuhiro Otomo drew a short story in DC's *Batman: Black & White,* while Yoshitaka Amano worked on several illustrated books, including DC's *Sandman: The Dream Hunters* and Marvel's *Elektra and Wolverine: The Redeemer.* Kia Asamiya actively sought work in American comics, including a stint as an artist on Marvel's *Uncanny X-Men* (most of his work here is collected in the 2003 graphic novel *Uncanny X-Men: Dominant Species*), as well as DC's *Batman: Child of Dreams,* which was serialized in the Japanese manga magazine *Magazine Z* prior to its American publication.

Unlike DC, which has a large line of non-superhero comics as well as the translated manga division CMX, Marvel is almost all superheroes; thus they have more aggressively courted Japanese-American superhero hybrids. Their kitschy 2002 Marvel Mangaverse line was created entirely by manga-influenced American artists, but they have also experimented with hiring authentic manga creators, such as bilingual writer Akira Yoshida (*Thor: Son of Asgard, Electra: The Hand,* and many others), artist Shin Nagasawa (*Wolverine: Soultaker*), and artist Makoto Nakatsuka (*X-Men: Ronin*). Printed in color and starring familiar Marvel characters, these stories are more American comics than manga. Tsutomu Nihei drew *Wolverine: Snikt!* (2003), transplanting Marvel's famous superhero into a cyberpunk world much like that of his manga *Blame!* In 2006 a

New Mangaverse limited series featured artwork by Tommy Ohtsuka, previously best known in the United States for his work on *Slayers Special*.

Just as American artists have been influenced by (or outright swiped from) manga, so Japanese artists have been inspired by American comics. Ryoichi Ikegami, one of the most realistic draftsmen in manga, was influenced by the 1970s comics of Neal Adams. Thinly disguised Marvel characters show up in the works of Nobuhiro Watsuki and Yasuhiro Nightow. Yukito Kishiro's *Ashen Victor* is an homage to Frank Miller (*Sin City, 300, Batman: The Dark Knight Returns*), while Kia Asamiya's *Steam Detectives* is one of many manga influenced by Mike Mignola (*Hellboy*).

Sentai (task force) TV shows, in which masked heroes in skintight costumes beat up bad guys, fill a similar niche among young children that superheroes do in America. From 1978 to 1981, Marvel co-produced several Japanese live-action *tokusatsu* TV shows with Toei (producers of the *Power Rangers*) in an attempt to popularize their characters. The fondly remembered first show, *Spider-Man,* retained the hero's traditional costume and powers but gave Spider-Man a giant robot; the later shows, such as *Battle Fever J* (intended as an *Avengers* adaptation), stripped away all evidence of Marvel characters, due to Toei's heavy-handed alterations. The moral of the story: America has no monopoly on messing with imported pop culture.

See also: PSYCHIC, TOKUSATSU.

Superhero Manga

Astra • Batman: Child of Dreams • Dame Dame Saito Nikki • Justice • The Mighty Bombshells • Spider-Man: The Manga • Warrior Nun Areala: The Manga • Witchblade Manga • X-Men: The Manga

Famous, popular adult women's comedy manga about "office ladies," Japanese white-collar women in their early twenties who do clerical work, serve tea, and (according to these strips) spend most of their spare time thinking about vacations, restaurants, boyfriends, and marriage. (A few women in management positions, and male employees, show up as well.) Although the world depicted may seem old-fashioned to Americans, the strips are an entertaining window into Japanese culture, the art is cute, and the jokes are funny.   ★★★

SUZUKA

(涼風) • Kouji Seo • Del Rey (2006–ongoing) • Kodansha (Weekly Shônen Magazine, 2004–ongoing) • 15+ volumes (ongoing) • Shônen, Sports, Romantic Comedy • 18+ (language, nudity, sexual situations)

Fifteen-year-old Yamato moves to his aunt's apartment complex (also a women's spa, with all the opportunities for nudity that implies), where he falls in love with his new neighbor Suzuka, a teenage track star. Soon he discovers that Suzuka has her own hidden insecurities, and when they start going to the same high school, he joins the track team and musters his courage to ask her out. A mostly serious boys' romance manga, *Suzuka* pays unusually strong attention to its sports subplots. The hero and heroine's story is well written, with believable relationship twists and turns instead of the usual flat line of unspoken crushes and unrequited love. As in most Boys' Love comedies, there's plenty of T&A (although no more than many titles rated 16+), but Suzuka herself is spared the indignity of getting her breasts exposed every other page—instead, that role falls to other characters, in particular two busty college students who also live in the apartment complex. The art is generic, with frankly weak character artwork but slick photorealistic backgrounds. ★★

SWAN

Swan—Hakuchô, "Swan" (Swan—白鳥) • Kyoko Ariyoshi • CMX (2005–ongoing) • Shueisha (Margaret, 1976–1981) • 21 volumes • Shôjo, Drama • All Ages

Doe-eyed Masumi struggles to become a prima ballerina like her dead, mysterious mother and prove the greatness of Japanese ballet on the world stage. Her journey leads her through one grueling dance competition after another and introduces her to an ever-expanding cast of friends, rivals, mentors, and love interests, most of whom have their own equally involved subplots. Unabashedly girly, *Swan* is an eye-catching confection of sweetness, sparkle, and huge, moist eyes. But beneath the endlessly falling flowers and feathers is a tough narrative center, with a focus on torturous training reminiscent of classic boys' sports manga. The intensely sincere dialogue likewise suggests a certain *Shônen Jump* quality: "It was you that told me ballet isn't about skill or interpretation—but *heart!*" *Swan* is clearly intended for preteens, but the skill and passion of its storytelling and the engrossing nature of its intricate soap-opera plot make it rewarding fare for readers of all ages. Above all, Ariyoshi's artwork is spectacular. The 1970s was a watershed decade for *shôjo* manga, and *Swan* represents some of the most beautiful work of that period: lush, inventive, collage-style pages that push the boundaries of comic-book layout without sacrificing clarity of storytelling. It's a visual tour de force. (SG) ★★★★

SWEAT AND HONEY

Sex no ato Otoko no Ko no Ase wa Hachimitsu no Nioi ga suru, "After Sex a Boy's Sweat Smells Like Honey" (セックスのあと男の子の汗はハチミツのにおいがする) • Mari Okazaki • Tokyopop (2005) • Shodensha (2002) • 1 volume • Jôsei, Drama • 16+ (nudity, sex, adult themes)

Kyoko Ariyoshi's *Swan*

One of two volumes in Tokyopop's "Passion Fruit" line (the other is *Galaxy Girl, Panda Boy*), *Sweat and Honey* is a collection of evocative short stories for adult readers. In the title story, a woman's relationship with men is destroyed by the Sapphic attitudes of the strange, catlike cousin who moves in with her. The longest story, "The Land Where Rain Falls," follows two girls who experiment furtively with lesbianism and incest until a more traditional teenage romance encroaches on their dreamy "kingdom of girls." Other stories involve a girl who grows out of the ground like a plant, an insecure teenager's obsession with her spinster career-girl neighbor, and a young music nerd's crush on an older woman. Okazaki's artwork is beautiful and expressive, with palpable texture and a hovering erotic musk, and she develops some ingenious visual touches. (SG) ★★★½

SWORD OF THE DARK ONES

Ragnarok (ラグナロク) • Kentaro Yasui (story), Tsukasa Kotobuki (art) • CMX (2005) • Kadokawa Shoten (Monthly Shônen Ace, 2000–2003) • 3 volumes • Shônen, Fantasy, Action • 18+ (language, graphic violence, nudity, sexual situations)

Manga adaptation of Kentaro Yasui's novels. In a vaguely Wild West fantasy future, mankind lives in fear (according to the narration, anyway) of Dark Ones, monsters of various types. Leroy, a sullen swordsman with a dark secret, wields Ragnarok, a talking sword, against assassins and an evil vampire. Tsukasa Kotobuki is a decent artist, but his angular, exaggerated body types (streamlined, perhaps, by his work as a video game character designer) can't save this predictable, poorly structured story. The art lacks detail; the fights are unexciting. The first printing of volume 1 was censored for nudity, which was restored in a second printing. ★

THE SWORD OF SHIBITO

Shibito no Ken, "Sword of Shibito" (しびとの剣) • Hideyuki Kikuchi (story), Missile Kakurai (art) • CPM (2004–ongoing) • Scholar Publishing/Sony Magazines/Gentosha (Comic Birz, 1998–2002) • (8 volumes) • Historical, Fantasy, Horror • 16+ (graphic violence)

Based on the untranslated novels by Hideyuki Kikuchi, *The Sword of Shibito* mixes sword-fighting carnage with the quiet creepiness of a classical ghost story. Kinzou, a middle-aged apothecary in feudal Japan, finds himself the unwilling traveling companion of Shibito, a one-hundred-year-old samurai resurrected in a Frankenstein-like undead body. The darkly *shôjo*-tinged art is fluid, reminiscent of Kei Toume, but the plot moves as slowly as Kinzou's wandering in the wilderness and the mute, emotionless Shibito makes a difficult center for the story. Although relatively conventional by Kikuchi's standards, it's a worthy B-list addition to the ranks of supernatural samurai manga. ★★½

TACTICS

Sakura Kinoshita, Kazuko Higashiyama • Tokyopop (2007–ongoing) • Square Enix/Mag Garden (Monthly G-Fantasy/Comic Blade Masamune, 2001–ongoing) • 8+ volumes (ongoing) • Occult, Fantasy • 13+

Kantarou, an adorably childlike folklore researcher and goblin hunter for hire, does his job with the help of two supernatural servants: Yoko, a fox spirit who takes the human form of a maid, and Haruka, a mighty spirit who appears as a tall, dark, handsome gentleman. Together they exorcise evil spirits and *tengu* (goblins), which mostly take the forms of normal people or cute abstract shapes. *Tactics* has clever plots and makes interesting use of Japanese folklore, but the series mostly focuses on the sweet, slightly suggestive relationship between Kan and Haruka: a little boy and his mature protector. The characters' faces have a typical anime-style look, but the simple art somehow evokes green forests and elaborate fabrics and quaint Japanese villages. No violence or ugliness intrudes on this perfect world, and little conflict either: it's an evocative, fluffy read, a sweet dessert of a manga. Prior to the Tokyopop edition, the first two volumes were published in 2004–2005 by ADV Manga. ★★★

TAIL OF THE MOON

Tsuki no Shippo, "Tail of the Moon" (月のしっぽ) • Rinko Ueda • Viz (2006–ongoing) • Shueisha (Margaret, 2002–ongoing) • 13+ volumes (ongoing) • Shôjo, Ninja, Romance, Action • 13+ (violence, partial nudity, sex)

In the days of the first Tokugawa shogun, being a ninja was illegal and harshly punished. Usagi is the granddaughter of the head of the Iga ninja clan; after years of failing the ninja test and goofing off, she's sent to serve her people by getting hitched and pregnant. Usagi is excited to be on her first mission, but the prospective groom is not at all interested. Usagi refuses to give up and swears to win him over. This of course involves many adventures and rivals, as Usagi and her love-to-be Hanzo face danger and political intrigue. Although Usagi is a goof, she is determined and brave, and she comes with an awesome sidekick, all of which save her from being annoying. The art is adorable and spirited, and there are lots of hot guys in kimonos or in all their bare-chested glory. A fun, sprightly read. (HS) ★★★

TAIMASHIN

Massatsu Note Taimashin, "Notebook of a Demon Killer: Exorcising Magic/Demon (Acupuncture) Needles" (魔殺ノート退魔針) • Hideyuki Kikuchi (story), Masaki Saitoh (art) • ADV (2004) • Gentosha (Comic Birz, 2001–2004) • 1 volume, suspended (6 volumes in Japan) • Seinen, Action, Horror • 18+ (graphic violence, nudity, sex)

Pulp horror based on a series of novels by Hideyuki Kikuchi. The handsome, androgynous Dr. Taima is a master of acupuncture whose needles can affect the *chi* of the very elements. With the help of his nurse assistant Togetsu, he fights revolting possessor-demons seemingly composed of naughty tentacles and oozing internal organs. The plot is set up as a sequel to H. P. Lovecraft's *The Dunwich Horror;* the characters even go from Japan to Lovecraft's fictional New England town of Dunwich. The scratchy, dark, dissolute-looking artwork (similar to *The Sword of Shibito*) helps sustain a mood of horror, although the plot drifts close to tentacle porn. ★★

THE TALE OF GENJI

Asaki Yumemishi, "(No More) Shallow Dreams to See" (あさきゆめみし) • Waki Yamato • Kodansha International (2000–2001) • Kodansha (Mimi/Mimi Excellent, 1979–1993) • 4 volumes, suspended (13 volumes in Japan) • Shôjo, Historical Romance • Unrated/13+ (sexual situations)

The Tale of Genji, written around 1021, is the oldest Japanese novel and sometimes considered the first psychological novel in the modern sense, concerned with characters' feelings as much as actions. The plot follows the birth and life of the nobleman Genji, the son of the emperor and a low-ranked concubine, who is raised without a mother but grows into a handsome man who excels at everything. Most of the plot involves his affairs with various upper-class ladies, playing the game of courtly love with sensitivity; both he and the female characters are given to introspection ("Will time really heal my pain? Will I ever be able to find happiness again?"). The tale has been adapted to manga many times, but this classic *shôjo* manga edition looks dated and fails to extract drama from the navel-gazing story. The art is bland, generic early-1980s *shôjo* artwork. A character chart in the back of the English edition is the only context provided for readers, and the English lettering is often confusingly placed in or outside the word balloons. The title of the manga is a reference to the Iroha, a famous Heian-era Japanese poem. ★★

TANPENSHU

Endo Hiroki Tanpenshu, "Hiroki Endo Short Works" (遠藤浩輝短編集) • Hiroki Endo • Dark Horse (2007) • Kodansha (Afternoon, 1998–2001) • 2 volumes • Seinen, Drama • 18+ (language, graphic violence, nudity)

Short story collection by Hiroki Endo, better known for his science fiction manga *Eden.* Like *Eden,* the stories frequently deal with psychological and philosophical themes. NR

TEKKON KINKREET: See *Black & White*

TELEPATHIC WANDERERS

Nanase: The Telepathic Wanderers • Yasutaka Tsutsui (story), Sayaka Yamazaki (art) • Tokyopop (2005) • Kodansha (Bessatsu Young Magazine, 2001–2003) • 4 volumes • Seinen, Psychic, Drama • 16+ (language, violence, nudity, sex)

An adaptation of Tsutsui's novel *Nanase Futatabi* (which was also made into a 1979 Japanese TV series), this is a well-plotted adult drama about how psychics might act in the real world. Nanase is a beautiful, somewhat distant woman who wanders Japan separated from humanity by her power of telepathy; she automatically senses nearby thoughts, which in the case of men are usually sexual (it's not intended as humor—it's just dryly realistic). For most of her life she thought she was the only one, but one day she encounters a young boy with telepathy like hers, and soon she gathers a small "family" of psychics with powers such as telekinesis and precognition. Loosely connected short mysteries lead up to a dark, violent thriller story line; the characters' powers and personalities are believable and logical throughout. Like the plot, the artwork is realistic, restrained, and suspensful.   ★★★½

TENCHI MUYÔ!: See *No Need for Tenchi!* and *The All-New Tenchi Muyô!*

TENCHI MUYÔ!: SASAMI STORIES

Tenchi Muyô! Ryo-Oh-Ki: Sasami Densetsu, "New No Need for Tenchi!/Unnecessary Tenchi! Ryo-Oh-Ki: The Legend of Sasami" (天地無用!魎皇鬼砂沙美伝説) • Hitoshi Okuda • Viz (2003) • Kadokawa Shoten (2002) • 1 volume • Shônen, Science Fiction, Romantic Comedy, Four-Panel • 13+ (violence, nudity, sexual situations)

Eight-year-old housekeeping prodigy Sasami is the most popular character in the *Tenchi Muyô!* series, perhaps because she embodies the *otaku* idea of the perfect woman: a prepubescent schoolgirl who doubles as a substitute mom. This special Sasami-themed anthology consists of three Sasami-oriented stories from the *No Need for Tenchi!* manga, plus *Tenchi, Heaven Forbid! G,* a four-panel gag strip that ran in the Pioneer LDC fan club newsletter. Like a lot of gag manga, the *Heaven Forbid!* strips alternate between amusing and baffling. The most entertaining element of the book is the addition of a sort of director's commentary, in which Okuda and Sasami chat about the comics via marginal notes. The commentary is often funnier than the actual manga, but, considering that the book is 80 percent reprint material, it's essential reading only for *Tenchi* completists and hard-core Sasami fans. (CT)   ★★

TENGAI RETROGICAL OR: HOW I LEARNED TO STOP WORRYING AND LOVE THE CRISIS

Tengai Retrogical, "Beyond the Heavens Retrogical" (天外レトロジカル OR: HOW I LEARNED TO STOP WORRYING AND LOVE THE CRISIS) • Rin Asano • ADV (2004) • Mag Garden (Comic Blade, 2002–2006) • 1 volume, suspended (6 volumes in Japan) • Fantasy • 13+ (mild violence)

Ryohei and his father are roped into becoming the managers of Tengai-ya, a mysterious row house surrounded by rumors of ghosts and sorcery. Once they get there, Ryohei falls into a pit, touches a buried meteorite, and awakens Anju, a little-girl-like creature who is an agent of the heavens, sent to debug the planet Earth by gathering data from certain objects with her magic jewel. If it sounds slightly confusing, that's how it reads too; *Tengai Retrogical* is part spooky mood piece, part sweet domestic story, but the plot and Anju's purpose are vague at best. At its best moments, it reads like a young-adult fantasy novel, but so much information is withheld from the reader that it never comes together, particularly not in the limited portion available in English. The art is pretty; the mood is gentle and restrained.   ★★½

TENJHO TENGE

Tenjô Tenge, "Heaven and Earth" (天上天下) • Oh! Great • CMX (2005–ongoing) • Shueisha (Ultra Jump, 1997–ongoing) • 15+ volumes (ongoing) • Seinen, Martial Arts, Drama • 13+/16+ (mild language, graphic violence, sex)

Drawn by ex-adult-comics-artist Oh! Great, *Tenjho Tenge* is all about the body: a combination of fighting game action and exquisitely drawn fetishism. When two young brawlers arrive at Todo Gakuen High School, they expect to become kings of the hill, but the nearly superhuman fighters of the Student Executive Committee viciously put the freshmen in their place. To stand a chance, Nagi and Bob (in a relatively decent role for a black character in manga) must swallow their pride and train under the Juken martial arts club, where Nagi attracts the attention of a beautiful but cursed swordswoman, Aya Natsume, and her older sister Maya. Homework and normal school drama have no place here; the school is a training ground and all the major characters are fighters, most of whom can use strange *ki* powers and rip bodies apart with their bare hands. The action scenes are incredible, not so much for the blow-by-blow choreography (as in, say, *Dragon Ball Z*) as for the jaw-dropping images: handsome men and beautiful women in deadly stare-downs, classrooms and other familiar surroundings ripped to shreds, phantasmal dragons and monstrous snakes that coil around the heroes as they unleash their abilities. (Admittedly, the early volumes have a few weak panels, but it quickly gets better.) Sarcastic humor and trash-talking aside, the plot is stone-cold serious; in fact, it's so brutal that the English edition of the manga is heavily censored. Although the Japanese series is aimed at older teens and adults, the early volumes of the English edition were cut to get a 13+ rating, from the very front cover of the first volume (on which the logo obscures the panty shot) to many, many scenes of nudity and the occasional middle finger. The decision is questionable since it is still graphically violent and has rape and sex scenes . . . only now the girls have bras on. However, the series is still enjoyable, and the censorship becomes less obtrusive in later volumes, eventually switching to a 16+ rating in volume 9. ★★★

TENRYU: THE DRAGON CYCLE

Tenryû the Dragon Cycle, "Heaven Dragon the Dragon Cycle" (天龍THE DRAGON CYCLE) • Sanami Matoh • CMX (2005–2006) • Akita Shoten (Bonita, 1999–2003) • 6 volumes • Shôjo, Fantasy, Adventure • 13+ (mild language, violence)

Seeking revenge against the evil lord Torao, the bandit warriors Hiryu and Ryukei team up with the princess Ryurei and discover that they are members of the "dragon clan," with the power to transform into giant Chinese-style dragons. The plot is told mostly through exposition; the characters seem to do nothing but camp out in the forest and talk, but despite dozens of pages of talking heads in cramped, rectangular panels, it's still unclear what's going on. The characters look exactly like the ones in Matoh's *By the Sword,* and although Matoh attempts to mix comedy with the action, the story is too weak to self-parody. The art improves slightly from volume 2 onward (the

first volume was drawn in 1996 for the now-defunct *Comic Nora,* after which Matoh put the project on hold for a few years), but it's still boring and confusing. ★

TENSHI JA NAI!!

Tenshi ja Nai!!, "I'm No Angel!" (天使じゃない!) • Takako Shigematsu • Go! Comi (2005–2007) • Akita Shoten (Princess, 2003–2006) • 8 volumes • Shôjo, Romantic Comedy • 16+ (mild language, mild violence, brief nudity, sexual situations)

Hikaru, a publicity-shy girl who was once a child model, discovers that her girls'-school roommate, Izumi, is more than a popular actress—she's actually a guy in disguise! With the help of his sword-wielding man-servant Yasukuni, Izumi blackmails Hikaru to keep his secret so he can earn money as an actress to pay his father's hospital bills. One of many *shôjo* manga about cross-dressing male models, *Tenshi ja Nai!!* is more of a true love triangle than most; rather than finding herself immediately drawn to her roommate, Hikaru instead falls in love with her twenty-three-year-old music teacher, yet *another* moody, standoffish guy. The plot twists are as unrealistic as the characters (one episode involves bank robbers), but the romance is entertaining in an over-the-top way; it's the kind of series where people wipe food off each other's faces and eat it seductively. Although the character art is stiff, the pages look nice, making good use of copious screentone, flowering plants, and sparkly effects. Trashy but enjoyable. ★★

TESTAROTHO

(テスタロト) • Kei Sanbe • CMX (2005–2006) • Kadokawa Shoten (Comic Dragon, 2001–2002) • 4 volumes • Shônen, Fantasy, Action-Adventure • 18+ (language, nudity, graphic violence)

In a pseudo-medieval setting of poverty and plague, a repressive church clamps down on heretics, using priest-assassins whom the common people call Testarotho. Leonedus, a self-mutilating, tormented Testarotho wielding a giant gun, and Father Garrincha, his one-eyed mentor, are caught in the church's power struggles. *Testarotho* has decent gory action scenes and wild camera angles, but the plot ends frustratingly on a cliff-hanger. Like many grim-and-gritty comics, the series vaguely attempts to address moral issues, but what sticks in the reader's mind are fight scenes, torture scenes, and big-breasted women getting their clothes ripped off. ★½

TETRAGRAMMATON LABYRINTH

Danzaisha—Tetragrammaton Labyrinth, "The One Who Judges—Tetragrammaton Labyrinth" (断罪者—Tetragrammaton Labyrinth) • Ei Itou • Seven Seas Entertainment (2007–ongoing) • Wani Books (Comic Gum, 2005–ongoing) • 4+ volumes (ongoing) • Seinen, Occult, Fantasy, Action • 16+

Sister Meg, a young nun, and Angela, a pretty girl with a scythe, fight evil in turn-of-the-century London. Cute anime-style gothic art with T&A and lesbian intimations. NR

THEY WERE ELEVEN: See *Four Shôjo Stories*

THOSE WHO HUNT ELVES

Elf wo Karu Monotachi, "Those Who Hunt Elves" (エルフを狩るモノたち) • Yu Yagami • ADV (2003–2004) • MediaWorks (Dengeki Gao!, 1995–2003) • 7 volumes, suspended (21 volumes in Japan) • Shônen, Fantasy, Comedy • 13+ (language, crude humor, mild violence, nudity)

With no explanation of how they got there, *Those Who Hunt Elves* jumps right into the action: three people from Earth (a burly martial artist, a teenage female military *otaku*, and an "Oscar-winning" Japanese actress) are stranded in an anything-goes fantasy world, where they must randomly strip female elves to find the fragments of the dimensional-travel spell imprinted on their skin. Oh, and they drive around in a tank, accompanied by an elf sorceress usually imprisoned in the form of a super-deformed dog. Considering the premise, the story has much less naked elf flesh than you'd expect; instead, the focus is on quirky anime-style humor, as the characters go from place to place encountering weird fantasy elements, hunting for modern-day necessities such as toilet paper, and only occasionally saving the world. The stories are hit-and-miss, sometimes cheesy, but the better ones have nice sitcom-esque punch lines. ★★½

THE TIME GUARDIAN

Toki no Mamorisha, "The Time Guardian" (時の守護者) • Daimuro Kishi (story), Tawao Ichinose (art) • CMX (2007–ongoing) • Akita Shoten (Princess, 2005–2006) • 2 volumes • Shôjo, Fantasy • All Ages

A girl named Miu stumbles into a mysterious pawnshop where time itself—memories, experiences, opportunities—is bought and sold. The owner recruits Miu as a part-time worker, allowing her to observe strange stories of time. NR

THE TIMES OF BOTCHAN

Bocchan no Jidai, "The Age/Era of Botchan" (坊ちゃんの時代) • Natsuo Sekikawa (story), Jiro Taniguchi (art) • Fanfare/Ponent Mon (2005–ongoing) • Futabasha (Weekly Manga Action, 1987–1997) • 10 volumes • Seinen, Historical Drama • Unrated/13+ (mild violence, adult themes)

The Times of Botchan is a literary experiment, an attempt at a dense historical novel in manga form. Set in 1905 Japan, its central character is the real-life writer Soseki Natsume, an alcoholic professor of English literature, who pours his ideas into a novel, *Botchan,* a thinly fictionalized account of his own mixed reactions to Japan's rapid modernization and Westernization. Natsume's drinking buddies include young writers, revolutionaries, and reactionaries, one of whom is passionately in love with a proto-feminist "modern woman," an affair that disrupts the men's world and turns them against one another. A glimpse of a complicated time period, *The Times of Botchan* can't escape a certain "Classics Illustrated" feel, like manga Cliff's Notes. The characters are more historical archetypes than individuals, many events are described in narration rather than shown, and the whole thing feels extremely condensed by manga standards. Furthermore, the female characters are merely ciphers. On the upside, Taniguchi's always reliable artwork re-creates Meiji-era Japan with fine-lined accuracy; he also does a masterly job with the characters' expressions, adding a great deal to what is basically a story of concepts rather than deeds. The plot is based on an untranslated novel, Seigai Ota's *Meiji Kenken Hikyu Roku*. Volumes 1 and 2 work together as a self-contained story; a new story begins in volume 3. ★★★

TIME TRAVELER AI

(タイムトラベラ愛) • Ai Ijima (story), Takeshi Take-bayashi (art) • CPM (1999–2002) • Gakken (GS Guys Special, 1994–1995) • 3 volumes • Sex Comedy • 18+ (language, nudity, sex)

Bikini-wearing real-life porn star Ai Ijima (who's also credited as writer) time-shifts whenever she gets sexually aroused, going to ancient Egypt, the Wild West, Atlantis, and so on. As a side effect of her time shifts, everyone around her has huge orgies. This pleasantly dumb sex comedy aims for laughs, with lots of joke sex ("I've assembled a hundred horny men who haven't had a woman for a long time") but no visible genitals; strangely, the result is a much less fetishistic tone than your typical *shônen* romantic comedy. The three volumes each stand on their own: volume 1 consists of classical historical settings, volume 2 is set in a *Waterworld*-like future, and volume 3, the silliest and least explicit, involves ninjas in feudal Japan. ★★

TOGARI

(トガリ) • Yoshinori Natsume • Viz (2007–ongoing) • Shogakukan (Weekly Shônen Sunday, 2000–2002) • 8 volumes • Shônen, Fantasy, Action • 16+ (violence)

Tobe, a dead villain from feudal Japan, is offered a chance to get out of hell if he can kill 108 evil spirits (Toga) in 108 days. Reborn in the present day, he starts his hunt for Toga . . . but is he ready for the baffling ways of the modern world? NR

TO HEART

(トゥハート) • Ukyou Takao • ADV (2004) • Media-Works (Dengeki Daioh, 1997–2000) • 3 volumes • Shônen, Video Game, Romance • All Ages

A manga adaptation of the wildly successful dating sim game of the same title. The male lead, Hiroyuki, is surrounded by an ever-expanding circle of cute girls with bland personalities and very mild problems. In each chapter, he meets a girl and solves her problem, usually just by saying a few kind words, inspiring paroxysms of tearful gratitude in both the girl herself and all the other girls who bear witness to his bargain-basement chivalry. Some of the girls incorporate fantasy elements—there's a witch, a psychokinetic, and a robot maid—but otherwise the setting is an ordinary Japanese high school, albeit one with almost no visible male students. Takao's artwork is crude and sparse. The hyper-innocent *moe* art style makes the characters, supposedly in their final years of high school, look like third-graders except when they're modeling swimwear. It's as calculated as a computer program, as damply sentimental as a wet teddy bear, and as soulless as either. (SG) ½

TOKYO BABYLON

(東京BABYLON) • CLAMP • Tokyopop (2004–2005) • Shinshokan (Wings, 1990–1993) • 7 volumes • Shiojo, Occult, Fantasy • 13+ (mild language, violence, mild sexual situations)

This prequel of sorts to *X/1999* is about Subaru Sumeragi, a teenage *onmyôji* who uses yin-yang magic to exorcise the restless sprits of early 1990s Tokyo. He is aided by his precocious sister Hokuto, who makes matching costumes for herself and Subaru, and by Seishiro Sakurazuka, a veterinarian who acts as chauffeur and moral support. What starts out as a fairly conventional episodic manga quickly takes a turn for the darker as Seishiro's true identity and nature come to the surface, building up to a tragic finale that is one of the most powerful scenes in CLAMP's body of work. *Tokyo Babylon* is also noteworthy as a trailblazing *shônen ai* series. Subaru and Seishiro's relationship,

TOKUSATSU (特撮)

Tokusatsu means "special effects" in Japanese. The term refers to all manner of illusion-based techniques used in film and television, ranging from miniatures, pyrotechnics, and opticals to the very latest in computer graphics.

But that all sounds a bit dry. In truth, the *tokusatsu* genre—as fans refer to it—is a colorful and explosive realm of wild monsters and bizarre superheroes. As with anime and manga, science fiction, fantasy, and horror are popular themes. But there is one crucial difference between *tokusatsu* and its 2-D cousins. Tokusatsu is rendered on film in live action by any means necessary. Thus, you have Godzilla, a giant monster who attacks Tokyo—an awesome idea and striking image—created by means of a man in a rubber suit pulverizing a balsa wood city.

Don't laugh or call it cheesy. Before the rise of anime and manga, *tokusatsu* was Japan's biggest pop culture export to the rest of the world. Millions know characters like Godzilla and Ultraman globally. Back in Japan, *tokusatsu* helped show the way for tie-ins among film, television, magazines, and merchandise, which have practically become an exact science in recent years. And throughout it all, manga has always been a very big part of the picture.

The Japanese golden age of special effects productions officially took off in 1954 with the release of Toho Studio's *Gojira*, which became a worldwide sensation when seen around the world as *Godzilla, King of the Monsters*. Several different manga adaptations of this pivotal title hit the market in 1958, by which time Toho was aggressively producing more and more *tokusatsu* films to meet the global demand for giant monsters and science fiction spectacle. Manga adaptations of these movies quickly became an essential part of their marketing in Japan.

1957 marked the debut of the first modern Japanese superhero: Super Giant (known abroad as Star Man), a caped wonder from the cosmos who repelled alien invaders in a series of crude low-budget adventures. The success of these Super Giant films (which in turn took their cues from the old American serials from Republic Pictures) inspired an avalanche of imitators who flooded the burgeoning Japanese mass media of movies, radio, television, and especially boys' magazines. One of the major contributors to this early era of *tokusatsu* heroes was manga artist Jiro Kuwata (later to create the famed *8 Man*), who drew the adventures of motorcycle-riding mystery man *Gekko Kamen* ("Moonlight Mask," 1958) and teen crime fighter *Maboroshi Tantei* ("Phantom Detective," 1957).

The next major turning point for the *tokusatsu* genre came in 1965 when a new television series, *Ultra Q*, began airing on TBS. This *Outer Limits*–like show, created by the special effects geniuses behind the *Godzilla* series, introduced a brand-new monster every week to viewers. *Ultra Q*, along with the continued popularity of *Godzilla*-style films, led to a full-scale phenomenon known as the *kaijû* boom or "monster boom." Children began rabidly collecting model kits, toys, and books about Japan's growing bestiary of colossal creatures. And soon, glossy glamour shots of monsters became mandatory for the covers of boys' magazines such as *Shônen King*, *Shônen Magazine*, and *Shônen Sunday*.

The burgeoning *kaijû* boom went supernova in 1966 with the arrival of the first *tokusatsu* show to air on TV in living color. *Ultraman* was designed as a sequel to *Ultra Q*, but it revolutionized and surpassed the giant-monster-of-the-week formula by adding an equally giant superhero to the mix. As before, manga were there to help capitalize on its success. *Weekly Shônen Magazine* began an official *Ultraman* adaptation in its pages, penned by an up-and-coming Kazuo Umezu (*The Drifting Classroom*). But Umezu's strange and morbid take on the material lasted only a few chapters before a more mainstream artist was brought in to replace him.

In the wake of *Ultraman*, television studios, manga artists, and publishers began forming alliances in earnest to crank out even more *tokusatsu* product. Artist Mitsuteru Yokoyama, who'd previously struck gold with *Tetsujin 28* (1956), aka "Gigantor," created both the science fiction ninja hero *Red Shadow* and *Giant Robo* (both 1967), aka "Johnny Sokko and his Flying Robot," for *Weekly Shônen Sunday* and Toei Studio's television division. Osamu Tezuka himself presided over the characters, story, and manga adaptation for the 1965 series *Magma Taishi* ("Ambassador Magma"), eventually exported to U.S. television as "Space Giants."

But the most influential artist to emerge from the manga-*tokusatsu* connection turned out to be one of Tezuka's contemporaries from the 1950s: Shotaro Ishinomori. Having already well established himself with the 1964 anime-manga hit *Cyborg 009*, Ishinomori spent 1970 helping to develop a *tokusatsu* show called *Kamen Rider* ("Masked Rider") for Toei TV. Like the protagonists of *009*, *Kamen Rider* was a cyborg at war with a secret evil organization bent on world domination. The difference was that he was a *henshin* (transforming) hero who changed from a normal human being into a mechanical marvel with the aid of a few dramatic poses and his trusty *henshin* belt (millions of plastic replicas of which were sold). Debuting on television in 1971, the series proved to be another unstoppable hit. Along with helping to create numerous *Kamen Rider* sequels that continue to this day, Ishinomori's fertile imagination also brought forth other *tokusatsu* staples such as *Kikaider*, *Robo Detective K*, *Henshin Ninja Arashi*, and *Inazuman*.

These new characters helped to inspire new kinds of children's magazines. The 1971 debut issue of *Terebi Magazine* ("TV Magazine") featured Kamen Rider on its cover. Designed as a kind of *TV Guide* for monster-and-hero-addicted kids, the bulk of the mag was made up of manga adaptations of the latest *tokusatsu* shows. Children quickly needed multiple magazines to stay on top of all that was going on in this increasingly crowded genre, and so competitors *Terebi-kun* and *Terebi-Land* were launched.

Creative manga artists were routinely hired by television companies to help dream up and design new heroes and monsters for them to fight. Some of the most interesting works from the hero boom of the early 1970s that graced both manga pages and TV screens include Kawauchi Kouhan's *Warrior of Love: Rainbow Man* (1972) and Souji Ushio (aka Tomio Sagisu)'s *Spectreman* (1971) and *Lion Maru* (1972). Ken Ishikawa, of Go Nagai's Dynamic Productions, penned a series of unrepentantly violent sequels to *Ultraman* along with creating the pro-wrestling superman *Aztekaiser* (1976). Even Saito Pro, of *Golgo 13* fame, got into the act by helping to make *Barom-1* (1972).

Although characters like Godzilla, Ultraman, and Kamen Rider were now firmly established in the public's imagination, there was still one major innovation that awaited the *tokusatsu* genre. Once again, it was Shotaro Ishinomori who dreamed it up. April 1975 marked the television debut of a new *tokusatsu* series that Ishinomori helped develop for Toei-TV: *Himitsu Sentai Goranger* ("Secret Task Force Goranger"). Essentially, it was the live-action debut of the five-multicolored-heroes formula that would prove crucial to countless anime and manga to this day. The resulting live-action shows that followed became generically known as *sentai* ("task force") and the sequels were legion. There were few innovations on Ishinomori's original plan until the addition of a giant robot to the heroes' arsenal in 1979's *Battle Fever J*. The resulting five-heroes-plus-robot plot made an equally big impact in anime. Already popular robot hero animation shows began increasing the numbers of their principal casts to meet the now requisite called-for quintet. Perhaps the best-known example of the *sentai* influence on anime can be seen in the U.S. hit *Voltron* (1984), which repeated the formula to a T.

But as the 1970s came to a close, the *tokusatsu* genre was facing lean times. The rising cost of production and the financial toil of the global energy crisis led to a massive decrease in the amount of film and television programs made in Japan. Godzilla went into hibernation, Ultraman became a short-lived anime, and *sentai* teams were among the few live-action heroes left for children to root for. The situation greatly improved during the 1980s, as Japan's economy began to pick up. New *tokusatsu* films and TV shows hit theaters and airwaves, although this wave lacked the manic variety common in the past. As the 1990s rolled around, *tokusatsu* was perhaps bigger than ever around the globe, thanks to the runaway success of the *Mighty Morphin' Power Rangers,* a re-edit of a direct sequel to Ishinomori's original *Goranger* series.

Today, publications such as the still-in-print *Terebi Magazine* and bestselling manga series including Kenichi Muraeda's 2001 *Kamen Rider Spirits* (with story duties credited to the now-deceased Shotaro Ishinomori) help keep *tokusatsu* a viable part of the Japanese pop culture spectrum. While Godzilla is currently taking another one of his periodic breathers, Ultraman, Kamen Rider, and *sentai* sequels continue to appear to both the delight of children and their nostalgic parents. (PM)

Tokusatsu Manga

Bio-Booster Armor Guyver • *Change Commander Goku* • *Cutie Honey '90* • *Cyborg 009* • *Dodekain* • *Dragon Voice* • *Duklyon: Clamp School Defenders* • *Electric Man Arrow* • *Excel Saga* • *Figure 17: Tsubasa & Hikaru* • *Godzilla* • *Gôjin* • *Hyper Dolls* • *Hyper Rune* • *Imperfect Hero* • *Junk: Record of the Last Hero* • *Kikaider Code 02* • *Masked Warrior X* • *Neon Genesis Evangelion* • *Silbuster* • *The Skull Man* • *Twin Signal* • *Ultraman Classic: Battle of the Ultra-Brothers*

although not consummated physically in any way, is a clear example of the *uke/seme* relationship and helped introduce *shônen ai* themes to western *otaku*. Though not as ornate as *X/1999*, *Tokyo Babylon* features striking artwork, with heavy use of black and frequent photo background to ground the series in a real place. In fact, the city of Tokyo is as big a character as the three humans. The spirits Subaru encounters embody the darker aspects of Tokyo's opulence and selfishness before the economic bust, which gives the series more gravity but also serves to date it quite a bit. The writing is sometimes heavy-handed and wields lengthy monologues too frequently and clumsily, but still, flaws and all, *Tokyo Babylon* is CLAMP's first really great work. (MT)

★★★

TOKYO BOYS & GIRLS

Tokyo Shônen Shôjo, "Tokyo Boys and Girls" (東京少年少女) • Miki Aihara • Viz (2005–2006) • Shogakukan (Betsucomi, 2004) • 5 volumes • Shôjo, Romance • 16+ (mild language, brief sex)

In her first year at a new high school, Mimori is caught between two guys: Haruta, a biker with bleached hair and a grudge against her, and Kuniyasu, a handsome and popular guy whom her best friend Takaichi is in love with. Meanwhile, Mimori's father is laid off, leading to problems at home. *Tokyo Boys & Girls* is a disappointingly weak love triangle with an unsatisfyingly open ending. Compared to Aihara's later *Hot Gimmick,* the art is less distinctive, and the emotional level isn't cranked up high enough to make the manipulative ride worthwhile. The early volumes include several unrelated short stories. ★½

TOKYO MEW MEW

(東京ミュウミュウ) • Reiko Yoshida (story), Mia Ikumi (art) • Tokyopop (2003–2004) • Kodansha (Nakayoshi, 2000–2003) • 7 volumes • Shôjo, Magical Girl, Fantasy • All Ages

An uninspired magical girl series tarted up with a vague, preachy environmental message. *Tokyo Mew Mew* was clearly designed by its publisher to ride the magical girl tsunami for all it was worth: the creators' marginal notes are filled with references to big book signings, photo shoots, and models hired to dress as the scantily clad preteen heroines. On a trip to a museum with her environmentally conscious crush Masaya, ditzy Ichigo is fused with the DNA of an endangered Japanese wildcat and develops wildcat-oriented superpowers. Well, not particularly wildcat-oriented, actually: one of the curiosities of the series is how lamely it follows up on its premise, giving Ichigo generic magical girl powers and a costume that makes her look like an ordinary housecat. One suspects that the creators weren't especially jazzed about the "endangered species" concept and just wanted to draw cute girls in animal-themed lingerie. Ichigo is soon joined by four other DNA-modified girls, all of whom are named after foods (in manga, a standard sign of creative bankruptcy) and endowed with powers that have nothing to do with their respective endangered species. It's clearly aimed at small children (and pervy middle-aged men), but no child should be subjected to anything this insipid. The story continues in *Tokyo Mew Mew a la Mode.* (SG) ★½

TOKYO MEW MEW A LA MODE

(東京ミュウミュウあ・ら・もーど) • Mia Ikumi • Tokyopop (2005) • Kodansha (Nakayoshi, 2003–2004) • 2 volumes • Shôjo, Magical Girl, Fantasy • All Ages

A short-lived sequel to *Tokyo Mew Mew,* introducing a new central character, Berry, and a new gang of villains, the gothic-styled Saint Rose Crusaders. With previous heroine Ichigo transferred to England, Berry takes over as leader of the team. The Mew Mews are now celebrities, ingeniously allowing for references to *Tokyo Mew Mew* fandom ("The members of Tokyo Mew Mew I used to watch on TV are now going to the same school as me?") and merchandise ("Is that a Tokyo Mew Mew cell phone strap?") within the manga itself. Even the villains' evil plan involves exploiting the team's popularity. Berry, an ordinary girl who not only joins Tokyo Mew Mew but gets better powers than the other members and is immediately placed in charge of them, is the type of transparent wish-fulfillment protagonist that fanfiction writers call a "Mary Sue." (SG) ★½

TOKYO TRIBES

Tokyo Tribe 2 • Santa Inoue • Tokyopop (2004–ongoing) • Shodensha (Boon, 1997–2006) • 12 volumes • Crime Drama • 16+ (constant language, graphic violence, explicit nudity, sex)

Originally published in a Japanese fashion magazine, this story of gang warfare, friendship, and action is a violently spirited homage to American rap and gangsta culture. The setting is very-near-future Tokyo, or rather a cross of Tokyo and urban America: guns are everywhere, cops are a joke, and everyone drives instead of taking the subway. Kai and Mera were once best friends, but fate conspired to make Mera the sadistic leader of the Bukuro Wu-Ronz gang, while Kai and his homies mostly play video games and chill at Penny's Diner. The schemes of

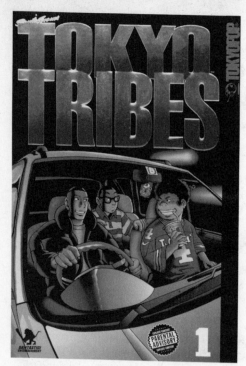

Santa Inoue's *Tokyo Tribes* © 1998 SANTASTIC! ENTERTAINMENT

Bubba, Mera's fat, revolting millionaire overlord, unleash a cycle of nearly superheroic violence, where characters kill one another with swords and baseball bats and race around the sewers and rooftops of Tokyo. Not just a gimmick or shock value (although there's plenty of shock value), *Tokyo Tribes* is a genuinely good story. The computer-toned art is vigorous, self-taught, and completely unique. (Inoue has real design sense, and in Japan he's merchandised himself and his manga for all it's worth, with clothes, action figures, accessories, and a series of manga soundtrack albums titled *Drivin' Wiz My Homies!*) The profane, slangy English rewrite fits perfectly. ★★★½

TOMIE

(富江) • Junji Ito • ComicsOne (2001) • Asahi Sonorama (Monthly Halloween/Nemuki, 1987–1997) • 2 volumes • Horror • Unrated/18+ (graphic violence, nudity)

Tomie, a malicious teenage girl, is actually a protean entity who cannot die, whose every dismembered piece regrows into a crawling, living portion of herself. Her beauty drives men to madness and murder, in an endless cycle of jealousy and violence. The first *Tomie* story was Junji Ito's first professional work, with rough but forceful art, and this series of vaguely interconnected horror stories shows Ito's artistic teething process (emphasis on the "teeth"). Although some stories tend toward relationship parody and black humor, the tone is generally dark; this is very physical horror, full of blood, gore, and grotesque transformations. Several of the stories have female protagonists, helping offset the title character, who embodies every negative stereotype of a beautiful woman. ★★★½

TORI KORO

Tori Koro, "Tri-Color" (トリコロ) • Hai Ran • DrMaster (2005) • Houbunsha (Manga Time Kirara/Manga Time Natural/Manga Time Special, 2002–2004) • 2 volumes • Moe, Four-Panel Comedy • 13+

Three unrelated teenage girls live together under the same roof, with one of the girls' mothers. It sounds like there should be some twist or some conflict, but that's really all there is; like *Azumanga Daioh,* but vastly inferior, it's a peephole into a girls-only world of daily life and conversational "was that a joke?" humor. The art is excessively stylized; with their huge pill-shaped eyes, the characters don't even look human. In 2006 the series was picked up by *Dengeki Daioh* magazine and is still being produced in Japan. ½

TO TERRA

Chikyû (Terra) he . . . , "To Terra" (地球へ) • Keiko Takemiya • Vertical (2007) • Asahi Sonorama (Manga Shônen, 1977–1980) • Shôjo, Psychic, Science Fiction, Drama • 3 volumes • All Ages

In the far future, environmental degradation forces humans to leave the planet Earth, retreating to space colonies where children are raised in test tubes. Many centuries later, a forbidden secret society of psychics, the Mu, arises in the inhumane, computer-controlled world of the colonies. Jomy Marcus Shin, a fourteen-year-old raised in the controlled world of a vast spaceship, is startled out of his normal life when he is chosen as the leader of the Mu and must guide a group of children on a journey back to Earth. A *shôjo* science fiction classic, with lavish, impressionistic artwork. Takemiya's art has a welcome cartoony sensibility, which helps humanize the characters. ★★★★

TOUGH

Koko Tekken-den Tough, "High School Iron Fist Legend Tough" (高校鉄拳伝タフ) • Tetsuya Saruwatari • Viz (2004–2006) • Shueisha (Young Jump, 1993–2003) • 6 volumes, suspended (42 volumes in Japan) • Seinen, Martial Arts • 18+ (language, graphic violence, nudity)

Kiichi "Kiibo" Miyazawa, teenage son of a martial arts champion, fights bloody battles with eight-foot-tall opponents from the worlds of karate, pro wrestling, boxing, and more. Tetsuya Saruwatari, the creator of the even gorier untranslated martial arts manga *Riki-Oh* (aka *The Story of Ricky*), here waters down his signature violence with a goofy protagonist (Kiibo is a luckless girl-chasing doofus) and juvenile comic relief (such as Kiibo's porn-addicted grandpa). The fight is still the thing, though, with wince-inducing clinical close-ups of smashed joints and mangled limbs, as the story struggles to maintain the pretense of sadistic anatomical plausibility. The art is manufactured and full of traced photos. The Viz edition consists of the "Shueisha Jump Remix" edition, containing 6 volumes' worth of stories selected from the original 42–volume run. ★★

TOWER OF THE FUTURE

Mirai no Utena, "Tower of the Future" (未来のうてな) • Saki Hiwatari • CMX (2006–ongoing) • Hakusensha (Hana to Yume, 1994–1999) • 11 volumes • Shôjo, Science Fiction, Romantic Drama • 13+ (mild violence, adult themes)

Takeru, a Japanese teenager who spends most of his time writing plots for a video RPG he dreams of making, has several problems. After the death of his mother, he finds out that he has a British half sister whom he

has never met. He has a crush on a girl, Ichigo, who has a disturbingly close relationship to her older brother. And lastly, a strange little kid, Zen, keeps pestering him about his personal life . . . and behaving as if he knows Takeru's future. Saki Hiwatari's follow-up to the deservedly popular *Please Save My Earth*, *Tower of the Future* has the same strong writing, great dialogue, and novel-like plot. However, Hiwatari may have been allowed to indulge herself a bit in the wake of her masterpiece: *Tower of the Future* has an *extremely* slow buildup, and it is many volumes before the relationship story begins to connect with the sci-fi elements behind the scenes. ★★★½

TOWN OF EVENING CALM, COUNTRY OF CHERRY BLOSSOMS

Yûnagi no Machi Sakura no Kuni, "Town of Evening Calm, Country of Cherry Blossoms" (夕凪の街桜の国) • Futabasha (Weekly Manga Action/ Manga Action, 2003–2004) • Historical Drama • 1 volume • Unrated/13+ (adult themes, corpses)

A beautiful mood manga and an understated antiwar statement, *Town of Evening Calm, Country of Cherry Blossoms* is a tribute to the city of Hiroshima, the artist's birthplace. The plot (a series of interconnected short stories) follows a few characters from 1955 to the modern era; in one scene, an old man sits and dreams of the past on a grassy, peaceful riverbank, and the next page shows him as a young man on the same site, when it was a postwar shantytown. The bombing itself is not shown, and unlike the melodramatic *Barefoot Gen*, there is little shock value—only a few far-off, almost surreal images of corpses and wreckage, like ghosts haunting the characters' lives. Dreamlike and evocative, the tales focus on love and loss, and the social ostracism suffered by victims of radiation sickness. The faintly *shôjo*-style, crosshatched artwork has lovely backgrounds. ★★★★

TRAIN MAN: A SHOJO MANGA

Densha Otoko: Bijo to Jûnjô Otaku Seinen no Net Hatsu Love Story, "Train Man: A Love Story from

YOU'RE THE CUTE ONE.

YOU CAN'T WRITE IN THE SAME STYLE YOU USED FOR THE SOCIAL AND POLITICAL STUFF.

FOR THE LIFESTYLE SECTION, WE NEED WRITING THAT'S PLAIN-SPOKEN... FRIENDLY.

WELL, MISS IWAYA...

SO YOU'RE SAYING YOU WANT ME TO REWRITE THE WHOLE THING?

the Net, of a Beautiful Woman and a Naïve Otaku Youth" (電車男—美女と純情ヲタク青年のネット発ラブストーリー) • Hitori Nakano (original story), Machiko Ocha (manga) • Del Rey (2006) • Kodansha (Dessert, 2005) • 1 volume • Shôjo, Romantic Comedy • 16+ (mild violence, mild sexual situations)

A spin-off of the smash hit book *Densha Otoko* by Hitori Nakano, this version is done in *shôjo* manga style, aimed at girls in their early teens. Although it tells the same story, it is the weakest of the three versions; the main character never seems believably nerdy and the ending is forced and overly sentimental. However, the translation notes are terrific and there is an excellent article at the end of the book on the Train Man phenomenon. See also *Densha Otoko* and *Train_Man: Densha Otoko*. (RB) ★★

TRAIN_MAN: DENSHA OTOKO

Densha Otoko: Net Hatsu no Kakuekiteisha no Love Story, "Train Man: A Local Train Love Story from the Net" (電車男—ネット発、各駅停車のラブ・

ストーリー) • Hitori Nakano (original story), Hidenori Hara (manga) • Viz (2006–2007) • Shogaku-kan (Weekly Young Sunday, 2005) • 3 volumes • Seinen, Romantic Comedy • 13+ (mild violence, mild sexual situations)

Spin-off of the smash hit book *Densha Otoko* by Hitori Nakano, this one in *seinen* style, aimed at late-high-school- and college-age men. Compared to *Train Man: A Shojo Manga*, the story is more heartfelt, the main character is more believable, and the story isn't as rushed. One drawback that may turn away younger manga fans is the distinctively old-school art, vaguely comparable to Rumiko Takahashi's *Maison Ikkoku*. See also *Densha Otoko* and *Train Man: A Shôjo Manga*. (RB) ★★★

TRAIN + TRAIN

Hideyuki Kurata (story), Tomomasa Takuma (art) • Go! Comi (2006–ongoing) • MediaWorks (Dengeki Daioh, 1999–2003) • 6 volumes • Shônen, Science Fiction, Action • 13+

From the author of *R.O.D* (*Read or Die*). On a distant planet, teenagers are enrolled in either the standard School Train or the Special Train, which takes them across the planet to a future of excitement and danger. Reiichi, a shy student, ends up on the wrong train after a run-in with a rebellious girl, and they travel toward adventure. NR

TRAMPS LIKE US

Kimi wa Pet, "You're a Pet/You're My Pet" (きみはペット) • Yayoi Ogawa • Tokyopop (2004–2008) • Kodansha (Kiss, 2000–2005) • 14 volumes • Jôsei, Romantic Comedy • 16+ (language, mild violence, infrequent nudity, sex)

Sumire, a tall, Harvard-educated journalist in her late twenties, has a problem: her job is stressful, she intimidates men, and as an unmarried professional woman in Japan, she must constantly deal with sexism and people's expectations about her future. When she finds a handsome, scruffy, shortish college-age man curled up in a cardboard box outside her apartment, she feeds him a meal and ends up letting him stay with

TRANSGENDER

"**I**s that a guy or a girl?" must rank just behind "Are these characters supposed to be white?" as the most commonly asked question by people unfamiliar with manga. Unlike the race question, gender confusion isn't an accident of the artwork; manga, with its idealized body types and faces, is the perfect mode of expression for the gender-bending streak in Japanese pop culture. If the American image of androgyny is campy like RuPaul or unappealing like the 1990s "Pat" skits on *Saturday Night Live,* the Japanese image is a cute, boyish girl or an alluring, long-haired *bishônen,* "beautiful boy."

Compared to stereotypical Western culture, where men are men and women are women, Japan has always had a fascination with gender ambiguity. In kabuki theater, female roles were (and still mostly are) played by men, as they were in Elizabethan England; *onnagata,* who specialize in playing women, are respected performers. Some bars feature male transvestites as bar hostesses; *okama,* a slang term for gay men (now considered pejorative), originally referred to these transvestites. (Such hostesses appear in *3x3 Eyes* and *Ouran High School Host Club.*) The famous Takarazuka Revue, founded in 1914 and still going strong, reversed the kabuki tradition by staging elaborate musicals with young women playing both male and female roles. *Visual kei* bands, similar to Western glam rock and extremely popular with teenage girls, often feature androgynous male leads. Images of campy drag queens do appear in manga, but they are rarer than in America.

Transgender themes in manga go back at least as far as Osamu Tezuka's *Princess Knight* (1953), whose cross-dressing heroine is born with the souls of both a girl and a boy, allowing her to take place in exciting adventures in a "man's world." The genre was further explored in *shôjo* manga of the 1970s, such as Riyoko Ikeda's classic *The Rose of Versailles* (1972) and Moto Hagio's *They Were Eleven* (1975). Soon previously macho *shônen* manga were getting into the act as well, mostly in the love comedy genre. (After all, transgenderism, like bisexuality, instantly doubles the potential number of romantic pairings.) Rumiko Takahashi's *Ranma 1/2* (1987) is one of the most famous *shônen* sex-change fantasies, starring a tough martial artist who changes into a buxom (but still tough) girl when splashed with cold water. Sharon Kinsella, in her book *Adult Manga: Culture and Power in Contemporary Japanese Society,* suggested that even the outwardly heterosexual harem fantasies of manga such as *Oh My Goddess!* (1988), in which a meek male character is surrounded by women, actually express a desire to become a girl, as if by proximity. But there is no shortage in manga of out-

Yes, that's a guy; Takako Shigematsu's *Tenshi Ja Nai!!*

right transvestites and cross-dressers (such as the protagonist of *Yubisaki Milk Tea*) and of characters who change gender due to magic, genetics, plastic surgery, or state of arousal.

Despite the popularity of transgendered characters in Japanese fiction and performance, gender roles in Japanese daily life are still clearly defined, and manga often reinforce traditional values. In stories as different as *Hana-Kimi* and *Ranma ½*, playing in the role of the opposite sex is basically a transitory phase on the road to adulthood; Ranma views his transgendered state as a weakness, and Mizuki in *Hana-Kimi* is incapable of expressing her affection for the boy she likes because she must pretend to be his male roommate. Side characters may express transgender leanings, but for the protagonists, the other gender's clothes (or skin) is often a source of trouble rather than pleasure. At best, it is a fleeting chance to be a "knight" as well as a "princess," made sweeter by its very briefness and artificiality. The few manga in which the characters embrace the change, such as *Futaba-kun Change!* and *Your and My Secret,* are the exception rather than the rule and are usually played for slapstick comedy. (On the other hand, hermaphrodites—*futanari*—frequently appear in adult manga, as in American pornography.)

In contrast to the countless imaginary ways of changing gender, actual medical transsexuals and hermaphrodites rarely appear as main characters in manga, apart from bit parts in series such as *IWGP* and *Gravitation,* and the protagonist of the ultimately conventional *The Day of Revolution.* Gender reassignment surgery was not performed in Japan until 1998, and it is still impossible to get one's gender legally changed on one's *jûminhyo* (resident card, the equivalent of a birth certificate).

Transgender Manga

Afterschool Nightmare • *A Cheeky Angel* • *Le Chevalier d'Eon* • *Chirality: To the Promised Land* • *The Day of Revolution* • *Four Shojo Stories* • *Fushigi Yûgi* • *Fushigi Yûgi: Genbu Kaiden* • *Futaba-kun Change* • *Girl Got Game* • *Hana-Kimi: For You in Full Blossom* • *Kedamono Damono* • *Lagoon Engine Einsatz* • *Magical x Miracle* • *Metamo Kiss* • *Moon Child* • *Murder Princess* • *Musashi No. 9* • *Paradise Kiss* • *Penguin Revolution* • *Pretty Face* • *Princess Knight* • *Princess Prince* • *Princess Princess* • *Ranma ½* • *The Rose of Versailles* • *Tenshi ja Nai!!* • *Until the Full Moon* • *W Juliet* • *Your and My Secret* • *Yubisaki Milk Tea*

her as her "pet," a role to which he happily agrees. While she lives and occasionally snuggles with her pet boy (who, it's eventually revealed, has a real life aside from playing video games in Sumire's apartment), she finds herself drawn back toward her ex-boyfriend Hasumi, who fits the traditional masculine stereotype of surpassing Sumire in three ways: he's taller, he's better-educated, and he has a higher salary. A role-reversal adult relationship story with a strong female lead, *Tramps Like Us* is well written enough to make up for its occasionally meandering plot and awkward leaps in the story. (Ogawa often builds to a dramatic moment and then defuses it by skipping forward in time, summarizing what happened in flashback.) The art is plain, and a few of the stories are frankly immature, such as when the characters get amnesia, investigate a ghost story, work at an amusement park, and so on. However, the dynamics of the three main characters carry the plot through these weak points. ★★★

TRANSLUCENT

Translucent: Kanojo wa Hantômei, "Translucent: The Girl Is Semitransparent" (トランスルーセント〜彼女は半透明) • Kazuhiro Okamoto • Dark Horse (2007–ongoing) • Media Factory (Comic Flapper, 2005–2006) • 5 volumes • Drama, Romance • All Ages

Shizuka, an introverted teenage girl, suffers from the rare disease known as "translucent syndrome," which causes her to become partially invisible. Her classmate Tadami tries to help her overcome her shyness. NR

TRASH

Sanami Matoh • Tokyopop (2006) • Biblos (Be x Boy, 2004) • Crime, Comedy • 1 volume • 16+ (language, mild violence)

Guy, Keith, Ginger, and their pet penguin Bobby are the Trash Company, a bunch of cool dudes (and the female brains of the outfit) who do odd jobs on the streets of New York. In the course of their sometimes criminal missions they encounter Will and Kate, two rich kids who soon become the stars of the story. Drawn from the same "prop closet" as Sanami Matoh's *Fake* and *RA-I, Trash* is a mix of crime-solving action and loudmouthed comedy. The jokes are bland and the story goes nowhere.　　★

TREASURE HUNTER

Hizenya Jûbei, "Jûbei, the Seeker of Riches" (肥前屋十兵衛) • Hitoshi Tomizawa • CPM (2003–2004) • Akita Shoten (Weekly Shônen Champion, 1995) • 3 volumes • Shônen, Fantasy, Adventure • 13+ (violence)

In a fantasy world, Jubei is a merchant-adventurer who rides a human-headed magic carpet and carries an assortment of bizarre, living tools. In a typically crazy plot, he is hired by a skeleton pirate to fetch the Figurehead of Souls, for which he must journey to Jelly Island and fight a giant dancing toad wearing a beret. A completely far-out *shônen* manga tall tale, *Treasure Hunter* is nothing if not imaginative, but the stretchy art is cluttered and muddy, and the nonstop weirdness gives the reader no point of reference. Except for a fondness for snakes, bugs,

Yasuhiro Nightow's *Trigun*

and grotesque transformations, Tomizawa's work is almost unrecognizable as being from the artist of *Alien Nine* (the latter being probably the result of a conscious decision to draw cuter).　　★★

TRIGUN

(トライガン) • Yasuhiro Nightow • Dark Horse (2003–2004) • Tokuma Shoten (Monthly Shônen Captain, 1995–1997) • 2 volumes • Shônen, Science Fiction, Action, Comedy • Unrated/13+ (language, graphic violence, partial nudity, brief mild sexual humor)

"Deep Space Planet Future Gun Action!" roars the cover text for both the English and Japanese editions of *Trigun,* an over-the-top Wild West science fiction comedy. The setting is a desert planet settled by stranded colonists from Earth, where "sand-steamers" roam the vast wastelands; the hero is Vash the Stampede, a seemingly innocuous guy in a bullet-riddled trench coat, who is reputed to have wiped out entire cities. As the insurance investigators sent to follow him soon discover, the dreaded Vash is in fact a friendly pacifist, who (like the hero of *Rurouni Kenshin*) always manages to incapacitate his opponents without killing them, no matter how much they try to provoke his bad side. Quiet *High Noon* moments punctuate bursts of slapstick action, with thousands of bullets Swiss-cheesing everything in sight and insanely exaggerated cyborg villains doing dastardly deeds. The manga ends abruptly with a lead-in to *Trigun Maximum*.

★★½

TRIGUN MAXIMUM

(トライガン・マキシマム) • Yasuhiro Nightow • Dark Horse (2004–ongoing) • Shônen Gahosha (Young King Ours, 1998–2007) • 13 volumes • Seinen, Science Fiction, Action, Comedy • Unrated/13+ (language, graphic violence, nudity)

Picking up two years after the original story, the continuation of *Trigun* sees Nightow flexing his artistic muscles. With the full extent of his powers now revealed, Vash travels the planet facing the Gung-Ho Guns, mercenaries serving the genocidal Knives, his evil brother. His traveling companion is Wolfwood, a cynical priest who runs an orphanage and carries a giant gun shaped like a cross; the two of them fight over spaghetti when not fighting grotesque, superpowered bad guys. The generic Western story lines of *Trigun* are here replaced with portentous foreshadowing and pure fight scenes, more influenced by the visuals-are-everything style of American superhero comics than the clarity-is-everything style of *shônen* manga. Nightow is clearly a massive fan of American comics, and his art combines Mike Mignola's strong black-and-white compositions with Geof Darrow's obsessively detailed linework and machinery. The plot is standard, and sometimes it's hard to tell what's going on, but it's always fun to look at. ★★★

TRINITY BLOOD

(トリニティ・ブラッド) • Sunao Yoshida (story), Thores Shibamoto (character design), Kiyo Kujyo (art) • Tokyopop (2006–ongoing) • Kadokawa Shoten (Asuka, 2004–ongoing) • 8+ volumes (ongoing) • Shôjo, Occult, Fantasy, Action • 16+ (violence)

Derivative but well-executed manga adaptation of the light novels by Sunao Yoshida. In a distantly postapocalyptic future, humans war with vampires, who have formed a militaristic society. On the humans' side is the Vatican, and their most powerful agent is Abel Nightroad, whose clumsy facade conceals a super-vampire priest who drinks the blood of other vampires. The manga adaptation is drawn in a slick anime-influenced style, with fists slamming and blood spurting in exaggerated action scenes. At the same time, it was printed in a *shôjo* magazine, so at times it makes good use of impressionistic *shôjo* page layouts. Unfortunately, character designs and style borrowed from *Trigun* and *Hellsing* leave the end product merely average. ★★

TSUBASA: RESERVOIR CHRONICLE

(ツバサ-RESERVoir CHRoNiCLE-) • CLAMP • Del Rey (2004–ongoing) • Kodansha (Weekly Shônen Magazine, 2003–ongoing) • 18+ volumes (ongoing) • Shônen, Fantasy, Adventure • 13+ (mild violence)

From their earliest *dôjinshi* works, CLAMP has always showed a proclivity for crossovers, but in 2003, with the simultaneous release of *Tsubasa: Reservoir Chronicle* and *xxxHOLiC,* CLAMP took the crossover to new heights. This manga, equivalent to DC's *Crisis on Infinite Earths,* reimagines the casts of almost every previous CLAMP manga as the inhabitants of various theme worlds such as Clow Country, Celes Country, and Piffle World. At the center of the story are Syaoran and Sakura of *Cardcaptor Sakura.* He's now an archaeologist and she's an amnesiac princess whose lost "feathers" are scattered throughout the many worlds. Syaoran travels from his fantasy world to the "real" world, where he makes a pact with Yuko, star of *xxxHOLiC,* to gain the ability to travel between worlds. This isn't the first time CLAMP has been serialized in a *shônen* anthology (that honor goes to *Angelic Layer*), but it is the first time they surrender their style to the boys' action comic format. The results are a mixed bag. Visually it's an amazing accomplishment—not nearly as luscious as the woodblock-inspired stylings of *xxxHOLiC,* but definitely featuring CLAMP's most dynamic action scenes. And even though CLAMP is recycling most of the characters, the designs look more unique than ever (check out the *Clamp in Wonderland* artwork to see just how similar many early CLAMP characters look next to one another). On the other hand, perhaps because CLAMP is emulating the *shônen* conventions, the characters in *Tsubasa* lack the range of expressions that the team is capable of. Although the manga does not require a familiarity with the referenced works, it certainly helps; CLAMP has a tendency to use insider knowledge about the past characters as a crutch for lazy characterization. Thankfully, Del Rey provides enough translation notes to help the uninitiated keep up. (MT)

★★★

TSUKUYOMI: MOON PHASE

Tsukuyomi, "Moon Poem" (月詠Moon Phase) • Keitaro Arima • Tokyopop (2006–ongoing) • Wani Books (Comic Gum, 1999–ongoing) • 12+ volumes (ongoing) • Seinen, Vampire, Action, Comedy • 13+ (mild language, violence, infrequent nudity, sexual situations)

"I want . . . to kiss . . . your neck." While visiting a castle in Germany, Kouhei, a Japanese photographer who works with occult investigators, encounters a strange little girl who bites him in the neck and drinks his blood. To the girl's surprise, Kouhei proves immune to her mind-control powers, so she follows him back to Japan and moves in with him and his folks. It soon turns out that Hazuki is a vampire who was imprisoned in the castle until Kouhei freed her, and as she hangs out with Kouhei and learns human values, her "relatives" from Germany send her fellow vampires to track her down and bring her back into the fold. Although the anime-style art is mediocre, the action scenes are satisfying and the plot proceeds logically, managing a good balance between romantic comedy and drama. Volume 4 of the English edition was censored, with nipples removed from a scene where a character is whipped and tortured; that scene plus the uneasy master-slave relationship between Kouhei and Hazuki stand out as reminders that, despite the cute art and cat-ear bonnets and generally mild tone, the series was intended for older teenage and adult men.

★★½

TUXEDO GIN

Tuxedo Gin: Ginji no Koi no Monogatari, "Tuxedo Gin: The Story of Ginji's Love" (タキシード銀-GINJIの恋の物語) • Tokihiko Matsuura • Viz (2003–2005) • Shogakukan (Weekly Shônen Sunday, 1997–2000) • 15 volumes • Shônen, Romantic Comedy • 16+ (mild language, crude humor, violence, nudity)

When tough guy Ginji dies in a motorcycle crash just before his date with his classmate Minako, he is reincarnated as a penguin, with the promise of coming back as his old self when his penguin life runs out. Soon he is Minako's pet penguin Gin . . . a boxing, skateboarding, snowboarding penguin with the ability to stare down human bad guys and to summon help from hordes of his penguin pals. And then there's also the fact that "from penguin height, I can peep at all the panties I want." A silly, macho romantic sitcom, *Tuxedo Gin* suffers from too many filler stories (Gin helps out a run-down boxing gym, Gin helps out as a delivery driver, Gin helps out with a kindergarten class, etc.) ("That penguin's passion has been an inspiration for Shosuke!"). Minako, a girl who has nothing better to do than wait for Ginji to reappear, exists mostly for T&A value and so that Gin can fend off her suitors. The plot is packed with cute talking animals—penguins, ospreys, walruses, koalas—and the best stories are those where Gin's penguin-ness is in the forefront, instead of the ones where he's just a sort of *chibi* guy in a Hawaiian shirt.

★★½

TWILIGHT OF THE DARK MASTER

Shihaisha no Tasogare, "Twilight of the Master/Ruler" (支配者の黄昏・Twilight of the Dark Master)

• Saki Okuse • DMP (2005) • Shinshokan (Wings, 1991) • 1 volume • Occult, Action • 18+ (language, nudity, sex, graphic violence)

Shinjuku, 2019: a new drug on the streets is turning men into cannibalistic killers who murder women. With the police unable to help, one of the surviving victims hires the mysterious Tsunami Shijo, a cool, psychic-powered detective who discovers that the answer lies with the *oni,* the horned devils of Japanese folklore. A 1980s urban-fantasy-horror manga in the style of Hideyuki Kiku-chi, *Twilight*'s demons, psychic battles, and dark conspiracies are all typical for the genre. The figure drawing is stiff, the buildings are drawn with screentone and rulers, and the whole thing suffers from lack of originality.

★

TWIN SIGNAL

Sachi Oshimizu • Media Blasters (2006–ongoing) • Enix (Monthly Shônen Gangan/Monthly G-Fantasy, 1992–2001) • Shônen, Action, Comedy • 1 volume, suspended (19 volumes in Japan) • All Ages (mild language, mild violence)

Children's gag/action manga set in the future with roly-poly police robots and robot wrestlers (not to mention vampires, monsters, beer-guzzling bionic alligators . . .). While visting the lab of his scientist grandfather Dr. Otoi, eleven-year-old Nobuhiko accidentally interferes with the creation of Signal, a heroic combat android with a big shock of spiky hair. Now, whenever Nobuhiko sneezes, Signal changes from a blustering superhero to a wimpy, chocolate-eating baby version of himself. Together, Nobuhiko and Signal go on wacky adventures and fight evil robots. Although the art is generic and the humor is strictly for kids, the flow of jokes is snappy.

★★

THE TWO FACES OF TOMORROW

Mirai no Futatsu no Kao, "Two Faces of Tomorrow" (未来の二つの顔) • James P. Hogan (original creator), Yukinobu Hoshino (manga) • Dark Horse (1997–1998) • Kodansha (1993–1994) • 1 volume • Science Fiction, Drama • Unrated/13+ (mild language, violence, brief nudity)

Speculative science fiction based on the 1979 novel by Western author James P. Hogan. Before committing to a worldwide computer systems upgrade, a multinational think tank launches a controlled experiment on a remote space station to see if their new level of artificial intelligence could evolve into a threat. A program is written to stimulate a survival instinct, and then the soldiers and scientists posted on the station provoke the computer to defend itself; soon they are struggling to keep up with its adaptations. *The Two Faces of Tomorrow* tackles the possible development of an A.I. with impressive logic and solid science, but the character drama is often sterile and the story loses some credibility points for its overly rational vision of humanity's future. (Billions spent on preventative measures? Scientific geniuses getting a place at the international policy-making table?) Hoshino's artwork shows superb draftsmanship, but it's also stiff; action scenes frequently have to be explained in dialogue after the fact. The ending, though, is satisfying. (JD)

★★★

ULTIMATE MUSCLE:
THE KINNIKUMAN LEGACY

Kinnikuman Nisei, "Muscleman Second Generation" (キン肉マンII世) • Yudetamago • Viz (2004–ongoing) • Shueisha (Weekly Playboy, 1998–2005) • 29 volumes • Seinen, Action, Comedy • 16+ (mild language, crude humor, violence, nudity)

Ultimate Muscle is the sequel to the untranslated *Kinnikuman* ("Muscleman"), a popular 1978–1987 manga that made it to America only through a line of tiny wrestling toys sold under the name M.U.S.C.L.E. In Japan, it's primarily a nostalgia property, aimed at Gen-Xers and written and drawn by the same team responsible for the original manga. Kid Muscle, the protagonist, is the son of King Muscle, hero of *Kinnikuman.* Mostly against his will, he becomes a super-human wrestler for the Muscle League and a defender of Earth. Most of the supporting characters are based on ideas from readers, and many of them are extremely silly (a wrestler who turns into a giant sneaker, a wrestler who's a walking toilet). Like many successful franchises designed for grade-schoolers, *Kinnikuman* is based on the winning combination of over-the-top violence and gross-out humor. But because the sequel is written for adults, it can fly even further past the boundaries of good taste, with no end of poop, pee, butts, boobs, erections, and severed limbs. In other words, it's lowbrow fun, just like real (i.e., fake) pro wrestling. The early volumes of the Viz edition are censored for nudity and scatological humor; the later volumes are uncensored. An untranslated sequel series began in 2005. ★★½

ULTRA CUTE

Urukyu (うるきゅー) • Nami Akimoto • Tokyopop (2006–2007) • Kodansha (Nakayoshi, 1999–2003) • 9 volumes • Shôjo, Romantic Comedy • All Ages (comic violence, mild sexual situations)

Ever since they were little, Ami and Noa have competed against each other for the same guy, and as a result, they've never had boyfriends. Then one day they meet Tamon and Tomohiro, two hot surfers who seem to be perfect—until Ami discovers that the guys are just playing them. "If you're really that upset, why don't you try to make me fall in love with you?" says Tamon, an unlikely challenge that triggers a predictable but occasionally amusing romantic comedy for young readers. (Even after discovering that Tamon is a jerk, Ami feels compelled to compete with Noa to see who can be more lovey-dovey with their respective boyfriends.) Generic art. ★½

ULTRAMAN CLASSIC: BATTLE OF THE ULTRA-BROTHERS

The Ultraman (ザ・ウルトラマン) • Mamoru Uchiyama • Viz (1994) • Shogakukan (Shôgaku Sannensei, 1975–1980) • 5 issues, suspended (4 volumes in Japan) • Tokusatsu, Action • Unrated/All Ages (mild violence, frequent death)

Moronic but mildly enjoyable adventures featuring the Ultra-Warriors, the numerous, spandex-clad residents of the Ultra-Homeworld (ruled over by the Ultra-Father and Ultra-Mother) and their awe-inspiring battles against outer-space menaces such as Jackal the Demon King (from the planet Jackal), the Pirates (of the planet Pirate), and King Vadar and his Vadarians. Surprisingly grim for a juvenile comic—nearly everyone on the Ultra-Homeworld is killed in the first issue, only to be resurrected later—*Ultraman Classic: Battle of the Ultra-Brothers* is the only example in English of Mamoru Uchiyama's huge catalog of *Ultraman* comics. Serious *Ultraman* fans might enjoy playing spot-the-Ultraman—Ace, Jack, Taro, Seven, Leo, and Zoffy all appear. (JD) ★★

ULTRA MANIAC

(ウルトラマニアック) • Wataru Yoshizumi • Viz (2005–2006) • Shueisha (Ribon, 2002–2004) • 5 volumes • Shôjo, Magical Girl, Romantic Comedy • All Ages

Wataru Yoshizumi writes in a straightforward but enjoyable manner, and *Ultra Maniac* is her take on the "teenage witch" formula. The twist in *Ultra Maniac* is that the witch isn't the main character; instead it's Ayu, a normal girl, who must deal with the well-intentioned meddling of her ditzy witch friend Nina. (In this story, witches are just ordinary folks from the Magic Kingdom, which despite its name is basically like any other foreign country and even has a "study abroad" office in Tokyo.) Using her magic PDA, Nina creates magic "love candy," a camera that shows you the other person's secret crush, and other spells with unforeseen side effects; however, the magic wackiness eventually takes second place to the romantic subplots. ★★★

UNTIL THE FULL MOON

Full Moon ni Sasayaite, "Whisper to Me on a Full Moon Night" (FULLMOONにささやいて) • Sanami Matoh • Broccoli (2004–2005) • Akita Shoten/Biblos (1993–1998) • 2 volumes • Shôjo, Romantic Comedy • 16+ (brief nudity, brief sex)

David, a vampire playboy, finds himself betrothed to his male childhood friend Marlo,

UNDERGROUND AND *GEKIGA* (アングラ・劇画)

"Burn your manga! . . . the programmed manga that's become commercial, the manga that lacks all originality, the calculated manga made to sell . . . and those interactive manga whose plots are determined by the readers' polls."

—Takeo Udagawa, *Manga Zombie*

Manga is a thriving industry, and bestselling manga artists share in the copyrights to their work, but no mainstream manga artist expects complete artistic freedom. The plots of most manga are essentially collaborations between the artist and his or her editor, and artists face tremendous pressure to take the story in the most commercial direction. Art styles, too, are subject to scrutiny; even in magazines that do not have clearly definable "house styles," the assistant/apprenticeship system, and general creative poverty, results in many manga looking alike. But in the shadow of the major Japanese publishers, an underground has always existed: artists who reject commercial success in order to pursue art for art's sake.

As in America, Japan's early underground comics were a conscious effort to produce comics for adults, within a market overwhelmingly aimed at children. Of the few manga artists drawing for adults in the 1950s, many of them worked in the *kashibonya* (book rental) market, where the pay was low but artists enjoyed greater freedom than in the mainstream children's magazines. *Kashibonya* anthologies with titles such as *Kage* ("shadow") and *Machi* ("street") focused on gritty urban stories influenced by current Japanese cinema and film noir. Yoshihiro Tatsumi coined a term for the movement: *gekiga* ("dramatic pictures"), as opposed to *manga* ("whimsical pictures"). At one level,

Junko Mizuno's hallucinatory *Pure Trance*

gekiga was a purely visual style, renouncing cartoony exaggeration in favor of realistic draftsmanship (such as the work of Goseki Kojima or even Katsuhiro Otomo). On the other hand, it meant serious adult fiction (or at least hard-boiled pulp fiction), often dealing with working-class subjects and hard-hitting social themes. A few artists, such as Takao Saito, still use the term *gekiga* to describe their own works, but today the techniques—though not the politics—of *gekiga* have diffused throughout mainstream adult manga.

One of the most successful *gekiga* artists was Sanpei Shirato, whose *Ninja Bugeichô* ("Ninja Military Chronicles," 1959–1962) used a historical ninja drama to explore themes of rebellion and class struggle. As rising prosperity brought an end to the blue-collar *kashibonya* market (most Japanese people could now afford to buy comics instead of renting them), the editor Katsuichi Nagai invited Shirato to join him in forming a new magazine devoted entirely to experimental works. In 1964 they founded *Garo,* Japan's first and longest-running underground manga magazine. Shirato's *Kamui Den* ("The Legend of Kamui"), an even more openly political ninja manga, was the magazine's first hit title, and throughout the 1960s *Garo* was a favorite of college students and the intelligentsia. In contrast to the intrusive editorial policies of most manga magazines, Nagai's *Garo* encouraged artistic experimentation. Inspired by *Garo,* in 1967 the famous manga artist Osamu Tezuka created his own avant-garde magazine, *Com,* in which he published new artists as well as a part of his epic *Phoenix.* Many artists who debuted in *Garo* and *Com* later went on to mainstream success, including Moto Hagio, Mitsuru Adachi, and Ryoichi Ikegami.

Japanese underground comics have a stunning range of style and subject matter. In the early years, many artists reacted against the macho realism of old-school *gekiga.* Yoshiharu Tsuge combined detailed, illustrative artwork with surrealism, a combination that influenced Kazuichi Hanawa. *Garo* and *Com* were among the first manga magazines to give equal time to male and female artists, and the underground produced the introspective, feminist work of Murasaki Yamada (in the 1970s) and the dreamlike manga of Yuko Tsuno (in the late 1980s). Other artists rebelled against visual polish itself, such as Terry Johnson, aka "King Terry," who founded the pop-art *heta-uma* ("bad-good") art style. While American underground comics often reveled in sex, drugs, and violence, Japanese comics had fewer taboos to shatter, one exception being World War II militarism and emperor worship, satirized in the decadent erotic horror comics of Suehiro Maruo and the pop-culture trash comics of Makoto Aida. Other artists broke less obvious taboos in their depiction of social relationships, such as the absurdist salaryman manga of Yoshikazu Ebisu and numerous semi-autobiographical manga ranging from the whimsical to the bleak.

However, the golden age of underground manga was short-lived. With the appearance of *seinen* magazines in the early 1970s, mainstream publishers offered higher-paying opportunities to draw comics for adults, and the counterculture audience was fading. *Com* folded in 1972, and when *The Legend of Kamui* ended in 1971, *Garo*'s circulation dwindled from 80,000 to a few thousand copies. Some experimental artists, such as Hideo Azuma and Naoki Yamamoto, worked in the relatively unrestricted world of sex comics (see the introduction to ADULT MANGA) until that market, too, became incorporated into the mainstream. The anti-establishment mood of the 1960s had died down, and for people who simply wanted to draw whatever they wanted without editorial interference, there was the *dōjinshi* self-publishing market, which grew massively in the 1980s. Several short-lived underground magazines came and went, such as *Comic Baku* (1984–1987) and the "comic new wave" magazine *Comic Are!* (1994–1996).

The 1990s saw a growing nostalgia for classic manga, from a time before multimedia tie-ins and readers' polls drained the medium of its individuality. In his untranslated book *Manga Zombie,* Takeo Udagawa sang the praises of "outlaw manga," which could have been released only by major publishers in the wild atmosphere of the 1960s and 1970s. Comics were newly appreciated as kitsch, epitomized by playful magazines such as the annual *Comic Cue* ("ultra super deluxe pop comix for entertainment"). Many of the best-known underground artists of the 1990s, such as Usamaru Furuya and Junko

Mizuno, had "cute" styles and savvy business sense, quite unlike the outsider artists often associated with underground comics. Even artists such as Nekojiru, who committed suicide in 1998, and the reclusive Yoshiharu Tsuge saw their work adapted into anime and live-action TV series. In the early 1990s, the legendary *Garo* was bought out by a software company, and after accusations of "selling out" and a brief stint as an online magazine, it finally ceased publication in 2002.

Today, a few Japanese magazines print what could be called underground manga. *Ax,* founded in 1998 by disgruntled ex-*Garo* editors, is the closest to the old-school underground tradition. Ohta Shuppan's *Manga Erotics* and *Manga Erotics F* publish artsy sex comics. Enterbrain's *Comic Beam* ("magazine for the comic freaks"), originally a video game manga magazine, prints an eclectic mix of material and has a circulation so low that they have resorted to "going out of business" scare tactics and begging to keep readers buying. The most "underground" magazines from major publishers are Shogakukan's monthly *Ikki* and Kodansha's *Comic Faust,* which publishes sex comics, science fiction, and more personal stories drawn in unusual art styles. Magazines such as *Ikki* are not expected to make money so much as to keep the goodwill of talented artists such as Iou Kuroda and Taiyo Matsumoto, who may one day produce a surprise hit or end up applying their talents to more mainstream series.

Several Japanese underground comics have been translated into English. In the 1980s, the comic magazine *Raw* translated short works by several artists, including Yoshiharu Tsuge, Shigeru Sugiura, and King Terry. Michio Hisauchi's art manga *Japan's Junglest Day* (1985) was published in the Japanese prose fiction anthology *Monkey Brain Sushi* (1991). *Comics Underground Japan* (1996) is the single best introduction to traditional Japanese underground comics, while *Secret Comics Japan* (2000) reprints slightly newer, more mainstream material. More recently, several underground manga were reprinted in *The Comics Journal Special Edition 2005,* as well as Yoshiharu Tsuge's classic *Nejishiki* ("Screw Style") in *The Comics Journal* #250.

In 2001, after many years living in Japan and drawing comics for a Japanese audience (such as the autobiographical meta-romance *Yukiko's Spinach*), the expatriate French artist Frédéric Boilet announced the manifesto of a new artistic movement: *nouvelle manga* ("new manga"). Dissatisfied by the genre-oriented nature of his native Franco-Belgian comics (as well as most translated manga), and inspired by manga about normal people and relationships, Boilet called for Japanese and European artists to work together to produce lyrical and realistic works about everyday life. Japanese artists associated with the movement range from *Garo* alumni Kan Takahama and Kiriko Nananan to established mainstream artists such as Jiro Taniguchi. Published in English by the UK-based Fanfare/Ponent Mon, *nouvelle manga* is one of the latest forms of the avant-garde.

Underground Manga

Abandon the Old in Tokyo • *Awabi* • *Bakune Young* • *Black & White* • *Blue* • *Blue Spring* • *Comics Underground Japan* • *Disappearance Diary* • *Doing Time* • *Even a Monkey Can Draw Manga* • *Japan as Viewed by 17 Creators* • *Junko Mizuno's Cinderalla* • *Junko Mizuno's Hansel and Gretel* • *Junko Mizuno's Princess Mermaid* • *Mariko Parade* • *Monokuro Kinderbook* • *No. 5* • *A Patch of Dreams* • *Pure Trance* • *The Push Man and Other Stories* • *Sake Jock* • *Secret Comics Japan* • *Sexy Voice and Robo* • *Short Cuts* • *The Walking Man* a half-vampire, half-werewolf whose only power is to turn into a woman on the night of the full moon. Various supernatural exes and family members interfere, but the two develop a loving, not quite gay relationship. Written with a wink and played for laughs, the story is light but charming. Sanami Matoh's art is in her usual awkward but distinctive big-jawed style. ★★

URBAN MIRAGE

Genwaku no Matenrô, "Dazzling Skyscrapers" (幻惑の摩天楼) • Udo Shinohara • ComicsOne (e-book, 2000) • Asahi Sonorama (Monthly Halloween, 1986–1991) • 2 volumes, suspended (5 volumes in Japan) • Shôjo, Horror, Drama • 13+ (graphic violence)

A collection of New York City tales revolving around Curt, a mysterious man with an affinity for the supernatural, and his female friends. Although the three main characters never purposely seek out the supernatural, they always end up fighting eerie threats, including werewolves, hypnotic cults, and spirit possessions. While many of the underlying concepts are unoriginal, *Urban Mirage* succeeds by setting these horror scenes alongside the heroes' everyday lives and romances. Sad to say, the plots and resolutions are often predictable, such as the chapters describing Curt's relationship to his evil nemesis Kyen, complete with vacant *yaoi* undertones. But when it works, such as in the cool story about a spirit hiding under bridges in Central Park and scarfing down dogs and kids (à la Pennywise in Stephen King's *It*), *Urban Mirage* provides easy and satisfying thrills. (RS) ★★½

UZUMAKI

Uzumaki, "Whirlpool/Spiral" (うずまき) • Junji Ito • Viz (2001–2002) • Shogakukan (Big Comic Spirits, 1998–1999) • 3 volumes • Seinen, Horror • 18+ (mild language, graphic violence)

The coastal town of Kurôzu-cho is haunted by increasingly bizarre and graphic spiral-related phenomena, starting with a single man's obsession and growing into an apocalypse of snails, twisted bodies, Medusa-like hair, and finally something almost too strange to imagine. Starting out as a series of short stories (connected by the common presence of gloomy teenage lovers Shuichi and Kirie), in its third volume *Uzumaki* develops a stronger plot, revealing (intentionally) Lovecraftian depths behind a typical Junji Ito "is it supposed to be funny or scary?" premise. While there are gory moments, violence is not the focus. Although some of the individual chapters are better than others, as a whole it works remarkably well: an elegant, sometimes blackly humorous story of dreamlike logic and nihilism. ★★★½

VAGABOND

(バガボンド) • Takehiko Inoue • Viz (2001–ongoing) • Kodansha (Morning, 1998–ongoing) • 25+ volumes (ongoing) • Seinen, Samurai, Drama • 18+ (language, graphic violence, nudity, sex)

A manga adaptation of the epic novel *Musashi* by Eiji Yoshikawa, *Vagabond* is the rare manga that spans its characters' entire lives and works together as a single powerful narrative. It is the story of Takezô, the teenage boy who becomes the great historical swordsman Miyamoto Musashi. Reviled as a beast and a demon, full of rage, Takezô goes out into the world wanting to become "invincible under the sun" . . . but this is *not* a *shônen* manga, where victory is inevitable, and as he fights and flees, gathers scars and enemies, he faces death and struggles toward transcendence. Many other characters have huge roles, especially Otsû, the girl Takezô grew up with, and Takezô's childhood friend Matahachi, who also admires the "way of the sword" but perpetually stumbles from cowardice, lust, and other human weaknesses. In volume 14, the series undergoes a huge shift away from the novel and tells the life story of Musashi's legendary archrival, Sasaki Kojiro, before finally returning to the original characters many volumes later. Inoue's artwork, while somewhat processed-looking, is incredibly accomplished: the characters' faces are individualistic, the computer-toned backgrounds are crisp and pure, and the action flows smoothly. More than just flesh-splitting battle scenes and mandala-like sequences of spiritual introspection, *Vagabond* seems to contain the entire world and span the entire human condition.

★★★★

VAIZARD

Michihiro Yoshida • ADV (2004) • Mag Garden (Comic Blade, 2003–2004) • 1 volume, suspended (3 volumes in Japan) • Shônen, Fantasy, Adventure • 16+ (language, violence, sexual situations)

In a world littered with mysterious ancient ruins, Vaizards are the all-purpose heroes responsible for keeping long-lost magic technology safely in the crypt. Everything about *Vaizard* is borrowed from other manga or anime, from the fights to the earnest, goofy, power-blasting *shônen*-manga hero and the glasses-wearing girl archaeologist he follows around. The art is ugly. For a similar plot set in the real world, see *Striker*.

½

THE VAMPIRE DAHLIA

Dahlia the Vampire • Narumi Kakinouchi • Studio Ironcat (2001) • Akita Shoten (Susperia/Susperia Mystery, 1995–2004) • 6 issues, suspended (2 volumes in Japan) • Shôjo, Horror • Unrated/13+ (graphic violence, mild sexual situations)

Lia D. Green, aka Dahlia, is a teenage vampire who dwells in a dark mansion and is the subject of whispered rumors from her classmates. Unlike Kakinouchi's better-known *Vampire Princess Miyu*, Dahlia is a traditional blood-drinking vampire of dubious morality, who, when she's not seducing victims while wearing a skimpy black girdle, performs in the school play in the role of Salome. More focused on atmosphere than plot, it's adequate but hardly groundbreaking *shôjo* horror with expressionistic artwork.

★★

VAMPIRE DOLL GUILT NA ZAN

(バンパイアドール・ギルナザン) • Erika Kari • Tokyopop (2006–ongoing) • Ichijinsha (Comic Zero-Sum, 2004–ongoing) • 4+ volumes (ongoing) • Comedy • 13+ (mild sexual situations)

Brooding exorcist Kyoji releases the lord of all vampires, Guilt-na-Zan, from within a magical cross because he wants to use him as a maid. In order to serve his particular brand of depravity and limit the power of this lord of darkness, Kyoji places Zan's soul into a full-sized wax doll of a cute schoolgirl. The vampire's fearsome magic now summons stuffed animals instead of creatures of the night. When Kyoji's twin brother, Kyoichi, shows up to steal some cursed family heirlooms, the manga dissolves into a series of uninspired gags. Some of the cute ideas could have found a home in a more substantial title but fail on their own. (SM)

★

VAMPIRE GAME

Kyûketsu Yûgi (Vampire Game), "Vampire Game" (吸血遊戯[ヴァンパイア・ゲーム]) • JUDAL • Tokyopop (2003–2006) • Shinshokan (Wings, 1996–2004) • 15 volumes • Shôjo, Comedy, Fantasy, Drama • 13+ (language, infrequent violence, mild sexual situations)

The evil vampire king Duzell, slain a hundred years ago by the valiant St. Phelios, is reincarnated . . . in the form of a tiny, cute-looking kitten-creature. Still plotting revenge on Phelios, who has been reincarnated in the form of one of his descendants, the kitten becomes the pet of Princess Ishtar, a spoiled, tomboyish noble who soon discovers Duzell's secret. But rather than trying to fight Duzell, Ishtar is more than happy to help him kill off some of her annoying relatives, and the two become allies, traveling from place to place seeking the reincarnation of Phelios so Duzell can kill him or her. Similar in style to *Dragon Knights*, *Vampire Game* is a long fantasy soap opera for young adults, with comic relief in the form of anachronistically modern, silly dialogue ("No matter how vamped out you look, you'll still always be my cuddly-wuddly little Duzie to me!"). Where *Dragon Knights* involves grandiose RPG-style quests and monster fighting, however, *Vampire Game* involves courtly intrigue and romance, a more successful fit for the relationship-focused *shôjo* style and the plain, even drab, artwork. Assassination and treachery are on everyone's lips, but little violence actually occurs; the story is more comedic than dark, and the vampires in *Vampire Game* are more like magical beings than evil bloodsuckers. The story is divided into story arcs of two or three volumes, a rambling road to a satisfying climax. ★★½

VAMPIRE KNIGHT

Vampire Kishi, "Vampire Knight" (ヴァンパイア騎士) • Matsuri Hino • Viz (2007–ongoing) • Hakusensha (LaLa, 2005–ongoing) • 5+ volumes (ongoing) • Shôjo, Vampire, Romance • Not Rated Yet (violence)

Yuki, a girl who was once saved from a vampire when she was young, now attends the elite Cross Academy, a boarding school where the "day class" of humans coexists uneasily with the "night class" of alluring, but not necessarily evil, vampires. Yuki and her partner, Zero, are the "guardians" in charge of maintaining the separation of the two worlds and the fragile truce between them . . . but will human prejudice and vampire hunger cause everything to end in a tragedy of blood and angst? A sinister gothic romance with dark secrets, guns, and fangs aplenty, *Vampire Knight* shows Matsuri Hino's affinity for baroque European settings. NR

VAMPIRE PRINCESS MIYU

Kyûketsuki Miyû (Vampire Miyu), "Vampire Princess Miyu" (吸血姫美夕(ヴァンパイアミユ)) • Narumi Kakinouchi (story and art), Toshiki Hirano (co-creator) • Studio Ironcat (2001–2004) • Akita Shoten (Susperia, 1988–2002) • 5 volumes, suspended (10 volumes in Japan) • Shôjo, Horror, Fantasy • Unrated/13+ (brief mild language, violence, brief sex)

A ghostly figure in her white kimono and red sash, Miyu—an ageless vampire girl—lives to banish *shinma* (god-demons), monsters who sometimes cause trouble in the human world. Her companion on her eternal duty (and presumably her lover) is Larva, an immortal *bishônen* who watches over her and conceals his beauty beneath robes and a mask. Originating as a nearly simultaneous manga and OAV series (the TV series came later), *Vampire Princess Miyu* was a *shôjo* horror hit of the late 1980s and the first of zillions of vampire manga by Kakinouchi. The manga is less polished than the anime; Kakinouchi's moody, expressionistic artwork, full of deep pools of blackness, frequently crosses the border between minimalism and hastiness. Faces are generic, linework is sparse, and the backgrounds consist of a few twisted branches and dreamscapes of crystal and mist. As Miyu defeats one dull supernatural being after another (in mediocre fight scenes), she intrudes in the tragic lives of human boys and girls, who sometimes survive the story and sometimes die at the hands of either the creatures or Miyu herself, who gladly tempts them with the "beautiful dream" of death. Alternately merciful and cold, human and inhuman, Miyu is a memorable protagonist, and some of the stories are interesting. The publication history is complicated; Kakinouchi drew the first volume in 1988–1989, took a break to draw *New Vampire Miyu* (which takes place between volumes 1 and 2 of *Vampire Princess Miyu*), and later returned to *Vampire Princess Miyu* in 1997. Prior to the Studio Ironcat release, 6 issues were published in monthly comic book format by Antarctic Press in the early 1990s. ★★

VAMPIRE YUI

Kyûketsuki Yui (Vampire Yui), "Vampire Princess Yui" (吸血姫夕維(ヴァンパイアゆい)) • Narumi Kakinouchi (story and art) • Studio Ironcat (2000–2003) • Akita Shoten (Susperia, 1989–1995) • 4 volumes, suspended (5 volumes in Japan) • Shôjo, Horror, Fantasy • Unrated/13+ (brief language, violence)

A spin-off of *Vampire Princess Miyu*, Yui reads like an attempt to re-create the *Miyu* mythos with a more human, sympathetic protagonist. Yui is a slightly ditzy girl who lives with her grandmother, blissfully unaware that she is the half-vampire heir of the *shi*, supernatural spirit creatures who dwell beneath a bloodred lake shrouded in cherry blossoms. When her powers come to life, she flees with her companion Nagi, a slightly older supernatural boy, and they wander from place to place and school to school, encountering victims of monsters, spirits, and ghostly possession (all of which are treated as pretty much the same thing). On the way, Yui searches for Miyu, the vampire who was instrumental in her making. The story sounds better in summary than it reads; it alternates confusingly between dreamy, atmospheric sequences, vampire melancholy ("You and I are monsters!"), and unexciting fight scenes with vaguely explained supernatural characters. There is no real ending, and the art is mediocre. Volume 5 was published in monthly comics format but never collected. An untranslated sequel ran from 2002 to 2005 in *Susperia Mystery*. ★½

VARIANTE

(ヴァリアンテ) • Igura Sugimoto • CMX (2007–ongoing) • Kadokawa Shoten (Dragon Age, 2004–2006) • 4 volumes • Shônen, Action, Horror • 18+ (graphic violence)

Aiko, a fifteen-year-old girl, is left for dead after horrible shapeless creatures kill her parents. But in the morgue she comes to life, shivering and afraid, her injured arm miraculously healed. And that's only the beginning of the changes taking place in her body.... Gruesome action bio-horror. NR

VENGER ROBO

Getter Robo Gô (ゲッターロボ號) • Go Nagai (original concept), Ken Ishikawa & Dynamic Production (story and art) • Viz (1993–1994) • Tokuma Shoten (Monthly Shônen Captain, 1991–1993) • 7 issues, suspended (7 volumes in Japan) • Shônen, Mecha, Action • Unrated/13+ (language, violence)

The Dinosaur Empire, a race of underground-dwelling humanoid lizards, decide one day that they'd like to live on the surface of the Earth again. The cities of the world are soon threatened by their giant machine-monsters. To combat this threat, Professor Saotome creates three giant robots that merge into one big robot, and finds a trio of wild young men to pilot this mechanical marvel. Originally created by Go Nagai and his main assistant, Ken Ishikawa, in 1974, *Getter Robo*

introduced the revolutionary concept of the combining-transforming robot, which set the precedent for everything from Voltron to the Transformers. Nagai and Ishikawa devoted themselves to cranking out *Getter Robo* sequels and spin-offs, such as 1991's *Venger Robo,* originally published in Japan as *Getter Robo Gô. Venger Robo* boasts a redesigned Getter Robo along with a new cast of pilots. Ishikawa's art is several shades slicker than the 1970s original, but the action remains very much the same. It's basically nonstop brawling paired with ridiculous dialogue like "All you need is love to pilot Venger Robo!" as buildings crumble and hundreds die. Sure, this is junk of the lowest order, but anyone with a sweet tooth for anarchic robot action and senseless violence will be handsomely rewarded. Several story points, characters, and designs were later recycled for the 1998 anime series *Getter Robo: Armageddon.* (PM) ★★★½

VENUS VERSUS VIRUS

Atsushi Suzumi • Seven Seas Entertainment (2007–ongoing) • MediaWorks (Dengeki Gao!, 2005–ongoing) • 3+ volumes (ongoing) • Shônen, Gothic, Horror, Fantasy • 16+

High-schooler Sumire Takahana has the special ability—or curse—to see malevolent beings known as Viruses. When she meets Lucia, a mysterious Gothic Lolita monster-killer for hire, the two of them team up to hunt down the evil Viruses who prey on innocent victims. NR

THE VENUS WARS

Venus Senki, "Venus War Record" (ヴイナス戦記) • Yoshikazu Yasuhiko (story and art) • Dark Horse (1991–1993) • Gakken (Comic Nora, 1987–1990) • 1 volume (4 volumes in Japan) • Science Fiction, Action, Drama • Unrated/16+ (mild language, nudity, sex, violence)

In 2003, a chance collision with a stray asteroid transforms Venus into a habitable planet, but within three generations, the new human population of Venus has moved from terraforming to war. Writer/artist Yasuhiko shows both sides of a brutal conflict between the neighboring city-states of Ishtar and Aphrodia, first with Ken Seno (original Japanese name: Hiro Seno), punk recruit to the Ishtar army's new motorcyle attack unit, and then Matthew Radom, an elite Aphrodian officer who becomes a pawn in a larger shell game of backstabbing politics, murder, and dangerous sexual relationships. Yasuhiko's skill in depicting everything from drama to comedy to breakneck action is at its height in this series: the combat sequences between massive tanks and agile battle bikes are genuinely pulse-pounding, as is the *Rollerball*-like battle bike stadium game played by Ken and his friends. Miranda, a Bodicea homage whose chariot-style motorbike has protruding blades on its wheels, is only one of a refreshing variety of spunky women in the story, and Rado, the oily social climber who is the main villain of the second part of the story, is a memorable creation. Unfortunately, only the first seven issues of Dark Horse's translation have been collected in graphic novel form, although 29 issues were published in total. The anime, also written and directed by Yasuhiko, departs significantly from the manga. (JD) ★★★★

VENUS WARS II: See *The Venus Wars*

VERSION

Hisashi Sakaguchi • Dark Horse (1992–1994) • Ushio Shuppansha (Comic Tom, 1989–1992) • 15 issues, suspended (3 volumes in Japan) • Science Fiction, Drama • Unrated/16+ (violence, nudity)

Unfinished (in the English edition) adventure tale about a computer chip that may have evolved into a new form of life. A Japanese detective is hired to find the chip's scientist creator, and the search takes him around the world with the scientist's daughter and her pet orangutan, encountering pirates, a sinister organization called the Order of Religio, and possibly the sentient chip itself in the form of a mermaid along the way. Some fascinating ruminations on the future of computers and biotech, and writer/artist

Sakaguchi's history as an animator shows in his accomplished art (he worked at Osamu Tezuka's Mushi Productions on *Astro Boy*, *Kimba the White Lion*, and *Princess Knight*, among others): his linework is refreshingly clean and decisive, with a preference for stark black and white, and his talent for caricature and fondness for unusual character types keeps the complicated story afloat. Unfortunately, the developing mystery is never resolved in Dark Horse's English release, nor have the available issues been collected. (JD) ★★

VERSUS: See *VS*.

VIDEO GIRL AI

Denei Shôjo (Video Girl), "Video Girl" (電英少女 [ビデオガルー]) • Masakazu Katsura • Viz (1998–2006) • Shueisha (Weekly Shônen Jump, 1989–1992) • 15 volumes • Shônen, Romance • 16+ (brief violence, nudity, frequent sexual situations)

After discovering that the girl he likes has a crush on his best friend, depressed teenage loser (and aspiring artist) Yota stumbles into a mysterious video store, where he rents a video with a cute girl on the cover. When he plays it, out of his TV emerges Video Girl Ai, a boyish girl on a mission to "cheer him up" and help him get a girlfriend. But due to a defect, Ai can feel human emotions, and so she falls in love with him herself, even though her "running time" is only a few weeks. *Video Girl Ai* distinguishes itself from the countless other *I Dream of Jeannie*–style wish-fulfillment manga by its dead seriousness (except for some comedy in the first volume): no other boys' manga so captures the angst, obsession, and turgid emotions of adolescence. At the same time, it's also incredibly pandering, with lavish, photorealistic close-ups of girls' butts, obviously the artist's favorite part of the anatomy. This combination of sensitive internal monologues and masturbation material ensured the series' popularity, making it basically a manga version of the how-to-date-girls books Yota is made fun of for reading. The cast of characters is tight, almost claustro-

VIDEO GAMES

Video games are Japan's only cultural export to surpass manga in influence and raw sales. While Japanese PC games have never succeeded in the American market, Japanese console games, handheld games, and arcade games dominate their Western competition. With the rise of Japanese video game companies such as Nintendo and Sega in the 1980s, followed in the 1990s by SNK's NeoGeo, NEC's TurboGrafx-16 (known in Japan as the PC Engine), and the Sony PlayStation, American gamers were increasingly exposed to manga-influenced themes and artwork.

Many of the most popular genres of video games were developed in Japan. Fighting games, such as Capcom's Street Fighter series, dominated arcades in the 1990s. When the fighting game fad ended, music and rhythm games such as Dance Dance Revolution and Beatmania helped revitalize the arcades, which were hurt by ever-growing competition from increasingly sophisticated home console games. Role-playing games (see the article on RPGs) were invented in America but developed along new lines in Japan, where the Final Fantasy and Dragon Quest series became bestsellers. Preferring story over action, Japanese fans were more receptive to simple multiple-choice adventure games, including "visual novels" such as *Lunar Legend Tsukihime* (2003), a genre considered too old-fashioned for American audiences.

A related genre is dating simulation games, also known as *bishôjo* ("beautiful girl") games or *galge* (girl games). In the typical *galge,* an unseen male protagonist talks to various girls (by choosing from various menu options) and, in the event of a happy ending, goes out with one of them. *Comic Party* (2001), *To Heart* (1997), *Sakura Taisen* (2002), and *Happy Lesson: Mama Teacher Is Wonderful!* (2003) are translated manga based on dating sims. Several Japanese magazines, such as *Comptiq* and its companion manga magazine *Comp Ace,* are devoted to these games, and pornographic versions enjoy a strong following. In so-called *naki games* (crying games), the focus is not on sex but melodrama: weepy stories involving girls who are blind or otherwise disabled. Dating sims for female players exist as well; La Corda d'Oro (2004), one of many, places its heroine in a music academy full of hot guys.

Since 1986, when Dragon Quest was popularized by articles in *Weekly Shônen Jump* magazine, Japanese manga publishers have embraced video games' "media mix" potential. Game tie-ins most often appear in *shônen* magazines for younger readers, such as *Corocoro Comic, Comic Bombom,* and *V-Jump, Shônen Jump*'s video game supplement. Shinseisha, publisher of the arcade game fan magazine *Gamest* and its companion *Comic Gamest,* published numerous video game manga before going bankrupt in 1999 along with the decline of the arcade market. (Masahiko Nakahira's *Street Fighter Alpha* and *Street Fighter III Ryu Final,* perhaps the best manga ever based on a fighting game, were published in *Gamest* magazine.) Square Enix, the video game publisher, also runs a successful manga line. The *dôjinshi* market overflows with game-based comics and fanzines; Mami Itoh (*Pilgrim Jäger*) got his start doing Capcom *dôjinshi.*

In America, Japanese console and arcade games played, and still play, a major role in popularizing manga and anime. In some cases, games based on manga were released in the United States before the manga itself, as in the case of the Nintendo games *Dragon Power* (1987; based on *Dragon Ball*) and *Golgo 13: Top Secret Episode*

(1988). Japanese games didn't familiarize Americans with specific manga so much as with the conventions of manga: the character designs, the occasionally risqué humor, even such simple things as the manga habit of filling a word balloon with ". . ." to indicate silence. American manga publishers tried to exploit this connection, such as with Viz's 1996 magazine *Game On! USA,* a short-lived anthology of fighting game manga. The American magazine *Nintendo Power* has run several colorized manga serials, including *Pokémon Mystery Dungeon, Super Mario Adventures, The Legend of Zelda: A Link to the Past, StarFox,* and *Super Metroid* (the latter two were never reprinted in graphic novel form). But Nintendo's biggest impact on the manga scene came in 1999, when the tremendous success of Pokémon introduced millions of American children to speed-lines, "big sweat drop behind the head," and other anime and manga conventions. From that point on, there was no turning back.

Many manga artists have worked in video game character design, including Tsukasa Kotobuki (Battle Arena Toshinden), Akira Toriyama (Dragon Quest, Blue Dragon, Tobal No.1), Kosuke Fujishima (Tales of Phantasia), Range Murata, Kenichi Sonoda, Yasuhiro Nightow (Gungrave), and Masamune Shirow. The illustrator Yoshitaka Amano is known primarily for his work on the Final Fantasy RPGs. And of course, like their Western comic artist counterparts, manga artists (at least those beneath a certain age) often tell stories of deadlines nearly missed because of video game playing.

Fighting Game Manga
Night Warriors: Darkstalkers' Revenge • Street Fighter II • Street Fighter II: The Animated Movie: Official Comic Adaptation • Street Fighter III Ryu Final • Street Fighter Alpha • Street Fighter Sakura Ganbaru! • Super Street Fighter II: Cammy

Dating Simulation Manga
Comic Party (CPM) • Comic Party (Tokyopop) • La Corda d'Oro • Gakuen Heaven (yaoi) • Galaxy Angel • Galaxy Angel II • Galaxy Angel Beta • Galaxy Angel Party • Happy Lesson: Mama Teacher Is Wonderful! • Sakura Taisen • To Heart

Other Game Manga
Culdcept • Devil May Cry 3 • Gunparade March • Gunparade March: A New Marching Song • Ichigeki Sacchu Hoihoi-san • Legendz • Lunar Legend Tsukihime • MegaMan NT Warrior • Mobile Suit Gundam: Blue Destiny • Mobile Suit Gundam: Lost War Chronicles • Onimusha: Night of Genesis • Super Mario Adventures

Video Game–Themed Manga
Gacha Gacha • Gacha Gacha: The Next Revolution • Popo Can • Tower of the Future

phobic, and apart from a dumb subplot involving an evil Video Girl with superpowers, the series always stays focused on their relationships. In short, it's some kind of shameless masterpiece. Volumes 14 and 15 are a separate story, "Video Girl Len," in which Yota plays only a minor role.   ★★★½

VIRTUAL BANG!

Ippongi Bang • Studio Ironcat (1998) • 5 issues • Otaku, Action, Romance, Comedy • Unrated/13+ (language, violence, sexual situations)

Spunky, fannish, silly short stories by 1980s cult *otaku* artist Ippongi Bang. (Probably the most memorable character is "Bangji Go," a bad-girl high school manga artist who's part angel and part werewolf.) The action is sometimes confusing and pointless, but die-hard Bang fans will enjoy the supplement, "Ipponji Bang's Campus Diary," which runs in issues 2–4. These charmingly goofy auto-biographical comics, drawn for *Fanroad* magazine in 1983, show Bang's life in agri-cultural college. ★★

THE VISION OF ESCAFLOWNE

Tenkû no Escaflowne, "Escaflowne of the Sky" (天空のエスカフローネ) • Hajime Yatate and Shoji Kawamori (original concept), Katsu Aki (manga) • Tokyopop (2003–2004) • Kadokawa Shoten (Monthly Shônen Ace, 1994–1998) • 8 volumes • Fantasy, Mecha, Adventure • 16+ (language, violence, nudity)

The 1996 anime series *Vision of Escaflowne* began with the boilerplate premise of a teen-age schoolgirl transported to a mystical world where handsome knights battle evil empires with sword-swinging giant robots, and then took it into wholly unexpected and original territory. As for Aki's manga adaptation . . . well, not so much. Because the manga serial began before the anime actually aired, based on early versions of the characters and plot, perhaps this is what *Escaflowne* could have been had it stayed strictly within genre boundaries. On its own terms it's actually pretty decent, with an adorably foul-mouthed and ill-tempered take on hero Van Fanel and an entertaining rogues' gallery of guest villains. Aki's anat-omy is shaky and his costume designs some-what eccentric—one imagines that the downward-pointing spikes attached to one gal's bustier would make it hazardous for her to cross her arms—but he tells his story with cheesy gusto and does a splendid job with the battling robots and the polluted in-dustrial landscape of the sinister Zaibach Empire. Just don't expect it to be anything like the anime. (MS) ★★½

THE VOICES OF A DISTANT STAR: HOSHI NO KOE

Hoshi no Koe, "Voices of a Star" (ほしのこえ) • Mizu Sahara • Tokyopop (2006) • Kodansha (Afternoon, 2005) • 1 volume • Science Fiction, Romance • 13+

The anime *Voices of a Distant Star* by Makoto Shinkai was a classic the moment it was completed in 2002. A romance of rare hon-esty, depth, and beauty, it tells of young as-tronaut Mikako and her attempt to remain connected to her Earth-bound male friend Noboru despite the tremendous distance between them. Mikako is sent on an explo-ration mission while Noboru remains an-chored to the Earth. Their only form of communication is a low-priority text mes-sage that travels at the speed of light, an ago-nizingly slow pace as Noboru and Mikako drift light-years apart. The literal distance between them serves as allegory for the emotional distance, but the unrelenting re-alism of the characterizations and the deftly chosen words are what make the greatest impact on the reader. The artwork is inten-tionally understated and graceful, with par-ticular respect given to the memories of the characters' time together. Few manga ever achieve such grace. (SM) ★★★½

VOYEUR

Nozokiya, "Voyeur Business" (のぞき屋) • Hideo Yamamoto • Viz (1997–1999) • Shogakukan (Young Sunday, 1992–1993) • 1 volume • Seinen, Psycho-logical, Crime, Thriller • Unrated/18+ (language, violence, nudity, graphic sex)

Suspicious that his girlfriend is cheating on him, Ko (an outwardly nice guy full of re-pressed rage) makes a dark partnership with a creepy voyeur wearing night-vision gog-gles. Yamamoto's artwork is incredibly rough, but his storytelling is good, and de-spite some clichéd "meditations on trust in the modern age," the manga has a tense Hitchcockian quality. The last eighty pages of the manga are a less effective sequel, in-volving a surveillance business hired to pro-tect a woman from a stalker (apparently as a dry run for *Voyeurs, Inc.*, although none of the same characters reappear). ★★½

VOYEURS, INC.

Shin Nozokiya, "New Voyeur Business" (新・のぞき屋) • Hideo Yamamoto • Viz (1999–2001) • Shogakukan (Young Sunday, 1994–1997) • 3 volumes, suspended (11 in Japan) • Seinen, Crime, Thriller • Unrated/18+ (language, crude humor, violence, nudity, graphic sex)

On the sordid streets of Tokyo, a team of surveillance experts—loudmouthed braggart Ken, horndog sidekick Smile, and all-business straight man Cho—hire out their investigative skills in sleazy cases of harassment and infidelity. A thematic sequel to *Voyeur, Voyeurs Inc.* keeps the dirty sex and barren urban setting but replaces the former's psychology with slapstick humor and boner jokes. Yamamoto's world is an ugly one, and he excels at depicting pathetic behavior and slimy, degrading evil. But *Voyeurs, Inc.,* is the Sistine Chapel compared to his untranslated manga *Koroshiya Ichi* ("Ichi the Killer"), whose live-action movie and anime versions are available in the United States. On the other hand, his attempts at drawing cute characters fail badly. The resulting mood of "Scooby-Doo meets schoolgirl prostitution meets cockroach porn" is purely for trash-culture lovers. Viz published only an early portion of the series. ★★

VS

Versus (VSバーサス) • Keiko Yamada • CMX (2006–2007) • Akita Shoten (Princess, 1999–2001) • 7 volumes • Shôjo, Music, Drama • 13+ (brief violence, brief nudity)

Reiji is a talented but arrogant prodigy at a Japanese music academy, driven by his desire to save his little sister from their alcoholic, abusive father. Trying to turn Reiji into a better violinist and a better person, the old maestro calls in twenty-eight-year-old Mitsuko, a loud, outspoken former female violinist who becomes Reiji's personal trainer. After many passionate arguments, Reiji and Mitsuko come to terms and work together in the world of classical music, a world of surprisingly intense rivalry. Enjoyably melodramatic in its best moments, *VS* is basically a character story of personal dramas, illustrated in a hyperactive style where attractive *shôjo* characters make melodramatic declarations surrounded by speedlines. ★★

THE WALKING MAN

Aruku Hito, "The Walking Man" (歩く人) • Jiro Taniguchi • Fanfare/Ponent Mon (2004) • Kodansha (Morning Special, 1990–1992) • 1 volume • Underground • Unrated/13+ (brief nudity)

This fascinating, mostly wordless art-manga has no plot in the conventional sense; instead, it follows an unnamed, middle-aged businessman on his pleasant walks through his neighborhood in Japan. Usually alone, occasionally accompanied by his dog or his wife, he walks through narrow streets and grassy lots, construction sites, and tree-lined paths, drawn with crisper detail than any photograph and a keen eye for the beauty of the suburban areas in which most of us live. The incidents on his walks reinforce the contemplative mood and a love of nature wherever you find it: climbing a tree, finding an unusual shell, catching glimpses of birds and animal life. Through dawn and dusk, snow and rain and hot summer days, Taniguchi creates a perfect microcosm of a peaceful world, which will make you want to put down the book and go outside (after you're done reading, that is). It's a successful artistic experiment, a glimpse of everyday life, and a rare example of manga as therapy (and manga as virtual reality). The book contains nothing objectionable, except for two very brief sequences in which the walking man is fully naked, in a swimming pool and in a bath. ★★★★

THE WALLFLOWER

Yamatonadeshiko Shichihenge, "The Transformation into the Ideal Japanese Woman" (ヤマトナデシコ七変化) • Tomoko Hayakawa • Del Rey (2005–ongoing) • Kodansha (Bessatsu Friend, 2000–ongoing) • 18+ volumes (ongoing) • Shôjo, Comedy

The gothic heroine and her beautiful boys: Tomoko Hayakawa's *The Wallflower*

• 16+ (mild language, violence, mild sexual situations)

Four hot guys + one homicidal/suicidal goth girl = comedy! Four upbeat teenage guys (who serve mostly as eye candy for the readers) are promised free rent in a mansion if they can turn their wealthy landlady's teenage niece into a "lady." But Sunako is more than a wallflower; she's "like a horror movie come to life," a slasher-movie-obsessed girl with sunken eyes and long black hair (like the ghost in *The Ring*) who's most happy when she's sitting in the dark talking to her collection of skeletons and anatomical models. *The Wallflower* is a *shôjo* sitcom inspired by things such as *The Nightmare Before Christmas, The Addams Family,* and Japanese visual rock bands. In true sitcom fashion, the characters' traits become only more exaggerated as the series goes on, and rather than Sunako becoming more "ladylike," she gets weirder and weirder. Surrounded by horror movies and

her unofficial harem, able to transform at will from a shy, childlike *chibi* form to an evilly beautiful woman who kicks ass with knives and chain saws—what more could a goth girl ask for? In short, it's a good gimmick supported by one very funny character. Unlike most manga artists, Hayakawa openly acknowledges that the less important characters are drawn by assistants, although the abrupt style changes make it obvious anyway. ★★★

THE WANDERER

Narumi Kakinouchi • Studio Ironcat (2003–2004) • Akita Shoten (Susperia, 1996–1997) • 2 volumes, suspended (3 volumes in Japan) • Shôjo, Occult • Unrated/13+ (mild language, violence)

Yet another spin-off of Kakinouchi's vampire mythos, *The Wanderer* stars Sei Kodô, a modern teenage boy vampire, who roams the Earth in search of his mistress Yui (from *Vampire Princess Yui*). In each story he encounters a different group of teenagers in a different supernatural situation (such as a young rival vampire lording it over a boys' school from within a moody pseudo-European castle). The better stories combine action with a decadent *bishônen* sensibility. The English rewrite makes the questionable but occasionally hilarious decision to render the hero's Kansai accent as a Texas drawl ("Ah dunno, hoss . . . been three days and we ain't seen hide nor hair of Osanai"). ★½

WARREN BUFFETT: AN ILLUSTRATED BIOGRAPHY OF THE WORLD'S MOST SUCCESSFUL INVESTOR

Manga Warren Buffett: Sekai Ichi Omoshiroi Tôshika no Sekai Ichi Môkaru Seikô no Rule, "Manga Warren Buffett: The World's Greatest Rules for Success in Making Money from the World's Most Interesting Investor" (マンガウォーレン・バフェット〜世界一おもしろい投資家の世界一もうかる成功のルール) • Ayano Morio • John Wiley & Sons (2004) • Pan Rolling (2003) • 1 volume • Biography • All Ages

A no-nonsense manga biography of billionaire investor and philanthropist Warren Buffett. Aimed at executives, the manga focuses on Buffett's theories of investing, interspersing stories of his greatest professional successes and failures with "Buffett's Rules for Success." But it's also an engaging portrait of a brainy idealist driven by passion for his chosen career. Morio's art is crude but charming; it's hard not to crack a smile at a panel of the young Buffett flipping out when first looking into Benjamin Graham's *The Intelligent Investor,* speedlines and sweat drops flying from his head. The English edition, published by a nonfiction book publisher as part of its line of investment advice books, features some weak lettering and touchup. Overall, however, this is a disarmingly engaging read. (SG) ★★★

WARRIOR NUN AREALA: THE MANGA

Run Ishida • Antarctic (2000) • Dôjinshi • Superhero, Action • 1 issue • 13+ (mild violence, thongs)

Translated *dôjinshi* based on Ben Dunn's *Warrior Nun Areala* superhero comics, starring scantily clad nuns who fight evil. The heroine this time is a Japanese warrior nun, Sakura, who fights a demoness at a Catholic girls' school. ★

WARRIORS OF TAO

To-Ma: A Fool over the Lonely Planet • Shinya Kuwahara • Tokyopop (2004–2005) • Kodansha (Young Magazine Uppers, 2001–2002) • 4 volumes • Seinen, Science Fiction, Horror, Battle • 18+ (language, extreme graphic violence, nudity, sex)

Extraterrestrial races plan to hold an intergalactic fighting tournament to decide which species will live and which will be eaten alive by monsters. Toma Suguri is one of the humans chosen to represent Earth; the battle will take place in Tao, a dimension of fighters, and the weapon of choice will be "codon," biomechanical attachments that allow the wielder to morph their flesh. Starting out as if it might be a seminormal fighting manga, *Warriors of Tao* quickly becomes *really* disgusting, with human bodies mutating into hideous bug-eyed cannibal blobs and ripping one another to pieces. The manga ends abruptly; the characters never even make it to the intergalactic tournament, or even meet any aliens, because the Earth team spends the entire story fighting with one another. (Apparently teamwork isn't our strong suit.) Weepy subplots amid the gore drag the rating even lower, although like *Arm of Kannon,* it's a worthy read for anyone who likes a good gross-out. ★½

WEATHER WOMAN

Otenki Oneesan, "Weather Woman" (お天気お姉さん) • Tetsu Adachi • CPM (2000) • Kodansha (Young Magazine, 1992–1994) • 1 volume, suspended (8 volumes in Japan) • Seinen, Comedy, Drama • Unrated/18+ (language, crude humor, nudity, sex)

A cold *seinen* satire of vicious and pathetic personalities, better known in America for the live-action movie adaptation. Minoru, an ugly young man with no job prospects, discovers one day that his high school crush—Keiko Nakadai—has become a popular TV weather woman by wearing tight outfits and lifting her skirt on the air. Getting a job at the studio, he becomes a bit player in the schemes of Keiko and her hypocritical female rival. The art is limber and grotesque, with quiet, gloomy scenes of city life, and some of the writing is memorable, such as Minoru's opening lines ("Don't any of you talk to me about looks . . . don't any of you talk to me about beautiful things!"). From there, it works its way to vibrators, laxatives, and explicit dominance-submission. Like *Voyeurs, Inc.,* but more depressing, it's filthy, dirty exploitation with a light wrapping of cynical sociological commentary . . . but for what it is, it's well done. ★★½

WEDDING PEACH

Ai Tenshi Densetsu Wedding Peach, "Love Angel Legend Wedding Peach" (愛天使伝説ウエディングピーチ) • Nao Yazawa (story and art), Sukehiro Tomita (original creator) • Viz (2003–2004) • Shogakukan (Ciao, 1994–1996) • 6 volumes • Shôjo, Magical Girl • 13+ (partial nudity)

Through the power of the goddess Aphrodite and the angels of heaven (the cosmology is a little confused), pubescent Momoko becomes the bridal-gowned superheroine Wedding Peach. Her friends become Angel

Lily and Angel Daisy, suited up as bridesmaids. *Wedding Peach* isn't remotely shy about being a calculated *Sailor Moon* doppelgänger and the core of a marketing blitzkrieg; in Japan, the manga was quickly followed by an anime, a video game, and a flood of tie-in merchandise. It's by-the-numbers magical girl material: Momoko is the standard dim-witted, klutzy heroine, and the story is one of those logic-skirting convenience plots where everything happens on school grounds and every major character turns out to have a backstory that plugs into the central conflict. The story builds up some steam in the later volumes but ends abruptly, with a truncated final battle and many apologetic notes from the author about running out of space. The wedding theme is bizarre, even setting aside the basic creepiness of preteens in bridal paraphernalia. The otherwise solid Viz translation features strange sound effects, such as "POLTER!" (a ceiling crumbling), "FUNKEL" (a glare), and "VERZWEI-FLUNG!" (a preteen boy burning in demonic flame). (CT) ★½

WEDDING PEACH: YOUNG LOVE

Ai Tenshi Densetsu Wedding Peach, "Love Angel Legend Wedding Peach" (愛天使伝説ウエディングピーチ) • Nao Yazawa (story and art), Sukehiro Tomita (original creator) • Viz (2004) • Shogakukan (Shogaku Sannensei, 1994–1996) • 1 volume • Shôjo, Magical Girl • 13+ (partial nudity)

Thought *Wedding Peach* was as dumbed down as a manga could get? Think again. This series, which ran at the same time as *Wedding Peach* in a magazine for younger readers, is the same licensable concept rewritten for a third-grade audience. The story lines are shorter and more episodic, the convoluted premise is streamlined, and some details are changed to bring the manga in line with the anime. The result is a more coherent but even blander product. The later chapters introduce major characters and plot points without explanation, the assumption being that the reader has already seen the anime. *Wedding Peach: Young Love* was never printed as a graphic novel in Japan; the sto-

ries were collected only in German and English. (CT) ★

WELCOME TO LODOSS ISLAND

Yôkoso Lodoss Tô he!, "Welcome to Lodoss Island!" (ようこそロードス島へ!) • Ryo Mizuno (story), Rei Hyakuyashiki (art) • CPM (2003) • Kadokawa Shoten (Monthly Shônen Ace, 1996–1999) • 2 volumes, suspended (3 volumes in Japan) • Four-Panel, Fantasy, Comedy • 13+ (partial nudity, mild sexual humor)

Super-deformed gag comics based on *Record of Lodoss War: The Grey Witch* and Ryo Mizuno's untranslated and never-animated novel *Record of Lodoss War: The Demon of Flame.* The first volume is mostly four-panel gag strips aimed at elementary school students, but the second volume (based on *The Demon of Flame*) turns into a comedic story manga, aimed at junior-high- or high-school-age readers of the novel. The art is ungainly, and the unfunny jokes often depend on dutifully footnoted Japanese puns. ★

WELCOME TO THE NHK

NHK ni Yôkoso!, "Welcome to the NHK!" (NHKにようこそ!) • Tatsuhiko Takimoto (story), Kendi Oiwa (art) • Tokyopop (2006–ongoing) • Kadokawa Shoten (Monthly Shônen Ace, 2004–ongoing) • 6+ volumes (ongoing) • Otaku, Comedy • 18+ (language, nudity, sexual situations, adult themes)

Manga about *otaku* culture are nothing new, but seldom has nerdiness been as savagely eviscerated as in this manga, a gonzo satire based on a light novel by Takimoto. *Welcome to the NHK* explores the sub-subculture of *hikikomori,* young people so withdrawn from mainstream society that they become total recluses. The protagonist, Satou, is an unemployed dropout holed up in a filthy apartment, where hallucinations brought on by cabin fever and mail-order drugs convince him that the Japanese broadcasting network NHK is engaged in a secret conspiracy to turn all Japanese citizens into *hikikomori* like himself. Satou has two contacts with the outside world: his neighbor Yamazaki, a porn addict ("This is my greatest desire! A sexy maid-robot! What are you waiting for, Sony?! Honda?!") who drags him ever deeper into *otaku* circles, and Misaki, a girl who uses Satou as a guinea pig in her ongoing experiments on *hikikomori*. This is not the cute, presentable portrayal of *otaku* seen in manga such as *Genshiken* or *Comic Party*. Instead, *Welcome to the NHK* Dumpster-dives into the darkest corners of the culture, exploring pornographic video games, maid cafés, online suicide pacts, pedophilia (Satou glimpses some nude pinups of teenage girls and slippery-slopes all the way down to hiding outside a kindergarten with a telephoto lens), and the general depravity and pathos of the extreme *otaku* lifestyle. It's ugly, cynical, dirty-minded, and hilarious. Oiwa has a clean, appealing art style but nonetheless delights in making Satou look absolutely wretched and disgusting. (SG) ★★★½

WHAT'S MICHAEL?

(ホワッツマイケル?) • Makoto Kobayashi • Dark Horse (1997–2006) • Kodansha (Morning, 1984–1995) • 11 volumes, suspended (9 longer volumes in Japan) • Pet, Comedy • All Ages

Michael, the archetypal cat, appears in various roles in these collections of humor strips, each about six pages long. In some, the cats are anthropomorphized (as in a parody of Michael Jackson's "Bad" video, or the "Planet of the Cats" story line), but in most of them, they're just pets, and the joke depends on their reliably catlike behavior and the reactions of the humans around him. The innovation of *What's Michael?* (although some cat fanatics may frown) is depicting cats not as secretly intelligent, cooler-than-thou houseguests, but as animals—lovable animals, but just animals—with curious, often predictable behavior. As a result, readers may find themselves wondering if cats really hate tangerines, and if it's really possible to grab a cat's tongue by coating your thumb with butter. Kobayashi's big-mouthed, big-jawed, goofy artwork is perfectly suited for these exaggerated, gentle, but not immature comedies; his cats are cute but not "anime-style." The Dark Horse edition reprints selected strips from the Japanese version, leaving out the more objectionable ones. Prior to the Dark Horse release, two volumes were published in the early 1990s by the now-defunct Eclipse Comics. ★★★½

WHISTLE!

(ホイッスル!) • Daisuke Higuchi • Viz (2005–2008) • Shueisha (Weekly Shônen Jump, 1998–2003) • 39 volumes • Shônen, Sports • All Ages

Daisuke Higuchi tapped into a rich vein of national pride when *Whistle!* debuted in 1998—the same year Japan qualified to play in the World Cup for the first time. The team failed to win a single game, but *Whistle!* went on to a long and successful run in the pages of *Weekly Shônen Jump*. The story follows the meteoric rise of soccer sensation Shô Kazamatsuri: a gifted, hardworking, and painfully earnest forward. After he is relegated to the bench at Musashinomori Junior High, Shô transfers to Josui Junior High, where he blossoms into a star player under the tutelage of former J-League great Shouju Matsushita. Along with standout teammates like Tatsuya Mizuno, a brilliant midfielder with daddy issues, and Shigeki Sato, a smarmy young runaway with killer instincts on the field, Shô eventually competes on the international stage against the finest players in the world. *Whistle!* works best when the players take to the soccer pitch: Higuchi's clear and elegant depictions of games—some of them consuming many chapters' worth of pages—make it easy to forget the bland, paint-by-numbers nature of the central story line. You can take comfort in the fact that when all the teen angst and touchy-feely team bonding get to be a bit too much, someone will always lace up his cleats and say, "Shut up and play." (RG) ★★½

WHO FIGHTER WITH HEART OF DARKNESS

Foo/Who Fighter with Heart of Darkness) (フー・ファイター With Heart of Darkness) • Seiho Takizawa • Dark Horse (2006) • Dai-Nippon Kaiga (Model Graphix, 2004) • 1 volume • Seinen, Military, Science Fiction • Unrated/13+ (mild language, brief graphic violence)

Seiho Takizawa is a detailed, realistic artist whose character art and military machinery resembles Katsuhiro Otomo's. Unfortunately, his plots are weak homages that bring nothing new to their source material, aside from being set in World War II Japan. In "Who Fighter" (a variant spelling of "foo fighters"), a Japanese fighter pilot encounters floating balls of light followed by even weirder signs of alien presences—animal mutilation, Men in Black, even the Mothman. At first promisingly creepy, the story adds up to little more than an excuse to draw various classic UFO phenomena. The second story, "Heart of Darkness," borrows predictably from *Apocalypse Now,* with a Japanese Imperial Army officer sent to the jungles of Burma to assassinate a rogue colonel. A very short third story tells the history of tanks in visual form. ★½

WILD 7

(ワイルド7) • Mikiya Mochizuki • ComicsOne (2001–2002) • Shônen Gahosha (Weekly Shônen King, 1969–1979) • 6 volumes, suspended (48 volumes in Japan) • Shônen, Crime, Political Drama • Unrated/13+ (language, crude humor, violence)

A pop-cultural artifact of revolutionary 1960s Japan, *Wild 7* combines the smiling attitude and art style of *Speed Racer* with the vaguely right-wing, vaguely antiestablishment violence of Sam Peckinpah or *Dirty Harry.* Recruited by a ruthless police officer who lost his faith in the system, the Wild 7 are motorcycle-riding ex-cons (one's a hippie, one's a reform-school kid, etc.) who ride souped-up bikes and kill bad guys with shotguns and sidecar-launched missiles. Their enemies include cigar-smoking evil lawyers, TV producers, and union leaders, as well as more ordinary foes such as the biker knights, who fight with lances. Considering that it's basically a kids' manga, the amorality and sadism are amazing, reaching a pinnacle in volume 3 when the villains force the hero's girlfriend into a panther suit so the hero can mistake her for a panther and whip her. The

near-constant action scenes are well drawn and still exciting despite their age. ★★★

WILD ACT

Rie Takada • Tokyopop (2003–2005) • Shogakukan (Shôjo Comic, 1998–2000) • 10 volumes • Shôjo, Action, Romantic Comedy • 16+ (nudity, sex, adult themes)

Yuniko is a teenage thief and martial artist who specializes in stealing memorabilia related to her favorite movie star, the late actor Akira Nanae. Her path crosses with that of handsome young actor Ryu Eba, and the two quickly pair up. A cross between a heist comedy and a backstage drama, with dollops of ridiculous *shôjo* melodrama (amnesia, long-lost children, even possible incest) tossed into the mix, *Wild Act* is a potluck of a manga. It succeeds mainly by being too good-humored to take any of its disparate elements too seriously. Takada has a cock-eyed sense of humor that livens up almost any scene: "Even though I thought his kiss might taste like cigarettes," Yuniko muses at one point, "it actually tasted like those ranch-flavored crackers." The spunky, devilish attitudes of the two leads—Yuniko cheerfully rappels off buildings and beats the stuffing out of would-be molesters, and Ryu goes along for the ride with gusto—is another key to the manga's charm. It's also interesting to read a *shôjo* manga in which the heroine actively enjoys sex, instead of taking the "I'll let him do it because I love him" attitude more common in *shôjo* heroines, and where the romantic relationship is treated as a source of strength for the characters, rather than their central problem. (SG) ★★★½

WILD ADAPTER

Kazuya Minekura • Tokyopop (2007–ongoing) • Tokuma Shoten (Chara, 2001–ongoing) • 5+ volumes (ongoing) • Action, Drama • 18+

Gang warfare, gambling, and mob hits are one thing, but young *yakuza* member Makoto Kubota draws the line when he comes across a lethal drug called Wild Adapter. With the help of a mysterious drifter, Kubota sets out to unravel the mystery of this killer drug. By the creator of *Saiyuki,* so naturally our young men are as pretty as they are dangerous. (MS) NR

WILD BOOGIE

Yancha Boogie, "Wild Boogie" (やんちゃブギ) • Tsutomu Shinohara • ComicsOne (e-book, 2000) • Sogo Tosho (1999) • 1 volume, suspended (many volumes in Japan) • Pachinko • 13+ (gambling)

Wild Boogie revolves around Takeshi and his exploits in Tokyo's grittier neighborhoods as he learns how to get big cash out of the newest Pachinslo (*pachinko* slot) machines. The story spends a lot of time talking technique and gets deep into specifics on how to beat the odds, identify high-return machines, and so on. It also takes the time to include plot details: love interests, a rotating ensemble of friends/rivals, and a subplot when Takeshi loses a bet and has to understudy in a local theater troupe. As with all hobbyist manga, however, the sport overrides the story. Hobbyist manga in Japan rely on being timely; publishing the stories years later, for readers who have no way to access the actual hobby and have never seen a *pachinko* slot machine in their life, seems unnecessary and pointless. Nevertheless, it still has value as a window into a huge genre of Japanese manga. (RS) ★★½

WILD COM.

Chônoryoku Rôdôtai Wild Com., "Psychic Squad Wild Com.," aka "Super Natural Powers Wild Com." (超能力労働隊スーパーナチュラルパワーズワイルドコム) • Yumi Tamura • Viz (2004) • Shogakukan (Betsucomi, 1999) • 1 volume • Shôjo, Psychic, Drama • 16+ (sexual situations, violence)

This short story collection is Tamura at her best, with well-constructed plots and her usual flowing, impressionistic artwork. The title story, "Wild Com.," reads like an *X-Men* homage, involving a rescue squad of young psychics operating from a headquarters beneath a pizza joint. "The Beasts of June," a hard-edged love story of crime, drugs, and kept women, shows how much better Tamura's *Chicago* could have been. Lastly, "The Eye of the Needle" is an uncharacteristically gruesome horror story. ★★★

WISH

(ウィッシュ) • CLAMP • Tokyopop (2002–2003) • Kadokawa Shoten (Mystery DX, 1995–1998) • 4 volumes • Shôjo, Romance, Fantasy • 13+

Kohaku, a kindhearted but accident-prone angel, comes to Earth in search of Hisui, one of the four angel masters, who has gone missing. No sooner does Kohaku arrive on our planet than the angel gets stuck in a tree and attacked by crows. Shuichiro Kudo, a handsome young doctor, rescues Kohaku and takes the angel home. Kohaku wants to repay the favor by granting Shuichiro a wish, but the successful doctor can think of nothing he wants that he can't get on his own. Unable to leave without repaying the debt, Kohaku sets up as Shuichiro's indefinite roommate until he can think of something to wish for. Soon devils, cat demons, and the wayward Hisui show up, and Shuichiro's home becomes the neutral ground in a brewing feud between heaven and hell over a star-crossed affair between Hisui and the son of Satan. Romantic comedy hijinks ensue! *Wish* is a gem of a series, a breezy breath of fresh air after the dense and dark artwork of *X/1999* and *Magic Knight Rayearth.* The art is by Tsubaki Nekoi, who has a gift for sweetness and *chibi* characters. The playful rivalry between Kohaku and Koryu, a spunky demon, yields many smiles, and the several romantic pairings, especially that of the leads, are sweet and tender. If the story sounds like a perfect setup for a *yaoi* romance, it's no coincidence. CLAMP, unabashed fans of same-sex romantic pairings, clearly had Boys' Love in mind when making this series, although *Wish* is more a *shônen ai* kindred spirit than the bona fide article, as Kohaku is a genderless tomboy and the romance is purely G-rated. At four volumes, *Wish* is a neat little package and a great "gateway drug" series for *shônen ai,* CLAMP, and *shôjo* manga in general. (MT) ★★★★

WITCHBLADE MANGA

Witchblade Takeru (ウィッチブレイド丈琉) • Yasuko Kobayashi (story), Kazasa Sumita (art) • Bandai/ Top Cow (2007) • Akita Shoten (Champion Red,

2006–2007) • 2 volumes • Seinen, Superhero, Horror • Not Rated Yet (extreme graphic violence, frequent partial nudity, sexual situations)

Licensed adaptation of Top Cow's *Witchblade* superhero comic. The plot has little relation to the 2004 anime series. Takeru, a high school girl raised in a Buddhist convent, has disturbing dreams and discovers that she is the chosen partner of the Witchblade, an ancient living weapon that comes to life in a mass of oily tentacles and squirms all over her body, turning her into a superpowered killing machine. Her opponents are the *oni*, traditional Japanese demons, and the fight scenes are filled with gore and torture. Just like the original American version, the transformed Takeru wears a skimpy bio-organic outfit that leaves nothing to the imagination; the only real difference is that in the manga version there are more exploitative camera angles and her body type is softer and curvier. The art (by *ero-manga* artist Kazasa Sumita) is attractive and detailed, and the mood is unrelentingly dark and suggestive, making for a better-than-average adaptation of a gritty superhero comic. The English edition is published in two formats: a colorized, left-to-right monthly comics version released by Top Cow, and a black-and-white, right-to-left graphic novel edition from Bandai, following the style of the original Japanese. **NR**

W JULIET

W Juliet, "Double Juliet" (Wジュリエット) • Emura • Viz (2004–2007) • Hakusensha (Hana to Yume, 1997–2003) • 14 volumes • Shôjo, Romantic Comedy • 13+ (mild language)

Ito Miura, a tall, butch, karate-fighting tomboy, makes friends with an attractive girl in her drama club, Makoto Amano. But Makoto has a secret: "she" is actually a boy disguised as a girl, as part of his father's bizarre condition to allow him to become an actor. Apart from the extremely shallow treatment of gender roles, the main problem with *W Juliet* is that the central relationship has no tension—the main characters quickly learn one another's secrets and obviously love one another. The slapstick sitcom plots merely involve school competitions or concealing the secret of Makoto's identity, which isn't hard since no one can recognize him without his wig. The acting theme is at the elementary school level, slightly younger than the intended audience. For slightly better versions of the same plot, see *Never Give Up* or *Nosatsu Junkie*. ★

WOLF'S RAIN

(ウルフズ・レイン) • Bones/Keiko Nobumoto (original creators), Iida Toshitsugu (story and art) • Viz (2004–2005) • Kodansha (Magazine Z, 2003–2004) • 2 volumes • Shônen, Postapocalyptic, Fantasy • 16+ (mild language, violence, nudity)

Adaptation of the anime series of the same name. On a postapocalyptic world similar to Earth, a group of wolves with the power to appear human search for a legendary lost paradise. In this grim future wolves are thought to have been hunted to extinction, and the pack of outcasts must overcome their differences if they are ever to survive the human attacks and find their promised land. Manga adaptations of anime often compress the story, but *Wolf's Rain* compacts a full 26 episodes into two manga volumes. Entire episodes take place within the span of 10–20 pages. Brevity aside, the art is barely adequate and at times not even that. In short, a transparent grab for cash. (RB) ★

THE WONDERFUL WORLD OF SAZAE-SAN

Sazae-san (サザエさん) • Machiko Hasegawa • Kodansha International (1997) • Various Newspapers (1946–1974) • 12 volumes • Four-Panel, Family, Comedy • All Ages

Sazae-san is the homegrown Japanese equivalent of *Blondie,* with which it competed, and won, for placement in Japanese newspapers after World War II. Sazae-san is a housewife and mother who lives with her husband, their child, and her parents in a traditional Japanese extended family. However, Hasegawa was Japan's first successful female cartoonist, and Sazae is a modern woman for her time and place (including her 1940s haircut); she takes charge in the household, and in the later strips voices support for the feminist movement. Although the characters never age, the strip follows topical events from the immediate postwar days, when food is scarce and American GIs drive through the streets, to later social phenomena such as hippies and *kyoiku mama,* "education mamas", obsessed with making sure their children get into a good college. The strip is of great cultural and historical importance; however, in the all-too-typical newspaper strip fashion, the jokes are generally mild chuckles for middle-aged and older readers. ★★½

THE WORLD EXISTS FOR ME

S to M no Sekai, "The World of S&M" (SとMの世界) • Be-PaPas (story), Chiho Saitou (art) • Tokyopop (2005–2006) • Kadokawa Shoten (Asuka, 2002) • 2 volumes • Shôjo, Historical Fantasy • 13+ (mild language, violence, brief nudity, sex)

Be-PaPas knew just what they were doing when they chose the Japanese title, but they probably hadn't planned out the plot. Half history lesson and half vaguely symbolic, bodice-ripping fantasy, the story follows Sekai (the name means "world"), a Japanese girl who is thrown back in time to Renaissance-era France in a train accident. Jumping from 1681 (when she encounters King Louis XIV) to 1440 (when she meets the infamous sadist Gilles de Rais), she is pursued across time by the sinister Machiavello, a handsome evil magician who looks just like the boy she loves in the present day. But what about the legend of two magic dolls named S and M? And the strange gem that embeds itself in her chest? And Sovieul, the wimpy time-traveling kid who starts the plot rolling? Who knows? The abrupt ending leaves almost every question unanswered. Saito's simplistic art is functional at best. ★½

THE WORLD OF NARUE

Narue no Sekai, "The World of Narue" (成恵の世界) • Tomohiro Marukawa • CPM (2004) • Kadokawa Shoten (Monthly Shônen Ace, 2000–2002) • 4 volumes, suspended (8 volumes in Japan) •

Shônen, Science Fiction, Romantic Comedy • 13+ (mild violence, mild sexual situations)

They're the perfect pair: Kazuto, a lovestruck anime fan, and his classmate Narue, a half-human alien girl who uses a teleportation hairband and other high-tech devices. Vaguely similar to *No Need for Tenchi!, The World of Narue* trades in most of *Tenchi's* sexual/romantic teases for light explorations of science fiction concepts, such as time travel. (The time travel machine powered by cats and mice is particularly charming.) The writing is above average for its genre, but the art is generic and the romantic leads are boring; as in many manga where the main character is a stand-in for the reader, the side characters are more interesting. ★★½

WORST

(ワースト) • Hiroshi Takahashi • DMP (2004) • Akita Shoten (Monthly Shônen Champion, 2002–ongoing) • 3 volumes, suspended (17+ volumes in Japan, ongoing) • Seinen, Martial Arts, Comedy • 16+ (language, violence)

Hana Tsukushima, a dorky-looking, polite hick with a shaved head, moves into a boardinghouse with four other juvenile delinquents, a bulldog named DeNiro, and the landlord's cross-dressing brother. When he reveals how strong he is, all the gangs of Suzuran Boys' High School—the "worst" high school in Japan—want to have him on their side. An old-school and oddly realistic high school fighting manga, *Worst* hardly even dwells on the fights, which are often off-screen, over in one punch, or both. Instead, the focus is on incidental, dry comedy and power struggles, set in an all-male world of broad-nosed, scarred, occasionally comedic tough guys. ★★★

WOUNDED MAN

Kizuoi Bito, "Wounded Man" (傷追い人) • Kazuo Koike (story), Ryoichi Ikegami (art) • ComicsOne (2001–2002) • Shogakukan (Big Comic Spirits, 1981–1986) • 7 volumes • Seinen, Action-Adventure • 18+ (language, graphic violence, constant nudity, frequent sex)

NHK newscaster Yuko makes for the jungles of Brazil in search of a big scoop that will make her famous. Instead she gets mixed up in a bad way with Keisuki Ibaraki, a "White Haired Demon" on a single-minded mission of revenge. Years earlier, Ibaraki was a football hero kidnapped and imprisoned by an evil organization known as G.P.X. ("God's Pornographic Films") who wanted to turn Keisuki into a blue-movie star against his will. After Keisuki's high school sweetheart commits suicide as a result of G.P.X.'s nefarious plan, he vows to get vengeance on them at all costs. But the cash-rich organization has vast resources, including a pair of murderously psychotic former Green Berets. Given its porno-movie-making villains and a hero who occasionally rapes people, this is easily the raunchiest of the Koike-Ikegami collaborations, and that is saying something. *Wounded Man* routinely depicts the sort of scenes unimaginable and impermissible in any other mass medium save manga. Ikegami's detailed art is in fine form throughout and even manages to put the sheen of respectability over Koike's joyfully raunchy, macho, and unnervingly well-researched scripts. (PM) ★★★★

X/1999

X • CLAMP • Viz (1996–2005) • Kadokawa Shoten (Asuka, 1992–2003) • 14 volumes • Shôjo, Psychic, Action • 16+ (mild language, graphic violence)

The end of the world draws near and the fate of the Earth is in the hands of Kamui Shiro, a young man with immense psychic powers. When he returns to Tokyo after a long absence to confront his destiny, he must choose to lead one of two factions toward two possible fates: the Seven Harbingers, who seek to destroy the Earth (or at least human civilization), and the Seven Seals, who seek to protect it. When Kamui makes his choice, the final battle approaches . . . and never arrives. Due to disputes with Kadokawa about the violence and CLAMP's reluctance to draw Tokyo's destruction after real-world earthquakes and terrorist attacks,

the series was put on indefinite hold. Four years later, CLAMP's signature series seems increasingly unlikely to reach the prophesied finale. Even without a proper ending, though, the series has a lot going for it. For one, it's absolutely gorgeous—never has Armageddon looked so lovely. CLAMP has a talent for swirling energy, shattering glass and buildings, crucifixion, and ribbons of blood, which they contrast beautifully with cascades of feathers and cherry blossoms. Maybe CLAMP goes a little overboard with their signature flourishes (okay, not maybe—definitely), but there is no denying that they make destruction look good. The storytelling isn't CLAMP's best—the series is anything but subtle, driving home its points in repetitive flashbacks, recaps, and iconography—but it is hard not to get swept up in the momentum toward the day of destiny. Even if the series never gets an ending in manga form, *X/1999* is still easy to recommend, and a must-read for fans of *Tokyo Babylon,* as the fates of Subaru and Seishiro are at last revealed. The Chairman and his Clamp School detective friends also make appearances, having matured into *bishônen* eye candy. (MT) ★★★½

×2 (TIMES TWO)

Kakeru Ni, "Times Two" (かけるに) • Shouko Akira • Viz (2004–2005) • Shogakukan (Betsucomi, 2002) • 1 volume • Shôjo, Romance • 13+ (mild language)

Mild, innocent high school love stories. In "Frequency," the only supernatural story, a girl gains the ability to hear her male classmate's thoughts. In "Baby Universe," a boy has a crush on a girl who may be dating an older man. Although the stories are sweet and restrained, the lack of overt comedy or melodrama makes the collection unmemorable. Of the several stories involving girls with crushes on guys, the best is "Love at First Touch." ★★

X-DAY

Kanojotachi no X-Day, "Their/The Women's X-Day" (彼女たちのエクス・デイ) • Setona Mizushiro • Tokyopop (2003) • Akita Shoten (Princess, 2002–2003) • 2 volumes • Shôjo, Drama • 16+ (language, violence, sexual situations)

"Let's blow the school to pieces." After one student in a high school chat room makes the suggestion, others agree. Soon, four conspirators—one of them a teacher—are plotting to build a bomb to blow up their school. Calling one another by their screen names, they meet after hours to trade bomb recipes, collect explosives, and understand one another's motivations for terrorism. The first volume, in which the four wounded, stressed-out souls grow closer while testing how far they're really willing to go, is stronger than the second volume, in which more predictable *shôjo*-manga relationship clichés rear their pretty heads. Despite its short-comings, *X-Day* has moments of beauty and keen observation that have earned it a devoted fan base in Japan. It also accurately depicts the power and fragility of online connections; a scene in which a lonely girl goes online at night just to watch her co-conspirators chat rings achingly true. Mizushiro's strong, elegantly composed art helps carry the story. Volume 2 also includes a bizarre bonus story, a sci-fi parable called "The Last Supper." (SG) ★★★

XENON: See *Heavy Metal Warrior Xenon*

X-KAI

(X-カイ) • Asami Tohjoh • Tokyopop (2006) • Homesha (Eyes, 1998–2000) • 2 volumes • Bishônen, Crime Drama • 16+ (language, brief graphic violence, nudity, sex)

Kai, aka Kaito Yagami, is a beautiful assassin who works at a flower shop and kills people to pay his older brother's medical bills. In his search for "someone to care for," he eventually adopts Renge, a child who was abused by priests. Quiet, predictable, and full of soppy sentiment, *X-Kai* has no purpose other than for readers to enjoy the angst-ridden, good-looking guys. The high-contrast, polished art is one of the manga's high points; the men have long bodies and bony hands. ★

X-MEN: THE MANGA

X-Men (エックス・メン) • various artists • Marvel (1998–1999) • Take Shobo (1994) • 26 issues • Superhero • Unrated/All Ages (mild violence)

A faithful adaptation of the 1990s *X-Men* American animated TV series (which aired in Japan), drawn in tag-team fashion by numerous artists who trade off with one another from chapter to chapter. The main weakness hard-core Marvel fans will notice is not the writing but the frequently lazy art, with huge sound effects and speedlines everywhere. (On the other hand, some of the artists are good, and Hirofumi Ichikawa turns in a very passable imitation of mid-1990s American comics.) Considering how many levels of translation it went through, the content holds up well. That said, the only thing that feels completely wrong is seeing the ever-regal Magneto sweat so much. The other artists include Rei Nakahara, Reiji Hagihara, and Miyako Kojima. (RM) ★★

XXXHOLIC

CLAMP • Del Rey (2004–ongoing) • Kodansha (Weekly Young Magazine, 2003–ongoing) • 10+ volumes (ongoing) • Seinen, Occult, Fantasy • 13+ (mild language, graphic violence)

In downtown Tokyo, nestled between skyscrapers, lies a quaint Victorian boutique where the beautiful and mysterious Yuko Ichihara sells magical trinkets and remedies for ailments psychological and supernatural . . . for a price. Watanuki Kimihiro is haunted by oppressive ghosts and spirits, so when Hitsuzen (kinda like fate) leads him to Yuko's shop, he jumps at a chance for a cure. In order to pay off the debt, Watanuki is roped into working as Yuko's servant, doing chores and cooking for the witchy woman and her spritely attendants, and assisting her in performing her business. As time goes on and the young man learns more and more about the secret workings of fate and the spirit world, it's clear that Watanuki is no mere servant but Yuko's apprentice. When he's not being dragged along on Yuko's business, Watanuki pines for the chipper but seemingly unlucky Himawari and argues with his "rival" Domeki, whom fate keeps throwing in his path. *xxxHOLiC* launched simultaneously with *Tsubasa: Reservoir Chronicle,* and the two series intersect from time to time, but *xxxHOLiC* is an independent entity, stylistically and tonally removed from its sister series. Visually, *xxxHOLiC* is closest to *Chobits,* but it's a huge leap forward in the team's technique and is absolutely one of the best-looking manga being drawn today. The character designs are uniformly top-notch, especially Yuko, whose goth-modern dresses and confident composure make her the sexiest character in CLAMP's catalog. The artists swap their trademark cherry blossoms and feathers for twisting, curling wisps of smoke, which, combined with the pale faces and heavy-lidded eyes of the protagonists, creates opium-den otherworldliness that perfectly complements the stories. CLAMP has mixed the modern and the supernatural before, most notably in *Tokyo Babylon,* but in *xxxHOLiC* they come closest to reaching a Miyazaki-like level of sublime beauty. The episodic story line has its misses, but they're far outweighed by solid hits. One of CLAMP's very best. (MT)

★★★½

YAKITATE!! JAPAN

Yakitate! Japan, "Fresh Baked!! Japan" (焼きたて!!ジャぱん) • Takashi Hashiguchi • Viz (2006–ongoing) • Shogakukan (Weekly Shônen Sunday, 2001–2007) • 26 volumes • Shônen, Cooking, Comedy • 16+ (crude humor, comic violence, occasional partial nudity, mild sexual situations)

Proving that you can make a melodramatic manga about anything, *Yakitate!! Japan* is the story of a teenage baker and his quest to make Japan's national bread, the equivalent of French bread or English muffins. If *Iron Wok Jan* could sort of pass as an earnest, trashy, old-school *shônen* manga, *Yakitate!! Japan* is its Cartoon Network Adult Swim equivalent—self-parodying, fully aware of its own calculated nuttiness, and full of horrible, wonderful puns. Kazuma Azuma, the naive, optimistic hero, moves to Tokyo to

work at the famous Pantasia bakery. When the manga begins, he doesn't even know what a croissant is, but that's okay because he's already invented almost all possible kinds of bread in his homemade baking experiments! The mouthwatering breads are more or less within the bounds of reality (volume 2 includes a genuine recipe for making bread in a rice cooker), but beyond that it's chaos—the plot revolves around a series of ludicrous baking tests and tournaments, with side characters such as Ken (Kazuma's muscular, Afro-sporting boss), Meister Kirisaki (the masked, caped manager of Pantasia), and even more freakish enemy bakers. The appealing, anime-style artwork is full of exaggerated facial expressions, cute girls, and the occasional gay joke. The English rewrite comes up with good equivalents for the Japanese puns, and for self-conscious wackiness, it doesn't get much better than this. ★★★½

YOKI KOTO KIKU

Yoki, Koto, Kiku. (ヨキ、コト、キク。) • Koge-Donbo • Broccoli (2006) • Broccoli (Comic Di Gi Charat, 2006) • 1 volume • Mystery, Comedy • 13+ (comic violence)

An *Addams Family*–esque sitcom set in 1936 Japan, *Yoki Koto Kiku* is a parody of Seishi Yokomizu's mystery novel *Inugami-ke no Ichizoku* ("The Inugami Clan"), although knowledge of this isn't necessary to enjoy the story. When their ancestor dies without leaving a will, three young siblings and the family maid stand to inherit a fortune. The adorably cute siblings immediately try to murder one another with random visual gags involving flying axes, needles, razor blades, and poison. Koge-Donbo's cute art-naive style is a blackly humorous contrast to the plot (although "plot" is putting it strongly; it's mostly a grab bag of retro in-jokes with appearances by various bizarre guest characters). ★★★

YOTSUBA&!

Yotsubato!, "Yotsuba and ———" (よつばと!) • Kiyohiko Azuma • ADV (2005–ongoing) • Media-

Works (Dengeki Daioh, 2003–ongoing) • 6+ volumes (ongoing) • Moe, Comedy • All Ages

The follow-up work by the creator of *Azumanga Daioh, Yotsuba&!* likewise features a cast of cute girls; simple, open artwork; and a focus on everyday whimsy and absurdity. The central character is six-year-old Yotsuba, a green-haired, wide-eyed girl who cheerfully wanders around the neighborhood, talks to the teenage girls next door, and gets hours of entertainment from a playground swing or a doorbell. As her adoptive single father (an apparently twenty-something slacker) approvingly says, "She can find happiness in anything!" Freed from the relatively dense joke demands of four-panel gag manga, Azuma takes it easy in *Yotsuba&!*, indulging in his trademark long pauses—the reaction shots where the non sequitur jokes sink in—and a peaceful mood. It's a light, feel-good manga, like an endless summer day; only the most cynical readers will wonder why this manga about little girls was serialized in a boys' magazine. ★★★

YOU & ME

Yû & Mii (優＆魅衣) • Hiroshi Aro • Studio Ironcat (2002) • Shueisha (Monthly Shônen Jump/Monthly Shônen Jump Original, 1983–1988) • 3 issues, suspended (8 volumes in Japan) • Shônen, Romantic Comedy • Unrated/16+ (nudity)

This obscure 1980s cult favorite crosses *Maison Ikkoku* with *Urusei Yatsura.* Nerdy high school student Yuu Aimu (a pun on "I'm you") moves into a boardinghouse where he meets various weirdos, including a cute girl ghost who haunts him. The slapstick comedy is dense and good-natured, and the eventual ending is actually touching, but unfortunately, only a tiny fraction of the series was translated. ★★½

THE YOUNG MAGICIAN

Shônen Mahôshi, "The Boy Magician" (少年魔法士) • Yuri Narushima • CMX (2005–ongoing) • Shinshokan (Wings, 1996–2005) • 13 volumes • Shôjo, Fantasy, Drama • 18+ (language, graphic violence, nudity)

Carno Guino is a teenage magician of incredible raw power, which stems from a demonic, dangerous source. Raised on the other side of the world, Ibuki Shikishima is a gifted young Shinto practitioner whose powers are less dramatic but in their own way may be even greater. When mighty clans of demons and wizards (including the Knights Templar) fight to control or destroy the two boys, they end up on the run together, trying to master their powers and simply live. Moody and slow-paced (Ibuki doesn't even show up until volume 2), *The Young Magician* is a powerful work of modern fantasy, despite the indifferent character artwork and minimalistic or absent backgrounds. Narushima more than makes up for this with excellent writing and imaginative page layouts, bringing to life the world of the story—or, as one character puts it, "the abyss of the dark arts." Like a good novel, it's difficult to put down. ★★★½

YOUR AND MY SECRET

Boku to Kanojo no XXX, "My and Her XXX" (僕と彼女のXXX) • Ai Morinaga • ADV (2004) • Mag Garden (Comic Blade, 2002–2005) • 1 volume, suspended (3 volumes in Japan) • Romantic Comedy • 13+ (partial nudity, sexual situations)

Akira Uehara, a shy *bishônen,* is caught in a mad scientist's experiment and switches bodies with the girl he likes: Nanako Momoi, a violent, masculine tomboy. The catch is that their personalities are both better suited to their new gender; Nanako soon discovers she loves being a man, and Uehara, who's slightly less thrilled with his new body, must watch in horror as his former guy friends hit on him and as Nanako starts working out and loses "his" virginity. Meanwhile, Uehara blushingly undergoes various trials of womanhood. Morinaga's *shôjo/shônen* hybrid art and comedy writing are solid, and the story flirts openly with gay/lesbian/transgender humor, although everything sexual happens offscreen. ★★★

YOU'RE UNDER ARREST!

Taiho Shichauzo, "You're Under Arrest/You're Busted!" (逮捕しちゃうぞ) • Kosuke Fujishima • Dark

Horse (1995–1999) • Kodansha (Morning Party Zôkan, 1986–1992) • 2 volumes, suspended (7 volumes in Japan) • Seinen, Police, Comedy • Unrated/13+ (brief nudity)

High-spirited but unfunny office comedy starring two female cops—one's reckless, the other's demure—who chase down panty thieves, speeders, and overenthusiastic paintball gamers. Fujishima's bright, anime-style artwork is pretty and detailed (particularly the cars and motorcycles, obviously his favorite thing to draw), but the stories are bland and unmemorable. The English edition of *You're Under Arrest!* does not start with volume 1 of the Japanese edition; instead, it reprints material from volumes 5 and 6, when Fujishima's art was slicker.

★★

YUBISAKI MILK TEA

Yubisaki Milk Tea, "Fingertip Milk Tea" (**ゆびさきミルクティー**) • Tomochika Miyano • Tokyopop (2006–ongoing) • Hakusensha (Young Animal, 2003–2006) • 7 volumes • Romance • 18+ (language, nudity, sexual situations)

One of the only manga to depict crossdressing in a semirealistic fashion, *Yubisaki Milk Tea* is the story of Yoshinori, a boy who acquires a fetish for photographing himself in women's clothing and fooling people by passing as female. At the same time, he likes girls, and he finds himself torn between two of them: his guarded classmate Kurokawa and his cute childhood friend Hidari, who's a little too young for him. But will Hidari open up to him only when he's disguised as Yuki? A generally well-plotted story, *Yubisaki Milk Tea* nevertheless stumbles in the first volume, in which too much happens and they have to retroactively take it back later; probably the series was intended as only a single volume but was extended due to reader demand. Miyano has a unique art style, realistic but soft, even tasteful; it's light on the typical breasts-and-panties *shônen* fanservice but sexualizes its characters in a subtler, arguably *moe* fashion. It's not a perfect manga, but it's unusually honest in expressing the blurred line between self-identity and sexual attraction.

★★★

YU-GI-OH!

Yu-Gi-Oh!, "Game King" (**遊☆戯☆王**) • Kazuki Takahashi • Viz (2002–2004) • Shueisha (Weekly Shônen Jump, 1996–2004) • 7 volumes • Shônen, Game, Battle • 13+ (violence)

Published in Japan as a single manga but split into three sections in the English edition, *Yu-Gi-Oh!* actually divides fairly well into three distinct parts. When he solves the Millennium Puzzle (an ancient Egyptian artifact), nerdy high school outcast Yugi awakens what seems to be another side of his personality: Yu-Gi-Oh, the King of Games, an unbeatable champion who challenges evildoers to magical Shadow Games where the loser suffers an ironically appropriate fate. A superhero-esque "revenge of the underdog" fantasy, the early volumes of *Yu-Gi-Oh!* (whose anime version was not shown on American TV) are remarkable for their cartoon viciousness: while almost no one actually dies, the endless army of bullies and jerks who pick on Yugi and his friends end up insane, blinded, deafened, blown up, and set on fire. (However, Yugi's malicious grin in the early chapters is soon replaced by the sternly disapproving look of a champion of justice.) The chapters are mostly disconnected episodes, based on different kinds of games from yo-yos to tabletop RPGs, but a few longer story arcs introduce recurring villains (such as Shadi, Bakura, and Kaiba) who have bigger roles in the later parts of the series. The story continues in *Yu-Gi-Oh!: Duelist* and concludes in *Yu-Gi-Oh!: Millennium World.* (AT)

★★

YU-GI-OH!: DUELIST

Yu-Gi-Oh!, "Game King" (**遊☆戯☆王**) • Kazuki Takahashi • Viz (2002–2007) • Shueisha (Weekly Shônen Jump, 1996–2004) • 24 volumes • Shônen, Game, Battle • 13+ (violence)

Picking up where the American TV series begins, *Yu-Gi-Oh!: Duelist* shows the evolution of *Yu-Gi-Oh!* into a franchise. The turning point was the Duel Monsters collectible card game; introduced in *Yu-Gi-Oh!* as a one-shot parody of *Magic: The Gathering*, it grew to dominate the series and was turned into a real-world card game, which eclipsed *Magic* in popularity. Thus, whereas the original *Yu-Gi-Oh!* involves a variety of games, *Yu-Gi-Oh!: Duelist* sees Yu-Gi-Oh mostly fighting his way through collectible card game tournaments against evil, sneering opponents. His goal: to discover his own lost identity, which is somehow linked to the world-famous card game, which is secretly of ancient Egyptian origin! The disconnect between collectible card game commercialism and weepy *shônen* melodrama (with many speeches about the value of friendship, etc.) makes *Yu-Gi-Oh!: Duelist* impossible for anyone over a certain age to enjoy nonironically. The monsters from the cards come to virtual reality life, and dastardly villains threaten our hero with various forms of (mostly) bloodless torture, but the gaming sequences can't help but get repetitive, since there's little tension about whether Yu-Gi-Oh will win. The awkward carnival funhouse artwork of the original *Yu-Gi-Oh!* is tamed, becoming more polished and less surprising. In Japan, *Yu-Gi-Oh!: Duelist* was published as volumes 8–31 of the 38-volume *Yu-Gi-Oh!* series. (AT)

★★

YU-GI-OH! GX

Yu-Gi-Oh! GX, "Game King GX" (遊☆戯☆王GX) • Kazuki Takahashi (story), Naoyuki Kageyama (art) • Viz (2006–ongoing) • Shueisha (V-Jump, 2006–ongoing) • 1+ volumes (ongoing) • Shônen, Game, Battle • 13+ (violence)

A sequel to *Yu-Gi-Oh!* drawn by a new artist and based on the anime of the same name, *Yu-Gi-Oh! GX* lacks the scraps of personality that gave the original its charm. Sometime after the events of *Yu-Gi-Oh!*, a Duel Monsters collectible card game academy has been founded, and the students compete among themselves for honor and rare cards. The title is short for "Generation Next." (AT)

NR

YU-GI-OH!: MILLENNIUM WORLD

Yu-Gi-Oh!, "Game King" (遊☆戯☆王) • Kazuki Takahashi • Viz (2002–2008) • Shueisha (Weekly Shônen Jump, 1996–2004) • 7 volumes • Shônen, Game, Battle • 13+ (violence)

Having gathered the three Egyptian God Cards and the seven Millennium Items, the spirit of Yu-Gi-Oh opens the mystical door to the World of Memories, and finds himself seemingly transported to ancient Egypt, reliving his life as the pharaoh three thousand years ago. There, he discovers the origin of the Millennium Items and much more, and must fight a last battle, while his modern-day friends (including Yugi, now a totally separate character) struggle to help him reach his "final destination." After the long slog of *Yu-Gi-Oh!: Duelist,* the climax of the *Yu-Gi-Oh!* series is surprisingly good, containing several real surprises and revealing in retrospect that the entire series was more deeply plotted than at first glance. Even Takahashi's artwork musters its strength for the conclusion, with startling splash pages and bold layouts. The finale is genuinely moving and deals with themes of parents and children, death and growing up. If you read any *Yu-Gi-Oh!,* read it through to the end. In Japan, *Yu-Gi-Oh!: Millennium World* was published as volumes 32–38 of the 38-volume *Yu-Gi-Oh!* series. (AT)

★★★

YURARA

Yurara no Tsuki, "Yurara's Moon" (ゆららの月) • Chika Shiomi • Viz (2007–2008) • Hakusensha (Bessatsu Hana to Yume, 2002–2005) • 5 volumes • Shôjo, Occult, Romance • 16+

Yurara, who is cursed with the ability to sense ghosts, develops a powerful split personality that is triggered whenever she's in mortal danger. How can she deal with the supernatural world while also trying to deal with boys?

NR

YUYU HAKUSHO

Yûyû Hakusho, "Poltergeist White Paper/Report") (幽☆遊☆白書) • Yoshihiro Togashi • Viz (2002–ongoing) • Shueisha (Weekly Shônen Jump, 1990–

YURI//LESBIAN (百合・レズビアン)

In contrast to *yaoi*'s tremendous popularity, lesbian manga remains a small subgenre, but one with arguably greater relevance to real lesbians than *yaoi* manga has to real gay men. The term *yuri* (lily) for "lesbian" originated in 1971 in a remark by Ito Bongaku, editor of the gay men's magazine *Barazoku* ("Rose Tribe"), who described lesbians as the "lily tribe" (*yurizoku*). Today, the English term *lesbian* (*rezubian*) is commonly used in Japan, but the term *yuri* survives to describe lesbian manga and anime.

The historical awareness of Japanese lesbians has followed the women's rights movement. Lesbian themes first began to surface in the 1920s in the works of feminist writers such as Nobuko Yoshiya. Lesbian activism began in the 1970s, at the same time as the explosion of psychological experimentation in *shôjo* manga led to lesbian-themed manga such as Ryoko Yamagishi's *Shiroi Heya no Futari* ("Two in a White Room") and Riyoko Ikeda's *Oniisama e* ("To My Dear Brother"). Like American gay narratives of the same period, the stories were angst-ridden and often ended in suicide and mental illness. But attitudes changed; coming-out books reached mainstream audiences in the 1980s and 1990s, and today Japan, particularly Tokyo, has a small but active lesbian scene.

As with *bishônen* manga—which hint at relationships between attractive young men—some of the most popular lesbian-themed manga merely suggest relationships between women, or are vague enough for fans to draw their own conclusions. Boys' manga such as *Bleach, Negima,* and *Azumanga Daioh* have learned to get titillation from lesbian crushes. In the early twentieth century lesbian relationships were often referred to as "S" (sister), reflecting the Japanese view that same-sex attraction was merely a platonic phase of adolescence; this attitude can be seen in one of the most popular modern *yuri* manga, the untranslated manga/novel series *Maria-sama ga Miteru* ("The Virgin Mary Is Watching"). Japanese pop culture takes it for granted that feminine girls will swoon over forceful women in men's clothes, such as the women who play men's roles in the all-female Takarazuka Revue (see the article on TRANSGENDER), or butch heroines in mainstream manga such as *The Rose of Versailles* and *Sailor Moon.* But even series that consciously flirt with lesbian subtext, such as *Revolutionary Girl Utena,* rarely "come out of the closet."

Rica Takashima's *Rica 'tte Kanji!* © R. Takashima, ALC Publishing. All Rights Reserved.

However, more openly lesbian and sexual material does exist, particularly in manga aimed at an older age group. *Jōsei* manga, such as the works of Mari Okazaki, Erica Sakurazawa, and Kiriko Nananan, often treat lesbian themes in an adult manner. No Japanese lesbian lifestyle magazine has lasted more than a few years, but the short-lived few, such as *Phryne, Anise,* and *Carmilla,* occasionally published manga (such as Rica Takashima's *Rica 'tte Kanji!*). In 2003 the *yaoi* publisher Magazine Magazine founded the quarterly magazine *Yuri Shimai* ("Lily Sisters"), the first ongoing magazine devoted to lesbian manga. *Yuri Shimai* was discontinued in 2005, only to be revived by Ichijinsha as *Yuri Hime* ("Yuri Princesses"). *Yuri Hime* attracts mostly female readers, but rarely deals with real-world issues such as coming out or homophobia. Girls' school stories are common, as are fantasy and science fiction *yuri* stories.

The term *yuri* itself has an uneasy blanket definition, covering both works aimed at actual lesbians (such as *Rica 'tte Kanji!*) and girl-girl manga usually aimed at men (such as *Kashimashi* and *Iono-sama Fanatics*). Some Japanese fans use the term Girls' Love (GL) in a conscious echo of the more established Boys' Love (BL) *yaoi* genre, while some American fans use the term *shōjo ai* (girls' love) for the same reason. To some male *otaku*, uncomfortable with their own bodies or their expected social role, *yuri* manga may be the natural extension of *moe* manga: love stories set in an all-girls world with no distracting male elements. Comparisons have been made with *yaoi* manga, although the evidence suggests that there are more actual lesbians among *yuri* readers than there are gay men among *yaoi* readers. Or perhaps, regardless of their own sexual orientation, female readers are more open to same-sex themes.

In America, lesbian-themed manga (together with the word *yuri*) were first promoted by a single grassroots company, ALC Publishing, which first published *dōjinshi* such as *Erica Tadeno: Works* and the Japanese-American anthology *Yuri Monogatari* ("Yuri Stories"). In 2003, ALC organized the first YuriCon, a convention devoted to *yuri* anime and manga, in New Jersey. The second YuriCon was held in Tokyo in 2005, bringing together Japanese and American fans and activists. Recognizing a growing market, in 2006 Seven Seas Entertainment announced their own *yuri* line, publishing more *otaku*-oriented works such as *Strawberry Panic!* (2005) and *The Last Uniform* (2005). *Yuri* manga seem certain to become more mainstream in America, but only time will tell its final form.

Lesbian Manga

Blue • Chirality: To the Promised Land • Erica Sakurazawa: Between the Sheets • Eriko Tadeno: Works • Iono-sama Fanatics • Kashimashi: Girl Meets Girl • The Last Uniform • Miyuki-chan in Wonderland • Revolutionary Girl Utena • Revolutionary Girl Utena: The Adolescence of Utena • Rica 'tte Kanji! • Strawberry Panic! • Sweat and Honey • Tetragrammaton Labyrinth

---

1994) • 19 volumes • Shōnen, Occult, Comedy, Battle • 13+ (mild language, graphic violence, mild sexual humor)

A typical *Shōnen Jump* manga that changed in reaction to readers' perceived tastes, *YuYu Hakusho* starts as a spooky, silly comedy and, around volume 3, turns into an increasingly violent but still silly fighting manga. When stereotypical teenage delinquent Yusuke Urameshi dies performing a good deed, he ends up doing odd jobs for the afterlife bureaucracy as a ghost, and eventually returns to Earth with supernatural powers. After undergoing martial arts training, he and his fellow reformed baddies—ugly dude Kuwabara, fire demon Hiei, and *bishônen* fox spirit Kurama—become heroes and enter long, drawn-out tournaments against armies of demons and monsters. An awkward mix of horror, comedy, and action, *YuYu Hakusho* is most interesting as a record of Togashi's artistic development, as he moves from an 1980s gag-manga style to something rougher, but also more vigorous and individualistic. The plot is formulaic, but the anything-goes spirit is endearing, and the series never entirely ceases being a comedy. The English rewrite accentuates the goofiness ("Holy cheese on rye!" "Nuts to you, Urameshi!"). Togashi's horror-movie-influenced visuals include some H. R. Giger–esque sexual imagery, some of which is censored in the English edition. ★★½

ZATCH BELL!

Konjiki no Gash!!, "Gash the Golden!" (金色のガッシュ!!) • Makoto Raiku • Viz (2005–ongoing) • Shogakukan (Weekly Shônen Sunday, 2001–ongoing) • 28+ volumes (ongoing) • Shônen, Fantasy, Comedy, Battle • 13+ (crude humor, violence)

Kiyo, an antisocial teenage genius, receives a gift from his father in England: Zatch ("Gash" in the original Japanese), a cheerful little kid with amnesia and huge marionette eyes, bearing a mysterious red book. As it turns out, Zatch isn't human—he's a Mamodo from an unearthly plane, sent to Earth along with ninety-nine of his fellows—and the spells in the book activate his hidden powers, turning him into a sort of walking weapon who shoots lightning bolts from his mouth. (In the original Japanese, the Mamodo are *mamono,* meaning "demons" or "monsters," but almost all traces of demonology were scrubbed clean of the idea long before it reached American shores.) A plot summary can't describe Raiku's spastic artwork, which brings the crude energy of gag manga to an extremely secondary *Shônen Jump*–style plot, in which Zatch and Kiyo make friends and fight bad guys so Zatch can become "a kind king" to his fellow Mamodo. The art mixes "ewww" ugliness with so-cute-it's-ugly ugliness (often both in the

same character), and the Mamodo vary in appearance between bug-eyed kids, *Pokémon,* and Muppets rejects. As the manga turns into an endless series of mostly disconnected fight scenes, what sticks in the older reader's mind is the comedy bits and the absurd but affectionate characters, such as cleft-chinned Italian pop star Parco Folgoré and Ponygon, a misbehavior-prone Mamodo whose master is named Kafka Sunbeam (or was in the Japanese edition—the English edition changes him to Kafk). At these times, the author seems to be enjoying himself the most. The English edition is censored for gun violence, sexual jokes, and Zatch's occasional habit of walking around naked. ★★½

ZIPANG

(ジパング) • Kaiji Kawaguchi • Kodansha International (2002)• Kodansha (Morning, 2000–ongoing) • 4 volumes, suspended (28+ volumes in Japan, ongoing) • Alternate History, Military • Unrated/16+ (mild language, graphic violence)

Kaiji Kawaguchi's thirty-million-copy-selling *The Silent Service* put him into the top rank of Japanese *seinen* artists when it ran in *Morning* magazine in the late 1980s and early 1990s. As a naval techno-thriller, it drew comparisons to Tom Clancy, but what makes Kawaguchi, and Japan, very different is the *lack* of superpower status, and a modern history that has seen neither conscription nor combat. Since Kawaguchi is out to draw cool weapons systems and battles at sea, it doesn't mean his storytelling is pacifist, but rather that he views war from an outsider's perspective, leaving him free to ask not only the small what-if questions but the big ones as well. *Zipang* is about both forms of the question, an alternate history saga in which the crew of the Japanese AEGIS missile cruiser *Mirai* time-slips back to 1942, when the conflict between America and Japan still hung in the balance. It sounds similar to the 1980 Kirk Douglas film *The Final Countdown,* but the cultural differences between Japan's naval forces of today and those they encounter during World War II are far greater—a downed imperial officer whom the *Mirai*'s crew rescues, thereby changing history, puts it well when he tells them, "I can see that you are 'Japanese' . . . but not in the same way I am." As Japan begins to build a missile defense system against North Korea and sends peacekeepers to Iraq, Kawaguchi uses *Zipang* to debate thoughtfully and humanely the future and past of an armed Japan, against the irresistible backdrop of an alternate World War II. (CGH)

★★★½

ZIPANGU NIGHT: See *Hino Horror, Vol. 13: Zipangu Night*

ZODIAC P.I.

Jûnikyu de Tsukamaete, "Catch Them with the Zodiac" (十二宮でつかまえて) • Natsumi Ando • Tokyopop (2003) • Kodansha (Nakayoshi, 2001–2003) • 4 volumes • Shôjo, Psychic, Magical Girl, Mystery • All Ages (brief violence, mild sexual situations)

Lili, the daughter of a cop, is a fourteen-year-old astrologer/detective; using the power of the magical Star Ring, she transforms into her secret identity, Spica, and summons the spirits of the stars to solve crimes (she calls out the suspects' birth dates, and the cute little spirits, who are named after constellations, perform horoscopes on them). The mostly self-contained cases range from murder mysteries to "who sent the love letter"; side characters include Lili's shy love interest, Hiromi, and her sexy rival, Sirius. It's formulaic stuff for very young readers, but the plots are lighthearted and the art is easy to follow. The extras include random astrology info (what color is "lucky" for what sign, etc.).

★★

ZOIDS CHAOTIC CENTURY

Kijû Shinseiki Zoido, "Machine Beast New Century Zoid" (機獣新世紀ゾイド) • Michiro Ueyama (story and art) • Viz (2002–2003) • Shogakukan (Corocoro Comic, 1999–2001) • 14 volumes • Shônen, Science Fiction, Mecha, Pet, Adventure • Unrated/All Ages (mild violence)

A manga published in parallel with the 1999 *Zoids* anime series (which was released in English under the title *Zoids Chaotic Cen-*

tury), using the same basic premise and cast of characters but taking the story in a different direction. On the war-torn planet Zi, where rival nations fight their battles with armies of biomechanical beasts known as Zoids, we meet a young man named Van who loves Zoids. Really, *really* loves Zoids. The result is a hybrid of *Gundam* and *Pokémon,* as our hero wanders the planet befriending robot animals and then piloting them in mecha battles. Van's Zoid-ophilia and relentless positive thinking make him a rather one-note character, but Ueyama does a great job building up an engaging cast of supporting characters, presenting nuanced political situations, and exploring the symbiotic relationships between the people of Zi and the Zoids on which they depend. Ueyama's art is also far better than in most tie-in comics aimed at younger audiences, showing a real knack for facial expressions and thrilling battle sequences. Despite the unpromising start, the somewhat abrupt ending of the story comes as a genuine disappointment. The English edition reprints the five-volume Japanese edition as fourteen short books, approximately eighty pages each. (MS)

★★★

ZOIDS NEW CENTURY

Zoido Shinseiki Slash Zero, "Zoid New Century Slash Zero") (ゾイド新世紀∅) • Makoto Mizobuchi • Viz (2002) • Shogakukan (Corocoro Comics Special, 2001) • 1 volume • Shônen, Science Fiction, Mecha, Sports, Action • Unrated/All Ages (mild violence)

This is the sort of thing that gives toy commercials a bad name. *Zoids New Century* is an absurdly compressed version of the 2001 anime series *Zoids New Century Slash Zero* (released in English as *Zoids New Century Zero*), which strips the story down to its simplest and most annoying essentials. Many years after the warring nations of the planet Zi settled their differences, their idle descendants use the mechanical beasts left over from the past conflicts to fight mock battles for sport. Our protagonist is Bit Cloud of Team Blitz, whose trusty Liger Zero somehow manages to win every battle without breaking a sweat, while the rest of the team gets taken hostage, giving the enemy players somebody to beat up on. Mizobuchi's artwork is competent but unexciting and gives the impression that Bit wins every duel by waving his Liger's claws at the camera and then posing in front of an explosion. The series was never collected in graphic novel form in Japan. (MS) ★

ZOMBIE POWDER

(ゾンビパウダー) • Tite Kubo • Viz (2006–2007) • Shueisha (Weekly Shônen Jump, 1999–2000) • 4 volumes • Shônen, Adventure • 16+ (mild language, violence)

In a vaguely Wild Western landscape, four outlaws—teenage Elwood, melon-breasted Wolfina, unassuming gunman C. T. Smith, and, last but not least, the invulnerable, chain-saw-wielding, bullet-catching Gamma Akutabi—search for the twelve rings that hold the powder of eternal life. *Zombie Powder* is essentially a rip-off of *Trigun,* down to individual panels and weaponry. Tite Kubo's snarky humor and love of strange imagery provide some reason to keep reading (check out the rock-poster title pages), but the fight scenes are boring and the overall mood is indulgent, mean-spirited, and far less funny than Kubo's later work, *Bleach.* Perhaps for that reason, the manga ends abruptly, apparently a victim of cancellation. Volumes 2–4 also contain clunky short stories from Kubo's early career. The series is mildly censored for near nudity. (AT) ★½

ZYWORD

(ガイオード) • Tamayo Akiyama • Tokyopop (2006) • Kadokawa Shoten (Monthly FanDela, 2005) • 1 volume • Shôjo, Fantasy, Adventure • 13+ (violence)

In Zyword, "the magical spell world controlled by chaos," the Kingdom of Araimel is suddenly cursed by evil forces. The mighty spell freezes all its citizens in eternal sleep, except for Luna and Roddy, boy and girl magicians, and Zera, a messenger from a neighboring kingdom who happens to be visiting. The three adventurers go on a quest through landscapes that look like vague chunks of screentone, fight monsters (which are equally poorly rendered), and utter generic RPG dialogue like "What? My red thunder spell didn't work?" Horrible, boring series that ends abruptly in what feels like the middle of the story. ½

YAOI REVIEWS

YAOI AND GAY MANGA

(やおい・ゲイ)

I made two guys go through something that's difficult for a straight couple so that's probably why I get letters saying "Being gay is good!" It's true a male and female are the norm in society so that's why I think a connection between two souls is more important than a physical connection.

—Kazuma Kodaka, *Kizuna*

Manga are filled with images of gay male lovers, but these are almost exclusively in comics created for and by straight women. In America, these comics are usually called *yaoi;* in Japan, they are called *yaoi* (a term that specifically refers to parody *dôjinshi*), *shônen ai* ("Boys' Love," an older term), or the current popular English term, Boys' Love (BL for short). On the most superficial level, *yaoi* can be compared to the fascination some straight men have with lesbians; but *yaoi* is a massively popular, complicated genre, ranging from hard-core sex to blushing romances, and its influence is felt in virtually all manga aimed at young women.

GAY MANGA

Historically, the Japanese attitude toward male homosexuality has been tolerant, even romantic; like warriors in ancient Greece, it was not uncommon for samurai to take male lovers. Imported Western morality caused homosexuality to be discreetly swept under the rug, but the general attitude remained that your sex life was your own business . . . as long as you did your duty to your family by getting married and having children, of course. In the 1990s, Japan, like America, underwent a so-called gay boom, with gay characters appearing on main-stream TV and in the public eye; the first Tokyo Lesbian Gay Parade took place in 1994. But social pressures, and a general Japanese attitude that private things should stay private, still make "coming out" less common than in America. Toru Yamazaki (*Octopus Girl*) is one of the few openly gay manga artists whose work has been translated, although his comics do not deal with gay themes. The English term "gay" (*gei*) is now preferred over the traditionally derogatory term "*okama.*"

Japanese comics aimed at a gay male audience are sometimes called *bara*, after *Barazoku* ("Rose Tribe"), a famous but now-defunct gay magazine, published from 1971 to 2004. *Bara* ("rose") became a synonym for gay, and so-called *bara* manga often appear as side features in Japanese gay magazines such as *Badi, Sabu,* and *G-Men*. Manga-only magazines aimed at gay men are periodically published, with names like *Pride, Baracomi,* and *Nikutaiha* ("Muscle Cult"), but most of these magazines last no more than a few issues, and none have ever been translated. A few translated *shôjo* manga deal with gay themes in a more or less realistic manner, including Fumi Yoshinaga's exceptional *Antique Bakery*, Akimi Yoshida's *Banana Fish*, *Erica Sakurazawa: Nothing but Loving You,* and Ai Yazawa's *Paradise Kiss*.

SHÔNEN AI

In the 1970s, a number of *shôjo* manga artists began to experiment with stories about teenage boys in love. Moto Hagio's *Jûichigatsu no Gymnasium* ("The November Gymnasium") and *Thomas no Shinzô* ("The Heart of Thomas") (1974), and Keiko Takemiya's *Kaze to Ki no Uta* ("The Song of the Wing and Trees") (1976), set the tone: angst-ridden tales of forbidden love in exotic European settings. Published in mainstream magazines such as *Shôjo Comic,* these so-called *shônen ai* (Boys' Love) stories struck a nerve, and soon specialty *shônen ai* manga magazines appeared, beginning with *June* (1978). With its emphasis on beauty and tragedy—which made the beauty all the more fleeting—the early *shônen ai* had a distinctly decadent, aesthetic sensibility. Although the stories often involved dark themes such as rape and suicide, the emphasis was not on realistic depictions of homosexuality and homophobia, but on idealized love and psychological themes such as the conflict between spirit and flesh. The genre was soon parodied, as in Yasuko Aoike's

From Eroica with Love (1976) and male artist Maya Mineo's *Pataliro!* (1979), a long-running gag manga starring a tiny, dumpy prince who thinks of himself as the greatest *bishônen* in the universe.

YAOI

The aesthetic *shônen ai* trend dwindled in the 1980s, only to be revived in fandom as a sort of self-parody: *yaoi.* Based on the first syllables of the joke phrase *ya-manashi, ochinashi, iminashi* ("No climax, no conclusion, no meaning"), *yaoi* filled the same role as "slash" fanfiction in the West, which placed male characters from pop culture in steamy gay situations (e.g., Kirk and Spock). Another half-joking explanation is that the term *yaoi* stands for *yamete, oshiri (ga) itai!* ("stop, my ass hurts!"). Originating as self-published *dôjinshi* sold at conventions such as Comic Market, *yaoi* based on popular *shônen* manga became one of the most popular *dôjinshi* genres. In the hands of *yaoi* artists, the friendship aesthetic of popular boys' manga such as *Dragon Ball* and *Captain Tsubasa* was easily pushed over the line into homosexuality. Some *yaoi* are merely suggestive, with nothing more than hand-holding or declarations of love, but others are extremely explicit. Ranging from humor to affectionate tributes to outright porn, *yaoi* attracted thousands of Japanese women to self-published comics, and frequently parodied the macho outlook of mainstream Japanese manga.

BOYS' LOVE

In the late 1980s, gay themes returned to professional comics. Yun Kouga's gentle sci-fi love story *Earthian* (1987), serialized in the minor magazine *Wings,* was popular, but an even more influential series was Minami Ozaki's *Zetsuai* ("Desperate Love") (1989) and its sequel, *Bronze,* the story of a jaded rock star and his obsession with a young soccer prodigy. Serialized in the bestselling magazine *Margaret,* it brought gay themes to a modern setting and also subjected its characters to unprecedented angst and torment, to violent passion and outbursts of savage jealousy. *Zetsuai* was almost relentlessly harsh, but Kazuma Kodaka's *Kizuna: Bonds of Love* (1992) swung between melodrama and humor. Both titles had their roots in *yaoi dôjinshi,* of mainstream soccer manga and *yakuza* manga, respectively. By the time of Sanami Matoh's *Fake* (1994) and Maki Murakami's *Gravitation* (1996), the formula was well established enough for self-parody, bringing a welcome playfulness back to the genre.

Boys' Love was now an established market; all the titles in the previous paragraph were successful enough to be animated. Nonetheless, Japan's largest publishers—Shueisha, Shogakukan, Kodansha, Hakusensha—shied away from the genre, leaving the field open to dozens of small publishers, who released specialty manga magazines such as *Craft, Chara,* and *Pierce.* Some of the more marginal *shôjo* magazines have companion Boys' Love magazines; Kadokawa Shoten's *Asuka* has *Ciel* and *Ciel Très Très,* and readers of Shinshokan's *Wings* can turn to *Dear Plus,* where the boy-boy action goes from implicit to explicit. The most popular are the monthly *Be x Boy* and its more explicit bimonthly companion, *Be x Boy Gold.* By the mid-2000s, the market was showing signs of a glut, and some publishers shifted toward gay prose novels.

Most modern Boys' Love manga are formulaic fantasy scenarios: idealized monogamous romances with little relation to actual gay men, typically one or two volumes long. (Some *yaoi* artists also draw for gay men's comics, and some men do read *yaoi,* but it's rare for manga artists to remark on it when they receive letters from men.) The majority of *yaoi* take place in a world without homophobia, and don't even use the word "gay"; in this way it's not different from typical love comedy manga, in which characters with same-sex crushes often say things like "I'm not gay, I just like so-and-so!" Sexual orientation is not an issue, let alone political statements, apart from a few exceptional titles such as Youka Nitta's *Embracing Love* (1999) and Maki Kanemaru and Yukine Honami's wishful short story *Kiss Scandal,* in which a bachelor American presidential candidate is caught sleeping with his secretary, only to be forgiven by the public because it's true love and Americans love gay people. Typically, the gay element is just strong enough to add the faintest hint of forbidden love; some titles flirt with other "forbidden" scenarios, such as pseudo-incest (usually stepbrother-stepbrother), rape, or borderline pedophilia, aka *shota.* (This side of *yaoi* must be seen in the context of straight male *lolicon* manga and the abusive behavior directed toward women in such *seinen* manga as Kazuo Koike's.) Unlike in most actual gay relationships, one party is almost always the pursuer (*seme*) and one party is the pursued (*uke*); the *seme-uke* relationship often conforms to stereotypical male-female roles, with the *uke* being shorter, cuter, and more passive. Some Boys' Love is comedic, some serious; some PG-rated, others graphically sexual; often the last story in a book will contain uncharacteristically explicit content, a bonus for readers who buy the graphic novel.

Many Japanese and American commentators have theorized about the appeal of Boys' Love. There are many lesbian Boys' Love fans, leading some to suspect that the genre is a "safe" expression of lesbian feelings. (Moto Hagio wrote the first draft of *Thomas no Shinzô* as a lesbian story involving girls but changed it because she felt it read better with male characters.) A more generally accepted explanation is that Boys' Love is a safe expression of feelings, period. Although most of the stories no longer take place in nineteenth-century European boys' schools, they deal with a type of sexuality that is still distant to most Japanese women, and, because it is seen from the perspective of the opposite sex, may always be essentially unknowable. Men in *yaoi* are both idealized and objectified; the readers can safely fantasize about handsome men, or fantasize about *being* men, projecting themselves into the *seme* or *uke* role as their secret heart desires. Men, after all, still enjoy privileges in Japanese society. Emotionally and physically (with their sleek, hairless bodies, unlike the typically muscular bodies in actual gay men's manga) the characters in *yaoi* manga combine male and female traits according to readers' desires, creating a sort of perfect hermaphroditic creature who happens to have a penis. Perhaps with gender roles, the grass is always greener on the other side; then again, you can't discount the sheer desire to see hot men making out with one another.

BISHÔNEN

Boys' Love books represent the purest and most formulaic of the genre, but even though gay stories rarely appear anymore in ordinary girls' manga magazines, there is considerable crossover with mainstream anime and manga. Stories involving teams of *bishônen* ("beautiful boys") who are devoted to one another to the point of ambiguity are often popular with female fans even when nothing overtly sexual happens. The 1995 hit anime *Gundam Wing* helped popularize *bishônen* in America. Even *shônen* manga artists acknowledge the genre. When Naruto accidentally kisses his rival Sasuke in the second chapter of *Naruto,* the scene was certainly intended not just as a joke but as a sly wink to female *Shônen Jump* readers (although *Shônen Jump* artists and editors would never admit it). In no time at all, the Japanese *dôjinshi* scene was rife with Naruto/Sasuke stories, doing their own part to contribute to the tremendous popularity of *Naruto.*

Yaoi is a relatively new manga genre in America and owes much of its success to online fandom. In 2001, the first annual "*Yaoi*-Con" took place in San Francisco; the first convention was so tightly knit that preregistered attendees' names were printed in the program book. ComicsOne translated a few *yaoi* in e-book format in 2000 (*Horizon Line* and *Lucky Star*), but it was not until 2004 that *yaoi* manga were translated in print and promoted by companies such as Digital Manga Publishing and Be Beautiful (a division of CPM). DramaQueen, Kitty Media (a division of Media Blasters), 801 Media (a more explicit imprint of Digital Manga Publishing), and BLU (a division of Tokyopop) soon entered the market, along with *yaoi*-influenced Korean comics and original comics by American and European artists. Some artists are as apolitical as their Japanese counterparts, while others, such as Abby Denson, consciously tackle homophobia, "coming out," and other real-world themes. The critical and commercial success of such movies as *Brokeback Mountain,* which was a hit in both America and Japan, suggests that the tastes for male-male romance may be universal, and that Boys' Love may be one of the most influential of modern-day manga genres.

Bishônen *Manga*

Aquarian Age: Juvenile Orion • Bus Gamer • Cipher • Clover • Descendants of Darkness • The Devil Does Exist • GATE • Hands Off! • Kamui • Mobile Suit Gundam Wing • Mobile Suit Gundam Wing: Battlefield of Pacifists • Mobile Suit Gundam Wing: Blind Target • Mobile Suit Gundam Wing: Endless Waltz • Mobile Suit Gundam Wing: Episode Zero • Mobile Suit Gundam Wing: Ground Zero • Ouran High School Host Club • Peace Maker • Peacemaker Kurogane • The Prince of Tennis • Saiyuki • Saiyuki Reload • Satisfaction Guaranteed • Seimaden • Sequence • Tactics • Urban Mirage • The Wallflower • The Wanderer • Wild Adapter • X-Kai

AFFAIR

Shiuko Kano • 801 Media (2007) • Tokuma Shoten (2005) • 1 volume • Yaoi • 18+ (nudity, graphic sex)

Steamy short stories about reunited friends, *yakuza* with more in common than their gangster ways, and a high-stakes mahjong game. (HS)   NR

AIJIN ICHIMANYEN

Aijin Ichimanen, "10,000 Yen Lover" (愛人いちまんえん) • Dr. Ten • DramaQueen (2007) • Kousai Shobo (2003) • 1 volume • Yaoi • 18+ (nudity, graphic sex)

A young homeless man is taken in by a stranger who plans to be his master. (HS)
                NR

ALCOHOL, SHIRT AND KISS

Sake to Y-shirt to Kiss, "Alcohol, Y-Shirt and Kiss" (酒とYシャツとキス) • Yuuko Kuwabara • DMP (2007) • Biblos (2004) • 1 volume • Yaoi, Contemporary • 18+ (nudity, graphic sex)

Naru plans to drink away the pain of a failed relationship with fellow detective Kita. But after a night of drowning sorrows, Naru wakes up in bed, naked with his booze buddy. (HS)   NR

ALLURE

Kowaku, "Allure" (ALLURE—蠱惑) • Yuri Ebihara • DramaQueen (2007) • Shinkôsha (2005) • 1 volume • Yaoi • 18+

Kai was blinded years ago in a freak accident, but even though he has had corneal implants he finds it impossible to focus on anyone but his handsome surgeon, Dr. Hizuki. (HS)   NR

ALMOST CRYING

Naichaisoyô, "Almost Crying" (泣いちゃいそうよ) • Mako Takahashi • DMP (2006) • Kaiohsha (2002) • 1 volume • Yaoi, Comedy • 16+ (sexual situations)

A collection of comedic, vaguely *shota* Boys' Love stories, where even the eighteen-year-old characters look about ten. The premises

Mako Takahashi's *Almost Crying* © Kaiohsha

are often imaginative and quirky, and the art is cute, but some readers may be creeped out by the character designs and the master-servant/stepbrother-stepbrother themes. The better stories include "The Mer-Prince" (a sequel to "The Little Mermaid"), "Celluloid Closet" (in which a doll-obsessed boy transfers his infatuation to another boy), and "Second Hand" (in which a girl gives her brother to her ex-boyfriend as a replacement). The only story with sex is the last one, "The Taste of First Love."   ★★½

ALONE IN MY KING'S HAREM

Harem de Hitori, "Alone in the Harem" (ハレムでひとり) • Lily Hoshino • DMP (2005) • Biblos (2004) • 1 volume • Yaoi, Fantasy • 18+ (mild language, nudity, graphic sex)

A collection of exquisite, baroque gay love stories set in fantastic settings. The main characters are mostly prisoners, concubines, and servants, but the well-written stories achieve a mood of dreamlike romance. Hoshino's stories are imaginative and her artwork is lovely, although her character designs represent the extreme of feminine *ukes;* with their long hair, small frames, and feminine clothes, they're virtually indistinguishable from prepubescent girls. The book would be suitable for a 16+ age rating except for the last two tales, which involve graphic sex and are set in the real world, breaking the mood that the other stories have established. ★★★½

ANGEL OR DEVIL?!

Ore no Tenshi wa Mayonaka Akuma, "My Angel Is a Devil at Midnight" (オレの天使は真夜中悪魔) • Jun Uzuki • DramaQueen (2007) • Ookura Shuppan (2005) • 1 volume • Yaoi • 18+

Under Mr. Fujiki's stern schoolteacher demeanor beats the heart of a man with a weakness for all things cute. Angelic, adorable transfer student Shiina is terrified by his new teacher, and Mr. Fujiki vows to change his intimidating ways. Then one night a devilish young man, answering to the name Shiina, steals a kiss from Mr. Fujiki. Are there two Shiinas? What's a hot teacher to do? (HS) NR

ANTIQUE BAKERY: See General Manga Reviews

THE ART OF LOVING

Renai Kôfukuron, "A Discourse on Love and Happiness" (恋愛幸福論) • Eiki Eiki • DMP (2006) • Shinshokan (2001) • 1 volume • Yaoi, Drama • 18+ (nudity, graphic sex)

Starting with a glimpse of its characters as adults, *The Art of Loving* changes perspective and flashes back to high school. Yutaka, a boy from a wealthy family, becomes obsessed with his rough but talented classmate Tohno, compulsively masturbating while thinking of Tohno as the "black stain" in his heart spreads further. Soon a disturbing opportunity arises for Yutaka to get what he wants. . . . As in *Dear Myself,* Eiki Eiki combines interesting story structures with psychological insights and dark themes, but in *The Art of Loving* the darkness seems to come more naturally from the story. Unfortu-

nately, the promising story is cut short by the cliff-hanger ending of volume 1; Eiki Eiki is slowly working on a second volume, but as of April 2007, it has yet to be published in Japan. ★★½

BANANA FISH: See General Manga Reviews

BECAUSE I'M A BOY!

Otoko no ko Dakara Ne, "Because I'm a Boy!" (男のコだからね) • Asia Watanabe • Kitty Media (2006) • Houbunsha (Hanaoto, 2003) • 1 volume • Yaoi • 18+ (nudity, graphic sex)

These short stories are disturbing in both content and art style. The men look superpervy, the boys look super-underage, everyone has weird lips, some of the FX look like nipples, and most of the sexual situations are highly questionable. For example, the young man who is in love with his guardian (his dead mother's last lover) and so screws the guardian's brother; the school doctor who screws the students, and then the science teacher who tries to stop him; the young man who lets his best friend practice S&M on him until he can't find sexual pleasure any other way. Lots of explicit sex, but very little in the way of satisfying story. (HS) ★★

BEYOND MY TOUCH

Meniha Sayakani Mienedomo, "Without Realizing Clearly/With Eyes However" (目にはさやかに見えねども) • Tomo Maeda • DMP (2005) • Shinshokan (2003) • 1 volume • Yaoi, Romantic, Comedy • 16+ (mild sexual situations)

Mizuno, a gloomy teenager who lives alone, finds himself haunted by his dead classmate Mamoru, a cheerful ghost bound to Earth by his desire to kiss Mizuno. *Beyond My Touch* reads like a *shônen ai* version of a boys' "housewife fantasy" manga, as Mamoru dotes on the disinterested Mizuno and attempts to cook and do chores despite being incorporeal. With only two characters and very little plot, the story is shallow but cute, and the main characters look girlish. Two short stories round out the book. The plot is almost sexless and is suitable for younger teenage readers. The title is a reference to a haiku by Fujiwara no Toshiyuki. ★★½

BLACK KNIGHT

Kuro no Kishi, "Black Knight" (黒の騎士) • Kai Tsurugi • BLU (2006–2007) • Biblos (Be x Boy, 2003–2005) • 3 volumes • Yaoi, Fantasy, Drama • 18+ (mild language, violence, nudity, sex)

Dense with courtly intrigue, which most readers will skim over to get to the love scenes, *Black Knight* is a well-drawn, well-written *shônen ai* manga in a vaguely European period setting. Chris Jeremy, the fragile prince of the Kingdom of Aran, goes to a military boarding school, where he meets his one true love, Zeke O'Brian, a gifted swordsman, hunter, and horseman. Zeke becomes part of Chris' royal guard, and the two enter a forbidden but tacitly accepted relationship. Perhaps the best part of the comic, however, is the art and the action scenes. The artwork is detailed and accurate, with forests, castles, and young men in knee-high boots and formal jackets—a sort of eighteenth- or nineteenth-century "man's world" of vaguely homosexual camaraderie that feels as if it could have really existed. It's light on the sex, however. ★★½

BOND(Z)

BONDZ • Touko Kawai • 801 Media (2007) • Biblos (2003) • 1 volume • Yaoi • 18+ (nudity, graphic sex)

It's not uncommon for friends to tumble into bed together after a night of boozing it up. But when both friends are guys who just happen to have girlfriends, the situation gets a little messy. (HS) NR

BROTHER

(ブラザー) • Yuzuha Ougi • DramaQueen (2005) • Kaiohsha (2004) • 1 volume, suspended (2 volumes in Japan) • Yaoi • 18+ (nudity, graphic sex)

Ougi's art style has a decadent sensibility: her male characters are masculine and strongly sexualized, with long, predatory faces and full lips, long bony fingers, and genitals so detailed they're almost scary.

Asuka, a twenty-something virgin, has been impotent ever since a long-ago summer when he was trapped in a confined space with his stepbrother for an entire afternoon. When his now grown-up stepbrother comes back into his life, their mutual feelings of shame turn into lust. After the plausibly twisted setup, the story follows a conventional Boys' Love development, showing the give-and-take of an idealized relationshi The art is distinctive, the sex extremely graphic. The second volume has not been translated, possibly because of a surprising downturn in Ougi's normally excellent art. ★★★

. . . BUT, I'M YOUR TEACHER

Seito no Shuchô ☆ *Kyoshi no Honbun,* "A Student's Work Is the Teacher's Duty" (生徒の主著☆教師の本分 . . . but, I'm Your teacher) • Row Takakura • Kitty Media (2006) • Biblos (2001) • 1 volume • Yaoi • 18+ (nudity, graphic sex)

A collection of short, explicit *yaoi* stories, delivering both the emotional and sexual money shots. In the first story, a student seduces his substitute teacher; other stories involve stepbrother-stepbrother pairings, a teenage prostitute, and two boyfriends taking care of a baby. The relationships are basically consensual and lighthearted (there's lots of blushing and tousled hair amid the bodily fluids), except for a single dark story about a photographer and his model. Takekura's art is polished, with a fine line and lots of screentone; her *ukes* tend to be girlish. ★★★

CAGE IN THE FINDER: See *Finder Series*

CAGE OF THORNS

Ibara no Ori, "Cage of Thorns" (荊の檻～いばらのおり) • Sonoko Sakuragawa • DramaQueen (2007) • Kaiohsha (2005) • 1 volume • Yaoi • 18+ (nudity, graphic sex)

Kujou Tsurugi, a young executive, is assaulted at an industry cocktail party. Katsuragi Takaya, the son of a parliamentarian, saves him . . . but he expects payment for his troubles. *Physical* payment. (HS) NR

CANTARELLA: See General Manga Reviews

CAN'T WIN WITH YOU

Kimi ni wa Kattenai!, "Can't Win with You!" (きみに
は勝てない!) • Satosumi Takaguchi (story), Yukine
Honami (art) • DMP (2007–2008) • Houbunsha
(Hanaoto, 2003–2004) • 3 volumes • Yaoi, Comedy
• 18+ (nudity, graphic sex)

Shuuju Academy is an elite school for young
men of aspirations. But once the lights go
out, their inhibitions drop! (HS)   NR

CASINO LILY

(カジノ・リリィ) • Youka Nitta • Be Beautiful (2007) •
Biblos (Be x Boy Gold, 1999) • 1 volume • Yaoi • 18+
(nudity, graphic sex)

Casino owner Kaoru and gambling prodigy
Yuri play a high-stakes game, but when Yuri
wins he declines Kaoru's fortune in favor of
his favors. (HS)   NR

CHALLENGERS

(チャレンジャーズ) • Hinako Takanaga • Drama-
Queen (2006–2007) • Hakusensha/Kaiohsha
(1996–2004) • 4 volumes • Yaoi, Comedy • 16+
(sexual situations)

Girlishly cute college student Tomoe moves
to Tokyo to attend an engineering program,
where he meets Mitsugu, a young salaryman
who develops a huge crush on him. Embar-
rassed to find himself liking a man, Mitsugu
offers Tomoe his spare room for rent but
can't resist hitting on him afterward, despite
the threat of murder by Tomoe's homophobic, protective older brother Souichi ("All
homos must die!"). *Challengers* is an entertaining *shônen ai* version of any number of
straight manga romantic comedies, with
Tomoe playing the oblivious girl who can't
possibly believe she's getting hit on, despite
innumerable kisses and close calls. The interior art is notably older and rougher than
Takanaga's *Little Butterfly,* with a retro 1980s–
1990s look in the early chapters. The first
volume was originally published by Hakusensha under the title *Gôkakukigan* ("Prayers
for Passing Marks").   ★★½

CLAN OF THE NAKAGAMIS

Nakagamike no Ichizoku, "Clan of the Nakagamis"
(仲神家の一族) • Homerun Ken • DMP (2006) • Biblos (2005) • 1 volume • Yaoi, Comedy • 16+ (sexual
situations)

Off-the-wall anime-style *shônen ai* comedy.
Haruka and Tokio (who's twenty-five but
looks underage) are a gay student-teacher
couple. When Haruka goes to Tokio's house,
he discovers that Tokio's family is a bunch of
creepy but beautiful weirdos (a cross-dressing
shôjo manga artist, uncannily youthful parents, etc.) who all have varying degrees of
unhealthy interest in their favorite son. Although no one quite takes their pants off,
high doses of taboo-relationship humor
and *dôjinshi*-esque absurdity make this a
fun title, particularly for high-level manga
fans who recognize all the genre in-jokes.
In any case, the art is attractive and the
jokes are well done. Among the also comedic side stories, the best involves two gay
teenagers preparing to have sex for the first
time.   ★★★

CLOSE THE LAST DOOR

Saigo no Door wa Shimero!, "Close the Last Door!"
(最後のドアを閉めろ!) • Yugi Yamada • DMP (2006–
2007) • Biblos (2001–2004) • 2 volumes • Salaryman, Yaoi • 18+ (nudity, graphic sex)

Nagai has loved Saitoh since they were in
college, but now that Saitoh is married,
Nagai plans to drown his sorrows in endless
cans of beer and Honda's willing, uncom-
mitted arms. Then Saitoh's bride runs off
with another man and Saitoh starts hitting
on him, and Honda's casual sex turns out to
mean a lot more than Nagai expected. Nagai
and Honda's relationship is intriguing, and
the story would do well to focus on it more.
Saitoh, the supposed love of Nagai's life, is
an annoyance who should just go away. It's
irritating that the author feels the need to
throw in girlfriends and wives, who don't
have much of a presence in the story except
to make the main characters "accidentally"
gay. The art is a bit odd, especially in the facial features, but it isn't off-putting so much
as dated. (HS)   ★★

CRIMSON SPELL

(クリムゾン・スペル) • Ayano Yamane • Kitty Media (2007–ongoing) • Tokuma Shoten (2005–ongoing) • 2+ volumes (ongoing) • Yaoi, Fantasy • 18+ (nudity, graphic sex)

To protect his people, Prince Bald must use a demonic sword that curses its bearer. The only one who can help Prince Bald lift the curse is the wizard Harvir . . . who has a special attraction to Bald. (HS)   NR

CRIMSON WIND

DUO BRAND. • DramaQueen (2007) • Ookura Shuppan (2005) • 1 volume • Yaoi, Fantasy • 18+ (nudity, graphic sex)

The prequel to *White Guardian* tells the story of how General Sei met his first lover, Governor Touri. As a new cadet, Sei wins a tournament and the eyes of the governor. (HS)   NR

THE DAY I BECOME A BUTTERFLY

Chô ni Naru Hi, "The Day I Become a Butterfly" (チョウになる日) • Sumomo Yumeka • DMP (2007) • Taiyoh Tosho (2003) • 1 volume • Yaoi, Drama • 16+ (sexual situations)

Uka is fifteen and dying from a terminal disease. Mikami is a sullen misanthrope who might have the power to hear death coming. Do they have a chance for a happy ending? (HS)   NR

DEAR MYSELF

Dear Myself (ディア・マイセルフ) • Eiki Eiki • DMP (2006) • Shinshokan (Dear Plus, 1998) • 1 volume • Yaoi • 16+ (mild language, mild sexual situations)

After two years of amnesia, teenage Hirofumi suddenly regains his memory, only to discover to his surprise that during the "lost" two years he picked up a gay boyfriend, Daigo. While Daigo pursues Hirofumi with an aggressive neediness that, in the real world, would justify counseling, Hirofumi reads his diary from his period of amnesia, which is written in the form of letters to his future self. The "lost time" premise is ingenious, and Hirofumi's "conversations with himself" are sensitively done ("I didn't plan to become gay . . . but if my heart's gonna pain me like this, what else can I do?"). But as the plot focuses more on Daigo, his troubled personality and rape attempts bring down the whole story ("Even if your *brain* doesn't remember, your *body* should, right?!"). The art is hasty and generic, the facial expressions are awkward. Ambitious but flawed. Continued in *World's End.* ★★½

DESIRE

Yabai Kimochi, "Forbidden Feelings/Feelings of Desire" (ヤバイ気持ち) • Maki Kazumi (story), Yukine Honami (art) • DMP (2004) • Tokuma Shoten (2001) • 1 volume • Yaoi • 18+ (mild language, partial nudity, sex)

A would-be realistic Boys' Love manga, *Desire* has frank sex talk and some effort to show how actual teenage boys might deal with homosexuality, but its realism is more on the level of lube than psychology. Toru, a short, blond artist, has a crush on his friend Ryoji, a tall, dark-haired boy who has had multiple casual girlfriends. Suddenly, Ryoji turns bi-curious and asks Toru if he wants to have sex, pressuring him and causing unexpected anxiety for Toru, who wants him but doesn't want to be just used. Honami draws nice, realistic male bodies and figures, offset by the stereotypical *seme-uke* character designs and bland, subdued facial expressions (which, admittedly, fit the characters' troubled and inscrutable personalities). Most Boys' Love manga never even use the term "homosexuality," but in this story, being gay is an act of both self-affirmation and surrender: "I am a deviant," Toru finally declares to himself with a slight smile, after endless pages of discomfort and anxiety. Later adapted into a novel by Maki Kazumi.   ★★

EARTHIAN

(アーシアン) • Yun Kouga • BLU (2005–2006) • Shinshokan (Wings/South, 1987–1995) • 4 volumes • Science Fiction, Yaoi, Romance • 16+ (mild language, violence, nudity, sexual situations)

For billions of years, Earth has been watched over by angels—actually aliens from the planet Eden—who count the pluses and minuses of humankind, debating whether the "earthian" (earthlings) should be allowed to exist. Two such angels are Chihaya and Kagetsuya, androgynous-looking male partners who must keep their growing attraction a secret . . . for the angel race is dying off, and homosexuality is punishable by death. ("What is the crime in loving someone?") Considered a classic manga of the 1980s and 1990s, *Earthian* reads like a bridge between the sci-fi *shônen ai* of the 1970s (*A, A'*) and more plotless, formulaic modern *yaoi*. The art is like a survey of *shôjo* styles from the period, eventually graceful (the attractive covers were drawn much later than the interiors), but never too strong on the backgrounds or distinguishing one character from another. Part of the action consists of different one-shot stories set on Earth—such as a major subplot involving cyborg "biohumanoids" in love—while the rest takes place on the angels' home world, where they look, dress, and act like humans in fruitless romantic triangles. The theme of forbidden love provides welcome tension to the main characters' relationship, but Chihaya and Kagetsuya's romance doesn't get moving until volume 3, when the love and the loosely sketched science fiction plotline both come to a climax. As a love story, it eventually works, but as a world-spanning drama, it's weak; perhaps the art—mostly just flowers and isolated human figures—doesn't provide enough sense of scale. Volume 4 consists of side stories, of which the best is "Secret Garden," which includes the series' only nude scenes; oddly, they're female. ★★½

EERIE QUEERIE: See General Manga Reviews

EMBRACING LOVE

Haru wo Daiteita, "Embrace the Spring" (春を抱いていた) • Youka Nitta • Be Beautiful (2005–2006) • Biblos (1999–2006) • 11 volumes • Yaoi, Performance, Drama • 18+ (nudity, graphic sex)

Iwaki, a straight porn star who is becoming insecure about his career future, sets his sights on a mainstream breakout rule: the movie adaptation of "Embracing Love," a novel-within-the-manga about gay porn stars and "homosexuality in today's society." While auditioning for the role, he has sex with a rival star, Katou, and the experience changes him, until he and Katou are openly gay lovers whose relationship is lapped up by the tabloid media. Compared to the typical *yaoi* title where the main characters are theoretically ordinary folks, the adult film industry setting gives *Embracing Love* a perfect excuse for hard-core sex scenes. Better still, the plot is written with media-savvy humor and even a certain amount of realism; Iwaki must "come out" to his homophobic family, and as Iwaki and Katou's relationship becomes more domestic, they consider marriage ("We might even hold a ceremony in America"). With hunky, adult characters, realistic sex scenes, and almost no elements of coercion, it's a sexy and well-written series; even actual gay men might enjoy it. ★★★★

EMPTY HEART

Empty Heart—Itsuwari no Koi Dakara, "Empty Heart—Because of False Love" (Empty Heart—偽りの恋だから) • Masara Minase • DramaQueen (2006) • Ookura Shuppan (2003) • 1 volume • Yaoi, Romance • 18+ (sexual situations)

Takumi has had a crush on art teacher Usami for years, but Usami only has eyes for Takumi's older brother Ryuuta. Now that Ryuuta is getting married, Takumi sees his chance to get with Usami, if only as a stand-in for Ryuuta. While this is another one of those "can't have the older brother, guess I'll bang the younger" setups, this manga takes care to really explore the emotions between Takumi and Usami, creating vivid characters and making the reader truly care about their blossoming relationship. It helps that the art is well done and that they are pretty, pretty boys with soulful eyes. This is a well-written story, and the only downfall is a translation that falls short; overuse of dialect and honorifics add to the clunkiness of the dialogue but can't take all the blame for disrupting the reading experience. (HS) ★★★½

FAKE: See General Manga Reviews

FAKE FUR

(フェイクファー) • Satomi Yamagata • DMP (2007) • Houbunsha (Hanaoto, 2004) • 1 volume • Yaoi • 18+

Sweet short stories about the trials and tribulations of falling in love. (HS)　　　NR

FINDER SERIES

Finder no Hyôteki, "Target in the Finder"; *Finder no Ori,* "Cage in the Finder"; *Finder no Sekiyoku,* "One Wing in the Finder" (ファインダーの標的・ファインダーの檻・ファインダーの隻翼) • Ayano Yamane • Be Beautiful (2004–2007) • Biblos (Be x Boy, 2002–2005) • 3 volumes • Yaoi, Crime Drama • 18+ (violence, nudity, graphic sex)

When photojournalist Akihito takes photos of the wrong criminals, he is captured, tied up, and raped by Asami, an impeccably dressed, dominant underworld boss who later saves his life. Considering that it involves graphic rape and S&M, *Finder Series* is written in an appropriately dark and brooding fashion. The side stories involve more conventional, even humorous pairings (although an element of coercion is often present), while the relatively sexless volume 2 consists mostly of a single dramatic story involving Asami and Fei Long, a Chinese Mafia boss. The art is a strong point: coolly attractive, with handsome, chiseled guys.

★★½

FROM EROICA WITH LOVE: See General Manga Reviews

GAKUEN HEAVEN

Gakuen Heaven, "School Heaven" (学園ヘヴン) • SPRAY (concept), You Higuri • BLU (2006–2007) • Biblos (Be x Boy, 2004–ongoing) • Yaoi, School, Romance • 5 volumes • 18+ (nudity, graphic sex)

Based on the video game Gakuen Heaven: Boy's Love Scramble! by Spray, *Gakuen Heaven* is the story of Keita and his unexpected transfer to the exclusive boys' school Bell Liberty Academy (BL Academy, ha ha). BL Academy is populated with only the

Masara Minase's *Empty Heart*

most accomplished boys, and so everyone wonders what the hell Keita is doing there. He's threatened with expulsion, and the only way to stay seems to be to win the director's MVP competition. With the campus king as his partner and his uncanny luck to guide him, Keita is sure to win the right to stay. The story seems intent on introducing the maximum amount of characters in the least amount of time and rushing into the nonsensical competition (even the characters remark on how weird it is). Keita and the king fall desperately in love after barely three days of acquaintanceship and consummate their lackluster relationship in a very forced (plotwise) sex scene on the beach. There's nothing wrong with the art, except for an overabundance of indistinguishable boys with long golden locks, but coupled with such a spastic story, it fails to hold the reader's attention. (HS)　　　★

IL GATTO SUL G

G Senjô no Neko, "The Cat of the G Chord" (G線上の猫) • Tooko Miyagi • DMP (2006) • Taiyoh Tosho

(Craft Original Comics Anthology, 2002–2005) • 2 volumes • Yaoi, Romance • 16+ (mild violence, sex)

One day, teenage Atsushi discovers an injured boy lying in front of his door: Riya, a talented but troubled violinist, who has developed a split personality disorder because of the pressures of his music. When his personality returns to normal, a suddenly shy Riya leaves Atsushi's apartment and rejects his offer of friendship, but finds himself coming back when he is sexually harassed by one of his male classmates. A restrained tale of *shônen ai* angst, *Il Gatto sul G* benefits from a slow pace and willingness to leave the characters' feelings unspoken. The art makes up in style for what it lacks in anatomical precision, with thin, frail-looking characters resembling those of Sumomo Yumeka. ★★½

GERARD & JACQUES

Gerard to Jacques, "Gerard and Jacques" (ジェラールとジャック Gerard et Jacques) • Fumi Yoshinaga • BLU (2006) • Biblos (Be x Boy, 1999–2001) • 2 volumes • Historical, Yaoi, Drama • 18+ (mild language, brief violence, nudity, graphic sex)

Fumi Yoshinaga is seemingly incapable of writing a boring story, and in *Gerard & Jacques* she manages to express the passion and decadence of revolutionary-era France and create a sexually sophisticated *yaoi* drama, with little more than talking heads and bodies on bedsheets. Jacques, an inexperienced teenage aristocrat sold to a brothel to pay his parents' debts, is purchased by Monsieur Gerard Anglade, a brusque, wealthy, self-made author with a distaste for aristocrats and a taste for young boys. "You filthy sodomite!" Jacques curses on their first encounter, but then Gerard pays for Jacques' freedom, to show the pampered boy that living in poverty is even worse than being a whore. Random chance, rather than romantic predestination, causes Jacques to be hired as a servant in Gerard's household, after which he grows into an adult without further interference from the older man. Then something happens, and both characters change in a way both believable and sympathetic. Excellent characterization and dialogue drive the plot, which, surprisingly, hinges on Gerard's past and his relationship with his dead wife. The sex scenes are explicit and varied. Highly recommended.

★★★★

GET YOU (WANTED MAN)

Get You Meshimase Kaitou, "Get You: I'll Catch the Phantom Thief" (GET YOU 召しませ怪盗) • Kusuko Asa • DramaQueen (2007) • Shinkôsha (2005) • 1 volume • Phantom, Thief, Yaoi • 18+ (nudity, graphic sex)

Detective Fujishina is determined to prove himself by catching society's bad boy du jour, the debonair thief Fox. But soon Fujishina's obsession with catching a thief becomes a desire to hold the man. (HS)   NR

GOLDEN CAIN

Kin no Cain, "Golden Cain" (金のカイン) • You Asagiri • Be Beautiful (2004) • Biblos (Be x Boy, 2003) • 1 volume • Yaoi • 18+ (mild violence, nudity, graphic sex)

Shun, a repressed student with feelings for his older brother, is nearly raped by satanists at a Black Sabbath, only to be rescued by Cain, a handsome model with golden hair. Cain, who speaks Vietnamese and studied in Britain ("the home of Oscar Wilde"), has sex with Shun outside, and then transfers to his high school to follow him around more. Despite lots of dirty talk ("Do you like the taste of sin?"), the main characters' relationship is mostly consensual, for a mood of intentionally over-the-top pornographic fun with lots of crudely drawn fingering. What seem to be unresolved plot elements involving Shun's brother are actually the result of censorship; several pages of incest-related sequences were removed from the English edition.   ★★

GORGEOUS CARAT

(ゴージャス・カラット) • You Higuri • BLU (2006–2007) • Shueisha (Eyes, 1999–2002) • 4 volumes • Yaoi, Historical, Crime Drama • 16+ (mild language, violence, sexual situations)

Set in turn-of-the-century Paris, *Gorgeous Carat* demonstrates You Higuri's flair for period settings; her detailed backgrounds and costumes give the series a lush, ornate look. (On the other hand, her character designs are attractive but relatively unmemorable.) Florian, an amethyst-eyed young man from an impoverished noble family, allows himself to be sold to a handsome moneylender, Ray Balzac Courland, who leads a double life as the mysterious top-hatted jewel thief Noir. Florian soon becomes an accomplice to Noir's band of thieves, but not before being tied up and whipped in the dungeon to show who's on top (the first of many indignities suffered by Florian, who generally plays the role of the swooning heroine of a Victorian bodice-ripper). Despite this and other darkly suggestive moments, the story is more an adventure manga than a *yaoi* manga; the stories are exciting treasure hunts in exotic settings such as the Eiffel Tower, the Paris catacombs, and the palaces of Morocco. Although the plots are simple, the combination of action and fin de siècle decadence is enjoyable. ★★★

GORGEOUS CARAT GALAXY

Gorgeous Carat Galaxy: Sei naru Kaibutsu no Mori, "The Forest of Holy Monsters" (ゴージャス・カラットGALAXY 聖なる怪物の森) • You Higuri • DMP (2006) • Gentosha (2004) • 1 volume • Historical, Yaoi, Mystery • 13+ (mild violence, mild sexual situations)

Stand-alone sequel to *Gorgeous Carat*. While visiting a castle to purchase artwork, handsome jewel thieves Florian and Ray Balzac (and their girl assistant Lila) are trapped for the night by a snowstorm. Soon the other guests in the castle start turning up dead, and a mystery ensues, involving Florian's childhood friend Eleonora, the niece of the castle's owner. A functional gothic mystery for young readers, *Gorgeous Carat Galaxy* has moments of atmosphere, but the art is slightly weaker than the original *Gorgeous Carat,* and the sexual element is even more subdued. ★★½

GRAVITATION: See General Manga Reviews

HERE COMES THE WOLF?!

Ookami ga Kuruzo!?, "Here Comes the Wolf?!" (オオカミが来るぞ!?) • Youichirou Kouga • DramaQueen (2007) • Ookura Shuppan (2005) • 1 volume • Yaoi • 18+

Naomichi loves his classmate Kaoru, but circumstances haven't been ideal for confessing his feelings. Nevertheless, Naomichi decides to declare his love to Kaoru only to have Kaoru's brother hit on him! (HS) NR

HERO HEEL

Hero Heel—Eiyû to Akkan, "The Hero and the Scoundrel" (HERO HEEL—英雄と悪漢) • Makoto Tateno • DMP (2006) • Biblos (2005–2007) • 1 volume • Yaoi, Showbiz, Romance • 18+ (nudity, graphic sex)

Set during the filming of a children's action show, *Hero Heel* is about new actor Minami and his slow realization that his veteran co-star is gay. At first, Minami is disturbed, but then he's jealous enough of Sawada's other lovers to blackmail him into bed. The setup of the story takes forever, with way too much time wasted on behind-the-scenes action that glosses over any interesting technical details while also delaying the sex until the last scene of the book. The art gets the job done, but Sawada's eyes are so far apart they look like they are migrating into his hair, and it's hard to take him seriously as a "demon of seduction." (HS) ★

HORIZON LINE

Suiheisen, "The Horizon" (水平線) • Ikue Ishida • ComicsOne (e-book, 2001) • Ookura Shuppan (1997) • 1 volume • Yaoi • 16+ (sexual situations)

This e-book contains four short stories, all of which are boring. The title story is about Sanpei and Tani, who work at a supermarket together. Sanpei gets promoted, Tani pouts and professes his love. Sanpei gets weirded out, Tani pouts and doesn't tell Sanpei that he's moving back home. They hook up. The other three stories ("Jack Pot," "Boys Just Want to Love," "Close to You") are equally lackluster. The writing has neither the sweetness of *shônen ai* nor the sex of *yaoi,* and even the angst seems halfhearted and unconvincing. The pages have been flipped and poorly touched up for the English version, though the art itself is merely inoffensive and bland. However, many of the characters are too similar in appearance, to the point that in one story the love rival and the lover look alike. (HS) ★

HYBRID CHILD

Hybrid Child (ハイブリッドチャイルド(Hybrid Child)) • Shungiku Nakamura • DMP (2006) • Biblos (2005) • 1 volume • Yaoi • 16+ (language, sexual situations)

A *yaoi* version of a *Chobits* or *Dolls* theme, these three boy-on-boy romances involve the "Hybrid Children," intelligent, articulate artificial humans who bond with their owners and grow in response to love. The art is on the bad side of generic, but the tragic, bittersweet stories have some emotional meat, the only weak link being the second story, which has uncomfortably pedophilic overtones. The time and technology are vague; the first two stories have a vaguely modern setting, but the third, a flashback involving the inventor of the Hybrid Children, appears to be set in samurai times. It's an interesting read, but the art doesn't inspire you to pick it up again, or to linger over the pages. ★★

I CAN'T STOP LOVING YOU!

Yannatchaukurai Aishiteru, "I Can't Stop Loving You" (やんなっちゃうくらい愛してる) • Row Takekura • Kitty Media (2006) • Biblos (2003–2004) • 2 volumes • Yaoi, Occult • 18+ (explicit sexual situations)

Kyouji is a Buddhist exorcist-in-training who can't see ghosts. Yu is Kyouji's boyfriend, who can. This seems like a perfect relationship, but Yu has superhuman strength that shows up at the worst possible moment—in the middle of sex. The chapters are episodic, detailing Kyouji and Yu's adventures as they liberate spirits, vanquish demons, and try desperately to get it on. Kyouji and Yu have been in love since they were kids, and their strong relationship is a

good anchor for this story, which blends humor, horror, sex, and love into a very enjoyable package. (HS) ★★★½

ICHIGENME . . . THE FIRST CLASS IS CIVIL LAW

Ichigenme wa Yaru Ki no Minpô, "The First Class Is Civil Law" (1限めはやる気の民法) • Fumi Yoshinaga • 801 Media (2007) • Biblos (1998–2002) • 2 volumes • Yaoi • 18+ (nudity, graphic sex)

Tamiya and Tohdou meet at Teinou University, a school for priviliged kids. After graduation, their friendship turns into something more. NR

INNOCENT BIRD

Na mo Naki Tori no Tobu Yoake, "The Nameless Bird Flies at Daybreak" (名も無き鳥の飛ぶ夜明け) • Hirotaka Kisaragi • BLU (2007) • Kadokawa Shoten (2002–2004) • 3 volumes • Yaoi, Supernatural • 18+

Karasu is an angel sent to return the demon Shirasagi to hell. But Shirasagi has renounced his demonic powers and is living as a priest. Can the two find love in each other's arms with the might of heaven and hell against them? (HS) NR

INVOKE

Kirico Hagashizato • DramaQueen (2007) • Shinkô-sha (2003) • 1 volume • Yaoi, Science Fiction • 18+

Kai gets a virtual reality machine that allows him to explore endless worlds and times. In this virtual realm, Kai meets a stranger who dazzles him with extreme pleasure. Now Kai must scour the virtual landscape for his mysterious stranger. (HS) NR

IN THE WALNUT

Kurumi no Naka, "In the Walnut" (胡桃の中) • Touko Kawai • DMP (2007) • Biblos (2002) • 1 volume • Yaoi, Romance • 16+ (sexual situations)

Hideo Tanizaki and Shoehi Nakai are both twenty-four years old and graduated from the same art school. But Hideo's taste for forging art is a difference that Tanizaki plans to correct as soon as possible. (HS) NR

JAZZ

(ジャズ) • Sakae Maeda (story), Tamotsu Takamure (art) • DMP (2005–2006) • Shinshokan (Dear Plus, 1999–2005) • 4 volumes • Yaoi, Drama • 18+ (mild violence, partial nudity, sex)

Narusawa, a handsome but lonely doctor, treats eighteen-year-old Naoki for asthma. In the course of a few pages, Naoki graduates from high school, invites his former doctor out to dinner, and then drugs and rapes him, calling out "Doc . . . I love you . . ." as sweaty hands clutch the bedcovers. *Jazz* (so named for a brand of cologne and jazz music) is a fast-paced Boys' Love story based on a series of novels by Sakae Maeda. Like *Passion* or the title story of . . . *But, I'm Your Teacher,* the teenager is the pursuing *seme,* and the older authority figure is a shy, demasculinized *uke.* In volume 2, Narusawa leaves Naoki to go to America, resulting in an interesting change in setting. However, the character relationships remain formulaic, and plot tension is provided mostly by Naoki's relapses and jealous arguments over tiny misunderstandings. ★½

J-BOY BY BIBLOS

Various artists • DMP (2006) • Biblos • 1 volume • Yaoi, Anthology • 18+

This anthology contains one-shots and spin-offs from the Japanese magazine *Junk Boy,* a companion to the leading *yaoi* magazines *Be x Boy* and *Be x Boy Gold.* Includes stories by Naduki Koujima (*Our Kingdom*), Ken Homerun (*Clan of the Nakagamis*), Haruka Minami, Kana Mizuki, Kyushu Danji, Natsuho Shino, etc. (HS) NR

THE JUDGED

Sabakareshi Mono, "The Judged" (裁かれし者) • Akira Honma • DramaQueen (2006) • Shinkôsha (2003) • 1 volume • Crime, Yaoi • 18+ (brief violence, partial nudity, sex)

Kyou Sugiura, a noble public prosecutor, becomes involved in the case of Tatsuki Toudou, a politician with cruelly chiseled features under suspicion of vague charges of

Akira Honma's *The Judged*

corruption. Soon it's revealed that the two young men went to the same orphanage, and Toudou still desires Sugiura, so badly that he will use his influence and threaten Sugiura's family in order to get him. By the end of the first chapter it's clear that this story could happen only in *yaoi*-land, but most of the time Honma's bold, realistic artwork maintains a serious, dramatic mood. Despite the dark nature of the central relationship (well served by the use of black spaces in the art), the sex scenes are discreet. Several lighter *yaoi* stories round out the volume. ★★

JUNE PRIDE

(6月の自尊心) • Shinobu Gotou (story), Kazumi Ooya (art) • BLU (2007) • Kadokawa Shoten (2001) • 1 volume • Yaoi • 18+

The first in the Takumi-kun series, self-contained stories based on novels by Shinobu Gotou. Takumi attends the prestigious Shidou boys' academy high in the mountains, where he dates the famous Giichi. But all is not well, for Takumi has a secret. . . . (HS)   NR

JUNJO ROMANTICA

Junjô Romantica, "Pure Romance" (純情ロマンチカ) • Shungiku Nakamura • BLU (2006–ongoing) • Kadokawa Shoten (Ciel/Ciel Très Très, 2003–ongoing) • 8+ volumes (ongoing) • Yaoi, School, Romance • 18+ (sexual situations)

Misaki's a terrible student who is failing his college entrance exams, so his brother sets him up with an old friend as a tutor. But Akihiro isn't your regular nerdy tutor—he's a silver-spoon-sucking, Boys' Love–writing crazy man. Misaki resents Akihiro for making his brother a character in a porn novel, but before he knows it Akihiro has changed main characters. Now Misaki must put up with Akihiro groping him on the page and in person! This manga has moments of sparkling comedy, with well-adapted one-liners and excerpts from Akihiro's Boys' Love novels. The art is also at its best when the characters are in amusing super-deformed mode. But the comedic moments come as little gems in a slag pile of otherwise tedious text. Also contains the short story "Junjô Egoist." (HS)   ★★½

JUNK!

(ジャンク) • Shushushu Sakurai • DramaQueen (2007) • Taiyoh Tosho (2006) • 1 volume • Yaoi, Science Fiction, Fantasy • 18+

Junk is a freelance special agent sent to meet with the leader of a group of heretics. What he finds is a beautiful young man who begs for his protection. Can Junk discover what's really going on before his mission ends his life? (HS)   NR

JUST MY LUCK

Bokura no Unsei, "Our Luck" (ぼくらの運勢) • Temari Matsumoto • BLU (2007) • Kadokawa Shoten (2003) • 1 volume • Yaoi • 18+ (nudity, graphic sex)

Contains the short stories "Our Luck," "The Uniform and You," "The Mechanism of Love," and "Uwasa no Futari." (HS)   NR

KIMI SHIRUYA—DOST THOU KNOW?

Kimi Shiruya, "Dost Thou Know?" (君知るや) • Satoru Ishihara • DMP (2005) • Shinshokan (Dear Plus, 2003) • 1 volume • Yaoi, Kendo, Romance • 16+ (mild sexual situations)

Tsurugi, from an upper-class family, and Katsuomi, whose father runs a fish store, are rivals at *kendo* (Japanese swordfighting). As they compete, Katsuomi finds himself attracted to his rival, while their two younger brothers also slip into a parallel romance-friendship. ("What if I fell in love with him . . . would my skill with the *shinai* beome dulled?") This athletic boy-on-boy romance takes the indirect road, with almost no humor and little overt sexuality: there's only the subtlest tug-of-war of dominance and submission, plus some phallic sword close-ups. The slightly flowery, stilted writing captures the yearning mood, but most *yaoi* fans will find it more boring than suggestive.   ★½

KISSING

(キシング) • Teiko Sasaki (story), Shoko Takaku (art) • DMP (2006) • Tokuma Shoten (2004) • 1 volume • Yaoi • 16+ (sexual situations)

Haru and Kazushi have been best friends for years and are so close that people joke that they are a couple. But when Kazushi pushes the boundaries of their relationship, Haru isn't sure that they can ever go back to being just friends. Another story about a dude who's totally straight until he gets the taste of the right man, *Kissing* is a pretty mediocre addition to the *yaoi* genre and is tame right up until the end, where a brief sex scene makes it a little racy for the "young adult" rating. (HS)   ★★

KIZUNA: BONDS OF LOVE

Kizuna, "Bonds" (KIZUNA-絆) • Kazuma Kodaka • Be Beautiful (2004–2005) • Biblos (Be x Boy Gold, 1992–ongoing) • 10+ volumes (ongoing) • Yaoi, Crime Drama • 18+ (language, violence, nudity, graphic sex)

A *yaoi yakuza* story (although of the four main characters, only one is a full-time gangster). Former high school lovers Kei and Ranmaru now live together: Kei is the illegitimate son of a *yakuza* boss, Ranmaru is a former *kendo* champion who lost the use of his sword hand in an accident. Kai, Kei's half brother, also lusts after Ranmaru, but his heart truly belongs to another. Drawn by a female artist who worked in boys' *yakuza* comics, *Kizuna* started out as a *dôjinshi* sex parody of her "straight" work. After volume 1's initial porno scenes and *kendo*-themed dominance-submission, the story gradually fleshes out the characters, leading up to a serious crime/relationship story in the later volumes. The story has the usual idealized relationships and meandering plot of Boys' Love comics, but the promising combination of gangster machismo and gay love is handled with humor, affection, and the occasional fraction of a nod to realism (homosexuality is at least mentioned by name, and in her author's notes, Kodaka talks about going to gay clubs with her gay male friends). The stiff, 1980s *shônen*-manga-style art is not a strong point of the series and is particularly inconsistent in the early volumes, with Ryoichi Ikegami–style tough guys standing alongside the baby-faced romantic leads. Brief scenes of an underage boy kissing an adult man were cut from the English edition. ★★½

KURASHINA-SENSEI'S PASSION

Shiritsu Shoei: Gakuen Danshi Kôtôbu Kurashina-sensei no Jûnan, "Shoei: Private Academy's Boys High School Section Kurashina-sensei's Passion" (私立翔瑛学園男子高等部倉科先生の受難) • Shino Natsuho • DMP (2007–ongoing) • Biblos (2004–ongoing) • 3+ volumes (ongoing) • Yaoi • 16+

Kurashina-sensei is a new teacher at the prestigious Shoei Academy, where he soon finds himself the love target of a group of sexually awakening young men. Whatever will he do? (HS)   NR

LAST PORTRAIT

Saigo no Shôzô, "Last Portrait" (最後の肖像) • Akira Honma • DramaQueen (2006) • Shinkôsha (2005) • 1 volume • Yaoi • 18+ (explicit sexual content)

Yamato works for his sister at the family company and covets her fiancé. The day before the wedding, Yamato declares his love and gets a surprising answer. Is he ready to face the consequences of his confession? Also contains the short story "Stairway to Heaven." (HS)   NR

LEVEL-C

Aoi Futaba, Kurenai Mitsuba • Kitty Media (2005–2006) • Biblos (1993–2003) • 6 volumes • Yaoi • 18+ (nudity, graphic sex)

Mizuki, a girlish teenage model, is picked up at a bar by Kazuomi, a bisexual adult businessman. Kazuomi soon moves into Mizuki's apartment and the two have lots and lots of consensual, monogamous gay sex. *Level-C* was originally a one-shot semi-humorous *dôjinshi* that was expanded to series length, and the creators tell it like it is in the authors' notes to volume 4: "We just wanted to create lots of sex scenes, so now we're struggling to create a story for it!" As a result, the series works as porn but fails when the authors attempt to tell a serious story; a few side characters come and go, and volume 3 has almost no sex for some reason, but Mizuki and Kazuomi's idealized May-September relationship never develops or changes. (In the original Japanese, Mizuki was in high school; the English edition changes him into a college student, but a few high school references remain.) Mizuki's huge girly eyes and petite figure instantly point him out as the *uke,* and the dialogue seems teasingly aware that he is the "woman" in the relationship ("I'll make sure you have multiple orgasms!" "I feel pregnant. How many times did we have sex?"). The upside is the basically warmhearted couple; the downside is the crude art.   ★★

LIES & KISSES

Uso to Kiss, "Lies and Kisses" (嘘とキス) • Masara Minase • DramaQueen (2005) • Ookura Shuppan (2005) • 1 volume • Yaoi • 18+ (sexual situations)

Tatsuya has been searching for his younger half brother, who disappeared years ago when their parents divorced. On the eve of

Hinako Takanaga's *Little Butterfly* © Kaiohsha

away from home to escape his abusive parents. Beautiful artwork, sympathetic characters, and strong, believable emotions make *Little Butterfly* one of the best slow-paced *shônen ai* titles. Although the main characters are standard types (tall, dark, and brooding; cute, blond, and innocent), the writing combines plausible human behavior with self-awareness of its genre; after making out with Nakahara for the first time, Kojima hugs one of his annoyed straight male classmates to see if it makes him feel the same way ("Did your heart pound? Did you feel dreamy?"). Although feverish with heart-pounding promise, the first volume is totally chaste; however, the later volumes become increasingly sexual.   ★★★½

LITTLE CRYBABY

Nakimushi na Little, "Little Crybaby" (泣き虫な リトル) • Keiko Kinoshita • DMP (2007) • Taiyoh Tosho (2004) • 1 volume • Yaoi • 16+ (sexual situations)

Kishino is the bumbling but cute guy everyone loves and Fujimoto is the campus ladies' man. What happens when these two fall in love? (HS)   NR

LORD OF SAL MANOR

Sarayashiki no Wakagimi, "The Young Lord of Sal Manor" (沙羅屋敷の若君) • Yutaka Nanten • Drama-Queen (2007) • Shinkôsha (2005) • 2 volumes • Yaoi • 18+

Orphaned Taro is suddenly brought to a wealthy mansion and told that he is the seventeenth viscount of Sal Manor! Takamori, steward to the previous viscount, takes Taro under his wing, but just as Taro gets used to his new life, strange things start to happen. . . .   NR

LOST BOYS

(ロストボーイズ) • Kaname Itsuki • DMP (2006) • Taiyoh Tosho (Craft Original Comic Anthology, 2004) • 1 volume • Yaoi • 16+ (mild language, brief sex)

A *shônen ai* play on *Peter Pan;* instead of leaving Neverland in search of a surrogate

some good news from his private investigator, Tatsuya stops at his favorite bar and finds his gaze drawn to the hot new waiter, Haru. They go home together for a night of passion, but the dawn reveals that Haru recognizes Tatsuya—as his older brother! The incest bait-and-switch game is already tired, and this manga does nothing to revive it. Tatsuya is a little creepy, Haru is accidentally gay (oops, I tripped, I'm gay!), and the dialogue is stilted and awkward. The art in theory is nice, but the character designs are almost identical to those in the vastly superior *Empty Heart* (right down to the stubbled tertiary character who gives questionable love advice). (HS)   ★★

LITTLE BUTTERFLY

(リトル・バタフライ) • Hinako Takanaga • DMP (2006–2007) • Kaiohsha (2001–2004) • 3 volumes • Yaoi • 18+ (nudity, sex)

On a school trip, innocent Kojima gets separated from the rest of the group and ends up alone with his classmate Nakahara, a handsome but depressed outcast planning to run mother and finding Wendy, the lost boys go in search of a father and find Mizuki, a Japanese teenager living in Britain. The most enjoyable thing about *Lost Boys* is how it craftily incorporates bits of the original story: Pan has become the cute and playful Air; his fairy protector, Reux, gets jealous of Mizuki just like the original Tinkerbell; and the pirate Captain Vanity, who shows up only briefly, is obsessed with Pan just like Captain Hook was. (Well, not *just* like Captain Hook was.) The central relationship is handled in a graceful, molestation-free fashion, although zippers come undone in the final story. (In her notes, the author apologizes to the readers for not including enough sex.) The story's weaknesses are its brevity and weak art. ★★½

LOVE A LA CARTE

Renai a la Carte, "Love a la Carte" (レンアイ・アラカルト!) • Haruka Minami • Be Beautiful (2007) • Biblos (Be x Boy Gold, 2003) • 1 volume • Yaoi • 18+ (nudity, graphic sex)

Izumi is a frequent model for the photography club, but the aloof Shinooka wants to take more than Izumi's picture. Will a group vacation turn into a hotbed of love? (HS) NR

LOVEHOLIC

Renai Chûdoku, "Loveholic/Love Addict" (恋愛中毒) • Touko Kawai • DMP (2007) • Biblos (2001–2004) • 2 volumes • Yaoi, Contemporary • 16+ (sexual situations)

Nishioka is a talented but selfish photographer and Matsukawa is the ad agency genius who makes Nishioka's work a hit. They may seem to be antagonistic, but in reality they share a burning love. (HS) NR

LOVE IS LIKE A HURRICANE

(恋はいつも嵐のように) (*Koi wa Itsumo Arashi no Youni*, "Love Is Always Like a Storm") • Tokiya Shimazaki • 801 Media (2007–2008) • Kousai Shobo (2001–2004) • 5 volumes • Yaoi • 18+ (nudity, graphic sex)

Explicit *yaoi* high school stories. In the first story, Mizuki is molested on the train on the way to school by the student body president, Azuma. Later, Azuma calls Mizuki to the office to confess his love. (HS) NR

LOVELESS: See General Manga Reviews

LOVELY SICK

(ラブリーシック) • Shoko Ohmine • DramaQueen (2006–ongoing) • Ookura Shuppan (2004–ongoing) • 3+ volumes (ongoing) • Yaoi • 18+ (nudity, graphic sex)

This is one of those stories that barely skirts the *shota* line. Akiyoshi's legs were terribly mangled in an accident that killed his parents, and his surgeon, Dr. Sumi, has more or less adopted him—and made Akiyoshi his lover. It's a really creepy power dynamic since Akiyoshi is so much younger and depends on Sumi for everything (home, medical care, parental authority). It's especially gross when Sumi brags to a colleague "how wonderful it is to have a kid who can't live without you." Remember, this is his lover Sumi is talking about, a child he has raised. Bad touch. (HS) ★

LOVE ME SINFULLY

Tsumi Bukaku Aishite yo, "Love Me Sinfully" (罪深く愛してよ) • Mio Tennouji • DramaQueen (2007) • Shinkôsha (2005) • 1 volume • Yaoi, Fantasy • 18+

Yuu has the misfortune of looking exactly like Prince Carlo of Qurdis, and the prince wants Yuu to act as a decoy. Yuu, afraid for his life, refuses. But when the prince's handsome bodyguard Brad offers to protect him with his life, Yuu finds his convictions slipping. (HS) NR

LOVE MODE

(ラブモド) • Yuki Shimizu • BLU (2006–ongoing) • Biblos (Be x Boy, 1995–2003) • 11 volumes • Yaoi, Drama • 18+ (language, violence, nudity, graphic sex)

A long-running Boys' Love manga of the 1990s, *Love Mode* focuses on a male escort club and its clients, mostly older men–younger men pairings. In the first volume's story, teenage Izumi is mistaken for a male escort and goes on a date with an adult man, Takamiya, waking up after a few too many drinks to find them having sex. He angrily lashes out at Takamiya (who is surprised and apologetic) and goes home, only to find himself unable to forget the incident and wondering, "I got turned gay?!" The art is extremely scrawly and unattractive, creating a dirty, ugly mood sometimes at odds with the stories. On the other hand, the writing is sometimes sharp, as in one scene when Izumi dreams of being raped, thus allowing the author to include a rape scene (and indicating Izumi's sexual orientation) without actually making Takamiya into a rapist. Humorous banana-eating scenes are also a plus.　　　　　　　　　　　　★★

LOVE PISTOLS

Sex Pistols • Tarako Kotobuki • BLU (2007–ongoing) • Biblos (2004–2005) • 4 volumes • Yaoi, Science Fiction, Fantasy, Comedy • 18+ (nudity, graphic sex)

What would happen if some people evolved from animals other than monkeys? Norio is about to find out, because it turns out he's one of them—with rare and ultradesirable DNA, and the way to pass it on is to get him pregnant! (HS)　　　　　　　　　NR

LOVE RECIPE

Kirico Higashizato • DMP (2007–ongoing) • Frontier Works (2005–ongoing) • 2+ volumes (ongoing) • Yaoi, Otaku, Comedy • 18+ (nudity, sex)

Young cutie Tomonori just landed a job as an editor for a Boys' Love magazine. He has to work his way up, starting out by checking drafts, editing scripts, and lettering. To add insult to injury, he has to ride herd on Sakurako Kakyoin, a male *yaoi* artist who is notorious for missing deadlines. (HS)　NR

LOVER'S FLAT

1k Apaato no Koi, "Love in the First Floor Apartment" (1Kアパートの恋) • Hyouta Fujiyama • DMP

(2007) • Frontier Works (2001) • 1 volume • Yaoi • 18+ (nudity, graphic sex)

A little too much holiday cheer leaves Natsu and Kouno dealing with a whole new type of morning-after Christmas. (HS)　　　NR

LUCKY STAR

Shiomi Kohara • ComicsOne (e-book, 2000) • Ookura Shuppan (1996) • 1 volume • Yaoi, Short Stories • 16+ (sexual situations)

Two of these stories are stand-alone businessmen romances, two are about twins who fall in love with their older brother, and two are set in a fantasy world. The stand-alones are so-so and not particularly inspired. But the related stories all feel as if they were given short shrift and would have benefited from being expanded into whole volumes. The story lines involving the twins rely heavily on the overused "incest—wait, adopted!" motif. The fantasy world has a lot of promise, but the characters deserve to be fleshed out more. The art is a little simplistic and dated, with plenty of mullets to go around. (HS)　　　　　　　　　★★

MANDAYUU & ME

Mandayuu to Ore, "Mandayuu and Me" (万太夫とオレ) • Shushushu Sakurai • DramaQueen (2006) • Biblos (2003) • 1 volume • Yaoi • 18+

Kyohei is a serious office worker, but his friend Mandayuu is an off-the-wall *hentai* artist who always manages to catch Kyohei up in his crazy schemes. (HS)　　　NR

MAN'S BEST FRIEND

Inu mo Arukeba Falling Love, "A Dog Only Has to Walk Around and It's Sure to Fall in Love" (犬も歩けばフォーリンラブ) • Kazusa Takashima • BLU (2006) • Biblos (Be x Boy Gold, 2000–2004) • 1 volume • Yaoi • 18+ (language, nudity, graphic sex)

The furry title story is the standout of this collection of early short stories by Kazusa Takashima. A leg-humping border collie transforms into a hot man with dog ears, a tail, and wild tangled hair that consummates its love with its owner (his response: "You have no idea how incredible this dog is!"). In the other stories, a college student is reunited with his childhood girlfriend only to realize it was a man all along, and a goldfish won at the fair turns into a boy. Good artwork and strong, sexy anatomy. The title is a pun on a Japanese saying, "A dog only has to walk around and it's sure to come across a stick." ★★★

MENKUI!

Menkui!, "Shallow/Superficial!" (メンクイ!) • Suzuki Tanaka • BLU (2006–2007) • Biblos (Be x Boy, 2000–2003) • 3 volumes • Yaoi, Comedy • 16+ (language, mild violence, sexual situations)

Teenage Kotori is a sucker for a guy with a pretty face. Despite his own average looks, he ends up going out with his hot classmate Kaname, a relationship that starts as discreet friendship and eventually gets to the point where they can't keep their hands off each other. ("Quit groping each other in front of me!" one of their friends complains.) Soon, other handsome guys start showing up to tempt Kotori's affections, including a ghost and an East Indian prince, but despite Kotori's *menkui* shallowness, the moral of the story is that he is always loyal to Kaname, the only guy he truly loves. This mostly sexless comedy has pleasantly simple artwork and a light touch (even an incest subplot can't bring down the story) but lacks any really memorable twists or images. ★★½

MIDARESOMENISHI:
A TALE OF SAMURAI LOVE

Midaresomenishi, "Unrest" (乱れそめにし) • Kazuma Kodaka • Be Beautiful (2007) • Take Shobo (Reijin, 1999) • 1 volume • Samurai, Yaoi • 18+ (nudity, graphic sex)

A lone samurai is determined to rescue his brother from the depraved grasp of a feudal lord, but instead becomes a captive to the sadistic lord. (HS) NR

MISSING ROAD

Shushushu Sakurai • DramaQueen (2007) • Taiyoh Tosho (2006) • 1 volume • Yaoi, Science Fiction • 18+

Set in the battlefields of a futuristic world, this is the story of Leo Bride, a member of an elite convict mercenary force, and his struggles to protect his cohorts from each other and a world that hates them. (HS) NR

MOON AND SANDALS

Tsuki to Sandals, "Moon and Sandals" (月とサンダル) • Fumi Yoshinaga • DMP (2007) • Houbunsha (Hanaoto, 1994–2000) • 2 volumes • Yaoi • 18+ (nudity, graphic sex)

Fumi Yoshinaga's debut work, *Moon and Sandals* is the story of Ida and Kobayashi, a high school teacher and student who find themselves drawn together. NR

MY DEAR SWEETHEART

Seika Kisaragi • DramaQueen (2007) • Ookura Shuppan (2005) • 1 volume • Yaoi • 18+

Akira and Ryou enjoy a playful relationship even though Akira works as an escort for Ryou's dad. But when Ryou is attacked, they are forced to realize that their feelings for each other are far from a game. (HS) NR

MY ONLY KING

Boku dake no Ôsama, "My Only King" (ボクだけの王さま) • Lily Hoshino • DMP (2005) • Kousai Shobo (2004) • 1 volume • Yaoi, Fantasy, Comedy • 16+ (brief partial nudity, sexual situations)

Kazuomi, a high school ladies' man, is accidentally imprinted (above his crotch) with the crest of a faraway fantasy kingdom, so Mewt, an extremely female-looking male sorcerer, travels through the dimensions to watch over him. Mewt disguises himself as a girl to attend Kazuomi's school and develops a crush on him, petulantly asking, "Am I that unappealing?" The chaste plot is silly but charming, and Hoshino's artwork is pretty. (However, readers may have varying reactions to the fact that her gay men look like long-haired, underage girls.) Several short stories round out the collection, some slightly more explicit than others; the best one is "The King and Rune," a disturbing but well-executed fairy tale about child slavery. ★★½

MY PARANOID NEXT DOOR NEIGHBOR

Tonari no Heya no Paranoia, "The Paranoia of my Neighbor's Room" (隣の部屋のパラノイア) • Kazuka Minami • 801 Media (2007) • Tokuma Shoten (2004) • 1 volume • Yaoi • 18+ (nudity, graphic sex)

Hokuto and Yukito were childhood friends . . . but to Yukito, it meant something more. For years, he tried to stay away from Hokuto, afraid of what might happen, but when they become seniors in high school, fate conspires to get them under the same roof. NR

NOT/LOVE

(ノット・ラブ) • Kano Miyamoto • DramaQueen (2007) • Ookura Shuppan (2003) • 1 volume • Yaoi • 18+

The angst-laden romance between a male prostitute and a detective. (HS)   NR

OMEN

Yôkan, "Premonition" (予感) • Makoto Tateno • DramaQueen (2007) • Ookura Shuppan (2003) • 1 volume • Yaoi • 18+

Akira, the lead vocalist for the hot band Charon, has youth, beauty, and fortune going for him. But the one thing he wants is Sunaga, a popular actor who is sending mixed messages. (HS)   NR

ONE WING IN THE FINDER: See *Finder Series*

ONLY THE RING FINGER KNOWS

Sono Yubi dake ga Shitteiru, "Only the Ring Finger Knows" (その指だけが知っている) • Satoru Kannagi (story), Hotaru Odagiri (art) • DMP (2004) • Tokuma Shoten (Chara, 2002) • 1 volume • Yaoi, Romance • 16+ (language, mild sexual situations)

Teenage Wataru discovers that he shares matching rings with his classmate Kazuki, an inscrutable upperclassman whom all the girls have crushes on (including, possibly, Wataru's own sister). Although Wataru initially thinks Kazuki's a jerk, he gradually comes to wonder if Kazuki's coldness isn't a mask for some stronger emotion . . . an emotion that he himself shares. Based on a series of novels by Satoru Kannagi, *Only the*

Ring Finger Knows is a tidily plotted *shônen ai* love story with basically sympathetic characters and initially plausible (yet in the end, of course, highly romanticized) behavior. Good beginner Boys' Love.   ★★★

ORDINARY CRUSH

Warito Yokuaru Danshikouteki Renaijijou, "The Love Affair(s) That Happen Relatively Often in Boys' Schools" (わりとよくある男子校的恋愛事情) • Hyouta Fujiyama • DMP (2007) • Frontier Works (2001–2003) • 2 volumes • Yaoi, Romance • 16+ (sexual situations)

Nanase and Heiji are the only straight guys in school, but a stray White Day exchange of chocolates might change all that! (HS) NR

ORGANIC SONS

(オーガニック・サンズ) • Mika Sadahiro • DramaQueen (2007) • Magazine Magazine (2005) • 1 volume • Yaoi • 18+

Life as a farmer isn't easy, as two friends learn when they move to the country. Despite the hardships, the two find solace in their love for each other. (HS)   NR

OTHELLO

Toui Hasumi • DMP (2007) • Ookura Shuppan (2002) • 1 volume • Yaoi, Romance, Drama • 16+

After Ayumi's twin brother dies in an accident, Ayumi tries to assume his honor-roll identity at school. But somehow, Ayumi has a hard time keeping up the ruse around his classmate Kirishima. Plus several short stories. (HS)   NR

OUR EVERLASTING

Keijijô na Bokura, "Metaphysical Us" (形而上なぼくら) • Toko Kawai • DMP (2005–2006) • Biblos (Be x Boy, 2000–2001) • 2 volumes • Yaoi • 18+ (language, partial nudity, sex)

Horyu, a college student who cares only about surfing and partying, finds himself attracted to a man for the first time: the studious, internally tormented Shouin. Despite rival gay suitors and conflicting plans for the future, their relationship blossoms into happy domesticity, with plenty of love and kisses, walks on the beach, and home-cooked meals. The story is told alternatingly from both characters' perspectives, and Shouin and Horyu are not entirely two-dimensional, but despite hints of drama (and one unnecessary nonconsensual scene), the plot ultimately takes the safest route and the sex scenes are unimpressive. The characters are drawn in a lanky, manly fashion. Several unrelated short stories are also included.   ★½

OUR KINGDOM

Bokura no Ôkoku, "Our Kingdom" (僕らの王国) • Naduki Koujima • DMP (2005–2006) • Biblos (Be x Boy, 2000–2005) • 6 volumes • Yaoi • 16+ (language, sex)

Akira, a fifteen-year-old orphan, is adopted by unexpectedly wealthy relatives and moves into the family mansion with another orphan: his half-American cousin, Rei. But Rei (like just about everyone in the story) is gay, and instead of competing with Akira over the massive family fortune, he hits on his flustered cousin and possessively protects him from the men who try to come between them. (They're just jealous, after all.) The plot sees Akira defending himself, not always successfully, against a number of would-be molesters of varying forcefulness. Although the pseudo-incestuous story is a page-turner, the art is stiff and the baby-faced character designs are crude. (The characters have flat faces with noses always seen from the wrong perspective.)   ★½

THE PARADISE ON THE HILL

Oka no Ue no Rakuen, "The Paradise on the Hill" (丘の上の楽園) • Momoko Tenzen • DMP (2007) • Taiyoh Tosho (Craft Original Comics Anthology, 2002) • 1 volume • Yaoi, Romance • 16+

Kijima is a teacher at an all-girls school, but it's not the sweet deal his friends all seem to think it is. The new PE teacher, Ono, has deflected some of the girlish attention, and Kijima finds himself as interested as the students in the shy young teacher. (HS)   NR

PASSION

Netsujyô, "Passion" (熱情) • Shinobu Gotoh (story), Shoko Takaku (art) • DMP (2005–2006) • Tokuma Shoten (Chara, 2002–2005) • 3 volumes • Yaoi • 18+ (language, nudity, sex)

Opening with a student raping his teacher, *Passion* is actually not an idealized-pair *shônen ai* sexfest, but an angsty, emotional drama like Shinobu Gotoh's other manga, *Time Lag* (but with a less gimmicky plot device). Hikaru, the student and aggressor, feels awkward and guilty for his attraction to his teacher, while the friendly but distant Mr. Shima agrees to secretly sleep with Hikaru until graduation but retains the paternal attitude of an adult educator ("If your final scores are higher than the previous exams, why don't we go out?"). Meanwhile, however, another male teacher also has feelings for Shima. A well-written example of its formula, with a few interesting surprises.   ★★★

PICNIC

(ピクニック) • Yugi Yamada • DMP (2007) • Houbunsha (Hanaoto, 2004) • 1 volume • Yaoi, Romance • 18+ (nudity, graphic sex)

Koreeda is on the rebound from breaking up with his long-term girlfriend, and looking for something different. When Noda, a buddy from college, offers a "friends with benefits" deal, Koreeda is ready to give it a try. (HS)   NR

PLAY BOY BLUES

P.B.B. (*Play Boy Blues*) (P.B.B. プレイボーイ ブルース) • Shiuko Kano • Be Beautiful (2005) • Biblos (Be x Boy, 2003–2005) • 1 volume, suspended (2 volumes in Japan) • Yaoi • 18+ (nudity, graphic sex)

Do you crave well-endowed, muscular, manly men in your *yaoi* manga? Shinobu and Junsuke are gay (or possibly bisexual) lovers in their early twenties, who work at a "host bar," where they play gigolo to young women. The story opens with Shinobu waking up in bed with a coworker, and later on he ends up with a woman in a hotel room. However, confusing storytelling dilutes the impact of the plot twists, and the result is like disconnected snapshots of a relationship mixed with sex scenes. Part of the problem may be that this does not include the very first chapter of *Play Boy Blues,* which was published as a one-shot in the back of Kano's untranslated construction-workers *yaoi* manga *Gaten na Aitsu* ("That Blue-Collar Guy") . . . , which, in turn, appears in a one-shot in the back of *Play Boy Blues* under the title "Manly Construction Training." ★★½

PLEASURE DOME

Kanrakukyû, "Pleasure Dome" (歓楽宮) • Megumu Minami • Kitty Media (2007) • Houbunsha (Hanaoto, 2000) • 1 volume • Yaoi, Science Fiction, Fantasy • 18+ (violence, nudity, graphic sex)

Bondage-oriented *yaoi* short stories in exotic settings: nineteenth-century India, medieval Europe, feudal Japan. NR

POISON CHERRY DRIVE

(ポイズン・チェリー・ドライブ) • Motoni Modoru • Kitty Media (2006) • Houbunsha (Hanaoto, 2005) • 1 volume • Yaoi • 18+ (nudity, graphic sex)

Nihongi was raped, after which he lost his memory and developed a phobia of naked men. He turns to Cherry Drive for help, a company of three men who will deflower you or enact vengeance rape for you, whichever you prefer. For the price of his body, Cherry Drive tracks down Nihongi's rapist, violates him, and gives pictures of the attack to Nihongi. When they show him the photos, they ask if it was worth it; he replies, "It was worth it. I was finally proud of myself." This is a terrible book with an ugly plot and art that in any other context might have been interesting but when coupled with such a bizarre take on rape comes off as creepy and deranged. 0 Stars

RIN

Rin, "Cold" (凛) • Satoru Kannagi (story), Yukine Honami (art) • DMP (2006–2007) • Tokuma Shoten (2002–2004) • 3 volumes • Yaoi, Romance • 16+ (mild sexual situations)

Katsura has turned to his older brother's best friend, Sou, for years, but now that they're in high school Katsura's need for Sou's hugs is beginning to raise eyebrows. After some confusion, the two realize that their love is more important than appearances, and embrace their new relationship. This story is refreshing in a lot of ways, especially in that Katsura and Sou's relationship undergoes a very realistic evolution. This isn't the surprise attack gayness that so often gets written about in *yaoi.* Katsura's family is very supportive of his decision, too, and he is comfortable discussing his feelings with his older brother and father (who is a househusband while his wife works). The art is a little sketchy and takes a backseat to the story (which is awkwardly translated at times) but serves the emotions of the characters well enough. (HS) ★★★½

RISING STORM

Arashi ga Oka, "Rising Storm" (嵐が丘) • Yuzuha Ougi • DramaQueen (2005) • Kaiohsha (2003) • 1 volume • Yaoi • 18+ (nudity, graphic sex)

You know it's hard *yaoi* when the line "Bend over" appears just a few pages into the book. Reona, a lean, well-built teenager, is hired to take care of the horses at the estate of an unbelievably, impossibly wealthy young gentleman, who "punishes" him for various infractions by caning his buttocks, then graduates to sex. This unreal, almost fairytale setting is the stage for "loving" dominance porn and deadpan jokes about the master's unbelievable wealth and power and the lengths he'll go to in order to keep Reona. The sex is rough and explicit—no shadowy "ghost penises" here! The combination of almost Suehiro Maruo–esque perversity and a giggly *yaoi* sensibility isn't for everyone, but Ougi's art style is undeniably unique. The Japanese title, *Arashi ga Oka,* is the same as the Japanese title for Emily Brontë's *Wuthering Heights.* ★★½

SAME CELL ORGANISM

Dô-Saibô Seibutsu, "Same Cell Organism" (同細胞 生物) • Sumomo Yumeka • DMP (2006) • Taiyoh

Tosho (Craft Original Comic Anthology, 2001) • 1 volume • Yaoi • 16+ (mild sexual situations)

More an art portfolio than a manga, *Same Cell Organism* is an anthology of several wistful vignettes, expressing the wish for eternal companionship with a lover who is like a part of yourself. The title story (and another story with identical characters) involves high school students, while another, more interesting story, "To Make an Angel," pairs a girlish, long-haired guy with an angel who has watched over him from heaven. Yumeka's heroes have lanky, almost anorexic bodies (in the 1990s fashion) and wind-blown hair, but the general plotlessness offsets the charm of the art, except for readers for whom the mere depiction of an idealized, static emotional state may be enough.

★★

SCENT OF TEMPTATION

Yūwaku no Kaori, "Scent of Temptation" (誘惑の香り) • Toyama Mako • DramaQueen (2007) • Magazine Magazine (2004) • 1 volume • Yaoi • 18+

Toshiya is a part-time barista who falls for one of the café regulars. But Kanae is so cool and beautiful, can he ever return Toshiya's affection? (HS) NR

SELFISH LOVE

Kunshusama no Koi wa Katte!, "The Monarch's Love Is Selfish!" (君主サマの恋は勝手!) • Naduki Koujima • Be Beautiful (2004) • Biblos (Be x Boy, 2001–2003) • 2 volumes • Yaoi • 18+ (mild violence, explicit sexual content)

Ryuya, a scholarship student at the highfalutin O-ha University, is pursued by Orito, the arrogant president of the honor society, who wants him for his vice president . . . and lover. ("Bastard! This is sexual harassment!" Ryuya cries, when not calling Orito a "freak" and a "disgusting pig.") Attempts at humor don't make up for the clichéd plot (midway between suggestive and hard-core) and Koujima's weak artwork (here's how you tell the characters apart: one guy's got white hair, one guy's got black hair, one guy's got screen-toned hair . . .). After there's already

been a rape scene, it probably shouldn't matter so much who kisses whom in the school play. In addition to changing O-ha from a high school to a college, the English edition omits a twelve-page underage sex story from volume 1. ½

SEVEN

(セブン) • Momoko Tensen • DMP (2007) • Taiyoh Tosho (Craft Original Comic Anthology, 2004) • 1 volume • Yaoi, Contemporary • 16+ (sexual situations)

Nana has no memory of his past before age twelve. Mitsusha is looking for his missing childhood friend. The two meet when a mutual friend insists Mitsusha crash at Nana's place. While Nana initially dislikes Mitsusha, he soon comes to love his houseguest. (HS) NR

SHINOBU KOKORO: HIDDEN HEART

Shinobu Kokoro Wa, "About/As for a Hidden Heart" (しのぶこころは) • Temari Matsumoto • BLU (2005) • Biblos (Be x Boy, 2004) • 1 volume • Ninja, Yaoi • 18+ (brief mild violence, nudity, graphic sex)

Unmemorable collection of adult *yaoi* stories centered around a small group of ninja (*shinobu,* the Japanese word used in the title, has the same root as *shinobi,* i.e., ninja). In the first, creepy scenario, an extremely young, vulnerable-looking rookie ninja is trained in the arts of seduction by his apparently thirty-something master ("That's a good boy . . ."); in the second scenario, two ninjas bond in the course of their duty. The stories are mostly sex, with the ninja theme providing only the bare outline of the relationships; even the generic costumes are barely drawn. A third scenario involves a teenage boy who sleeps with a handsome snow spirit. ★

SHOUT OUT LOUD!

Sakende Yaruze, "Shout Out Loud!" (叫んでやるぜ!) • Yuki Shimizu • BLU (2006–2007) • Kadokawa Shoten (1995–1999) • 5 volumes • Yaoi, Comedy, Drama • 16+ (language, partial nudity, sexual situations)

Hisae Shino, a sensitive, baby-faced thirty-three-year-old anime voice actor, has a problem: he's typecast as the *uke* (bottom) in Boys' Love drama CDs, his male costars are hitting on him, and the entire studio is a hotbed of undercover gayness. If that wasn't enough, Shino is suddenly reunited with his long-lost teenage son, Tsukaya, who is fine with his dad's roles in kiddie anime but less comfortable with having to protect his own father from lusty guys. *Shout Out Loud!* is a witty *yaoi* title that satirizes the genre at the same time as it satirizes anime voice acting. The humor is dialogue-driven and understated, with office comedy alternating with family drama, as Shino tries to be a good father and steer his son through his own crises. (Unlike some *yaoi* manga, there's no incest theme.) It's not as surprising and dense with humor as *Antique Bakery* (the closest comparison), but it's a well-written title with surprising plot developments and intelligent dialogue. ★★★★

THE SKY OVER MY SPECTACLES

Meganegoshi no Sora Wa, "The Sky over My Spectacles" (眼鏡越しの空は) • Mio Tennohji • 801 Media (2007) • Biblos (2005) • 1 volume • Yaoi • 18+ (nudity, graphic sex)

Azuma has a serious specs fetish, but even he draws the line at guys—until he sees über-serious Sorachi asleep in his glasses and can't resist kissing him. Azuma's attracted to Sorachi only because of the glasses thing, right? (HS) NR

SKYSCRAPERS OF OZ

Oz no Matenrô, "Skyscrapers of Oz" (オズの摩天楼) • Yoshino Somei (story), Row Takekura (art) • Kitty Media (2004) • Tokuma Shoten (2001) • 1 volume • Yaoi, Detective, Drama • 18+ (language, mild violence, nudity, graphic sex)

Based on the novel by Yoshino Somei, this *yaoi* crime drama manages to combine a decent plot, good art, and explicit sex scenes. (They aren't really worked into the plot; it's more like the main character tries to move the story along while the side characters get

it on like rabbits.) Three gay detectives—they also apparently do mundane things such as housecleaning, but not on-screen—are hired to seduce and bring down Yu Kaito, a young man apparently responsible for wrecking a marriage. Uptight, morally responsible Mari performs the classic private eye role, while Mari's girlish little brother Miyuki spends most of the manga in bed with Yoichi, the third detective. (Miyuki gives off faint incest vibes, but Mari isn't having any of it.) Takakura's detailed, realistic art gives the manga a sleek, hard-boiled quality. ★★½

SLEEPING FLOWER

Nemureru Hana, "Sleeping Flower" (眠れる花) • Yuuri Ebihara • DramaQueen (2007) • Shinkôsha (2006) • 1 volume • Yaoi • 18+

Masami's fiancée insists that they hire Haruji to do the floral arrangements for their wedding. But Masami finds himself paying more attention to the handsome florist's body than the bouquets. (HS) NR

SOLFEGE

(ソルフェージュ) • Fumi Yoshinaga • DMP (2007) • Houbunsha (Hanaoto, 1996–1998) • 1 volume • Yaoi • 18+ (nudity, graphic sex)

Kugayama is a music teacher with great talent and privilege but little passion for life. When an ex-student requests his help in studying for a prestigious music school's entrance exam, his youth and enthusiasm awaken feelings in Kugayama that he never thought possible. NR

SOUND OF MY VOICE

Boku no Koe, "My Voice" (僕の声) • Youka Nitta • Be Beautiful (2006) • Biblos (Be x Boy Gold, 2004) • 1 volume • Performance, Yaoi • 18+ (nudity, graphic sex)

A young voice actor wants to succeed in the industry but chokes when he gets his big chance. Will his senior actors teach him the ropes and take him in hand—literally? (HS) NR

SWEET REVOLUTION

Binetsu Kakumei, "Sweet Revolution" (微熱革命) • Serubo Suzuki (story), Yukine Honami (art) • DMP (2006) • Houbunsha (Hanaoto, 2000) • 1 volume • Fantasy, Yaoi, Romance • 18+ (partial nudity, brief sex)

When he tries to protect a male transfer student from bullying, Kouhei sees something he shouldn't have, and discovers that Tatsuki and Ohta have a master-servant sexual relationship. Not only that, they're visitors from another realm, an ancient Japanese fantasy world where Tatsuki is the successor to the throne and Ohta is his loyal vassal. An element of forbidden love gives *Sweet Revolution* some sting (Tatsuki is under pressure to take a wife and continue the family line), but the plot is slight, the dominance elements are creepy, and there is little character development or even sex. The fantasy bits are largely irrelevant, except for one fanfic-esque excuse to get naked ("Oh, that. That was just purification. It's easier to absorb *chi* through physical contact"). Also includes "An Unseen Force," another light supernatural *yaoi* story. ★

SWEET WHISPER

Akutai wa Toiki to Mazariau, "Insults Mixed with Sighs" (悪態は吐息とまざりあう) • Hyouta Fujiyama • DMP (2007) • Biblos (2005) • 1 volume • Yaoi • 18+ (nudity, graphic sex)

Natsume, a salesman, makes an "inserting" deal with college kid Touji after some stalking, some handcuffs, and a night spent in jail. (HS) NR

TARGET IN THE FINDER: See *Finder Series*

THUNDERBOLT BOYS EXCITE

Chôhatsu~Denkô Sekka Boys, "Exciting~ Thunderbolt Flash Boys" (挑発~電光石火BOYS) • Asami Tojo • Kitty Media (2007) • Houbunsha (Hanaoto, 2004–2005) • 2 volumes • Yaoi • 18+ (nudity, graphic sex)

Kodaka and Ritsu work together as models, and Kodaka wants to become worthy of his friend. When Kodaka enlists the aid of Ritsu's valet, the training sessions turn out a little steamier than he anticipated! (HS) NR

TIME LAG

Time Lag (タイムラグ) • Shinobu Gotoh (story), Hotaru Odagiri (art) • DMP (2006) • Tokuma Shoten (1999–2000) • 1 volume • Yaoi • 16+ (mild sexual situations)

Boys' Love triangle based on the young-adult novel by Hotaru Odagiri. After repeatedly confessing his love to track star Shirou and repeatedly being rejected, Satoru is propositioned by Seiichi, his editor at the school newspaper. But can he give up on Shirou? Although *Time Lag* has moments of real romantic anxiety, its genius is in coming up with one of the most unlikely, but entertaining, romantic wish-fulfillment scenarios imaginable. Despite the 16+ rating, the book has nothing unsuitable for younger teens. ★★★

THE TYRANT FALLS IN LOVE

Koi suru Bo-kun, "Bo-kun in Love" (恋する暴君) • Hinako Takanaga • DramaQueen (2007–ongoing) • Kaiohsha (2005–ongoing) • 3+ volumes (ongoing) • Yaoi, Romance • 18+

Morinaga is in love with his homophobic upperclass schoolmate Tatsumi, whose hot ass is a major boy magnet. Morinaga despairs of ever getting in his true love's pants, but when the opportunity arises, will he leap on the chance? (HS) NR

LA VIE EN ROSE

(ラ・ヴィ・アン・ローズ) • Sakura Yamada • DMP (2007) • Tokyo Mangasha (2005) • 1 volume • Yaoi • 18+

Short story collection. Includes "Goodbye Baby," about a high school student whose friends are drifting away from him and toward each other, and "Love Novelist," about a romance author whose top-selling new book is secretly about his feelings for his best friend. (HS) NR

VIRGIN SOIL

Hanairo Virgin Soil, "Flower-colored Virgin Soil" (花色バージンソイル) • Haruka Minami • Be Beautiful (2007) • Biblos (Be x Boy Gold, 2005) • 1 volume • Yaoi • 18+ (nudity, graphic sex)

Model Nagise is given a wonderful chance to be the face of a hot new product. The only problem is he has to pose nude. To help him get ready for the shoot, Fumitaka offers his apartment and his skills in the bedroom. (HS)   NR

VIRTUOSO DI AMORE

Netsujô no Virtuoso, "Virtuoso of Passion" (熱情の ヴィルトゥオーソ) • Uki Ogasawara • DramaQueen (2006) • Shinkôsha (2004) • 1 volume • Yaoi • 18+ (nudity, graphic sex)

Pianist Kenzo doesn't have to think twice when wealthy eccentric Lorenzo Carlucci offers to be his patron, but he has plenty of opportunity to regret his decision as their stubborn natures rub each other the wrong way. But soon their bitter enmity turns to burning desire. (HS)   NR

WAGAMAMA KITCHEN

Wagamama Kitchen, "Whimsical Kitchen" (わがままキッチン) • Kaori Monchi • DMP (2007) • Biblos (2005) • 1 volume • Yaoi, Romance • 18+

Kumaki is a salaryman with the appearance of a lady-killer, but in reality he keeps falling for straight men. Naoto, an artist, is the latest object of his affection. Can Kumaki win his love, or will this be another in a long line of disappointments? (HS)   NR

WARU

Waru, "Bad" (悪) • Yukari Hashida • DMP (2007) • Ookura Shuppan (2002) • 1 volume • Yaoi, Contemporary • 18+

Bad boy Jou does the baddest thing ever when he kidnaps the son of a parliamentarian. In the midst of their adventure, the two end up falling in love. (HS)   NR

WE ARE THE NAKED JEWELS CORPORATION

Warera Takarara Corporation Ôki na Vibe no Sha no Shita De, "We Are the Takarara Corporation: In the House of Vibes" (われら宝裸コーポレーション －大きなバイブの舎の下で－) • Shushushu Sakurai • DramaQueen (2007) • Magazine Magazine (Pierce, 2001–2003) • 2 volumes • Yaoi, Salaryman, Comedy • 18+ (nudity, graphic sex)

Okazaki and Fujishima love their jobs and will go to any lengths to make sure their product is the best. Good news for the lovers of the world, since the men work at Japan's number one vibrator company! Join the adventure to find the perfect piece to add to their line! (HS)   NR

WHITE GUARDIAN

DUO BRAND. • DramaQueen (2006) • Kousai Shobo (2003) • 1 volume • Yaoi • 18+ (brief violence, nudity, graphic sex)

While fighting a naval engagement in tall ships at sea, young soldier Linth Highwind is saved—and then raped—by the famous General Sei, a scarred, stubbly older man with long hair. Linth then reveals that he is in fact the crown prince of the kingdom, and asks a repentant Sei to become his bodyguard and accompany him back to the palace. *White Guardian* is a plotless *yaoi* manga that jumps almost instantly into bloody rape (which in turn is forgiven immediately). The anatomy is stiff, and the art overuses tone and computer color (on the color pages). Includes a brief preview of the artists' related story *Crimson Wind*.   ★

WILD ROCK

(ワイルド・ロック) • Kazusa Takashima • BLU (2006) • Biblos (2002) • 1 volume • Yaoi, Prehistorical, Romance • 18+ (nudity, graphic sex)

Yuuen's clan has long been losing game animals to the Lakeside clan, and now Yuuen's father has a crafty plan—delicate Yuuen will dress like a girl and get Emba, the heir to the Lakeside clan, to fall in love with him. Yuuen reluctantly complies, but when he finds himself falling for the rugged Emba, he calls off the ruse. But Emba, who always knew Yuuen was a man, risks the wrath of both their clans to claim his love. This is very much a *yaoi* romance novel, an unapologetically fun read in an exotic setting with hot men in loincloths. The art is enjoyable as well, fully realizing the fantasy setting and lovingly detailing the characters. Also contains a short story about Emba and Yuuen's fathers, "Innocent Lies." ★★★★

WORDS OF DEVOTION

Ai no Kotodama, "Words of Love" (愛の言霊) • Keiko Konno • DMP (2007) • Frontier Works (2003–2004) • 2 volumes • Yaoi • 18+ (nudity, graphic sex)

When Tachibana and Otani graduated from high school they were finally able to confess their love and are now happily living together. But when former classmate Yuki shows up, all of Otani's old suspicions rear up. Is he right to be so nervous? (HS)   NR

WORLD'S END

Eiki Eiki • DMP (2007) • Shinshokan (Dear Plus, 1999) • 1 volume • Yaoi, Drama • 16+ (language, sexual situatons)

The sequel to Eiki Eiki's *Dear Myself.* (HS) NR

WORTHLESS LOVE

Rokudenashi no Koi, "Good-for-Nothing Love" (ろくでなしの恋) • Yuuya • DramaQueen (2006–ongoing) • Kaiohsha (2004–ongoing) • 3+ volumes (ongoing) • Performance, Yaoi • 18+

Misaki lives aimlessly until one night a theater performance changes his life. Now he has a goal, to get into the troupe, but his pretty looks turn out to be his downfall. Misaki is determined to wear them down, especially the charismatic lead actor Kuroda. (HS)   NR

YEBISU CELEBRITIES

(YEBISUセレブリティーズ) • Shinri Fuwa (story), Kaoru Iwamoto (art) • Be Beautiful (2006) • Biblos (Be x Boy, 2006) • 3 volumes • Yaoi • 18+ (nudity, graphic sex)

Haruka is the newest employee at the prestigious design firm Yebisu Graphics and bears the brunt of his boss's bad humor—and passions. (HS)   NR

YELLOW

Makoto Tateno • DMP (2005–2006) • Biblos (2002–2004) • 4 volumes • Crime, Yaoi, Action • 18+ (language, mild violence, nudity, sex)

Two hot male undercover agents, the gay Goh and the ostensibly straight Taki, live together and work together on drug busts. *Yellow* is a dumbed-down version of *Fake* (or an "only the good stuff" version of *Fake,* depending on your tastes). The focus is not on the improbable, clichéd detective cases but on "When are they going to have sex?" In a typical scene, Goh starts groping Taki's ass, and Taki sticks a gun in his face . . . but with a smile! The men are masculine-looking (by *yaoi* standards) and the formula delivers the desired fanservice, but the character interaction is weak and the plot is derivative. The title refers to yellow traffic lights (in the sense of "proceed at your own risk," not "slow down"). ★★

YOU AND HARUJION

Kimi to Harujion, "You and Harujion" (君とハルジオン) • Keiko Kinoshita • DMP (2006) • Taiyoh Tosho (Craft Original Comic Anthology, 2004) • 1 volume • Yaoi • 16+ (mild language, mild sexual situations)

After his father's death leaves him an orphan, teenage Haru is unexpectedly sheltered by an adult lawyer, Senoh, who keeps vultures away from the estate and eventually offers Haru a place to live. Up until the last twenty pages or so, *You and Harujion* could be a psychological story about a conflicted father figure with partly pure, partly impure motivations. ("Haru's future isn't with some thirty-something man! He'll fall in love with some pretty girl, get married, have children, and be happy! *As he should!*") But this is a Boys' Love manga, so it crosses over the line, not into on-screen sex but into something beyond a platonic relationship. The mood is bittersweet, and the writing is subdued enough that one wishes the story wasn't confined by its genre. ★★½

YOUR HONEST DECEIT

Kimi no Tsuku to Hontô • (君のつく嘘と本当) • Sakufu Ajimine • DramaQueen (2006–2007) • Shinkôsha (2004–2005) • 2 volumes • Yaoi • 18+ (nudity, graphic sex)

Kitahara is a lawyer who has never considered sex with a man until his cute paralegal Kuze started coming on to him. Now Kitahara finds himself trying to deal with a new office romance and his shocking new feelings. The art is bland, with some hilarious porn face shots, and everyone's eyes make them look consumptive. Also includes the connected short stories "Hunny Bunny" and "Cutie Bunny." (HS) ★

ADULT REVIEWS

ADULT MANGA

(成年・エロ漫画)

Bisexual fairies copulating with horny insects. Nurses seducing hermaphrodite schoolgirls. Tentacle monsters probing the orifices of teenage warriors. The world of adult erotic manga can seem like a print bacchanal, an omnivorous orgy in screentone and ink . . . and that's only the material deemed palatable for Western mores. Between the diversity of fetishes and the sheer proliferation of titles, it's tempting to imagine that Japan has a laissez-faire attitude toward the depiction of sex in its comics. After all, eroticism is a given across the manga spectrum, from the panty shots dotting boys' manga to the angst-ridden *bishônen* that make teenage girls' hearts skip. Adult manga are merely the logical, extreme consequence of this hothouse atmosphere, and it may seem that as long as artists and publishers pay lip service to obscenity laws, they will be left alone. The reality is more complex and far less benevolent.

The Japanese attitude toward adult manga is a complex and contradictory one, difficult to untangle. To avoid confusion, it is vital to differentiate adult manga from the related categories of *seinen* (young men's) and *jôsei* (women's) manga. These categories of manga all contain work that fits the classic definition of pornography—narratives pivoting on sexual acts that are meant to stimulate—but only adult manga bear the stigma of the term. T&A is a regular component of many *seinen* and *jôsei* series, and sex is not uncommon. Throughout the genres' history there have been series that pushed the envelope in terms of explicitness (Naoki Yamamoto's *Dance Till Tomorrow*) or contentious subject matter (Haruko Kashiwagi's *Inu* includes bestiality), but the majority of works are no worse than what you would find in an R-rated movie or late-night cable series. This doesn't mean such series are immune to being caught up in the "harmful manga" hysteria that seems to sweep the nation at least once a decade, but ultimately *seinen* and *jôsei* are accepted parts of the manga landscape. There are also soft-core manga magazines, such as Futabasha's *Men's Young,* that walk a razor's edge between *seinen* and adult manga. Sex scenes are frequent (once per chapter on average) and more graphic, with frontal nudity and ejaculation common. Minor restraints—broad censoring of genitalia, a dearth of gynecological close-ups—allow these manga to avoid an 18+ label and to be sold in mainstream outlets.

And adult manga? It's the equivalent of hard-core pornography in public perception if not always in content (only in the 1990s was the bulk of erotica explicit enough to earn the designation). "Pure" adult sex manga are known in Japan as *ero-manga* (erotic manga) or *seinen* manga ("adult manga," written with different kanji characters than *seinen* meaning "young men," to the confusion of English speakers). Like pornography in the West, it's an omnipresent part of popular culture, but not something the average person is going to champion or boast about reading—or drawing (hence the wealth of clever pseudonyms used by artists). Despite many of manga's most acclaimed creators passing through its ranks, there has always been an unsavory air surrounding the whole business, a disreputable aura. With adult manga treading water in recent years, such derision may seem deserved, but at its aesthetic peak, the genre boasted a rebel spirit and iconoclastic attitude, and provided a haven for artists to experiment and innovate.

EARLY ADULT MANGA

The prehistory of adult manga is found in postwar manga's back alleys, in the rental-market *gekiga* and the early men's magazines. With the era's mainstream manga anthologies catering to children, these formats provided the sole avenue for open depictions of sex. By the mid-1960s, *gekiga* had matured and blossomed into the avant-garde manga movement embodied by *Garo* (1964) and *COM* (1967), while *Heibon Punch* (1965) brought a needed touch of class to men's magazines. The venerable *Manga Action* was founded in 1967, paving the way for the first wave of *seinen* magazines, such as *Young Comic* (1967) and *Big Comic* (1968), which employed sex as a marketing tool to woo its audience.

Seinen pioneer Kazuhiko Miyaya (*Ningyo Densetsu,* "Mermaid Legend") is considered the crucial figure in establishing sex as an accepted part of mainstream manga. Oscillating between pop culture–drenched coming-of-age tales and more straightforward macho genre exercises, Miyaya, as one fan put it, "made comics cool." Another critical figure was the late Kazuo Kamimura (*Lady Snowblood*). Dubbed "the Showa master painter," Kamimura's art graced numerous *seinen* covers while his stories broke ground in portraying homosexuality, lesbianism, and incest.

Between the success of *seinen* and the increasing vulgarity of *shônen* manga thanks to the likes of Go Nagai and George Akiyama, manga sexuality percolated throughout the early 1970s. It was inevitable that a magazine devoted exclusively to adult manga would appear. That magazine was *Manga Erotopia,* founded in 1973 with future manga historian and playwright Ei Takatori at the helm as editor. Its breakout star was twenty-four-year-old Masaru Sakaki, whose meticulously rendered voluptuous women proved such a hit that an entire series of special issues (*Ai to Yume,* "Love and Dreams") was devoted to his work. Sakai and *Young Comic*'s Takashi Ishii would be the avatars for a new movement called *ero-gekiga,* or more pejoratively *sanryû gekiga* (third-rate *gekiga*).

Following *Erotopia*'s success, a deluge of adult manga magazines appeared. To paraphrase famous manga editor Carl Gustav Horn on the soft-core adult anime *Cream Lemon,* the late 1970s were the "boogie nights" of adult manga. Contributors to the new magazines included *Garo* habitués in need of a paycheck, hungry young hopefuls, and mainstream veterans looking for a little breathing room. Editors were intellectuals with literary aspirations who gave the artists their head: As long as each issue had the requisite nudie photographs and modicum of sex, artists were free to do as they pleased. Most seized the opportunity.

The magazine that best encapsulates the anarchic ethos of the era is *Manga Alice* (1976). Unlike its brethren, *Alice* was distributed exclusively via vending machines, a tactic that would prove appealing to publishers seeking to avoid police hassles. Its editor, future sci-fi novelist and critic Takeshi Kamewada, posed nude within its pages and cultivated an aesthetic closer to the arthouse than the grindhouse. Future luminaries including Yoko Kondo and Hisashi Sakaguchi were regulars. In 1979 the magazine scored a coup when one of its serials, Hideo Azuma's *Fujori Nikki* ("Absurdity Diary"), won the prestigious Seiun Award for Best Manga.

Alice was not alone in showcasing rising stars. *Sanryû gekiga* contributors ranged from mavericks Michio Hisauchi and Shinchi Abe to gag legend Yasuji Tanioka to future critics (Jun Ishikawa), musicians (Keizo Miyanishi), and even a cult actor (Tomoroh Taguchi of *Tetsuo the Iron Man* fame).

In spite of its attempts at alternate distribution routes and grudging acquiescence to laws against the depiction of genitalia, adult magazines could not avoid run-ins with the law. There were several censorship incidents in the 1978–1979 period, with the 1978 bust of *Manga Erogenika* often cited as a downward turn for *ero-gekiga*'s fortunes. However, it was not the police or bluenoses who sounded the death knell for the rambunctious movement, but an unlikely figure: a little cartoon girl.

ANIME AND *LOLICON*

Throughout the 1980s, the entire manga industry seemed engaged in a mass sing-along of "Thank Heaven for Little Girls." Theories abound as to why *lolicon,* a fetish absent from *ero-gekiga* and the related *bishôjo* genre, overtook adult manga in a coup and soon penetrated the mainstream of Japanese pop culture. Much of the credit (or blame) can be laid at the feet of one man: Hideo Azuma, known as the father of *lolicon* and *bishôjo* manga. Already a decade-long veteran with numerous *shônen* and *seinen* series under his belt, Azuma combined a pared-down cartoony style inspired by Osamu Tezuka and other old-school masters with absurdist gags and satirical sex. Like Robert Crumb, Azuma created art in which the combination of nostalgic, accessible images with taboo-breaking subject matter proved irresistible to artists and audiences alike. As Tomo Machiyama has observed, Azuma's *lolicon* manga brought to the surface the latent sexuality many fans found in the prepubescent heroines of Tezuka and Hayao Miyazaki. Azuma's only work available in English is the non-adult, autobiographical *Disappearance Diary* (2005).

In 1979, Azuma instigated a *lolicon* anthology within the nascent *dôjinshi* community. The year 1980 would be *lolicon's annus mirabilis,* as Azuma's appearances in the vending-machine magazine *Shôjo Alice* (English subtitle: "Alice in Pornography. With Lolita") broke the movement to a wider audience. By year's end the manga magazine *OUT* ran a special on the "lolicon virus." In 1982, fellow *lolicon* traveler Aki Uchiyama's perverse, diaper-fixated series *Andoro Trio* began its run in *Weekly Shônen Champion* while the movement gained its flagship magazine in *Lemon People.*

Lolicon's unprecedented spread was bolstered by the burgeoning market for adult anime videos. Works by Uchiyama and Fumio Nakajima were among the earliest *hentai* anime, while the trail-blazing *Cream Lemon,* which began in 1984, appropriated *lolicon* tropes. Another factor in *lolicon's* rise to the top was audience buying habits. Critic Kaoru Nagayama has observed that while *ero-gekiga* readers were reluctant to shell out cash for collections of individual artists' manga (hence the paucity of graphic novels from that era), *lolicon* fans were ravenous for books by their favorite creators, putting more money in the pockets of publishers and artists. Despite the name of the genre, not all *lolicon* manga actually involved young girls—some stories simply applied a cute, infantile, anime-influenced art style to adult sexual situations.

While *lolicon* had a stranglehold on Japan's collective conscience, it was not the only significant development in the 1980s. *Ero-gekiga* had ceded the limelight, but it never died, and some of the decade's most important creators, among them Naoki Yamamoto, combined *lolicon* and *ero-gekiga* styles to arrive at a new, darker hybrid.

Toshio Maeda's *Urotsukidôji: Legend of the Overfiend* (1986) spawned tentacle manga, one of the more novel attempts to evade obscenity laws by drawing monstrous pseudopods instead of male genitalia. Despite its popularity, its impact was far greater on anime—and American perceptions of adult anime—than on manga in the long run.

Female artists also made their first significant dent in adult manga. Some commentators have suggested that their "cuter" art styles contributed to the *lolicon* trend. Today, a significant number of adult manga artists are female, with translated examples including work by Akira Gajou, Akiko Fujii, and Kengo Yonekura. That's not including the countless explicit *yaoi* manga and straight sex comics aimed at adult women. The first women's adult manga, known as *redicomi* (ladies' comics), appeared at the start of the 1980s, while the likes of Kyoko Okazaki and Shungiku Uchida laid the foundation for modern *jôsei* manga.

MODERN ADULT MANGA

In 1989 the outcry against manga in the wake of the Tsutomu Miyazaki murders (see OTAKU) dealt adult manga a devastating blow. The most immediate effect was the implementation of warning labels forbidding adult manga from being sold to minors. This only inspired a ratcheting up in the extremity of sexual content. Rape, violence, and misogyny have always peppered erotic manga, but whether due to increased competition from adult anime, video games, and the Internet, or a symptom of pornography's worldwide dash toward the gutter, recent adult manga seems intent on being as repugnant as possible. Gone are the days when *tankôbon* covers portrayed coy housewives and naughty schoolgirls lifting their tops or skirts: Female characters are now so drenched in bodily fluids it looks as if they were dipped in mayonnaise. Publishers began to target niche markets, churning out anthologies devoted to particular fetishes, from threesomes to older women to gym bloomers.

Some of the more popular specialty genres include:

Bakunyu (large breasts)—Buxom women have always been a staple of adult manga, although they were eclipsed by the *lolicon* craze. Big busts made a comeback in the 1990s, with cup sizes growing ever more outrageous, and are now the norm in non-*bishôjo* erotica. Tohru Nishimaski's *Blue Eyes* is a representative example.

Incest—The perennial pornographic theme has skyrocketed in popularity in the past decade, with series including Wolf Ogami's *Super Taboo* and innumerable anthologies dedicated to the subject. Mother/son and sister/brother are the most prevalent combos.

Cosplay—From nurses and maids to cat-girls and bunny-girls, adult manga does its part for today's working woman. Whole anthologies are devoted to occupations such as waitresses and stewardesses, in addition to garden-variety schoolgirls and office ladies.

Futanari (hermaphrodites, "she-males")— *Futanari* were to the 1990s what *loli-con* was to the 1980s: a seemingly minority-taste kink that quickly became a pervasive part of the industry, cross-pollinating every genre from *seinen* to *redicomi*. Toshiki Yui (*Hot Tails*) is the best-known exponent in the West.

Ero-Guro ("erotic-grotesque")—The blood-soaked, dark-humored genre dates back to iconoclasts such as Kazuichi Hanawa and Toshio Saeki in the 1970s. It reached its aesthetic peak in the 1980s with the likes of Suehiro Maruo and Jun Hayami. Recent practitioners have included Shintaro Kago (whose work is published in *Secret Comics Japan*), Mukade Meribe, and Waita Uziga, who has gone so beyond the pale in his depiction of sexual violence that he's inspired a new coinage: snuff manga.

There have also been some promising aesthetic and financial developments. *Ero-gekiga* underwent a welcome revival, with many of its architects finally receiving their due. Ota Shuppan's *Erotics* (1999) and *Erotics F* (2001) combine the all-inclusive ethos of the old adult magazines with an alternative manga sensibility and offer a reliable space for artists wishing to portray sex in a mature fashion. Beginning with Antarctic Press's Venus imprint in 1994, adult manga finally made inroads into the American comics market in the 1990s, achieving a foothold with Eros Comix's Mangerotica imprint (another project of Toren Smith's Studio Proteus). Other companies that have dabbled or specialized in adult manga include Radio Comix, Studio Ironcat, and Icarus Publishing. However, the growth of online sites offering downloads of translated and raw scans places the future of English-language adult manga in question, as do the censorship hassles faced by companies releasing the more extreme works (Creation Books had to publish its Jun Hayami compilation *Beauty Labyrinth of Razors* online after every printer turned it down).

As the *sanryû gekiga* become collector's items and the glory days of adult manga fodder for history books, one may wonder: Has the genre's artistic flame been extinguished? Have the innovators and firebrands abandoned the field—or have they simply moved to another medium? A fan of a contemporary erotic manga artist known for harsh, disturbing work dismissed his latest book as compromised: he had to dilute his vision so as not to alienate readers. However, he continues to draw personal work within the *dôjinshi* community. It is no coincidence that many of the most important adult artists in recent years have strong ties to the *dôjinshi* community. Like the old adult magazines, the format encourages experimentation and boasts its own subculture. With its limited audience and distribution, preponderance of parodies, and lack of quality filters, *dôjinshi* may not be the ideal medium for artistry—but neither were the vending machines. Adult manga has shown a remarkable ability to survive and thrive in the most hostile environments, with its best work often created in the shadows. (CV)

ADVENTURE KID

(アドベンチャーKID) • Toshio Maeda • Manga 18 (2002–2003) • Wani Magazine (1988) • 4 volumes • Science Fiction, Fantasy, Horror, Adult • 18+ (graphic violence, nudity, graphic sex)

A kid is next to a computer when it explodes, and before long he and his girlfriend are sucked into the digital world and dumped into the past—in the middle of a World War II battlefield. A bunch of delinquents follow them in and fight off the evil, lecherous American soldiers. It turns out the computer was haunted by a mad scientist and the only way to escape is to go back in time and stop him from entering the machine. But then all the dead solders start moving again—they're zombies! Meanwhile, the kid's fat father has sex with a bunch of women. Back to the action! The kids are transported to a fantasy realm based on a video game where they fight/seduce demons to escape. As you can probably tell, this manga is more interested in not making sense than anything else. There are plenty of sexy women and frequent (but brief) sexual interludes, but really it's just a weird mix of video game references, zombies, *yakuza* wanna-bes, and demon sex. (DG) ★★★

AKUMA-SHE: See *Wingbird*

ALICE IN SEXLAND

Alice First • Mashumaro Jyuubaori • Eros Mang-Erotica (2001–2004) • Angel Shuppan (1999) • 15 issues • Fantasy, Adult • 18+ (nudity, graphic sex)

Alice in Sexland is pretty straightforward: take *Alice in Wonderland* and turn it into a giant, nonstop orgy. All of the classic characters are here, but almost invariably recast as women using magic to grow the appropriate equipment for the job. The art is simple, clean, and effective, while the tone remains fun and lighthearted with the exception of Alice's tragic past and a surprisingly dark twist ending. The second volume was translated under the title *Alice in Sexland Extreme.* (DG) ★★★

ALICE IN SEXLAND EXTREME: See *Alice in Sexland*

AMAZING STRIP

Ippongi Bang • Antarctic/Venus (1994) • 2 volumes • Fantasy, Comedy, Adult • 18+ (brief violence, nudity, sex)

Ippongi Bang's work has the imagination, the good-natured humor, and the short attention span of a college fanzine. *Amazing Strip,* perhaps her best translated comic, is a series of short stories about Taima "Timer" Kawasaki, a motorcycle-riding guitarist, and his bandmates Ralph and Nami, who are lovable rebels just like him. Together, they encounter science fiction scenarios that usually involve both music and sex; Timer sleeps with ghosts, angels, and "sound beings," although he has less luck with normal women. The lighthearted stories could only be told with Bang's action-packed, cartoony art style; exaggerated poses and extreme camera angles abound, and the characters are a cross between the gangly tough guys and girls of the 1970s and the chubby, big-eyed heroes of 1980s anime. The sex scenes, while not frequent or explicit enough to really qualify as ero-manga, are fun and loving; when the characters get busy, flowers and cascades of light obscure their genitals, and they spend lots of time lying in bed together afterward. The dialogue ranges from silly, dirty humor to trippy cosmic thoughts about music, and it's hard not to love a sex comic that uses the sound effect "FINISH!" ★★★½

ANY WAY I WANT IT

Omô ga mama ni . . . , "Any Way I Want It" (想うがままに . . .) • Kei Matsuzawa • Icarus Publishing (2006) • Akaneshinsha (2004) • 1 volume • Adult • 18+ (nudity, graphic sex)

Based solely on adult manga, one would think that sex is a violent, forceful thing that happens only when someone traps and forces someone else into it, whether it's teachers and students, brothers and sisters, the rich and the poor, or anyone else. *Any Way I Want It* uses all these standard plots, although it's never really rape so much as victims being caught giving in to their lusts. The art is good and the premises range wide enough to hit most nonviolent fetishes, but it all ends up being predictable and pedestrian. It works for anyone looking for something a bit beyond simply consensual stories but afraid of the darker side of adult manga; just don't expect any new positions and ideas. (DG) ★★★

ANZU: THE SHARDS OF MEMORY

Anzu: Kioku no Hakuhen, "Anzu: The Shards of Memory" (ANZU〜記憶の薄片〜) • Kirikaze • Icarus Publishing (2007) • France Shoin (2004) • 1 volume • Occult, Adult • 18+ (nudity, graphic sex)

When a popular student commits suicide, Anzu's repressed psychic powers are triggered, unleashing visions of a brutal rape from centuries past. As memories of past lives resurface, Anzu's little sister Kaede becomes the target of dark forces. Will the ancient tragedy repeat itself? And what about their cross-dressing classmate Akimoto?
NR

BANG'S SEXPLOSION!

Ippongi Bang • Studio Ironcat/Sexy Fruit (1999) • 1 issue • Adult • 18+ (nudity, graphic sex)

One-shot adult manga by cult 1980s *otaku* artist Ippongi Bang. NR

BATTLE BINDER PLUS

Battle Binder Plus—Kekkôsôkô Karon, "Binding Armor Karon" (BATTLE BINDER PLUS—結合装甲カローン) • Rulia 046 • Antarctic/Venus (1994–1995) • Hit Shuppansha (1992) • Science Fiction, Yuri, Action, Adult • 18+ (violence, nudity, graphic sex)

It might start as a sci-fi story of cyborg combat and rampant lesbian sex in the future, but *Battle Binder Plus* quickly leaves all the sex behind. The first few chapters feature our heroine getting naked and engaging in sexual showdowns with a variety of beautiful female criminals before transforming into a giant armored robot and killing everyone, but eventually the whole sex pretense is abandoned entirely in favor of getting right into the cyber-suit power armor combat. Not that there aren't plenty of nude reaction shots, but it's more about blowing things up than blowjobs by that point. The mechanical designs and landscapes are good, but the humans just don't measure up (and the artist skips more than one frame, jokingly apologizing for being lazy). In the end, the entire thing was probably just written as an excuse to draw a destroyed skyscraper on the moon and have a hot chick in power armor fight herself. (DG) ★★

BEAUTY LABYRINTH OF RAZORS

Jun Hayami • Creation Books (2006) • Ota Shuppan (2000–2001) • 1 volume • Erotic-grotesque • 18+ (language, extreme graphic violence, nudity, graphic sex)

For more than two decades Jun Hayami has reigned as the standard-bearer for the extreme outer edge of erotic-grotesque manga, as renowned for his literary and artistic qualities as for the reams of inventively violated and butchered women (and the occasional man) who populate his oeuvre. Hayami's metaphysical aspirations and notion of cosmic evil can be laughably adolescent, but his best work is hard to dismiss. Mourning a schoolgirl-hooker's murder even as he wallows in her evisceration, juxtaposing grim gallows humor with flare-ups of moral revulsion, his work is so feverish and anguished that it often teeters on the brink of complete incoherence. The most controlled, subversive, and pleasurable of the dozen stories here are the two episodes from his infamous "Jun series." These pseudo-autobiographical portraits of the artist as a young degenerate, suggesting R. Crumb or Joe Matt as redrawn by S. Clay Wilson, are as hilarious as they are appalling. Not a translation of any one Japanese book, *Beauty Labyrinth of Razors* gathers assorted Hayami material dating back to the 1980s, primarily drawn from his untranslated collections *Love Letter from Kanata* ("Love Letter from Far Away") and *Jigoku no Communication* ("A Hell of Communication"). (CV) ★★★

BIZZARIAN

(ビザリアン) • Senno Knife • Studio Ironcat (2000–2001) • Tsukasa (1993) • 8 issues • Science Fiction, Adult • 18+ (nudity, graphic sex)

The most comedic of Senno Knife's many translated adult manga, this series focuses on science fiction stories, schoolgirls suddenly turned into nymphos, and other "bizarre" scenarios. The amusing time-travel plotlines are the highlights of this series (though the living alien dildo is also creative), but the sex scenes are brief and lacking in detail, so the series fails as a sex comic. The writing is mediocre and the characters are undeveloped. (JW) ★★½

BLUE EYES

Blue Eyes (ブルー・アイズ) • Tohru Nishimaki • Icarus Publishing (2004–ongoing) • Hit Shuppansha (1996–ongoing) • 4+ volumes (ongoing) • Adult • 18+ (nudity, graphic sex)

A rarity in adult manga, Blue Eyes actually has a continuing story line instead of being a collection of one-shot sex stories that are done as soon as the characters themselves are. As the story moves along, the protagonist adds more and more gigantic-breasted women to his stable of conquests. The art is extremely simplistic and amateurish, to the point that there's no way to tell when the main story ends and the side stories begin; it all looks alike. (DG) ★

LA BLUE GIRL: THE ORIGINAL MANGA

Injû Gakuen: La Blue Girl, "Lascivious Beast School: La Blue Girl" (淫獣学園La Blue Girl) • Toshio Maeda • Manga 18 (2002–2004) • Leed Publishing (1989–1992) • 6 volumes • Ninja, Tentacle, Adult • 18+ (graphic violence, nudity, graphic sex)

In many ways it's anime and manga boiled down to their most striking components: magical schoolgirl ninjas fighting tentacle demon monsters (and getting raped all along the way). Oftentimes hilarious in its sheer absurdity, Maeda's extremely realistic artwork really brings it to life. However, while he may be a master at drawing beautiful and realistically proportioned women, he's pretty terrible at giving any sense of motion—everyone always looks like they're standing around, posing for a clichéd art lesson about drawing nude figures. Like most of his work, the plot gets a lot more attention than in most adult manga—not that it honestly matters, however, as it's really all about the gorgeous women and the newest stupid secret ninja technique they have to use to escape from the clutches of the latest nympho nether creature. A La Blue Girl licensed comic adaptation by American artists, produced in the late 1990s, was titled simply La Blue Girl and is sometimes mistaken for this series. (DG) ★★★★

BOMBSHELL BOOBIES

Bakunyûdô, "The Way of Huge Breasts/Bombshell Breasts" (爆乳道) • Yukio Yukimino • Red Light Manga (2001) • Tokyo Sanseisha (2000) • 1 volume • Adult • 18+ (nudity, graphic sex)

Adult short story collection, named after Yukimino's favorite fetish; the Japanese title, "Bakunyûdô," is also the name of his Web site. NR

BONDAGE FAIRIES

Insect Hunter (インセクト・ハンター) • Kondom • Eros MangErotica (1996–2006) • Kuboama (Lemon Kids, 1990–1991; also published in other magazines) • 5 volumes (ongoing) • Fantasy, Comedy, Adult • 18+ (nudity, graphic sex)

One of the first hit translated adult manga, the classic Bondage Fairies was originally released by Antarctic Press in the early 1990s, then reprinted and continued by Eros. The fantasy-porn story follows Pfil and Pamela, two tiny fairies in skimpy outfits, as they carry out their duties as "Hunters," protectors of forest creatures. Naturally, sex is the answer to all problems, and sexy-innocent Pfil finds herself all too often "giving it up" for the sake of forestkind. The series features unforgivingly graphic sex with creepy-crawlies, the ickier the better. In brief, all the men are talking animals or insects: the heroines are raped by beetles! Molested by crayfish! They even have consensual sex with

The New Bondage Fairies by Kondom *New Bondage Fairies* © 1996 Kondom

bats! And yet they usually retain their self-respect, don't get battered or *bukkake*d, and end up punishing the bad guys afterward. The female characters look cute in a typically 1980s style, but the wildlife artwork is surprisingly accurate; the bugs may talk, but they're totally non-anthropomorphic except for their penises. Though the "bestiality" may turn off some, it's a rewarding adult comedy with likable characters and enough bizarre sex scenes to make even the most jaded reader think, "How'd he come up with *that*?" Like many adult manga, different parts of the story have been printed under several different names: in chronological order, it runs *The Original Bondage Fairies* (a revised edition of the material originally published by Antarctic Press), *The New Bondage Fairies*, *Bondage Fairies: Fairy Fetish*, and *Bondage Fairies Extreme*. As of April 2007, *Bondage Fairies Extreme* has not been collected in graphic novel form. (JW)

★★★★

BONDAGE FAIRIES EXTREME: See *Bondage Fairies*

CHIRALITY: TO THE PROMISED LAND: See General Manga Reviews

CO-ED SEXXTASY

Nagi-chan no Yuutsu, "Nagi-chan's Melancholy" (凪ちゃんのゆううつ) • Makoto Fujisaki • Eros MangErotica (2000–2004) • Fujimi Shuppan (1996–1997) • 2 volumes • Adult • 18+ (nudity, graphic sex)

This is a rare beast among adult manga: a continuous erotic story about several adults in consensual, monogamous, *happy* relationships. *Co-ed Sexxtasy* has a great deal more story and characterization than you'd expect. Each chapter revolves around a big sex scene (often involving anal sex or doing it outside) but manages to squeeze in enough dialogue and plot to actually build a believable and (relatively) realistic relationship among the two main couples. Hell, it even ends with a happy ending about the triumph of true love. It's a rare thing to see a romantic and healthy relationship capped off with powerful sex. If the art was a bit better, it would be perfect; the sex is illustrated beautifully, but faces don't get as much attention. (DG)

★★★★

COUNCIL OF CARNALITY UNLIMITED

Bonnô Seitokai Unlimited, "Carnality Council Unlimited" (煩悩生徒会UNLIMITED) • Yanagi Yuki • Icarus Publishing (2006) • Akaneshinsha (2003) • 1 volume • Adult • 18+ (nudity, graphic sex)

Satou joins the student council to pursue the girl he loves, the sex-crazed Shimizu.

NR

COUNTDOWN: SEX BOMBS

Count Down • Hiroyuki Utatane • Eros MangErotica (1995–1996) • Fujimi Shuppan (1992) • 1 volume • Adult • 18+ (nudity, graphic sex)

Countdown: Sex Bombs is a classic—the anime adaptation was one of the first adult anime brought to the United States. This collection includes a number of different short stories, most of them involving some sort of violation of normal gender roles—lots of cross-dressing, hermaphrodites, and female domination. The androgynous characters are right at home in Utatane's extravagant art style. The stories are varied and erotic (it's less explicit than many' more recent adult manga, thus making it more effective). The most remarkable one is a short piece featuring a sinuous dragon drawn in an evocative, almost Zen ink painting style. (DG)　★★★

DANCE TILL TOMORROW: See General Manga Reviews

DEMON BEAST INVASION: THE ORIGINAL MANGA

Yōjū Kyōshitsu, "Monster/Demon Classroom" (妖獣教室) • Toshio Maeda • Manga 18 • Wani Magazine (1989) • 2 volumes • Tentacle, Horror, Adult • 18+ (nudity, graphic sex)

Another infamous tentacle romp from the troubled mind that produced *Urotsukidoji: Legend of the Overfiend.* Aliens/monsters invade from another planet/dimension and take over our world by raping and impregnating as many schoolgirls (and some teachers) as possible. The series is filled with gorgeous women (usually half nude), ugly human men, hideous demonic creatures with pulsating, prehensile phalluses, and completely nonsensical plot twists and revelations. It isn't all tentacle rape, surprisingly enough. There are interludes of human lovemaking as well, and Maeda renders his women with exquisite care. The art is somewhat static and the frequent sex scenes are brief but disturbing. However, the insane light-speed pace at which the plot moves along, introducing new plotlines and developments only to destroy them on the next page, keeps you from taking anything too seriously. It's just beautiful women, strange monsters, and lots of sex and violence. A *Demon Beast Invasion* licensed comic adaptation by American artists, produced in the late 1990s, was titled simply *Demon Beast Invasion* and is sometimes mistaken for this series. (DG)　★★★★

DIMPLES DOWN BELOW

Kokan ni Ekubo, "Dimples Between the Legs" (股間にエクボ) • Yukio Yukimino • Red Light Manga (2001) • Tokyo Sanseisha (1998) • 1 volume • Adult • 18+ (nudity, graphic sex)

Adult short story collection.　NR

DOMIN-8 ME!

Take on Me • Sessyu Takemura • Eros MangErotica (2007) • Core Magazine (2004) • 1 volume • Adult • 18+ (nudity, graphic sex)

Slick, polished, and arousing artwork mixed with a good sense of framing and inventive camera angles aren't the only things that separate this adult manga from the rest. A manga featuring mild domination and sexual experimentation entirely featuring willing participants, ones in a long-term relationship no less? Unheard of! Then there's the irreverent sense of humor inherent in the premise of a short, childlike man having sex with a much taller and older-looking classmate whose adult sister looks like a child (and is still a virgin at twenty-six to boot). The necessary fetishes are indulged but it all comes off as just so much *fun* it's impossible not to want some yourself. (DG)　★★★★

EDEN

(エデン) • Senno Knife • Studio Ironcat (2002) • Cybele Shuppan (1994–1997) • 4 issues (5 volumes in Japan) • Historical, Adult • 18+ (nudity, graphic sex)

In Japan, *Eden* is one of Senno Knife's best-known series, but only a small portion has been translated. (Ironcat's plans to do a graphic novel series were cut short by the company's collapse.) Set in early-twentieth-century prewar Japan, the mood is one of period elegance and decadence: brothels, bathhouses, kimono-clad girls, and pretty boys with long flowing locks. Knife creates a *shôjo* manga atmosphere of sweet romance and cherry blossoms, mixed with sexual slavery and "what the butler saw" perversion. But this isn't a vicious Suehiro Maruo assault on the hypocrisy of the past; it's a gentle tribute, almost an erotic fairy tale.

Unfortunately, the art is weak and the actual stories are forgettable. (JW) ★★½

EIKEN: See General Manga Reviews

EMBLEM

Kei Taniguchi • Antarctic/Venus (1994–1995) • Hit Shuppansha (1993) • 8 issues • Adult • 18+ (nudity, graphic sex)

In the lumpy, ugly-faced, tiny-headed-but-giant-eyed world of *Emblem,* sex never ends well. Whether it's a dominatrix being killed by her possessive slaves, a student publicly beaten and exposed by her teacher, a cheating wife killing her husband for insurance money, or some punks kidnapping and raping a random girl, the world is full only of pain. The sex rapidly transitions from uncomfortable to stomach-churning as the series becomes more about torture than actual sex. Even when it's relatively normal, the art ensures that it doesn't get anywhere near arousing. (DG) ★

FAIR SKINNED BEAUTY

Irojiro Ojô-san, "Fair-skinned Young Lady" (色白 お嬢さん) • Yukio Yukimino • Red Light Manga (2002) • Tokyo Sanseisha (1999) • 1 volume • Adult • 18+ (nudity, graphic sex)

Short adult stories in everyday settings, with an emphasis on big-breasted women. NR

FANTASY FIGHTERS

Phoenix Papa (フェニックス・パパ) • Koh Kawarajima • Manga 18 (2002) • France Shoin (1996) • 1 volume • Science Fiction, Comedy, Action, Adult • 18+ (violence, nudity, graphic sex)

Everyone knows that the rich rape the poor, but rarely has it been so graphically (and absurdly) demonstrated as here. A poor girl's father is nearly killed after a fight with some mutant delinquents and is now kept alive only by a coin-operated life support machine. How does his daughter pay for it? By being the sex slave for the evil rich boy who led the gang of mutants. That's when things get interesting. The girl's father is used in an experimental program to create super-soldiers for the rich (androids for the bourgeois—thus he's a "bourgeroid"), so he escapes to rescue her. But it turns out that the father of the rich boy tried to stop his son from defiling her and committed suicide in atonement—only to be brought back as a bourgeroid himself! Now the two old men/cyborgs must fight (after traveling through a secret tunnel hidden in the bathtub). The art may be a cheap copy of Satoshi Urushihara and the sex boring, but the bizarre story and sheer absurdity of the dialogue gets high marks. (DG) ★★★★

FEMME KABUKI

Nozomu Tamaki • Studio Ironcat/Sexy Fruit (1998–1999) • Futabasha • 9 issues • Historical, Adult • 18+ (nudity, graphic sex)

It's rare to find adult manga that's accessible to both male and female audiences, is well drawn, and features an enjoyable story to boot. Set in Tokugawa-era Japan, *Femme Kabuki* stars a troupe of spunky female erotic performers struggling to keep their act on the road in a time when women are forbidden to perform in the theater. Relying on their wits and sexual charms to stay alive, they are joined by handsome swordsman-in-disguise Sojiro, who adopts a secret identity to get close to Oshizu, the lovely performer he saves from police capture. Romantic comedy complications abound: Will Sojiro ever reveal his true identity as the one Oshizu truly loves? Or will they continue to bicker and torture each other with sexual tension? The adult content is woven smoothly into the story line. (JW) ★★★★

FLASH BANG!

Roshutsu de Pon!, "Exposure de Pon!" (露出で PON!) • Yoshitatsu Kiichigono • Icarus Publishing (2007) • France Shoin (2003) • 1 volume • Adult • 18+ (nudity, graphic sex)

Adult short stories with a theme of exhibitionism. Strip down in public, smile, and say cheese! NR

GIRLS OF VEROTIK: See *Wingbird*

THE GOD OF SEX²

Love Love Kami-sama, "Love Love God" (ラブラブ
カミさま) • Kazuki Taniuchi • Eros MangErotica
(1997–1998) • Core Magazine (1996) • 5 issues •
Science Fiction, Comedy, Adult • 18+ (nudity,
graphic sex)

With terrible art and limited, simple sex, all
The God of Sex has going for it is comedy.
Aliens with remarkable sexual organs and
unwilling cyborg sex-machines/superhe-
roes have humorous adventures, frequently
getting naked in the process and maybe
even getting it on. In addition to being ugly,
however, it doesn't have enough straight-
up sex to really be satisfying as an adult
manga. At the same time it goes beyond the
line of simple ribald humor and has too
much sex to just laugh at. It ends up satisfying nothing, despite amusing moments.
(DG)   ★★

GORGON

(ゴルゴーン) • Chouji Maboroshi • Antarctic/Venus
(1996) • Fujimi Shuppan (1992) • 5 issues • Fantasy, RPG, Adult • 18+ (nudity, graphic sex)

Best described as Dungeons & Dragons
fanporn, set in a fantasy world filled with
skeletons, werewolves, mages, liches, and
vampires—and they all want money, XP, and
sex. The actual explicit moments are relatively infrequent; most of the manga is spent
on big explosions, monsters, and the comedic bumbling of the Misfortune sisters.
Thankfully, the art is good enough to carry
the series, despite too many dark spaces and
ink on the page. The gaming in-jokes fly fast
and furious; to non-gamers, on the other
hand, this is just an average fantasy comedy
with sex scenes. (DG)   ★★★

H-BOMB

Various artists • Antarctic/Venus (1993) • 1 issue •
Adult, Dôjinshi • 18+ (nudity, graphic sex)

Short-lived collection of Japanese adult
dôjinshi, the X-rated companion to Antarctic
Press's *Dôjinshi: The World of Japanese Fanzines.*   NR

HEARTBROKEN ANGELS: See General
Manga Reviews

HEART CORE

(ハートコア) • Protonsaurus • Studio Ironcat (2002–
2003) • Issuisha (1999) • 4 issues • Adult • 18+ (nudity, graphic sex)

Heart Core hides one or two halfway amusing ideas behind a flood of truly terrible,
amateurish artwork—and that's really the
best that can be said about it, though it at
least avoids the usual traps of rape and scat.
The short stories involve many kinds of fantasies, generally involving older women and
younger men/boys; the most notable include
sex using eggs (raw and cooked), a video
game that uses a naked robot girl as the con-
troller, and a game of *Pokémon* where the
players bet sex instead of money. It's all
rather predictable and poorly drawn, but at
least the ideas are amusing. What is perhaps
most disappointing is that the background
homages to things such as *Star Trek Voyager*
and *Pokémon* prove that the artist actually *can*
draw when he wants to. (DG)   ★

HEAT

Heat—Unmei no Rin, "Heat: Wheel of Fate" (HEAT-
運命の輪) • Makoto Fujisaki • Icarus Publishing
(2007) • Akaneshinsha (2005) • 1 volume • Adult •
18+ (nudity, graphic sex)

Adult short stories from the creator of *Co-ed
Sexxtasy.*   NR

HOT TAILS

Junction (ジャンクション) • Toshiki Yui • Eros Mang-
Erotica (1996–1998) • Byakuya Shobo (1993–
1994) • 2 volumes • Fantasy, Adult • 18+ (nudity,
graphic sex)

Toshiki Yui has been an adult manga king for
a long time and it's clear why: no one else
comes close to his mix of sex, humor, and
bizarre imagination. He simply lets his id
run wild, and we get stories that are as surreal as they are sexual: lovers conjured from
the blood of a lust-induced nosebleed; aliens
from the future who kidnap girls for sex in

their dreams; flying fantasy worlds populated with dragons, wizards, dinosaur cops,
and lecherous gnomes. His art is still a bit
unpolished and busy in these older stories,
but his style is undeniable. The art is gorgeous, the ladies are sexy, and the premises
too bizarre not to enjoy. (DG)   ★★★★

HOT TAILS EXTREME: See *Wingding Orgy*

IGRAT X: See *Wingbird*

I LOVE YOU

Lei Nekojima • Studio Ironcat/Sexy Fruit (2003) •
Cybele Shuppan (1996) • 3 issues (1 volume in
Japan) • Science Fiction, Furry, Adult • 18+ (nudity,
graphic sex)

A twenty-year-old (the author is *very* insis-
tent on his age) guy wakes up with an egg on
his chest and out pops a cat-girl (apparently
his daughter—somehow) that he has to
teach how to feel true love. That means he
has to have uncomfortable not-quite-incest
sex with her. Cue lots of raunchy jokes about
how the cat-girl doesn't know any better
and how alien space food is revolting—the
real focus of the manga. The art is actually
good, though at times overwrought and difficult to follow. (DG)   ★★★

IMMORAL ANGEL

Lemming Kyôsôkyôku, "Lemming Mad Dash
Melody/Lemming Concert" (レミング狂走曲) • Koh
Kawarajima • Manga 18 (2002) • France Shoin
(1997) • 3 volumes • Occult, Horror, Adult • 18+ (nudity, graphic sex)

Koh Kawarajima desperately wants to draw
like Satoshi Urushihara. While it only ends
up reaching the level of pretty good fan art
in that regard, this still places it well above
most other adult manga out there. The other
striking feature about *Immoral Angel* is its
bizarre, dead-serious plot about lemmings,
the Hill of Golgotha, immortality, and
creepy rats with glowing eyes. The sex is all
rape at the hands of an insane lunatic–cum–
newborn god and it isn't the lighthearted
"she learned to like it despite herself" kind

either; it's deeply traumatic and leads to the
girl's complete mental breakdown. A man
rapes a girl, ruins her life, dies, becomes a
god, and rapes her some more. There is no
happiness here, just pseudo-religious blath-
ering about divinity and lots of crying. The
Japanese title is a pun. (DG)   ★★

INNOCENCE

(イノセンス) • Kamogawa Tanuki • Icarus Publishing
(2005) • France Shoin (1999) • 1 volume • 18+ (nudity, graphic sex)

From the giant-headed and silken-haired
school of art, *Innocence* is the usual stock of
staple adult manga fetishes: student-teacher
relationships, blackmail rape that the victim
ends up enjoying, feminine domination,
hermaphrodites, and "Was it all a dream?"
with a recurring theme of incest. The girls
tend to be old sister types who end up with
a short, scrawny nancy-boy—and love it.
The formula does get mixed up a bit in the
final story, where the author amusingly plays
around with repeated scenes and flashbacks,
but the sex itself is constrained by the format. The art, all-important for adult manga,
is generic: big eyes, big hair, big heads.
(DG)   ★★

JAPANESE EROTICISM: A LANGUAGE
GUIDE TO CURRENT COMICS

Hajime Tarumoto, Aoi Makita, Yutaro Kosuge, Jack
Seward (ed) • Yugen Press (1993) • 1 volume •
Adult Manga Language Guide • 18+ (nudity,
graphic sex)

This hard-to-find collection contains four
short bilingual adult manga, presented with
footnotes and articles on the field. The stories include Hajime Tarumoto's "Brother
and Sister Slaves" and "Heartful Hard Play,"
Aoi Makita's *futanari* story "The Angels Will
Not Stop," and Yutaro Kosuge's "All Is
Vanity," an adult *dôjinshi*. The existence of
this well-researched book is all the more incredible as it was put together with wry
humor by linguist Jack Seward, the author
of countless books on Japan. (He began
studying Japanese in the military during

World War II, and in 1986 he was awarded the Order of the Sacred Treasure, Third Class, by Emperor Hirohito for his efforts to deepen cross-cultural understanding.) In a format similar to the defunct *Mangajin* magazine, the entertaining stories also serve as a straight-faced tutorial on the uses of language in erotic manga. A rarity; although written before most academic analysis of manga, it almost serves as a parody of the field. ★★★★

JUICY FRUITS

Yumisuke Kotoyoshi • Icarus Publishing (2007) • Akaneshinsha (2004) • 1 volume • Adult • 18+ (nudity, graphic sex)

Adult short story collection. NR

KAERIMICHI: THE ROAD HOME

Kaerimichi, "The Road Back/The Road Home" (帰り道) • Tahichi Yamada • Icarus Publishing (2006) • Akaneshinsha (2003) • 1 volume • Adult • 18+ (nudity, graphic sex)

Adult short stories. A bored housewife and a delivery man experiment with anal play and dildos, a warped young man confines his sister in her room in order to psychologically dominate her, and more. NR

LEGEND OF LEMNEAR: See General Manga Reviews

LEGEND OF THE OVERFIEND: See *Urotsukidoji: Legend of the Overfiend*

LOVE TOUCH

Akira Gajou • Studio Ironcat/Sexy Fruit (1999) • Video Shuppan (1993) • 5 issues • Adult • 18+ (nudity, graphic sex)

Another entrant into the category of terrible fan art that somehow got published, *Love Touch* begins with a sense of humor but quickly loses it amid jumbled, incompetent storytelling and art that degenerates to the point where it is almost impossible to distinguish characters from one another. As it progresses, the series becomes more focused on relationships than just straight-up sex (but it never does either well). The art is simple, but still manages to end up a cluttered mess without any real sense of eroticism, aside from the fact that people are naked and (might be) having sex. (DG) ★

LUCK OF THE DRAW

TRUMP • Radio Comix (2001) • Dôjinshi • 1 issue • Furry, Adult • 18+ (mild violence, nudity, graphic sex)

Furry adult one-shot featuring TRUMP's signature voluptuous, big-booty dog-women and animal-women, with human male partners. NR

LUST

Ori, "Lust" (澱) • Tenjiku Ronin • Eros MangErotica (1997–2002) • Core Magazine (1996) • 1 volume • Occult, Adult • 18+ (nudity, graphic sex)

Supernatural tales with a heavy dose of sex: a lustful spirit whose desires are satisfied by a mountain hermit, a promiscuous woman whose exploits are remotely observed by her psychic and bedridden brother, and (the creepiest story) a timid voyeur who fades farther and farther into shadow until the only one who can feel his touch is the cruel object of his desire. The art is suitably dark and realistic, frequently looking like artist's sketches. The plot takes center stage right along with the sex, and generally tries to make some statement or give some insight into human nature. Additional material was published in monthly comics form but never collected. (DG) ★★

MASQUERADE

(マスカレード) • Takushi Fukada • Icarus Publishing (2006) • France Shoin (2002) • 1 volume • Adult • 18+ (nudity, graphic sex)

Adult short story collection. A young widow offers her body to kidnappers in order to protect her stepdaughter! A teen idol is kidnapped, raped, and forced to become a submissive sex slave! All this, plus text-message cell phone sex and more. NR

MELTY FEELING

Kibun ga Melty, "Melty Feeling" (気分がメルティ) • Antarctic/Venus (1996–1997) • Tsukasa (1993) • 4 issues • Adult • 18+ (nudity, graphic sex)

It is a mystery why an adult manga this ugly got published. Maybe it's the *Lupin III* reference with a panty thief or the story about a teacher using wild sex to reform a delinquent student, but even that doesn't manage to work past the artwork (The eyes! The hideous, hideous *eyes!*) and raise the manga past the level of completely terrible. Average sex with terrible artwork makes for a terrible adult manga. (DG)   ★

MESSIAH

Aki Kyouma • Verotik (1997) • 1 issue • Adult, Science Fiction, Fantasy, Action • 18+ (mild violence, nudity, graphic sex)

A muscular, superhero-like figure, his flesh entirely concealed in black leather, fights mutant insect-women and subdues them with dildos and enemas. Good action scenes and attractive artwork (computer-colorized in the English edition) make for a surprisingly gore-free, good-looking "story" of speedlines and slimy leakage. The dialogue is minimal, almost surreal, and in a comic moment, one of the women's human sex partners speaks for the reader: "What the hell was *that*?!"   ★★½

MIDARA

Midara, "Lewd/Bawdy" • Yumisuke Kotoyoshi • Icarus Publishing (2006) • Akaneshinsha (2003) • 1 volume • Adult • 18+ (nudity, graphic sex)

A collection of five short stories: the fantasy of what every fanboy always wanted *Tomb Raider* to be, a cop willing to do *anything* to protect the innocent, a sex robot, a lesson on swimming in a G-string, and even some honest-to-goodness consensual lovin'. The stories are well developed by adult manga standards and the art is superb. The creator clearly loves the female form and experiments with a wide variety of poses and points of view. It doesn't always work (or

follow rules of anatomy), but the sense of energy more than overcomes any failings in realism. (DG)   ★★★

MIDNIGHT PANTHER: See General Manga Reviews

MIKU'S SEXUAL ORGY DIARY

Miku no Yokuyonikki, "Miku's Sexual Orgy Diary" (ミクの乱交日記) • Fujio Okamoto • Icarus Publishing (2006) • Kuboama (2001) • 1 volume • Adult • 18+ (nudity, graphic sex)

The same formula is repeated in each of this story's nine chapters: a bunch of creepy old men/virgins forcibly violate Miku while she halfheartedly protests, then bemoans her fate and laments that if she were to get pregnant she wouldn't know who the father was. She never raises her voice, however, nor does she ever make a single move to resist. Wash, rinse, and repeat. As the volume progresses, it just gets creepier as she marries the first old lecher who took her and falls in "love" with him and all the friends he keeps bringing over for her to pleasure. The art is terrible, except for Miku's "talents and abilities," with which the artist clearly takes loving care. (DG)   ★

MILK MAMA

(ミルクママ) • Yukiyanagi • Eros MangErotica (2007) • Fujimi Shuppan (2005) • 1 volume • Adult • 18+ (nudity, graphic sex)

High school senior Hiroyuki is still drinking his mother's breast milk every morning, at her request. Can he keep it on the level of nursing and avoid his forbidden passion for his incredibly well-endowed, lactating mother?   NR

MISTY GIRL EXTREME

Misty Girl • Eros MangErotica (1997–2003) • Fujimi Shuppan (1991) • 1 volume • Fantasy, Adult • 18+ (nudity, graphic sex)

While Toshiki Yui's art is still unpolished and somewhat busy in this early work, his stories still have an energy and inventiveness beyond the simple sex. This is a collection of five stories: a hermaphrodite in a Catholic school for girls, a bizarre fantasy world where police and machines run on sex, a mage who summons a demon to give her the ultimate pleasure, a woman from a land where everyone goes into a maddening heat at the same time, and a short bit about a train ride every teenage boy wishes he could take once. Through it all the artist's distinctive style shines through and the sex is actually much more suggestive than explicit, making it all the more powerful. (DG)   ★★★★

MR. ARASHI'S AMAZING FREAK SHOW

Shôjo Tsubaki, "Camellia Girl" (少女椿) • Suehiro Maruo • Blast Books (1992) • Seirindo (1984) • 1 volume • Erotic-grotesque • 18+ (graphic violence, nudity, graphic sex)

Midori, the heroine, is a twelve-year-old orphan forced to work in a freak show, where she is exploited, bullied, and sexually abused by the other performers. Things improve for her when a dwarf who is a magician joins the show, rapidly becoming the star, and makes Midori his assistant and lover (the latter by implication). But her happiness may be only temporary . . . In Maruo's hands this plot becomes both a horror story and a parody of *shôjo* manga. But the plot is secondary to Maruo's finely detailed, classically composed art, which is by turns beautiful, grotesque, and horrific. While this book is not nearly as extreme as the stories collected in *Ultra Gash Inferno,* some of the images are quite disturbing, such as the book's second panel, a beautifully composed picture of Midori biting the head off a chicken. (AS)

★★★★

THE NEW BONDAGE FAIRIES: See *Bondage Fairies*

NIPPLE MAGICIAN

Kouzou Shimokata • White Lightning Productions (2004) • 4 issues • Adult • 18+ (nudity, graphic sex)

"Waltraute von Kielmanzueicke, International High-class Callgirl Guild" agent, at-

tempts to stop scientist Yosuke Enomoto from developing a serum that turns women into sex slaves. A crudely drawn series composed of big boobs and no plot, the grotesque art is likely to turn off all but the most breast-fetishistic readers. (JW)   ½

OGENKI CLINIC

Ogenki Clinic, "Feel-good Clinic" (お元気クリニック) • Studio Ironcat (1997–2003) • Akita Shoten (Play Comic, 1987–1994) • 4 volumes, suspended (9 volumes in Japan) • Comedy, Adult • 18+ (nudity, graphic sex)

Not so much about sex as it is a raunchy comedy where the punch line to every joke invariably involves bizarre sex. The art isn't particularly good, looking more ridiculous than sexy, but that fits the general tone of the series. It's rarely arousing, but instead it's simply amusing to watch the parade of sexual dysfunction that marches through the sex clinic—all of which can be cured by the liberal application of intercourse. The manga is way over the top, never taking itself seriously and just reveling in the joys of the flesh, no matter how dirty, silly, or stupid they may be. It does explore territory that might make some uncomfortable, such as male bisexuality, transgenderism, and male anal intercourse. Although only four English graphic novels were released, the entire series was translated in monthly comics format. (DG)   ★★★

OH MY!

Iya!, "No!" (いやっ) • Protonsaurus • Studio Ironcat/ Sexy Fruit (2002) • Issuisha (1993) • 1 issue • Adult • 18+ (nudity, graphic sex)

The best that can be said about *Oh My!* is that it is cute, once or twice. Everything else is terrible. Stories of incest and inappropriate student-teacher relationships might be worth the time if the art wasn't entirely abysmal, amateurish sketches—and if it didn't go to such great pains to try to convince the reader that the clearly underage girls are *eighteen* and *just about to graduate from college.* (DG)   ★

Kengo Yonekura's *Pink Sniper* Pink Sniper © 2002
Kengo Yonekura

THE ORIGINAL BONDAGE FAIRIES: See *Bondage Fairies*

PATCHWORK

(パッチワーク) • Rego Yokoi • Icarus Publishing (2006) • Akaneshinsha (2003) • 1 volume • Adult • 18+ (nudity, graphic sex)

A collection of short stories differentiated from other adult manga only by inconsequential details: instead of a cat-girl, there's a bunny-girl. Instead of selling herself (and liking it) for the school tennis club, it's the communication club. It's not the art teacher seducing students, it's the drama teacher (who has an obsession with dolls and puppets). The best is a twist on the classic she-male: a boy has sex with an elf who then steals his penis/turns him into a girl and has sex with him using his own member. Aside from a habit of letting noses disappear, the art is very average, as is the sex. (DG) ★★

PATRIOT

Mashumaru Jyuubaori • Icarus Publishing (2006) • Akaneshinsha (2004) • 1 volume • Adult • 18+ (nudity, graphic sex)

Short stories with a uniformly dark feel. Most of the stories feature the male protagonist (often a younger brother) raping women (usually sisters or mothers) until they are so overcome with passion and lust that he has "trained" them to be dripping sluts. Even the few consensual stories feature women who are slaves to their passions. The art is actually promising, showing not only real talent but also a surprising range of style. Unfortunately, it's also cramped, making it hard to see what's going on much of the time. (DG) ★★

PET HUMILIATION DIARY

Aigan Ryôjoku Sho, "Pet Humiliation Paper" (愛玩凌辱書) • Gorou Horikawa • Icarus Publishing (2007) • Akaneshinsha (1999) • 1 volume • Adult • 18+ (nudity, violence, graphic sex)

Bondage-themed short stories by the artist of *Slave Contract.* NR

PHEROMONE ON THE STREET CORNER

Machikado Pheromone, "Street Corner Pheromone" (街角フェロモン) • Yukio Yukimino • Red Light Manga (2001) • Tokyo Sanseisha (2000) • 1 volume • Adult • 18+ (nudity, graphic sex)

It's almost impossible to live up to the promise of a title like that, but it certainly tries hard. Despite terrible art (featuring big eyes with small, lumpy heads) the stories are a good mix of sexy and completely bonkers. The premises range from the almost tame "sex while his girlfriend is asleep in a drunken stupor" to the bizarre "girl trying to find her pet snake who only comes out to watch sex, and then getting bitten" to the completely unintelligible "stalker forces a girl afraid of heights to have sex on a high-dive board, making her use her vagina to get a grip so she doesn't fall." It really is a shame that the art is so poor; it doesn't matter how weird the story or sexy the pose if everyone in an adult manga is simply ugly. (DG) ★★

PINK SNIPER

(ピンクスナイパー) • Kengo Yonekura • Eros MangErotica (2006) • Core Magazine (2002) • 1 volume • Furry, Adult • 18+ (nudity, graphic sex)

Titillatingly well drawn, *Pink Sniper* is set in a high school of humans and anthro-humans (teenagers with cat ears, cow horns, etc.), where unsuspecting students find themselves at the mercy of the wildly sexual school nurse. Each story gets to the goods pretty quickly, the comedy keeps everything in good spirits, and the otherworldly sexual antics keep the, uh, meat of the manga going. The story and writing aren't bad, but they're secondary; Yonekura's awesome art does all the work for her. (JW) ★★★★

PLASTIC LITTLE: CAPTAIN'S LOG: See General Manga Reviews

PRINCESS OF DARKNESS

(プリンセスオブダークネス) • Yuichiro Tanuma • Eros MangErotica (1995–2001) • Byakuya Shobo (1990) • 1 volume • Fantasy, Horror, Adult • 18+ (nudity, graphic sex)

While each chapter follows the same formula—normal, everyday schoolgirl Maki is raped, summons demon, and exacts revenge—readers familiar with H. P. Lovecraft will giggle themselves silly every time Maki summons her demonic servant, El Hazzared. The demon appears to be bound to a book (or *is* the book—it's not entirely clear) and is the faithful servant of the owner. The story ultimately culminates in Maki discovering her own tremendous inner powers, battling bizarre demons, and finding true love. The art's a bit rough and dated, with the usual adult manga conceit that the women are all beautiful and the men ugly. Despite repeated rape and plenty of naked women, the sex never really seems to be the center of attention; the sex scenes are quick and disjointed. (DG) ★★

RELISH

Yutakamaru Kagura • Icarus Publishing (2006) • Akaneshinsha (2002) • 1 volume • Adult • 18+ (nudity, graphic sex)

This is pretty much standard adult manga: pure and wholesome women are forced (either physically, emotionally, or just tricked) into outrageous sexual situations only to discover that they are slaves to their passions. *Relish* touches on a number of common fetishes as well, from student-teacher relationships to incest to hermaphrodites to squirting breast milk. Its most unique story involves a messiah come down from heaven to help purge men of evil thoughts—by fulfilling their desires, of course. There is really nothing new here; the story lines are just setups for clichéd sex and the art is notable only in that it's not as bad as most of its peers. (DG) ★★

RHAPSODY

Kyôshikoku (Rhapsody), "Rhapsody" (狂詩曲 Rhapsody) • Yuuki Ryo • Red Light Manga (2001) • Tokyo Sanseisha (2000) • 1 volume • Adult • 18+ (nudity, graphic sex)

Rhapsody's main tale is an incest story with a dark twist, as the sister of the pair becomes more and more possessive and manipulative. Confusingly, that graphic and extreme story is followed by an almost sexless budding romance between two schoolgirls before the volume plunges back into the usual domain of adult manga: bondage, rape, improbable threesomes, and creative use of milk. It's a bit better than average, however; the art is consistent and the writing is as concerned with the scenario setup as with the actual sexual consummation. (DG) ★★★

S&M UNIVERSITY

Injû Gakudan, "S&M University" (淫縛学艶) • Nariaki Funabori • Eros MangErotica (2001–2003) • Core Magazine (2000) • 1 volume • Adult • 18+ (nudity, graphic sex)

This is exactly as the title describes: domination, rape, bondage, and blackmail at school (though it's clearly a high school, not a university or college). The story is a common adult manga plot: a completely vile man rapes and abuses women until they snap and realize that they truly love the humiliation he heaps upon them. The clichéd and repulsive premise aside, the art is actually quite good. Detailed and stylish, the women and sex are very arousing if you can get beyond the constant abuse and statements that there is no such thing as true love and people are just flesh to be used and tossed aside. (DG) ★★★

SATANIKA X: See *Wingbird*

SCHOOL ZONE

Akiko Fujii, Michio Akiyama • Red Light Manga (2001) • Wani Magazine (2000–2001) • 1 volume, suspended (2 volumes in Japan) • Adult • 18+ (nudity, graphic sex)

Straightforward sexy-schoolteacher fluff, each story focusing on different characters presumably from the same high school. Teachers do students, students do teachers, teachers do teachers . . . no combination is left behind. In one of the more creative stories, a female teacher uses sex toys underneath her prim school attire while class is in session. Standard fare in both art and plot. (JW) ★★

SECRET PLOT

NeWMeN • Eros MangErotica (1997–2001) • Fujimi Shuppan (1995) • 2 volumes • Adult • 18+ (nudity, graphic sex)

Just about every red-blooded young man wishes he went to a school like this. Filled with nymphomaniac teachers and nerdy kids with more natural sexual prowess than they knew, this classic adult manga is largely straightforward fantasy fulfillment, despite brief detours into cross-gender and vaguely homoerotic territory. The art is often rushed but the artist slows down when it matters, giving loving attention to the sex scenes. The sex is not only passionate and varied but also consensual (albeit with some browbeating) and pleasurable. *Secret Plot* has a surpris-

ing sense of humor as well; it doesn't take itself too seriously but still manages to pull off being sexy. The second half of the series was published under the name *Secret Plot Deep*. As of April 2007, *Secret Plot Deep* has not been collected into graphic novel form. (DG) ★★★

SECRET PLOT DEEP: See *Secret Plot*

SEPIA

(セピア) • Senno Knife • Studio Ironcat/Sexy Fruit (2000) • Cybele Shuppan (1993) • 5 issues • Occult, Adult • 18+ (nudity, graphic sex)

Erotic stories with the theme of ghosts and the supernatural. Genre-hopping artist Senno Knife has done pure horror work (see *Mantis Woman*), but these stories focus on mystical, almost fairy-tale erotica rather than outright scares. Shipwrecked men are entertained by sexually voracious women on mysterious islands; ghosts are summoned and exorcised; strange fantasies are lived out. Unfortunately, Knife's vaguely *shôjo* art is stiff and old-fashioned, and the sex scenes are weak; fans of romance or Japanese mythology will enjoy *Sepia* more than people approaching it as a porn comic. (JW) ★★

SEXCAPADES

Hotaru Kibun, "Hotaru's Feelings" (ほたるきぶん) • Jiro Chiba • Eros MangErotica (1996–2004) • Core Magazine (1995) • 1 volume • Adult • 18+ (nudity, graphic sex)

What starts out as a lighthearted story about a nympho with the worst luck in the world and her lover (and the spirit of her dead dog watching over her like a guardian angel) gets progressively more serious over the course of this adult manga. The man is married and has a young daughter. Later he has another affair with a different woman. His wife resents him and blames him for ruining her life and acting career, but refuses to divorce him—or let him see his kid. The nympho's luck worsens when she gets raped, only to reveal that she was raped as a child and her mother blamed her for all her problems. Bouts of sex that are supposed to "make me forget about all the pain" are liberally scattered throughout. In the end it swings back to the light, everyone living happily ever after without bothering to resolve anything. The art is cute and energetic, if amateurish at times. The problem is that although he's a nice guy most of the time, it's impossible to forgive the male lead for cheating on three women at once and pretty much abandoning his daughter. (DG)   ★★

SEXHIBITION

Suehirogari • Eros MangErotica (1995–1997) • Core Magazine (1993–1994) • 1 volume • Adult • 18+ (nudity, graphic sex)

The contents of this manga match the title: they're centered around domination, exhibition, and voyeurism. A few of the stories explore the wonders of the Internet and VR, but most of them are more straightforward tales of lusty women being exposed and used in public at the will of their male masters, culminating in multiple-partner orgies. There's a stepfather seducing a family, friends training and swapping partners, and even a game of strip tennis gone terribly, terribly right. Thankfully, despite the consistent theme of domination, the stories aren't dark at all. As unrealistic as each scenario might be, they're always consensual, without the "rape you till you like it" conceit. The art is simple and somewhat rough at times, but overall it's pretty good. The stories also spend time setting up each scenario instead of just jumping in headfirst, making up for the relatively reserved artwork. (DG)   ★★

THE SEX-PHILES

Benkyo Tamaoki • Eros MangErotica (1999–2004) • 3 volumes • Adult • 18+ (nudity, graphic sex)

This short story collection is a rarity in adult manga: consensual sexual relations between adults, with glimpses at healthy relationships as well. It's got a lot of the usual fare (hermaphrodites, water sports, incest), but the closest it comes to the dark side is a story about a Valley girl succubus seducing a cloistered priest. The artwork is unique, com-

Benkyo Tamaoki's *The Sex-Philes* Sex-Philes © 2003 Benkyo Tamaoki.

bining realism with the impression of an inspired sketch, and the characters often have anomalies such as tattoos and piercings. This is cartoon porn for adults who have actually had sex—it's about adults who *want* to have sex with each other, and enjoy it, and while the actual sex isn't particularly inventive, the characters' sense of life more than makes up for it. The English edition, titled *The Sex-Philes,* compiles three separate short story collections published by Issuisha in 1995 and 1996: *Porno Bakate de Tsutakamaete* ("Catcher in the Porno"), *Hanaji Buu* ("Nosebleed Spurt"), and *Eroi Hon* ("Erotic Book"). (DG)   ★★★★

SEX WARRIOR ISANE EXTREME

Isane Hound/Isane Break Away • Okawari • Eros MangErotica (2003–2006) • Fujimi Shuppan (1999) • 2 volumes • Science Fiction, Adult • 18+ (violence, nudity, graphic sex)

After a disaster changes the Earth's orbit and destroys the seasons, the world falls into sin and ruin: sex in the streets and chaos in the wind. Isane is a laconic warrior who goes about taking care of the degenerates and undesirables of the world one public rape-show at a time, all of it part of a grand plan to save the world. His primary weapon is a malleable artificial arm complete with claws and tentacles and mind-controlling pseudopods. The sex is usually not as directly abusive as one might imagine from the premise and the art manages to be quite provocative, despite being uneven and difficult to follow in places. The second volume, published in Japan as *Isane Break Away,* was published in English as *Sex Warrior Isane XXX.* (DG)

★★★

SEX WARRIOR ISANE XXX: See *Sex Warrior Isane Extreme*

SHEILA'S DIARY

Sheila Nikki, "Sheila's Diary" (シーラ日記) • Ryo Yuuki • Red Light Manga (2001–2002) • Tokyo Sanseisha (1998) • 3 volumes • Adult • 18+ (nudity, graphic sex)

A standard coerced-sex/rape/humilation story in which the victim (of course) ultimately discovers that she loves it. It's spiced up a bit with some piercings and characters who are more realistically endowed than the average adult manga star—and the original idea that instead of a creepy stranger/brother/father/boyfriend dominating some hapless girl, it's a goddess who has come to Earth to make a pliable sex slave out of a Japanese schoolgirl. In addition, despite involving domination and forced sex, it's never really mean-spirited. The sex slave may be shocked or profess her opposition, but she never actually weeps or ends up traumatized, unlike many other stories of this type. That puts this just a bit above average; not great, but certainly less uncomfortable than most of its fellows. (DG)

★★★

SILKY WHIP

Oh! Great • Eros MangErotica (1998–2004) • 2 volumes • Action, Adult • 18+ (violence, nudity, graphic sex)

This is exactly what you would expect from the famous Oh! Great, who got his start with adult manga before moving on to legitimacy with *Air Gear* and *Tenjho Tenge:* gorgeous ladies, bad-ass guys, and killer robots engage in sexual relations and lots of destructive fighting. The sex and action are mixed about 50/50 here, with stories about professional thieves, crime lords, alien magicians, and superpowered combat cyborgs. The tone is rather dark, the sex and violence mixing freely (even drifting beyond rape into bestiality). This is its biggest flaw, but it's also punctuated with moments of humor and tenderness. Oh! Great experiments with several slightly different art styles, but he is always a master of alluring women. The initial *Silky Whip* series was continued under the name *Silky Whip Extreme.* Together, they compile three separate short story collections published by Core Magazine between 1996 and 1998: *Engine Room, Five,* and *Junk Story.* Additional material was published in monthly comics format but never collected. (DG)

★★★

SILKY WHIP EXTREME: See *Silky Whip*

SLAVE CONTRACT

Reizoku Keiyakusho, "Subordination Contract" (隷属契約書) • Gorou Horikawa • Icarus Publishing (2006) • Akaneshinsha (1994) • 1 volume • Adult • 18+ (violence, nudity, graphic sex)

A wasteland of humiliation and emotional trauma. Pure girls (students, cops, figure skaters, nuns) are raped and abused by fat, ugly men until they either die inside or convince themselves that it's what they always wanted. And the ugliness isn't restricted to the subject matter; the art is terrible. Unless you want scat porn with girls being tied up and raped by fat, warty slobs, there's nothing here. (DG)

0 Stars

SLUT GIRL

Slut Onna, "Slut Woman" (スラット女) • Isutoshi • Eros MangErotica Comix (2000–2005) • Fujimi Shuppan (1999) • 1 volume • Comedy, Adult • 18+ (nudity, graphic sex)

Slut Girl boasts some of the most distinctive and expressive artwork in any translated adult manga. The title character is Sayoko, a lustful freeloader who constantly tries to make an easy fortune but instead keeps running into her equally gorgeous and sex-hungry friends. The hapless guy she's staying with reaps the benefits. It's not just the luscious ladies that make the manga so good, it's the constant humor. The story lines are played up for comedic payoff, and you can't help but laugh at the characters' facial expressions. (DG)　　　　★★★★

SPACE DREAMS

Harumi Shimamoto • Studio Ironcat/Sexy Fruit (1998) • 5 issues • Science Fiction, Adult • 18+ (nudity, graphic sex)

Nympho space merchants, oversexed angels, and randy witches happily romp through the pages of this adult manga. The real appeal of the series is the art, which, while barely above the amateur level, has a great sense of humor. Though roughly drawn, the super-deformed segments and bizarre facial expressions liven up otherwise boring sex scenes. While not good enough to seek out, it's decent, silly porn. (DG)

★★★

THE SPIRIT OF CAPITALISM

Shihonshugi no Seishin, "The Spirit of Capitalism" (資本主義の精神) • Maguro Teikoku • Icarus Publishing (2007) • Akaneshinsha (2004) • 1 volume • Salaryman, Adult • 18+ (nudity, graphic sex)

They say it's bad to date your coworkers . . . but casual sex is okay, right? The sordid sexual adventures of two young OLs ("office ladies"). The title is a reference to Max Weber's *The Protestant Ethic and the Spirit of Capitalism.*　　　　NR

SPUNKY KNIGHT

Punky Knight • Kozo Yohei • Eros MangErotica (1996–2006) • Akaneshinsha (1995–ongoing) • 1 volume • Fantasy, Adult • 18+ (nudity, graphic sex)

This is an X-rated Dungeons & Dragons. A chain-mail-bikini-clad adventuress fights

Isutoshi's *Slut Girl Slut Girl* © 2000 Isutoshi

evil with only her sword and feminine wiles. This generally involves killing lots of orcs and then having wild sex with the evil mastermind (often an evil magician or lustful demon) before soundly defeating him— often through simply having a greater sexual appetite. The art develops dramatically over the course of the series as the spunky knight herself changes from a typical fantasy woman warrior into a well-endowed and big-boned pseudo-hermaphrodite. That slow transition may take the series into unsettling territory for some, but it's still a very good adult fantasy manga. The series was continued under the names *Spunky Knight Extreme* and *Spunky Knight XXX* (in that order). As of April 2007, *Spunky Knight Extreme* and *Spunky Knight XXX* have not been collected in graphic novel form. (DG)　　★★★

SPUNKY KNIGHT EXTREME: See *Spunky Knight*

SPUNKY KNIGHT XXX: See *Spunky Knight*

SUPERFIST AYUMI

Punky Knight • Kozo Yohei • Eros MangErotica (1996–2007) • Akaneshinsha (1995–2005) • 3 issues • Yuri, Martial Arts, Adult • 18+ (nudity, graphic sex)

It starts out as a story about a lesbian karate master, with art vaguely reminiscent of Toshiki Yui, but quickly grows into its own as the art style develops into something more "plus-sized." The women aren't obese, just well endowed, plump, and maybe even a bit thunder-thighed. At the same time, the plot drifts away from a dialogue-heavy lesbian romp (using Ayumi's "superfist" just as expected) to more typical *futanari* (she-male) manga. The art is quite good, especially for those who prefer women with some meat on their bones instead of waifs or *lolicon*. In Japan, the material was originally printed as a portion of *Punky Knight* (English title *Spunky Knight*). (DG) ★★★

SUPER TABOO

Super Family Complex (SUPERファミリーコンプレックス) • Wolf Ogami • Eros MangErotica (1996–2007) • Fujimi Shuppan (1993) • 4 volumes • Adult • 18+ (nudity, graphic sex)

All about the "ultimate taboo," this is the story of Yuu and the epic battle of reason versus instinct as he just can't stop himself from helping himself to his mother and sister. There are a few side stories (also usually about incest), but the central focus is on the family affair. The art and the sex are both extremely simple and straightforward—the character designs could have come out of a Sunday paper. The manga stands out with the humorous battles between personified reason and instinct that always take place in Yuu's mind before he inevitably gives in to lust. That sense of humor pervades the entire manga, keeping it from being just a simply drawn romp between family members. The original Japanese title is a pun on "Super Famicom," the Japanese name for Super Nintendo. In English, the series was published under the names *Super Taboo, Super Taboo Extreme,* and *Super Taboo XXX* (in that order). As of April 2007, *Super Taboo XXX* has not been collected in graphic novel form. (DG) ★★

SUPER TABOO EXTREME: See *Super Taboo*

SUPER TABOO XXX: See *Super Taboo*

SWING OUT SISTERS

Taro Shinonome • Icarus Publishing (2007) • Akaneshinsha (2005) • 1 volume • Adult • 18+ (nudity, graphic sex)

It's an incestravaganza! Well, if you like Faulkneresque brother-sister action, at least. Two sisters—one a motherly housekeeper, the other an aggressive tomboy—vie for their brother's affection. NR

TABOO DISTRICT

Kinryoku—Taboo, "Forbidden Area/Sanctuary—Taboo" (禁猟区—TABOO) • Yuuki • Icarus Publishing (2007) • France Shoin (2004) • 1 volume • Adult • 18+ (nudity, graphic sex)

Adult short story collection. NR

TEMPTATION

Yūwaku (Erotic Eccentric), "Temptation (Erotic Eccentric" (誘惑(エロティックエキセントリック)) • Hiroyuki Utatane • Eros MangErotica (1994–1996) • Akaneshinsha (1993) • 1 volume • Adult • 18+ (graphic violence, nudity, graphic sex)

Utatane's art is gorgeous, his women are sexy, and his sex is exciting, but the stories of *Temptation* are inexorably tied to violence and deep emotional trauma. The sex isn't meant to simply arouse so much as it is a showcase of dominance and a way to reveal the deep emotional scars exhibited by virtually all the characters. Here, dominance is not an expression of love or even pleasure; it goes hand in hand with insecurity, abuse, unrequited love, confusion about identity, and even a basic inability to relate to other people. Plenty of sex, psychoanalysis, angst, and blurred gender roles. (DG) ★★

TIME TRAVELER AI: See General Manga Reviews

ULTRA GASH INFERNO

Suehiro Maruo • Creation Books (2001) • Seirindo (1981–1993) • 1 volume • Erotic-grotesque • 18+ (language, extreme graphic violence, nudity, graphic sex)

Suehiro Maruo is a leading practicioner of *ero-guro* (erotic-grotesque) manga, and this collection of eight short stories and one novelette illustrates why. These grotesque, often surreal stories, frequently set in Taisho-era prewar Japan, graphically depict horrific violence and perverse sexual acts of every kind. In "Sewer Boy," perhaps the book's best story, the title character's mother abandons him as a baby by dropping him into a toilet (really a hole in the floor). He survives and becomes an adolescent living in the sewers, who pulls women down through the toilets and rapes them. In contrast to the extreme subject matter, Maruo's art is realistic, detailed, and often beautiful, as are his composition and visual storytelling. Collectively these stories present a powerful vision of human cruelty. (AS) ★★★★

UROTSUKIDOJI: LEGEND OF THE OVERFIEND

Chôjin Densetsu Urotsukidôji, "Super God Legend Urotsukidoji/Loitering Boy" (超神伝説うろつき童子) • Toshio Maeda • Manga 18 (2002–2003) • Wani Magazine (1986) • 6 volumes • Fantasy, Horror, Tentacle, Adult • 18+ (violence, nudity, graphic sex)

Overfiend is one of those names that is known far beyond the bounds of anime and manga. Infamous for its violence, sexuality, and the frequent mixing of the two through liberal application of tentacled demons, it is actually surprisingly tame by modern adult manga standards. There's plenty of sex and violence, but it's less frequent and less graphic than readers might expect. The very static and Western-influenced art is rough and inconsistent except where it really matters: the naked female form. Like most of Maeda's work, the story is as important as the sex—and pretty much incomprehensible. Subplots appear and disappear with blinding speed, but the core follows a jack-ass of a demon infiltrating a school to find the reincarnation of the most powerful demon ever. This, of course, involves lots of random psychic battles, flying through the night sky, and sweaty demon rape. (DG) ★★★

VALKYR

(ワルキューレ) • Senno Knife • Studio Ironcat (1999) • Kubo Shoten (1989) • 6 issues, suspended (2 volumes in Japan) • Mecha, Romance • 18+ (violence, nudity, graphic sex)

Soapy android sex slavery by multigenre artist Senno Knife, set in a futuristic dark city with the presence of Nazi overlords adding to the mood of sinister decadence. Ichizuki, a kimono-clad android prostitute, searches for the root of her existence while mysterious men in suits debate the morality of human-robot technology. Hot on Ichizu's trail are the city's secret police, the Gestapo, run by tall-booted Nazi bombshell Maria. Predictable writing and expressionless characters squander a decent science fiction concept, and the sex scenes are few and far between. The most attractive visuals, frankly, are Maria's fetishistic Nazi outfits. As usual for Knife, the sex is not particularly graphic, no matter what the characters do; the girls have doll-like, nearly blank crotches. (JW) ★★

VANITY ANGEL

Antarctic/Venus (1994–1995) • Fujimi Shuppan (1992) • 6 issues • Yuri, Adult • 18+ (nudity, graphic sex)

Two beautiful friends who are *really* close have fantastic adventures through time and space—whenever one of them gets sexually aroused, she flies around with terrific speed and power. Fighting aliens, messing with ancient history, the two girls will do anything in their never-ending quest to win the hearts of the men they love. The plot is (obviously) very, very silly. There is also plenty of lesbian lovin', but the plot takes higher prominence than in most modern adult manga. The heroines do more than travel across the universe and have sex (though not *much* more). (DG) ★★★

VENUS DOMINA: See *Wingbird*

VOICE OF SUBMISSION

Voice • Mashumaro Jyuubaori • Eros MangErotica (1998–2004) • Mediax (1996–2001) • 2 volumes • Adult • 18+ (nudity, graphic sex)

Contrary to the title, this isn't *all* about BDSM. It's got its fair share of rape, bondage, sadomasochism, humiliation, and ball gags, but it also has just as many mainstream sexual situations. The art is fantastic, showing surprising variety and impressive growth over the series. The female form is beautifully rendered and sex is nothing if not extremely passionate throughout. The manga is at its best, however, when it's funny; the best short stories involve sexual experimentation among cavemen and a drunken sleepover gone terribly, terribly right. While the beginning is a collection of short stories, the second volume turns to an ongoing plot revolving around rape, incest, and domination; it's as disturbing as it is erotic. The second half of the series was published under the name *Voice of Submission II: Gehenna.* (DG) ★★★★

VOICE OF SUBMISSION II: GEHENNA: See *Voice of Submission*

WERE-SLUT

Henshin! Tonari no Kimiko-san, "Transformation! Neighbor Kimiko-san/Next Door Kimiko-san" (変身!となりの公魅子さん) • Jiro Chiba • Eros MangErotica (2001–2004) • Angel Shuppan (1999) • 1 volume • Fantasy, Adult • 18+ (nudity, graphic sex)

Kimiko has the Beauty Stone, a pill that makes her totally gorgeous—but has the terrible side effect of also making her an uncontrollable nympho slut. Despite being in a loving relationship, she finds herself compelled to travel the town at night for further gratification. Lonely men can summon her by waving a strip of unused condoms around in an abandoned street. And thus the legend

of the were-slut grows. The art is cute sometimes, but very simple and often off-model. The actual sex is pretty much by the numbers. (DG) ★★

WILD ZOO

Naginata Matsurino • Radio Comix (2000–2001) • 8 issues • Furry, Adult • 18+ (mild violence, nudity, graphic sex)

A straightforward furry sex comic about Lord Amon, a muscular anthropomorphic wolf-man, and the submissive furry females who love him. A perfunctory, somewhat sadistic plot and crude artwork make *Wild Zoo* of interest mostly to furry fans, although the female characters, unlike the more animalistic males, have mostly human faces. (JW) ★½

WINGBIRD

Various titles • Verotik • Fantasy, Adult • 18+ (nudity, graphic sex)

The *dôjinshi* artist Wingbird is primarily known in the United States for his work on Glen Danzig's Verotik line of erotic horror/superhero comics, mostly in the late 1990s. His translated work includes several one-shot comics based on Danzig's Verotik characters (*Akuma-She, Girls of Verotik, Igrat X, Satanika X, Girls of Verotik*), two pinup books (*Wingbird: Black and White Bondage* and *Wingbird Portfolio*), and two one-shot collections of original stories and pinups. His original stories (*Wingbird Special* and *Wingbird Returns*) are standard porn scenarios about mammoth-breasted, wasp-waisted, salivating anime-style girls in bondage gear, getting lashed and wearing lots of leather. With the exception of *Wingbird: Black and White Bondage,* all his work is computer-colored in the English editions. NR

WINGBIRD: BLACK AND WHITE BONDAGE: See *Wingbird*

WINGBIRD RETURNS: See *Wingbird*

WINGBIRD SPECIAL: See *Wingbird*

WINGDING ORGY

Wingding Party (ウィンディング・パーティー) • Toshiki Yui • Eros MangErotica (1997–2005) • Souryusha (2001) • 1 volume • Fantasy, Adult • 18+ (nudity, graphic sex)

Keisuke's girlfriend doesn't want to have sex, and his sexual frustration manifests in the form of a succubus, Ruki. Attempts to exorcise the demoness result only in more sex with Keisuke, his girlfriend, and everyone else in sight. Due to the success of Yui's previous manga *Hot Tails, Wingding Orgy* was released in English under the title *Wingding Orgy: Hot Tails Extreme,* although there is no connection between the two series. NR

Afterword

A book like this is necessarily a snapshot of time; manga publishers continue to translate and localize titles, and trends come and go. Many classic works from the 1980s and earlier are still untranslated or available only in rare bilingual editions, despite the efforts of publishers such as Vertical and CMX. Meanwhile, the manga market marches on, following new trends such as *yuri, yaoi,* and *moe* manga, the ever-present anime tie-ins, and an ever-growing number of recent *shôjo* and *shônen* titles, often licensed the moment they begin to show signs of popularity in Japan.

The rise of electronic media, together with used-book stores and manga cafés, continues to change the Japanese manga market. Many manga are now available as "print on demand" and e-books, sometimes released simultaneously with print editions. The Internet and blogging have also changed manga; numerous Japanese Internet phenomena such as *Oniyome Nikki* ("Demon Wife Diary") and *Densha Otoko* have been adapted into books, manga, and live-action movies. Cell phones and PDAs have eaten up much of the commute time once spent on manga magazines; some people, such as *shôjo* manga scholar Matt Thorn, believe that all printed magazines will vanish within ten years and be replaced by online comics and mobile technologies such as handheld e-book readers using "electronic paper."

But manga itself are still popular; despite slumping magazine sales, graphic novel sales are higher than ever. Traditional Japanese bookstores are doing poorly, but fan-oriented niche stores such as Tora no Ana are thriving. In 2007 the venture publisher Digima launched *Comic Gumbo,* the first free weekly manga magazine, planning to make money through graphic novel sales, licensing, subscription-based online archives, and product placement. Major companies have launched online manga magazines, such as Futabasha's *Comic Seed!* and Softbank's *Shônen Blood.* Leiji Matsumoto, Maki Murakami, and Takehiko Inoue are some of the many manga artists who have experimented with online comics. Most artists and publishers view the Internet with optimism, despite concerns about piracy. Although this book is necessarily print-centric, it is an open secret that many untranslated manga, including ones discussed in this book, are available on the Internet in fan-produced scanslations. In 2006, uclick mobile announced the American license of Hisao Tamaki and Naoyuki Sakai's sci-fi story *Guilstein,* the first manga translated specifically for distribution on cell phone.

Although this book describes many of the most popular Japanese manga magazines, and a few untranslated artists, to go into depth about either would fill a whole book in itself. A separate book could also be written about the thousands of English-language creators producing manga-inspired works in the small press and online. In America, the cultural melting pot of manga-influenced Korean, American, and European comics may produce a market where most fans do not even consider or recognize a comic's country of origin, a situation actively desired by some "global manga" publishers. It is to be hoped that such a market has a broad definition of "manga-style," with room for *seinen, jôsei,* and underground-style works aimed at adult readers, as well as the big-eyed *shôjo* and *shônen* works most Americans associate with manga and anime. As this book has tried to show, Japanese comics have too much variety to be pinned down to any particular style or look, and many American comic artists, such as Frank Miller, Colleen Doran, and Paul Pope, do not wear their manga influence on their sleeve.

Everyone's tastes are different, but as the author and coordinator of this book, I have tried to recognize exceptional manga in both story and artwork. The former are more uncommon; you can hire assistants to help you draw, and most artists become polished after drawing a few thousand pages, but truly original stories are rare in any medium, and well-written cliff-hangers and soap operas are rarer than they appear to be. Manga is a mass medium, like movies or TV; we can't always expect more from it, but we shouldn't expect less.

—*Jason Thompson*
January 2007

Check out http://www.delreymanga.com/mangaguide for periodic online updates to the book.

AGE RATINGS

Sadism, cannibalism, bestiality. Crude eroticism. Torturing, killing, kidnapping. Monsters, madmen, creatures half-brute, half-human. Raw melodrama; tales of crimes and criminals; extravagant exploits in strange lands and on other planets; pirate stories . . . All these, day after day, week after week . . .

—John K. Ryan, "Are the Comics Moral?" *Forum,* May 1936,
describing then-current American newspaper comic strips

CONTENT AND CENSORSHIP

Japanese pop culture, including manga, has different standards for violent and risqué material than exist in the United States. The Japanese PTA and other groups do protest "objectionable" manga, and individual manga magazines have guidelines for what they will and will not publish, but the guidelines are lenient compared to American TV or movies. Manga has been censored as long as it has been translated, beginning with a nude bathing scene in the first issue of *Mai the Psychic Girl* in 1987

Ken Akamatsu's *Love Hina,* a fanservice love-comedy manga

(the scene was restored for the graphic novel). At the same time, American fans have complained about changes and alterations for as long as translations have existed; the first letter column in *Justy* (1988–1989) is filled entirely with letters complaining about name changes such as "Cosmo Police" to "Galactic Patrol" and "Justy Kaizad" to "Justy Starflare."

As with prose books, there is no central ratings authority for manga, like the MPAA for movies or the ESRB for video games. (The Comics Code, created in 1954 to monitor comics for such things as torture, profanity, vampires, and werewolves, is now a vestigial organization ignored by almost all comics publishers.) Different manga companies follow their own internal guidelines, sometimes with input from bookstore chains and other large buyers. Titles with graphic adult content are frequently sold shrink-wrapped, sometimes with a "parental advisory" sticker. (In Japan, all manga are sold shrink-wrapped, but not for content reasons; it's to keep people from reading it at the bookstore.) In short, manga censorship in

America is primarily "economic censorship," self-imposed by the desire to sell more copies. American editions of manga have been censored not only for sex and violence (*Tenjho Tenge, Shadow Star*) but for cruelty to animals (*JoJo's Bizarre Adventure*), crucifixion scenes (*Fullmetal Alchemist*), potentially racist imagery (*Dragon Ball*), drug references (*Shaman King*), unauthorized drawings of brand-name products and sportswear (too many manga to count), and even underage cigarette smoking (*Hikaru no Go*). At the same time, equally explicit manga may go uncensored, simply because the publisher is willing to forgo major sales outlets such as Scholastic or Wal-Mart.

As manga become more popular and widely available in America, major American publishers have become more cautious, fearing controversy. No one wants a repeat of what happened in the United Kingdom in the early 1990s, where explicit adult anime such as *Uro-*

The characters get ready for the big *dôjinshi* convention in Shimoku Kio's *Genshiken*.

tsukidoji: Legend of the Overfiend were picked up by the media and caused all manga and anime to be stereotyped as pornography. And yet, to many fans, the very Japaneseness of manga—its status as a product of a different culture with different standards—is part of its appeal. Because manga is both a mainstream business and the focus of intense fandom, American publishers must often walk a fine line between angering fans and publishing potentially offensive material.

SEX AND SEXISM

Japanese taboos against nudity are not as strong as they are in America. A nude hot spring or public bath is an innocent place in a real-life Japanese context (although not always in manga). Comics for adults may contain sex scenes, and *shônen* and *seinen* comics often include fan service in the form of nudity or panty-exposing up-the-skirt camera angles, included as a "service" to male readers. *Shôjo* manga generally have more discreet visuals, but stories may involve sex. *Yaoi* manga range from suggestive to explicit, often in the course of a few pages. Repressed sexual desire sometimes erupts from male characters in the form of gushing nosebleeds, a classic manga comedy symbol that says to any Japanese reader "he's turned on," just as a dark cloud over a character's head means "he's in a bad mood" in American comics terminology.

Generally speaking, Americans are not shocked so much by sex in manga as by sex in manga aimed at teenagers, a gray area alien to American pop culture. (Movies such as *Porky's* and *American Pie* may be surreptitiously watched by teenagers, but they are officially rated R.) *Shôjo* and *shônen* magazines do occasionally receive phone calls from angry parents, and so each magazine has its own internal guidelines. In some cases, these guidelines have become stricter over the years; for instance, *Weekly Shônen Jump* used to show full topless nudity in series such as *Video Girl Ai* and *I"s,* but today its most explicit images are the occasional girls in bras or swimsuits, in series such as *Strawberry 100%.* One compromise is to show breasts without nipples, like a body stocking, as seen in anime and manga such as *No Need for Tenchi!* (Perhaps the excuse is that all the women in the story are aliens.) English labeling is inconsistent, and much depends on the artist and target audience. The girls' comic *Sensual Phrase* is rated 18+ for nudity and on-screen sex (really just embraces under the bedsheets) but is less explicit than the technically sexless titillation in *Video Girl Ai* or *Mahoromatic,* 16+ titles aimed at teenage boys.

Another issue is sexism. Voyeurism, "dirty old men," and accidental (or intentional) breast groping are common images in *shônen* and *seinen* manga and are generally treated as comedy. As with other objectionable content, the treatment of women in manga reflects Japanese culture; Japanese women did not acquire the right to vote until 1945, anonymous sexual harassment in crowded trains used to be a major problem, and although the term *sekuhara* (sexual harassment) became a buzzword in the late 1980s, conditions for women in the workplace are still dubious. Feminist groups such as the Society for the Protection of Women have campaigned against sexism and violence against women, and against pornographic manga, which often contains images of rape.

Freedom of expression is guaranteed by the postwar Japanese constitution, but depictions of sex and nudity are governed by Article 175 of the Japanese Penal Code, which threatens fines and imprisonment for anyone who sells or distributes obscene material. For decades, the vague term *obscenity* was defined by the presence or absence of one thing: pubic hair. Movies, photographs, and manga containing pubic hair were dutifully censored, the offending genitals covered with white or black bars (in the case of manga) or digital mosaic (in the case of movies). The single-minded focus on genitals allowed inventively obscene and bizarre acts to go uncensored as long as no hair was visible. Some blame the hair obsession for the Japanese *lolicon* trend, in which manga artists drew increasingly young-looking female characters—because if they didn't have any pubic hair, it was all right to show them naked. In the 1980s, the restrictions on pubic hair gradually eased, and in the early 1990s there was a boom in photos of "hair nudes." However, the genitals themselves could still not be clearly shown, even in Japanese adult comics. (In English editions of Japanese adult manga, the genitals have generally been redrawn, either by American artists or by the original Japanese artists.)

Today, even a quick glance at many *seinen* or *yaoi* titles will show that Japanese obscenity laws are nebulous at best. However, this hasn't stopped periodic witch hunts and public outcries against explicit manga. Since 1964, the so-called Youth Ordinance (technically a local measure, albeit one adopted by almost every local government body in Japan) has forbidden the sale of "harmful materials" to those under eighteen years old. Numerous local organizations with names such as the Tokyo Mothers' Society, the Parents' Society for the Protection of Children, and the Society for the Protection of Children from Pornographic Manga act as manga watchdogs, pressuring politicians to pass local ordinances prohibiting the sale of specific manga. A number of governmental and quasi-governmental organizations, such as the Youth Policy Unit and the National Assembly for Youth Development, process the information on a national level, making lists, exerting pressure on publishers, and encouraging local organizations to act. One major censorship epidemic occurred in the years following the 1989 arrest of the child murderer Tsutomu Miyazaki, who was found in possession of *lolicon* manga. Numerous popular manga have been pressured into ceasing publication over the years, including Go Nagai's *Harenchi Gakuen* ("Shameless School"), Haruka Inui's *Ogenki Clinic,* and U-Jin's *Angel: High School Bad Boys and Girls Story.* In 2002, Yûji Suwa's adult manga *Misshitsu* ("Honey Room") became the first manga ever actually charged with obscenity under Japanese law. Fines were imposed, although a potential prison sentence was suspended. As *Misshitsu* was hardly more explicit than many other adult titles, the question remains whether it was merely chosen as a scapegoat to have a chilling effect on other adult publishers.

As of 2006, the latest controversies involve sexed-up *shôjo* manga for teenagers and *moe* manga, the latter considered by some to be a "plausible deniability" evolution of *lolicon.* (See the OTAKU article.) In May 2006, *jôsei* manga artist Mimei Sakamoto tore into *moe* in an interview with the newsmagazine *Shûkan Bunshun:* "This fetish you call 'moe' is a pedophiliac fetish . . . in other countries, they'd call what you're fantasizing over 'child pornography' and you'd all be arrested." In November 2006, Takehana Yukata, director of the National Police Agency for Community Safety, proposed a nationwide ban on sexually explicit games, manga, and anime involving children, an expansion of Japan's existing 1999 law against real-life child pornography. Such a ban could theoretically affect even mildly sexual *shôjo* manga, and even in America, such bans have run up against First Amendment concerns, so the future remains in doubt. In addition, the manga industry has its share of free-speech firebrands, such as Yoshinori Kobayashi, and manga artists have their own organizations, such as the Society to Protect the Freedom of Expression in Manga, which generally promotes self-regulation.

RACIAL ISSUES

Japan is an ethnically homogenous country; more than 98 percent of the population is ethnically Japanese, with the largest minority groups being Koreans, Chinese, Filipinos, and South Americans. Most Japanese people have little day-to-day contact with foreigners or people of other races, and as a result, Japanese pop culture—including manga—sometimes contains racially insensitive images.

A common misperception of Americans encountering manga for the first time is that the characters look "white." This assumption says more about the self-centeredness of white Americans than about the intentions of manga artists. Manga characters have large eyes mostly due to the influence of Osamu Tezuka, who was influenced by Western animation such as that of Walt Disney. Light-colored hair developed as a way to differentiate between different characters in black and white, and rather than mimicking real-world blondes and brunettes, it soon spun off into the increasingly fanciful pink, red, green, and blue hair seen in anime. While postwar Japanese fashion has occasionally pursued Western ideals of beauty, the truth is that most *shôjo* and *shônen* manga characters are cartoon characters who resemble no particular race known to humanity; Japanese see this "default" race as being Japanese, while people from other races may see themselves reflected. (Actual Caucasians are often drawn with freckles, wavy blond hair, and big noses.) Some more detailed, realistic artists draw more obviously Japanese characters; examples include Masakazu Katsura and Katsuhiro Otomo.

Generally, characters of different races are almost indistinguishable in manga, as long as they're supposed to be attractive, but negative images do exist, often echoing Western stereotypes. Chinese, Koreans, and other Asians are occasionally drawn with buck teeth and slant eyes. Sexy "China girls" with *cheongsam* dresses and bad accents appear in manga such as *3x3 Eyes, Spirit of Wonder,* and *Ranma ½.* Stereotypes of African Americans are even more common. When Commodore Perry's crew met with Japanese delegates in 1854, the first official diplomacy between America and Japan, they entertained their guests with a "minstrel show." People of African descent are sometimes drawn as "blackface" caricatures with huge white lips on dark skin, a style used by Shotaro Ishinomori and Osamu Tezuka. Recent examples include minor characters in *Moon Child, Arm of Kannon,* and *Baron Gong Battle,* as well as heroic characters such as Joco (originally named "Chocolove") in *Shaman King* and Mr. Popo in *Dragon Ball* (both of whose faces were redrawn in the English editions). On the other hand, nine times out of ten, manga characters with Afros (such as Tsukasa in *Boys over Flowers*) or dark skin are supposed to be ethnic Japanese with tans and permed hair. However, this does not excuse the fact that such characters are often stereotyped as thugs, or sluts in the case of the artificially tanned, bleached-blond girls of *ganguro* fashion. The traditional Japanese ideal of beauty is light-skinned; *Peach Girl* depicts a Japanese heroine who is discriminated against for her dark skin color.

Racist imagery in manga is usually the result of ignorance rather than malice. Members of other ethnic groups living in Japan, as well as Japanese liberals, have campaigned for better representation. In 1988 the Association to Stop Racism Against Blacks, a tiny organization originating from a single Japanese family, began a campaign against racist imagery such as the *Little Black Sambo* children's book (then widely available in Japan) and negative stereotypes of black characters in manga. Although some artists complained about "political correctness," the campaign took hold, with support from American black civil rights organizations. Today, artists and their editors are more sensitive to the way their comics depict foreigners. In addition, hip-hop culture has taken hold of Japan, as it has done throughout the Western world. Santa Inoue's *Tokyo Tribes* reverses the usual style in which Japanese people are drawn in manga; the heroes are ethnically Japanese, but the reader could be forgiven for asking, "Are these characters supposed to be black?"

VIOLENCE

Shônen and *seinen* manga are full of fight scenes, and blood and gore are not uncommon, although the violence is more stylized than realistic. In keeping with the common Japanese self-image that Japanese culture is "wet" (i.e., emotional and sentimental), characters in boys' manga such as *One Piece* show their self-sacrifice by losing gallons of blood and weeping buckets of tears, but they're usually fine by the end of the chapter. The actual body counts are rarely higher than in an American action movie, and the bad guys are as often forgiven as punished. Publishers also impose restrictions; in the notes to *Zombie Powder,* Tite Kubo complains that he had to make "a ton of changes" to a scene in which a character is tortured. On the other hand, *seinen* manga, particularly horror manga, and some especially gory boys' manga, such as *JoJo's Bizarre Adventure,* may involve mutilation and mass slaughter on the level of the most explicit horror movies.

Violence is a secondary concern for Japanese media critics and censors, partly because Japan itself has such a low crime rate, and the violence in manga and anime is seen as pure fantasy. Still, now-classic series such as Sanpei Shirato's *Ninja Bugeichô* ("Ninja Military Chronicles") and Tetsuya Chiba and Asao Takamori's boxing comic *Ashita no Jo* ("Tomorrow's Joe") were attacked for violence and general inappropriateness, forcing the cancellation of the latter. (Both comics were also embraced by the left wing for their radical themes, which contributed to their condemnation.) Although manga such as *GTO* reveal that the Japanese public has many of the same anxieties about youth violence as Americans, extremely strict gun control laws make gun violence and school shootings almost unheard of. In *Gals!*

the characters undergo bag and uniform checks, but they're checking for knives, not guns. On the other hand, the bloodless fistfights and bullying bad guys frequently shown in *shônen* manga are themselves beyond the level of American children's TV programming, which forbids showing any blows to the face.

CRUDE HUMOR

Bathroom humor is universal, and occasionally appears in *shônen* and *seinen* manga. Few comics reach the level of Kazuyoshi Torii's untranslated *Toilet Hakase* ("Professor Toilet," 1970), whose title character solves scatological ailments and works in a toilet-shaped laboratory, but stylized dollops of poo, looking like soft-serve ice cream, occasionally appear in gag manga. Akira Toriyama's essentially charming children's manga *Dr. Slump* (1980) became famous for its toilet humor: aliens with heads shaped like butts, talking poo with little arms and legs and faces, and the heroine's habit of running around waving a piece of poo on a stick. Most manga are more restrained, if they include crude humor at all.

PROFANITY

Profanity in translated manga is largely the result of English editing decisions. Although some manga authors invent colorful insults, typical Japanese insults such as *temee, bakayaro, onore,* and *kisama* have no specific meaning and could be translated as "jerk," "bastard," or "why, you lousy . . . ," depending on the context and feel of the story. Likewise, the common Japanese term *kuso* could be translated as "poo," "crap," or "shit." Japanese people are aware of English swear words and sometimes use them for humorous effect, as in *JoJo's Bizarre Adventure* and *Eyeshield 21* (in which English profanity in the original version was censored for the translated edition). "The finger" is considered a lighthearted, rascally gesture in Japan and is sometimes censored in English editions of manga.

RELIGIOUS IMAGERY

See the article on OCCULT AND RELIGION.

LIST OF CONTENT GUIDELINES

With a few exceptions, these guidelines are used to describe all objectionable content in this book. In some cases the content may be listed as "brief" (one or two instances), "infrequent," "frequent," or "constant."

- Mild language ("crap," "damn," "bastard," "bitch")
- Language ("fuck," "shit," "asshole")

- Crude humor
- Mild violence (bloodless fistfights, slapping, punching)
- Violence
- Graphic violence (dismemberment, extreme blood loss)
- Extreme graphic violence
- Partial nudity (including breasts without nipples)
- Nudity (topless or full nudity)
- Mild sexual situations (suggestive dialogue, implied relationships)
- Sexual situations (may include breast grabbing, sexual humor)
- Sex
- Graphic sex (genitalia and pubic hair may be visible)
- Adult themes (incest, drugs, suicide, etc.)

AGE RATINGS USED IN THIS BOOK

As each publisher's guidelines are different (and older titles often have no age rating on the cover), concerned individuals should read the manga themselves if they have any doubts. In the case of titles that have no clearly visible rating, *Manga: The Complete Guide* lists the titles as "unrated" and has attempted to assign an appropriate rating.

All Ages
(A, Y, Youth, 7+, 10+)

In movie terms, All Ages titles would qualify for a PG or G rating. Some titles may contain blood, violence, or crude humor. *Manga: The Complete Guide* does not distinguish between All Ages and the 7+ or 10+ ratings used by some publishers.

For Ages 13+
(T, Teen)

These titles would generally qualify for a PG or PG-13 rating. The level of violence may be higher, and there may be profanity, offscreen sex, or sexual humor.

For Ages 16+
(T+, OT, Older Teen)

These titles occupy a vast gray area from PG-13 to R. Profanity, graphic violence, and on-screen (but not explicit) sex may occur. Some American publishers assign this rating, or 18+ ratings, for thematic content such as drugs and suicide.

For Ages 18+
(*M, Mature Readers*)

These titles generally correspond to a hard R rating, or in the case of adult and *yaoi* manga, an NC-17. They may contain graphic violence, explicit sex, or extremely strong language and adult themes.

THE JAPANESE LANGUAGE

Thanks to translators and publishers everywhere, you don't need to know Japanese to read manga, but a little knowledge can provide interesting insights. (Needless to say, this appendix has space enough to cover only the most basic concepts.) In the 1980s and 1990s, most English-language manga publishers used a combination of literal translators and rewriters, whose job was to make the translation smoother and the dialogue more colloquial. Early rewriters were mostly American comics industry professionals, such as Gerard Jones, Fred Burke, James Hudnall, and Marv Wolfman. Whether out of fidelity to the original text or to save money, the current trend is away from rewriters and toward more pared-down, literal translations, but some rewriters are still known for bringing a distinct style to the manga they work on, including Kelly Sue DeConnick, Carl Gustav Horn, and Keith Giffen.

The written Japanese language uses three separate sets of characters: kanji, hiragana, and katakana (the latter two collectively known as *kana*). In addition, because English is a required course in most Japanese schools, most Japanese people are familiar with *rômaji* (the Latin alphabet used in English and other Western languages).

KANJI (漢字)

Kanji translates to "Chinese characters"—specifically "Han characters," referring to China's Han dynasty (206 B.C– A.D. 220), when the modern-day Chinese writing system was developed. Kanji were imported to Japan (by way of Korea) between the sixth and eighth centuries A.D. They were the first writing system used in Japan. Adopting kanji did not mean adopting the Chinese spoken language, because *kanji* primarily encode meaning, not sound. For instance, the kanji for "dragon" (龍) is pronounced "ryû" in Japanese and "long" in Chinese. Because many kanji are the same in Chinese, Japanese, and Korean, readers of any of the three languages can read a little bit of the others—but the spoken languages have almost nothing in common.

More than five thousand kanji are used in Japan; children are expected to know about two thousand common kanji by the end of high school to have basic reading proficiency. However, due to the differences in pronunciation, grammar, and usage between Chinese and Japanese, it is impossible to write a normal Japanese sentence with kanji alone. The same kanji can often be pronounced several different ways or used in several different contexts. Major differences in meaning and inflection, as well as conjunctions and other words for which there are no kanji, are conveyed with Japan's phonetic languages: hiragana and katakana.

HIRAGANA (ひらがな)

Hiragana was developed in Japan sometime after A.D. 800 as a phonetic language for handwriting and personal documents. They originated as simplified kanji, but compared to the thousands of kanji, there are only forty-six hiragana, each one expressing a different sound. A few markers and combinations of hiragana up the total number of sounds to 104: for instance, "chi" (ち) plus a small "ya" (や) makes the sound "cha" (ちゃ). The entire Japanese language can be expressed with these sounds, and so long as hiragana are provided in the text, Japanese speakers always know how a word should be spoken. (In other words, you can't really write intentionally unpronounceable words like "Mxyzpltk" and "Cthulhu" in Japanese.) Hiragana encode sound, not meaning.

Hiragana is the most commonly used script in manga. Because it's possible to write Japanese entirely in hiragana, the choice of how much kanji to use is one way to choose between formal and informal writing. For instance, *yami* ("dark") has the same meaning whether it's written in kanji (闇) or in hiragana (やみ). Manga for younger readers usually has few kanji.

KATAKANA (カタカナ)

Last, but not least for English readers, is the angular, even simpler-looking katakana, also developed sometime after A.D. 800. Each one of the 104 katakana characters corresponds to a hiragana character and expresses the same sound, but katakana are used primarily in phonetic spellings of foreign names and words, such as *jump* (ジャンプ). They make strange words stand out. Katakana usually indicate that the sound is emphasized or somehow unusual; thus, it is often used in manga to indicate when foreigners or other strange-sounding characters such as robots and aliens are speaking. Katakana are also frequently used in sound effects. A long dash (—) indicates that the sound is drawn out.

FURIGANA (振り仮名)

Furigana, also known as *rubi* or *yomigana,* aren't an alphabet of their own; they're the training wheels for Japanese readers who don't know all their kanji yet. In manga for younger readers, all kanji have tiny hiragana or katakana letters printed alongside them, showing how the kanji is pronounced. These are *furigana.* If readers don't recognize the meaning of the kanji, they can read the *furigana* phonetically. Although even grown-up manga sometimes use *furigana* for particularly obscure words, they are used mostly in children's manga. In fact, the strictest technical difference between a *seinen* or *jôsei* magazine and a *shônen* or *shôjo* magazine is that the former do not have *furigana.*

Furigana are also a handy way to encode double meanings, such as puns or translations of foreign words. For instance, the original Japanese title of Etsuko Ikeda and Yuho Ashibe's *Bride of Deimos* (悪魔の花嫁) uses the *furigana* for "Deimos" (デイモス) over the kanji meaning *akuma,* or "devil" (悪魔). Thus, the Japanese reader knows that Deimos is, for all intents and purposes, the devil. An example of a pun meaning is the Japanese title of Kazuya Minekura's *Saiyuki* (最遊記), a semimodernized, semiserious version of the classic Chinese novel *Saiyuki* (西遊記). The *sai* (西) in the original Chinese version means "West," so the original title is *Journey to the West;* but the *sai* (最) in Minekura's version means "long" or "far." Thus the title of Minekura's version could be translated as *Journey to the Extreme.*

HIRAGANA

わ wa	や ya	ら ra	ま ma	ぱ pa	ば ba	は ha	な na	だ da	た ta	ざ za	さ sa	が ga	か ka		あ a
		り ri	み mi	ぴ pi	び bi	ひ hi	に ni	ぢ ji★	ち chi	じ ji	し shi	ぎ gi	き ki		い i
ん n	ゆ yu	る ru	む mu	ぷ pu	ぶ bu	ふ fu	ぬ nu	づ zu★	つ tsu	ず zu	す su	ぐ gu	く ku		う u
		れ re	め me	ぺ pe	べ be	へ he	ね ne	で de	て te	ぜ ze	せ se	げ ge	け ke		え e
を wo	よ yo	ろ ro	も mo	ぽ po	ぼ bo	ほ ho	の no	ど do	と to	ぞ zo	そ so	ご go	こ ko		お o
		りゃ rya	みゃ mya	ぴゃ pya	びゃ bya	ひゃ hya	にゃ nya	ぢゃ ja★		じゃ ja	しゃ sha	ぎゃ gya	きゃ kya		
		りゅ ryu	みゅ myu	ぴゅ pyu	びゅ byu	ひゅ hyu	にゅ nyu	ぢゅ ju★	ちゅ chu	じゅ ju	しゅ shu	ぎゅ gyu	きゅ kyu		
		りょ ryo	みょ myo	ぴょ pyo	びょ byo	ひょ hyo	にょ nyo	ぢょ jo★	ちょ cho	じょ jo	しょ sho	ぎょ gyo	きょ kyo		

KATAKANA

ワ wa	ヤ ya	ラ ra	マ ma	パ pa	バ ba	ハ ha	ナ na	ダ da	タ ta	ザ za	サ sa	ガ ga	カ ka		ア a
		リ ri	ミ mi	ピ pi	ビ bi	ヒ hi	ニ ni	ヂ ji★	チ chi	ジ ji	シ shi	ギ gi	キ ki	イ i	
ン n	ユ yu	ル ru	ム mu	プ pu	ブ bu	フ fu	ヌ nu	ヅ zu★	ツ tsu	ズ zu	ス su	グ gu	ク ku	ウ u	
		レ re	メ me	ペ pe	ベ be	ヘ he	ネ ne	デ de	テ te	ゼ ze	セ se	ゲ ge	ケ ke	エ e	
ヲ wo	ヨ yo	ロ ro	モ mo	ポ po	ボ bo	ホ ho	ノ no	ド do	ト to	ゾ zo	ソ so	ゴ go	コ ko	オ o	
		リャ rya	ミャ mya	ピャ pya	ビャ bya	ヒャ hya	ニャ nya	ヂャ ja★		ジャ ja	シャ sha	ギャ gya	キャ kya		
		リュ ryu	ミュ myu	ピュ pyu	ビュ byu	ヒュ hyu	ニュ nyu	ヂュ ju★	チュ chu	ジュ ju	シュ shu	ギュ gyu	キュ kyu		
		リョ ryo	ミョ myo	ピョ pyo	ビョ byo	ヒョ hyo	ニョ nyo	ヂョ jo★	チョ cho	ジョ jo	ショ sho	ギョ gyo	キョ kyo		

MODERN ADDITIONS TO KATAKANA

	ヴャ vya		ファ fa		ツァ tsa		ヴァ va
ウィ wi			フィ fi	ディ di	ツィ tsi	ズィ zi	スィ si	グィ gwi	クィ kwi	ヴィ vi
	ヴュ vyu			ドゥ du	トゥ tu			ヴ vu
ウェ we	イェ ye		フェ fe		ツェ tse	ジェ je	シェ she	グェ gwe	クェ kwe	ヴェ ve
ウォ wo	ヴョ vyo		フォ fo		ツォ tso			グォ gwo	クォ kwo	ヴォ vo
					チェ che		
			フュ fyu	デュ dyu	テュ tyu		

Additional header entries: グヮ/グァ gwa, クヮ/クァ kwa — グィ gwi, クィ kwi — グェ gwe, クェ kwe — グォ gwo, クォ kwo

Indicates deprecated or unused

SOME COMMON KANJI

Many kanji have different meanings and pronunciations when used in different combinations; this lists only a few common usages found in manga titles. For instance, in casual conversation, the word *shin* ("new") is usually spoken as *atarashii* (新しい).

花	*hana*	flower
天	*ten*	heaven
世界	*sekai*	world
犬	*inu*	dog
大	*dai* or *tai*	big
王	*ô*	king
新	*shin*	new
少女	*shôjo*	girl
少年	*shônen*	boy
美	*bi* or *mi*	beautiful (often used in *bishôjo* and *bishônen*)
忍	*shinobi*	shinobi
忍者	*ninja*	ninja
魔	*ma*	(evil) magic or demon
魔物	*mamono*	monster or demon

JAPANESE PRONUNCIATION

The most basic rule in pronouncing Japanese is that each vowel sound is a separate syllable, and each syllable is spoken distinctly from the others. Consonants (including sounds that are written with two English consonants, such as "sh" and "ch") are always followed by a vowel; with the exception of "n," there are no Japanese syllables that end on a consonant. For instance, *Hanaukyo Maid Team* is pronounced "Ha-na-u-kyo" rather than "Hanau-kyo" or "Hanauky-o" or "Hanauk-yo." *Aishiteruze Baby* is pronounced "Ai-shi-te-ru-ze." *Tsubasa: Reservoir Chronicle* is pronounced "Tsu-ba-sa." *Ranma ½* is pronounced "Ran-ma." Each syllable is equally stressed.

Japanese vowel sounds have often been compared to Spanish. "L" and "r" sounds are nearly identical in Japanese; so are "b" and "v." Vowel sounds are always pronounced the same:

JAPANESE VOWEL SOUNDS

a   as in "raw"

i   as in "bee"

u   as in "zoo"

e   as in "end"

o   as in "no"

Long vowels, in which the sound stays the same but is longer in duration, are sometimes indicated by a circumflex (ˆ) or a macron (˜). The most common example of this is the long "o" in the words *shôjo* and *shônen,* which are variably written as *shôjo, shōjo,* and *shoujo.* Technically, none is incorrect, but the third spelling might lead to the incorrect assumption that the word rhymes with the English word *you,* or that the "u" is pronounced separately from the "o." For that reason, this book uses circumflexes and the spellings *shôjo* and *shônen.* For titles of translated manga, however, we use the same spelling as the English edition.

Like American advertisers playing with the words *samurai* or *wasabi,* manga titles often include English (or French or German) words, usually for their cool factor (i.e. *Fake, Othello, Sailor Moon*). These words are generally written in katakana, but there is no formal system for determining how foreign words are "spelled" in katakana, so the same word may be written with slightly different katakana. For clarity, all non-Japanese words (or made-up non-Japanese words) written in katakana are spelled by their "intended" English spelling, rather than a phonetic transliteration (i.e., "Gundam" instead of "Gandamu"). In Japanese, the solitary letter "z" is usually pronounced "zet" (e.g., *Dragon Ball Z*). The letter "x" is usually silent (e.g., *Hunter x Hunter* is pronounced simply "Hunter Hunter.")

Japanese speakers often casually abbreviate long titles into a few syllables, and this is sometimes followed by English-language publishers (i.e., *Saikano* instead of *Saishu Heiki Kanojo* ("Ultimate Weapon Girlfriend") or *Pokémon* instead of *Pocket Monsters*).

NAMES AND HONORIFICS

Except when indicated, *Manga: The Complete Guide* lists Japanese names in the English fashion: personal name first, family name last. Almost all manga publishers do the same.

Japanese names often contain meanings that, depending on the translation, may be lost on English readers. For instance, Aya, the heroine of *Ceres: Celestial Legend,* is named with the word *ayashi* ("bewitching") in the series' Japanese title, *Ayashi no*

Ceres ("Bewitching Ceres"). In real-life Japan, it'd be an unusual name, but not by manga standards. Puns are popular in Japanese humor, and characters in children's or comedy manga are often named after food or other objects, without any deep meaning beyond creating a memorable name. Often English words are used, as in *Dragon Ball Z* (where otherwise intimidating characters are named after dairy products and vegetables) and *Ranma ½* (where all the Chinese characters are named after hair care products). This pun practice dates back a long time, even to classics such as *The Wonderful World of Sazae-san* (1946), whose main characters are named after Japanese words for seafood.

English-language manga publishers increasingly assume reader familiarity with the Japanese system of honorifics (*-chan, -kun, -san, -sempai,* etc.), although many publishers still exclude honorifics or rewrite them into the dialogue (i.e. "the great Piccolo" instead of *Piccolo-sama*). Honorifics sometimes appear in book titles, such as *Guru Guru Pon-chan* and *Mystical Prince Yoshida-kun*.

SOUND EFFECTS

Generally speaking, manga use more sound effects than American comics. In addition to the sound of actual events, such as a heartbeat ("DOKI DOKI") or a beep ("PII"), manga sound effects often serve as a "soundtrack," with nonliteral dramatic noises such as "DON" (often a sort of "Ta-da!") and "GO GO GO" (a rumbling sound sometimes used to indicate rising tension). Manga often employ sound effects for things American comics would leave blank, such as "SHIIIN" (the sound of silence) or "NIKO" (a smile).

Some English editions of manga have fully translated sound effects, while others have marginal English translations next to the Japanese FX, or a sound effects glossary in the back of the book, or no translations at all. Interestingly, sound effects typically read from left to right, even in the original right-to-left Japanese editions.

READING RIGHT TO LEFT

The Japanese language traditionally reads right to left, and most manga are drawn in right-to-left format. For years, this was considered one of the greatest obstacles to the American acceptance of manga, and so American publishers "flipped" the artwork, mirror-imaging it to read left to right for the convenience of English readers. (Most Japanese readers are used to reading in both directions; since World War II, Japanese product labels, book covers, and movie posters are typically printed left to right, as are translations of American comics.) Many Japanese artists were unhappy with the results and refused to allow their work to be printed left to right, believing that it made it look bad, like a photograph taken from an unflattering angle. (For the same reason, some comic artists examine their art in a mirror before the final draft.) Other artists compromised by rearranging the panels on the page to read from left to right; however, within the individual panels, the natural order of the dialogue and action was still the other way around.

For many years, only a few rare titles were published fully right to left, but in 2002 Tokyopop started an aggressive campaign to popularize "unflipped" manga, based on the idea that it represents the artist's original intentions. The plan was a huge success, and "unflipped" manga are now standard. This book does not differentiate between formats, on the basis that—as for Japanese readers—it shouldn't make a difference. Basically, almost all titles published before 2002 are left to right, and almost all titles published from 2002 onward are right to left. Some older titles, such as *Peach Girl* and *Maison Ikkoku,* have been printed in both formats in subsequent editions.

A few manga, such as *Apocalypse Meow,* were drawn left to right for a consciously "Western" effect, or because they were printed in a magazine that reads in the Western fashion. Other examples of original left-to-right manga include *Kingdom Hearts, Madara, Lagoon Engine Einsatz,* and *Record of Lodoss War: The Lady of Pharis.*

GLOSSARY

ANIME (アニメ)—The Japanese word for animation from all countries, *anime* is usually used in an English context to refer to Japanese animation specifically. Theatrical anime existed before World War II; the first anime TV series appeared in the early 1960s, and the first direct-to-video animation (OAVs) in the mid-1980s. Manga series have always been adapted into anime, and vice versa. In the case of OAVs and movies based on manga, the plots often have to be compressed for the anime version, but in the case of long-running TV series such as *Dragon Ball Z,* in which the anime version is produced nearly simultaneously with the manga, the anime often contains new story lines intended to kill time while they wait for the manga artist to get farther along in the story. Japan has several anime magazines aimed at hard-core fans, including *Animedia, Animage,* and *Newtype,* which has an English counterpart, *Newtype USA.* This book sometimes uses the term "anime style" to refer to a popular style of character design that arose in anime and that now dominates manga aimed at younger readers: cute, attractive characters with big, bright eyes, spiky or otherwise exaggerated hair, and clean, simple (and thus easy-to-animate) linework.

***BESSATSU* (別冊)**—"Supplement." Often used in the titles of manga magazines, such as *Bessatsu Margaret* or *Betsucomi* (an abbreviation for *Bessatsu Shôjo Comic*).

BISHÔJO (美少女)—"Beautiful girl." In manga and anime, refers to any boys' series in which the focus is on attractive women.

BISHÔNEN (美少年)—"Beautiful boy." In manga and anime, refers to male characters with a handsome yet often slightly androgynous look, as well as any girls' manga involving attractive boys in sexually ambiguous situations. *Bishi* or *bishie* for short. See the introduction to YAOI.

BOYS' LOVE (BL)—Popular subgenre of *shôjo* manga involving romances between handsome men. See the introduction to YAOI.

BUNKOBAN (文庫本)—Pocket edition, sometimes *bunko* for short. A small, compact Japanese book size, approximately 4 by 6 inches, often used for reprints of manga. *Bunkoban* are considered a "prestige format"; generally, most manga are initially published in *tankôbon* size and only later repackaged as *bunkoban* if sales warrant. In addition to being smaller than *tankôbon, bunkoban* usually have more pages, typically 300–400 compared to 200 pages in the average *tankôbon.* Because of this difference in page counts, a series that is 15 volumes long in *tankôbon* edition may be only 10 volumes in *bunkoban* edition, and so forth. *Bunkoban* sometimes use higher-quality paper than *tankôbon.* Like *tankôbon,* they are usually softcover with dust jackets. Dark Horse's editions of *Lone Wolf and Cub, Samurai Executioner,* and *Path of the Assassin* are printed in *bunkoban* format.

CHIBI (ちび)—Slang for "short person" or "child." In anime, manga, and Japanese video games, *chibi* refers to cartoony, babylike, super-cute character designs in which the character's head and body are approximately equal in size. Some manga are drawn entirely in this style, but more often it is used together with more realistic proportions for comic relief.

COMIC (コミック)—The English term *comic* is widely used in Japan, where it can refer to comics from any country, not specifically American or English-language comics. It appears in the titles of many manga magazines, such as *Big Comic* and *Shôjo Comic.* This book occasionally uses the word *comic* in a general sense for both American and Japanese comics, but reserves the term "monthly comics" or "issues" for American-style comic book pamphlets. American comic book issues are typically twenty-four to forty-eight pages in length.

COSPLAY (コスプレ)—Short for "costume play." Popular fan pastime of dressing up in (and often making) costumes, often based on popular anime, manga, or video game characters.

DÔJINSHI (同人誌)—"Same-person publications," i.e., self-published works aimed at fellow fans. In an English context, the term *dôjinshi* usually refers to self-published manga, although the term also covers small-press novels, video games, art books, and other crafts and merchandise. *Dôjinshi* comics are generally fan tributes or parodies of existing works, and "anthology comics" such as *Di Gi Charat* and *Gunparade March: A New Marching Song* often have a similar style, although technically they are not *dôjinshi* because they are produced by large publishers. See the article on DÔJINSHI.

ERO-MANGA (エロ漫画)—The most common Japanese term for adult manga, in the sexual sense. The term *ero* is short for *erotic*.

ETCHI (エッチ)—Based on the Japanese pronunciation of the letter *H,* this term refers to sexual material, specifically in anime and manga. In Japanese, it is also used as a pseudonym for sex itself. The exact origin of the term is unknown, although it is believed to be short for *hentai*.

FANSERVICE (ファンサービス)—"A service to the fans." Also known as a "service cut" or simply "service," this Japanese term typically refers to any sexually suggestive "eye candy" or nudity, particularly material that has nothing to do with the story (such as camera angles that expose a girl's panties in an otherwise serious scene). Some boys' manga have so much fanservice that they are referred to as "fanservice manga." In a more general sense, it also refers to in-jokes and other material intended to amuse the audience. See the article on ROMANCE.

FOUR-PANEL MANGA (4コマ)—Also known as *yon-koma* manga. Short Japanese comics, usually four panels long, comparable to American newspaper comic strips. See the article on FOUR-PANEL MANGA.

FURRY—An American comics term referring to anthropomorphic animal characters, or characters with animal features such as cat ears, dog ears, tails, etc. (Examples in manga include *Hyper Police, Fantastic Panic, Inuyasha, Free Collars Kingdom,* and many of the comics of Ippongi Bang and Johji Manabe.) Relatively uncommon in manga apart from the occasional cat-girl, it generally has no deeper meaning than cuteness value.

GAG MANGA (ギャグ漫画)—Japanese term for any purely humor-oriented, basically plotless manga. See the article on COMEDY AND GAG.

GAIDEN (外伝)—Side story. Literally meaning "outside legend," it is often used in Japanese titles to indicate a sequel or noncanonical spin-off. For instance, the original Japanese title of *Mars: Horse with No Name* is *Mars Gaiden: Namae no nai Uma* ("Mars Side Story: Horse with No Name").

GEKIGA (劇画)—"Dramatic pictures." A term promoted by certain Japanese artists in the 1960s as a more sophisticated, adult alternative to *manga*. Today, some artists may identify their work as *gekiga,* but for most people the *gekiga* genre is merely an old-fashioned style of manga. See the article on UNDERGROUND AND GEKIGA.

GEKKAN (月刊)—Monthly. Often used in the titles of manga magazines, such as *Gekkan Shônen* magazine ("Monthly Shônen" magazine). In this book, the English term *monthly* is generally used in place of *gekkan*.

GRAPHIC NOVEL—English term referring to any comic (or, by extension, manga) published in softcover or hardcover book format. The term first arose in the 1970s and is sometimes used to refer specifically to comics with a strong novel-like narrative, as opposed to collections of short stories or four-panel manga. (The term "trade paperback" is used for these types of softcover comic collections.) The term "graphic novel" is often used to describe the various Japanese manga formats known as *bunkoban, tankôbon,* and *wideban.*

HENTAI (変態)—"Abnormal." In colloquial Japanese, a derogatory term meaning "weirdo" or "pervert." In English fandom, *hentai* refers to explicitly pornographic anime and manga, although the term is not used this way in Japan. See the introduction to ADULT MANGA.

HIRAGANA (ひらがな)—See Appendix B, on the Japanese language.

JIDAI-GEKI (時代劇)—Period drama. Refers to manga, movies, or other media set in Japanese history, typically but not always samurai dramas set in the Edo era. See the article on JAPANESE HISTORY.

JÔSEI (女性)—Women. Refers to manga aimed at adult women. See the article on JÔSEI.

KAIJÛ (怪獣)—"Mysterious creature." Usually used to refer to giant monsters in the style of Godzilla and Gamera. See the article on TOKUSATSU.

KANJI (漢字)—See Appendix B, on the Japanese language.

KANZENBAN (完全版)—Complete edition. Like *bunkoban* and *wideban, kanzenban* is a format into which bestselling manga are sometimes reprinted after first appearing as *tankôbon.* Compared to *tankôbon, kanzenban* editions are usually bigger (typically 300–400 pages), printed on higher-quality paper, and include bonus materials not available in the original, such as color pages or notes from the artist. They may be hardcover or sold in box sets. The term *aizôban* ("collector's edition") is sometimes used for much the same format.

KASHIBONYA (貸し本屋)—Rental bookshops. A common manga venue from the immediate postwar period through the 1960s, particularly around Osaka, *kashibonya* rented hardcover, durable manga for a fee. Manga artists working in the *kashibonya* market had lower pay and greater freedom, and experimented with adult themes and realistic artwork before their fellow artists in the children's magazine market centered in Tokyo. Rising prosperity gradually put an end to *kashibonya,* as citizens chose to buy manga instead of renting.

KATAKANA (カタカナ)—See Appendix B, on the Japanese language.

KAWAII (かわいい)—Cute. A term often applied to anime and manga characters.

KI (気)—A broad term that usually means energy or spirit. In Chinese, it is pronounced *chi* or *qi.* In anime and manga *ki* is most often used in its martial arts context, in which it describes the natural energy produced by all living things, which can be manipulated by disciplined martial artists. See the article on MARTIAL ARTS.

LIGHT NOVELS (ライト・ノベル)—Short novels aimed at a young adult audience, typically with illustrations, "light novels" became popular in Japan beginning in the 1980s. Some are original works, some are stories based on anime or manga (often with a few pages of drawings by the original manga artist), and some are reprints of works originally serialized in Japanese young adult fiction magazines, such as *The Sneaker, Dragon Magazine, Cobalt,* and *Novel Japan.* An increasing number of American manga publishers also translate light novels, including Viz, Tokyopop, Seven Seas, DMP, and Dark Horse.

LOLICON (ロリコン)—Short for "Lolita complex." A Japanese trend dating back to the early 1980s, *lolicon* refers to sexually suggestive material involving underage (or young-looking) female characters. Its influence can also be seen in a common art style in which female characters (who may be adult) are drawn with "cute" faces and childlike features. See the article on OTAKU and the introduction to ADULT MANGA.

MANGA (漫画)—"Whimsical pictures." The Japanese word for comics from all countries, *manga* is usually used in an English context to refer to Japanese comics, or to comics drawn in a Japanese style. This book uses the term *manga* exclusively for comics drawn in Japan for Japanese audiences.

MANGAKA (漫画家)—Manga creator. This book generally uses the English terms "manga artist" and "manga author" instead of *mangaka*.

MANHUA (漫画)—Chinese comics. The word comes from the same Chinese characters as the word *manga*. Small amounts of manhua have been published in America since the 1980s; current publishers include HK Comics and DrMaster. Most translated *manhua* are full-color martial arts, science fiction, or historical action comics, very distinct from manga, although a few, such as I-Huan's *Real Fake Princess,* are drawn in black-and-white, manga-influenced style. Wendy Siuyi Wong's book *Hong Kong Comics* is an excellent introduction to the medium.

MANHWA (漫画)—Korean comics. The word comes from the same Chinese characters as the word *manga*. Also spelled *manwha* in English. Most *manhwa* are drawn in black and white in a style heavily influenced by Japanese comics, although they can be distinguished from manga by the artists' names and the fact that Korean, unlike Japanese, reads left to right. The first high-profile translated *manhwa* was ComicsOne's *Redmoon* in 2001. Today, many publishers translate *manhwa,* including DrMaster, CPM, ADV, Ice Kunion, Tokyopop, Dark Horse, Infinity Studios, and Netcomics.

MECHA (メカ)—Short for *mechanical,* the term refers to all sorts of machines, including military tanks, planes, and ships and fantastic science fiction machinery such as spaceships and giant robots. Often used to refer to robots specifically. See the article on MECHA AND ROBOTS.

MOE (萌え)—"To sprout," in the sense of sprouting plants. In the 1990s the term *moe* became slang for a particular type of manga, anime, and pop-culture obsession focused on cute, young, or underage girls. The difference between *moe* and *lolicon* is that *moe* is ostensibly platonic idol worship and focuses on nonsexual, often domestic situations: "cuteness for cuteness' sake." In a broader sense, *moe* can also be used to mean any kind of passionate fandom; to quote Kirico Higashizato's *Love Recipe,* "Enthusiasm, love and other emotions add up and become *moe.*" See the article on OTAKU.

OAV—Original animated video. Direct-to-video anime first appeared in the mid-1980s; the new medium allowed studios to target more niche audiences (such as science fiction, fantasy, adult anime, etc.) and allowed smaller studios to break into the anime business. Also known as OVA (original video animation).

OEL MANGA—Original English-language manga. Like "manga-style," the term refers to manga-influenced comics drawn by American or other English-language artists. A related term is *OGL* (original global manga), typically used for manga-style works by European and South American artists. Manga-influenced comics have been a recognized style in American comics since the early 1980s, although their numbers have boomed in recent years, partly thanks to heavy promotion by publishers such as Tokyopop and Seven Seas Entertainment.

OMAKE (お負け)—Extra or bonus. In manga, refers to short bonus materials printed at the end of the book or between chapters, which were not printed in the original magazine serialization version. *Omake* manga are often self-parodies or in-jokes aimed at fans.

OTAKU (オタク)—Literally meaning "house" (in the sense of "household," or "you and yours"), *otaku* is a formal masculine pronoun in Japanese.

OVA—Original video animation. Variant term for OAV.

PACHINKO—A popular Japanese pastime similar to vertical pinball machines. Most *pachinko* machines also incorporate elements from slot machines and are sometimes known as *pachisuro* (*pachinko* slots). Invented sometime after World War II, they are found in "*pachinko* parlors" throughout Japan, where people play for prizes or tokens (often surreptitiously exchanged for money in a form of quasi-legal gambling). See the article on GAMES AND HOBBIES.

REDICOMI (レディコミ)—Ladies' comics. Originally used to refer to all *jôsei* manga (manga for adult women), the term later acquired the more narrow meaning of sex comics aimed at women. The terms *jôsei* and *redicomi* are still sometimes used interchangeably in Japan.

RPG—Role-playing game. Originating in the 1970s with pen-and-paper games such as Dungeons & Dragons, the term is now mostly used to describe video games such as *Dragon Quest, Final Fantasy,* and *Worlds of Warcraft.* See the article on RPGs.

SALARYMAN (サラリーマン)—White-collar worker. The term has negative connotations of being a wage slave but is also ironically embraced. See the article on SALARYMAN.

SCREENTONE (スクリーントーン)—Generally called "tone" in Japan, screentone is the dot patterns used by manga artists to achieve patterns and textures. Originally screentone was manually applied using adhesive plastic overlays, but now many artists use computer software for the same effect.

SEINEN (成年)—Adult. Despite sounding the same as *seinen* ("young man"), the written form is differerent, and this usage refers only to adults. It is one of the terms used in Japan to refer to adult sex comics; the Japanese term *seinen comic* (adult comic) even appears as a playful design element on the covers of old Eros MangErotica graphic novels. Except in specific cases such as in the introduction to ADULT MANGA, this book uses the term *seinen* exclusively in the sense of "young man."

SEINEN (青年)—Young man. Despite the implications of youth, the term *seinen manga* usually refers to all manga aimed at male readers in their late teens to adulthood. See the article on SEINEN.

SENTAI (戦隊)—Literally meaning "task force" or "regiment," the term's military meaning is now secondary to a genre of Japanese TV shows featuring teams of colorfully costumed, masked heroes. See the article on TOKUSATSU.

SHIN (新)—New. Often used in Japanese titles to indicate a sequel. For instance, the original Japanese title of *The All-New No Need for Tenchi!* is *Shin Tenchi Muyô!* ("New Tenchi Muyô!").

SHÔJO (少女)—Girl. Refers to manga aimed at girls. See the article on SHÔJO.

SHÔNEN (少年)—Boy. Refers to manga aimed at boys. See the article on SHÔNEN.

SHÔNEN AI (少年愛)—Boys' Love. A popular subgenre of *shôjo* manga involving romances between handsome men and/or teenage boys; in Japan, the term *shônen ai* usually refers to the early examples of the genre, published in the 1970s. See the introduction to YAOI.

SHOTA (ショタ)—Also known as *shotacon.* Short for "Shotarô complex" (a reference to Shôtaro, the young hero of Mitsuteru Yokoyama's manga series *Tetsujin 28–gô,* aka *Gigantor*). The gender-reversed equivalent of *lolicon,* it refers to sexually suggestive material involving underage (or young-looking) male characters.

SHÛKAN (週刊)—Weekly. Often used in the titles of manga magazines, such as *Shûkan Shônen Jump* ("Weekly Shônen Jump"). In this book, the English term *weekly* is generally used in place of *shûkan.*

STORY MANGA—Manga with an ongoing plot, as distinct from gag manga.

SUPER-DEFORMED—*SD* for short. Older term for *chibi,* most popular in the 1980s and 1990s.

TANKÔBON (単行本)—Literally meaning "stand-alone book," *tankôbon* are the format in which most manga is sold in Japan: small paperback books, often 4.375 by 6.875 inches and 200 pages long. Almost all *tankôbon* are softcover with dust jackets. Although most manga is originally printed in short installments in anthology magazines, they are usually collected afterward in the form of one or several *tankôbon* (except in the cases of extremely unpopular series, which may last only a few magazine installments and never be reprinted). Although manga magazines are usually thrown away after being read, *tankôbon* and other book editions often go into multiple printings and have a long shelf life. Sufficiently popular titles are often reprinted years later in other formats, such as *kanzenban, bunkoban,* and *wideban.* Most translated manga is published in *tankôbon* format.

TOKUSATSU (特撮)—Special effects. A term used in Japanese movies and TV shows, short for *tokushu satsuei* ("special photography"). In the broad sense, *tokusatsu* refers to all Japanese special effects features, but it is often used specifically to refer to the science fiction, *kaijû,* and *sentai* genres. See the article on TOKU-SATSU.

WIDEBAN (ワイド本)—Wide edition. Like *bunkoban* and *kanzenban, wideban* is a format into which bestselling manga are sometimes reprinted after first appearing as *tankôbon.* As the name implies, "wide" manga are generally printed larger than the original *tankôbon* edition. Unlike *kanzenban,* however, the emphasis is on being big and cheap; they are usually softcover and are not printed on especially high-quality paper. The page count per volume ranges as high as one thousand.

YANKII (ヤンキ)—A blue-collar subculture of juvenile delinquents mostly from the 1970s and 1980s, known for their loud, rebellious attitude, fistfighting, smoking, and wild haircuts (such as the 1950s-style greaser look often seen in older *shônen* manga such as *YuYu Hakusho*). The term *yankii* has a complicated origin but is related to the English term *Yankee,* with its connotations of American boorishness. See the article on CRIME AND YAKUZA.

YAOI (やおい)—Slang term for *dôjinshi* parody comics, usually drawn by women, in which male characters from anime and manga series are in love or have sex with one another. In English, the term is often used to describe all manga romances between handsome men. See the introduction to YAOI.

YOUNG (ヤング)—A common English loan word, referring to people in their late teens to very early twenties. Usually used in the titles of young men's manga magazines such as *Young Jump* and *Young Sunday,* it also refers to young women, as seen in magazine titles such as *Feel Young* and *Young You.*

YURI (百合)—Lily; slang term for lesbian. See the article on YURI/LESBIAN.

ZÔKAN (増刊)—Special edition. Often used to refer to one-shots and spin-offs of manga magazines, such as *Morning Party Zôkan.*

BIBLIOGRAPHY

Allison, Anne. *Permitted and Prohibited Desires: Mothers, Comics and Censorship in Japan.* Berkeley: University of California Press, 2000.

Apostolou, John L., and Martin H. Greenberg, eds. *The Best Japanese Science Fiction Stories.* New York: Barricade Books, 1997.

Birnbaum, Alfred, ed. *Monkey Brain Sushi: New Tastes in Japanese Fiction.* Tokyo: Kodansha International, 1991.

Buruma, Ian. *Behind the Mask.* New York: Random House, 1984.

Clute, John, and John Grant. *The Encyclopedia of Fantasy.* New York: St. Martin's Press, 1997.

Clute, John, and Peter Nicholls, eds. *The Encyclopedia of Science Fiction.* New York: St. Martin's Press, 1993.

Gravett, Paul. *Manga: 60 Years of Japanese Comics.* New York: Collins Design, 2004.

Herbert, Rosemary. *The Oxford Companion to Crime and Mystery Writing.* New York: Oxford University Press, 1999.

Jones, Mason, Patrick Macias, Carl Gustav Horn, and Yuji Oniki. *Japan Edge: The Insider's Guide to Japanese Pop Subculture.* San Francisco: Cadence Books, 1999.

Kanemitsu, Dan. *Storm Front Journal #0, "Doujinshi: The Alternative Publishing Medium of Japan."* Minneapolis: Studio Revolution USA, 1998.

Kinsella, Sharon. *Adult Manga: Culture & Power in Contemporary Japanese Society*. Honolulu: University of Hawai'i Press, 2000.

Kohler, Chris. *Power Up: How Japanese Video Games Gave the World an Extra Life*. Indianapolis: BradyGAMES Publishing, 2005.

Macias, Patrick. *Cruising the Anime City: An Otaku Guide to Neo-Tokyo*. Berkeley: Stone Bridge Press, 2004.

Macias, Patrick. *Tokyoscope: The Japanese Cult Film Companion*. San Francisco: Cadence Books, 2001.

Masanao, Amano, and Julius Wiedemann, eds. *Manga Design*. Köln: Taschen, 2004.

Poitras, Gilles. *The Anime Companion*. Berkeley: Stone Bridge Press, 1999.

Quigley, Kevin, ed. *Comics Underground Japan*. New York: Blast Books, 1996.

Schodt, Frederik L. *Dreamland Japan: Writings on Modern Manga*. Berkeley: Stone Bridge Press, 1996.

Schodt, Frederik L. *Manga! Manga! The World of Japanese Comics*. Tokyo: Kodansha International, 1983.

Sheff, David. *Game Over: How Nintendo Zapped an American Industry, Captured Your Dollars, and Enslaved Your Children*. New York: Random House, 1993.

Shiratori, Chikao, ed. *Secret Comics Japan*. San Francisco: Cadence Books, 2000.

Silverman, Laura K., ed. *Bringing Home the Sushi: An Inside Look at Japanese Business Through Business Comics*. Atlanta: Mangajin, 1995.

Smith, Toren. "Miso Horny: Sex in Japanese Comics." *The Comics Journal* (April 1991): pp. 111–115.

The Society for the Study of Manga Techniques. *How to Draw Manga: Volume 1: Compiling Characters*. Tokyo: Graphic-sha Publishing Co., 1999.

Takekuma, Kentaro, and Koji Aihara. *Even a Monkey Can Draw Manga*. San Francisco: Viz Communications, 2002.

ARTIST INDEX

The artist index is focused on individuals; it excludes organizations and companies (such as Gainax or Bandai Games), with the exception of artist studios (such as Akame Productions). It includes all artists, writers, and other creative staff listed in the manga reviews, including Western collaborators, but not Western creators of other material (movies, books) that was adapted into manga without the creator's input. Authors of *yaoi* and adult manga are listed here along with mainstream manga creators. Writers whose translated work appears only in small stories in anthologies are not listed, so many of the contributors to *Comics Underground Japan, Secret Comics Japan, Bringing Home the Sushi,* and *J-Boy by Biblos* are not included on this list.

Most manga artists use pen names; real names are listed when possible. Following the example of nearly all manga publishers, names are written in the English style: personal name first, family name last. The exception is nonstandard pen names such as Tori Miki, Mario Kaneda, and Rikdo Koshi. In cases where the manga artist's name has been printed on books in the Japanese style (or both ways, as in the Gutsoon and Viz editions of Takehiko Inoue's work) both versions are listed. Several CMX books switch from Japanese-style to English-style names in the middle of the series.

Only translated work is listed; many classic artists, such as Go Nagai, Osamu Tezuka, Moto Hagio, and Shotaro Ishinomori, have many more untranslated series.

Manga artists' Web sites may contain adult content; browser caution is advised.

Mitsuru Adachi (1951–)
Short Program

Tetsu Adachi (1968–)
Weather Woman (1992)

Toka Adachi
Alive (2003) (art)

Tadashi Agi (aka Seimaru Amagi, Yuya Aoki)
Getbackers (1999) (story) (as Yuya Aoki)
Remote (2002) (story) (as Seimaru Amagi)

Yu Aida
Gunslinger Girl (2002)

Koji Aihara (1963–)
Even a Monkey Can Draw Manga (1989) (art)

Miki Aihara
http://www.betsucomi.shogakukan.co.jp/talk/aihara.html
Hot Gimmick (2000)
Tokyo Boys & Girls (2004)

Yu Aikawa
http://www.geocities.jp/ao_m_glory/index.html
Dark Edge (1999)

Sakufu Ajimine
Your Honest Deceit (2004) (*yaoi*)

Satoru Akahori (1965–)
http://www.i-poli.com/
Sorcerer Hunters (1993) (story)
Saber Marionette J (1996) (original creator)
Abenobashi: Magical Shopping Arcade (2002) (story)
Kashimashi: Girl Meets Girl (2004) (story)

Ken Akamatsu (1968–)
http://www.ailove.net
A.I. Love You (1994)
Love Hina (1998)
Negima!: Master Negi Magi (2003)

Akame Productions
Collective name for Sanpei Shirato's studio of assistants. Formed in 1963.
The Legend of Kamui Perfect Collection (1981)

Kazuki Akane
Heat Guy J (2002) (original story) (with Satelight)

Fujio Akatsuka (1935–)
http://www.koredeiinoda.net/
Akko-Chan's Got a Secret! (1962)
The Genius Bakabon (1967)

Katsu Aki (1961–)
The Vision of Escaflowne (1995) (manga)
Psychic Academy (1999)

Akikan
Onegai Twins (2005) (art)

Nami Akimoto (1960–)
Miracle Girls (1991)
Ultra Cute (1999)

Yasushi Akimoto (1956–)
One Missed Call (story)

Matsuri Akino
Petshop of Horrors (1995)
Kamen Tantei (1998)
Genju no Seiza (2000)

Shouko Akira (aka Shoko Akira)
Shôjo Beat's Manga Artist Academy (2000) (contributor)
X2 (2002)

Yoshinobu Akita (1973–)
http://www.motsunabenohigan.jp/
Orphen (1998) (story)

Michio Akiyama
School Zone (adult)

Tamayo Akiyama
http://www.interq.or.jp/hot/paururun/
Mouryou Kiden: Legend of the Nymph (1994)
Hyper Rune (1996)

Secret Chaser (1999)
Zyword (2005)

Risu Akizuki (1957–)
Survival in the Office: The Evolution of Japanese Working Women (1989)
Bringing Home the Sushi (contributor)

Ryo Akizuki
http://www.scn-net.ne.jp/~ryoji/
Stellvia (2003) (art)

Seimaru Amagi: See Tadashi Agi.

Sumiko Amakawa
Cross (1997)

Akira Amano (1973–)
Reborn! (2004)

Kozue Amano (1974–)
http://ariapokoten.sakura.ne.jp/
Aqua (2001)
Aria (2002)

Shiro Amano (1976–)
Kingdom Hearts (2003)
Kingdom Hearts: Chain of Memories (2005)

Natsumi Ando
Zodiac P.I. (2001)

Moyoco Anno (1971–)
http://www.annomoyoco.com/
Happy Mania (1995)
Flowers & Bees (2000)
Sugar Sugar Rune (2003)

Nobuyuki Anzai (1972–)
Flame of Recca (1995)
Mär (2003)

Haruka Aoi
A Little Snow Fairy Sugar (2001) (creator)

Yasuko Aoike (1948–)
http://www.aoikeyasuko.com/
From Eroica with Love (1976)

Takao Aoki
Beyblade (1999)

Tetsuya Aoki
Angel's Wing

Yuya Aoki: See Tadashi Agi.

Gosho Aoyama (1963–)
Case Closed (1994)

Kiyoko Arai
Beauty Pop (2003)

Rui Araizumi (1966–)
Slayers Medieval Mayhem (1995) (art)
Slayers Super-Explosive Demon Story (1995) (character design)
Slayers Special (2000) (character design)
Slayers Premium (2002) (character design)

Hiromu Arakawa (1973–)
Fullmetal Alchemist (2002)

Hirohiko Araki (1959–)
Baoh (1984)
Jojo's Bizarre Adventure (1987)

Hitoshi Ariga (1972–)
http://www.ancient.co.jp/~ariga/
The Big O (1999)

Keitaro Arima (1969–)
http://www.waruwaru.com/
Tsukuyomi: Moon Phase (1999)

Sena Aritou
IWGP: Ikebukuro West Gate Park (2001) (art)

Kyoko Ariyoshi (1950–)
Swan (1976)

Hiroshi Aro (1959–)
You & Me (1983)
Futaba-Kun Change (1990)

Kusuko Asa
Get You (Wanted Man) (2005) (*yaoi*)

Sakura Asagi
Mobile Suit Gundam Wing: Blind Target (1999) (art)

Yu Asagiri
http://www.asagiriyu.to/
  Midnight Panther (1994)
  Golden Cain (2003) (*yaoi*)

Yuzuno Asaki: See Asaki Yuzuno.

George Asakura
http://www.jazze7.com/
  A Perfect Day for Love Letters (1998)

Kia Asamiya (1963–)
http://www.tron.co.jp/
Studied animation at the Tokyo Designer
Institute and went on to work as an
animator and character designer under the
name Michitaka Kikuchi. Debuted as a
manga artist with *Vagrants* in *Comptiq*
magazine in 1986. His anime character
design work includes *Sonic Soldier Borgman,*
Detonator Orgun, and *Hades Project Zeorymer,*
and his work as an American comics artist
includes DC's *Batman: Child of Dreams,*
Dark Horse's *Hellboy: Weird Tales,* and
Marvel's *Uncanny X-Men.*
  Silent Möbius (1988)
  Gunhed (1989)
  Dark Angel (1990)
  Möbius Klein (1994)
  Steam Detectives (1994)
  Nadesico (1996)
  Corrector Yui (1999) (story)
  Star Wars Episode I: The Phantom Menace
    (1999) (art)
  Batman: Child of Dreams (2000)
  Dark Angel: Phoenix Resurrection
    (2001)
  Junk: Record of the Last Hero (2004)

Kaori Asano
  Vanity Angel (1992) (adult)

Rin Asano
http://www8.plala.or.jp/rin-a/
  Tengai Retrogical or: How I Learned to
    Stop Worrying and Love the Crisis
    (2002)

Misuzu Asaoka
  Glass Wings (2003)

Yuho Ashibe
http://www.air-castle.com/suishoukyu/
  Bride of Deimos (1975) (art)
  Darkside Blues (1988) (art)

Hinako Ashihara
  Forbidden Dance (1997)
  SOS (2003)

Mio Aso
  Keiji (1990) (scriptwriter)

Atelier Lana
Also known as Kazuaki Ishida.
  Star Trekker (1985)
  The Amazing Adventures of Professor Jones

Chuck Austen
  Boys of Summer (story)

Rando Ayamine (1974–)
  Getbackers (1999) (art)

Ran Ayanaga
http://members.jcom.home.ne.
jp/0724236901/
  R.O.D (2003) (art)

Hideo Azuma (1950–)
http://azumahideo.nobody.jp/
  Disappearance Diary (2005)

Kiyohiko Azuma (1968–)
http://azumakiyohiko.com/
  Azumanga Daioh (1999)
  Yotsuba&! (2003)

Mayumi Azuma (1975–)
  Elemental Gelade (2002)

Yukinobu Azumi
  Scrapped Princess (2002) (character
    design)

Ippongi Bang (1965–)
http://homepage2.nifty.com/~bang/
Self-proclaimed "Manga Empress of all the
Asias," a *dôjinshi* artist, and popular female
otaku star due to her flamboyant personality,
cosplaying, and willingness to print scantily
clad photos of herself. In the 1980s, while

in agricultural college, she contributed to Japanese fan magazines such as *Fanroad*. She eventually formed Studio Do-Do, a group of artists including Masayuki Fujihara, Mio Odagi, and Hiroshi Yakumo. She has also released records and CD-ROMs and acted in several films, including the *ExorSister* series of adult movies. A Catholic, she spent some time doing charity work in Bolivia.

F-III Bandit (1992) (adult)
Amazing Strip (adult)
Bang's Sexplosion! (adult)
Change Commander Goku
Dark Tales of Daily Horror
Doctor!
Ippongi Bang's Canvas Diary
Virtual Bang!

Barasui (1980–)
http://bara.sakura.ne.jp/
Strawberry Marshmallow (2001)

Ashura Benimaru: See Benimaru Itoh.

Be-Papas
http://www.jrt.co.jp/yos/ikuniweb/
Revolutionary Girl Utena (1996) (concept)
Revolutionary Girl Utena: The Adolescence of Utena (1999) (concept)
The World Exists for Me (2002) (story)

BH SNOW+CLINIC
The pen name of Botan Hanayashiki, used specifically for *A Little Snow Fairy Sugar.*
A Little Snow Fairy Sugar (2001) (art)

Frédéric Boilet (1960–)
www.boilet.net
Mariko Parade (2003) (collaborator) (with Kan Takahama)
Japan as Viewed by 17 Creators (2005) (contributor)

DUO BRAND.: See under D.

Buronson (1947–)
Manga writer also known as Yoshiyuki Okamura (his real name) and Sho Fumimura.

Fist of the North Star (1983) (story)
King of Wolves (1989) (story)
Sanctuary (1990) (story) (as Sho Fumimura)
Japan (1992) (story)
Strain (1997) (story)
Fist of the Blue Sky (2001) (adviser)

Suguro Chayamachi
http://www.geocities.co.jp/AnimeComic-Pen/6785/
Devil May Cry 3 (2005)

Taro Chiaki
http://prelude.moo.jp/
Puri Puri (2004)

Jiro Chiba
Also known as Hiroyuki Takizawa.
Sexcapades (1995) (adult)
Were-Slut (1999) (adult)

Katsuhiko Chiba
Mobile Suit Gundam Wing: Battlefield of Pacifists (1997) (scenario)

Tomohiro Chiba
http://www.studioorphee.net/blog/
Mobile Suit Gundam: Blue Destiny (1997) (cooperation)
Mobile Suit Gundam: Lost War Chronicles (2002) (story) (with Bandai Games Inc.)
Mobile Suit Gundam Seed Astray (2003) (story)
Mobile Suit Gundam Seed Astray R (2003) (story)
Mobile Suit Gundam Seed X Astray (2004) (story)

Nanae Chrono (1980–)
Peace Maker (1999)
Peacemaker Kurogane (2002)

CLAMP
http://www.clamp-net.com/
Collective pen name of a popular group of female manga artists. The group began in 1989 as a *dōjinshi* circle of twelve friends, but soon the group was reduced to four members who remain today: Ageha Ôkawa,

Mokona, Tsubaki Nekoi, and Satsuki Igarashi. (To commemorate their fifteenth anniversary in 2004, they changed their pen names; these are the most recent versions.) Their pen name, in their own words meaning "a bunch of potatoes," is a misspelling of "clump." Former CLAMP members include Tamayo Akiyama (*Hyper Rune*) and Leeza Sei, aka Iba Takeo (untranslated *Tasogare no Rakuen*).

Man of Many Faces (1989)
RG Veda (1989)
Tokyo Babylon (1990)
Duklyon: Clamp School Defenders (1991)
Clamp School Detectives (1992)
The Legend of Chun Hyang (1992)
Shirahime-Syo: Snow Goddess Tales (1992)
X/1999 (1992)
Magic Knight Rayearth (1993)
Miyuki-Chan in Wonderland (1993)
The One I Love (1993)
Wish (1995)
Cardcaptor Sakura (1996)
Clover (1997)
Angelic Layer (1999)
Suki (1999)
Chobits (2000)
Legal Drug (2000)
Tsubasa: Reservoir Chronicle (2003)
xxxHOLiC (2003)

Cuvie
http://cuvie.hp.infoseek.co.jp/
Dorothea (2006)

Ryusei Deguchi
http://www.t3.rim.or.jp/~ryuse/
Abenobashi: Magical Shopping Arcade (2002) (art)

Bow Ditama
Mahoromatic (1998) (art)

Sharman DiVono
Samurai, Son of Death (story)

DJ Milky
Princess Ai (2004) (co-creator and co-scripter)
Juror 13 (story)

Koge-Donbo: See under K.

Dr. Ten
http://www.k2.dion.ne.jp/~dr.ten/
Aijin Ichimanyen (2003) (*yaoi*)

Jo Duffy
Nestrobber (1992)

DUO BRAND.
http://home8.highway.ne.jp/DUOBRAND/main.htm
Pen name for two manga artists: Haruka Akatsuki and Nobuyoshi Watanabe.
White Guardian (2003) (*yaoi*)
Crimson Wind (2005) (*yaoi*)

Dynamic Production
Collective name for Go Nagai's studio of assistants.
Devilman (1972) (with Go Nagai)
Venger Robo (1991) (story and art) (with Ken Ishikawa)
Cutey Honey '90 (1992) (with Go Nagai)

Yuri Ebihara
http://www.y-ebihara.com/
Allure (2005) (*yaoi*)
Sleeping Flower (2006) (*yaoi*)

Eiki Eiki
http://www.kozouya.com/
Dear Myself (1998) (*yaoi*)
World's End (1999) (*yaoi*)
The Art of Loving (2001) (*yaoi*)

Emura
W Juliet (1997)

Hiroki Endo (1970–)
Eden: It's an Endless World! (1997)
Tanpenshu (1998)

Minari Endo
http://www.minariendou.com/
Dazzle (1999)

Hiroyuki Etoh (1971–)
Gadget (2002)

Miyabi Fujieda (1975–)
http://www.moonphase.jp/
    Di Gi Charat vol. 1 (2000)
      (contributor)
    Di Gi Charat Theater: Dejiko's Summer
      Vacation (contributor)
    Iono-sama Fanatics (2005)

Toru Fujieda
http://t-mania.chu.jp/
    Oyayubihime Infinity (2003)

Masayuki Fujihara (1963–)
http://www.geocities.co.jp/
AnimeComic/2414/
    Masked Warrior X (1988)
    Dodekain (1992)

Akiko Fujii
    School Zone (adult)

Mihona Fujii (1974–)
    Gals! (1999)

Takuya Fujima
http://www.geocities.jp/fujima040/
    Deus Vitae (2000)
    Free Collars Kingdom (2002)

Moyamu Fujino (1982–)
http://www.mag-garden.co.jp/officialwebc/
moniwa/TOP.htm
    The First King Adventure (2002)

Fujiko Fujio
    Doraemon: Gadget Cat from the Future
      (1970)

Makoto Fujisaki
    Co-Ed Sexxtasy (1996) (adult)
    Heat (2005) (adult)

Ryu Fujisaki
    Hoshin Engi (1996)

Tohru Fujisawa (1967–)
    GTO: The Early Years—Shonan Junai-
      Gumi (1990)
    GTO (1997)
    Rose Hip Zero (2005)

Kosuke Fujishima (1964–)
    You're Under Arrest! (1986)
    Oh My Goddess! (1988)
    Sakura Taisen (2002) (character
      design)
    Oh My Goddess!: Adventures of the Mini-
      Goddesses

Maki Fujita
http://kumato.cool.ne.jp/
    Kids Joker (1998)
    Platinum Garden (2001)

Kamui Fujiwara (1959–)
http://www004.upp.so-net.ne.jp/studio2b/
    Raika (1987) (art) (with Studio 2B)
    Hellhounds: Panzer Cops (1988) (art)
      (with Studio 2B)

Hyouta Fujiyama
http://www.din.or.jp/~yuc/
    Lover's Flat (2001) (*yaoi*)
    Ordinary Crush (2001) (*yaoi*)
    Sweet Whisper (2005) (*yaoi*)

Kairi Fujiyama
    Dragon Eye (2005)

Takushi Fukada
http://www1–1.kcn.ne.jp/~t-fkd/
    Masquerade (2002) (adult)

Tsubasa Fukuchi (1980–)
    The Law of Ueki (2001)

Haruka Fukushima
http://www.roo.to/haruca/
    Instant Teen: Just Add Nuts (2000)
    Kedamono Damono (2004)

Ryoko Fukuyama
http://ryoco.net/
    Nosatsu Junkie (2004)

Sho Fumimura: See Buronson.

Kou Fumizuki
http://www.little-cotton.com/
    Ai Yori Aoshi (1998)

Nariaki Funabori
http://tamana.cside21.com/
    S&M University (2000) (adult)

Usamaru Furuya (1968–)
    Short Cuts (1998)
    Secret Comics Japan (contributor)

Kan Furuyama
    Samurai Legend (1992) (story)

Aoi Futaba
http://www.twincastle.com/
    Level-C (1993) (*yaoi*)

Shinri Fuwa
http://www3.plala.or.jp/TPP/
    Yebisu Celebrities (2006) (*yaoi*) (story)

Reku Fuyunagi
http://www3.to/raytrec
    Mobile Suit Gundam Wing: Ground Zero
        (1998) (story and art)

Akira Gajou (aka Akira Gatjaw)
    Love Touch (1993) (adult)

Ganbear
Also known as Satoru Yamasaki.
    Fantastic Panic

Shouji Gatou
http://www.gatoh.com/
    Full Metal Panic! (2000) (story)
    Full Metal Panic Overload (2000)
        (story)

Sakurako Gokurakuin
http://sumire.sakura.ne.jp/~heaven/
    Aquarian Age: Juvenile Orion (2001)
    Category: Freaks (2002)

Keiji Goto (1968–)
http://goto.cute.or.jp/
    Gatekeepers (1999) (manga)

Shinobu Gotoh (aka Shinobu Gotou)
http://www2.gol.com/users/bee/
    Time Lag (1999) (*yaoi*) (story)
    June Pride (2001) (*yaoi*) (story)
    Passion (2002) (*yaoi*) (story)

Masaru Gotsubo
    Samurai Champloo (2004) (story and art)

Alan Grant (1949–)
http://www.rengamedia.com/
    Psychonauts (1990) (story) (with Tony
        Luke)

Nankin Gureko: See Gureko Nankin.

Shuzilow Ha (1966–)
http://www.aya.or.jp/~tetrapod/HA/DATA/
index.html
    Alice in Lostworld

Moto Hagio (1949–)
Vastly influential *shôjo* manga artist, known
for her novelistic plotting. Debuted in 1969
with *Lulu to Mimi* in *Nakayoshi*. Her first
major hit was *Po no Ichizoku* (1972), a
vampire story. Her works often combine
mystery, science fiction, and psychological
elements. In works such as *Jûichigatsu no
Gymnasium* (1971) and *Thomas no Shinzô*
(1974), she depicted romantic, traumatic
relationships between androgynous boys,
making her one of the founders of the
shônen ai genre. Her short story "Hanshin"
(1984) was published in English in *The
Comics Journal* no. 269 (2005), along with a
lengthy interview.
    A, A' (1981)
    Four Shôjo Stories

Kazushi Hagiwara (1963–)
http://basta.gangz.com/
    Bastard!!: Heavy Metal Dark Fantasy
        (1988)

Hai Ran
http://homepage2.nifty.com/ceramicgirlie/
    Tori Koro (2002)

Mera Hakamada
http://mera.hacca.jp/
    The Last Uniform (2005)

Maki Hakoda
http://www.mag-garden.co.jp/officialwebc/
r2/atogaki-web.htm
    R² [*Rise R to the Second Power*] (2002)

Tatsuya Hamazaki
.Hack//Legend of the Twilight (2002)
(story)

Yoko Hanabusa
http://homepage2.nifty.com/lady/
Harlequin Pink: Idol Dreams (1998) (art)

Pink Hanamori
Pichi Pichi Pitch: Mermaid Melody (2002)
(art)

Kazuichi Hanawa (1947–)
Comics Underground Japan (contributor)
Doing Time (1998)

Botan Hanayashiki: See BH
SNOW+CLINIC.

Hidenori Hara (1961–)
Train_Man: Densha Otoko (2005)
(manga)

Tetsuo Hara (1961–)
http://www.haratetsuo.com/
Fist of the North Star (1983) (art)
Keiji (1990) (art)
Fist of the Blue Sky (2001) (art)

Show-Tarou Harada
Nananana (2002)

Tachiri Haruko: See Haruko Tachiri.

Makoto Haruno
Legendz (2003) (art)

Machiko Hasegawa (1920–1992)
http://www.hasegawamachiko.jp/
The Wonderful World of Sazae-San
(1946)
Granny Mischief (1966)

Yukari Hashida
Waru (2002) (yaoi)

Takashi Hashiguchi (1967–)
Yakitate!! Japan (2001)

Takako Hashimoto
Harlequin Violet: Response (1999) (art)

Toui Hasumi
http://homepage2.nifty.com/hasumi-toui/
Othello (2002) (yaoi)

Kenjiro Hata
http://websunday.net/backstage/hata.html
Hayate the Combat Butler (2004)

Bisco Hatori
Millennium Snow (2001)
Ouran High School Host Club (2003)

Akiko Hatsu (1959–)
http://www003.upp.so-net.ne.jp/
namibanpa/
Devil in the Water (1992)
Mourning of Autumn Rain (1992)

Tomoko Hayakawa
The Wallflower (2000)

Jun Hayami
Beauty Labyrinth of Razors (2000) (adult)

Fumino Hayashi
http://serpent.exblog.jp/
Neon Genesis Evangelion: Angelic Days
(2003) (art)

Shizuru Hayashiya
http://csx.jp/~jd-mh/2006/index.html
Sister Red (2001)
Onegai Teacher (2002)
Gunparade March: A New Marching Song
(2003) (contributor)

Hekaton
Disgaea 2 (2006)

Yoshiki Hidaka (1935–)
The First President of Japan (1998)
(story)

Kazuko Higashiyama
http://tactics.moo.jp/
Tactics (2001)

Kirico Higashizato
http://www.digital-comic.com/kirico/
Invoke (2003) (yaoi)
Love Recipe (2005) (yaoi)

Daisuke Higuchi
Whistle! (1998)

You Higuri
http://www.diana.dti.ne.jp/~higuri/
Seimaden (1994)
Gorgeous Carat (1999) (*yaoi*)
Cantarella (2000)
Gakuen Heaven (2004) (*yaoi*)
Gorgeous Carat Galaxy (2004) (*yaoi*)

Kyoko Hikawa
From Far Away (1991)

Hina
Di Gi Charat Theatre: Leave It to Piyoko! (2002) (story and art)

Hideshi Hino (1946–)
Horror manga artist whose troubled postwar childhood is often referenced in his work; he was born in Manchuria to Japanese immigrant laborers, who were forced to flee to Japan due to the postwar anti-Japanese sentiment. Debuted in 1967, his early work appeared in underground magazines such as *COM* and *Garo*. Wrote, directed, and starred in several of the 1980s "guinea pig" splatter horror movies. One of his short stories also appeared in the 1999 international comics anthology *Comix 2000*.
Hell Baby (1982)
Panorama of Hell (1983)
Hino Horror, Vol. 1: The Red Snake (1985)
Hino Horror, Vol. 2: The Bug Boy (1975)
Hino Horror, Vols. 3–4: Oninbo and the Bugs from Hell (1987)
Hino Horror, Vol. 5: Living Corpse (1986)
Hino Horror, Vol. 6: Black Cat (1979)
Hino Horror, Vols. 7–8: The Collection (1996)
Hino Horror, Vol. 9: Ghost School
Hino Horror, Vol. 10: Death's Reflection
Hino Horror, Vol. 11: Gallery of Horrors (1998)
Hino Horror, Vol. 12: Mystique Mandala of Hell (1982)

Hino Horror, Vol. 13: Zipangu Night (1997)
Hino Horror, Vol. 14: Skin and Bone (1997)
Comics Underground Japan (contributor)
Lullabies from Hell (2004)

Matsuri Hino
Merupuri: Märchen Prince (2002)
Vampire Knight (2005)

Aoi Hiragi
Baron: The Cat Returns (2002)

Kazumasa Hirai (1938–)
http://www.wolfguy.com
Spider-Man: The Manga (1970) (story assistance)

Rin Hirai
Legendz (2003) (story)

Kohta Hirano (1973–)
http://www.geocities.jp/hirano73714/
Hellsing (1998)

Toshihiro Hirano: See Toshiki Hirano.

Toshiki Hirano (1956–)
Anime director, animator, and character designer. Officially changed his name from Toshihiro Hirano in 1997. Married to Narumi Kakinouchi.
Golden Warrior Iczer-One (1986) (creator and some art)
New Vampire Miyu (1992) (co-creator)
Vampire Princess Miyu (1988) (co-creator)

Hiroshi Hirata (1937–)
http://www2.wbs.ne.jp/~tesh/
Satsuma Gishiden: The Legend of the Satsuma Samurai (1977)
Manga (contributor)
Samurai, Son of Death (1987) (art)

Ohji Hiroi: See Hiroi Oji.

Kenshi Hirokane (1947–)
Division Chief Kosaku Shima (1992)
Bringing Home the Sushi (contributor)

Shin-Ichi Hiromoto (1966–)
http://members.jcom.home.ne.jp/
mangaforce/
  Star Wars: Return of the Jedi (1998) (art)
  Stone (2001)

Mihoko Hirose
  Harlequin Violet: Blind Date (2003) (art)

Tamakoshi Hiroyuki: See Hiroyuki
Tamakoshi.

Yasuda Hitoshi: See Hitoshi Yasuda.

Saki Hiwatari (1961–)
  Please Save My Earth (1987)
  Tower of the Future (1994)

Tsukasa Hojo (1959–)
http://www.hojo-tsukasa.com/
  City Hunter (1985)

Yukine Honami
  Sweet Revolution (2000) (*yaoi*) (art)
  Desire (2001) (*yaoi*) (art)
  Rin (2002) (*yaoi*) (art)
  Can't Win with You (2003) (*yaoi*) (art)
  J-Boy by Biblos (*yaoi*) (contributor)

Keiko Honda (1962–)
  Over the Rainbow (1998)

Akira Honma
  The Judged (2003) (*yaoi*)
  Last Portrait (2005) (*yaoi*)

Nobu Horie (1955–)
  Fist of the Blue Sky (2001) (story)

Gorou Horikawa
http://mujin.m78.com/horikawagorou.htm
  Slave Contract (1994) (adult)
  Pet Humiliation Diary (1999) (adult)

Horumarin
  Medabots (1999)

Misao Hoshiai
  Harlequin Pink: The Bachelor Prince (2001)
  (art)

Harlequin Violet: Holding on to Alex (2002)
  (art)

Katsura Hoshino (1980–)
  D.Gray-Man (2004)

Lily Hoshino
  Alone in My King's Harem (2004)
  (*yaoi*)
  My Only King (2004) (*yaoi*)

Memi Hoshino
http://www.hoshino-memi.com/
  Dream Hotel

Yukinobu Hoshino (1954–)
  Saber Tiger (1980)
  2001 Nights (1984)
  The Two Faces of Tomorrow (1993)
  (manga)
  Manga (contributor)

Shin-Ichi Hosoma
  Demon City Hunter (1986) (art)
  Demon Palace Babylon (2001) (art)
  Demon City Shinjuku (2002) (art)

Fujihiko Hosono
  Crusher Joe (1979) (art)

Yumi Hotta (1957–)
  Hikaru no Go (1998) (story)

Rei Hyakuyashiki
http://www.geocities.jp/yashiki100/
  Welcome to Lodoss Island (1996) (art)

Tawao Ichinose
http://blog.goo.ne.jp/ichinosetamao
  The Time Guardian (2005) (art)

Rei Idumi: See Rei Izumi.

Haruko Iida
  Crescent Moon (1999) (art)

Iida Toshitsugu
  Wolf's Rain (2003) (story and art)

Hiroyuki Iizuka
> *Shôjo Beat's Manga Artist Academy* (2000)
> (concept)

Ai Iijima (1972–)
http://ameblo.jp/iijimaai/
> *Time Traveler Ai* (1994) (story)

Etsuko Ikeda
> *Bride of Deimos* (1975) (story)

Riyoko Ikeda (1947–)
http://www.ikeda-riyoko-pro.com/
> *The Rose of Versailles* (1972)

Ryoichi Ikegami (1944–)
Debuted in 1971. An Ikegami short story in the underground manga magazine *Garo* attracted the attention of Shigeru Mizuki, who asked Ikegami to become his assistant. Ikegami always works with a writer, typically on men's adventure stories. His almost photorealistic art style, influenced by American comic artist Neal Adams, attracted incredible attention in *shônen* and *seinen* magazines in the 1970s and 1980s.
> *Spider-Man: The Manga* (1970) (story
>   and art)
> *Wounded Man* (1981) (art)
> *Mai the Psychic Girl* (1985) (art)
> *Crying Freeman* (1986) (art)
> *Offered* (1989) (art)
> *Sanctuary* (1990) (art)
> *Samurai Crusader* (1991) (art)
> *Strain* (1997) (art)

Satomi Ikezawa
http://home.f02.itscom.net/ikezawa/
> *Guru Guru Pon-chan* (1997)
> *Othello* (2002)

Mia Ikumi
http://www.ikumimi.com/
> *Tokyo Mew Mew* (2000) (art)
> *Tokyo Mew Mew a la Mode* (2003)

Yasuhiro Imagawa (1961–)
> *Seven of Seven* (2002) (story)

Yasue Imai
> *B.B. Explosion* (1997)

Koji Inada
> *Beet the Vandel Buster* (2004) (art)

Shiho Inada
http://inadaya.net/
> *Ghost Hunt* (1998) (artist)

Misao Inagaki (1975–)
http://www3.to/misarin
> *The Ring* (1999) (art)

Riichiro Inagaki (1976–)
http://www7a.biglobe.ne.jp/~reach/
> *Eyeshield 21* (2002) (story)

Kazuro Inoue (1970–)
http://websunday.net/backstage/inoue.html
> *Midori Days* (2003)

Santa Inoue (1968–)
http://www.santa.co.jp
Cousin of Taiyo Matsumoto (*Black & White*).
> *Neighbor #13* (1993)
> *Tokyo Tribes* (1997)

Sora Inoue (1972–)
> *Samurai Girl Real Bout High School* (1998)
>   (art)

Takehiko Inoue (1967–)
http://www.itplanning.co.jp/
> *Slam Dunk* (1990)
> *Vagabond* (1998)

Haruka Inui
> *Ogenki Clinic* (1987) (adult)

Sekihiko Inui
> *Comic Party* (Tokyopop) (2001)
> *Gunparade March: A New Marching Song*
>   (2003) (contributor)
> *Murder Princess* (2005)

Kanako Inuki
http://jmac.dma-j.net/inuki/
> *School Zone* (1996)

Bang Ippongi: See Ippongi Bang.

Ikue Ishida
   Horizon Line (1997) (*yaoi*)

Ira Ishida (1960–)
   IWGP: Ikebukuro West Gate Park (2001)
   (story)

Run Ishida
   Night Warriors: Darkstalkers' Revenge
   Warrior Nun Areala: The Manga

Satoru Ishihara
   Kimi Shiruya—Dost Thou Know? (2003)
   (*yaoi*)

Tsunekazu Ishihara (1957–)
   Magical Pokémon Journey (1997) (original
   creator) (with Satoshi Tajiri)
   Pokémon: The Electric Tale of Pikachu
   (1997) (original creator) (with
   Satoshi Tajiri)
   Pokémon Adventures (original creator)
   (with Satoshi Tajiri)

Ken Ishikawa (1948–2006)
   Venger Robo (1991) (story and art) (with
   Dynamic Production)

Yûjin Ishikawa
   The Mighty Bombshells

Shotaro Ishimori: See Shôtarô Ishinomori.

Shôtarô Ishinomori (1938–1998)
http://www.ishimoripro.com
Famed manga artist; also the creator of
many live-action *tokusatsu* superheroes
including *Kamen Rider* and *Himitsu Sentai
Goranger.* Debuted in 1954 in *Manga Shônen.*
A fan of Osamu Tezuka, he briefly worked
as his assistant on *Astro Boy,* and for a time
in the 1950s he lived in the legendary
Tokiwaso apartment building with Osamu
Tezuka, Fujio F. Fujiko, and other creators.
In addition to children's robot and hero
series, he also worked on realistic grown-up
manga such as the long-running *Hotel.* His
assistants have included Go Nagai and
Keiko Takemiya.

Cyborg 009 (1964)
*Japan Inc.: An Introduction to Japanese
   Economics* (The Comic Book) (1986)
The Legend of Zelda: A Link to the Past
   (1992)
The Skull Man (1998) (original concept
   and story)
Kikaider Code 02 (2000) (story)

Isutoshi
http://www.ls-mk.bb4u.ne.jp/~th03/
   Slut Girl (1999) (adult)

Masahiro Itabashi
http://www.shuwatch.com/
   Boys Be (1997) (story)

Keisuke Itagaki (1957–)
   Baki the Grappler (1991)

Shuho Itahashi (1954–)
http://www1.odn.ne.jp/~cdc52120/
   Cyber 7 (1986)

Akihiro Ito
http://www.ipc-tokai.or.jp/~ssuzuki/itoh/
   Mega Comics (contributor)
   Geobreeders (1997)

Junji Ito (1963–)
   Museum of Terror (1987)
   Tomie (1987)
   Flesh Colored Horror (1988)
   Uzumaki (1998)
   Gyo (2000)

Noizi Ito
   Shakugan no Shana (2005) (character
   design)

Ashura Itoh: See Benimaru Itoh.

Benimaru Itoh
Commonly known by the alias Ashura
Itoh; Viz credited him as Ashura Benimaru
on *Pokémon: Pikachu Meets the Press.*
   Pokémon: Pikachu Meets the Press (art)

Ikuko Itoh
   Princess Tutu (2002) (story) (with
   Junichi Satoh)

Kako Itoh
http://www.246.ne.jp/~i-kako/
Harlequin Pink: A Girl in a Million (2003)
(art)

Mami Itoh
Pilgrim Jäger (2002) (art)

Sei Itoh
Monster Collection: The Girl Who Can Deal with Magic Monsters (1998) (story and art)

Shimpei Itoh (1960–)
http://www.hyperdolls.com
Married to Mio Odagi.
Hyper Dolls (1995)

Ei Itou
http://candypot-web.hp.infoseek.co.jp/
Tetragrammaton Labyrinth (2005)

Kaname Itsuki
Lost Boys (2004) (*yaoi*)

Hitoshi Iwaaki
Parasyte (1990)

Yuji Iwahara
http://www2.tky.3web.ne.jp/~lobo/
Chikyu Misaki (2001)
King of Thorn (2002)

Kaoru Iwamoto
Yebisu Celebrities (2006) (*yaoi*) (art)

Masakazu Iwasaki
Popo Can (2003)

Masatsugu Iwase
Mobile Suit Gundam Seed (2003) (art)
Mobile Suit Gundam Seed Destiny (2005) (art)

Kazuhisa Iwata (1960–)
http://owl.or.tv/
Godzilla (1985)

Yutaka Izubuchi (1958–
Rahxephon (2001) (original creator) (with Bones)

Kaneyoshi Izumi
Doubt!! (2002)

Rei Izumi
http://www1.ttcn.ne.jp/~izumiya/
.Hack//Legend of the Twilight (2002) (art)
Hibiki's Magic (2004) (art)

Ueno Jiro: See Jiro Ueno.

Gerard Jones (1957–)
http://www.gerardjones.com/
Pokémon: Pikachu Meets the Press (story)

JUDAL
Vampire Game (1996)

Mashumaro Jyuubaori
Voice of Submission (1996) (adult)
Alice in Sexland (1999) (adult)
Patriot (2004) (adult)

Kouhei Kadono (1968–)
Boogiepop Dual: Loser's Circus (1999) (original creator)
Boogiepop Doesn't Laugh (2000) (original creator)

Yuna Kagesaki (1973–)
Chibi Vampire (2003)

Naoyuki Kageyama
Yu-Gi-Oh! GX (2006) (art)

Yutakamaru Kagura
Relish (2002) (adult)

Tachibana Kaimu: See Kaimu Tachibana.

Sousuke Kaise
Grenadier (2002)

Kaishaku
http://www.toshima.ne.jp/~kaishaku/
Collective pseudonym for two manga artists, Hitoshi Ota and Terumasa Shichinohe.
Steel Angel Kurumi (1998)

Key Princess Story: Eternal Alice Rondo
  (2004)

Kengo Kaji
http://www.kengo.co.jp/
  Lycanthrope Leo (1991) (story)

Narumi Kakinouchi (1962–)
www.aprildd.co.jp/~kakinouchi/
  Vampire Princess Miyu (1988) (story and art)
  My Code Name Is Charmer (1990) (story and art)
  Vampire Yui (1990)
  New Vampire Miyu (1992) (story and art)
  The Vampire Dahlia (1996)
  The Wanderer (1996)
  Juline (1997)
  Shaolin Sisters (1999)
  Shaolin Sisters: Reborn (2001)

Hideki Kakinuma (DARTS)
  Junk Force (2002) (story)

Missile Kakurai
http://mimi.chips.jp/
  The Sword of Shibito (1998) (art)

Akimine Kamijyo (1975–)
  Samurai Deeper Kyo (1999)

Kazuo Kamimura (1940–1986)
  Lady Snowblood (1972) (art)

Yoko Kamio (1966–)
  Boys over Flowers (1992)

Kanan
  Galaxy Angel (2001) (manga)
  Galaxy Angel Beta (2004) (manga)
  Galaxy Angel II (2005) (story and art)
  Galaxy Angel Party

Yozaburo Kanari (1965–)
  Kindaichi Case Files (1992) (story)

Akira Kanbe
http://www.fwinc.jp/daria/profile/kanbe&f.
html
  Mobile Suit Gundam Wing: Episode Zero
  (1997) (art)

Mario Kaneda
http://mario.parfait.ne.jp/
  Girls Bravo (2000)

Atsushi Kaneko (1966–)
  Bambi and Her Pink Gun (1998)

Shinya Kaneko
  Culdcept (1999) (manga)

Yukio Kanesada
http://ykcomic.vvv.boo.jp/
  Kamikaze Girls (2004) (art)

Satoru Kannagi
http://www.s-kannagi.net/top.htm
  Only the Ring Finger Knows (2002)
  (*yaoi*) (story)
  Rin (2002) (*yaoi*) (story)

Aya Kanno (1980–)
http://saraba.kill.jp/
  Soul Rescue (2001)

Shiuko Kano
http://www.studioe-kennel.com/
  Play Boy Blues (2003) (*yaoi*)

Yasuhiro Kano (1970–)
  Pretty Face (2002)

Hajime Kanzaka (1964–)
  Slayers Medieval Mayhem (1995)
  (story)
  Slayers Super-Explosive Demon Story
  (1995) (story)
  Slayers Special (2000) (story)
  Slayers Premium (2002) (story)

Masaomi Kanzaki (1964–)
http://www.masaomi-kanzaki.com/
  Heavy Metal Warrior Xenon (1986)
  Gun Crisis (1991)
  Gun Crisis: Deadly Curve (1991)
  Street Fighter II (1993)
  Flag Fighters (1995)
  Ironcat (1996)

Erika Kari
http://www2.tokai.or.jp/erieri/
  Vampire Doll Guilt Na Zan (2004)

Jinsei Kataoka
http://www.lungpeng.com/kataoka/
  Eureka Seven (2005) (story and art) (with
  Kazuma Kondou)

Kyoichi Katayama (1959–)
  Socrates in Love (2004) (original creator)

Aki Katsu: See Katsu Aki.

Kasane Katsumoto
  Hands Off! (1998)

Asuka Katsura
http://www.lungpeng.com/asuka/
  La Portrait de Petite Cossette (2004) (art)

Masakazu Katsura (1962–)
http://k2r.main.jp/
  Shadow Lady (1989)
  Video Girl Ai (1989)
  I"s (1997)

Yukimaru Katsura
http://yukipaco.s19.xrea.com/
  Kashimashi: Girl Meets Girl (2004) (art)

Izumi Kawachi
http://www2.gol.com/users/takapon/
  Enchanter (2003)

Kaiji Kawaguchi (1948–)
  *Eagle: The Making of an Asian-American
  President* (1997)
  Zipang (2000)

Yumiko Kawahara (1960–)
  Dolls (1994)

Chigusa Kawai
  La Esperança (2000)

Ritsuko Kawai (1964–)
  *The Adventures of Hamtaro: A House for
  Hamtaro* (1997)

Toko Kawai (aka Touko Kawai)
  Our Everlasting (2000) (*yaoi*)
  Loveholic (2001) (*yaoi*)
  In the Walnut (2002) (*yaoi*)
  Bond(z) (2003) (*yaoi*)

Junko Kawakami
  Galaxy Girl, Panda Boy (2002)

Shoji Kawamori (1960–)
  The Vision of Escaflowne (1995) (original
  concept) (with Hajime Yatate)

Koh Kawarajima (1963–)
http://www.henreikai.com/
  Fantasy Fighters (1996) (adult)
  Immoral Angel (1997) (adult)

Tadashi Kawashima
  Alive (2003) (original story)

Yoshio Kawashima
http://www.kawashimayoshio.com/
  How to "Read" Manga: Gloom Party
  (1995)

Mizuki Kawashita
  Strawberry 100% (2002)

Kazumi Kazui
  Socrates in Love (2004) (art)

Maki Kazumi
  Desire (2001) (*yaoi*) (story)

Umekawa Kazumi: See Kazumi Umekawa.

Yuana Kazumi
http://home.s01.itscom.net/yuana/
  Flower of the Deep Sleep (2002)

Daiji Kazumine (1935–)
http://jmac.dma-j.net/minesan/index.html
  Electric Man Arrow (1964)

Sanbe Kei: See Kei Sanbe.

Ryu Keiichiro: See Keiichiro Ryu.

Itagaki Keisuke: See Keisuke Itagaki.

Homerun Ken
http://www003.upp.so-net.ne.jp/hedgehog/
Collective pseudonym of two manga artists,
Norikazu Akira and Makoto Minami.
  Clan of the Nakagamis (2005) (*yaoi*)
  J-Boy by Biblos (*yaoi*) (contributor)

Yusuke Ken
Junk Force (2002) (art)

Sato Ken-etsu
My-HIME (2004) (art)

Yoshitatsu Kiichigono
Flash Bang! (2003) (adult)

Hideyuki Kikuchi (1949–)
Demon City Hunter (1986) (story)
Darkside Blues (1988) (story)
The Sword of Shibito (1998) (story)
Demon Palace Babylon (2001) (story)
Taimashin (2001) (story)
Demon City Shinjuku (2002) (story)

Masahiko Kikuni (1958–)
http://www.kunikikuni.com/
Heartbroken Angels (1988)

Michiyo Kikuta
Mamotte! Lollipop (2002)

Sakurako Kimino
Strawberry Panic! (2005) (story)

Noboru Kimura
My-HIME (2004) (story)

Keiko Kinoshita
Little Crybaby (2004) (*yaoi*)
You and Harujion (2004) (*yaoi*)

Sakura Kinoshita
http://tactics.moo.jp/
Tactics (2001)
The Mythical Detective Loki Ragnarok (2002)

Yu Kinutani (1962–)
Shion: Blade of the Minstrel (1988)

Shimoku Kio (1974–)
Genshiken (2002)

Yuki Kiriga
Di Gi Charat Theater: Dejiko's Adventure (2000) (story and art)

Kirikaze
Anzu: The Shards of Memory (2004) (adult)

Takeru Kirishima
Kanna (2001)

Hirotaka Kisaragi
Gate (2002)
Innocent Bird (2002) (*yaoi*)

Seika Kisaragi
http://web2.incl.ne.jp/kisa/
My Dear Sweetheart (2005) (*yaoi*)

Daimuro Kishi
The Time Guardian (2005) (story)

Masashi Kishimoto (1974–)
Naruto (1999)

Seishi Kishimoto (1974–)
Twin brother of Masashi Kishimoto.
O-Parts Hunter (2002)

Yukito Kishiro (1967–)
http://www.yukito.com/
Battle Angel Alita (1990)
Ashen Victor (1995)
Aqua Knight (1998)
Battle Angel Alita: Last Order (2000)

Naoe Kita
The Empty Empire (1994)

Mohiro Kitoh (1966–)
http://www.geocities.jp/nahoowner/mono/p_top.htm
Shadow Star (1998)

Tennouji Kitsune: See Kitsune Tennouji.

Henry (Yoshitaka) Kiyama (1885–1951)
The Four Immigrants Manga (1931)

Senno Knife (1960–)
http://www.ceres.dti.ne.jp/~nekoi/
Valkyr (1989) (adult)

Bizzarian (1993) (adult)
Sepia (1993) (adult)
Eden (1994) (adult)
Mantis Woman (2000)

Jin Kobayashi (1977–)
School Rumble (2002)

Makoto Kobayashi (1958–)
What's Michael? (1984)
Club 9 (1992)

Miyuki Kobayashi
Kitchen Princess (2004)

Motofumi Kobayashi (1951–)
http://www.genbun.net/
Psychonauts (1990) (art)
Apocalypse Meow (1991)

Toshihiko Kobayashi
Pastel (2002)

Yasuko Kobayashi (1965–)
Witchblade Manga (2006) (story)

Kazuma Kodaka (1969–)
http://k2c.pinky.ne.jp/
Kizuna: Bonds of Love (1992) (*yaoi*)
Midaresomenishi: A Tale of Samurai Love
(1999) (*yaoi*)

Nao Kodaka
Kilala Princess (2005) (art)

Ryoichi Koga
Ninin Ga Shinobuden (2000)

Koge-Donbo (1976–)
http://koge.kokage.cc/
Pita-Ten (1999)
Di Gi Charat (2000)
Di Gi Charat Theater: Dejiko's Adventure
(2000) (original concept)
A Little Snow Fairy Sugar (2001)
(character designs)
Di Gi Charat Theatre: Leave It to Piyoko!
(2002) (original concept)
Digiko's Champion Cup Theatre
(2002)
Kamichama Karin (2002)

Kon Kon Kokon (2006)
Yoki Koto Kiku (2006)
*Di Gi Charat Theater: Dejiko's Summer
Vacation*
*Di Gi Charat Theater: Piyoko Is Number
One!*

Shiomi Kohara
Lucky Star (1996) (*yaoi*)

Kazuo Koike (1936–)
http://www.koikekazuo.jp/
Prolific and influential manga author, a
pupil of historical novelist and playwright
Kiichiro Yamate. In 1968 he joined Takao
Saito's studio as a scriptwriter, but soon left
to work on his own manga with a variety
of talented artists. In 1977 he set up *Koike
Kazuo Gekiga Sonjuku,* a course intended
to teach manga writing and art basics to
aspiring professionals; his students have
included Rumiko Takahashi, Tetsuo Hara,
Keisuke Itagaki, Kazuya Kudo, Takayuki
Yamaguchi, Naoki Yamamoto, Kengo Kaji,
Atsushi Yamamoto, and Yuji Horii (the
creator of the *Dragon Quest* video game
series). His hobbies include golf and
samurai swords, which he has indulged by
founding the golf magazine *Albatross View*
and the samurai manga magazine *Comic
Ran.*
Lone Wolf and Cub (1970) (story)
Lady Snowblood (1972) (story)
Samurai Executioner (1972) (story)
Path of the Assassin (1978) (story)
Wounded Man (1981) (story)
Crying Freeman (1986) (story)
Offered (1989) (story)

Goseki Kojima (1928–2000)
Lone Wolf and Cub (1970) (art)
Samurai Executioner (1972) (art)
Path of the Assassin (1978) (art)

Eiji Komato
http://www.alpha-net.ne.jp/users2/co2a/
Junk Force (2002) (character design)

Kazuhisa Kondo (1959–)
Mobile Suit Gundam 0079 (1994) (story
and art)

Yutaka Kondo
    Gôjin (art)

Kondom
Also known as Teruo Kakuta.
    Bondage Fairies (1990) (adult)

Kazuma Kondou
    Eureka Seven (2005) (story and art)
        (with Jinsei Kataoka)

Keiko Konno
    Words of Devotion (2003) (yaoi)

Takeshi Konomi (1970–)
    The Prince of Tennis (1999)

Rikdo Koshi (1970–)
http://www.rikudoukan.com/
    Excel Saga (1997)

Tetsuya Koshiba
    Remote (2002) (art)

Yua Kotegawa (1975–)
http://www.bekkoame.ne.jp/ro/gj13041/
    Anne Freaks (2000)
    Line (2003)

Tarako Kotobuki
    Love Pistols (2004) (yaoi)

Tsukasa Kotobuki (1970–)
    Saber Marionette J (1996) (character
        design)
    Sword of the Dark Ones (2001) (art)
    Mechanical Man Blues

Yumisuke Kotoyoshi
http://home10.highway.ne.jp/HATAHATA/
    Saber Marionette J (1996) (story and art)
    Midara (2003) (adult)
    Juicy Fruits (2004) (adult)

Youichirou Kouga
    Here Comes the Wolf?! (2005) (yaoi)

Yun Kouga (1965–)
http://www.kokonoe.com
    Earthian (1987) (yaoi)
    Loveless (2002)

Naduki Koujima
    Our Kingdom (2000) (yaoi)
    Selfish Love (2001) (yaoi)
    J-Boy by Biblos (yaoi) (contributor)

Fumiyo Kouno (1968–)
    *Town of Evening Calm, Country of Cherry
        Blossoms* (2003)

Satomi Kubo
http://www.mag-garden.co.jp/officialwebc/
kubosatomi/top.htm
    Kagerou-Nostalgia: The Resurrection
        (2002)

Tite Kubo (1977–)
    Zombie Powder (1999)
    Bleach (2001)

Kazuya Kudo
    Mai the Psychic Girl (1985) (story)
    Pineapple Army (1985) (story)

Toshiki Kudo
    Star Wars: The Empire Strikes Back (1998)
        (art)

Cain Kuga
    Cowboy Bebop: Shooting Star (1998) (story
        and art)

Misaho Kujiradou
    Princess Ai (2004) (co-scripter and art)

Kiyo Kujyo
    Trinity Blood (2004) (art)

Yuichi Kumakura (1971–)
    Jing: King of Bandits (1995)
    Jing: King of Bandits: Twilight Tales
        (1999)

Azusa Kunihiro
    Seven of Seven (2002) (art)

Hideyuki Kurata (1968–)
http://homepage3.nifty.com/YO-SKE/diary.
html
    Train + Train (1999) (story)
    R.O.D (2000) (story)
    R.O.D (2003) (story)

Yuki Kure
La Corda d'Oro (2004)

Shinsuke Kurihashi
Infinite Ryvius (2000) (manga)
Maniac Road (2002)
Pretty Maniacs (2004)

Iou Kuroda (1971–)
Sexy Voice and Robo (2000)

Yosuke Kuroda (1968–)
Infinite Ryvius (2000) (construction)
Scryed (2001) (story)

Masami Kurumada (1953–)
http://www5e.biglobe.ne.jp/~saint/
Knights of the Zodiac (1986)
B'TX (1995)

Hidenori Kusaka
Pokémon Adventures (story)

Yuuya Kusaka
Orphen (1998) (original character design)

Nari Kusakawa
http://lotus.her.jp/
The Recipe for Gertrude (2001)

Mizuho Kusanagi (1972–)
Mugen Spiral (2004)

Maki Kusumoto
Dolis (1998)

Kei Kusunoki (1966–)
http://www.ngy1.1st.ne.jp/~k2office/
Twin sister of Kaoru Ohashi.
Ogre Slayer (1992)
Sengoku Nights (1999) (co-creator)
Diabolo (2001)
Innocent W (2004)

Yuuko Kuwabara
Alcohol, Shirt and Kiss (2004) (yaoi)

Shinya Kuwahara
Warriors of Tao (2001)

Jiro Kuwata
Speed Racer: The Original Manga (art)

Noriko Kuwata
888 (2001)

Ariyoshi Kyoko: See Kyoko Ariyoshi.

Aki Kyouma
Messiah (adult)

Courtney Love
Princess Ai (2004) (co-creator)

Tony Luke
http://www.rengamedia.com/
Psychonauts (1990) (story) (with Alan Grant)

Chouji Maboroshi
Gorgon (1992) (adult)

Jun Maeda (1975–)
Hibiki's Magic (2004) (story)

Sakae Maeda
Jazz (1999) (yaoi) (story)

Tomo Maeda
http://kurozakana.gozaru.jp/top.html
Black Sun, Silver Moon (2002)
Beyond My Touch (2003) (yaoi)

Toshio Maeda (1953–)
Urotsukidoji: Legend of the Overfiend (1986) (adult)
Adventure Kid (1988) (adult)
Demon Beast Invasion: The Original Manga (1989) (adult)
La Blue Girl: The Original Manga (1989) (adult)

Takeshi Maekawa (1960–)
Ironfist (1983)

Teikoku Maguro
The Spirit of Capitalism (2004) (adult)

Majiko!
St. Lunatic High School (2004)

Yoko Maki
Aishiteruze Baby (2002)

Toyama Mako
Scent of Temptation (2004) (*yaoi*)

Niwano Makoto: See Makoto Niwano.

Komashi Mamiya
Melty Feeling (1993) (adult)

Johji Manabe (1964–)
http://www.katsudon.com/
Outlanders (1985)
Caravan Kidd (1987)
Drakuun (1988)

Shohei Manabe
http://www.showhey.com/
Smuggler (2000)
Dead End (2001)

Tomohiro Marukawa
The World of Narue (2000)

Suehiro Maruo (1956–)
http://www.maruojigoku.com
Ultra Gash Inferno (1981) (adult)
Mr. Arashi's Amazing Freak Show (1984) (adult)
Comics Underground Japan (contributor)

Ikku Masa
Sakura Taisen (2002) (art)

Itabashi Masahiro: See Masahiro Itabashi.

Hiro Mashima (1977–)
Rave Master (1998)

Mato
http://www1.odn.ne.jp/ginta/mato/
Pokémon Adventures (1997) (art)

Sanami Matoh (1969–)
http://www.sanami-matoh.com
Fake (1994)
Ra-I (1995)
Until the Full Moon (1998)

Tenryu: The Dragon Cycle (1999)
By the Sword (2000)
Trash (2004)

Hiro Matsuba (1971–)
More Starlight to Your Heart (2002)

Tokamura Matsuda
Crescent Moon (1999) (story) (with Red Company)

Leiji Matsumoto (1938–)
http://www.leiji-matsumoto.ne.jp/
http://ginga999.shogakukan.co.jp/
Galaxy Express 999 (1996)

Makoto Matsumoto
My Dearest Devil Princess (2004) (story)

Taiyo Matsumoto (1967–)
http://www.shogakukan.co.jp/taiyo/
Cousin of Santa Inoue (*Tokyo Tribes*).
Black & White (1993)
Blue Spring (1993)
No. 5 (2000)
Japan as Viewed by 17 Creators (2005) (contributor)

Temari Matsumoto
http://homepage3.nifty.com/hensyoku/temariindex.html
Just My Luck (2003) (*yaoi*)
Shinobu Kokoro: Hidden Heart (2004) (*yaoi*)

Tomo Matsumoto
Beauty Is the Beast (2002)

Toyokazu Matsunaga
Bakune Young (1993)

Naginata Matsurino
Wild Zoo (adult)

Yoko Matsushita
Descendants of Darkness (1994)

Tokihiko Matsuura (1968–)
Tuxedo Gin (1997)

Seiji Matsuyama
http://den.blog.ocn.ne.jp/
Eiken (2001)

Kei Matsuzawa
Any Way I Want It (2004) (adult)

Mari Matsuzawa
Hinadori Girl (2003)

Mattsuu
http://www2.ttcn.ne.jp/~yakin-dx/
He Is My Master (2002) (story)

Kenichi Matukawa
Junk Force (2002) (mechanical design)

MEE (1963–)
Hyper Police (1994)

MEIMU (1963–)
The Ring Vol. 2 (1999) (art)
The Ring Vol. 4: Birthday (1999) (art)
Kikaider Code 02 (2000) (art)
Ju-On Vol. 2 (2003) (art)
Dark Water (art)

Mitsukazu Mihara (1970–)
Mitsukazu Mihara: IC in a Sunflower
  (1994)
Doll (2000)
Mitsukazu Mihara: R.I.P. ("Requiem in
  Phonybrian") (2000)
Mitsukazu Mihara: Beautiful People
  (2001)
Mitsukazu Mihara: Haunted House
  (2002)
Mitsukazu Mihara: The Embalmer
  (2003)

Fujii Mihona: See Mihona Fujii.

Natsumi Mikai
+*Anima* (2001)

Rei Mikamoto
http://www.zombieyareiko.com/
Reiko the Zombie Shop (1999)

Tori Miki: See under T.

Haruhiko Mikimoto (1959–)
http://www.mikimotoharuhiko.com/
Marionette Generation (1989)
Baby Birth (2001) (art)
Mobile Suit Gundam: Ecole du Ciel (2002)
  (story and art)

Ryoji Minagawa (1964–)
http://www.otyanoma.net/~valensia/
Striker (1988) (art)
Project Arms (1997) (art)

Haruka Minami
Love a la Carte (2003) (*yaoi*)
Virgin Soil (2005) (*yaoi*)
J-Boy by Biblos (*yaoi*) (contributor)

Kazuka Minami
My Paranoid Next Door Neighbor (2004)
  (*yaoi*)

Megumi Minami
http://www.minamimegumu.net/
Pleasure Dome (2000) (*yaoi*)

Masara Minase
Empty Heart (2003) (*yaoi*)
Lies & Kisses (2005) (*yaoi*)

Suu Minazuki
Judas (2004)

Nobuaki Minegishi
Old Boy (1996) (art)

Kazuya Minekura (1975–)
http://www.minekura.com/
Saiyuki (1997)
Bus Gamer (2001)
Wild Adapter (2001)
Saiyuki Reload (2002)

Sakurano Minene: See Minene Sakurano.

Aso Mio: See Mio Aso.

Kurenai Mitsuba
http://www.twincastle.com/
Level-C (1993) (*yaoi*)
Let's Do It (2003) (*yaoi*)

Takanashi Mitsuba: See Mitsuba Takanashi.

Yasunori Mitsunaga
  Princess Resurrection (2005)

Ryu Mitsuse (1928–1999)
  Andromeda Stories (1980) (story)

Kentaro Miura (1966–)
  Berserk (1989)
  King of Wolves (1989) (art)
  Japan (1992) (art)

Tooko Miyagi
  http://www7a.biglobe.ne.jp/
  ~hatsunetsuweb/
  Il Gatto Sul G (2002) (*yaoi*)

Wasoh Miyakoshi
  http://blog.zaq.ne.jp/turezuremiyakoshikun/
  Seikai Trilogy (1999) (art, vol. 3)

Kano Miyamoto
  Not/Love (2003) (*yaoi*)

Yuki Miyamoto
  Café Kichijouji De (2000) (original
  concept)

Tomochika Miyano
  Yubisaki Milk Tea (2003)

Gaku Miyao (1959–)
  Kazan (1997)

Kaho Miyasaka
  http://www.k-miyasaka.com
  Kare First Love (2002)

Miki Miyashita
  http://www.saturn.dti.ne.jp/~m-miki/
  Maburaho (2003) (art)

Hayao Miyazaki (1941–)
  http://www.ntv.co.jp/ghibli/
  Famous animator and animation director,
  founder of Studio Ghibli (with his
  colleague Isao Takahata). His films,
  including *Princess Mononoke* and *Spirited
  Away,* have been some of the biggest hits in
Japanese box-office history. His work
frequently grapples with environmentalist
and anti-war themes. In addition to
Nausicaä, his manga work includes a brief
15-page color manga, *Hikoutei Jidai* ("The
Age of the Flying Boat"), which was
printed in Japan in *Model Graphix* magazine
in 1989 and later in *Hayao Miyazaki's
Daydream Note* in 1997. It became the basis
of his movie *Porco Rosso.* This manga was
released by Viz in 1993 in *Animerica*
magazine vol. 1, nos. 5–7, under the title
"Crimson Pig: The Age of the Flying
Boat."
  Nausicaä of the Valley of the Wind (1982)

Yuki Miyoshi
  Samurai Shodown (1995) (art)

Takahashi Miyuki: See Miyuki Takahashi.

Makoto Mizobuchi
  Zoids New Century (2001)
  Pokémon Mystery Dungeon (2006)

Hakase Mizuki
  The Demon Ororon (1998)

Sakura Mizuki
  The Ring Vol. 3: Spiral (1999) (art)

Shigeru Mizuki (1922–)
  http://www.japro.com/mizuki/
  Gegege no Kitaro (1965)

Shioko Mizuki
  http://www.shioko.com
  Crossroad (2003)

Takehito Mizuki
  http://yui.sakura.ne.jp/
  Indian Summer (2004)

Junko Mizuno (1973–)
  http://www.mizuno-junko.com
  Pure Trance (1998)
  Secret Comics Japan (contributor)
  Junko Mizuno's Cinderalla (2000)
  Junko Mizuno's Hansel and Gretel (2000)
  Junko Mizuno's Princess Mermaid (2002)

Ryo Mizuno (1963–)
http://www.mizunoryo.com/
  Record of Lodoss War: The Grey Witch
    (1994) (story)
  Record of Lodoss War: The Lady of Pharis
    (1994) (story)
  Welcome to Lodoss Island (1996) (story)
  Record of Lodoss War: Chronicles of the
    Heroic Knight (1997) (story)
  Record of Lodoss War: Deedlit's Tale (1998)
    (story)
  Louie the Rune Soldier (2000) (story)
  Galaxy Angel (2001) (supervisor)
  Galaxy Angel Beta (2004) (supervisor)

Ryou Mizuno: See Ryo Mizuno.

Setona Mizushiro
  X-Day (2002)
  Afterschool Nightmare (2004)

Yuzu Mizutani
  Magical x Miracle (2002)

Mikiya Mochizuki (1938–)
http://www.mangazoo.jp/studio/mochizuki/
  Wild 7 (1969)

Minetaro Mochizuki (1964–)
  Dragon Head (1994)

Motoni Modoru: See Modoru Motoni.

Reiko Momochi
  Confidential Confessions (1998)
  Confidential Confessions: Deai (2003)

Haruhiko Momokawa
  The Good Witch of the West (2004) (art)

Takeaki Momose
  Rahxephon (2001) (story and art)

Kaori Monchi
http://www.shion.sakura.ne.jp/~monchi/
index.htm
  Wagamama Kitchen (2005) (*yaoi*)

Mook (1977–)
http://mook-tv.com/
  Cosplay Koromo-chan (2001)

Pita-Ten Official Fan Book, Vol. 1 (2002)
    (contributor)

Jinpachi Mori (1958–)
  Benkei in New York (1991) (story)

Kaoru Mori (1978–)
http://pine.zero.ad.jp/~zad98677/
  Emma (2002)

Kotaro Mori
http://hanginthere.cool.ne.jp/
  Stray Little Devil (2004)

Shinnosuke Mori
  Gunparade March: A New Marching Song
    (2003) (contributor)
  Happy Lesson: Mama Teacher Is Wonderful!
    (2003) (art)

Yasuhiro Moriki
  Golden Warrior Iczer-One (1986) (primary
    art duties)

Yo Morimoto
  Seraphic Feather (1994) (story, vols. 1–2)

Ai Morinaga
  Duck Prince (2001)
  Your and My Secret (2002)
  Strawberry-Chan (2004)
  My Heavenly Hockey Club (2005)

Ayano Morio
http://www.jade.dti.ne.jp/~ayanosun/
  Warren Buffett: An Illustrated Biography of
    the World's Most Successful Investor
    (2003)

Hiroyuki Morioka (1962–)
  Seikai Trilogy (1999) (original creator)

Morishige
  Hanaukyo Maid Team (2001)

Daisuke Moriyama (1971–)
  Chrono Crusade (1998)

Yuji Moriyama
  All Purpose Cultural Cat Girl Nuku Nuku
    (1990)

Modoru Motoni

http://www1.seaple.icc.ne.jp/lovin/motoni.html

Dog Style (2005) (*yaoi*)

Poison Cherry Drive (2005) (*yaoi*)

Maki Murakami

http://crocodile.jeez.jp/

Gravitation (1996)

Kanpai! (2001)

Gamerz Heaven (2003)

Yusuke Murata (1978–)

Eyeshield 21 (2002) (art)

Wataru Murayama

http://water-run.main.jp/

Desert Coral (2002)

Hiromu Mutou

Never Give Up (1999)

Go Nagai (1945–)

http://www.mazingerz.com/GO.html

Hugely influential manga artist known for capturing the spirit of adolescent rebellion and chaos in his simply drawn manga generally about giant robots, naked or near-naked women, rampaging monsters, and the end of the world. Former assistant to Shotaro Ishinomori. Debuted in 1967 with a gag manga in *Bokura* magazine, then in 1968 was picked up by *Weekly Shônen Jump* for the school comedy *Harenchi Gakuen* ("Shameless School"). In 1970, founded his studio Dynamic Production and went on to create legendary manga such as *Mazinger Z, Devilman, Violence Jack,* and *Cutey Honey.* He was profiled in Marvel Comics' *Epic Illustrated No. 18* (1980), for which he drew an original story. His primary assistant, until his early death, was Ken Ishikawa.

Devilman (1972) (with Dynamic Production)

Venger Robo (1991) (original concept)

Cutey Honey '90 (1992) (with Dynamic Production)

Mazinger

Tomohiro Nagai

http://www013.upp.so-net.ne.jp/kumateishoku/

Full Metal Panic Overload (2000) (art)

Mamoru Nagano (1960–)

http://automaticflowers.ne.jp/

Five Star Stories (1986)

Takumi Nagayasu (1949–)

The Legend of Mother Sarah: Tunnel Town (1990) (art)

Aya Nakahara

Love♥Com (2001)

Guy Nakahira

Figure 17: Tsubasa & Hikaru (2001) (story and art)

Masahiko Nakahira

http://www.bekkoame.ne.jp/~n-masahiko/

Super Street Fighter II: Cammy (1994)

Street Fighter Alpha (1995)

Street Fighter Sakura Ganbaru! (1996)

Street Fighter III Ryu Final (1997)

Hisaya Nakajo

http://www.wild-vanilla.com

Hana-Kimi: For You in Full Blossom (1996)

Shungiku Nakamura

Junjo Romantica (2003) (*yaoi*)

Hybrid Child (2005) (*yaoi*)

Yoshiki Nakamura

Skip Beat! (2002)

Katsuwo Nakane

Hurrah! Sailor (2004)

Tatsurou Nakanishi

Dream Gold: Knights in the Dark City (2003)

Hitori Nakano

Collective pseudonym for the Internet community that put together the bestselling 2004 book *Train Man.*

*Densha Otoko: The Story of the Train Man
    Who Fell in Love with a Girl* (2005)
    (original story)
Train Man: A Shôjo Manga (2005) (original
    story)
Train_Man: Densha Otoko (2005) (original
    story)

Makoto Nakatsuka
Juror 13 (art)

Bunjuro Nakayama (1964–)
Mahoromatic (1998) (story)

Tow Nakazaki
Et Cetera (1997)

Keiji Nakazawa (1939–)
Barefoot Gen (1972)

Shingo Nanami
http://www.sn-1.com/
Kamui (2001)

Kiriko Nananan (1972–)
Blue (1996)
Sake Jock (contributor)
Secret Comics Japan (contributor)

Aoi Nanase (1972–)
http://www.aoinanase.gr.jp/
Angel/Dust (2001)
Angel/Dust Neo (2003)

Kyoichi Nanatsuki
http://www006.upp.so-net.ne.jp/Nanatsuki/
Samurai Shodown (1995) (story)
Project Arms (1997) (story)

Gureko Nankin
http://gureko.fc2web.com/
Imperfect Hero (2002)

Yutaka Nanten
Cowboy Bebop (1999) (art)
Lord of Sal Manor (2005) (*yaoi*)

Minako Narita (1960–)
Cipher (1985)

Kaori Naruse
Pretear: The New Legend of Snow White
    (2000) (manga)

Yuri Narushima
http://www.naruri.com/
The Young Magician (1996)
Planet Ladder (1998)

Yukie Nasu (1965–)
Here Is Greenwood (1986)

Shino Natsuho
Kurashina-sensei's Passion (2004)
    (*yaoi*)

Yoshinori Natsume
Togari (2000)

Masato Natsumoto
*Record of Lodoss War: Chronicles of the Heroic
    Knight* (1997) (art)
Mobile Suit Gundam: Lost War Chronicles
    (2002) (art)

Kyoko Negishi
Café Kichijouji De (2000) (story and
    art)

Lei Nekojima
I Love You (1996) (adult)

Maika Netsu
My Dearest Devil Princess (2004) (art)

NeWMeN
http://www.k2.dion.ne.jp/~nhp/
Secret Plot (1995) (adult)

Yasuhiro Nightow (1967–)
http://www.din.or.jp/~nightow/
Trigun (1995)
Trigun Maximum (1998)

Tsutomu Nihei (1971–)
Blame! (1997)

Tomoko Ninomiya (1969–)
http://www.din.or.jp/~nino/
Nodame Cantabile (2001)

Keiko Nishi (1966–)
Four Shôjo Stories
Love Song

Tohru Nishimaki
http://www.d-lovers.x0.com/
Blue Eyes (1996) (adult)

Hiroyuki Nishimori (1963–)
A Cheeky Angel (1999)

Yuriko Nishiyama
Harlem Beat (1994)
Dragon Voice (2001)

Youka Nitta (1971–)
http://www3.to/harudaki/
Casino Lily (1999) (*yaoi*)
Embracing Love (1999) (*yaoi*)
Sound of My Voice (2004) (*yaoi*)

Makoto Niwano (1964–)
Bomber Girl (1994)

Horie Nobu: See Nobu Horie.

Keiko Nobumoto
Wolf's Rain (2003) (original creator)
    (with Bones)

Eiji Nonaka (1965–)
Cromartie High School (2001)

Kuwata Noriko: See Noriko Kuwata.

Charlie Nozawa
Super Mario Adventures (1992) (art)

Miho Obana (1970–)
Kodocha (1994)

Takeshi Obata (1969–)
Hikaru no Go (1998) (art)
Death Note (2004) (art)

Machiko Ocha
Train Man: A Shôjo Manga (2005) (manga)

Yoshihiko Ochi (1961–)
http://twinshot.sakura.ne.jp/
Record of Lodoss War: The Grey Witch (1994) (art)

Eiichiro Oda (1975–)
One Piece (1997)

Hideji Oda (1962–)
www.odahideji.com
A Patch of Dreams (2005)

Mio Odagi
http://www.ksky.ne.jp/~mio/index.html
Married to Shimpei Itoh.
Magical Mates (1995)

Hotaru Odagiri
Time Lag (1999) (*yaoi*) (art)
Only the Ring Finger Knows (2002) (*yaoi*)
    (art)

Wolf Ogami
Super Taboo (1993) (adult)

Uki Ogasawara
http://homepage3.nifty.com/l-graph/
Virtuoso di Amore (2004) (*yaoi*)

Kouji Ogata
Boogiepop Doesn't Laugh (2000) (art)

Yayoi Ogawa
http://www.linkclub.or.jp/~asasin/
Tramps Like Us (2000)

Chiaki Ogishima
Heat Guy J (2002) (story and art)

Noriko Ogiwara (1959–)
http://andante-d.way-nifty.com/blog/
The Good Witch of the West (2004) (story)

Oh! Great (1972–)
Tenjho Tenge (1997)
Air Gear (2002)
Silky Whip (adult)

Kaoru Ohashi
http://www.ngy1.1st.ne.jp/~k2office/
Twin sister of Kei Kusunoki.
Sengoku Nights (1999) (co-creator)
Diabolo (2001)

Tsugumi Ohba
Death Note (2004) (story)

Mineko Ohkami
http://neko.g-com.ne.jp/mineko/
Dragon Knights (1990)

Shoko Ohmine
Lovely Sick (2004) (*yaoi*)

Mitsuru Ohsaki
Onimusha: Night of Genesis (2005)

Tommy Ohtsuka
http://www.amy.hi-ho.ne.jp/tommy-
ohtsuka/welcome.htm
Slayers Special (2000) (art)
Slayers Premium (2002) (art)

Kenichi Oishi
Astra (1999) (script)

Kendi Oiwa
Welcome to the NHK (2004) (art)

Hiroi Oji (1954–)
Samurai Crusader (1991) (story)
Sakura Taisen (2002) (story)

Fujio Okamoto
Miku's Sexual Orgy Diary (2001) (adult)

Kazuhiro Okamoto
Translucent (2005)

Keiko Okamoto
http://www.netlaputa.ne.jp/~kiriko/
Corrector Yui (1999) (art)

Eriko Okamura
Nurse Call

Kenji Okamura
Lycanthrope Leo (1991) (art)

Yoshiyuki Okamura: See Buronson.

Kunio Okawara (1947–)
Gundam the Origin (2001) (mechanical
design)

Okawari
Sex Warrior Isane Extreme (1999)
(adult)

Mari Okazaki
Sweat and Honey (2002)

Tsuguo Okazaki
Justy (1981)
Ragnarok Guy (1984)
Super Dimensional Fortress Macross II
(1992) (art)

Hitoshi Okuda
No Need for Tenchi! (1994)
The All-New Tenchi Muyô! (2001)
Tenchi Muyô!: Sasami Stories (2002)

Saki Okuse (1966–)
Twilight of the Dark Master (1991)
Blood Sucker: Legend of Zipangu (2001)
(story)

Ray Omishi
Sorcerer Hunters (1993) (art)

Akemi Omode (1968–)
Mobile Suit Gundam Wing: Blind Target
(1999) (story)

Sora Omote
Metamo Kiss (2003)

Fuyumi Ono (1960–)
Ghost Hunt (1998) (creator)

Kôsei Ono (1939–)
Spider-Man: The Manga (1970) (story
assistance)

Toshihiro Ono (1965–)
Justice (contributor)
Pokémon: The Electric Tale of Pikachu
(1997) (story and art)
Seikai Trilogy (1999) (art, vols. 1–2)

Yoichiro Ono
Revenge of Mouflon (2002) (art)

Kazumi Ooya
http://kohjin.hp.infoseek.co.jp/oya/oya-
enter.htm
June Pride (2001) (*yaoi*) (art)

Mamoru Oshii (1951–)
Hellhounds: Panzer Cops (1988) (story)

Towa Oshima (1979–)
http://towa-o.com/
High School Girls (2001)

Sachi Oshimizu
Twin Signal (1992)

Katsuhiro Otomo (1954–)
Manga artist who has mostly turned his
talents to the anime industry, working in a
variety of creative roles on anime such as
Roujin Z, Spriggan, Metropolis, and *Steamboy.*
Influenced by French artist Moebius, his
incredibly realistic and detailed artwork
raised the bar for manga in the 1980s. A
short story by Otomo appeared in issue no.
4 of DC Comics' *Batman Black & White*
(1996).
Domu: A Child's Dream (1980)
Akira (1982)
The Legend of Mother Sarah: Tunnel Town
(1990) (story)
Memories (1990)
Manga (contributor)

Otsuichi (1978–)
Calling You: Kimi Ni Shika Kikoenai
(2003) (story)

Eiji Otsuka (1958–)
Madara (1987) (story)
MPD Psycho (1997) (story)
The Kurosagi Corpse Delivery Service
(2002) (story)

Hiroki Otsuka (1974–)
http://www.hirokiotsuka.com/
Boys of Summer (art)

Yuzuha Ougi
Rising Storm (2003) (*yaoi*)
Brother (2004) (*yaoi*)

Keiko Oyama
http://www.mdilab.co.jp/officeo/index.htm
Iron Wok Jan (1995) (supervisor)

Kaori Ozaki
http://www.ne.jp/asahi/innocent/bad/
Immortal Rain (1999)

Peach-Pit
http://p-pit.net/
Collective pen name for two manga artists,
Banri Sendô and Shibuko Ebara.
Di Gi Charat vol. 2 (2000)
(contributor)
DearS (2001)
Rozen Maiden (2002)
Shugo Chara! (2006)

Please!
http://www.please-please.jp/
Onegai Teacher (2002) (original creator)
Onegai Twins (2005) (original creator)

Protonsaurus
Oh My! (1993) (adult)
Heart Core (1999) (adult)

Monkey Punch (1937–)
http://www.monkeypunch.com
Lupin III (1967)
Lupin III: World's Most Wanted (1977)

PURE
Pixy Junket (1992)

Marimo Ragawa
http://www.ragawa.co.jp
Baby & Me (1991)

Makoto Raiku (1974–)
Zatch Bell! (2001)

Hai Ran: See under H.

Shibata Renzaburo: See Renzaburo
Shibata.

Miki Rinno
http://blog.livedoor.jp/barck/archives/cat_
50003822.html
Ju-On (2003) (art)

Jerry Robinson (1922–)
Astra (1999) (original concept and
story)

Tenjiku Ronin: See under T.

Rulia 046
Battle Binder Plus (1992) (adult)

Yuuki Ryo: See Ryo Yuuki.

Keiichiro Ryu
Keiji (1990) (story)

Tsugihara Ryuji: See Ryuji Tsugihara.

Ryukihei
Dragon Wars: The Tale of Lufiak Duell
(1989)
Stainless Steel Armadillo

Mika Sadahiro
Organic Sons (2005) (*yaoi*)

Yoshiyuki Sadamoto (1962–)
Neon Genesis Evangelion (1995) (story
and art)

Jun Sadogawa
Noodle Fighter Miki (2002)

Ryo Saenagi
Satisfaction Guaranteed (1999)
Sequence (2003)

Ikkou Sahara
Credited as Kazumitsu Sahara in early
issues of *Silbuster*.
Silbuster

Mizu Sahara
The Voices of a Distant Star: Hoshi no Koe
(2005)

Reiji Saiga
Samurai Girl Real Bout High School (1998)
(story)

Shinji Saijyo
http://homepage2.nifty.com/malimiki/sinji/
Iron Wok Jan (1995) (story and art)

Chiho Saito (1967–)
Revolutionary Girl Utena (1996) (art)

*Revolutionary Girl Utena: The Adolescence
of Utena* (1999) (art)
The World Exists for Me (2002) (art)

Takao Saito (1936–)
http://www.saito-pro.co.jp/
Golgo 13 (1969)

Tomoyuki Saito
Dame Dame Saito Nikki (2000)

Misaki Saitoh
http://www.linkclub.or.jp/~misaki-2/
Taimashin (2001) (art)

Hisashi Sakaguchi (1946–1995)
http://homepage3.nifty.com/stp/sakaguchi/
Version (1991)

Takayuki Sakai
*Street Fighter II: The Animated Movie:
Official Comic Adaptation*

Ichiro Sakaki
http://www.ugougo.net
Scrapped Princess (2002) (original creator
and story)

Maya Sakamoto
Nestrobber (1992)

Harold Sakuishi (1969–)
http://www.ne.jp/asahi/hp/belfacs/
Beck: Mongolian Chop Squad (2000)

Ken-ichi Sakura
Dragon Drive (2001)

Sonoko Sakuragawa
http://www.fwinc.jp/daria/profile/
sakuragawa&f.html
Cage of Thorns (2005) (*yaoi*)

Yukiya Sakuragi
Inubaka: Crazy for Dogs (2004)

Ami Sakurai
Made in Heaven (2003) (story)

Shushushu Sakurai
http://webs.to/noreset

We Are the Naked Jewels Corporation
(2001) (*yaoi*)
Mandayuu & Me (2003) (*yaoi*)
Junk! (2006) (*yaoi*)
Missing Road (2006) (*yaoi*)

Gokurakuin Sakurako: See Sakurako
Gokurakuin.

Kanoko Sakurakoji
Backstage Prince (2004)

Minene Sakurano
http://www.mag-garden.co.jp/officialwebc/
sakuranosono/
Guardian Angel Getten (1996)

Erica Sakurazawa (1963–)
http://www.shu-cream.com/erica_01.html
Erica Sakurazawa: The Rules of Love (1993)
Erica Sakurazawa: Nothing but Loving You
(1994)
Erica Sakurazawa: Between the Sheets
(1995)
Erica Sakurazawa: Angel (1999)
Erica Sakurazawa: Angel Nest (1999)
Erica Sakurazawa: The Aromatic Bitters
(2002)

Hiroaki Samura (1970–)
Blade of the Immortal (1993)
Ohikkoshi (2001)

Hiroyuki Sanadura
Gunparade March (2001) (story and art)

Kei Sanbe
http://www.interq.or.jp/pink/dantyo-/
Testarotho (2001)
Kamiyadori (2004)

Riku Sanjo
Beet the Vandel Buster (2004) (story)

Tetsuya Saruwatari (1958–)
Tough (1993)

Akane Sasaki (1979–)
http://www003.upso-net.ne.jp/kaponco/
tohtml
Princess Ninja Scroll Tenka Musô (2002)

Mutsumi Sasaki
http://www.ne.jp/asahi/hp/belfacs/
Happy Lesson: Mama Teacher Is Wonderful!
(2003) (story)

Teiko Sasaki
Kissing (2004) (*yaoi*) (story)

Sasakishonen
http://www004.upp.so-net.ne.jp/sumicco/
Lunar Legend Tsukihime (2003) (art)

Ayato Sasakura
Shakugan no Shana (2005) (art)

Jun Sasameyuki
http://fairlady.ciao.jp/
Louie the Rune Soldier (2000) (art)

Fumiya Sato
Kindaichi Case Files (1992) (art)

Junichi Sato (aka Jun-ichi Satou)
Pretear: The New Legend of Snow White
(2000) (original creator)
Princess Tutu (2002) (story) (with Ikuko
Itoh)

Kenichi Sato (1956–)
New Lanchester Strategy (1990) (art)

Shio Sato (1950–)
Four Shôjo Stories

Shiki Satoshi: See Satoshi Shiki.

Hajime Sawada
Orphen (1998) (art)

Yoshio Sawai (1977–)
Bobobo-bo Bo-bobo (2001)

SAYA
Central City

Yoshinori Sayama
Mobile Suit Gundam: Ecole du Ciel (2002)
(mechanical design)

Akira Segami
Kagetora (2001)

Masaki Segawa
http://homepage1.nifty.com/segawa-page/
Basilisk (2003) (art)

Takahiro Seguchi
http://www16.plala.or.jp/the552/
Enmusu: Picture Scroll to Promote Love
(2002)

Itoh Sei: See Sei Itoh.

Shizuru Seino
http://shizuru.milkcafe.to/
Girl Got Game (1999)
Heaven!! (2003)

Natsuo Sekikawa
Hotel Harbour View (1985) (story)
The Times of Botchan (1987) (story)

Kouji Seo
http://www.kyowakoku.jp/dandei/
Suzuka (2004)

Naoki Serizawa
http://www.geocities.jp/
naokiserizawaofficialsite/
Samurai Man (2002)

Narumi Seto
Otogi Zoshi (2004)

Shamneko
Because I'm the Goddess (2003)

Thores Shibamoto
Trinity Blood (2004) (character design)

Masahiro Shibata (1949–)
http://www.linkclub.or.jp/~shakan/
Sarai (1998)

Renzaburo Shibata (1917–1978)
Nemuri Kyoshiro (2001) (original creator)

Takako Shigematsu
http://www5b.biglobe.ne.jp/~taka_s/
Tenshi Ja Nai!! (2003)

Shuichi Shigeno
Initial D (1995)

Mayumi Shihou
One Missed Call (art)

Satoshi Shiki
http://www.wrenchstudio.gr.jp/
Riot (1993)
Kami-Kaze (1997)
Daphne in the Brilliant Blue (2004)

Shikidouji
Full Metal Panic! (2000) (character
design)
Full Metal Panic Overload (2000)
(character design)

Harumi Shimamoto
Space Dreams (adult)

Kazuhiko Shimamoto
The Skull Man (1998) (art)

Tokiya Shimazaki
Love Is Like a Hurricane (2001) (*yaoi*)

Aki Shimizu
http://www.hige-system.com
Blood Sucker: Legend of Zipangu (2001)
(art)
Qwan (2002)
Suikoden III: The Successor of Fate (2002)

Reiko Shimizu
Moon Child (1988)

Takashi Shimizu (1972–)
Ju-On (2003) (story)
Ju-On Vol. 2 (2003) (story)

Toshimitsu Shimizu (1959–)
http://www.lares.dti.ne.jp/~reirei/
Maico 2010 (1997)
Red Prowling Devil (1999)

Yuki Shimizu
Love Mode (1995) (*yaoi*)

Yoshiaki Shimojo
Bass Master Ranmaru (art)

Kouzou Shimokata
Nipple Magician (adult)

Kio Shimoku: See Shimoku Kio.

Arashi Shindo
Disgaea (2003)

Mayu Shinjo (1973–)
http://www.mayutan.com/
Sensual Phrase (1997)
Shojo Beat's Manga Artist Academy (2000)
(contributor)

Chie Shinohara
Red River (1995)
Shojo Beat's Manga Artist Academy (2000)
(contributor)

Tsutomu Shinohara
Wild Boogie (1999)

Udo Shinohara
Urban Mirage (1986)

Mizuo Shinonome
Princess Tutu (2002) (art)
Chibimono (2005)

Taro Shinonome
Swing Out Sisters (2005) (adult)

Shinsei Shinsei
Collective pen name for the authors
and artists of Tokyopop's *Star Trek: The
Manga*.
Star Trek: The Manga

Kaoru Shintani (1951–)
http://www.area88.jp/
Area 88 (1979)

Chika Shiomi
http://www.katch.ne.jp/~shiomi/
Canon (1994)
Night of the Beasts (1996)
Yurara (2002)

Yuji Shiozaki (1967–)
Battle Vixens (2000)
Battle Club (2004)

Shuri Shiozu
Eerie Queerie (1998)

Sanpei Shirato (1932–)
The Legend of Kamui Perfect Collection
(1981)

Masamune Shirow (1961–)
Former Japanese high school teacher
turned cyberpunk science fiction manga
artist. Debuted in 1983 with *Black Magic
M-66* (for which he later directed and
wrote the anime adaptation); his early
works were published in *otaku*-oriented
manga and anime magazines such as
B-Club, Anime V, and *Comic Box.* In recent
years, Shirow has essentially abandoned
manga in favor of anime and video game
character design and pinup artwork,
typified by his *Intron Depot* series of art
books. The artist Pure was his assistant.
Black Magic (1983)
Appleseed (1985)
Dominion (1985)
Ghost in the Shell (1989)
Orion (1990)
*Ghost in the Shell 1.5: Human-Error
Processor* (1991)
*Ghost in the Shell Volume 2: Man-Machine
Interface* (1991)

Kyoko Shitou (1961–)
http://homepage.mac.com/rumakarl/
Blue Inferior
Key to the Kingdom (2003)

Kouyu Shurei
Alichino (1998)

Masahito Soda (1968–)
http://www.sodamasahito.jp/
Firefighter: Daigo of Fire Company M (1995)

Yoshino Somei
http://www.kumahige.net/
Skyscrapers of Oz (2001) (*yaoi*) (story)

Kenichi Sonoda (1962–)
Gunsmith Cats (1991)
Cannon God Exaxxion (1998)
Gunsmith Cats: Burst (2005)

Hideaki Sorachi (1979–)
Gintama (2004)

Fuyumi Soryo (1959–)
Mars (1995)
Mars: Horse with No Name (1999)
ES (2001)

Haruo Sotozaki
Coyote Ragtime Show (2006) (manga design)

SPRAY
Gakuen Heaven (2004) (*yaoi*) (concept)

Studio 2B
Collective pen name for Kamui Fujiwara's assistants.
Raika (1987) (art) (with Kamui Fujiwara)
Hellhounds: Panzer Cops (1988) (art) (with Kamui Fujiwara)

Suehirogari
Sexhibition (1993) (adult)

Kumiko Suekane
http://super.main.jp/
Once Upon a Glashma (2006)

Keiko Suenobu
Life (2002)

Igura Sugimoto
Variante (2004)

Yukiru Sugisaki
http://arecacatechu.jp/
D.N.Angel (1997)
The Candidate for Goddess (1997)
Brain Powered (1998) (art)
Rizelmine (2000)
Lagoon Engine (2002)
Lagoon Engine Einsatz (2004)

Katsuyuki Sumisawa
Mobile Suit Gundam Wing: Episode Zero (1997) (story)

Kazasa Sumita (aka Kazuasa Sumita)
http://www.slpinfo.net/
Witchblade Manga (2006) (art)

Yumeka Sumomo: See Sumomo Yumeka.

Amu Sumoto
Shojo Beat's Manga Artist Academy (2000) (primary art)

Aya Suzuka
My Code Name Is Charmer (1990) (original creator)

Jiro Suzuki
http://www2.ttcn.ne.jp/~yakin-dx/
Sota-kun no Akihabara Funtoki (2001)

Koji Suzuki (1957–)
The Ring (1999) (original novel)
The Ring Vol. 2 (1999) (original novel)
The Ring Vol. 3: Spiral (1999) (original novel)
The Ring Vol. 4: Birthday (1999) (original novel)
Dark Water (story)

Serubo Suzuki
Sweet Revolution (2000) (*yaoi*) (story)

Toshimichi Suzuki
AD Police (1989) (story)

Yasushi Suzuki
Purgatory Kabuki

Atsushi Suzumi
http://www.h5.dion.ne.jp/~as-as/
Venus Versus Virus (2005)

Kaimu Tachibana
http://hw001.gate01.com/himuronosakura/
Pieces of a Spiral (1992)

Yutaka Tachibana
Gatcha Gacha (2001)

Megumi Tachikawa
http://www6.plala.or.jp/mts/

Saint Tail (1994)
Dream Saga (1997)
Mink (2000)

Haruko Tachiri
Panku Ponk (1983)

Eriko Tadeno
Eriko Tadeno: Works (1994)

Yoshihisa Tagami (1958–)
Grey (1985)
Frontier Line (1987)
Horobi (1987)

Masayuki Taguchi
Baron Gong Battle (1997)
Battle Royale (2000) (art)

Sho-u Tajima (1966–)
http://d-arkweb.com/sho-u/
Madara (1987) (art)
MPD Psycho (1997) (art)

Satoshi Tajiri (1965–)
Magical Pokémon Journey (1997) (original
    creator) (with Tsunekazu Ishihara)
Pokémon: The Electric Tale of Pikachu
    (1997) (original creator) (with
    Tsunekazu Ishihara)
Pokémon Adventures (1997) (original
    creator) (with Tsunekazu Ishihara)

Haruka Takachiho (1951–)
http://www.takachiho-haruka.com/
Crusher Joe (1979) (story)

Rie Takada
Wild Act (1998)
Shojo Beat's Manga Artist Academy (2000)
    (contributor)
Happy Hustle High (2003)
Punch! (2005)

Yuzo Takada (1963–)
3x3 Eyes (1987)
All Purpose Cultural Cat Girl Nuku Nuku
    (1990)

Ryou Takagi
The Devil Within (2003)

Satosumi Takaguchi (1957–)
http://www.takaguchi.net/
Shout Out Loud! (1995) (*yaoi*)
Can't Win with You (2003) (*yaoi*)
    (story)

Kan Takahama (1977–)
http://takahamak.exblog.jp/
Monokuro Kinderbook (2001)
Mariko Parade (2003) (collaborator) (with
    Frédéric Boilet)
Awabi (2004)
Japan as Viewed by 17 Creators
    (contributor)

Hiroshi Takahashi (1965–)
Worst (2002)

Hiroshi Takahashi
Also known as Yo Takahashi. Not the same
as the creator of *Worst*.
The Ring (1999) (script)
The Ring Vol. 2 (1999) (script)

Kazuki Takahashi (1963–)
Yu-Gi-Oh! (1996)
Yu-Gi-Oh!: Duelist (1996)
Yu-Gi-Oh!: Millennium World (1996)
Yu-Gi-Oh! GX (2006) (story)

Mako Takahashi
Almost Crying (2002) (*yaoi*)

Miyuki Takahashi
http://miyuki.iii.co.jp/
Musashi No. 9 (1996)

Rumiko Takahashi (1957–)
Attended Kazuo Koike's *Gekiga Sonjuku*
manga artists' academy. Former assistant
to Kazuo Umezu. Debuted in 1978 with
several short stories and her first major
hit, the influential *Urusei Yatsura*, which
combined science fiction, Japanese
mythology, gag manga, and romantic
comedy elements. The first female manga
artist to find major success drawing *shônen*
and *seinen* manga, she is said to be one
of the wealthiest women in Japan. Her
assistants have included Akimine Kamijyô
(*Samurai Deeper Kyo*).

Lum★Urusei Yatsura (1978)
Maison Ikkoku (1980)
Mermaid Saga (1984)
One Pound Gospel (1987)
Ranma ½ (1987)
Inuyasha (1996)
Rumic Theater
Rumic World Trilogy

Shin Takahashi (1967–)
http://www.sinpre.com/
Saikano (2000)

Taiga Takahashi
Bass Master Ranmaru (1999) (story)

Tutomu Takahashi (1965–)
http://tao-69.com/
Ice Blade (1992)

Yasuchiro Takahashi
Shakugan no Shana (2005) (original
 creator)

Yoshihiro Takahashi (1953–)
http://www.nihonbungeisha.co.jp/weed/
Ginga Legend Weed (1995)

Shoko Takaku
http://blog.livedoor.jp/slo0902/
Passion (2002) (*yaoi*) (art)
Kissing (2004) (*yaoi*) (art)

Koushun Takami (1969–)
Battle Royale (2000) (story)

Ryo Takamisaki
Megaman NT Warrior (2001)

Tamotsu Takamure
Jazz (1999) (*yaoi*) (art)

Hinako Takanaga
http://cgi2.it-serve.ne.jp/~anaguranz/
Challengers (1996) (*yaoi*)
Little Butterfly (2001) (*yaoi*)
The Tyrant Falls in Love (2005) (*yaoi*)

Mitsuba Takanashi
The Devil Does Exist (1998)
Crimson Hero (2002)

Masayuki Takano
http://www.h5.dion.ne.jp/~mtaka/
Boogiepop Dual: Loser's Circus (1999) (art)
Blood Alone (2004)

Ukyou Takao
http://park15.wakwak.com/~mamagult/
To Heart (1997)

Hiroshi Takashige
Striker (1988) (story)

Kazusa Takashima
http://www.kazusa-t.com/
Man's Best Friend (2000) (*yaoi*)
Wild Rock (2002) (*yaoi*)

Rica Takashima
Rica 'tte Kanji! (1995)

Natsuki Takaya (1973–)
http://www.hakusensha.co.jp/furuba/
Fruits Basket (1998)

Yoshiki Takaya (1960–)
Bio-Booster Armor Guyver (1985)

Kazumasa Takayama
Chronowar (1995)

Mizuho Takayama (1964–)
Mobile Suit Gundam: Blue Destiny (1997)
 (story and art)

Takeshi Takebayashi (1962–)
http://ttake.com/
Time Traveler Ai (1994) (art)
Maxion (1996)

Toshiya Takeda
Seraphic Feather (1994) (story, vols. 3+)

Inoue Takehiko: See Takehiko Inoue.

Hiroyuki Takei (1972–)
Shaman King (1998)

Kentaro Takekuma (1960–)
http://takekuma.cocolog-nifty.com/
Even a Monkey Can Draw Manga (1989)
 (story)

Super Mario Adventures (1992)
(story)

Row Takekura
. . . *But, I'm Your Teacher* (2001) (*yaoi*)
Skyscrapers of Oz (2001) (*yaoi*) (art)
I Can't Stop Loving You! (2003) (*yaoi*)

Keiko Takemiya (1950–)
http://www.tra-pro.com/
To Terra (1977)
Andromeda Stories (1980) (art)

Novala Takemoto
http://www.novala.net
Kamikaze Girls (2004) (story)

Sessyu Takemura
http://homepage2.nifty.com/sessyu/
Domin-8 Me! (2004) (adult)

Kana Takeuchi
Death Trance

Mick Takeuchi
http://id74.net/
Her Majesty's Dog (2000)

Naoko Takeuchi (1967–)
Married to Yoshihiro Togashi.
Sailor Moon (1992)

Tony Takezaki (1963–)
http://www.threeweb.ad.jp/~tonitake/
AD Police (1989) (art)
Genocyber (1991)

Tatsuhiko Takimoto (1978–)
http://www.boiledeggs.com/index.html
Welcome to the NHK (2004) (story)

Kazuho Takizawa
Gôjin (story)

Seiho Takizawa
Who Fighter with Heart of Darkness
(2004)

Tomomasa Takuma (1972–)
http://www1.pos.to/~takuma/
Train + Train (1999) (art)

Namuchi Takumi
http://karen.saiin.net/~muchi/
Strawberry Panic! (2005) (art)

Hisao Tamaki
Star Wars: A New Hope (1997) (art)
Astrider Hugo (1999)

Nozomu Tamaki
Femme Kabuki (adult)

Hiroyuki Tamakoshi
http://www16.ocn.ne.jp/~tamaya/frame/
Boys Be (1997) (art)
Gacha Gacha (2002)
Gacha Gacha: The Next Revolution
(2002)

Benkyo Tamaoki (1973–)
http://get-ugly.jp/pornostar/
Blood: The Last Vampire 2002 (2001)
The Sex-Philes (adult)

Yumi Tamura
http://www02.so-net.ne.jp/~tamura-y/
index.html
Basara (1990)
Wild Com. (1999)
Chicago (2000)

Yellow Tanabe
http://www.websunday.net/backstage/
tanabe.html
Kekkaishi (2003)

Kunihiko Tanaka (1970–)
http://www3.tky.3web.ne.jp/~r4kmt/
Ichigeki Sacchu Hoihoi-san (2004)

Masashi Tanaka (1962–)
Gon (1991)

Meca Tanaka
Omukae Desu (1999)
Pearl Pink (2002)

Rika Tanaka
Kilala Princess (2005) (story)

Shojin Tanaka
Astra (1999) (art)

Suzuki Tanaka
   Menkui! (2000) (*yaoi*)

Arina Tanemura (1978–)
http://arina.lolipop.jp/
   Kamikaze Kaito Jeanne (1998)
   Full Moon O Sagashite (2002)
   Gentleman's Alliance (2005)

Jiro Taniguchi (1947–)
http://www.jiro-taniguchi-fan.com/
   Hotel Harbour View (1985) (art)
   The Times of Botchan (1987) (art)
   The Walking Man (1990)
   Benkei in New York (1991) (art)
   Samurai Legend (1992) (art)
   Japan as Viewed by 17 Creators
      (contributor)

Kei Taniguchi
http://mizunotawamure.web.infoseek.co.jp/
   Emblem (1993) (adult)

Tomoko Taniguchi
http://www.h6.dion.ne.jp/~tomoko-t/
index.html
   Let's Stay Together Forever (1987)
   Aquarium (1990)
   Miss Me? (1991)
   Just a Girl (1992)
   Popcorn Romance (1992)
   Call Me Princess (1993)
   Princess Prince (1994)
   Spellbound: The Magic of Love

Hitoshi Tanimura (1953–)
http://www.donquihote.jp/
   High School Agent (1987)

Kazuki Taniuchi
   The God of Sex (1996) (adult)

Kamogawa Tanuki
http://www.interq.or.jp/pink/kamogawa/
   Innocence (1999) (adult)

Yuichiro Tanuma
   Princess of Darkness (1990) (adult)

Chiaki Taro: See Taro Chiaki.

Tartan Check
   Coyote Ragtime Show (2006) (art)

Takuya Tashiro
   Najica Blitz Tactics (2001) (manga)

Makoto Tateno
http://www.netlaputa.ne.jp/~tenhou/
   Yellow (2002) (*yaoi*)
   Omen (2003) (*yaoi*)
   Hero Heel (2005) (*yaoi*)

Retsu Tateo
http://www.tt.rim.or.jp/~tateotch/
   Full Metal Panic! (2000) (art)

Yoshihiro Tatsumi (1935–)
   The Push Man and Other Stories (1969)
   Abandon the Old in Tokyo (1970)

Maguro Teikoku: See Teikoku Maguro.

Dr. Ten: See under "D."

Tenjiku Ronin
   Lust (1996) (adult)

Mio Tennohji (aka Mio Tennouji)
   Love Me Sinfully (2005) (*yaoi*)
   The Sky over My Spectacles (2005) (*yaoi*)

Kitsune Tennouji
http://www.lifox.co.jp/
   Orfina (1994)

Momoko Tensen
   The Paradise on the Hill (2002) (*yaoi*)
   Seven (2004) (*yaoi*)

Katsuya Terada (1963–)
http://www.t3.rim.or.jp/~terra/
   Katsuya Terada's The Monkey King
      (1995)

Buichi Terasawa (1955–)
http://www.buichi.com
   Cobra (1977)
   Goku: Midnight Eye (1987)
   Kabuto (1987)

Yû Terashima
Raika (1987) (story)

Hara Tetsuo: See Tetsuo Hara.

Osamu Tezuka (1928–1989)
http://www.tezuka.co.jp
Known as the God of Manga, Osamu
Tezuka is considered the most influential
of all postwar manga artists. Originally a
medical student, he was trained as a
physician before debuting as a manga artist
in 1946. In the 1950s, he briefly lived in the
same apartment complex as several other
important artists, including Shotaro
Ishinomori, Fujio Akatsuka, and Fujiko F.
Fujio. In 1961 he founded his own
animation company, Mushi Productions,
and began to experiment with anime as
well. His former assistants include Shotaro
Ishinomori and Buichi Terasawa. Manga
scholar Frederik Schodt devotes a lengthy
chapter to Tezuka in his book *Dreamland
Japan,* and a portion of Tezuka's *Phoenix* is
translated in Schodt's *Manga! Manga! The
World of Japanese Comics.*
Lost World (1948)
Metropolis (1949)
Nextworld (1951)
Astro Boy (1952)
Phoenix (1956)
Princess Knight (1963)
Ode to Kirihito (1968)
Apollo's Song (1970)
Buddha (1972)
Black Jack (1973)
MW (1976)
Adolf (1983)

Yasunari Toda (1970–)
http://tamtamx.hp.infoseek.co.jp/
toda~index.htm
Scryed (2001) (art)
Mobile Suit Gundam Seed Astray R (2003)
(art)

Seiuchiroh Todono
http://www.mag-garden.co.jp/officialwebc/
taimanndaimao/daimao_top.htm
Daemon Hunters: Hymn for the Dead
(2002)

Yoshihiro Togashi (1966–)
Married to Naoko Takeuchi.
YuYu Hakusho (1990)
Hunter x Hunter (1998)

Asami Tohjoh (aka Asami Tojo)
http://tojo-asami.com/
X-Kai (1998)
Thunderbolt Boys Excite (2004) (*yaoi*)

Koichi Tokita (1961–)
http://www2.hi-nobori.net/tokita/
Mobile Fighter G Gundam (1994) (art)
Mobile Suit Gundam Wing (1995) (art)
*Mobile Suit Gundam Wing: Battlefield of
Pacifists* (1997) (art)
Mobile Suit Gundam Wing: Endless Waltz
(1997) (art)
Mobile Suit Gundam: The Last Outpost
(1997) (story and art)
Mobile Suit Gundam Seed Astray (2003)
(art)
Mobile Suit Gundam Seed X Astray (2004)
(art)

Yoshiyuki Tomino (1941–)
Mobile Fighter G Gundam (1994) (original
story) (with Hajime Yatate)
Mobile Suit Gundam 0079 (1994)
(original story) (with Hajime Yatate)
Mobile Suit Gundam Wing (1995)
(original story) (with Hajime Yatate)
Mobile Suit Gundam: Blue Destiny
(1997) (original story) (with Hajime
Yatate)
Mobile Suit Gundam: The Last Outpost
(1997) (original story) (with Hajime
Yatate)
*Mobile Suit Gundam Wing: Battlefield of
Pacifists* (1997) (original story) (with
Hajime Yatate)
Mobile Suit Gundam Wing: Endless Waltz
(1997) (original story) (with Hajime
Yatate)
Mobile Suit Gundam Wing: Episode Zero
(1997) (original story) (with Hajime
Yatate)
Brain Powered (1998) (original story)
Mobile Suit Gundam Wing: Ground Zero
(1998) (original story) (with Hajime
Yatate)

Mobile Suit Gundam Wing: Blind Target (1999) (original story) (with Hajime Yatate)

Gundam the Origin (2001) (original story) (with Hajime Yatate)

Mobile Suit Gundam: Ecole du Ciel (2002) (original story) (with Hajime Yatate)

Mobile Suit Gundam: Lost War Chronicles (2002) (original story) (with Hajime Yatate)

Mobile Suit Gundam Seed (2003) (original story) (with Hajime Yatate)

Mobile Suit Gundam Seed Astray (2003) (original story) (with Hajime Yatate)

Mobile Suit Gundam Seed Astray R (2003) (original story) (with Hajime Yatate)

Mobile Suit Gundam Seed X Astray (2004) (original story) (with Hajime Yatate)

Mobile Suit Gundam Seed Destiny (2005) (original story) (with Hajime Yatate)

Sukehiro Tomita (1948–)
Super Dimensional Fortress Macross II (1992) (original script)
Wedding Peach (1994) (original creator)
Wedding Peach: Young Love (1994) (original creator)
Baby Birth (2001) (story)

Hitoshi Tomizawa
http://www.jah.ne.jp/~lucky/fss.html
Treasure Hunter (1995)
Alien Nine (1998)
Alien Nine: Emulators (2003)

Tori Miki (1958–)
Anywhere but Here (1988)

Akira Toriyama (1955–)
Famous creator of some of the most popular *Weekly Shônen Jump* manga ever; debuted in 1978. Originally a gag manga artist (*Dr. Slump*), he achieved even greater fame for martial arts stories (*Dragon Ball* and *Dragon Ball Z*). Known for doing almost all his art himself, with few assistants. His non-manga work includes children's books (untranslated *Toccio the*

Angel) and video game character designs (*Dragon Quest, Chrono Trigger,* the Tobal fighting game series). Friends with Masakazu Katsura.
Dr. Slump (1980)
Dragon Ball (1984)
Dragon Ball Z (1984)
Sand Land (2000)

Hirano Toshihiro: See Toshiki Hirano.

Iida Toshitsugu: See Toshitsugu Iida.

Kei Toume
Kuro Gane (1996)
Lament of the Lamb (1996)

Ema Toyama
http://emaema.sakura.ne.jp/
Pixie Pop: Gokkun Pucho (2004)

Minoru Toyoda (1971–)
http://members.edogawa.home.ne.jp/poo1007/
Love Roma (2002)

TRUMP
Luck of the Draw (adult)

Asu Tsubaki
http://members.jcom.home.ne.jp/fusianasan
He Is My Master (2002) (art)

Hidetomo Tsubura (1964–)
El-Hazard: The Magnificent World (1995)

Garon Tsuchiya
Old Boy (1996) (story)

Shigeru Tsuchiyama (1950–)
Pachinko Player (1999)

Masami Tsuda (1970–)
Kare Kano: His and Her Circumstances (1996)

Mikiyo Tsuda
http://www.kozouya.com/
The Day of Revolution (1999)
Princess Princess (2002)

Ryuji Tsugihara (1958–)
The First President of Japan (1998) (art)

Hojo Tsukasa: See Tsukasa Hojo.

Toshihiko Tsukiji
http://t-tsukiji.info/
Maburaho (2003) (original creator)

Yumi Tsukirino
Magical Pokémon Journey (1997) (story and art)

Sakura Tsukuba
Land of the Blindfolded (1996)
Penguin Revolution (2004)

Kai Tsurugi
http://www2.ttcn.ne.jp/~crushers/
Black Knight (2003) (*yaoi*)

Kenji Tsuruta (1961–)
http://www2.odn.ne.jp/ihatov/SBC/
Spirit of Wonder (1986)

Yasutaka Tsutsui (1934–)
http://www.jali.or.jp/tti/
Telepathic Wanderers (2001) (story)

Setsuri Tsuzuki
http://setsuri.raindrop.jp/
Broken Angels (1999)
Calling You: Kimi Ni Shika Kikoenai (2003) (art)

Siro Tunasima (1978–)
http://k2bat.cool.ne.jp/
Jinki: Extend (2002)

Toh Ubukata (1977–)
http://www.kh.rim.or.jp/~tow/
Also known as Tow Ubukata.
Pilgrim Jäger (2002) (story)
Le Chevalier d'Eon (2005) (original story)

Mamoru Uchiyama (1949–)
Ultraman Classic: Battle of the Ultra-Brothers (1975)

Hajime Ueda
FLCL (2000) (art)
Q-Ko-chan: The Earth Invader Girl (2002)

Masashi Ueda (1947–)
Kobo the Li'l Rascal (1982)

Miwa Ueda
http://www.yomogi.sakura.ne.jp/~peach/
Peach Girl (1997)
Peach Girl: Sae's Story (2004)

Rinko Ueda
Tail of the Moon (2002)

Jiro Ueno
Revenge of Mouflon (2002) (story)

Michiro Ueyama (1970–)
http://homepage3.nifty.com/ueyamam/
Brother of Tetsuro Ueyama.
Zoids Chaotic Century (1999)

Tetsuro Ueyama (1973–)
http://homepage3.nifty.com/ueyamam/
Brother of Michiro Ueyama.
Metal Guardian Faust (1994)

Hiroki Ugawa
http://hiruko.cool.ne.jp/
Standard Blue (1998)
Shrine of the Morning Mist (2000)

Kazumi Umekawa (1972–)
http://kazumiu.m78.com
Bow Wow Wata (2001)

Yukari Umezawa (1973–)
http://www.yukari.gr.jp/
Hikaru No Go (1998) (Go consultant)

Kazuo Umezu (1936–)
http://umezz.com/jp/
Japan's most influential horror manga artist; he is also well known for his slapstick children's humor manga, such as *Again* (1970) and *Makoto-chan* (1976). Debuted in 1955 working in a variety of genres in both *shôjo* and *shônen* manga. From the 1970s to the 1990s, he became famous for his horror manga, which became increasingly gory

and explicit, culminating in the nightmarish *Fourteen* (1990). During and after *Makoto-chan*'s run, he cultivated a public image as a lovable eccentric and became the front man of the short-lived Makoto-chan Band. Rumiko Takahashi briefly served as his assistant.

> *Orochi: Blood* (1969)
> *The Drifting Classroom* (1972)
> *Scary Book*

Naoki Urasawa (1960–)
> *Pineapple Army* (1985) (art)
> *Monster* (1994)

Yuki Urushibara (1974–)
> *Mushishi* (1999)

Satoshi Urushihara (1966–)
http://www.earthwork.ne.jp/
> *Legend of Lemnear* (1991) (art)
> *Plastic Little: Captain's Log* (1994)
> *Chirality: To the Promised Land* (1995)

Yoshito Usui (1958–)
> *Crayon Shinchan* (1990)

Hiroyuki Utatane (1966–)
> *Countdown: Sex Bombs* (1992) (adult)
> *Temptation* (1993) (adult)
> *Seraphic Feather* (1994) (art)

Jun Uzuki
http://www3.to/uzukijun/
> *Angel or Devil?!* (2005) (*yaoi*)

Asia Watanabe
http://www.watanabe-asia.com/top.html
> *Because I'm a Boy!* (2003) (*yaoi*)

Shinichiro Watanabe (1965–)
> *Cowboy Bebop* (1999) (cooperation) (with Sunrise)

Taeko Watanabe (1960–)
> *Kaze Hikaru* (1997)

Wataru Watanabe
http://mypage.odn.ne.jp/home/ seihukunuidara/

> *Densha Otoko: The Story of the Train Man Who Fell in Love with a Girl* (2005) (manga)

Yoshitomo Watanabe
> *Beyond the Beyond* (2004)

Nozomi Watase
http://www.geocities.jp/n_watase/
> *Brigadoon* (2000) (manga)

Yuu Watase (1970–)
http://www.y-watase.com/
Popular *shôjo* manga artist who often works in the fantasy and science fiction genres. Debuted in 1989 with *Pajama de Ojama* ("An Intrusion in Pajamas"). Member of the Soka Gakkai religion.

> *Fushigi Yûgi: The Mysterious Play* (1992)
> *Ceres: Celestial Legend* (1996)
> *Imadoki! Nowadays* (2000)
> *Shojo Beat's Manga Artist Academy* (2000) (contributor)
> *Alice 19th* (2001)
> *Absolute Boyfriend* (2003)
> *Fushigi Yûgi Genbu Kaiden* (2004)

Kaworu Watashiya (1972–)
http://homepage2.nifty.com/ WATASHIYAKAWORU/
> *Nymphet* (2005)

Nobuhiro Watsuki (1970–)
> *Rurouni Kenshin* (1994)
> *Buso Renkin* (2003)

Wingbird
> *Akuma-She*
> *Girls of Verotik*
> *Igrat X*
> *Satanika X*
> *Venus Domina*
> *Wingbird: Black and White Bondage*
> *Wingbird Returns*
> *Wingbird Special*

Go Yabuki
http://www13.plala.or.jp/tibi2001/
> *Scrapped Princess* (2002) (art)

Kentaro Yabuki (1980–)
  Black Cat (Viz) (2000)

Yu Yagami (1969–)
  Those Who Hunt Elves (1995)

Norihiro Yagi
  Claymore (2001)

Hiroshi Yakumo
  Hurricane Girls

Akihiro Yamada (1957–)
http://www1.odn.ne.jp/yamada-kirakuya/
  Lost Continent (1990)
  Record of Lodoss War: The Lady of Pharis
    (1994) (art)

Fûtaro Yamada (1922–2001)
  Basilisk (2003) (original creator)

Keiko Yamada
  Go Go Heaven!! (1994)
  VS (1999)

Norie Yamada
  Someday's Dreamers (2002) (story and
    original creator)
  Someday's Dreamers: Spellbound (2004)
    (story)

Sakurako Yamada
http://micromacro.cool.ne.jp/
  La Vie en Rose (2005) (*yaoi*)

Shutaro Yamada
http://yamasyu.fc2web.com/
  Loan Wolf (1999)
  R.O.D (2000) (art)

Tahichi Yamada
  Kaerimichi: The Road Home (2003)
    (adult)

Yugi Yamada
  Close the Last Door (2001) (*yaoi*)
  Picnic (2004) (*yaoi*)

Hiromi Yamafuji
  Monsters, Inc.

Satomi Yamagata
http://sumomo.upper.jp/agate/agate-set.
html
  Fake Fur (2004) (*yaoi*)

Hiroshi Yamaguchi (1964–)
  Gatekeepers (1999) (original story)

Masakazu Yamaguchi
http://www.asahi-net.or.jp/~zb7m-ymgc/
  Arm of Kannon (2001)

Takayuki Yamaguchi (1966–)
  Apocalypse Zero (1994)

Hideo Yamamoto (1968–)
http://www.yamapro.com/
  Voyeur (1992)
  Voyeurs, Inc. (1994)

Naoki Yamamoto (1960–)
http://www.yamamotonaoki.com/
  Dance Till Tomorrow (1989)

Hajime Yamamura (1968–)
  Kamunagara: Rebirth of the Demonslayer
    (2000)

Ayano Yamane
  Finder Series (2002) (*yaoi*)
  Crimson Spell (2005) (*yaoi*)

Satoru Yamasaki: See Ganbear.

Tomomi Yamashita
http://www3.plala.or.jp/nuttoyou/tytop.
html
  Apothecarius Argentum (2004)

Waki Yamato (1948–)
  The Tale of Genji (1979)

Housui Yamazaki
  The Kurosagi Corpse Delivery Service
    (2002) (art)
  Mail (2004)

Sayaka Yamazaki (1974–)
http://blogs.yahoo.co.jp/yamazaki_pro
  Telepathic Wanderers (2001) (art)

Toru Yamazaki (1969–)
http://www.toguro.com/home.html
Octopus Girl (1994)

Yoshihiro Yanagawa
http://slow-slow.hp.infoseek.co.jp/
Nemuri Kyoshiro (2001) (art)

Shinichi Yano (1949–)
New Lanchester Strategy (1990) (script)

Yukari Yashiki
Made in Heaven (2003) (art)

Hitoshi Yasuda (1950–)
*Monster Collection: The Girl Who Can Deal
with Magic Monsters* (1998) (original
concept) (with Group SNE)

Yoshikazu Yasuhiko (1947–)
http://www.asahi-net.or.jp/~sj2n-skrb/yas/
The Rebel Sword (1986)
The Venus Wars (1987)
Joan (1995)
Jesus (1997)
Gundam the Origin (2001) (story and art)

Moriki Yasuhiro: See Yasuhiro Moriki.

Kentaro Yasui (1972–)
http://homepage3.nifty.com/logical/hobby-
yasui.html
Sword of the Dark Ones (2001) (story)

Aoike Yasuko: See Yasuko Aoike.

Hajime Yatate
Collective pseudonym for the staff of the
anime studio Sunrise; seen on the credits of
virtually all manga based on Sunrise anime
properties.
Mobile Fighter G Gundam (1994) (original
story) (with Yoshiyuki Tomino)
Mobile Suit Gundam 0079 (1994)
(original story) (with Yoshiyuki
Tomino)
Mobile Suit Gundam Wing (1995)
(original story) (with Yoshiyuki
Tomino)
The Vision of Escaflowne (1995) (original
concept) (with Shoji Kawamori)

Mobile Suit Gundam: Blue Destiny (1997)
(original story) (with Yoshiyuki
Tomino)
Mobile Suit Gundam: The Last Outpost
(1997) (original story) (with
Yoshiyuki Tomino)
*Mobile Suit Gundam Wing: Battlefield of
Pacifists* (1997) (original story) (with
Yoshiyuki Tomino)
Mobile Suit Gundam Wing: Endless Waltz
(1997) (original story) (with
Yoshiyuki Tomino)
Mobile Suit Gundam Wing: Episode Zero
(1997) (original story) (with
Yoshiyuki Tomino)
Cowboy Bebop: Shooting Star (1998)
(original concept) (with Sunrise)
Mobile Suit Gundam Wing: Ground Zero
(1998) (original story) (with
Yoshiyuki Tomino)
The Big O (1999) (original concept)
Cowboy Bebop (1999) (story)
Mobile Suit Gundam Wing: Blind Target
(1999) (original story) (with
Yoshiyuki Tomino)
Brigadoon (2000) (original concept) (with
Yoshitomo Yonetani)
Infinite Ryvius (2000) (original story)
Gundam the Origin (2001) (original story)
(with Yoshiyuki Tomino)
Mobile Suit Gundam: Ecole du Ciel (2002)
(original story) (with Yoshiyuki
Tomino)
Mobile Suit Gundam: Lost War Chronicles
(2002) (original story) (with
Yoshiyuki Tomino)
Mobile Suit Gundam Seed (2003)
(original story) (with Yoshiyuki
Tomino)
Mobile Suit Gundam Seed Astray (2003)
(original story) (with Yoshiyuki
Tomino)
Mobile Suit Gundam Seed Astray R (2003)
(original story) (with Yoshiyuki
Tomino)
Mobile Suit Gundam Seed X Astray (2004)
(original story) (with Yoshiyuki
Tomino)
Mobile Suit Gundam Seed Destiny (2005)
(original story) (with Yoshiyuki
Tomino)

Ai Yazawa (1967–)
Paradise Kiss (1999)
Nana (2002)

Nao Yazawa
http://www.geocities.jp/yazawanet/index.
html
Wedding Peach (1994) (story and art)
Wedding Peach: Young Love (1994) (story
and art)

Kozo Yohei
http://www.sumomo.sakura.ne.jp/~youhei/
Spunky Knight (1995) (adult)
Superfist Ayumi (1995) (adult)

Ono Yoichiro: See Yoichiro Ono.

Rego Yokoi
http://www.onoma.jp/index.shtml
Patchwork (2003) (adult)

Mamoru Yokota
http://park19.wakwak.com/~myf/yokota/
Louie the Rune Soldier (2000) (character
design)

Michiko Yokote
Pichi Pichi Pitch: Mermaid Melody (2002)
(story)

Akira Yokoyama
Project X—The Challengers (2003)

Kengo Yonekura
http://members3.jcom.home.ne.jp/
feemour/
Pink Sniper (2002) (adult)

Yoshitomo Yonetani (1963–)
Brigadoon (2000) (original concept) (with
Hajime Yatate)

Setsuko Yoneyama
Record of Lodoss War: Deedlit's Tale (1998)
(art)

Akimi Yoshida (1956–)
Banana Fish (1985)

Michihiro Yoshida
Vaizard (2003)

Reiko Yoshida
Tokyo Mew Mew (2000) (story)

Sunao Yoshida (1969–2004)
Trinity Blood (2004) (story)

Tatsuo Yoshida (1932–1977)
Speed Racer: The Original Manga

Yanagawa Yoshihiro: See Yoshihiro
Yanagawa.

Kinji Yoshimoto (1966–)
http://www.earthwork.ne.jp/
Legend of Lemnear (1991) (story)

Natsuki Yoshimura (1978–)
http://www.mag-garden.co.jp/officialwebc/
Yoshimura/index.htm
Mystical Prince Yoshida-kun (2002)

Aya Yoshinaga
Seikai Trilogy (1999) (composition)

Fumi Yoshinaga (1971–)
Moon and Sandals (1994) (*yaoi*)
Solfege (1996) (*yaoi*)
Ichigenme . . . the First Class Is Civil Law
(1998) (*yaoi*)
Gerard & Jacques (1999) (*yaoi*)
Antique Bakery (2000)
Flower of Life (2004)

Shoko Yoshinaka
Slayers Super-Explosive Demon Story
(1995) (art)

Akihito Yoshitomi
http://homepage3.nifty.com/garigarikun/
Eat-Man (1996)
Ray (2003)

Mine Yoshizaki (1971–)
http://mnet.nicomi.com/
Sgt. Frog (1999)

Kumichi Yoshizuki
http://www.tuchinoko.com/
    Someday's Dreamers (2002) (art)
    Someday's Dreamers: Spellbound (2004)
      (art)

Wataru Yoshizumi (1963–)
    Marmalade Boy (1992)
    Ultra Maniac (2002)

Higuri You: See You Higuri.

Yudetamago
Collective pen name of Yoshinori Nakai
(1961–) and Takashi Shimada (1960–).
    Ultimate Muscle: The Kinnikuman Legacy
      (1998)

Toshiki Yui
http://www.yui-toshiki.com/shed/
    Misty Girl Extreme (1991) (adult)
    Hot Tails (1993) (adult)
    Wingding Orgy (2001) (adult)

Satol Yuiga
http://www.radial-r.jp/
    E's (1997)

Iwahara Yuji: See Yuji Iwahara.

Kaori Yuki
    The Cain Saga (1991)
    Angel Sanctuary (1994)
    Godchild (2001)

Masami Yuki (1957–)
http://www.yuukimasami.com
    Mobile Police Patlabor (1988)

Nobuteru Yuki (1962–)
http://www.ac.cyberhome.ne.jp/~say/hall.
html
    Heat Guy J (2002) (character design)

Yukio Yukimino
http://www.h2.dion.ne.jp/~yukimino/
    Dimples Down Below (1998) (adult)
    Fair Skinned Beauty (1999) (adult)
    Bombshell Boobies (2000) (adult)
    Pheromone on the Street Corner (2000)
      (adult)

Makoto Yukimura (1976–)
    Planetes (2001)

Yukiyanagi (aka Yanagi Yuki)
http://white.sakura.ne.jp/~tezawari/
    Council of Carnality Unlimited (2003)
      (adult)
    Milk Mama (2005) (adult)

Kiriko Yumeji
http://homepage3.nifty.com/ATOMIC/
HOME.html
    Le Chevalier d'Eon (2005) (art)

Sumomo Yumeka (aka Yumeka Sumomo)
http://www5e.biglobe.ne.jp/~sasshi-/
    Same Cell Organism (2001) (*yaoi*)
    The Day I Became a Butterfly (2003)
      (*yaoi*)

Ako Yutenji
    Liling-Po (1997)

Yuuki
http://pss.skr.jp/yuuki/
    Taboo District (2004) (adult)

Ryo Yuuki
http://www.ryo-yuuki.com
    Sheila's Diary (1998) (adult)
    Rhapsody (2000) (adult)

Yuuya
    Worthless Love (2004) (*yaoi*)

Asaki Yuzuno
http://www.closetchild.net/ë
    Neconoclasm (2005)

Various artists
    Justice (1981)
    X-Men: The Manga (1994)
    Di Gi Charat (2000)
    Edu-Manga (2000)
    Shojo Beat's Manga Artist Academy (2000)
    Comic Party (CPM) (2001)
    Pita-Ten Official Fan Book (2002)
    Gunparade March: A New Marching Song
      (2003)
    Bringing Home the Sushi
    Comics Underground Japan

ABOUT THE AUTHOR

JASON THOMPSON was born in 1974 in San Francisco. From 1996 to 2006 he worked as an editor at Viz Media LLC, where he supervised the English editions of manga such as *Dragon Ball Z, Naruto, Yu-Gi-Oh!, Uzumaki* and *Shaman King*. As the first editor of *Shonen Jump,* he helped launch Japan's number one manga magazine in America. His writings on manga have appeared in *Otaku USA, The Comics Journal, Animerica,* and *Pulp*. His web-comic The Stiff appears on the comics Web site http://www.girlamatic.com.

THANK YOU FOR BUYING

MANGA: THE COMPLETE GUIDE

—

THIS EXHAUSTIVE REFERENCE GUIDE IS AS COMPLETE AS WE COULD MAKE IT, BUT EVEN IN THE TIME SINCE THE BOOK WENT TO THE PRINTER AND MADE IT TO BOOKSTORE SHELVES, STILL MORE NEW MANGA SERIES HAVE LAUNCHED IN AMERICA. FOR UPDATES TO THE GUIDE, PLEASE VISIT OUR WEBSITE AT WWW.DELREYMANGA.COM/MANGAGUIDE.